The fun, fast, and easy way to get productive online

Que's Official

Internet Yellow Pages
2005 EDITION

Joe Kraynak

800 East 96th Street
Indianapolis, Indiana 46240

QUE'S OFFICIAL INTERNET YELLOW PAGES, 2005 EDITION

Copyright © 2005 by Que Publishing

International Standard Book Number: 0-7897-3252-1

Library of Congress Catalog Card Number: 2004107053

Printed in the United States of America

First Printing: August 2004

07   06   05   04   4   3   2   1

TRADEMARKS

WARNING AND DISCLAIMER

BULK SALES

Que Publishing offers excellent discounts on this book when ordered in quantity for bulk purchases or special sales. For more information, please contact

U.S. Corporate and Government Sales

1-800-382-3419

corpsales@pearsontechgroup.com

For sales outside the U.S., please contact

International Sales

international@pearsoned.com

Associate Publisher
Greg Wiegand

Acquisitions Editor
Stephanie J. McComb

Development Editor
Mark Cierzniak

Managing Editor
Charlotte Clapp

Project Editor
Tonya Simpson

Production Editor
Seth Kerney

Indexer
Chris Barrick

Technical Editor
Mark Cierzniak

Publishing Coordinator
Sharry Lee Gregory

Interior Designer
Anne Jones

Cover Designer
Dan Armstrong

Page Layout
Bronkella Publishing

TABLE OF CONTENTS

About the Author

Joe Kraynak has taught hundreds of thousands of novice computer users how to master their computers and their software. His long list of computer books includes *Easy Internet, The Complete Idiot's Guide to Computer Basics, Using and Upgrading PCs,* and *Absolute Beginner's Guide to Excel 2003.* Joe's wide range of computer and training experience have helped him develop a strong commitment to making computers, software, and the Internet more easily accessible to users of all levels of experience.

WE WANT TO HEAR FROM YOU!

As the reader of this book, *you* are our most important critic and commentator. We value your opinion and want to know what we're doing right, what we could do better, what areas you'd like to see us publish in, and any other words of wisdom you're willing to pass our way.

As an associate publisher for Que, I welcome your comments. You can email or write me directly to let me know what you did or didn't like about this book—as well as what we can do to make our books better.

Please note that I cannot help you with technical problems related to the topic of this book. We do have a User Services group, however, where I will forward specific technical questions related to the book.

When you write, please be sure to include this book's title and author as well as your name, email address, and phone number. I will carefully review your comments and share them with the author and editors who worked on the book.

Email: feedback@quepublishing.com

Mail: Greg Wiegand
           Associate Publisher
           Que Publishing
           800 East 96th Street
           Indianapolis, IN 46240 USA

For more information about this book or another Que title, visit our Web site at www.quepublishing.com. Type the ISBN (0789732521) or the title of a book in the Search field to find the page you're looking for.

THE SECRETS OF SUCCESSFUL SEARCHING

by Michael Miller

The most common activity for web users isn't online shopping or auctions, and it isn't downloading MP3 files, and it isn't even playing online games or viewing dirty pictures. No, the most common web-based activity is *searching*. That's because the Web is big and disorganized, so you have to actively search for just about anything you want to find. The reality is that most users spend at least part of every Internet session searching for some type of information—and hating every minute of it!

There are a number of perfectly valid reasons people hate searching the Web. First, searching isn't easy—or, at least, it's not always intuitive. Second, it isn't immediately gratifying, because you seldom find what you're looking for. (On the first try, anyway.) And third, it isn't fun—unless you're one of those odd birds who thinks thumbing back and forth through the cross references in an encyclopedia is a blast.

Those objections aside, you're still forced to search the Web for the information you want. Fortunately, the more you know about *how* and *where* to search, the more likely it is you'll find what you're looking for, fast.

THE NEEDLE IN THE HAYSTACK PROBLEM

Here's something you need to know: Web searching is more an art than a science. You need to develop a *feel* for how and where to search; following a set of hard and fast rules won't always deliver the best results. That's because every search site not only operates differently, but also contains a different set of data; entering the same identical query at different sites more often than not produces wildly different results.

So, even though the act of searching is deceptively easy (just enter a query in a search box and click a button), finding useful information is hard. Of course, it doesn't help that the Internet is big—really, *really* big—more than 80 billion documents and growing! With these numbers, your odds of finding a single page of information on the Web are in the neighborhood of 80 billion to one.

The size problem is compounded by the fact that information online is not stored or organized in any logical fashion. You have to realize that the Internet itself is not run or managed by any central organization; the Web is nothing more than a collection of millions of individual computers, all connected by a bunch of wires crisscrossing the globe. Nobody is in charge; therefore, everybody has to manage his or her own computers and servers with no rules or regulations for guidance.

In addition, there are no standards or guidelines for laying out web pages so that certain types of information are always presented the same way, using the same words, positioned in the same place. There is no guarantee that the topic described in a web page's title is even mentioned in the text of the page. There is no assurance that a page that was on the Web yesterday will still be there tomorrow.

In short, the Web is a mess.

THE ART OF SEARCHING

Not surprisingly, there have been several attempts over the years to organize this mess we call the Internet. This book, *Que's Official Internet Yellow Pages*, is one such attempt. However, as helpful as this book is, all attempts to organize the Internet ultimately fall short, simply because the Internet is *so* big and *so* disorganized and growing *so* fast. Even the best attempts (and I view this book as one of the best) can document only a small part of the Internet; literally billions of other web pages go undocumented.

So, when you're looking for something on the Internet, you should first go to a good printed directory, such as this book. But if you can't find what you're looking for there—or if you're looking for even more current information—where do you turn?

You are now faced with the prospect of *searching the Internet*. But if there are no rules for *storing* information on the Internet, what procedures can you follow when you're *searching* for information?

To get good results—results that zero in precisely on the information you want, without throwing in pages and pages of irrelevant data—you need to know the right way to search. And the right way to search is all about asking the right questions.

Imagine you're a detective questioning a suspect, and you have only a limited number of questions you can ask. Do you waste a question by asking, "Where were you on the night of the crime?" The suspect can answer that question many different ways, most of them vague: "California." "Home." "Out." "Someplace better than here."

A better question is one that is more precise, and allows less latitude in the way it is answered. "Were you at 1234 Berrywood Lane on the night of the crime?" For this question, there are only two acceptable answers: "Yes" or "No." Either of these answers will give you the information you're looking for, with no chance for evasion or misinterpretation.

Searching the Web is like playing detective. Ask the right questions, and you get useful answers. Ask vague questions, and you get useless answers.

Effective searching requires a combination of innate ability, productive habits, and specific skills. It also helps to have a kind of "sixth sense" about where to look for information, and a lot of patience to make it through those long stretches when you can't seem to find anything useful, no matter how hard you try.

In other words, successful searching is a blend of art and science, of intuition and expertise—something some are born with, and others have to learn.

THE DIFFERENCE BETWEEN SEARCH ENGINES AND DIRECTORIES—AND WHY YOU SHOULD CARE

There are hundreds of websites that enable you to search the Internet for various types of information. The best of these sites are among the most popular sites on the Web, period—even though each of these sites approaches the search problem in its own unique fashion.

Directories: Manually Cataloging Web Pages

One approach to organizing the Web is to physically look at each web page and stick each one into a hand-picked category. After you collect enough web pages, you have something called a *directory*. Directories can be very appealing, because they enable you to browse for a website by category, often finding what you didn't know you were really looking for. Most directories also provide a Search box for searching for specific sites in the directory.

A directory doesn't search the Web; in fact, a directory catalogs only a very small part of the Web. But a directory is very organized, and very easy to use, and lots and lots of people use web directories every day.

In fact, one of the most popular websites today is a directory. Yahoo! catalogs close to two million individual websites in its well-organized directory, and people seem to like it—even though Yahoo!'s directory content represents less than 1/10 of 1% of the total number of pages currently published on the Web.

Many directories are very specialized—designed to be used by people sharing a common interest or having a special need. For example, Education Planet (http://www.educationplanet.com/) catalogs information and websites specifically for teachers.

Search Engines: Scouring the Web, Automatically

It's important to note that a directory is *not* a search engine. A *search engine* is not powered by human hands; instead, a search engine uses a special type of software program (called a *spider* or *crawler*) to roam the Web automatically, feeding what it finds back to a massive bank of computers. These computers hold *indexes* of the Web. In some cases, entire web pages are indexed; in other cases, only the titles and important words on a page are indexed. (Different search engines operate differently, you see.)

In any case, as the spiders and crawlers operate like little robot web surfers, the computers back at home base create a huge index (or database) of what was found. The largest search engine index (Google) contains more than 6 billion entries—which still leaves the vast majority of the Web untouched and unavailable to searchers.

When you go to a search engine, you enter a *query* into a search box on the home page. This query represents, to the best of your descriptive ability, the specific information that you're looking for. When you click the Search button, your query is sent to the search engine's index—*not* out to the Internet itself. (You never actually search the Web itself; you search only the index that was created by the spiders crawling the Web.) The search engine then creates a list of pages *in its index* that match, to one degree or another, the query that you entered.

And that's how you get results from a search engine.

Directories or Search Engines: Which Is Better?

So, which is better, a directory or a search engine? What is better for you depends on what you want:

- If you want the *most* results, use a search engine. (A search engine's automatic index is *much* bigger than a manually constructed directory.)
- If you want the *best* hand-picked results, use a directory. (People generally make better decisions than machines.)
- If you want the most *current* results, use a search engine. (Search engine bots crawl the Web daily; it takes time for human beings to manually enter and delete directory entries.)
- If you want the *best-organized* results, use a directory. (Human editors are best at sorting the results into the proper categories.)

It's tempting to say that search engines deliver quantity, and directories deliver quality, but that isn't always the case. Some of the best and most powerful search engines—such as Google—can deliver quality results matching or besting those from the top directories. And, to complicate matters even further, many search engine sites include web directories as part of their services—and the major directories often include search engine add-ons. It's all very confusing.

WHERE TO SEARCH

There are, by several counts, more than 200 separate search engines and directories on the Internet. With that many options available, you almost need a search engine to search for a search engine!

If you go by usage trends, however, you end up with a couple of big search sites and then a long list of "other" sites. The Big Two are a search engine and a directory—Google and Yahoo! The "other" category includes all the other sites.

Google

The most popular search engine today is Google (www.google.com). Google offers a huge search index (more than six billion entries), highly relevant search results, extremely fast searches, and a variety of specialty searches.

The basic Google search page is extremely simple; you get a search box and a Google Search button. You also get an I'm Feeling Lucky button, which will take you directly to the first listing on the Google results page. (I don't recommend feeling lucky; it's better to view a variety of result listings, just to get a feel for what else is available.)

In addition to its main web search, Google also offers the following specialty searches, all available from tabs on the main page:

- **Images**—This option lets you search for pictures and graphics. Because a normal text-based search typically ignores pictures in its results, you can use this search when you're looking for specific types of images.
- **Groups**—This option lets you search the Internet's Usenet newsgroup archives. You can search the entire archive, or narrow your search by date or newsgroup.
- **Directory**—This option bypasses the Google search engine to provide hand-picked results from the Open Directory. This is one of Google's best-kept secrets because the Open Directory is arguably the best directory on the Web.
- **News**—This page gathers the top news stories from more than 4,500 news sources on the Web and presents you with a front page, headline "newspaper." Here, you can keep yourself informed about U.S. and world news, sports, business, entertainment, and health.
- **Froogle**—A search engine specifically for online shopping. Froogle lets you search thousand of online stores for the lowest prices on items you want to buy.

You can perform either simple or advanced searches from Google's main page, using the wildcards, modifiers, and Boolean operators discussed later in this foreword. Even easier, you can click the Advanced Search link and use the form-based features on Google's Advanced Search page. Here, you can fine-tune your search by language, date, file format, domain, or keyword. (If your search turns up pages from foreign-language sources, many times, Google provides a link for translating the page!)

Google also offers filtered searches via its SafeSearch feature. SafeSearch is a great way for kids to search the Web; when it's activated, inappropriate content is filtered from Google's normal search results. (You activate SafeSearch from the Advanced Search page or by clicking the **Preferences** link on Google's home page.) And, Google has its own search Toolbar that you can add to your desktop! Click the **more** link on Google's opening page to access links to the toolbar and learn more about other features and tools.

Google features some advanced search operators that can really optimize the results it returns:

- **cache:** shows the version of the web page that Google has in its cache. For example, cache:www.foxnews.com shows the snapshot of the Fox News web page that Google took when it indexed the site. (Note that there is no space between "cache:" and the site's address.)
- **link:** shows all sites that link to the specified site. Type **link:** immediately followed the by the site's address—no spaces.
- **related:** shows all pages that have similar data to the specified page.
- **info:** displays any information that Google has about the specified web page.
- **define:** displays a definition for the specified word.

- **stocks:** displays the current price of a stock for the specified ticker symbol.
- **site:** limits the search to a specific domain. For example, if you search for **caribbean cruise site:www.carnival.com**, Google searches only the www.carnival.com sites for "caribbean cruise."
- **allintitle:** shows only those pages that have in their title all the search words you entered. For example, allintitle: stand up comedy looks only for pages that have "stand," "up," and "comedy" in their titles. Without this, Google searches for pages that have the specified words anywhere in their title or text.
- **intitle:** shows only those pages that have the word directly following "intitle:" in their title. For example, intitle:holistic medicine finds only pages that have "holistic" in their title and "medicine" in their title or anywhere else on the page. Note that no space can be between "intitle:" and the key word.
- **allinurl:** shows only those pages that have in their URL (page address) all the search words you entered. For example, allinurl: jazz club looks only for pages that have "jazz" and "club" in their URL.
- **inurl:** shows only those pages that have the word directly following "inurl:" in their URL. For example, inurl:coaching soccer finds only pages that have "coaching" in their URL and "soccer" in their URL, title, or anywhere else on the page. Note that no space can be between "inurl:" and the keyword.

For additional details on how to properly enter these operators and limitations to them, go to http://www.google.com/help/operators.html.

Yahoo!

Yahoo! (www.yahoo.com) is one of the most popular sites on the entire Internet. It's a fully featured portal, complete with all sorts of services and information; it's also home of the most popular directory on the Web.

The Yahoo! directory contains close to two million hand-picked listings, organized by category. The Yahoo! directory is popular because it's so easy to use; you can search the directory for specific information, or just click through the hierarchy of topics until you find the site or page you need.

Yahoo! supplements its directory listings from results from its own search engine, which is pretty good. To access the directory results only, click the Directory link at the top of the search results page.

Everybody Else

When it comes to the "other" search sites, the best of the rest tend to be defined by their convenience rather than their results. That's because most of these other sites (such as Yahoo!, actually) are really full-service *portals* that offer search features, rather than dedicated search engines. (Of course, Yahoo! is a portal, too, so being a portal isn't necessarily a negative.)

That doesn't mean that these sites don't give good results; some are almost as good as Google, and most are better than Yahoo! But most of these sites probably wouldn't get much traffic at all if it weren't for all the other information and services they offer, so searching is definitely an auxiliary function.

Just what are these "other" sites? Here's an alphabetical list of the most popular of these second-level search options:

- **About.com (www.about.com)**—In the recent past About.com has become less of a general search site and more of a collection of articles and links. The site is organized into thousands of major categories managed by human "guides"; the site has a strong editorial voice and includes more than a quarter million proprietary articles.
- **AllTheWeb (www.alltheweb.com)**—AllTheWeb is the official site for the FAST search engine, which rivals Google in terms of size and speed. It also offers separate MP3, FTP, news, picture, and video searches.
- **AltaVista (www.altavista.com)**—AltaVista used to be a major search player, but revolving-door management resulted in a strategy du jour that tried to turn the site into (alternately) a consumer-level portal and a professional-level search tool. Today, AltaVista is back in the search engine–only business, with an index bigger than all its competitors save Google. In addition to normal text searches, AltaVista also offers audio, video, image, and news searches, and it includes a directory listing.
- **AOL Search (search.aol.com)**—AOL Search is a big deal only because it's the default search for America Online subscribers—and there are a lot of AOL subscribers. Search results are powered by Google. AOL Search also features a directory, listing sites by category, like Yahoo!
- **Ask Jeeves (www.ask.com)**—Ask Jeeves got its start as a "natural language" search engine that let you ask questions in plain English. That didn't work too well, so today Ask Jeeves offers more traditional search index results, as well as picture, product, and news searches.
- **HotBot (www.hotbot.com)**—HotBot used to be a major contender in the search engine wars but in recent years has been eclipsed by Google's strength and power. It's still a relatively big and relatively fast search engine, and also offers buttons for searching Lycos, Google, or Ask Jeeves.
- **LookSmart (www.looksmart.com)**—LookSmart is a directory that's a little larger than Yahoo! but not quite as big as the Open Directory. It employs paid editors to create its listings.
- **MSN Search (search.msn.com)**—This is the default search engine for Microsoft's MSN online service—and is also the default search engine when you use the search feature of the Internet Explorer web browser. Microsoft is in the process of introducing its own proprietary search technology, so look for big things from this site in the future.

- **Open Directory (www.dmoz.org)**—The Open Directory is the largest directory on the Web, with more than 3 million edited listings. The Open Directory is unique in that it's a public project. Through the collective efforts of more than 10,000 users, the Open Directory can catalog many more sites than can be cataloged by a small staff of paid workers, such as the staff at Yahoo!
- **Teoma (www.teoma.com)**—Most search sites gauge a website's relevance by the number of other sites that link to this site. In other words, when you search for a site, the site at the top of the list is the one that matches your search term and has the most sites linking to it. Teoma takes a different strategy, measuring relevance by the number of *like sites* that link to the website. This provides a much more targeted search that returns links to more relevant sites.

You'll also find a number of search engines that let you search multiple search engines and directories from a single page—which is called a *metasearch*. The top metasearchers include Beaucoup (www.beaucoup.com), CNET's Search.com (www.search.com), Dogpile (www.dogpile.com), GoGettem (www.gogettem.com), Mamma (www.mamma.com), MetaCrawler (www.metacrawler.com), WebCrawler (www.webcrawler.com), and WebTaxi (www.webtaxi.com).

Other Types of Search

While we're on the topic of professional search sites, you should make note of three other paid search sites. Dialog (www.dialogweb.com), Lexis-Nexis (www.lexis-nexis.com), and ProQuest Direct (www.proquest.com) are all well known and well regarded in the professional research world, and worth your attention if you want results beyond what you can achieve with Google or Yahoo!

If you'd rather not spend any cash, consider searching one of the Internet's many library-related websites. These sites include both the online arms of traditional libraries and the new generation of completely digital web-based libraries, such as Argus Clearinghouse (www.clearinghouse.net), Berkeley Digital Library SunSITE (sunsite.berkeley.edu), Internet Public Library (www.ipl.org), Library of Congress (lcweb.loc.gov), the New York Public Library Digital Library Collections (digital.nypl.org), and Refdesk.com (www.refdesk.com).

For that matter, several online encyclopedias are good sources for a variety of information. These sites include versions of traditional encyclopedias as well as completely new web-based encyclopedias, such as Encarta Online (encarta.msn.com), Encyclopaedia Britannica Online (www.eb.com), and Encyclopedia.com (www.encyclopedia.com). Many of these sites require paid subscriptions to access all available content.

If you're looking for people or places, consider using a dedicated online people finder site. These sites feature directories of phone numbers, street addresses, and email addresses, and include AnyWho (www.anywho.com), Bigfoot (www.bigfoot.com), InfoSpace (www.infospace.com), Switchboard (www.switchboard.com), The Ultimates (www.theultimates.com),

WhoWhere (www.whowhere.lycos.com), and Yahoo! People Search (people.yahoo.com).

HOW TO SEARCH

Every search site you visit works in a slightly different way, using a slightly different logic (and technological infrastructure) to perform its search operations. To master the intricacies of every single search site would appear to be an insurmountable task.

Fortunately, some common logic is used in almost all the major search sites. This logic is represented by a series of commands, modifiers, and operators that work in similar fashion across most search engines and directories. If you can master these basic skills, you'll be 80% of the way there in mastering each individual site.

Here are the general steps you should follow wherever you choose to search:

1. Start by thinking about what you want to find. What words best describe the information or concept you're looking for? What alternative words might some use instead? Can you *exclude* any words from your search to better define your query?

2. Determine *where* you should perform your search. Do you need the power of a Google or the better-qualified results of a Yahoo!? Should you use topic-specific sites instead of these general sites?

3. Construct your query. If at all possible, try to use modifiers and Boolean expressions to better qualify your search. Use as many keywords as you need—the more, the better. If appropriate (and available), use the site's advanced search page or mode.

4. Click the Search button to perform the search.

5. Evaluate the matches on the search results page. If the initial results are not to your liking, refine your query and search again—or switch to a more appropriate search site.

6. Select the matching pages that you want to view and begin clicking through to those pages.

7. Save the information that best meets your needs.

The bottom line? Think more *before* you search and spend more time learning from your results afterward.

FIVE TIPS FOR MORE EFFECTIVE SEARCHING

Savvy searchers approach their task quite seriously. Smart searching involves more than just entering a few keywords in a search box; thought needs to be given as to how to construct the query, what words to use, and what operators and modifiers can be employed to help narrow the search results.

If you want to improve your search results—both in terms of effectiveness and efficiency—learn from these tips, garnered from search professionals across the Internet.

Tip #1: Think Like the Creators

Websites are created by human beings. That isn't necessarily a good thing, because human beings are less than logical—and less than perfect.

To look for information created and managed by a human being, you have to *think* like that human being. Did the person writing about Internet Explorer call it *Internet Explorer* or *Microsoft Internet Explorer* or just *Explorer* or *IE* or *IE6* (including the version number), or was it simply called a *browser* or a *web browser* or even (somewhat incorrectly) a *navigator*? You see, any or all of those words and phrases could have been used to refer to the single thing you thought you were looking for. If all you do is look for *one* of these words or phrases, you could skip right over important information that happened to use a slightly different word or phrase.

The best search engines in the world can't anticipate human beings who use alternative words or (heaven forbid!) use the wrong words by mistake, or even misspell the right words. But you must somehow learn to overcome these human shortcomings if you're to find all the information you want to find.

You have to learn how to think like the people who created and organized the information you're looking for. If you're looking for old plastic model kits, you have to realize that some people call them *kits* and some call them *model kits* and some call them *plastic model kits* and some call them *models* and some call them by name (*Aurora model kits*) and some call them *ready-to-assemble kits* and some even have poor spelling skills and call them *modal kits*.

When you construct your queries, think through all the different ways people refer to the topic you're looking for. Think like the people who put the information together, like the people who create the web pages. *Visualize* the results you'd like to find and what they might look like on a web page. Then, and only then, should you construct your query, using the keywords and operators and modifiers you need to return the results you visualized. Master this skill, and you'll almost always find what you want.

Tip #2: Use the Right Words

When you construct your query, you do so by using one or more *keywords*. Keywords are what search engines look for when they process your query. Your keywords are compared to the index or directory of web pages accessible to the search engine; the more keywords found on a web page, the better the match.

You should choose keywords that best describe the information you're looking for—using as many keywords as you need. Don't be afraid of using too many keywords; in fact, using too *few* keywords is a common fault of many novice searchers. The more words you use, the better idea the search engine has of what you're looking for. Think of it as describing something to a friend—the more descriptive you are (that is, the more words you use), the better picture your friend has of what you're talking about.

It's exactly the same way when you "talk" to a search engine.

If you're looking for a thing or place, choose keywords that describe that thing or place, in as much detail as possible. For example, if you're looking for a car, one of your first keywords would, of course, be **car**. But you probably know what general type of car you're looking for—let's say it's a *sports* car—so you might enhance your query to read **sports car**. You might even know that you want to find a *foreign* sports car, so you change your query to read **foreign sports car**. And if you're looking for a classic model, your query could be expanded to **classic foreign sports car**. As you can see, the better your description (using more keywords), the better the search engine can "understand" what you're searching for.

If you're looking for a concept or idea, you should choose keywords that best help people understand that concept or idea. This often means using additional keywords that help to impart the meaning of the concept. Let's say you want to search for information about senior citizens, so your initial query would be **senior citizens**. What other words could you use to describe the concept of senior citizens? How about words such as *elderly, old,* or *retired*? If these words help describe your concept, add them to your search, like this: **senior citizens elderly old retired**. Trust me—adding keywords such as these will result in more targeted searches and higher-quality results.

One other point to keep in mind: Think about alternative ways to say what it is that you're looking for. (In other words, think about *synonyms*!) If you're looking for a *car*, you also could be looking for a *vehicle* or an *automobile* or an *auto* or *transportation*. It doesn't take a search guru to realize that searching for **car vehicle automobile auto transportation** will generate more targeted results than simply searching for **car**.

Tip #3: When You Don't Know the Right Words, Use Wildcards

What if you're not quite sure of which word form to use? For example, would the best results come from looking for *auto, automobile,* or *automotive*? Many search sites let you use *wildcards* to "stand in" for parts of a word that you're not quite sure about. In most instances, the asterisk character (*) is used as a wildcard to match any character or group of characters, from its particular position in the word to the end of that word. So, in our previous example, entering **auto*** would return all three words—*auto, automobile,* and *automotive*.

Wildcards are very powerful tools to use in your Internet searches. I like to use them when searching for people and I'm not totally sure of their names. For example, if I'm searching for someone whose name might be Sherry or Sheryl or Sherylyn, I just enter **sher*** and I'll get all three names back in my results. To take it even further, if all I knew is that the person's name started with an *s*, I'd enter **s***—and get back Sherry and Susan and Samantha as matches.

Wildcards also can return unpredictable results. Let's say you're looking for Monty Python, but you're not sure whether Monty is spelled *Monty* or *Montey*, so you search for **mon***. Unfortunately, this wildcard matches a large number of *mon* words, including Monty—and *money, monsters,* and *Mongolia*. In other words, if you go too broad on your wildcards, you'll find a lot more than what you were initially looking for.

Tip #4: Modify Your Words with +, -, and " "

A *modifier* is a symbol that causes a search engine to do something special with the word directly following the symbol. Three modifiers are used almost universally in the search engine community:

- + (always include the following keyword). Use the + modifier when a keyword *must* be included for a match. As an example, searching for **+monty +python** will return Monty Python pages or pages about pythons owned by guys named Monty—because any matching page must include both the words, but not necessarily in any order.

- - (always *exclude* the following keyword). Use the - modifier when a keyword must *never* be part of a match. For example, searching for **+monty -python** will return pages about guys named Monty but will *not* return pages about Monty Python—because you're *excluding* "python" pages from your results.

- " " (always search for the exact phrase within the quotation marks). Use the " " modifier to search for the precise keywords in the prescribed order. As an example, searching for **"monty python"** will return pages only about the British comedy troupe Monty Python—you're searching for both the words, in order, right next to each other.

Of these three modifiers, I find quotation marks to be the most useful. Whenever you're searching for an exact phrase, just put it between quotation marks, and you'll get more accurate results than if you listed the words individually.

Tip #5: Use OR, AND, and NOT in a Boolean Search

Modifiers are nice, but they're not always the most *flexible* way to modify your query. The preferred parameters for serious online searching are called *Boolean operators*.

Here are the most common Boolean operators you'll be able to use at most search sites:

- **OR** (A match must contain *either* of the words to be TRUE.) Searching for **monty OR python** will return pages about guys named Monty or pythons or Monty Python. With an OR search, you're searching for *either* monty *or* python, so both words don't have to appear on the same page together to make a match. The more words connected by OR operators, the less precise your search, but the more matches you'll receive.

- **AND** (A match must contain *both* words to be TRUE.) Searching for **monty AND python** will return Monty Python pages or pages about pythons owned by guys named Monty, but *not* pages that include only one of the two words. The more words connected by AND operators, the more precise your search, and the fewer matches you'll receive. (Remember, however, that in an AND search, you're searching for both the words, but *not necessarily in order.* If you want to search for both words in order, next to each other, you will want to search for the exact phrase by putting the phrase inside quotation marks, like this: **"monty python".**)

- **NOT** (A match must *exclude* the next word to be TRUE.) Searching for **monty NOT python** will return pages about guys named Monty but will *not* return pages about Monty Python—because you're *excluding* "python" pages from your results. (*NOTE: At some search engines, this operator must be used in the form AND NOT.*)

True Boolean searching also lets you use parentheses, much like you would in a mathematical equation, to group portions of queries together to create more complicated searches. For example, let's say you wanted to search for all pages about balls that were red or blue but not large. The search would look like this:

balls AND (red OR blue) NOT large

There are a handful of other Boolean operators, such as ADJ or NEAR or FAR, that have to do with *adjacency*—how close words are to each other. However, very, *very* few search engines use these adjacency operators, so you probably won't have much of an opportunity to use them.

Note that not all search sites allow Boolean searching, and even those that do might limit Boolean searching to their advanced search page. For example, Google lets you use the OR operator, but not AND or NOT. (With Google, you use + and - instead of AND and NOT.)

In addition, not every search site implements Boolean searching in exactly the same way. For example, some sites use AND NOT instead of the more common NOT operator. Because of these differences, it's a good idea to read the Help files at a search site before you attempt Boolean searching.

A Bonus Tip—Search for Other Places to Search

Here's a sixth tip, at no extra charge. Given that even the biggest search engines index only a fraction of the total Internet, sometimes you have to turn to proprietary sites to find specific data. For example, if you're looking for a recent news story, you're better off searching a newspaper or magazine's online archives than you are trying to find that information at Google or Yahoo! Or, if you're looking for medical information, you can probably find the information you want faster and easier at one of the many online health sites.

Here's a real-world example. My brother was thinking about buying a new home and wanted to know the original selling price of a particular home in a nearby neighborhood. In the offline world, this information is typically recorded by some county government office and sometimes listed in the local newspaper. It made sense, then, to search these entities online.

The problem is, we didn't know where to search. So, we turned to Google, and searched for **broward county property values**. (My brother lives in Broward County, Florida.) One of the first results was the Broward County Property Appraiser's Network, which

enabled my brother to search for properties by street address, owner name, or subdivision. Using this topic-specific site, my brother quickly found the information he was looking for—which he couldn't have found at Google or any of the other generalist search sites.

So, it pays to use your normal search engines to search for more specific directories of information. And the more specific the information you're looking for, the more likely it is you'll have to perform a "double search" in this fashion.

SAFE SEARCHING FOR CHILDREN

If you have children, be sure to monitor their activity on the Internet. Even when kids are not looking for adult content, it can pop up on screen and either upset them or encourage them to explore further. In either case, you, as a parent or guardian, need to be aware of what's going on. You should also encourage your children, especially young children, to use child-safe search directories. These directories enable you to search, but the search returns links to only those sites that are appropriate for kids. Here are some of the better web directories for kids:

- **Yahooligans!** at www.yahooligans.com is the child-friendly version of Yahoo! Parents and teachers can find useful tips at this site for ensuring their children and students explore the Internet safely.

- **Google Safe Search** at www.google.com/preferences.html enables parents and guardians to set options that filter out most of the undesirable content.

- **Ask Jeeves Kids** at www.ajkids.com provides a kid-friendly version of Ask Jeeves, enabling children to type in their questions and find safe answers. This site also features a reference library to help kids with their homework and some safe games to play when they need a break.

- **Education World** at www.education-world.com provides a directory of more than 500,000 resources that are safe for kids to explore. This site is more focused on teachers, but kids can find plenty of good information here.

- **Kids Click** at sunsite.berkeley.edu/KidsClick!/ is a simple web directory that organizes sites by categories, including Facts & Reference, Health & Family, and Popular Entertainments.

A FINAL WORD ABOUT SEARCHING

You hold in your hands one of the best available guides to the Internet. *Que's Official Internet Yellow Pages, 2005 Edition* catalogs thousands of the best sites on the Web, and is a great first place to look when you're searching for information. I especially like the fact that you can use this book to find the *best* sites in any given category; it's more than a simple site listing. There's a good chance you'll find exactly what you want listed in this book and never have to use a web search engine or directory.

If you do need to use a search site, however, be smart about it. Construct an intelligent and sophisticated query and use the same query on multiple search sites. Examine your results and learn from them to fine-tune your query. Don't limit yourself in where you search or how you search; try new sites and new methods with regularity.

Above all, maintain a sense of curiosity. Don't stop looking with the first page you visit. When you visit a web page, look for links on that page to other pages. Follow those links and then follow the next set of links. Always be on the lookout for good sources of information, no matter where they might come from. You'll be surprised just how much information you can find, if you're only open to finding it!

> Michael Miller is the author of Que's *Absolute Beginner's Guide to eBay, Absolute Beginner's Guide to Computer Basics, The Complete Idiot's Guide to Online Search Secrets, Bargain Hunter's Secrets to Online Shopping,* and more than 50 other bestselling how-to books. Mr. Miller is known for his ability to explain complicated subjects to the average consumer; he has established a reputation for practical advice, accuracy, and an unerring empathy for the needs of his readers.
>
> A publishing industry professional since 1987, Mr. Miller is currently president of The Molehill Group, offering writing and consulting services on a variety of topics. More information about Mr. Miller and The Molehill Group can be found at www.molehillgroup.com.

BLOGS, POP UPS, AND MOBILE INTERNET OPTIONS

by Joe Kraynak

The Web is constantly evolving, presenting users with new tools, new forms of expression, and new annoyances. Since the first edition of the *Internet Yellow Pages*, the Web has seen the introduction and explosive growth of blogs, easier mobile access via cell phones, and the escalation of unsolicited advertising via pop-up ads. The following sections provide the information you need to keep abreast of the latest, most significant developments and enhance your web browsing experience by reducing the number of ads that pop up on your screen.

BLOGS ARE WEBSITES, TOO

Short for *weblog, blogs* are personal journals that enable individuals to voice their opinions and insights, keep an online journal of their lives, or enable families and other groups to stay in touch. Blogging hosts provide all the tools and instructions a user needs to create a blog online and update it in a matter of minutes. This enables even the least tech-savvy web users to establish a presence on the Web.

In section B, look for the section on Blogging. We have included a list of blogging hosts that can help you create and manage your own blog, a list of blog directories that can help you sift through the thousands of excellent blogs already running on the Web, and lists of some excellent blogs that you might find intriguing.

BLOCKING POP-UPS

The commercialization of the Web has enhanced it a great deal by providing a profit motive that has generated the investment and innovation required to seed its growth. However, it has also inspired some companies to attempt to force-feed unsolicited advertisements to web users. Many of the most annoying ads are in the form of *pop-ups*, ads that automatically appear in separate windows or boxes on your computer screen.

Pop-ups come from two sources:

- Pop-up software and/or spyware that is installed on your computer with or without your knowledge. Some sites automatically install software on your computer that can track your web browsing habits, or they automatically call for pop-ups as you browse. Web users often unwittingly install adware on their own computers when they install a "free" game or other software from a website on their computers.
- Websites themselves often are programmed to generate pop-ups. You just open the site or click a particular link, and the pop-up appears.

If pop-ups are driving you crazy, you need to attack the problem using two utilities: a spyware remover and a pop-up blocker. You can download two freeware programs on the Web at Tucows (www.tucows.com) that, together, can prevent at least 90 percent of the pop-ups on your computer:

- **Spybot Search and Destroy** removes spyware. Install the software and run it every week or so to remove any spyware installed on your computer. (Ad-aware is another excellent utility, which you can download from www.lavasoftusa.com.) Research any companies that offer heavily advertised adware or spyware removal utilities before purchasing any of them. They are often scams.
- **12Ghosts Popup Killer** blocks most pop-ups that websites try to automatically display on your screen. The only mild inconvenience this adds is that if you click a link for a site and the link is set up to open in a separate window, 12Ghosts prevents it from opening; to get the window to open, you simply hold down the Ctrl key while clicking. The Google and MSN toolbars and other specialized browser add-on toolbars also offer pop-up blocking.

WIRELESS WEB PRIMER

More and more people are beginning to access the Web and their email by way of wireless connections, using their Internet-enabled cell phones or personal digital assistants (PDAs). With one of these handheld devices, a user can connect to a wireless-web–enabled site to obtain news, weather reports, stock prices, sports scores, driving directions, and other information from the Web. The following sections provide a brief introduction to the wireless web and explain how to access some of the more popular search sites, directories, and wireless-web–enabled sites on the Internet.

What Is the Wireless Web?

If you saw a cell phone or PDA advertisement that touted the device as *wireless Internet-ready* or *web-enabled*, you might envision a phone or PDA that displays miniature web pages in their full glory—colorful, graphic, animated, and interactive. If you purchased one of these devices based on this common misconception, you will be sorely disappointed.

The wireless web is anything but graphic and interactive. It is primarily text-based. When you connect to a wireless website using a cell phone, for example, a short menu appears on the screen, enabling you to pick a command by pressing a particular button on the phone's keypad. The phone's display is capable of displaying only a few lines of text at the very most.

When you "surf" the wireless-web, you are actually surfing a different, smaller Web than the Web you surf using your computer. The wireless Web comprises text-only web pages composed according to the Wireless Application Protocol (WAP) standards. These web pages are actually scaled-down, text-based versions of the pages you would access using your computer. The wireless Web is not designed for leisurely browsing of mass amounts of data, graphics, music clips, videos, and animation. It is more useful for obtaining small bits of data when you're on the go—sports scores, local weather updates, phone numbers and addresses you may have forgotten to bring along, headline news, stock prices, current flight information, driving directions, and so on.

Accessing the Wireless Web Via Menus

Most web-enabled cell phone providers feature their own directories of sites that you can access via a text-based menu system. For example, Sprint PCS web-enabled phones come complete with a mini web browser that you access using the phone's menu system. When you choose the browser or web option from the phone's opening menu, the browser appears and displays a menu that includes options such as 1. Google, 2. Bookmarks, 3. Shopping, 4. Finance, 5. News, and 6. Weather. Using your phone's keypad, you simply press the number next to the desired option and follow the trail of menus to the desired destination.

Accessing Wireless Web Directories and Search Engines

Many of the same companies that feature website directories and search engines feature wireless web versions of their services as well. These so-called *portals* filter out all the standard websites, providing you with links to only those sites that are wireless-web–friendly. The following list provides the names and addresses of some of the most useful wireless web portals:

- **Awooga** (wap.awooga.com) provides news, sports scores, entertainment suggestions, business news, weather reports, and a TV guide. Ananova, the company that manages the mobile Internet service directory, also offers WAP hosting and email.

- **MoPilot** (mopilot.com/wml/index.wml) displays an opening menu that contains options for accessing the dating pilot, search engine, chat areas and other fun stuff, mail, and a any account management tools you might need. Check in, it's free!

- **MSN Mobile** (mobile.msn.com) provides you with a scaled-down version of several of the Microsoft Network's most powerful tools, including MSN Messenger and Hotmail. MSN Mobile also features access to MSNBC News, ESPN sports, movie times, restaurant listings, a searchable yellow pages directory, and various online games.

- **Google Wireless** (Google or www.google.com/wml www.google.com/jsky or www.google.com/imode or www.google.com/palm) enables you to use Google's search engine to locate wireless websites that match your query. Choose Search Options and choose Mobile Web to search only wireless websites. Type your query using your wireless device's keypad; on a cell phone, press 0 for a space between words or a 1 to insert a quotation mark.

- **Yahoo! Mobile** (wap.yahoo.com) enables you to check your Yahoo! email, use Messenger, check your calendar or address book, obtain headline news and weather reports, and check stock prices and sports scores. Yahoo! mobile is best used in tandem with a standard computer. Use the computer to set up and manage your Yahoo! account and specify the type of content you want to access when you're on the road.

- **Newsvendor Headlines** (wap.newsvendor.com) features news and information from around the world. The opening menu contains options for checking out world elections, TV guide (Tuner), information about WAP in Ireland, the Google search engine, various news services, the BBC TV listings, and BBC radio listings.

- **go2online** (wap.go2online.com) is one of the more unique online directories, acting as a yellow pages directory for your cell phone or PDA. Do you want to know the movie times at a local theater? Then select Movies, pick the movie you want to see, enter your ZIP code to find out where it's playing, and select the desired theater to view a list of show times. go2online can help you locate malls and local businesses, find out the current weather conditions, and even locate restaurants. Businesses must pay to be listed, so this site is very commercialized, but it's pretty cool nevertheless.

- **Mobone.com** (wap.mobone.com) features a directory of more than 1,000 of the best wireless websites in the world. Mobone leans toward the European market, where the wireless web is more fully developed and used. This site is updated by users who submit and describe the sites.

- **m-central.com** (wap.m-central.com) is another wireless web directory that caters more to the European user. m-central.com features a collection of its favorite links (called m-links), m-go (for pulling up a specific page by entering its address), m-mylinks (for bookmarking your favorite pages), m-find (to search for wireless web pages), m-translate (to translate a word or phrase from a dozen different languages), m-cocktail (to view a recipe for your favorite alcoholic beverage), and dozens of other m-categories to search.

Although you can connect to and search many of these directories from your cell phone or PDA, a better way to use one of these directories or search engines is to search for and research wireless websites using your computer and then bookmark the sites on your cell phone or PDA. (For example, instead of using your cell phone to go to mobile.msn.com, use the web browser on your computer to go to mobile.msn.com, and search its mobile Internet directory to find sites.) This saves you the time and aggravation of using your cell phone or PDA's slow connection, dinky display, and clunky navigational tools to track down sites. Most wireless services charge by the minute, whether you use your device to talk on the phone or browse the Web.

Keeping Up on Late-Breaking News, Weather, and Sports

Many websites that support the wireless web also feature *alerts*—short text messages that deliver late-breaking news, weather, sports scores, and other tidbits to your phone while you're on the road. For example, if you're on a business trip and are following the World Series, you might want to check the latest scores as runners are batted in.

To receive alerts, you must register at the site that offers the alerts you want and specify your preferences. You typically do this using your computer. For example, at Yahoo! Mobile (mobile.yahoo.com), you log on and then click the Alerts link to display a list of items for which you can request alerts—Breaking News, Email, Auction, Sports, Horoscope, Stocks, and Weather. Next, you specify the device type (cell phone, PDA, or pager) and device name and the number of times you want to be alerted during the day (from 5 to 30 times). Yahoo! Mobile then prompts you to specify your phone's email address or your cell phone provider and your phone's 10-digit phone number. The service then sends your phone a confirmation code, which you must enter to confirm the alert. Other sites feature similar procedures for requesting alerts.

Top Wireless Websites

Although you can scan and browse wireless web directories and use wireless web search engines to track down hundreds of wireless-web–enabled sites, this book is dedicated to sorting out the fluff and pointing out the best sites on the Web. For a list of wireless-web-enabled sites, flip to section W and look for the "Wireless Websites" section.

HOW THIS BOOK IS DESIGNED

Here's a quick look at a few structural features designed to help you get the most out of the book.

[Best] This icon identifies THE best website in any given category. If you have time to visit only one site in a category, look for the Best of the Best!

($) The e-commerce icon identifies sites that process online transactions. If you're looking to purchase something from the Internet, be sure to look for listings with this icon.

★★★★★ The usability icon is designed to help you find the sites that are the easiest to navigate. Look for a ranking of five stars and you've found the most user-friendly of sites; find a site ranked one star and be prepared to spend some time finding the information you want.

The child-rating icons are designed to help you find sites that are appropriate for and appealing to children in specified age groups. Look for:

[0-8]
for kids 0–8,

[9-13]
for kids 9–13,

[14-18]
for teenagers 14–18,

[All]
for kids of all ages, or

Not for kids
for sites that include content inappropriate for children (violence, drugs, racism, or adult content).

If a site has no rating, it generally poses no risk to kids, but it won't appeal to most kids, either.

WARNING:

Although we made every attempt possible to identify child-friendly sites and sites that children should not visit, ratings are not always reliable. Sometimes a site will lose the right to use a particular address, and a company will purchase the address and use it for a site that contains content inappropriate for children. In addition, some sites may include links that point to other sites that have unsuitable content. Every parent should monitor his or her child's activity on the Internet and consider using monitoring or censoring software, such as CyberPatrol, to filter out inappropriate content. However, even censoring software is not foolproof.

ABORTION

abort.com

http://www.abortionclinic.org

★★★★

Not for kids

Reproductive choices and information. Users can search for providers of various reproductive services, including adoption, abortion (medical or surgical), or family planning.

Abortion Clinics On-Line

http://gynpages.com/ACOL/choice.html

★★★★★

Not for kids

Abortion Clinics On-Line (ACOL) is a directory service composed of providers of abortion and other reproductive healthcare. On this site, you'll find abortion rights articles, feedback on clinics, and a vehicle for listing a clinic in ACOL.

ACLU Reproductive Rights

http://www.aclu.org/issues/reproduct/hmrr.html

★★★★★

Not for kids

Plenty of information about the ACLU's position on reproductive freedom, including regularly updated news on abortion, court cases, legislation, recommended book list, ACLU materials on abortion, and links to other sites.

Ask Noah About: Pregnancy, Fertility, Infertility, Contraception

http://www.noah-health.org/english/pregnancy/pregnancy.html

★★★

14-18

Extremely comprehensive site provided by New York Online Access to Health (NOAH). Information is provided on virtually any and every topic or question you might have regarding reproduction and parenting. The site has a no-frills look but is well organized and chock-full of useful information.

EngenderHealth

http://www.engenderhealth.org/

★★★

Not for kids

This site focuses on a wide range of topics dealing with women's healthcare, including family planning, contraception, post-abortion care, and sexually transmitted diseases.

Ethics Updates

http://ethics.acusd.edu/Applied/abortion/

★★★★★

Not for kids

A comprehensive resource of information regarding current legislation on abortion, public opinion poll results and statistics, and links to other websites about abortion.

A
B
C
D
E
F
G
H
I
J
K
L
M
N
O
P
Q
R
S
T
U
V
W
X
Y
Z

Marie Stopes International

http://www.mariestopes.org.uk

★★★★★

👫 Not for kids

This site covers abortion and reproductive health from A to Z, including countries offering the Marie Stopes services; obtaining an abortion in the United Kingdom, Ireland, or overseas; and an abortion FAQ. Additional information covers breast healthcare, contraception, infectious diseases, and more.

NARAL Pro-Choice California

http://www.choice.org/

★★★★

👫 Not for kids

NARAL Pro-Choice California is dedicated to keeping voters in California informed about the reproductive rights they have in the state of California. Voters who want to support pro-choice legislation and candidates can visit this site for information.

National Abortion and Reproductive Rights Action League

http://www.naral.org/

💲

★★★★

👫 Not for kids

This site offers a pro-choice perspective on abortion and allows you to join the advocacy group. You can contribute your efforts and make donations to help ensure that women have a choice.

National Abortion Federation

http://www.prochoice.org/

★★★★★

👫 Not for kids

This site is divided into the following categories: Abortion Fact Sheets, If You're Pregnant, Voices of Choice, Clinic Violence, Media Center, Legal Issues, Get Involved, Take Action, Contributions, and Join NAF.

National Right to Life

http://www.nrlc.org/

★★★★

👫 Not for kids

This site offers a pro-life perspective on abortion and other right-to-life issues. This organization is one of the largest pro-life groups in the United States. The site includes information about what you can do to help support the cause and allows you to add your email address to its mailing list.

[Best] Planned Parenthood Federation of America, Inc.

http://www.plannedparenthood.org/

💲

★★★★★

👫 14-18

A source for sexual health information for women. Topics covered include abortion, birth control, brochures and products, parenting and pregnancy, pro-choice advocacy, women's health, and more. You'll also find links, fact sheets, FAQs, a guide for parents, job listings, and a nurse practitioner program. The online store offers books and pamphlets about Planned Parenthood as well as branded items such as T-shirts and coffee cups. Spanish translations are also available. Excellent content combined with an easily navigable format make this a hands-down choice for Best of the Best.

Planned Parenthood Golden Gate

http://www.ppgg.org

★★★★★

 14-18

Home of the. largest not-for-profit birth-control and reproductive healthcare organizations in the world. This site is devoted to helping educate women, men, and teenagers make responsible decisions about their own sexuality and reproductive choices. Learn more about Planned Parenthood's medical services and education programs, shop its secure online store, donate online, or learn how to become a Planned Parenthood activist.

Teenwire

http://www.teenwire.com/

★★★★★

 14-18

Planned Parenthood designed this site to answer the questions and concerns of teens and their families. It addresses birth control for teens, body changes, dating and relationships, staying healthy, testing your sex IQ, and helps you figure out what to do if you're pregnant.

A
B
C
D
E
F
G
H
I
J
K
L
M
N
O
P
Q
R
S
T
U
V
W
X
Y
Z

A
B
C
D
E
F
G
H
I
J
K
L
M
N
O
P
Q
R
S
T
U
V
W
X
Y
Z

ACTIVISM

AlterNet

http://www.alternet.org

★★★★

Online magazine dedicated to strengthening and supporting independent, alternative journalism. Site features news, investigative articles, and opinions on a range of topics covering everything from environmental and political issues to cultural trends, technology, and sexuality.

The Committee to Free Lori Berenson

http://www.freelori.org

★★★★

Lori Berenson is a United States citizen currently serving a 20-year sentence as a political prisoner in Cajamarca, Peru. This site provides information about Lori Berenson and her case and encourages visitors to help free Lori Berenson by donating money and joining the letter-writing campaign. This site also provides information about other political prisoners being held in Peruvian jails.

CorpWatch.org

http://www.corpwatch.org

★★★★★

Home of the CorpWatch.org corporation watchdog group, dedicated to ensuring that large corporations follow ethical business, political, and environmental practices. Visit this site to learn more about CorpWatch.org's campaigns, activities, issues, and research.

Freemuse

http://www.freemuse.org

★★★

Freemuse is an independent, international organization devoted to protecting freedom of expression for composers and musicians. Learn more about censorship in music and why Freemuse is of the opinion that censorship is detrimental. You can also learn more about what various artists think about censorship and how you can become more involved in the organization.

Best | Idealist.org

http://www.idealist.org

★★★★★

Home of Action Without Borders, a worldwide network of individuals and organizations devoted to promoting freedom and human dignity throughout the world. Features an excellent directory of activist organizations, lists of jobs and volunteer opportunities, available services and resources, and much more. If you're looking for ways to make the world a better place to live, check out this site.

PETA.org

http://www.peta.org

★★★★

Home of People for the Ethical Treatment of Animals (PETA), this site provides a list of action alerts—specific causes for which PETA needs your immediate support. Also features a list of PETA campaigns, information on how to live in greater harmony with animals, and a PETA mall where you can shop for books, clothing, and other items online.

Indybay.org

http://www.indybay.org/

★★★★★

This independent media center strives to provide independent media makers with an infrastructure for distributing their ideas, visions, and creations in whatever form of media they choose to express themselves. This group is also dedicated to helping fight against exploitation and oppression. Site features information and support for a wide variety of issues, including the environment, arts, poverty, globalization, and war.

They Rule

http://theyrule.net

★★★★

If you suspect that a handful of powerful corporate leaders control most of the world's resources, this site will confirm your suspicions. They Rule provides a virtual map of the most powerful corporate leaders in the world and shows how they are all interconnected in a mass conspiracy to control the world's economies and resources.

tolerance.org

http://www.tolerance.org

★★★★★

Dedicated to promoting greater understanding and tolerance of diverse groups of people, this site provides information on how to combat hate and intolerance in our daily lives. Includes articles on hate and hate crimes, studies on hate and racial bias, information on gay rights, and advice on how to track hate groups.

A World Connected

http://www.aworldconnected.com/

★★★★★

A World Connected is dedicated to fostering an environment that encourages open discussion about the need for true globalization of the world economy to help citizens of underdeveloped countries achieve some degree of prosperity. Site features articles, stories, and discussions. Visitors can also choose to get involved to make a difference.

A
B
C
D
E
F
G
H
I
J
K
L
M
N
O
P
Q
R
S
T
U
V
W
X
Y
Z

ADD/ADHD

A.D.D. Clinic

http://www.addclinic.com/

★★★★

Visit this site to learn more about the treatment of ADD/ADHD; associated conditions, such as Tourette's syndrome; ways to distinguish between ADHD and bipolar disorder; and many other issues surrounding the condition.

A.D.D. Warehouse

http://www.addwarehouse.com/

★★★★

This site features an online catalog of books, videos, training tools, games, and assessment products on ADD and ADHD and related problems for parents, educators, health professionals, children, and adults.

ADD FAQ

http://www3.sympatico.ca/frankk/body.html

★★★★

This frequently asked questions (FAQ) list addresses the background, testing, treatments, and resources dealing with Attention Deficit Disorder. This is a great place to start researching ADD.

ADD/ADHD Links Pages

http://user.cybrzn.com/~kenyonck/add/Links/

★★★★

This page offers myriad annotated and categorized ADD/ADHD links as well as a link to a page with all the links listed alphabetically. The list includes links to sites about different facets of living with ADD/ADHD.

ADDitude.com

http://www.additudemag.com/

★★★★★

Home of *ADDitude* magazine, where you can find information about ADD in adults and children from experts and from those who are dealing with this condition themselves or with a family member.

ADHDNews.Com

http://www.adhdnews.com/

★★★

This site offers a wide variety of information on ADD/ADHD for parents, adults, and teachers in coping with the disorder. The monthly online newsletter *ADDed Attractions* is available at the site. The site also offers additional information specifically for adults and parents, as well as access to the most up-to-date ADD/ADHD research.

CHADD: Children and Adults with Attention-Deficit/Hyperactivity Disorder

http://www.chadd.org/index.htm

★★★★

Sponsored by CHADD, the nation's leading nonprofit ADHD group, this site features the latest information about ADHD diagnosis, treatment, and legislation. You can find the answers to most of your questions in CHADD's FAQ, sign up for its newsletter, become a member, or even find out about local CHADD support groups.

Christian ADHD Alternative Treatment List

http://www.christianadhd.com

★★★★

This online support group and resource center provides information for those suffering from ADD, ADHD, and related psychological illnesses and for the guardians or parents of ADHD children. It provides a Christian perspective that reassures visitors that their illness is not a punishment for something they've done.

Internet Special Education Resources

http://www.iser.com/

★★★★

This site focuses on helping parents find local special education professionals who can help with learning disabilities and Attention Deficit Disorder assessment, therapy, advocacy, and other special needs.

Best National Attention Deficit Disorder Association

http://www.add.org/

⑤

★★★★★

This extremely comprehensive site on the topic of ADD includes the following categories: ADD Information, ABC's of ADD, ADD Research, ADD Treatment, ADD Coaching, Books on ADD, Family Issues, Kid's Area, Legal Issues, School & ADD, Support Groups, Teen's Area, Web Sites, Women & ADD, Work & Career, ADD Interviews, Creative Corner, Myth of the Week, Personal Stories, and ADD Book Store. If you or a loved one suffers from ADD or ADHD, bookmark this Best of the Best site now.

A
B
C
D
E
F
G
H
I
J
K
L
M
N
O
P
Q
R
S
T
U
V
W
X
Y
Z

A
B
C
D
E
F
G
H
I
J
K
L
M
N
O
P
Q
R
S
T
U
V
W
X
Y
Z

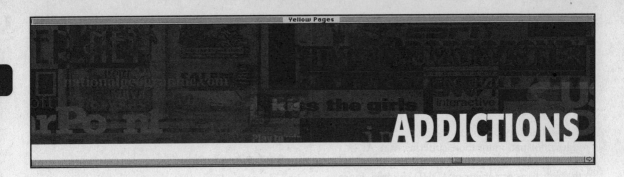

ADDICTIONS

Addictions & More

http://www.addictions.net/

★★★

Developed to provide information and education about addictions, discussions on the site center on drug and alcohol abuse, eating disorders, gambling, and ADD/ADHD. Within each area, you can find an abundance of information about coping and treating such illnesses. Identifying and treating denial, for example, is one topic addressed.

Web of Addictions

http://www.well.com/user/woa/

★★★

With a goal of providing accurate information about alcohol and other addictions, this site offers factual information about the prevalence of addiction, treatment, local meetings and groups, places to get help, and an in-depth look at related issues associated with addiction.

DRUGS

Drugnet

http://www.drugnet.net

★★★★

Dedicated to treating and preventing drug abuse, this site offers prototype assessment tools, online training, help in preparing research grants related to drug abuse, as well as access to databases with prevention and treatment guidelines and tools. Chat and discussion opportunities also are available.

Narcotics Anonymous

http://www.na.org

★★★★

Serving as a resource primarily for health professionals, Narcotics Anonymous provides plenty of resource material, including reports, periodicals, and access to a database of past publications and news.

EATING DISORDERS

American Anorexia Bulimia Association of Philadelphia

http://www.aabaphila.org/

★★★

Great resource for individuals confronting eating disorders. Also contains information for professionals who treat eating disorders and information for friends and families who are affected.

Anorexia Causes

http://www.noah-health.org/english/illness/mentalhealth/eatingdisorders.html#Anorexia

★★★

This site describes the factors likely to perpetuate anorexia nervosa and bulimia.

Anorexic Web

http://www.anorexicweb.com

★★★

👥 14-18

Designed and written by a recovering anorexic, the site aims to provide understanding to those fighting eating disorders through information, photos, and reflective poems. Unlike more medically oriented sites, this one speaks directly to those afflicted with eating disorders. And, because this site has been developed by a recovering anorexic, it provides a non-judgmental forum that is highly empathetic.

Binge Eating Disorders

http://www.niddk.nih.gov/health/nutrit/pubs/binge.htm

★★★★

This site addresses binge eating disorders by providing information to help identify the problem. Directions on getting help are also provided.

Body Image

http://www.gwu.edu/~cade/bodyimage.htm

★★★★

This site provides information on body image problems that are at the root of eating disorders. It also offers information on helping to deal with body image problems.

Center for Eating Disorders

http://www.eating-disorders.com/

★★★★

A resource for gathering information on eating disorders. Includes FAQs and discussion groups for the eating disorder sufferer. Questions asked here are answered.

Eating Disorder Recovery Online

http://www.edrecovery.com

★★★★

Offers the latest information on eating disorders, including what they are, who has them, what the causes are, what the warning signs are, and what to do if you or someone you know shows signs of having an eating disorder; also provides a set of guidelines for family members. The site offers a quiz that indicates whether you, a relative, or a friend might be suffering from an eating disorder. Also offers an online consulting service for those who do not have access to traditional therapy.

Eating Disorder Site

http://closetoyou.org/eatingdisorders/

★★★★

This site provides information to help recognize if you or someone you know has a problem with eating. At the end of each brief article is a list of local organizations available to help individuals cope and treat their illness.

Eating Disorders Association (EDA)

http://www.edauk.com/

★★★★

Very informative site for both young and older people who suffer from or are interested in learning more about eating disorders. Provides a cool interactive flip-card tool for determining if you have an eating disorder and provides general information about the various eating disorders. Features some poetry and other inspirational material plus links to other resources.

Eating Disorders Resource Centre

http://www.uq.net.au/eda/documents/start.html

★★★★

This site provides information about eating disorders and periodic newsletters about treatment options.

IAEDP: International Association of Eating Disorders Professionals

http://www.iaedp.com/

★★★

This site serves as a helpful resource for professionals who treat patients suffering from eating disorders. The site offers a calendar of events, links, and conference opportunities. You can also learn how to become IAEDP certified.

Mental Health Net

http://eatingdisorders.mentalhelp.net/

★★★★

Learn about symptoms, treatments, online resources, organizations, and research materials related to eating disorders.

A
B
C
D
E
F
G
H
I
J
K
L
M
N
O
P
Q
R
S
T
U
V
W
X
Y
Z

A
B
C
D
E
F
G
H
I
J
K
L
M
N
O
P
Q
R
S
T
U
V
W
X
Y
Z

The Renfrew Center Foundation

http://www.renfrew.org/

★★★★

Get answers to your questions about eating disorders, downloadable educational materials, information about treatment options and current research studies, and view a list of recommended books and other resources. You can even submit a question online.

 Best ### Something Fishy

http://www.something-fishy.org/

⑤

★★★★★

A site chock-full of information related to symptoms, treatments, variations on eating disorders (EDs), and physical problems as a result of EDs, as well as advice for doctors, friends, and family members to help those struggling with the disorder. You can buy music and other small gift-type items. A percentage of the proceeds from every sale goes to support nonprofit organizations.

Stay Healthy

http://www.uhs.net/wcservices/womens/
psychological/eatingdisorders/eating.htm

★★★

An excellent information resource for anorexia and bulimia disorders as well as other health-related topics. A calendar of events and classes is also provided.

STOP SMOKING

Action on Smoking and Health (ASH)

http://ash.org/

★★★

ASH is the nation's oldest and largest antismoking organization, providing visitors to its site with information on nonsmokers' rights, the health risks of smoking—to smokers and nonsmokers—and legislative updates. The tone is definitely antismoking, with a slant toward lawsuits to protect nonsmokers' rights. This is a membership-based site.

CDC's Tobacco Info-Quit Site

http://www.cdc.gov/tobacco/quit/quittip.htm

★★★★

Five tips on quitting, plus plenty of links to related information, including Surgeon General's reports, educational resources, smoking-cessation tools, and health databases.

Definition of Nicotine Dependence

http://www.mayoclinic.org/ndc-rst/

★★★★

This page, part of the Mayo Clinic's site, provides a clear explanation of nicotine dependence and provides several options to help you quit.

How to Quit Smoking

http://www.hoptechno.com/book43.htm

★★★

A booklet on how to stop smoking published by the U.S. Department of Health and Human Services.

National Center for Tobacco-Free Kids

http://tobaccofreekids.org/

★★★★

 9-13

Information on anti-tobacco campaigns, including "Mission Possible," a call to kids to play an active role in the antismoking campaign. The site also presents press releases and news items, fact sheets, and information on each state's efforts against tobacco.

Nicorette

http://www.nicorette.com

⑤

★★★★★

From the makers of Nicorette gum, this site offers a quiz, hints on how to quit, and FAQs. You can purchase Nicorette online here.

Nicotine Anonymous

http://www.nicotine-anonymous.org

⑤

★★★★

Nicotine Anonymous provides support for people wanting to quit smoking and live free of nicotine.

Quit Smoking Cigarettes

http://www.megalink.net/~dale/quitcigs.html

★★★

Links and text on the misery of smoking, nicotine addiction, stories from people who have quit smoking, and more.

Quit Smoking Support.com

http://www.quitsmokingsupport.com

★★★★★

This site lists more than 40 sites that offer tips and articles to help quit smoking. Recommended stop-smoking products are advertised on this page.

The QuitNet

http://www.quitnet.org/qn_main.jtml

★★★★

QuitNet provides a collection of online resources, news, and guides for individuals who want to quit smoking. You can buy T-shirts and sweatshirts with the QuitNet logo. Links to your favorite retail for prescription drugs to help you quit smoking are also provided.

QuitSmoking.com

http://www.quitsmoking.com/

★★★★

Billed as "The Quit Smoking Company," QuitSmoking.com is the place to go for smoking-cessation products. Here, you will find the largest collection of nicotine substitutes, vitamins, books, tapes, and even T-shirts. This site also features stop-smoking methods, articles, and FAQs.

Smoke-Free Families

http://www.smokefreefamilies.org/

★★★

Smoke-Free Families is dedicated to encouraging and helping pregnant women to stop smoking. Provides a link for emailing a supportive card to a pregnant smoker.

SUBSTANCE ABUSE AND RECOVERY

12 Step Cyber Café

http://www.12steps.org/

★★★★

Find recovery resources for addictions of all kinds. This site focuses on the 12 Step program made famous by Alcoholics Anonymous. The 12 Steps are applicable to any type of addiction, and this site helps you to see that and apply it in your situation.

Addiction Resource Guide

http://www.addictionresourceguide.com/

★★★★

The primary purpose of this site is to provide a comprehensive listing of addiction treatment facilities, but the online guide to treatment options and alternatives is a useful resource as well.

Al-Anon

http://www.al-anon.org/

★★★★

Al-Anon is a self-help recovery program for family and friends of alcoholics. Included here is a program overview and a list of contacts and events. Subscribe to *The Forum*, Al-Anon's monthly magazine, at this site.

Alateen

http://www.al-anon.org/alateen.html

★★★★

 9-13

Alateen provides support and information for young people whose lives have been affected by someone else's alcoholism. Includes information on meetings, a list of literature, and facts about Alateen.

A B C D E F G H I J K L M N O P Q R S T U V W X Y Z

A
B
C
D
E
F
G
H
I
J
K
L
M
N
O
P
Q
R
S
T
U
V
W
X
Y
Z

Alcoholics Anonymous

http://www.alcoholics-anonymous.org/

★★★★★

From the home page, choose the English, Spanish, or French version of the text, and continue. You'll find 12 questions you can answer to help determine whether AA might be helpful. You'll also find local contact information and a special section for professionals.

Betty Ford Center

http://www.bettyfordcenter.org/

★★★★

Betty Ford Center is the first and most famous of addiction treatment centers. Here, you'll find information about the inpatient and outpatient programs at the Betty Ford Center. You can also find information on a codependency treatment plan, along with news of upcoming events.

Cenikor Foundation, Inc.

http://www.cenikor.org/

★★★

A nonprofit organization with a focus on assisting people in developing skills they need to live a lifestyle free from substance abuse. Provides free residential, treatment, education, and prevention services to people over the age of 18.

Close to Home Online

http://www.pbs.org/wnet/closetohome/

★★★

👥 14-18

An in-depth web companion to the Bill Moyer's PBS series on addiction. It includes addiction information, personal accounts, legislative news, a chat room, and a listing for resources and help.

D.A.R.E.

http://www.dare.org/

★★★★★

 All

This is the home page of the Drug Abuse Resistance Education (DARE) organization. It offers information for kids, parents, and educators. Find out how law enforcement is cooperating in your community and elsewhere to stop drugs. This is a family-friendly site.

Drinking: A Student's Guide

http://www.mcneese.edu/community/alcohol/help.html

★★★★

👥 14-18

This is a fun site about a serious topic. Aimed at high school and college students, the site presents the facts about binge drinking, alcohol and health, and alcohol and drugs. After reading all the facts, you can do the self-assessment to determine whether you're at risk. If so, the site offers an extensive list of resources to contact.

DrinkWise

http://www.med.umich.edu/drinkwise/

★★★★

An educational program that helps people reduce alcohol consumption. Includes a self-evaluation form and phone number to contact DrinkWise for more information.

Get It Straight: The Facts About Drugs

http://www.usdoj.gov/dea/pubs/straight/cover.htm

★★★★★

 9-13

A drug-prevention book targeted at kids, put out by the Drug Enforcement Administration. Provides serious resources and information about the laws related to drugs and drug abuse.

Grant Me the Serenity...

http://open-mind.org/

★★★★

Dedicated to individuals who are wrestling with all types of addictions, this site provides hundreds of links to the best resources on the Web. It also features motivational quotes, an online bulletin board, lists of support groups, and an online store where you can purchase recovery-related books and gifts.

Indiana Prevention Resource Center

http://www.drugs.indiana.edu/

★★★★

Indiana University's Prevention Resource Center is a clearinghouse for prevention-oriented technical assistance and information about alcohol, tobacco, and other drugs. The site has statistics, publications, a search engine, and a library.

Join Together Online

http://www.jointogether.org/

★★★★

Join Together Online is a national resource center for communities working to reduce substance abuse and gun violence. The site includes policy alerts, news updates, discussion boards, fact sheets, a calendar of events, a directory of national organizations, and more.

The Marijuana Anonymous World Services

http://www.marijuana-anonymous.org/

★★★★

Learn the facts about marijuana addiction. Take the quiz to find out whether you need help. Learn the 12 steps for recovery. Benefit from the shared experiences of others. Find out how to join Marijuana Anonymous.

National Institute on Drug Abuse

http://www.nida.nih.gov/

★★★★★

The National Institute on Drug Abuse, established in 1974, works on research and programs to prevent and treat drug addiction. The site features information on the organization including its programs and publications on drug abuse.

Partnership for a Drug-Free America

http://www.drugfreeamerica.org/

★★★★

👥 9-13

A searchable database of drug information makes this site one of the best places to start researching addictions to specific drugs. It also includes answers to frequently asked questions about drugs, a section of advice for parents, and a page specifically directed at teens.

Prevention Online

http://www.health.org/

★★★★★

👥 9-13

Provides information for those people battling substance abuse, or who know someone battling substance abuse. Press releases, publications, forums, and calendars of upcoming events are all available, including several publications for kids age 8 and older, though parents or teachers may want to go online to retrieve the material.

Sober Vacations International

http://www.sobervacations.com/

★★★

Two brothers, one a recovering alcoholic and the other recovering from drug use, sponsor sober group vacations for others. Check it out and join them for fun in the sun that includes speakers and workshops.

Sobriety and Recovery Resources

http://www.recoveryresources.org/

★★★★

A great Alcoholics Anonymous (AA)–related site with many personal stories from individuals struggling with addiction and recovery, as well as treatment information and encouragement. Links to online recovery resources are helpful, as is the listing of local addiction treatment organizations.

A
B
C
D
E
F
G
H
I
J
K
L
M
N
O
P
Q
R
S
T
U
V
W
X
Y
Z

ADOPTION

Adopting.com

http://www.adopting.com

★★★

The goal of this site is to assist prospective adoptive parents with the adoption process. This includes providing information on making contact with adoption agencies, support groups, and access to a waiting-child database.

Adopting.org

http://www.adopting.org/

★★★★

Billed as a community adoption site, it allows visitors to gain access to information on the adoption process, resources, and available children and families interested in adoption.

Adoption

http://www.adopt.net

★★★★

Read frequently asked questions regarding adoption, look at profiles of prospective adoptive parents, and learn more about the process of adoption at this site, provided by an attorney who specializes in helping families adopt.

Adoption Advocates: Adoption Policy Resource Center

http://www.fpsol.com/adoption/advocates.html

★★★

Provides federal and state legislative news and analysis (including statutes and court decisions), adoption assistance (subsidy) information resources, legal resources, and advocacy sources.

Adoption Benefits: Employers as Partners in Family Building

http://www.adopting.org/employer.html

★★★★★

Provides information about company-sponsored adoption benefit plans, including who is eligible for benefits, how company-sponsored benefit plans actually work, what expenses are covered and when they are paid, what types of adoption benefit plans cover, and whether adoption leaves of absence are available from the workplace. Also provides a list of companies that offer adoption benefits, as well as other adoption-assistance programs. If you are considering adopting a child, this is a great place to go to learn about company-sponsored benefits.

Adoption.com

http://www.adoption.com/

★★★★

📰 Not for kids

Offers information about alternatives to abortion, such as adoption and single parenting, and provides chat rooms and counseling. You can buy books about adoption and childrearing, as well as toys and other items for your adopted child.

Adoption Counselor

http://www.adoptioncounselor.com

★★★

Visitors can search. by state to find a qualified adoption counselor at this site, as well as participate in online chats, and link to other adoption-related sites to find adoption agencies and attorneys. You can buy toys, books, jewelry, and many other items from the online store.

Adoption International Program

http://www.adoption-service.com

★★★

Adoption International Program is an adoption agency specializing in the placement of children from Russia, Romania, Uzbekistan, and other Eastern European countries. The site provides information about this international adoption program and the process of adopting a child from one of these countries.

Adoption on the Usenet

http://www.webcom.com/kmc/adoption/faqs.html

★★★

This comprehensive site contains tons of important information for those searching for birth parents, children, or siblings. You can find book lists (with reviews), legislative information, newsgroups (such as alt.adoption), and a list of support groups (broken down by country and state). This site also contains links to must-read information if you are considering the use of a searcher in your quest.

Adoption Search

http://www.adoptionsearch.com

★★★★

This adoption-focused search engine enables users to quickly locate information on adoption resources, as well as parenting, birth registries, health, infertility, and pregnancy.

Adoption Travel

http://www.adoptiontravel.com

★★★★

Potential adoptive parents intending to adopt internationally will find the links to country-specific travel and adoption sites very helpful. Advice from parents who have already adopted on what to bring, what to expect, and so on is especially useful.

AdoptioNetwork

http://www.adoption.org/

★★★

Volunteers drive this information resource for the adoption community. Provides information that encompasses the broad scope of adoption, including lists of agencies and photo listings, legal resources, information about international adoptions, FAQs for children about adoption, a walk-through of the adoption home study process, and much more.

Adoption Shop

http://www.adoptionshop.com/

★★★★★

Billed as the world's largest adoption store, this site specializes in books, videos, and tapes about the adoption experience, but it also carries essential kids stuff, such as baby clothes, games, and toys. A pay service enables you to perform a search for a child's (or adult's) birth parents.

Adoption Today Magazine

http://www.fosteringfamiliestoday.com/adoptinfo.html

★★★★

Adoption magazine that offers a wide variety of articles covering everything from adopting a child to building a multicultural atmosphere in your home where children from all countries will feel welcome. This site gives nothing away for free, but it does enable you to sign up for a subscription to the magazine and order back issues online.

Alliance for Children

http://www.allforchildren.org/

★★★

Provides information about the Ecuador Adoption Program, the Romania Adoption Program, the China Adoption Program, and programs in many other countries. Also includes a list of criteria that adoptive parents must satisfy.

A
B
C
D
E
F
G
H
I
J
K
L
M
N
O
P
Q
R
S
T
U
V
W
X
Y
Z

A
B
C
D
E
F
G
H
I
J
K
L
M
N
O
P
Q
R
S
T
U
V
W
X
Y
Z

AMREX: Adoption Management Resource EXpertise

http://www.amrex.org/

★★★

This multiagency adoption organization has pooled its resources and database of waiting children to help professional adoption experts locate children for their clients. In addition to providing tools for adoption professionals, AMREX provides a referral service to help adoptive parents locate an adoption agency.

Holt International Children's Services

http://www.holtintl.org/

★★★★

Provides information and support for birth parents and adoptive parents, information and resources for professionals in the adoption field, and links to other websites that provide information about adoption. The site is very current thanks to weekly updates. You can buy books, T-shirts, and calendars through the online store.

Independent Adoption Center: Open Adoptions for Birth Mothers and Parents

http://www.adoptionhelp.org/

★★★

The site boasts that the Independent Adoption Center is the largest nonprofit open-adoption program in the United States, with offices on the West Coast, the East Coast, and the Midwest, and almost two decades of experience with open adoption. The site is inviting and offers a wealth of information and resources about open adoption.

National Adoption Center

http://www.adopt.org/

★★★★

A national program, in the United States, that pairs up homeless children with parents who are looking to adopt. Also includes information on legislation, the adoption process, lists of adoption agencies and organizations, conferences and seminars, and other material pertinent to all aspects of adoption. The Waiting Children link displays pictures and biographies of children currently waiting for a family to adopt them.

National Adoption Clearinghouse

http://naic.acf.hhs.gov/

★★★★★

Managed by the U.S. Department of Health and Human Services Administration for Children & Families, this site features a collection of information and resources for all aspects of the adoption process. Here you can find a national adoption directory, a list of adoption professionals, information on tracking down birth parents, information on how to prepare to become an adoptive parent, and much more. This site's basic design makes it easy to access its vast store of information, earning it our choice as Best of the Best.

National Council for Single Adoptive Parents

http://www.adopting.org/ncsap.html

★★★

The National Council for Single Adoptive Parents, a member of the Joint Council on International Children's Services and the North American Council on Adoptable Children, was founded by single adoptive parents in 1973 to inform and assist single people in the United States who want to adopt. This site contains some information about and a link to order the group's publication, *The Handbook for Single Adoptive Parents*. Site also includes a brief FAQ.

Our Chinese Daughters

http://www.ocdf.org/

★★★★

This site is dedicated to supporting any and all efforts (travel grants, scholarships, and so on) that encourage single mothers to adopt from China and that benefit the children they adopt.

Para Mim

http://www.limiar.org/para_mim/welcome.html

★★★★

👫 All

Correspond online with adopted kids from Brazil. Para Mim is a service of LIMIAR, an organization that advocates and assists Brazilian children who need families, and unadoptable children with their various needs.

Precious in HIS Sight (Internet Adoption Photo Listing)

http://www.precious.org/

★★★★

This site contains a photo listing of more than 500 children from 15 countries available for international adoption, as well as a collection of adoption information (including a FAQ) and links to other sites for adoptive parents. You can sort the children in the listings by multiple criteria. In addition, you can select to view a list of agencies with accounts and email all of them at once.

Treasure Maps

http://www.amberskyline.com/treasuremaps/

★★★

Great site with many tools for searching and tracking your family history—especially useful for searching for birth families. This site contains helpful tools, a tutorial on the U.S. federal census, research outlines, and collections of compiled and original family records.

A
B
C
D
E
F
G
H
I
J
K
L
M
N
O
P
Q
R
S
T
U
V
W
X
Y
Z

A
B
C
D
E
F
G
H
I
J
K
L
M
N
O
P
Q
R
S
T
U
V
W
X
Y
Z

Yellow Pages

ADVICE

All Experts

http://www.allexperts.com

★★★★

Ask a question of a volunteer expert on virtually any topic, from arts and entertainment to relationships to business, and more for free. This site is organized by category, so you can quickly browse for the desired topic and then submit your question. The site covers virtually every topic—from automobiles to television shows. If you can't find your answer here, you may not be able to find it anywhere!

Ask a Chef

http://www.askachef.com/

★★★★

When you need some professional cooking advice, turn to Ask a Chef, where you can read through recent questions and answers or post a question to have it answered via email. This site also features plenty of original recipes.

Ask Dr. Tracy

http://www.loveadvice.com/

★★★

This site is the home of Dr. Tracy Cabot's online encyclopedia of answers to all your questions concerning intimate relationships. Learn when to try to work out your problems and when to let go; how to find the right person for you; how to build a loving relationship; and much more. Dr. Tracy is a world famous author who has appeared on *Oprah* and several other TV talk shows.

Ask an Expert

http://www.askanexpert.com

★★★

 All

At this site, find an expert who has volunteered to answer your questions. Search the site for an appropriate expert to respond to your query and then be connected to the expert's website to learn more about your area of interest, as well as ask your question.

Ask the Hog

http://www.hogwild.net/askhog/askhog.htm

★★★

👥 14-18

Ask the Hog takes a lighthearted approach to advice columns. Yes, the Hog does answer personal questions and provides some sage advice, but the Hog pulls no punches, and most Hog opinions are packed with punchy, politically incorrect, and pungent language. Not for prudes or young children.

〔Best〕 Daily Candy

http://www.dailycandy.com/

★★★★★

👥 All

For advice on fashion, food, and fun, turn to Daily Candy, where you can find cutting edge information on the current social scene. Here, you can learn which jeans are the hottest on the market, where to score a pair of the hippest shoes that haven't yet hit the market, what to read, which movies are must-sees, and which concerts to attend. Read about the latest beauty tips and hairstyles. Sign up for the newsletter to get the latest advice via email or visit this site to explore some of the slightly older recommendations. This well-designed site is packed with good, solid advice that makes it our pick for Best of the Best.

Dear Abby

http://www.uexpress.com/dearabby/

★★★★

 14-18

Write to Dear Abby, read her latest column, or search past columns in the archive at this site, where you also can buy books by Abigail Van Buren.

Dr. Laura

http://www.drlaura.com/main/

$

★★★★★

When you're having trouble with a relationship, see what Dr. Laura has to say about it, and don't expect a sugar-coated answer! This popular radio and TV personality shoots straight from the hip to tell you just what *you* need to do to fix your relationship. Here, you can learn more about Dr. Laura, read her advice, listen to her show, get tips for working at home, shop online for Dr. Laura's books and other merchandise, and much more.

Dr. Ruth Online!

http://www.drruth.com

★★★★

 Not for kids

Ask Dr. Ruth your own questions about sex, or take a look at recent questions posed by others. You can also find a sex tips section and the results of sex polls.

drDrew

http://www.drdrew.com/

$

★★★★★

 14-18

Learn more about sex, health, and relationships, from the co-host of MTV's *Loveline*, Dr. Drew. Submit questions, and participate in online communities with concerns about a wide range of personal health issues.

Everything2

http://www.everything2.com/

★★★★

 Not for kids

At Everything2, you can find discussions on every topic imaginable—some light and funny, some deep and intriguing, and some just plain pointless.

Experts Exchange

http://www.experts-exchange.com/

★★★★★

Computer experts who want to barter their expertise for the knowledge of others in the field should check out this site. Here, you can offer advice to earn points that enable you to "buy" advice from other experts.

Femina

http://femina.cybergrrl.com/

$

★★★★★

This women-only site features information, resources, and advice dealing exclusively with female issues. The site is a web directory of women-friendly sites that contain information primarily targeting the female crowd. Here you can check out Femina's site of the month, read the latest women's news, submit an article, check the calendar, or add an event.

Go Ask Alice!

http://www.goaskalice.columbia.edu/

★★★★

 Not for kids

Alice! is the Columbia University Health Service's online nurse, essentially. Designed to provide health information, Ask Alice can field questions for most health-related topics. You can Ask Alice! a health question, search past Q&As, or search Alice!'s database for health information on your own. Some areas of this site are appropriate for children, but others are strictly off limits.

A
B
C
D
E
F
G
H
I
J
K
L
M
N
O
P
Q
R
S
T
U
V
W
X
Y
Z

A
B
C
D
E
F
G
H
I
J
K
L
M
N
O
P
Q
R
S
T
U
V
W
X
Y
Z

KnowledgeHound

http://www.knowledgehound.com/

★★★★★

This searchable directory of how-to sites is the ultimate guide for the do-it-yourselfer. Here you can learn everything from how to care for a baby to how to cook with solar energy. Categories include Animals, Cooking, Environment, Arts & Humanities, Money & Law, and much more.

The Women's Network

http://www.ivillage.com/work/boards/

★★★★

Visit the Women's Network to get advice from online experts on the topics of relationships, sex, and career at this site, as well as join in chats and message boards for more discussion.

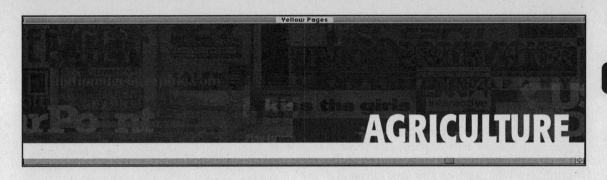

AGRICULTURE

Agricultural Network Information Center (AgNIC)

http://www.agnic.org/

★★★★

Listing of resources and activities for the agricultural community. The site provides links to universities and institutions providing online reference assistance, including listservs, newsgroups, products and services, and frequently asked questions.

Agriculture in the Classroom

http://www.agclassroom.org/

★★★★

 All

A fun website designed to help kids and teachers learn more about the critical role of agriculture in our economy and society. A great place for teachers to learn about hands-on projects for teaching students about agricultural topics.

[Best] @griculture Online

http://www.agriculture.com/

$

★★★★★

Read legislative news, market news, news from around the world, technology news, weather forecasts, and more. Clearly organized and visually attractive, this site is packed with all the most current information available for farmers and others who are devoted to agriculture and agribusiness. If you're a farmer or in the farming industry, be sure to bookmark this Best of the Best site, and visit it daily.

AgWeb

http://www.agweb.com/

★★★★

Information on farming industry topics, headline news (updated twice daily), lists of upcoming industry events, and a variety of farm-related links, including a list of handy links to weather forecast sites. Includes industry financial information such as investment news.

American Dairy Science Association (ADSA)

http://www.adsa.org

★★★★

This site posts information about association meetings and articles from the *Journal of Dairy Science* (including an index that is searchable by author or content) and instructions on submitting manuscript for publication. Also includes links to other dairy- and agriculture-related sites.

American Egg Board

http://www.aeb.org

★★★★

 All

Devoted to egg lovers, this site offers recipes, FAQs about eggs, nutrition information, and industry facts and statistics. Excellent site for both kids and adults.

American Farm Bureau: Voice of Agriculture

http://www.fb.com/

★★★★

Provides links to agricultural, ranching, and farm-related sites, as well as state and county farm bureaus. Also offers links to national and rural news, educational materials, agricultural legislation, and bulletin boards where members of the agricultural community share information and ideas.

A
B
C
D
E
F
G
H
I
J
K
L
M
N
O
P
Q
R
S
T
U
V
W
X
Y
Z

American Farmland Trust

http://www.farmland.org/

★★★★

The American Farmland Trust is concerned with preserving farmland and wildlife habitats. The trust's site includes statistics on the loss of farmland to urban sprawl and details on what users can do, as well as links to related resources and other organizations. The site is kept very current.

Beef Home Page

http://www.beef.org/

★★★★

This is the home page of the National Cattlemen's Beef Association. The site is inviting and oriented primarily toward consumers interested in beef information, although the site contains information that might interest people in the industry. Categories of information include Nutrition, Kitchen (cooking), Food Safety, Shopping, Beef Production, Research, New Products, and News.

Ceres Online

http://www.ceresgroup.com/col/

★★★★

Ceres Online specializes in providing information for agriculture professionals. The site's search functions enable users to connect to other professionals in the agriculture industry. Other site features include a calendar database that lists hundreds of upcoming events and weather maps that include world, national, and hot-spot information.

The Coop: Resources on Raising Chickens

http://www.the-coop.org/index.html

★★★

Your key to the online poultry community, The Coop is an extensive resource center on raising chickens, ducks, geese, turkeys, and other domestic and wild birds. The Coop also includes a bulletin board where you can read questions and replies dealing with several topics on raising poultry.

DirectAg.com

http://www.directag.com

★★★★★

Farmers looking for information on ag news, up-to-date ag prices, and weather should stop by DirectAg. The Experts tab provides options for submitting a question to the Virtual Dairy Expert or the Livestock Advisor. The Finances tab enables you to apply for a farm loan online.

Economic Research Service (USDA)

http://www.ers.usda.gov/

★★★★

Provides economic and social science information and analysis for public and private decisions on agriculture, food, natural resources, and rural America. It features reports, catalogs, publications, USDA data statistics, and employment opportunities. Also offers other agriculture-related links. This site is updated every weekday.

Farm Safety 4 Just Kids

http://www.fs4jk.org/

★★★★

 All

This site advocates farm safety and the prevention of farm-related injuries. Here, you'll find information on membership and becoming a sponsor, chapter listings, Dr. Danger's safety tips, and a catalog of items to help teach kids about farm safety. The kids' section is graphical and fun.

FarmCredit

http://www.farmcredit.com/

★★★

Home of Farm Credit Services is a national network of providers of interactive financial solutions for the agricultural community. If you're looking for a farm loan, this site helps you locate companies that service your part of the country.

Farmland Information Center

http://www.farmlandinfo.org/

★★★★

This site is devoted to individuals interested in agriculture, and contains information about upcoming events and legislation, literature, Internet resources, farm statistics (U.S., by state), and an agricultural library. While this book was being revised, the Farmland Information Library was being redesigned, and promises to present a more robust and attractive site.

Gempler's

http://www.gemplers.com/

★★★★★

At Gemplers.com, you can search the secure online store for thousands of hard-to-find products for agriculture, horticulture, and grounds maintenance.

GrainGenes

http://wheat.pw.usda.gov/index.shtml

★★★★

This database, sponsored by the USDA, provides molecular and phenotypic information on wheat, barley, rye, oats, and sugarcane.

John Deere–Agricultural Equipment

http://www.deere.com/

★★★★★

Offers product information on the entire John Deere farm machinery line, as well as other Deere products. Includes lists of dealers in the United States and Canada.

Kansas City Board of Trade (Kansas City, Missouri)

http://www.kcbt.com/

★★★★

Provides detailed articles about wheat and natural gas futures, historical and trading information, membership information, and links to other exchange centers. This site is also packed with futures trading charts, calendars, and quotes.

National Agricultural Library (NAL)

http://www.nalusda.gov/

★★★★★

Part of the USDA, this site is a resource for ag research, education, and applied agriculture. It contains a huge collection of downloadable agricultural images, as well as government documents, access to assistance from special research sites, and links to other Internet agriculture sites. In addition, its AGRICOLA database provides millions of agriculture-related citations from publications.

National Corn Growers Association (NCGA)

http://www.ncga.com/

★★★★

This site contains interesting statistics on corn crops, news and headlines for corn growers, a searchable archive of past news articles, and announcements of upcoming industry trade shows.

National Pork Producers Council

http://www.nppc.org/

★★★★

Includes current news, articles of interest, market summaries, and information on such topics as government regulation and swine care. The Producers link enables you to connect to discussion forums, weather reports, and information about pork markets.

Small Farm Today Magazine

http://www.smallfarmtoday.com/

★★★

Small Farm Today is dedicated to the preservation and promotion of small farming, rural living, community, and agricultural entrepreneurship. This site focuses on issues relating to small farms (179 acres or less in size, or earning $50,000 or less in gross income per year). Here, you can find articles on alternative farming, such as growing high-value crops, raising unusual livestock, and direct marketing.

A
B
C
D
E
F
G
H
I
J
K
L
M
N
O
P
Q
R
S
T
U
V
W
X
Y
Z

Sunkist

http://www.sunkist.com

★★★★

 All

Visit the Sunkist Growers site for historical information about citrus growing and corporate goings-on, such as job openings and the most recent annual report. You can purchase food service equipment such as juicers from the business-to-business online store. Features a Sunkist Kids area, where kids can play and learn at the same time.

Today's Market Prices

http://www.todaymarket.com/

Ⓢ

★★★★

Listing of worldwide wholesale market prices on fruits and vegetables. Product prices reported by product and location of origin; the site features an extensive searchable index. You'll also find links to university and government agriculture, horticulture, agronomy, biology, and other related departments.

USDA (United States Department of Agriculture)

http://www.usda.gov

★★★★

Contains information about USDA programs, news releases, current events, and legislation dealing with the agricultural industry. Also contains employment lists and links.

ALLERGIES

Allegra: Allergy Answer Site

http://www.allegra.com

★★★★

Devoted to allergy sufferers everywhere, this site offers tips for relief from allergy discomfort, Allegra product information, and an allergy tip of the day. Sponsored by Aventis Pharmaceuticals.

Allergies Book Store

http://wellnessbooks.com/allergies/

★★★★

A comprehensive resource to health and wellness books on allergies of all kinds. Using this site, you can read informative book reviews and order books online via Amazon.com.

Allergy, Asthma, and Allerpet

http://www.allerpet.com/

★★★★

Allerpet markets products designed to substantially reduce the level of pet-related allergens in the home. The company offers a lot of useful information covering nearly everything related to allergies. Site categories include Allergy Questions/Answers, Allergy Facts and Fiction, Allergy Supply Sources, Allerpet Products, Allerpet Literature, Allerpet vs. Washing, Allerpet Clinical Studies, Pet Related Allergy Sites, Allergy and Asthma Sites, and Allergy and Asthma Articles.

Allergy Asthma Technology Ltd.

http://www.allergyasthmatech.com/allergyasthmatech/default.asp

★★★

A supplier of medically approved and fully tested products for allergy and asthma sufferers. Information on causes and diagnoses, as well as treatments available to patients, consumers, physicians, and kids.

[Best] Allergy Info

http://www.allergy-info.com

★★★★★

Sponsored by the manufacturers of ZYRTEC, this site promises to provide helpful tips for managing indoor and outdoor allergy suffering. Learn how to manage your allergies with a combination of allergy medication, environmental changes, and other treatments. The site provides excellent general information about allergies, as well. This site's excellent collection of information and its easily accessible design make it well deserving as the Best of the Best.

The Allergy Store

http://www.foryourallergy.com/

★★★★

This site provides information on allergies, asthma, and sinus problems, as well as product resources for people who have allergies to pollen, pets, mold, house dust, and dust mites.

A
B
C
D
E
F
G
H
I
J
K
L
M
N
O
P
Q
R
S
T
U
V
W
X
Y
Z

Allernet: All About Allergy

http://www.allernet.com/

★★★

Defines what causes allergies, and offers national allergy forecasts, a newsletter, and answers to frequently asked questions. Links to other websites and tips to find a specialist also are included.

American Academy of Allergy, Asthma, & Immunology Online

http://www.aaaai.org/

★★★★

The AAAAI is the definitive medical organization for allergy, asthma, and immunology information. The academy's website allows you to search the site, refer to its Physician Referral Directory, and consult its Patient/Public Resource Center and Media Information Hub. The content and structure of this site is such that it is a physician resource, too.

Asthma and Allergy Information and Research (AAIR)

http://www.users.globalnet.co.uk/~aair/

★★★

Provides information for patients and parents of patients on a wide range of allergy and asthma topics. This site contains few graphics, so it loads quickly; it's full of information to address all your questions.

Dust Free

http://www.dustfree.com/

★★★★

A resource for purchasing electrostatic air filters, antimicrobial UV light systems, room air cleaners, and other allergy products.

Food Allergy Network

http://www.foodallergy.org

★★★★

This site aims to further the understanding of food allergies, offering FAQs, updates, a searchable database, access to recipes and research reports, as well as a daily allergy alert.

HealthSquare.com: Asthma and Allergies

http://www.healthsquare.com/ftana.htm

★★★★★

With dozens of links to asthma and allergy information, this site is a great place for asthma and allergy sufferers to learn more about their condition and treatment options. This site provides information on everything from general issues to specific treatments and tips that can help relieve suffering immediately.

National Institute of Allergy and Infectious Diseases

http://www.niaid.nih.gov/default.htm

★★★★

NIAID's mission is to support research aimed at developing better ways to diagnose, treat, and prevent the many infectious, immunologic, and allergic diseases that afflict people worldwide. NIAID's site enables users to search for information about any related topic as well as to access information about current research activities.

Pollen

http://www.pollen.com

★★★

Anyone who is plagued by airborne allergies will love being able to access up-to-the-minute allergy forecasts for cities across the United States. Check out the pollen count for virtually any U.S. city at this site. You can also sign up to have allergy alerts emailed to you every morning.

Priorities

http://store.yahoo.com/priorities-online/

★★★★★

This site offers a complete line of medically tested allergy control products, all proven effective in protecting you from allergens, asthma triggers, and airborne irritants. Includes a "How to Create an Allergen-Free Home" guide.

ALTERNATIVE MEDICINE

AlternativeDr.com

http://www.alternativedr.com/

★★★★

This site features links for Conditions and Treatments, Drug Interactions, Alternative Therapies, Herbs, Drugs, Supplements, a Practitioners' Directory, a list of Medical Terms, and alternative medicine Forums (discussion groups). You can choose to browse conditions listed alphabetically or research them by symptoms or by the affected body part. Also provides reviews of books.

Alternative Medicine

http://www.alternativemedicine.com

★★★★

Check out alternative health products, find alternative treatments for various conditions, catch up on the latest news about alternative therapies, find local providers through the online Practitioner's Yellow Pages, or locate an alternative health clinic near you. The Products tab contains links to various alternative health products.

The Alternative Medicine Home Page

http://www.pitt.edu/~cbw/altm.html

★★★

A good starting point for any search on alternative health medicine and therapies, this site features dozens of links to the best resources, including Internet resources, mailing lists, databases, government resources, and practitioners' directories.

American Holistic Health Association

http://ahha.org/

★★★

Dedicated to promoting holistic health (health of the mind, body, and spirit), this site features self-help articles, a searchable index of holistic health practitioners, and tips on living a healthy lifestyle.

Ayurveda Yoga Ultra-Nutrition

http://www.ayurvedaonline.com/

★★★★

Ayurveda means "science of life." It is a natural medicine tradition that has helped millions of people feel healthier and more alive for the last 50 centuries. Mentioned in Dr. Deepak Chopra's book *Perfect Health*, Ayurveda considers that each of us is a unique individual with a unique mind-body type. Visit this site to learn more about the Ayurvedic therapeutic health plan and to order products online.

ChiLel-Qigong

http://www.chilel-qigong.com/

★★★★

Visitors can subscribe or read excerpts from the current and past issues of the *ChiLel-QiGong News!* magazine. Other selection options include World's Largest Medicineless Hospital, Miracles of Natural Healing, Certification Program, Workshops and Retreats, Books and Tapes, ChiLel Methods, and more.

A
B
C
D
E
F
G
H
I
J
K
L
M
N
O
P
Q
R
S
T
U
V
W
X
Y
Z

Explore Publications

http://www.explorepub.com/

Written for medical professionals and researchers, *Explore Magazine* provides information and reports on alternative and holistic medicine, nutritional therapies, homeopathy, and energy medicine. Learn about topics in the current issue or scan topics in past issues.

HANS: The Health Action Network Society

http://www.hans.org/

★★★

This site covers current issues such as acupuncture, chiropractic topics, diseases, fluoride, mercury fillings, food irradiation, pesticides, vitamins, and water.

He@lth At Health, Inc.

http://www.athealth.com/Consumer/Farticles/
Anderson.html

Offers all sorts of resources and links to articles on various health conditions. Well worth reading is *Biofeedback: Managing Stress with Biofeedback* by Arne Anderson, BA, BCIAC. This article covers the methods and instruments used in biofeedback.

Health News

http://www.altmedicine.com

★★★

Offering the most up-to-date news and information about alternative medicine, this site covers a variety of approaches, counseling visitors to be cautious when reading about untried or unproven methods.

HealthWorld Online

http://www.healthy.net

HealthWorld contains links to a wide variety of healthcare topics covering everything from mainstream medicine to alternative therapies. Turn to the experts at this site for answers to your alternative medicine questions, or rely on the resource center for information. You can also participate in online discussions and sign up for the free newsletter. The opening page displays a virtual HealthWorld that makes navigating to the desired area fun and easy.

HealthWWWeb: Choices for Health

http://www.healthwwweb.com/tools.html

Dedicated to empowering patients to manage their own health, this site features everything from general information about healthy living to more specific articles on herbs and homeopathy.

Life Matters

http://www.lifematters.com/

These pages are designed for easy access and reading with many interactive features on such topics as counseling, biofeedback, physical education, Tai Chi, and Pilates. Excellent information on managing and relieving stress.

National Center for Complementary and Alternative Medicine

http://nccam.nih.gov/

★★★★

Get information on the NCCAM, which identifies and evaluates unconventional healthcare practices. You'll find the latest information on research, training, education, and development for complementary and alternative medicine. Investigate areas such as alternative therapies, bioelectromagnetics applications, diet/nutrition/lifestyle changes, herbal medicine, manual healing methods, mind/body interventions, and pharmacological/biological treatments. Also includes a FAQ.

Natural Health and Longevity Resource Center

http://www.all-natural.com/index.html

★★★

Provides alternative and holistic approaches to healing and the exposure of health hazards in modern society. You'll get information on articles, health news updates, nutrition, recommended books, and links to other health sites. Includes an herbal reference library.

Qi: The Journal of Traditional Eastern Health & Fitness

http://www.qi-journal.com/

 $

★★★

Browse through articles on acupuncture, meditation, Qigong, Tai Chi, yoga, TCM, herbs, and health exercises or shop for herbs, books, and other alternative health products at the online store.

WholeHealthMD

http://www.wholehealthmd.com/

 $

★★★★★

WholeHealthMD.com takes a holistic, preventive approach to healthcare by focusing on all aspects of human health. Here, you can find information on proper nutrition, nutritional supplements and vitamins, WholeHealth complementary treatments for specific conditions, expert opinions, a reference library, and the latest health news. This site offers a comprehensive list of supplements and herbs, explaining what each of them does, any interactions they might cause, and precautions.

ACUPUNCTURE

Acupuncture/Acupressure Internet Resources

http://www.holisticmed.com/www/acupuncture.html

★★★★

Huge collection of links to various acupuncture and acupressure sites on the Web.

Best Acupuncture.com

http://www.acupuncture.com/

★★★★★

This site features information for the practitioner, student, and patient in different areas of traditional Chinese medicine. Also provides current events and news concerning laws that affect the practice of traditional Chinese medicine. Here, you can research various Chinese medical practices, including acupuncture, Chinese herbal medicine, Qi Gong, Tui Na, Dietetics, and more. Excellent sources for research and a comprehensive FAQ.

American Academy of Medical Acupuncture

http://www.medicalacupuncture.org/

 $

★★★★

Approaching acupuncture from a Western perspective, this site provides information on the role of acupuncture in traditional Western medicine. Also features a directory of acupuncturists.

American Acupuncture

http://www.americanacupuncture.com/

★★★

Visit this site for information on incorporating alternative oriental medicine with Western living. Learn how to address such problems as smoking, weight gain, and addictions through acupuncture.

American College of Acupuncture & Oriental Medicine

http://www.acaom.edu/

★★★★

ACAOM's vision is to strengthen the role of acupuncture and Oriental medicine in providing complementary healthcare delivery in the United States. Using this site, you can find out how to become a trained, nationally certified health practitioner in the diagnosis and treatment of health problems based on theories and principles of acupuncture and Oriental medicine.

A
B
C
D
E
F
G
H
I
J
K
L
M
N
O
P
Q
R
S
T
U
V
W
X
Y
Z

A
B
C
D
E
F
G
H
I
J
K
L
M
N
O
P
Q
R
S
T
U
V
W
X
Y
Z

Blue Poppy Press

http://www.bluepoppy.com/

★★★

Established in 1982, Blue Poppy is the largest publisher of books about acupuncture and Chinese medicine. Here, you can purchase books, oils, herbs, and other products; research the Disease Database and other resources; and read a list of FAQs. By registering, you can gain access to the Practitioner's Store.

BuyAMag: Acupuncture Supplies

http://www.acupuncture-healing.com/

★★★

A one-stop shop for the acupuncture professional, BuyAMag features acupuncture charts, models, needles, and educational CDs. BuyAMag is also a great place to shop for magnets, herbs, and other alternative healthcare products.

China Guide

http://www.china-guide.com/

★★★

The China Guide offers acupuncture books and software, the most authoritative audio-visual teaching materials, and an online source of information related to Chinese culture.

National Certification Commission for Acupuncture and Oriental Medicine

http://www.nccaom.org/

★★★

If you want to become an acupuncture practitioner or administer Chinese medicine legally, visit this site to learn how to become certified. Here, you can learn about state regulations and requirements, certification programs, exam dates and deadlines, and other information you need to become a qualified, certified practitioner. Patients can visit this site to find a certified acupuncturist.

Veterinary Acupuncture Page

http://users.med.auth.gr/~karanik/english/veter.htm

★★★

If acupuncture is good enough for humans, it's good enough for your dog or cat… or maybe even that racehorse you're betting on. Learn more about how acupuncture is used to treat animals. This is an excellent site for veterinarians who are studying acupuncture to learn more about the procedure.

AROMATHERAPY

AGORA

http://www.nature-helps.com/agora/agora.html

★★★

Learn more about the use of essential aromatherapy oils for healing and well-being by reading the articles available at this site.

Amateur Aromatherapy

http://www.smellyonline.com/

★★★★

The site is designed as an introduction to aromatherapy for the inexperienced. Here, you can learn the properties and uses of various oils, the chemistry behind them, and various massage techniques. The site also features dozens of recipes for therapeutic scents.

Aromatherapy: Essential Oils Guide

http://www.aromatherapy-essential-oils-guide.com/

★★★★

Learn descriptions of essential oils and symptoms that can be reduced through their use. Includes an excellent introduction to aromatherapy, instructions, cautions, a list of essential oils, and a symptoms list.

AromaWeb

http://www.aromaweb.com/

★★★★

Read articles about aromatherapy, scan product information and suppliers online, and find aromatherapy books through this resourceful and attractive site. This site also features an excellent collection of recipes.

Bird's Encyclopedia of Aromatherapy

http://www.imm.org.pl/bird/list1.htm

★★★

A huge directory that explains the medical benefits of various essential oils. Lavender, for example, can aid in digestion, genitourinary functions, and circulation, as well as help skin/hair damage and muscle tension.

  ## Great Expectations

http://www.galaxymall.com/aromatherapy/health/index.html

★★★★

A great site for understanding which types of oils impact ailments and to help prepare healing mixtures. Check out the Aromatherapy Essential Oil Recipes link. Recipes are divided into a number of categories, from medicinal to facial care, foot care, massage, and cosmetic, to name just a few. Although this site is not the most attractive of the bunch, it's packed with excellent resources for beginner and expert alike.

Kevala Centre: Aromatherapy Information

http://www.kevala.co.uk/aromatherapy/

★★★★

Here, you can read a prospectus for an accredited diploma course in aromatherapy and learn more about the basics of aromatherapy, essential oils and their correct usage, and massage blends.

National Association for Holistic Aromatherapy

http://www.naha.org/

$

★★★★

The National Association for Holistic Aromatherapy is dedicated to "enhancing public awareness of the benefits of true aromatherapy." This organization also promotes the study and attempts to raise the academic standards in aromatherapy education and practice. Here, you can learn more about the medicinal qualities of aromatherapy.

A World of Aromatherapy

http://www.aworldofaromatherapy.com/

★★★★★

This well-organized site starts with the history of aromatherapy, teaches you the basics, provides information about the various oils, and then shows you how to use the oils to treat both the mind and body. You can also sign up for a free monthly newsletter.

CHIROPRACTIC

American Chiropractic Association

http://www.amerchiro.org/

★★★

The official site of the largest professional organization in the world representing the interests of chiropractors, this site provides information for chiropractors, patients, and insurers; access to its publications; educational materials for consumers; updates concerning legislation; and products for chiropractic doctors to purchase.

Back Pain Resource Center

http://www.backpainreliefonline.com

★★★

Those living with back pain might find relief through information available at this site, as well as products to aid in reducing discomfort. Links to other sites and a newsletter are other useful tools here.

Chiropractic in Canada

http://www.ccachiro.org/

★★★

This site is the official home page of the Canadian Chiropractic Association. It provides the general public with valuable information about chiropractic healthcare.

Chiropractic Internet Resources

http://www.holisticmed.com/www/chiropractic.html

★★★

A list of chiropractic links can help you find a local practitioner, read about chiropractic care, contact related healthcare organizations, and participate in discussion forums.

A B C D E F G H I J K L M N O P Q R S T U V W X Y Z

A
B
C
D
E
F
G
H
I
J
K
L
M
N
O
P
Q
R
S
T
U
V
W
X
Y
Z

Chiropractic Online Today

http://www.chiro-online.com/

★★★

A "news-zine" for the chiropractic profession and the healthcare community.

The Chiropractic Resource Organization

http://www.chiro.org/

★★★

This site is maintained by and for chiropractors and provides dozens of links to useful resources. Also provides information on nutrition, acupuncture, and pediatrics.

Chiropractic SOAP Notes

http://www.clinicpro.com/soap.htm

★★★★

With Chiropractic SOAP Notes software, you can record exam/X-ray results for those patients whose records you need on file, or you can create a full-blown narrative report of your initial exam and X-ray findings for the acting insurance company, attorney, or work comp board. Download a working trial version and check it out for yourself, or order a SOAP Notes trial on CD.

Chiropractor Directory

http://www.chiropractordirectory.com/

★★★

This site offers a free search to find a chiropractor in your area by ZIP code, links to insurance companies and workers compensation information, and chiropractic facts section.

Chiropractor Finder

http://www.chiropractor-finder.com/

★★★

Free online referral service for chiropractors, acupuncture practitioners, massage therapists, nutritionists, and other medical professionals. You must submit your name, email address, phone number, and a description of your problem. A representative will then contact you with details.

ChiroStore Online

http://www.chirostore.com/

★★★★

ChiroStore provides chiropractic and health products for chiropractors and the general public.

ChiroWeb

http://www.chiroweb.com/

★★★★

Of potential interest to chiropractors, chiropractic students, and consumers, this site provides discussion forums, news and information, a database of chiropractic colleges, and links to other resources.

International Chiropractors Association

http://www.chiropractic.org/

★★★★

If you are a chiropractic doctor or student, you will find this site useful. It contains news and information relating to chiropractic topics, details about continuing education programs, and the latest developments in legislation. Consumers can click the Chiropractic Information link for more general information about chiropractic services.

Best MyBackStore.com

http://www.backworld.ca/mbs.asp

★★★★★

Back World specializes in selling products specifically for people suffering from back or neck pain. This includes home seating solutions and office seating solutions, as well as all those products to help deal with back problems. This site offers sales in Canadian dollars as well as American dollars. If you're looking for products to help your back—at home, in the office, or on the road—this is your one-stop shop.

Spine-Health.com

http://www.spine-health.com

★★★

Read about back pain symptoms, causes, and treatments at this well-organized site.

SpineUniverse.com

http://www.spineuniverse.com/

★★★★★

Excellent site for both patients and professionals who must deal with back pain. This site provides everything you need to know about diagnoses, treatment options, new technologies, and preventive care.

HOMEOPATHY

abc Homeopathy

http://www.abchomeopathy.com/

★★★★

This site consists of three basic elements—an introduction to homeopathy and homeopathics, a remedy finder, and links to online stores where you can purchase homeopathic products. Near the bottom of the opening page is a list of the most common homeopathic remedies.

Finding Professional Homeopathic Care

http://www.homeopathic.com/procare/index.html

$

★★★

Dana Ullman, one of the leading spokespeople for homeopathy, has put together this excellent FAQ page on finding a homeopathic practitioner.

Homeopathic Information Center

http://www.healthy.net/clinic/therapy/homeopat/info/index.html

$

★★★

Use the site index for finding information on homeopathy information, events, news, and suppliers. Shop the online store for various natural remedies, treatments, and other products.

Homeopathic Treatments

http://www.homeopathic.com/ailments/index.html

★★★

This site provides homeopathic treatments for a wide variety of specific maladies. Includes a category of treatments for children's health.

Homeopathic FAQs

http://www.elixirs.com/faq.htm

$

★★★

A complete guide to homeopathic remedies. This site provides answers to frequently asked questions (FAQs) about homeopathic remedies.

Homeopathy Home Page

http://www.homeopathyhome.com/

★★★

This page is a central jumping-off point, aiming to provide links to every related resource available on the alternative medical practice of homeopathy. Provides links to various retail sites as well.

Homeopathy Internet Resources

http://www.holisticmed.com/www/homeopathy.html

★★★

A lengthy list of homeopathic links that are organized by the type of site they lead to. This site includes addresses for mailing lists as well.

Homeopathy Online

http://www.lyghtforce.com/HomeopathyOnline/

★★★★★

An international journal of homeopathic medicine for lay persons, students, and practitioners alike. Begins with a foreword and cover story, proceeds through the basic philosophy of homeopathy, provides a background on how some homeopathic treatments are discovered, and provides some case reviews.

A B C D E F G H I J K L M N O P Q R S T U V W X Y Z

A
B
C
D
E
F
G
H
I
J
K
L
M
N
O
P
Q
R
S
T
U
V
W
X
Y
Z

National Center for Homeopathy (NCH)

http://www.homeopathic.org/

★★★★

At the NCH site, visitors can learn about membership and catch up on recent research results, as well as look at a copy of the center's media kit, which features articles about homeopathy in the news. You can also search the NCH directory for a certified homeopathic practitioner.

What Are Homeopathic Medicines?

http://www.arnica.com/homeo/homeopath1.html

★★★

This somewhat limited site briefly reviews what homeopathic medicines are and how to use them effectively.

HYPNOTHERAPY

Center for Hypnotherapy

http://www.hypnotherapycenter.com/

★★★

This site provides information about becoming a certified hypnotherapist plus links to available books and videos.

Clinical Hypnosis

http://www.athealth.com/Consumer/FArticles/Pearson.html

★★★

An article on understanding clinical hypnotherapy by Judith E. Pearson, Ph.D.

HypnoGenesis

http://www.hypnos.co.uk/hypnomag/articles.htm

★★★

Plenty of excellent articles to keep you busy reading for quite some time, all formatted for easy reading. *HypnoGenesis* is a magazine for hypnosis and hypnotherapy.

Hypnosis.com

http://www.hypnosis.com/

★★★

The official website of the American Board of Hypnotherapy, this site is designed with the hypnotist in mind. Here, you can find links to certification programs, hypnosis scripts and books, convention and conference dates, and hypnosis FAQs.

Hypnotica

http://www.bcx.net/hypnosis/

★★★

This is an excellent site for information on self-hypnosis. You can learn how to induce hypnosis and how to harness it to accomplish the things you want to do, and it is free.

Hypnotism Education Website

http://www.wayneperkins.net/

★★★

 Not for kids

Home of Wayne Perkins, stage hypnotist, this site provides background information about the various uses of hypnotism along with information on how to learn more from Wayne Perkins himself and have him give a performance at your next event. Also provides some free articles and other resources that visitors might find helpful.

MAGNET THERAPY

Magnet-Therapy.com

http://www.magnet-therapy.com/

★★★

This magnet-therapy.com superstore features a wide selection of products, including magnetic jewelry, mattresses, and individual magnets—very little information about magnet therapy, however.

Promagnet

http://www.promagnet.com/

★★★

This magnet store features a wide selection of magnets, books about magnet therapy, and testimonials from satisfied customers.

Quackwatch: Magnet Therapy

http://www.quackwatch.com/04ConsumerEducation/QA/magnet.html

★★★

Skeptical about magnet therapy? Then check out this article by Stephen Barrett, M.D. Here, Dr. Barrett questions the effectiveness of magnet therapy.

MASSAGE

American Massage Therapy Association

http://www.amtamassage.org/

★★★

This site gives you the opportunity to learn more about the AMTA, an association that represents more than 46,000 massage therapists in 30 countries.

Associated Bodywork and Massage Professionals

http://www.abmp.com/

★★★★

ABMP has 15 years' experience serving the massage therapy profession and more than 40,000 active members. Find out about becoming a member and learn about bodywork, massage, and somatic therapies. Read the current issue of *Bodywork & Massage* magazine or browse through the archive of hundreds of articles on massage.

Body Therapy Associates

http://www.gotyourback.com/

★★★★

Massage tables, ergonomic chairs, natural bedding products, treatment chairs, inversion systems, and more.

Bodywork and Massage Information

http://www.gems4friends.com/massage.html

★★★

Learn about the various types of massages, tips for getting the most out of a massage, and links to other massage websites. You can also register for a free newsletter.

Bodywork.com

http://www.bodywork.com/

★★★

Massage tables, lotions, oils, spa and salon products, and medical and chiropractic supplies.

Illustrated Guide to Muscle and Clinical Massage Therapy

http://danke.com/Orthodoc/

★★★★

Presented by the Pain and Posture Clinic, this site offers animated guides to massage. A unique and informative site, though it looks a little plain at first glance. Links to Amazon.com to purchase recommended books.

Living Earth Crafts

http://www.livingearthcrafts.com/

★★★★

Providing massage and spa tables and bodywork supplies for more than two decades.

Massage Magazine

http://www.massagemag.com/

★★★★

Home of *Massage Magazine*, the self-proclaimed "definitive massage and touch-therapy resource for practitioners, instructors, students and consumers." Here, you can read articles from the current and past issues, find schools that teach various massage and touch therapy techniques, and find links to dozens of additional massage resources.

A
B
C
D
E
F
G
H
I
J
K
L
M
N
O
P
Q
R
S
T
U
V
W
X
Y
Z

A
B
C
D
E
F
G
H
I
J
K
L
M
N
O
P
Q
R
S
T
U
V
W
X
Y
Z

Massage Network

http://massagenetwork.com/

★★★★

Find a massage therapist near you through a searchable database at this site, where you can also read FAQs about massage and locate recommended books on the subject. Links where you can purchase retail merchandise.

Massage Therapy

http://www.massagetherapy.com/

$

★★★★★

Excellent site for learning more about massage therapy and careers in massage therapy. If you are looking for a massage therapist near you, the search tool at this site enables you to search not only by location, but also by type of massage—for example, reflexology, hydrotherapy, or healing touch.

Massage Today

http://www.massagetoday.com/

$

★★★★

This site features news stories and articles about massage and enables you to search for a massage therapist near you, learn more about the benefits of massage therapy, and even submit a question to have it answered by a qualified massage therapist. You can join discussion forums to learn even more.

Massage Warehouse

http://www.massagewarehouse.com/

$

★★★★

Owned and operated by massage therapists, Massage Warehouse features thousands of massage supplies. Whether you're shopping for a new massage table or massage chair, or looking for massage creams, oils, lotions, sheets, anatomical charts, books, tapes, or virtually anything related to massage, you've come to the right place.

MassageNet

http://www.massagenet.com/

★★★

A comprehensive directory of massage therapists throughout the United States plus links to books, articles, massage training, and other resources.

NaturalHealers

http://www.naturalhealers.com/

★★★

If alternative or natural health professions interest you, visit this site for information on schools and programs, and certification and licensing requirements.

SomaZen

http://www.somazen.com/

★★★

This site is intended to stimulate communication and understanding of the healing and spiritual growth of the human body/mind.

Utah College of Massage Therapy

http://www.ucmt.com/

★★★

Provides training in massage therapy, acupressure, shiatsu, reflexology, rolfing, and much more.

ALZHEIMER'S

Ageless Design, Inc.

http://www.agelessdesign.com

★★★★

An education, information, and consultation service company founded to help seniors have what they really want—a home that is easy to live in and that accommodates the difficulties associated with growing older. Using Ageless Design's site, you can learn how to modify a home to care for a loved one with Alzheimer's, and access unique ideas and products that embrace the special needs of people as they age.

Alzheimer Research Forum

http://www.alzforum.org/

★★★★

The Alzheimer's Research Forum is a nonprofit organization that promotes collaboration of Alzheimer's researchers worldwide to hasten development of new ways to prevent and treat the disease. Well-known science writer June Kinoshita, a consulting editor of the journal *Science*, manages the site.

Alzheimer Society of Canada

http://www.alzheimer.ca/

★★★★

Provides information about care, research, and programs to help those affected by the disease. This site also features a creative area, where Alzheimer's patients and their friends and family members have posted short stories, poems, and artwork. Discussion forums are available to exchange information with others who are dealing with Alzheimer's disease in their lives.

Alzheimer's Association

http://www.alz.org/

★★★★★

Superb site. Attractive, well laid-out, and very comprehensive, including FAQs, resources on medical issues relating to Alzheimer's (such as steps for proper diagnosis and current/future treatment options), updates on advances and legislation, and information about finding a local chapter. This site is designed for Alzheimer's patients, family caregivers, professional caregivers, and researchers.

Alzheimer's Disease Education and Referral Center

http://www.alzheimers.org

★★★★

Sponsored by the National Institute on Aging, this site answers questions about Alzheimer's, offers research reports and publications on the disease, and responds to email queries. You will find a list of government resources and services, too.

Alzheimer's: Coping

http://www.geocities.com/HotSprings/3004/

★★★

Journal and resources from a woman (Denise Cooper) who provides ongoing care to her mother. Very well done. She not only shares her personal experience but also provides links to all sorts of things that others going through this situation will find very helpful.

A
B
C
D
E
F
G
H
I
J
K
L
M
N
O
P
Q
R
S
T
U
V
W
X
Y
Z

Alzheimer's Disease International

http://www.alz.co.uk/

★★★★

Internet home of Alzheimer's Disease International provides information about the possible causes of Alzheimer's disease, ways it is diagnosed, and common treatments. It also provides a list of frequently asked questions, information for caregivers, and a directory of Alzheimer's associations around the world.

Alzheimer's Society

http://www.alzheimers.org.uk/

★★★★

The Alzheimer's Society is the U.K.'s leading care and research charity for people with all forms of dementia and their caregivers.

Alzheimer's Watch

http://www.go60.com/go60alzheimers.htm

★★★★

Part of the Go60.com seniors site, this section offers information about Alzheimer's, as well as the latest medical breakthroughs and developments.

ALZwell Caregiver

http://www.alzwell.com

★★★

Designed for caregivers of patients suffering from dementia, this site offers information and support, as well as a place to vent. A nice, safe place to escape for those coping with caring for someone with Alzheimer's.

Geriatric Video Productions

http://www.geriatricvideo.com/

★★★★

Since 1991, Geriatric Video Productions has been producing and distributing video programs in the fields of geriatric healthcare education. Clients include nursing homes, hospitals, universities, community colleges, hospice programs, home health programs, and Alzheimer organizations. The company's videos have received numerous prestigious awards.

⟦Best⟧ Healthy Aging, Geriatrics, and Elderly Care

http://www.healthandage.com/

★★★★★

The Novartis Foundation for Gerontological Research supports education and innovation in healthy aging, geriatrics, and the care of elderly people. This site includes a Reuters Health Information news feed, which provides both healthcare professionals and patients with late-breaking health news. When you don't know where to turn for the latest information on aging and healthcare for the elderly, this is the place to start.

National Library of Medicine (NLM)

http://www.ncbi.nlm.nih.gov/PubMed/

★★★★

NLM's search service enables users to access the 9 million citations in MedLine and Pre-MedLine (with links to participating online journals) and other related databases. By entering "Alzheimer's," you will access virtually anything published on the topic.

Senior Care

http://www.retirementdirectory.com/

★★★★

A nationwide directory of nursing homes, assisted living, Alzheimer facilities, and hospices, complete with links to email addresses and websites. Your ability to search by state makes this site especially helpful.

AMUSEMENT AND THEME PARKS

Adventure City

http://www.adventurecity.com/

★★★★

 0-8

This affordable California theme park is built especially for younger kids. The site contains information about the available rides, petting farm, shows, and so on. You can also print coupons from this site.

Anheuser-Busch Theme Parks

http://www.4adventure.com/

★★★★★

 All

Contains links to all Anheuser-Busch parks across America, including Sea World, Busch Gardens, Water Country USA, Adventure Island, Discovery Cove, and Sesame Place. They're all over the country; one surely is located near you. Buy your tickets online, too!

Canobie Lake Park

http://www.canobie.com/

★★★★

All

Canobie Lake Park is a family-oriented amusement park located in Salem, New Hampshire. This site offers a detailed description of the park's rides, shows, hours, and rates. Canobie Lake Park offers more than 45 rides, including 4 coasters.

Cedar Point

http://www.cedarpoint.com/

★★★★

 All

This 364-acre amusement park/resort located in Ohio claims to host the largest collection of rides (69) and roller coasters (15) in the world. You gotta see it to believe it. This site gives you a bird's-eye view of all the attractions along with the opportunity to buy tickets online, get information on resorts, and lots more.

Coney Island

http://www.brooklynonline.com/coneyisland/

★★★

All

Brooklyn's famous national treasure, where the concept of the roller coaster originated. The site says that nothing will "scare the willies out of you" like the Cyclone, the famous 80-year-old coaster.

A
B
C
D
E
F
G
H
I
J
K
L
M
N
O
P
Q
R
S
T
U
V
W
X
Y
Z

  Disney.com—The Web Site for Families

http://disney.go.com/

★★★★★

 All

Contains links to all things Disney, which by now is more than just a cute little mouse. Includes information about its theme parks as well as movies, the TV channel, videos, books, its cruise line, and much more. This site also features a games area where kids can play online video games, and a music area for playing audio clips. If you have a credit card, you can even shop online for Disney trinkets and apparel. If you're looking for the best theme parks in the world and are leaning toward taking your family on a Disney adventure, introduce your entire family to this site. You can plan your trip and figure out the best places to go, and your kids can find plenty to keep them busily entertained.

Frontier Movie Town

http://www.onlinepages.net/frontier_movie_town/

★★★

All

This site tells you what you can expect to find when you visit Frontier Movie Town. You'll read about the cowboy-style dining, old-time Frontier Photography, the Western Heritage Museum, the gift shop, and the movie sets. At Frontier Movie Town, you can create and film your own Western!

Great Escape and Splashwater Kingdom

http://www.sixflags.com/greatescape/

★★★★

All

This Lake George, New York, theme park contains more than 125 rides, shows, and attractions. For roller coaster enthusiasts, the site boasts of the Comet, which was rated the best wooden coaster by readers of *Inside Track* magazine.

Hershey Park

http://www.hersheypark.com/

★★★★★

 All

Recently named the number one amusement park in the northeast by readers of *FamilyFun* magazine, Hershey Park has more than 60 rides, including 9 roller coasters, 7 water rides, and 20 kiddie rides, plus professional shows, concerts, talent shows, and other entertainment. Here, you can find information about the park and its features, along with driving directions, information about food and lodging, and admission prices.

LEGOLAND California

http://www.lego.com/legoland/california/

★★★

All

LEGOLAND California is LEGO's newest theme park. Visit the site to get a park tour, plan your visit, learn about upcoming special events, find out what's new, and link to other LEGO parks or to LEGO's toy site.

LibertyLand

http://www.libertyland.com/

★★★

All

Located in Memphis, Tennessee, LibertyLand is home to one of the oldest all-horse carousels, as well as the Zippin Pippin, Elvis' favorite ride.

New England Association of Amusement Parks

http://www.neaapa.com/

★★★

Trade association that supports amusement parks, attractions, and vendors. This site is your source for information about amusement parks, shows, family entertainment centers, and more in Connecticut, Maine, Massachusetts, New Hampshire, and Rhode Island.

Paramount's Great America

http://www.pgathrills.com/

★★★★★

 All

This official site provides a virtual tour of the park and its attractions. Also contains employment and season ticket information, as well as a section about what's new.

Paramount's Kings Island

http://www.pki.com/

★★★★★

 All

Visit the amusement park choice of the Brady Bunch! (Remember the infamous tube mix-up?) Take an online tour of the park and discover the latest live stage shows.

Sea World

http://www.seaworld.com

★★★★★

 All

Get park information for one of several Sea World locations, order tickets online, and investigate new attractions.

Six Flags Theme Parks

http://www.sixflags.com/

★★★★★

 All

The largest regional theme park company in the world, with 30 parks in the United States, 1 in Mexico, and 9 in Europe. According to the site, "85% of all Americans live within just a day's drive from a Six Flags Theme Park." Click Pick a Park and then click any of the dots on the globe to view detailed information about that particular Six Flags park or property.

Theme Park Review

http://www.themeparkreview.com/

★★★

 14-18

Contains a photo gallery, video clips, and trip reports from some of the world's best theme parks and roller coasters. You can order full-length videos of Robb Alvey's latest coaster season.

Universal Studios

http://themeparks.universalstudios.com/

★★★★★

 All

Click the link for one of four Universal Studio Theme Parks: Orlando, Hollywood, Japan, or Spain. Check out park hours and new rides and attractions, buy merchandise, and order tickets online. This site also features a game area, where kids can play video games online.

Utah Fun Dome

http://www.fundome.com/

★★★★

 All

The Utah Fun Dome is an incredible 200,000 square-foot indoor family entertainment center located in beautiful Salt Lake City, Utah. This site gives you the scoop on all the attractions: a 32-lane bowling alley, skating rink, laser tag arena, special effects 3D theater, miniature golf course, an arcade, a handcrafted carousel, two motion simulators, race cars, and bungee jumping. Offers detailed descriptions of attractions as well as hours of operation and information for making party reservations.

A B C D E F G H I J K L M N O P Q R S T U V W X Y Z

A
B
C
D
E
F
G
H
I
J
K
L
M
N
O
P
Q
R
S
T
U
V
W
X
Y
Z

Walt Disney World

http://disneyworld.disney.go.com/waltdisneyworld/
index

★★★★★

 All

Everything you need to plan your magical Walt Disney World Resort vacation is right here. Click the Parks & More link to review a list of Disney Theme Parks and then click the park you want to tour. Use the navigation bar that runs down the left side of the screen to find what you want. Order admission tickets online, check out FAQs and special events, review resort and spa options, and lots, lots more!

Related Sites

http://www.adventurelanding.com

http://www.casinopier-waterworks.com/

http://www.napavalley.com/napavalley/outdoor/
marinewo/marinewo.html

http://www.holidayworld.com/

http://www.knotts.com/

http://www.kingsdominion.com/

http://www.santasvillage.com/

ANTIQUES

100s of Antiques and Collectibles
http://cgi.tias.com/showcase/

★★★★

If you are looking for a specific item, this site enables you to run a search, and the results tell you which online dealers or galleries have the item in stock. Searches might take three forms: Quick, Complete, and Auction.

Antique.com
http://www.antiqnet.com/

★★★★★

This site's modern design makes it easy to navigate this company's extensive collection of fine antiques. Here, you can find antique advertisements, architecture, books, clocks, furniture, glass, jewelry, pottery, silverware, textiles, watches, and much more. If you have a specific item in mind, use the Search box to track it down. Crystal clear graphics make it easy to see just what you're getting.

The Antiques Council
http://www.antiquescouncil.com

★★★

The Antiques Council is an association of professional antique dealers, formed to educate the public about antiques, promote high standards, and provide show management services for charities.

Antiques on the Farmington
http://antiquesonfarmington.com

★★★

A multi-dealer shop specializing in furniture, lighting, linens, silver, china, glassware, clocks, art, jewelry, books, ephemera, toys, and Civil War items, complete with online ordering.

Antiques Roadshow
http://www.pbs.org/wgbh/pages/roadshow/

★★★★★

Even if you're an inexperienced antiquer, PBS's *Antiques Roadshow* is a great show and website to visit to learn from the experts. The show comes to cities around the country to meet with the locals and appraise their items. The show's experts not only spot the real antiques but make a point to appraise fake items so you, the viewer, will learn what to look for in your antiquing jaunts. Check out the appraisal contest. You can buy books and videos about antiques through the online store.

Artnet.com
http://www.artnet.com

★★★★★

Artnet has an extensive listing of art galleries and artists, in addition to offering online auctions of fine artwork. This site also offers research tools and *Artnet* magazine information.

A
B
C
D
E
F
G
H
I
J
K
L
M
N
O
P
Q
R
S
T
U
V
W
X
Y
Z

Augie's 45 RPM Vinyl Record Sale

http://www.augiesrecords.com

★★★★

Augie has been collecting records since the 1950s, so it is not surprising that you have your choice from 6,000 titles. An alphabetic index lists all the titles he has available.

Related Sites

http://www.all-vinyl.com/

http://www.infinityrecords.net/

 Circline

http://www.circline.com

★★★★★

Billing itself as "the marketplace of the world's finest art, antiques, and dealers," Circline enables users to search an extensive database of dealers and available inventory to find just the right piece of art or antique. A section on learning about antiques is helpful for the neophyte collector. Excellent site for beginners and experts alike.

Dismuke's Virtual Talking Machine

http://www.dismuke.org/

★★★★★

This site features Real Audio recordings of vintage music from the early 20th Century to spur interest in this largely forgotten era of American pop culture. Here you can listen to the private collection of Dismuke's 78 rpm records. Tune in to Dismuke Radio to listen to vintage pop and jazz from 1925 to 1935. Listen to Dismuke's "Hit of the Week," or bop to the vintage dance, jazz, and vocals of the "Roaring '20s through the Great Depression and the dawn of World War II." Well done!

Early American History Auctions, Inc.

http://www.earlyamerican.com/

★★★

The online site for the EAHA specializes in antique Americana, such as maps, Civil War memorabilia, newspapers, coins, and so on. Check out the price list of current items and submit a bid, either by email, fax, or snail mail. You can submit payments online using PayPal.

Eureka, I Found It!

http://www.eureka-i-found-it.com/

★★★★

This site offers very unusual items for sale, such as signed vintage costume jewelry, toy sewing machines, toy steam engines, and vintage fans. You can submit payments online using PayPal.

Finer Times

http://www.finertimes.com/

★★★★★

Finer Times features an incredible selection of vintage timepieces—over 400 personally selected wrist and pocket watches, as well as accessories that can enhance your collection. Discussion board helps you get in touch with others who collect vintage timepieces.

ICollector.com

http://www.icollector.com/

★★★★

Bid on items from more than 350 auction houses and dealers worldwide or search auction house catalogs for upcoming sales around the world. Search a selection of archived catalogs from auction house sales since 1994 and find out about dealers and galleries, related associations, and publications. Go to the Community section to meet other collectors, participate in live chats with industry experts and celebrities, or check out the selection of exhibitions.

Maine Antique Digest

http://www.maineantiquedigest.com

★★★★

The web supplement to the print publication, this site offers articles, news, a dealer directory, price database, directory of appraisers, and antique discussion forum. Auction and show ads on the site will alert you to upcoming events.

Medical Antiques Online

http://www.antiquemed.com/

★★★

This site is dedicated to the stethoscope. Not only can you purchase antique stethoscopes here, but you can also read historic articles, speeches, and essays about these medical instruments. The site also contains links to other medical antique dealers.

Newel

http://www.newel.com/

★★★★★

Search the entire inventory of Newel antiques or study along with the tutorial to get started.

Political Parade

http://www.politicalparade.com/buy_page.htm

★★★

Whether you collect presidential campaign buttons, posters, pins, flags, plates, or whatnot, this site covers it. Whether you want to buy, sell, or just learn about collecting political memorabilia, this is the site for you.

Tias

http://www.tias.com/

★★★★★

Tias is an online mall where collectors can advertise their shops. Think of it as a directory of online antique dealers.

ARCHITECTURE

A
B
C
D
E
F
G
H
I
J
K
L
M
N
O
P
Q
R
S
T
U
V
W
X
Y
Z

The American Institute of Architects

http://www.aia.org/

★★★★

The collective voice of America's architects, this organization has advanced the profession since 1857. The website serves 58,000 members and provides information on their mission statement, history, events, chapter offices, and member services. The information for consumers includes help in finding a local architectural firm for a particular project.

Arch Inform

http://www.archinform.net

★★★★

An international architectural database consisting of 11,000 plus projects, some built and some unrealized.

Architects USA

http://www.architectsusa.com

★★★★

A directory listing more than 20,000 architectural firms in the United States.

Architectural Research Institute

http://www.architect.org

★★★

This think tank provides information to help city planners and developers make the decisions necessary to build more livable cities and neighborhoods.

Best Architecture.com

http://www.architecture.com

★★★★★

Internet home of the Royal Institute of British Architects (RIBA), this site is dedicated to further the cause of architecture in Britain and internationally. Here, you will find abundant resources relating to architecture, including articles, reference libraries, links to great buildings, information on what an architect does and how to become an architect, a searchable directory of architects, and links to architectural museums. Architects and students can also learn how to submit an entry for the RIBA Award. Excellent site and very easy to navigate.

Architecture Magazine

http://www.architecturemag.com

★★★★

Review back issues of this monthly magazine for the architecture industry, subscribe to the magazine, enroll for online courses, search for job openings or building services, or read one of several current articles on design and culture issues.

Architecture Schools

http://www.acsa-arch.org

★★★

Prospective architectural students will want to visit this site to learn about architecture programs and the application process, and to obtain information about and deadlines for upcoming design competitions.

Bricsnet

http://www.aecinfo.ca

★★★★

A great business-to-business site for architects and builders, this site enables architects and builders to track down the materials they need for a particular job. Here, you can find everything from building specs and computer-aided design details to concrete mixtures, insulation, windows, and even furnishings. Site enables you to request information from dozens of companies via email.

Design Basics Home Online Planbook

http://www.designbasics.com

★★★★★

Design Basics, Inc. provides single-family home plans with available technical support and custom design options. Build your dream home with plans that are also marketed through catalogs, newsstand magazines, and home building industry trade publications. Decorative home accessories are available in the Web Store, making this a one-stop, comprehensive site for people seeking to build and decorate their own homes.

First Source Exchange

http://www.cmdfirstsource.com/

★★★★★

A comprehensive architectural site designed to help architects develop accurate construction documents, including plans and estimates. First Source Exchange provides a collection of tools and resources to deliver essential product information, early-planning project leads, reliable cost data, an online library of state and local building codes, and industry news from respected industry sources.

Frank Lloyd Wright: Official Web Site

http://www.cmgww.com/historic/flw/bio.html

★★★★★

Check out the life and works of the most famous architect in the world. Here you can read a brief biography of Frank Lloyd Wright, scan a brief list of his major accomplishments, view photographs of his most beautiful buildings, and read some of his intriguing quotes. To order books or videos about Frank Lloyd Wright, click the Library link and click the item you want to order; this takes you to Amazon.com, where you can place your order.

McGraw/Baldwin Architecture

http://www.mbarch.com

★★★

Advertises the San Diego–based firm that offers services in project management.

Metropolis Magazine

http://metropolismag.com

★★★★

A look at architectural, furniture, clothing, and other design disciplines in a changing world. Check out events and exhibitions, read articles, and subscribe. Also features a great collection of photos showcasing some very cool home and office furniture and accessories.

Plan Net

http://www.plannet.com/

★★★

An informational site about architecture, which includes the Daily Plan Net, the Studio, the Library, the Showcase, and a Net Index. Vital product information, CAD demos, and architectural forums are all included.

The Pritzker Architecture Prize

http://www.pritzkerprize.com/

★★★

The Pritzker Architecture Prize, sponsored by the Hyatt Foundation, is the world's most prestigious architecture award. Learn about its Laureates and about its international traveling exhibition, "The Art of Architecture."

A
B
C
D
E
F
G
H
I
J
K
L
M
N
O
P
Q
R
S
T
U
V
W
X
Y
Z

A
B
C
D
E
F
G
H
I
J
K
L
M
N
O
P
Q
R
S
T
U
V
W
X
Y
Z

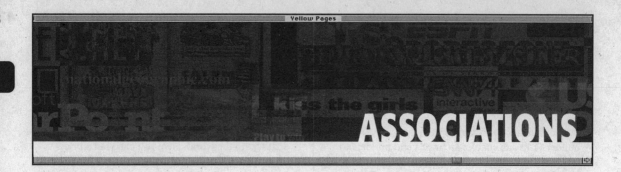

ASSOCIATIONS

Directory of Associations

http://www.marketingsource.com/associations/

★★★

Search this global database of professional and trade associations and not-for-profit organizations. You can view a sample listing for free, but you must become a member to search the complete directory of more than 35,000 associations and organizations.

National Council of Nonprofit Associations

http://www.ncna.org/

★★★

Find the nonprofit organizations in your area through the state listings at this site, which consists of more than 21,000 members in 37 states.

 Rotary International

http://www.rotary.org/

★★★★★

Are you a business leader searching for something more to life? Do you want to give back to your community and make the world a better place? Then consider becoming a Rotarian. Rotary International is a worldwide organization of business and professional leaders who provide humanitarian services and uphold high ethical standards in their profession. Their well-designed website is packed with information about the organization and ways you can become a member. Find a Rotary chapter in your area, learn about Rotary initiatives, download forms and information, and become a member.

BUSINESS

American Management Association

http://www.amanet.org/index.htm

★★★★

Get a listing of self-paced learning opportunities, seminars, and conferences; review AMA books and publications. This site is a good starting point for learning about the function of management.

American Small Business Association

http://www.asbdc-us.org/

★★★

This site acts as a kiosk for all the development resources you will need to start and manage your small business. Provides information and contacts in many different areas of business management, along with valuable government resources. A great place to network.

Direct Marketing Association

http://www.the-dma.org/

★★★★

Learn more about the field of direct marketing by reading industry news briefs and surveying information of particular interest to consumers, agencies, or catalogers. The Direct Marketing Association claims a membership base of more than 4,700 companies.

Financial Management Association

http://www.fma.org

★★★

The FMA is dedicated to "developing and disseminating knowledge about financial decision making." FMA members get conference, placement, publication information, and special services.

International Association of Convention and Visitor Bureaus

http://www.iacvb.org/

★★★

Home of the "world's largest association of convention and visitor bureaus," this association serves more than 1,200 members in nearly 500 organizations in 30 countries. Designed for meeting planners, this website enables planners to check out potential convention sites online, purchase contact lists and publications, and obtain other valuable resources.

International Business Forum

http://www.ibf.com/ba/ibba.htm

★★★

Find links to business and professional associations internationally, as well as chambers of commerce.

EDUCATION

American Library Association

http://www.ala.org/

★★★

Keep up with ALA news, check on library job opportunities, read about upcoming events and conferences, and investigate the ALA library.

National Head Start Association

http://www2.acf.dhhs.gov/programs/hsb/

★★★★

This private not-for-profit education initiative gives children from low-income families a jump on education during their formative years (ages birth to 5 years). Learn about upcoming conferences, get up-to-date government guidelines and statistics, and enter contests online.

Institute of Educational Sciences

http://www.ed.gov/offices/IES/

★★★★

Initiated on November 5, 2002, when President Bush signed into law the *Education Sciences Reform Act of 2002*, the Institute of Education Sciences focuses on "evidence-based" education. Funding opportunities listed on this site are a great starting point for early childhood educators. FAQs, research updates, and publications are also available.

National PTA

http://www.pta.org

★★★★

This home for the National Parents and Teachers Association provides links to child advocacy sites, updates to legislative activity, and bulletin boards. Excellent articles for parents on becoming more involved in their children's lives and helping their children succeed in school.

REAL ESTATE

American Homeowners Association

http://www.ahahome.com

★★★★

This site offers real estate and home-related information, products, mortgage audits, and other services. Don't miss the Top 10 Home Buying Tips and Top Home Buying Mistakes. The site also features coupons, hotel discounts, vision discounts, and plenty of tips to help homeowners save money.

American Society of Home Inspectors

http://www.ashi.com

★★★★

This site tells you how to choose a qualified home inspector and what to expect from a home inspection. It also provides a list of frequently asked questions and a searchable directory of qualified home inspectors. This is an excellent site for homebuyers and home inspectors alike.

Institute of Real Estate Management

http://www.irem.org

★★★★

Property management professionals can learn about upcoming meetings and conventions, search the online database, and order IREM's publications on property management.

A B C D E F G H I J K L M N O P Q R S T U V W X Y Z

Mortgage Bankers Association of America

http://www.mbaa.org

★★★★

A complete resource for mortgage bankers. Read mortgage industry news, review a calendar of upcoming meetings, check the job board, and stay current using industry resources available on the site.

National Association of Realtors

http://www.realtor.com

★★★★★

Find a home, find a neighborhood, and find a realtor using this large, popular real estate site with a searchable database of more than 1,200,000 homes nationwide—an eye-catching and easy-to-follow site. Although you cannot shop directly here, clicking one of the product or shopping links takes you to Homestore.com, where you can place orders online.

WOMEN

American Business Women's Association

http://www.abwahq.org

★★★

Official site for the ABWA containing news, event dates, and organizational information.

American Nurses Association

http://www.nursingworld.org

★★★

A professional organization that fosters the high standards of the nursing practice and protects nurses' rights in the workplace.

National Association for Female Executives

http://www.nafe.com

★★★

Resources and services through education, networking, and public advocacy to empower its members to achieve career success and financial security.

National Association of Women in Construction

http://www.nawic.org

★★★★

Dedicated to helping women succeed in the construction industry, this site provides information on educational programs and legislation. Membership information is available at this site, as well as information on upcoming events, SIC code index, and helpful construction links.

ASTRONOMY

Adler Planetarium and Astronomy Museum

http://www.adlerplanetarium.org/

★★★★★

 All

Located in Chicago, on the shores of Lake Michigan, the Adler Planetarium and Astronomy Museum is one of the premier astronomy museums in the United States. Here, you can find the latest astronomy news and information, a skywatcher's guide, ideas for family fun, a visitor's guide, and much more. You can even shop the museum store online.

Amazing Space

http://amazing-space.stsci.edu/

★★★★★

 All

Designed for classroom use, Amazing Space provides a collection of interactive web-based activities to teach students various topics, such as understanding light and how black holes function. Some cool features, such as Planet Impact; where you can smash a comet into the planet Jupiter, make this site well worth a visit.

American Astronomical Society

http://www.aas,org/

★★★★★

Provides general astronomy information of interest to professionals and amateur enthusiasts. Maintains links to other astronomy resources on the Net.

Astro!nfo

http://www.astroinfo.org/english.php

★★★★

Check out the most recent astronomical events compliments of the Swiss Astronomical Society. When you reach the site, click the Planetarium tab to view the English version. At the top of the resulting page, click the Calendar link to view descriptions of celestial events on a given date, or click the desired heavenly body (Sun, Moon, Planets, Comets, and so on) to view dates on which you can witness events.

Astronomy HyperText Book

http://zebu.uoregon.edu/text.html

★★★

A hypertextual astronomy textbook written at the college level. Contains interactive information about astronomy. Also offers links to sites that offer astronomy assistance.

Astronomy Magazine

http://www.astronomy.com/home.asp

★★★★★

 9-13

This site contains an almanac of current sky happenings, a calendar of star parties, directories of planetariums and clubs, a well-stocked photo library, as well as product reviews on telescopes and binoculars. Well designed, this site is a pleasure to explore. Although not much at this site is designed specifically to appeal to kids, amateur astronomers will find many of the articles fascinating and comprehensible.

A
B
C
D
E
F
G
H
I
J
K
L
M
N
O
P
Q
R
S
T
U
V
W
X
Y
Z

Astronomy Now On-Line

http://www.astronomynow.com/

★★★★

👥 9-13

Check out late-breaking stories about the most significant astronomical events and space missions. The Breaking News area is the site's main feature, providing very current stories on astronomical events and space exploration. You can click the Store link to shop for calendars, books, T-shirts, patches, and other items. You can try clicking the Night Sky link, but last I checked, the page was last updated two years ago. Likewise, the Index and Resources areas have been "under construction" for at least a year.

Astronomy Picture of the Day

http://antwrp.gsfc.nasa.gov/apod/astropix.html

★★★★

An up-to-date picture of a particular celestial body or scene, complete with a brief description of the photo or explanation of the phenomenon it represents. You can also search through the archive for past pictures of the day by clicking the Calendar, Search, or Index link.

Bad Astronomy

http://www.badastronomy.com/

★★★

The advice not to believe everything you hear or read applies to the sciences as well, including astronomy. Here, you can read about common misconceptions and claims about space and find out the truth. For example, few people realize that there is no "dark side of the moon."

Caltech Space Society

http://www.seds.org/seds/chapters/css/CSS.html

★★★

Provides information about space-related projects, such as conferences and educational programs that are open to the public.

CCD Images of Galaxies

http://zebu.uoregon.edu/galaxy.html

★★★

Presents a collection of images, specializing in photographs of galaxies. Also offers educational resources.

Chandra X-Ray Observatory

http://chandra.harvard.edu/

★★★★★

👥 All

This is the home of NASA's Chandra X-Ray Observatory, where you can learn everything from the basics of X-Ray astronomy to the intricacies of how Chandra functions. View digital images of Chandra's discoveries, learn about galactic navigation, track Chandra's progress, submit a question to one of NASA's experts, and play interactive games online.

Comet Observation

http://encke.jpl.nasa.gov/

★★★

Archive with hundreds of comet images, news on current comets, light curves, ephemerides, and definitions.

Compton Gamma Ray Observatory

http://cossc.gsfc.nasa.gov/cossc/cossc.html

★★★

Learn about the Compton Gamma Ray Observatory, NASA's second project in its Great Observatories program. Whereas NASA's first project, the Hubble telescope, was designed to observe visible objects, the Compton Gamma Ray Observatory is designed to observe invisible energy fields.

Constellation X

http://constellation.gsfc.nasa.gov

★★★★★

👥 9-13

This site offers information on studies of black holes and the life cycles of matter throughout the universe using a network of powerful X-ray telescopes. A very cool welcome screen, excellent graphics and video clips, and clear descriptions of various astronomical phenomena combine to make this one of the most intriguing astronomy sites in the group.

Earth & Sky

http://www.earthsky.com/

★★★★★

👫 9-13

Internet home of the popular *Earth & Sky* radio program, a science program created by Deborah Byrd and Joel Block for kids. Each program is one and a half minutes long and provides a brief explanation of a particular science topic. Here, you can replay the radio shows and/or read along with the scripts. Teachers can visit this site to obtain lesson plans and other resources, and anyone can shop online for calendars, books, and software. Kids should check out the Activities area for games and quizzes.

Eclipse Information

http://members.iinet.net.au/~homer/eclipse/

★★★★★

This site focuses on solar and lunar eclipses around the world, with detailed diagrams showing the path of the eclipse as it will be seen around the world. On the left side of the opening page is a navigation bar that provides links to more than 20 additional pages that deal with other celestial events plus links to several news filters and more than a dozen other astronomy-related sites.

The Event Inventor: Web Sites for Space Mission Projects

http://kyes-world.com/spacesites.htm

★★★

👫 9-13

Consider this site a launch pad for online space exploration. This site provides several links to interesting astronomy and space travel sites around the Web, especially sites that appeal to younger space enthusiasts.

High Energy Astrophysics Science Archive Research Center

http://heasarc.gsfc.nasa.gov/docs/HEASARC_HOME_PAGE.html

★★★★

Contains general information on supernovae, X-ray binaries, and black holes. This site is definitely for the more advanced astronomers.

Best HubbleSite

http://www.hubblesite.org/

$

★★★★★

This is the home of NASA's Hubble telescope, where you can explore the heavens through the incredible photos that the Hubble telescope has sent back to earth. View digital images of Hubble's discoveries, read expert analysis of those discoveries, learn about the technology that powers the Hubble telescope and its digital imaging and transmission capabilities, play games, check out the reference desk, and explore Hubble's future. Site is easy to navigate, packed with great information and dazzling graphics, and is accessible and interesting to astronomers at all levels of learning, making this our universal pick for Best of the Best in Astronomy!

International Astronomical Union

http://www.iau.org/

★★★

Contains access to current and past bulletins, as well as reports posted by association members.

The Long Duration Exposure Facility

http://setas-www.larc.nasa.gov/LDEF/index.html

★★★

This site is primarily designed to provide engineers with information about space environments to help them design spaceships and plan missions. The LDEF satellite, which contained 57 experiments, spent 69 months studying various aspects of the environment in space.

A B C D E F G H I J K L M N O P Q R S T U V W X Y Z

A
B
C
D
E
F
G
H
I
J
K
L
M
N
O
P
Q
R
S
T
U
V
W
X
Y
Z

Mount Wilson Observatory

http://www.mtwilson.edu/

★★★

Overviews several ongoing astronomy projects using innovative techniques and modern detectors. Provides information for professionals, amateurs, tourists, and educators from its location just outside Pasadena, California.

NASA Earth Observatory

http://earthobservatory.nasa.gov

★★★★★

This public access site is designed to provide visitors with current satellite images and information about the earth—mainly its environment and how environmental changes are affecting the landscape.

NASA HumanSpaceflight

http://spaceflight.nasa.gov/

★★★★

Study the history of NASA's space missions from Mercury to the present, get real-time data on sighting opportunities, track the orbit of NASA spacecraft, obtain detailed information about the space station and space shuttle programs, check out NASA's photo gallery, and much more.

NASAKIDS

http://kids.msfc.nasa.gov/

★★★★★

 All

This site from NASA is designed specifically to appeal to kids. Here, children can view NASA cartoons, learn about rockets and airplanes, explore the Milky Way and other celestial frontiers, tour the astronaut's living space, play games and animations, and much more. For kids who are interested in space, there's no better site on the Web.

Related Sites
http://www.nsip.net
http://www.thursdaysclassroom.com

National Geographic Star Journey

http://www.nationalgeographic.com/stars/

★★★★

9-13

View the nighttime sky using the online sky chart, complete with images from the Hubble telescope. You can also set your own course to investigate the heavens. Although you cannot shop directly at this site, it displays a link to National Geographic's online store. Older children who are interested in astronomy may find some of the information here very interesting and clearly presented.

Planetary Sciences at NSSDC

http://nssdc.gsfc.nasa.gov/planetary/planetary_home.html/Element of the National Space Science Data Center (NSSDC)/

★★★

NSSDC provides online information about NASA and non-NASA data as well as information about spacecraft and experiments that generate NASA space science data. Here, you can find details about specific space exploration missions plus links to planetary events and other astronomy sites.

Purdue SEDS (Students for the Exploration and Development of Space)

http://roger.ecn.purdue.edu/~seds/

★★★

14-18

Provides information about the Purdue Students for the Exploration and Development of Space (SEDS) group and serves as a place to discuss space exploration and development. This site is more for Purdue SEDS members than for the general public. For a friendlier SEDS site, check out the following entry.

SEDS Internet Space Warehouse

http://www.seds.org/

★★★

[♟] 14-18

The home of Students for the Exploration and Development of Space (SEDS), this site is dedicated to building enthusiasm for space exploration in younger generations. Contains many links to space resources on the Internet, a few multimedia documents, and information about the organization. It's a good place to share enthusiasm for model rocketry, as well.

Sky & Telescope

http://www.skypub.com/

$

★★★★

This site offers information from current and back issues of *Sky and Telescope* magazine as well as links to information that can help you set up your own observatory, including news reports about up and coming astronomical events and information on how to take pictures through your telescope.

Solar System Live

http://www.fourmilab.ch/solar/solar.html

★★★

Allows you to view a model of the solar system. Offers adjustable settings so you can see how the solar system would be at any given time or on any given date.

Star Stuff

http://www.starstuff.com/

★★★★

[♟] 9-13

"For astronomy students of all ages," Star Stuff is an excellent resource for learning about the universe and solar system, complete with images located in the Planets for Kids section.

StarWorlds–Astronomy and Related Organizations

http://cdsweb.u-strasbg.fr/~heck/sfworlds.htm

★★★

Furnishes a searchable listing of the addresses of organizations, institutions, associations, companies, and other groups involved in astronomy and related space sciences.

Views of the Solar System

http://www.solarviews.com/eng/homepage.htm

$

★★★★

Features a vivid multimedia tour of the solar system. Contains images and information about the sun, planets, moons, asteroids, comets, and meteoroids. You can purchase books and equipment with which to view the planets here.

Web Nebulae

http://seds.lpl.arizona.edu/billa/twn/

★★★

Contains a collection of images of various objects in our galaxy. Includes images and explains how to classify nebulae.

Welcome to Loch Ness Productions

http://www.lochness.com/

$

★★★★

[♟] All

Specializes in producing planetarium program materials. Includes access to samples of planetarium music and art, as well as a listing of planetariums around the world.

A
B
C
D
E
F
G
H
I
J
K
L
M
N
O
P
Q
R
S
T
U
V
W
X
Y
Z

A
B
C
D
E
F
G
H
I
J
K
L
M
N
O
P
Q
R
S
T
U
V
W
X
Y
Z

AUCTIONS

Amazon Auctions

http://s1.amazon.com/

★★★★★

Visit Amazon's newest addition—an auction area, where you can scout for deals on everything from antiques to jewelry to clothing, even automotive parts and accessories. For those users looking to simplify their life, Amazon Auctions also accepts items for sale. For an additional fee, Amazon will cross-sell your item on the Amazon website, which puts your products in front of millions of potential buyers.

Andalé

http://www.andale.com

★★★★

This auction management site is designed for auction sellers who want to save time and money in listing their products and services at online auction sites. In other words, Andalé acts as a middleman between auctioneers and online auctions, such as Amazon and eBay.

Auction Patrol

http://www.auctionpatrol.com

★★★★

Search several auction sites through this site, including Amazon, eBay, Sotheby's, and Yahoo!, or use the free online web tools to manage the auction of items online. For buyers and sellers, this site provides a directory of more than 600 auction resources, software tools, and auction sites.

AuctionAddict.com

http://www.auctionaddict.com/

★★★★

AuctionAddict.com is designed as a meeting place for buyers and sellers. Sellers can put individual items up for sale, create their own storefronts and market items at a fixed price, or designate them for an online auction where prospective buyers can bid.

AuctionPage Auctions

http://auctionpage.com/

★★★★

Relatively small auction site that enables you to put items on the auction block or bid on items. Main categories are Collectibles, Antiques, Computers, Software, and Merchandise. You can also post news of your own auctions and services here.

Bidders Edge

http://www.bidxs.com/be/

★★★★

Search for auction bargains through this auction portal. This site allows you to search more than 500 auction sites for things you need. You can make quick side-by-side comparisons of the products available.

Bottomdollar.com

http://www.bottomdollar.com/

★★★★★

Compare prices from a long list of online merchants and auctions before making a purchase. Visitors can save plenty of money by checking prices here first. Most of the real deals are for used versions of the products.

CNet Auctions

http://auctions.cnet.com

★★★★★

This site is a great place to find computers and peripheral devices for sale by auction. The auction interface is excellent and easy to use.

 eBay

http://www.ebay.com

$

★★★★★

It's the world's largest trading online community. Bid on millions of items from books, to computer products, to antiques. Join millions of registered (and eager) users who frequent this site, and test your expertise at finding the best deals on the Internet. By some counts, eBay is the busiest site on the Internet, possibly the largest free market in the world. Because of its incredible popularity and its ease of use, this is truly the Best of the Best.

InetAuction

http://www.softglobe.com

★★★★

Auctioneers and auction managers should check out this site. For $1,000 per event day plus a 3.5–5% cut of the proceeds, you can use InetAuction software to host a traditional auction online. You interact with the bidders just as you would at a live auction.

Internet Auction List

http://www.internetauctionlist.com/

★★★★

Click a category (art, military memorabilia, horses and livestock, and many more) and choose from dozens of online auctions. Go to the calendar and see which auctions are being held on a particular date. Check for links to other auction sites or subscribe to the free newsletter. This is the most complete list of auctions available on the Web.

MastroNet, Inc.

http://www.mastronet.com/

★★★★★

This site specializes in niche auctions—one-of-a-kind collectibles, such as the football that Emmitt Smith carried when he surpassed Walter Payton as the all-time leading rusher in NFL history. This auction site deals mostly in sports collectibles, but you can find other rare items here, as well.

Priceline.com

http://www.priceline.com

★★★★★

Name your price for airline tickets, hotel rooms, cars, and mortgage rates on this site. Priceline then approaches potential sellers who might be willing to fulfill your request. Many users have reported saving hundreds of dollars on plane tickets using this site.

Sotheby's

http://www.sothebys.com

★★★★★

This, as you might expect, is a classy web page. Read about upcoming auctions or results of recent auctions, browse or order catalogs, or browse the categories of collections that are currently being auctioned. Sotheby's online auction is managed by eBay.

uBid

http://www.ubid.com/

★★★★★

A huge auction site featuring every imaginable product. The opening page displays thumbnail photos of products, and the navigation bar on the left side of the page makes it easy to browse available items.

A B C D E F G H I J K L M N O P Q R S T U V W X Y Z

Vendio Productions

http://www.vendio.com/

★★★

If you're looking to sell products on the Web, either through fixed pricing or auctions, Vendio can help you set up an automated system for promoting, selling, and distributing your products online.

Yahoo! Auctions

http://auctions.shopping.yahoo.com/

★★★★★

Yahoo! was a little late in entering the auction arena, but now it has a fairly decent auction site, where you can sell or bid on items in dozens of categories ranging from Art to Automobiles to Video Games. You can easily navigate the site and find items you want to bid on.

ZDNet Auctions

http://auctions.zdnet.com/

★★★★★

An auction site with a full range of services. You can buy, sell, search for items, create watchlists, and more at this site. Check out the computers and computer accessories.

Related Sites
http://www.usaweb.com/
http://www.myitem.com/
http://www.auctiontalk.com/

AUTO RACING

Andretti Home Page

http://www.andretti.com

★★★★

View photos of the drivers in action and read personal profiles of Mario, Michael, Jeff, and Marco. And if you enjoy that, join the fan club! At this site, you can also download Andretti wallpaper for your computer's desktop.

Cart.com

http://www.cart.com

★★★★

At this comprehensive site from Championship Auto Racing Teams, visitors can find out just about anything about racing teams, drivers, past and future events, and results.

CATCHFENCE.com

http://www.catchfence.com

★★★★

From headline racing news to race information and explanations, this site is a one-stop racing library. Also includes chat rooms and a message board, so you can share your racing enthusiasm with fellow fans.

Honda Racing

http://www.hondaracing.com

★★★★

Find out what's going on this week at the track and enjoy racing images here, where you can also learn more about drivers and their cars. You can purchase Honda caps and T-shirts through the online store.

Indy Racing League

http://www.indyracingleague.com/

★★★★

Dedicated to Indy Racing League (IRL) fans, this site provides a schedule of events, complete with information about how to tune in to races on TV or radio. You can also check the point totals to find out where your driver is in the standings and check out the latest headlines.

KartingForum.com

http://kartingforum.com/

★★★

 14-18

Go-kart racing fans can stay in touch with other participants through this friendly site that features plenty of discussion opportunities as well as news. This site also offers auctions and classifieds where you can see what is being offered for sale.

Motor Sports on the Internet

http://www.online96.com/sports/auto.html

★★★

You'll find a list of auto racing links on this site. Links include F1 racing, NASCAR, racing teams, and other racing resources.

A
B
C
D
E
F
G
H
I
J
K
L
M
N
O
P
Q
R
S
T
U
V
W
X
Y
Z

Motorsports Hall of Fame

http://www.mshf.com/

★★★★★

Dedicated to preserving the legacy of the "Heroes of Horsepower," the Motorsports Hall of Fame of America houses more than 40 racing and high-performance vehicles, including various types of cars, trucks, boats, motorcycles, air racers, and even racing snowmobiles. Click the Museum link to explore a small selection of the museum's offerings. Check out the list of Hall of Fame Inductees to read biographies of your favorite drivers.

My Brickyard: Brickyard 400

http://my.brickyard.com

★★★★

Get the latest information about NASCAR and one of its premier events: the Brickyard 400. Check out the schedule of events, a collection of audio and video clips, and an online racing game. You can even sign up for mobile updates or shop online at the gift shop.

NHRA Online

http://www.nhra.com

★★★★

Follow the progress of your favorite racers in the National Hot Rod Association, or get up-to-date news and information on upcoming races.

Racecar

http://www.racecar.co.uk

★★★★★

Racecar creates websites for a number of companies in the specialty auto field. This site features stories from around the world related to various car races and racing leagues, including F1 and Le Mans.

Speednet

http://www.starnews.com/sports/racing/

★★★

Covers the latest racing news for IRL, CART, Formula 1, and NASCAR. View schedules, reviews, racing results, and statistics. Visit the fan forum to read messages from fellow fans or post your own messages.

Best Winston Cup

http://www.nascar.com/series/wc/index.html

★★★★★

 9-13

Packed with the latest articles and information about NASCAR's Winston Cup Series, this site serves up a feast of information about drivers, teams, statistics, sponsors, and history. If you're a NASCAR novice, click the Know Your NASCAR link to get up to speed. Seasoned fans will find plenty of features to keep them interested as well. Though this site is not designed for kids, it features some cool racing video games that kids (and adults) can play on the computer.

FORMULA ONE

Atlas F1

http://www.atlasf1.com

★★★★

For in-depth coverage of events, racing enthusiasts will want to visit this online magazine, which also provides daily news updates. With stats and commentary, this is one of the richest sites for Formula 1 content. Buy T-shirts and posters and other photo memorabilia through the online store.

Formula1.com

http://www.formula1.com/

★★★★★

👥 9-13

This "unofficial" site is packed with information about F1 drivers, teams, history, stats, schedules, and news. Click the Fun tab to race around a virtual track, join in a fantasy racing competition, or download an F1 screensaver. Racing fans will love to listen in on audio feeds from races and watch videos from live events on the audio/video section of the site.

ITV Formula 1

http://www.itv-f1.com/

★★★★

ITV is the largest commercial television network in the United Kingdom. ITV's F1 site provides in-depth coverage and lots of photos related to F1 racing, including coverage of teams, drivers, and pit crews.

News on F1

http://www.newsonf1.com/

★★★

Detailed racing information and driver updates are featured here, as are current standings and team information.

Shell-Ferrari

http://www.shellmotorsport.com/ferrari/index.html

★★★★★

👥 9-13

If you want a history of Formula 1, pre- and post-race reports, and car statistics, come to this site sponsored by Shell-Ferrari. Very cool, well-designed site. Special games area encourages children and adults to get behind the wheel for some virtual car racing excitement.

AUTOMOBILE CLUBS AND ORGANIZATIONS

AAA Online

http://www.aaa.com/

★★★★★

Go directly to your state's "Triple A" office by entering your ZIP or Postal code in the AAA website. In addition to information about AAA's famous Triptiks and the 24/365 road service that offers car lockout help, jump starts, and fixed flats, find out about travel reservations and discounts, domestic and international tours, and $1,000 arrest bonds. If there's one auto club site you should visit, this is it.

The Antique Automobile Club of America

http://www.aaca.org/

★★★★

The AACA is not just for people who like old cars. Actually, this club wants to preserve and celebrate all modes of "self-propelled vehicle," which is any vehicle meant to carry people and that runs on gasoline, diesel, steam, or electricity. Founded in 1935, the AACA has more than 400 chapters all over the world, and its website is exhaustive in its coverage of history, legislation, film and video, museums, links, and much more.

CHVA (Contemporary Historical Vehicle Association): Arizona Chapter

http://www.theriver.com/Public/chva/index.htm

★★★

The Contemporary Historical Vehicle Association is a club dedicated to the preservation of vehicles from the Action Era (any car 25 years old or older) back to 1928.

The Electric Auto Association

http://www.eaaev.org/

★★★

The EAA is a nonprofit organization dedicated to the advancement and adoption of the electricity-powered car. The principle of the EAA is that electric vehicles (EVs) are more efficient and better for the planet than those that run on standard fossil fuel. A long list of links to other EV-related sites is provided.

The National Motorists Association

http://www.motorists.com/

★★★★

The NMA exists to protect your rights as a driving citizen. Among its many services, the NMA lobbies for sensible road traffic laws and engineering, argues for your right to drive whatever you want, helps you fight tickets, and opposes camera-based enforcement, as well as speed traps designed to generate revenue. Don't leave without clicking the Fight Your Traffic Ticket button and reading through the tips on how to avoid getting a ticket.

The Sports Car Club of America

http://www.scca.org

★★★★

If you've ever driven down the street and made car racing noises to yourself, the SCCA is the club for you. You are encouraged not only to love sports cars and racing, but to enter racing school and go racing yourself. This site provides a huge list of pro and amateur races and other events. Do you have a teenager with a heavy foot? How about entering him or her in the Speed Freakz program?

Women's Auto Help Center

http://www.mpilla.com/images/ford/wac_home/wac_home.html

★★★★

At Women's Auto Help Center you will find more articles and help than you can shake a stick shift at. Excellent information on car care for both men and women.

A
B
C
D
E
F
G
H
I
J
K
L
M
N
O
P
Q
R
S
T
U
V
W
X
Y
Z

A
B
C
D
E
F
G
H
I
J
K
L
M
N
O
P
Q
R
S
T
U
V
W
X
Y
Z

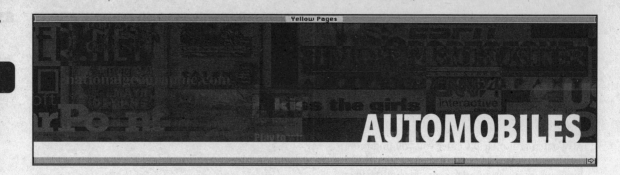

AUTOMOBILES

BUYING ONLINE

Auto Stop

http://www.theautostop.com/

★★★

Auto Stop is an auto-buying service that guarantees low, competitive prices on both new and previously owned vehicles. Within 48 hours after you choose the vehicle you want, Auto Stop's nearest subscribing dealership calls you with a quote, guaranteed to be fleet price, not retail price. You also have access to a large database of classifieds for used vehicles.

Related Sites
http://www.aiada.org/
http://www.auto.com/
http://www.myclassiccar.com/
http://www.autoexchange.com/

Auto World

http://www.autoworld.com/

★★★★

Unlike the Kelley Blue Book (a competitor of Auto World), Auto World updates its Vehicle Information and Pricing Service on a daily basis and takes into account variations in regional pricing. In addition to dynamic pricing reports, you can get a quote on a car or read tips on buying a car.

AutoBuyingTips

http://autobuyingtips.com/

★★★★

Consult this resource when buying your next car or extended warranty. Includes resources on loans, warranties, insurance, dealer costs, and even a place to get quotes. An excellent site to consult.

Autobytel.com

http://www.autobytel.com

★★★★

Buy or sell your car here, in addition to researching dealers, models, invoice pricing, Blue Book value, warranties, and dealer incentives. You can also apply for financing and insurance online.

AutoTrader.com

http://www.autotrader.com

★★★★

If you're looking for a used car, you'll want to search this database of more than 2 million used cars being sold by private individuals and dealers across the country. You can also limit your search geographically.

autoweb.com

http://www.autoweb.com/

★★★

A subsidiary of Autobytel.com, Autoweb brings you an online "auto superstore." Not only can you browse the Virtual Lot, but you also can check the Kelley Blue Book value, search the database of dealers for your ideal car, get an insurance quote for your vehicle, and offer your own review of cars you've test-driven.

Carprice.com

http://www.carprice.com/

★★★★★

Carprice.com is a search engine designed specifically to find vehicles (new and used) over the Internet. You simply specify the car you want and the desired options and enter your ZIP code. For new cars, the search turns up the manufacturer's suggested retail price and the invoice price; you can then fill out a form to have a local dealer contact you. For used cars, the search displays the asking price and a link for contacting the seller.

ConsumerGuide.com

http://www.consumerguide.com/

★★★★★

Consumer Guide has been providing sage advice to consumers for more than 30 years, and now provides this advice online at this site. Here, you can obtain quotes on new car prices from dealers in your area, determine the trade-in value of your old vehicle, and even check the history of a used vehicle via its Vehicle Identification Number (VIN). Site features some informative articles, as well.

Cars.com

http://www.cars.com

★★★★

Get the background information on used cars for sale at the site, or research new car performance and pricing and then get an online quote.

CarsDirect.com

http://www.carsdirect.com

★★★★

Search and compare new car alternatives that meet your needs, then get an online price quote, and arrange for delivery. For $25, you can list your car for sale online for as long as it takes to sell the car.

CarSmart.com

http://www.carsmart.com/

★★★

Check Consumers Guide reports on cars of interest and then search the database of available used cars, or get a quote on a new one. You can locate specific cars and dealers from the site. You can also do a lemon-check, using a vehicle's vehicle identification number (VIN), to ensure you don't get stuck with a defective vehicle. When you find a new car, you can sell your old car here, too.

DealerNet

http://www.dealernet.com/

★★★★

A very comprehensive guide to buying a car via the Internet. Enter your specific search criteria on the make, model, year, price range, and dealership location of your desired vehicle, and DealerNet gives you a list of options. You can also check out New Car Test Reviews or go to a chat room and discuss automotive topics with other auto lovers.

Edmund's Automobiles Buying Guides

http://www.edmunds.com/

★★★★★

The place to go when thinking of buying a new or used car. A multitude of information is available, including price guides, dealer cost information, buyer advice and recommendations, recall information, and much, much more.

Kelley Blue Book

http://www.kbb.com/

★★★★★

Before you sell a car or purchase a used car, you should check its "blue book" value, and Kelley Blue Book is the standard nearly all auto dealers use to determine the value of a used car. At this site, you can plug in a few details, including the make, model, and year of the car and its condition to see the blue book value for yourself. This site is packed with information and tips about buying new and used cars and provides all the tools you need to finance and purchase a car online.

B C D E F G H I J K L M N O P Q R S T U V W X Y Z

A
B
C
D
E
F
G
H
I
J
K
L
M
N
O
P
Q
R
S
T
U
V
W
X
Y
Z

LeaseGuide.com

http://www.leaseguide.com/

★★★★

If you're debating whether to purchase or lease your next car, this site provides all the information you need to make a good decision. You can even plug numbers into the lease calculator to take a quick look at the bottom line.

Microsoft Autos

http://autos.msn.com/

★★★★★

Yep, Bill Gates is selling cars, too. Microsoft's Autos offers new and used car information, interactive classifieds, 360-degree views of cars and trucks (inside and out), Kelley Blue Book pricing reports, reliability ratings, side-by-side comparisons, and news and advice on car-related issues.

Newspaper Advertising

http://www.newspapers.com/npcom1.htm

★★★

If you are interested in selling rather than buying a vehicle, you could try listing your vehicle in your local newspaper online. This site provides entry into numerous newspaper sites nationwide.

Stoneage

http://www.stoneage.com/

★★★★

Stoneage specializes in putting consumers in touch with new and used car dealers and sellers over the Internet. Find a specific dealer in your area and schedule an appointment or ask for a quick quote. Before buying that used car, purchase a vehicle history report for $14.95 (or 20 reports for $19.95)—first one's free. Learn the benefits of extending that manufacturer's warranty. For one fee, get the three major credit reports in one easy-to-read report.

Related Sites
http://www.motorzoo.com/
http://classifieds.yahoo.com/auto.html

CLASSIC CARS

Auto Restorer On-Line

http://www.autorestorer.com/

★★★

Get inspired by stories and photos of successful restoration projects, and then investigate how to do it yourself through Q&As and message boards from those who've done it.

Classic Car Source

http://www.classicar.com/

★★★★★

For car lovers interested in bonding with fellow classic car buffs, this site has a community spirit combined with articles, photographs, chat, auctions, message boards, and restoration help.

Classic Car-Nection

http://www.car-nection.com/

★★★★

Need parts for your car? Then search the online classifieds here in search of your missing link. Or place an ad for available parts and cars for those in need.

Classic Showcase

http://www.classicshowcase.com/

★★★

This classic car dealer specializes in the sale of sports cars and hard-to-find classics, as well as restoration of some vehicles. Check the vehicle inventory if you're in the market, or contact the dealer about buying a vehicle you might want to sell.

Hemmings Motor News

http://www.hmn.com/

★★★★★

Hemmings Motor News is the authority on classic collector cars. Check out this site for classifieds, upcoming events, and links to museums, dealers, parts locators, and much more.

Model T Ford Club

http://www.modelt.org/

★★★★

Learn more about Model Ts at this site, where you can also find out about the Model T club and search the database for information on the car's history and manufacture.

Pontiac Server

http://www.pontiacserver.com/

★★★★

Pontiac Server is created and maintained by a guy named Rich, who wanted to share his enthusiasm about classic Pontiacs with other enthusiasts. This site, dedicated to Tempests, GTOs, Grand Prix's, and Firebirds, includes photo albums, classic ads, classic road tests, and links to other classic Pontiac sites.

INFORMATION

AutoAdvice.com

http://www.autoadvice.com

★★★

This site walks you through the whole process of researching a new car, selling your old one, and negotiating with dealers.

Car Buying Tips

http://www.carbuyingtips.com

★★★

With information provided at this site, you should be able to negotiate a car purchase without falling victim to common scams.

Carfax Lemon Check

http://www.carfax.com/

★★★★★

An essential resource for anyone thinking of buying a used car. Enter the car's vehicle identification number (VIN) at the site and find out whether the car has been labeled a lemon, or one with repeated problems, free. If you like the service, you can look up additional VINs for $19.99 (or $27.99 for unlimited reports).

CarInfo.com

http://www.carinfo.com

★★★★

Learn the secrets of a successful lease or purchase from consumer advocate Mark Eskeldson. Mark also provides information on how to avoid being ripped off by inscrutable auto mechanics.

MANUFACTURERS

Acura

http://www.acura.com/

★★★★★

The classy Acura has become an urban status symbol, and you can find out why on this page. It provides information about the newest models, searching for Acuras online, plus service and benefit information for current owners.

Audi

http://www.audiusa.com

★★★★★

The sleek home page highlights the design, performance, technology, and safety features that go into making Audi vehicles premium products. Search online for a new or used Audi, locate a dealer, and even check out Audi's contribution to motorsports.

Austin Healey

http://www.healey.org/

★★★

Home of the Austin Healey club. Here, you can locate other Austin Healey owners worldwide, learn about planned excursions and trips, and view car images and links to other Healey-related sites.

A
B
C
D
E
F
G
H
I
J
K
L
M
N
O
P
Q
R
S
T
U
V
W
X
Y
Z

BMW of North America

http://www.bmwusa.com

★★★★★

Whether you're a current BMW owner or a wannabe, you'll find plenty of information at this site. Learn about the new models by clicking Choose a Model, or visit the pre-owned area to find out how you can acquire a gently used BMW. You can even check out BMW motorcycles.

Buick

http://www.buick.com

★★★★★

Request a brochure, find a dealer nearby, purchase Buick merchandise, learn about Buick's involvement with charity events and golf tournaments, or buy a car online. Lots of information is available in a neatly laid-out site.

Cadillac

http://www.cadillac.com

★★★★★

Check out the Interactive Module on this site and experience the 360-degree video that will make you feel like you're in a Cadillac. You can also learn more about available models and order yours online.

Chevrolet

http://www.chevrolet.com

★★★★★

Gather information on Chevy cars and trucks on this site, learn about special offers, view brochures, and find a local dealer.

Daihatsu

http://www.daihatsu.com/

★★★★

Daihatsu specializes in designing and manufacturing compact, energy-efficient vehicles. To enter the showroom, click the On-Line Catalogues link. Click Motor Show to view a list of automobile shows where you can find Daihatsu vehicles on display. You can also read Daihatsu's environmental reports and information about its industrial engines.

DaimlerChrysler

http://www3.daimlerchrysler.com

★★★★★

Your one-stop shopping spot for all the models made by DaimlerChrysler Corporation, including Dodge, Chrysler, Jeep, and Mercedes-Benz. Click the Products link and then click the logo for the desired model to browse available vehicles, or click Research & Technology to view the latest automotive improvements. Some of the manufacturer sites that are part of DaimlerChrysler enable you to shop online for accessories.

Ford Motor Company

http://www.ford.com/en/default.htm

★★★★

Here's the master page from which you can access all the model-specific pages for vehicles made by the Ford Motor Company. They include Ford, Lincoln, Mazda, Mercury, Volvo, Aston Martin, and Jaguar. Click the Services link for information on caring for and servicing your vehicle.

General Motors

http://www.gm.com

★★★★★

This page is the jumping-off point for individual websites for the various models made by General Motors, including Chevrolet, GMC, Buick, Holden, Isuzu, Opel, Pontiac, Saab, Saturn, Chevy Trucks, Cadillac, Vauxhall, and Oldsmobile. This site also features links for pages on safety issues, innovations, parts and service, and other GM products and services.

Honda

http://www.honda.com/

★★★★★

Check out all the latest Honda and Acura models here, locate nearby dealers, and visit the Honda corporate headquarters, all in one trip. This site also features links to other Honda products, including motorcycles, power equipment, personal watercraft, and boat engines. Click Honda Automobiles and then click the Build Your Honda link to start shopping for a Honda vehicle online, or simply click the desired model to get started.

Best Hummer

http://www.hummer.com

★★★★★

This militaristic site stresses durability and strength just by its design, which fits the product well. Look at the photo gallery, check out current models, and learn the history of the Hummer. A cool interactive tool enables you to build your dream Hummer online and immediately experience the sensation of sticker shock.

Hyundai Motor Company

http://www.hmc.co.kr/

★★★★★

This easy-to-navigate site offers profiles on the new Hyundai models, a company profile, and current company news. A great place to check out the various Hyundai models and get a ballpark figure on the price.

Isuzu

http://www.isuzu.com/

★★★

Comparatively speaking, this site is fairly basic. Click the desired model for a brief description of it and links for checking out the vehicle's features, specifications, and comparisons to other vehicles in its class. You can also build a custom Isuzu online, request a brochure, or view 360-degree images of the various models.

Lexus

http://www.lexus.com/

★★★★★

With a focus on its newest models, Lexus offers information on all its vehicles, providing stunning photography and information. As with other manufacturer sites, you can tour the showroom, locate a dealer near you, search a database of preowned Lexuses, and build a custom Lexus online.

Mazda

http://www.mazdausa.com/

★★★★★

Learn all about the latest Mazda models in this online showroom and participate in Mazda's current sweepstakes to win a new car. If you own a Mazda, you can enter the members-only area, which offers news about your vehicle, plus driving, safety, and maintenance tips. Zoom zoom!

Mercedes-Benz

http://www.mercedes-benz.com

★★★★★

Learn all about the various models of Mercedes-Benz vehicles, locate a dealer, and read what others have to say about Mercedes performance.

Mercury

http://www.mercuryvehicles.com

★★★★★

View current Mercury models, get a glimpse of next year's models, and arrange for a test drive at this site.

Mini Cooper

http://www.mini.co.uk/

★★★★★

If you own a Mini Cooper or are one of many drivers who dream of owning one, visit the official Mini Cooper home page. Here, you can check out the latest models, learn how to find a good used Mini Cooper, and shop for some nifty accessories.

Mitsubishi Motors

http://www.mitsubishi-motors.co.jp

★★★★★

Mitsubishi Motors presents dealer listings, financing information, model specifications, and motorsports information. Click the link for the desired model to research its design and features, and build a custom vehicle online to estimate its full cost.

A B C D E F G H I J K L M N O P Q R S T U V W X Y Z

A
B
C
D
E
F
G
H
I
J
K
L
M
N
O
P
Q
R
S
T
U
V
W
X
Y
Z

Nissan

http://www.nissandriven.com/

★★★★★

Learn about special offers available to potential Nissan owners and fully research all Nissan models at this sleek website. Financing information is also available online, making your shopping experience more convenient.

Porsche

http://www.porsche.com

★★★★★

In addition to scoping out luscious models of Porsche engineering, you can also learn about the company's involvement with international motorsports. Catch up on race news and plan for upcoming events with the help of the Race Dates calendar. Current Porsche owners will want to check out the local Porsche clubs and visit the online shopping pages. Beautiful photography throughout the site.

Rolls-Royce

http://www.rolls-roycemotorcars.com/

★★★

Unlike most other car websites, the Rolls-Royce Motor Cars site provides much more information about the Rolls-Royce Phantom, its history, and production process. However, you can also locate worldwide dealers here, too.

Saab

http://www.saabusa.com

$

★★★★★

Explore Saab's current models, learn about upcoming announcements, and hear about Saab services.

Saturn

http://www.saturn.com/

★★★★★

Home of the no-haggle policy, this Saturn site allows you to research various models and build a custom package online. And, because the price is nonnegotiable, you can be assured that the price you see online is the price the dealer is going to quote you. To find a Saturn dealer near you, click Retailers and enter your ZIP code.

Subaru

http://www.subaru.com

★★★★★

Learn about Subaru's newest vehicles, locate a dealer near you, and take a look at MSRP. You'll also find in-depth information on the company's all-wheel driving system plus industry reviews.

Toyota

http://www.toyota.com/

★★★★★

Configure a new Toyota, locate a used one, or just browse the news and corporate information at Toyota's website. Owners can access a special area of the site by entering their Toyota VIN. And information about future Toyota vehicles is available, for those visitors just starting to consider a new purchase.

Volkswagen

http://www.vw.com

$

★★★★★

This Volkswagen site is fun and active, geared to the young and hip web audience. The specs are not terribly detailed, but there's enough to point you toward your local dealer for more information.

Volvo

http://new.volvocars.com/

★★★★★

Visit the official Volvo site to browse the online showroom, build a custom Volvo, check out pre-owned Volvos, and find a dealer near you. Volvo owners can visit the site to obtain additional information about caring for and servicing their vehicles.

REPAIR

ALLDATA Auto Repair Site

http://www.alldata.com/

★★★

Publisher of electronic automotive diagnostic and repair information for professional mechanics and consumers.

A
B
C
D
E
F
G
H
I
J
K
L
M
N
O
P
Q
R
S
T
U
V
W
X
Y
Z

AUTOSHOP Online

http://www.autoshop-online.com

★★★★

For a better understanding of your car's major internal systems, go through Automotive 101, the online tutorial. Then check on preventive tips and helpful hints to keep your car running.

Bob Hewitt's (Misterfixit's) Autorepair Page

http://www.MisterFixit.com/autorepr.htm

★★★

In addition to auto repair links provided at this site, you'll find helpful and humorous stories about mysterious auto problems encountered by fellow car owners. It's obvious that Bob Hewitt has spent a few hours under the hood of his own vehicles.

The Body Shop, Inc.

http://www.thebodyshopinc.com

★★★★

If you live in the Chicagoland area and you have a fender bender that you want fixed right, check out The Body Shop, Inc., a body shop that not only offers free estimates, expert collision and paint workmanship, and paintless dent removal, but also professional detailing, to make your car, van, or SUV look like new.

Car Care Council

http://www.carcarecouncil.org/

★★★★★

Perhaps the most complete list of preventive maintenance tips on and off the Web. Just don't anticipate the opportunity to ask questions; the site is dedicated to keeping you out of trouble in the first place. This site provides some excellent information in an easily accessible format.

Car Talk

http://cartalk.cars.com/

★★★★★

The funniest show on radio. This is not a dead-serious "Whom do I call when the fan belt breaks in the middle of Death Valley?" site, but you'll find helpful material between the gags. Listen to the show for more information.

Chilton's Online

http://www.chiltonsonline.com/

★★★★

If you're looking for the authoritative book on repairing your own vehicle, visit this site to find the book you need. Chilton's is the largest publisher of automobile repair manuals and has earned a stellar reputation for its consistent quality and accuracy.

Discount Auto Repair Manuals

http://www.discountautorepairmanuals.com/

★★★★

Order the Haynes Auto Repair Manual for your vehicle from this site. These manuals are written with the do-it-yourselfer in mind.

DoItYourself.com: Auto Repair and Care Tips

http://doityourself.com/auto/

★★★★

Designed specifically for do-it-yourselfers, this site provides basic instructions on a wide range of auto-care topics covering everything from purchasing a new car to dealing with roadside emergencies. Cartoony illustrations help clarify the more technically heavy material.

Factory Auto Manuals

http://www.factoryautomanuals.com/

★★★★

If you're trying to work on a vintage vehicle but can't find a service manual to refer to, check out this site.

Family Car

http://www.familycar.com

★★★★

Dedicated to the proper selection and care of the family vehicle, this site also provides driving tips and news. You can even learn how to become a better driver.

A
B
C
D
E
F
G
H
I
J
K
L
M
N
O
P
Q
R
S
T
U
V
W
X
Y
Z

Nutz and Boltz

http://www.motorminute.com/

★★★

Baltimore radio show on car care, with "live" play-backs of previous programs. The paid newsletter includes a vast amount of information. If auto maintenance takes up a major portion of your life, this could be an excellent value.

Weekend Mechanics Club

http://www.weekendmechanicsclub.com

★★★

People planning to do maintenance or repair work on their car will want to visit this site for help in locating stores, parts, and helpful tips to make the job go more smoothly.

The Workshop

http://www.users.bigpond.com/jack_stands/

★★★

Car and motorbike owners will want to turn to the Workshop for tips and advice on proper repair work.

Yahoo! Autos

http://autos.yahoo.com/repair/tree/0.html

★★★★

Yahoo!'s auto repair site is unique, in that it leads you step-by-step through the process of troubleshooting and diagnosing your car's problem. If your car has a problem you can see, hear, feel, or smell, you can find the cause right here.

AVIATION

ACES HIGH: The Finest in Aviation Photography

http://www.aviationphoto.com

★★★

Whether for personal enjoyment or to spice up a presentation, look at this site for downloading aviation photography. This site also offers tips for taking your own photographs.

Air Affair

http://www.airaffair.com/

★★★

Focuses on different types of flying machines. Includes a calendar of flying shows, a listing of aviation fuel prices, and an aviation library.

Air Combat USA

http://www.aircombatusa.com/

★★★★★

Find out how you can fly actual air-to-air combat in a real, state-of-the-art military aircraft! You don't even need a pilot's license. If you've been a student of aerial warfare for years and have only dreamed of taking a seat behind the wheel of a real warplane, check out this site!

Air Force Link

http://www.af.mil/

★★★★

The official U.S. Air Force site offers timely news, information on career opportunities, and exciting aviation images.

Air Safe

http://www.airsafe.com

★★★★

A treasure trove of information, for fearful flyers, about flying safely—whether that means identifying the safest airline, aircraft, or airport—and tips for having a safe, comfortable flight.

Aircraft Images Archive

http://www.cs.ruu.nl/pub/AIRCRAFT-IMAGES/

★★★

Collection of pictures of mainly military aircraft. All photos are in JPEG format.

Aircraft Museum

http://www.aircraftmuseum.com/

★★★★

This online aircraft museum features many of the most well-known aircraft of the jet age, including fighters, bombers, maritime aircraft, and passenger jets. The sites feature aircraft, information about designs, and a question and answer area. The Shop link connects to an Amazon-powered shopping site, where you can purchase books and other items.

Amelia Earhart

http://www.ellensplace.net/ae_eyrs.html

★★★★

Interested in Amelia Earhart? This site provides a nice biography detailing her life from her youth until her last flight. It also has some interesting pictures.

A
B
C
D
E
F
G
H
I
J
K
L
M
N
O
P
Q
R
S
T
U
V
W
X
Y
Z

Aviation Archives

http://www.aviationarchives.com

★★★★

This organization's goal is to help veterans, veterans' families, and others learn and understand what happened to missing crews. Guests can order missing air crew reports, mission reports, squadron histories, and many other pieces of information for $30 and up, depending on the complexity of the report.

Aviation Museum Locator

http://www.aero-web.org/museums/museums.htm

★★★★

If you're looking for an aviation museum in Canada or the United States, visit this site to pinpoint their locations. The site lists Canadian provinces and U.S. states that you can click to find nearby aviation museums. (You can't click the points on the map.) For each museum, the site displays its address, a map showing its location, and a visitor ranking.

AVWeb

http://www.avweb.com

★★★★

An Internet aviation magazine featuring up-to-the-minute aviation news, articles by top aviation writers, links to online shopping, and a searchable aviation database.

Banyan Air Service

http://www.banyanair.com/

★★★

This is a good place to look if your airplane needs servicing. Banyan does several kinds of repairs as well as sells parts.

Basics of Space Flight Learners' Workbook

http://www.jpl.nasa.gov/basics/

★★★★

Provides orientation to space flight and related topics, including the solar system, gravity and mechanics, interplanetary trajectories, orbits, electromagnetic phenomena, spacecraft types, telecommunications, onboard subsystems, navigation, and phases of flight.

The Boeing Home Page

http://www.boeing.com/

★★★★★

Home page for the world's largest producer of commercial jetliners. Provides information on employment opportunities and company news as well as background information and facts about the company's families of airplanes. Contains interesting, downloadable pictures of its airplanes.

Canova Aviation Publications

http://www.canovair.com/

★★★

This page offers aviation publications intended to help train professional pilots. Simulator profiles, system schematics, and other topics are covered.

Delta SkyLinks Home Page

http://www.delta.com/

★★★★

Loads of useful information for those interested in flying with Delta. You can check flight schedules, reserve tickets, or just read news about the company.

Embry-Riddle Aeronautical University

http://www.db.erau.edu/

★★★

Learn about the world's largest aeronautical university. This site contains admission information, research opportunities, and a virtual tour of the campus.

Embry-Riddle Aeronautical University Virtual Library

http://www.embryriddle.edu/libraries/virtual/

★★★

This site covers practically every imaginable aspect of aviation. It is a library containing links to hundreds of other related sites. This would be an excellent place to begin a search into the area of aviation.

FAA

http://www.faa.gov

★★★★

 All

The home of the Federal Aviation Administration (FAA), this site is an excellent resource for both pilots and passengers. Here, you can check on flight safety, advisories, and airport status. Passengers should check out the Traveler Briefing area for travel tips and other information. You can also determine the steps you need to take to become a pilot, air traffic controller, security screener, or other airline professional. Kids should click the Kids link to access coloring books, word games, and ideas for experiments.

Fear of Flying

http://www.fearofflying.com/fear.htm

$

★★★

If you are among the 50 million Americans who have given up flying, fly with anxiety, or have never flown, Seminars On Aeroanxiety Relief (SOAR) is here to help you overcome your fear of flying. You must pay for the course, but success is 100% guaranteed.

Flight Safety

http://www.flightsafety.org

$

★★★

Read about aviation safety, stay updated on safety statistics and reports, and search for scheduled upcoming events.

Helicopter Adventures, Inc.

http://www.heli.com/

★★★

Learn about this helicopter flight-training school and how you can learn to fly helicopters. This site also contains several links to other helicopter-related sites.

Landings

http://www.landings.com/aviation.html

★★★★

Excellent and informative site that provides a wide variety of aviation information for all levels, including recent news items and editorials.

Lockheed Martin

http://www.lmasc.com/

★★★★★

 All

This beautifully designed site provides information about the Lockheed Martin company, its airplanes (in the Hangar section), press releases, and more. The Kids' Wing area features an interactive model airplane, a flight simulation that demonstrates the forces that act on an aircraft, and a chart that compares the time it would take to travel from one city to another by running, speeding in a Porsche, flying in a 747, or flying in an F22 Raptor. Very well-designed site.

NASA Home Page

http://www.nasa.gov/

★★★★★

Acts as the starting point for all of NASA's web-based information. Offers links to resources, including space shuttle information, home pages for the NASA centers around the country, space images, and educational resources.

NASA Television

http://btree.lerc.nasa.gov/NASA_TV/NASA_TV.html

★★★

Helps visitors learn how to access live images and audio from NASA using RealPlayer or CU-SeeMe software. Provides links for obtaining the required software.

National Aeronautic Association

http://www.naa-usa.org/website/

★★★★

The NAA's home page states that "by promoting safety, rights of access, and better public understanding of aviation and air sports, the NAA is not only for the experienced pilot, but for aviation enthusiasts of all kinds." See the NAA home page to learn about the association and how to become a member.

A
B
C
D
E
F
G
H
I
J
K
L
M
N
O
P
Q
R
S
T
U
V
W
X
Y
Z

A
B
C
D
E
F
G
H
I
J
K
L
M
N
O
P
Q
R
S
T
U
V
W
X
Y
Z

Pilot Shop

http://www.aipilotshop.com/

★★★

Offers a wide range of pilot supplies from several manufacturers. Pictures and descriptions of goods are available as well as an online order form.

Smithsonian National Air and Space Museum

http://www.nasm.si.edu/

★★★★★

 9-13

This site features a robust collection of online versions of the museum's most popular exhibits. There's no replacement for visiting the museum in person, but this is pretty close. An excellent tool for parents and teachers to introduce kids to the wonderful world of flight.

Student Pilot

http://www.studentpilot.com

★★★★

This one-stop teaching tool for student pilots online teaches visitors everything they need to know to pursue their dreams of becoming a pilot. Use the interactive section to run through FAA Test Prep with an online coach.

Student Pilot Network

http://www.ufly.com

★★★

Learn about flight schools, read interviews with pilots, and purchase instructional books on piloting and flying from this instructional and inspirational site. You can also purchase navigational and safety equipment through the online store.

The Ultralight Home Page

http://www.ultralighthomepage.com/

★★★

This site is intended to make it easy for people to learn more about flying ultralights. It does a fine job of this and even contains links to other ultralight pages.

United Airlines

http://www.ual.com/

★★★★

Check flight schedules or reserve tickets. You can also learn some background information about the company. Check out the company's Mileage Plus program to see how you can earn free miles.

X Prize

http://www.xprize.com/

★★★★★

Do you want to take a chance to win 10 million dollars building a space taxi? Well, that's what the X Prize challenge is all about. If you and your team of experts can design and build a spacecraft that can carry three people safely to an altitude of 1,000 kilometers, return to earth, and complete the same trip within two weeks, you walk away with the prize. The X Prize project is designed to encourage inventors to develop technology that will build a future space tourism industry.

BABIES

A
B
C
D
E
F
G
H
I
J
K
L
M
N
O
P
Q
R
S
T
U
V
W
X
Y
Z

4Babies

http://4babies.4anything.com/

★★★★★

Learn how to take care of your baby, from choosing a cradle to preparing nutritious meals. Parental pointers and safety tips are also available at this site.

American Academy of Pediatrics

http://www.aap.org/

★★★★★

Offers information relating to the mental, physical, and social health of infants through young adults. A searchable, easy-to-navigate site filled with valuable information for parents and pediatric professionals.

Babies Online

http://www.babiesonline.com

★★★★

Excellent links for finding baby freebies, preparing for your baby's arrival, and obtaining printable baby product coupons. You can even enter your baby in a cute-baby contest! Message boards provide a way to communicate with other parents and expectant mothers and fathers.

Babies "R" Us

http://www.babiesrus.com

★★★★★

Possibly the biggest baby store in the world, Babies "R" Us carries just about every baby product imaginable, from pacifiers and rattles to baby backpacks and cribs. You can also register online to make it easier for friends and family to buy you what you need for the new addition to your family. This site also features some useful articles on baby care, including a tutorial on how to clip your baby's nails and care for your baby's belly button. Amazon.com handles the orders, so you can be assured of receiving quality service.

Babies Today Online

http://babiestoday.com

★★★★

A community for new and new-again parents full of information to guide parents through the formative years of their child's life. The site is organized by development stages, starting out with preconception topics and going all the way up to the teenage years. You can enter your baby's birthday to find out his or her exact age and flip through a series of daily facts and information for each day of the first year of your baby's life.

A
B
C
D
E
F
G
H
I
J
K
L
M
N
O
P
Q
R
S
T
U
V
W
X
Y
Z

Baby Bag Online

http://www.babybag.com

 $

★★★★

Catch up on product recalls and warnings, download baby food recipes, and check baby product reviews. You also can access a wealth of information in just about any baby-related category imaginable. Lots of good information on nutrition, plus quizzes and informative articles.

Baby Center

http://www.babycenter.com

 $

★★★★★

A shopping site, owned by Johnson & Johnson, dedicated to providing all you'll need for your baby, from clothing to nursery furniture to car seats, strollers, and toys. Personalize the site by entering your baby's birthday and your email address, to have the site display information specifically related to your child's current developmental stage. You can go directly to the shopping area by visiting http://store.babycenter.com.

Baby Namer

http://www.babynamer.com

★★★

Search for the perfect name for your baby from more than 23,000 options based on panelists' favorites, popularity, meaning, or historical significance.

Baby Names

http://www.babynames.com

★★★★

Check out the results of recent polls regarding baby names before searching the names database. Learn which names visitors love and hate, as well as the most popular this year. An excellent site to browse when you have no idea what to name your baby.

Baby Place

http://www.baby-place.com

★★★★

Offers baby and parenting information, including pregnancy and birth FAQs, parenting FAQs, baby care, and even some baby jokes. Also gives links to baby-related newsgroups, sites offering services to new and expectant parents, and the Baby Place Store. Though you cannot purchase products directly from Baby Place, it offers plenty of links that take you to other online baby supply stores. A good jumping-off point for additional baby information.

Baby Workshop

http://www.sesameworkshop.org/babyworkshop/

★★★★

 0-8

Find age-customized advice for parents and babies up to two years, as well as activities parents and babies can enjoy. Covers baby stages from 0 to 24 months and includes a checklist for new parents, a list of tips, and a complete library of articles covering everything from breastfeeding to behavior and cognitive development.

⌐Best¬ Baby Zone

http://babyzone.com/

★★★★★

 0-8

This comprehensive site covers the three stages of a parent's development: preconception, pregnancy, and parenting. The Member (My Baby) Zone enables pregnant mothers to keep a journal of their pregnancy online and allows parents to create online photo albums and track events. The Regions area provides pertinent information based on where you live or where you plan to travel. The Community Zone provides chat rooms and message boards where you can keep in touch with other parents. This site is packed with links to other useful pregnancy and parenting sites and features links to money-saving coupons and product offers as well. New parents will soon realize why we picked this site as the Best of the Best.

Babyworld Home Page

http://www.babyworld.co.uk

★★★★★

An excellent site containing a wealth of information on childcare, pregnancy, birth, and baby products. You could easily spend all afternoon exploring the related pages and links that include everything from information on fertility to recipes for homemade baby food.

Crying Babies

http://www.crying-babies.com

★★★

This site is devoted to helping parents resolve their newborn's colic by learning what causes it and what can be done about it. You can purchase Tummy Calm, a natural product that reportedly works quickly to relieve newborn colic, as well as other natural products for your baby.

Pampers Parenting Institute

http://us.pampers.com

★★★★★

Get parenting help from experts and learn more about taking care of children up to age four. Don't miss the Playing Center, where you can learn ways to stimulate your child's mind through creative games and activities. This site is sponsored by Procter & Gamble.

ParentsPlace.com

http://www.parentsplace.com/

★★★★★

Learn everything from how to improve your conception odds to how to baby-proof your home. Find information about the development of your baby from birth to one-year-old, as well as tips for caring for and interacting with your child. Weekly newsletters are posted at this site, and message boards and chats are available. You can even test your baby knowledge by taking an online quiz.

A
B
C
D
E
F
G
H
I
J
K
L
M
N
O
P
Q
R
S
T
U
V
W
X
Y
Z

Yellow Pages

BACKGROUND CHECKS

Background Check Gateway

http://www.backgroundcheckgateway.com/

★★★★★

Entering into a personal or business relationship with someone is always risky, but you can feel more comfortable if you know that the person you're dealing with has a clean background. The Background Check Gateway provides the services you need to track down friends, classmates, or relatives; research the background of a prospective mate, employee, business associate, or tenant; and protect your identity.

CheckMate

http://www.infotel.net/checkmate/

★★★

If you're single and dating, before you get serious and if you have any doubts, it's a good idea to make sure the person you're about to get serious with is presenting himself or herself accurately. At CheckMate, you can order up a background check and rule out any undesirable prospects.

Choice Point

http://www.choicepointinc.com/

★★★★★

Choice Point is dedicated to helping businesses and the government screen out applicants by verifying credentials and providing background checks of prospective employees. Visit this site to learn more about the service and what it has to offer.

Docusearch

http://www.docusearch.com/

★★★★★

Docusearch is an investigative service that can check the identity, reputation, conduct, affiliations, associations, movements, and whereabouts of potential business partners, suspicious employees, prospective spouses, and relatives-to-be. You specify the purpose of the investigation, the person(s) you want investigated, and the types of services you want, and when the investigation is complete, the results are posted on a secure server for you to view.

 ## KnowX

http://www.knowx.com/

★★★★★

KnowX.com is a searchable public records database that can help users track down old friends and classmates; verify credentials; and perform background checks on prospective employees, mates, and others. System is easy to navigate and offers several levels of access depending on the required depth of the search.

BALLOONING

The Balloon Federation of America

http://www.bfa.net/

★★★★

👥 14-18

This American ballooning organization's site includes membership information, events, competition standings, and products for sale—all geared to the experienced balloonist and junior balloonist. Basic site layout places all resources right at your fingertips.

Ballooning International

http://www.ballooning.net/

★★★

👥 14-18

Contains information, reports, and photographs of various balloon races around the world, including hot air balloons, gas balloons, and experimental balloons.

Balloon Life Magazine

http://www.balloonlife.com/bl.htm

★★★

This site doesn't provide much in the way of free information; you must subscribe to the magazine to access most of the content. However, subscribers will find a wealth of information about ballooning, including articles on insurance, photography, special events, and contests. Be aware that you cannot subscribe from the website but must email the subscription department.

Balloon Pages on the World Wide Web

http://www.euronet.nl/users/jdewilde/

★★★

👥 14-18

A comprehensive list of web addresses for all things related to ballooning. From here, you can jump to sites for various "Around the World" attempts, as well as to several pages of ballooning history, advice, and photography. Excellent site to start your exploration of ballooning.

Battle Creek's Field of Flight

http://www.bcballoons.com/

★★★

If available, this site provides a complete program, schedule, and entry forms for this prestigious Battle Creek ballooning competition. If this information is not yet available, you can still visit the site to view photographs of the previous year's competition.

🎈Best🎈 Hot Air Ballooning

http://www.launch.net

💲

★★★★★

👥 14-18

Locate a ride or festival, learn how to become a pilot, place a classified ad for balloon parts and accessories, or just sign up for the online newsletter at the site. This is a great site to learn more about ballooning as a recreational activity and a sport. At the top of the page is a navigation bar containing links to balloon rides, festivals, and weather reports. Along the left side of the page are several buttons that lead to discussions of balloon basics, balloon questions and answers, balloon ride promotional deals, a pilot's corner, and a pilot's shop. If you have time to visit only one balloon site, this is where you should land.

A
B
C
D
E
F
G
H
I
J
K
L
M
N
O
P
Q
R
S
T
U
V
W
X
Y
Z

Hot Air Balloons USA

http://www.hot-airballoons.com/

★★★

👥 14-18

A colorful, complete, and thoroughly enjoyable site. Features an interactive "Take a Cyber-Ride" balloon ride expedition, a mall area for shopping for balloon-related items, and a map showing balloon ride vendors all over the United States. Though the site has a link for the Balloon Store, the trails of links that lead to the various stores are dead ends.

Jet Stream Information

http://virga.sfsu.edu/crws/jetstream.html

★★★

View images of the jet stream over the Eastern Pacific, Northern hemisphere, or North America and track the latest jet stream analysis prepared by the San Francisco State University Meteorology department. Excellent site for balloonists who are planning a flight.

National Scientific Balloon Facility

http://www.nsbf.nasa.gov

★★★★★

The NSBF is a NASA facility managed by the Physical Science Lab of New Mexico State University. It launches, tracks, and recovers scientific balloon experiments all over the world, and this page shows some of its PR materials and photographs. This site offers great information and photos and a layout that makes it one of the more attractive of the ballooning sites.

Quest TV

http://www.quest-tv.com

★★★★

👥 14-18

The one-hour documentary *Around the World by Balloon* tracks teams racing to travel the globe. Use Quest TV's website to read profiles of each race team and their respective balloons, as well as to link to other ballooning sites. This site is a little dated, since the challenge was finally met on March 20, 1999, by Bertran Piccard of Switzerland and Brian Jones of Britain, but some of the diagrams of the balloons and capsules are still quite fascinating.

Related Site

http://www.pbs.org/wgbh/nova/balloon/

World Balloon Corporation

http://www.worldballoon.com/

★★★

A must-bookmark site for the serious balloon enthusiast, this New Mexico–based company sells and repairs balloon equipment, prints banners for the balloons (as well as for aircraft towing, buildings, and so on), and even manages balloon events. Some cool balloon designs you must see to believe.

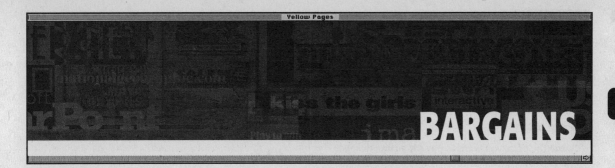

BARGAINS

A
B
C
D
E
F
G
H
I
J
K
L
M
N
O
P
Q
R
S
T
U
V
W
X
Y
Z

Airfare.com

http://www.airfare.com/

★★★★

Get up to 60% off on published ticket prices for major airlines, car rental agencies, and hotels. Just plug in your departure and destination points and specify your dates to have Airfare.com track down the best prices.

Amazing-Bargains

http://www.amazing-bargains.com

★★★★

View bargains by category or by store. You'll find everything from books to jewelry to office supplies, all reduced in price. You cannot order products from this site; the links carry you to any of several online stores where you can purchase the products listed.

Birkenstock Express

http://www.birkenstockexpress.com/Discounts/sale.cfm

★★★★

Birkenstock Express Online has two types of bargains to offer: regular stock items at reduced prices and lists of discontinued or "as is" items at even better prices.

Bridal Bargains

http://www.windsorpeak.com/bridalbargains/default.html

★★★

Order the Bridal Bargains book or just browse through the overview, tips, or articles at this site. A mailbag with letters from other customers gives an insight on the book and wedding-related topics.

ItsRainingBargains

http://www.itsrainingbargains.com/

★★★★

Opening page features today's top bargains and provides a list of categories you can browse for additional deals, including Art, Baby, Computers, Electronics, Furniture, and Sporting Goods. On the right side of the page is a long list of retailers that display products on this site.

LowerMyBills.com

http://www.lowermybills.com/

★★★★★

Dedicated to providing a single site where you can lower your unavoidable bills in several budget categories, LowerMyBills.com is a free service that helps you find the best prices for long-distance telephone service, automobile and homeowner's insurance, loan rates, cell phone rates, credit card rates, and much more.

⌐Best⌐ Overstock.com

http://www.overstock.com

★★★★★

Save as much as 70% by buying manufacturers' overstock and discontinued items at this site. Products in inventory change daily, so visitors are encouraged to check back often or to sign up for the overstock newsletter. With its huge collection of overstock items updated daily and its easy-to-use format, this site is the hands-down winner as the Best of the Best.

A
B
C
D
E
F
G
H
I
J
K
L
M
N
O
P
Q
R
S
T
U
V
W
X
Y
Z

Priceline.com

http://www.priceline.com

★★★★★

Name the price you want to pay for airline tickets and travel accommodations, as well as cars and groceries, and Priceline negotiates on your behalf to get a bargain from the original manufacturer. Manufacturers won't always accept your bid for their products or services, but it's worth a shot! If they do, you can save tens or even thousands of dollars.

SalesCircular.com

http://www.salescircular.com

★★★★

Instead of sifting through tons of sales circulars each week to track down a bargain locally, visit this website, click on your state, and find out which department stores have the best deals on items you need. You can also download and print valuable coupons from this site.

techbargains.com

http://www.techbargains.com/

★★★★

Features a search tool that tracks down the best deals on computers, hardware, digital cameras, CD and DVD players and recorders, and other electronic equipment and gadgets. Links to other sites where you can place your order. If you're an electronics gadget guy or gal, bookmark this site!

UsedMusicExchange.com

http://www.usedmusicexchange.com/

★★★

Buy or sell used CDs. Rummage through the bargain bin for the real deals, search for a specific artist or album, or browse for music by genre. You can even download free music clips.

COUPONS

car-pons.com

http://www.car-pons.com/

★★★

Dedicated to distributing coupons for automobile services, this site features coupons for oil changes, tune-ups, tires, and other auto maintenance and repair jobs.

Cents Off

http://www.centsoff.com/

★★★★★

Buy just the coupons you want in whatever amount you choose, and they'll be mailed to you for a fee. These are the standard Sunday paper coupons.

 ## Cool Savings

http://www.coolsavings.com

★★★★★

Register to be notified of major retailers' sales. Plus the Cool Savings site offers lots of inside scoops on rebates as well as coupons to print out, all for free. If you're tired of flipping through the Sunday paper in search of coupons and special deals, register here to gain access to coupons you know you can use. This site is well designed, making it easy to locate the best deals around.

Coupon Pages

http://www.couponpages.com

★★★★

The current focus of this site is on coupons for local businesses, supermarkets, car rental agencies, fast food restaurants, retail stores, casinos, and much, much more!

CouponSurfer

http://www.couponsurfer.com

★★★★

Visit this site for personalized coupons at national stores or for major brands. Browse categories such as baby items, books, health and beauty, or sports, and then look at coupons available toward a purchase.

Daily e-Deals

http://www.dailyedeals.com

★★★★

A great site to find online shopping bargains, online coupons, and free stuff available on the Internet. You'll save a lot of time and effort with deals you wouldn't find anywhere else. And to keep up to date on the latest and greatest bargains, join the mailing list.

GoodBazaar.com

http://www.goodbazaar.com/

★★★

GoodBazaar.com features online coupons, discounts, Internet bargains, rebates, bargain shopping, daily deals, promotions, personal finance specials, credit card deals, travel discount coupons, free stuff, freebies, and more. Links for obtaining coupons in dozens of categories.

Hot Coupons

http://www.hotcoupons.com/

★★★★

Stop by this site, which provides coupons you can use on products and services you use every day near your home, office, or when you travel. Join the Hot Coupons savers' club and receive coupon deals in your local area.

Jason Higley's TouristFlorida.com

http://www.touristflorida.com/

★★★

Planning a trip to Florida? Then visit this site to pick up coupons for some of the major attractions, including Sea World, Busch Gardens, and Universal Studios Theme Park.

Motel Coupons

http://motel-coupons.com/

★★★★

When planning your next road trip, check out this site for deals on motel rooms. On the opening page, click the state you plan to visit and then follow the trail of links to pull up a list of coupons for motels in a specific region.

MyCoupons

http://www.mycoupons.com

★★★★

The purpose of MyCoupons/DirectCoupons is to save you the time of surfing the Net for hours looking for savings. You can register for a free 30-day trial or upgrade your membership to receive special products and services. Lots of great coupons delivered right to your email box.

RedTagDeals.com

http://www.redtagdeals.com/

★★★★

Huge, searchable, and browsable collection of coupons, specials, rebates, and other money-saving deals for dozens of categories, including automobiles, entertainment, apparel, books, long-distance telephone service, and much more.

U-pons

http://www.upons.com/

★★★

U-pons specializes in grocery store coupons for some of the major supermarkets, including Kroger, Giant Eagle, and Dillons. If you like to grocery shop at these stores, you can find a good collection of coupons to save you money, right here.

ValPak

http://www.valpak.com

★★★★

The ValPak folks send you that blue envelope of savings every month. They now offer coupons online as well.

FREEBIES

#1 Free Stuff

http://www.1freestuff.com

★★★★

This site is an index of free and trial offers available on the Internet. Select a category or check out the most popular free items to start your search.

A
B
C
D
E
F
G
H
I
J
K
L
M
N
O
P
Q
R
S
T
U
V
W
X
Y
Z

100 Hot Free Stuff

http://www.100hotfreestuff.com

★★★

Sign up for the Free Stuff newsletter to get regular notice of new freebies on the Internet. When you subscribe, you check a box next to each type of freebie you want to be notified about in several categories, including Beauty, Computers, Health, Sports, Entertainment, and so on. When freebies are available, you receive a newsletter via email letting you know about them.

Absolutely Freebies

http://www.absolutelyfreebies.com/

★★★

A free stuff guide for webmasters and general Net surfers. Includes web space, free classifieds, screensavers, greeting cards, sweepstakes, clip art, and more.

CheapFree

http://www.cheapfree.com

★★★★★

Get free stuff—some are great and others are junk—through this site, which also features links to sites offering even more free stuff. Very cool graphics make this one of the more attractive freebie sites to visit.

[Best] Freaky Freddies Free Funhouse

http://www.freakyfreddies.com/

★★★★★

With the motto "If it ain't free, it's not for me," Freaky Freddy greets you with a stack of freebies, coupons, and special offers from hundreds of leading manufacturers and dealers. Free stuff for everyone, including free chocolate! This site is updated daily and features more than 70 categories of freebies. Sign up for Freaky Freddy's daily or weekly newsletter to keep up on the latest deals. Its excellent collection of freebies and devotion to keeping visitors informed about the latest deals combine to make this the Best of the Best.

The Free Site

http://www.thefreesite.com/

★★★★★

Huge resource for finding freebies, especially those relating to computers and the Internet, including products and services, graphics, samples, games, email accounts, technical support, and much more.

Free Site X

http://www.freesitex.com/

★★★★

Offers an incredible array of free stuff and looks to be well maintained. You can find free stuff ranging from free clothing to free software. More than 100 free offers!

FreeShop.com

http://www.freeshop.com

★★★★★

Check out hundreds of offers of free stuff and free trials, organized by categories such as auto, swimwear, entertainment, and travel. Lots of links to free catalogs, but the free product offering is a little light.

refundsweepers.com

http://www.refundsweepers.com

★★★★★

Search the site for freebies on clothing, food, and jewelry. You can also sign up for coupons, rebates, and special deals, as well as find information about good deals on low-interest credit cards. Many links kick you out to other sites where you can obtain freebies.

Seasonal Freebies on the Web

http://www.thefreesite.com/Seasonal_Freebies/

★★★★

A unique collection of freebies organized by holiday. Here, you can find freebies for Christmas, Valentine's Day, Halloween, April Fool's day, and more.

Tonsforfree.com

http://tonsforfree.com/

★★★

This site offers several categories of freebies, including free games, websites, screensavers, books, clothes, food, and movies. You can check out some freebies at the website, but for the good stuff, register for the newsletter. Many links at the site are outdated.

BASEBALL

American League Web Sites

$

★★★★

All

Anaheim Angels	http://anaheim.angels.mlb.com/
Baltimore Orioles	http://baltimore.orioles.mlb.com/
Boston Red Sox	http://boston.redsox.mlb.com/
Chicago White Sox	http://chicago.whitesox.mlb.com/
Cleveland Indians	http://cleveland.indians.mlb.com/
Detroit Tigers	http://detroit.tigers.mlb.com/
Kansas City Royals	http://kansascity.royals.mlb.com/
Minnesota Twins	http://minnesota.twins.mlb.com/
New York Yankees	http://newyork.yankees.mlb.com/
Oakland Athletics	http://oakland.athletics.mlb.com/
Seattle Mariners	http://seattle.mariners.mlb.com/
Tampa Bay Devil Rays	http://tampabay.devilrays.mlb.com/
Texas Rangers	http://texas.rangers.mlb.com/
Toronto Blue Jays	http://toronto.bluejays.mlb.com/

National League Web Sites

$

★★★★

All

Arizona Diamondbacks	http://arizona.diamondbacks.mlb.com/
Atlanta Braves	http://atlanta.braves.mlb.com/
Chicago Cubs	http://chicago.cubs.mlb.com/
Cincinnati Reds	http://cincinnati.reds.mlb.com/
Colorado Rockies	http://colorado.rockies.mlb.com/
Florida Marlins	http://florida.marlins.mlb.com/
Houston Astros	http://houston.astros.mlb.com/
Los Angeles Dodgers	http://losangeles.dodgers.mlb.com/
Milwaukee Brewers	http://milwaukee.brewers.mlb.com/
Montreal Expos	http://montreal.expos.mlb.com/
New York Mets	http://newyork.mets.mlb.com/
Philadelphia Phillies	http://philadelphia.phillies.mlb.com/
Pittsburgh Pirates	http://pittsburg.pirates.mlb.com/
San Diego Padres	http://sandiego.padres.mlb.com/
San Francisco Giants	http://sanfrancisco.giants.mlb.com/
St. Louis Cardinals	http://stlouis.cardinals.mlb.com/

A
B
C
D
E
F
G
H
I
J
K
L
M
N
O
P
Q
R
S
T
U
V
W
X
Y
Z

Babe Ruth League

http://www.baberuthleague.org

★★★★

 All

Play Babe Ruth Home Run Derby or learn all about the Babe Ruth League's history, divisions, and camps.

Baseball Almanac

http://baseball-almanac.com/

★★★

 All

Students of the game will want to visit this site, providing a veritable encyclopedia of baseball facts and figures. Here, you can read about baseball legends, get the scores of every All-Star Game, view hitting and pitching charts, and play games.

Baseball Archive

www.baseball1.com

★★★★★

The Baseball Archive features the largest collection of baseball statistics available, covering the history of baseball from 1871 to the end of the previously completed season. If you're into baseball trivia, this is the site to test your knowledge and expand it. If you're not into baseball, this is a good place to start becoming more interested as you explore its history.

Baseball Links

http://www.baseball-links.com/

★★★★

Skilton's Baseball Links is a comprehensive collection of links to baseball-related resources, containing more than 10,000 unique links. Check out baseball equipment, read daily analyses of player performance, participate in reader polls, and much more on this site for baseball fanatics.

Baseball-Reference

http://baseball-reference.com/

★★★★★

If you want to know something about baseball, past or present, and you're not really sure where to turn, turn here. This site features player and team statistics, records, league leaders, awards, Hall of Fame information, manager bios, team schedules, and much more. You will find some links to other great baseball sites, as well.

Baseball Think Factory

http://www.baseballthinkfactory.com/

★★★★★

Founded by Jim Furtado and Sean Forman, the Baseball Think Factory addresses a wide range of baseball interests and information through four distinct areas: Baseball-Reference.com, BaseballPrimer.com, BaseballNewstand.com, and BaseballStuff.com. Baseball-Reference.com includes statistics from 1871 to the present for players, teams, and leagues and includes a Baseball Travel Guide to help you track down events near you. BaseballPrimer.com offers inside information and commentary from the authors of this site to keep the thinking fan thinking. BaseballNewstand.com collects all the latest news and information about each team from various sources across the country to place *all* of the information available for your favorite team in one location. And BaseballStuff.com provides links and additional information that you might find useful, or at least interesting.

Little League Online

http://www.littleleague.org/

★★★★

 All

Provides lists of past state champions and a Little League World Series link that details the happenings of that event. Information on summer camps is provided, along with an online shop where you can purchase gifts and equipment. A great place for parents and coaches to learn the rules and pick up coaching tips.

Major League Baseball

http://mlb.mlb.com/

★★★★★

 All

Official site of Major League Baseball contains an up-to-date scoreboard, daily video of an amazing play, and a section for kids. Also included are links to individual player stats and career highlights, as well as links to each team's home page. Perhaps best of all, when the players or umpires strike, the site still works!

National Baseball Hall of Fame

http://www.baseballhalloffame.org/

★★★★★

 All

The Hall of Fame site provides admission prices and hours of operation. You can link to directions on how to get to Cooperstown, access the Hall of Fame newsletter *Around the Horn*, and view online special exhibits.

Spring Training Yearbook Online

http://www.springtrainingmagazine.com

★★★

 9-13

Spring Training Online is a guide to baseball's exhibition season and spring training camps, including day-by-day team schedules.

USA Today: Baseball Weekly

http://www.usatoday.com/sports/baseball/front.htm

★★★★

 All

This site features just about everything a Major League Baseball fan could ever want: the latest scores and game highlights, league standings, statistics, schedules, rosters, trades, fantasy baseball games, and much more. Check this site frequently for updates on game scores, stats, team match-ups, and baseball news.

A
B
C
D
E
F
G
H
I
J
K
L
M
N
O
P
Q
R
S
T
U
V
W
X
Y
Z

BASKETBALL

A
B
C
D
E
F
G
H
I
J
K
L
M
N
O
P
Q
R
S
T
U
V
W
X
Y
Z

Basketball Daily

http://www.basketballdaily.com/

★★★★★

👫 9-13

Check out the daily basketball scores and game summaries at this site. On weekends and during the playoffs, this site is packed with information. On off days, you'll find little to keep you going.

The Basketball Highway

http://www.bbhighway.com/

★★★★★

This is the site of the Coaches and Basketball Professional's Home Page, which exists to help coaches improve their game. They might search the site for specific topics, jump to other basketball pages, and learn more about the CIRN database.

Coaching Well Basketball Journal

http://www.havenport.com/hosa/cjournal.html

★★★

If your kid just volunteered you to coach the neighborhood basketball team, this site should be your first stop on your journey to becoming coach of the year. Here, you can find strategies, drills, skills lessons, practice plans, and other information you need to become a successful coach.

Full Court Press

http://www.fullcourt.com/

★★★★

👫 14-18

Full Court Press covers women's basketball at the high school, college, professional, and international levels. The site is full of articles about players, teams, conferences, and coaches.

Harlem Globetrotters Online

http://www.harlemglobetrotters.com/

★★★★★

👫 All

The Globetrotters have been beating the Washington Generals (and entertaining us along the way) for decades, and now you can find them on the Web. This site covers the history, current schedule, information about the team members, and all things Globetrotter. Special kids area includes puzzles and games and information on how to sign up for the Globetrotters' basketball camp.

Journal of Basketball Studies

http://www.rawbw.com/~deano/

★★★★

The *Journal* is one of the most detailed publications that studies the science of professional sports. On one hand, it's a wonderful tool for students to learn the use of statistics in a practical, fun environment; on the other, the articles are interesting, regardless of their purpose.

Naismith Memorial Basketball Hall of Fame

http://www.hoophall.com/

★★★★★

👫 9-13

This is the official online site for the Naismith Memorial Basketball Hall of Fame in Springfield, Massachusetts. You can find museum information, as well as a detailed biography on the game's creator, James Naismith. Be sure to check out all the items that you can buy from the Hall of Fame gift store, from books to gift items.

National Wheelchair Basketball Association

http://www.nwba.org/

★★★★

The NWBA consists of 185 teams with more than 2,000 athletes, which adds up to a lot of wheels! The association has teams for men, women, students, and children of all ages. The website has a team directory, the official rules, the history of wheelchair basketball, and more.

 Best ## National Basketball Association

http://www.nba.com/

★★★★★

 9-13

This Internet home of the National Basketball Association features the latest scores and reports about your favorite professional basketball teams and players. Here, you find links to the NBA, Jr. NBA, the WNBA (Women's National Basketball Association), and the Jr. WNBA. Each of these links takes you to a page devoted to the selected league, and each page contains links for the teams, players, news, statistics, standings, scores, schedules, transactions, and more. If you're a professional basketball fan, you'll find that this site or one it links to has everything you want.

NBA Eastern Conference Web Sites

★★★★★

9-13

Atlanta Hawks	http://www.nba.com/hawks/
Boston Celtics	http://www.nba.com/celtics/
Chicago Bulls	http://www.nba.com/bulls/
Cleveland Cavaliers	http://www.nba.com/cavs/
Detroit Pistons	http://www.nba.com/pistons/
Indiana Pacers	http://www.nba.com/pacers/
New Jersey Nets	http://www.nba.com/nets/
New Orleans Hornets	http://www.nba.com/hornets/
New York Knicks	http://www.nba.com/knicks/
Miami Heat	http://www.nba.com/heat/
Milwaukee Bucks	http://www.nba.com/bucks/
Orlando Magic	http://www.nba.com/magic/
Philadelphia 76ers	http://www.nba.com/sixers/
Toronto Raptors	http://www.nba.com/raptors/
Washington Wizards	http://www.nba.com/wizards/

NBA Western Conference Web Sites

★★★★★

 9-13

Dallas Mavericks	http://www.nba.com/mavericks/
Denver Nuggets	http://www.nba.com/nuggets/
Golden State Warriors	http://www.nba.com/warriors/
Houston Rockets	http://www.nba.com/rockets/
Los Angeles Clippers	http://www.nba.com/clippers/
Los Angeles Lakers	http://www.nba.com/lakers/
Minnesota Timberwolves	http://www.nba.com/timberwolves/
Phoenix Suns	http://www.nba.com/suns/
Portland Trail Blazers	http://www.nba.com/blazers/
Sacramento Kings	http://www.nba.com/kings/
San Antonio Spurs	http://www.nba.com/spurs/
Seattle SuperSonics	http://www.nba.com/sonics/
Utah Jazz	http://www.nba.com/jazz/
Memphis Grizzlies	http://www.nba.com/grizzlies/

NCAA Sports: Home of the Final Four

http://www.ncaasports.com/

★★★★★

 14-18

Watch live video from your favorite NCAA team's participation in the Final Four Championship, or if your team didn't make it, keep up on men's and women's team news. You can also buy Final Four merchandise at the site to show your spirit.

Related Kids Site
http://kids.ncaasports.com

SlamOnline

http://www.slamonline.com/

★★★

The abridged version of the regular magazine, *SlamOnline* contains the best articles from the latest edition. You can also subscribe to nine issues yearly from this site's secure server. Be sure to check out the "free issues" offer!

A B C D E F G H I J K L M N O P Q R S T U V W X Y Z

A
B
C
D
E
F
G
H
I
J
K
L
M
N
O
P
Q
R
S
T
U
V
W
X
Y
Z

Sports Fans Message Boards

http://www.sportsfansofamerica.com/Interactive/
Boards/main1.htm

★★★

A forum for those who love to discuss and critique basketball, its players, coaches, and referees as much as they love to watch the games. This site features message boards for the most popular sports. Scroll down the page to access the basketball message boards.

USA Basketball

http://www.usabasketball.com/

★★★★

USA Basketball is the governing body of men's and women's basketball in the United States and is recognized by the International Basketball Federation and the U.S. Olympic Committee. The organization selects and trains USA teams for national and international play. Its website offers a FAQ, news releases, photos, links, schedules, athlete bios, and much more. If you like to keep abreast of the top up-and-coming basketball players in the nation, bookmark this site and visit it often.

USBasket

http://www.usbasket.com/

★★★★★

USBasket is part of Eurobasket, a group that's devoted to providing the most in-depth coverage of basketball-related news and information from around the world. This site covers all aspects of United States basketball—the NCAA and NBA, plus U.S. players who play professionally and semi-professionally in other countries. Great site for fans, players, and agents.

Women's National Basketball Association

http://www.wnba.com

★★★★★

Check out the scoreboard for the latest results of WNBA play at the official site. You also can chat with players during frequent online chat sessions, get the latest WNBA news, review the upcoming season's schedule, and buy tickets.

WNBA Eastern Conference Web Sites

★★★★★

👫 9-13

Charlotte Sting	http://www.wnba.com/sting/
Connecticut Sun	http://www.wnba.com/sun/
Detroit Shock	http://www.wnba.com/shock/
Houston Comets	http://www.wnba.com/comets/
Indiana Fever	http://www.wnba.com/fever/
Los Angeles Sparks	http://www.wnba.com/sparks/
Minnesota Lynx	http://www.wnba.com/lynx/
New York Liberty	http://www.wnba.com/liberty/
Phoenix Mercury	http://www.wnba.com/mercury/
Sacramento Monarchs	http://www.wnba.com/monarchs/
San Antonio Silverstars	http://www.wnba.com/silverstars/
Seattle Storm	http://www.wnba.com/storm/
Washington Mystics	http://www.wnba.com/mystics/

BEER

A
B
C
D
E
F
G
H
I
J
K
L
M
N
O
P
Q
R
S
T
U
V
W
X
Y
Z

1-800-MICROBREW

http://www.800-microbrew.com/

★★★

 Not for kids

This microbrew-of-the-month club promises each member will receive 12 bottles of fine microbrew each month (6 from two different breweries). The site also contains recipes for such delicacies as cheesy beer bread and beef braised in igloo ale.

Ale Street News

http://www.alestreetnews.com

★★★★

 Not for kids

Find out about upcoming brew events "Hoppenings" and stay current on beer-related news at this site, which also features links to Pubcrawler, a database that allows you to search for breweries, pubs, and bars in the United States.

All About Beer

http://www.allaboutbeer.com

★★★★

 Not for kids

This is the Internet home of *All About Beer* magazine, which is packed with beer news, opinions, ratings, home-brew secrets, international beers, and much more. Plenty of articles are available in this site.

Related Sites

http://www.beerparadise.ltd.uk/

http://www.hogshead.com/

http://www.alaskanbeer.com/

Badger Brewery

http://www.badgerbrewery.com/

★★★★

 Not for kids

This site reveals Badger Brewery and its beers. You can view the brewing process, learn about the ingredients Badger uses in its beers, and even go on a virtual pub walk. Click the Ecard link to send a friend a custom greeting card from Badger Brewery. A very quaint site.

Beamish & Crawford Brewery

http://www.beamish.ie

★★★★

 Not for kids

The Beamish & Crawford Brewery has been brewing Beamish Genuine Irish Stout in Cork for more than 200 years. The site contains, among other things, a movie file about the brewery plus wallpaper and a screensaver to "Beamish" your computer.

BeerBooks.com

http://www.beerbooks.com/

★★★★

 Not for kids

Tired of drinking beer brewed by others? Then brew your own with the help of BeerBooks.com's hefty collection of beer books and videos. Here, you can purchase almost any book published on the topic of beer, from tasting and cooking with beer to brewing your own concoctions. Pick from a wide selection of recipe books as well.

A
B
C
D
E
F
G
H
I
J
K
L
M
N
O
P
Q
R
S
T
U
V
W
X
Y
Z

Beer Hunter

http://www.beerhunter.com

★★★★★

 Not for kids

Learn how to taste beer, learn about beer from around the world, and get updates on the Michael Jackson (the beer hunter) World Beer Tour. Michael Jackson himself answers questions with his beer FAQ.

Beer Info

http://www.beerinfo.com

★★★

Not for kids

If you're looking for a beer information source, you should start here, where you can search for facts about your favorite brew. A rather dry site, but full of information nonetheless.

Beer Me!

http://www.beerme.com/

★★★★

Not for kids

Meet The Good Soldier Svejk on this website (formerly called Beer Is My Life), and learn all about home brewing as well as the fine art of pub crawling. Offerings here are humorous and informative at the same time. Features links for Regional Brewery Guides, Beer List, Beer Styles, a Beer Library, and much more.

Brew Hut

http://www.thebrewhut.com/

$

★★★

Not for kids

This homebrew supply warehouse, which claims to be the most comprehensive on the Web, features a complete line of beer- and wine-making supplies.

Bud Online

http://www.budweiser.com/

 $

★★★★★

Not for kids

A colorful, innovative site from Budweiser, the King of Beers. Features information on the history of beer and how Budweiser is improving the quality of beer. Order Budweiser paraphernalia, check out the latest Budweiser sponsored/endorsed events, and download Budweiser screensavers or wallpaper. This site even "cards" you before allowing you to enter.

Guinness

http://www.guinness.ie/

 $

★★★★★

Not for kids

This high-tech site invites you to visit St. James' Gate, the home of Guinness beer. Learn about the beer, the can, and much more. You can even download a Guinness screensaver. Don't miss the Pearls of Wisdom link, where you can learn some beer trivia and read up on some bizarre facts.

Heineken

http://www.Heineken.com

★★★★★

Not for kids

Provides history of the Heineken brewery and offers a virtual tour. Send customized email postcards and e-invitations and participate in Heineken's online game to win prizes.

Leinenkugel's Leinie Lodge

http://www.leinie.com/splashscreen.asp

 $

★★★★★

Not for kids

Learn all about this Wisconsin brew and other specialties in the Leinenkugel family of beers. Purchase T-shirts, sweatshirts, hats, and other promotional items from the online gift shop.

Beer, Beer, and More Beer Home Brewing Supplies

http://www.morebeer.com/

★★★★

 Not for kids

Pick up everything you need to turn your home into the neighborhood brewery. Here, you'll find home brewing kits, ingredients, dispensing equipment, and other home brewing essentials.

Pabst Brewing Company

http://www.pabst.com/

★★★★★

Not for kids

Provides a history of beer in general as well as of this brewing company, one of the oldest in America, and currently one of the most popular "retro" beers. Also under the Pabst umbrella are Olympia, Hamm's, Pearl, and other labels. Click the **Beer 101** link to learn about the brewing process. You can check out the gift store for promotional items sporting the names and logos of several popular brands of beer, including Old Milwaukee, Old Style, Schlitz, and Rainier. However, at the time of this writing, you couldn't purchase items online.

The Pub Brewing Company

http://www.pubbrewing.com/

★★★

  Not for kids

Thinking about opening your own brew pub? This is the company to show you the ropes. It provides lay-outs, equipment, installation, training, inspections, and more. Your comprehensive guide to getting into the brew business.

Best RealBeer.com: The Beer Portal

http://www.realbeer.com

★★★★★

  Not for kids

The quintessential site for home brewers and micro-breweries alike. Host to three beer-of-the-month clubs, plus more than 150,000 pages about beer, this site appeals to the most enthusiastic beer lovers on the Web. With a huge cache of links to other related websites and places where you can purchase special brews, this site is truly the Best of the Best when it comes to breweries.

Redhook Ale Brewery

http://www.redhook.com/

★★★★

 Not for kids

Provides information on the Washington state–based microbrewery that has begun to make its existence known nationwide for its diversity and excellence. Take a virtual tour of the brewery and evaluate the stock value of this up-and-coming brewery. Purchase T-shirts, hats, glasses, mugs, and more from the online gift store.

Sam Adams

http://www.samadams.com

★★★★★

 Not for kids

The definitive guide to the different styles of Samuel Adams Beers; learn the history, brewing, and flavor characteristics of Sam Adams' hand-crafted beers. Order items including mugs, steins, hats, T-shirts, and more from the online store or download the Sam Adams animated screen saver!

Siebel Institute of Technology

http://www.siebelinstitute.com/

★★★★

 Not for kids

The classes many college students dream about are offered at this brewing training establishment. Take courses such as Sensory Evaluation of Beer, Advanced Brewery Technology, or Yeast Management Workshop. Lab services also are offered, and you can consult the institute's newsletter.

Related Sites

http://www.shenandoahbrewing.com/

http://www.sierra-nevada.com/

A B C D E F G H I J K L M N O P Q R S T U V W X Y Z

96

A
B
C
D
E
F
G
H
I
J
K
L
M
N
O
P
Q
R
S
T
U
V
W
X
Y
Z

BICYCLES

Bicycling Magazine
http://www.bicyclingmagazine.com/

★★★★★

 9-13

Tour information, events, product reviews, techniques, and more. Whether you enjoy tinkering with your bike or you just like to ride, you'll find plenty of useful information at this site. Also contains links to other great bicycling sites.

Bike Lane
http://www.bikelane.com

★★★★

Great links to manufacturer sites, custom frame builders, magazines, and the latest news in competitive biking.

Best Bike Ride Online
http://www.bikeride.com

★★★★★

 9-13

An exceptional bicycling web directory that features links to hundreds of resources, including regional clubs, manufacturers, retailers, racing events, mountain biking, training, coaching, and more. And if you run out of links to click, you can check out the newsgroups to find messages posted by other bicycling enthusiasts.

Cambria Bicycle Outfitters
http://www.cambriabike.com/

★★★★★

Cambria stocks everything imaginable for the avid bicyclist, including parts, tires, tools, bags, carriers, apparel, and even food. Before your next tour, check out this site to make sure you're properly equipped.

Cannondale
http://www.cannondale.com

★★★★★

Check out Cannondale's listing of awesome mountain bikes as well as other Cannondale products. Site also features owner's manuals, kit lists, tech notes, bicycle safety information, and much more.

Cycling Web
http://www.cyclingweb.com/

★★★★

Cycling fans will want to check out this site for the latest news about races, teams, and cyclists.

International Mountain Bicycling Association
http://www.altrec.com/shop/dir/cycle/

★★★★

Provides action alerts, trail care, and other information from a group aiming to promote environmentally responsible mountain biking.

Performance Bicycles

http://www.performancebike.com/

★★★★

In the 1980s, Garry and Sharon Snook began Performance, Inc. in the basement of their home in Chapel Hill, North Carolina. It has since grown into the nation's leading bicycle mail order and retail company.

Schwinn

http://www.schwinn.com

★★★★

Anyone considering buying a Schwinn bike or exercise equipment will want to stop by here to research each model, locate a dealer, and hear about how the Schwinn racing team is doing this year. If you already own a Schwinn bike, you can register for your warranty online, download a replacement owner's manual, or find a dealer near you.

Shimano

http://bike.shimano.com/

★★★★★

 9-13

Learn more about the ins and outs of Shimano racing technology at this site, where you'll learn why so many professional racers choose to ride Shimano bicycles. This site also helps you locate a local dealer and contact customer support. Very well-designed site.

Specialized

http://www.specialized.com

★★★★★

9-13

This site is packed with racing news and cycling tips. You can shop for bikes and accessories online or access owner's manuals and obtain tech support. Features a very useful and thorough glossary of many of the more technical terms you will encounter in the world of bicycling.

Tour de France

http://www.letour.fr

★★★★

Search the archives to learn more about past winners of the Tour de France at this bilingual official site, which will also track the progress of this year's racers online. Click the link for your preferred language: English or French.

Trails from Rails

http://www.trailsfromrails.com/

★★★★★

Find the best bike trails across the United States. This site provides a list of trails that are paved with asphalt, concrete, or crushed limestone/gravel—trails that are suitable for touring or cross-bikes. Many of the trails are also open to hikers, cross-country skiers, snowmobilers, and roller bladers. Most trails pass through small towns, giving riders a bit of the local flavor as well as some outdoor adventure.

VBT

http://www.vbt.com

★★★★

You'll consider cycling through Europe after visiting this page, which will tell you about upcoming tours, equipment, and tour leaders.

VeloNews Interactive

http://www.velonews.com

★★★

A journal of competitive cycling. Offers news, Tour de France information, and links to other pages. Stay up to date on racing news or get training tips at this site.

Virtual Bike Barn

http://www.bikebarn.com/

★★★

9-13

A great starting point for information about everything from bike repair and safety to bicycle magazines, newsgroups, and clubs. Includes a good collection of links to other premier bicycling sites and includes information about kids' bikes.

A B C D E F G H I J K L M N O P Q R S T U V W X Y Z

A
B
C
D
E
F
G
H
I
J
K
L
M
N
O
P
Q
R
S
T
U
V
W
X
Y
Z

MAINTENANCE AND REPAIR

Barnett Bicycle Institute

http://www.bbinstitute.com/

★★★

Barnett Bicycle Institute, a school founded by John Barnett, offers classes in bicycle mechanics and materials for bicycle repair shops. You can read a sample chapter of the 1,000-page *Barnett's Manual* for the most comprehensive guide to bicycle repair and maintenance or purchase a copy of the manual online

Bicycle Tune-up and Repair

http://members.aol.com/biketune/

★★★★

This site features a free bicycle repair tutorial plus other informative lessons on various ways to make money with bicycles, how to weld, how to start and manage a bicycle repair business, and much more. A nice glossary of terms also is available and even a 20-question bicycle repair quiz.

Harris Cyclery

http://sheldonbrown.com/repair/

★★★★

A great site for learning how to repair your bicycle. Merchandise also available by ordering via email, fax, phone, or standard mail. Be sure to read the articles written by Sheldon Brown while you're at this site.

MOUNTAIN BIKING

Adventure Cycling Association

http://adv-cycling.org/

★★★★

👫 14-18

This site features a touring map, a list of events, online catalogs, articles on biking, a list of bargains, a guide to cross-country adventures, and details on how to become a member of Adventure Cycling Association. You can even use the online version of the *Cyclist's Yellow Pages* to find bicycle stores and resources near you.

Aegis Bicycles

http://www.aegisbicycles.com/

★★★★

👫 14-18

Technical details about the carbon fiber bicycle frames and forks created by Aegis, plus tips on bicycle fit and details on Aegis dealers throughout the United States.

Analytic Cycling

http://www.analyticcycling.com/

★★★★

👫 14-18

Cyclists can chart speed, equipment performance, and more with this service, which allows riders to enter their data into predetermined formulas. Excellent site for competitive cyclists—very techie.

Bianchi

http://www.bianchi/com

$

★★★★

👫 14-18

Get information about the Bianchi line of bikes and accessories, championship biking event results, magazines, and advice from expert bikers.

Big Island Mountain Biking Trail Guide

http://www.interpac.net/~mtbike/bigmap.html

★★★

👫 14-18

A clickable map of Hawaii's big island allows users to access information on bike trail distances, difficulty levels, elevations, and estimated riding times.

Competitive Cyclist
http://www.competitivecyclist.com/

★★★★

 14-18

A complete inventory of cycling products for the serious competitor, including bicycles, frames, components, clothing, and more. If you're looking to build your own custom bike or have it built for you, this is the site for you. Excellent selection combined with superior service make this a great place to shop.

Cyclingnews.com
http://www.cyclingnews.com/

★★★★★

 14-18

If you like to follow bicycle races, this is the place for it. Cyclingnews.com is packed with the latest news and information about bicycle races from around the world. Read about the latest races and racers, check the racing calendar, browse the photo index, and much more.

Diamondback Bikes
http://www.diamondback.com/

★★★★

 All

Since 1977, Diamondback has been producing quality mountain and BMX bicycles. You can get detailed descriptions of all models, read tech specs, and also see available accessories. A special section just for kids lets them shop for a new bike online, too!

Dictionary of Mountain Bike Slang
http://world.std.com/~jimf/biking/slang.html

★★★

 14-18

If you're going to ride like a mountain biker, you should learn to talk like one, too. Check out this site to view a list of mountain biking slang terms and their definitions.

Dirt Camp
http://www.mountainworkshop.com/dirt_camp

★★★★

 All

This is the site for America's only national, award-winning mountain biking instructional and guide program. With more than 10,000 guests to date from nearly 50 states and overseas, Dirt Camp is for enthusiasts of all ages and abilities. This is a great source for mountain biking adventures.

Gearhead
http://www.gearhead.com/gearhead/

★★★

 14-18

Gearhead cyber-zine offers some scant commentary, news, and other information for visitors interested in mountain biking. *Gearhead*'s website is primarily useful for its many message boards where beginning and advanced gearheads can keep in touch and trade tips and advice.

International Mountain Bicycling Association
http://www.imba.com/

★★★★★

14-18

The International Mountain Bicycling Association (IMBA) is dedicated to "enhancing and improving trail opportunities for mountain bikers worldwide." This group claims a membership of more than 32,000 riders worldwide and 450 bicycling clubs. Here, you can learn about the organization and its projects, read the rules of the trails, and learn what you can do to help.

Marin Mountain Bikes
http://www.marinbikes.com/

★★★★

14-18

Marin Mountain Bikes provides technical specifications of its product line at this site. Information on the design and construction of Marin bikes is included.

A B C D E F G H I J K L M N O P Q R S T U V W X Y Z

Merlin Bicycles

http://www.merlinbike.com/

★★★★★

👥 14-18

Merlin Bicycles builds mountain bikes as well as road bicycles. Check out this site to see the latest models as well as current apparel available. Very high-tech, cutting-edge bikes and equipment.

Mountain Bike Daily

http://www.mountainbike.com/

★★★★

👥 14-18

A trail finder, details on bike gear, updates on racing news, and product reviews are listed here. If you're a biking enthusiast, you'll want to bookmark this site for return visits.

Mountain Bike Trailsource

http://www.trailsource.com/biking/index.asp

★★★★

👥 14-18

Adventure travel guide to 3,000 biking single tracks in more than 100 countries around the globe. Just click on the map to find mountain bike trails where you want to go.

Mountain Biking

http://mtb.live.com/

★★★

👥 14-18

"The Internet's mountain bike park," covers places to ride, racing, biking advice, online magazines and stories, humor, and more.

Mountain Cycle

http://www.mountaincycle.com/

$

★★★

👥 14-18

Great site for browsing through a collection of high-end mountain bikes. Choose a bike type, make, and model, and then customize by selecting the desired options. You can even purchase your bike online and have it delivered to your home.

MTBR.com: The Ultimate Mountain Biking Resource

http://www.mtbr.com/

$

★★★★

👥 14-18

A guide developed by mountain bikers for mountain bikers, delivering user-provided reviews of mountain bike products, news, and tips. This site has 50,000 product reviews and brings together 30,000 riders daily (or so MTBR.com claims). Excellent directory of Internet resources on biking.

Roadcycling.com

http://www.roadcycling.com/

$

★★★

👥 14-18

Cycling news, events, standings, product reviews, merchandise, books, training, teams, and more. Register for the free newsletter.

Rocky Mountain Bicycles

http://www.bikes.com/

★★★★

👥 14-18

Overviews of the mountain bikes created by Rocky Mountain Bicycles, plus team profiles, photos, and action video clips.

Santa Cruz Bicycles

http://www.santacruzmtb.com/

$

★★★★

👥 14-18

Technical details and reviews of Santa Cruz mountain bikes, plus a color picker that allows potential buyers to envision the bike of their dreams. You can shop online for T-shirts, shorts, and other apparel.

Spokeswomen
http://www.spokeswomen.com/

★★★

👫 14-18

This site offers information about Spokeswomen's mountain biking camps for women in Whistler, British Columbia.

Trails.com
http://www.trails.com

$

★★★★★

👫 14-18

Chosen as Forbes West of the West, this site offers locations and ideas for mountain biking trips, as well as hiking, paddling, and skiing excursions. If you have a bike and think there's no place to ride it, check out this site. It features biking trails throughout the United States and Canada and is very easy to search. The cost is about $40 per year.

Trek Bicycle Corporation
http://www.trekbikes.com/

$

★★★★★

👫 All

Trek offers information about its bicycles and accessories here. You can also find your local Trek dealer or read the latest Trek news. Kids area has safety tips, instructions on how to select a bike, and tips for riding together as a family.

Western Spirit Cycling
http://www.westernspirit.com/

$

★★★★

👫 14-18

Operates mountain bike tours in Utah, Colorado, Idaho, and Arizona. Includes photos and tour information. Learn about the various bike tours available and then sign up for a trip online.

A B C D E F G H I J K L M N O P Q R S T U V W X Y Z

A B C D E F G H I J K L M N O P Q R S T U V W X Y Z

BILLIARDS

American Poolplayers Association

http://www.poolplayers.com/

★★★★

Geared primarily toward the competition-minded player, this site offers complete rules for the games of 8-ball and 9-ball, plus an opportunity to join the APA or start up an APA tournament franchise. Also includes a link to *American Poolplayer Magazine* articles.

Billiard Congress of America

http://www.bca-pool.com/

★★★

 All

The Billiard Congress of America is the governing body for the sport of pocket billiards in North America. Its site is primarily educational, providing official rules and guidelines for equipment, but you can also join the organization and read about its publications.

Billiard Info

http://www.billiardinfoline.com

★★★

Find places to play local tournaments and catch up on billiard-related news. Provides several links to online billiard shops, where you can purchase cues and other billiards products.

Billiard Pro Shop, Inc.

http://www.billiardpro.com/

$

★★★

Purchase the very finest cues, cases, and table fabrics at this online store. This equipment is pricey ($200 and up for a cue), but if billiards is your life, this can be a great place to shop online.

Billiards Digest Interactive

http://www.billiardsdigest.com/

$

★★★★

The online complement to the most comprehensive magazine in billiards. Rather than replacing the magazine, the site offers features that supplement the paper copy, such as coverage of upcoming tournaments, chat rooms, and opinion polls. Several links to billiard-supply retailers. Order your subscription online.

Best Brunswick

http://www.brunswick-billiards.com

★★★★★

 All

Product information and dealer locations can be found at this manufacturer site, as well as information about what makes a Brunswick table different. Great place to learn the basic rules that govern the most common games, including 8-ball, 9-ball, and straight pool. For the best information about billiards presented in the most easily accessible format, visit this site.

Pool Hall

http://www.poolhall.com

$

★★★★

Find a pool hall in your area by searching the state listings of pool halls here, shop at the pro shop, or check up on pool tournaments. Also offers some useful instructions and tips on how to play.

Shooters Billiard

http://www.shootersbilliards.com

★★★

Buy pool cues and accessories at discount prices from this billiards dealer. Most major manufacturers represented.

U.S. Billiard Association

http://www.uscarom.org

★★★★

Find a billiard hall near you, read past issues of the organization newsletter, and hear about upcoming tournaments. Click the Instruction link to brush up on the rules of the game, get tips from the pros, and learn the do's and don'ts of practicing. Clicking the **Room Directory** calls up a list of pool halls organized by state. Not the most intuitive site to navigate, but lots of good information.

Women's Professional Billiard Association

http://www.wpba.com

★★★★★

Read the biographies of leading players, check up on their current rankings, and find out when the next competition is being held. A good history of the game along with a bullet list of rules for 9-ball and classic billiards. Attractive site.

A
B
C
D
E
F
G
H
I
J
K
L
M
N
O
P
Q
R
S
T
U
V
W
X
Y
Z

104

A
B
C
D
E
F
G
H
I
J
K
L
M
N
O
P
Q
R
S
T
U
V
W
X
Y
Z

BINGO

Bingo Bugle Online Newspaper

http://www.bingobugle.com/

★★★★

 Not for kids

The definitive resource for the Bingo enthusiast. Here, you'll find plenty of links to articles about online gaming, plus links to the best gaming sites on the Web. Play bingo, slot machines, Keno, and other gambling games. Bingo Bugle also offers its own (no-wager) games, just in case you want to play for fun.

Bingo Gala

http://www.bingogala.com/

★★★★★

 Not for kids

Bingo Gala is one of the premier bingo sites on the Web. New games start every 3 to 5 minutes. Just register online, deposit at least ten bucks into your account (via credit card), pick your card, and join in the next game. Play at your own risk.

Bingos.com

http://www.bingovegas.com/

★★★★★

 Not for kids

Play bingo and other games on the Internet at the Net's premier online casino—Bingos.com. Well-designed for navigation, this site makes losing money almost too easy.

Bingo Novelty World

http://www.bingonoveltyworld.com/shopping/

★★★★

 Not for kids

If you're running your own Bingo night, look to this site as a resource for all your bingo needs: ink daubers, cards, waiters, cups, mugs, and can coolers, all for the bingo enthusiast.

Bingo Online

http://www.bingoonline.com/

★★★★★

 Not for kids

Play free bingo games for fun, or for cash and prizes, 24 hours a day, 7 days a week. To play for cash, click the **Sign Up** link on the opening page and follow the onscreen instructions to register.

CyberBingo

http://www.cyberbingo.net/

★★★★★

 Not for kids

Billed as America's first and largest bingo network, CyberBingo has been named Top Bingo Site by *Gambling Online Magazine*. Join thousands of other players in the largest bingo hall on the Internet.

DaboInk

http://www.daboink.com/

★★★

 Not for kids

This site is aimed at wholesale distributors, not retail customers. It describes the variety of Bingo markers DaboInk offers. This company has been manufacturing Bingo markers since 1962.

Instant Bingo

http://www.instantbingo.com/

★★★★

 Not for kids

Play for fun, points, or cash at this online gaming site. Players can enter weekly drawings and win merchandise, prizes, and special offers.

Which Bingo

http://www.whichbingo.com/

★★★★

 Not for kids

Games, newsletters, and bingo news are all available here. This site features links to both land-based and online games. Merchandise and equipment can be found as well as links to other bingo sites. An incredible directory of bingo games and resources.

A
B
C
D
E
F
G
H
I
J
K
L
M
N
O
P
Q
R
S
T
U
V
W
X
Y
Z

106

A
B
C
D
E
F
G
H
I
J
K
L
M
N
O
P
Q
R
S
T
U
V
W
X
Y
Z

BIRDS

American Birding Association

http://www.americanbirding.org/

★★★★

Dedicated to increasing the knowledge, skills, and enjoyment of birding and to contributing to bird conservation, the American Birding Association's home page features links to publications, programs, tours, conventions, and other birding resources. Also helps you locate restaurants near birding hotspots.

The Aviary

http://www.theaviary.com

★★★★

All

For people interested in birding or companion birds, this site is a great resource. Find out more about a particular species, as well as how to attract them and care for them.

Backyard Birding

http://www.bcpl.net/~tross/by/backyard.html

★★★

All

The Baltimore Bird Club has designed a site that helps you attract birds to your yard. It addresses plants birds prefer, food and habitat questions, information from seasoned backyard birders, and a good collection of links to related websites.

The Baltimore Bird Club

http://baltimorebirdclub.org/

★★★

 All

This site is not just for Maryland residents. It contains rare bird alerts posted for the entire East Coast region, links to bird societies, and an extensive list of additional sites on the adventures of birding in America.

Bird Breeder

http://www.animalnetwork.com/birds/

★★★★

A monthly online magazine devoted to the care of exotic birds, providing helpful hints from fellow bird lovers and a vet. Species descriptions, an online photo gallery, and behavior and training areas make this site a must-visit for bird owners.

Bird Song Matcher

http://www.virtualbirder.com/vbirder/matcher/matcherDirs/SONG/

★★★★

All

Test your bird knowledge with this site's bird identification game. The game gets tricky when you are dealing with multiple habitats and multiple bird species indigenous to any one habitat. To hear and see all the birds, you'll have to play several games.

Best Bird Watchers Digest

http://www.birdwatchersdigest.com

$

★★★★★

 All

For bird watchers everywhere, this site provides advice on bird watching from the experts, whether you're watching birds from exotic locations or just out your back window. You can also learn about bird gardening, identification, and new birding products. Purchase binoculars, paintings, CDs, books, and other items online. Packed with useful information about bird watching in an easy-to-access format, this site is an easy pick as the Best of the Best.

Birder

http://www.birder.com

$

★★★★

Enjoy virtual birding if you don't have access to local birds or make plans for a birdwatching vacation from this site, which emphasizes the sale of birdwatching equipment, books, and other products.

Birding.com

http://www.birding.com

$

★★★★

 All

A site that has a section specifically for beginning birders, Birding.com also lists bird records, birding hot spots, organizations, and links to other resources of potential interest. You can shop online for binoculars, bird feeders, bird houses, books, and just about anything an avid birder could ever want.

Birding in British Columbia

http://www.birding.bc.ca

★★★★

 All

Very current site devoted to birding and ecological sites in British Columbia, Canada. Read birding articles, check out field reports from other birders, get visitor and weather information, and try some links to other birding sites in British Columbia.

Birds n Ways

http://www.birdsnway.com/

$

★★★★

 All

Look to Birds n Ways for pet parrots, exotic birds, bird supplies, and pet bird information; it's a complete guide to pet parrots and exotic birds on the Net! You'll find information on dozens of varieties of birds, as well as information on e-zines, chats, bird shows, and more!

Caring for Your New Bird

http://www.ddc.com/~kjohnson/birdcare.htm

★★★

 All

This 23-page e-book includes information such as listings at local pet stores, mail-order supply catalogs, veterinarians, and bird clubs. Includes information on choosing breeders and a bird; surviving the first few days; handling your new bird; addressing issues related to household safety, nutrition, diseases, and injuries; and more.

Cockatiel Society

http://www.acstiels.com

$

★★★

The official site of the American Cockatiel Society, which features information for other clubs, upcoming shows, articles, and photos. Dedicated to both cockatiel owners and professional breeders, this site offers a small selection of articles from the *A.C.S. Magazine*.

The Fabulous Kakapo (Strigops Habroptilus)

http://www.kakapo.net/

★★★★

 All

Focuses on the kakapo bird, a rare nocturnal, flightless parrot that's native to New Zealand. Once prevalent throughout the area, the kakapo population is slowly diminishing; there are only about 62 left. This site details how New Zealanders are working to help the population recover.

A B C D E F G H I J K L M N O P Q R S T U V W X Y Z

A
B
C
D
E
F
G
H
I
J
K
L
M
N
O
P
Q
R
S
T
U
V
W
X
Y
Z

Field Guides

http://www.fieldguides.com

★★★★

👥 All

Look into birding tours around the world or in your area at this site, which provides information on upcoming tours and guides to help you make your decision.

Finch World

http://www.finchworld.com

★★★★

👥 All

A finch search engine complete with directories of bird lovers and breeders, as well as articles on various finch species. Links to Amazon.com for books and videos on finches.

Hot Spots for Birders

http://www.birder.com/birding/hotspots/index.html

★★★

👥 All

This site is exactly what its title suggests: A list of the best sites around the world for viewing birds in their natural habitats.

Majestic Macaws

http://www.exoticbird.com

★★★★

👥 All

Excellent site for macaw owners and admirers. Learn all about the health, behavior, and care for the exotic macaw. The help desk provides excellent information on treating injuries and illnesses, and the Parrot Humor link provides a nice touch. The site also has links for macaw food recipes, supplies, books, breeders, and more.

National Audubon Society

http://www.audubon.org

★★★★★

👥 All

This site, the home page of the National Audubon Society, provides information on the conservation issues and programs the society is currently working on. Those campaigns currently target the marine ecosystems of the world and bird sanctuaries that protect wildlife habitats, including legislation affecting wetlands. Some excellent information on how to increase biodiversity in your own backyard.

Northern Prairie Wildlife Research Center

http://www.npwrc.usgs.gov/resource/tools/ndblinds/ndblinds.htm

★★★

👥 All

Detailed plans for do-it-yourselfers interested in building nest structures and feeders. You can even learn how to build your own bat house.

Optics for Birding

http://www.optics4birding.com/

★★★

👥 All

This site is designed to educate those who want to buy optics (binoculars and telescopes, primarily). Although the target audience is those who enjoy watching birds, much of the information is generally applicable. This site contains reviews of optical equipment, FAQs, and manufacturer contacts, and allows you to search for a topic.

PETBird

http://www.upatsix.com/

★★★★

👥 All

Introduces aviary practices; provides FAQs; and offers links to numerous breeders, vendors, artists, and avian associations. Check out the Fun and Games section to rate your bird addiction, share your favorite bird names, or check out a colorful photo album.

Peterson Online Birds

http://www.houghtonmifflinbooks.com/peterson/

★★★★

All

Where do you begin when you want to identify a new bird? To narrow down the possibilities quickly, first put the bird into one of Peterson's eight visual categories. This site also offers birding links and resources, a skill builder section, a calendar of bird-related events and spectacles, a bird watcher's digest, a bird identification area, and more. Easy-to-navigate site.

Seed Preferences

http://www.birdware.com/schart.htm

★★★

All

So, what food do you put in what feeder to attract that bird? Find out here.

Wild Birds Unlimited

http://www.wbu.com

$

★★★★★

All

Wild Birds Unlimited is the first and largest franchise system of retail stores catering to the backyard bird-feeding hobbyist. Find all kinds of seed, bird feeders, bird houses, nesting boxes, books, and more at this one-stop shopping site. Email questions directly to the experts.

Wildbird ID Charts and Posters

http://www.chartingnature.com/

★★★

All

Definitely will appeal to bird lovers, but also to all wildlife enthusiasts. Sells wildlife posters; wildlife identification charts; and wildlife pictures, prints, and gifts. You'll find Nature Discovery's complete line of biologically exact wildlife identification and art products.

Winging It Post Office

http://birding.miningco.com/hobbies/birding/
library/blcard.htm?pid=2804&cob=home

★★★

All

Free Internet postcards of wild birds and butterflies. Send or pick up a free postcard with a bird theme!

A
B
C
D
E
F
G
H
I
J
K
L
M
N
O
P
Q
R
S
T
U
V
W
X
Y
Z

BLOGS

DIRECTORIES AND SEARCH ENGINES

Blogarama
http://www.blogarama.com/

★★★★★

Blogarama features a respectable directory of more than 8,000 blogs, which you can browse by category or search for specifically by name or type. Also lists sites by Most Cool, Most Popular, and Highly Rated.

BlogWise
http://www.blogwise.com/

★★★★

Here you will find an extensive directory of more than 16,000 blogs sorted by popularity and browse-able by keyword. If you have your own blog, you can register it here.

Globe of Blogs
http://www.globeofblogs.com/

★★★★

This site functions as a directory of blogs that you can browse by topic, title, or author. If you have a blog, you can visit this site to register it and have it included in the directory.

LA Blogs
http://www.lablogs.com/

★★★

If you live in Los Angeles or are just curious as to what the LA crowd has to say, visit LA Blogs. This self-proclaimed "blog of blogs" provides a loosely organized directory of blogs that relate to life in Los Angeles.

Longhorn Blogs
http://www.longhornblogs.com/

★★★★★

Are you interested in learning and discussing the latest news and information about Microsoft's new version of Windows, code-named Longhorn? Then check out this site, which provides links to 50 of the best Longhorn blogs.

Root Blog
http://www.rootblog.com/

★★★★

This blog search engine lists over a dozen categories of blogs, including multiple subcategories that can help narrow your search. Also provides a search box for tracking down specific blogs or types of blogs. You can register your own blog to have it included on this site.

Related Sites
http://www.blogsearchengine.com/
http://www.blogscanada.ca/directory/default.asp
http://directory.etalkinghead.com/

Wizbang Blog Awards
http://wizbangblog.com/poll.php

★★★★★

Excellent directory of the Best of the Best blogs, as voted by users like you.

BLOG HOSTING

Blog-City.com
http://www.blog-city.com/

★★★★

At Blog-City.com, you can sign up for free blog hosting, so you can create and maintain your own blog. Blog-City.com also features access to several blogs, so you can see how they work. For about $2.50 per month, you can upgrade to premium service for advanced features such as taking online polls, password-protecting your blog entries, and keeping an online photo album.

Blogger
http://www.blogger.com/

★★★★★

Publish your thoughts and insights on the Web for the general public to read or ponder. At Blogger, you can create your own *blog* (short for web log) and publish messages simply by completing a form. Blogger also offers a feature that enables you to use a web-based cell phone to record and post your messages when you're on the go; visitors to your blog can then listen to your recorded messages.

Blogging Network
http://www.bloggingnetwork.com/

★★★★

If the general public finds your words of wisdom valuable, people will be willing to pay you for sharing your opinions and insights. At Blogging Network, you can publish your thoughts online and get paid every time someone clicks a link to read one of your articles. The service charges visitors $2.99 per month for access to all blogs and then divvies up the money among all writers based on each writer's popularity. The more people read your writing, the more you earn.

LiveJournal
http://www.livejournal.com/

★★★★★

LiveJournal is a blog hosting service that enables you to create and update your own blog, check out other blogs in the community, and share your interests with other bloggers. Visit this site to take a free tour of the service and find out what it has to offer.

Movable Type
http://www.movabletype.org

★★★★★

Movable Type is a program that installs on your web server, and provides you with the tools you need to create and manage your blog. To use Movable Type, you need to know how to install and configure the software on your web server. At the Movable Type site, you can learn how to access the TypePad service, which provides an easier way for most users to create and manage their blogs. Its powerful tools and useful information make this the Best of the Best Blog Site.

Salon.com Blogs
http://www.salon.com/blogs/

★★★★

For about $40 per year, you can obtain the software and service you need to create and host your own blog. Free 30-day trial is available. This site also features a clear explanation of blogs.

TypePad
http://www.typepad.com

★★★★★

TypePad is a powerful blogging host that gives users a comprehensive set of features and tools to publish and update their blogs right on the Web. You don't need to install or configure a separate program on you computer. Service costs about $5 per month.

A
B
C
D
E
F
G
H
I
J
K
L
M
N
O
P
Q
R
S
T
U
V
W
X
Y
Z

Xanga

`http://www.xanga.com`

★★★★

Xanga offers a free blogging service that's pretty basic. For as low as $2 per month (if you pay up front for a 2-year subscription), you can upgrade to the premium service and get powerful tools for creating and updating your site online, so you don't need to install any special software or learn complicated website management software.

SAMPLE BLOGS

Celebrity

Bill Maher	`http://www.safesearching.com/billmaher/blog/`
Dave Barry	`http://davebarry.blogspot.com`
Melanie Griffith	`http://www.melaniegriffith.com/in2mec/intimacy_firstpeek.html`
Moby Tour Diary	`http://www.moby.com/cms/viewalldiary.asp`
Sheryl Crow	`http://www.sherylcrow.com/pictures/diary/diary_index.html`
Wil Wheaton	`http://www.wilwheaton.net`
William Gibson	`http://www.williamgibsonbooks.com/blog/blog.asp`
Gossip Columnist	`http://gossiplist.com/blog/`

Cooking

Cooking with Amy	`http://cookingwithamy.blogspot.com/`
Deus Ex Culina	`http://deusexculina.robsama.com/`
Food Basics	`http://wolves.typepad.com/food_basics/`
Food Goat	`http://foodgoat.blogspot.com/`
Lapin Gourmand	`http://www.lapingourmand.com/`
Radical Chef	`http://cooking.houseonahill.net/`
The Julie/Julia Project	`http://blogs.salon.com/0001399/`

Economic

Angry Bear	`http://www.angrybear.blogspot.com/`
ArgMax	`http://www.argmax.com`
EconLog (Arnold King)	`http://econlog.econlib.org`
Institutional Economics	`http://www.institutional-economics.com`
Knowledge Problem	`http://www.knowledgeproblem.com`
Technical Outlook	`http://technicaloutlook.blogspot.com/`
Winter Speak	`http://www.winterspeak.com`

Health and Medicine

Family Medicine Notes	`http://www.docnotes.net`
GirlFit	`http://www.girlfit.com/`
GruntDoc	`http://www.gruntdoc.com`
In The Pipeline	`http://www.corante.com/pipeline`
Living Code	`http://www.corante.com/livingcode`
Medpundit	`http://www.medpundit.blogspot.com`
The Birdhouse (Mental Health)	`http://www.bookblogs.com/piercingtheveil/`

Humor

Allah Is in the House	`http://www.allahpundit.com/`
BoingBoing	`http://www.boingboing.net/`
IMAO	`http://imao.us/`
JWalk Blog	`http://www.j-walkblog.com/blog/`
Museum of Hoaxes	`http://www.museumofhoaxes.com/`
ScrappleFace	`http://www.scrappleface.com/`
Wit and Wisdom	`http://wittandwisdom.blogs.com/home/`

Media

BlogCritics. org	http://blogcritics.org
Gawker	http://www.gawker.com
I Want Media	http://www.iwantmedia.com
Media Relations	http://after-words.org/mr/
MetaFilter	http://www.metafilter.com
Popism	http://popism.blogspot.com/
Poynter Online	http://poynter.org/

Movies

Addicted to Movies	http://www.aggressivegirl.blogger.com.br/
DVD Verdict	http://www.dvdverdict.com
FilmFodder	http://www.filmfodder.com/
MilkPlus	http://www.milkplus.blogspot.com/
The Matrix	http://thereisno-spoon.blogspot.com/
MovieBlog	http://www.rickmcginnis.com/movieblog/
RottenTomatoes	http://www.rottentomatoes.com

Personal

Amanita	http://journal.amanita.net/
Beli-Blog	http://belicove.com
Dr. Frank's What's-It	http://www.doktorfrank.com/
Kid's Corner	http://kidjacque.blogspot.com/
Leslie Katz	http://www.lesliekatz.com/
Mike Little's Journalized	http://zed1.com/journalized/
Milk and Cookies	http://www.milkandcookies.com/
Nino Nano Speed	http://www.ninonanospeed.com/
Wizbang!	http://wizbangblog.com/

Photo

Catherine Jamieson	http://www.catherinejamieson.com
Daily Dose Of Imagery	http://wvs.topleftpixel.com
A Day In The Life	http://www.adayinthelife.org
if i only knew	http://www.idared.net/
Quarlo	http://www.quarlo.com
Ten Years Of My Life	http://www.tenyearsofmylife.com
The Coyote's Bark	http://www.idared.net/
Two Lane Love	http://ridingduo.tripod.com/blog.html

Political

Blog for America	http://blogforamerica.com/
Citizen Smash, the Indepundit	http://www.lt-smash.us
Decembrist	http://markschmitt.typepad.com
Electablog	http://www.electablog.com
The Manifest Border	http://www.manifestborder.com/
Musings…	http://www.enterstageright.com/cgi-bin/gm/
PoliBlog	http://www.poliblogger.com
Suburban Guerilla	http://www.suburbanguerrilla.blogspot.com/
Wonkette!	http:// www.wonkette.com

Sports

BadJocks. com	http://www.badjocks.com
fanblogs	http://www.fanblogs.com
Kwacky's Konfessional	http://kwacky.blogspot.com/
Off Wing Opinion	http://www.ericmcerlain.com/offwingopinion
Replacement Level Yankees	http://www.yankeefan.blogspot.com
SportsInfoBlog	http://sparcinfo.blogspot.com/
TheHardTruth	http:// thehardtruth.blogspot.com/

A
B
C
D
E
F
G
H
I
J
K
L
M
N
O
P
Q
R
S
T
U
V
W
X
Y
Z

Tech

Geek News Central	`http://www.geeknewscentral.com/`
Gizmodo	`http://www.gizmodo.com`
InternetNexus	`http://www.internet-nexus.com/`
kuro5hin	`http://www.kuro5hin.org`
Life in Slow Lane	`http://www.jke.it/blogdata/`
Reiter's Wireless Weblog	`http://reiter.weblogger.com`
Tech Dirt	`http://www.techdirt.com`
Technically Speaking	`http://tech-is-in.blogspot.com/`

Travel

Achikochi	`http://www.vincentvds.net/blog/index.html`
Bike to Shine	`http://www.biketoshine.com/postings.html`
Ed's Gone South	`http://www.edsgonesouth.com/blog/`
FourOnTour	`http://geocities.com/fourontour/`
GlobalWalk	`http://www.globalwalk.org`
HoboTraveler	`http://www.hobotraveler.com/blogger.html`
Tim Leffel's Cheapest Destinations	`http://blogs.booklocker.com/travel/`
Vagabonding	`http://www.vagabonding.com/`

War

Back to Iraq	`http://www.back-to-iraq.com/`
Daily Kos	`http://www.dailykos.com/`
Tacitus	`http://tacitus.org/`
Where is Raed?	`http://dear_raed.blogspot.com/`
Vodka Pundit	`http://vodkapundit.com/`
Stand Down	`http://www.nowarblog.org/`
NationalSecurityBlog	`http://www.nationalsecurityblog.com/`
Inside VC's War Blog	`http://blogs.insidevc.com/0000008/`

BOATS AND SAILING

1001 Boats for Sale

http://www.1001boats.com/

★★★

Search a large photo database of powerboats and sailboats from across the USA to find the boat of your dreams. There is no commission to sellers, although there is a minimal listing fee.

American Sail Training Association

http://tallships.sailtraining.org/

★★★

ASTA's site outlines all that the association offers in the way of Tall Ships sail training, sea education, and sailing travel adventures. It promotes the association's book, newsletter, and benefits of membership, too. You'll find detailed information about vessels, scholarships, ship events, and much more.

American Sailing Association

http://www.american-sailing.com/

★★★

Aspiring sailors will likely find a school near them—no matter where they live—that is staffed by instructors who have earned ASA certification through rigorous training and studies.

Boating 4 Kids

http://www.gomilpitas.com/homeschooling/explore/boating.htm

★★★★★

 All

For kids who are interested in learning about building, navigating, and controlling a boat, this is where you should start. Site features a directory of other sites where kids can learn how to build a milk carton boat, paddle a canoe, practice water safety, sail a boat, and much more.

Boat Owner's World

http://www.boatownersworld.com/

★★★★

If you have a boat but need stuff for it, this is the place for you. This site specializes in supplies and accessories, including boat covers, mooring, trailers, and camping gear.

BoatSafeKids

http://boatsafe.com/kids/

★★★★

 All

An extremely informative site for kids about boats and boating that features their questions and then answers from experts. The site also offers a boat safety checklist for adults.

A
B
C
D
E
F
G
H
I
J
K
L
M
N
O
P
Q
R
S
T
U
V
W
X
Y
Z

BoatShow

http://www.boatshow.com/

★★★

At this online boat show billed as the biggest on the Web, visitors can search for available boats or learn about new boats from the manufacturers, just as at a live show. The site also offers an online sailing lesson and links to merchandise. Covers both sailboats and powerboats.

David Dellenbaugh's Speed and Smarts

http://speedandsmarts.com/

★★★

This page, by an ex-America's Cup sailor, has all the tips and techniques you need to learn to sail faster, based on Dellenbaugh's monthly newsletter of the same name.

[Best] Internet Boats

http://www.internetboats.com/

★★★

Find more than $100 million worth of boats, yachts, cabin cruisers, specialty boats, classic wood boats, sailboats, anything that travels on water and all for sale on Internet Boats! This is your source for buying, selling, and locating any type of new or used watercraft!

Mark Rosenstein's Sailing Page

http://www.apparent-wind.com/sailing-page.html

★★★★

An extensive sailing directory where you can get the latest sailing news, information about maritime museums and magazines, individual stories from around the world, and much more.

Sailboats Inc.

http://www.sailboats-inc.com/

★★★★

Anyone considering purchasing a big boat might want to investigate a three-day cruise and seminar from Sailboats Direct. This site will tell you all about the course and what you can expect. And, when you complete the course, be sure to come back here to shop for a yacht and learn about available marina services.

Sailing

http://www.sailnet.com/sailing/

★★★★

The online version of the magazine. Read back issues, as well as the current one. Leave messages on the Message Center and surf through the many sailing links.

Sailing Alternatives

http://www.sailingalternatives.org/

★★★★

Sailing Alternatives is an organization dedicated to helping disabled (and "abled") persons sail on ships appropriately modified or otherwise fitted. Physical therapy and rehab are integrated with the sailing as needed.

Sea-Doo

http://www.seadoo.com/

★★★★★

In the market for a boat? Sea-Doo has a wide selection of unique designs to tempt your pocketbook, from the 5-person to the 12-person Islandia. The online showroom has a sleek design to match the beauty of Sea-Doo's watercraft.

United States Power Squadrons Web Page

http://www.usps.org/

★★★★

Presents USPS, a private boating organization. Focuses on USPS's Basic Boating Course and the purpose of the club. Provides a FAQ, link, and tells how to locate a squadron near you.

USAuctions.com

http://www.usauctions.com/

★★★

A live 24-hour auction site that specializes in boats and other watercraft.

U.S. Sailing

http://www.ussailing.org/

★★★★

9-13

The home page of the official governing body of the sport of sailing in America. The United States Sailing Association features information on sailing publications, racing events and schedules, educational courses, Olympic sailing, and more. Includes excellent information for aspiring young sailors and offers links to other youth-related boating sites.

Yachtingnet

http://www.yachtingnet.com/

★★★

A complete online boating guide that provides marine forecasts for your ZIP code, as well as information on new boats, helpful gear and apparel, a database of available boats, and a community of fellow boaters.

Related Sites

http://www.sailing.org/

http://www.boating.co.nz/sailing/

A B C D E F G H I J K L M N O P Q R S T U V W X Y Z

BOOKS

Abe Books

http://www.abebooks.com/

★★★★★

If you're looking for hard-to-find books or collectible books, visit Abe Books online. This site is designed to make it easy to browse or to search for specific titles and authors. Abe Books also provides tools for those who have rare books that they want to sell.

Banned Books Online

http://digital.library.upenn.edu/books/
banned-books.html

★★★

 Not for kids

Banned Books Online celebrates the freedom to read. You'll find links to e-texts on the Web featuring authors who have at one time been banned in America and elsewhere. The books range from *Candide* to *Huckleberry Finn*. Also present is some censorship history of the books featured on the page and commentary on banning and censorship attempts currently underway.

Bookbinding: A Tutorial

http://www.cs.uiowa.edu/~jones/book/

★★★

An instruction guide to repairing books that might be falling apart, this site has been carefully researched and represents the work of a true bibliophile.

BookCrossing

http://www.bookcrossing.com/

★★★★★

Do you like to share books with others and meet people who love the same books? Then check out BookCrossing, where you can review your favorite books, tag them, release them into the wild, and track their journeys to readers in your community or around the world. When someone finds a book you released, by leaving it somewhere or donating it to a library or other organization, the person can sign on to BookCrossing and report finding the book. If the person enters a journal entry about the book, BookCrossing notifies you by email, so you can read the entry. BookCrossing's goal is to turn the whole world into a great big library.

BookSite

http://www.booksite.com/

★★★

BookSite's goal is to make it easy and affordable for independent booksellers to add the Web to their overall marketing strategy. Interested? Visit this site for suggestions and detailed information.

BookWire

http://www.bookwire.com/

★★★★

BookWire is the book industry's most comprehensive and thorough online information source. BookWire's content includes timely book industry news, features, reviews, original fiction, guides to literary events, author interviews, thousands of annotated links to book-related sites, and more.

Children's Literature Web Guide (CLWG)

http://www.acs.ucalgary.ca/~dkbrown/

★★★★

👫 All

Must-visit site for anyone interested in great books for kids. The Children's Literature Web Guide is an attempt to gather and categorize the growing number of Internet resources related to books for children and young adults. The ideal audience for this site is teachers, librarians, parents, book professionals, and KIDS!

City Lights Bookstore

http://www.citylights.com/

★★★★★

Creative and innovative site representing the historic City Lights Bookstore, founded by poet Lawrence Ferlinghetti, in San Francisco's North Beach area. This site offers cutting-edge literature and books on compelling social and political issues. Whether you're interested in the Beat Generation or the latest cutting-edge literary works, this is the place to track down copies of your favorite books.

Conservation OnLine

http://palimpsest.stanford.edu/

★★★

A guide to preserving books, articles, pictures, and other media for professionals and amateurs alike. This site is dedicated to the preservation of information of many media.

Great Books Foundation

http://www.greatbooks.org/

★★★

👫 All

Interested in starting a reading discussion group? Visit this site for information about this nonprofit organization's approach. Headquartered in Chicago, Great Books publishes reading series for children and adults and conducts training in the Shared Inquiry method. Includes link to Junior Great Books, for K–12 readers.

Best 🗒 Harry Potter (Scholastic Books)

http://www.scholastic.com/harrypotter/home.asp

★★★★★

👫 All

Harry Potter fans should check out this site for information about the books, a reference guide, a discussion forum, games, a portrait gallery, a downloadable screensaver, and much more. Near the top of the page is a navigation bar that enables visitors to view other features of the Scholastic Books site. This site is beautifully designed, easy to navigate, and engaging for all ages.

Related Site
http://www.fictionalley.org/

Henry Miller Library

http://www.henrymiller.org

⑤

★★★★

👫 Not for kids

Peruse rare Miller books, literature, an online bookstore, a gallery, interactive forums, and more at the online home of the Henry Miller Library, located in Big Sur, California.

A Hundred Highlights from the Koninklijke Bibliotheek

http://www.kb.nl/kb/100hoogte/menu-tours-en.html

★★★

This large Dutch library has a searchable index of resources. It also contains many pictures that were either created specifically for the library or archived at the library. This library mainly houses older books, and its site enables the library to bring them to the public in a way that makes them less vulnerable to battery and the caustic effects of being in the open.

Zanadu Comics

http://www.zanaducomics.com/

★★★★

👫 Not for kids

Specializes in alternative and mainstream comics, graphic novels, and more. Features reviews by staff and customers, promotions, and a virtual catalog.

A
B
C
D
E
F
G
H
I
J
K
L
M
N
O
P
Q
R
S
T
U
V
W
X
Y
Z

A B C D E F G H I J K L M N O P Q R S T U V W X Y Z

AUDIO BOOKS

Audible
http://www.audible.com/

★★★★★

If you like to listen to books being read to you as you travel, exercise, or relax, but you don't like to mess with tapes or CDs, check out Audible's collection of downloadable audio books. You can download the audio file to your computer and then burn it to a CD, transfer it to an MP3 player or Pocket PC, and then carry the book with you wherever you go. If you become a member, you can download a set number of books every month for a monthly fee. You have 18,000 books to choose from.

Audio Books on Compact Disc
http://www.abcdinc.com/

★★★

Browse the large selection of books on CD, which are available at a 20% discount.

Audiobooks.com
http://www.audiobooks.com

★★★★

Search the database of a wide variety of audiobooks and place your order online.

AudioBooks Online
http://www.audiobooksonline.com/

★★★★

Another audiobook site that features books on tapes and CDs and downloadable MP3 files.

AudioLiterature
http://www.audiouniverse.com

★★★

Organized similar to Amazon.com, AudioUniverse advertises thousands of audio books at its site, at up to 50% off the retail price.

Books on Tape
http://www.booksontape.com/

★★★★★

One of the very few audiobook sites that lets you rent rather than buy tapes. You can also listen to audio clips of certain selections at the site. With its huge collection of audio samples, audio books for purchase, and easy navigation, this site is an easy pick for Best of the Best.

BOOK REVIEWS

Atlantic Online
http://www.theatlantic.com/books/

★★★★★

Visit Atlantic Online for book reviews, author interviews, information about new releases, and more. Excellent resource for learning about the latest in the literary world.

BookHive
http://www.bookhive.org/
★★★★★
👥 All

BookHive is designed to help teachers, parents, and kids from reading age to about 12 years old to find quality books and literature. This site is attractive, especially for kids, and includes several valuable features, such as a recommended book list, Zinger Tales (audio books), Find a Book (which helps you search for books by category), and Fun Activities (where you can play games online).

Booklist
http://www.ala.org/booklist/
★★★★

The online counterpart to the American Library Association's publication, *Booklist*, the website offers new reviews every two weeks on adult, children's, and reference books. Visitors will also find feature articles, author interviews, bibliographies, book-related essays by well-known writers, and several columns.

BookPage

http://www.bookpage.com/

★★★★

This site offers monthly book reviews of the latest in new fiction, nonfiction, business, children's, spoken audio, and how-to books. Reviews are available online, and the print version is purchased by booksellers and libraries to distribute to their patrons. The site also conducts interviews with authors.

Bookspot

http://www.bookspot.com

★★★★★

👪 All

Get recommendations on good books by looking at recent award-winning titles, reviewed works, and popular selections. Links to many online bookstores.

Boston Book Review

http://www.bookwire.com/bookwire/bbr/bbr-home.html

★★★

Providing scholarly commentary on contemporary literary works, the Boston Book Review site is the online companion to the print edition. Fiction, poetry, interviews, and essays are evaluated by well-respected experts and educators.

Related Site

http://www.bookwire.com/bookwire/bbr/children/children.html

The Scoop

http://www.friend.ly.net/scoop/

★★★

👪 All

Provides reviews of popular activities and adventure books for children. Site includes biographies of authors and illustrators, author interviews, and links to other sites. You can shop for books through links to Amazon.com.

CompBookReview.com

http://www.compbookreview.com/

★★★

Find the best computer books and buy them online at this site, which helps to sift through the thousands of computer programming, design, and application titles to recommend the best.

New York Review of Books

http://www.nybooks.com

★★★★★

The online version of the popular print publication that seeks to discuss important contemporary literary works and issues.

New York Times Book Review

http://www.nytimes.com/pages/books/index.html

★★★★★

Extensive book reviews from the *New York Times* book reviewers. Forums, reading groups, and first chapters are offered.

BOOKSTORES

Adler's Foreign Books

http://www.afb-adlers.com/

★★★

Adler's Foreign Books imports and distributes French, Spanish, German, Italian, and Portuguese language books in the United States. It also supplies books in Chinese and Russian. Adler's has an estimated 18,000 foreign titles in its inventory, making it one of the largest foreign book distributors in the United States. Its inventory consists primarily of novels, anthologies of both prose and poetry, literature, history, philosophy, language-learning resources, dictionaries, and other reference materials.

A
B
C
D
E
F
G
H
I
J
K
L
M
N
O
P
Q
R
S
T
U
V
W
X
Y
Z

Adventurous Traveler Bookstore

http://adventuroustraveler.com

★★★★

This site is the outdoor person's dream. Here you'll find books on fishing, hunting, hiking, and outdoor adventure. Learn the basics of backpacking, knot tying, fly-fishing, and kayaking with this wide assortment of outdoor books.

Alibris

http://www.alibris.com

★★★★★

Browse titles from a wide variety of categories and then rely on Alibris to find them for you. The company specializes in tracking down those hard-to-find books.

Antiquarian Booksellers' Association of America (ABAA)

http://abaa.org

★★★

Specializes in rare and antiquarian books, maps, and prints. Provides a search service by specialty and location, catalogs and links to other services for more than 330 dealers online, current information on book fairs nationwide, links to online public access catalogs at libraries worldwide, and articles of interest to booksellers and book collectors from the *ABAA Newsletter.*

Astrology et al Bookstore

http://www.astrologyetal.com/

★★★

Features online catalog of astrology, occult, pagan, UFO, metaphysical, and other related titles. Includes a listing of out-of-print and hard-to-find books the bookstore has in stock.

Barnes & Noble.com

http://www.bn.com

★★★★★

Visit the online version of the popular Barnes & Noble bookstore and search its inventory for new and out-of-print titles. Order online and have the book you want delivered right to your door. Barnes & Noble also carries audio CDs, VHS and DVD videos, and software.

Be Creative Bookstore

http://www.becreativebooks.com/

★★★

Specializing in knitting, quilting, cross-stitching, and other arts and crafts, this online bookseller features a varied assortment of books.

BookCloseOuts.com

http://www.bookcloseouts.com/bc/home.asp

★★★★

The online division of one of the largest closeout/remainder bookstores in North America. The parent company (Book Depot) has been in business for years; the company offers more than five million books at blowout prices. Because it features closeouts exclusively, you might not find today's bestsellers, but you will find books on your favorite subjects and by your favorite authors—at super cheap prices!

BookFinder.com

http://www.bookfinder.com

★★★★

Anyone looking for a new, used, out-of-print, or first-edition copy of a particular title might want to start with Book Finder. The option to request a first edition is unique to this site and might be of interest to book collectors.

Books for Cooks

http://www.books-for-cooks.com/

★★★★

The Internet extension of a family-run cookbook store. This site features thousands of cookbooks, organized into more than 140 cooking categories. From Pacific Rim cooking to chocolate desserts to diabetic meals to garnishing ideas, this site has something for everyone. Each title includes a picture of the cover and a brief description. A recipe symbol tells you that a sample recipe is attached for you to try. New recipes are added to the site every week.

Borders.com

http://www.borders.com/

★★★★★

Connects you to the Amazon/Borders team site, where you can search the largest collection of books and magazines and order them online. Also provides a list of Borders bookstore locations and events.

Bud Plant Illustrated Books

http://www.bpib.com/

★★★

This company's niche is illustrative, cartooning, comic, reference, and how-to art books from the 1880s to 1990s. It also specializes in books about illustrators. Orders can be placed via email, fax, telephone, or regular mail.

East Bay Book Search

http://www.eastbaybooks.com/

★★★★

Billed as the "World's Premier Book Search Service," East Bay Book Search can track down rare and out-of-print books. Call the toll-free number or fill out the online search form, and a representative will contact you with search results.

Guidon Books

http://www.guidon.com/

★★★★

Online site for Guidon Books, a 35-year-old book-seller located in Scottsdale, Arizona. The store's claim to fame is an extensive collection of new and out-of-print books on the American Civil War, Western Americana, Lincoln, Custer, and American Indian history and arts and crafts, too. You can place your order by phone, email, fax, or regular mail, but no online sales are currently available.

Know Knew Books Online

http://www.knowknew.com/

★★★

Have you been looking for that special first-edition Ayn Rand forever? Know Knew Books has collectible books in many categories: art and photography, fiction, history, Westerns, music, humor, children's, science fiction, and more. Let this company help you find the book that you're looking for, and then you can order via email, phone, or regular mail.

L'Art Medical Antiquarian Books

http://www.xs4all.nl/~artmed/

★★★

The history of medicine, antique books, and a place to register a wish list for certain titles. This site contains links to a mailing list and the Netherlands Antiquarian Bookseller's Network. Also provides a searchable database for antique maps and prints. The database lists more than 4,000,000 books and 200,000 maps and prints.

LawCatalog.com

http://www.lawcatalog.com/

★★★★

A one-stop legal resource service for lawyers and law students. You can find casebooks and supplements, legal references, study guides, and tools for managing your legal practice. Fifty years of experience helping lawyers and law students excel.

A B C D E F G H I J K L M N O P Q R S T U V W X Y Z

A
B
C
D
E
F
G
H
I
J
K
L
M
N
O
P
Q
R
S
T
U
V
W
X
Y
Z

Loganberry Books

http://www.logan.com/loganberry/

★★★★

This bookstore offers book-of-the-month clubs specializing in women's, children's, arts, and out-of-print books. Choose the club that is right for you. The store will also do book searches.

Midnight Special Bookstore

http://msbooks.com/

★★★★

An independent social and cultural bookstore featuring political, social science, history, and related books; weekly events; video; and web connections. Provides access to other independent bookstores. Asks you to bypass the chains and support the independents.

Moe's Books

http://www.moesbooks.com/

★★★

Contains more than 100,000 volumes in stock at a discount. Includes rare children's books, hard-to-find import titles, new books, remainder books, and used books. Also offers free searches if you can't find the book you want.

The Old Bookroom

http://www.oldbookroom.com/

★★★

A secondhand and antiquarian bookshop specializing in books, prints, and maps on Asia, Africa, and the Middle East.

Powell's Books

http://www.powells.com/

★★★★★

Powell's Bookstore has a long history, from its humble beginnings in Chicago to its expansion in Portland, Oregon. Although shopping online cannot replace the experience of browsing the aisles of Powell's outstanding collection of new and used books, this site provides a little of the flavor along with some powerful tools for tracking down rare, out-of-print books or even the more popular fare. Within two years of the origin of this website, Powell's entire inventory was online! Check it out here.

Publisher Direct Online Bookstore

http://www.pdbookstore.com/

★★★★

Find deals on a wide assortment of titles, including biographies, novels, computer books, religious writings, and more. Not a huge selection of books but great prices.

WordsWorth Books

http://ishop.wordsworth.com/

★★★★★

Besides offering a wonderful selection of books at a discounted price, WordsWorth Books is a book lover's dream, with its book selection of the day; interviews with authors; great selection of children's books; contests for adults and children; autographed copies of books; the independent bestseller list; and all literary award winners, for fiction, nonfiction, and children's literature.

BOOKS ONLINE

Amazon.com

http://www.amazon.com/

★★★★★

Touted as the "Earth's Biggest Bookstore" and one of the largest online shopping centers, Amazon.com offers millions of books, CDs, audiobooks, DVDs, computer games, and more. If you want a book and can't find it anywhere else, check out Amazon.com.

Best Book Buys

http://www.bestwebbuys.com/books/

★★★★★

Find the lowest prices for any book imaginable. Search for the book you want. Best Book Buys locates the book at several online bookstores and displays a list, showing which bookstore offers the best deal. Simply click the link for the desired store and order the book. Search includes new and used copies.

Bigwords.com

http://www.bigwords.com/

★★★

Specializing in college textbooks, Bigwords buys and sells used textbooks for less.

Books A Million

http://www.booksamillion.com/

★★★★★

This online bookstore advertises discounts of 20–55% off retail book prices, which can be found at its brick-and-mortar locations as well. Search the database to find the title you're looking for.

BookSelecta

http://www.bookselecta.com/

★★★

Download electronic versions of books to read on your computer. With text-to-speech software, you can even have your computer "read" the book to you. Some free books, including *The Red Badge of Courage* and *Aesop's Fables*. Most e-books for purchase cost less than half the price of the printed versions.

Deseret Books

http://deseretbook.com/

★★★

Deseret Book Company presents four publishing imprints: Deseret Book, Bookcraft, Eagle Gate, and Shadow Mountain. The company's mission is to provide products that strengthen individuals, families, and society.

The eBook Directory

http://www.ebookdirectory.com/

★★★★

Links to thousands of electronic books, many of which are self-published. Learn how to publish your own e-books online, too.

Fatbrain.com

http://www.fatbrain.com

★★★★

Unlike other online booksellers that focus on popular consumer titles, Fatbrain serves the business and technology professional. Books, training materials, and print-on-demand documents are available on computer, science, technology, medicine, finance, and business topics.

A
B
C
D
E
F
G
H
I
J
K
L
M
N
O
P
Q
R
S
T
U
V
W
X
Y
Z

NetLibrary

http://www.netlibrary.com

★★★★★

NetLibrary is a collection of electronic versions of books, some of which are available to read free and others available for purchase. After locating an e-book at NetLibrary, visitors have the option of either purchasing or borrowing the e-book. By borrowing an e-book, users have exclusive access to the book during the checkout period (no one else can borrow the same book unless there are multiple copies). e-books are automatically checked back in to the NetLibrary collection when the checkout period expires. Some free e-books are available in the Reading Room.

Online Books

http://digital.library.upenn.edu/books/

★★★★

Here is a remarkable collection of books on the Web: 18,000+ listings with an index searchable by author or title. For just browsing, try the subject listing and view the scores of timeless and copyright-free great works, with an especially strong showing in philosophy, religion, and history.

Project Gutenberg

http://www.gutenberg.net

★★★

Search the archives of Project Gutenberg to find e-texts in the public domain that are available free for download. Great collection of classic literature and reference books for free!

A Sherlockian Holmepage

http://www.sherlockian.net/

★★★

Contains many links to electronic Holmes and Conan Doyle resources.

PUBLISHERS

Association of American Publishers

http://www.publishers.org

★★★★

The Association of American Publishers (AAP), with some 310 members located throughout the United States, is the principal trade association of the book publishing industry. AAP members publish hardcover and paperback books in every field: fiction, general nonfiction, poetry, children's literature, textbooks, reference works, Bibles, and other religious books and scientific, medical, technical, professional, and scholarly books and journals.

Books AtoZ

http://www.booksatoz.com/

★★★

Books AtoZ brings together in one place all the vendors needed to publish a book. Its specialty is helping self and small publishers with layout, printing, marketing, and fulfillment. In addition, this site provides award-winning information and links on publishing.

Books @ Random

http://www.randomhouse.com/

★★★

 All

Home of Random House, Inc. Use this site to access its library, bookseller, and teacher services, or browse for books by the subject that interests you. Includes links to other Random House pages that feature titles for kids of every age group.

Canadian Publishers' Council

http://www.pubcouncil.ca

★★★

Association representing book publishers in Canada since 1910. This site includes links to publishing-related sites, FAQs, industry studies, and statistics and information on copyright.

Houghton Mifflin Company

http://www.hmco.com/

★★★

Houghton Mifflin Company online. Houghton Mifflin publishes educational books and materials for elementary through college levels; its site includes links to subsidiaries.

Kane/Miller Book Publishing

http://www.kanemiller.com

★★★

 0-8

Kane/Miller translates children's books from foreign languages to make them available to English-speaking children. Here, you can browse through the collection of children's titles (for ages 0 to 9) or search for a specific book.

Mage Publishers Digital Catalog

http://www.mage.com/

★★★

Publisher of Persian literature and culture in the English language. Order from the company's catalog—even books out of print.

McGraw-Hill Bookstore

http://www.bookstore.mcgraw-hill.com/

★★★★

 All

This bookstore offers a huge selection of science and technical, reference, professional, business, and computer books from all publishers—not just McGraw-Hill. Kids and parents should click the McGraw-Hill Children's Publishing link for information about children's books.

Best Pearson Technology Group

http://www.pearsonptg.com/

★★★★★

Search Pearson Technology Group's vast collection of professional, technology, and computer books. Searchable collections of reference content, books and software for sale, links to valuable third-party sites, and related resources covering the topics business and technology professionals are looking for. Here, you can find books on business, computers, engineering, science, and vocational skills. The top imprints in the business call this site home, including Addison-Wesley Professional, Adobe Press, PeachPit Press, Que, New Riders, Sams, Cisco Press, and more.

Perseus Books Group

http://www.perseusbooksgroup.com/

★★★

Specializing in nonfiction books on topics ranging from psychology and sociology to politics and public policy, this site provides links to the various imprints that make up Perseus Books Group. Imprints include CounterPoint Press, Basic Books, Public Affairs, and Westview Press.

Publishers Marketing Association (PMA) Online

http://www.pma-online.org/

★★★

This trade association represents independent publishers of books, audio, video, and CDs. Find member directories, information, discussion forums, and more.

Publishers Weekly

http://www.publishersweekly.com

★★★★★

International news source for book publishers and sellers features reviews of the latest books, bestseller lists, trade information, and much more. If you're in the publishing business, bookmark this site and visit often.

A
B
C
D
E
F
G
H
I
J
K
L
M
N
O
P
Q
R
S
T
U
V
W
X
Y
Z

A
B
C
D
E
F
G
H
I
J
K
L
M
N
O
P
Q
R
S
T
U
V
W
X
Y
Z

Pubnet

http://www.pubnet.org

★★★

Pubnet links more than 3,000 booksellers nationwide to more than 80 publishers to help booksellers stock their shelves and control their inventories. Pubnet streamlines the ordering process, giving booksellers more time to spend with their customers.

Time Life

http://www.timelife.com

★★★★

👫 All

Explore the many products Time Life offers in books, music, and videos. The Kids area includes books and recordings for kids from birth up to age 12.

BOWLING

Amateur Bowling Tournaments

http://www.bowling300.com/

★★★

If you're a bowler and want to find a tournament to participate in, check out this Official Page of Amateur Bowling.

AMF Bowling Worldwide

http://www.amf.com/

★★★★★

AMF is the largest company in the world that is focused solely on bowling. Check out AMF's site for more information on the company, its bowling centers, and its products; tips from the pros; fun and games; product reviews; and more.

Bowl.com

http://www.bowl.com/templates/BowlDotCom/index.html

★★★★

All

Industry news, feature stories, events, tournaments and results, games, trivia, newsletter, tips, links to shopping sites, and more. Check out the tabs near the top of the page for links to various bowling associations. Links to some junior bowling sites for the younger crowd.

Bowling.com

http://www.bowling.com/

★★★★★

9-13

Complete line of bowling equipment, including balls, bags, shoes, and shirts from all the major manufacturers. Includes special area for kids.

Bowlers Journal International

http://www.bowlersjournal.com/

★★★

Launched in February 1998, the Bowlers Journal International website has set out to complement its print counterpart by making many of its monthly columns, instructional articles, and tournament insights available to the online reader.

Bowling Digest

http://www.centurysports.net/bowling/

★★★

An online magazine that spotlights professional bowling, including articles, columns, a scoreboard, and classified ads.

Bowling This Month Magazine

http://www.bowlingthismonth.com

★★★★

Bowling This Month magazine. is for serious bowlers who want to improve their scores. It provides the most up-to-date technical information available on subjects ranging from advanced technique through lane play to balls and ball motion. Topics include: comprehensive new equipment reviews, lane play, ball motion and reaction, tips to improve mechanics, mental conditioning, physical conditioning, and an updated ball comparison chart."

Bowling World

http://www.bowlingworld.com/

★★★

Bowling World's website contains a reproduction of the printed version of the Bowling World Newspaper, which has been covering the world of bowling for 36 years.

A B C D E F G H I J K L M N O P Q R S T U V W X Y Z

A
B
C
D
E
F
G
H
I
J
K
L
M
N
O
P
Q
R
S
T
U
V
W
X
Y
Z

Bowling Zone

http://www.bowlingzone.com/

★★★★★

With more than 1,300 linked sites, you can find directions to lanes, scores and stats, PBA players' home pages, clinics and instruction, and international organizations and associations.

Brunswick Online

http://www.brunswickbowling.com/

★★★★★

Whether you're interested in building a bowling alley or just building your average, this site points the way. Find out about the Brunswick products that can help. You can also play a Blockbuster Bowling online game (if your browser supports Shockwave).

Dick Ritger Bowling Camps

http://www.ritgerbowlingcamp.com/

★★★

Information about a training camp that bowlers can attend to help improve their game. Summer and winter sessions are offered, plus instructor certification.

International Bowling Museum and Hall of Fame

http://www.bowlingmuseum.com/

★★★★

The International Bowling Museum and Hall of Fame is a facility located in downtown St. Louis. This site includes information about the history of the sport (starting in ancient Egyptian times), weekly trivia, and a museum shop where you can purchase clothing and novelty items online.

Kegler Bowler Tournament Guide

http://www.kegler.com/

★★★

Get information on all sorts of tournaments for all ages and sexes, including World Team challenge events and the Team USA coaching certification schedule.

LeagueSecretary.com

http://www.leaguesecretary.com/

★★★★★

LeagueSecretary.com is the only site that can generate Interactive Standing sheets and provide your bowlers with a graphical image of the bowlers' historical records. This is the only site that provides total integration between a leading software product, CDE Software BLS, and the Internet.

PBA News: Yahoo! Sports

http://fullcoverage.yahoo.com/fc/ysports/pba

$

★★★★

Bowling news and commentary covering Professional Bowlers Association tours, bowlers, and results. Links for leaderboards, statistics, and season schedules make this a great site for bowing fans.

Best PBA Tour

http://www.pba.com/

★★★★★

The official site of the Professional Bowlers Association tour, this site profiles the key competitors, provides updated scores and standings, and lets you know when various bowling tournaments will be broadcast on television.

Related Sites

http://www.icubed.com/users/allereb/faq3.html

http://www.igbo.org/

http://dir.yahoo.com/Recreation/sports/bowling/

Young American Bowling Alliance

http://www.bowl.com/bowl/yaba/index.html

★★★★★

👥 All

The website for young bowlers, this site is maintained by Bowl.com and is the top bowling site for young bowlers. It features news, tournaments and results, coaching tips, bowling tips and rules, and a fun and games section. Several links to online stores that carry bowling equipment, apparel, and novelty items.

BOXING

Boxing: CBS SportsLine

http://cbs.sportsline.com/boxing

★★★★★

A well-designed online newspaper from CBS Sports that focuses on professional boxing. Includes articles and current scores, as well as photos from major competitions.

Boxing Game

http://www.boxinggame.com

★★★

Do you yearn to be a boxing manager but question your ability to make a living at it? If so, this site might be for you. Join the site and create your own stable of fighters. Then follow their careers as they punch their way through a season of fights. The site informs you five days prior to each bout, so you have a chance to check out your fighter's opponent and come up with a fight strategy. After each fight (you need not be present), you receive a blow-by-blow description of how your fighter fared.

Boxing Monthly

http://www.boxing-monthly.co.uk/

★★★

Sample articles from the current print issue of this popular boxing magazine, plus information about subscribing.

The Boxing Times

http://www.boxingtimes.com/

★★★★

Excellent source for fight previews, fight analyses, columns, and world rankings. You can also visit the archives for reports from past fights. Though you cannot purchase products directly from this site, it provides a link to Amazon.com, which makes the transition from browsing to shopping nearly transparent.

Cyber Boxing Zone

http://cyberboxingzone.com/boxing/cyber.htm

★★★★★

The Cyber Boxing Zone offers late-breaking boxing news, bout previews, and a lineage of past to present champions in classes ranging from the straw-weights to heavyweights. You will also find the *CBZ Boxing Encyclopedia*, a book and video store, and *Cyber Boxing Journal*.

[Best] Doghouse Boxing

http://www.doghouseboxing.com

★★★★★

Updated daily, this site is the source of the freshest boxing news on the Internet. Packed with boxing articles, fight schedules, and a good dose of humor, this site promises to keep boxing fans entertained for hours. This sites clean design, unpretentious presentation of the information, and informative, engaging (and free) articles made it a hands-down pick for Best of the Best!

ESPN.com Boxing

http://espn.go.com/boxing/

★★★★★

The latest boxing news stories from ESPN. Updated daily, this is your best source for up-to-the-minute coverage. Home of *Friday Night Fights* with Max Kellerman.

HBO Boxing

http://www.maxboxing.com/

★★★

All the latest HBO boxing news, updated fight schedules, announcements, and more. Includes free boxing screensavers.

International Boxing Hall of Fame

http://www.ibhof.com/

★★★★

An attractive tribute to the great fighters in boxing history, this site spotlights many boxing legends and provides information about the newest inductees.

International Female Boxers Association

http://www.ifba.com/

★★★

Dedicated to promoting the sport of female boxing, this site provides a list of boxing champions, rankings, and fight results, plus a schedule of upcoming events. Check out the photo library for pictures of your favorite female fighters in action.

Max Boxing

http://www.maxboxing.com/

★★★★★

This site has almost everything a boxing fan could ever dream of: up-to-the-minute-news, fight schedules, video coverage, fight picks, profiles, message boards, a trivia quiz, and much more. This site even contains a link you can click to place a bet on your favorite fighter… or at least the one you think will win the fight. Some good stuff for free, but to access the good stuff, it'll cost you—about $5 a month.

Oscar De La Hoya

http://www.oscardelahoya.com/

★★★★★

The official online channel for this world champion boxer. The site includes fan club information, news, a calendar listing upcoming fights, photos, and much more.

Showtime Championship Boxing

http://www.sho.com/site/boxing/home.do

★★★★

Showtime's pay-per-view boxing matches are some of the best spectacles in boxing. Check this site for Showtime's fight schedule, biographies of Showtime boxers, and descriptions of past fights. You can even submit a question to Showtime's boxing expert and view video clips of great knockouts.

Top Rank

http://www.toprank.com/

★★★

Top Rank is the promotion firm run by Don King's chief rival, boxing impresario Bob Arum. Find out what it takes to be a fighter; tune in for a live Netcast of the next big boxing event; check out the men who made boxing what it is; keep track of fight schedules; and view results, records, and rankings. You can even shop online for Top Rank apparel.

USA Boxing

http://www.usaboxing.org/

★★★★

Home of the United States' national governing body for Olympic-style boxing, which is a member of the International Amateur Boxing Association (AIBA). This site provides news, information about the boxers representing the United States, event announcements, rankings, and more.

BUSINESS

411.com

http://www.411.com/

★★★★

Find anyone, locate a business, find a ZIP code, perform a trademark search, compare phone rates, and more at this convenient and informative site. Easy to navigate.

555-1212.com

http://www.555-1212.com/

★★★

Find a product, service, company, or organization that has a presence on the Web.

@Brint.com

http://www.brint.com/

★★★

This business research site specializes in management and technology concerns. The searchable database provides access to hundreds of full-text articles and research papers on topics such as outsourcing, virtual corporations, online commerce, and more.

All Business Network

http://www.all-biz.com/

★★★★

The All Business Network has links to hundreds of online publications, business directories, job banks, accounting resources, professional reference materials, economic reports, and other websites relating to business.

BigBook

http://www.bigbook.com/

★★★★

This site allows you to conduct a quick search on virtually any U.S. company. It provides addresses, phone numbers, profile information, and maps indicating where the businesses are located.

Bigfoot

http://bigfoot.com/

★★★★★

Fast telephone, address, email, and home page finder. Accepts queries in several languages.

Businesstravelnet.com

http://www.businesstravelnet.com/

★★★★

A first-class website for people accustomed to flying first class. If your business means travel, Businesstravelnet.com has lots of useful resources.

The BizWiz

http://www.clickit.com/touch/bizwiz.htm

★★★

With 300,000+ members, BizWiz is one of the largest business-to-business service companies on the Web. Designed to put businesses in contact with one another, the site is searchable by category and keyword.

A
B
C
D
E
F
G
H
I
J
K
L
M
N
O
P
Q
R
S
T
U
V
W
X
Y
Z

Business 2.0

http://www.business2.com/

★★★★★

Business magazine that highlights the most innovative and successful businesses and reveals the secrets of their success. Also provides useful insights and shows how to put the best business strategies into action.

Business.com

http://www.business.com/

★★★★★

Comprehensive, browsable, or searchable business directory that helps you or your company find the products and services you need. The opening page acts as the directory, but don't miss the other two tabs: **News** and **Jobs**. Together, the three pages provide a very comprehensive collection of links for all areas of business.

BusinessWeek.com

http://www.businessweek.com/

★★★★★

Home of *BusinessWeek* magazine, this site features a daily briefing, investment information, small business tips, career information, and industry news. Also features some pay services, including investment services, databases, and reprints.

Business Wire

http://www.businesswire.com/

★★★

Business Wire has the latest international press releases related to business and marketing, updated hourly. Visitors can also search for more information by name or state.

CorporateInformation

http://www.corporateinformation.com/

★★★★★

An online directory of corporate information resources organized by country. Searches more than 350,000 company profiles, 20,000 of which are analyzed at this site.

Dun & Bradstreet

http://www.dnb.com/

★★★

Home of the leading provider of business information, this site is essentially a marketing service for Dun & Bradstreet's business advice. Database tracks more than 70 million companies worldwide.

Esselte

http://www.esselte.com/

★★★

Home of the leading office supplies manufacturer in the world, claiming an annual sales of more than $1 billion. Here, office supply stores can learn more about the products and services that Esselte has to offer.

Fast Company

http://www.fastcompany.com

★★★★★

Online magazine focusing on business innovation, creativity, and productive practices in the workplace. This site features a wide range of articles on how to find a job, keep a job, and climb the corporate ladder. Also provides information on how to establish a business on the Web, how to become an effective manager, and much more. Excellent content presented in an easily accessible format.

⌐Best⌐ Forbes Online

http://www.forbes.com/

★★★★★

Technology, investing, media, and politics are all covered in this site from Forbes publications. You'll also find articles on companies, entrepreneurs, the economy, and the world's wealthiest people. The site features easy navigation, the latest financial news, and a good collection of personal finance tools, making it the Best of the Best business site on the Web.

Fortune.com

http://www.fortune.com/

★★★★★

The online version of *Fortune* magazine offers feature articles, personal computing and finance sections, and other business and finance-related information and news.

Harvard Business Online

http://harvardbusinessonline.hbsp.harvard.edu

★★★★★

Harvard Business Online focuses on the issues confronting top managers in today's business environment. The site offers ideas, research, and subscription information. Shop for publications online that have to do with important business topics, such as communication, finances, leadership, innovation, sales, and management.

Hoover's Online

http://www.hoovers.com/

★★★★★

Free access to business directories with operations and products, financials, officers, and competitors. Links for investing, sales prospecting, jobs, marketing, competitive research, and more. Links to other sites where you can purchase company reports online.

The Industry Standard

http://www.thestandard.com

★★★★

The Industry Standard aims to be the single source for critical, timely information about the Internet economy. When you need to know the latest, most significant information about what's happening in the world of technology and the Internet, this is the place to go.

InfoSpace.com

http://www.infospace.com/

★★★★

One of the best people-finder directories, including a global telephone and address search, email lookup, and reverse lookup.

IOMA'S Business Management Supersite

http://www.ioma.com/

★★★

The Institute of Management & Administration's site. Managers and executives can access newsletters and archived articles covering the topics of business and management, as well as a business directory of links to other pertinent sites.

Infobel: Telephone Directories

http://www.infobel.com/teldir/default.asp

★★★★

Links to online phone books worldwide, including white pages, yellow pages, business directories, email addresses, and fax numbers.

LEXIS-NEXIS Communication Center

http://www.lexis-nexis.com/

★★★

LexisNexis online is a legal research system, launched in 1973 that many law firms and businesses have found to be indispensable in helping them resolve any corporate legal issues.

Lycos Small Business Company Research

http://www.tripod.lycos.com/smallbiz/index.html

★★★

Visitors to this site can access several articles on how to start and manage a small business.

A
B
C
D
E
F
G
H
I
J
K
L
M
N
O
P
Q
R
S
T
U
V
W
X
Y
Z

OneSource

http://www.onesource.com/

★★★★

Dedicated to delivering corporate, industry, financial, and market information to professionals who need to keep abreast of the latest business data. Compiles data from more than 25 information providers, drawing from more than 2,500 sources. For a fixed annual subscription price, you can access the OneSource database over the Internet using a standard web browser.

STAT-USA

http://www.stat-usa.gov/

★★★★

Provides statistical releases, export and trade databases and information, and domestic economic databases and information. Some free information, but for the good stuff, you must pay an annual $175 subscription fee.

Related Sites

http://www.usitc.gov/tr/tr.htm

http://dir.yahoo.com/Business_and_Economy/Trade/

http://ibc.katz.pitt.edu/

Switchboard: The Internet Directory

http://www.switchboard.com/

★★★★★

Offers all kinds of lookup features. You can find a person, a business listing, an email address, maps and directions, or you can search the Web.

The TechExpo on WWW

http://www.techexpo.com/

★★★

Provides information about high-technology companies in the areas of engineering and life sciences. Includes information on their products and services, societies, universities, magazines, and newsletters.

Tradeshow List

http://www.internettradeshowlist.com/

★★★★

International directory of tradeshows organized by category and by date. Click the desired category, such as Finance or Software, to view a list of upcoming tradeshows in the category or click a date on the calendar to view a list of the major tradeshows on that date.

Travel-Watch

http://www.travel-watch.com/airphones.htm

★★★

An extensive directory listing the reservation and frequent flyer phone numbers for just about every airline in the world.

Web100: Big Business on the Web

http://www.metamoney.com/w100/

★★★★

This site contains a list of the 100 largest U.S. companies that have a presence on the Internet. It also has links to each company and a list of the 100 largest companies in the world.

WhoWhere?!

http://www.whowhere.lycos.com/

★★★

WhoWhere features telephone listings, email addresses, personal home pages, and business URLs. Also listings for U.S. government employees, Internet phones, and more.

Related Sites

American International Group, Inc.	http://www.aig.com
AT&T Corporation	http://www.att.com/
Bank of America Corporation	http://www.bankamerica.com
Boeing	http://www.boeing.com
Chase Manhattan Corporation	http://www.chase.com
Citigroup	http://www.citi.com
Coca-Cola Company	http://www.cocacola.com
DuPont	http://www.dupont.com
Federal Express Corporation	http://www.federalexpress.com
Ford Motor Company	http://www.ford.com/
General Electric Company	http://www.ge.com
General Motors	http://www.gm.com
Goodyear Tire and Rubber Company	http://www.goodyear.com
Hewlett-Packard Company	http://www.hp.com
IBM Corporation	http://www.ibm.com
Intel Corporation	http://www.intel.com
Kmart Corporation	http://www.kmart.com
Lucent Technologies	http://www.lucent.com
Merck & Co.	http://www.merck.com
MCI WorldCom, Inc.	http://www.mciworldcom.com
Merrill Lynch	http://www.ml.com
Microsoft Corporation	http://www.microsoft.com
Mobil	http://www.mobil.com
Motorola	http://www.motorola.com/
The Procter & Gamble Company	http://www.pg.com
Prudential Insurance Company of America	http://www.prudential.com
Sears, Roebuck & Company	http://www.sears.com
State Farm Insurance Companies	http://www.statefarm.com
SBC Communications	http://www.sbc.com
Texaco	http://www.texaco.com
TIAA-CREF	http://www.tiaa-cref.org
United Parcel Service of America, Inc. (UPS)	http://www.ups.com
Verizon	http://www22.verizon.com
Wal-Mart Stores, Inc.	http://www.wal-mart.com
The Walt Disney Company	http://www.disney.com

FRANCHISING

American Association of Franchisees & Dealers
http://www.aafd.org/

★★★★

This organization represents the rights of both franchisees and dealers. Here you can learn about upcoming events, read some free publications online, order other publications from the bookstore, and become a member.

Be The Boss
http://www.betheboss.com/
★★★★

Visit this site to post a franchise opportunity or to investigate an opportunity. Lots of information, including alphabetical and category listings, and features with detailed information on specific franchises.

BizBuySell
http://www.bizbuysell.com/
★★★★

Looking to buy a business? Good chance you'll find one here at BizBuySell. From restaurants in California to auto shops in Florida, you can search more than 20,000 businesses currently for sale. New businesses are added every weekday. Get notified about new listings by email. It's free! Selling your biz? Visit the Sell area. Post a free ad. New to franchising? Read the Buyer's Guide section.

Canadian Business Franchise Magazine
http://www.cgb.ca/

★★★★

Latest news, tips, and features on franchising in Canada. You can subscribe to the magazine and order other publications online.

A
B
C
D
E
F
G
H
I
J
K
L
M
N
O
P
Q
R
S
T
U
V
W
X
Y
Z

Centercourt

http://www.centercourt.com/

★★★★

Covers franchises in the United States, Canada, Colombia, Peru, Venezuela, and the United Kingdom. Get information on the latest trends, check out their business showcase section, search their database for details on franchises that interest you. You'll also find a section devoted to classifieds; another offering products and services to purchase; and one offering marketing, legal, and operational tips.

EntreMKT

http://www.entremkt.com/

★★★

Provides information for franchisers and prospective franchisees. EntreMKT encourages you to "sign our guest book" so you can receive its email newsletter.

Federal Trade Commission: Franchises and Business Opportunities

http://www.ftc.gov/bcp/franchise/netfran.htm

★★★

This site has lots of information, including a FAQ section, Guide to the FTC Franchise Rule, consumer alerts, Before You Buy pamphlets, state disclosure requirements, and more.

Franchise Doctor

http://www.franchisedoc.com

★★★★

Take the free FranchiseFit Entrepreneurial Survey before you invest in a franchise to see whether you're really meant to be a franchisee. The franchise reviews are very helpful, as are the newsletter and the articles related to franchise opportunities.

Franchise Expo

http://www.franchiseexpo.com

★★★

If you're thinking about buying a franchise, you might want to attend one of MFV's franchise expos (held across the country) to learn more about the process and the potential for success. Visit the site to find the show schedule.

The Franchise Handbook On-Line

http://www.franchise1.com/

★★★

Features various franchises and offers a directory of franchise opportunities, industry news, and articles. Order a subscription online.

The Franchise Registry

http://www.franchiseregistry.com/

★★★

Hosted for the U.S. Small Business Administration by FRANdata. The registry lists names of franchise companies whose franchisees enjoy the benefits of a streamlined review process for SBA loan applications.

Franchise Solutions

http://www.franchisesolutions.com/

★★★★

Franchise Solutions has been featured in *Entrepreneur Magazine, USA TODAY, Nation's Business*, and on CNBC. Find franchise and business opportunities at this site. Good collection of articles, tips, and advice from franchise experts, along with a FAQ, glossary, and suggested reading list.

Franchise Update

http://www.franchise-update.com

★★★★

Check out articles about franchising, find experienced franchise attorneys, and learn more about available franchises at the site.

Franchise.com

http://www.franchise1.com

★★★★★

Learn more about available franchise opportunities or advertise your franchise to potential buyers at this site, which aims to connect franchise buyers and sellers, as well as anyone thinking of starting one.

Franchise Zone by Entrepreneur.com

http://www.entrepreneur.com/Franchise_Zone/

★★★★★

Dedicated to linking enthusiastic entrepreneurs with the top franchises, this site provides all the information you need to find the best franchises and become a successful franchisee. How-to articles, advice from experts, and lists of the top franchises in various categories make this the first site to turn for those considering the purchase of a franchise. Don't miss the article on How to Buy a Franchise.

Franchising.org

http://www.franchising.org/

★★★

Get help dealing with the paperwork and regulations associated with franchising. Get valuable information you need, whether you are considering purchasing a franchising opportunity or franchising your current business.

FRANInfo

http://www.franinfo.com/

★★★★

Information about franchising and whether you're suited for it, lists of available franchises, and existing franchise operations for sale. Some excellent resources on the history of franchising and what it's all about, plus a guide to selecting the right franchise for you. Great place for when you're just starting to consider becoming a franchise owner.

FranNet: The Franchise Connection

http://www.frannet.com/

★★★★

This site represents a network of franchise consultants who try to match you to the right opportunity. Their services are free because they are paid by the companies they represent. Find out about whom they represent and what they have to offer you.

International Franchise Association

http://www.franchise.org/

$

★★★

Membership organization of franchisers, franchisees, and suppliers. Provides a franchise directory, information on how to build your franchise, a resource center, and bookstore.

US Business Exchange

http://www.usbx.com/

★★★★

Apply online to search large databases of U.S. businesses for sale and business buyers, or post your own listing. Links to U.S. and worldwide brokers here, too. Some of the businesses for sale have classified ads, which provide contact information; for other businesses, the contact information is available only if you're a paying member.

HOME-BASED BUSINESS

Jim Blasingame: The Small-Business Advocate

http://www.jbsba.com/

★★★★★

Jim Blasingame is a renowned small-business advocate and syndicated talk-show host who has assembled the largest community of small-business experts in the world. He refers to this group as the Brain Trust, and he interviews one of them every 30 minutes on his show. This site contains a wealth of information and advice for small-business owners and entrepreneurs.

 Bizy Moms

http://www.bizymoms.com/

★★★★★

Business ideas, recommended books and resources, and work-at-home scams and how to avoid them. Be sure to sign up for the free newsletter that's sent once a week. And don't forget to check out the message board for more ideas on a variety of topics! If you weren't busy before you visited this site, this place can keep you busy for days.

A B C D E F G H I J K L M N O P Q R S T U V W X Y Z

A
B
C
D
E
F
G
H
I
J
K
L
M
N
O
P
Q
R
S
T
U
V
W
X
Y
Z

Business@Home

http://www.gohome.com/

★★★

Online e-zine for home business and self-employment. Articles include topics such as marketing success and how to incorporate your home business.

Entrepreneurial Parent

http://www.en-parent.com/

★★★★

A resource for home-based entrepreneurs and career professionals who are looking for alternative work options. Free membership and newsletter.

Getting New Business Ideas

http://www.planware.org/ideas.htm

★★★★

A seven-step process for developing ideas for a business. These seven simple steps take you through the initial search for business ideas through copyrighting and legal stuff. Links to free business planning and financing software.

Home Business Journal

http://www.homebizjour.com/

★★★★

This online magazine offers home business owners information about taxes, as well as tips for running a successful home-based business.

Home Office Means Entrepreneurs

http://www.varzari.com/home/

★★★

A Canadian association for home-based businesses. Offers support and information to help home-based businesses in Alberta, Canada.

Homeworking.com

http://www.homeworking.com/

★★★

Focusing on the work-at-homer and the work-at-homer wannabe, this site provides a thorough list of viable opportunities and the tips and tools required to succeed. Don't miss the section on scams.

HomeWorks Home Page

http://homeworks.com/

★★★

Website of Paul and Sarah Edwards, authors of *Working From Home*; includes articles, advice, a forum, and links.

National Association of Home-Based Businesses

http://www.usahomebusiness.com/

★★★★

Links and resources from the National Association of Home-Based Businesses (NAHBB). Click the link for 50 State Companion Sites to find local resources.

Outsource 2000

http://www.outsource2000.org/

★★★★

Outsource 2000 provides plenty of ideas for people who are considering the telecommuting lifestyle. Site features job listings, scam searches, a list of featured employers, and more. You need to subscribe for most of the good stuff.

Pros and Cons of Working at Home

http://www.homebasedwork.com/advantages.html

★★★

This article presents a clear discussion of the good sides and bad sides of working at home.

Quatloos

http://www.quatloos.com/

★★★★★

Thinking of buying into a franchise or investing in a promising business opportunity? Check out Quatloos before you lay out any cash. Here you can learn about and avoid some of the most sinister scams—tax scams, general fraud, investment fraud, and more.

Small & Home Based Business Links

http://www.bizoffice.com/

★★★

Directory to references, news, services, opportunities, and programs.

WorkAtHomeindex.net

http://www.work-at-home-index.net/

★★★★

A human-edited directory of home business opportunities designed to help entrepreneurs find quality opportunities and the tools and resources they need to build a successful home-based business.

YourHomeBiz

http://www.yourhomebiz.com/

★★★

An e-zine that helps you start, grow, and succeed in your own home-based business.

INTERNATIONAL BUSINESS

Australian Department of Foreign Affairs and Trade

http://www.dfat.gov.au/

★★★

Australian business information site managed by the Australian government. Here, you can brush up on Australian foreign policy, obtain travel advice, and research global issues that affect Australia and its businesses.

BISNIS

http://www.bisnis.doc.gov/

★★★★★

BISNIS is "the U.S. Government's primary market information center for U.S. companies exploring business opportunities in Russia and other newly independent states." U.S. companies use BISNIS to access the latest market reports, news, and developments; gather export and investment leads; and learn strategies for doing business in the NIS.

Bureau of Export Administration

http://www.bxa.doc.gov/

★★★

Governs export licenses from the United States, commodity classifications, and commodity jurisdiction.

China Online

http://www.chinaonline.com/

★★★★★

China's Ministry of Information Industry. You'll also find a business-to-business portal. Site is designed to serve English-speaking visitors and includes a wealth of information for anyone who does business or is considering doing business in China. Articles cover all sections of economy, including Agriculture, Automotive, Black Market, Consumer Goods, Media, and more.

Crossborder

http://www.crossborder.com/

★★★

Focuses on international tax planning and transactions. Choose United States, Canada, or International.

Export-Import Bank of the United States

http://www.exim.gov/

★★★

An independent U.S. government agency that helps finance the overseas sales of U.S. goods and services. In more than 65 years, Export-Import Bank has supported more than $400 billion in U.S. exports.

Federation of International Trade Associations

http://www.fita.org/index.html

★★★★

The Federation of International Trade Associations (FITA), founded in 1984, "fosters international trade by strengthening the role of local, regional, and national associations throughout the United States, Mexico and Canada that have an international mission." FITA is made up of a membership of more than 450 independent international associations.

A B C D E F G H I J K L M N O P Q R S T U V W X Y Z

A
B
C
D
E
F
G
H
I
J
K
L
M
N
O
P
Q
R
S
T
U
V
W
X
Y
Z

FinFacts

http://www.finfacts.ie/

★★★

Extensive information on Irish finance and business.

globalEDGE

http://globaledge.msu.edu/ibrd/ibrd.asp

★★★★

Maintained by the Michigan State University Center for International Business Education and Research (CIBER), this site serves as an index of business, economics, trade, marketing, and government sites with an international focus. If you're thinking of expanding or moving your business to another country, you will find the information at this site most valuable.

Global Marketing Discussion List

http://glreach.com/gbc/index.php3

★★★★

Dedicated to providing advice to companies on how to address and tap the world market. Specializes in globalization via the Web, showing clients how to make better use of languages, increase traffic from foreign countries, respond promptly to requests from foreign customers, and manage the details of currency exchanges and distribution.

Infonation

http://www.un.org/Pubs/CyberSchoolBus/infonation/e_infonation.htm

★★★★★

👥 All

Interested in statistics? This is the site for you. Compare data within the countries of the United Nations, including urban growth, top exports, and threatened species. A great resource for adults and kids.

Related Site
http://www.cia.gov/cia/publications/factbook/

International Business Forum

http://www.ibf.com/

★★★

Provides links to information about international business opportunities, resources, advertisement agencies, and much more.

International Monetary Fund

http://www.imf.org/

★★★★

A cooperative institution that 184 countries have voluntarily joined to maintain a stable system of buying and selling their currencies so that payments in foreign money can take place between countries smoothly and without delay.

[Best] The Internationalist

http://www.internationalist.com/

★★★★★

The source for books, directories, publications, reports, maps on international business, import/export, and more. Very nice site—colorful, easy to navigate, and loaded with choices. Provides links to Amazon.com and other retailers.

International Trade Center

http://www.intracen.org/

★★★★

Home of the ITC, a group dedicated to supporting developing countries and transition economies achieve a goal of sustainable growth. ITC provides information, maps, and services designed specifically to help developing economies better expedite exports and imports.

JETRO (Japan External Trade Organizations)

http://www.jetro.go.jp/

★★★★

A nonprofit, Japanese government–related organization dedicated to promoting mutually beneficial trade and economic relations between Japan and other nations.

Latin Trade

http://www.latintrade.com/

★★★★

Business source for Latin America. Excellent, up-to-date articles, a business-to-business directory, and other resources make this site a must-visit for anyone doing business or planning to do business in Latin America.

NEWSWEEK International Business Resource

http://www.newsweek-int.com/

★★★★★

Newsweek's International news site, where you can read the latest news from around the world.

OverseasJobs.com

http://www.overseasjobs.com/

★★★★

Does the prospect of international travel appeal to you? Then consider looking for a job in a foreign country. Here, you can search for jobs by keyword or browse openings in a particular location. You can even post your resume to advertise your qualifications to prospective employers.

Regional and Country Information

http://www.usitc.gov/tr/REGION3.HTM

★★★★

Trade resources by country—from the U.S. International Trade Commission.

Tilburg University Marketing Journals

http://www.tilburguniversity.nl/faculties/few/
marketing/links/journal1.html

★★★★

Long list of links that point to various marketing journals on the Web, including national and international journals.

United Nations Economic Social Commission for Asia and the Pacific

http://www.unescap.org/

★★★★★

Home of the United Nations Economic and Social Commission for Asia and the Pacific (ESCAP), this site is dedicated to promoting economic and social development in Asia and the Pacific. Here, you can learn about the commission and read various reports.

U.S. International Trade Commission

http://www.usitc.gov/

★★★

An independent, quasi-judicial federal agency that provides objective trade expertise to both the legislative and executive branches of government; determines the impact of imports on U.S. industries; and directs actions against certain unfair trade practices, such as patent, trademark, and copyright infringement.

United Nations and Business

http://www.un.org/partners/business/index.asp

★★★

Procurement information, statistics, and publications in five business categories. See the role that the United Nations plays in helping developing countries and improving economic globalization.

United States Council for International Business

http://www.uscib.org/

★★★★

The United States Council for International Business encourages and assists companies to succeed abroad by joining "together with like-minded firms to influence laws, rules and policies that may undermine U.S. competitiveness, wherever they may be." In other words, this organization helps U.S. companies break down trade barriers in other countries.

United States Trade Representative

http://www.ustr.gov/

★★★★★

Responsible for developing and coordinating U.S. international trade, commodity, and direct investment policy, and leading or directing negotiations with other countries on such matters.

Web India

http://www.webindia.com/

★★★★

Provides information about doing business with companies in India, plus plenty of links to online stores. Web India's mission is to help its clients set up businesses that take advantage of globalization via the Internet.

A B C D E F G H I J K L M N O P Q R S T U V W X Y Z

World Bank Group

http://www.worldbank.org/

★★★★

Offers loans, advice, and an array of customized resources to more than 100 developing countries and countries in transition. Also helps finance disease control and eradication efforts in under-developed countries.

World Trade Organization

http://www.wto.org/

★★★★

The only international organization dealing with the global rules of trade between nations. Its main function is to ensure that trade flows as smoothly, predictably, and freely as possible.

PATENT INFORMATION

All About Trademarks

http://www.ggmark.com/

★★★

This directory offers an overview of trademarks and their use. You'll also find links to federal and international laws, journals, and organizations.

American Intellectual Property Law Association (AIPLA)

http://www.aipla.org/

★★★

The American Intellectual Property Law Association guide to patent harmonization, committee reports, and Congressional testimony.

American Patent and Trademark Law Center

http://www.patentpending.com/

★★★★

Some useful information about patents and how to obtain a patent from certified patent attorneys.

The British Library: Patents

http://www.bl.uk/services/information/patents.html

★★★★★

Excellent site maintained by the British Library to help users fully exploit the world's greatest patent resources. Explains what a patent is and how to go about getting something patented. Also provides information on how to search for trademarks and registered designs.

Delphion Intellectual Property Network

http://www.delphion.com/

★★★★

Subscription service that provides a comprehensive database of more than U.S. patent descriptions dating back to 1971. Subscribers can search for patent information that can help them generate new ideas and gain a competitive edge in the marketplace.

General Information Concerning Patents

http://www.uspto.gov/web/offices/pac/doc/general/

★★★★

All

Provides general information about applying for and granting patents in non-technical language. Intended for inventors, students, and prospective applicants for patents.

Intellectual Property

http://www.lectlaw.com/tinp.htm

★★★

Articles on patenting your invention, the impact of GATT on patent tactics, trademark information, and Internet domain names.

Intellectual Property Mall

http://www.ipmall.fplc.edu/

★★★★

This comprehensive directory includes a guide to intellectual property sites and links to related resources. Also features some information on copyright laws.

Kid's Cafe: Patents & Inventions

http://kids.patentcafe.com/index.asp

★★★★★

👥 All

One of the best invention/patent sites on the Web for novice innovators of all ages, this site is specifically designed for kids. Provides information on how to invent, famous inventors, and discoveries. Also provides a Patent-O-Pedia with links to other invention resources.

KuesterLaw Resource

http://www.kuesterlaw.com/

★★★★

Directory to intellectual property law, with links to statutes, journals, organizations, government agencies, and case law. Covers patent, copyright, and trademark law. Excellent information for beginners, plus some interesting descriptions of actual court cases.

Patent Act

http://www4.law.cornell.edu/uscode/35/

★★★★

Text of the Patent Act, covering patentability of inventions, grants of patents, protection, and rights.

Patent and Trademark Office

http://www.uspto.gov/

★★★★

👥 All

Official site for searching the U.S. patent database. Includes international treaties, statutes, and patent news. Young inventors should check out http://www.uspto.gov/go/kids/ for access to a special kids area where they can learn about inventions, inventors, and patents and play some cool games online.

Patent Law Links

http://www.patentlawlinks.com/

★★★★

Great place to learn patent law. An impressive collection of links grouped in categories including Case Law, Statutes & Limitations, Journals, Patent Offices, Patent Law Firms, and more.

SMALL BUSINESS—PRODUCTS AND SERVICES

AllBusiness.com

http://www.allbusiness.com

★★★★

AllBusiness wants to be the resource for small business owners and has compiled a wide range of online services to make it easier for business owners to focus on their companies. Although there is a range of services available, from developing a human resource manual to designing an e-commerce venture, there are costs involved.

American Express Small Business Central

http://www.americanexpress.com/smallbusiness/

★★★★★

One of the best features of American Express' small business section is the interactive tools section, where you can create a business plan with guidance from AMEX experts free. And there are expert columnists, too, providing helpful tips and ideas to make you more successful.

CenterBeam

http://www.centerbeam.com

★★★★★

Small businesses in need of sophisticated computing systems might want to check out CenterBeam for subscription computing services. Rather than invest in equipment, companies can pay a monthly fee to CenterBeam to provide what is needed.

eFax.com

http://www.efax.com

★★★★

People who are away from their faxes and telephones frequently might want to sign up for free efax service that accepts incoming faxes and then converts them to an email message. The same is true of voice mail messages. Be able to pick up your faxes and voice mail messages from your computer wherever you are.

A
B
C
D
E
F
G
H
I
J
K
L
M
N
O
P
Q
R
S
T
U
V
W
X
Y
Z

Entrepreneur.com

http://www.entrepreneur.com/

★★★★★

Excellent resource for small-business owners, Entrepreneur.com features a good collection of articles and tips from the experts, plus hundreds of links to other small-business resources on the Web. For additional help, check out the message boards and the Ask the Experts area.

Microsoft bCentral

http://www.bcentral.com/

★★★★★

The focus of bCentral is helping companies set up and run a business website, which Microsoft makes very attractive by offering a $24.95-per-month deal. But there's more than just website development information here; business owners can get advice on just about every aspect of running a business.

NASE (National Association for the Self-Employed)

http://www.nase.org/

★★★★★

NASE is an association of small-business owners and self-employed individuals. Its website provides access to excellent information and advice. NASE supports self-employed workers by offering its own health insurance and providing referrals to other companies that can help you save money and manage your business.

Office.com

http://www.office.com

★★★★★

Office.com provides news and industry updates, as well as outsourcing assistance to business owners. The main focus is on keeping owners up to date on industry happenings.

Onvia

http://www.onvia.com/

★★★

Subscribe to Onvia's customized daily report filled with projects and new business opportunities. This newsletter goes out to thousands of consultants, contractors, suppliers, and service providers every day.

Small Business Administration

http://www.sba.gov/

★★★★★

Before you decide to quit your day job and start your own business, visit this site from the United States government's Small Business Administration. Here, you can learn how to start your own business and finance it. The site also provides information on business opportunities, local SBA offices, laws and regulations, and much more.

Stamps.com

http://www.stamps.com

★★★

Tired of standing in line at the Post Office? Then download stamps.com's free software and print postage right from your printer. The amount of your postage will be deducted from your prepaid account, and a small monthly service fee of 10% will be added—a minimum of $1.99 to a maximum of $19.99.

United States Post Office

http://www.usps.com

★★★★★

Use the Post Office's online ordering system and have postage stamps delivered to your door. No more waiting in line at the post office for all your stamp and postal needs.

SMALL BUSINESS— WEBSTOREFRONT SUPPORT

Bigstep.com

http://go.bigstep.com/

★★★

Bigstep is a great, free way to build a website yourself (with help from Bigstep) and then host and manage it. E-commerce capabilities can be added in, and follow-up tools, such as newsletters, can also be used. An excellent, low-cost way to get on the Web!

EarthLink Business

http://www.earthlink.net/business/

★★★★★

Rely on EarthLink for a variety of business/ e-commerce services, such as setting up an intranet, providing web hosting, or holding an online meeting. You can also stay abreast of Internet news with regular online updates at the site. Plenty of services, but it's hard to know where to start.

Freemerchant.com

http://www.freemerchant.com

★★★

Freemerchant offers free auction site–building capabilities, as well as shopping cart features to help build your online business. You can also build in free traffic trackers.

PayPal

http://www.paypal.com

★★★★★

If you're planning on opening your own store on the Web but you're not sure how to take orders and collect payments, go to PayPal. PayPal can add a payment option to your site that allows users to pay you via PayPal. It costs you about 30 cents plus 2.2% of each transaction. More than 3 million businesses use PayPal.

TopHosts.com

http://www.tophosts.com/

★★★

Great place to shop for web hosting services.

CAMPING

A B C D E F G H I J K L M N O P Q R S T U V W X Y Z

Adventure Network

http://www.adventurenetwork.com/

★★★★

Planning a camping trip? Then you'll want to take down some suggestions for activities from Adventure Net, which also offers camping FAQs, product recommendations, and a "fabrics glossary." Who knew fabrics could be so important?! But to a camper faced with rain, they make all the difference in the world.

Best Altrec.com

http://www.altrec.com/

$

★★★★★

Shop here for hiking, camping, climbing, cycling, paddling, fly-fishing, snow skiing, and running gear. Whichever outdoor activity interests you, you can find all the gear you need at this site. Attractive and well-organized site makes it easy to find equipment and supplies.

American Camping Association

http://www.acacamps.org/

★★★

All

Families can find a camp by searching the camp directory, and camp directors can find tips and suggestions for improving the quality of a camp here. The site also offers product suggestions and information about joining the ACA.

American Park Network—Camping

http://www.americanparknetwork.com/activity/camping.html

★★★

All

Planning a camping trip to a national park? Check here first for site availability, park activities, fees, and much more. Camping in some national parks requires reservations, and you'll find contact information here. Some park campgrounds are available on a first-come, first-served basis, and this site provides information on how to make sure you get a spot.

Related Sites

http://www.geocities.com/Yosemite/Trails/2400/

http://www.gorefabrics.com/

Benz Campground Directory

http://www.bisdirectory.com/camping/

★★★

An extensive campgrounds and camping directory for the United States, Canada, and Mexico. Links to other pertinent sites.

Camp-A-Roo

http://www.camp-a-roo.com/

★★★★

Camping and hiking information with specific tips for parents wanting to camp with their children.

Camp Channel

http://www.campchannel.com

★★★★★

 9-13

Looking for a summer camp for your child? Then tune in to the Camp Channel. Here, you can search through a huge database of summer camps by theme and geographical location. Covers camps in the United States and all over the world. Visit the Camp Store for links to other sites that sell camping gear. Very attractive site, easy to navigate.

Campground Directory

http://www.gocampingamerica.com

★★★★★

 All

Find a campground or RV park quickly and easily using the searchable directory or pull-down menus. Special kids area is full of activities to keep kids busy on long trips, and includes safety tips and campfire recipes.

The Camping Source

http://thecampingsource.com/

$

★★★

The place on the Internet to find anything that has to do with camping: clothes, recipes, tents, backpacks, equipment for sale, trailers, RV shows, RV dealers, RV classifieds, weather, links, and more!

Camping-USA

http://www.camping-usa.com/

★★★

Searchable index of campground directories, resources for RVers, and other camping information.

Camping World Online

http://www.campingworld.com/

$

★★★★

Camping World is a leading supplier of products for RVs in particular and camping in general. Use this site to order a free catalog, check out products, get special online bargains, or find the Camping World store closest to you. You'll also find links to some other great camping websites.

CampNet America

http://www.kiz.com/campnet/html/campnet.htm

★★★

A huge library of links to campgrounds, suppliers, RV information, and camping and travel information. The online bookstore links to Amazon.com, where you can order books on various camping topics.

Christian Camping International

http://cci.gospelcom.net/ccihome/

$

★★★★

This nonprofit service provides information on more than 1,000 Christian campgrounds, retreats, conference centers, and outdoor adventures nationwide. Information about all these services can be obtained free via CCI's website. Whether you are an outdoor enthusiast or someone who thinks roughing it is a nice beachside hotel room, you ought to check out this resource.

Coleman.com

http://www.coleman.com/

$

★★★★★

Besides descriptions of Coleman products you can buy online, you'll find advice on how to prepare for a camping trip, how to set up camp, where to go, how to cook meals in the great outdoors, and more.

Equipped to Survive

http://www.equipped.com/

$

★★★

A comprehensive guide to the selection and use of survival gear, from the pages of *Equipped to Survive*.

Get Knotted

http://www.mistral.co.uk/42brghtn/knots/42ktmenu.html

★★★

 All

Animated knots for scouts, plus the do's and don'ts of knot tying. Not the glitziest site of the lot, but if you need to tie something, this site can show you 15 ways to do it.

A B C D E F G H I J K L M N O P Q R S T U V W X Y Z

A
B
C
D
E
F
G
H
I
J
K
L
M
N
O
P
Q
R
S
T
U
V
W
X
Y
Z

GORP: Great Outdoor Recreation Pages

http://www.gorp.com/

★★★★★

So, what do people actually do when they camp? Learn about all the great outdoor activities here: fishing, hiking, canoeing, bicycling, and more. Learn about little-known and uncrowded camping places in national, and some state, parks and forests. Ever wonder how those campground hosts got their jobs? Click on Jobs in the Outdoors for links to dream jobs. You can purchase books, maps, and outdoor gear, and even plan your trips or purchase packaged outings through the online store.

Kids Camps

http://www.kidscamps.com/

★★★★

 All

If you're looking for a camp for your child this summer, you're sure to find one here. Using topics broken down by interest, such as sports, arts, academics, and special needs, families can locate day and residential camps nationwide. You can also apply for a loan to send your kid to camp. Results of your loan application are known within minutes. This site is designed more for parents than for kids, but kids can look for camps as well.

KOA Homepage

http://www.koakampgrounds.com/

★★★★

If you like plenty of luxury while you're camping—hot showers, recreation rooms, convenience stores—KOA is the way to go. Check here for a list of the KOA campgrounds across North America, an explanation of the different ways to camp at a KOA, a list of services available, and, if you're looking for an enjoyable and profitable way to earn your living, ways to open a KOA of your very own.

L.L. Bean Welcome Page

http://www.llbean.com/

★★★★★

Keeping warm is a primary concern when you're camping, and L.L. Bean is the place to go for warm (and stylish) clothes, snowshoes, and more. Order a free catalog, check out the online product guide, and use the park search page. With hundreds of national and state parks, forests, and wildlife refuges, it's a handy tool.

Minnesota State Parks

http://www.dnr.state.mn.us/state_parks/index.html

★★★★

If we had to pick only one state to highlight in the camping section, Minnesota would be the one. Whether on the prairie, in a hardwood forest, or near the Great Lakes, Minnesota state parks offer every possible camping experience, from canoeing and portaging the Boundary Waters, to just sitting outside your RV listening to the wolves howl. Find the park you'd like to visit and make your reservations—all at this site.

Nature Rangers

http://www.naturerangers.com/

★★★★

 All

Whether you're looking for the latest children's high-performance outdoor clothing and equipment; locations of the best spots to camp, hike, or kayak; or you just want to share ideas and experiences with other outdoor moms, dads, and kids, Nature Rangers is the place!

Ocean City, MD's Frontier Town Campground

http://www.frontiertown.com/

★★★

 0-8

Here's a unique family camping experience. This campground features more than 500 sites, a pizza parlor, and access to many area attractions, including golf courses and harness racing.

Outdoor Action

http://www.princeton.edu/~oa/index.shtml

★★★★

 14-18

Princeton University provides this site, which you should check before undertaking any kind of wilderness trip. Loaded with places to go and things to do, the site is equally jam-packed with safety and health facts. A comprehensive site for outdoors folk to visit.

Summer Camps

http://www.summercamps.com

★★★

 All

Search a national database of kids' summer camps to find the setting that fits your child's interests and needs, as well as your pocketbook.

Visit Your National Parks

http://www.nps.gov/parks.html

★★★★

This is an official National Park Service page. Learn about the national parks, pick one that is right for your camping needs, find out what the fees are, and make reservations. The site features a park of the month and a guide to lesser-known parks, along with lots of useful and up-to-date information.

BACKPACKING

Backpacker.com

http://www.bpbasecamp.com/

$

★★★★

This is the home of *Backpacker* magazine, where you can learn about every aspect of backpacking, including gear you need to pack, interesting destinations, and skills and techniques. You can connect with other backpacking enthusiasts in the Community area, shop online, or even subscribe to the magazine online. Site also includes a link to *AnyPlace Wild* TV with John Viehman, who can lead you on a series of adventures in the wilderness.

Eastern Mountain Sports

http://www.emsonline.com

$

★★★★

Great place to shop for camping gear and equipment for hiking, climbing, kayaking, and other outdoor adventure activities. Click the Adventure Travel link to plan an outdoor vacation. Subscribe to the EMS newsletter for the most up-to-date information.

Leave No Trace

http://www.lnt.org/

$

★★★★

The Leave No Trace Center for Outdoor Ethics is a "non-profit organization dedicated to promoting and inspiring responsible outdoor recreation through education, research, and partnerships." This site provides tips on how to interact with nature without leaving your human footprint behind in the form of litter, noise, erosion, or anything else that can damage the pristine environment you visit.

The Lightweight Backpacker

http://www.backpacking.net

★★★

Find useful information on researching and purchasing lightweight backpacking gear here. You can also read contributions from visitors dedicated to making backpacking safer and more fun.

Susan and Bob's Place

http://www.kwagunt.net/

★★★

Check out the trip descriptions and reports from the United States, Mexico, New Zealand, and other destinations. Ask for a copy of the quarterly adventure travel newsletter.

A B C D E F G H I J K L M N O P Q R S T U V W X Y Z

A
B
C
D
E
F
G
H
I
J
K
L
M
N
O
P
Q
R
S
T
U
V
W
X
Y
Z

HIKING

Alpina Sports

http://www.alpinasports.com

★★★

Get information about Alpina Sports' range of hiking and skiing products here.

America's Roof

http://www.americasroof.com

★★★★

View a map of the United States or the world to identify the highest points in the world that you might want to hike. In addition to helping you find places to hike, this site helps you catch up on hiking news and register online for upcoming events.

American Hiking Society

http://www.americanhiking.org/

★★★

News and information from an organization dedicated to promoting hiking and establishing, protecting, and maintaining foot trails in America.

American Long Distance Hiking Association West

http://www.aldhawest.org/

★★★

This site supports hikers by providing information about trails, equipment to take, and recipes divided by meal type; it also provides tips on how to avoid common hiking problems, such as giardia. You'll even find a listing of the Triple Crown members—those who have completed all three of the 2000-mile trails.

American Volkssports Association

http://www.ava.org/

★★★★

The American Volkssport Association is a non-profit group that encourages people to "walk scenic trails at your own pace for health, fitness, and fun." AVA has a network of 350 walking clubs that collectively organize more than 3,000 annual walking events in all 50 states. They occasionally organize biking, skiing, and swimming events, as well.

Appalachian National Scenic Trail

http://www.nps.gov/appa/

★★★

This is the National Park's Service website for the famous Appalachian Trail, which is 2,167 miles long and traverses 14 states. The site offers basic information about hiking the trail and provides addresses you can write to for more information. Link to information about Shenandoah and Great Smoky Mountains National Park hiking as well. You can buy books, posters, decals, and other merchandise through the online store.

AZ Central

http://www.azcentral.com/travel/arizona/outdoors/

★★★★

This site provides a ton of information about trails and outdoor activities in Arizona. Good place to pick up coupons for your trip, too!

Barefoot Hikers

http://www.barefooters.org/hikers/

★★★

Home of the barefoot hikers, where you can kick off your shoes and hike the way Mother Nature intended you to.

The Camping and Hiking Emporium

http://www.tgoemall.com/ecamping.htm

★★★★

Index of camping and hiking supply websites organized by category (Tents, Sleeping Bags, Apparel, Flashlights, Shoes, and Food).

CyberBlaze

http://www.cyberhikes.com/cyblink/

★★★

CyberBlaze will blaze a trail to other websites where the hiking or outdoor enthusiast can find virtual hiking experiences for some of the most scenic hiking trails around the world.

GearShopping.com, Great Outdoor Apparel

http://www.tgoemall.com/mallodappar.htm

★★★

Find all the clothing and accessories you'll ever need for hiking and other outdoor activities.

 ### GORP–Great Outdoor Recreation Page

http://www.gorp.com/gorp/activity/hiking.htm

★★★★★

Find trails, vacations, books, and more at this comprehensive site. Online discussions about hiking-related topics, news, and equipment-selection tips help to keep you informed about hiking and the great outdoors. Links to retail merchants where you can buy equipment, books, and maps. Pop-up ads can become a little annoying, but except for that slight drawback, this is an excellent site. On your first visit to this site, you'll quickly realize why it's the Best of the Best.

Kings Canyon and Sequoia Wilderness Hikes

http://sierrahiker.home.comcast.net/index.html

★★★

Gives reports, tips, and links to hiking in the Sierra Nevada mountains. The site's author offers trip logs (mileage, number of days a trek takes to hike, and personal experiences on the trail) and photographs. You can also send an electronic postcard from this site; each postcard has a beautiful scenic view from a hiking spot in the mountains.

The Lightweight Gear Shop

http://www.backpacking.net/gearshop.html

★★★★

The key to any successful backpacking trip is the packing, and the secret is to pack light. At the Lightweight Gear Shop, you can find products to lighten your load.

Mainelyhiking.com

http://www.mainelyhiking.com

★★★

A complete guide to hiking trails in Maine and New Hampshire, with information and photos of all the mountains, ticket information, maps, weather reports, calendars, and much more to help you plan a trip to the state.

Newfoundland Backcountry

http://www.stemnet.nf.ca/~cpelley/

★★★

Opens with beautiful, full-color photos of the mountains in Newfoundland. You can select from a panel of trails and hiking places to get more information.

Seagull Outfitters: Minnesota Fishing Trips

http://www.seagulloutfitters.com/canpac.htm

★★★

Explore the Land of 10,000 lakes and experience some of the best fishing ever in the upper Midwest and Canada by having Seagull Outfitters manage your trip. You bring your clothes, fishing gear, and a camera, and Seagull Outfitters takes care of the rest.

Superior Hiking Trail

http://www.shta.org/

★★★

The Superior Hiking Trail is a long-distance footpath modeled after the Appalachian Trail that follows the shore of Lake Superior in northeastern Minnesota. It was conceived by a group of visionaries in the mid-1980s who banded together to form the Superior Hiking Trail Association.

Trailplace

http://www.trailplace.com

★★★★

Find out what an Appalachian Trail "thru-hiker" is and learn about the amazing Appalachian Trail at this site.

A
B
C
D
E
F
G
H
I
J
K
L
M
N
O
P
Q
R
S
T
U
V
W
X
Y
Z

**A
B
C
D
E
F
G
H
I
J
K
L
M
N
O
P
Q
R
S
T
U
V
W
X
Y
Z**

Washington Trails Association

http://www.wta.org/

★★★★

This site provides a hiking guide, photos, chat, trip reports, and more. You can see recent trail reports with up-to-date conditions. You can buy memberships, books, and maps through the online store.

Yosemite Trails Pack Station

http://www.sierranet.net/web/highsierrapackers/yth.htm

★★★

A nice site if you want to learn about trips through the Yosemite Trails on horseback. A variety of rides are available, and large groups are welcome. Wagon rides and horsemanship camps are also offered.

Related Sites

http://www.webwalking.com/hiking.html

http://www.canyondreams.com/

http://www.discoveralberta.com/moonshadow/

http://www.traildatabase.org/

http://www.worldwidequest.com/

CANADA

Air Canada

http://www.aircanada.ca/

★★★★★

Home of Canada's official airline, this site enables you to plan a trip, book a flight, and find out about any special rates that are available.

Canada

http://canada.gc.ca/

★★★★

The Government of Canada's official site, which contains information on the country and provides access to government publications.

Best Canada.com

http://www.canada.com/home/

$

★★★★★

The premier site for Canada and everything Canadian, this site provides information about all of Canada's major cities, including Calgary, Edmonton, Winnipeg, Toronto, Montreal, and Ottawa. Here, you can find the latest local, national, and international news; obtain weather reports; check out the latest sports scores; and keep abreast of the latest news in business and finance. Whether you live in Canada or just plan a visit to this great country, bookmark this Best of the Best site and visit it daily!

Canadian Resource Page

http://www.cs.cmu.edu/Web/Unofficial/Canadiana/README.html

★★★

A host of links to everything Canadian, from facts and figures to travel and tourism to history and news.

Montreal Official Tourist Info

http://www.tourism-montreal.org/

★★★★★

Visit more than 80 Montreal sites and locations via QuickTime videos on the site and learn more about visiting and staying in Montreal at this friendly site.

moreMontreal.com

http://www.moremontreal.com/

★★★★★

This exhaustive list of how to get to Montreal and what to do after you're there contains information on what to see and where to eat and sleep. Details are divided by district and category of activity.

Ontario Science Centre

http://www.ontariosciencecentre.ca/

★★★★★

All

Get the details regarding more than 800 exhibits at this child-oriented museum, as well as directions, pricing, and facility rental information. Explore the robot zoo, take nature walks, test your knowledge with online trivia games, and check out some of the museum's other exhibits at this site. Online games, travel exhibits, ideas for science projects, and more designed especially for kids.

A
B
C
D
E
F
G
H
I
J
K
L
M
N
O
P
Q
R
S
T
U
V
W
X
Y
Z

Paramount Canada's Wonderland

http://www.canadas-wonderland.com/visit.jsp

★★★★

 All

Find out how to get to this theme park and where to stay after you're there. The park offers more than 60 rides and shows on its 330-acre grounds. Twenty acres are devoted to its water park. You can buy a season pass through the online store.

Toronto.com

http://www.toronto.com/

★★★★★

Learn more about this city to the north, including upcoming performances and concerts, restaurant suggestions, shopping and fashion guidance, and news.

Winnipeg Blue Bombers

http://www.bluebombers.com/

★★★★★

Fans of the Blue Bombers football team can stay current on trades and new team members at this site, where you can also request tickets.

Yahoo! Canada

http://ca.yahoo.com/

★★★★★

The Canadian version of the Yahoo! search engine, which provides results from Canadian businesses and organizations.

CANCER

American Cancer Society

http://www.cancer.org

★★★★★

Online support resources include information on a wide variety of programs such as the Great American Smokeout, the Breast Cancer Network, and Man to Man prostate cancer information. You can buy books about cancer and coping with it through the online bookstore.

Avon: The Crusade

http://www.avoncompany.com/women/avoncrusade/

★★★★★

Avon touts itself as the largest corporate supporter of breast health programs in America. This site gives information about Avon's Breast Cancer Awareness Crusade, which is targeted at providing women—particularly low-income, minority, and older women—direct access to breast cancer education and early-detection screening services, at little or no cost. Find out how much has been raised to date and what grants have been awarded as a result.

Breast Cancer Action

http://www.bcaction.org

★★★★★

Home of one of the most popular and powerful breast cancer action groups, this site is designed to inform and empower breast cancer patients and others concerned about breast cancer. Learn about the latest preventions and treatments as well as political issues that should concern all citizens.

Breast Cancer Net

http://www.breastcancer.net/

★★★

Daily news service on breast cancer research and treatment. Thorough, well-written. From WebFeats Inc.

Cancer Detection and Prevention

http://www.cancerprev.org/

★★★★

Established by the International Society for Preventive Oncology, this site provides information on the activities of *The Cancer Detection and Prevention Journal*, including the biannual symposia, a searchable database of abstracts published in the journal, and links to other research sources. Primarily for health professionals.

Cancer Directory

http://www.welcomefunds.com/cancer-links.htm

★★★★

Alphabetical list of dozens of the top websites focusing on cancer risks, treatments, drugs, and support.

Cancer Facts

http://www.cancerfacts.com/

★★★★★

This site provides information on various types of cancer and the latest treatments. It features the NexProfiler Tools for Cancer to help those with cancer and their family members and caregivers to find the best treatment plans available. Site also features news, profiles, and links to support groups.

A
B
C
D
E
F
G
H
I
J
K
L
M
N
O
P
Q
R
S
T
U
V
W
X
Y
Z

Cancer Group Institute

http://www.cancergroup.com/

★★★★

Read about the causes and treatments of virtually every type of known cancer here. Excellent collection of articles on the latest breakthroughs in cancer research and treatments.

Best Cancer411.com

http://www.cancer411.com/

★★★★★

The Mission of the Rory Foundation and the Joyce Foundation is to "increase public awareness of and access to alternative and conventional choices available for the treatment of cancer." Take advantage of this tremendous library of cancer information and resources collected and made available by these two foundations. Learn about the latest treatment options, even if they're not promoted by the mainstream medical community. This is *the* site to go for the latest information in cancer research and treatments.

CancerBACUP

http://www.bacup.org.uk/

★★★★

Find specific information on types of cancer and their treatment at this site, designed for people facing cancer, their family, friends, and health professionals. Learn whether there are local cancer centers in your area.

CancerKids

http://www.cancerkids.org/

★★★★

 All

Exceptional electronic support for kids with cancer and their families through personal websites and mailing lists. Provides a place where kids who have cancer can post their own web pages.

CancerNews on the Net

http://www.cancernews.com/

★★★★★

This site provides patients and their families the latest news on cancer diagnosis, treatment, and prevention. Features a new calendar of upcoming events and a newsletter distributed via email.

CanTeen

http://www.canteen.com.au/

★★★★

👥 9-13

A peer support organization run by teenage cancer patients in Australia. A shining example of how online support should work. The Sony Foundation of Australia sponsors this site.

Childhood Cancer Center

http://www.patientcenters.com/childcancer/

★★★

Review O'Reilly and Associates guides to childhood cancer and check out other resources dealing with childhood cancer and ways to discuss cancer with children. Deal with common issues relating to childhood cancer, find support groups, and start researching here. This site is designed more for parents than children.

Community Breast Health Project

http://www-med.stanford.edu/CBHP/

★★★★

Nonprofit project aimed at offering information and support. In addition to learning more about the organization, visitors can access a variety of breast cancer–specific links as well as general cancer links. The site categorizes links, making it easy for you to find exactly what you're looking for.

Faces of Hope

http://www.facesofhope.org

★★★★★

First of its kind site in that it offers private one-on-one Internet mentoring and support to newly diagnosed breast cancer patients through its mentor-matching program. Visitors can read the stories of breast cancer survivors and access a message board offering breast cancer information resources. Designed to give hope to women with breast cancer.

National Cancer Institute

http://newscenter.cancer.gov/

★★★★★

The National Cancer Institute (NCI) coordinates the government's cancer research program. It is located just outside Washington, D.C., in Bethesda, Maryland. NCI's website is for cancer patients, the public, and the mass media; on it, you will find news and information on many of its programs and resources, general cancer information, and news about clinical trials.

National Coalition for Cancer Research

http://www.cancercoalition.org/

★★★

National Coalition for Cancer Research is a "nonprofit organization, comprising 26 national organizations, dedicated to the eradication of cancer through a vigorous public and privately-supported research effort." This site contains information about briefings that the organization has presented to Congress, including *Childhood Cancer: What We Must Do for Our Children*. Also provides general information about cancer research.

OncoLink: University of Pennsylvania Cancer Center Resources

http://oncolink.upenn.edu/

★★★★★

A comprehensive site for cancer patients and professionals that provides information on many types of cancer, treatments, new drug treatments, clinical trials, the social and emotional aspects of coping with the disease, and FAQs.

Prostate Cancer and Health Resources

http://www.prostate.com/

★★★★★

Not for kids

You'll find a thorough explanation of the functions of the prostate, as well as information on how to keep the prostate healthy, and alternative treatments for people diagnosed with prostate diseases.

Susan G. Komen Breast Cancer Foundation

http://www.komen.org

$

★★★★★

A site from the Susan G. Komen Foundation dedicated to detailing research, community projects, and news about breast cancer prevention and control.

Testicular Cancer Resource Center

http://www.acor.org/diseases/TC/

★★★★

Not for kids

A wealth of information about testicular cancer—diagnosing, treating, and recovering from it.

A
B
C
D
E
F
G
H
I
J
K
L
M
N
O
P
Q
R
S
T
U
V
W
X
Y
Z

160

A
B
C
D
E
F
G
H
I
J
K
L
M
N
O
P
Q
R
S
T
U
V
W
X
Y
Z

CANDY

Abbott's Caramels

http://www.abbottscandy.com

★★★★

One of the best caramel candies you will ever have! The buttery treats are available with or without nuts, so be sure to try both.

Altoids

http://www.altoids.com

★★★★

9-13

A fun site for this strong flavored peppermint candy. Enter the Free $50 contest, listen to tunes, or check out results of the Altoids survey. Some online games for kids.

Bubblegum

http://www.bubblegum.com

★★★★★

All

At this site geared squarely at kids and preteens, you can learn more than you ever wanted to know about various Armurol bubblegum products, as well as entertain yourself. One of the coolest areas is the "Your Room" section where you can build your own room, complete with games, activities, homework helpers, and a personal journal.

Candy Cottage Company, Inc.

http://www.ultimatepretzel.com/

★★★

Chocolate manufacturing company that manufactures only high-quality chocolate products, including the Ultimate Pretzel line—sometimes copied but never duplicated.

Candy Direct: World's Largest

http://www.candydirect.com/

★★★★

Search for past candy favorites deeply missed or make new discoveries. Thousands of selections available. Great place for schools or sports concessions stands to order candy in bulk. Also features candy bouquets.

Candy's Apples

http://www.candysapples.com/

★★★★

Gourmet caramel-coated Granny Smith apples with cashews, peanut butter, almonds, pistachios, walnuts, Heath bars, macadamias, pecans, and drizzled with chocolates.

Candy USA

http://www.candyusa.org/

★★★★

 All

Home page of the largest organization of candy producers, this site features candy history, statistics, information about health and nutrition, candy FAQs, information about chocolate, candy trivia, a special kids area, and more. The kids area is designed for a younger crowd.

Chocoholic

http://www.chocoholic.com

★★★

Sign up for the reminder service at this site to have plenty of time to order chocolate for a special occasion, which, to chocolate lovers, is any day ending in *y*. The site features a huge selection of top-quality chocolate, which can be ordered at the site or won through one of the contests.

Fannie May Candies

http://www.fanniemay.com/

★★★

Home of Fannie May Candies, whose motto "Make the best quality candy possible and always sell it fresh" is still at work today. Order a box of chocolates online and have it delivered to your door.

Godiva Chocolatier

http://www.godiva.com/godiva/

★★★★★

Offering some of the best chocolate in the world, this site enables you to order online or to locate the Godiva retailer nearest you. Even the graphics make your mouth water. Definitely a stop for chocoholics with discriminating taste.

Goody Goody Gum Drop

http://www.goodygumdrop.com/

★★★★

Welcome to the Wisconsin Dells Candy Stores, where you can order fudge, chocolates, and gourmet candies online or through an 800 number.

Hershey Chocolate North America

http://www.hersheys.com/

★★★★★

 All

Includes information on Hershey's chocolate, as well as pasta, Hershey's grocery, and an online cookbook. Special area for children of all ages, called Kidz Town, features games, recipes for cooking with candy, and candy quizzes.

Hometown Favorites

http://www.hometownfavorites.com

★★★★

If you're longing for candies and food from the '40s, '50s, or '60s, chances are good that this online store carries it and can ship it to you. Search by brand name or type of food to find your old favorites.

Kailua Candy Company

http://www.kailua-candy.com/

★★★★

The Kailua Candy Company has been handcrafting fine chocolate candies in its Kona kitchen since 1977. Use the secure order form to order candies online!

 LifeSavers

http://www.candystand.com

★★★★★

 All

Enjoy lots of great games and visit the virtual theme park, all of which are designed to get you hungry for Lifesavers products. Targeted toward children, but fun for adults, too.

A
B
C
D
E
F
G
H
I
J
K
L
M
N
O
P
Q
R
S
T
U
V
W
X
Y
Z

Name That Candybar

http://www.smm.org/sln/tf/c/crosssection/
namethatbar.html

★★★

 All

Shows cross-sections of various candybars, prompting you to guess the name of each bar.

Nestle

http://www.nestle.com/html/brands/chocolate.asp

★★★★

 All

Home of Nestle chocolates, this site provides a brief description of Nestle's candy products, but not much else. If you're looking for chocolate fun, Hershey's website is much tastier.

PEZ Candy

http://www.pez.com/

★★★★

 All

Home of PEZ Candy, this site dispenses a good collection of information about this famous candy and its dispensers. Learn the history of PEZ, shop at the online store, play games, or register for the PEZ Collectors newsletter.

Sugarcraft

http://www.sugarcraft.com/

★★★

Candy-making supplies including bags, molds, coatings, brushes, and much more for sale online.

The Ultimate Bad Candy Web Site

http://www.bad-candy.com

★★★★★

 14-18

Dedicated to the eradication of bad candy products, such as Circus Peanuts, this site is the funniest of the candy sites. The humor is directed more at adults and older kids who have had memorable experiences of eating bad candy.

CASINOS

Atlantis

http://www.atlantiscasino.com

★★★

 Not for kids

Search this Reno, Nevada, casino's site to find out about upcoming conventions, hotel services, special rates, and recent winners.

Bay 101 Club

http://www.bay101.com

★★★

 Not for kids

Learn more about this San José club's facilities, find out about upcoming tournaments, and make plans for your next trip here.

British Casino Association

http://www.britishcasinoassociation.org.uk/

★★★★

 Not for kids

The BCA is the casino industry's trade association in Great Britain, representing 90 percent of Britain's casinos. Read up on the gaming regulations of the industry in this country, which are considered to be the most strictly regulated in the world.

Caesar's Resorts

http://www.caesars.com/corporate/

★★★★★

 Not for kids

Caesars Entertainment, Inc. is one of the world's leading gambling and gaming companies in the world, claiming $4.5 billion in annual net revenue. It has "29 properties in five countries on four continents, 29,000 hotel rooms, two million square feet of casino space and 54,000 employees, the Caesars portfolio is unequaled in the industry." If you like to gamble or simply find the aura of the casino exhilarating, you'll find this to be the web equivalent. It contains links to all of the Caesar's Resorts, plus information on responsible gaming. Very glitzy design that's easy to navigate.

Casino Center

http://www.casinocenter.com/

★★★★

 Not for kids

If you're a gaming enthusiast, you need to bookmark this comprehensive site. Brush up on your gaming strategies with the online gaming magazine, find information on hundreds of casinos across the country from an extensive database, and learn the rules of all the casino games from Keno to blackjack. Also, you can check out current stock prices and company news from the industry's publicly owned companies. You can buy merchandise from the online gift store or indulge in a magazine subscription.

A
B
C
D
E
F
G
H
I
J
K
L
M
N
O
P
Q
R
S
T
U
V
W
X
Y
Z

Casino City

http://www.casinocity.com/

★★★★

 Not for kids

This glitzy site makes you feel like you're on the Strip in Vegas. Browse the bookstore and order online, search the casino database, try your hand at the Virtual Casino, or go to Wall Street and take a gamble on gaming stocks. And for the diehard enthusiast, the site lists a Who's Who of casino executives.

Related Site
http://www.casinomagic.com/

Casino Int'l

http://www.casino-int.com

$

★★★

 Not for kids

Play at this online casino for real money or play offline just for fun. Casino games and slot machines are available. Order a free CD or download the required software to start playing.

The Casino Net

http://www.the-casino-net.com/

$

★★★★

 Not for kids

A comprehensive directory of casinos and casino-related news. Search the casino database by location, name, or type of game. Visit casinos located around the world or in your backyard, and even make reservations online. Also, read up on the latest in gaming news. Fill out the guest book and enter yourself in a weekly prize drawing. You can buy books and videos on different casino games through the online gift store.

Casinos

http://www.casino-on-net.com

★★★★

 Not for kids

Enjoy virtual reality technology that helps you feel as though you're in a real casino and play alone against the computer or at an open table with up to two friends. The betting is real, though.

Cliff Castle Casino

http://www.cliffcastle.com/

★★★★★

Arizona casino that's designed to appeal not only to gamblers but to families as well. The site features information about the casino and a Family Fun link where kids can learn more about what the casino has to offer them.

Gold Club Casino

http://www.goldclubcasino.com

★★★

 Not for kids

Play for real or for practice here at this online casino, where you can play multiplayer games by downloading the casino software.

Golden Nugget

http://www.goldennugget.com

★★★★

 Not for kids

Find out all you wanted to know about this Las Vegas landmark casino. Make reservations at this hotel online. The site also provides links to affiliated establishments.

Golden Palace

http://www.goldenpalace.com

★★★★

 Not for kids

Links to free online casino games can be found here, as well as the opportunity to gamble for real money.

La Cabana: Aruba Resort and Casino

http://www.lacabana.com/

$

★★★

Gamble or just relax in this beautiful beach resort in Aruba. Check out the games available in the casino such as bingo and online poker, the late-night snack menu, the lounge, and area shopping.

Mississippi Casinos

http://www.mississippicasinos.com/

★★★

Thirteen casinos populate the Mississippi Gulf Coast. Discount gaming vacation packages and free stuff are for the taking, and this is the place to cash in. Also, check out the area weather, maps, entertainment, and golf opportunities. You'll also find links to Mississippi's Memphis-area casinos and some gambling games you can play for fun or for real.

Park Place Entertainment

http://www.ballys.com/

★★★★★

Bally's Hotels and Casinos of Las Vegas, Atlantic City, New Orleans, and Mississippi can all be accessed here. You can find room rates, casino information, entertainment schedules, and more for each of these Bally's resorts.

Player's Edge

http://www.playersedge.com/

★★★★★

 Not for kids

Player's Edge is an e-zine devoted to gaming and casino issues. Features cover various industry topics, specific casinos, and even book reviews. Visit the Ask the Pro column for answers to your gambling questions. You can also download freeware and check the odds on different sporting events.

Sands Hotel and Casino

http://www.acsands.com/

★★★★

 Not for kids

One of Atlantic City's best casinos comes to your desktop. This resort offers the latest games, world-class performers, and high-quality dining. Reservations are just a mouse click away. If you're feeling lucky, enter the online sweepstakes to win a BMW, or check out the company's financial report and job opportunities.

Spirit Mountain Casino

http://www.spirit-mountain.com/

★★★

 Not for kids

This casino, offering the best in casino games and entertainment, is operated by the Confederated Tribes of the Grand Ronde Community of Oregon and is located well away from the bustle of the city. Check out the complimentary shuttle bus service from Portland and Salem. There's also an interesting page covering where and how casino revenues are being invested in the community.

Trump Casino

http://www.trumpindiana.com/

$

★★★★★

Visit Trump Casino, a mega-yacht just outside Chicago, in northwest Indiana. In addition to travel packages and casino information, find out about the Trump Club, a way to redeem instant cash, complimentary meals, Trump products, and more.

A B C D E F G H I J K L M N O P Q R S T U V W X Y Z

Yellow Pages

CHEERLEADING

About: Cheerleading

http://cheerleading.about.com/

★★★★

About's cheerleading site contains dozens of links to articles and resources focused on cheerleading. Learn cheers and chants, jumps, pyramid formations, stunts, and more. Information for coaches and fundraising ideas are also available here.

American Cheerleader Magazine

http://www.americancheerleader.com/

★★★★

👥 9-13

Excellent articles about cheerleading, covering both novice and advanced techniques. Links to other cheerleading and dance resources. Younger cheerleaders should check out the sister site, American Cheerleader Junior.

American Cheerleader Junior Magazine

http://americancheerleaderjunior.com/

💲

★★★★★

👥 9-13

Cheerleading site for younger cheerleaders—between the ages of 7 and 12. Provides a spirit shop, message boards, articles from the magazine, and other features.

Cheerleader Central

http://www.cheerleader.com/

💲

★★★

This site specializes in selling cheerleader merchandise and licensed NFL cheerleader apparel for women and girls. You can also join the Cheerleader Central mailing list, where you can find out when and where professional cheerleading squads will be making appearances.

CheerPlace.com

http://www.cheerplace.com/

★★★★

👥 All

Excellent articles about cheerleading, categorized by Stretching, Motions, Jumps, Stunting, Formations, Cheers and Chants, and Try-out Tips. Communicate with other cheerleading enthusiasts via the message boards or just pick up some cheerleading clip art and cheer signs. Great site for cheerleaders and coaches.

EssesCo Athletic and Cheerleading Supply

http://www.essesco.com/cheerindex.htm

★★★

An online catalog for cheerleading and sports supplies. View full-color pictures illustrating the company's line of uniforms, shoes, pom-poms, warm-up gear, jackets, and more.

RAMGraphics: Spiritwear

http://www.ramgraphics.com/

★★★★

Spiritwear offers a wide range of cheerleading apparel that you can order online. Choose from the cheerleading line of products including special camp packs and cheer accessories, or have products custom-made for your squad. Inventory reduction items are available through the Closeouts page.

Team Cheer Online

http://www.teamcheer.com/

★★★★

 14-18

Whether you want pom-poms, jackets, team bags, or cheer shoes, Team Cheer Online offers competitive pricing based on volume (the more you buy, the better price you get). Browse the online catalog and call (toll free), fax, or mail in your order. The only drawback is that you can't place your order online; otherwise, this site is one of the best.

U.S. Open: Cheerleading Competition

http://www.uscheerleading.com/

★★★

Learn about and register for the U.S. Open Cheerleading and Dance competitions. Questions about rates, regulations, registration, and accommodations are all answered here.

Varsity.com

http://www.varsity.com/

★★★★★

 All

Top site for cheerleaders, offering links for coaches, cheerleaders, parents, and anyone else who is involved or interested in cheerleading. Find out about school traditions, learn tips and techniques, find out about fundraising and scholarships, check out camps and clinics, and much more. Special area for cheerleading coaches. Fun and games area provides a little extra diversion online. Clothing, books, videos, and other items are available at the online store.

Related Sites

http://www.cheeracf.com/

http://www.cheerleading.net/

CHILD ABUSE AND MISSING CHILDREN

Abuse-Excuse.com

http://www.abuse-excuse.com

★★★★

If you have been falsely accused of abusing a child, visit this site for help. Dean Tong, internationally known family rights and forensic consultant on child abuse, domestic violence, and child custody cases, manages this site, where he provides useful resources for those who have been falsely accused.

Bikers Against Child Abuse

http://www.bacausa.com/

★★★

 All

Dedicated to creating safer environments for abused children, Bikers Against Child Abuse hosts this site for member information and news. Click Links for a great list of sites where you can go for additional information or click Newsletter to view news reports about BACA activism. Good list of links to cool sites for kids.

Child Abuse Prevention Month

http://www.phgsc.org/child_abuse_prevention_month.htm

★★★

This site is a terrific resource for information on child abuse, incest, adult support, and so on. Select from the following categories: Abuse and Protection Child Abuse; Abuse/Incest Support; Adult Survivors of Child Sexual Abuse: Major Cases; An Orthodox View on Child Abuse; Characteristics of Families Experiencing Violence; Child Abuse Bookmarks; Child Sexual Abuse; Domestic Violence Linked to Child Abuse; Hidden Bruises; National Committee to Prevent Child Abuse Home Page; Preventing Child Abuse; Secrecy of Child Sexual Abuse; Signs of Child Abuse; Some Great Child Abuse Survivor Resources; Voices In Action; What Makes the Disabled Child at Risk for Child Abuse?; and You Can Prevent Child Abuse.

childabuse.org

http://www.childabuse.org/

Ⓢ

★★★

All

Dedicated to ending child neglect and abuse, this site is focused on increasing awareness of the problems, informing parents of their responsibilities, and keeping children aware of their rights.

Child Abuse Prevention Network

http://child-abuse.com/

★★★

This site is dedicated to enhancing Internet resources for the prevention of child abuse and neglect. Offers a list of state-level programs on the prevention of child abuse, an electronic newsletter that keeps you up to date on site developments, and links to other helpful sites.

Child CyberSEARCH Canada

http://www.childcybersearch.com/

★★★★

Canadian site that provides a database of missing children; a list of Canada's missing children agencies; and a library that contains helpful tips, pamphlets, and special-interest articles about missing children, childcare, and parenting. Mostly geared toward Canadians, but some information is universal.

Child Search: National Missing Children's Center

http://www.childsearch.org/

★★★

Provides support services for people whose children are missing, such as crisis counseling, search assistance, and photo distribution assistance. Also provides photo-listings of missing children, child ID kits, and safety tips for parents.

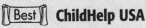 **ChildHelp USA**

http://www.childhelpusa.org/

★★★★★

 All

ChildHelp USA is dedicated to meeting the physical, emotional, educational, and spiritual needs of abused and neglected children, focusing efforts and resources upon treatment, prevention, and research. ChildHelp operates the ChildHelp National Child Abuse Hotline, 1-800-4-A-CHILD; residential treatment villages and group homes for severely abused children; foster family agencies; advocacy centers to reduce the intake-processing trauma for severely abused children; community outreach; and education programs. At least 85 cents of every dollar spent goes directly to its programs benefiting children. Now donations can be made online using a Visa or MasterCard. Special area just for kids.

Child Lures Prevention

http://www.childlures.com/

★★★

Dedicated to increasing the awareness of child exploitation and helping parents, schools, and communities prevent it, this site provides information about the various Child Lure Prevention programs, which you can order online.

Children's House in Cyberspace

http://www.child-abuse.com/childhouse/

★★★

This site is an interactive resource center—a meeting place for the exchange of information that serves the well-being of children. Offers workshops and training, information resources on the well-being of children, information about early childhood, and a spot about children's rights.

Children's Safety Network Home Page

http://www.edc.org/HHD/csn/

★★★★

Contains publications and resources produced by CSN and other EDC injury prevention projects; they include text in HTML format that can be viewed, downloaded, and printed directly from this site.

Code Alert

http://codeamber.org/

★★★★

The AMBER alert is. system that coordinates the efforts of law enforcement and the media to broadcast and track down children who are suspected of being abducted. This site is the web extension of the AMBER system.

National Center for Missing and Exploited Children

http://www.missingkids.org/

★★★★

Site of a private, nonprofit organization working in cooperation with the U.S. Department of Justice dedicated to the search for missing children and pursuit of child protection. Offers training for those involved in child protection and recovery, search assistance to those looking for missing children, and publications and resources pertinent to the safety of children. Also provides access to a missing children database.

National Clearinghouse on Child Abuse and Neglect Information

http://nccanch.acf.hhs.gov/

★★★★

A service of the Children's Bureau, Administration for Children and Families, the Department of Health and Human Services. The National Clearinghouse on Child Abuse and Neglect is a national resource for professionals seeking information on the prevention, identification, and treatment of child abuse and neglect and related child-welfare issues.

A
B
C
D
E
F
G
H
I
J
K
L
M
N
O
P
Q
R
S
T
U
V
W
X
Y
Z

A
B
C
D
E
F
G
H
I
J
K
L
M
N
O
P
Q
R
S
T
U
V
W
X
Y
Z

National Data Archive on Child Abuse and Neglect

http://www.ndacan.cornell.edu/

★★★★

Promotes the scholarly exchange of data on child abuse and neglect among researchers. This site provides access to databases that store child mistreatment research results. More for professionals than for parents or children.

Pandora's Box: The Secrecy of Child Sexual Abuse

http://www.prevent-abuse-now.com/

★★★★

Extremely comprehensive and current site offering information about preventing the sexual abuse of children, lists of other resources, statistics, news, publications, newsletters, legal information, guides for getting involved, recovery information, and more.

Parents for Megan's Law

http://www.parentsformeganslaw.com

★★★

Learn tips for preventing abuse and access limited New York state and national databases of sex offenders to find out who's in your area. More information about Megan's Law is also available to help you understand how to protect your children.

The Polly Klaas Foundation

http://www.pollyklaas.org/

★★★★

Named after an abducted and murdered child, this site has pictures of and information about missing children. It also has relevant information on how to keep your children safe and how to educate the public.

Prevent Child Abuse America

http://www.preventchildabuse.org/

★★★★★

Home of Prevent Child Abuse America, working since 1972 toward "building awareness, providing education and inspiring hope to everyone involved in the effort to prevent the abuse and neglect of our nation's children." Here, you can learn more about the organization and its programs.

SOC-UM: Safeguarding Our Children-United Mothers Organization

http://www.soc-um.org/

★★★★

Dedicated to safeguarding children both online and off, this site is an excellent resource for the prevention of child sexual abuse and violence. Provides links for education, prevention, and pedophile information and a collection of links to state sex-offender registries.

Stop Child Abuse Now

http://www.efn.org/~scan/

★★★★

Uses personal stories and pleas designed to prevent the vicious cycle of child abuse. Also includes links on domestic violence, child abuse, help for the battered and abused, help for children, help for abusers, and art as therapy.

When Love Hurts

http://www.dvirc.org.au/whenlove/

★★★

This outstanding resource is a guide for girls but contains information for everyone—particularly the respect checklist and the information on how abuse affects you.

CHILDCARE

AFDS, Inc.

http://www.afds.com/

★★★★

The American Federation of Daycare Services, Inc., provides liability insurance for in-home daycare providers. You can research insurance plans and get an online price quote on this site.

Bright Beginnings Family Child Care

http://www.juliefcc.com

★★★

Originally created by Julie to promote her daycare business, this site now offers information that's useful for any parent who's shopping for daycare and for daycare providers. This site stands as an excellent model of a website for small businesses: attractive and easy to navigate.

Best ChildCareAware

http://www.childcareaware.org/

★★★★★

This site is dedicated to helping parents locate quality childcare facilities near them. Features articles on how to evaluate a childcare provider, types of care, and five steps to choosing a provider. Also features a search tool to help locate providers or childcare referral services in or near your ZIP code area.

Child Care PPIN (Parent Provider Information Network)

http://childcare-ppin.com/

★★★

👫 All

Includes information and articles from *Child Care Provider Magazine* on various health issues as well as a discussion forum to share ideas and problems. You can buy children's books, posters, and reproductions of paintings featured on the site through the online outlet. Kids can click the Fun Stuff link to access a list of more than a dozen links to fun sites on the Web.

Daycare Providers Home Page

http://www.icomm.ca/daycare/

★★★

A good directory of sites for anyone interested in daycare. Established by one provider to share techniques, ideas, problems, and solutions, this site offers a wealth of information and resources, including a mailing list, a variety of craft and activity ideas, and links to a host of daycare-related sites—sites for preschool development, preschool activities, daycare businesses and daycare software, and many, many more.

DaycareUniverse.com

http://www.daycareuniverse.com/

★★★★

Dedicated to providing daycare centers with connections to the products, resources, and information needed to provide quality daycare, this site features articles, product reviews, and a robust collection of links to additional resources.

A
B
C
D
E
F
G
H
I
J
K
L
M
N
O
P
Q
R
S
T
U
V
W
X
Y
Z

drSpock.com

http://www.drspock.com

★★★★★

Staying in the spirit of the late world-renowned pediatrician, Dr. Benjamin Spock, this site is dedicated to providing parents with the expert information they need to raise healthy, happy children. Search this site for medical information, product alerts, and parenting advice from some of the world's top experts in childcare.

Idea Box: Early Childhood Education

http://www.theideabox.com/

★★★

👫 All

The Idea Box site offers early childhood education and activity resources. It contains an extensive set of educational tools, activities, recipes, and other early childhood learning resources. A parenting message board and teacher-to-teacher discussion group area are also provided.

Individual States' Childcare Licensure Regulations

http://nrc.uchsc.edu/STATES/states.htm

★★★★

Just what the title suggests. Click your state to access the childcare licensure regulations that apply. The site lists each regulation and provides a full-text document so you can read the actual regulation. As indicated, the information is specific to each state. Use this site to set up your own childcare facility or to see what your state does to ensure the safety and well-being of your child.

Kiddie Campus U

http://www.kiddiecampus.com

★★★★

👫 0-8

Kiddie Campus U owns and operates daycare centers in the New York area. In addition to the KCU program and consulting options, the site serves as a primer for daycare considerations and includes a number of kiddie links and resources for the care provider. Preschool kids should click the Kids Links link to view a list of fun places on the Web.

MomsView.com

http://www.momsview.com/

★★★

Freebies and coupons for a wide selection of products for parents and children (mostly babies).

Monday Morning Moms

http://www.MondayAm.com/MondayMorning.html

★★★★

Monday Morning Moms provides paperwork and management support for childcare providers and their employers. This company helps working parents find quality care, complete the tax paperwork in support of the care provider, and monitor provider activities to ensure quality. This site explains Monday Morning Moms' services in detail.

NAEYC Accredited Centers

http://www.naeyc.org/accreditation/

★★★

The National Academy of Early Childhood Programs, a division of NAEYC, administers a national, voluntary, professionally sponsored accreditation system for all types of preschools, kindergartens, childcare centers, and school-age childcare programs. To date, more than 8,000 programs serving more than 700,000 children have achieved NAEYC accreditation. NAEYC-accredited programs have demonstrated a commitment to providing high-quality programs for young children and their families. Find the accredited centers closest to you by selecting Accredited Center Search.

National Child Care Information Center (NCCIC)

http://nccic.org/

★★★

The National Child Care Information Center (NCCIC) was established to complement, enhance, and promote childcare linkages and to serve as a mechanism for supporting quality, comprehensive services for children and families. NCCIC is supported by a contract from the U.S. Department of Health and Human Services; the Administration for Children and Families; the Administration on Children, Youth, and Families; and the Child Care Bureau.

National Network for Child Care (NNCC)

http://www.nncc.org/

★★★★

This site is packed with quality resources that all have been hand-picked and reviewed by knowledgeable staff members. You can also sign up at the site to receive a newsletter or be included on a listserv mailing list.

National Resource Center for Health and Safety in Child Care (NRC)

http://nrc.uchsc.edu/

★★★

Home of The National Resource Center located at the University of Colorado Health Sciences Center in Denver, Colorado, and funded by the Maternal and Child Health Bureau, U.S. Department of Health and Human Services. NRC's primary mission is to promote health and safety in out-of-home childcare settings throughout the nation.

Related Sites

http://www.geocities.com/Heartland/Plains/1231/

http://mdchildcare.org/childcareexperts/

http://www.childrensdefense.org/

http://childcare.net/

A
B
C
D
E
F
G
H
I
J
K
L
M
N
O
P
Q
R
S
T
U
V
W
X
Y
Z

CIGARS

Antique Carta

http://www.antiquecarta.com/cigcat99.htm

★★★

⌘ Not for kids

Nicely organized, large online catalog of cigar labels. You can purchase labels by mailing in an order form with a check or money order.

⌐Best⌐ Cigar Aficionado

http://www.cigaraficionado.com/

$

★★★★★

⌘ Not for kids

If you love cigars, you'll love this site. Features of cigar ratings, searchable directory of local retailers, restaurants that are cigar-friendly, people highlighted on the covers of *Cigar Aficionado* magazine, a *Cigar Aficionado* magazine archive, a list of drinks that go well with a good cigar, and much more.

Cigar.com

http://www.cigar.com/

$

★★★★★

⌘ Not for kids

Excellent online store that carries a diverse collection of the finest cigars, humidors, and accessories. To sample cigars, consider joining the Cigar of the Month Club. Site also features some great gift ideas.

CigarAntiques.com

http://www.cigarantiques.com/

★★★

⌘ Not for kids

This searchable directory provides links to various resources on the Web for everything from automobiles and hobbies to cooking and fitness. If you want information specifically concerning cigars, click the Cigars link near the top of the page to access a robust collection of links to online cigar stores.

Cigar Friendly.com

http://www.cigarfriendly.com

★★★★

⌘ Not for kids

Locate cigar-friendly restaurants and lounges in your city and nationwide by searching the online directory, and then order your favorite brand there.

Cigar Nexus

http://www.cigarnexus.com/

★★★★★

⌘ Not for kids

Read unbiased cigar reviews before you buy your next set of cigars, enjoy cigar-related articles, and enter contests to win free cigars here. You'll find more information about cigars than you ever thought possible.

eBay's Tobacciana

http://listings.ebay.com/aw/listings/list/
category986/index.html

★★★

 Not for kids

Online cigar collectibles auctions—thousands of items.

Framing Artistry: Cigar Label Art

http://www.anzack.com/

★★★

 Not for kids

Books about collecting and pricing cigar label art, plus a private sale of antique cigar labels.

Tobacciana and Tobacco Advertising

http://www.the-forum.com/ephemera/tobacco.htm

★★★★

 Not for kids

Fabulous collection of cigar- and tobacco-related antiques that can be purchased online.

Vintage Lighters

http://www.vintagelighters.com/merchant2/
merchant.mvc

★★★

 Not for kids

Great selection of vintage lighters, including hard-to-find Zippos. Go to this site even if you don't need a lighter; it's fun to see the pictures of these unusual lighters!

A
B
C
D
E
F
G
H
I
J
K
L
M
N
O
P
Q
R
S
T
U
V
W
X
Y
Z

CIVIL RIGHTS

 The American Civil Liberties Union

`http://www.aclu.org/`

★★★★

Lots of information about this powerful organization, which champions the rights of individuals. Read about the issues that threaten our freedoms and rights and get on an alert list that warns you of events that threaten our liberties so you can participate. Learn about the latest legal cases in areas ranging from racial preferences to the separation of church and state. You can buy "liberty" items such as tote bags and T-shirts through the online store. For information on current civil rights issues and cases, no site is better than this!

American Civil Rights Institute

`http://www.acri.org/`

★★★

A nonprofit site dedicated to increasing awareness of racial and gender preferences. Includes links to book reviews, speeches, news, legislation, and other civil rights sites.

Amnesty International

`http://www.amnesty.org/`

★★★★

Amnesty International is a worldwide campaigning movement that works to promote all the human rights enshrined in the Universal Declaration of Human Rights and other international standards. In particular, Amnesty International campaigns to free all prisoners of conscience; ensure fair and prompt trials for political prisoners; abolish the death penalty, torture, and other cruel treatment of prisoners; end political killings and "disappearances"; and oppose human rights abuses by opposition groups.

Cato Institute

`http://www.cato.org`

★★★★★

Dedicated to promoting the "traditional American principles of limited government, individual liberty, free markets and peace," the Cato Institute seeks to inspire intelligent citizens to take a more active role in improving the United States government. This site provides information about the Cato Institute and its programs, events, experts, and publications.

Civil Rights Division (of the Department of Justice)

`http://www.usdoj.gov/crt/crt-home.html`

★★★

This site provides an overview of the U.S. Department of Justice's Civil Rights Division, along with a list of section sites within the division, a reading room, press releases, speeches, and more concerning the division's work on civil rights issues. Updated regularly.

Constitutional Rights Foundation

`http://www.crf-usa.org/`

★★★

 14-18

Constitutional Rights Foundation (CRF) is a nonprofit, nonpartisan, community-based organization dedicated to educating America's young people about the importance of civic participation in a democratic society. This website explains the organization's publications, events, and programs. High school sophomores or juniors can learn more about the youth intern program here.

Greensboro Justice Fund

http://www.gjf.org/

★★★

Named after the 1979 Greensboro Massacre, the Greensboro Justice Fund provides grants to individuals and groups fighting bigotry in the South today. You can find out how to apply for a grant here or view a list of current and past grant recipients.

Historic Audio Archives

http://www.webcorp.com/civilrights/

★★★

Subtitled "Voices of the Civil Rights Era," this site provides RealAudio clips of famous civil rights speeches, including those by Martin Luther King, Jr., and Malcolm X.

Law Research: The United States Department of Justice

http://www.lawresearch.com/v2/cusdoj.htm

★★★

A huge collection of links to every imaginable division of the Department of Justice.

Related Sites

http://www.cccr.org/

http://www.freedomhouse.org/

http://www.acrc1.org/

http://www.law.ucla.edu/faculty/volokh/ccri.htm

http://www.ceousa.org/

Leadership Conference on Civil Rights

http://www.civilrights.org/

★★★

Home to both the Leadership Conference on Civil Rights and the Leadership Conference Educational Fund, this site explains both organizations and provides a wealth of information and links.

Minority Rights Group International

http://www.minorityrights.org/

★★★★

An international nongovernmental organization that promotes the rights of ethnic, linguistic, and religious minorities.

National Civil Rights Museum

http://www.civilrightsmuseum.org/

★★★★

👫 9-13

A collection of civil rights artifacts, including Dr. Martin Luther King Jr.'s speeches and replicas of civil rights monuments. No specific areas for children, but kids will find some good educational information at this site.

Office of Civil Rights: U.S. Department of Education

http://www.ed.gov/about/offices/list/ocr/index.html

★★★★★

👫 14-18

Do you know your civil rights? You should, and with this site, there's no excuse for any citizen not to know his or her civil rights. This U.S. Department of Education site keeps you informed. Very easy to navigate.

United States Commission on Civil Rights

http://www.usccr.gov/

★★★★

The United States Commission on Civil Rights (USCCR) is an independent, bipartisan, fact-finding agency of the executive branch. Check out its publications, regional office locations, and information about filing a complaint.

CENSORSHIP

Electronic Frontier Foundation

http://www.eff.org/

★★★★★

One of the premier sites dealing with electronically relayed free speech and press, it contains extensive material and global links covering this issue and is the origin of the Blue Ribbon icon of support for the cause. This site, which was started to promote free speech on the Internet, continues to address the most current threats to free speech, including antiterrorism and privacy issues that arose as a result of the 9-11 tragedy.

A B C D E F G H I J K L M N O P Q R S T U V W X Y Z

A
B
C
D
E
F
G
H
I
J
K
L
M
N
O
P
Q
R
S
T
U
V
W
X
Y
Z

Center for Democracy and Technology

http://www.cdt.org/speech/

★★★★

The Center for Democracy and Technology works to "promote democratic values and constitutional liberties in the digital age." Visit this site to learn the basic issues revolving around free speech and the Internet, including pending legislation, the child online protection act, spam, and more.

Citizens Internet Empowerment Coalition

http://www.ciec.org/

★★★★

Rulings and reactions from involved officials and concerned observers regarding the Communications Decency Act. The CIEC came together to fight Congress' first attempt at restricting communications on the Internet. Now the site is maintained only as a historical resource for this landmark case.

Related Site
http://cctr.umkc.edu/~bhugh/indecent.html

Freedom of Expression Links

http://www.efc.ca/pages/chronicle/censor.html

★★★★

A big list of interesting sites that deal with freedom of ideas and expression, including organizations, documents, legal cases, and newsgroups. Focuses mostly on the issue of censorship.

Index on Censorship

http://www.indexonline.org/

★★★

 Not for kids

The most recent and back issues of this magazine are available in their entirety online. Look here for well-written articles on the ramifications of freedom of speech in our everyday lives.

National Coalition Against Censorship

http://www.ncac.org/

★★★★★

National Coalition Against Censorship is a group that fights for freedom of speech in the United States. Here, you can learn more about the coalition, read articles about cases and issues, and check up on action alerts.

CLASSIFIEDS

A–Z Free Classifieds

http://www.freeclassifieds.com/

★★★

You can view ads via an index or area code, place an ad (free), or review the statistics area, which tells you the number of hits per category per month. Categories range from Business Services to Child Care to Dance Instruction.

AdQuest 3D

http://www.adquest.com/

★★★★

This site provides a searchable index of more than 100,000 ads in more than 600 publications. One of the most thorough, up-to-date, and easy-to-navigate classified indexes around.

AllAbout Center

http://www.icemall.com/allabout/inmark.html

★★★

The free classifieds section of this site includes links to various other free classifieds sections, regional and national, as well as ads of its own. This is a good point of entry if you are looking for a ton of classified sites.

BuySellBid

http://www.buysellbid.com

★★★★

Place online classified ads for virtually anything that you want to sell, from car parts to timeshares in Bermuda. Or search the database to find bargains up for sale or bid.

Classifieds2000

http://www.infospace.com/info.cls2k/?ran=1780

★★★★★

Formerly Excite Classifieds, Classifieds2000 is a directory of classifieds from millions of publications and online resources. You can search by entering the item you are looking for or clicking on a product category. You can also sign up for email notification when a new listing that matches your interests is added.

EP.com Classifieds

http://ep.com/

★★★★

Network of classified ad sites that provides increased exposure for its advertisers. Users can post ads on this site to have them listed on thousands of classified ads sites. Become a Gold Member to gain increased exposure for your ads.

Recycler.com

http://www.recycler.com/

★★★★★

Recycler.com enables visitors to browse through more than 100,000 new classified ads each week organized by category, including animals, antiques, computers, travel, and more. You can also submit your own ads free to have them included on the site and in the Recycler paper. Become a member for access to premier services and to give your ads better placement.

A
B
C
D
E
F
G
H
I
J
K
L
M
N
O
P
Q
R
S
T
U
V
W
X
Y
Z

Best Trader Online

http://www.traderonline.com/

★★★★★

TraderOnline.com is a collection of more than 20 high-traffic websites receiving millions of visitors each month, and is a division of Trader Publishing Company, publisher of classifieds and editorial magazines with an emphasis on bringing buyers and sellers together efficiently. The publications cover a diverse mix of categories such as automobiles, trucks, heavy equipment, boats, motorcycles, aircraft and general merchandise, jobs, homes, and apartments. TraderOnline.com collects fresh data from each of Trader's more than 650 weekly and 14 monthly classifieds publications and posts this data to the Internet every day.

Yahoo! Classifieds

http://classifieds.yahoo.com/

★★★★★

Post a full-page ad on the Internet complete with graphics for less than the $10 you would pay for a newspaper ad. Your ad remains online for three weeks (21 days).

COACHING SPORTS

 Coaching Corner

http://www.thecoachingcorner.com/

★★★★★

When you're called on to coach your kid's team, whether it's baseball, basketball, football, or soccer, this is the first place you need to visit for basic coaching techniques, information, tips, and suggestions on how to do it right. The goal of this service is "to enable youth sport coaches to be better informed, more organized and more professional in their communications and interactions with their players, parents and association," and they do a great job of meeting this goal.

eTeamz

http://www.eteamz.com/

★★★★

Giving your team a presence on the Web helps you keep in touch with both players and parents and gives your team a sense of pride. This site is home to more than 1.5 million teams. If you're not interested in building a website for your team, you can visit this site to see what it has to offer for more than 80 sports. For example, the soccer area contains coaching tips, drills, and a whiteboard. Tips are not available for every sport listed.

Football Drills

http://www.footballdrills.com/

★★★★★

Football coaches will love this site, where they can find football drills for every position from linebacker to quarterback. Drills are free for registered users (free registration). You can also purchase Teamanizer software for additional drills and tips.

SoccerROM

http://www.soccerrom.com/

★★★★

Although soccer coaching requires some attention to strategy, skills and techniques are what really matter on the playing field, and this site provides the suggestions and tips that coaches at all levels need to help their players hone their skills. If you're coaching soccer and need some drills, this is the place to go. Plenty of free features are available, but for the really good stuff, you need to subscribe for about $35 per year. Site also features some team management tools.

WebBall

http://www.webball.com/

★★★★★

 All

Coaching baseball has never been easier with WebBall at your side. Site opens with page that displays several tabs for coaching, hitting, pitching, catching, infield, outfield, and youth. Drills, conditioning exercises, strategies, and tips are all discussed here. If you're coaching younger kids, you'll find plenty of tips for helping them keep their heads in the game.

A B C D E F G H I J K L M N O P Q R S T U V W X Y Z

COLLECTING

Beckett Collectibles Online

http://www.beckett.com/

★★★★★

Specializing in sports cards and memorabilia, this site claims more than 10 million items for sale through a network of dealers. In addition to making purchases and trades, you can also learn more about the value of cards and purchase related products, such as binders and books.

CollectingChannel.com

http://www.collectingchannel.com

★★★★★

Have a passion for artwork? Or maybe bridal cake figurines? No matter what you enjoy collecting, you'll have fun chatting with fellow collectors and learning more about your hobby at CollectingChannel, which links dealers and collectors of a vast array of items.

Collectors.org

http://www.collectors.org/

★★★★

This is the Official website for the National Association of Collectors and the Association of Collecting Clubs. Site features a good directory of collecting sites along with a calendars of upcoming events.

Collector Man

http://www.collectorman.com/

★★★★★

Collector Man buys, sells, and trades in a wide variety of collectibles, including action figures, piggy banks, Flintstones items, LPs, and posters. Check out his site to learn more. This is a great site to go for help in identifying just what you have and trying to figure out what it's worth.

Collectors Universe

http://www.collectors.com

★★★★

If you collect autographs, coins, currency, sports memorabilia, or stamps, you'll want to check out Collectors Universe for more information and authentication services. Using the searchable price guide, you can determine what your item is worth, too.

Curioscape

http://www.curioscape.com

★★★★

Unlike other online auction sites, Curioscape is a directory of more than 13,000 independently owned shops that carry antiques and collectibles. The sites have all been checked by the staff to make sure they are reputable and are within the right category. You can also advertise your wares at the site for a minimal investment.

Internet Collectibles Awards

http://www.collectiblenet.com

★★★

This site enables visitors to vote on their favorite collectibles sites on the Internet. Although the site seems a little out of date, it does provide links to many sites that just might have the collectible you're looking for. Links are organized into categories, including Art, Beanie Babies, Dolls, Stamps, and Toys.

Mr. Baseball

http://www.mrbaseball.com

★★★

Gain an appreciation for the history of baseball and track down baseball memorabilia all at the same site.

BEANIE BABIES

Beanie Babies Official Club

http://www.beaniebabiesofficialclub.com/

⑤

★★★★★

👥 All

Ty Corporation's official Beanie Babies club features members-only special offers, newsletter, "Pin-Demonian" trading, a message board, FAQs, and access to the BBOC online store. Even features Color Me Beanie for creating your own custom Beanie Baby.

Beanie Babies: Wholesale and Retail

http://www.barrysbeanies.com/

⑤

★★★★

👥 All

Barry Stein has been selling Beanie Babies on the Internet since 1997 and features a huge collection of Beanie Babies at this site. When he's not selling Beanie Babies on eBay, Barry's selling Beanie Babies here.

 Ty's Beanie Site

http://www.ty.com/

⑤

★★★★★

 All

The official home of Beanie Babies, this site is offered in four languages (English, Spanish, French, and Japanese) and is organized into several sections, including Boppers, Beanie Kids, Beanie Buddies, Attic Treasures, and Baby Ty. Includes a Funorama where kids can play games, Beanie Greetings you can email to friends and family, and a Tyfolio that helps you catalogue your collection. Shop online at the Ty store. Lots more here, too.

COINS

American Numismatic Association

http://www.money.org/

⑤

★★★★

 9-13

The ANA, a nonprofit, educational organization chartered by Congress, is dedicated to the collection and study of coins, paper money, tokens, and medals, and was created for the benefit of its members and the numismatic community. The association provides a comprehensive site with links, articles, online exhibits, educational programs, and much more. Special area for young collectors as well.

American Numismatic Association's Coin Club Site

http://www.money.org/clublist.html

★★★★

A website dedicated to promoting the hobby of coin collecting. You'll find access to community coin clubs and numismatic organizations nationwide.

A B C D E F G H I J K L M N O P Q R S T U V W X Y Z

A B C D E F G H I J K L M N O P Q R S T U V W X Y Z

Centerville Coin and Jewelry Connection

http://www.centercoin.com/

Ⓢ

★★★

Excellent site for buying coin collecting supplies, gifts, starter kits, and jewelry.

Coin Club

http://www.coinclub.com

★★★

Have a question about numismatics? This is the site to go to. You'll find pricing information, dealer directories, bulletin boards, and chat. You can also link to other coin-related sites.

Coin Collecting FAQ

http://www.telesphere.com/ts/coins/faq.html

★★★

This FAQ addresses a few of the most commonly asked questions about coin collecting. Find out what your coins are worth. What are the risks in collecting coins as investments? Which are better, rare coins or bullion coins?

Coin Gallery

http://www.coin-gallery.com

★★★

Search the many categories of coin information at this site, which boasts access to rare coin dealers, books and magazines, major coin shows, and auctions, as well as articles and exhibit details.

Coin Library

http://www.coinlibrary.com/

★★★

The Coin Library is an online resource for information about numismatics, the study and collecting of coins, medals, tokens, and paper money. The "Numismatics in the News" section holds the text of newspaper articles relating to American coinage, from colonial times to the present.

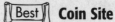 **Coin Site**

http://www.coinsite.com

★★★★★

 9-13

View images of coins for sale, ask the coin doctor a question that's been perplexing you, search the database of coins for sale, and track down up-to-date information on what your coins are worth. Some fun stuff is available, such as the coin quizzes, that will appeal to young coin collectors. This site is operated by a couple of nationally renowned numismatists who have a thorough knowledge of the hobby. This site is packed with useful information and is one of the easiest sites in this group to navigate.

Coin Shows

http://www.coinshows.com/

★★★

More than 500 worldwide coin shows are listed here. Since 1996, users from 82 countries have accessed this site. Find the region you're interested in (U.S., Canada, or International) and click on the state or country that interests you.

Coin World

http://www.coinworld.com

★★★★★

Here's the online version of the print publication, providing a searchable database of thousands of coins for sale. Catch current news and information about the world of numismatics. Get a preview of upcoming state quarter designs being considered. Links to online stores where you can shop for coins and coin collecting supplies.

CoinGrading.com: A Comprehensive Guide to Grading Your Coins

http://www.coingrading.com/

★★★

Grade your coins with confidence with free advice from experienced numismatist Jim Halperin.

CoinLink Numismatic and Rare Coins Index

http://www.coinlink.com/

★★★★★

Large rare coin index with links to more than 800 numismatic sites. Piles of links to sites dealing with currency exchange, gold prices, ancient coins, statehood quarters, and exonumia (coin-like objects, such as tokens and medals). Sites are rated, providing links to only the best resources.

Coin Universe Price Guide

http://www.pcgs.com/prices/

★★★

Find out how much your coins are worth. This site provides a price guide, updated daily by coin experts, for all U.S. coins. Very detailed information presented in a clear way.

Coins at Sammler.com

http://www.sammler.com/coins/

★★★

A lot of information about German coins, ancient coins, and world coins.

Forum Ancient Coins

http://www.ancient-coin-forum.com/

★★★★

This site not only sells coins, but also provides coin collectors, history buffs, and students a fun and informative place to explore and learn about ancient history, as well as coin collecting. All sales are guaranteed.

Heritage Rare Coin Gallery

http://www.heritagecoin.com/

★★★★★

World's largest numismatic dealer and auctioneer. Go online to view the $20 million inventory, but that's just the beginning: This site is chock-full of information and neat coin stuff to see and learn about. Participate in online auctions and maintain a list of coins you want. The site will notify you when items on your want list become available.

NumisMedia–Numismatic Interactive Network

http://www.numismedia.com/

★★★★★

Register to bid for NumisMedia online auctions, offering rare coins supplied by the member dealers of NumisMedia. Featured coin auctions close every Monday through Friday between 6:00 p.m. and 7:00 p.m. Eastern time (or five minutes after the last bid), and coins in all categories are available 24 hours a day, 7 days a week.

The United States Mint

http://www.usmint.gov/

★★★★

👥 9-13

View all U.S. Mint products, see coin production, find fun facts about the mint, and lots more. My son loved the section on the United States Mint 50 States Quarters Program, which described how a series of five quarters with new reverses will be issued each year from 1999 through 2008, celebrating each of the 50 states of the Union (the coins will be issued in the sequence in which the states became part of the United States of America). You can see the current year's five quarters (front and back), learn about each state and when it joined the Union, and also view the 10-year Schedule of Quarters. You can also learn about the New Nickels program.

DOLLS

Alexander Doll Company

http://www.alexanderdoll.com/

★★★★

👥 All

This manufacturer of Madame Alexander dolls since 1923 has established a presence on the Internet with this website. Here, you can flip through doll catalogs, check out the new chic collection, purchase new releases of the latest dolls, visit the doll hospital, and locate other places to purchase these classic dolls.

A B C D E F G H I J K L M N O P Q R S T U V W X Y Z

A B C D E F G H I J K L M N O P Q R S T U V W X Y Z

American Girl

http://www.americangirl.com/

★★★★★

 All

American Girls dolls and clothing allow young ladies to select a doll that matches their personalities. Girls can even order clothing if they would like to dress up like their dolls! Young girls and their mothers often plan special trips to the American Girl stores to bond through shopping.

Best Barbie.com

http://www.barbie.com/

★★★★★

 All

Barbie isn't just in toy stores anymore. You can now find her on the Web, where you can even go shopping with her. This site is beautifully designed and offers tons of fun stuff and freebies. Kids can play games online, keep a calendar, and even register to tell friends and relatives which Barbie dolls and accessories they want. Kids can even download Barbie wallpaper and screensavers for their computers. Special area for parents as well.

Barbie Sites
http://www.joeslist.com/
http://www.dollhabit.com/
http://www.dsdolls.com/
http://www.katyskollectibles.com/
http://www.dollhotline.com/
http://www.mikelman.com/

collectiblestoday.com

http://www.collectiblestoday.com/

★★★★

Great site for finding all sorts of collectibles, including dolls. Special categories for angel figurines, Ashton Tate dolls, Barbies, Madame Alexander dolls, porcelain dolls, and more.

Corolle Dolls

http://www.liveandlearn.com/corolle/

★★★★

Home of dolls by Corolle of France. The babies are fabulous. The heads, hands, and feet are vinyl, and the bodies are soft and weighted so that you think you're holding a little baby. They are sized for little mommies and come in adorable outfits. The best part about this site is the discounted prices! Corolle dolls can be hard to find in stores, so why not get them via the Internet at discounted prices?

Dollsville

http://www.dollsville.com/

★★★

Dolls and bears both are featured on this colorful website. Current dolls and retired collectibles are available here.

GADCO: The Great American Doll Company

http://www.greatdolls.com/

★★★

GADCO has been designing and manufacturing some of the most prestigious dolls in the world for many years. Here, you can order a catalog and find out information on how to place an order.

iQVC.com Shopping Home Page

http://www.qvc.com/

★★★★★

For those who love collector dolls, enjoy iQVC's corner of doll heaven. Here, you can browse through handcrafted dolls of fine porcelain, cloth, vinyl, and more. You'll find dolls by some of the world's most respected doll artists—Goebel, Madame Alexander, Lloyd Middleton, Precious Moments, and more. With so many choices, iQVC is a treasure trove for novices and experienced collectors alike. When you reach the QVC home page, click **Toys**, **Crafts & Leisure**, **Collectibles**, **Dolls**.

Madeline Dolls

http://www.liveandlearn.com/madeline.htm

★★★

Madeline doll fans will find everything Madeline that they could want.

MarieDollFriends!

http://www.mariedollfriends.com/

★★★

This site is for all Marie Osmond doll collectors. It contains a new message board, a free online auction, a chat room, and more.

minishop.com

http://www.mottsminis.com/

★★★★

A good source for dolls, dollhouses, miniature furniture, building components, landscaping accessories, porcelain doll china, and other miniature accessories. One-stop shop for building, decorating, and furnishing miniature dollhouses.

Raggedy Ann and Andy Museum

http://www.raggedyann-museum.org/

★★★★

This is the official website of the Johnny Gruelle Raggedy Ann & Andy Museum in Arcola, Illinois. Here, you can obtain information about the museum, learn the history of Raggedy Ann and Andy, read up on Johnny Gruelle, and even check out what's offered at the museum's gift shop.

The United Federation of Doll Clubs, Inc.

http://www.ufdc.org/

★★★★

UFDC is a nonprofit corporation aimed at creating, stimulating, and maintaining a national interest in all matters pertaining to doll collecting, and promoting and assisting in the preservation of historical documents pertaining to dolls.

Yahoo! Auctions: Dolls

http://auctions.yahoo.com/25864-category.html

★★★★

Bid on and sell dolls at Yahoo! Auctions.

HOT WHEELS AND MATCHBOX CARS AND TRUCKS

Hot Wheels

http://www.hotwheels.com/

★★★★★

 All

This official home of Hot Wheels cars and trucks enables visitors to browse through a huge collection of cars and trucks, tracks, helicopters, airplanes, games, and accessories. Links to Amazon.com for shopping. An innovative navigation system allows you to browse by toy or by age group. Links to other cool Hot Wheels sites as well.

Hot Wheels @ netfix.com

http://www.netfix.com/hotwheels/

★★★

Excellent site for beginning and seasoned Hot Wheels collectors. Beginners should check out the Starting Collecting Tips link to learn how to start their collection. Check out the Collector Series for a quick view of how various collections are organized. Most of this site is devoted to sharing information about the author's collection and generating some interest from other avid Hot Wheels collectors.

Matchbox

http://www.matchbox.com/

★★★★★

All

This official home of Matchbox cars and trucks enables visitors to browse through a huge collection of cars, trucks, and other Matchbox toys. Links to Toys "R" Us and Wal-Mart for shopping. Links to other cool Matchbox sites, as well. Separate sites are accessible from the home page—a site for kids and a site for collectors.

A B C D E F G H I J K L M N O P Q R S T U V W X Y Z

A
B
C
D
E
F
G
H
I
J
K
L
M
N
O
P
Q
R
S
T
U
V
W
X
Y
Z

Matchbox Shop

http://www.matchboxshop.com/

★★★★

 All

Shop for and purchase Matchbox cars and trucks online. Separate shopping site for kids and collectors.

Matchbox Models of Yesteryear FAQs

http://robbinsplace.com/moy/frames/FAQ.htm

★★★

Excellent introduction to the art of collecting Matchbox cars and trucks, this site provides answers to the most commonly asked questions.

POSTERS

AllPosters.com

http://www.allposters.com/

★★★★★

Billing itself as the "World's Largest Poster and Print Store," AllPosters.com does feature a hefty collection of posters. If you're looking for a poster or print of your favorite movie, movie star, musician, fine art painting or drawing, or a photo, go to AllPosters.com and track it down… or just tour the gallery. It really is an amazing collection!

Chisholm-Larsson Vintage Posters

http://www.chisholm-poster.com/

★★★★

Search this collection of more than 27,000 vintage posters, and purchase them online. This site is more for collectors who know what they're looking for. You can browse new acquisitions by category.

PosterGroup.com

http://www.postergroup.com/

★★★★★

This site features an incredible collection of vintage posters that is both searchable and browsable. Browse by size, price, artist, or category, including Liquor, Food & Beverages, Entertainment, Travel, Transportation, War & Military, Sports, and Original Art. Crystal clear digital images show you just what each of these beautiful posters looks like.

Posters, Inc. Historical Posters

http://www.postersinc.com/

★★★★★

This site specializes in historical posters, prints, and postcards—especially items with a patriotic, military, and/or political theme. If you're looking for posters or other graphics from World War I, World War II, the Korean War, the Civil War, and the 60s, this is the place to go.

Rick's Movie Graphics and Posters

http://www.ricksmovie.com/

★★★★★

Have you ever gone to a movie and wondered if you could get one of those cool posters they have hanging at the theater? Well, wonder no more. At Rick's Movie Graphics and Posters, you can order the poster you want and have it delivered to your door. This site has a vast collection of posters and other graphics for new and old movies alike and for thousands of popular celebrities.

STAMPS

American Philatelic Society

http://www.stamps.org/

⑤

★★★★★

 9-13

This well-designed site features the American Philatelic Society's journal, a dealer locator, a searchable library catalog, a printable membership application, extensive information on the basics of stamp collecting, and details on its expert service. If you're interested in stamp collecting, whether you are a novice or an expert, bookmark this site and visit it often. This site is packed with the most useful information you'll find on the subject of stamp collecting, making it a sure winner of the Best of the Best designation. Special area where kids can learn the basics of stamp collecting.

Antarctic Philately

http://www.south-pole.com/homepage.html

★★★★

This site is dedicated to the stamps, postal history, and heroic explorers of the great white continent and its surrounding islands.

AskPhil

http://www.askphil.org/

★★★★

Sponsored by The Collectors Club of Chicago, AskPhil (short for AskPhilatelic) provides an excellent resource for stamp collectors. Here, you can learn stamp collecting from the experts. Offers a tremendous collection of resources for novice stamp collectors, a Q&A list, and the AskPhil Academy, where you can take online courses.

British Library Philatelic Collections

http://www.bl.uk/collections/philatelic

★★★★

Details on United Kingdom's National Philatelic Collections are featured here, including the Crown Agents Collection, Board of Inland Revenue, and Foreign Office Collection.

British North America Philatelic Society Stamp Collecting for Kids

http://www.bnaps.org/stamps4kids/

★★★★

9-13

This stamp collecting site for kids is great for all ages of stamp collectors. Covers teens, preteens, and parents, and provides instructions on how to get started, what to collect, and how to judge the condition of a stamp. Also features a list of multiple-choice questions and an area where you can submit a question via email.

Joseph Luft's Philatelic Resources on the Web

http://www.execpc.com/~joeluft/resource.html

★★★

Extensive inventory of links to stamp collecting resources: supplies, shows, dealers, image collections, software, auctions, and individual collectors. Frequently updated.

Linn's Stamp News

http://www.linns.com/

★★★

The largest weekly publication of its kind in the world. Its online edition features answers to frequently asked questions on philately, news updates, a reference area, and a classified ads section. Some good information for beginners.

Open Source Directory of Philatelic Sites

http://dmoz.org/Recreation/Collecting/Stamps/

★★★★

The Open Source directory has a category devoted to stamp collecting. You can find hundreds of listings for philatelic sites.

Philatelic.com

http://www.philatelic.com/

★★★★

Visit the online mall to shop for stamps for your collection or jump into online chat to talk about stamp collecting. A good place to start networking and learning about stamp collecting. Also features an online bulletin board, cheap classified ads, an email network, and a comprehensive directory of additional resources.

A
B
C
D
E
F
G
H
I
J
K
L
M
N
O
P
Q
R
S
T
U
V
W
X
Y
Z

A
B
C
D
E
F
G
H
I
J
K
L
M
N
O
P
Q
R
S
T
U
V
W
X
Y
Z

philbasner.com

http://www.philbansner.com/

★★★★

This site for serious stamp collectors provides a wealth of information plus an excellent search tool for tracking down and ordering rare stamps.

S.C. Virtes Stamps

http://www.scvs.com/stamp/

★★★★

Catering to novice and advanced collectors, this site includes classifieds, a beginners' corner, and an extensive list of stamp inscriptions. Click the link to shop the Scott Virtes Stamps at eBay.

Stamp Collectors Organizations

http://www.stampshows.com/clubs.html

★★★

From the Stamp Yellow Pages, a list of the world's stamp collecting organizations from the Aerogramme Society to the Welsh Philatelic Society.

Stamp Finder.com

http://www.stampfinder.com

★★★★★

Find stamps and supplies, buy entire stamp collections, check out the calendar of events, browse the classifieds, and much more. In addition to searching for particular stamps of interest, you can register a "want list," to alert other collectors to your needs. You can also download stamp collecting software and review news about upcoming events. Affiliate programs are also available.

Stamp Shows

http://www.stampshows.com/

★★★

Locate stamp shows anywhere in the world from this directory. Stamp shows are grouped by country and state. Also the home of the Stamp Yellow Pages Directory, where you can find hundreds of links to postal authorities, stamp stores, kids sites, restoration services, publications, and much more.

U.S. Mints

http://www.best.com/~mleon/usmints.html

★★★

Private page listing U.S. stamps for sale. Sorted into early twentieth century, 1929 to the present, and airmail stamps.

United States Postal Service

http://shop.usps.com/

★★★★

Buy stamps online and have them delivered to your door. Collector's Corner keeps you informed with its Release Schedule, Stamp Collecting FAQ, and Philatelic glossary.

Virtual Stamp Club

http://www.virtualstampclub.com/

★★★★

News, message boards, and chat rooms to keep stamp collectors in touch with one another and informed about the latest stamps being issued worldwide. Some excellent, very current articles.

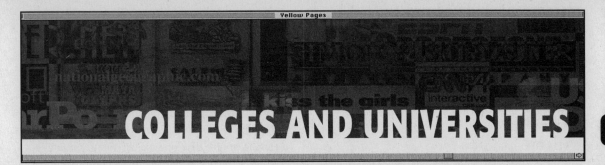

COLLEGES AND UNIVERSITIES

A
B
C
D
E
F
G
H
I
J
K
L
M
N
O
P
Q
R
S
T
U
V
W
X
Y
Z

ACT

http://www.act.org

★★★★

 14-18

Learn more about the ACT, buy products to help you prepare for it, and register for upcoming tests online. In addition to providing information for students, the site also provides information for educators and parents on helping students prepare.

All About College

http://www.allaboutcollege.com

★★★

 14-18

Search the college database to find links to just about every university in the United States, Canada, and several other countries. While there, you'll also be able to find admission office addresses, so you can request an application. You'll find financial aid information and details about study abroad, too.

American Colleges and Universities

http://www.globalcomputing.com/university.htm

★★★

 14-18

This site is a fast and easy way to get more information about a specific U.S. college. Type in the first letter or click on the state in which the college is located, and you'll be given a complete listing of colleges starting with the same letter or in the state you clicked. Then you can click on the college's name and be linked to the college's website. Recommended for checking out colleges in a particular area.

Art, Culinary, and Music Colleges

http://www.ulinks.com/list/art.html

★★★

14-18

A list of specialized art, music, and cooking colleges.

Braintrack

http://www.braintrack.com

★★★

14-18

Looking internationally for a college? This site provides links to more than 7,100 colleges in 192 countries.

College Board

http://www.collegeboard.org/

★★★★★

14-18

Students planning to apply to college and teachers who want to help them do well on the SAT should visit this site to learn more about the test, take practice tests, find out about upcoming dates and locations, and register for the test.

A
B
C
D
E
F
G
H
I
J
K
L
M
N
O
P
Q
R
S
T
U
V
W
X
Y
Z

College Club.com

http://www.collegeclub.com

★★★★

👥 14-18

Want to meet and chat with fellow college students from across the country or in the next dorm? College club is an online chat room and place to express your opinions. You can also send online greeting cards, read articles pertinent to college life, find a compatible roommate, and check out some student deals on everything from spring break apparel to a new car. (This site is designed to help businesses keep in touch with the student market.)

College Links

http://home.nycap.rr.com/nis/linksto.htm

★★★★

👥 14-18

You'll find a large number of links to college home pages, making your college-selection process a tad easier.

College View College Search

http://www.collegeview.com/

★★★★

👥 14-18

Check out hundreds of colleges using College View's virtual tours or just search for a college using its database. You can also collect financial aid information and enter a contest to win a $1,000 scholarship. You'll find plenty of college-related articles and an "Ask the Experts" section for those questions you need answers to. Check out the shopping links!

FreSch!

http://www.freschinfo.com/index.phtml

★★★

👥 14-18

Free scholarship search service with a searchable database of available scholarships, tips on applying, and information about student loans.

HowtoStudy.com

http://www.howtostudy.com/

★★★

👥 All

Having trouble developing good note-taking skills and study habits? This site provides dozens of links to some of the best study techniques and tips on the Web. Also provides links to sites where you can learn how to reduce stress and test anxiety and improve your memory.

Mapping Your Future

http://www.mapping-your-future.org

★★★★★

👥 14-18

Having trouble narrowing down your choice of potential colleges? Mapping Your Future might be able to help, with its 10 Steps to Selecting a College. You can also receive counseling on financial aid packages and what you can afford here. Great place for parents and students to start planning for the college years.

mtvU

http://www.mtvu.com/

★★★★★

👥 14-18

Former home of the College Television Network, this site is dedicated to covering lifestyle-oriented programming and experiences that tap into the fabric of the college audience, the trends, the culture, and the issues relevant to their lives. mtvU is the largest television network just for college students; it broadcasts to more than 720 colleges across the country, with a combined enrollment of 5.5 million.

Music Schools

http://stimpy.music.ua.edu/features/addresses.html

★★★★

👥 14-18

Take a look at this database of more than 900 music schools and colleges if you're considering an education in music.

Petersons.com: The College Channel

http://www.petersons.com/

★★★★★

 14-18

A resource of online course offerings from colleges and universities nationwide. Find out what courses and degrees are available online, or search by institution. Then request scholarship information online, too. Educators can find out more about distance learning, how to develop an online curriculum, and how to market such offerings to students.

Princeton Review Rankings

http://www.princetonreview.com/college/

★★★★★

 14-18

This complete ranking of colleges provides feedback on various colleges' overall educational program. You enter the college name and receive a ranking report.

Ulinks

http://www.ulinks.com/

★★★

 14-18

Considering colleges only in a particular state or area? This directory will make your search much easier.

Universities Worldwide

http://geowww.uibk.ac.at/univ/

★★★

 14-18

A huge searchable index to colleges and universities worldwide providing links to 6,797 universities in 177 countries throughout the world. Click the desired country, enter a keyword (such as music, art, or chemistry), and start the search.

Women's Colleges

http://www.ulinks.com/list/women.html

★★★★

 14-18

A complete listing of women's colleges can be found here for easy reference.

 Xap

http://www.xap.com/

★★★★★

Xap is a full-featured college-selection and financial aid center that assists high school student and their parents and counselors weave their way through the college selection and financial assistance process, and even through career planning. Xap gets its edge by partnering directly with associations and institutions of higher learning to develop regional, university-approved *mentor* websites. Mentor sites use the Internet to guide students through the comparison, selection, admission, and financial aid stages of preparing for college. The site is attractive, easy to navigate, packed with useful tools, and well deserving of our Best of the Best award.

FINANCIAL AID AND SCHOLARSHIPS

Access Group

http://www.accessgroup.org

★★★

 14-18

A no-nonsense site that offers educational loan financing. Search the school database to confirm that your college is eligible and then complete the application online.

Citibank StudentLoan.com

http://www.studentloan.com

★★★★

 14-18

Information for high school students on selecting a college and estimating financial aid need, for college students on repaying their student loans, and for parents on how much their child might qualify for. A student loan application can be completed online here, too. Special offers are also listed for current college students.

A
B
C
D
E
F
G
H
I
J
K
L
M
N
O
P
Q
R
S
T
U
V
W
X
Y
Z

**A
B
C
D
E
F
G
H
I
J
K
L
M
N
O
P
Q
R
S
T
U
V
W
X
Y
Z**

College Is Possible

http://www.collegeispossible.org/

★★★

👥 14-18

You'll find basic facts about college prices and student aid at this site, which is full of statistics regarding what typical students receive in the way of financial aid at state and private schools. Students can learn some general guidelines regarding what to expect in the way of assistance by visiting this site.

Best eStudentLoan.com

http://www.estudentloan.com

★★★★★

👥 14-18

Compare student loans online to find the best deal for you. After completing the online application, you will be provided with 12 loan programs that meet your criteria. After you've selected one, you can complete the loan application online, too. This one-stop approach to student loans makes this site an easy choice for the Best of the Best designation.

FastAID Free Scholarship Search

http://www.fastap.org/fastap/

★★★

👥 14-18

The authors of *The Scholarship Book* have set up a free database of scholarships, which you can search to find scholarships for which you qualify.

fastWEB! (Financial Aid Search Through the Web)

http://www.fastweb.com/

★★★★

👥 14-18

At this site you'll gain access to fastWEB's database of more than 600,000 scholarships worth more than $1 billion. By registering, you get regular updates on scholarships of interest. Come back regularly for information on hot new awards and updates on current scholarships. In the More About Local and Federal Aid section, you can learn about other loan, work-study, and grant programs.

FinAid!

http://www.finaid.org

★★★★★

👥 14-18

A huge site with information about applying to college and financing it. You can locate scholarships; calculate what you'll need to attend; learn about other ways to finance your studies, such as military service; and download financial aid application forms.

Financial Aid Links

http://www.collegeview.com/finaid/

★★★

👥 14-18

Excellent introduction to financial aid describes what it is and various types of financial aid. The site also offers a scholarship directory and an ask-the-expert service.

Financial Aid Resource Center

http://www.theoldschool.org/

★★★

👥 14-18

At this site, you can learn about basic forms of financial aid, loans and lenders, and general sources of financial aid. You'll also find free financial aid databases to search for potential scholarships and grants for college.

Financing Education

http://iiswinprd03.petersons.com/finaid/

★★★★

👥 14-18

Learn all about negotiating tactics, scholarship myths, trends in financial aid, and much more at this comprehensive site.

Free Application for Federal Student Aid

http://www.ed.gov/offices/OSFAP/Students/apply/express.html

★★★

👥 14-18

Complete the U.S. Department of Education's Free Application for Federal Student Aid (FAFSA) at this government location.

FreSch!

http://www.freschinfo.com/index.phtml

★★★

†† 14-18

FreSch! has a database of more than 5,000 organizations and foundations that offer scholarships, representing approximately 500,000 awards. Start by reading tips for qualifying for scholarships and then search the free scholarship database to locate scholarships you might want to apply for. You'll also find information about contests through which you can earn even more money for school.

The Princeton Review

http://www.embark.com

★★★★★

†† 14-18

One-stop information and resource center for helping students research institutes of higher education, prepare for entrance, explore financing options, and apply for admission and financial aid. Also provides services for colleges and universities to help in recruiting top students and services for businesses to locate qualified college graduates. High school counselors of college-bound students will want to check out this site as well.

Scholarship Page

http://www.scholarship-page.com

★★★

†† 14-18

Search or browse this scholarship database to find potential scholarships you qualify for. Not the most up to date.

Scholarships

http://www.scholarships.com/

★★★

†† 14-18

Here, you'll find links for information on scholarships, financial aid, funding resources, and grants.

SRN Express

http://www.srnexpress.com

★★★

†† 14-18

Search the SRN database of more than 8,000 programs representing 150,000 scholarship awards. A free private scholarship resource worth checking out.

Student Financial Assistance

http://studentaid.ed.gov/

★★★★★

†† 14-18

SFA is one of the largest sources of student aid in America, providing more than $40 billion a year in grants, loans, and work-study assistance. Here, you'll find help for every stage of the financial aid process, whether you're in school or out of school. If you or your child is planning on attending college, this should be one of your first stops.

TGWorks

http://www.tgslc.org/

★★★

†† 14-18

This site offers more than just a loan application, although loan calculators and information about repayment are available. In addition, you can search the database of colleges and find out more about available financial aid packages.

United Negro College Fund

http://www.uncf.org

★★★★

†† 14-18

Download program and scholarship information to learn more about money available through the United Negro College Fund. You'll find information about qualifying for a scholarship, as well as background facts about the organization itself.

A B C D E F G H I J K L M N O P Q R S T U V W X Y Z

A
B
C
D
E
F
G
H
I
J
K
L
M
N
O
P
Q
R
S
T
U
V
W
X
Y
Z

Welcome to the Harry Truman Scholarship Foundation

http://www.truman.gov/

★★★★

👥 14-18

The Truman Scholarship is a highly competitive, merit-based award offered to U.S. citizens and U.S. nationals who want to go to graduate school in preparation for a career in public service. The scholarship offers recognition of outstanding potential as a leader in public service and membership in a community of persons devoted to helping others and to improving the environment.

Wyoming Student Loan Corporation

http://www.wslc.com/

★★★

👥 14-18

Learn about the general sources of financial aid—from the government, to the colleges themselves, to private organizations with scholarship programs.

Yahoo! Education: Financial Aid: College Aid Offices

http://dir.yahoo.com/Education/financial_aid/

★★★

👥 14-18

Offers links to the college aid office for each university in the United States. You'll get information on all the financial aid opportunities at each university.

Related Sites
http://cbweb10p.collegeboard.org/fundfinder/html/fundfind01.html
http://www.scholarships4college.com/
http://www.college-scholarships.com/
http://www.finaid.org/
http://www.nsf.gov/home/grants.htm
http://www.universitysports.com/
http://www.iie.org/fulbright/

GRADUATE SCHOOLS

U.S. News and World Report Best Graduate Schools Rankings

http://www.usnews.com/usnews/edu/beyond/bcrank.htm/

★★★

U.S. News online ranks graduate programs annually to help you evaluate academic quality.

Accepted.com

http://www.accepted.com/

★★★★

On this website, you will find comprehensive advice on the writing tasks associated with applying to graduate and professional schools, as well as general information on the admissions process. You can read articles on the writing tasks specific to your specialty or review sample essays. Also find out which books will really help you through the admissions derby. To keep abreast of admissions news, the latest tips, and developments at Accepted.com, sign up for the free monthly newsletter, *Accepted.com Odds 'N Ends*.

Advice for Undergraduates Considering Graduate School

http://www.acm.org/crossroads/xrds3-4/gradschool.html

★★★★

A nice overview of the process of evaluating whether attending grad school is a smart move for undergraduates to make. Takes into account interests, ambitions, and career goals.

All About Grad School

http://www.allaboutgradschool.com/

★★★★

Provides a comprehensive geographic directory of graduate schools in the United States. Click one of four categories (Business Schools, Engineering Schools, Law Schools, or Medical Schools), and you'll be linked to an alphabetic list of states. Click on your state, and you'll find an alphabetic list of graduate schools with links to all of them (and email addresses, too).

Council of Graduate Schools

http://www.cgsnet.org/

★★★

The "Resources for Students" section provides information on selecting a graduate school, financing graduate education, and the timetable for applying.

EDUFAX

http://www.edufax.com

★★★

Provides individualized counseling for educational placement from preschool through graduate school, for reentry and adult learners, and for the American and international student. Network actively with admissions professionals from schools in the USA and around the world to keep abreast of what is current and appropriate for each applicant.

ETS Net

http://www.ets.org/

★★★

Educational Testing Service Network provides information about college and graduate school admissions and placement tests, with links to AP, GRE, GMAT, SAT, The Praxis Series, and TOEFL sites, as well as other educational resources. ETS Net provides sample test questions, test preparation, and test registration. This site also contains information on ETS research initiatives, teacher certification, college planning, financial aid, and links to college and university sites.

Gradschools.com

http://www.gradschools.com/

★★★

With more than 50,000 free program listings, this site claims it is "The most comprehensive online source of graduate school information." Click the Search function, select a program category, and see a list of not only U.S. programs, but international programs, too.

Graduate Guide

http://www.graduateguide.com/

★★★

Searchable directory of graduate schools and schools that offer distance-learning opportunities.

GradView

http://www.gradview.com/

★★★★★

A site devoted to helping students get into and successfully completing a graduate school program, with help for taking graduate entrance exams, studying, and securing financial aid. Comprehensive and easy to navigate.

GRE Online

http://www.gre.org/

★★★★

Learn about registering and taking the GRE in your area, and take practice tests to boost your confidence and point out your weak spots.

Kaplan Online

http://www1.kaplan.com/

★★★★★

As far as testing goes, this site holds the top online spot for information and service. Good site if you are in admissions counseling, student services, advising, or if you're trying to find some good information on graduate school testing for yourself. You can shop for and order test preparation books and software from this site.

Lawschool.com

http://www.lawschool.com/

★★★★

One-stop resource center for law school students. Features everything from law school rankings to bar exam information, plus links to a law book library and law fiction.

A
B
C
D
E
F
G
H
I
J
K
L
M
N
O
P
Q
R
S
T
U
V
W
X
Y
Z

A
B
C
D
E
F
G
H
I
J
K
L
M
N
O
P
Q
R
S
T
U
V
W
X
Y
Z

MBA Exchange

http://www.mbaexchange.com/

★★★

Consultation service for MBA applicants. Monitors and evaluates the top MBA programs and provides applicants with the assistance they need to compete for entrance.

Petersons.com

http://www.petersons.com/gradchannel/

★★★★★

Peterson's site features the capability to search specific programs and also offers links to the Access Group, as well as test preparation tips. The online store contains hundreds of Peterson's titles.

Pre-Law: How to Get into Law School

http://www.hollins.edu/undergrad/prelaw/pre-law.htm

★★★

A guide to preparing for entrance into law school.

U.S. News Online: Graduate School

http://www.usnews.com/usnews/edu/grad/grhome.htm

★★★

The magazine that brings you those famous yearly rankings of U.S. colleges and universities also offers a broad and helpful primer on higher education and careers.

COMICS, CARTOONS, AND ANIMATION

A
B
C
D
E
F
G
H
I
J
K
L
M
N
O
P
Q
R
S
T
U
V
W
X
Y
Z

The 86th Floor

http://members.aol.com/the86floor/

★★★

Provides an online site for fans of the pulp fiction and comic book hero Doc Savage. Includes Doc Savage news, information, a virtual comic, and much more.

Animation Art

http://www.ara-animation.com/misc.htm

★★★★★

 All

Billed as "The Best Animation Art Gallery on the Web," Animation Art features an enormous collection of still shots and animations. Search by artist, animated series, or company (Marvel, Disney, and so on). Or just flip through the many tabbed pages: Cartoon Network, Disney, Talking Art, Fine Art & Photography, Vintage Animation, and so on. You can purchase images and learn about licensing online.

Animation Library

http://www.animationlibrary.com/

★★★★

Collection of more than 13,000 animated clips you can download for use on your web pages, organized by category to make them easy to find.

Animation World Network

http://www.awn.com/index.php3

★★★★

Anyone interested in animation should check out this site! It includes links to *Animation World Magazine*; a career connection; and an animation village, gallery, and vault. Links to all kinds of animation-related products.

Archie

http://www.archiecomics.com/

★★★

 All

Archie and the gang from Riverdale High School are featured prominently at this Archie Comics site. You'll find Jughead, Betty, and Veronica here in the "Today's Comic," section with Archie. And you'll also find games, the latest comics, puzzles, and contests.

Batman Superman Adventures

http://www.batman-superman.com/

★★★★★

 All

Warner Brothers Kids brings you this site, which provides information about the new Batman Adventures and Superman Adventures cartoons. Here, you can learn more about the heroes and villains who do battle on the shows, check out the multimedia libraries, and play some games online. Fans of all ages will love this site.

Calvin and Hobbes

http://www.ucomics.com/calvinandhobbes/

★★★★

 All

If you like the comic strip, you'll be in heaven when you hit this site. Initially, you're greeted by today's strip, but a calendar below the strip lets you flip through an entire gallery of Calvin and Hobbes episodes. Peruse the book list and then examine the latest Calvin and Hobbes picture books. This site also includes icons and desktop patterns, a popularity poll, a random picture generator, links to newsgroups, and interviews with the creator, Bill Watterson. Although this site is unofficial, it is incredibly thorough.

A
B
C
D
E
F
G
H
I
J
K
L
M
N
O
P
Q
R
S
T
U
V
W
X
Y
Z

The Cartoon Factory

http://www.cartoon-factory.com/

★★★★★

 All

Search for your favorite cartoon at this fun site. This resource guides you through the Net directly to the characters and cartoons you want to view. You can even order brief animations online.

CartooNet

http://www.cartoonet.org

★★★

Editors looking for illustrators and cartoonists will find this site a big help. And illustrators looking to showcase their work can do so by joining the site. Search based on topic or style to find a cartoon that meets your needs.

Related Site
http://www.cs.uidaho.edu/~frincke/misc/cartoons.html

Best Cartoon Network.com

http://www.cartoonnetwork.com/

★★★★★

 All

The official website of *Dexter's Laboratory*, *Scooby-Doo*, the *Power-Puff Girls*, *Samurai Jack*, and other favorites. Here, you can find loads of games to play online, visit your favorite cartoon character, and check on program times. Includes an online store where you can shop for books, videos, apparel, toys, games, collectibles, and other items.

Chuck Jones Web Site

www.chuckjones.com

★★★★★

Check out the official site of the late Chuck Jones, the famous Warner Brothers/Loony Tunes animator and animation director. At this site, you can read about Mr. Jones and his many famous cartoon characters. This is an exceptionally well-constructed site, both visually and content-wise.

Comic Book Movies

http://www.efavata.com/CBM/

★★★★★

For those who follow movies based on comic books, this site is a must-visit. Here, you find the latest information and gossip about comic book movies, including who's slated to play your favorite heroes, heroines, and villains; how successful or unsuccessful a particular movie is; where you can find trailers; and more.

Comic Book Resources

http://www.comicbookresources.com

★★★★★

9-13

Nice site that includes special sections with hundreds of links regarding Marvel, DC, Dark Horse, miscellaneous, independent, and self-published comics.

Computer Graphics World

http://cgw.pennnet.com/home.cfm

★★★★

Home of *Computer Graphics World* magazine, a good source for industry news and product information. Don't miss the Graphics Gallery (under Special Features).

Dark Horse Comics Home Page

http://www.dhorse.com/

★★★★★

9-13

Provides news, information, artwork, and upcoming release information for Dark Horse Comics, publisher of *Star Wars*, *Aliens*, and many more titles. Includes many different articles about Dark Horse titles and artists.

DC Comics

http://www.dccomics.com

★★★★

9-13

Download the latest cover images from DC comic books, watch QuickTime movies of some of your favorite characters, follow links to other sites where you can buy comic merchandise, and join a chat to discuss your love of comic books.

Diamond Comic Distributor, Inc.

http://www.diamondcomics.com/

★★★

 All

This comic distributor's online page has comic news, previews, and a catalog. Find out many interesting facts at this fun page!

Digital Webbing

http://www.digitalwebbing.com/

★★★★★

Great source for finding comic book–related websites and information. Includes an extensive database of comic book websites, news, interviews, previews, and talent search area.

Disney.com

http://disney.go.com/

★★★★★

A great website for families to explore together! Has links to some of Disney's best known cartoons, along with activities for kids and families. Also has a Disney shop online.

The Dreaming

http://www.holycow.com/dreaming/

★★★

Provides a fan page dedicated to the comic writing of Neil Gaiman and fantasy titles such as *The Sandman*. Includes graphics, articles, interviews, and much more.

EX: The Online World of Anime and Manga

http://www.ex.org/

★★★★

All

Provides an online magazine dedicated to Japanese anime and manga. Includes back issue and subscription information. EX features many different articles, pictures, and much more dealing with anime.

iCOMICS

http://www.icomics.com/

★★★

9-13

Keep up on the latest comics at this site, where you can read the review of the day or peruse the archive of reviews.

Iguana's Comic Book Café

http://www.go2iguanas.com/

★★★★★

This café is a gaming and comic book mail-order service. Also specializes in toys, Beanie Babies, and manga videos.

International Museum of Cartoon Art

http://www.cartoon.org/

★★★★

All

Internet home of the International Museum of Cartoon Art represents the work of artists from more than 50 countries and has a huge collection of original drawings, books, videos, interviews, and other items related to comic book illustrations and animations. Here, you can check out some select items and learn more about your favorite cartoonist.

Karmatoons

http://www.karmatoons.com/

★★★

14-18

Anyone interested in considering a career in animation will want to take Doug Compton's "Drawing for Classical Animation" mini-course at his website. Read about his career and see samples of his work here, too.

Kids' Cool Animation

http://www.kaleidoscapes.com/kc_intro.html

★★★

9-13

Create your own animations through tutorials and other links at this fun site. View animations of other visitors.

A
B
C
D
E
F
G
H
I
J
K
L
M
N
O
P
Q
R
S
T
U
V
W
X
Y
Z

Marvel Comics

http://www.marvel.com/

★★★★★

 9-13

The home of Spiderman, the Hulk, Captain America, and other famous heroes, this site is marvelous! Here, you can learn about your favorite Marvel comic books, preview upcoming issues, shop online, and register to win free comic books. Some excellent free downloads and brilliant graphics. Bravo, Marvel!

MTNCartoons

http://www.mtncartoons.com

★★★

See the work of cartoonist Marc Tyler Nobleman at his site, where you can also purchase rights to feature his work.

Related Site
http://www.cybercomm.net/~dano/toontown.html

Official Peanuts Website

http://www.snoopy.com

★★★★

 All

Kids can play the Peanuts trivia game and color in the coloring book, while adults might want to read more about Peanuts' creator, the late Charles Schulz. There is also a comic archive to find past strips. Shopping link to SnoopyStore.com.

The Simpsons

http://www.thesimpsons.com/

★★★★★

Explore Springfield using the virtual map and view the latest antics of Homer and Bart. Meet the voice actors, guest stars, and show's creator. Get character bios, view episode descriptions, and share your enthusiasm for the show with other fans. Excellent site!

Small Press Comics Chat

http://www.sentex.net/~sardine/small.press.html

★★★★

Provides information, articles, reviews, and a discussion room about small press and independent comics. Includes links to artist and other related small press comic sites. Also includes information about how to publish your own comics.

South Park

http://www.comedycentral.com/tv_shows/southpark/

★★★★

 Not for kids

Home of Comedy Central's South Park cartoon. View a trailer of the latest South Park movie, submit your vote in this week's poll, or buy South Park memorabilia online. Kids like this animated cartoon, but it's not really suitable for kids. I'm not sure it's even suitable for adults.

Spiderman: The Amazing Spiderman Page

http://www.msu.edu/user/haleysco/spiderman/

★★★

 All

Provides an unofficial fan page dedicated to Marvel Comics' Spiderman. Includes artwork, news, and an interview with Marvel Comics' guru Stan Lee.

Related Site
http://spiderman.sonypictures.com/

Sponge Bob Square Pants

http://www.nick.com/all_nick/tv_supersites/spongebob/

★★★★★

 All

Follow the antics of Sponge Bob Square Pants and his fellow silly sea creatures online at Nickelodeon's official Sponge Bob website. Here, you can solve a crossword puzzle, play a boating game, feed the anchovies, download a screensaver, view a talking cast picture, and more. Excellent site for young kids, but older fans will like it too.

Super Marketing: Ads from the Comic Books

http://www.steveconley.com/supermarketing.htm

★★★★★

This site is dedicated to the classic ads that appeared in golden and silver age comics. Ads for such things as the Hypno-coin, six tapes for $1.49, and much more are quite humorous.

WebComics

http://www.webcomics.com/

★★★★

Huge collection of links to comics on the Web. Features include WebComic of the Day, WebComic of the Week, Top 30 Toons, and a discussion area.

Wolverine's REALM

http://wolverine.x-knights.com/

★★★★★

👫 All

Provides an unofficial fan page for Marvel Comics' character Wolverine. Includes facts, origin information, artwork, fan pictures, and much more.

Related Site
http://www.cartoonsforum.com/

A
B
C
D
E
F
G
H
I
J
K
L
M
N
O
P
Q
R
S
T
U
V
W
X
Y
Z

A
B
C
D
E
F
G
H
I
J
K
L
M
N
O
P
Q
R
S
T
U
V
W
X
Y
Z

Yellow Pages

COMPUTERS

BUYING/INFORMATION RESOURCES

Chumbo.com

http://www.chumbo.com

★★★★

Search for the software you want by category or product name and then purchase it at the site. Great place to find deals on audio CDs and video DVDs, too.

CNET

http://cnet.com

★★★★★

Get hardware and software reviews here before you buy, compare prices from various suppliers, and catch up on tech news. You can also download freeware, learn more about website building, and lots more at this popular site.

Related Site
http://shopper.cnet.com/

CompUSA.com

http://www.compusa.com/

★★★★

Get advice on which computer products to buy and then buy them online from CompUSA. You can also download software here.

egghead

http://www.egghead.com

★★★★★

At Amazon.com-powered egghead.com, check out a wide selection of Egghead products. Browse by category, check out some great deals, or view the list of 100 top electronics devices.

MSN Tech

http://tech.msn.com/

★★★★★

MSN's tech site is packed with excellent information and resources for PC/Windows users of all levels of experience. Includes product reviews, downloads, how-to instructions, news, trends, virus and security information, and much more.

Outpost.com

http://www.outpost.com

★★★★

Search for products by brand name or type and then search the bargain basement for overstocks, or bid on what you want at outpost auctions. Besides computing equipment and electronics, you can also shop for books, cameras, and seasonal gifts.

PC Connection

http://www.pcconnection.com

★★★★

Scout hot deals and bargains before placing your order online at PC Connection, where your order will be shipped overnight. A nice perk of shopping here.

Smart Computing

http://www.smartcomputing.com/

★★★★★

Home page of *Smart Computing* magazine, one of the most popular computer magazines for beginning-level PC users, features articles, techniques, and tricks for using and optimizing PCs. Subscribers can log on for additional features.

ZDNet

http://www.zdnet.com

★★★★

Read industry news, download useful software, scan product reviews, and go shopping for hardware and software at affiliate sites.

ZDNet Shopper

http://shopper-zdnet.com.com/

★★★★

Browse dozens of hardware and software categories for the items you need, read product reviews and recommendations, and learn how to shop for various computer products.

COMPUTER COMPANIES: HARDWARE AND SOFTWARE

Acer America on the Web

http://www.acer.com/aac/

★★★

Home page for Acer North America. Acer manufactures personal computer clones. The Acer America site provides online shopping, FAQs, and information about the Acer Group, including employment opportunities.

Apache Digital Corporation

http://www.apache.com/

★★★★

Provides information on ALPHA-based, NeXTSTEP, Linux/BSD Unix, Windows NT, SPARC-based, and other custom-design systems sold by Apache. Also provides online custom design form, company background, policies, and additional detailed product information.

Apple Computer Home Page

http://www.apple.com/

★★★★★

Apple now provides an online storefront where you can purchase customized hardware configurations of your favorite Macintosh models. Provides information on Apple's latest products and also supplies software updates. Check out this site for the latest on Apple technology.

Compaq Access

http://www.compaq.com/

★★★★

Access Compaq's Web services for corporate information, worldwide service center directories, technical support, and press releases on Compaq's newest web servers and pricing. Don't forget to check out the online store, where you can buy Compaq computers and accessories.

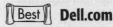 Dell.com

http://www.dell.com/

★★★★★

This site provides secure online shopping for Dell personal computer products. You can custom configure a system and buy it online. The site also lets you search for information by type of user, as well as provides the standard corporate information. And, if you own a Dell computer, this site features excellent online technical support that can help you solve most of the problems you might encounter with it. Excellent site design and comprehensive information make this an easy Best of the Best selection.

A
B
C
D
E
F
G
H
I
J
K
L
M
N
O
P
Q
R
S
T
U
V
W
X
Y
Z

A
B
C
D
E
F
G
H
I
J
K
L
M
N
O
P
Q
R
S
T
U
V
W
X
Y
Z

Gateway

http://www.gateway.com/

★★★★★

Gateway's site is designed for easy navigation. The opening screen displays three basic options: At Home, At Work, and Support. If you're looking for a computer for your home or home-based business, click the At Home link and start shopping. Business users should click the At Work link to shop for computers and other products designed for business applications. You can configure and purchase a computer online from this site. The site also provides access to technical support and corporate information.

Hewlett-Packard

http://www.hp.com/

★★★★

The leader in desktop hardware and network servers provides a multilingual website that is much more international than most other computer manufacturers. Jump from this site to learn about HP's Latin American division, its newest systems in other countries, and technical information on HP printers.

IBM Corporation

http://www.ibm.com

★★★★★

Here, you can reach all of IBM's myriad divisions from the home page. You can also read about IBM systems solutions via articles. Take online training courses, attend real-time seminars, or chat with people with similar interests. An extensive search engine is also provided for navigating this very large corporate site. Take advantage of IBM's Buy Today, Ship Today purchase program.

Intel

http://www.intel.com/

★★★★★

This site provides all the information you ever wanted to know about Intel's integrated circuits, and especially its latest processor. The site showcases software running on Intel-based hardware and hardware implementations, and it offers business opportunities as well as the standard technical support and news briefs.

MPC

http://www.buympc.com/

★★★★

Less popular than Gateway and Dell, this online computer store (formerly Micron PC) has been providing quality products and service to its customers for just as long. Shop online or obtain technical support and downloads for a Micron or MPC PC you already own.

Motorola

http://www.motorola.com

★★★

Manufacturer of PowerPC chips and other integrated circuits, as well as computers and peripherals. The Motorola home page provides information about the corporation, its products, divisions, and activities. Great starting point for obtaining technical support for Motorola products.

MACINTOSH

Apple Links

http://www.applelinks.com

★★★

News, reviews, buyers' guides, and Mac information all in one place. Many links to retail sites.

Everything Mac

http://www.everythingmac.com

★★★

In addition to finding the Top 100 Mac links, you'll find articles and other Mac-related resources to help you get the most out of your computer. Get help from other users in the online forums.

Mac Addict

http://www.macaddict.com

★★★★

Sign up for the Mac Addict newsletter, jump into some discussions to share and gather Mac information, and stay tuned for up-to-date news and rumors.

Mac Central/Macworld/MacWEEK

http://maccentral.macworld.com/

★★★★★

Macintosh industry news, product reviews, newsletters, and forums. Search for the best deals on Mac hardware and software with Macworld's Pricefinder. If you're a Mac enthusiast, this place is a great hangout.

Mac Design Online

http://www.macdesignonline.com/

★★★★★

Involved in the graphics industry? Mac Design is devoted to covering Macintosh graphics, multimedia, and web issues specifically for Macs.

MacGamer.com

http://www.macgamer.com/

★★★★★

Game reviews, previews, interviews, editorials, and downloads for Macintosh games. Join an online discussion of your favorite Mac games and find deals and freebies.

Mac Home

http://www.machome.com

★★★★★

Looking for a Mac product review? You'll find more than 1,000 from the pages of *MacHome* magazine here, as well as downloadable software, updates, and tips. Subscribe to the magazine online.

Macintosh News Network

http://www.macnn.com/

★★★★

Excellent source for Macintosh news, reviews, discussion, tips, troubleshooting, links, and reviews. Tracks and reports on the latest developments in the industry. Great resource for Mac IT professionals.

Mac Update

http://www.macupdate.com

★★★★

Download Macintosh software and games here. Links to additional Mac-related resources.

Macs Only!

http://www.macsonly.com

★★★

You'll find an impressive list of hands-on product reviews, all the Mac news you'll probably need, editorial commentary, and Mac links.

MacTech

http://www.mactech.com

★★★

Geared more toward Mac programmers, MacTech provides product reviews and news, web and multimedia programming information, and networking guidance.

TidBITS

http://www.tidbits.com

★★★

TidBITS is an email publication devoted to helping Mac users make better use of their computers. Sign up for a free subscription.

Ultimate Mac

http://www.ultimatemac.com

★★★★★

Named to several "Best of …" reports because of the comprehensive approach to Macintosh information, this site bills itself as "The BIGGEST, UGLIEST, and MOST USEFUL Macintosh Page on the Web." For beginners and programmers alike, the Ultimate Macintosh provides answers to user questions, downloadable software, product and software reviews, and just about anything else you need to know about the Mac.

A
B
C
D
E
F
G
H
I
J
K
L
M
N
O
P
Q
R
S
T
U
V
W
X
Y
Z

A
B
C
D
E
F
G
H
I
J
K
L
M
N
O
P
Q
R
S
T
U
V
W
X
Y
Z

PCs

Annoyances.org

http://annoyances.org/

★★★★★

This site shines the spotlight on the most annoying computer and software features you might encounter, including Microsoft Office's Clippit. This site lists the top Windows annoyances and provides instructions on how to avoid them. Additional information is available for tweaking the Windows Registry, customizing the desktop, improving performance, and much more.

GoToMyPC

http://www.gotomypc.com

★★★★★

Online service that enables you to connect to and use your desktop computer from any Internet-connected computer in the world via a secure connection. If you frequently find yourself on the road without access to the programs and documents you need to survive, connect to this site to sign up for a free trial.

Laptop Buyer's Guide

http://www.infohq.com/Computer/LaptopGuide.htm

★★★

Shopping for a new laptop or notebook computer? Read this guide first to find out what you need to consider.

Microsoft Product Support Services

http://support.microsoft.com/

★★★★★

If you have a PC that runs any version of Windows and any other Microsoft product, such as Microsoft Office, bookmark this site. Here, you'll find a searchable knowledgebase where you can find answers to most of your technical support questions. Simply click the Search the Knowledgebase link, select the product that's giving you trouble, type a few key words that describe the problem, and click Go.

PC Guide

http://www.pcguide.com

★★★★

Everything you always wanted to know about PCs, from how a PC works to troubleshooting common problems. Provides a useful PC buyer's guide and information on how to care for and optimize your system. Plain presentation, but excellent content and easy to navigate.

PC Tech Guide

http://www.pctechguide.com

★★★

Learn more about how PC hardware functions here, where a PC enthusiast works to share his knowledge.

PC World

http://www.pcworld.com

★★★★★

Get PC help, downloads, news about the most popular software, as well as reviews of the best PCs, accessories, and software.

Windows

http://www.microsoft.com/windows/

★★★★

Windows product downloads, tips, and support are all available here.

[Best] WinPlanet

http://www.winplanet.com/

★★★★★

Premium site for all topics related to Microsoft Windows and Windows applications. Take an online tutorial to learn a new skill, pick up some tips and tricks, and learn how to customize Windows with some tech-savvy tweaks. Excellent collection of downloadable shareware and updated drivers. When you want to learn more about your computer's operating system, this is the place to go.

Winsite

http://www.winsite.com

★★★

Download usable files, share tips, and browse the hottest PC sites via this site.

Related Sites

http://www.mywindows.com/

http://www.windrivers.com/

http://www.globalvillage.com/

Woody's Watch

http://www.woodyswatch.com/

★★★★

Woody Leonhard, Microsoft Office expert, features Office advice, troubleshooting, and tips via his newsletter, which you can subscribe to at this site. Newsletter features no-nonsense, unbiased advice from the world's leading experts on Microsoft Office products.

PROGRAMMING LANGUAGES

Active State

http://www.activestate.com

★★★★

Produces Perl scripting software for web developers. The site provides software purchases and support to Perl programmers.

Amzi! Prolog+ Logic Server

http://www.amzi.com/

★★★★

Produces Amzi! Prolog+ Logic Server, a software add-on you embed in C++ and other programming languages to create logic-based intelligent agents and intelligent components, which are used in software that relies on artificial intelligence. Amzi!'s products assist programmers who need to create software that configures, schedules, diagnoses, advises, recognizes, lays out, plans, understands, or teaches. Downloadable demos and tutorials are provided to show how this Prolog-based programming language works.

ASP 101

http://www.asp101.com/

★★★★★

Whether you've just started learning Active Server Pages programming or consider yourself a pro, you can find something that's new and informative at this site. Includes lessons and tutorials, sample code, news, resources, and links to other ASP-related sites.

ASP Alliance

http://www.aspalliance.com/

★★★★

Founded in 1997, the ASP Alliance has grown to include more than one hundred contributors and more than 1,000 articles related to ASP programming. The site supports forums and has spawned several related sites. Visit to obtain free tutorials, articles, resources, and code snippets or to connect with other ASP enthusiasts.

ASP Free

http://www.aspfree.com/

★★★★

This site, presented in any of six languages, is packed with articles, news, and development updates relating to ASP programming. Includes ASP code and examples.

ASP Resource Index

http://www.learnasp.com/chaz/

★★★★

Well-stocked inventory of ASP sites and resources organized into categories, including Applications, ASP Web Hosting, ASP.NET Directories, and Tutorials & Code Snips.

BD Software

http://www.bdsoft.com/

★★★

Delivers expert, hands-on training seminars in C++, Java, C, and Unix-related topics onsite. Seminars focus on critical, practical programming language issues.

A B C D E F G H I J K L M N O P Q R S T U V W X Y Z

A
B
C
D
E
F
G
H
I
J
K
L
M
N
O
P
Q
R
S
T
U
V
W
X
Y
Z

Borland C++

http://info.borland.com/devsupport/borlandcpp/

★★★

Borland C++ 5 is one of the top-selling C++ programs on the market. This website includes press releases about Borland C++, the latest patches for various versions of C++, technical support information, and bug information. It also includes a link to other sites devoted to Borland C++.

Builder.com

http://builder.com.com/

★★★★★

CNET maintains this resource dedicated to helping users build better websites. Topics include web authoring and scripting, graphics, and design. User can download tools and participate in user forums.

C/C++: Learn C/C++ Today

http://www.cyberdiem.com/vin/learn.html

★★★

Provides a brief introduction to C and C++ and features links to several online tutorials with a brief description of each tutorial.

Related Site
http://www.cs.mun.ca/~donald/bsc/node6.html

CGI Extremes

http://www.cgiextremes.com/

★★★★

This site provides an accurate and up-to-date database of more than 2,100 CGI scripts for web programmers. Descriptions, ratings, and user feedback are provided for each script to help programmers make an informed choice.

CGI Resource Index

http://cgi.resourceindex.com/

★★★★

Dedicated to the CGI programmer, this site contains thousands of links to CGI scripts, documentation, books, programmers, and even jobs.

COBOL

http://www.cobolreport.com/

★★★★

An organization of hardware manufacturers and COBOL software developers that provides information about COBOL developments. Read book reviews, visit COBOL University, work through an online tutorial, and obtain the latest COBOL news and developments.

Code Guru

http://www.codeguru.com

★★★

Get the latest information and tips for .NET, C++, Java, Visual Basic, JavaScript, and XML as well as access to discussion forums and other programmers who can answer your questions. Links to Fatbrain where you can purchase book titles.

developers.net: Jobs for Technical Professionals

http://www.developers.net/

★★★★

Put your programming skills to work and earn a pretty good living. This site provides a long and up-to-date list of openings for programmers and other technical professionals.

EarthWeb

http://www.earthweb.com/

 $

★★★★★

Comprehensive collection of the latest information and resources for IT professionals, programmers, webmasters, and others interested in computer technology.

eXtreme Programming

http://www.extremeprogramming.org/

★★★

Learn the basics of Extreme Programming (XP)—the "deliberate and disciplined approach to software development." Learn when to use this approach, how to get started, and where to find out more information about it.

Related Site
http://www.xprogramming.com/

Free Compilers and Interpreters

http://www.idiom.com/free-compilers/

★★★

Enter the name of the free (public-domain) compiler, compiler generator, interpreter, or assembler you need, and the search engine will find it. You can also search by category.

The Haskell Home Page

http://haskell.org/

★★★

General-purpose, purely functional programming language. A functional language, as opposed to an imperative language such as C, simplifies programming by focusing on the evaluation of expressions rather than on executing specific commands. The Haskell 98 Report and the Haskell 98Library Report define the language and can be accessed on the website or downloaded. A tutorial is also available.

Hotscripts.com

http://www.hotscripts.com/

★★★★

With links to thousands of web programming resources in more than 1,000 categories, Hotscripts.com is one of the best places for webmasters and programmers to find what they need to enhance their sites. Hotscripts.com evaluates resources and presents a collection of the best resources on the Web.

HTML Goodies

http://htmlgoodies.earthweb.com/

★★★★★

Programmers will find the tutorials and primers a great start to learning more about various programming tools, including HTML, JavaScript, ASP, Perl, and CGI. Visitors can also ask questions of experts and search the site for more information.

HTML Center

http://www.htmlcenter.com

★★★★

Learn about HTML, Java, JavaScript, Flash, and more. Online tutorials teach the basics, product reviews evaluate the best HTML authoring software, help forums answer your questions. Shop online via Amazon.com.

HTML Guru

http://www.htmlguru.com

★★★★

An unusual site that demonstrates what is possible with dynamic HTML programming through reference material and tutorials.

HTML Help

http://www.htmlhelp.com

★★★

Great tools and guidelines available for programmers and designers here, as well as FAQs and informative articles.

JavaScripts

http://webdeveloper.earthweb.com/webjs/

★★★

In addition to typical FAQs and free newsletters, users can access and download more than 5,000 JavaScripts at this site.

java.sun.com

http://java.sun.com/

★★★★★

Maintained by Sun Microsystems, this site is the official home of Java. Here, you will find the latest news and information about Java, downloads, tutorials, code samples, support, and much more. If you program in Java, you will definitely want to bookmark this site.

Linux Planet

http://www.linuxplanet.com/

★★★★★

Huge collection of information and resources about the Linux operating system. Here, you will find discussion groups, distributors, opinions, reports, reviews, and tutorials. If you're planning on ditching Windows and using Linux instead or if you are programming for Linux, check out this site before you proceed.

A B C D E F G H I J K L M N O P Q R S T U V W X Y Z

A
B
C
D
E
F
G
H
I
J
K
L
M
N
O
P
Q
R
S
T
U
V
W
X
Y
Z

MSDN Online

http://msdn.microsoft.com/

★★★★★

Resources, downloads, magazines, and more are available at this comprehensive site. Microsoft Developers Network (MSDN) is a resource site for programmers and developers. Links to additional information about .NET technology.

PC AI: The Dylan Programming Language

http://www.pcai.com/web/ai_info/pcai_dylan.html

★★★

Dylan is an object-oriented programming language currently being developed by Apple. This site offers links to sites with information about Dylan, Dylan vendors, Dylan FAQs, and Dylan newsgroups.

Pennington/XTRAN

http://www.pennington.com/xtran.htm

★★★

Pennington Systems Incorporated developed XTRAN, an expert system that provides translation, analysis, re-engineering, standardization, and code generation. XTRAN's rules language is like C in syntax but is similar to Lisp in semantics.

Related Sites

http://www.acm.org/sigplan/

http://www.math.uio.no/doc/gnu/emacs/program_modes.html

Perl: CPAN Comprehensive Perl Archive Network

http://www.cpan.org/

★★★★★

Comprehensive collection of links to the best Perl resources on the Web. Locate Perl source code, modules, and scripts; research documentation; and find answers to the most common questions.

Perl Resources and Reviews: Diving for Perl

http://www.possibility.com/Perl/

★★★

Interested in learning Perl? Then start with this introduction to Perl put together by one of its most enthusiastic advocates. Lots of links to the best Perl resources on the Web.

Perl.com

http://www.perl.com/

★★★★

O'Reilly and Associates Perl site is the premier site for learning about Perl. Provides links for documentation, training, downloads, books, FAQs and other resources focusing on Perl.

Programmers' Heaven

http://www.programmersheaven.com/

★★★★★

Online resource for beginner to expert programmers. Download source code and files for various programming languages or order them on CD-ROM. You'll also find more than 26,000 links to programming-related sites. Subscribe to the mailing list to receive email updates.

Quadralay's C++ Archive

http://www.austinlinks.com/CPlusPlus/

★★★★

Quadralay is a developer of software products that produce and distribute documents in standard electronic formats. This site includes a number of links that point to C++ programming information. You can find links to guides for understanding Microsoft Foundation Classes (MFCs), get a list of C++ library archives, and access career resource links. The Learn C++ section includes a number of links to books, tutorials, and classes that will help you understand C++ better.

Related Sites

http://www.cs.arizona.edu/sr/

http://www.research.att.com/~bs/C++.html

Webmonkey

http://hotwired.lycos.com/webmonkey/

★★★★

A great list of how-to libraries for topics ranging from e-commerce to authoring, design, multimedia, programming, and more. Excellent resource for web developers.

SOFTWARE—ANTIVIRUS

Dr. Solomon

http://www.drsolomon.com

 $

★★★★★

Learn more about Dr. Solomon's Virex product and then order it online.

McAfee.com

http://www.mcafee.com

 $

★★★★★

Get new virus alerts at McAfee, as well as help buying, installing, and running its VirusScan software, as well as instruction in eliminating existing viruses on your system. Also features a searchable database of viruses, to help you determine if a virus warning is a hoax and to learn more about a particular virus and how to eliminate it from your computer.

Symantec

http://www.norton.com

 $

★★★★★

Buy Norton AntiVirus here, learn about protecting your system from viruses and other threats, and download virus definition updates (if you own the program).

SOFTWARE—DOWNLOADS

5 Star

http://www.5star-shareware.com

★★★

Check the laundry list of types of shareware available for download, or read the expert recommendations before making your selection.

32 Bit-ServerFiles.com

http://www.32bit.com

★★★

A great site for locating networking and Internet security shareware and downloading it, as well as finding out about new software additions. Search the database by type of software or by the most popular.

DemoNet

http://www.demonet.com/

★★★

Commercial software index. Browse through detailed information for more than 47,000 titles, and download free demos of products.

Download.com

http://www.download.com

★★★★★

Download software for virtually any application—virus protection, productivity, multimedia, and more.

freshmeat.net

http://freshmeat.net/

★★★★

freshmeat maintains the Web's largest index of open-source Unix and cross-platform software and Palm OS software. Each entry contains a description of the software, a link for finding out more about it and download it, and a brief history of the product's development. If you're looking for Linux software, this should be your first stop.

Happy Puppy

http://www.happypuppy.com

★★★★★

This gaming site provides shareware games and reviews for a wide variety of games for Mac and PC. Subscribe to the newsletter to keep abreast of the latest news and reviews.

A
B
C
D
E
F
G
H
I
J
K
L
M
N
O
P
Q
R
S
T
U
V
W
X
Y
Z

A
B
D
E
F
G
H
I
J
K
L
M
N
O
P
Q
R
S
T
U
V
W
X
Y
Z

Mac Surfer

http://www.macsurfer.com/

★★★

Weekly directory of free and demo Mac software available on the Web. Features links to other Mac-related resources.

Jumbo!

http://www.jumbo.com/

★★★★

Huge collection of freeware and shareware for download organized by categories, including Internet, MP3 Players, Utilities, Wallpaper, Business, Drivers, and more. Excellent descriptions and reviews of each available program.

Network ICE Corporation

http://www.networkice.com/downloads/blackice_defender.html

★★★★★

Protect your computer and files from potential hack attacks by downloading Black Ice Defender, a personal firewall. Tech support and customer service are also available on this site.

Qwerks

http://www.qwerks.com/

★★★★

This site helps smaller software manufacturers get their products into the hands of users like you. The site exposes you to a wide variety of software. To get started, you can go to See What's Hot, New Products, or Do A Search. Read a description, order it online, and download it immediately.

Tucows

http://www.tucows.com/

★★★★★

One of the largest, most popular shareware/freeware sites, Tucows features more than 30,000 software titles for the Macintosh operating system, Windows, Linux, OS/2, and others. Ranks, describes, and reviews each program in its collection. Here, you can find Internet programs, computer utilities, games, themes, multimedia players, and more.

SnapFiles

http://www.snapfiles.com/

★★★★★

Formerly WebAttack.com, this site features one of the "world's largest Internet related software collection." It also features a good collection of software that is not related to the Internet. SnapFiles is unique in that it reviews and rates all shareware that is submitted before making it available to users. This site is nicely designed, easy to use, and provides excellent descriptions of the available software.

SOFTWARE—MISCELLANEOUS

2020 Software.com

http://www.20-20.com/

★★★

Your Internet source for accounting software ranging in price from $99–$250,000. Products are grouped into low-end, mid-range, and high-end. Online shopping is available via AccountingShop.com.

Adobe

http://www.adobe.com/products/

★★★★

Product feature information for Adobe software products, including PageMaker, Acrobat, and Photoshop. Great place to find shareware versions of Adobe products, order products online, and obtain technical support.

Family Tree Maker Online

http://www.familytreemaker.com/

★★★★★

An online genealogy library, genealogy lessons, columns featuring researching techniques, and tips on how to trace immigrant origins. Buy genealogy software and family archive CDs online.

Help-Site Computer Manuals

http://help-site.com/

★★★

Links to 365 online manuals pertaining to DOS, Windows, the Internet, networking, Unix, and programming.

International Data Group

http://www.idg.com/

★★★★★

Publisher of magazines such as *ComputerWorld/ InfoWorld*, *PC World*, *Network World*, *MacWorld*, *Channel World*, and *Specialty*. Find links to each of these publications. Many feature software previews, reviews, and recommendations.

Laurie McCanna's Photoshop, Corel, Painter, and Paintshop Pro Tips

http://www.mccannas.com/pshop/menu.htm

★★★★

This site features tips and tutorials for Photoshop, Corel, Painter, and Paintshop Pro users. A multitude of examples for the applications that are offered.

New Breed Software

http://www.newbreedsoftware.com

★★★

New Breed creates open source software for a variety of platforms, including Windows, Macintosh, Linux, Unix, BeOS, and PDAs and video game systems. Products range from games to applications to programming libraries.

Web Copier

http://www.maximumsoft.com

★★★

Web Copier is a powerful offline browser that records websites and stores them on your hard drive until you are ready to view them. Save time by storing records locally before referencing them.

ZDNet

http://downloads-zdnet.com.com/

★★★★

Demos and downloads site for *ZD Internet* magazine, providing Internet applets, demos, product reviews, and free software for all platforms. Updated weekly.

TROUBLESHOOTING

5 Star Support

http://www.5starsupport.com/

★★★★

At this site, volunteer technical support personnel help users resolve computer and software issues for free. Get free technical support, meet the techs, visit the solution center, or sign up for the free newsletter. You can also donate your time or money to keep the service running.

ActiveWindows

http://www.activewin.com

★★★★

ActiveWindows is packed with up-to-date news regarding most aspects of the computer industry, including Macintosh and PC hardware, MacOS and Windows, DVD technology, and DirectX. Includes interviews, downloads, reviews, tech tips, and more.

Answers That Work

http://www.answersthatwork.com/

★★★★★

Answers That Work is an online helpdesk that can assist you in solving both hardware and software issues. Registered users can submit a query. Unregistered users must browse through the task list directory to find a topic that matches their specific problems.

AppleCare Technical Support

http://www.info.apple.com/

★★★★★

Apple Computer's technical support site features free downloads and patches and answers to common questions. Check out products and services, search the knowledgebase, download files, check out the discussion groups, or find online user manuals.

Related Site
http://www.apple.com/support/

A
B
C
D
E
F
G
H
I
J
K
L
M
N
O
P
Q
R
S
T
U
V
W
X
Y
Z

A
B
C
D
E
F
G
H
I
J
K
L
M
N
O
P
Q
R
S
T
U
V
W
X
Y
Z

AskDrTech

http://www.askdrtech.com/

★★★★

For about eight bucks a day, you can get expert technical support over the phone for all of your computer questions and problems 24 hours a day, 7 days a week. At this site, you can learn more about the service and sign up. Both Mac and PC tech support is available.

Help2go

http://www.help2go.com

★★★★

Get free computer advice in the form of helpful articles at this site, which also offers to answer your first live question free if the articles don't do it—through Expertcity.

MacFixIt

http://www.macfixit.com

★★★

Mac owners who have encountered a problem they can't solve should head to MacFixIt, where they can participate in forums, read archived articles that might answer questions, look at a troubleshooting report, or download shareware and freeware designed to correct bugs.

PC Pitstop

http://www.pcpitstop.com/

★★★★★

Have an automated technician check your PC for problems and help you optimize your system. PC Pitstop checks to see whether your computer is vulnerable to attacks from viruses or hackers, determines if the hard drive has enough space and is fast enough, checks the memory, reports on the speed of your Internet connection, and much more. Very cool tool for tuning up a PC.

SoftwareLifeTips.com

http://software.lifetips.com/

★★★★★

Provides tips for using several software applications, including Excel, PowerPoint, AutoCAD, Word, Outlook, and Windows. Site enables users to submit questions to online "gurus" to have those questions answered.

Tech Support Guy

http://www.helponthe.net/

★★★

Online forum where users with computer or software problems can post questions to have them answered by more experienced users, or the pros themselves.

VirtualDr

http://www.virtualdr.com/

★★★★

Dedicated to providing computer users the tools and information they need to maintain their computers and troubleshoot problems. Tutorials on how to keep your computer running correctly and forums where you might be able to find the answer to your problem.

CONSUMER ISSUES

A B C D E F G H I J K L M N O P Q R S T U V W X Y Z

Better Business Bureau

http://www.bbb.org/

★★★★

The Better Business Bureau allows visitors to access a database of business and consumer alerts. Visitors can also file a complaint with the BBB, find an office, and learn about membership and various BBB programs. You can also check the BBB's database to determine whether a particular online store is a safe place to shop.

Bicycle Helmet Safety Institute Home Page

http://www.bhsi.org/

★★★★

The helmet advocacy program for the Washington Area Bicyclist Association. You'll find a consumer pamphlet, a toolkit for organizing bicycle helmet programs, plus the latest issue of *The Helmet Update*, a newsletter devoted to discussing helmet news.

The Consumer Law Page

http://consumerlawpage.com/

★★★★

Provides information related to consumer law. Offers articles on topics such as insurance fraud and product liability; brochures on topics such as automobiles, funerals, and banking; and useful links to other resources related to consumer law.

Related Site
http://www.epic.org/

Consumer World

http://www.consumerworld.org/

★★★★★

Find 2,000 Internet consumer resources from reporting fraud to looking for the best airfare. Search the database for your specific consumer issue. Read the latest consumer news.

ConsumerLine

http://www.ftc.gov/ftc/consumer.htm

★★★★★

The Office of Consumer and Business Education of the Bureau of Consumer Protection operates this online service. Find published articles on various consumer issues (in English or Spanish), read about current consumer problems, report a consumer complaint, or check out educational campaigns.

Corporate Watch

http://www.corpwatch.org/

★★★★

Website designed for investigating corporate activity. Get the hottest consumer news, learn about the organization's latest campaigns, and learn the research techniques needed to dig up dirt on your favorite company.

The Dental Consumer Advisor

http://www.toothinfo.com/

★★★★★

Useful and practical information on dental issues. You'll find dental terminology, information on insurance, and information on finding a dentist. Write about your own dental experiences or ask the advisor questions. Extensive list of links related to dentistry.

FDA Consumer Magazine

http://www.fda.gov/fdac/

★★★★

Publication of the U.S. Food and Drug Administration; includes reports of unsafe or worthless products. Electronic copies are available through the website, or you can subscribe to the magazine by sending in the online form. Archives can be searched at this site as well.

A
B
C
D
E
F
G
H
I
J
K
L
M
N
O
P
Q
R
S
T
U
V
W
X
Y
Z

 Federal Citizen Information Center

http://www.pueblo.gsa.gov/

★★★★★

👥 All

Access 200 federal publications regarding consumer issues. A catalog offers information on a wide range of areas, such as cars, healthcare, food, travel, and children. You can also order the entire catalog of publications. Because this site features an easy way to obtain some of the most useful government publications for the average citizen, we've chosen to award it the Best of the Best award for this category. Also features a fun area where kids can play.

Foundation for Taxpayer and Consumer Rights

http://www.consumerwatchdog.org/

★★★★★

Company dedicated to protecting the rights of the consumer, taxpayer, and medical patient. Find out the latest in consumer news and events, or search for your area of interest. You can even donate funds or volunteer to help out the cause. Don't miss *The Whistleblower*, "The newsletter that addresses the corporate and governmental crises of today and blows the whistle on the brewing fiascos of tomorrow."

Internet ScamBusters

http://www.scambusters.com/

★★★★

Free online newsletter dedicated to exposing Internet fraud and protecting consumers from misinformation and hype. Subscribe to the newsletter, share your own Internet scam experience, or enter the Internet ScamBusting Contest.

National Consumer Protection Week

http://www.consumer.gov/ncpw/

★★★★

👥 9-13

Find out when National Consumer Protection Week will be celebrated this year and pick up tips on securing your personal information and safety. Site also includes links for young people.

National Consumers League

http://www.natlconsumersleague.org/

★★★★

Founded in 1899, this advocacy group represents consumers on workplace and marketplace issues. Find out the latest on consumer scams. Learn how to become an NCL member and when and where the NCL's next event is scheduled.

The National Fraud Information Center

http://www.fraud.org/

★★★★★

Originally formed in 1992 to battle telemarketing fraud, the NFIC now has a toll-free hotline for reporting telemarketing fraud, asking for advice about telemarketing calls, and investigating Internet fraud. The website also offers a section on fraud targeting the elderly.

The PIRGs: Fighting for Consumers

http://www.pirg.org/consumer/

★★★

The Public Interest Research Group battles against consumer abuses. Some of the group's campaigns are against rising bank fees, credit company errors and abuses, dangerous products, and the tobacco industry's marketing to children.

U.S. Consumer Product Safety Commission

http://www.cpsc.gov/

★★★★

👥 All

Protects Americans against possible injury and death caused by consumer products. If you have had an experience with an unsafe product, report it on the Talk to Us page. Check out the latest recalled products. You'll find a special 4 Kids page that addresses issues such as the risks of scooters, the importance of wearing bike helmets, and tips for playing baseball safely. Some fun stuff for kids, too.

Related Sites

http://www.sec.gov/consumer/cyberfr.htm

http://www.nhtsa.dot.gov/cars/problems/

COOKING AND RECIPES

About: Low Fat Cooking

http://lowfatcooking.about.com/

★★★

Recipes and techniques to help you prepare low-fat meals.

Art of Eating

http://www.artofeating.com

★★★

You'll consider subscribing to this quarterly print publication after reading the description on the website. *The Art of Eating* is about the best food and wine—what they are, how they are produced, where to find them (the farms, markets, shops, restaurants).

Bread

http://www.cs.cmu.edu/~mjw/recipes/bread/bread.html

★★★

Provides an index of bread recipes, including recipes for bagels, biscuits, scones, and pretzels.

CheeseNet

http://cheesenet.wgx.com/

★★★★★

👥 All

The graphics-rich cheese bible of the Web—ways to make it, its history, the different variations, a picture gallery, cheese literature, and cheese language. Features a cheese-making demonstration and free consultation with Dr. Emory K. Cheese. Though not designed for kids, this site will appeal to visitors of all ages.

Chef Talk

http://www.cheftalk.com

★★★★

Turn to this site to learn all about cooking from the professionals. Culinary 101 offers lessons from the experts themselves, who also offer some of the best new recipes around. You can also sign up to receive free Chef Talk updates via email.

Chile Pepper Magazine

http://www.chilepepper.com/

★★★★

Chile pepper culture, recipes, restaurants, botany, and chat.

Christiane's Collection of Cooking Recipes of Chemists and Physicists

http://chris_fra.tripod.com/recipes/

★★★

Contains easy-to-make and inexpensive recipes collected by German chemists and physicists. Recipes are available in both English and German. Includes a metric conversion chart.

Cookbooks Online Recipe Database

http://www.cook-books.com/reg.htm

★★★★★

Cookbooks Online recipe database is the largest recipe database on the Web. If you're looking for recipes, this is the place to start!

A
B
C
D
E
F
G
H
I
J
K
L
M
N
O
P
Q
R
S
T
U
V
W
X
Y
Z

Cooking.com

http://www.cooking.com

$

★★★★★

The weekly menu planner and menu of the day are two of the most helpful items on this site, which also offers every conceivable cooking utensil and piece of equipment for sale to help you cook up those meals.

The Cooking Couple Clubhouse

http://www.cookingcouple.com

★★★★

 Not for kids

Jump out of the frying pan and into the fire with the best-selling cooking couple on a website dedicated to food, romance, love, and lust.

Cooking Light

http://www.cookinglight.com/

★★★★

Not for kids

Learn how to cook and eat lighter meals. Includes a Cooking 101 tutorial, recipes for some tasty dishes, menu and meal planning guides, bulletin boards, surveys, and more. Excellent site includes fantastic pictures showing how a dish *should* look when it's ready to be served.

Cooks Online

http://www.cooksillustrated.com

★★★★★

Calling itself the "Consumer Reports of Cooking," this site does a good job of evaluating cookware and testing recipes for its members, who can also find cookbook reviews and helpful cooking tips.

Creole and Cajun Recipe Page

http://www.gumbopages.com/

★★★★

Mark Twain once said, "New Orleans food is as delicious as the less criminal forms of sin." He'd love this site. It features a comprehensive guide with recipes that distinguish the fine art of New Orleans Cajun and Creole cuisine. Also contains links to several online cookbooks and food-related sites.

Culinary Schools

http://www.starchefs.com/community/html/schools.shtml

★★★

Lists culinary schools in the United States and describes programs offered.

Culinary World Tour

http://gumbopages.com/world-food.html

★★★

Provides a nice representation of international recipes ranging from African Bobotie, a curried bread custard with lamb, to Kloi Buad Chi, a dessert from Thailand.

Dinner Co-Op

http://dinnercoop.cs.cmu.edu/dinnercoop/

★★★★

This site offers more than your run-of-the mill food-related site. More than 750 recipes plus 3,000 links to sites concentrating on recipes, culinary education, restaurant reviews, and online food stores. Well organized and useful—definitely worth a bookmark!

Dole's Healthy Foods & Recipes

http://www.dole.com/health/index.jsp

★★★★

All

Encourages kids to prepare their own healthy snacks with fruits and vegetables. Includes recipes for fruity breakfast parfait, ABC vegetable soup, crispy winter vegetable salad, and more than a dozen other healthy snacks and meals.

Best Epicurious

http://eat.epicurious.com/

$

★★★★★

Boasting a 16,000 plus collection of recipes for meals and cocktails from *Bon Appetit* and *Gourmet* magazines, this site acts as your electronic cookbook. Search for a specific recipe or search by food, such as asparagus or chicken. Site also features a restaurant guide, travel guide, and online shopping. Advertises food, wine, cooking, and travel products. And if that's not enough, the site's design and tantalizing photos will almost make your mouth water!

Fabulous Foods

http://www.fabulousfoods.com

★★★★★

Looking for some low-carb recipes to help you lose some weight? This site has several sets of recipes for people watching what they eat. It also offers primers on types of food, describing how to prepare it and providing recipes to follow. Meet celebrity chefs and pick up some special-occasion menus.

FatFree Vegetarian Mailing List Archive

http://www.fatfree.com/

★★★

Contains 4,667 fat-free and low-fat vegetarian recipes that can be accessed from a searchable archive. Also contains links to other low-fat/vegetarian-oriented Internet resources.

Filipino Cuisine

http://www.tribo.org/filipinofood/

★★★★

Provides information on Filipino restaurants, cookbooks, recipes, and substitutions for hard-to-find ingredients. Also contains links to other Filipino cooking–related sites.

Food Network

http://www.foodnetwork.com/

★★★★★

Home of Iron Chef America, Boy Meets Grill, and dozens of other gourmet cooking, food, and drink shows, the Food Network provides culinary information and resources for those who truly enjoy and appreciate fine cuisine.

Food Resource

http://www.orst.edu/food-resource/food.html

★★★

A comprehensive index of food-related sites. Choose from a plethora of links to recipe sites, restaurant databases, colorful images of food, sites on culinary education, and anything else even remotely connected with food.

Food TV Network

http://www.foodtv.com/

★★★★★

Incredible collection of cooking information and resources, including the Cooking 101 tutorial, recipe and menu search, links to celebrity chefs (including Emeril), live chats, video clips, and much more.

Friends and Partners Kitchen

http://www.friends-partners.org/friends/life/kitchen/index.html

★★★

 All

Offers American, Russian, and international cuisine recipes. Also supports an international chef chat room for culinary tips and treasures. Contains links to other online cookbooks and an area just for kids.

FYNet's Collection of Malaysian Recipes

http://ucsee.eecs.berkeley.edu/~soh/recipe.html

★★★

Looking to try something a little different? Try this site, which contains links to four Internet recipe sources of Malaysian cuisine.

Kosher Express

http://www.koshercooking.com/

★★★

A generous collection of Kosher recipes for Passover. Also contains links to Usenet Kosher recipe archives.

Mama's Cookbook

http://www.eat.com/

★★★★★

 All

A graphics-rich collection of Italian-style recipes using Ragu products. Contains a pasta and cooking glossary for those just starting to cook.

A
B
C
D
E
F
G
H
I
J
K
L
M
N
O
P
Q
R
S
T
U
V
W
X
Y
Z

Medieval/Renaissance Food Home Page

http://www.pbm.com/~lindahl/food.html

★★★

Offers references and recipes for anyone who wants to make a medieval feast or sample medieval cooking just for one's self. Includes references for European and Islamic dishes.

Mushroom Recipes

http://www.mushroomfest.com/recipes.htm

★★★★

Excellent collection of mushroom facts and recipes. Find out how mushrooms grow and how to handle mushrooms properly. Explains mushroom varieties and basic preparation of mushrooms. Includes a mushroom recipe of the month, recipes for mushroom appetizers, and nutritional information.

National Pork Producer's Council

http://www.nppc.org/

★★★★

Find out all there is to know about "the other white meat," including industry facts, health statistics, and pig facts.

New England Lobster

http://www.877givelobster.com

★★★★

Offers fresh lobster, guaranteed overnight delivery. Provides online ordering through a secure server. Be sure to check out the extensive indexed collection of seafood recipes.

Pasta Home Page

http://www.ilovepasta.org/

★★★★

Answers to frequently asked questions about pasta, information about the National Pasta Association and its brands, pasta nutritional information, information about various pasta shapes and which sauces to use them with, and several pasta recipes.

Pedro's Kitchen

http://www.toucansolutions.com/pedro/

★★★

A collection of authentic Brazilian recipes from a self-proclaimed Renaissance man.

Prevention.com

http://www.prevention.com

★★★★

From *Prevention*'s Healthy Ideas; includes nutrition news and a "healthy" collection of recipes. When you get to Prevention.com's home page, click the Food & Nutrition tab.

Recipe Archive Index

http://www.cs.cmu.edu/~mjw/recipes/

★★★

A master recipe archive ranging from crock pot recipes to ethnic dishes collected by Amy Gale. Hundreds of recipes in dozens of categories.

Rhubarb Compendium

http://www.rhubarbinfo.com

★★★

The history and description of rhubarb; how to grow, harvest, store, and use rhubarb; tons of rhubarb recipes; and a rhubarb photo gallery.

Stuart's Chinese Recipes

http://www.dcs.gla.ac.uk/~blairsa/Chinese_Recipes.html

★★★★

An impressive collection of Chinese food recipes gathered from submissions by visitors of the site. Visitors are encouraged to add their Chinese culinary wisdom to the present collection.

TexMex

http://www.texmex.net/Rotel/main.htm

★★★

Provides a collection of traditional TexMex recipes. A good foundation of dishes sure to please the palate suited for spicy food.

Top Secret Recipes

http://www.topsecretrecipes.com/

Top Secret Recipes on the Web is the world's only website that brings you original custom recipes that have been created from scratch in the test kitchen of the guy who has devoted the past decade to kitchen cloning. Links to online shopping.

Tuscany Italian Cooking

http://www.umberto.com/

From Umberto's Kitchen. Italian cuisine is so popular because it is accompanied by lots of hospitality, fun, wine, and people. The site includes a cookbook and recipe of the month.

Williams-Sonoma

http://www.williams-sonoma.com

★★★★★

Well-stocked online store for serious chefs and gourmets features cookware, dinnerware, cutlery, electronic appliances, and much more. The site also features gift ideas, recipes, and wedding gift registries.

A
B
C
D
E
F
G
H
I
J

Q
R
S
T
U
V
W
X
Y
Z

A B C D E F G H I J K L M N O P Q R S T U V W X Y Z

CRAFTS AND HOBBIES

Arts and Crafts Society

http://www.arts-crafts.com/

★★★★

In the spirit of the societies created during the early twentieth century in response to the Arts & Crafts Movement, this site has been created to provide an online "home" for the present-day Arts & Crafts Movement community. If you aren't sure what the Arts & Crafts Movement is/was, check out the Archives for more information. Links to artisans and publications.

Aunt Annie's Crafts

http://www.auntannie.com/

★★★★

Takes the craft how-to book one step further by putting it on the Web and taking advantage of the flexibility that the Internet offers. New craft projects every week.

Candle Projects

http://members.iinet.net.au/~campbell1/projects.htm

★★★

This page has many project ideas, including water balloon candles, fruit candles, and many more.

Children's Crafts Recipes

http://members.aol.com/MISSolgita/recipies.html

★★★

 All

Recipes for different kinds of dough, paint, silly putty, and even ice cream! A little messy, but fun.

Craft Fairs Online

http://www.craftsfaironline.com/

★★★★

Craft-y people will be delighted to see so many links—to artists, fairs, supplies, publications, newsgroups, software, and more.

Craft Ideas.com

http://www.craftideas.com/

★★★

Get craft project ideas here, as well as access to craft supplies. You'll also find auctions of popular crafting, stitching, and painting supplies, books, and magazines here, through Amazon.com.

Do-It-Yourself Network

http://www.diynet.com

★★★★★

Huge collection of projects complete with step-by-step instructions for the do-it-yourselfer. Projects include everything from creating your own party favors to weatherproofing your home. If you're handy around the house or you just enjoy doing creative projects on your own, you'll find plenty to keep you busy.

Joseph Wu's Origami Page

http://www.origami.as/

★★★★★

This site features the origami art of Joseph Wu, along with links to sites where you can find other origami creations and instructions. Crisp, clear photos of some of these amazing creations will inspire awe in some visitors and the desire to create in others.

Mother's Home

http://www.mothers-home.com/

★★★

 All

A virtual home with several rooms for creative activities and crafts. Each room is packed with links that direct your browser to other sites on the Web. Some fun activity ideas just for kids.

ReadyMade

http://www.readymademag.com/

$

★★★★★

This site is "for people who like to make stuff." Here you can find articles from the magazine, along with a store where you can buy plans and kits for many of the projects. ReadyMade can show you how to make everything from posters to your own modular dwelling! Subscribe online, sample the current issue, dig through the archives, read and post messages in the forums, and much more. When you're ready make something with your own two hands, visit ReadyMade.

HOBBY SHOPS AND CRAFT STORES

A2Z Hobbies

http://www.a2zhobbies.com/

$

★★★★

Find all the kits and supplies you need to fuel your enthusiasm for remote-controlled airplanes, model rocketry, pine cars, plastic models, and model trains. You won't find candles, lace, or floral arrangements at this shop.

A.C. Moore Home Page

http://www.acmoore.com

★★★

 All

Site of A.C. Moore, an arts, crafts, and floral shop. The site features a store locator, handy information about individual stores, projects to dig into, a Kids Club for fun, and a Teachers Club offering discounts to teachers. Features some great craft ideas just for kids, too.

Art Glass World

http://www.artglassworld.com/

★★★★

A searchable site specializing in stained art and art glass. See visitors' glass artwork or display your own at the Visitors Gallery. Grab some free patterns, order stained-glass books, find a list of suppliers, join a live chat, locate retail stores, discover what's new in glass art, peruse glass art magazines, and dig into the Q&A section.

Basketpatterns.com

http://www.basketpatterns.com/

★★★

Using an online shopping-cart system, you can purchase basket patterns, as well as basket-weaving tools, accessories, and books. You can also order finished baskets. The site also supplies some basketry-related links.

Crafts Etc!

http://www.craftsetc.com/

★★★★

Find the kits and supplies you need for your arts and crafts projects and order them online.

eHobbies

http://www.ehobbies.com

$

★★★★

Looking to develop a hobby? You'll find plenty of ideas, expert advice, and product information to get you in the right direction. There are also contests and products to order.

A B C D E F G H I J K L M N O P Q R S T U V W X Y Z

A
B
C
D
E
F
G
H
I
J
K
L
M
N
O
P
Q
R
S
T
U
V
W
X
Y
Z

 Fabri-Centers

http://www.joann.com/

⑤

★★★★★

Site for Jo-Ann, ClothWorld, and New York Fabrics and Crafts stores. Find your local store, enter a drawing, subscribe to the store newsletter, visit the investor relations page, find out about in-store specials, or post a message in Message Central to ask questions or share tips. Best of all, visit the creative center for loads of crafts and sewing ideas and information. This one-stop kiosk for everything related to fabrics and crafts is an easy choice for the Best of the Best award.

Hobby Lobby Home Page

http://www.hobbylobby.com/

★★★

 All

Hobby Lobby's searchable Internet catalog is a good way to get details on the products you're interested in or just browse for ideas. You'll find lots of other things to check out, including weekly specials, television goings-on, craft projects, store locations and information, affiliated companies, and visitors' correspondence. You can even print an Internet coupon and take it to the store on your next visit or shop online at Hobby Lobby's affiliate store, Crafts Etc!

HOBBYLINC

http://www.hobbylinc.com/

⑤

★★★★★

 9-13

A full resource of hobby supplies—more than 10,000 items available. View an extensive graphical catalog and take advantage of links, hints for hobbyists, biweekly specials, and educational information about various hobbies. Place or check the status of your order. Online gift certificates available for gift-giving.

Michael's: The Arts and Crafts Store

http://www.michaels.com

★★★★★

 All

At this site, you can get craft tips and new project ideas, find out about upcoming store activities, have fun on the Kids Club pages, join in the online activities and interactive crafts, find the Michael's store nearest you, or even find investor information. Kids Club features activities, crafts, events, and games that appeal to younger kids.

R/C Web Directory

http://www.towerhobbies.com/rcweb.html

⑤

★★★

For radio-controlled vehicles and aircraft enthusiasts. This site offers kit sales, tips, and advice.

Active Videos

http://www.activevideos.com/

★★★

 All

Huge collection of dance and exercise videos. Dance videos available for all types of dancing, including ballet, ballroom dancing, belly dancing, clogging, exotic dancing, and tap dancing. Click the Kids Dance & Exercise link to access a selection for younger dancers.

C.L.O.G.

http://www.clog.org/

★★★

Home of the National Clogging Association, this site features information about the Association and its conventions, national competitions, lists of certified instructors, and more. Not much for the general public about clogging, but cloggers and clogging instructors will find plenty.

Related Sites
http://members.aol.com/mdevin/clogtext.html
http://members.tripod.com/~clogging/index.html
http://www.texas-clogging.com/

Dance Art

http://www.danceart.com

★★★★

14-18

Combining art and dance news and education, Dance Art is geared to lovers of art and dance, as well as teachers and parents. Hear about interesting productions, read about upcoming exhibits and competitions, and stay in touch with fellow aficionados. Message boards for girl dancers are rated PG-13. Shop link takes you to a store that apparently lets you shop online, but when I visited it, the store had no products.

Dance Jump

http://artworks.qtime.com/dance/

★★★★

Find links to every kind of performance dancing you can imagine, as well as links to dance performers, magazines, institutions, art, and schools.

Dance Magazine

http://www.dancemagazine.com/

★★★★

Highlights of the current print issue of *Dance Magazine*, plus links, reviews, and editorials.

Dance Online

http://www.danceonline.com

★★★

Check news and reviews of NYC performances at Dance Online, which also offers Web versions of performances and feature articles.

A
B
C
D
E
F
G
H
I
J
K
L
M
N
O
P
Q
R
S
T
U
V
W
X
Y
Z

Dance Pages

http://www.dancepages.com

★★★

This dance site provides a variety of resources for dancers covering everything from dance techniques and tips to identifying and treating eating disorders in dancers. The site also contains a motivational column and advice from dancers making a living in the dance world.

Dance Spirit

http://www.dancespirit.com

★★★

Find out "what's up in dance," use the dance directory, learn about fundraising, and pick up some dance pointers. Developed by the publishers of *Dance Spirit* magazine.

Dance Teacher Magazine

http://www.dance-teacher.com/

★★★★

Samples from the current issue, plus a library of back issues to peruse and writers' guidelines for article submissions. A great resource for any dance instructor.

Related Sites
http://www.linedancefun.com/
http://www.bacds.org/

Dancer Online

http://www.danceronline.com

★★★

Internet home of *Dancer* magazine, this site provides access for subscribers to articles and archives covering everything from fashion to yoga. Sign up for a free subscription to check out what this site has to offer. Shop at the Dancer Mall, where you can find links to several online dance stores. Links to other dance sites are also available here.

Dancer's Delight

http://www.msu.edu/user/okumurak/

★★★

All about hip-hop and house dancing. Contains descriptions, history, and pictures of different styles of dancing such as B-boying (break dancing), locking, popping, house, hip-hop, and capoeira. Discusses famous dancers and the international dancing scene as well.

Dancing Deep in the Heart of Texas

http://members.aol.com/CactusStar/home.htm

★★★★

Covers many issues related to square dancing and country-western dancing in Texas and is hosted by two instructor/dancers. Definitions of square dancing, related sites, good nightclubs in Texas, and top ten line dances of the week are just a few of the features at this site.

Irish Set Dancing in Milwaukee

http://www.c7r.com/setdance/index.html

★★★

This site explains set dancing and its background and history. Find special events, instructors, and dance studios in Milwaukee that teach set dancing.

Latin Music Online

http://www.lamusica.com/

★★★

Learn about Latin dancing and music, including club, concert, and tour guides for the United States and Europe. Includes resources to find dance classes, books, radio, and TV shows. Covers Latin music and dancing in the news and provides live chat areas. Links to Amazon.com for online shopping.

Luna Kids Dance Programs

http://www.lunakidsdance.com/

★★★

 All

Luna Kids Dance offers programs to teach young children how to express themselves through dance. Visit this site to learn more about the programs available for kids. This site is designed more for teachers and parents, but kids can check out what the programs have to offer for them.

Pow Wow Dancing

http://www.powwows.com/

★★★

Learn about this Native American form of dancing in all its various forms. Learn about the etiquette, the instruments (drums), and the songs used in Pow Wow dancing as well. Includes calendar of events, too.

Shapiro and Smith Dance Company

http://shapiroandsmithdance.org/

★★★

Learn all about this New York City–based dance company that specializes in athletic-oriented artistic dance. The site includes a newsletter, reviews, gallery, and schedule of performances. The company is composed of seven members.

 Best **Voice of Dance**

http://www.voiceofdance.org

$

★★★★★

Providing "the latest on news, events, and just plain fun stuff," this site has it all. From learning a new dance step to finding out about upcoming performances of virtually any major dance organization, staying current with dance news, reading reviews and commentary, and purchasing dance products, you'll find it here.

BALLET

100 Common Ballet Terms Defined

http://www.panix.com/~twp/dance/dicty.htm

★★★

If you're learning ballet, but your dance instructor seems to be speaking a foreign language, check out this ballet dictionary for a list of terms and definitions.

American Ballet Theatre

http://www.abt.org/

★★★★

An information site for this touring classical dance company. Includes performance schedules, photos, and information about the ballets performed and the dancers in the company.

ballet.co

http://www.ballet.co.uk/

★★★★★

The most comprehensive ballet website, this site features information and resources on all things related to ballet and dance in the United Kingdom and throughout the world. The Magazine section is updated monthly and features the latest reviews, interviews, articles on the history of ballet, and regular columns by choreographers Christopher Hampson and Cathy Marston. You can also access articles from past issues of the magazine. The Updates area keeps you abreast of the latest happenings in the world of ballet, and the Postings page lets you communicate with other ballet enthusiasts. You can also register for a free weekly newsletter.

CyberDance: Ballet on the Web

http://www.cyberdance.org/

★★★★

A collection of more than 3,500 links to dance-related websites (classical ballet and modern dance). Also features links to stores on the Web that carry dancewear, jewelry, and other accessories.

New York City Ballet

http://www.nycballet.com

★★★★★

You'll find a fun take on ballet through trivia questions and games at the NYC Ballet site, which also features the standard information on getting tickets, planning trips to performances, and buying NYC Ballet merchandise. You can also read about the history of the organization and catch up on troupe members.

A
B
C
D
E
F
G
H
I
J
K
L
M
N
O
P
Q
R
S
T
U
V
W
X
Y
Z

San Francisco Ballet

http://www.sfballet.org

★★★★

Find out about the upcoming repertory season of the SF Ballet. Also, discover opportunities to study dance with the dancers, learn how to support the organization, and get tickets to performances.

BALLROOM DANCING

Ballroom Dancers.com

http://www.ballroomdancers.com/

★★★

Learn dances from the waltz to the rumba at this site. You can purchase videos and CDs here and can also "try before you buy" by listening to the music before ordering it.

The Ballroom Dancing Pages

http://www.quasarvideo.co.uk/new/

★★★★

Includes information about the Blackpool dance festival, variations of ballroom dancing (modern versus Latin American), and links to other ballroom dancing sites. You can order videos and CDs on this site as well.

Dance Directory–Ballroom

http://www.sapphireswan.com/dance/ballroom.htm

★★★

Search links organized by type of dance on this large site devoted to all kinds of dance. Leans toward ballroom dance.

DanceTV

http://www.dancetv.com

★★★

Learn to ballroom dance online with the Ballroom Dance Group's free online dance tutorials. Videos and CDs also available.

History of Modern Ballroom Dancing

http://linus.socs.uts.edu.au/~don/pubs/modern.html

★★★

Read about the origins of ballroom dancing while learning the appropriate hand and feet placement for each of the five ballroom dances.

Much Ado About Ballroom Dancing

http://www.outdancing.com/Ballroom/

★★★

You'll find pointers on learning ballroom dance, choosing shoes, finding dance music, following proper dance etiquette, and more. Click Ask a Dance Question to find answers to commonly asked questions.

DARTS

American Darts Organization

http://www.cyberdarts.com

★★★

This is the official website of the American Darts Organization, which was incorporated in 1975. General information, tournament rules and calendar, bylaws, and member list are all available here.

Crow's Dart Page

http://www.crowsdarts.com/

★★★★

Tremendous site! Covers the basics, equipment, strategy, tips and articles, links, stuff for your league, tournament information, dart stuff, dart chat rooms, dart graphics and cartoons, and more. The site might be a bit out of date when you visit because the creator is moving to Belgium, but he promises to update the site after he gets settled in.

Cyber/Darts

http://www.cyberdarts.com/

★★★★

A treasure trove of information about rules, places to play, tournaments, and organizations related to darts all in one place. A great starting place to learn more about darts.

Dartbase.com

http://www.dartbase.com/

★★★

A simple guide to all the basics of darts—from rules to equipment—as well as a place to chat with fellow dart enthusiasts.

Best Darts Directory

http://dartplayer.net/

★★★★★

This is a great site for everything darts. Here, you'll find information and links to everything you ever wanted to know about the game of darts. Meet other dart players from around the world and participate in online discussions and chats. Find places that are dart-friendly near you. An easily accessible layout combined with comprehensive links make this an easy choice for Best of the Best.

Smilie Darts

http://www.smiliegames.com/darts/

★★★★★

👥 9-13

Pick a single or multi-player game and enjoy an online game of darts. You can get help on how to play and see who are the best players.

World Darts Federation

www.dartswdf.com

★★★★

Fifty-five countries are represented on this site, which is the home of the World Darts Federation. Learn the rules and regulations of the game, check out the various tournaments, check out the history pages, and access dozens of links to various dart organizations from around the world.

Related Sites

http://www.dannyveghs.com/darts.htm

http://www.geocities.com/Colosseum/7114/

http://www.shootersedge.com/dartgame.html

DATING

2ofaKind Online

http://www.2ofakind.com/

★★★★

Not for kids

Soulmates and perfect pen pals connect by using more than 150 match options, match analysis reports, anonymous email, and free registration. This is not your typical personals service!

Checkmate

http://www.checkmate1.com/

$

★★★

Not for kids

Checkmate was the first Internet Background Resource designed especially for dating singles. Use a Social Security number and address, and you're on your way to checking your potential date's or mate's background.

Christian Matchmaker

http://www.christian.matchmaker.com/

★★★

Not for kids

Christian Matchmaker provides a place for Christians to find friends, mates, love, romance, and personals. Give yourself a half hour to fill out the registration/profile form. It is extensive.

DatingClub.com

http://datingclub.com/

★★★

Not for kids

Search the records of 1.5 million singles to try and find your match or post your profile and photo for free to have others check out you.

Dating Sites

http://www.datingsitesguide.com

★★★

Not for kids

To increase your odds of finding someone to date, search here for dating sites to visit. You'll find many sites with profiles of potential matches.

eCRUSH

http://www.ecrush.com/

★★★★

Not for kids

eCRUSH will send whomever you choose a confidential email telling them that someone has listed them and inviting them to register their own eCRUSHes. When they do, eCRUSH will see whether there's a match. If there is, you'll both be invited to the match lounge. If not…they'll never know who eCRUSHed them! Lots of fun stuff at this site!

Friendster

http://www.friendster.com/

$

★★★★★

Friendster combines the power of Internet dating with the concept of networking to help you find a suitable date. With Friendster, you create a profile and then invite your friends to create profiles and invite their friends to join. Assuming your friends join and add their friends, you create a network of prospective daters, to whom you are already related in some way. When you check a person's profile, you can also see what others have to say about him or her.

The Internet Personals

http://www.montagar.com/personals/

★★★

Not for kids

The Internet Personals puts your personal ad on the World Wide Web. You can search the ads to select only those people in your age range, area, and other personal preferences. Alternatively, you can place your own ad so others can find you. It's free to browse and place ads.

LoveCity

http://www.lovecity.com/

★★★★

Not for kids

This dating site has been online since 1996 and has been accessed more than 100 MILLION times. Basic design makes it easy to search for potential dates by state.

Best Match.com

http://www.match.com/

★★★★★

 Not for kids

Millions of singles worldwide have used the services of Match.com. Match.com strives to provide a safe and easy way for members to meet other quality singles on the Web. After you create your own unique profile, Match.com's superior matching technology provides you with instantaneous matches based on your pre-selected dating criteria. It's fast, convenient, and simple to use. Whether you're looking for an activity partner, a casual date, or a lifelong companion, Match.com just might have the person for you. You can search free, but if you want to contact members, you must register and pay about $11 to $25 per month, depending on the subscription package.

A B C D E F G H I J K L M N O P Q R S T U V W X Y Z

A
B
C
D
E
F
G
H
I
J
K
L
M
N
O
P
Q
R
S
T
U
V
W
X
Y
Z

DEAFNESS

Alexander Graham Bell Association for Deaf and Hard of Hearing

http://www.agbell.org/

★★★★★

Learn more about membership benefits of this international organization, which was established to serve parents of deaf and hard-of-hearing children. You'll find information on local chapters, publications, and financial assistance here.

ASL Access

http://www.aslaccess.org/

★★★★

Information about American Sign Language videos and how to order them is available here, as well as information about supporting the group's efforts to get more ASL videos into public libraries.

ASL Fingerspelling

http://www.where.com/scott.net/asl/

★★★★★

All

A great fingerspelling dictionary is available here, as well as a converter, which provides the correct fingerspelling for any word you type into the directory. You can also take a quiz to test your knowledge.

ASL Spelling Study: The Alphabet

http://www.duber.com/CALL/asl.html

★★★★

A very cool finger spelling training tool. You'll need Shockwave to start and a quick mouse finger to successfully complete the test.

Association of Late-Deafened Adults (ALDA)

http://www.alda.org/

★★★

Find out more about local chapters of this organization for people who gained language skills before becoming deaf and chat online with other ALDA members.

Captioned Media Program

http://www.cfv.org/

★★★★

CMP lends open captioned videos to members who complete an application form, enabling them to borrow videos on a wide variety of topics, for school, entertainment, or information.

Communications Unlimited

http://www.communltd.net/

$

★★★★

Communications Unlimited is a deaf-owned business that sells telecommunications (TTYs/TDDs—text telephones) equipment and notification alerts, amplified telephones, and assistive listening devices for the deaf and hard-of-hearing community. Search the online product catalog to find what you need.

DeafandHH.com

http://www.deafandhh.com/

★★★★

Extensive information and resource kiosk for health professionals, patients, and families dealing with hearing loss.

Deaf Chat

http://www.deafchat.com

★★★★

A chat community that brings together deaf, hard of hearing, and hearing individuals to discuss issues, share information, trade jokes, or talk about whatever's on their mind without fear of harassment. The Deaf Chat monitor makes sure of that.

deafkids.com

http://www.deafkids.com/

★★★

👥 All

Designed as a fun place for deaf and hard of hearing children, 17 years old and younger, to meet and chat.

Deaf Library

http://www.deaflibrary.org

★★★

Created by a Yale doctoral candidate in deaf culture, the deaf resource library is an online collection of reference material and links intended to educate and inform people about deaf cultures in the United States and Japan.

Deaf Resources

http://www.deafresources.com/

💲

★★★★★

This site offers a variety of home décor items and gifts using ASL as the theme. Baby blankets, for example, are embroidered with the ASL sign for "I love you." You'll find jewelry, jackets, videos, tote bags, and many other interesting items.

DeafZONE

http://www.deafzone.com/

★★★★★

Chat rooms, links, current events, and information on a wide variety of topics ranging from ADA laws to a workshop calendar. Find relay services and interpreters on this site. It even has a page with some hilarious jokes contributed by members. If you're deaf and you feel all alone, visit this site to tap the vast resources for the deaf and to make some friends along the way.

Gallaudet University, Washington, D.C.

http://www.gallaudet.edu/

★★★★

The world's only four-year university for deaf and hard of hearing undergraduate students.

GG Wiz's FingerSpeller

http://www.iwaynet.net/~ggwiz/asl/

★★★★★

This is a must-see site. Type a phrase and see it finger spelled, and test your reading skills with hidden phrases.

HandSpeak

http://www.handspeak.com/

★★★★

HandSpeak is the largest, fast-growing visual language dictionary online. Check out the baby and international signs, as well as ways to use sign language with animals. This is a very cool site with lots of good information and ideas.

Helen Keller National Center for Deaf-Blind Youth

http://www.helenkeller.org/national/

★★★★

The Helen Keller Center provides evaluation and training in vocational skills, adaptive technology and computer skills, orientation and mobility, independent living, communication, speech-language skills, creative arts, and fitness and leisure activities for deaf-blind youth. Learn more about the center and its work here.

[Best] National Association of the Deaf (NAD)

http://www.nad.org

★★★★★

👥 14-18

This national nonprofit organization provides grass-roots advocacy and empowerment for deaf individuals, captioned media, certification of American Sign Language professionals and interpreters, deafness-related information and publications, legal assistance, and policy development and research. The group also works to improve awareness of issues specific to deaf individuals. This site's straightforward presentation and excellent information combine to make it the best resource for hearing impaired people on the Web.

A B C D E F G H I J K L M N O P Q R S T U V W X Y Z

A
B
C
D
E
F
G
H
I
J
K
L
M
N
O
P
Q
R
S
T
U
V
W
X
Y
Z

National Institute on Deafness and Other Communication Disorders

http://www.nidcd.nih.gov/

★★★★★

Robust collection of information and resources for those suffering from hearing loss and for physicians and other health professionals. Includes links for information directed toward parents, children, and teachers. Plus Spanish translations of much of the material.

Oral Deaf Education

http://www.oraldeafed.org/

★★★★

Home to the Oral Deaf Education website. ODF's position is that deaf children can learn to talk by using the hearing technology options available today and the instruction provided at ODF schools. You will find specific information about these schools and their programs and services, and other information on oral deaf education in its library. Use the Search or the What's New page to find a specific topic.

Self Help for Hard of Hearing People (SHHH)

http://www.shhh.org/

★★★

Get answers to your questions about hearing loss, as well as information about this national organization.

SignWritingSite

http://www.signwriting.org

★★★★★

 All

Learn more about SignWriting, which enables people to read and learn using sign language, including taking lessons and joining in discussion forums about its use. There is a search engine and online library for further research and learning.

World Deaf Connect

http://www.deafconnect.com/

★★★

A listing of more than 16,500 email addresses of deaf persons to help you connect with others. Click on the map, go to the country you want, and get a list of emails for that area. Also search the World Deaf Directory for all sorts of businesses, services, schools, clubs, and so on.

Zoos Software

http://www.zoosware.com/

★★★★

Learning American Sign Language (ASL) is now easier with this software package for Palm devices. The software enables you to study the sign language alphabets and numbers at your own pace. After you're more familiar, you can type in the words, and PalmASL will show them to you using American Sign Language.

DEATH AND DYING

A
B
C
D
E
F
G
H
I
J
K
L
M
N
O
P
Q
R
S
T
U
V
W
X
Y
Z

Euthanasia World Directory

http://www.finalexit.org/

★★★

Includes pages on the Euthanasia Research and Guidance Organization; the World Federation of Right to Die Societies; and acts, laws, and news about euthanasia.

GriefNet

http://griefnet.org/

★★★★

GriefNet is an Internet community of persons dealing with grief, death, and major loss providing an integrated approach to online grief support. GriefNet is supervised by Cendra (ken'dra) Lynn, Ph.D., a clinical grief psychologist, death educator, and traumatologist.

Growth House

http://www.growthhouse.org/

★★★

Find resources for hospice and home care, palliative care, and pain management here, as well as plenty of information about end of life care, major illnesses, and grief and bereavement. Created as a link between hospice and end of life organizations, this site is a great resource.

Hospice Foundation of America

http://www.hospicefoundation.org/

⑤

★★★★★

Learn all about hospice and how it works, as well as read articles on grieving and loss. News archives contain information on death, and events such as teleconferences enable individuals to deal with the prospect of someone close to them dying.

 Hospice Net

http://www.hospicenet.org/

★★★★★

 All

Find a hospice location near you and learn more about the hospice concept at Hospice Net. Also, learn more about the role of caregiver, the bereavement process, and what patients can do to control how they die. A comprehensive site with information for just about everyone who faces losing a loved one. Though this site does not contain an area specifically for children, it does contain a Children area, where parents can learn how to communicate with their children about death and dying.

Hospice Web

http://www.hospiceweb.com/

★★★★

Find answers to your questions about hospice here and find a hospice near you through the hospice search engine. For questions not answered in the FAQ section, you can get an email response.

International Association for Near-Death Studies

http://www.iands.org/

★★★

For those with an interest in near-death experiences, those who have had near-death experiences, and those who research the phenomenon.

Internet Cremation Society

http://www.cremation.org/

★★★

Contains links to cremation providers and societies, scattering options, and U.S. and Canadian society participants. Features an online bookstore that links to Amazon.com for online transactions.

A B C D E F G H I J K L M N O P Q R S T U V W X Y Z

KIDSAID

`http://kidsaid.com/`

★★★

  All

This site provides a safe environment for kids and their parents to find information and ask questions about how to deal with the death of a loved one and how to help someone else deal with the grieving process. Features a question and answer area, a collection of games, poetry and stories submitted by visitors, and much more.

National Hospice and Palliative Care Organization

`http://www.nhpco.org`

★★★★

Gain an understanding of hospice and palliative care at this nonprofit organization's site, which provides a central contact point for end of life organizations nationwide. You can search for a hospice near you and stay current on end of life issues at this site.

Sociology of Death and Dying

`http://www.trinity.edu/~mkearl/death.html`

★★★

Contains pages dealing with the ways people die, death across cultures and time, death and religion, and moral debates.

Summum Mummification

`http://www.summum.org/mummification/`

★★★

Offers ideas on modern mummification, a philosophical examination of mummification, and pet memorials.

Related Site
`http://summum.kids.us/`

DEBT MANAGEMENT

A B C **D** E F G H I J K L M N O P Q R S T U V W X Y Z

123Debt.com
http://www.123debt.com/

★★★★★

Buried in debt? Then visit this site for the information and tools you need to dig yourself out and strengthen your financial position. This site features a host of credit and debt calculators, along with articles on credit cards, credit reports, credit scoring, debt consolidation, and refinancing.

About: Credit/Debt Management
http://personalcredit.about.com/

★★★★

Provides budget worksheets; debt-reduction advice; and information on family finances, refinancing, taxes, retirement planning, and everything else you need to know about personal finance. Links to online financial services for obtaining credit reports and financial counseling.

American Consumer Credit Counseling
http://www.consumercredit.com/

★★★★

A nonprofit organization dedicated to helping people who are having money trouble or considering bankruptcy regain control of their financial lives.

American Debt Management Services
http://www.americandebt.com/

★★★

The world's largest nonprofit debt management organization can help you become debt free! American Debt Management Services, Inc., debt consolidation is supported mainly by voluntary donations, contributions, and community grants. ADMS debt consolidation services has received a nonprofit status from the Internal Revenue Service. And ADMS debt consolidation is licensed under Article 12-C of the New York State Banking Department, one of only 12 companies to receive this license.

The Center for Debt Management
http://center4debtmanagement.com/

★★★★★

Free debt counseling through a nonprofit agency. Reduce your payments, lower your interest, and stop late fees. This well-organized and user-friendly site provides 500 pages of information about debt consolidation, lending sources, credit repair, legal resources, and lots more! Its focus is primarily consumer debt and money management. If you owe money and are having panic attacks trying to figure out how you're going to pay off your debts, this is the Best of the Best site to learn about your options.

Consumer Credit Counseling by Springboard
http://www.credit.org/

★★★★★

A helpful resource for people struggling to stay afloat financially. Individuals can get budget counseling and debt management assistance online, as well as access several tools for analyzing mortgage, car loan, and credit card debt.

A
B
C
D
E
F
G
H
I
J
K
L
M
N
O
P
Q
R
S
T
U
V
W
X
Y
Z

Credit411: Credit Reports and Credit Monitoring Online

http://www.credit411.com/

★★★★

For $34.95, you receive a credit report containing information from three agencies: Experian, Trans Union, and Equifax. Free customer advisory hotline assistance is included.

Debt Counselors of America

http://www.dca.org/

★★★★

DCA is a nonprofit organization, providing confidential help free or at a low cost to individuals seeking assistance. It is supported mainly by contributions from consumers, financial institutions, citizens, and merchants. As a DCA client or creditor, you can access and manage your account 24 hours a day on DCA's secure website. When you visit the site, you will find a huge amount of information.

Debt Laws

http://www.consumercreditcounseling.net/debt-laws.htm

★★★

What you and "they" can and cannot do, as set out in the Fair Debt Collection Practices Act.

Department of Veterans Affairs Debt Management

http://www.va.gov/debtman/

★★★

Information for people who owe debts to the Department of Veterans Affairs.

Dig Yourself out of Debt

http://denver.bcentral.com/denver/stories/1997/07/07/smallb4.html

★★★

Rid yourself of credit card debt and get your financial life back in order with help from this site.

InfoHQ Online CPA

http://www.infohq.com/CPA/OnlineCPA.htm

★★★

Original articles and advice on mortgages and refinancing, income taxes, and debt management. Personal financial questions are answered for a small fee.

iVillage Money: Personal Finance for Women

http://www.ivillage.com/money/

★★★★★

Free tax advice, three-step plan for eliminating debt, budgeting tutorial, divorce survival guide, investment basics, plus plenty of money-saving tips. Includes quizzes for testing your knowledge of personal finance topics, financial calculators, and Q&A sessions with financial experts. Supposedly directed toward women, but very useful for anyone who needs to take control of his or her personal finances.

Money Management International

http://www.moneymanagement.org/

★★★★★

When you're in debt and don't know where to turn, look to this site for help. Money Management International is a "nonprofit, community service organization that provides professional financial guidance, counseling, community-wide educational programs, debt management assistance, and debt consolidated loans to consumers." At this site, you will find money management advice, calculators, and other tools to help you manage your money and reduce your debt.

MSN Money: Savings and Debt Management

http://moneycentral.msn.com/smartbuy/home.asp

★★★★★

MSN Money features several tools to help you analyze your credit, manage your debts, and reign in your expenses. The Debt Evaluation calculator can help you determine if your ratio of debt to income is manageable or too high. You can also take a credit quiz to determine just how credit savvy you are.

National Foundation for Credit Counseling

http://www.nfcc.org/

★★★★

National organization that sets debt-reduction and credit counseling training standards and guidelines for companies that provide credit counseling to consumers. Consumers can find some information about reducing debt and managing their credit.

Related Site
http://www.debtadvice.org/

Ten Strategies to Reduce Your Debt

http://moneycentral.msn.com/articles/smartbuy/debt/1330.asp

★★★★

The average American pays more than $1,000 a year in interest fees to carry a balance of $8,500 on two to three bank credit cards, according to recent estimates. And credit card companies are tacking on new fees and raising interest rates that make it even more expensive. Learn 10 winning strategies for paying down your credit card debt.

U.S. National Debt Clock

http://www.brillig.com/debt_clock/

★★★★

The National Debt Clock keeps a running total of outstanding public debt as well as provides an explanation of the problem and links to sites that discuss the subject and propose solutions.

BANKRUPTCY

American Bankruptcy Institute

http://www.abiworld.org

★★★

ABI World offers up-to-date bankruptcy news, statistics, legislative updates, and information on how to file for bankruptcy.

Bankruptcy: An Overview

http://www.law.cornell.edu/topics/bankruptcy.html

★★★★

This introduction to bankruptcy is provided by Cornell Law School. Includes links to sources mentioned in the introduction and to other helpful bankruptcy sites on the Web.

Bankruptcy FAQ by Swiggart and Agin

http://www.lawtrove.com/bkfaq/

★★★

Find the answers to the most common questions about bankruptcy, such as what it means to file bankruptcy, what the various kinds are and how they affect your assets, and how long a bankruptcy stays on your records. A simple but informative site.

Related Site
http://www.lawtrove.com/bankruptcy/

Bankruptcy FAQs

http://www.nolo.com/encyclopedia/articles/dc/bankruptcy_faq.html

$ ★★★

When, if ever, is claiming bankruptcy the best policy? Find out here.

Bankruptcy Reform Act of 1994

http://www.creditinfocenter.com/bankruptcy/bankref9.shtml

$ ★★★

Complete information regarding the act and how it affects small businesses and consumers.

InterNet Bankruptcy Law Library

http://bankrupt.com/

★★★★

Provides information about various large companies in the United States that are facing bankruptcy or are currently having serious financial problems. Includes a library of books and periodicals related to struggling businesses, and features a list of local bankruptcy rules organized by state.

A B C D E F G H I J K L M N O P Q R S T U V W X Y Z

A
B
C
D
E
F
G
H
I
J
K
L
M
N
O
P
Q
R
S
T
U
V
W
X
Y
Z

CREDIT CARDS

American Express

http://www.americanexpress.com

★★★★★

Apply online for an American Express card, find out how the card can save you money, and learn about other financial services. This site provides features for individuals, small businesses, corporations, and merchants.

CardWeb

http://www.cardweb.com/cardtrak/

★★★★

Get the latest news on credit card deals and usage from this site, which has areas for consumers and business professionals in the credit industry.

Credit Card Goodies

http://www.creditcardgoodies.com/

★★★★★

If you like to reap rewards from using credit cards but you pay your balance in full when you receive your bill, visit this site to learn which credit cards can deliver you the greatest benefits. If you carry a balance, the best card for you is the card that delivers the lowest interest rate, which you can find through other debt management sites, such as 123Debt.com.

Getsmart.com

https://www.getsmart.com/

★★★

Shop mortgages, credit cards, loans, and savings products at this site, which provides up-to-date rates and information. You can also enroll in a service for paying your bills online.

MasterCard

http://www.mastercard.com

★★★★★

MasterCard's home page offers help in finding a card, emergency services for information on reporting a lost or stolen card, an ATM finder, a list of special offers, a consumer education area, and more. You can apply online at this site for a MasterCard credit card.

Visa

http://www.visa.com

★★★★★

Home of the International Visa site, where you can click a country to jump to the Visa site in that locale. Here, you can apply for a Visa credit card, obtain information about special deals, and even pick up a few tips on managing your credit. Designed for individuals, small businesses, corporations, and merchants. If you lose your card, you can also visit this site to obtain a toll-free number to call to report it missing.

DEPRESSION

Coping with Depression Fallout

http://www.depressionfallout.com/

★★★

Learning how to cope with someone who is depressed and how it affects you is the focus of this site, which is based heavily on the book, *How You Can Survive When They're Depressed*. Not a lot of information, but one of the few sites to recognize the impact depression has on others.

Depressed Anonymous

http://www.depressedanon.com/

★★★

Depressed Anonymous was formed to provide therapeutic resources for depressed individuals of all ages. Check out the newsletter for mental health professionals and depressed or recovering individuals. Practice the 12-step program to recovery.

Depression-net

http://www.depression-net.com/

★★★

Learn how common depression is, what you can do about it, and what typical treatments are. For both medical professionals and the general public.

Depression Is an Illness, Not a State of Mind

http://www.geocities.com/HotSprings/Villa/5712/

★★★

For those under age 30. Personal experiences, support groups, suggestions for what to do if you have depression, questions and answers, help in choosing therapy.

Dr. Ivan's Depression Central

http://www.psycom.net/depression.central.html

★★★★

Mood disorders information site, with links both on- and offsite. If you have a question about depression or any related disorder, you will probably find the answer here.

Best National Depressive and Manic-Depressive Association

http://www.ndmda.org/

★★★★★

Find information about clinical depression, dysthymic disorder, major depression, bipolar disorder, treatments, as well as self-help resources online. Read general articles about depression and other mood disorders, find a local support group, or research a specific topic. You can also buy books from the online store. Whether you're suffering from clinical depression or have a loved one who suffers from a serious psychiatric disorder, this is the best place to start your research.

National Institute of Mental Health: Depression

http://www.nimh.nih.gov/HealthInformation/Depressionmenu.cfm

★★★★★

9-13

Read the National Institute of Mental Health (NIMH) brochure on depression and how to deal with it. This brochure provides descriptions of and treatments for major depression, dysthymia, and bipolar disorder (manic depression) for both the depressed person and those around him or her. This site also provides links to additional resources and to a special area for kids.

A B C D E F G H I J K L M N O P Q R S T U V W X Y Z

A
B
C
D
E
F
G
H
I
J
K
L
M
N
O
P
Q
R
S
T
U
V
W
X
Y
Z

Pendulum Resources: The Bipolar Disorder Port

http://www.pendulum.org/

★★★★★

A departure point for learning everything you need to know about bipolar disorder (manic depression). Find out about the diagnostic criteria for bipolar disorder, the latest medications and treatments, and ongoing studies. Includes links to other sites, books, articles, and even some jokes.

Psychology Information Online

http://www.psychologyinfo.com/depression/

★★★★

Plenty of information about the symptoms of depression, causes, treatments, as well as descriptions of the many types of depression. Also, find out how common it is in various groups, such as in women and teenagers.

SUICIDE PREVENTION

@Health Suicide Newsletter

http://www.athealth.com/Practitioner/Newsletter/FPN_3_14.html

★★★

Resources for mental health professionals, patients, and families about early detection of depression and suicide prevention.

AFSP

http://www.afsp.org/

★★★★

The American Foundation for Suicide Prevention funds research, education, and treatment programs. The site includes such categories as Depression, Survivor Support, and Assisted Suicide.

Before You Kill Yourself

http://www.glyphmedia.com/host/darklight/suicide.htm

★★★

Read what Renee Lucero, a psychiatric nurse, would have to say to anyone contemplating suicide, given the opportunity. Appears as reprinted in "Dear Ann Landers," December 12, 1995.

Befrienders International

http://www.befrienders.org/

★★★

Locate one of the 350 Befrienders centers worldwide providing a sympathetic ear and suicide intervention based on listening therapy. Articles on helping a suicidal friend or family member, warning signs of suicide, suicide statistics, and more.

Community Lifelines

http://www3.sympatico.ca/masecard/

★★★★

Online brochures cover such issues as dealing with suicidal thoughts, helping a depressed person, and coping with grief in the aftermath.

Covenant House

http://www.covenanthouse.org/nineline/kid.html

★★★

9-13

Young people can contact the telephone advice line and locate help centers across the country, and parents can also get assistance.

Depression and Suicide Help Links

http://www.terraworld.net/npd/suicidelinks.htm

★★★

Provides links to resources, organizations, and medical information.

Don't Quit

http://www.lollie.com/dontquit.html

★★★

Encouragement to keep going even when you feel like quitting. Worth printing out and rereading each time you feel like you can't go on.

Preventing Adolescent Suicide

http://www.ace-network.com/whatsnew.htm

★★★

Explore the options for school and community programs designed to identify and help youth, from America's Continuing Education Network.

Preventing Teen Suicide

http://www.aap.org/advocacy/childhealthmonth/
prevteensuicide.htm

Created by the American Academy of Pediatrics, this article describes some of the early warning signs of teenagers at risk and tells how to approach the topic when discussing it with teenagers.

Rainbows of Hope

http://enchantedwings.freeservers.com/suicide.html

 Not for kids

Collection of links to other sites that provide information on depression, suicide, self-harm, abuse, eating disorders, and other topics that deal with the darker side of human existence.

SAVE: Suicide Help

http://www.save.org/

Practical advice for dealing with suicidal feelings, helping someone who is suicidal, and dealing with the grief when someone close to you commits suicide. Hosted by Suicide Awareness Voices of Education (SAVE).

SFSP: Suicide Prevention

http://www.sfsuicide.org/

★★★★

Home of San Francisco Suicide Prevention, the oldest crisis hotline in America. Choose Suicide Facts and then click Myth or Fact Quiz for a series of statements and see how much you really know about spotting the warning signs for suicide. A 24-hour telephone crisis line is available.

Suicidal.com

http://suicidal.com/

★★★★

Offers depression and suicide FAQs, information about prevention and care, treatment advice, poetry, and links on suicide and depression.

Suicide Information and Prevention

http://yellowribbon.org/suicide.html

Helpful information on how to prevent suicide.

Suicide Prevention Advocacy Network

http://www.spanusa.org/

★★★

Join the national campaign to reduce suicide rates. Find out how to be a community organizer and read the SPANUSA newsletter.

Suicide: Read This First

http://www.metanoia.org/suicide/

★★★★★

Addresses the causes behind suicidal thoughts and offers suggestions on how to overcome them. Links to sites from suicide prevention organizations are included.

Yellow Ribbon Suicide Prevention Program

http://www.yellowribbon.org/

★★★★★

 9-13

This site is for both parents and teens, but the program is designed for young people. It teaches teens how to recognize the symptoms of depression in their friends and gives them ideas what they can do to help their friends get the help they need.

A
B
C
D
E
F
G
H
I
J
K
L
M
N
O
P
Q
R
S
T
U
V
W
X
Y
Z

A
B
C
D
E
F
G
H
I
J
K
L
M
N
O
P
Q
R
S
T
U
V
W
X
Y
Z

DIABETES

[Best] ADA

http://www.diabetes.org/

★★★★★

The American Diabetes Association website offers the latest information on diabetes and living with the disease. The American Diabetes Association is the nation's leading voluntary health organization supporting diabetes research, information, and advocacy. The association supports an affiliated office in every region of the country, providing services to more than 800 communities. If you or a loved one suffers from diabetes, make this Best of the Best site your first stop to learning more about the disease and available treatments. Also features an online bookstore.

ADA Recipe of the Day

http://www.diabetes.org/recipeoftheday.jsp

★★★

A recipe every day from the American Diabetes Association.

Children with Diabetes Recipes

http://www.childrenwithdiabetes.com/d_08_200.htm

★★★★

 All

Readers' favorite recipes with a special emphasis on recipes for children with diabetes. Each is on its own page so you can easily print a copy.

Children with Diabetes Online Community

http://www.childrenwithdiabetes.com/

★★★

 All

An online community for kids, families, and adults with diabetes, featuring message boards, chat rooms, and questions and answers from medical professionals.

Diabetes Insight

http://www.diabetes-insight.info/

★★★★

A wonderful site for those recently diagnosed with diabetes, as well as those who have been living with the disease. An email support group and online forum are just a couple of features of this comprehensive site.

Diabetes Interview World

http://www.diabetesworld.com/

★★★

Home page for *Diabetes Interview* newspaper, which features stories about issues that matter to those suffering with diabetes: "cutting-edge diabetes research, hard-hitting investigative reports, and illuminating features about how people with diabetes grapple with day-to-day problems." Features comics as well.

Diabetes Mall

http://www.diabetesnet.com

Ⓢ

★★★★

Find out about clinical trials in your area, as well as diabetes news, delicious recipes, and books on the topic of managing your diabetes. Lots of links to other diabetes sites, too.

Diabetes News

http://www.diabetesnews.com/

★★★

Provides the latest-breaking news about diabetes and related subjects as well as links of particular interest to diabetics.

Diabetic Gourmet Magazine

http://diabeticgourmet.com/

★★★★

Search the recipe archives of *Diabetic Gourmet Magazine* for all diabetic recipes. The site also provides a great resource for additional information on diabetes, including the Diabetes 101 tutorial, tips on health living and exercise, and forums where you can communicate with others who suffer from diabetes and related conditions.

Diabetic Testing Supplies by Mail: Diabetes Home Care

http://www.diabeteshomecare.com/

★★★★

A full line of diabetic testing supplies sent priority mail to your home, including blood glucose monitors, test strips, lancets and lancet devices, from several manufacturers. Shipping is always free, and you can order online or by calling the toll-free 800 line.

Gourmet Connection Network

http://gourmetconnection.com/

★★★★

Learn how to cook healthy meals, whether you suffer from diabetes or not. Diabetes headlines, cooking tips, and recipes.

Joslin Diabetes Center

http://www.joslin.harvard.edu/

$

★★★★★

Joslin is the only U.S. medical center dedicated solely to diabetes treatment, research, cure, and education. On its site, you'll find news, lifestyle and nutrition information, discussion groups, a directory of nationwide affiliates, and more.

Kids Learn About Diabetes

http://www.kidslearnaboutdiabetes.org/

★★★★★

All

This site, designed specifically for kids, begins with an explanation of diabetes and provides links to topics that address Complications, Testing, Shots, Diet, Balance, Activities, Feelings, and The Future. Also provides a place where kids can chat. Nicely designed and packed with excellent information.

Medical Alert Charms for Children

http://www.missbrooke.com/

$

★★★★

One of the few sources of medical IDs for children and teens.

National Institute of Diabetes & Digestive & Kidney Disorders

http://www.niddk.nih.gov/

★★★★

A component of the United States National Institutes of Health, this site is packed with information about diabetes and other major health issues. Under Health Information, click Diabetes to access Diabetes topics, research, publications, and additional resources.

Online Diabetes Resources

http://www.mendosa.com/faq.htm

★★★★

A comprehensive listing of diabetes resources on the Net, such as email mailing lists, Usenet newsgroups, organizations and charities, and much more.

A B C D E F G H I J K L M N O P Q R S T U V W X Y Z

DIET AND NUTRITION

American Dietetic Association

http://www.eatright.org/

★★★★

This site contains information about this organization and its efforts to promote good nutrition. You'll find nutrition resources, a searchable database of registered dietitians, home food safety information, publications for consumers and dietetic professionals, lots of links, and more.

American Health and Nutrition, Inc.

http://www.organictrading.com/

★★★

This site is a resource center for certified organic commodities. It provides product information, a list of distributors, and a certification overview. Products are available through distributors only—not to retailers or the public.

American Heart Association

http://www.americanheart.org/

★★★★★

Better food habits can help you reduce your risk for heart attack. This comprehensive site offers a healthful eating plan as a means for choosing the right foods to eat and preparing foods in a healthy way. One of the better sites for nutrition information. After opening the home page, click the Healthy Lifestyle link to access the nutrition page.

Arbor Nutrition Guide

http://www.arborcom.com/

★★★

Arbor Nutrition Guide features a search engine, articles on food science, a "Site of the Week," details on dietitians, special diets, clinical aspects of diets, journals and newsletters on the topic, articles on food and agriculture, and related links.

Ask the Dietitian

http://www.dietitian.com/

★★★★★

Ask the Dietitian is an advice column hosted by registered dietitian Joanne Larsen. Topics discussed range from nutrition and vitamin-related issues to eating disorders such as anorexia. Check out the Healthy Body Calculator to determine your target weight and nutritional and exercise needs.

Blonz Guide to Nutrition, Food, and Health Resources

http://blonz.com/

★★★★

Dr. Ed Blonz, a nutritionist and syndicated newspaper columnist, offers this collection of websites about food, nutrition, and health. Provides link to Amazon.com to purchase Dr. Blonz's books.

Center for Food Safety and Applied Nutrition

http://vm.cfsan.fda.gov/list.html

★★★

This FDA site describes cosmetics, food additives and pesticides, labeling, press releases, women's health, and much more. Also includes a seafood hotline.

Center for Science in the Public Interest

http://www.cspinet.org/

★★★★★

 All

The CSPI website features health-related newsletters, nutrition quizzes, updates on health news, and an archive of its reports and press releases. The page also includes links to other health-related sites. Kids should click the Kids Stuff link to go to an area designed specifically for the younger crowd.

Consumer Information Center: Food

http://www.pueblo.gsa.gov/food.htm

⑤

★★★

This consumer information catalog presents a series of free or low-cost publications. Topics include buying fresh produce and roasting a turkey.

DietSite.com

http://www.dietsite.com/

★★★★★

Excellent site provides general information on healthy diets. Nutrition topics for disease prevention, performance improvements in sports, nutrition facts, diet news, and alternative diets. Also features free diet and recipe analysis and tools for tracking your weight and exercise.

Dole 5 a Day

http://www.dole5aday.com/

★★★★★

 All

A graphics-rich site devoted to the health and nutrition benefits of fruits and vegetables. A fantastic educational tool for teachers and parents and a fun place for kids to learn about nutrition. Sponsored by the Dole Food Company.

eDiets

http://www.ediets.com/

★★★★★

eDiets has a goal of "building a global online diet, fitness, and motivation destination to provide consumers with solutions that help them realize life's full potential." With more than 1 million members since its inception in 1997, eDiets is well on its way to meeting its goal and helping visitors define and achieve their fitness goals.

Fast Food Facts

http://www.olen.com/food/

★★★★

This interactive food finder gives the nutritional breakdown on some fast foods. Users can type in the restaurant name and the menu item, and Fast Food Facts will go to work.

FDA Center for Food Safety and Applied Nutrition

http://www.mothernature.com/

★★★★

The Center for Food Safety and Applied Nutrition, known as CFSAN, is one of six centers that carry out the mission of the Food and Drug Administration (FDA)—to ensure the safety of foods, cosmetics, drugs, and other related products in the United States. Here, you can find information about the center and the issues it is addressing along with plenty of consumer information.

Feingold Association of the United States

http://www.feingold.org/

★★★★

This site offers information about the connection between diet and behavior. Get details on the Feingold nutrition program and take advantage of all the resources and links, too. Definitely worth investigating if you are dealing with a diagnosis of ADD, ADHD, or asthma.

A B C D E F G H I J K L M N O P Q R S T U V W X Y Z

A
B
C
D
E
F
G
H
I
J
K
L
M
N
O
P
Q
R
S
T
U
V
W
X
Y
Z

Food and Nutrition Library

http://www.lib.vt.edu/subjects/nutr/

★★★

Updated monthly, this site addresses issues in nutrition and food production. Links to dozens of databases and other resources on the Web.

The FOOD Museum

http://www.foodmuseum.com/

★★★

The FOOD Museum is a collection of artifacts, ideas, facts, and fun. Community, school, and commercial educational programs related to food are vitally informative and interesting. Arrange for a program to be presented or museum artifacts to be exhibited anywhere in the world.

Food Pyramid

http://schoolmeals.nal.usda.gov/

★★★

Click the pyramid and find out what to eat daily. Provides a nutritional breakdown of food groups and a guide to servings.

Food Safety, Nutrition, and Preparation

http://lancaster.unl.edu/food/index.htm

★★★★

University of Nebraska Cooperative Extension in Lancaster County brings you this site edited and updated by Alice Henneman, MS, RD & Extension Educator. This site contains a hefty collection of cooking tips, nutrition advice, and general nutrition information.

Healthfinder

http://www.healthfinder.gov/

★★★★★

 All

Browse this vast archive of health and nutrition information or search for a specific topic. If you have time for only one site, start here! Also features a site just for kids—click the KIDS link.

LifeClinic

http://www.lifeclinic.com/focus/nutrition/

★★★★★

Devoted to empowering individuals to manage their own health through nutrition, preventive care, and fitness, this site offers a wealth of information on healthy living. Visit the nutrition center to research vitamins, minerals, nutrients, and other diet-related topics. You can also track your exercise and nutrition online. Excellent site.

Macrobiotics Online

http://www.macrobiotics.org/

★★★

Find out about macrobiotics and the role of this diet in healing. Read case histories, browse through articles, get recipes, and even shop for organic products from the online catalog. This site also promotes the Kushi Institute's Way to Health Program.

Mayo Clinic Nutrition Center

http://www.mayohealth.org/home

★★★★★

Everything from quick breakfasts to elegant dinners, soups, sauces, and baked goods. Mayo Clinic registered dietitians take your recipes and make them healthier by reducing the calories, fat and salt—but not the taste.

Meals for You

http://www.mealsforyou.com/

★★★★★

Fabulous recipe site. Calculator enables you to customize recipes based on the number of servings. Nutrition-conscious visitors will especially like the fact that each recipe is accompanied by complete nutritional information. The site also contains special sections devoted to dietary exchange information and recipes grouped by nutrition content and popularity.

Mike's Calories and Fat Gram Chart

http://www.ntwrks.com/~mikev/

★★★

One of the Internet's best one-stop resources for diet, nutrition, and health information. This site has been given an award by *The Los Angeles Times*, recognizing its value to the paper's readership.

NutriBase

http://www.nutribase.com/

★★★★

If you're looking for a software diet and fitness manager for personal or family use, visit this site and take a look at the options NutriBase offers. The prices range from $24.95 to $2,495.00. The higher-priced software packages are oriented to professional/clinical use.

Nutrition Explorations

http://www.nutritionexplorations.org/

★★★★★

All

Maintained by the National Dairy Council, this fun site helps kids, teachers, parents, and families learn more about nutrition. Family Food Guide presents the food guide pyramid, recipes for families on the go, kids recipes, an ask-the-expert feature, and much more. Some excellent teaching tools for educators and a link to a special site just for kids.

NutritionFocus.com

http://nutritionfocus.com/

★★★★

A nutrition and wellness portal that aims to pull together everything you need to know about combining nutrition, vitamins, supplements, and exercise to be healthier.

 Nutrition.gov

http://www.nutrition.gov/

★★★★★

A new federal resource, this site provides easy access to all online federal government information on nutrition. Obtain government information on nutrition, healthy eating, physical activity, and food safety. Provides accurate scientific information on nutrition and dietary guidance. When you're ready to start eating a more nutritional diet, this Best of the Best site is the first place you should visit.

Prevention's Healthy Ideas

http://www.prevention.com

★★★★★

Contains news and information about nutrition, natural healing, weight loss, fitness techniques, tips on healthy cooking, and lifestyle-related articles from *Prevention* magazine.

Self Magazine

http://www.self.com/

★★★★

Home of *Self* magazine. Visitors to this site can calculate their body fat percentage, ideal weight, and daily nutritional requirements. Users can also create their own personalized diet plan and take a health risk assessment quiz. Tips on health and nutrition are also included, plus dozens of health-related articles and a food fact finder that displays the bad news on the fat content of thousands of popular foods.

Tufts University Nutrition Navigator

http://navigator.tufts.edu/

★★★★

Directory of nutrition sites organized by category, including Women, Men, Family Seniors, General Nutrition, and Health Professionals. Each listing in the directory contains a link to the site, a rating of the site, and a brief description of what the site has to offer.

A
B
C
D
E
F
G
H
I
J
K
L
M
N
O
P
Q
R
S
T
U
V
W
X
Y
Z

Yellow Pages

DINOSAURS

 Best **BBC Walking with Dinosaurs**

http://www.bbc.co.uk/dinosaurs/

★★★★★

👥 All

Excellent site features dinosaur chronology, fact files, articles and reports from the experts, dinosaur games and quizzes, and much more. Great place to learn about life on our planet during prehistoric times. Excellent graphics combined with comprehensive information make this an easy Best of the Best pick.

Dinosaur National Monument

http://dinosaur.areaparks.com/

★★★

The Dinosaur National Monument is located in northwest Colorado and northeast Utah, straddling the border of these states. About two thirds of the park is in Colorado. Dinosaur Park spans 210,000 acres, offering plenty of room for you to find solitude, view magnificent scenery, hike a wild landscape, and renew your relationship with nature. The Dinosaur Quarry Visitor Center is the area of the park where dinosaur bones can be seen.

Dinosauria

http://www.dinosauria.com

★★★★

👥 9-13

Dinosaur dictionaries, maps, and enthusiastic discussions among those experienced in dinosaur facts and lore as well as new fanatics. Lots of information, much of which is presented to help clear up misconceptions about dinosaurs.

Discovering Dinosaurs

http://dinosaurs.eb.com/dinosaurs/index2.html

★★★★★

👥 9-13

Discovering Dinosaurs explores our evolving conceptions of these extraordinary creatures. Trace the great dinosaur debate through time by traveling down through each color-coded theme. The historical exploration of not only the scientific discoveries and the dinosaurs themselves but also the interpretation of those discoveries put in chronological order teaches us about the evolution of the current scientific theories as well as the steps in the evolution of life on earth.

Dinosaurs in Hawaii

http://www.hcc.hawaii.edu/dinos/dinos.1.html

★★★

👥 9-13

Visit Honolulu Community College and check out its collection of dinosaur fossils.

Extinctions.com

http://www.extinctions.com/

💲

★★★★

👥 9-13

Huge collection of the most popular fossils for sale and show. Shop the Web store for related merchandise. Secure online ordering.

Field Museum of Natural History

http://www.fmnh.org/

★★★★★

 9-13

Internet home of the Field Museum of Natural History in Chicago, Illinois, this site features online versions of many of the exhibits along with information about the museum. While you're here, be sure to say hello to Sue, "the world's largest, most complete, and best preserved Tyrannosaurus rex."

The Lost World of Dinosaurs

http://www.id.iit.edu/~doe/alphadmo_07a/dinosaur.html

★★★★

 9-13

High school students in Bellevue, Washington, maintain this bulletin board for elementary students to post messages, ask questions, or make comments on any topic dealing with dinosaurs. Students are also asked to make submissions to the newsletter, *Prehistoric Post*. You'll also find an online dictionary of terms used on the website and links to other sites.

NMNH Dinosaur Home Page

http://www.nmnh.si.edu/paleo/dino/

★★★★★

 9-13

National Museum of Natural History dinosaurs. Learn about a dinosaur bone injury, view some "mummified" dinosaur skin impressions, learn about herbivore versus carnivore teeth, examine the brain cavity of a Triceratops, and much more.

Sue at the Field Museum

http://www.fmnh.org/sue/

★★★★★

9-13

Sue has her own website. Learn about the largest, most complete Tyrannosaurus rex, view an online image gallery, check out Sue's timeline, and find the answers to the most frequently asked questions.

Zoom Dinosaurs

http://www.zoomdinosaurs.com/

★★★★

9-13

Zoom Dinosaurs is a comprehensive online hypertext book about dinosaurs. It is designed for students of all ages and levels of comprehension. It has an easy-to-use structure that allows readers to start at a basic level on each topic and then to progress to much more advanced information as desired simply by clicking on links.

A
B
C
D
E
F
G
H
I
J
K
L
M
N
O
P
Q
R
S
T
U
V
W
X
Y
Z

A
B
C
D
E
F
G
H
I
J
K
L
M
N
O
P
Q
R
S
T
U
V
W
X
Y
Z

DIVORCE AND CUSTODY

Children's Rights Council

http://www.gocrc.com/

★★★★★

Site of Children's Rights Council (CRC), a national, nonprofit, tax-exempt children's rights organization based in Washington, D.C. Provides information about children's rights, legislation regarding children's rights, and data on the state and national levels.

DivorceBusting.com

http://www.weiner-davis.com/

★★★★

Before you file for divorce, visit Michele Weiner-Davis's DivorceBusting.com to learn how to put love back in your marriage. Information about Michele's books and seminars, plus some free advice from Michele herself.

Divorce Care Home Page

http://www.divorcecare.com/

★★★★

Site of the Divorce Care support group. Provides a list of Divorce Care support groups in your area; resources for self-help; and information on children and divorce, financial survival, and more. Links to the HelpCenter bookstore, where you can shop for books about divorce.

Divorce Online

http://www.divorceonline.com/

★★★

An electronic resource for people involved in divorce. Offers free articles and information on divorce-related topics and contains a professional referral section to help locate professional assistance near you. Also contains a FAQ section that applies to divorce.

Divorce Source

http://www.divorcesource.com/

★★★★

Check out state divorce laws, bulletin board forums, live chat rooms, article archives, family law links, divorce publications, and the Divorce Dictionary. To date, almost 5 million people have visited this site, which was established in 1997.

[Best] DivorceNet

http://www.divorcenet.com/

★★★★★

Contains FAQs with the most common questions pertaining to divorce and family law, an online newsletter and index, a state-by-state resource center, an interactive bulletin board, international and national laws pertaining to child abduction along with a link to the U.S. State Department, and more. Also contains helpful information regarding child custody and child support. Whether you're divorced, going through divorce proceedings, or are considering divorce, this site has the information you need in an easy-to-find format.

DivorceWizards

http://www.divorcewizards.com/

★★★★

Getting divorced has never been easier. At DivorceWizards, you can get divorced online, as long as it's an uncontested divorce. Just pick a desired divorce package and follow the onscreen instructions. The site also provides useful information on choosing the right type of divorce for you: paralegal, mediation, or litigation. Also features articles on how to protect yourself financially.

FamilyLaw.org

http://www.familylaw.org/

★★★★

Comprehensive list of links to other sites that primarily cover child-custody issues. Features family law code by state, a directory of lawyers, and thousands of articles relating to child custody cases.

SmartDivorce.com

http://www.smartdivorce.com/

★★★★

Home of Broken Heart Publishing, which specializes in books on divorce, relationships, and marriage-enhancement topics. Before, during, or after a divorce, visit this site to gather the information you need to make wise decisions and cope with situations over which you have no control. Scroll down the page to check out the Divorce HotTips Archives, where you can find great articles, such as Dirty Divorce Tricks.

Split-Up

http://www.splitup.com/

★★★★★

Features software for divorced individuals, those seeking divorce, and those currently living through divorce proceedings. Here, you can find divorce calculators, a divorce primer, coping tips, legal links, and financial advice. State links also provided.

CHILD SUPPORT

ACES: Association for Children for Enforcement of Support

http://www.childsupport-aces.org/

★★★

A nonprofit child support organization that works to improve child support enforcement, to educate about legal rights and remedies, and to promote public awareness about the plight of affected children.

Alliance for Noncustodial Parents Rights

http://www.ancpr.org/

★★★

Dedicated to preserving and promoting the civil and inalienable human rights of noncustodial parents.

American Coalition for Fathers and Children

http://www.acfc.org/

★★★★

The aim of this site is to educate fathers about their rights, help them avoid becoming deadbeat dads, and make sure all parties in a dispute are treated fairly. ACFC believes that "children need both parents."

Child Support Central

http://www.wwlia.org/

★★★

This site enables visitors to support payment advocacy and provides a list of professional and state resources that assist in child support collection and location of deadbeat parents. Also provides a list of the top 20 deadbeat parents for each state.

Child Support Enforcement (CSE)

http://www.supportkids.com/

★★★★

The nation's largest and most experienced private company helping parents collect court-ordered child support. Claims a 90% success rate.

Child Support Intervention

http://www.deadbeatparent.com/

★★★

CSI claims to be the only "true child support enforcement agency" in the world. With a success rate of more than 78%, CSI is recognized as the most aggressive, results-oriented child support agency in the world. No fees are required up-front.

A B C D E F G H I J K L M N O P Q R S T U V W X Y Z

A
B
C
D
E
F
G
H
I
J
K
L
M
N
O
P
Q
R
S
T
U
V
W
X
Y
Z

Child Support Law at freeadvice.com

http://freeadvice.com/law/547us.htm

★★★★

Find answers from top lawyers about child support, attorneys, and lawyers who can help you with a legal claim or problem in family law.

Federal Office of Child Support Enforcement

http://www.acf.dhhs.gov/programs/cse/

★★★★

Provides helpful information about the child support system, including basic child support program facts, newsletters and announcements, recent policy documents, and the opportunity to offer feedback. Be sure to visit the External Information link for information about child support guidelines specific to your state.

Mothers Against Fathers In Arrears (MAFIA)

http://www.mafia-usa.com/

★★★

This organization strives to draw the attention of Congress, state legislatures, and public agencies to the concerns of custodial parents. Includes a rogues gallery and a message board.

NCSEA: National Child Support Enforcement Association

http://www.ncsea.org/

★★★★

Brings together professionals from all aspects of the nation's child support program, including public and private sectors, state and local agencies, judges and court administrators, prosecutors and private attorneys. The goal is to protect the well-being of children through effective child support enforcement.

SupportGuidelines.com

http://www.supportguidelines.com/

★★★

The comprehensive resource for interpreting and applying child support guidelines in the United States. Intended primarily to help attorneys research the most current guidelines, this site does offer some useful information for individuals who are curious to learn more about child support guidelines.

DOMESTIC VIOLENCE

End Abuse

http://endabuse.org/

★★★★★

 14-18

This site is devoted to fighting all forms of family violence. Here, you can learn more about various programs that are available, read news stories relating to family violence issues, check out celebrities in the Hall of Fame and Hall of Shame, and access additional information and resources.

For Your Healing

http://www.foryourhealing.com/

★★★

 Not for kids

This site is an extension of the monthly newsletter for women in recovery from sexual abuse. Created by a survivor of childhood sexual abuse, this site offers writings from both the site owner and site visitors. Audiotapes can be purchased from this site.

National Coalition Against Domestic Violence

http://www.ncadv.org

★★★★

 14-18

The National Coalition Against Domestic Violence offers public education and advocates for social change.

National Council of Child Abuse and Family Violence

http://nccafv.org/

★★★

 14-18

Latest news and reports from the NCCAFV on child abuse and family violence. Learn how to report suspected cases of abuse and check for announcements of upcoming conferences.

National Domestic Violence Hotline

http://www.ndvh.org/

★★★

14-18

A project of Texas Council on Family Violence, this national hotline provides a way for victims of domestic violence to get help. Features a database of more than 4,000 shelters and service providers across the United States, Puerto Rico, Alaska, Hawaii, and the U.S. Virgin Islands.

National Network to End Domestic Violence

http://www.nnedv.org

★★★★

14-18

Offers up-to-date facts about domestic violence and training and education for advocates.

A B C D E F G H I J K L M N O P Q R S T U V W X Y Z

Office on Violence Against Women
http://www.ojp.usdoj.gov/vawo/

★★★★★

👫 14-18

Since its inception in 1995, the Office on Violence Against Women has "handled the Department of Justice's legal and policy issues regarding violence against women, coordinated departmental efforts, provided national and international leadership, received international visitors interested in learning about the federal government's role in addressing violence against women, and responded to requests for information regarding violence against women." Visit this site to learn more, and to get law enforcement help, if you need it.

Related Sites
http://www.nccn.net/~dvcoaltn/
http://www.now.org/issues/violence/

Post-Traumatic Stress Disorder Bibliography
http://www.dcha.org/EP/Guides/PTSD%20Bibliography.htm

★★★

👫 14-18

A current annotated list of books and articles that relate to post-traumatic stress disorder.

A Safe Place
http://www.asafeplacedvs.org/

★★★

👫 14-18

Supportive services for battered women and their children in the Northern California East Bay region. The agency works to decrease the number of women and children returning to violent relationships and educate the community on issues surrounding domestic violence.

Suggested Readings on Domestic Violence
http://www.cybergrrl.com/views/dv/index.shtml/bib.html

★★★

👫 Not for kids

This site offers links to books that deal with domestic violence and gay/lesbian battering. Also has links to SafetyNet Home page and Cybergrrl.

United States Domestic Violence Hotlines
http://www.ndvh.org/

★★★

👫 14-18

This site provides national toll-free hotline numbers you can call at any time of day or night for help.

〚Best〛 Victim Services Domestic Violence Shelter Tour and Information Site
http://www.dvsheltertour.org/

★★★★★

👫 14-18

An outstanding resource for referrals to local help for victims of domestic violence from all over the world. This site also includes information and a children's art gallery. If you or someone you know is a victim of domestic violence, and you don't know where to turn, turn here.

Woman's Resource Network (WRN): Domestic Violence/Abuse Resources
http://www.womanet.org/frame/violence.html

★★★

👫 14-18

This site is a complete resource for women, with information for women of all ages and life stages. This particular page has links to resources for women with abuse and violence issues in their lives. These resources include information and support for rape, violence, emotional abuse, and child abuse. This site also contains a listing of phone numbers that may be helpful as well. Special Teen area addresses issues that commonly affect teenage girls.

E-COMMERCE

Beginner's Guide to E-Commerce

http://www.nightcats.com/sales/free.html

★★★★

E-commerce and all its jargon can be confusing. This site offers a little help sorting it all out, including information in the following categories: Definition of Terms, Facts About Accepting Credit Cards Online, and E-Commerce Solutions Compared.

Biz Report

http://www.bizreport.com

★★★

Get today's Internet news or search the archives for background information on e-commerce. Also, get information on careers and opinions.

Center for Research in Electronic Commerce

http://cism.bus.utexas.edu/

★★★★

News about e-commerce from the academic world from the University of Texas at Austin, a leading center for research and education in the area of e-commerce.

CommerceNet

http://www.commerce.net

★★★★

The site for members of this Internet industry association provides research reports, some of which are free; a searchable database of articles; and information about upcoming conferences.

E-Biz

http://www.wired.com/news/ebiz/

★★★

The latest e-commerce news is here at Wired's news section, the online version of the print publication. Learn about Internet successes and failures so that you don't become one of the latter.

E-Commerce Guide

http://ecommerce.internet.com/how/

★★★★

Provides instructions, tips, and advice relating to various e-commerce topics, including how to build an e-commerce site, how to attract and keep customers, and how to get paid. Additional tabs at this site enable you to read e-commerce news and book reviews, research companies, and join discussion groups.

E-Commerce Guidebook

http://www.online-commerce.com/

★★★

A step-by-step guide to the process of becoming e-commerce enabled. An excellent introduction to the subject.

E-Commerce Tax News

http://www.ecommercetax.com/

★★★

States have not yet agreed on a way to collect sales tax on Internet transactions, but they continue to try. Learn more about the latest developments here.

A
B
C
D
E
F
G
H
I
J
K
L
M
N
O
P
Q
R
S
T
U
V
W
X
Y
Z

 E-Commerce Times

http://www.ecommercetimes.com

★★★★★

Lots of e-commerce news and discussions, as well as a free newsletter, offered either on a daily or weekly basis, to keep you updated. The information is categorized into current events or news, marketing, opinions, special reports, industry reports, and emerging technology, to name a few. Even includes a cartoon. You can readily access stock quotes and watch the tech market from this site. For the latest in e-commerce, you can find no better site.

E-Commerce Tutorial

http://hotwired.lycos.com/webmonkey/e-business/tutorials/tutorial3.html

★★★★

This site features an online tutorial that covers the five areas on which you must focus to build a successful e-business—Making a Plan, Sales Techniques, Online Transactions, Software Solutions, and Attracting Customers. Each lesson consists of approximately 3 to 6 sections.

eMarketer.com

http://www.emarketer.com/

★★★★

Home of the world's leading provider of e-business statistics. Subscribe and order reports online.

Federal Trade Commission's E-Commerce Publications

http://www.ftc.gov/bcp/menu-internet.htm

★★★★

Complete list of publications from the Federal Trade Commission that apply to transactions on the Internet and other issues regarding privacy, security, and protecting children on the Internet. Includes information on scams, spam, pyramid schemes, and online investments, to name only a few.

FreeMerchant.com

http://www.freemerchant.com/

★★★★

One of the largest e-commerce providers in the world, FreeMerchant.com is home to a mega-mall of online stores. At FreeMerchant.com, you can set up your own store, locate vendors to stock your "shelves," and have a FreeMerchant design specialist build your store for you.

Guide to E-Commerce

http://www.ilr.cornell.edu/library/subjectGuides/ecommerce.html

★★★★

Directory of e-commerce resources on the Web that are arranged in a way to provide an overview of e-commerce. Provides a brief introduction to e-commerce and links to other sites in the following categories: General Sites, Industry Associations and Organizations, International, Legal Resources, Online News and Journal Sources, and U.S. Government Sites.

Internet.com

http://www.internet.com/

★★★★

Excellent source of news and commentary on electronic commerce and the Internet in general.

InternetNews.com

http://www.internetnews.com/ec-news/

★★★

Check the latest Internet news and how Internet stocks are faring.

Jupiter Direct Research

http://www.jupiterdirect.com

★★★★

Internet business research firm that provides listings of hundreds of research reports with discounts off the purchase of virtually all of them. Be forewarned, however; the reports aren't cheap.

Marketing Tips

http://www.canadaone.com/technology/
smallbizstrat060898.html

★★★★

Maps out a strategy for small business online marketing efforts and campaigns. From CanadaOne.

NetBusiness

http://www.techweb.com/netbiz

★★★★

Read helpful articles on designing a website that works, such as "Avoid 10 Fatal Web Storefront Mistakes"; ask e-commerce questions of the experts; and read about case studies.

PayPal

http://www.paypal.com

★★★★★

One of the fastest growing e-commerce sites on the Web, PayPal is a service that handles credit card transactions for small businesses. If you have a mom-and-pop operation and you want a simple way to enable your customers to order and pay for products on the Web, check out PayPal.

SmallBiz

http://content.techweb.com/smallbiz/

★★★★

Devoted to giving small businesses an edge on the Internet, this site features a small collection of articles addressing the concerns of small-business owners. Also provides a section on public relations and forums where you can network online.

Wired.com

http://www.wired.com

★★★★

Find the latest Internet news here, as well as international news, along with information on e-commerce court decisions and timely issues.

ZDNet's E-Business

http://techupdate.zdnet.com/

★★★★

Resource for the latest e-business news and information. When you reach ZDNet's home page, click the eBusiness tab to access information relating to e-commerce. Links to B2B (business-to-business), B2C (business-to-consumer), and CRM (customer relations management). Software solutions for managing various aspects of e-commerce.

Wilson: Web Marketing and E-Commerce

http://www.wilsonweb.com/

★★★★

Excellent resource for information on how to market products and services on the Web. Obtain marketing advice from one of the top Web marketers, Dr. Ralph Wilson. Site includes tools for searching Dr. Wilson's articles and for searching an archive of thousands of Web marketing articles. You'll find plenty of useful information at this site.

A
B
C
D
E
F
G
H
I
J
K
L
M
N
O
P
Q
R
S
T
U
V
W
X
Y
Z

EDUCATION

CONTINUING EDUCATION

American Association for Adult and Continuing Education

http://www.iacet.org/

★★★

Home of the nation's premier organization dedicated to enhancing the field of adult learning. The American Association for Adult and Continuing Education has members from 60 affiliates and 40 nations in fields that include secondary and post-secondary education, business and labor, military and government, and community-based organizations. Here, you can learn more about the organization and what it has to offer.

Automotive Management Institute (AMIONLINE)

http://www.amionline.org/

★★★★

Members of the automotive service industry can find out about AMI's continuing education programs at AMIONLINE. Check the calendar of upcoming AMI events or the catalog for specific coursework offered.

Biomedical Communications

http://www.biomedical-communications.com/

★★★★

Offers continuing medical education (CME) programs and training materials for the following areas of medicine: colposcopy, cervical intraepithelial neoplasia, gynecology, laser surgery, electrosurgery, and abnormal pap smears. Shop the mall for books, videos, and CD-ROMs related to your area.

CEB: Continuing Education for the Bar

http://www.iacet.org/

★★★★★

This site is created and maintained by lawyers for lawyers in California. The site features legal resources online and on CDs, access to online legal publications, and continuing education seminars. Must subscribe for the good stuff, but some samples and free trials are available.

Colorado School of Mines Special Programs and Continuing Education

http://www.mines.edu/Outreach/Cont_Ed/

★★★

Conferences and programs offered to chosen off-campus groups. Topics include mine safety and health, environmental issues, and industrial minerals processing. Some of the courses include post-conference online discussion. Distance-learning available.

Dalhousie University Maritime School of Social Work Continuing Education Program

http://is.dal.ca/~schsw/coned/

★★★★

Serves the need for social work continuing education in the maritime provinces and concentrates on the Nova Scotia area. Welcomes American and Canadian students. Check out the workshops and certificate programs available.

DenTrek: Global Online Dental Education Network

http://www.dentrek.com/

★★★★★

Extensive catalog of education programs and courses in dentistry. Some free tutorials and demos.

Foundations in Continuing Education

http://www.fice.com

★★★

Foundations in Continuing Education provides quality, self-study (home-study) continuing education for dental professionals. ADA CERP-recognized provider. AGD national sponsor. Courses approved by DANB.

Institute of Continuing Legal Education

http://www.icle.org/

★★★★

Offers continuing legal education programs for lawyers in Michigan. Approved continuing legal education (CLE) sponsor; gain CLE credits by attending ICLE's seminars. Click the Seminars tab to search for a seminar in your area of specialty. Also provides useful research tools.

JASON

http://www.jasonproject.org

★★★★

Brainchild of Dr. Robert Ballard, who discovered the wreck of the RMS Titanic in 1986, this site is dedicated to providing an avenue for students to perform field work online through various expeditions. Also provides continuing education opportunities for teachers.

LearnWell: Online Continuing Education in Nursing

http://www.ce5.com/

★★★★

Short courses for nursing professionals and other medical professionals. The entire process is done online: Select a course; study the material; participate in interactive cases; print, fill out, and mail in the online test form with your $15 fee; and await your results (two weeks). If given a passing score, you receive your continuing education certificate in the mail.

MarcoPolo

http://www.marcopolo-education.org/

★★★★★

MarcoPolo is an excellent resource for K–12 teachers. This program provides teachers with lesson plans, classroom activities and materials, links to valuable content, and powerful search tools. MarcoPolo even provides teacher guides for elementary and secondary school teachers that give additional instructions on how to use MarcoPolo effectively in their classrooms. Visit this site for more information.

NYU's School of Continuing Education

http://www.scps.nyu.edu/

★★★

NYU's School of Continuing Education offers more than 2,000 credit and noncredit courses in more than 100 fields for adults to advance their careers, enhance their lives, and keep ahead of a constantly changing world.

Professional Social Workers: Continuing Education

http://www.brynmawr.edu/socialwork/CE/

★★★★

License renewal, tuition, transportation information—all you need to know about continuing education options for social workers at Bryn Mawr College in Bryn Mawr, Pennsylvania. Gives a detailed list of registration information needed and where to send that information.

A B C D E F G H I J K L M N O P Q R S T U V W X Y Z

Students Against Testing

http://www.nomoretests.com

★★★

Do you hate standardized tests? Then visit this site to learn how to protest and boycott testing at your school. Features top 10 reasons to oppose standardized tests, 101 better things to do besides taking standardized tests, personal accounts of actual protests, and more.

University of Berkley: College Without Classes

http://www.berkley-u.edu

★★★

Alternative education, adult distance learning (correspondence school). No residency. Earn college degrees without classroom work. Low tuition, credit for life experience.

University of Connecticut: Division of Extended and Continuing Education

http://continuingstudies.uconn.edu/

★★★★

The Division of Extended and Continuing Education provides educational opportunities for professionals, adult learners, and traditional students. The school provides certificate, degree, credit, and noncredit courses.

University of Missouri-Rolla Continuing Education

http://www.umr.edu/~conted/

★★★

Offers continuing education courses and conferences sponsored by the University of Missouri-Rolla in countless disciplines: civil and electrical engineering, mining, asphalt, concrete, geotechnical engineering, explosives, earthquakes, machine foundation, and numerous others.

University of Nevada, Reno: Division of Continuing Education

http://extendedstudies.unr.edu/

★★★

Serving all of your continuing education needs, the DCE at UNR offers courses in gaming management, professional development, correspondence study…the list goes on.

University of North Alabama Continuing Education

http://www.una.edu/conted/

★★★★

The Continuing Education department of UNA offers a wide variety of courses for adults, youth, and various professions, including accounting and auditing, nursing, human resources and personnel, industrial hygiene/occupational health and safety, and quality improvement. Alternatively, check out the many courses designed for the person who simply wants to learn a new skill such as gardening or using a computer.

Western CPE: Continuing Education for Accountants CPA

http://www.westerncpe.com/

★★★

Sponsored by the University of Montana, this organization teaches courses to accountants seeking continuing professional education. Courses are either conducted in a resort setting or are self-study programs.

Related Sites

http://www.baylor.edu/cont_ed/

http://www.cll.purdue.edu/

http://www.dce.ksu.edu/

http://www.sjcme.edu/gps/

DISTANCE LEARNING

American Institute for Paralegal Studies

http://www.aips.com/

★★★★

Paralegal students at the American Institute can attend its nationally accredited program via computer-mediated distance learning, the Institute's unique interactive learning environment.

College Courses Offered at a Distance

http://www.dlrn.org/adult/index.html

★★★

This site takes you through Internet and non-Internet resources for finding out who offers college courses via distance education technologies.

Distance Education Clearinghouse

http://www.uwex.edu/disted/

★★★★

This University of Wisconsin site offers distance education news, highlights, resources, course descriptions, information on technologies, and more. Also features definitions, a glossary, and overviews of distance learning, so you will know what to expect.

Distance Learning Course Finder

http://www.dlcoursefinder.com/

★★★★

This site helps users track down distance-learning courses on the Internet by entering the course name or keyword, the subject, and/or the name of the institution offering the course.

Distance Learning on the Net

http://www.hoyle.com/

★★★★★

Glenn Hoyle is the creator and manager of this excellent directory of distance-learning programs offered on the Internet. Browse the directory by category to find a list of the best distance-learning providers in that category along with a brief description of each provider and a link to its site.

Distance Learning Resource Network

http://www.dlrn.org/

★★★★

The Distance Learning Resource Network (DLRN), located at WestEd (San Francisco, CA), is the dissemination project for the U.S. Department of Education Star Schools Program. Provides directories of distance-learning programs grouped by K–12, Adult Learners, and Educators. Also provides information for teachers on how to put together an effective online course.

Florida's CAMPUS

http://www.floridavirtualcampus.org/

★★★

A clearinghouse for distance-learning resources in the state of Florida.

IdiotBooks.com

http://www.idiotbooks.com/
idiotdummybooksforeignlanguage.html

$

★★★

Teach yourself a foreign language using one or more of the books featured at this Amazon.com affiliate. Select a title and then order it through the link to Amazon.

H. Wayne Huizenga School of Business and Entrepreneurship

http://www.huizenga.nova.edu/

★★★★

Internationally accredited, online MBA combining convenient Internet-based learning technologies, doctoral faculty, and years of experience in distance education.

Online Education

http://www.mindedge.com/

★★★★

Provides a listing of online courses, degrees, and certificates offered by accredited colleges and universities. Pick from Find A Course, Get A Degree, or Get A Certificate. Search thousands of courses offered by dozens of fully accredited schools.

A B C D E F G H I J K L M N O P Q R S T U V W X Y Z

A
B
C
D
E
F
G
H
I
J
K
L
M
N
O
P
Q
R
S
T
U
V
W
X
Y
Z

Petersons.com: The Lifelong Learning Channel

http://www.petersons.com/distancelearning/

 $

★★★★

Comprehensive distance-learning resource brought to you by Peterson's—the world's largest education information and services provider.

TEAMS Distance Learning

http://teams.lacoe.edu/

★★★★★

TEAMS Distance Learning provides interactive distance-learning programs for K–12 classes. A studio teacher runs the class from a remote location, while the classroom teacher and the students watch, listen, and ask questions. Visit this site to learn more about the available programs and how TEAMS works.

Technology Enhanced Learning and Research (TELR) at Ohio State University

http://telr.ohio-state.edu/

★★★★

Distance-learning courses, seminars, videotapes, and other resources developed and created by faculty at Ohio State and other institutions.

TeleClass4U.com

http://www.teleclass4u.com/

★★★★

TeleClass4U is a place where instructors, coaches, authors, and experts from many fields teach the skills, provide the education and training, and answer your questions—over the phone.

University of Maryland University College

http://www.umuc.edu/distance/

★★★★★

University of Maryland University College (UMUC) has a long tradition in distance learning—more than 25 years. It has perhaps the largest enrollment in the world with its more than 110,423 online course enrollments, and if you visit this site, you will understand why. The online university features BA programs in 15 areas of study, MA programs in 10 areas, and certifications in many others. The site is easy to navigate, and the online instructions are straightforward. Reading materials are available online and students can order books online, as well. Excellent, accessible site for any students seeking a higher education online.

Virtual School for the Gifted

http://www.vsg.edu.au/

★★★★

 9-13

An excellent supplement to a gifted student's education, this site provides nine-week courses for grades 4–8+. Students can build their understanding of math, science, English, history, and computing through a variety of courses.

World Lecture Hall

http://www.utexas.edu/world/lecture/

★★★

World Lecture Hall is an index of pages created by faculty worldwide who are using the Web to deliver free class materials.

FOREIGN LANGUAGES

Learn a Language with Eloquence

http://www.elok.com/

 $

★★★

Learn Spanish, German, French, English, or other languages online or with the help of conventional study materials, such as books and tapes.

Learn Spanish Online

http://www.studyspanish.com/

★★★

Take Spanish lessons online, complete tests, and keep track of your own report card. Plenty of tools and information for free. Premium services (for about $10–$15 per month) provide you with additional tests, resources, and study guides.

National K–12 Foreign Language Resource Center

http://www.educ.iastate.edu/nflrc/

★★★

Foreign language teachers will want to frequent this site for information on new approaches and technologies for use in teaching K–12 students foreign languages. There is currently information on upcoming conferences and projects underway, with plans to add an extensive listing of successful course guides.

TranslationExperts.com

http://www.tranexp.com/InterTran/
FreeTranslation.html

★★★★★

This site features various translations tools, including NeuroTran (for translating websites and email), InteractiveTran (for translating words and phrases you type), PalmTran and PocketTran (a translator and dictionary for Palm or PocketPC computers), InterTran (for translating websites), and MobileTran (a translator and dictionary for cell phones).

World Language Resources

http://www.worldlanguage.com/

★★★★

More than 725 languages are supported through products available at this site, from dictionaries to spell checkers to videos and other teaching tools.

INTERNATIONAL EDUCATION

AFS Intercultural Programs

http://www.afs.org/

★★★

This nonprofit organization offers intercultural learning opportunities through its international student exchange programs. The site offers information on AFS programs, current AFS news, links, and more.

American Councils for International Education

http://www.actr.org/

★★★

The American Council is devoted to improving education, professional training, and research within and about the Russian-speaking world, including both the Russian Federation and the many non-Russian cultures of central and eastern Europe.

Boston College Center for International Higher Education

http://www.bc.edu/bc_org/avp/soe/cihe/index.html

★★★

The Boston College Center for International Higher Education provides information and support for international initiatives in higher education, including links to other international education websites and centers, and publications.

The Digital Education Network's EduFind

http://www.edufind.com/

★★★

This site provides a wide range of resources for students and professionals interested in international education. Many schools offering courses to international students are featured on the site, and information can be found on language schools, universities, business schools, colleges, and vocational schools all over the world. The site also hosts a number of award-winning learning resources, such as the Online English Grammar and the ELT/TEFL Centre.

A B C D E F G H I J K L M N O P Q R S T U V W X Y Z

A
B
C
D
E
F
G
H
I
J
K
L
M
N
O
P
Q
R
S
T
U
V
W
X
Y
Z

Institute of International Education

http://www.iie.org/

★★★★

Learn about the IIE's educational exchange and training programs. Special sections cover information on fellowships and sponsored programs.

International Education and Graduate Programs Service: U.S. Department of Education

http://www.ed.gov/about/offices/list/ous/international/index.html

★★★

Provides domestic international education programs, along with overseas and graduate programs.

International Education Finance Corporation

http://www.iefc.com/

★★★

This site offers information on IEFC foreign study financial loan programs.

The International Education Site

http://www.intstudy.com/

★★★★

Students interested in studying abroad should visit this site. Find details on colleges and universities, course options, chat with other students worldwide, and take advantage of the free application service.

NAFSA: Association of International Educators

http://www.nafsa.org

★★★

This site offers information about this association and its activities promoting international educational opportunities.

Quaker Information Center

http://www.quakerinfo.org/

★★★

Great site to visit for a list of links to organizations that match students to suitable international exchange/study abroad programs. Click on a link and see a description of the organization and complete contact information.

Rotary International Eastern States Student EXchange Program, Inc. (ESSEX)

http://www.exchangestudent.org/

★★★★

Find out about Rotary International's student year abroad youth study programs.

Study Abroad Directory

http://www.studyabroad.com/

Ⓢ

★★★

Listing of more than 1,000 study abroad programs. The site offers links to a marketplace of related products and services. It also offers recommended reading and several sections that provide information on every aspect of choosing a study abroad program.

University of Oregon International Community

http://oip.uoregon.edu/

★★★

A good place to visit for its content on international education and exchange offices; international student organizations; its overseas study program; international student offices and so on in various universities, colleges, and schools.

World Education Guide

http://www.asiadragons.com/education/europe/

★★★

Links to websites of all countries offering international education.

K–12

ALA Resources for Parents and Kids

http://www.ala.org/parents/

 $

★★★★

 All

This educational site, which is maintained by the American Library Association, includes Internet guides for kids and teens, book lists, and links to hundreds of recommended sites for kids.

American School Directory

http://www.asd.com/

★★★

A resource for information on K–12 schools in the United States. Any school in America might post specific information at no cost, and visitors can search the database by name or location. Bulletin board enables students, parents, and teachers to post messages.

Apple: K–12 Education

http://www.apple.com/education/k12/

 $

★★★

Apple Computer's education site provides information and news about various programs Apple Computer and its associates offer for teachers of K–12 students. Excellent source for school administrators and teachers who are incorporating technology into their classrooms.

ArtsEdge Network

http://artsedge.kennedy-center.org/

★★★★★

The National Arts and Education Information Network focuses on using technology to increase access to arts resources and increase arts education in the K–12 school environment. Features an online newsletter, an information gallery, curriculum guides, and links to other arts-related online information.

Awesome Library

http://www.awesomelibrary.org/

★★★★

 All

Contains 22,000 carefully reviewed resources, including the top 5% in education. Pick the category that applies to you (Teacher, Parent, Kid, Teen, Librarian, or Community) and see an "Awesome Library" designed for your needs.

ClassroomConnectDirect.com

http://www.classroomdirect.com/

 $

★★★★

Offering a wide selection of classroom activities, software, and supplies at reasonable prices, this is a one-stop shopping site for classroom teachers.

Council of the Great City Schools Online

http://www.cgcs.org

★★★

Nonprofit organization that represents the nation's largest public school systems. Links to local chapter pages.

[Best] Discovery Channel School

http://www.school.discovery.com/

 $

★★★★★

 All

From The Discovery Channel, resources for teachers of science, humanities, and social studies. Includes lesson plans, email lists, and a schedule of upcoming science specials. You can buy educational and stimulating toys and gifts for children including telescopes, dinosaurs, videos, and books through the online store. Students area provides homework and study help and tips, a weekly brain booster quiz, a clip art gallery, puzzles, and science fair project ideas. Special area for parents and homeschoolers provides additional teaching resources. This Best of the Best site is packed with useful information and tools for everyone involved in the teaching/learning process!

A B C D E F G H I J K L M N O P Q R S T U V W X Y Z

A
B
C
D
E
F
G
H
I
J
K
L
M
N
O
P
Q
R
S
T
U
V
W
X
Y
Z

Education Index

http://www.educationindex.com/

★★★★★

†† All

Huge collection of links to the best education-based websites. Browse by subject or life stage, hang out in the Coffee Shop with your pals, or play around with Web Weasel.

EducationJobs.com

http://www.educationjobs.com/

$

★★★★

An employment resource for jobs in the education field providing services to school systems, teachers, and administrators. Premium package, offering lifetime access to the database, for $19.95.

Education: K–12 Articles

http://www.kidsource.com/kidsource/pages/ed.k12.html

★★★

The number-one concern of many parents who visit KidSource Online is how to help their children do better in school. These articles do just that. They are focused on specific subjects, skills, or lessons for children in grades K–12.

Education Week News

http://www.edweek.org/

★★★★

Featuring the latest news relating to education in America, this site keeps teachers, administrators, and parents informed of legislation and other happenings in the world of education. Links to *Teacher Magazine*, special reports, and state education numbers and statistics.

EduHound

http://www.eduhound.com/

★★★★★

†† All

Huge searchable directory of educational resources for K–12. Sites are organized into dozens of categories, including Administration, Animals, Back to School, Culture, Marine Life, and World & Countries. Special areas include Clip Art for Kids, Schools on the Web, Classrooms on the Web, Weekly Spotlight, and EduHound Weekly (a newsletter for educators. Teachers, parents, homeschoolers, and students will all want to bookmark this site.

Global Online Adventure Learning Site

http://www.goals.com/classrm/classfrm.htm

★★★★

†† All

Tune in to learn more about adventures in progress or already completed by people around the world. Learn about actual ocean-crossings, bike trips, and hiking treks being undertaken and transmitted to this site, which aims to teach kids about science, nature, and technology.

Global Schoolhouse at Lightspan.com

http://www.gsn.org/

★★★

This site provides communication tools, professional development tools, and a place to access collaborative projects. Features such as a discussion board and mailing lists can be found here.

Infomine: Instructional Resources

http://infomine.ucr.edu/

★★★★

†† 14-18

More than 30 librarians from the University of California and other universities and colleges have contributed to building INFOMINE, which is a goldmine of resources and information relevant to faculty, students, and research staff at the university level.

Interactive Educational Simulations

http://www.simulations.com/

★★★

This site contains a growing list of educational projects aimed at K–12 schools. Its goal: to provide the best in interactive simulations and stress higher-level thinking skills.

International Society for Technology in Education

http://www.iste.org/

★★★

The International Society for Technology in Education (ISTE) is the largest teacher-based, non-profit organization in the field of educational technology. Its mission is to help K–12 classroom teachers and administrators share effective methods for enhancing student learning through the use of new classroom technologies.

Kids of America Safe Search

http://www.kidsofamerica.com/

★★★★★

 All

Searchable directory of websites that are safe for kids of all ages to visit. Kids search the directory as they would search any directory, such as Google or Yahoo!, but the search tool returns links only for child-safe sites.

Related Sites
http://www.lycoszone.com/
http://www.super-kids.com/
http://www.yahooligans.com/
http://sunsite.berkeley.edu/KidsClick!
http://www.route616.com/

KidsBank.com

http://www.kidsbank.com/

★★★★

 All

KidsBank.Com is a tutorial website developed by Sovereign Bank that explains the fundamentals of money and banking to children. The site provides parents with information and a place to share with kids to aid their understanding of the benefits of saving.

Kindergarten Connection

http://www.kconnect.com/

★★★★

Provides resources for the primary school educator. Offers teacher tips, lesson plans, book reviews, and links to other related sites.

Microsoft Education

http://www.microsoft.com/education/

★★★★★

The Microsoft Education website is an online resource for school technology coordinators and educators. Offers articles, solutions, ideas, and resources for schools building connected learning communities and integrating technology in the classroom.

Mr. Dowling's Virtual Classroom

http://www.mrdowling.com/

★★★★

 All

This site was created by Mr. Dowling, a sixth-grade geography teacher. He presents a variety of historical and geographical topics that students, educators, and parents can utilize. Homework assignments are also included here.

NASA John C. Stennis Space Center Education and University Affairs

http://wwwedu.ssc.nasa.gov/

★★★★

A broad-spectrum collection of K–12 and other educational WWW resources, with special focus toward space and aerospace studies. Includes teacher resources, lesson plans, and links to many other education-related topics.

National Association for the Education of Young Children

http://www.naeyc.org/

★★★

This group promotes early childhood education, and its site contains educational activities teachers or parents can use, articles on childcare, a membership form, and a catalog. Must place orders via fax, phone, or standard mail.

A B C D E F G H I J K L M N O P Q R S T U V W X Y Z

A
B
C
D
E
F
G
H
I
J
K
L
M
N
O
P
Q
R
S
T
U
V
W
X
Y
Z

National Education Association

http://www.nea.org/

★★★★

The National Education Association is an organization representing the interests of the public school system. This site contains information about the organization, its publications, and legislative activities. Offers education resources, links to grant information, teacher-specific resources, parenting resources, and lots more.

Newbery Medal

http://www.ala.org/ala/alsc/awardsscholarships/
literaryawds/newberymedal/newberymedal.htm

★★★★

This annual award is given for excellence in American children's literature. Find information about the award, a printable list of past winners, and detailed information on award-winning and honor books. You can purchase books, jewelry, posters, and cards through the online store.

On2

http://www.pbs.org/newshour/extra/

★★★

 9-13

The Public Broadcasting Service provides this bimonthly magazine aimed at elementary and junior high students. It features world news, science and technology updates, and real-life accounts from people in the news. You can buy books and videos from the online store.

Online Teaching: Examples and Articles

http://www.unl.edu/websat/disted.html

★★★

The site includes courses using the Internet for communication and research or displaying the results of research. Also find online class resources.

Questacon: The National Science and Technology Center

http://www.questacon.edu.au

★★★★★

 All

This site is a scientific learning show for kids. It includes online games that teach scientific concepts and theories, a virtual tour of the center in Australia, and features that focus on international science events. You can purchase T-shirts and thought-provoking gifts for children from the online store.

Questia: World's Largest Online Library

http://www.questia.com/

★★★★★

All

Subscribe to this library to place a huge collection of books, magazines, journals, newspapers, and encyclopedias right at your fingertips. Some good free samples, too.

Resources for Early Childhood Educators

http://eceresources.iwarp.com/

★★★

Contains links to sites providing early childhood education resources and information. Features lesson plans submitted by readers and other resources for teachers. Lots of annoying pop-up ads make this site tough to navigate.

Scholastic.com

http://www.scholastic.com/

★★★★★

All

The home of the largest publisher of children's books in the world, including the *Harry Potter* series, Scholastic.com provides an excellent learning kiosk for parents, teachers, and children. Scholastic's goal is to instill the love of reading and learning for lifelong pleasure in all children. This site is well designed and packed with high-quality content.

The Science Source

http://thesciencesource.com/

★★★★★

Manufactures and sells more than 300 items for teaching physics, physical science, chemistry, biology, environmental science, and design technology. High-quality innovative science and technology teaching materials.

World Almanac for Kids

http://www.worldalmanacforkids.com/

★★★★★

 All

World Almanac for Kids is an excellent site for kids to visit to learn more about the world, including its animals, its history, human inventions, religions, populations, and much more. Plenty of games to help kids learn while having fun.

K–12—EDUCATIONAL TELEVISION

Bill Nye the Science Guy's Nye Labs Online

http://www.billnye.com

★★★★★

 All

The website for one of the hippest geeks on television, Bill Nye. Entertaining as well as educational, Bill Nye the Science Guy's website has listings, a search mechanism, and other goodies.

Biography

http://www.biography.com/

★★★★★

A website based on the A&E program of the same name. The Biography website has a 25,000-person search engine, quizzes and games, and chapters from published biographies of important people. You can also get VDO clips and a calendar of upcoming programs. You can buy books, videos, and posters from the online store.

Cable in the Classroom

http://www.ciconline.com/

★★★★★

Can television be educational? Find out what the cable industry thinks and see what it has to offer in the way of educational programming. Teachers are especially welcome at this site, where they can find details about various educational shows available through the Cable in the Classroom initiative.

ChannelOne.com

http://channelone.com/

★★★★★

 14-18

Home of the Channel One Network, a cable television network that broadcasts news stories and current events to middle school, junior high, and high school students from around the world. Here, you can find some of the top stories along with quizzes and other resources. Also features message boards and polls.

Children's Television Workshop

http://www.sesameworkshop.org/

★★★★★

 All

Offers many features for kids and parents alike, including a lineup of *Sesame Street*'s new season, ratings of various children's television shows for parents, information about the *Ghost Writer* series (among others), and online games galore for children. The parents' section includes discussions on child development, education, product reviews, behavior and discipline, and others. Parents of young children should not miss this site.

Related Sites
http://www.greentv.org/
http://www.ket.org/

A
B
C
D
E
F
G
H
I
J
K
L
M
N
O
P
Q
R
S
T
U
V
W
X
Y
Z

The Discovery Channel

http://www.discovery.com

★★★★★

 All

Cable channel covering history, technology, nature, exploration, and science-related issues. The site has special feature sections and "did you know" facts that make it a unique experience. Includes the standard programming schedules and sections on kid-related programming.

The Learning Channel

http://tlc.com/

★★★★

 All

Cable channel devoted to programming about history, science, and world culture, as well as commercial-free programs for preschoolers. Site includes programming schedules and information about upcoming shows. Shopping links take you to the Discovery Store.

PBS Online

http://www.pbs.org/whatson/kidschannel/calendar.html

★★★

 All

Check out what's on PBS television for kids. Click a date on the calendar, search for a specific show, or browse a list of shows from A to Z.

Schoolhouse Rock

http://disney.go.com/disneyvideos/animatedfilms/schoolhouserock/

★★★★

Remember these campy '70s edu-cartoons? Well, so does Disney. Soon you will be able to purchase a DVD with all your favorite *Schoolhouse Rock* cartoons. For now, however, you can cast a vote for your favorite tune here at Disney's Schoolhouse Rock site.

Stephen Hawking's Universe

http://www.pbs.org/wnet/hawking/

★★★★

 14-18

This PBS show addresses the big bang theories, why the universe is the way it is, where we come from, and other cosmic questions in an entertaining way accessible to all adult audiences. The site includes a schedule of programs, teacher's guide, and a Strange Stuff Explained section, which discusses black holes and antimatter, among other topics.

Street Cents Online

http://cbc.ca/streetcents/

★★★

 9-13

Tied to the Canadian television show *Street Cents*, which teaches young people how to be informed consumers. Covers all the highlights of the week's program and also offers an essay contest.

Termite Television Collective

http://www.termite.org/

★★★

14-18

The Termite TV Collective is a Philadelphia-based concern that produces a show called *This Is Only A Test*, a cable access series that confronts social issues through a low-budget, documentary approach. The website includes, among other things, an episode guide.

Related Sites

http://www.mpbc.org/

http://www.pbs.org/teachersource/

K–12–HOMEWORK HELP

About Schools

http://www.aboutschool.com/

★★★★★

👥 All

Excellent and extensive directory of resources for K–12 students, parents, and teachers. Resources are broken down by grade level: Preschool, Kindergarten, Grades 1–3, Grades 4–6, Grades 7–8, and High School. Within each category are subcategories for each subject, including reading, writing, arithmetic, chemistry, and so on.

Atlapedia Online

http://www.atlapedia.com/

★★★

👥 9-13

A virtual world almanac of planetary proportions, Atlapedia Online provides facts and vital statistics for every country on the globe.

bigchalk.com

http://www.bigchalk.com/

★★★★★

👥 All

bigchalk provides education materials to librarians, students, and teachers in more than 43,000 schools across the country. At the top of the bigchalk home page is a Homework Central search tool for obtaining homework help in nearly every subject based on grade: K–5, 6–8, and 9–12. You can also browse for homework help by clicking the link for the desired grade level near the top of the page.

B.J. Pinchbeck's Homework Helper

http://school.discovery.com/homeworkhelp/bjpinchbeck/

💲

★★★★

👥 All

B.J. "Beege" Pinchbeck is a Pennsylvania teenager who, with Dad's help, maintains this rich and handy K–12 educational reference directory.

California State Science Fair

http://www.usc.edu/CSSF/Resources/GettingStarted.html

★★★★

👥 9-13

A great supporting resource for any student considering entering a science fair, and for any parent who's been requested to help. You'll find ideas for getting started, information about judging, and plenty of other science links to look through.

Dictionary.com

http://www.dictionary.com/

💲

★★★★★

👥 All

A complete resource library on the Web, this site features a searchable dictionary, thesaurus, medical dictionary, translator, grammar and style guide, and foreign language dictionaries. Toss those tomes in a tomb, and look stuff up online!

The Great Globe Gallery

http://hum.amu.edu.pl/~zbzw/glob/glob1.htm

★★★★★

👥 All

The Great Globe Gallery puts a global spin on geographic visualization with its assortment of swirling globes and other Earthy depictions.

Grolier's Online: The American Presidency

http://gi.grolier.com/presidents/preshome.html

★★★★

👥 All

The American Presidency at Grolier Online Encyclopedia presents a history of presidents, the presidency, politics, and related subjects.

Homework Helper Page

http://www.geocities.com/Athens/Parthenon/7726/

★★★★

👥 All

This page was created for all students on the Web by a Collingwood, West Vancouver, parent. This site is a great place to research K–12 materials. Also be sure to investigate the "enrichment" websites, which are continually updated.

A B C D E F G H I J K L M N O P Q R S T U V W X Y Z

Best Homework Spot

http://www.homeworkspot.com/

★★★★★

 All

Excellent directory of homework help sites provides links to homework sites in nearly every subject area grouped by class level: Elementary, Middle, and High School. Also provides links to reference materials and sites for parents and teachers. If you need help with your homework, this is the best place to start looking.

Info Zone

http://www.assd.winnipeg.mb.ca/infozone/

★★★★

 All

Fresh from the Assiniboine South School Division in Winnipeg, Manitoba, Canada, comes the Info Zone, a terrific site that uses Internet resources to guide kids through the basics of research.

Jiskha Homework Help

http://www.jiskha.com/

★★★★★

 All

Find answers to your questions about nearly every school-related topic here. This site offers help for Art, Computers, English, Foreign Languages, Math, Science, and more. Most answers are in the form of essays written by experts. You can submit a question or join a discussion group to find your answer or browse through the topics in a particular subject area.

Merriam-Webster Online

http://www.m-w.com/home.htm

★★★

 All

You can look up words in the *Merriam-Webster Dictionary* and build your vocabulary in other ways via this generous English language reference site.

Ms. Smith's English Page

http://home.earthlink.net/~jesmith/

★★★★

 9-13

Here's an excellent example of how educators can use a personal home page to enhance their curriculum while gaining instant credibility among teacher-phobic, techno-savvy middle school students.

Refdesk.com

http://www.refdesk.com/

★★★★★

This site provides daily tidbits of information, from historical trivia to astronomical facts. You'll also find a crossword and quote of the day.

Time for Kids

http://www.timeforkids.com/

★★★★★

 9-13

Time magazine's edition for kids online. Students can browse articles on current events or search past issues for specific topics. Links for teachers and parents, as well.

WebMuseum, Paris

http://www.ibiblio.org/wm/

★★★★

All

Through this site, visitors can learn about and experience fine art from a number of museums. See famous and not-so-famous paintings from your computer!

White House for Kids

http://www.whitehouse.gov/kids/

★★★

All

This White House for Kids site provides information about the President of the United States and First Lady, and the Vice President and his wife. You can view a reading list for various age groups, take a tour of the White House with the President's pets, test your knowledge with a history quiz, and more.

Young Investor

http://www.younginvestor.com

★★★★★

👥 9-13

Tomorrow's moguls can learn money fundamentals and investing at this clever, colorful financial education site from Liberty Financial of Boston (which offers mutual funds geared to young people).

K–12—MONTESSORI EDUCATION

American Montessori Consulting

http://www.amonco.org/

★★★

An index of resources for American Montessori Consulting, with everything from home schooling information to creating your own beginning reading books. You get information about Montessori for preschoolers and elementary-age children, and you find links to sites for children, parents, and recommended educational sites.

American Montessori Society

http://www.amshq.org/

★★★★

The official AMS site has everything you need to know about Montessori education. Learn what Montessori education is all about, how effective it is, what goes on in the Montessori classroom, and how Montessori programs work in public schools.

The Center for Contemporary Montessori Programs

http://paradox.stkate.edu/montessori/

★★★★

This site offers information about The Center for Contemporary Montessori Programs' teacher education programs, which are American Montessori Society affiliated. You can get course descriptions and check out links to other Montessori sites.

The Children's Montessori Independent School

http://www1.xe.net/isnet/cmis/

★★★

Learn about the Children's Montessori Independent School and about Montessori education principles at this site, where you'll also find other education links.

International Montessori Society

http://trust.wdn.com/ims/

★★★★

Learn what Montessori education is all about. Request Montessori publications and get information on the society's Montessori teacher education program. Find out which schools are recognized by the International Montessori Accreditation Council (IMAC). If you'd like to, you can even join the society by filling out a simple form; when you join, you receive valuable information and materials about Montessori education.

The Materials Company of Boston

http://www.thematerialscompany.com/

💲

★★★★

This site offers Montessori teaching materials at low prices. It has a Montessori consultant on staff to answer any of your questions. You can buy everything from math beads to furniture.

The Montessori Centre International Site

http://www.montessori.ac.uk/

★★★

This site offers a list of Montessori schools, information about Montessori seminars and workshops, Montessori software, furniture, job listings, and much more. You can also get advice on starting your own Montessori school.

Related Site
http://bcn.boulder.co.us/univ_school/montess/

A B C D E F G H I J K L M N O P Q R S T U V W X Y Z

A
B
C
D
E
F
G
H
I
J
K
L
M
N
O
P
Q
R
S
T
U
V
W
X
Y
Z

Montessori Education Centers Associated (MECA)

http://www.meca-seton.com/

★★★

MECA is a teacher education program for Montessori teachers and administrators for children 0 to 6 years old. Learn about MECA's paraprofessional program for administrators, parents, and assistants, and register for training programs. Discover what fun MECA's summer camp holds for children, with camping for children 0 to 9 years.

The Montessori Foundation

http://www.montessori.org/

★★★★

Read about the Montessori Foundation and its purpose, learn about the variety of Montessori schools in America, and subscribe to *Tomorrow's Child*, a magazine for Montessori parents and educators. Check out the Montessori school directory, where you can search for Montessori schools around the world. You can add your school to the directory, too. Visit the Montessori Foundation Bookstore, where you can order original works of Maria Montessori translated into English (order form is not secure).

Montessori Resources on the Web

http://www.ccma.ca/ccma/montrsrc.htm

★★★★

This site provides searchable information about Montessori programs and training sites, as well as related educational associations.

K–12—PRIVATE EDUCATION

Catholic Education Network

http://www.catholic.org/cen/

★★★★

Developments in Catholic education, with an index of schools online and a list of upcoming conferences.

Choosing a School

http://www.nysais.org/family/choosingaschool.html

★★★★

This site should be a first stop for parents beginning the school-selection process. Includes information on how to select schools, how to narrow the choices, and how the schools choose the students. Also provides information on what to do if your child is not admitted.

Eschoolsearch.com

http://www.eschoolsearch.com/

★★★★★

Search this directory of more than 30,000 private schools (elementary through high school) by city, state, school type, and/or grade. Schools can register here to be added to the directory.

Independent Schools Association of the Central States

http://www.isacs.org/

★★★★

This site is designed to provide administrators, teachers, trustees, parents, and students with answers to all their independent school questions. Includes a searchable database of private schools, market research services, a career center, a recommended reading list, and more.

National Association of Independent Schools

http://www.nais.org/

★★★

Representing more than 1,100 pre-collegiate day and boarding schools worldwide, the NAIS provides leadership and works to preserve the independence of its members. Here, you can search for schools, learn about financing resources, check on upcoming conferences, and research legislation relating to independent schools.

Parochial School World Directory

http://www.parochial.com/

★★★

Lists parochial (Catholic) schools by state and country, although the list of schools is not comprehensive. Also includes links to suppliers of Catholic school uniforms.

Parochial/U.S. Book Covers

http://www.usbookcovers.com/index.html

★★★★

Since 1951, Parochial/U.S. Book Covers has been supplying private and public schools with book covers and folders free. Advertisers, not schools, pay the cost.

Peterson's Education Center

http://www.petersons.com/pschools/

★★★★★

Find private secondary schools by name, location, or type of program. Or identify schools to meet your child's special needs. A rich database of information, including help on financing a private education. You can purchase books about colleges, find out how to apply, and locate information to help you prepare for college through the online store.

Private Education Loan Resources

http://apollo.gmu.edu/finaid/htmldocs/privloan.html

★★★★

Many organizations accessible via the World Wide Web provide private education loan-funding options for parents, undergraduates, graduates, and professional students. Learn about Sallie Mae, Nellie Mae, and TERI loans, as well as several others.

Resources for Christian Teachers

http://www.teacherhelp.org/

★★★

Christian school teachers can find numerous resources for use in the classroom here, including worksheets, lesson plans, and ideas for activities.

Student Loans and Education Financing

http://www.gateloan.com/

★★★★

This site provides information about student loans and financing education. Even offers a place to apply online.

TABS—The Association of Boarding Schools

http://www.schools.com/

★★★★

This site provides answers to questions you may have about boarding schools. It also provides the means to find a boarding school and a common application form to start the process. International opportunities are also presented.

K–12—PUBLIC EDUCATION

Public Education Network

http://www.publiceducation.org/

★★★

The goal of this organization is to marshal support for improving the quality of education in public schools. Find out how to join, how you can support its efforts, and what can be done in your area.

National Association of State Boards of Education

http://www.nasbe.org/

★★★

This organization is dedicated to helping school boards of education establish high standards across the nation. Here, you can find news about educational issues and the various projects that the NASBE is involved in.

The Story of Public Education

http://www.pbs.org/kcet/publicschool/

★★★★★

All

PBS special that examines the history of public education in the United States and the innovators who changed the course of public education.

A
B
C
D
E
F
G
H
I
J
K
L
M
N
O
P
Q
R
S
T
U
V
W
X
Y
Z

PRESCHOOL

Chateau Meddybemps

http://www.meddybemps.com/

★★★★

👫 0-8

A whimsical site for parents and young children. The offerings for preschoolers include a list of the best books for preschoolers and young readers and fun learning activities designed to develop math, observation, memory, and reasoning skills.

Early Childhood Educators' and Family Web Corner

http://users.stargate.net/~cokids/

★★★

👫 0-8

This site, which bills itself as "the place for all things early childhood," deals with items of interest to early-childhood educators and parents of young children. Offers articles, education debate, family pages, teacher pages, ChildChat sessions, and lots of links. Links to online stores that carry early education products.

Early Childhood.com

http://www.earlychildhood.com/

💲

★★★★

Offers information for those who are interested in improving the education and experiences of young children. Take advantage of articles and other resources, seek advice from the experts, add to your collection of creative projects, and share your ideas with others in the early-childhood community. You can buy arts and crafts supplies and play equipment for your school or center through the online store.

Education World

http://www.education-world.com/

★★★★★

👫 All

Education World's stated goal is "to make it easy for educators to integrate the Internet into the class-room." The site offers articles, lesson plans, school information, employment listings, links, and other resources for educators of preschoolers through older children. Offers a search engine that searches 500,000 education-specific sites that are safe for kids.

Everything Preschool

http://www.everythingpreschool.com/

★★★★★

If you're a preschool teacher or are homeschooling your child, you will want to visit this site often. It features a vast collection of resources for teaching preschool children, including lesson plans, alphabet ideas, bulletin boards, recipes, songs, games, coloring pages, and holiday calendars.

Family Education Network

http://www.familyeducation.com

★★★★★

A resource for families to find out more about encouraging children to learn. You'll find child development Q&As, links to other educational sites, ideas to get your child to read, and many other useful ideas for helping your child get ready for and succeed at school. You can buy books, videos, software, toys, and games through various vendors who advertise at this site. The site provides links categorized by age group—Young Kids (0–8), Kids (9–13), and Teens (14–18).

Idea Box: Early Childhood Education and Activity Resources

http://www.theideabox.com/

💲

★★★

👫 0-8

A bright, informative site that focuses on the education of young children. This site is filled with goodies such as projects and games, printable pages, kids' recipes, online stories, links for children, and "Idea Box Talk."

Institute of Educational Services

http://www.ed.gov/about/offices/list/ies/index.html

★★★★

The institute sponsors various research projects on early childhood. Find out about IES, its research and development centers, its research and demonstration projects, and get IES news or check out the list of related resources.

KinderCare

http://www.kindercare.com/

★★★★

The largest preschool and childcare company in the United States. You can learn about KinderCare and its programs, tour a center online, or find a facility near you.

The Perpetual Preschool

http://www.perpetualpreschool.com/

★★★★

Excellent collection of resources and ideas for preschool teachers. This site offers an incredible array of themes for nearly every occasion, learning center ideas, teacher tips, playtime ideas, and even a directory of stores where you can purchase equipment and supplies.

PreschoolEducation.com

http://www.preschooleducation.com/

★★★★

This site provides a collection of resources for preschool teachers, including art and craft ideas, software and book reviews, calendars, snack ideas, plays, and much more. The pop-up ads can be annoying, but the site does provide some excellent resources for preschool teachers.

Preschool Page

http://www.kidsource.com/kidsource/pages/Preschoolers.html

★★★★

The Preschool area of KidsSource Online offers articles that provide information, tips, and suggested activities for children ages 3 to 6. Although part of the site's focus is on education, it also covers safety, recalls, new product information, health, and nutrition.

ReadyWeb Home Page

http://readyweb.crc.uiuc.edu/

★★★★

Information and resources sponsored by the ERIC Clearinghouse on Elementary and Early Childhood Education. Look into getting your child ready for school by turning to these U.S. Department of Education publications.

SuperKids Software Review

http://www.superkids.com/aweb/pages/reviews/early/3/elmopre/merge.shtml

★★★★★

Provides full reviews of educational software for early learners and older students. The reviews are written by teams of parents, teachers, and kids. Summary ratings of the titles include educational value, kid appeal, and ease of use.

RESOURCES

Adult Education

http://galaxy.einet.net/galaxy/Social-Sciences/Education/Adult-Education.html

★★★

Offers links to several resources on adult education. Enables the combination of distance education, adult education, and the Internet to deliver instruction. Invites contributions to the collection of resources.

AskTheBrain

http://www.askthebrain.com/

★★★★★

AskTheBrain is an online encyclopedia/directory that serves up answers about more than 200,000 interesting topics. When you can't find whatever you are looking for using one of the main search engines on the Web, Ask The Brain!

A
B
C
D
E
F
G
H
I
J
K
L
M
N
O
P
Q
R
S
T
U
V
W
X
Y
Z

Benjamin Franklin: Glimpses of the Man

http://sln.fi.edu/franklin/rotten.html

★★★★

 All

Provides multimedia information about Ben Franklin by using pictures, documents, and movies. Covers his family, inventions, diplomacy, philosophy, and leadership. Provides a bibliography for further study of Franklin, his accomplishments, and the time period.

Biology (Science)

http://galaxy.einet.net/galaxy/Science/Biology.html

★★★★

Offers links to all things scientific that might be of use to K–12 teachers or university teachers and students. Categorizes sections by subset of biology, most recent additions, software, and collections, to name a few.

CALI: The Center for Computer-Assisted Legal Instruction

http://cali.org/

★★★★

Nonprofit consortium of more than 155 U.S. law schools. Supports the production, distribution, and use of computer-based instructional materials.

The Comer School Development Program

http://info.med.yale.edu/comer/

★★★★

Provides information about the School Development Program, a national school reform project directed by James P. Comer, M.D., the renowned child psychiatrist at the Yale Child Study Center.

Community Learning Network

http://www.cln.org/cln.html

★★★★

👥 14-18

Shares information about educationally relevant Internet resources. Click the Subject Areas link to explore resources by subject or click Teachers & Tech to improve your computer skills. The Kids Stuff area provides some fun online activities for students.

Cornell Theory Center Math and Science Gateway

http://www.tc.cornell.edu:80/Edu/MathSciGateway/

★★★★

Provides links to resources in mathematics and science for educators and students in grades 9–12. Divides the resources into standard subject areas and includes links to online field trips and museums. Also offers journal and research articles.

Council for Exceptional Children

http://www.cec.sped.org

★★★★

Parents of exceptional children, whether they are physically challenged or gifted, might want to learn more about the work of this organization, which aims to improve the quality of services provided to these students. The site contains legislative information, a clearinghouse of information on the subject, and discussion forums to link parents and educators on this issue.

Faculty of Food, Clothing and Hospitality Management

http://www.hollings.mmu.ac.uk/

★★★

Details courses, staff, students, and the work done in this department. Contains examples of designs produced by students and staff and also details some of the conferences and shows scheduled.

The Digital Frog

http://www.digitalfrog.com/

★★★★

Focuses on producing high-quality educational software. Features The Digital Frog CD-ROM. Describes DFI and contains a full-featured Web version of The Digital Frog. You can order products online via email, but the site does not offer an online order form.

Educational Learning Systems
http://216.185.138.165/

★★★

This Flash-enabled site provides information on ELS's educational software products. These products cover subjects in reading, math, language arts, and science for schools in Florida and Georgia. Includes products for nonreaders to help development of reading skills.

Educause
http://www.educause.edu/

 $

★★★★

Offers searchable archives of *EDUCOM Review*, archives of the LISTSERV EDUPAGE, and other online documents. Supports EDUCOM's focus on educational technology in higher education. Also offers links to several other telecom/educational technology–related sites and programs. You can subscribe to various periodicals online.

Encarta
http://encarta.msn.com/

 $

★★★★★

Encarta online places a reference library right at your fingertips. Here, you can find the award-winning Encarta encyclopedia, a dictionary, a world atlas, quizzes, homework help, and areas for aspiring college students, college students, grad students, and more.

United Nations Cyberschool Bus
http://cyberschoolbus.un.org

★★★★★

 All

The next time you or your child needs to do a report on a specific country, this is the first site you should visit. Compare data within the countries of the United Nations, including urban growth, top exports, and threatened species. A great resource for adults and kids.

infoplease.com
http://www.infoplease.com/

★★★★★

 All

A huge library of reference material, including biographies, history, government facts, atlases, almanacs, encyclopedias, dictionaries, current events, and more.

Kid Info
http://www.kidinfo.com/

★★★★

 All

A great resource for young students, this site features a Student Index, where you can find homework help, a comprehensive list of reference resources, educational search engines, and some fun links to keep from frying your brain cells. Also includes resource centers for parents, teachers, and younger students. Most links take you to other sites.

The Math Forum
http://mathforum.org/

★★★★

 All

Focuses on math education. Offers links to resources such as the Coalition of Essential Schools, a Web-based lesson on vectors, a geometry LISTSERV, and more. Also offers a section on projects for students, such as "Ask Dr. Math."

MATHMOL: K–12 Mathematics and Molecules
http://www.nyu.edu/pages/mathmol/

★★★

 All

Provides students, teachers, and the general public information about the rapidly growing field of molecular modeling. Also provides K–12 students with basic concepts in mathematics and their connection to molecular modeling. Contains supporting materials for this project, such as a hypermedia textbook, a library of 3D molecular models, and online challenges for students.

A B C D E F G H I J K L M N O P Q R S T U V W X Y Z

A
B
C
D
E
F
G
H
I
J
K
L
M
N
O
P
Q
R
S
T
U
V
W
X
Y
Z

The Media Literacy Online Project

http://interact.uoregon.edu/MediaLit/HomePage

★★★

Provides information and resources to educators, producers, students, parents, and others interested in the influence of electronic media on children, youth, and adults. Contains a database on media literacy and links to Internet resources related to the topic.

Midlink Magazine

http://www.cs.ucf.edu/~MidLink/index.html

★★★★

👫 All

Midlink Magazine features educational projects by students aged 8–18 as a means of recognizing exemplary work and setting an example for other schools and students. You'll find articles, teacher resources, and a list of schools looking to establish collaborative ties with others around the world.

Mount St. Helens

http://volcano.und.nodak.edu/vwdocs/msh/

★★★★

👫 All

Provides image maps of more than 1,490 still images of the mountain before, during, and after the eruption. Provides information about the people, Mount St. Helens and other volcanoes, other Mount St. Helens resources, plants and animals, and curriculum. Link to the Mount St. Helens Volcano Gift Shop.

NASA Education Sites

http://quest.arc.nasa.gov/

★★★★

👫 All

Offers a collection of servers specifically geared for teachers, students, and administrators, as well as a selection of math and science education resources, connectivity to numerous education servers, journals, and grant and project participation information.

Peterson's Education Center

http://www.petersons.com

 $

★★★★★

Seeks to catalog all United States K–12 schools, colleges, and universities, both public and private, as well as community and technical colleges. Links to study guides for passing standardized tests, plus some free tips, strategies, and sample questions. Some excellent information on career and college planning.

Pitsco's Ask An Expert

http://www.askanexpert.com/

★★★★

👫 All

If you or your students have a question they'd like answered, head to this site to search for a qualified expert to answer it. After you've found one, go to that site to determine whether the answer is there. If not, use email to pose the question directly. Each month there is a featured expert, too.

scifair.org

http://www.scifair.org/

★★★★

👫 9-13

Are you having trouble coming up with an idea for a science fair project? Then scifair.org can help. Step-by-step instructions explain how to think of a unique idea on your own. If you're really stuck, you can find dozens of ideas in the Idea Bank or see what other budding scientists are up to on the Idea Board. Tips on using the scientific method, writing your report, and putting together a killer display.

Second Nature

http://www.secondnature.org/

★★★★

Nonprofit environmental organization that helps institutions of learning—such as colleges and universities—produce graduates who will become environmental leaders. Provides information about Second Nature's unique educational philosophy.

The Tecla Home Page

http://www.sgci.mec.es/uk/Pub/tecla.html

★★★★

Text magazine written for learners and teachers of Spanish, produced weekly during the school year. Provides text in Spanish, with vocabulary listed below the text.

Tutor.com

http://tutor.com/

★★★★

Tutor.com provides products and services for library systems, schools, and communities to help deliver information, resources, and assistance to students. It also provides a subscription service that features individual tutoring for students (but not for free).

Videodiscovery

http://www.videodiscovery.com/

★★★★

Provides information about interactive CD-ROM and laserdisc multimedia for science and math education, plus cool science facts, a guide to Internet education resources, educational technology primers, and more.

Voice of the Shuttle

http://vos.ucsb.edu/

★★★★★

📇 All

The Voice of the Shuttle began in late 1994 to introduce humanities students and teachers at the University of California, Santa Barbara, to the Web. Since then, it has gone public and draws general-interest visitors and hard-core researchers alike. This site features an annotated directory to the best humanities-related information and resources on the Web.

The Washington Center for Internships and Academic Seminars

http://www.twc.edu/

★★★★

📇 14-18

Proposes the idea that the key to student success is active involvement in the educational process. Provides internships and academic seminar programs to college students that challenge them personally and professionally. Students apply academic theory through practical experience, discover their professional strengths and weaknesses, question chosen career paths, interact with students from across the country, and develop a broad sense of civic and professional responsibility.

Web of On-line Dictionaries

http://www.yourdictionary.com/

★★★★★

📇 All

This website lists free and subscription online dictionaries and thesauri containing words and phrases to help students locate the best word to use.

A
B
C
D
E
F
G
H
I
J
K
L
M
N
O
P
Q
R
S
T
U
V
W
X
Y
Z

A
B
C
D
E
F
G
H
I
J
K
L
M
N
O
P
Q
R
S
T
U
V
W
X
Y
Z

ELECTRONICS

Alpine of America

http://www.alpine1.com/

★★★

Known for its high-end car stereos and speakers, Alpine also has a full product line of CD changers, head units (components that combine CD and cassette players, receivers, equalizers, and more), and auto security systems. Get full product features and links to Alpine sites in other countries.

AMDEX

http://www.unbeatable.com/

★★★★

AMDEX boasts more than 10,000 products ready to ship. Find an extensive catalog of consumer electronics, from palmtop computers to karaoke machines to camcorders. Order before 4:00 p.m., and your shipment will be sent out the same day.

Audio Ideas Guide

http://www.audio-ideas.com/

★★★★

Read audio and video product reviews by category or brand, and search the archives for back issues of this print magazine.

Audio Video News

http://www.audiovideonews.com

★★★★

For a look at audio, video, and home electronics news, new products, and upcoming electronics events, this site is a quick read.

Best Buy

http://www.bestbuy.com

★★★★★

The number one specialty retailer of consumer electronics, personal computers, entertainment software, and appliances in the United States. Compare products, get coupons and rebate forms, shop, and rent DVDs online.

Bose Corporation

http://www.bose.com

★★★★

One of the leaders in high-end consumer audio, Bose prides itself on using nonconventional thinking and products to solve conventional problems. Here, you'll find company history, current news and contests, and a secure site where you can purchase popular Bose models.

Cambridge SoundWorks

http://www.hifi.com/

★★★★

Get help choosing the best audio or home theater product, or go straight to the special deals and find out how much you can save.

Circuit City

http://www.circuitcity.com/

★★★★★

This consumer electronics retailer offers products in a number of categories, including home video and audio, car audio, digital cameras, phones, games, computers, and movie and music titles. Before buying, however, you'll want to read purchasing tips, check out product comparisons, and scan online reviews.

Crutchfield

http://www.crutchfield.com

★★★★★

This well-known home and car electronics catalog has gone online, offering products for sale via the Internet. A huge selection of products is available at competitive prices. Crutchfield has a solid reputation for quality and service, offering free shipping, 30-day moneyback guarantee, free shipping on returns, free technical support, free car stereo installation kits, expert advice on what to buy, and more.

Dynamism.com

http://www.dynamism.com/

★★★★★

If you're looking for the latest, greatest, coolest, cutting-edge electronics gizmos on the market, Dynamism can help you find (and purchase) them online.

eCoustics.com

http://ecoustics.com/

★★★★★

eCoustics.com specializes in home theater and hi-fi systems and provides everything you need to know in terms of instructions, product reviews to help you determine what you need, and how to assemble a killer home-entertainment center. This site also features other consumer electronic equipment, including digital cameras, MP3 players, car audio equipment, notebook computers, and much more. This site features an excellent collection of articles from some of the top consumer electronics magazines.

Electronics.cnet.com

http://electronics.cnet.com

★★★★★

Get gift ideas, read product reviews, find out which are editors' choices, and select from a long list of product categories—from TVs to DVD players to MP3 players, digital cameras, handheld devices, and much more. Current information presented in an easily accessible format makes this an easy pick for the Best of the Best award.

Home Theater Magazine

http://www.hometheatermag.com/

★★★★

Devoted to keeping home theater enthusiasts informed of the latest technology, this magazine serves a huge selection of articles and product reviews. If you're a home theater novice, click the Home Theater 101 link to learn the basics. You can even subscribe to the magazine online.

IEEE Home Page

http://www.ieee.org

★★★★

Home of the Institute of Electrical and Electronics Engineers, this site holds a great deal of information about the institute itself, its publications, the events it sponsors, and the ever-growing list of standards that it develops and supports. Find regional chapters and learn about training and career development programs through the organization.

Jerry Raskin's Needle Doctor

http://www.needledoctor.com/

★★★★

Just because digital is the latest thing doesn't mean that analog is dead. The Needle Doctor specializes in keeping the vinyl sound alive with catalogs of new turntables, needles, cartridges, and belts. You're not the only one out there still listening to records.

A
B
C
D
E
F
G
H
I
J
K
L
M
N
O
P
Q
R
S
T
U
V
W
X
Y
Z

Mega Hertz

http://www.megahz.com/

★★★

Mega Hertz specializes in the broadcasting and receiving end of the electronics spectrum. Products include amps, antennas, demodulators, satellite receivers, and TVs and monitors.

Nextag

http://www.nextag.com

★★★★

When you know which electronic gadget you want, visit Nextag and search for the best price. Nextag does the comparison shopping for you, quoting you the best price on a particular product, including tax and shipping. Now that's quality service!

Phone Scoop

http://www.phonescoop.com/

⑤

★★★★★

Finding the right cell phone and carrier can be a nightmare, but Phone Scoop can help. This site helps shoppers track down the perfect cell phone and comparison-shop for carriers. Expert reviews plus online forums can help you find the right phone/carrier combination for your needs.

Radio Shack

http://www.radioshack.com/

⑤

★★★★★

Radio Shack is still one of the leaders in consumer electronics. Find out about its many products, including minisatellite TVs, toys, cellular services, and home security. Also get the details on the international franchise program and employment opportunities.

Satellite Broadcasting and Communications Association

http://www.sbca.com

★★★

If you're interested in a digital satellite for your home but don't know where to begin, start here. The SBCA represents all parts of the home satellite industry. Check out the section about finding a good satellite dealer in your area and browse through the extensive glossary of DTH (direct-to-home) terms.

ShopNow

http://www.internetmall.com/

⑤

★★★★★

Huge online mall where you can shop for just about anything at hundreds of stores. When you reach the mall, click the Electronics link to view links for various electronics shops in the mall.

SoundStage

http://www.sstage.com

★★★★

The online magazine for high-end music and audio fans provides product and album reviews to guide you to your purchases. Plenty of links to manufacturers and retailers.

Tek Discount Warehouse

http://www.discountwarehouse.com/

⑤

★★★★★

Tek offers an enormous supply of appliances and electronics and promises a substantial savings from the manufacturer's suggested retail price. Products include stereo (home, car, and personal), microwaves, electric razors, camcorders, fax machines, telephones, copiers, digital cameras, vacuum cleaners, and much more. Order online or use the toll-free telephone number. The company promises quick ship times and a variety of payment methods.

EMERGENCY SERVICES

Abbey Group Consulting

http://www.abbeygroup.com/

★★★★

The Abbey Group provides consulting services in the public safety areas of fire services and law enforcement. Services include hazardous materials management systems, EMS reporting systems, and wireless on-the-job computing solutions.

AfterDisaster

http://www.afterdisaster.com/

★★★★

If your home or business has been damaged by fire, flood, or other natural disaster, this group promises to get you back on your feet as soon as possible while minimizing your loss and downtime. Specializing in responding to fire and water damage, the company has skills in drying documents, deodorizing, treating mold/mildew, getting clean water to your site, and much more.

American College of Emergency Physicians

http://www.acep.org/

★★★★

This site holds a warehouse of information about the ACEP, its policies and guidelines, and current news. Features a large "members-only" section, but much of it is focused on nonmembers as well. Find out about ACEP's views on managed care and other current concerns, as well as membership and dues information for doctors, residents, and medical school students.

⟦Best⟧ American Red Cross

http://www.redcross.org/

★★★★★

The jewel in the emergency services crown, the Red Cross exists to aid disaster victims and help people prevent and prepare for emergencies. Find out about the organization's current interests, locations in which it is currently helping disaster victims, and volunteer opportunities. Whether you're a victim of a terrible tragedy or are looking for a way to contribute to your community and lessen someone else's suffering, this site is a must-visit.

Computer Emergency Response Team

http://www.cert.org

★★★★

A site that tracks and reports on threats to computer security, such as viruses and worms.

Emergency Preparedness Information eXchange

http://epix.hazard.net/

★★★

Promotes the exchange of ideas about the prevention of, preparation for, and recovery from natural and sociotechnological disasters.

Event Medical Services, Inc.

http://www.eventmedical.com/

★★★★

EMS sets up shop at conventions, sporting events, private parties, and wherever else you need its services (as long as you're in California). Fully insured, EMS promises to take the worry away from hosting major events. It also carries a full line of emergency equipment and products.

A
B
C
D
E
F
G
H
I
J
K
L
M
N
O
P
Q
R
S
T
U
V
W
X
Y
Z

FireFighting.Com

http://www.firefighting.com/

★★★★

This jam-packed, energized site is like a giant recreation room for emergency-service workers of all flavors. Featuring news, articles, links, a chat area, and even poetry and other writing, FireFighting.Com caters mostly to firefighters, but it will also interest law enforcement workers, EMTs, and other public safety professionals.

Lifesaving Resources

http://www.lifesaving.com/

★★★★

Dedicated to the prevention of drowning and aquatic injuries, this site is a resource for lifeguards and other safety and rescue professionals. Articles on aquatic safety and rescue, information about upcoming seminars and training courses, case studies, online shopping, and much more. Very comprehensive site.

Related Sites

http://www.lifesaving.org/

http://www.americancpr.com/

http://www.worldwideaquatics.com/lifeguards.htm

Medic Aid Response Systems

http://www.medicaid-canada.com/

★★★

Based in Halifax, Nova Scotia, Medic Aid is a Canadian distributor of medical alarms. Search the products catalog, which includes a special health watch that notifies you when you need to take your medicine, and find an office near you with the store locator.

Mountain Rescue Association

http://www.mra.org/

★★★★

A volunteer organization that provides mountain safety education and volunteers for search-and-rescue operations.

Paramedic

http://www.paramedic.com/

★★★★

This site's goal is to be a resource to paramedics and those interested in paramedicine. Includes articles, news, research tools, educational links, list of top EMS sites, and online forums. Shop online for books and emergency equipment.

Rock-N-Rescue

http://www.rocknrescue.com/

★★★★

This company specializes in equipment for the narrow field of rock climbing and rope rescue. Browse the large catalog of ascending and rappelling devices, ropes and pulleys, and media resources. Whether your need is industrial, sports-based, or for a rescue squad, this site has what you need.

Related Sites

http://www.911.com

http://www.aaa.com/

http://www.geocities.com/Heartland/Plains/7841/

http://www.hurstjaws.com/

http://www.land-shark.com/

http://www.rescuebreather.com/

http://www.viking-life.com/usr/viking/vikingdotcom.nsf

ENVIRONMENTAL AND GLOBAL ISSUES

CONSERVATION

Arbor Day Foundation

http://www.arborday.com

★★★★★

Learn how you can help the environment by planting a tree in your community. Learn about the many Arbor Day programs for supplying trees to communities and educating the population about the importance of trees. You can find out what kinds of trees will do well in your area just by entering your ZIP code. You can order a wide variety of trees from this site at discount prices, with proceeds going to the foundation. Make a difference in your community by checking out this site.

Atlantic Salmon Federation

http://www.asf.ca/

★★★★

As if the salmon of North America didn't have enough trouble swimming upstream, now they have to contend with the possibility of extinction. The ASF's goal is to find solutions to all issues that could possibly affect the salmon's survival.

Bat Conservation

http://www.batconservation.org/

★★★★

 All

This site has information about bats and a section for kids to visit. You can adopt a bat and provide for its care. The Organization for Bat Conservation cares for orphaned and injured bats including those on the endangered species list. You'll find an online gift store where you can purchase shirts and even a bat detector.

The Butterfly Web Site: Conservation and Ecology

http://butterflywebsite.com

★★★★

 All

Provides articles calling for the conservation of butterflies, lists of butterfly gardens around the world, tips for attracting various types of butterflies, a well-stocked photo gallery, and much more. Plenty of links to related sites, plus online shopping through The Nature Store.

Center for Plant Conservation

http://www.mobot.org/CPC/welcome.html

★★★

Gives information about the Center for Plant Conservation located at the Missouri Botanical Garden. The center's primary focus is the conservation of plants in the United States. This site is primarily informational and gives links to other cooperating sites.

Conservation Breeding Specialist Group

http://www.cbsg.org/

★★★★

A conservation group whose mission is "to assist conservation of threatened animal and plant species through scientific management of small populations in wild habitats, with linkage to captive populations where needed." Check out this site to learn more about the group's programs and publications, read the current issue of its newsletter, or find out how you can assist. Global Zoo Directory lists zoos throughout the world.

A
B
C
D
E
F
G
H
I
J
K
L
M
N
O
P
Q
R
S
T
U
V
W
X
Y
Z

Conservation International

http://www.conservation.org/

★★★★

Learn all about the company that works in rainforests, coastal and coral reef systems, dry forests, deserts, and wastelands in more than 22 countries. Also, find out what you can do to assist actor Harrison Ford, Intel Chairman/CEO Gordon Moore, and the rest of CI in their ongoing fight to conserve our environment.

The Coral Reef Alliance

http://www.coralreefalliance.org/

★★★

[👫] All

This site is the diving-in point for an alliance made up of snorkelers, divers, and others who realize the value of our coral reefs and are working to preserve them. The alliance sponsors a number of conservation projects for which you can sign up online.

[Best] **Earth Island**

http://www.earthisland.org/

$

★★★★★

Earth Island is an organization dedicated to conserving, preserving, and restoring Earth's environment and biodiversity by encouraging people around the world to play an active role. Earth Island also educates visitors on the various threats to our environment and potential ways to reverse the degradation of our natural habitats. Here you can find a wide range of activities and projects to get involved in. If you don't see a conservation or preservation program that you are interested in, this Best of the Best site provides the information, resources, and contacts you need to start your own.

Endangered Species

http://eelink.net/EndSpp/

★★★

[👫] All

Huge directory of links to information and resources about endangered species. Here you can find everything from a comprehensive list of endangered species to organizations around the world that are working to preserve species. Great site for teachers, parents, and students.

Environmental Education Resources

http://eelink.net/

★★★

[👫] All

The goal of the EE-Link is to contribute to the protection and conservation of endangered flora and fauna. This site is not really designed for kids, but it does provide a collection of links to child-related resources.

Friends of the Earth International

http://www.foei.org/

★★★

A worldwide federation of national environmental organizations concerned with the preservation of the earth's ecological, cultural, and ethnic diversity. Read about ongoing campaigns and programs and link to other conservation sites.

green home

http://www.greenhome.com

$

★★★★

Are you trying to live a more environmentally conscious lifestyle? Then look no further. At green home, you can find all the information and products you need to live a life that's environment-friendly. Products include items for conserving water, composting waste, recycling materials, and conserving energy. You can also shop for organic pesticides and herbicides, environmentally friendly cleaning solutions, products made from recycled materials, and much more.

International Palm Society

http://www.palms.org/

$

★★★

The IPS is a group consisting of thousands of members in more than 80 countries dedicated to the study, culture, and preservation of palm trees around the world. This website provides general information about the society, membership information, and an image gallery and offers access to several palm-oriented publications.

International Rivers Network

http://www.irn.org/

★★★

Works to halt the construction of destructive river development projects and to promote sound river management options worldwide.

International Wildlife Coalition

http://www.iwc.org/

★★★★

 All

Concerned with saving endangered species, protecting wild animals, and preserving habitats and the environment. Kids should click the Inch in a Pinch link to tour the world of endangered habitats with the inchworm, Inch in a Pinch.

Land Trust Alliance

http://www.lta.org/

★★★

Learn what a land trust is, why it is so important, and what the most recent news is related to land protection and conservation. You'll also find public policy information and upcoming conferences and training related to land trusts. If you own land and would like to preserve it, this is a great place to learn how to obtain government resources for conservation.

League of Conservation Voters

http://www.lcv.org/

★★★

The League of Conservation Voters believes that the best way to achieve environmental results is through successful environmental legislation. The organization's goal is to elect members to Congress who truly care about the environment. It provides a scorecard that lets the public know how the House and Senate rate in environmental voting, in addition to providing a means to contact representatives to let them know that you care and are watching them.

MrSolar.com

http://www.mrsolar.com/

★★★★

MrSolar.com was started by a man in Utah who, along with his wife, has been living on solar energy for more than 20 years. His goal is to help everyone become as self-sufficient as he and his wife have been. Now the site acts as an information center and online store, where you can learn how to harness energy from the sun, wind, and water for yourself.

National Association of Service and Conservation Corps

http://www.nascc.org

★★★

The National Association of Service and Conservation Corps (NASCC) is the membership organization for youth corps programs. NASCC serves as an advocate, central reference point, and source of assistance for the growing number of state and local youth corps around the country.

National Audubon Society

http://www.audubon.org/

★★★★★

 All

Get background information on the society, its namesake John James Audubon, and his natural art. Find your local chapter and get membership information. You can even join online.

National Oceanic and Atmospheric Administration

http://www.noaa.gov

★★★★★

 All

Get the full story, complete with pictures, of some of the nation's natural disasters, from tornadoes in the Midwest to forest fires burning out of control on the West Coast. The NOAA has pictures and information on what's going on. An educational site with great pictures.

A B C D E F G H I J K L M N O P Q R S T U V W X Y Z

A
B
C
D
E
F
G
H
I
J
K
L
M
N
O
P
Q
R
S
T
U
V
W
X
Y
Z

National Recreation and Park Association (NRPA)

http://www.activeparks.org/

★★★

Home page of the National Recreation and Park Association (NRPA). NRPA is committed to advancing parks, recreation, and environmental conservation efforts that enhance the quality of life for all people. Link to the Active store provides online shopping.

National Safety Council

http://www.nsc.org

★★★

Read reports on public safety and find out how to avoid or lessen the most common injuries. You'll find an online library of information on safety at home and in the workplace, as well as special sections containing information on home and work hazards.

National Wildlife Federation

http://www.nwf.org/

★★★★★

 All

Remember *Ranger Rick* magazine? Well, it's still being published by the NWF, which works to protect and teach people about nature and wildlife. At the site, you can learn about the work of this organization and ways to support it. You can also order publications such as *Ranger Rick* and introduce kids to the KidZone, where they'll learn more about the wild.

The Nature Conservancy

http://nature.org/

★★★

 All

The Nature Conservancy puts an emphasis on saving entire habitats, including both plants and animals. Learn about its activities and programs and how you can join the organization in its conservation efforts. A very colorfully designed page.

The Ocean Alliance

http://www.oceanalliance.org/

★★★★★

 All

Concerned with protecting and conserving whales through research and international education initiatives. Though not designed for young children, some kids who are interested in whales and conservation issues will find this site fascinating.

RAINFORESTWEB.ORG

http://www.rainforestweb.org/

★★★★

 All

Works to protect Earth's rainforests by providing a comprehensive resource bank for concerned citizens, companies, and institutions. This is a great place for students to learn more about rainforests and why they are important.

Renewable Energy Policy Project

http://www.crest.org/

★★★★

Home of the Center for Renewable Energy and Sustainable Technology (CREST), this site is a treasure trove of information about renewable energy resources, such as sun, wind, water, and hydroelectric resources.

Sea Shepherd Conservation Society

http://www.seashepherd.org/

★★★

Works to defend the world's marine wildlife through the research, investigation, and video-documentation of violations of international laws, regulations, and treaties.

Surfrider Foundation USA

http://www.surfrider.org

★★★

This grassroots eco-surf organization is dedicated to the preservation of biological diversity on our coasts. It emphasizes low-impact "surfaris" and environmental education among surfers and others to maintain a synergy between man and beach.

USDA—Natural Resources Conservation Service

http://www.nrcs.usda.gov/

★★★★

The NRCS helps private landowners develop conservation systems suited to their land. It also works with rural and urban communities alike to reduce erosion, conserve water, and solve other resource problems.

Wildlife Conservation Society/Bronx Zoo

http://www.wcs.org

★★★★

 All

The Wildlife Conservation Society, headquartered at the Bronx Zoo, is dedicated to the conservation of wildlife around the world.

World Conservation Monitoring Centre

http://www.unep-wcmc.org/

★★★

Provides information services on conservation and sustainable use of the world's living resources, and helps others to develop information systems of their own.

World Wildlife Fund

http://www.wwf.org/

★★★★

 All

Dedicated to protecting the world's threatened wildlife and the biological resources they depend on. Features some information and games that appeal directly to kids.

ECOLOGY

Abbey's Web

http://www.abbeyweb.net/abbey.html

★★★★

Site honors the militant environmentalist Edward Abbey and provides information about his writings and current ecological causes he promoted. The site also contains interesting links to outdoor photos and more.

Cliff Ecology Research Group

http://www.uoguelph.ca/botany/research/cerg/index.html

★★★

A group of ecologists dedicated to the study of cliffs. Learn about ancient cedars on cliffs, effects of human trampling, and cryptoendolithic organisms.

Coastal America Partnership National Web Site

http://www.coastalamerica.gov

★★★★

The Coastal America program is a collaborative effort between organizations to protect the ecological systems and wildlife of America's coastal regions. This site provides general information on the program itself, publications, information centers, and success stories.

Earth Vision

http://www.earthvision.net/

★★★

Whether you are a staunch environmentalist, armchair trout fisherman, or CEO, you'll appreciate the news, content, and organization this site provides.

Earthwatch

http://www.earthwatch.org/

★★★★

A nonprofit membership organization that sponsors scientific field research projects. Read about the planned field research projects or participate online via expedition photos, reports, and online lessons. Membership information is also available at the site.

EcoFuture

http://www.ecofuture.org/

★★★

An environmental site that features readings, inspirational quotes, a list of upcoming events, and a list of things that you can do today to help keep our Earth beautiful and healthy.

A B C D E F G H I J K L M N O P Q R S T U V W X Y Z

A
B
C
D
E
F
G
H
I
J
K
L
M
N
O
P
Q
R
S
T
U
V
W
X
Y
Z

Eco-Pros

http://www.eco-pros.com/

★★★

 All

An educational but alarming site about the state our planet is in, including the loss of plant and animal species, air pollution, global warming, and more. The site explains what's happening and why, and what we can do to stop it. You'll find lots of links to other ecology sites, as well as sections on specific ecological topics.

Ecologia

http://www.ecologia.org/

★★★★

ECOlogists Linked for Organizing Grassroots Initiatives and Action is a group "replacing cold war competition with environmental cooperation." Headquartered in the United States, this group's mission is to provide assistance to environmental groups in the former Soviet Union, Eurasia, and the United States.

Ecology.com

http://www.ecology.com/

Ⓢ

★★★★★

 All

Home of Ecology Communications, Incorporated (ECI), a broadcasting company specializing in programs about ecology. Here, you will find the latest news, featured stories, quotes, links, and other resources dealing with ecological issues. Links to Amazon.com for books and videos.

Related Site
http://www.ecologyfund.com/

Greenpeace

http://www.greenpeace.org/

★★★★★

 All

Promoter of biodiversity and enemy of ecological and environmental pollution, Greenpeace and its links are accessible through this site. Links include the biodiversity campaign, the North Sea oil rig tour, a hot page, and more.

Home Energy Saver

http://www.homeenergysaver.lbl.gov/

Ⓢ

★★★★★

Visit this site to learn how you can cut down on energy consumption in your home. Simply enter your ZIP Code and complete a brief survey to obtain a list of ideas on how you can trim your home heating bill and conserve electrical consumption.

International Center for Tropical Ecology

http://www.umsl.edu/~biology/icte/

★★★

Combining the expertise of ecologists and systematists from both the University of Missouri–St. Louis and the Missouri Botanical Garden, the ICTE promotes research and education in biodiversity, conservation, and the sustainable use of tropical ecosystems.

International Ecotourism Society

http://www.ecotourism.org/

★★★

Provides resources for travelers who want to be environmentally responsible. Learn how to tour intriguing ecological areas without destroying natural habitats.

Sierra Club

http://www.sierraclub.org/

Ⓢ

★★★★★

 All

Home page for the nonprofit public interest conservation organization. The site focuses on activist news, current critical "ecoregions," and the Sierra Club National Outings Program, as well as an internal Sierra Club search engine.

U.S. Fish and Wildlife Service–National Wetlands Inventory

http://www.fws.gov/

★★★★

 All

Provides a list of the national wetlands and news related to them. Nineteen files are available for downloading, including a list of plant species that are found in wetlands. Also contains links to product information, ecology, and educator information.

Virtual Library of Ecology & Biodiversity

http://conbio.net/vl/

★★★

 All

Information related to ecology and biodiversity has been cataloged here and made available to the general public. Search the database for anything related to ecology and biodiversity.

World Forum for Acoustic Ecology

http://interact.uoregon.edu/MediaLit/WFAE/home/index.html

★★★

Seeks to investigate natural and human-made soundscapes. Offers links to sound resources and links to the online discussion forum.

PRESERVATION

The Air & Waste Management Association

http://www.awma.org/

★★★

The AWMA's purpose is "to enhance environmental knowledge and provide quality information on which to base environmental decisions." At the association's home site, you can find information on becoming a member and a calendar of events that includes annual meetings and workshops. Potential environmental scholars can find a list of schools that offer advanced degrees in environmental science here.

Environmental Defense Fund

http://www.environmentaldefense.org/

★★★

The group that formed in 1967 to fight the use of DDT is still going, and is more than 300,000 strong. The group needs your help in addressing what it feels are critical environmental issues; check out this site to find out what those issues are and what you can do.

Environmental Explorers Club

http://www.epa.gov/kids/

★★★★★

 All

The United States Environmental Protection Agency's kids site provides information for students, teachers, and parents; a place where kids can submit questions; an art room; a science room; a game room; an area with information on trash and recycling; and much more. Great place for kids to learn about our environment and what they can do to help keep it clean.

Environmental Protection Agency's Office of Water

http://www.epa.gov/ow/

★★★★

This beautifully produced site explores American water resources with an emphasis on the quality of our nation's water, and features powerful searching, imagery, animation, kids' pages, valuable publications, and informative hot links. See also the entry for the "United States Environmental Protection Agency" later in this section.

National Center for Preservation Technology and Training

http://www.ncptt.nps.gov/

★★★

Dedicated to the preservation of prehistoric and historic resources. This site attempts to further the technology and techniques of preservation and conservation by offering grants to study new methods and to provide training. You can apply for grants from the site. You can also request free publications from this site.

A
B
C
D
E
F
G
H
I
J
K
L
M
N
O
P
Q
R
S
T
U
V
W
X
Y
Z

A
B
C
D
E
F
G
H
I
J
K
L
M
N
O
P
Q
R
S
T
U
V
W
X
Y
Z

Rainforest Preservation Foundation

http://www.flash.net/~rpf/

★★★★

The Rainforest Preservation Foundation is a non-profit organization and a federally registered 501(c)(3) charity that is dedicated to preserving vast areas of rainforest in the Amazon basin.

United States Environmental Protection Agency

http://www.epa.gov/

★★★

At the EPA home page, you can access documents such as official EPA press releases, the *EPA Journal,* and more. All EPA programs are documented online, from Acid Rain to Wetlands. Through this page, you can send your comments directly to the EPA, as well as apply for employment.

The Whale Museum's Orca Adoption Program

http://whale-museum.org

($)

★★★★★

 All

What better way to "save the whales" than to adopt one? By adopting Ralph, Saratoga, Missy, Princess Angeline, Deadhead, Raven, or any of the number of orcas that swim the waters of Puget Sound and southern British Columbia, you'll be supporting orca research and education.

RECYCLING

Bureau of International Recycling (BIR)

http://www.bir.org/

★★★

Represents the world's recycling industry. Find out about recycling publications, organizations, and events.

Computer Recycling

http://www.usedcomputer.com/nonprof.html

★★★

Computers are packed with hazardous materials, so don't dump your old computer in the trash. This site shows you where to take your old PC to have it recycled. You might even get a tax credit!

Freecycle

http://www.freecycle.org/

★★★★★

If you want to get rid of something but don't want to go through the hassle of trying to sell it or dump it, consider *freecycling* it. At Freecycle, you can give and receive, but you cannot buy or sell. This site places you in contact with the Freecycle organization in your area, where you can post your goods to give to charity organizations or anyone who's willing to take it off your hands.

Global Recycling Network

http://grn.com/

★★★

This site is dedicated to providing recycling information and supports the work of recyclers nationwide by helping to advertise the network's services. In addition to a company directory, you'll find a commodity pricing section, recycling news, resource library, and news and events sections.

GREENGUIDE: Reduce/Reuse/Recycle

http://www.pnl.gov/esp/greenguide/appe.html

★★★★

The table on this page provides valuable information on how to reduce consumption, reuse frequently discarded items, and recycle materials that can be reprocessed. It also contains special handling instructions for materials from batteries to wood pallets.

Internet Consumer Recycling Guide

http://www.obviously.com/recycle/

★★★

This recycling guide provides a starting point for consumers in the USA and Canada searching the Net for recycling information. The information is for regular folks with regular household quantities of materials to recycle.

Recycle City

http://www.epa.gov/recyclecity/

★★★★★

 All

United States Environmental Protection Agency's site teaches kids about recycling to conserve resources and keep our environment clean. Visit Recycle Town to see how its citizens reduce use, re-use wastes, and recycle. Play the Dumptown game. Find out where trash ends up. And learn more about recycling than you ever imagined.

Recycler's World

http://www.recycle.net/

★★★★

This trading site offers links to recycling associations, publications, traders and recyclers, equipment, brokerage group services, and more. You'll find pages for every possible recyclable material, from automotive parts to wood and plastics. The site even has a section for organic and food waste recycling.

Recycling Today Magazine

http://www.recyclingtoday.com/

★★★

Find articles covering the recycling world as well as commodity prices, a searchable archive, and discussion board.

Shred-It Mobile Paper Shredding and Recycling

http://www.shredit.com/

★★★

Provides onsite shredding and recycling services to businesses and individuals nationwide. Information request form provided.

WebDirectory: Recycling

http://www.webdirectory.com/Recycling/

★★★★

WebDirectory covers businesses recycling glass, paper, computer products, and other materials.

A
B
C
D
E
F
G
H
I
J
K
L
M
N
O
P
Q
R
S
T
U
V
W
X
Y
Z

A
B
C
D
E
F
G
H
I
J
K
L
M
N
O
P
Q
R
S
T
U
V
W
X
Y
Z

ETIQUETTE

Dance Floor Etiquette

http://homepages.apci.net/~drdeyne/flooretq.htm

★★★

Provides a diagram of a dance floor with the dance areas outlined (line dances, flow dances, swing dances, and more).

Etiquette International

http://www.etiquetteintl.com/

★★★

Etiquette International provides information and workshops for companies and individuals to boost their knowledge of business etiquette, entertaining, and international protocol. Read testimonials from past seminar participants and get detailed descriptions of the available seminars.

| Best | Good Housekeeping Advice

http://magazines.ivillage.com/goodhousekeeping/experts/peggy

$

★★★★★

This is the index site for several *Good Housekeeping* advice columns, including Peggy Post's "Etiquette for Today." Search the list by topic or just scroll through all the questions. If you have a question of your own, send it to Peggy via email. When you're ready to learn more about etiquette, there's no better site to start.

International Protocol and Business Etiquette Training for Executives

http://www.lettgroup.com/

★★★

The Lett Group runs seminars which teach that one way to beat your competitors is to outclass them. Find details on seminars that are up to five days long and cover topics such as introductions, business meals, telephone skills, and many more.

Miss Manners

http://www.washingtonpost.com/wp-dyn/style/columns/missmanners/

★★★★★

Miss Manners has been teaching us how to behave for years, and continues to keep us updated on what's considered rude and distasteful as our culture changes. Here, you can search the archive or Miss Manners' latest recommendations to readers.

Mr. Golf Etiquette

http://www.mrgolf.com/

★★★★

Promising to "make an asset" of himself, Mr. Golf set up this site to help you do your part in keeping golf a game of ladies and gentlemen. Read current or archived "Ask Mr. Golf" columns, or play a game in which you're shown a picture and challenged to determine the golfing etiquette rule being violated.

National League of Junior Cotillions

http://www.nljc.com/

This North Carolina–based organization trains and licenses those who want to offer cotillion programs in their local areas. The groups teach young people the basics of etiquette, ethics, and good behavior to give them a head start at building character and confidence. Check out the Q&A section or find out how to start a program in your area.

Netiquette Home Page

http://www.albion.com/netiquette/index.html

★★★★

This site features excerpts from Virginia Shea's book *Netiquette*. Read the 10 core rules of the Internet, take a Netiquette quiz, and even join a mailing list to stay current on the newest ways to be polite online.

Related Site

http://www.phish.net/discussion/netiquette.html

The Original Tipping Page

http://www.tipping.org/TopPage.shtml

★★★★★

How much do you tip a skycap at the airport? This site gives recommended tipping standards for 10 different service categories, covering dozens of different service workers and situations. Includes ushers at sports arenas, manicurists, cruise ship cabin boys, and much more. New software for Palm computers is equipped with a tip calculator.

Pachter & Associates

http://www.pachter.com/

Pachter & Associates specializes in corporate training and keynote speakers dedicated to etiquette, communication, and assertiveness in business. The site also boasts a large selection of related books and audiotapes that you can order by mail or fax.

Table Manners

http://www.sneakykitchen.com/Ideas/table_manners.htm

This site is dedicated to helping family members eat a healthy meal without causing a major scene. You'll find recipes, articles on encouraging good table manners, helpful hints, and additional resources available here. For a good laugh, take the table manners quiz.

U.S. Flag Code

http://suvcw.org/flag.htm

Part of the Sons of Union Veterans of the Civil War site, this page reprints Chapter 10 of Title 36 of the United States Code. Included in this document are occasions to display, methods to properly raise and lower the flag, and proper disposal of old flags.

Related Sites

http://www.templetons.com/brad/emily.html

http://www.etiquettesurvival.com/

A B C D E F G H I J K L M N O P Q R S T U V W X Y Z

EXERCISE AND FITNESS

24HourFitness

http://www.24hourfitness.com

★★★

You'll find a wealth of information that changes daily on fitness, sport, nutrition, and health with world-wide links. A community of persons committed to active and healthy living.

Aerobics and Fitness Association

http://www.afaa.com/

★★★★

Starting a healthy exercise program is the focus of this site, which covers proper nutrition, equipment, goal setting, and safety. You'll also learn how to select the best instructor for yourself.

Benefits of Regular Physical Activity

http://www.healthclubs.com/benefits/

★★★

Explore the possible positive effects of regular exercise.

Exercise at Work

http://www.fitnesszone.co.za/exercise1.htm

★★★

Some more great things you can do at work to make work easier and your body better.

Muscle Physiology

http://muscle.ucsd.edu/

★★★★

This site will give you an overview of everything you'd want to know about the physiology of muscles. It contains links to articles about specific aspects of muscle physiology. Presented by the University of California, San Diego.

National Institute on Aging

http://www.nia.nih.gov/

★★★

The National Institute on Aging offers the inspiration and information on this site for people over age 60 regarding the benefits of exercise to the heart, mood, and confidence. Sample strength-training plans are also provided, as are helpful hints on beginning exercise routines and other resources.

NISMAT Exercise Physiology Center

http://www.nismat.org/physcor/

★★★

Home of the Nicholas Institute of Sports Medicine and Athletic Trauma, this site provides information and links to resources on exercise physiology, nutrition, physical therapy, and athletic training.

Office Exercise

http://www.green-office.com/info/dyk_exercise.htm

★★★

List of exercises you can do in your office to stay fit and prevent repetitive stress injuries.

Physician and Sportsmedicine Online

http://www.physsportsmed.com

★★★★

Developed primarily for athletes, this site features help in finding sports medicine doctors and clinics, back issues of useful fitness articles, and tips on preventing and treating common injuries. Female athletes will find guidance specific to their needs, as will overweight exercisers and individuals going through rehabilitation.

Stretching: Do It, But Do It Right

http://www.coastside.net/USERS/runner/articles/stretch2.html

★★★

Excellent article on stretching correctly.

Why Exercise Is Cool

http://kidshealth.org/kid/stay_healthy/fit/work_it_out.html

★★★★

 0-8

Article for kids on why it's cool to exercise. The home of this page, http://kidshealth.org/kid/, provides additional information for kids about health issues that relate directly to them.

CROSS-COUNTRY RUNNING

Cool Running

http://www.coolrunning.com/

★★★★

Comprehensive site showing the latest running news, calendar of running events, and race results. You'll find a Runner's Voice page where a successful runner is interviewed each month (you can listen with RealAudio). You can also find out about racing locations and events around the world.

Dr. Pribut's Running Injuries Page

http://www.drpribut.com/sports/sportframe.html

★★★

Dr. Stephen Pribut, D.P.M. (a podiatrist) from Washington D.C., offers his expertise on various running injuries, ways to avoid them, and methods used to treat them. He also shares tips on what to look for in a good running shoe and a good sports physician.

KidsRunning.com

http://www.kidsrunning.com/

★★★★

 All

Site that encourages kids of all ages to start running for their health and well-being. Presented by *Runner's World* magazine.

Men's Cross Country–NCAA Championships

http://www.ncaachampionships.com/cross/mcross/

★★★

You'll find schedules and results for just about every NCAA cross country match, as well as links to many other men's sports.

Road Race Management

http://www.rrm.com/

★★★

Information, products, and services for race directors and race enthusiasts. Read about what others are doing in the Race Directors' Survey or register for the next Race Directors' Meeting and Trade Exhibit. Check out the Race Director Tip of the Week.

Road Runners Club of America

http://www.rrca.org/

★★★

The RRCA is a national association of not-for-profit running clubs, the largest grassroots running organization in America. Find out how your club can join. Clubs and events are listed by state. Check out the many programs the association sponsors and publications it produces.

A B C D E F G H I J K L M N O P Q R S T U V W X Y Z

A B C D E F G H I J K L M N O P Q R S T U V W X Y Z

RunMichigan
http://www.runmichigan.com/

★★★

 14-18

Resource for Michigan runners. View results for regional, state, and local meets of all levels. Check out marathon results and photos. Look at the race calendar of upcoming events. Search the site for your specific interest.

Run the Planet
http://www.runtheplanet.com

★★★

A site for runners by runners that provides information on places to run and upcoming races all over the world. Just choose your country, state, and city to view a hefty collection of information about running in your area.

USATF on the Web
http://www.usatf.org/

★★★

Chosen for Lycos' Top 5% of the Web award, this site is home of USA Track and Field, the national governing body for track and field, long-distance running, race walking, and cross country. USATF's 100,000+ members are from clubs, colleges and universities, schools, and other organizations across the country. You can search the site for just about anything related to running.

FITNESS

Bally Total Fitness
http://www.ballyfitness.com/

$

★★★★

From the largest commercial fitness center in the world comes this site, where you can read articles on various fitness-related topics, see what Bally has to offer, find a Bally fitness center near you, and create an online fitness log. Links to Bally Total Fitness store, where you can purchase exercise equipment, clothing, and other items.

Fitness Fundamentals
http://www.bodytrends.com/fitfund.htm

★★★

Guidelines for personal exercise programs developed by the President's Council on Physical Fitness and Sports.

Fitness Jumpsite
http://primusweb.com/fitnesspartner/

★★★★

Two certified personal trainers provide quality fitness, health, and nutrition information for anyone interested in getting in shape. The online fitness library offers effective training ideas, proper techniques, books, and fitness news. You'll also find discussion areas, bulletin boards, and a handy calorie calculator.

Best Fitness Online
http://www.fitnessonline.com/

★★★★★

The online home of Weider Productions, Inc., publisher of *Flex*, *Men's Fitness*, *Natural Health*, and other magazines, this site features an incredible wealth of information organized in an easy-to-navigate format. Links to exercise, nutrition, and health lead to articles on each subject. An online trainer, fitness calculators, and forums make this the best fitness site on the Web.

Fitness Zone
http://www.fitnesszone.com

★★★★★

The Fitness Zone offers weekly fitness articles, chat areas, discussions, a library, and FAQs. Visitors can also shop online for fitness equipment, from weights to treadmills and everything in between. And for those of you looking to upgrade your equipment or get into a new sport, the classified ads can help you sell off what you don't want.

Health and Fitness

http://k2.kirtland.cc.mi.us/~balbachl/fitness.htm

★★★

This page contains practical advice about fitness training, as well as links to other fitness resources, forums, and related information. You'll also find fun facts and information on how to determine whether an exercise program meets your needs and learn how many calories you burn with a multitude of activities. Warm-up tips and a fitness dictionary are also available.

Jorge Cruise 8 Minute Weight Loss

http://www.jorgecruise.com/

★★★

A weekly Webcast on a variety of fitness and weight-loss topics ranging from burning fat to preparing psychologically for fitness.

Men's Fitness.com

http://www.mensfitness.com/

★★★★

 Not for kids

Home of *Men's Fitness* magazine, dedicated to delivering the latest information on fitness for men, including diet, weight lifting, health, and gear.

NetSweat

http://www.netsweat.com/

★★★★

Termed a "gold mine" for gathering useful information on exercise and nutrition through a plethora of links. You can also find a fitness instructor, create a fitness plan, place classified ads, and review a site of the month.

Physical Activity and Weight Control

http://www.niddk.nih.gov/health/nutrit/pubs/physact.htm

★★★

 14-18

The weight-control information network explains the health benefits of exercising and provides tips on safe and successful physical activities.

President's Council on Physical Fitness and Exercise

http://www.fitness.gov/

★★★★

 All

Learn about the President's Challenge to all Americans, especially children, to get fit and stay fit. This site includes quick references for parents, teachers, coaches, and kids, along with a well-stocked reference library of the council's publications.

RUNNING

1st Place Sports

http://www.1stplacesports.com/

★★★

This site focuses on distance running in Jacksonville, Florida. It has training plans, race results, event schedules, and online entry forms.

American Running Association

http://www.americanrunning.org/

★★★★

 14-18

Good site to visit for exercise information. You'll find sections devoted to nutrition information, injury prevention, rehabilitation, health care, strength training, weight management, equipment, and more. A free monthly newsletter is also available.

American Track & Field

http://www.american-trackandfield.com/

★★★★

14-18

This racing magazine provides an event calendar, race results, training tips, regional and national racing news, and links to related resources.

A B C D E F G H I J K L M N O P Q R S T U V W X Y Z

A
B
C
D
E
F
G
H
I
J
K
L
M
N
O
P
Q
R
S
T
U
V
W
X
Y
Z

Boston Athletic Association

http://www.bostonmarathon.org/

★★★

👥 14-18

This official site has information about the annual Boston Marathon, press releases, profiles, a history of the race, and links to related sites (Boston travel and tourism, and so on).

The Boston Globe's Boston.com: Boston Marathon

http://www.boston.com/marathon/

★★★

👥 14-18

Coverage of the Boston Marathon. Also includes a course map, runner profiles, a history of the event, and related links. Presented by *The Boston Globe*.

Dead Runners Society

http://storm.cadcam.iupui.edu/drs/drs.html

★★★

Discussion group (LISTSERV DRS) for people who like to talk about running. With further resources and commercial sites listed.

FogDog Sports: Running Store

http://www.fogdog.com/home/index.jsp

$

★★★★

Browse the range of sporting goods, including name-brand footwear and running books, and place an order.

How to Run Your First 50-Miler

http://www.oceansofenergy.com/howtorun.htm

★★★

👥 14-18

Oceans of Energy magazine gives advice on running marathons and ultra-marathons. Includes tips from veteran runners.

i-run.com

http://www.i-run.com/

★★★★

👥 14-18

A Web-based running log with a collection of calculators that can help runners in calculating pace, distance, race performance, and more.

Stan Jensen's Home Page

http://www.run100s.com/

★★★

👥 14-18

A dedicated ultra-runner who competes in 100-mile races presents photos, results, and related links. Includes links to a race calendar and training tips.

Kick!

http://www.kicksports.com/

★★★★

👥 14-18

Online resource exclusively devoted to running. It includes a guide to the basics, training ideas, injury treatment and prevention information, advice on nutrition, pointers on choosing running gear, and a schedule of more than 1,300 U.S. races. For beginners as well as experienced runners.

Lake Tahoe Marathon

http://www.laketahoemarathon.com/

★★★

👥 14-18

Information for competitors and spectators at this running and walking event held on Columbus Day weekend.

Marathon & Beyond

http://www.marathonandbeyond.com/

$

★★★

👥 14-18

This bimonthly magazine covers marathons and ultra-running, with editorials, article previews, and reader feedback. Includes several running links.

New York City Marathon

http://www.nyrrc.org/nyrrc/marathon/index.html

★★★★★

♦♦ 14-18

New York Road Runners Club maintains this site with information on the New York City Marathon. It includes application information, a course description, advice on how to train for a marathon, and more.

ontherun.com

http://www.ontherun.com/

★★★

♦♦ 14-18

This resource for long-distance runners includes a searchable marathon calendar, race photos and results, entry forms, and a directory of clubs. Links to online stores that carry running gear and apparel.

Portland Marathon

http://www.portlandmarathon.org/

★★★

♦♦ 14-18

Details about the Portland Marathon, including online registration, a calendar of related events, souvenirs, and results.

Raid Gauloises

http://www.raidgauloises.com/

★★★

♦♦ 14-18

The Raid Gauloises is a multisport adventure race that is held in a different part of the world each year. Its site has information about the current race, a history of the past races, and information about the spirit of the competition.

Road Running Information Center

http://www.usaldr.org/

★★★★★

♦♦ 14-18

Sponsored by the USA Track & Field organization, this site provides running news, records, rankings, and statistics.

The Runner's Resource

http://www.geocities.com/Colosseum/4258/running/

★★★

♦♦ 14-18

A teenage cross-country runner offers training and nutrition advice for high school competitors. Features a racing strategy guide and links to online running charts and calculators.

The Runner's Schedule

http://www.theschedule.com/

★★★

♦♦ 14-18

This running and racing magazine lets visitors search for event locations, dates, and results. Find subscription information and several running resources.

Runner's Web

http://www.runnersweb.com/running.html

★★★★

♦♦ 14-18

Resource for runners. Links to magazines, downloadable software, race results, sports medicine sites, and more.

Runner's World Online

http://www.runnersworld.com

★★★★

♦♦ 14-18

Runners will turn to this site for calendars of road races and marathons, as well as hyperlinks to other running sites to assist in training for such events. You'll also find nutrition advice, daily running news, a bookstore, recent road and track results, and home remedies for common running conditions.

Running Times

http://www.runningtimes.com/

★★★★★

♦♦ 14-18

Home of *Running Times* magazine, this site features articles about runners, running, running races, training tools, shoe reviews, city guides, marathon directories, women's races, coaching tips, and more.

A B C D E F G H I J K L M N O P Q R S T U V W X Y Z

A
B
C
D
E
F
G
H
I
J
K
L
M
N
O
P
Q
R
S
T
U
V
W
X
Y
Z

Running, Walking, and Fitness Publications

http://www.teamoregon.com/~teamore/publications/mags.html

★★★

👥 14-18

Useful way of finding print and online publications. Contact details are listed geographically.

Running Network

http://www.runningnetwork.com/

★★★★

👥 14-18

Provides a national event calendar, editorials, current news, shoe reviews, results, and links to related pages.

The Running Page

http://www.runningpage.com

★★★

👥 14-18

Check for information about upcoming races or find race results, places to run in the United States, and running products and magazines.

Running Room Online

http://www.runningroom.com/

★★★

👥 14-18

Features news articles, race calendars, running and training tips, online registration, and links to other running-oriented sites on the Internet. Monthly events calendar and store locations are also featured at this site.

Terry Fox Foundation

http://www.terryfoxrun.org/

★★★★★

👥 14-18

The Terry Fox Foundation offers pledge and participation information for this annual Canadian cancer research benefit. Also includes a brief biography of Terry Fox and information about the foundation.

Track & Field News

http://www.trackandfieldnews.com/

★★★

👥 14-18

Internet version of the print publication lists results and rankings of professional and collegiate track and field athletes. View past issues.

Venue Sports Inc.

http://www.venuesports.com/

$

★★★★

👥 14-18

Browse or order from the comprehensive catalog of running and track shoes and gear for serious athletes.

WomenRunners.com

http://www.womenrunners.com/

★★★★★

👥 14-18

Special running site for women runners who run not only for the fitness aspect of it, but also for the power it instills in them. Here, women can find special training tips, stretches, and other information that deals specifically with issues relating to women runners. Site also provides areas where you can learn about upcoming races, check race results, follow the progress of your favorite women runners, and learn about new products.

WALKING

American Volkssport Association

http://www.ava.org

★★★

Association of pedestrian activist groups in the USA.

BioMechanics Magazine
http://www.biomech.com/

★★★★

Online magazine from the editors of *BioMechanics Magazine*, with articles on feet, knees, shoes, walking, and other sports. Some unique articles on the study of physical movement that are completely unrelated to exercise.

Hiking and Walking Home Page
http://www.webwalking.com/hiking.html

★★★★

News, hiking and walking clubs, places to go, boots and shoes to wear, walking tips, and more.

Kids Walk to School
http://www.cdc.gov/nccdphp/dnpa/kidswalk/

★★★★★

All

This site, created by the United States Centers for Disease Control, encourages kids to walk to school as part of an exercise program to keep our kids fit. In a time when kids are becoming more and more sedentary, this is just the approach we need.

Racewalk.com
http://www.racewalk.com

★★★★

Official race walking home page of USATF provides information to start and improve your walking program, walking events, and products.

SlimStep
http://www.slimstep.com/

★★★

Home page for SlimStep, an electronic device that fits in the palm of your hand and measures your total percentage of body fat, determines an exercise plan to reduce that percentage, and tracks your progress.

The Walking Connection
http://www.walkingconnection.com/

★★★★★

Home of *Walking Connection* magazine, which features articles about walking for exercise and pleasure. Includes articles on walking, training regimens, walking tips, suggested places to walk, walking vacations, treatments for walking injuries, and much more.

Walking Shop
http://www.walkingshop.com/

★★★

Online store for walkers carries men's and women's shoes, apparel, and accessories.

The Walking Site
http://www.thewalkingsite.com/

★★★★★

This site provides a list of resources for walkers of all fitness levels, especially beginners, and is maintained by an active, enthusiastic walker and marathon walking coach. The site features sections on power walking, race walking, marathon walking, injuries, stretching, nutrition, treadmill walking, and much more. Also includes information about various walking clubs.

Walking Works
http://www.walking.org/

★★★

Become fit and trim, both physically and spiritually, by getting out of the office, off the couch, and walking your worries away. Here, you can find information that explains why walking works to alleviate stress in your life and makes you feel stronger and more aware.

A
B
C
D
E
F
G
H
I
J
K
L
M
N
O
P
Q
R
S
T
U
V
W
X
Y
Z

WEIGHTLIFTING AND BODYBUILDING

Bodybuilding Weightlifting Directory

http://bodybuilding-directory.net/

★★★

Learn about routines and training tips, drugs and supplements, and nutrition, as well as links to other bodybuilding sites. This site also offers opportunities to post messages to the boards, join a mailing list, and list upcoming events in the calendar.

Gold's Gym

http://www.goldsgym.com/

★★★★

Official site of Gold's Gym, this site features articles on fitness and nutrition, a newsletter, discussion areas, and a tool for finding a Gold's Gym near you.

[Best] International Powerlifting Federation

http://www.powerlifting-ipf.com/

★★★★★

Everything a powerlifter needs to know about training, competition, and classification. A great site with tons of links! This site includes a link to the technical rulebook in PDF format as well as information on refereeing. There is information on the federation, including the constitution and the bylaws.

International Weightlifting Federation

http://www.iwf.net

★★★★

Information about upcoming events, publications, officials, and more. One of the more glitzy weightlifting sites covered here.

Muscle Media

http://www.musclemedia.com/

★★★★

Home of *Muscle Media* magazine, this site features articles on body building, health, and nutrition.

Powerlifting.com

http://www.powerlifting.com/

★★★

A gateway site that points to almost every imaginable powerlifting site on the Web. Includes federations, match results, how-tos, and lots more.

USA Weightlifting

http://www.usaweightlifting.org/

★★★★★

Home of the National Governing Body (NGB) for Olympic weightlifting in the United States, USAW is a member of the United States Olympic Committee (USOC) and a member of the International Weightlifting Federation (IWF). Here, you can learn more about the organization and the weightlifting competitions it sponsors. Also features information about USAW weightlifters, weightlifting basics, and links to other resources.

Related Site

http://www.qwa.org/

Weights.net

http://www.weightsnet.com/

★★★

 Not for kids

An interactive daily discussion group for people interested in weightlifting. You can browse daily archives or contribute to today's discussion. The online store shuffles you off to Amazon.com, where you can purchase books, videos, and other items online.

Weighty Matters

http://staff.washington.edu/griffin/weights.html

★★★

A collection of articles and thoughts on techniques and exercises in bodybuilding.

Related Sites

http://www.cyberpump.com/
http://www.ironmanmagazine.com/
http://ageless-athletes.com/
http://www.nasa-sports.com/
http://www.strengthtech.com/
http://www.geocities.com/Colosseum/Field/7342/

EXTREME SPORTS

 **Boardz**

http://www.boardz.com

★★★★★

👥 14-18

Boardz is an online board sports magazine providing entertainment and information for board riders of all kinds, including snowboarders, skateboarders, surfers, skiers, and wakeboarders. In addition to chat and sports-specific information, you can also find surf forecasts and snow reports. Boarders visiting this site will soon realize just why it's the Best of the Best.

Eco-Challenge

http://www.ecochallenge.com

★★★

Watch the progress of this year's Eco-Challenge participants as they traverse Fiji. Eco-Challenge is an expedition race that runs for 6–10 days, with teams of 4 participants traveling 300 miles, 24 hours a day.

EXPN Extreme Sports

http://expn.go.com/

★★★

👥 14-18

ESPN's extreme sports site. Find continuously updated news about extreme sports here.

Extreme Sports Online

http://www.xtsports.com/

★★★★

👥 14-18

If you're interested in biking or kayaking in Charlottesville, VA, check out this site. Here you can find out where to go to rent kayaks or mountain bikes and take kayaking classes. Some good general information on choosing the right bike or kayak.

Heckler Magazine

http://www.heckler.com/ramps/index.html

★★★

👥 14-18

Devoted to serious skateboarders, Heckler's website features biographical articles on some of skateboarding's most intriguing characters, plus reviews of musical bands and skate parks. Check out the Ramp Plans tab for tips on creating your own skateboard ramps.

Hyperski Online

http://www.hyperski.com/

★★★★

👥 14-18

This online e-zine covers ski conditions, equipment, resorts, lessons, and other helpful information for those extremists looking for a skiing or snowboarding adventure. Heli-skiing is also a topic of discussion.

The Maui Windsurfing Report

http://www.maui.net/~mauiwind/MWR/

★★★★

The MWR is the center of windsurfing on the WWW. Offers action photos, news and views, contests to win a sail, and weather reports.

A
B
C
D
E
F
G
H
I
J
K
L
M
N
O
P
Q
R
S
T
U
V
W
X
Y
Z

Outside Online

http://outside.away.com/

★★★★★

Outside Online is the place to go when you're inside and have the urge to set out on an adventure in the great outdoors. Here you can explore travel opportunities, pick up some great fitness facts, learn new extreme sport techniques and tips, and gear up for your next adventure. You can also check the profiles of your favorite extreme sport athletes.

Parachute Industry Association

http://www.pia.com/

★★★★

The objectives of the Parachute Industry Association are to advance and promote the growth, development, and safety of parachuting and to engage and serve participants in the parachute industry. The PIA consists of companies and individuals united by a common desire to improve business opportunities in this segment of aviation. Site contains PIA publications, parachuting Yellow Pages, a product listing, meeting schedule, and more.

Sailboard Vacations

http://www.sailboardvacations.com/

★★★

Serves as a travel agency for windsurfers. Offers detailed travel information on the finest windsurfing spots. Features the latest in quality windsurfing equipment from Mistral. Provides information on how to windsurf.

Sandboard Magazine

http://www.sandboard.com/

 14-18

Hear all about the sport of riding snowboards over sand dunes, buy equipment, jump into a chat, get the latest sports news, and watch video clips of sandboarders in action.

Xtreme Sports of New York

http://www.xtremesports.com/

★★★

 14-18

Articles, news, and events about Xtreme sports in New York and the northeastern United States. Includes BMX biking, hang gliding, climbing, sky diving, wakeboarding, skiing, and much more.

HANGLIDING AND PARAGLIDING

A–Z of Paragliding

http://www.paragliding.net/

★★★★

Sensibly categorized, this site contains a useful collection of links and an excellent general paragliding resource.

Adventure Productions

http://www.adventurep.com/

★★★★★

Do you want to learn how to fly an ultralight? Paraglide? Hang glide? Trike? Then this is the place to go for training materials. Based in Reno, Nevada, Adventure Productions offers a variety of videos, CDs, books, and pilot tools designed to help pilots and flight students to take off.

All About Hang Gliding

http://www.all-about-hang-gliding.com/

★★★★★

Comprehensive resource for learning everything you need to know to begin hang gliding and improve your technique and enjoyment of hang gliding. Great collection of books, CDs, and videos you can purchase online. Includes a Getting Started FAQ, photo and video galleries, a list of places to fly organized by state, lists of clubs and organizations, and much more.

BHPA

http://www.bhpa.co.uk/

★★★

At this site, you'll find information about the British Hang Gliding and Paragliding Association.

Big Air International ParaGliding

http://www.bigairparagliding.com/

★★★

This U.S.–based site, maintained by Kinsley Wong, is for the international paragliding community.

Hang Gliding and Hang Gliders

http://www.hang-gliding.net/

★★★

Article on hang gliding which answers most of the questions that anyone who considers hang gliding should ask. Clears up many misconceptions about hang gliding.

How Hang Gliding Works

http://www.howstuffworks.com/hang-gliding.htm

★★★★

Ever wonder how a hang glider remains suspended in the air? Well, this site has the answers. Learn how a hang glider flies and the equipment that's required, and check out a description of a sample flight. Provides links to other related resources as well.

San Francisco Hang Gliding Center

http://www.sfhanggliding.com/

★★★

Planning a trip to San Francisco? Then check out the site of the San Francisco Hang Gliding Center, where you can take lessons on hang gliding or aquagliding (hang gliding over the water).

Sydney Hang Gliding Centre

http://www.hanggliding.com.au/

★★★★

Home of Sydney's first and only full-time hang gliding centre, where you can learn about tandem hang gliding training, the various courses available, and the equipment you need. Also features a Stories area and a Photograph Gallery, where you can get a small taste of the experience.

United States Hang Gliding Association

http://www.ushga.org/

★★★★

The association's web page provides plenty of useful information for the hang gliding professional, including the latest in regulations and details on pilot ratings (how to earn your rating, available endorsements, and so on), as well as information on membership benefits, local USHGA chapters, and upcoming competitions and other events.

Related Sites

http://www.hang-gliding.com/

http://www.birdsinparadise.com/

http://www.wallaby.com/

SKATEBOARDING

AKA: GIRL SKATER

http://www.girlskater.com/

★★★★

👥 14-18

Do you think that skateboarding is just for boys? Then visit this site to have your misconception shattered. These girls can ride, and they have the photos and video footage to prove it.

DansWORLD Skateboarding

http://www.cps.msu.edu/~dunhamda/dw/dansworld.html

★★★

👥 14-18

Dan's site is a world of photos, articles, and commentary. Even the nonskater can appreciate the "wisdom" of the *Zen of Skateboarding*.

Northern California Downhill Skateboarding Association

http://www.ncdsa.com/

★★★

👥 14-18

The NCDSA is dedicated to a different vein of skateboarding called *longboarding*. The site has articles, chat groups, organization links, equipment, pictures, riding techniques, and more.

A
B
C
D
E
F
G
H
I
J
K
L
M
N
O
P
Q
R
S
T
U
V
W
X
Y
Z

A
B
C
D
E
F
G
H
I
J
K
L
M
N
O
P
Q
R
S
T
U
V
W
X
Y
Z

RampPlans.org

http://www.rampplans.org/

★★★

♐ 14-18

Free ramp plans for skateboarding, BMX, or whatever extreme sport you're into, plus a FAQ list.

Skateboard.com

http://www.skateboard.com/

$

★★★★★

♐ 14-18

More than a skateboard store, this site features articles, photos, and stories to keep skateboarders informed and entertained. Beginners should check out Skate 101, where they can pick up a few pointers from the pros. When it's too wet or too cold to skateboard, check out the Hangout, where you can pick up some free desktop wallpaper, check out the message boards, or chat live with other enthusiasts.

Skateboarding.com

http://www.skateboarding.com/

$

★★★★★

♐ 14-18

This thorough site offers many entertaining articles, skate park lists, upcoming events, classifieds, ramp plans, and a huge array of relevant skate links.

Skateboardlink.com

http://skateboardlink.com/

★★★

♐ 14-18

A good collection of feature articles, skateboarder profiles, and action photos for the skateboard enthusiast. Some links to online stores, where you can purchase videos and other items. Click the Skatepark Directory link for a comprehensive list of skate parks broken down by state.

Skateboard Science

http://www.exploratorium.edu/skateboarding/

★★★

♐ 14-18

In 1999, the Exploratorium presented Skateboard Science—"a live webcast from the Phyllis C. Wattis Webcast Studio at the Exploratorium." As skateboard riders performed their stunts, physicist Paul Doherty explained the physics behind this extreme sport. Here, you can retrieve the webcast from the archives and learn more about the physics of skateboarding.

Skatepark.org

http://www.skatepark.org/

★★★★

♐ 14-18

Not just another skate page, Skatepark.org actually has a cause! If you are working to ensure the legalization of skateboarding in your town or want to build a skate park, come here first to get the latest tips, success stories, and other useful links.

Tum Yeto

http://www.tumyeto.com/

★★★★

♐ Not for kids

Tum Yeto is a commercial skateboarding concern that is mentioned in a several other websites. It offers links to companies that make products that this organization and all serious skaters approve of. Some material at this site is inappropriate for young children.

Related Sites

http://www.souldoubt.com/

http://www.rollercycle.com/

SKYDIVING

 DropZone

http://www.dropzone.com/

★★★★★

When looking for skydiving information on the Web, this is the first site you should drop in on. Here, you'll find an incredible collection of articles and interviews on skydiving, profiles of skydivers, a list of drop zones, photo and video galleries, discussion forums, a calendar of events and upcoming competitions, and even an auction site where you can buy and sell equipment.

International Parachuting Commission

http://www.fai.org/parachuting/

★★★

Home of the governing body of official skydiving activities, including world records and international competitions. Here, you can keep abreast of news relating to the commission and of its progress in getting parachuting accepted as an Olympic sport.

National Skydiving League

http://www.skyleague.com/

★★★★

Various teams from around the country have websites you can access through this site. You can also access the latest news, information, and products offered by the NSL.

SkyDance SkyDiving

http://www.skydance.net/

★★★

Here, you can find out where to learn to dive and how much any level of dive will cost. The site provides an online newsletter, a list of related skydiving sites, and memorable images to download.

Skydive!

http://www.afn.org/skydive/

★★★★★

 14-18

This excellent resource for skydiving enthusiasts is full of photos, FAQs, recommended places to skydive, skydiving humor, the sport's history and culture, the latest safety and equipment, training, links to other skydivers, and more. Also includes specific skydiving disciplines such as BASE jumping, paraskiing, relative work and canopy relative work, freestyle, VRW, and sit-flying. It is one of the most extensive websites available on skydiving and definitely a "don't miss" for any serious skydiver.

SkyDive WWW

http://www.skydivewww.com

★★★

Comprehensive skydiving resource, including articles, worldwide drop-zone listings, and photos.

Skydiving Fatalities

http://www.skydivenet.com/fatalities/

★★★

Incident reports from the United States and around the world. This page is maintained in the hope that lessons learned will save lives.

Skydiving Magazine

http://www.skydivingmagazine.com/index.htm

★★★

This home of *Skydiving Magazine* offers little for free from the magazine, but it does feature a subscription order form (not secure), a place to post questions about the sport, and an extensive directory of other useful skydiving sites.

Skydiving Organizations

http://www.afn.org/skydive/org/

★★★

Links to skydiving/parachuting organizations throughout the world.

A B C D E F G H I J K L M N O P Q R S T U V W X Y Z

A B C D E F G H I J K L M N O P Q R S T U V W X Y Z

SkyPeople
http://www.parachutehistory.com/sp/index.php

★★★★

A directory of skydivers across the country and a huge list of other skydiving links. An exhaustive resource for a variety of skydiving information. Visit this site and cruise the links.

United States Parachute Association
http://www.uspa.org/

★★★★

Another great resource for skydivers. This national organization's site promotes parachuting issues in government and legal matters. The site contains safety information, training advisories, details of competitions around the world, and USPA membership information.

Related Sites

http://www.cspa.ca/

http://members.aol.com/christskyd/

http://www.systemstech.com/paramain.htm

http://www.skydiveu.com/

http://www.skydive.ie/

SNOWBOARDING

About Snowboarding
http://www-acc.scu.edu/~lthrasher/

★★★

14-18

Do you want to learn about snowboarding? Then this is the place to start. Brush up on the history of snowboarding, learn snowboarding basics, and even study snowboarding terminology. If you already know the basics, you can pick up a few tricks here and even check out some action photos.

Burton Snowboards
http://www.burton.com/

★★★

14-18

Need gear or clothing for your next snowboarding run? Backhill has one of the most extensive selections of technical gear. You can request a catalog if you prefer to order by phone, or have fun participating in a backhill online contest.

Board the World
http://www.boardtheworld.com/

★★★

14-18

A complete snowboarding site, offering techniques and tips to improve your form, resort reviews, weather reports, and clothing shopping all in one place.

Ski Central
http://skicentral.com/

★★★

14-18

See the views at 220 mountains via snowcams and catch up on ski and snowboarding news, techniques, tips, and trip-planning advice. Links to stores where you can shop for ski and snowboarding equipment online.

SnowboarderREVIEW.com
http://www.snowboarderreview.com

★★★

14-18

What's the latest buzz about new products coming on the market and what do you think of some of the existing gear? Learn more about upcoming events and new product introductions here, where your product reviews and opinions are welcome. You'll also find the standard information on sporting news and snow reports.

Snowboarding.com
http://www.solsnowboarding.com/

★★★★★

14-18

Thinking of working on your technique this summer? Go to the directories to find instruction and camps to improve your form. You can also stop by the chat room, where top boarders are often scheduled for discussions. Plenty of articles, news, and information on weather, resorts, heli service, and gear. How To section is especially useful for beginners.

Snowboarding2.com

http://www.snowboarding2.com/

★★★★

 14-18

Post pictures of yourself in action and check snow-cams in place at resorts across the country, including images of competitors at recent competitions. Product reviews, gear shopping, and news and weather reports are also available here.

Transworld Snowboarding

http://www.transworldsnowboarding.com/snow/

★★★★

 14-18

Online magazine only for the most serious snow-boarders. Check out the feature articles, buyers' guides, instructions and tips, resort and travel guides, and announcements about the various snow-boarding competitions. You can also check out some cool snowboarding video games and shop online.

A
B
C
D
E
F
G
H
I
J
K
L
M
N
O
P
Q
R
S
T
U
V
W
X
Y
Z

Yellow Pages

EYE CARE

〖Best〗 American Academy of Ophthalmology

http://www.aao.org/

★★★★★

This site provides all the information you will need in the field of eye care—from finding an ophthalmologist near you, to keeping up with recent news stories pertaining to your eyesight, to career options for students interested in the field. You can also purchase educational modules for ophthalmologists as well as other doctors and allied healthcare workers on CD-ROM or in print through the online store. Other items available for purchase include kits to start your own practice.

Blind Links

http://www.seidata.com/~marriage/rblind.html

★★★

Hundreds of resources for those facing potential blindness, such as links to advocacy groups, employment, medicine, Braille, training, and assistance, as well as links to libraries for the blind and the Braille Monitor.

Computers and Eyestrain

http://www.mayohealth.org/home?id=HQ00462

★★★

Strategies for reducing eyestrain from computer usage are provided here, as well as suggestions for eliminating the discomfort associated with this common problem.

EyeCancer Network

http://www.eyecancer.com/

★★★

Educational website designed to inform visitors about the diagnosis and treatment of various types of eye cancer.

Eye Care Links

http://www.west.net/~seeintl/eyecare.html

★★★★

Easy-to-navigate and comprehensive directory of eye care websites. Sites are grouped by categories, including conjunctivitis, glaucoma, eye safety, macular degeneration, and vision tests.

Eye Search

http://www.eyesearch.com/

★★★★

You'll find more than you could imagine about eye care, diseases (complete with images), surgeries, what an eye exam looks like, and a directory of eye care specialists. You can also purchase contacts online.

Eyeglasses.com

http://www.eyeglasses.com/

★★★★

Learn how to choose eyewear that complements your face here, where you'll find many frames and lenses to choose from, including many by well-known designers. You can buy glasses including prescription lenses here.

Eye Injury First Aid

http://eyeinjury.com/firstaid.html

★★★

Brief list of emergency procedures for treating traumatized eyes. Covers everything from specks in the eye to chemical burns.

Eyesite

http://www.eyedoc.com

★★★

Eyesite is the location for eye care providers and consumers to obtain current information on contact lenses, fashion eyewear, instruments, equipment, services, eye care products, and eye health. This site promotes interaction among consumers, eye care providers, and the eye care industry.

Financial Aid for Eye Care

http://www.nei.nih.gov/health/financialaid.htm

★★★

Information on organizations that fund eye care treatments is available at this site.

Finding an Eye Care Professional

http://www.nei.nih.gov/health/findprofessional.htm

★★★★

General strategies and information resources suggested for identifying a qualified eye care professional appropriate for your particular vision situation are provided at this site.

Glaucoma Research Foundation

http://www.glaucoma.org

★★★

This site offers important information about the leading cause of blindness (glaucoma) through sections on research, hot topics, and a discussion forum.

Macular Degeneration Foundation

http://www.eyesight.org/

★★★★

Learn about what macular degeneration is, what causes it, and what research is being conducted to find out about it.

National Eye Institute

http://www.nei.nih.gov

★★★

Visitors will find comprehensive information about eye diseases, including diagrams of healthy and diseased eyes. Suitable for consumers and professionals, this site is objective and helpful. Additional links to other eye care organizations are also available.

Prevent Blindness America

http://www.preventblindness.org/

★★★★

Preventing blindness often starts by recognizing when there is a problem with your eyes. So, one of the best tools available at this site is an eye test you can take. You'll also find information about eye health and safety for adults and children.

A
B
C
D
E
F
G
H
I
J
K
L
M
N
O
P
Q
R
S
T
U
V
W
X
Y
Z

A B C D E F G H I J K L M N O P Q R S T U V W X Y Z

FASHION

BIG Magazine

http://www.bigmagazine.com/

★★★★★

BIG Magazine showcases the work of fashion designers, photographers, art directors, editors, and other creative individuals. Each edition is a special event that challenges the creators to envision and produce something unique and visually stimulating.

Colette

http://www.colette.fr/

★★★★

This site, available in both French and English, introduces you to tasteful clothing, contemporary design objects, make-up, music, and literature, and anything else Colette considers to be "in."

ELLE.com

http://www.elle.com/

★★★★★

Not for kids

Self-described as a "complement and counterpart to the magazine," this French fashion site provides a more intellectual, sophisticated approach to fashion, beauty, and style. In addition to being packed with beauty and fashion tips, ELLE.com goes behind the scenes in the fashion industry to provide readers with hands-on techniques and the best fashion secrets. The Shop link provides links to other sites where you can purchase items online.

Fashion Net

http://www.fashion.net/

★★★★

Comprehensive online directory to fashion sites, designer websites, fashion magazines, and online stores.

Hint Fashion Magazine

http://www.hintmag.com

Not for kids

This cutting-edge fashion magazine features interviews with the top fashion designers, articles about various fashion shows, photos by top fashion photographers, columns, message boards, and more. Requires online registration for access to most of the good stuff.

Issey Miyake

http://www.isseymiyake.com/

★★★★

This Flash-enabled site features a virtual fashion show that might not be the most intuitive to navigate, but features impressive graphics. Connect to this home page, click the desired season, and then point and click to move through the fashion show. Don't expect any buttons or onscreen clues—just point and click.

Self Esteem Clothing

http://www.selfesteemclothing.com/

★★★★

 14-18

Teens and tweens clothing manufacturer that designs clothes to improve teenagers' self-esteem. Here, you can check out the latest teen fashions, read articles about fashion issues, and even get some help with your homework. Also provides links to several online stores that carry Self Esteem clothing.

SoWear

http://www.sowear.com

★★★★

Not for kids

Home of the SoWear fashion collective, this site provides designers, stylists, photographers, and hair and makeup artists with a way to "connect, collaborate, and explore available resources."

STYLE.com

http://www.style.com

$

★★★★★

14-18

Home of *Vogue* magazine's online fashion forum, this site features fashion advice for the chic. Includes information on the latest styles, model and celebrity profiles, and fashion tips. Visit this site to keep up on the latest fashion and lifestyle trends.

Style at TeenPeople.com

http://www.teenpeople.com/teenpeople/style/

★★★★

14-18

Home of *Teen People* magazine's style area, this site provides articles about celebrities that teenagers are interested in, along with information about fashion, beauty, fitness, and nutrition.

Vogue

http://www.vogue.com/

★★★★

14-18

Home of *Vogue* magazine, one of the top style magazines in the world. Here, you can find the current feature article, the latest fashion news and talk, and the editor's picks. The site also offers links to nutrition, fitness, and weight loss information.

Best ZOOZOOM.com Magazine

http://www.zoozoom.com

★★★★★

Intriguing, refreshing online fashion magazine goes beyond fashion to explore the interconnectedness of art, culture, society, and other human factors in the evolution of fashion. Very cutting edge, this site presents various fashion concepts and designs in slide-show format. Also features profiles of some of the top fashion designers. Easy pick for the Best of the Best award.

322

A B C D E F G H I J K L M N O P Q R S T U V W X Y Z

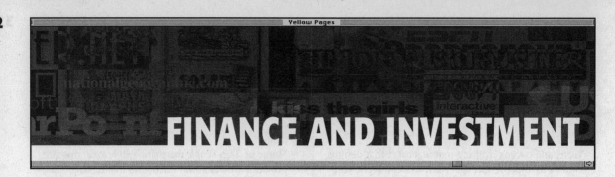

FINANCE AND INVESTMENT

About Credit

http://credit.about.com/

★★★★★

Learn how high-interest loans can torpedo your personal finances. Reduce and eliminate your personal debt by budgeting and consolidation. Huge collection of articles dealing not only with credit management but also with personal and family finances, living a frugal lifestyle, investing, and planning for retirement.

Related Sites
http://financialplan.about.com/mbody.htm
http://retireplan.about.com/mbody.htm
http://economics.about.com/mbody.htm
http://beginnersinvest.about.com/mbody.htm
http://mutualfunds.about.com/mbody.htm

CreditReport.com

http://www.creditreport.com/

★★★★★

Want to know what your bank and mortgage company already know about your finances? Then order a credit report. For about $30, you can order a report online and view the report right on your computer or receive it through the mail. Credit reports can reveal discrepancies between your records and the records of credit card companies and other credit institutions. They might even show if someone else is charging purchases using your name and Social Security number!

iVillage Money

http://www.ivillage.com/money/

★★★★

Outstanding collection of articles relating to various money-management topics. Here, you'll find expert tax advice, tips for reducing or eliminating debt, suggestions on how to survive a divorce, steps for creating a budget, investment strategies, advice from experts, and a robust collection of financial calculators.

Microsoft Money Central's Planning Section

http://moneycentral.msn.com/planning/home.asp

★★★★★

Learn how to budget, plan for retirement, stash away some cash for junior's college tuition, and shop for homeowner's insurance.

Best Money Magazine's Money 101 Tutorial

http://money.cnn.com/pf/101/

★★★★★

Money magazine's step-by-step tutorial on how to take control of your personal finances consists of 23 lessons covering everything from drawing up a budget to investing in stocks. Learn how to plan for retirement, save for a child's education, finance a new home, reduce your tax burden, and much more. When you decide to start taking control of your finances, be sure to bookmark this site, and return to it often for advice and ideas.

Personal Budgeting

http://www.personal-budget-planning-saving-money.com/

★★★★

If the concept of budgeting frightens you, visit this Personal Budgeting site, which makes budgeting seem like child's play. Covers budgeting basics, tips, pitfalls to avoid, money-saving tips, and much more.

Quicken.com

http://www.quicken.com

★★★★

Home of Intuit's Quicken, the most popular personal finance management program on the market. Here, you'll find articles on buying a new home, refinancing, planning for retirement, and preparing your taxes. Advanced features enable you to create an investment portfolio so that you can constantly monitor how your investments are doing. You can also research specific investment vehicles, get up-to-date alerts and news, and update personal files created using Quicken to monitor your investments.

Smart Money's Personal Finance

http://www.smartmoney.com/pf/

★★★

Smart Money magazine's website provides a decent collection of articles about sticky financial issues, such as divorce issues, estate planning, and the question of whether you should buy or lease your next car. Also features a collection of tools and worksheets to help you play with actual numbers.

BANKING

 Best | **Bank of America**

http://www.bankofamerica.com/

★★★★★

Bank of America is a full-service bank that provides its customers with online savings and checking accounts, credit cards, loans and mortgages, investment information and opportunities, and much more, plus educational information and resources to help them manage their finances more intelligently. This site is attractive, well organized, and packed with useful information, products, and services, making it our choice as Best of the Best banking website.

Citibank

http://www.citibank.com/

★★★★★

Tired of calling your bank every time you need information about your account, or want to make a transfer? Then consider banking online at Citibank. From the home page, you can see what types of products and services Citibank has to offer: savings and checking accounts, online bill payment, credit cards, loans and mortgages, investment opportunities, and more.

EH.net

http://eh.net/

★★★★★

Excellent site featuring information about economics and finance. The How Much Is That? feature is particularly interesting, providing statistics on the history of inflation, the fluctuating value of the dollar, changes in the price of gold, and much more. This site is managed by Economic History Services, which supports the study and teaching of economic history.

A B C D E F G H I J K L M N O P Q R S T U V W X Y Z

A
B
C
D
E
F
G
H
I
J
K
L
M
N
O
P
Q
R
S
T
U
V
W
X
Y
Z

E*TRADE Banking

https://bankus.etrade.com/

★★★★

E*TRADE provides all the banking services normally available—checking and savings accounts, online transfers, money market accounts, CDs, and credit cards. And, if you can keep a minimum balance of $5,000, most of the services are free. In addition, E*TRADE will refund any ATM charges you pay when getting cash from any ATM! Online bill payment is available through Bill Pay.

EverBank

http://www.everbank.com/

★★★★★

EverBank is one of the fastest growing banks in the nation, due in part to its customer bill of rights. Here you will find all the products and services you expect, along with higher than average investment returns on savings, checking, and money market accounts. Visit this site to see what EverBank has to offer, and if you like what you see, open an account today.

NetBank

http://www.netbank.com/

★★★★★

With the motto "No branches means better value," NetBank explains why it can offer such low fees and high interest rates on its customers' accounts. NetBank offers the usual banking services and accounts, but also offers loans, financial planning, investments, and insurance to provide for all of your financial needs. Site is attractive and easy to navigate.

Wells Fargo

http://www.wellsfargo.com/

★★★★

Wells Fargo offers a complete line of banking products and services, including online banking, bill pay, ATM withdrawals, check cards, savings accounts, and CDs. In addition, it features loans and credit, investment options, and insurance. No matter what your financial needs, Wells Fargo has a product or service that can meet it.

Other Online Banks
http://www.americanexpress.com/banking
http://www.ascenciabank.com
http://www.boh.com
http://www.bankone.com
http://www.chase.com
http://www.commerceonline.com
http://www.53.com
http://www.fleet.com
http://www.huntington.com

BONDS

Best Bond Market Association

http://www.investinginbonds.com

★★★★★

Read about what percentage of your portfolio should be in bonds, run through the investors' checklist to determine whether you should invest in bonds, learn about the different types of bonds, and stay updated on current bond prices at this site. If the stock market frightens you or you're just looking for investments that are a little less risky, this is the site for you.

Bonds Online

http://www.bonds-online.com/

★★★★★

Extensive market information for tax-free municipal bonds, treasury/savings bonds, corporate, bond funds, and brokers. Bond investment information is available from the Bond Professor. Link to Bondpage.com where members can trade bonds online.

Brady Net

http://www.bradynet.com

★★★

Find out the top gainers and losers in the bond market, stay up on bond prices and fluctuations worldwide, participate in market discussions, and read investing opinions. Open an account and trade online.

Briefing.com

http://www.briefing.com

$

★★★

Get free, live market analyses several times a day on stocks and bonds, as well as a stock and bond calendar and splits calendar. Subscriptions available for premium services, such as stock analysis.

CNNfn Bond Center

http://money.cnn.com/markets/bondcenter/

★★★★

Get the latest rates, short-term rates, and more information on municipal and corporate bonds.

ConvertBond.com

http://www.convertbond.com

★★★

You'll find news and information on the financial markets here, as well as a place to research your investments, chart them, and run through online tutorials to learn more about the intricacies of bonds. A division of Morgan Stanley & Company, Incorporated.

INVESTMENT CLUBS

Bivio

http://www.bivio.com/

$

★★★★

Bivio is a web-delivered application that enables groups of individual investors to create and manage their own investment clubs online, kind of like creating your own personal mutual fund. The name Bivio is derived from the Latin *bivium*, "where two roads meet."

InvestClub

http://www.yourinvestmentclub.com/

★★★

Free investment management software for individuals and investment clubs.

Investment Club Introduction

http://www.better-investing.org/articles/web/5184/

★★★

It doesn't get any better than this. Use this outline to introduce your friends and relatives to investment clubs. Includes a forum for discussing investment club-related topics.

Investment Club Central

http://www.iclubcentral.com

★★★

A comprehensive directory of investment club and NAIC-related resources for anyone considering joining an investment club or anyone in need of additional assistance in managing or participating in an existing one. From research sources to accounting software for finance management, this site has more information than you'll probably ever need.

Investment Clubs

http://www.investorguide.com/clubs.html

★★★★

InvestorGuide is the leading guide to investing on the Web; this page covers investment clubs (NAIC, online clubs, and more). For services that *InvestorGuide* does not provide, it displays links to other investment services.

Motley Fool's Guide to Investment Clubs

http://www.fool.com/InvestmentClub/
InvestmentClubIntroduction.htm

$

★★★★★

Excellent tutorial on investment clubs by two savvy but motley fools. Explains what an investment club is, why such clubs are useful, how to join an existing club or create your own, and much more. Even discusses potential pitfalls. A must-read for anyone considering joining an investment club.

A
B
C
D
E
F
G
H
I
J
K
L
M
N
O
P
Q
R
S
T
U
V
W
X
Y
Z

A
B
C
D
E
F
G
H
I
J
K
L
M
N
O
P
Q
R
S
T
U
V
W
X
Y
Z

U.S. Securities and Exchange Commission

http://www.sec.gov/investor/pubs/invclub.htm

★★★

Learn the basics about investment clubs and find out whether your investment club needs to register with the SEC.

Yahoo! Finance: Investment Clubs

http://biz.yahoo.com/edu/ed_clubs.html

★★★★

Excellent introduction to investment clubs both online and offline. Here, you can find a description of investment clubs, instructions on how to start a club, a list of pitfalls to avoid, tips on running successful meetings, and more.

Your Investment Club

http://www.yourinvestmentclub.com/

★★★

Information and resources for individual investors and investment clubs. Site contents are designed to empower investors and make them more independent. Learn the basics of investing and check out the online financial calculators to better understand your finances.

Zillions: Investment Clubs for Kids

http://www.zillions.org/Features/Invest/invest01.html

★★★★

 All

Information for kids about investment options, investing, and starting an investment club. The site also features a stock market quiz, examples of a few real investment clubs run by kids, and general information about the stock markets.

INVESTMENT INFORMATION

10K Wizard

http://www.10kwizard.com

★★★★★

Online financial toolbox packed with utilities designed to gather data concerning various companies whose stock is traded publicly. 10K Wizard, originally designed to help users search the SEC database, provides additional search tools for grabbing data from a multitude of online databases. Other products include the Portfolio Wizard, for helping you track your stocks, and a free trial of Hoover's Online, for gaining additional insights from professional analysts.

Accel Partners

http://www.accel.com

★★★

Accel Partners invests in entrepreneurial companies of selected technology-driven markets. The site provides information on the company's background, its investment strategy, and resources for entrepreneurs.

BenefitsLink

http://www.benefitslink.com

★★★

This site specializes in employee benefits compliance information. Articles and links provide access to useful information regarding compliance matters.

Biospace

http://www.biospace.com/

★★★★★

If you focus your investing on biotech companies, Biospace can help provide the information and analysis you need to make more educated decisions. Check out specific biotech companies by name, read late-breaking biotech news and results of clinical trials, and check out the investor newsletters.

BusinessWeek Online Personal Investor

http://www.businessweek.com/investor/index.html

★★★

Take a look at the free daily stock report to see what the analysts are watching.

BuySide

http://www.buyside.com/default.asp

★★★

BuySide provides Corporate Annual Reports, 10-Q's, and 10-K's, and serves as a launching pad to all other financial services on the Net. The site also provides investors with investment ideas and free stock quotes. There are individual listings for each American stock market.

CBS MarketWatch

http://cbs.marketwatch.com/

★★★★★

Home of the CBS stock market news and information service, this site provides feature stories about high-profile companies, plus access to stock quotes, personal finance information, investor tools, and research.

CyberFund

http://www.cyberfund.com

★★★

The CyberFund Investment Account program is a managed investment advisory service of Hammer Capital Management, Inc. It is designed to participate in the growth of the computer, telecommunications, and advancing technology industries. It invests only in publicly traded companies listed on the major U.S. and foreign stock exchanges.

Ethical Investments

http://www.ethicalinvestments.co.uk/

★★★★

A site offering advice to individuals, small businesses, and other organizations that want ethical considerations to have a bearing on their investment decisions. Provides information on companies with good environmental records.

Fantasy Stock Market

http://www.fantasystockmarket.com/

★★★★

 All

Online fantasy stock market game that's fun for investors of any age. You get $100,000 of play money to start the game, and, as you trade, you can check your profit or loss at any time. You compete against other online investors. This site also features information on how to invest wisely and some useful investment calculators.

Financial Engines

http://www.financialengines.com

★★★★

Co-founded and chaired by Bill Sharpe, Financial Engines is a financial service company devoted to helping financial institutions, employers, and financial advisers make sound investment decisions for their clients. Here, you can learn more about the company and its products, and by registering, you gain access to some very valuable online tools. Go through the Financial Forecast to learn more about where you stand and what you can expect to need for your retirement, and then collect information on how you should be investing to meet your future needs.

Financial Times

http://news.ft.com/home/us

★★★★★

This site is packed with late-breaking business news from around the world. Get the scoop on what OPEC is up to, how the dollar stacks up against the euro, and how business is doing in the Pacific Rim. Excellent reports, commentary, and analysis!

A B C D E F G H I J K L M N O P Q R S T U V W X Y Z

A
B
C
D
E
F
G
H
I
J
K
L
M
N
O
P
Q
R
S
T
U
V
W
X
Y
Z

FleetKids

http://www.fleetkids.com/

★★★★★

 All

This is a great site for kids and novice investors alike to learn the basics of investing and test their skills without the risk of losing money. Sign up to compete with other investors for bragging rights, or play one of the many online money games. Also features a lounge for parents and teachers that provides tips on teaching youngsters about money.

GreenMoneyJournal Online Guide

http://www.greenmoneyjournal.com/

★★★★

An information resource from the *GreenMoney Journal* for people interested in socially and environmentally responsible business, investing, and consumer resources. Information on companies' environmental track records is available, along with tips for socially responsible investing.

Hoover's Online

http://www.hoovers.com

★★★★★

A great research tool for investors. Hoover's provides company profiles plus free access to records on public and private companies. Here, you can find out how well a company has done in the past.

InterQuote

http://www.interquote.com

★★★

Provides a collection of affordable Internet-based financial information services, including real-time, delayed, and end-of-day information on stocks, options, indices, mutual funds, and futures from most U.S. and Canadian exchanges.

Investopedia

http://www.investopedia.com/

★★★★★

Are you thinking about investing? Have you started investing but you really don't feel very comfortable yet? Then check out Investopedia, the online encyclopedia where you can take a tutorial on the basics, move up to more advanced topics, peruse an assortment of investment information and tips, access free tools and calculators, play an investment game, test your knowledge with quizzes, and much more.

Investor's Business Daily

http://www.investors.com/

★★★★★

Investor's Business Daily is a magazine focusing on issues important to today's investor. On this site you can read today's issue. IBD also offers access to a free online IBD investment education course.

Kiplinger

http://kiplinger.com/

★★★★★

Kiplinger puts financial events in perspective on a daily basis. Stock quotes, mutual fund rankings, financial FAQs, financial calculators, and interactive resources are available.

Lycos Finance

http://finance.lycos.com/

★★★

Provides financial market data to the Internet community, including current quotes on stocks, options, commodity futures, mutual funds, and bonds. Also provides business news, market analysis and commentary, fundamental data, and company profiles.

Market Digest Online

http://www.marketdigestonline.com/

★★★

Presents a daily financial newsletter that offers the opinions and recommendations of successful stock market experts. Contains information on stocks, bonds, options, futures, securities, gold, the NYSE, and American and NASDAQ stock exchanges, as well as Dow Jones, over the counter, and Canadian stocks.

Marketocracy

http://www.marketocracy.com/

★★★★★

Find out when and what the top investors are buying, and follow their lead by subscribing to Marketocracy. Here, you can obtain alerts about which stocks to buy that often goes against the current trend.

Money Central

http://moneycentral.msn.com/investor/home.asp

★★★★

Geared for subscribers, this site provides helpful investing information to nonsubscribers as well, although not as detailed as the subscriber data. Use Microsoft Investor to get up-to-date company information, news, and stock market quotes.

Money Magazine

http://money.cnn.com

★★★★

From the editors of CNN and *Money* magazine, this site features an up-to-the-minute overview of the day's stock markets. Includes business news and events likely to affect the day's stock prices, plus some informative articles on personal finance.

Morgan Stanley

http://www.morganstanley.com

★★★

Provides real-time quotes, information on portfolio accounting, financial calculators, news, and research. Also offers information on local Morgan Stanley offices, as well as a link to Morgan Stanley Client Serv, where you can buy, sell, and move your Morgan Stanley investments online.

Motley Fool

http://www.fool.com/

★★★★★

The Motley Fool is a well-known online financial forum originating on America Online. This is the Motley Fool's home on the Web. The Fool provides individual investors with investment tips and advice. The Motley Fool website offers The Fool's School, an online investment guide that is subtitled "13 Steps to Investing Foolishly." When you're ready to start investing "foolishly," visit this Best of the Best site.

mPowerCafe

http://www.mpowercafe.com/

★★★

Take an interactive course called Wall Street 101 (on the Investing tab) to better understand investing, then check out the FAQs regarding 401Ks, and learn about new investing options when it comes to your 401K, as well as ask questions of the experts. A site with information for beginners as well as advanced investors.

Olsen & Associates

http://www.olsen.ch/

★★★

Provides economic research in the field of financial markets. Specializes in the forecasting and historical analysis of foreign exchange rates. Also provides trading models and a currency ranking analysis.

A B C D E F G H I J K L M N O P Q R S T U V W X Y Z

A
B
C
D
E
F
G
H
I
J
K
L
M
N
O
P
Q
R
S
T
U
V
W
X
Y
Z

Prophet.net

http://www.prophet.net/

★★★★★

Prophet.net has a reputation as one of the leading sites for providing technical analysis of stocks. Tim Knight, founder of Prophet.net, has based the system he created on his own investment approach to combine the power of software with the immediacy of streaming data and the availability of the Web to help investors achieve consistent profits in an inconsistent market. Sign up for a free 7-day trial to see what Prophet.net has to offer.

Red Herring

http://www.redherring.com/

★★★★

Provides recent stock market information and in-depth analysis on the forces driving innovation, technology, entrepreneurship, and financial markets. Categories include daily stock charts, bimonthly mutual fund charts, and top stocks.

Reuters Investor

http://www.investor.reuters.com/

★★★★★

Excellent information and resource site for investors to check stock prices, check late-breaking news, track stock performance, and research potential investment opportunities. Reuters has a long history and a solid reputation for providing accurate, timely information, which is crucial to helping investors make the right decisions. Registration is free, but access to the better research data and analyses will cost you.

RiskGrades

http://www.riskgrades.com/

★★★★★

How risky are those investments you're making or thinking about making? Here you can run your stock symbols through the system and have them graded from 0 (no risk) to 10,000 (roll-the-dice risky). Find out how your stocks would fare in a crisis.

SEC EDGAR Database

http://www.sec.gov/edgar.shtml

★★★

EDGAR, which stands for Electronic Data Gathering, Analysis, and Retrieval, is an online database of company financial information provided by the Securities and Exchange Commission. Provides access to company SEC filings, earning reports, and so on.

The Siegel Group, Inc.

http://www.fredsiegel.com

★★★

Specializes in providing financial news analysis and consulting to the broadcast media, primarily to local radio and television affiliates of the national networks. Includes links to several sites that provide commentary about activity in the financial markets.

Silicon Investor

http://www.siliconinvestor.com/index.gsp

★★★★

Consists of five innovative areas for technology investors: Stocktalk, Market Tools, Market Insight, Customize, and Portfolio. These areas enable you to participate in discussion forums, create individual charts and comparison charts, view company profiles, get quotes and other financial information, and track your portfolio.

The Stock Market Game

http://www.smgww.org/

★★★★

 All

Stock market game created and maintained by the Securities Industry Foundation for Economic Education (SIFEE), an affiliate of the Securities Industry Association. This game is intended for use in schools, primarily for grades 4–12, to help teach children and teenagers about money and investments.

Stocks.com: The Trader's Financial Resource Guide

http://www.stocks.com/

★★★

Serves as a financial resource guide to sites dealing with stocks, currencies, exchanges, banks, brokers, mortgages, futures, newspapers, sports pages, research, and search utilities.

Stock-Track Portfolio Simulations

http://www.stocktrak.com/

★★★★

 14-18

Put together your own investment portfolio and track its progress online. The portfolio simulator costs about $19 per account and is used primarily in high schools, colleges, and other schools to provide a relatively safe place for investors to get some hands-on trading without losing any real money.

TheStreet.com

http://thestreet.com

★★★★

Free services at The Street include market reports, commentary, news, and research access, but you'll have to pay a fee to get live market updates and stock analyses.

ValueEngine.com

http://www.valuengine.com/

★★★★★

ValueEngine.com provides the same stock valuation, risk management, and forecasting technology to individual investors that professional investors have been using for years. Here, you can check the valuations of stocks you own or plan on buying to evaluate potential risk, check breaking news, and obtain detailed analysis of various stocks. You can also access tools for tracking your portfolio.

Wall Street City

http://www.wallstreetcity.com

★★★★★

Telescan's Wall Street City is a next-generation financial website, where you can get the answers to your investment questions. Custom design your own stock and mutual fund searches with the most powerful search engine in the world, covering more than 700 different criteria. You can access real-time and delayed quotes on more than 300,000 domestic and international securities, and run full technical analysis on stock graphs from 1 day to 23 years.

Yahoo! Finance

http://finance.yahoo.com

★★★★

Provides financial data for investors, including current quotes on stocks, options, commodity futures, mutual funds, and bonds. Also provides business news, market analysis and commentary, financial data, and company profiles. Excellent place to check the latest market overview and see what other investors have to say about market trends.

Yodlee

http://www.yodlee.com

★★★★

Yodlee is a company that specializes in account aggregation—providing consumers with single-site access to all their accounts, including bank accounts, investment accounts, insurance, and so on. Yodlee is a third-party provider of account aggregation for banks, insurance companies, and financial institutions, so average users like you and me won't have much direct contact with Yodlee.

IPOs

Alert-IPO!

http://www.alertipo.com/cgi-bin/ai.exe

★★★★

Subscribe to IPO alert to keep track of IPOs, or scan the database of close to 4,000 IPO filings from more than 1,500 underwriters to find potential IPOs of interest.

A
B
C
D
E
F
G
H
I
J
K
L
M
N
O
P
Q
R
S
T
U
V
W
X
Y
Z

A
B
C
D
E
F
G
H
I
J
K
L
M
N
O
P
Q
R
S
T
U
V
W
X
Y
Z

IPO Home

http://www.ipohome.com/default.asp

★★★★

Like other IPO sites, this site provides a ton of information about upcoming IPOs, planned pricing, and rankings of past performers to give you a sense of how IPOs typically perform. Stay up to date with breaking IPO news, too. And research companies of interest.

IPO Monitor

http://www.ipomonitor.com/

★★★

Complete IPO tracker can notify you of the most recent IPO filings and any withdrawals from the IPO listing, provides a calendar showing when IPOs are scheduled to go public, supplies price information for IPOs, and provides tools for tracking the performance of IPOs after they're listed on the market.

MUTUAL FUND SELECTION

Fundalarm

http://fundalarm.com

★★★★

With the mission of helping investors know when to sell their mutual funds, Fundalarm tracks mutual fund performance, offers performance commentary, and alerts investors to "3-alarm" funds—those that have underperformed for 12 months, 3 years, and 5 years. A good site to check when you're wondering whether it's time to sell.

iDayo Investor

http://www.idayo.com/

★★★

iDayo Investor is an Application Service Provider (ASP), delivering unique financial content to professional money managers, financial planners, stockbrokers, and others in the business of providing investment services. Check out the iDayo indicator for some fresh stock tips.

Morningstar

http://www.morningstar.com

★★★★

Start at Morningstar University to find answers to all your investing and mutual fund questions and then check the Fund Quickranks for ideas of which stocks and mutual funds are performing the best. You can also do more in-depth research on funds, read up on previous Morningstar reports, and track your portfolio. For about $100 annually, you can subscribe to Morningstar to take advantage of premium services.

Mutual Fund Investor

http://www.mfea.com

★★★★★

Find funds that cost less than $50 or the ones that have the lowest minimum investment with the help of the Mutual Fund Education Alliance. You can also use online calculators to estimate what you'll need for your retirement or other major purchases, such as your child's college education. With information on how to get started with very little money down, this site is one of the better ones.

Personal Fund

http://personalfund.com

★★★★

Find the fund that best meets your needs—whether it's for a high-yield investment or no taxes. Find out how your funds compare cost-wise and sign up for Andrew Tobias's regular mutual fund newsletter.

MUTUAL FUNDS

American Century Investments

http://www.americancentury.com

★★★

A site for information on mutual funds managed by American Century Investments. Includes an online portfolio tracker that you can use to track your portfolio. Educational materials to help you determine and work toward your financial goals are also available, along with fund profiles and historical performance information.

Brill's Mutual Funds Interactive

http://www.brill.com/features.html

★★★★★

Features articles on what's happening in the mutual fund industry, including topics such as "Investing for Retirement" and "The Best Choices in Variable Annuities."

Calvert

http://www.calvertgroup.com

★★★

People who want to invest in socially responsible funds will want to learn more about Calvert. One of the interesting features at this site is a service that tells you what your existing mutual funds invest in (which stocks they hold). If your current fund owns companies you think are less than great corporate citizens, you can do research to find alternatives through Calvert's family of socially responsible funds.

Dreyfus Corporation

http://www.dreyfus.com

★★★★★

The Dreyfus Online Information Center provides listings and descriptions of some of the mutual funds offered by Dreyfus, along with the Dreyfus services. The site provides information that can help investors get a clearer sense of the direction to take to meet their investment objectives. In addition to general information on investing, you'll also find current economic commentaries on the financial markets updated weekly by Dreyfus portfolio managers.

Fidelity

http://www.fidelity.com/

★★★

A comprehensive site full of investment information. Fidelity provides services to the personal and institutional investor. Fidelity is a well-known and trusted investment firm, and its site is worthwhile reading for anyone wanting to use Fidelity's services.

Invesco

http://www.invesco.com/

★★★

Invesco investors can check their accounts online, and visitors can investigate the performance and ranking of Invesco funds. The Education Center has some great tutorials on the basics of investing, investing for women, and mutual fund basics, and it provides tools and calculators for checking out various investing options.

Janus Funds

http://ww4.janus.com/

★★★★★

Janus Funds provides access to information on the funds the company manages. You can check your funds' latest share price and account value 24 hours a day, 7 days a week. You can also find projected year-end dividends for each fund. All account information is accessed through security-enhanced web pages utilizing SSL.

ProFunds

http://www.profunds.com/

★★★★★

ProFunds features some of the top-rated funds in 2003 (according to Morningstar). At this site, you can obtain ProFunds overviews, profiles, prices, and performance statistics for the various mutual funds.

Putnam Investments

http://www.putnaminvestments.com

★★★★★

Get the latest news on new Putnam funds, decide whether a Roth IRA is for you, and find out how well your Putnam investment is doing.

Scudder Investments

http://www.scudder.com/

★★★

Provides information on all mutual funds managed by Scudder, Stevens & Clark. The site allows users to create a personalized page to access all the information available on the site. Fund performance, daily prices, interactive worksheets, and fund prospectuses are offered. Includes an informative retirement-planning section.

A
B
C
D
E
F
G
H
I
J
K
L
M
N
O
P
Q
R
S
T
U
V
W
X
Y
Z

A
B
C
D
E
F
G
H
I
J
K
L
M
N
O
P
Q
R
S
T
U
V
W
X
Y
Z

Strong Funds

http://www.estrong.com/

★★★★

Information for anyone interested in the Strong family of mutual funds. Fund-performance information and portfolio-management tips are available. Strong also offers retirement investing help and general investment help with Strong's Learning Center.

TCW Mutual Funds

http://www.tcw.com/

★★★★

For more than 30 years, TCW has been providing investment management services. TCW specializes in managing taxable and tax-free monies for pension and profit-sharing funds, retirement/health and welfare funds, public employee retirement funds, financial institutions, endowments, and foundations. TCW also offers a family of no-load mutual funds, called TCW Galileo funds.

T. Rowe Price

http://www.troweprice.com

★★★★

Use the T. Rowe Price investment service to track down the fund that's right for you and then track its performance at the site. Small business owners, investment advisors, and people planning for retirement might want to look into the specialized sections on the individual investing needs of these groups of people.

U.S. Global Investors

http://www.usfunds.com/

★★★

Information on investment opportunities in U.S. no-load mutual funds. Includes investment research reports, daily fund prices, weekly investor alert, prospectuses, and shareholder reports.

Vanguard

http://www.vanguard.com

★★★★

Learn about investing, develop a personal financial plan, search for a mutual fund, and check pricing and performance here at Vanguard's site. You can also do more research and get news updates.

ONLINE TRADING

About Online Trading

http://www.about-online-trading.com/

★★★

Presents a trading guide and software to assist investors. Covers details from the initial home setup of software to track your investments to advanced strategies for purchase and sale of stocks, bonds, and other investments.

American Express Financial Direct

http://www.americanexpress.com/direct

★★★★★

Trade online using the brokerage services of American Express. Fees per trade vary depending on your account balance and the number of shares traded. At this site, you can also conduct research and stay updated on market moves.

[Best] Ameritrade

http://www.ameritrade.com

★★★★★

Ameritrade provides quotes, account access, and online trading for independent investors. Ameritrade also provides discount brokering services. Though this site lacks some of the in-depth research tools you might find from some of the more professional investment services, such as Schwab, Ameritrade makes online stock transactions easy and relatively inexpensive at $10.99 per trade.

CyberTrader

http://www.cybertrader.com/jump/main/

★★★★

A full-featured investment program and service for cutting-edge trading on the NASDAQ and listed NYSE stocks. Supports real-time trading as low as $9.95 per trade (minimum of 20 trades).

E*Trade

http://www.etrade.com/

★★★★★

E*Trade is another online trading service geared toward the individual investor. With E*Trade, you can buy and sell securities online for NYSE, AMEX, and NASDAQ. Stock performance information and company information are available. $9.99 per trade.

Firstrade

http://www.firstrade.com/

★★★★

Offering trades for as low as $6.95, Firstrade is one of the least-expensive online investing services on the Internet. Its research tools are a little sparse, but if you subscribe to an investment information newsletter already and just need a vehicle for placing trades, this might be the place for you.

FOLIOfn

http://www.foliofn.com/

★★★★★

FOLIOfn is an online broker that uses a slightly different model for its investors, enabling investors to create a diversified portfolio for less in trading costs. Ready-to-go portfolios allow you to purchase a collection of securities (typically 30–50 different securities) for the price of a single trade. For a monthly fee of about $20, you get unlimited trading to create a custom portfolio, or you can trade for about $4 per transaction. Check out this site to learn more.

HARRISdirect

http://www.harrisdirect.com/

★★★★★

HARRISdirect is one of the most popular financial sites on the Net. HARRISdirect offers online trading, real-time quotes and news, research, and portfolio tracking. At $20 per trade, commissions using HARRISdirect are higher than some services, but HARRISdirect features more information and research tools than other services.

iDS Finance

http://www.idsfinance.com/

★★★★★

If you're looking to invest in the Asian markets, this might be the site you're looking for. iDS Finance provides news, research, investment tools, and analysis of companies that you might have trouble finding anywhere else.

The Internet and Online Trading

http://www.sec.gov/investor/online.shtml

★★★★

Created and maintained by the U.S. Securities and Exchange Commission (SEC), this site provides important information to help online traders avoid scams and other pitfalls of online investing and speculating. The site provides information about pump-and-dump schemes, pre-IPO investing, and more.

Merrill Lynch Direct

http://www.mldirect.ml.com/

★★★★

Receive stock opinions and recommendations from Merrill Lynch analysts, and then execute stock trades for $29.95, or do some more research on your own. Access free S&P reports; get free real-time stock quotes; and check into the performance of stocks, bonds, and mutual funds.

Morgan Stanley

http://www.morganstanley.com/

★★★★★

A nice all-around solid site, with online trading available, as well as educational tools, mutual fund research, IPO information, market news, and the option to open a free, no-fee IRA. On this site, you can also track your checking and savings accounts as well as your credit cards.

Online Trading Academy

http://www.tradingacademy.com/

★★★★

Do you want to try your hand at day trading? Then check out this site, where you can find courses, books, and other training materials to bring you up to speed. Free Direct Access Training workshop.

A B C D E **F** G H I J K L M N O P Q R S T U V W X Y Z

A
B
C
D
E
F
G
H
I
J
K
L
M
N
O
P
Q
R
S
T
U
V
W
X
Y
Z

Schwab Online Investing

http://www.schwab.com/

★★★★

This online trading service from Charles Schwab offers discount brokering services to individual investors. Trading online with Schwab offers convenience and control, at stock commissions of $29.95. You'll also find an extensive listing of mutual funds.

Scottrade

http://www.scottrade.com/

★★★★★

Another online trading site, where you can place market orders for as low as $7 per trade.

TD Waterhouse

http://www.tdwaterhouse.com

★★★

Before trading online, do some research and take the mini-courses on tax planning, college planning, and retirement planning. Trade online for as low as $9.95 per trade. Trades by phone are more expensive.

Trading Direct

http://www.tradingdirect.com

★★★

Trade any number of shares for $9.95 via the Internet; the cost is higher if you trade by phone. The site also provides research and information about the various types of trading accounts available.

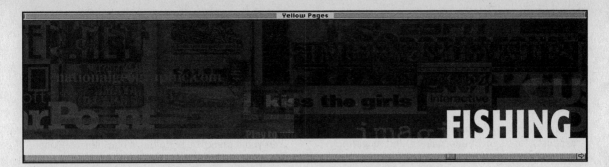

FISHING

Bass Fishing Network

http://www.bassfishingnetwork.com/

★★★

You'll find lots of message boards devoted to discussing the how-tos of catching more bass. You can also post pictures of your latest catch. Be sure to check out the Sell/Swap section to see whether another fisherman has something you need.

Bass Pro Shops

http://www.basspro-shops.com/

★★★

Shop online for fishing equipment and boats.

Boundary Waters Fishing Tips

http://www.boundarywaters.com/FishingGenTips.html

★★★

If you're planning a fishing trip to northern Minnesota, drop by this site to pick up a few tips on fishing the land of 10,000 lakes. Here, you'll learn the basic habits of the most common game fish in the area: smallmouth bass, northern pike, walleye, and lake trout.

eders.com

http://www.eders.com/

★★★★★

Choose to learn more about salt- or freshwater fishing through forums and tips at this site, which also has an extensive online catalog of fishing and hunting gear. Check out the huge online shopping area! Categories including Archery, Clothing, Camping, and Marine make it easy to browse the aisles and find what you need.

Field & Stream Online

http://www.fieldandstream.com/

★★★★

This popular magazine has set up a very extensive site that features a Q&A section, RealAudio fishing tips, and current articles. Search the large reference section for a vast selection of books, tips, and charts to prepare yourself for a successful fishing trip. You can even search the fish database to get information specific to the type of fish you want to catch.

Fish & Game Finder Magazine

http://www.fishandgame.com/

★★★

Read the latest news about fishing and hunting. Plan your next fishing vacation with the help of vendors and site sponsors. Stay current with the latest articles, columns, and product reviews.

The Fishing Network

http://www.the-fishing-network.com/

★★★★

Fishing reports from around the world, weather reports, a reference library, a calendar of events, chat rooms, bulletin boards, and a community of fellow anglers. What more could an angler want, except for a new bass boat?

Fishing Secrets

http://www.fishingsecrets.com

★★★

A group of Florida fishermen compiled this collection of fishing reports, tips, and related links that cover aspects of many types of fishing. Post a message on the board about a particular fishing trip you've had or feel free to ask for help from the site's regular visitors.

A
B
C
D
E
F
G
H
I
J
K
L
M
N
O
P
Q
R
S
T
U
V
W
X
Y
Z

FishingWorld.com

http://www.fishingworld.com

★★★

Offers all types of fishing information, services, products, tournament information, and magazines, and serves as a place to visit other fishermen.

GORP: Great Outdoor Recreation Pages

http://www.gorp.com/gorp/activity/fishing.htm

★★★

This site details the fishing hotspots across the United States and throughout the world. Prepare for your trip by visiting GORP's many links to tackle, apparel, and freeze-dried food vendors.

Grossenbacher Guides

http://www.grossenbacherguides.com/

★★★

Let Brian and Jenny Grossenbacher plan your next fly-fishing excursion in Southwest Montana. The site features information on traditional trips, specialty trips, and women-only fishing trips, along with a section on current conditions and a section with answers to FAQs.

Gulf Coast Angler's Association

http://www.gcaa.com/

★★★★

This group exists to help you plan the perfect fishing vacation. The site contains links and information about marinas, guides, bait and tackle, weather, and tides and currents in the Gulf states.

Kids Fishing Corner

http://www.fishing-hunting.com/kidsfishing/

★★★★

 All

This fishing page, designed specifically for kids, features online fishing games, instructions on how to tie knots, and areas where kids can submit fishing photos and fish stories.

Related Sites

http://groups.msn.com/FishinKids/
_homepage.msnw?pgmarket=en-us

http://www.fishing-hunting.com/kidsfishing/zebco.htm

http://www.fishing-hunting.com/kidsfishing/
airandjair.htm

King Crow

http://www.fishandgame.com/kingcrow/

★★★

King Crow makes fishing houses that are so luxurious you'll think you're pulling a bluegill from your living room floor. These houses are bigger than a college dorm room and, based on the pictures, quite a bit nicer.

⌐Best⌐ Land Big Fish

http://www.landbigfish.com/

★★★★★

Land Big Fish is dedicated to fostering a community of fishing enthusiasts to share information and stories, locate hot fishing holes, and learn new techniques. The information you find here covers salt water and freshwater fishing and puts you in touch with other anglers and the best fishing retailers in North America. Site features a home page with current articles, an online tackle shop, an outdoor business locator, and the LBF fishing library. You can even print up a few fishing recipes to take on your next trip! This site's attractive, easy-to-navigate design and huge collection of useful information lands it our Best of the Best fishing site award.

Nautical Net

http://www.nauticalnet.com

★★★

A recreational water sports site that contains a tackle shop, marine electronics, boat brokers and manufacturers, clubs, fishing reports, nautical links, weather and ocean information, clubs and associations, nautical events, and links to charter boats.

Nor'east Saltwater Online

http://www.noreast.com

★★★★

Avid fishers will want to sign up for the free fishing report to be emailed to them daily. Tune in to Nor'east Sportfishing Web Radio, send a friend a fishing postcard, read how-to articles, and check out the current issue of the *Nor'east Saltwater* magazine. You'll also find fishing reports, sport fishing news, new product information, boats for charter, party boat schedules, a weekly saltwater fly-fishing column, editorials, reader feedback, classifieds, and more.

Ol' Paw's Fishin' Page
http://www.pagebiz.com/pawfish.html

★★★

This site is an angler's dream database that claims to have more than 700 links. Categories include Radio and TV Shows; Fishing Magazines; and Links for the Americas, New Zealand, and All Points In Between. You'll also find plenty of information about bait, flies, and tackle. The site also contains links to dozens of newsgroups and bulletin boards.

Saltwater Sportsman
http://www.saltwatersportsman.com/saltwater/

★★★★

Tired of fishing for bluegills? Then hook up with the Saltwater Sportsman site to fish for saltwater trophy fish, including marlin and striped bass.

United States Fish and Wildlife Service
http://www.fws.gov/

★★★★★

The FWS, a division of the Department of the Interior, created this site to tell you a little about itself. Find out what the group does to protect endangered species and learn what the government—and you—can do to keep your old fishing hole clean and healthy.

Virtual Flyshop
http://www.flyshop.com/

★★★

Online version of the print publication *Fly Fisherman*. Find fly fishing how-tos, search for fly shops, read fly-fishing articles, check out the classifieds, and lots more.

Walleye Central
http://walleyecentral.com/

★★★

A site that caters exclusively to walleye fishermen. Find out about walleye software, chat with other walleye lovers, and sign up for *Walleye Central* magazine. Get tips from the world's best walleye fishermen.

Related Sites
http://www.igfa.org/
http://www.fishufa.com/
http://www.worldwidefishing.com/
http://www.fishingthenorthwest.com/
http://www.scottyusa.com/

A
B
C
D
E
F
G
H
I
J
K
L
M
N
O
P
Q
R
S
T
U
V
W
X
Y
Z

FOOD AND DRINK

BevNet

http://www.bevnet.com

★★★★

The Beverage Network is the premier beverage site. It has reviews of hundreds of different beverages, as well as industry news and classifieds.

Carnegie Deli Cheesecake

http://www.carnegiedeli.com/

★★★★

When you order a cheesecake from New York's famed Carnegie Deli, all other cheesecakes will pale by comparison.

Coca-Cola

http://www.coca-cola.com

★★★★★

 All

Provides information about the most renowned soft drink company. Buy, sell, and trade Coca-Cola paraphernalia online. Check out Coca-Cola–sponsored sporting events. See how Coca-Cola is doing in the business world before you decide to buy some stock in soft drinks. Also features some cool fun and games that kids of all ages will enjoy.

Fiery Foods Supersite

http://www.fiery-foods.com/

★★★

Your direct line to products, shows, magazines, and how-tos having to do with spicy hot foods. Links to Amazon.com for books and videos.

Food Resources

http://www.unlv.edu/Tourism/catres.html

★★★★★

A collection of useful food links for caterers, chefs, and hospitality-management students. Links to www.recipecenter.com for an excellent collection of recipes and to www.amazon.com for books.

Fresh Food Co.

http://www.freshfood.co.uk/

★★★★

Organics on the World Wide Web. The Fresh Food Co. delivers the finest-quality organic foods to your door, nationwide, in Great Britain and Northern Ireland.

Girl Scout Cookie Time

http://www.ptgirlscouts.org/cookie.htm

★★★

Never miss out on Girl Scout cookies again. Order them here online! The downside: The store is not open year round.

Global Gourmet

http://www.globalgourmet.com/

★★★

Online food magazine with lots of links.

Live Lobsters and Clambakes

http://www.lobsterclambake.com/

★★★★★

Live lobsters and clambakes shipped overnight via Federal Express.

Mimi's Cyber Kitchen

http://www.cyber-kitchen.com/

★★★★

Large, comprehensive food and cooking site with links to thousands of other food-related sites, also includes Mimi's tried-and-true recipes, a recipe-exchange bulletin board, and cyber greeting cards.

Moxie Collector's Page

http://www.xensei.com/users/iraseski/

★★★

Learn all there is to know about the first soft drink, which was endorsed by Ted Williams and remains a staple in most New England refrigerators. The only commercial product to become synonymous with a personal attribute, Moxie even played a role in history.

Omaha Steaks

http://www.omahasteaks.com/

★★★

Omaha Steaks has earned a reputation for offering first-rate steaks, meats, and other gourmet foods. Check out specials, purchase steaks, or enter to win some. You can also choose to learn more about the company, find and exchange recipes, and get all sorts of facts on preparing and storing Omaha steaks.

ONTHERAIL

http://www.ontherail.com

★★★★

Created and maintained by two former restaurateurs, this site features an online magazine packed with articles for restaurant owners and workers. Learn everything from where to shop for goods to how to design and build your own kitchen. Restaurant owners will want to bookmark this site for quick return visits.

Perrier

http://www.perrier.com/

★★★★

Nature's original beverage refresher in bottled form. Perrier's site provides information about the company and offers a gallery of Perrier ads from which you can download an image to use as your desktop wallpaper or send as an online greeting card.

Pickles, Peppers, Pots & Pans

http://www.p4online.com/

★★★★★

Cooking and specialty foods superstore. Featuring Calphalon, ScanPan, AllClad, Wustof, Essence of Emeril, and much more.

Restaurant-Store.com

http://www.restaurant-store.com/

★★★★

The company behind this site, Westchester Restaurant Supply, has sold cookware, cutlery, and other cooking products at wholesale prices for more than 70 years. This site offers cookware from AllClad; cutlery from J.A. Henckels, Wusthof-Trident, Dexter Russell, and Mundial; and appliances from KitchenAid and Cuisinart. You can also take advantage of the site's bridal registry service, register to win free cookware, purchase gift certificates, check out specials, and find out about the company's Buyer's Club.

Smucker's

http://www.smuckers.com/

★★★★

 All

This site features Smucker's Products, Smucker's Kitchen (recipes), Smucker's Smiles (fun and games), A Family Company (Smucker's history), and Smucker's Store (where you can shop online).

Snapple

http://www.snapple.com/

★★★★★

 All

Snapple's site offers information on its current and future flavored beverages—"Made from the best stuff on earth." Enter your personal Snapple story in the online Snapple contest, shop for Snapple gear, play a fun online game, or just drop in to experience a very cool website design.

A B C D E F G H I J K L M N O P Q R S T U V W X Y Z

A
B
C
D
E
F
G
H
I
J
K
L
M
N
O
P
Q
R
S
T
U
V
W
X
Y
Z

Sunrise Gourmet Foods

http://www.sunrisegourmet.com/

★★★★

The pictures alone will make you wish you could reach into your monitor and sample this site's wares. Gourmet foods, baked goods, and gifts. Online shopping with secure server.

[Best] Wet Planet Beverages

http://www.wetplanet.com/

★★★★★

 Not for kids

One of the best wet sites on the Web. With the advantage of having a computer-oriented core audience of jacked-up geeks, Global Beverage presents a Java-powered site featuring information on its carbonated beverages: Jolt, Pirate's Keg, DNA, and more. Its excellent product line, excellent site design, and incredible graphics combine to make this the best food and drink site on the Web.

ALCOHOL

Addy Bassin's MacArthur Beverages, Inc.

http://www.bassins.com

★★★

 Not for kids

One of the largest wine retailers in the world. Offers phone and fax ordering of a huge selection of French, American, and European wines featured on its site. Wines are organized into one of these three categories and then listed alphabetically by type, making this site very user-friendly.

Alcome Ltd.

http://alcome.com/default.htm

$

★★★

Not for kids

Alcome, located in Cyprus, can supply any quantity of whisky, vodka, gin, dark and white rum, and brandy, as well as glass bottles and jars.

BarMeister.com: The Drink Recipes

http://www.barmeister.com/drinks.html

★★★★

Not for kids

Hundreds of the best drink recipes from A to Z, traditional as well as new. Excellent collection of drinking games, plus a top 10 list of drinks and games. Links to Amazon.com for book sales.

Cocktail Magazine

http://www.cocktail.com/

★★★★

Not for kids

Test your drink knowledge with a quick quiz, brush up on some cocktail alchemy, see what drinks are in season, jump to other mixology sites, and get some expert advice from Miss Cocktail. Includes back issues of the e-zine.

Intoximeters Inc. Drink Wheel Page

http://www.intox.com/wheel/drinkwheel.asp

★★★★

Not for kids

Intoximeters Inc. hosts this site, which is designed to encourage the responsible use of alcohol. This company's specialty is in providing blood and breath alcohol testing. Click on the Drink Wheel option for an online simulated version. In addition to finding information on this company and its products, you'll also find a list of annotated links to lots of other drug or alcohol awareness and prevention resources.

Jack Daniels

http://www.jackdaniels.com

$

★★★★

Not for kids

Visit the famous Tennessee distillery online and learn about the Jack Daniels distilling process. Online store for purchasing Jack Daniels merchandise. This site "cards" you.

Jim Beam
http://www.jimbeam.com/

★★★★★

 Not for kids

Play the Find Jim Beam game. Try out some of the drink recipes, including the holiday drinks. Read the history of Jim Beam Bourbon. You can even buy Jim Beam–related merchandise online. Download some cool Jim Beam wallpaper or just hang out and play a game. This site "cards" you.

MixedDrink.com
http://www.mixed-drink.com/

★★★★★

 Not for kids

Don't know how to mix your favorite drink? This site offers a comprehensive guide to making and serving mixed drinks.

The Pierre Smirnoff Company
http://www.smirnoff.com/

★★★★★

  Not for kids

Try one of the Smirnoff cocktail recipes. Learn about the history of Smirnoff, the distillation process, and the ingredients. Read about the relationship of James Bond with Smirnoff by viewing downloadable files. Submit stories about the hippest place you've found to sample Smirnoff, your favorite Smirnoff combinations, or where in the world you have enjoyed your Smirnoff and what you were doing at the time. Must promise you're of drinking age to enter.

Plowed Society Single Malt Scotch Page
http://www.single-malt.com/

★★★

  Not for kids

This website describes and rates approximately 30 single malt scotches. It includes a brief history of the people and their organizations. Also includes several anecdotes about their experiences and words of wisdom to those first-time scotch drinkers or experienced imbibers.

Spitzy.net
http://www.spitzy.net/

★★★

 Not for kids

Huge collection of drink recipes, though each recipe is not very detailed. Vote for your favorite recipe or upload recipes for your own concoctions.

The Webtender: Bartender's Handbook
http://www.webtender.com/

★★★★

 Not for kids

This comprehensive source includes general information about mixology, tips for setting up a bar, mixing terms, bar measurements, recipes for alcoholic and nonalcoholic drinks, suggestions for punch garnishes, information about glassware, anti-hangover tips, and drinking games.

Related Sites
http://www.bushmills.com/
http://www.canadianmist.com/
http://www.cutty-sark.co.uk/
http://www.grand-marnier.com/
http://www.fujipub.com/scotchmalt/

World's Best Bars
http://www.worldsbestbars.com/

★★★★★

Tour the world's best bars from Amsterdam to Zurich and read reviews from people who actually frequent these bars. Just pull up this site, click the name of a city on the list, click the name of a bar or club, and read the reviews.

A
B
C
D
E
F
G
H
I
J
K
L
M
N
O
P
Q
R
S
T
U
V
W
X
Y
Z

COFFEES AND TEAS

Bella Italia

http://www.bella-italia.com/

★★★★

Bella Italia offers unique products direct from Italy. The company's selection extends well beyond coffee items. You'll find a complete line of coffee makers, grinders, and accessories at Italian prices (with approximate U.S. dollar equivalent). Click on La Gondola to shop.

Cafe Maison Coffee Roasters

http://gourmetcoffeeroaster.com/

★★★★★

What makes Cafe Maison gourmet coffees different from all other coffee roasters? They adhere to the 21 Day Rule, telling you the exact date of the roast and reminding you that coffee is fresh for only 21 days after roasting. Plus, Cafe Maison uses only authentic extracts and essences to flavor its coffee—never sugar syrups! Select the Coffee Roastery option, and you'll be guided through the process of ordering your own custom-roasted coffee.

China Mist Tea Company

http://www.chinamist.com

★★★★

Retail store over the Internet that offers many types of iced teas, especially green teas.

CoffeeAM.com

http://store.yahoo.com/cjgo/

★★★★

This company promotes itself as the Internet's largest coffee store. It will roast and ship your coffee when you order it, which guarantees you the freshest product available. CoffeeAM.com guarantees every purchase. In addition to coffees and teas, you will also find syrups and sauces, chai, coffee candies, biscotti, equipment, and accessories.

CoolBrew Coffee from the New Orleans Coffee Company

http://www.coolbrew.com/

★★★

Features concentrated, cold-filtered, gourmet coffee extract.

Fortunes Coffee Roasters

http://www.fortunescoffee.com

★★★

At this site you'll find coffee, tea, flavored syrups, cocoa, and other coffee additives, as well as equipment available for order.

Java Hut

http://www.javahut.com/

★★★

Delivers whole bean coffee right to your door. Offers more than 15 distinctive roasts, straights, and blends. Gift boxes are available.

Kona Coffee Times

http://www.coffeetimes.com/

★★★★

Kona Coffee Times is Hawaii's purveyor of fresh-roasted 100% Kona coffee and Hawaiian mail order gifts. Publishing since 1993 and roasting mail order coffee since 1994, Coffee Times is a proponent for the preservation of 100% Kona coffee and an advocate for truth in labeling for all 100% Hawaiian-made products. You also get a free gift for mentioning that you found this site on the Internet when making an order.

Orleans Coffee Exchange

http://www.orleanscoffee.com

★★★★

Gourmet coffee from the heart of the French Quarter. Orleans Coffee offers a free pound of java with every order of five pounds or more.

Peet's Coffee & Tea

http://www.peets.com/

★★★★★

Order online for home delivery. Visitors to this site can browse through journal entries from travel writers as they search for fine coffees and teas. Also includes a page called Coffee Wisdom for tips on how to brew the best cup of java possible.

Sally's Place

http://www.sallys-place.com/beverages/coffee/coffee.htm

★★★

Insights into coffee shops and cafés around the world. Suggestions on brewing the best coffee. Even includes a definition of coffee buzzwords for confused novices. Links to retail sites.

Starbucks

http://www.starbucks.com/default.asp

★★★★★

Use this fun and funky site, which is for coffee lovers only, to find out the history of Starbucks, check out job opportunities, shop online, check out ice creams and other "beyond the bean" products, locate a store near you, visit the FAQ spot, and more.

Related Sites

http://www.coffee-ent.com/

http://www.coffeeadagio.com/

http://www.coffeereview.com/

ORGANIC FOODS

Cascadian Farm

http://www.cfarm.com/

★★★

Locate stores carrying the Cascadian Farm brand name of organic foods, search for recipes to make the most of your vegetables, and learn why organic food is such a good idea.

Eden Foods

http://www.edenfoods.com/

★★★★

Home of one of the most successful organic food suppliers in the United States. This site features recipes for appetizers, main courses, healthy beverages, condiments, salads, soups, and desserts. Enter your ZIP Code to find a health food store near you that carries Eden Foods products.

GAIAM.com Lifestyle Company

http://www.gaiam.com/

★★★★★

This site sells natural and organic foods and beverages, as well as healthcare products, while offering information on the benefit of such purchases. You'll also find a database to research organic products and issues. A nicely designed site.

Maine Organic Farmers and Gardeners Association

http://www.mofga.org/food.html

★★★

Read why organically grown food is better, what the certified organic standards are, who the growers are, and where you can buy Maine certified organic products.

National Organic Program

http://www.ams.usda.gov/nop/

★★★

USDA-maintained site of the NOP, whose purpose is to set standards for organic farming and handling of organic foods. Here, you can read up on the rules and recommendations in English, Spanish, and Japanese. Some good consumer information on what organic food labels really mean.

Organic Alliance

http://www.organic.org/

★★★

A nonprofit organization that promotes organic produce. Find organic farmers, locate recipes, and read up-to-date organic news.

A B C D E F G H I J K L M N O P Q R S T U V W X Y Z

A
B
C
D
E
F
G
H
I
J
K
L
M
N
O
P
Q
R
S
T
U
V
W
X
Y
Z

Organic Coffee

http://www.urthcaffe.com/organic/organic.html

★★★

Urth Caffe grows organic coffee using sustainable agriculture techniques. That's good for all of us.

Organic Consumers Association

http://www.organicconsumers.org/

★★★★

Learn all about the hazards of genetically engineered food, as well as diseases and food-related problems at this site, which aims to encourage consumption of organic foods. You can search the site for keywords and find vendors that sell pure food. Organic food activists will love this site.

Organic Food

http://www.organicfood.co.uk/

★★★

The Organic Food website is a resource for consumers of organic food as well as the organic industry as a whole, with articles from the organic food federation, the official UK certification body.

Organic Food Labeling

http://www.islandscene.com/food/1999/990203/food_labels/

★★★★

A discussion of what organic really means as far as labels go.

Organic Gardening Magazine

http://www.organicgardening.com/

★★★★

The online version of this print favorite. Get news on organic issues in the Watchdog section, learn the secrets of growing favorite plants and flowers organically, and search for organic solutions to age-old gardening problems.

Organic Online

http://www.organiconline.com.sg/

★★★

If you're looking for organic foods, try this online retailer, which is based in Singapore.

Organic Trade Association

http://www.ota.com/

★★★★

The Organic Trade Association (OTA) is a national association representing the organic industry in Canada and the United States. Growers, shippers, processors, and more will find the site useful in learning about organic trends, finding upcoming events, and staying on top of industry happenings.

Organic Wine

http://www.ecowine.com/

★★★

Do you really want to ingest pesticides, insecticides, herbicides, fungicides, and synthetic chemicals? Read all about the benefits of organically grown grapes and the wine that results.

SunOrganic Farm

http://www.sunorganic.com/

★★★★

Order organic foods online and have them delivered to your door. Online catalog features baking ingredients, whole-grain foods, dates, honey, beans, lentils, seeds, coffees, broths, and much more.

Walnut Acres

http://www.walnutacres.com/

★★★

Walnut Acres is a crusader in organic farming. Here, you can find a list of places where you can purchase its delicious foods.

SOY PRODUCTS

NoSoy

http://www.geocities.com/HotSprings/4620/

★★★

Soy beans and soy products may be a panacea for some people, but for those who suffer from soy allergies, soy can be the bane of their existence. Here, you can see the other side of the soy debate, learn about restaurants that serve soy-laced foods, and explore articles debunking many health claims for soy.

Overview of Soy Products

http://www.talksoy.com

★★★

You'll find buying and cooking tips, storage advice, nutritional information, and more about some of the most popular soy products, including tofu, soy milk, soy flour, and many others.

Soy.com

http://www.soy.com/

★★★

Heard the hype about soy and wondering whether any of it's true? Check out the research section here to decide for yourself. There is also soy news and product information. You can sign up for a free soy newsletter, and soon you'll be able to buy products online.

Soy and Human Health

http://www.ag.uiuc.edu/~stratsoy/expert/
askhealth.html

★★★

Comprehensive FAQs on the benefits of increasing your soy consumption.

A Superfood Called Soy—The Top 10 Benefits

http://www.healthybiz2000.com/soy.html

★★★

Read about the benefits of soy and scan the database of information about isoflavones to learn which products have the highest concentration.

WINES

Ambrosia

http://www.ambrosiawine.com/

★★★

 Not for kids

Check out the top 10 purchased wines, talk wine with other wine lovers, and order wine from the site or request a catalog.

Bordeaux

http://www.bordeaux.com/

★★★★

 Not for kids

Take a tour of the Bordeaux countryside and learn how this wine is made. Find tips on enjoying Bordeaux wine and hosting a wine-tasting party. Learn what restaurants are "Bordeaux-friendly" and how to read a Bordeaux wine label. Also, learn the basics of grape varieties (Merlot, Cabernet, Semillon, and so on) and investigate the buyer's guide and vintage chart, as well as recipes for French cuisine. Or, check out the glossary of basic wine terms.

Buyers and Cellars Wine Education

http://www.wineeducation.com/

★★★

 Not for kids

This site focuses on wine education. It helps you gain the confidence to enjoy wine and feel comfortable ordering it. You'll learn how to find bargain wines, distinguish the characteristics of different grapes, determine the correct temperature to serve wine, and more.

Edgerton's Wine Price File

http://www.wineprices.com

★★★★

 Not for kids

This site showcases software for serious wine collectors to help manage wine inventory and keep track of aging. Software includes a wine database, a view of your cellar, and The Wine Price File book for sale online.

Fetzer Vineyards

http://www.fetzer.com/

★★★★

 Not for kids

This producer of organically farmed wines is the sixth largest premium winery in the country. In addition to checking out Fetzer's wine, you can find out more about its environmental policies.

A
B
C
D
E
F
G
H
I
J
K
L
M
N
O
P
Q
R
S
T
U
V
W
X
Y
Z

A
B
C
D
E
F
G
H
I
J
K
L
M
N
O
P
Q
R
S
T
U
V
W
X
Y
Z

Fine Wine Diary

http://www.finewinediary.com/

★★★

 Not for kids

A wine lover's paradise. This wine guide to France highlights all the best vineyards. Maps identify wine-producing regions and link you to specific descriptions and history.

Food and Wine Access

http://www.foodandwineaccess.com/

★★★★

 Not for kids

Keep abreast of upcoming wine-tasting events and festivals, read wine and restaurant reviews, and get the low-down on past events.

Food & Wine Magazine

http://www.foodandwine.com/

★★★★★

 Not for kids

You can find wines, foods, recipes, and more at this colorful, comprehensive site. Be sure to check out the store where you can purchase everything from mustard to cookbooks.

Geerlings & Wade

http://www.geerwade.com/gw/default.asp

★★★★

 Not for kids

Select a wine by region, flavor, or price and then purchase it from this site, which also offers accessories and wine gifts.

Global Wine Club

http://www.clubsofamerica.com

★★★

 Not for kids

Part of the Clubs of America series. With each month's shipment, clients receive two different bottles of rare wine, many from small award-winning wineries around the world. Included in each shipment is *Wine Expeditions*, the Club newsletter, offering insights on the monthly selections. You'll also have an opportunity to order your favorite wines at discounted prices.

Gruppo Italiano Vini

http://www.gruppoitalianovini.com/

★★★★★

 Not for kids

This company not only produces and distributes Italian wine, it also manages historic wine cellars. See where the cellars are located on a map of Italy and read about company news and information.

Internet Guide to Wine and Frequently Asked Questions

http://www.sbwines.com/usenet_winefaq//

★★★★

 Not for kids

Read a general introduction about what wine is. Learn how wine is made, aged, and stored. Learn the proper way to drink wine and get tips on buying wine. Check out the varieties of wine and tour wine countries in France, California, and Canada.

Into Wine

http://www.intowine.com

★★★★★

 Not for kids

Introduction to the wonderful world of wines, this site provides information on various wine regions, explains how wine is made, provides instructions on how to properly store wine, shows you how to enjoy wine, and more.

K&L Wine Merchants

http://www.klwines.com

★★★★★

 Not for kids

Named as the best wine shop on the Internet by *Money* magazine and one of the top 10 wine retailers in the nation by the publishers of the *Wine Spectator*.

Kahn's Fine Wines

http://www.kahnsfinewines.com/

★★★★

 Not for kids

Wines, gourmet foods, cigars, and more can all be ordered online from this wonderful website. Kahn's Fine Wines, which has been a retail liquor and wine business in Indianapolis for more than 20 years, now specializes in fine wine. This site is truly a treat.

Kendall Jackson Wineries

http://www.kj.com

★★★

 Not for kids

Newest wine releases, reviews, awards, guest columns, and the newly updated K-J current events calendar.

Marilyn Merlot

http://www.marilynmerlot.com/

★★★★

 Not for kids

Order special collector's editions of Marilyn Merlot wines. You can purchase these wines online, but the price is pretty steep—some sell for more than $600 per bottle!

Merryvale Vineyards

http://www.merryvale.com

★★★

 Not for kids

Features articles, reviews, recipes, and wine pairings. Click the Fun Stuff link for e-postcards, the wine trivia challenge, and weekend wine events.

Napa Valley Virtual Visit

http://www.napavalley.com/

★★★★

 Not for kids

Explore various Napa Valley wineries or purchase wines and wine-management software. This site provides sightseeing, dining, and catering ideas, as well as current events. If you're looking to make a real visit, check out the information about accommodations. Also contains links to other Valley sites.

Peter Ruhrberg's German Wine Page

http://www.winepage.de/

★★★

 Not for kids

Excellent introduction including tips on decoding German wine labels, and information on growing regions, grape varieties, and vintages.

[Best] Robin Garr's Wine Lovers Page

http://www.wine-lovers-page.com/

★★★★★

 Not for kids

Frequently updated notes and advice on wines of good value are backed by an online wine-tasting tutorial, wine FAQs, vintage charts, interactive discussions, and more. Click the Wine Chat link to learn about upcoming chat sessions with respected wine connoisseurs. Wine questionnaire, wine lexicon, winegrape glossary, and other resources make this the most comprehensive wine site on the Web.

A B C D E F G H I J K L M N O P Q R S T U V W X Y Z

A
B
C
D
E
F
G
H
I
J
K
L
M
N
O
P
Q
R
S
T
U
V
W
X
Y
Z

Silver Spirits Monthly

http://www.silver-spirits.com/

★★★

⚑ Not for kids

This site contains a newsletter published monthly by owner Barry Silver that showcases what's best in new and current wine releases. Provides links to domestic wines and wines from other countries. Sign up for the mailing list to be eligible for discounts.

SmartWine Online

http://winebusiness.com/

★★★

⚑ Not for kids

Claiming to be the largest wine-related site on the Web, SmartWine Online provides links to a variety of sites devoted to wine. Peruse some wine-tasting notes before you imbibe, select the best wine to complement your meal, glean some health facts about wine, and find out about the wine industry.

Spanish Wines

http://www.spanishwinesonline.co.uk/

 $

★★★★

⚑ Not for kids

Spanish wines, profiles, vintages, storage tips, and common wine terms.

Sutter Home

http://www.sutterhome.com

 $

★★★★

⚑ Not for kids

Screensaver, recipes, contests, history, and How to Drink Wine: An Interactive Guide. The online store contains not only wines but also clothing and wine accessory gifts.

Taste Tour Home Page

http://www.winetaste.com/

 $

★★★★

⚑ Not for kids

Your guide for gaining "instant wine expertise." Have to entertain clients or impress your stuffy boss? The *TasteTour WineGuides* can get you through. These quick wine references contain all you need to know and can be ordered from this site.

Vampire Vineyards

http://www.vampirewine.com/

$

★★★★★

⚑ Not for kids

The Vampire line of wines is imported from Transylvania, Romania, and includes Merlot, Pinot Grigio, Pinot Noir, Sauvignon Blanc, and Cabernet Sauvignon. You also can purchase unique Vampire Vineyards merchandise, including posters, baseball hats, T-shirts, and wine glasses.

Vergina Imports, Inc.

http://www.greekwines.com/

★★★

⚑ Not for kids

This Canadian company imports Greek wines and spirits. Learn about Greek vineyards, read the company's profile, and view a list of the award-winning wines this company sells.

Vins de Bordeaux

http://www.vins-bordeaux.fr/

★★★

 Not for kids

Tips on how to enjoy Bordeaux wine and how to have your own wine-tasting party! How the wine is made, what restaurants are "Bordeaux-friendly," and how to read a Bordeaux wine label.

Wine Access

http://www.wineaccess.com/pvt/my-wineaccess.tcl

★★★★

 Not for kids

A complete guide for all wine lovers. Extensive information highlighted by a wine selection tool. Designed for everyone from the experienced collector to the interested beginner. Check out the list of top-rated wines and the Q&A list, and put together your own wine portfolio.

The Wine Broker

http://www.winebroker.com

★★★★

 Not for kids

Contains wine and wine-related information for all types of wine lovers, from casual to connoisseur. The site offers holiday gift packages, a monthly wine club, a list of rare wines, and more.

Wine Enthusiast

http://www.wineenthusiast.com/

★★★★★

 Not for kids

This site sells wine-related accessories, from cellars to corkscrews to cigars. Of course, it also sells wine itself, including specials and samplers. Sign up for a free catalog.

Wine on the Web: The Talking Wine Magazine

http://www.wineontheweb.com

★★★★

 Not for kids

Independent, international Internet publication with vintage charts, a searchable and alphabetized database, and wine news. Includes columns by The Flying Wine Man and The American Wine Guy. Devoted to helping wine consumers find the best wines in their price range. Site is very up to date.

Wine Searcher

http://www.wine-searcher.com/

★★★★

 Not for kids

Wine-searcher is designed to help wine enthusiasts find reputable Web-based dealers that carry their favorite wines. Merchants place their lists on Wine-searcher so the wines can be more easily found via this site than with traditional Internet searches. Each offer is dated and is either updated or removed at regular intervals.

Wine Spectator

http://www.winespectator.com

★★★★★

 Not for kids

Find answers to nearly every question you can think up about wine and wine tasting. You'll find a searchable database of wine information, wine ratings, news, a library, and forums. Links to retail sites that specialize in wine and wine-related products.

WINE: UC Davis Department of Viticulture and Enology

http://wineserver.ucdavis.edu

★★★★

 Not for kids

The home page of the Department of Viticulture and Enology at UC Davis, the oldest wine and grape research institution in the world, offers information about wine science, home winemaking, wine extension classes, wine literature, wine weather, wine aroma, wine URLs, wine and health, wine and travel, and more.

Wine.com

http://www.wine.com/

★★★★★

 Not for kids

Home to the largest wine retailer in the United States, Wine.com features a huge wine cellar with a selection of more than 5,000 wines. Here, you can find wine reviews, a FAQ list, accessories, gift certificates, special deals, and more.

A
B
C
D
E
F
G
H
I
J
K
L
M
N
O
P
Q
R
S
T
U
V
W
X
Y
Z

A
B
C
D
E
F
G
H
I
J
K
L
M
N
O
P
Q
R
S
T
U
V
W
X
Y
Z

Wine Messenger

http://www.winemessenger.com

★★★

 Not for kids

A wine retailer that features wines from small grow-ers all over the world. Some excellent general infor-mation about wines and wine tasting.

Wines on the Internet

http://www.wines.com/

★★★★★

 Not for kids

An excellent resource for wine-related topics. Provides links to online wineries and vineyards, fea-tures a virtual tasting room, and includes other notes of interest for the connoisseur and novice wine drinker alike. Also details upcoming events for wine enthusiasts and links to reputable online wine sellers.

Zachys Online

http://www.zachys.com/

★★★★★

This online wine cellar features a huge collection of the finest wines in the world. This site features a searchable wine index, gifts and accessories, auctions, and special events. You can even ask for help in selecting a particular wine.

Related Sites
http://www.americanwineries.org/
http://www.invinoveritas.com/
http://www.wonderwine.com/
http://www.wineaustralia.com.au/

FOOTBALL

Best National Football League

http://www.nfl.com

★★★★★

 All

Get the latest information on every team, every player, and every game from the official NFL site. You can find statistics and scores, play fantasy football online, and even sign up for the official NFL email newsletter. Ticket information is also available, although tickets to games are not available from this site. You can even get information about international NFL. Links to other football-related sites. For the best that football has to offer, this is the site for you.

AFC Web Sites

Baltimore Ravens	http://www.ravenszone.net/
Buffalo Bills	http://www.buffalobills.com/
Cincinnati Bengals	http://www.bengals.com/
Cleveland Browns	http://www.clevelandbrowns.com/
Denver Broncos	http://www.denverbroncos.com/
Houston Texans	http://www.houstontexans.com/
Indianapolis Colts	http://www.colts.com/
Jacksonville Jaguars	http://www.jaguars.com/
Kansas City Chiefs	http://www.kcchiefs.com/
Miami Dolphins	http://www.miamidolphins.com/
New England Patriots	http://www.patriots.com/
New York Jets	http://www.newyorkjets.com/
Oakland Raiders	http://www.raiders.com/
Pittsburgh Steelers	http://www.steelers.com/
San Diego Chargers	http://www.chargers.com/
Tennessee Titans	http://www.titansonline.com/

NFC Web Sites

Arizona Cardinals	http://www.azcardinals.com/
Atlanta Falcons	http://www.atlantafalcons.com/
Carolina Panthers	http://www.panthers.com/
Chicago Bears	http://www.chicagobears.com/
Dallas Cowboys	http://www.dallascowboys.com/
Detroit Lions	http://www.detroitlions.com/
Green Bay Packers	http://www.packers.com/
Minnesota Vikings	http://www.vikings.com/
New Orleans Saints	http://www.neworleanssaints.com/
New York Giants	http://www.giants.com/
Philadelphia Eagles	http://www.philadelphiaeagles.com/
San Francisco 49ers	http://www.sf49ers.com/
St. Louis Rams	http://www.stlouisrams.com/
Seattle Seahawks	http://www.seahawks.com/
Tampa Bay Buccaneers	http://www.buccaneers.com/
Washington Redskins	http://www.redskins.com/

NFLPlayers.com

http://www.nflplayers.com/

★★★

 All

Check out the web page of your favorite players and contemplate who the unsung heroes have been this past season, as well as the draft favorites for the upcoming year.

Pro Football Hall of Fame

http://www.profootballhof.com/

$

★★★★

 All

Find out more about hall of famers and learn about the annual Hall of Fame Game. You'll also find information about pro football history. The Hall of Fame store offers many interesting items for sale.

FOREIGN POLICY

American Diplomacy

http://www.unc.edu/depts/diplomat/

★★★

14-18

An electronic journal of commentary, analysis, and research on American foreign policy and its practice. Published with the cooperation of the Triangle Institute for Security Studies.

American Foreign Service Association

http://www.afsa.org/

★★★

The website of AFSA, the professional association of U.S. Foreign Service, is an excellent resource for those interested in diplomacy and international affairs. The site includes educational programs, reference materials, publications, speakers, conferences, and more.

Best Carnegie Council on Ethics and International Affairs

http://www.cceia.org

$

★★★★★

Carnegie Council is an independent, nonpartisan, nonprofit organization dedicated to increasing the understanding of ethics and international affairs. Obtain edited transcripts and articles from the Council's "Ethics & International Affairs" publication, access interviews and book reviews, check out the online forums, and much more. You can order past issues and other publications online. This site's excellent design and top-notch information make it an easy choice as Best of the Best.

The Center for Security Policy

http://www.centerforsecuritypolicy.org/

★★★★

The purpose of the nonprofit, nonpartisan Center for Security Policy is to stimulate and inform the national and international debate about all aspects of security policy—notably those policies bearing on the foreign, defense, economic, financial, and technological interests of the United States.

Department of Foreign Affairs–Dublin, Ireland

http://www.irlgov.ie/iveagh/

★★★

Advises the government on all aspects of Ireland's external relations and acts as the channel of official communications with foreign governments and international organizations.

embassy.org

http://www.embassy.org/

★★★★

14-18

embassy.org is a connection to most of the U.S.–based embassies and consulates. Features a searchable diplomacy database with more than 50,000 addresses, phone numbers, and email addresses of diplomatic posts worldwide. This feature will be implemented online. embassy.org focuses on websites maintained by foreign representations all over the world.

NATO: The North Atlantic Treaty Organization

http://www.nato.int/

★★★★

👫 14-18

This site offers, in part, a short history of the alliance and a brief introduction to its main policies. A guide to NATO's structure, and its members and partners, as well as staff vacancies. A complete archive of all official documents and both general and specific NATO publications.

The United Nations

http://www.un.org/

★★★★★

👫 14-18

Home page of the United Nations. Six languages to choose from and five categories of information to select from: Peace and Security, International Law, Humanitarian Affairs, Human Rights, and Economic and Social Development. Find out more about every facet of the UN.

U.S. Agency for International Development

http://www.usaid.gov/

★★★

👫 14-18

Investigate U.S. Aid budget numbers, learn about countries currently being aided by the United States, and get background economic research on various countries and regions.

Women In International Security (WIIS)

http://wiis.georgetown.edu/

★★★★

The official home page of Women In International Security (WIIS), dedicated to enhancing opportunities for women working in foreign and defense policies. An international, nonprofit, nonpartisan network and educational program, WIIS is open to both men and women at all stages of their careers.

A
B
C
D
E
F
G
H
I
J
K
L
M
N
O
P
Q
R
S
T
U
V
W
X
Y
Z

FRUGAL SPENDING

A B C D E F G H I J K L M N O P Q R S T U V W X Y Z

About Frugality

http://frugalliving.miningco.com/

★★★★

Huge collection of resources on how to trim expenses and live on less income. Everything from saving on groceries to trimming the high costs of pet care.

BetterBudgeting.com

http://www.betterbudgeting.com/

★★★★

This site provides loads of tips and techniques for making a living on whatever you earn. Learn about debt consolidation, budgeting, cooking frugally, avoiding impulse buying, and much more. Lots of free information, but the subscription promises even more money-saving suggestions.

[Best] Cheapskate Monthly

http://www.cheapskatemonthly.com/

★★★★★

Get your daily tip for debt-free living at this site, which also features a radio interview with author Mary Hunt, the editor-in-cheap. By joining the site and buying a subscription to her debt-free living newsletter, you'll also gain access to discussion boards and get even more information about saving money. You can purchase books written by Hunt and other money experts that offer more creative ways to live a frugal life. When you're ready to cut your expenses and live a simpler life, there's no better site for you.

The Dollar Stretcher

http://www.stretcher.com/

★★★

A weekly online newsletter with tons of articles and information about frugal living. This site's motto is "living better…for less." Frugal living hints are available in a vast number of categories, including coupons, food, medical care, debt, hobbies, pets, children, auto care, retirement, and many others.

eSmarts Newsletter

http://www.esmarts.com/

★★★★★

Each week, eSmarts publishes a newsletter full of great Internet deals, including new online shopping secrets, Internet coupons, and general shopping tips. By reading this newsletter every week, you can save hundreds, even thousands, of dollars a year.

Found Money Saving Tips

http://money.mpr.org/cgi-bin/foundmoney.pl

★★★

List of tips and tricks to help you save organized by categories including Automobile, Banking, Grocery, and Shopping, to name a few.

Frugal Family Network

http://www.frugalfamilynetwork.com/

★★★

Learn how to "live creatively within your financial means," and have fun doing it. Angie Zilewski and Deana Ricks, authors of *Cheap Talk with the Frugal Friends*, teach you how to stretch a dollar and provide tips and links to other resources that show you how to save money on groceries, bills, insurance, and more. Learn how to pinch pennies and live a less stressful life.

The Frugal Shopper

http://www.thefrugalshopper.com/

Find articles on how to save money on your daily expenses. Provides information on freebies and special offers, coupons, rebates, and other money-saving stuff.

Julie's Frugal Tips

http://www.brightok.net/~neilmayo/

Read the tip of the week for saving money and find a long list of links to sites that specialize in frugal living.

Living the Cottage Life Frugally

http://www.littlecountryvillage.com/index.shtml

This site invites you to sign up for a monthly email publication called *Heart & Home*. It promises to deliver "exciting articles on frugal living, homesteading, how-to articles, gardening, recipes, farming, cheap building methods, decorating, self-sufficiency, home business, being prepared, and more!"

Money Master's Website

http://members.aol.com/Moneymstr/

Anyone struggling with money management issues will want to visit this site for an excellent primer on budgeting and many ideas for cutting costs in many areas, from insurance to clothing to food and more.

Swapping Services: Neighbors Meeting Needs

http://www.coopamerica.org/individual/Marketplace/IMMMswap.htm

Find out how a neighborhood-swapping group got started, how it works, and how to start your own variation.

A B C D E F G H I J K L M N O P Q R S T U V W X Y Z

358

Yellow PagesYellow Pages

FUN SITES

Access Project

http://www.accessproject.net/

★★★★★

This unique art project beams a spotlight and sound on selected individuals and enables viewers to watch the individuals as they react to the experience. The viewers themselves pick a person they want to spotlight. They can then watch as the person tries to avoid the spotlight or decides to perform for this audience that he or she does not see. Is it art or just a silly prank? You decide.

AhaJokes.com

http://www.ahajokes.com/

★★★

14-18

Huge collection of clean jokes organized by categories. Some people might find the ethnic jokes offensive, but the collection does a fair job of insulting all races and nationalities equally. Some of the jokes are not intended for young children, though many are.

Al Lowe's Humor Site

http://www.allowe.com/

★★★★★

14-18

Al Lowe, creator of Leisure Suit Larry, calls this site home. Here you can find sight gags, audio and video humor, text jokes, Leisure Suit Larry and Freddy Phargas games, free game and screensaver downloads, information about Al Lowe, and much more. All very funny and entertaining.

Baby Boomer Headquarters

http://www.bbhq.com/

★★★

Exactly who are the boomers? Use this site to try your hand at some trivia and check out statistics and resources. You'll love those posted stories of lost youth, too.

Burning Man

http://www.burningman.com

★★★★★

Not for kids

Home of Burning Man, the famous and infamous annual personal-expression-art-fair-and-mayhem ritual, where more than 25,000 participants gather in the desert every summer to form an interactive community, in which participants do some pretty weird stuff. Visit this site to learn more about Burning Man and what it means to its various participants.

Boxerjam

http://www.boxerjam.com/

★★★

Not for kids

Play word games and puzzles, and answer trivia questions to qualify for prizes. Lots of games and ways to amuse yourself. Kids would love this site, as well, but don't send your kid here with your credit card. The site does promote gambling.

Caricature Zone

http://www.magixl.com/

★★★★★

 All

This site features a huge collection of caricatures of the rich and famous organized by categories, including political figures, actors and actresses, rock stars, and famous athletes. Check out the gallery, generate your own caricature online, email a greeting card, download clip art and wallpaper, or shop online. The whole site has a cartoony look and feel, but it's very easy to get around and offers an extensive collection of valuable freebies.

Comedy Central

http://www.comedycentral.com/

★★★

 Not for kids

Visit the home of Comedy Central, the irreverent TV network responsible for such shows as *South Park* and *The Man Show*. Here, you can check the TV listings for your favorite show, enter contests, play games, or just waste time. Call me a prude, but I don't recommend this site for kids.

Communimage

http://www.communimage.ch/

★★★★★

This is the ultimate mosaic, a global visual dialog in which users from all over the world paste their own photos, paintings, drawings, and other eye candy. This site stitches them all together to create an intriguing image that visitors can zoom in on to explore in greater detail.

Cool Site of the Day

http://cool.infi.net

★★★

Connects you to the cool site of the day on the Internet, determined by the moderator. This works better than a random-site connector because the sites are more likely to be pretty cool.

CyberCafés

http://www.netcafes.com/

★★★★

Where are the coolest Internet cafés around the world? Offers a database of 4,211 Internet cafés in 149 countries. To find a café, search by city or country name, and click on the map. Café listings are very comprehensive.

Dane Cook

http://www.danecook.com/

★★★★★

 Not for kids

Dane Cook is a hilarious stand-up comedian well known to fans of Comedy Central. Here, you can listen to portions of Dane Cook's edgy stand-up routine, view short cartoons, chat online, follow his tour, shop online, and much more. Very cool design and plenty of material to keep you entertained.

Deep Cold

http://www.deepcold.com/

★★★

Fascinating look at the space race of the Cold War era. Check out the renditions of how these spacecrafts might look today and find out what software was used for the artwork. Government stories, too.

Formilab

http://fourmilab.ch/

★★★★★

This site, created and maintained by John Walker (the founder of Autodesk), features an eclectic collection of free books, articles, images, and software. Here you will find utilities for Windows, Unix, and Palm operating systems, science facts, science fiction, humor, and more.

A
B
C
D
E
F
G
H
I
J
K
L
M
N
O
P
Q
R
S
T
U
V
W
X
Y
Z

A
B
C
D
E
F
G
H
I
J
K
L
M
N
O
P
Q
R
S
T
U
V
W
X
Y
Z

Fortean Times

http://www.forteantimes.com/

★★★★

This site chronicles some of the strange phenomena occurring in the world today, combing various news sources to bring you the stranger stories of the day. The day we visited the site, we found a story on how to reduce dog flatulence (from a local ABC news station out of Toledo, Ohio), photos of camel spiders from Baghdad (at www.snopes.com), and a story from *The Union* about a murder suspect who claimed he was fleeing aliens. When the daily news no longer interests you, visit this site to get a different perspective on what's newsworthy.

Fray

http://www.fray.com/

★★★★★

Fray features a collection of personal stories from visitors around the world. Visit this site to read stories and to post your own story in reply. Fray challenges people everywhere to live an interesting life and then have something to say about it. After you've done that, come back and tell the world about it at Fray.

FunnyJokes.com

http://www.funnyjokes.com

★★★

 Not for kids

Need a good laugh? Check out this site for some of the best jokes on the Internet. Special category for Dirty Jokes, so keep the kids away.

Fun Zone

http://www.afunzone.com/

★★★★

Huge directory of fun websites, including a daily brain teaser, top 100 game sites, trivia zone, cartoon zone, IQ tests, and puzzles.

George Coates Performance Works

http://www.georgecoates.org/

★★★

Need a diversion? Hop over to this site, which provides you with some crazy wisdom to get you through the day.

Ghost Sites

http://disobey.com/ghostsites/

★★★★★

Ever wonder where one of your favorite sites disappeared to? Well, it may have died and ended up haunting the Ghost Sites page, "Where Dead Web Sites Live On." Here, you can check out the last days of a website to find out what caused its demise, or to simply wonder what happened. This site acts as a museum of dead sites, displaying the final screens of a website just before the lights went out.

Glass Wings

http://www.glasswings.com.au

★★★

A site whose stated purpose is "to have fun, help improve the state of the world, inform, and provide an interesting and useful commercial site." Provides a collection of links and a search site only for fun and non–business-oriented stuff. Includes links to other humorous sites. A special area for kids is available at http://kids.glasswings.com.au/, but some other links at this site are definitely not for kids.

Insultmonger

http://www.insultmonger.com/

★★★★★

 Not for kids

Looking for some soul-searing insults? Then this is the place for you. This site features a swearasaurus where you can learn to cuss in over 100 different languages, a random insult generator, an advice column, a joke index, a game arcade, and much more to keep you laughing.

It Seems Like Yesterday

http://www.itseemslikeyesterday.com/

★★★

Baby boomers can relive the 1960s or 1970s here, where sections of the site are devoted to each decade, as well as boomers and the atomic age. This quarterly magazine's chock-full of memories for boomers. Get featured articles on important news events from that time period, lifestyles, factoids, athletes, and celebrities. Play the crossword game or send a friend an electronic postcard with a '60s or '70s theme.

Kids World 2000: Cool Sites Just for Kids

http://www.now2000.com/bigkidnetwork/
otherkidssites.html

★★★

👥 All

Links to all kinds of sites of interest to children.
Includes links to Planet Zoom, CyberAngels Internet
Safety Patrol, and The Headbone Zone.

Marshall Brain's How Stuff Works

http://www.howstuffworks.com/

★★★★

👥 All

Ever wanted to know how a car engine works? Or how
toilets work? Well, the articles on this site are sure to
answer many of your "How does that work?" questions.

Microsoft TerraServer

http://terraserver.homeadvisor.msn.com/

★★★

Find your home town's satellite image! Just type in
your area and get a high-resolution photo. Zoom in,
zoom out, or shift directions. Check out famous places
such as Candlestick Park, Mount St. Helens, or the
Kremlin in Moscow. If you get turned around, click on
Street Map.

Payphone Project

http://www.payphone-project.com/

★★★★

A site featuring payphones all over the United States,
Canada, and even overseas. You can call Florida,
Switzerland, Romania, or even the Eiffel Tower, if
you dare. Whether it's informative or strictly for
laughs, you'll get a kick out of this site.

SlashNOT

http://www.slashnot.com/

★★★★★

Slashdot.org is the news site for nerds, dedicated to
keeping geeks all around the world informed of the
latest developments in Linux, Windows, Mac OS,
and Bill Gates. This site is dedicated to undercutting
the importance of everything related to computer
technology. Here, you can learn about the new
Microsoft .LIP server, the new religious sect formed
by Linux users, and studies on the environmental
impact of satire. If you're fed up with techno-hype,
visit this site for a healthy dose of techno-humor.

spamradio

http://www.spamradio.com

★★★

👥 Not for kids

An online service that transforms junk email messages into audio broadcasts, so all those interested
can tune in to a steady barrage of junk mail. Why?

Stupid.com

http://stupid.com/

★★★★★

Stupid candy, stupid games, stupid toys, and stupid
gifts… if you're looking for something stupid to buy
for yourself, a friend, or a relative, look to
Stupid.com. This site features the stupidest products
imaginable, complete with product reviews. Best of
all, you can purchase them online, so you won't look
stupid in public.

Uncle Roy All Around You

http://www.uncleroyallaroundyou.co.uk/

★★★★★

Uncle Roy All Around You is a computer game that
combines reality with virtual reality. Street players
with handheld computers comb the streets of a real
city looking for Uncle Roy. Online players assist in
the search by following a virtual map of the same
area. They provide instructions to their teammates
on the street, working together to reach the secret
destination in 60 minutes or less.

A
B
C
D
E
F
G
H
I
J
K
L
M
N
O
P
Q
R
S
T
U
V
W
X
Y
Z

A
B
C
D
E
F
G
H
I
J
K
L
M
N
O
P
Q
R
S
T
U
V
W
X
Y
Z

WebCounter Top Sites

http://www.digits.com/top/

★★★★

🚸 Not for kids

Listing of top sites ranked by the number of hits they receive per day. You'll find a Top 10 list and a Top 100 list. You'll also find an alphabetical listing and a listing of adult theme sites.

Worth1000

http://www.worth1000.com/

★★★★★

A picture used to be worth a hundred words, but here it's worth a thousand. This site features an online contest where photographers can submit phony photos to compete with others online. Each contest has a theme. For example, Supernatural Phenomena 2 calls for contestants to submit photographs that demonstrate a supernatural phenomenon, such as spoon bending, levitation, a religious miracle, or some other supernatural hoax. You can browse through submitted photos or enter your own photo in one of the many contests.

GAMES AND PUZZLES

1MoreGame.com

http://1moregame.com/

★★★★★

This site features an arcade with more than 15 Java games, including Wuzzler (Foosball), Tiny Pinball, Cybercourt (Tennis), and Speedbiker. You can log in as GUEST using the password GUEST, or register to have your scores saved and compete with other players. Excellent graphics and very responsive controls.

3D Realms

http://www.3drealms.com

★★★★

 14-18

Download shareware games like Duke Nukem and Max Payne, as well as many, many others, and get daily updates on gaming industry news here.

Activision

http://www.activision.com

$

★★★

14-18

Check out all the games you can buy from this site, including the new Star Trek series, Quake, and several games from Cabela's, as well as Disney and Shanghai.

Adrenaline Vault

http://www.avault.com

★★★★

14-18

Read reviews about gaming software, download demos of upcoming offerings, and stay current on game news at this site.

American Crossword Puzzle Tournament

http://www.crosswordtournament.com

★★★

All

Get more information about this annual event, directed by *New York Times* Crossword Puzzle Editor, Will Shortz. It is the nation's oldest and largest crossword competition with contestants attempting to solve eight crosswords created just for the tournament. Scoring is based on accuracy and speed, and prizes are awarded in more than 20 categories. Special section for kids 5 to 11 years old features puzzles, riddles, brain teasers, and more.

Apple Corps

http://apple-corps.westnet.com/apple_corps.2.html

★★★★★

0-8

The game you lost all the pieces to as a child is back. Mr./Mrs. Potato Head is here, under an online, non-copyrighted form, except now s/he's an apple. You can place eyes, nose, teeth, mouth, whatever, onto the apple. A new twist is also available: Change the vegetable if you like.

A B C D E F **G** H I J K L M N O P Q R S T U V W X Y Z

Ariel's Simpsons Trivia Quiz

http://www.geocities.com/Athens/1530/simptriv.html

★★★

👥 14-18

Provides an online trivia quiz about the popular television show *The Simpsons*. Includes many different questions and links to other related sites.

Backgammon

http://www.bkgm.com/motif.html

★★★★

👥 All

Home of Motif Backgammon, a Java application that will serve as your opponent. Newcomers to the game can learn how to play in the extensive "rules" area.

Backgammon Galore

http://www.bkgm.com/

★★★★

👥 All

Play and learn about backgammon at this site for game enthusiasts. You can also find newsgroup information and links to other related sites.

Banja

http://www.banja.com

💲

★★★★★

👥 All

In this intriguing online, role-playing game, you take on the identity of Banja the Rasta, a hip islander who makes his way around a semi-inhabited island looking for hidden passages, useful tools, and other things that might make his adventure more rewarding. Check out this site and join in the fun!

Boxerjam.com

http://www.boxerjam.com/

★★★★★

👥 Not for kids

Online game site where you can play against the computer or against other people at the site. Compete on virtual game shows, play solitaire, or try your hand at some puzzles. Some games are for kids, but gambling is definitely encouraged here.

BrettspielWelt

http://www.brettspielwelt.de/

★★★★★

This is one of the best sites on the Web for playing computer games, especially if you can read German. English speaking players can go to http://brettspielwelt.info/ for help on navigating the German site.

Caissa's Web Home Page

http://caissa.com/

★★★

👥 All

Provides a page where Caissa members can play chess live over the Internet. Includes membership rules and information.

Case's Ladder: Multiplayer Gaming League

http://www.igl.net

★★★

👥 All

Play one of more than 100 games through this multiplayer gaming league by registering and choosing from a lengthy list of games. More than 4 million registered users. Kids can play here, too, but a parent should approve the registration first.

Chinook

http://www.cs.ualberta.ca/~chinook/

★★★★★

👥 All

If checkers is your game, Chinook is your website. Beat Chinook and you will have outmaneuvered the world man-machine checkers champion. Good collection of links to other checkers sites as well.

ClueMaster

http://www.cluemaster.com

💲

★★★★

👥 All

If you're a word puzzle fanatic, you'll want to visit this site for hundreds of free puzzles to solve, as well as the ability to archive puzzles in progress.

The Daily 100

http://www.80s.com/Entertainment/Movies/Daily100/

★★★★

👥 14-18

A fantastic site featuring 1980s movie trivia. The site provides the clip; you provide the actor, movie, and year it debuted. The site keeps track of players; that is, it's a contest. Closed on weekends.

EA.com

http://www.ea.com/

★★★★★

👥 All

Home of Electronic Arts, producers of some of the most popular video games, this site provides information about EA's product line. Plus you'll find gobs of free games divided into categories that include everything from board games and bingo to online video games and trivia contests.

Fin, Fur, and Feather Bureau of Investigation

http://www.fffbi.com/

💲

★★★★★

👥 9-13

This site encourages kids 8 to 13 years old to explore the world and its many cultures. Stories, humor, and oddball characters combine to keep visitors amused and entertained as they set out on various missions around the world.

FreeArcade.com

http://ww12.freearcade.com/

★★★★

👥 14-18

Great place to play free Java-based arcade games, including Nineball, SuperDunk Basketball, Mower Mole, and Javanoid. Puzzle games and board games also featured. Some pop-up ads may not be suitable for young children.

Freecell.com

http://www.freecell.com/

💲

★★★★

👥 14-18

Are you a self-proclaimed Freecell junkie? Then this is the site for you. Study the finer points of Freecell, play Freecell online, get Freecell for your Palm Pilot, shop for Freecell paraphernalia, or learn how to get the monkey off your back with the 12-step recovery plan.

The Fruit Game

http://www.2020tech.com/fruit/

★★★★★

👥 All

Offers the challenging fruit game. Players remove fruit from the screen; the last player to remove fruit wins. Try this mathematical adventure. Great for parents and kids, students and teachers.

G4 Media Network

http://www.g4media.com/

★★★★

👥 14-18

Television network devoted to computer games provides articles, tips, tricks, and reviews of some of the most popular computer games on the market.

Gamasutra

http://www.gamasutra.com

💲

★★★★★

👥 14-18

Catering to the game developer, this site is designed for serious video game players and creators. Here, you can learn about the latest trends in video games, find out more about what game players want, pick up some new design techniques, learn about the latest programs and technologies, and much more.

A B C D E F **G** H I J K L M N O P Q R S T U V W X Y Z

A
B
C
D
E
F
G
H
I
J
K
L
M
N
O
P
Q
R
S
T
U
V
W
X
Y
Z

[Best] Games Domain

http://www.gamesdomain.com

★★★★★

👥 14-18

Download demos, read news and interviews with leading game programmers as well as game reviews, and chat with fellow gamers here. You can also find cheats to a number of games, as well as find links to official game pages. Many online games are available here, too. Overall, this is a jam-packed site for the avid gamer, an easy Best of the Best pick! Some content will appeal to younger players, but some of the games covered here can be a little suggestive and/or violent.

GamesIndustries.biz

http://www.gamesindustry.biz/

★★★★★

Keep up on the latest developments in the video game industry at this site. Here, you can read game reviews, check out game charts and planned release dates, check stock prices for the top game companies, and even look for a job in the industry. This site features plenty of current articles to keep any game enthusiast well informed.

Gamespot

http://www.gamespot.com/

★★★★★

👥 14-18

For all-around gamers who aren't devoted to any particular system, Gamespot features a little of everything: news, reviews, previews, surveys, contests, downloads, and more. Links to online stores where you can compare prices for various games and game gear. Some material appeals to younger players, as well, but some suggestive and violent games are covered here. Parents should visit the site first.

GameSpy

http://www.gamespy.com

★★★★★

👥 14-18

This site plays host to a huge collection of multiplayer arcade games and a popular gaming community. Join more than 4.4 million members worldwide playing nearly 300 of today's hottest games!

Gamesville

http://www.gamesville.lycos.com/

★★★★★

👥 Not for kids

Gamesville is a huge online gaming site, where visitors can play games against the computer or against each other. Play for cash prizes or play for fun. Plenty of links to online casinos, too. Some games will appeal to children, but gambling is promoted.

Homers

http://www.vicious-arrogance.com/Homers/

★★★

👥 14-18

This site is an online game that requires you to put Homer Simpson's head on straight, among other games. Includes rules and links to other online games. Some areas of this site may be suitable for younger children.

IGN

http://www.ign.com

$

★★★★★

👥 14-18

News, codes, reviews, previews, features, releases, hardware, contests, a game store, affiliates, links to magazine subscriptions, and more. This site is geared for serious gamers and contains some material that is not suitable for younger children.

Internet Chess Club

http://www.chessclub.com

★★★★

👥 All

Register to play chess against other players at this site, where you can also search for game strategies and learn from grandmasters and international masters. Parents may want to supervise the registration for younger players.

Kids Domain Online Games
http://www.kidsdomain.com/games/

★★★★

👥 0-8

Wide selection of games designed for fun and for educational purposes. Most games are for elementary-school kids. Plenty of trivia games that not only ask questions but present interesting facts in an engaging format. Excellent site for parents to introduce to their children.

Manic Maze
http://www.worldvillage.com/maze.htm

★★★

👥 All

Interactive online maze featuring prizes and other fun stuff. Check out some other fantastic links while you're at it. Many games will appeal to kids of all ages, but most are directed at the younger crowd.

Monopoly
http://www.monopoly.com

★★★★

👥 All

Pick up tips on winning at Monopoly, find out about upcoming Monopoly tournaments, learn about game news—such as a new token—and see the latest Monopoly merchandise at this site devoted to the famed board game.

MSN Game Zone
http://zone.msn.com/

★★★★★

👥 All

Microsoft's gift to the gaming community, this high-tech site serves up a huge collection of free games broken down into categories, including Puzzle Games, Word & Trivia, Card & Board, Zone Casino, Racing & Sports, and Kids' Zone. Free downloads and chat area populated by a very active community of gamers make this one of the best sites to play games on the Web.

Multi-Player Online Games Directory
http://www.mpogd.com/

★★★★

👥 14-18

A guide to the best multiplayer games. Game titles are broken down into categories ranging from action to sports. Game of the month poll helps you quickly identify the most popular games, and news headlines keep you abreast of the latest information in the online gaming world. Game reviews and other resources are also available.

Netbaby
http://www.netbabyworld.com

★★★★

👥 0-8

Online gaming community where little kids can hang out and play interactive video games against other players from all over the world. All games are free and clean—no sexuality or violence.

NovaLogic
http://www.novalogic.com

💲

★★★★

👥 14-18

Download war game demos such as Delta Force, Comanche, and Tachyon; and purchase the ones you like. You'll also find gaming news and announcements to keep you up-to-speed on up-and-coming games.

Official Worldwide Scrabble Home Page
http://www.mattelscrabble.com/

★★★★

👥 All

Get help forming words with the anagram builder and double-check words in the online Scrabble dictionary. The site also offers tips for improving your score and for playing with kids. In need of your own Scrabble game? Check out all your Scrabble options and find your nearest retailer.

A B C D E F **G** H I J K L M N O P Q R S T U V W X Y Z

PlaySite Games

http://www.playsite.com/index.gsp

★★★

👥 14-18

Board games, card games, and word games. This site is for you if you are looking to play backgammon, chess, checkers, hex, mancala, reversi, renju, hearts, spades, euchre, cribbage, bridge, or tanglewood. Step-by-step instructions are available for each game; you'll also find a FAQ section, tournaments, rankings, and more. Can't find someone up for a game? Choose an opponent among the unmatched players. You might end up playing against someone on the other side of the world. Some pop-up ads may not be suitable for young children.

Pogo.com

http://www.pogo.com/

★★★★

👥 14-18

This site features a wide range of online games you can play against the computer or against other players. Play card and board games, sports games, word and trivia games, casino games, and more. Most games are suitable for all ages, but some games do encourage gambling.

PopCap Games

http://www.popcap.com

★★★★

👥 All

Online game room where you can play a collection of simple, yet deeply layered games that will challenge your coordination and your intellect. All games are Java-based, so you need not download any additional software to play them; they play right inside your Web browser. Also features downloadable games for Palm computers.

Puzz.com

http://www.puzz.com/

★★★

👥 14-18

Your resource for puzzles, IQ tests, and trivia. Like thinking under pressure? Give the trivia games a whirl. Think you have a really high IQ? Try the intelligence test. If strategy's your thing, check out the games. Not a very polished site, but it's packed with links to some great online games.

Puzzability

http://www.puzzability.com

★★★

👥 All

Try solving a variety of puzzles at this site, which is actually a marketing tool for this puzzle-building company.

Puzzle Buffs

http://www.puzzlebuffs.com

💲

★★★

👥 All

Scrambl-Gram's website, where you can check out a wide selection of crossword books and other types of puzzle books, solve some sample puzzles, enter the weekly online crossword puzzle contest for fun and prizes, and even visit the Puzzle Museum.

SegaNet

http://www.sega.com/

💲

★★★★

👥 All

Sega's game site features articles about a variety of its games, plus some free mini-games you can play online, downloadable wallpaper and movie clips, and a discussion forum where you can trade secrets with other gamers and share your enthusiasm for playing.

Shockwave Games

http://www.shockwave.com/sw/games/

★★★★★

 All

Shockwave is famous for animating Web pages, so it should be no surprise that game developers are drawn to it. Here, you can play a wide selection of Shockwave games, everything from puzzles and parlor games to arcade games and interactive shoot-'em-ups. Some games may be too violent for younger children, but many are directed specifically at the younger crowd.

Samorost

http://analogik.org/samorost.asp

★★★★★

Give your brain a workout at this site, where you need to figure out just where to click to progress through seven levels and eventually complete your mission. Very cool 3D graphics and animation.

Star Wars Galaxies

http://starwarsgalaxies.station.sony.com/

★★★★★

This site features Sony's *Star Wars Galaxies* multiplayer online role-playing game based on the *Star Wars* classics. At this site, you can find support and updates, connect with other players and fans, check for new releases, and much more.

There

http://www.there.com/

★★★★★

There is an online chat area and game room, where you can hook up with other players from around the world, chat, and play games all at the same time. You start by creating your own avatar to represent you online. You get to choose the avatar's facial features, body shape, clothing, hairstyle, and other features and accessories, and then explore the 3D world of There, where you are guaranteed to meet someone new every time you sign on.

Thinks.com

http://www.thinks.com

★★★★

👥 14-18

This U.K.-based site calls itself "The Fun and Games for Playful Brains" site, offering visitors daily crosswords of all kinds, word contests, and plenty of other puzzles and games to make you think. Links to some cash games where gambling is promoted.

Trivia Company's Trivia Wars

http://www.triviawars.com/

★★★★

👥 14-18

Sharpen your wits, trivia junkies, for here is your site. Cruise through this site if you know everything about nothing important. Some questions here will stump all challengers.

The Ultimate Oracle: Pray Before the Head of Bob

http://www.resort.com/~banshee/Misc/8ball/

★★★

The online version of the legendary Magic Eight Ball. Ask Bob any question, and you are sure to get a response. You can even ask in several different languages.

Velvet-Strike

http://www.opensorcery.net/velvet-strike/

★★★★★

Velvet-Strike features a collection of virtual spray paints that you can use in the video game *Counter-Strike* to paint anti-war slogans and graffiti on the backgrounds. Here you can download spray paints, submit your own spray paints, and check out videos and screenshots of the spray paints in action.

A
B
C
D
E
F
G
H
I
J
K
L
M
N
O
P
Q
R
S
T
U
V
W
X
Y
Z

A
B
C
D
E
F
G
H
I
J
K
L
M
N
O
P
Q
R
S
T
U
V
W
X
Y
Z

VOG: Video Online Gamers

http://www.vogclub.com/

★★★

👥 All

Multiplayer game site where you can pull up a chair and play chess, checkers, backgammon, hearts, and more games against other visitors. Tournaments available, too. Though VOG provides an excellent selection of online games, you won't find as many players as you would on a more popular site, such as Yahoo! Games.

WebBattleship

http://www.head-crash.com/battle/

★★★★

👥 All

The online version of the classic game, except you cannot choose where you want to place your battleships. Always entertaining, and the computer is pretty formidable.

Who Wants to Be a Millionaire?

http://abc.abcnews.go.com/primetime/millionaire/millionaire_home.html

★★★★★

👥 All

Play the online version of this popular TV game show and find out how to earn a spot as a contestant.

Wizards of the Coast, Inc.

http://www.wizards.com/

$

★★★★

👥 All

Provides information for Wizards of the Coast, producers of the popular card game *Magic: The Gathering* and a series of *Harry Potter* games. This site includes information about Magic and other games produced by the Wizards, as well as company background and news.

World Village Games

http://www.worldvillage.com/wvgames/index.html

★★★★

👥 9-13

A handful of online games designed to keep you entertained for hours. Great selection for young players.

WWW Interactive Online Crossword

http://www.philly.com/mld/philly/entertainment/comics/

★★★

👥 All

An online crossword puzzle brought to you by the Philadelphia newspapers. Choose from a slew of previous newspaper puzzles put online to play. You can even choose an "easy" mode. Other games are available here, as well.

Yahoo! Games

http://games.yahoo.com

★★★★★

👥 All

Excellent collection of multiplayer games. A very populous and active group of online gamers make this one of the best places to hang out and play checkers, chess, blackjack, poker, fantasy sports, and dozens of other games.

Yohoho! Puzzle Pirates

http://www.puzzlepirates.com/

$

★★★★★

Join an online community of Buccaneers to solve several puzzles in your quest for treasure. As you set sail and cruise the high seas, this site launches appropriate puzzle games to challenge you and the rest of the crew. Solve the puzzle, and the site bestows great riches upon you and your mates.

CHEAT CODES

1UP.com

http://www.1up.com/

★★★★★

1UP.com is a Ziff-Davis site that features video game cheats along with game news, previews, reviews, techniques, and tips from some of the top gaming magazines, including *Computer Gaming World*, *Electronic Gaming Monthly*, *GMR*, *Official U.S. PlayStation Magazine*, and *Xbox Nation*.

Cheat Code Central

http://www.cheatcc.com

★★★

 14-18

Claiming to be the largest computer game help site in the world for Sony PlayStation, PlayStation 2, Nintendo 64, Sega Dreamcast, Game Boy, GameCube, Xbox, and PC, Cheat Code Central provides gamers with cheat codes, Game Shark codes, strategy guides, and saved game files for thousands of video games. Lots of pop-up ads.

Cheaters Krypt

http://www.cheaterskrypt.com/

★★★

 14-18

You'll find cheat codes, tips, and hints for winning at more than 1,400 Xbox and PC games here.

Freaky Cheats

http://www.freakycheats.com/index2.asp

★★★★

 14-18

Hundreds of cheats for PC, Xbox, Sega Dreamcast, GameCube, N64, and Playstation systems.

GameCheats.net

http://gamecheats.net/

★★★

 14-18

Comprehensive directory of Xbox cheat sites on the Web. Links to Ace Cheats, AreaGaming, Cheaters Planet, and more.

GameCube Code Center

http://www.gamecubecc.com/

★★★★

Cheats, codes, and FAQs for Nintendo's GameCube system. Online store links to Amazon.com for purchasing games.

Related Sites

http://hardman_5.tripod.com/cubecentral2/index.html

http://cubed.nu/

Gamesearcher.com

http://cheats.gamez.com/

★★★

Be sure you have the latest cheat codes for PlayStation, Dreamcast, Nintendo 64, and PC games, which are listed here. You can search by game or type to find tips, tricks, patches, and training.

GameWinners.com

http://www.gamewinners.com/

★★★★★

 14-18

One of the most informative video game help sites on the Web, tips for more than 18,500 games played on nearly 50 different game systems. Features cheats, hints, FAQs, strategy guides, and gameshark codes. Links to game books and game stores for online shopping.

N64 Code Center

http://www.thegamingonline.com/N64/Codes/home.htm

★★★

If you're looking for a Nintendo 64 cheat code, this site probably has it. You'll also find game reviews. Very well-stocked collection of game cheats.

A
B
C
D
E
F
G
H
I
J
K
L
M
N
O
P
Q
R
S
T
U
V
W
X
Y
Z

GARDENING AND LANDSCAPING

3D Garden Composer

http://www.gardencomposer.com/

★★★

Home page of one of the best gardening and land-scaping programs on the market. 3D Garden Composer helps you design your garden on your computer and provides an encyclopedia covering more than 9,000 plants. At this site, you can view demos of the program, check out a photo gallery, and even order the program online.

A.M. Leonard

http://www.Amleonard.com

★★★

A.M. Leonard offers a huge selection of gardening-related equipment and paraphernalia, from irrigation to cleaning supplies, fertilizers, knives, and much more. A comprehensive selection of gardening prod-ucts!

American Association of Botanical Gardens and Arboreta (AABGA)

http://www.aabga.org

★★★

The American Association of Botanical Gardens and Arboreta (AABGA) is the professional association for public gardens in North America. Currently, the AABGA has more than 400 institutional members and almost 3,000 individual members. The AABGA publishes a monthly newsletter and the quarterly journal, *Public Garden*, along with a variety of other publications, and sponsors eight regional and one national conference each year.

American Horticultural Society

http://www.ahs.org/

★★★★

This site, for the horticulture connoisseur, provides links to several articles from *The American Gardener*. Membership in the AHL and a subscription to *The American Gardener* permit you to order several vari-eties of seeds free in the month of January. Members are graced with many other privileges as well.

American Rose Society

http://www.ars.org

★★★★

If you're a rose lover, you'll want to consider joining this nonprofit organization, which is dedicated to the enjoyment, enhancement, and promotion of this flower. In addition to providing plenty of informa-tion about the thousands of varieties of roses, the site also offers answers to your rose-related questions, information on upcoming floral competitions, and membership FAQs.

Better Homes and Gardens Online Garden Page

http://www.bhg.com/bhg/gardening/

★★★★

This site offers a garden forum with questions and answers, some great long articles, shorter handy tips, and even how-to videos. Plant Hardiness and First Frost maps allow you to click on your state and can be magnified right down to your county.

Botanique

http://www.botanique.com

★★★

Offers a list of gardens you can visit throughout the United States and Canada. You can also follow the calendar of North American garden events. Guaranteed to make your next trip a flower-friendly road trip.

Botany.com

http://www.botany.com/

★★★★

An encyclopedia of plants. Each entry provides a description of the plant, instructions on how to grow the plant, and information on how to propagate the plant.

 Best **Burpee Seeds Home Page**

http://www.garden.com/

★★★★★

More than 12,000 products—plants, flowers, gardening supplies, accessories, and gifts. Gardening tips, an online magazine, and a 24-hour chat are also available. Membership and monthly newsletter are free. Whether you're a novice or expert gardener, you will find plenty to satisfy you at this Best of the Best site.

Butterfly Gardening

http://www.butterflyworld.com/

★★★★

Home of Butterfly World, the first and largest butterfly house in the United States. Take a virtual walk through the gardens, shop the online store, or learn how to help the campaign by creating butterfly-friendly environments.

Container Garden Guide

http://www.gardenguides.com/TipsandTechniques/container.htm

★★★★

Succinct guide to growing a garden on your porch or patio.

Cortesia Sanctuary and Center

http://www.cortesia.org/

★★★★

This site is divided into five sections: The Cortesia Sanctuary Project (everything you need to know about creating a sanctuary), The Sanctuary Garden (gardening, garden products/books, garden inspiration, flower essences, composting, and so on), Music, Inspiration, and Publications & Products.

The Creative Gardener

http://www.creativegardener.com/

★★★

This is Lynn Purse's site. She is well known among daylily lovers for her expertise at creating landscapes incorporating this beloved plant. A plant gallery, foliage gallery, and many worthwhile and informative articles are included.

Developing the Landscape Plan

http://muextension.missouri.edu/xplor/agguides/hort/g06901.htm

★★★

Pointers to keep in mind while drawing up your own plan for your yard.

Earthly Goods Online

http://www.earthlygoods.com/

★★★★★

Earthly Goods is a supplier of wildflower seeds, wildflower seed mixtures, and grass seeds. Advice on growing from seeds, garden planning, and online ordering are a few of its features. Earthly Goods offers custom seed packets for advertising, fundraising, and special promotions.

A B C D E F **G** H I J K L M N O P Q R S T U V W X Y Z

A
B
C
D
E
F
G
H
I
J
K
L
M
N
O
P
Q
R
S
T
U
V
W
X
Y
Z

EPA Green Landscaping with Native Plants

http://www.epa.gov/greenacres/

★★★

This site encourages everyone—from home gardeners to facilities managers at corporations—to consider adding native plants and wildflowers to a garden to beautify the environment and to attract butterflies and other animals and insects. To accomplish this, the site has helpful how-to information, an ask-the-expert area, and basic information on why native plants are so great.

Fine Gardening Online

http://www.taunton.com/finegardening/index.asp

★★★

Excellent gardening site that features articles on all aspects of gardening, including design, annuals, perennials, trees and shrubs, vegetables, container gardening, skills and techniques, and more. You can read articles online, order back issues of the magazine, and even view a few video tips.

The Garden Gate

http://garden-gate.prairienet.org/

★★★

Online books, magazines, catalogs, and catalog information, as well as online sources for gardening books. Enough glossaries, FAQs, special topic WWW pages, collections, and plant lists to keep info-junkies busy. Shop 'til your mouse goes belly-up. Find out how to stop killing houseplants, indoor plants, tropicals, and greenhouse plants. Go around the world for a virtual garden tour of botanical gardens, greenhouses, and private gardens. Also Usenet newsgroups, a "holding bed" for new links, and resources for gardeners in East Central Illinois.

Gardener's Supply Company

http://www.gardeners.com/

★★★★★

Huge mail-order gardening store now has a website where you can place your order online. Carries a wide variety of gardening tools and accessories designed to simplify your gardening experience, make it more enjoyable, and beautify your garden.

GardenGuides

http://www.gardenguides.com/

★★★★

Guides to herbs, bulbs, perennials, and annuals cover both basic information and interesting tidbits to help you appreciate what you plant. An easy-to-use site that new gardeners especially will find invaluable.

GardenNet

http://www.gardennet.com/

★★★★

Comprehensive directory of websites that feature gardening information and products. Links are grouped by individual plant names, plant groups, equipment and products, gardening types (for example, Bonsai or Urban), general information, events, and services. Excellent place to start your search.

Gardenscape

http://www.gardenscape.on.ca/

★★★★★

At this site you can find an excellent collection of innovative garden products and accessories, including tools from companies such as Felco, Fiskars, Haws, and Dramm, and a unique line of gifts for gardeners.

GardenWeb

http://www.gardenweb.com/

★★★

GardenWeb is the largest gardening site on the Web, including forums, events, directories, contests, and catalogs.

Jeff Chorba Landscape Design

http://home.ptd.net/~jchorba/

★★★

Provides design and horticultural documents, links to related landscaping sites, a future site for a BBS connection, and a photo gallery of various landscape designs.

Kidsgardening.com
http://www.kidsgardening.com/

★★★★★

 All

Created and maintained by the National Gardening Association, this site is dedicated to getting children involved in the wonderful world of gardening. Includes a Kidsgarden store, lesson plans for teachers, ideas for gardening activities, and a list of frequently asked questions (along with their answers).

Kids Valley Garden
http://www.raw-connections.com/garden/

★★★

 All

Website designed to encourage kids to get outside and plant their own vegetable and flower gardens. Includes information on planning and planting a garden, keeping plants healthy, and showing your plants.

Landscaping for Energy Efficiency
http://www.eren.doe.gov/erec/factsheets/landscape.html

★★★

Are you looking for cost-effective yet eye-pleasing ways to lower your energy bills? This site gives advice on how to plant trees, shrubs, vines, grasses, and hedges for reducing heating and cooling costs, while also bringing other improvements to your community.

Landscaping to Attract Birds
http://www.bcpl.net/~tross/by/attract.html

★★★

Tells visitors how to plant birdbaths and feeders and situate trees and flowers to attract the denizens of the air. Also contains descriptions of the benefits of landscaping for birds, plants for wild birds, and information for getting started, as well as a reading list.

Missouri Botanical Garden
http://www.mobot.org/

★★★★

 All

The MBG's website contains beautiful photographs of some of the many rare plants grown at its greenhouse. Information is also available from the research division in the field of biodiversity. A collection of online books is also accessible.

Museum of Garden History
http://www.cix.co.uk/~museumgh/

★★★

Take a virtual tour through garden history. Enjoy the profile of Gertrude Jekyll, garden designer extraordinaire.

National Gardening Association
http://www.garden.org

★★★★★

Gardeners will find the FAQs, tips, and reminders a great help, although the NGA was originally established to help foster gardening as a pastime. At the site, you'll find information on gardening programs in schools, available gardening grants, and other ways that the organization can help.

New Jersey Weed Gallery
http://www.rce.rutgers.edu/weeds/

★★★★★

From Barnyardgrass to Yellow Rocket, an award-winning weed identification site from Rutgers University.

New Plant Page
http://members.tripod.com/~Hatch_L/genera.html

★★★

Want the very latest plants? Here is a complete listing of all the newest ornamentals—with sources and a garden dictionary. The cultivar name thesaurus enables you to look up a plant by its official name and find a grower. In some cases, a request for a grower appears instead. Definitely worth a visit.

A B C D E F G H I J K L M N O P Q R S T U V W X Y Z

A
B
C
D
E
F
G
H
I
J
K
L
M
N
O
P
Q
R
S
T
U
V
W
X
Y
Z

Organic Gardening

http://www.organicgardening.com

★★★

Get a free copy of the *Organic Gardening Almanac* by subscribing to the free almanac newsletter at this site, where you'll also learn the basics of organic gardening and ways to get started, as well as hints for solving common organic gardening problems.

Perennials

http://www76.pair.com/mikron/garden/perenn.htm

★★★

A practical definition of perennials and the reasons you should work them into your design. There's a sample plan, too.

The Potting Shed

http://www.etera.com/

★★★★★

A free online gardening magazine containing information for the novice and the advanced gardener alike, including tips and how-to illustrations. You can buy everything from herbs to perennials here. This site is owned and operated by plant retailer, Etera.

Residential Landscaping

http://ipm.ncsu.edu/urban/horticulture/res_landscaping.html

★★★

Develop a plot plan, conduct a site analysis, and learn basic landscape design concepts.

Rhododendron and Azalea Page

http://www.users.fast.net/~shenning/rhody.html

★★★★

Ever wanted to know more about the pretty Rhododendron or the gorgeous Azalea? Then this site is just for you. Learn more about these particular flowers, the many varieties, ways to care for them; and check out the links to other gardening sites.

Selecting the Correct Garden Tool

http://www.ipm.iastate.edu/ipm/hortnews/1992/3-18-1992/tools.html

★★★

An Iowa State University article on choosing and using the proper tools.

Smith & Hawken

http://www.smithandhawken.com/

★★★★

Smith & Hawken sells well-built gardening tools and products so as to encourage gardening and preserve natural resources. The products are beautiful, as is the site. A good place to start if you're looking for a new garden trowel or teak bench.

Strawberry Web Ring

http://f.webring.com/hub?ring=strawberry

★★★

Dedicated to bringing together all websites with a recognizable connection to this most wonderful berry. Find sites that contain strawberry recipes, strawberry gardening information, and any other strawberry trivia or facts. Companies and individuals that use the strawberry as a symbol or name are also included.

Tom Clothier's Garden Walk and Talk

http://tomclothier.hort.net/

★★★

This is a green-thumb site for beginning gardeners. Tom Clothier believes in growing everything from seed. His site includes great tips on planting and propagating, and many worthwhile articles on pest control, soil manufacturing, and other important topics. Take a tour of Tom's garden through the years to see the results of his practical advice.

University of Delaware Botanic Gardens

http://ag.udel.edu/udbg/

★★★

Tour the gardens of the University of Delaware. The tour includes eight different gardens. Descriptions of plants that are contained in the gardens are available.

Weekend Gardener

http://www.chestnut-sw.com/weekend.htm

★★★★★

This site bills itself as the "Practical Horticulture for Busy People" site and contains everything from weather links to garden calendars and seed starting. The Weekend Gardener area has sections on starting your vegetable, flower, and herb seeds, plus a valuable calendar for when to do what. Participate in some interesting gardening forums on a wide variety of topics. Designed for the busy gardener.

Wildflower and Prairie Grass Seed

http://www.prairiefrontier.com/

★★★★

Purchase seeds and plants for the prairies here, and you'll also get all the information you need to help you to create your own. Helpful information from basic definitions to how-to articles, and a question-and-answer area. If you're interested in prairie plants or plantings, this is a great first stop.

LAWN CARE

CyberLawn

http://opei.mow.org/

★★★★

A mega-database of outdoor equipment, including reviews and guides on the use and maintenance of lawn mowers and other outdoor power equipment. Excellent list of earth-friendly yard-care tips, plus information on mower safety and links to related websites.

Organic Lawn Care

http://www.richsoil.com/lawn/

★★★

Learn how to reduce or eliminate your lawn's addiction to expensive and environmentally harmful chemicals.

Scotts Lawncare Page

http://www.scotts.com/

★★★

The home of Scotts fertilizers, this site shows you how to maintain your lawn's health through the proper use of chemical fertilizers. Some excellent information on the basics of seeding, mowing, and watering. Provides a maintenance schedule showing when you should fertilize.

Yardcare.com

http://www.yardcare.com/

★★★★

All your lawn care questions are answered at this site created and maintained by Toro. Learn everything from selecting grass seed to setting your mower to the proper height. Tips for controlling weeds, revitalizing a dying lawn, dealing with grubs and other pests, and reducing lawn maintenance.

ORCHIDS

1-888-Orchids.com

http://www.1888orchids.com/

★★★★★

Buy orchids, orchid books, orchid supplies, orchid pots, orchid baskets, and anything else related to orchids at this site.

All About Orchids

http://www.orchid.org.uk/contents.htm

★★★

Everything you need. to know about orchids and how to grow them is right here. Includes information about culturing orchids, tips on avoiding and solving problems, the story of how orchids evolved, and pictures of orchids. Also provides links to nurseries, societies, and shows.

A B C D E F G H I J K L M N O P Q R S T U V W X Y Z

A
B
C
D
E
F
G
H
I
J
K
L
M
N
O
P
Q
R
S
T
U
V
W
X
Y
Z

The American Orchid Society

http://www.orchidweb.org

★★★★

Anyone interested in trying to grow orchids will want to visit this site for guidance in creating conditions suitable for orchid growing. You'll also find information on upcoming orchid events, publications, research, and a discussion forum.

Orchid Mania

http://www.orchids.org

★★★

This site is dedicated to support of AIDS work through the sale and growing of orchids. You'll find information on the plant and upcoming events where they will be sold.

TREES

American Forests

http://www.americanforests.org

★★★

This nonprofit organization is dedicated to reforestation, as well as the preservation of the nation's forests. Learn how to become part of the group's efforts to plant 20 million trees and why this effort is so important. You'll also find interesting information on historical trees.

Bonsai: The Art of Growing Trees in Miniature

http://home.hiwaay.net/~fjw/bonsai1.htm

★★★

Instructions and tips on the art of growing and sculpturing Bonsai trees.

Champion Tree Project

http://www.championtrees.org

★★★

Learn what makes a tree a champion, where such trees are located, and what we can do to foster the growth of more champions.

TreeHelp.com

http://www.treehelp.com/

★★★★

Everything you need to know about caring for mature trees, including how to prune trees, identify and treat diseases, prevent insect infestations, and much more. This site also offers a selection of tree care products.

GAY/LESBIAN/BISEXUAL/TRANS

AltSex

http://www.altsex.org/

★★★

 Not for kids

A wealth of information about sexual and gender issues, such as homosexuality and heterosexuality, transgender, and transsexuality. Many articles and resource pages and links.

BiCafe

http://www.bicafe.com/

★★★★

 Not for kids

Social site for the bisexual community.

Gay.com

http://www.gay.com/

★★★★

 Not for kids

A news, information, and chat site for gay, lesbian, and transgender individuals. Links to stores where you can shop online.

GayWired.com

http://www.gaywired.com/

★★★★★

 Not for kids

One of the best sites focusing on the gay lifestyle, this site is packed with news, articles, profiles, travel information, business and financial information, and more. Read the latest on fitting into the gay culture or shop online.

PlanetOut

http://www.planetout.com/

★★★★★

 Not for kids

Premier gay and lesbian website, features articles, photos, video clips, and products for the gay and lesbian community. By joining PlanetOut, you can post messages in numerous forums, chat online, create a member profile (with or without a photo of yourself), and subscribe to free newsletters.

COLLEGES AND UNIVERSITIES

Harvard Gay & Lesbian Caucus

http://www.hglc.org/hglc/

★★★★

 Not for kids

Harvard Gay & Lesbian Caucus members include more than 2,200 gay, lesbian, and bisexual Harvard and Radcliffe alums, faculty, and staff. This site, run primarily for caucus members, details the organization's goals and activities.

Related Sites
http://www.columbia.edu/cu/gables/
http://www.gwu.edu/~lgba/
http://www.lgbtcampus.org/
http://www.northwestern.edu/gluu/

A B C D E F G H I J K L M N O P Q R S T U V W X Y Z

A
B
C
D
E
F
G
H
I
J
K
L
M
N
O
P
Q
R
S
T
U
V
W
X
Y
Z

!OutProud! College Resources

http://www.outproud.org/

★★★

⚌ Not for kids

Intended to provide a range of tools for college and university students, educators, and administrators to assist in making them a nurturing environment for lesbigay youth and a safe place for staff to work.

Pride Alliance of Princeton University

http://www.princeton.edu/~pride/home.html

★★★

⚌ Not for kids

A colorful and attractive site with information for gay/lesbian students and alumni, an online edition of a gay newspaper, a list of campus meetings, and a lot more.

Purdue's LesBiGay Network

http://expert.cc.purdue.edu/~triangle/

★★★

⚌ Not for kids

Meeting schedules and upcoming campus events for Purdue University's gay, lesbian, and bisexual support organizations.

Related Links
http://expert.cc.purdue.edu/%7Epea/
http://expert.cc.purdue.edu/%7Edlp/

CRISIS INTERVENTION AND COUNSELING

AVP: New York City Gay and Lesbian Anti-Violence Project

http://www.avp.org/

★★★★

⚌ Not for kids

New York City–based organization that combats violence against gays and lesbians, provides support for victims, and does what it can to catch criminals. This organization has a 24-hour hotline for victims to call to report crimes.

Community United Against Violence

http://www.cuav.org/

★★★

⚌ Not for kids

Community United Against Violence (CUAV) is a nonprofit agency that addresses and prevents hate violence directed at lesbians, gay men, bisexuals, and transgender persons. CUAV also provides services to gay men who are battered by their partners. CUAV offers crisis intervention, short-term counseling, advocacy with the criminal justice system, support groups, and a 24-hour CrisisLine.

The Gay and Lesbian National Hotline

http://www.glnh.org/

★★★★★

⚌ Not for kids

A nonprofit organization dedicated to meeting the needs of the gay and lesbian community by offering free and totally anonymous information, referrals, and peer counseling. Offers a toll-free phone number that anyone can call for gay/lesbian support and information. You can also submit email from this website and get a confidential reply.

Youth Assistance Organization (a.k.a. Youth Action Online)

http://www.youth.org/

★★★★

⚌ Not for kids

Youth Assistance Organization is a service run by volunteers, created to help self-identifying gay, lesbian, bisexual, and questioning youth. YAO exists to provide young people with a safe space online to be themselves. This pages contain links to useful sites and a FAQ devoted to questions such as "I think I might be gay; what do I do?"

Related Site
http://www.montrosecounselingcenter.org/

GAYS AND LESBIANS OF COLOR

The Blacklist

http://www.blackstripe.com/blacklist/

★★★★

Not for kids

A resource site for the writings of gay, lesbian, bisexual, and transgendered people of African descent. It contains an excellent bibliography of writings, in many cases with Web links. Shop for books and purchase them at Amazon.com.

People of Color

http://www.glbt.com/pages/org/poc.html

★★★

Not for kids

This site focuses specifically on addressing the needs of "people of color" who are part of the gay, lesbian, bisexual, transgendered community of Minneapolis and St. Paul, Minnesota.

GENERAL INFORMATION AND LINKS

Answers to Your Questions About Sexual Orientation and Homosexuality

http://www.apa.org/pubinfo/answers.html

★★★

Not for kids

This site for the American Psychological Association provides just plain answers to the most common questions about sexual orientation. Text format, very readable, fact-based, and backed up with hard clinical research—but not overly medical in tone.

The Bisexual Resource Center

http://www.biresource.org

★★★

Not for kids

A great list of links to other sites of interest to bisexuals.

Gay Men's Health Crisis

http://www.gmhc.org/

★★★★★

Not for kids

Find out more about the nation's oldest and largest not-for-profit AIDS organization: Gay Men's Health Crisis (GMHC), founded in 1981. Learn how you can get involved, get resources for support, access its AIDS Library, read about GMHC's latest efforts, and more.

GayScape

http://www.gayscape.com/

★★★★★

Not for kids

Specialized search tool for gay, lesbian, bisexual, and transgender sites on the Web. This search index lists more than 68,000 sites.

The Lesbian History Project

http://www-lib.usc.edu/~retter/main.html

★★★

Not for kids

Site dedicated to recording, archiving, and publicizing work on lesbian history in any geographic area or time period, with an emphasis on lesbians of color in general and Southern California in particular.

PrideLinks.com

http://www.pridelinks.com/

★★★★

Not for kids

Bills itself as "The Internet's premiere gay, lesbian, bi, and trans search engine." And with more than 8,000 links, this site lives up to its reputation. If you are looking for links, resources, information, support, or just fun, start here.

Queer Resources Directory (QRD)

http://www.qrd.org/qrd/

★★★★★

Not for kids

Widely thought to be the biggest and best gay and lesbian information source on the Internet, the Queer Resources Directory breaks down all kinds of resource information into easy-to-understand categories. You can surf the categories or jump directly to the Resource Tree (http://www.qrd.org/qrd/www/tree.html).

A
B
C
D
E
F
G
H
I
J
K
L
M
N
O
P
Q
R
S
T
U
V
W
X
Y
Z

A
B
C
D
E
F
G
H
I
J
K
L
M
N
O
P
Q
R
S
T
U
V
W
X
Y
Z

QWorld

http://www.qworld.org/

★★★

Not for kids

All the standard fare you would expect from a site (news, politics, opinions, and so on) plus a few interesting extras, such as downloadable queer-themed sound files and icons, and live chat rooms.

Related Sites

http://members.aol.com/detroit209/

http://www.outaustin.org/

http://www.oglpc.org/

http://valogcabin.org/

HOME AND FAMILY

Custom Jewelry Design: Commitment Rings

http://www.sumiche.com/

★★★

Not for kids

Handcrafted jewelry online (gallery/catalog).

Family Diversity Projects Inc.

http://www.familydiv.org/

★★★★

Not for kids

Family Diversity Projects is a nonprofit organization founded in 1996 by photographer Gigi Kaeser and writer Peggy Gillespie. Since that time, they've toured with their four traveling photo-text exhibits around the country to great acclaim. In addition, the book *Of Many Colors: Portraits of Multiracial Families*, (UMass Press, 1997) has been published; along with *Love Makes a Family: Portraits of Lesbian, Gay, Bisexual, and Transgender Parents and Their Families*, (UMass Press, 1999). Family Diversity Projects also provides speakers and workshop leaders for conferences and exhibit venues.

Family Pride Coalition

http://www.familypride.org/

★★★★

Not for kids

Dedicated to advancing "the well-being of lesbian, gay, bisexual and transgendered parents and their families through mutual support, community collaboration, and public understanding." Here, you can find links to events, programs, libraries, and other sources for helping families succeed.

Freedom To Marry

http://www.freedomtomarry.org/

★★★

Not for kids

A broadly based national group committed to organizing, educating, and advocating the freedom to marry for same-gender couples.

Lesbian Mothers Support Society

http://www.lesbian.org/lesbian-moms/

★★★

Not for kids

Lesbian Mothers Support Society (LMSS) is a Canadian nonprofit group that provides peer support for lesbian parents (biological and nonbiological) and their children, as well as those lesbians considering parenthood. Great links to reference articles of interest to lesbian parents.

[Best] Parents, Families, and Friends of Lesbians and Gays (PFLAG)

http://www.pflag.org/

★★★★★

Not for kids

PFLAG promotes the health and well-being of gay, lesbian, and bisexual persons, as well as their families and friends, through support, education, and advocacy. This organization provides counseling to help straight family and friends accept and support their gay and lesbian loved ones, and organizes grassroots efforts to end discriminatory practices toward gays and lesbians. This site's excellent design and content combine to make it an easy Best of the Best pick.

Partners Task Force for Gay and Lesbian Couples

http://www.buddybuddy.com/

★★★★

 Not for kids

Information and resources for gay and lesbian couples seeking ways to ensure their rights as a family. Includes discussion of marriage laws, surveys, legal information, and political news.

MEDIA AND CULTURE

Dyke TV

http://www.dyketv.org/

★★★

 Not for kids

A weekly show produced by lesbians for lesbians, the show mixes news, commentary, and the arts. Lesbian filmmakers all around the country are encouraged to help create the public access show's segments. You can order tapes of past shows as well as Dyke TV hats and T-shirts.

GALA: The Gay and Lesbian Association of Choruses

http://www.galachoruses.org/

★★★

 Not for kids

This umbrella organization unites and supports gay and lesbian choral groups all over the United States. It holds a yearly choral festival, which you can read about (as well as other activities) on this page.

Gay/Lesbian/Bisexual Television Characters

http://home.cc.umanitoba.ca/%7Ewyatt/
tv-char2000s.html

★★★

 Not for kids

This amazingly comprehensive list catalogs gay, lesbian, and bisexual television characters on 23 networks worldwide, from 1961 to the present.

Hothead Paisan

http://www.marystreet.com/HH

★★★

 Not for kids

The home page for an outrageous lesbian cartoon strip that plays out the notion, "What if a radical lesbian feminist suddenly went crazy and said and did everything she wanted to?" A must-read for any lesbian fed up with the patriarchy.

In The Life TV.org

http://www.inthelifetv.org/

★★★★

 Not for kids

A national television series in a news magazine format that reports on gay and lesbian issues and culture. Broadcasts on more than 130 public television stations nationwide, including all the top 20 viewer markets, reaching more than 1,000,000 viewers per episode.

International Association of Gay Square Dance Clubs

http://www.iagsdc.org/

★★★★

 Not for kids

The IAGSDC is the International Association of Gay Square Dance Clubs, a lesbian and gay organization that is the umbrella organization for gay square dance clubs in the United States, Canada, and Australia, formed by and for lesbians and gay men in their community and for their friends.

International Gay Rodeo Association

http://www.igra.com/

★★★★

 Not for kids

The gay rodeo association holds its own rodeos all over the country, including not only gay meccas such as Los Angeles and Washington, D.C., but smaller cities such as Billings, Montana, and Omaha, Nebraska. Get the full touring schedule here and find out how to become a member.

A
B
C
D
E
F
G
H
I
J
K
L
M
N
O
P
Q
R
S
T
U
V
W
X
Y
Z

A
B
C
D
E
F
G
H
I
J
K
L
M
N
O
P
Q
R
S
T
U
V
W
X
Y
Z

The Isle of Lesbos

http://www.sappho.com/

★★★★

🚸 Not for kids

Well-designed pages of poetry, art, and links to other lesbian-related sites. Coverage of Sapphic poetry is extensive.

Lesbian and Gay Bands of America

http://www.gaybands.org/

★★★★

🚸 Not for kids

Lesbian and Gay Bands of America (LGBA) is the national musical organization composed of concert and marching bands from cities across America. Find out here about the 22 member bands and their parade and concert appearances.

Women in the Arts

http://wiaonline.org/

💲

★★★★★

🚸 Not for kids

WIA is the organization that produces the National Women's Music Festival, the oldest and largest all-indoor festival of women's music and culture (primarily lesbian) each June. Find out what it has in store for this year's festival and learn more about this nonprofit organization.

POLITICAL AND LEGAL ISSUES

American Civil Liberties Union–Lesbian and Gay Rights

http://www.aclu.org/issues/gay/hmgl.html

★★★★★

🚸 Not for kids

A whole branch of the ACLU is devoted to lesbian and gay rights, and this section of the ACLU website provides updates on recent court rulings and bills coming up in Congress. You'll also find information about joining the ACLU here.

Gay and Lesbian Activist Alliance

http://www.glaa.org/

★★★

🚸 Not for kids

The Gay and Lesbian Activist Alliance of Washington, D.C., has been fighting for equal rights for gays and lesbians since 1971. Read up on the alliance's projects past and present and its testimony at hearings. Includes links to additional resources, including a FAQ.

Gay and Lesbian Alliance Against Defamation (GLAAD)

http://www.glaad.org/

💲

★★★★★

🚸 Not for kids

GLAAD bills itself as "your online resource for promoting fair, accurate, and inclusive representation as a means of challenging discrimination based on sexual orientation or identity." If you or a gay or lesbian person you know has been the victim of discrimination or abuse, this is the group to contact to find out what you can do.

Gay Rights Newstrove

http://gayrights.newstrove.com/

★★★

🚸 Not for kids

Late-breaking news from around the country dealing with gay and lesbian rights.

Human Rights Campaign

http://www.hrc.org/

★★★★★

🚸 Not for kids

The Human Rights Campaign is the United States' largest lesbian and gay political organization. It works to end discrimination, secure equal rights, and protect the health and safety of all Americans. This good-looking site contains a lot of political news for anyone interested in gay and lesbian issues.

National Gay and Lesbian Task Force (NGLTF)

http://www.ngltf.org/

★★★★

 Not for kids

NGLTF is a leading progressive civil rights organization that, since its inception in 1973, has been at the forefront of every major initiative for lesbian, gay, bisexual, and transgender rights. This organization is at work at national, state, and local levels, combating anti-gay violence, battling Radical Right anti-gay legislative and ballot measures, advocating an end to job discrimination, working to repeal sodomy laws, demanding an effective governmental response to HIV and reform of the healthcare system, and much more.

National Lesbian and Gay Law Association

http://www.nlgla.org/

★★★

 Not for kids

The National Lesbian and Gay Law Association (NLGLA) is a national association of lawyers, judges, and other legal professionals, law students and affiliated lesbian, gay, bisexual, and transgender legal organizations.

PUBLICATIONS

The Advocate

http://www.advocate.com/

★★★★★

 Not for kids

One of the oldest and most respected gay magazines. You can browse article summaries for the current issue here (but you have to buy the print edition for the full text) and participate in *The Advocate*'s latest poll.

Anything That Moves

http://www.anythingthatmoves.com/

★★★

Not for kids

A publication for bisexuals, including comics, fiction, poetry, articles, and more.

Girlfriends Magazine

http://www.girlfriendsmag.com/

★★★★★

 Not for kids

A national lesbian magazine. Each issue is loaded with coverage of culture, politics, and sexuality from a lesbian perspective. You can sample all that analog stuff here, but take time to enjoy the Web-only content, too. If you're missing a special *Girlfriends* back issue, you can get a copy at the online store. Ask Dr. Dyke your health questions or get advice in the Kiss and Tell area.

Lavender Magazine Online

http://www.lavendermagazine.com/

★★★★

Not for kids

A very cool and slick online magazine for the Twin Cities gay, lesbian, bisexual, and transgender community. Nice graphics and plenty of articles.

POZ Publishing, LLC.

http://poz.com

★★★

 Not for kids

Choose from any of these publications: *POZ, MAMM,* and *POZ En Español. POZ* is a publication for people who are HIV-positive, targeted primarily toward gay men. This very slick, graphical site contains the full contents of the current newsstand issue, including most graphics.

Sapphic Ink: A Lesbian Literary Journal

http://www.lesbian.org/sapphic-ink/

★★★

 Not for kids

Fiction, poetry, and book reviews by, for, and about lesbians.

Whosoever

http://www.whosoever.org/

★★★★

 Not for kids

A great magazine for gay, lesbian, bisexual, and transgender Christians, it includes theological articles, inspiration, and political action alerts.

A
B
C
D
E
F
G
H
I
J
K
L
M
N
O
P
Q
R
S
T
U
V
W
X
Y
Z

RELIGION

Affirmation: Gay and Lesbian Mormons

http://www.affirmation.org/

★★★

🏃 Not for kids

With chapters around the world, Affirmation serves the needs of gays, lesbians, and bisexuals and their supportive family and friends through social and educational activities. This site includes news, events, and support resources.

AXIOS: Eastern and Orthodox Gay and Lesbian Christians

http://qrd.tcp.com/qrd/www/orgs/axios/

★★★

🏃 Not for kids

A page with many links to information about AXIOS and the Orthodox church in general, including information about same-sex unions in history. Back issues of newsletters available.

Dignity/USA

http://www.dignityusa.org/

★★★★

🏃 Not for kids

Dignity is an international organization for gay, lesbian, and bisexual Roman Catholics. There are chapters in most major cities. Visit Dignity's website to learn about ongoing projects, news, worship, and liturgy. Check the FAQ list to learn more.

Ontario Consultants on Religious Tolerance

http://www.religioustolerance.org/ocrt_hp.htm

★★★

🏃 Not for kids

A very interesting site that compares and explains the varying levels of tolerance and acceptance for gays and lesbians in almost every religion you have ever heard of (and some that you probably haven't).

Rainbow Wind: Lesbigay Pagans

http://users.aol.com/RainbowWind/rbwintr.htm

★★★★

🏃 Not for kids

Support information for gay and lesbian pagans of all denominations. Includes information about *Rainbow Wind Magazine* and links to other queer pagan sites.

Seventh Day Adventist Kinship International

http://www.sdakinship.org/

★★★

🏃 Not for kids

Seventh Day Adventist Kinship International, Inc., is a support group that ministers to the spiritual, emotional, social, and physical well-being of Seventh-Day Adventist lesbians, gays, bisexuals, and their families and friends. SDA Kinship facilitates and promotes the understanding and affirmation of homosexual and bisexual Adventists among themselves and within the Seventh-Day Adventist community through education, advocacy, and reconciliation.

Unitarian Universalist Association

http://www.uua.org/main.html

★★★★★

🏃 Not for kids

The Unitarian Universalist Church is a "big tent" group that welcomes a wide variety of believers, including gay and lesbian people of all beliefs. Find out more about this organization at this page.

United Church of Christ

http://www.ucc.org/

★★★

🏃 Not for kids

A lot of general information about the United Church of Christ here, including its organization, beliefs, and member churches.

Universal Fellowship of Metropolitan Community Churches

http://www.ufmcc.com/

★★★

 Not for kids

MCC is a church fellowship designed specifically to minister to the spiritual needs of gay and lesbian people. This page directs you to its ministries all over the world.

Related Sites
http://www.clgs.org/
http://www.dioceseofnewark.org/theoasis/

TRANSGENDER

FTM International

http://ftmi.org/

★★★

 Not for kids

A peer support group for female-to-male transvestites and transsexuals. It offers information and networking for women who are exploring their gender identity issues, or who need a safe place to explore their male personae, as well as for men who are in the process of transition or who have completed the change. The group also provides educational services to the general public on transgender issues.

Intersex Society of North America (ISNA)

http://www.isna.org/

★★★

 Not for kids

Support and advocacy group for intersexuals, defined here as "individuals born with anatomy or physiology which differs from cultural ideals of male and female." Very heavy on medical terminology; parents who are concerned about dealing with these issues should find this site enlightening but might need a medical dictionary.

Susan's Place Transgender Resources

http://www.susans.org/

★★★

 Not for kids

Transgender forums and directory designed to help the transgender community find the help and resources they need. Links are grouped into several categories, including Activism, Articles, Cross Dressing, Hate Crimes, Surgery, and Shopping.

The TransGender Guide

http://www.tgguide.com/

★★★

Not for kids

Put together by a cross-section of folks from around the country (okay, pun intentional), this site features chat rooms, plenty of shopping and other resources, personals, anonymous newsletters and mailing lists. Support and information for those who need help in coming out to their family, learning about their rights, or dealing with emotional issues.

TRAVEL

Damron Lesbian and Gay Travel Guides

http://www.damron.com/

★★★

 Not for kids

Damron is a gay-owned/operated travel company offering exclusively gay vacation packages as well as traditional travel-related services (such as airline tickets and hotel/car reservations). Damron bills itself as "your one-stop travel consultant for business and vacation."

A B C D E F G H I J K L M N O P Q R S T U V W X Y Z

A
B
C
D
E
F
G
H
I
J
K
L
M
N
O
P
Q
R
S
T
U
V
W
X
Y
Z

Olivia Travel

http://www.olivia.com/

★★★

Not for kids

Olivia Travel hosts cruises and all-inclusive vacations for women only. Find your latest cruise and vacation information here, request a brochure, and (at selected times) enter a sweepstakes to win a free cruise.

Related Sites

http://www.abovebeyondtours.com/

http://www.alysonadventures.com/

http://www.journeysbysea.com/

http://www.gay-travel.com/

http://www.discoveryvallarta.com/guide.html

http://www.venture-out.com/

GENEALOGY

A Barrel of Genealogy Links

http://cpcug.org/user/jlacombe/mark.html

★★★

An amazing listing of links to resources that can help you in your efforts to track down historical family information.

Ancestry.com

http://www.ancestry.com/search/main.htm

 ⑤

★★★★

Looking for someone? You have several options at Ancestry.com. You can access some free search databases or become a member for $59.95 ($19.95 quarterly) and access all its databases. This site includes the Social Security Death Index, AIS Census Records Index, global searching, maps, books, and much more.

Beginner's Guide to Family History Research

http://www.arkansasresearch.com/guide.html

★★★★

If you can't even spell the word g-e-n-e-a-l-o-g-y, this is the place for you to start. Everyone has ancestors, and if you're wondering who yours are, it's time to get involved in family history and genealogy research.

Canadian Genealogical Projects Registry

http://www.afhs.ab.ca/registry/

★★★

Canadian (not just Albertan) genealogy extraction, transcription, and indexing projects are listed. Here, you will find more than 10,000 links to data housed online.

Cool Site of the Month for Genealogists

http://www.rootsweb.com/~cogenweb/comain.htm

★★★

The Colorado Genealogy Society sponsors this site, which provides links to sites that are not widely known to genealogists working on the Web, provide an example of good genealogical work, or contain valuable information for genealogists.

Cyndi's List of Genealogy Sites on the Web

http://www.cyndislist.com/howto.htm

★★★★

Great index of Genealogy sites on the Web, listing everything from beginner's guides and books to articles on using maps and microfiche. The links on this site comprise a veritable course on teaching visitors how to become genealogy experts.

Ellis Island

http://www.ellisisland.org

⑤

★★★★★

👥 14-18

If one of your ancestors passed through Ellis Island or the Port of New York on his or her way to becoming a United States citizen, chances are this website can turn up a record of that person's arrival. At this site, you can search for and (optionally) purchase passenger documents that record a relation's arrival in the States. You can even build a family scrapbook online to share with other visitors or check out some family scrapbooks that other people have already constructed.

A
B
C
D
E
F
G
H
I
J
K
L
M
N
O
P
Q
R
S
T
U
V
W
X
Y
Z

 Everton's Genealogical Helper

http://www.everton.com/

$

★★★★★

Search the genealogical database, buy products to help you in your research efforts, check out thousands of links listed here, and get help from others who've been at their search longer than you have. This site is packed with information and resources for novice and expert genealogists alike, making it our choice as the best genealogy site in the group.

Family Search

http://www.familysearch.org/

$

★★★★

This is the site to visit if you are looking for the largest collection of genealogical information in the world. The site was created by The Church of Jesus Christ of Latter-Day Saints and contains links to 400 million names of people dating back to the 1500s. In many cases, you'll find family pedigree charts. The church hopes to help its Mormon members find their ancestors so that they might be baptized by proxy and embrace their faith in the afterlife.

FamilyTreeMaker.com

http://familytreemaker.genealogy.com/

$

★★★★★

 All

In addition to searchable databases and family-finder information, you can also access how-to information to help in your search and buy genealogical products and reference material. FamilyTreeMaker is one of the most popular programs around for researching family history and constructing family trees.

Find a Friend

http://www.findafriend.com

$

★★★

Looking for that long-lost family member? This site will help you find him or her. You can search by name; if you have a birth date, last known address, and specific location, that will narrow the search. There is a charge for this service.

The Genealogy Home Page

http://www.genhomepage.com/

★★★★

This extensive set of pages offers information about maps and geography, communication with other genealogists, a compendium of genealogy databases, a list of other genealogy home pages, and other genealogy resources both in North America and around the world.

Genealogy Instruction Beginners, Teenagers, and Kids

http://home.earthlink.net/~howardorjeff/instruct.htm

★★★★

 All

Instructions for beginners, kids, and teenagers. This site is for people interested in getting started doing research on their family's history, whether they're beginning genealogists, adults, teens, or youngsters.

Genealogy Resources on the Internet

http://www-personal.umich.edu/~cgaunt/gen_int1.html

★★★

Chris Gaunt and John Fuller, creators of this site, offer a comprehensive list of genealogy information accessible through mailing lists, newsgroups, Telnet, email, FTP, Gopher, and World Wide Web sites.

GenForum

http://genforum.genealogy.com/

$

★★★

Provides more than 5,000 discussion forums devoted to specific surnames, countries, and ethnicities, as well as general genealogical topics.

GenGateway.com

http://www.gengateway.com/

★★★

Conduct free surname searches, access family name databases, chat, and search gateways to get started.

German Genealogy Resources

http://www.germanroots.com/

★★★★

Do you have some German blood in your family? Then check out this site, where you can track down links to your Germanic ancestry.

JewishGen: The Home of Jewish Genealogy

http://www.jewishgen.org/

★★★★

For people researching their Jewish ancestry, this nonprofit site offers a family finder database of 250,000 names and towns, access to discussion groups, and infolinks.

Kindred Konnections

http://www.kindredkonnections.com/

★★★

Genealogy and family history research. The site contains thousands of genealogy databases displayed as pedigree-linked trees. The archive also contains selected genealogy census, birth, marriage, and death records. The free area has the genealogy Social Security Death Index (SSDI), the genealogy Cornwall census, and the index to a 27-million–name genealogical database.

Murphy's Massive Irish MIDI Page

http://irish.teledyn.com/?section=Geneology

★★★

This is a great site where you can access links to find your Irish ancestry.

National Archives and Records Administration: Genealogy Page

http://www.nara.gov/genealogy/genindex.html

★★★★

NARA offers online microfilm catalogs, which are also available for purchase. The microfilms are available for census records, military service records, and immigrant and passenger arrival records. These records can be used for genealogical research.

Origins.net

http://www.origins.net/

★★★★

Are you descended from British royalty? Search the records at this site to find out. Here, you can search Scots, Irish, and English records, including census data, Griffith's valuations, ships' passenger lists, church records, convict records, and more. Click the How to Trace Your Family History link to learn the seven steps of an effective search, even if you're not Irish, Scottish, or English.

RootsWeb

http://www.rootsweb.com/

★★★

The RootsWeb project has two missions: to make large volumes of data available to the online genealogical community at minimal cost and to provide support services to online genealogical activities, such as Usenet newsgroup moderation, mailing list maintenance, surname list generation, and so on.

Treasure Maps: The "How-To" Genealogy Site

http://www.amberskyline.com/treasuremaps/

★★★

Offering a wealth of information about researching family history, this site features tips for newcomers to genealogy and tells you what to do if you hit a wall in your research.

Vital Records Information: United States

http://vitalrec.com/

★★★

This page contains information about where to obtain vital records from each state, territory, and county of the United States.

Related Sites

http://www.eogn.com/home/
http://www.ctssar.org/
http://www.geo.ed.ac.uk/home/scotland/genealogy.html
http://www.ngsgenealogy.org/

GEOGRAPHY

Association of American Geographers

http://www.aag.org/

★★★

Association of American Geographers (AAG) is a scientific and educational society founded in 1904. Its 6,500 members share interests in the theory, methods, and practice of geography. The AAG conducts educational and research projects that further its interests and programs.

Chesapeake Bay Program

http://www.epa.gov/r3chespk/

★★★

This page contains information on the health and history of the Chesapeake Bay waterway, featuring trends in pollution and restoration projects that are underway. Also contains links to scientific data and research about the bay and other bay resources.

CIA World Factbook

http://www.cia.gov/cia/publications/factbook/

★★★★★

All

One of the CIA's best kept secrets is its World Factbook, which provides detailed information about various regions, countries, islands, and areas around the world. If you're planning a trip to a particular country or are doing a report about a country, check here for the latest information. Great site for kids to visit when they're doing their geography homework.

Department of Geography: Syracuse University

http://www.maxwell.syr.edu/geo/Default.htm

★★★

Covers the department, faculty, degree programs, and area information. Addresses all the topics someone considering Syracuse University for studying geography would want to know.

FirstGov for Kids: Geography

http://www.kids.gov/k_geography.htm

★★★★

All

The Federal Citizen Information Center provides this useful site to help kids find out about certain regions, countries, and cities; investigate volcanoes, rain forests, and other geographical features; view pictures of the earth from space; and much more. Provides links to additional resources.

GeoCommunity

http://data.geocomm.com/

$

★★★★

Free access to the largest Geographical Information Systems database on the Internet.

Geographic Nameserver

http://geonames.usgs.gov/

★★★

Provides geographic information about a specific location, including county, state, country, population, area code, latitude, longitude, and elevation.

Geography at the University of Buffalo

http://www.geog.buffalo.edu/

★★★★

Wondering what geography is and why geography could be a possible focus of undergraduate or graduate study? This site addresses both of these questions, as well as describes what the Geography department at UB has to offer in four different concentrations: Cartography and GIS, Urban and Regional Analysis, Physical Geography and Environmental Systems, and International Business and World Trade. Also find out what geographers do after they get their degree.

Geography World

http://members.aol.com/bowermanb/101.html

★★★★★

Plenty of information for students studying geography—from homework help to background information on cultures and history of countries around the world. You'll also find climate, conservation, and calendar information, as well as geography games to enjoy.

GIS WWW Resource List

http://www.geo.ed.ac.uk/home/giswww.html

★★★

Geographical Information Systems' (GIS) index of World Wide Web servers that are likely to be of interest to the GIS community.

GPS Primer

http://www.aero.org/publications/GPSPRIMER/

★★★★

Learn about global positioning systems and how you can use them to navigate the globe.

Related Site
http://www.howstuffworks.com/gps.htm

How Far Is It?

http://www.indo.com/distance/

★★★★

 All

Find the latitude and longitude of two cities by typing in two locations and then learn how many miles the two cities are from each other.

 National Geographic

http://www.nationalgeographic.com/

★★★★★

 All

Learn geography from the experts. Home of *National Geographic*, the magazine that has traveled the world and taught children and adults to appreciate geography, nature, and various cultures for decades. Here, you will find online versions of National Geographic's award-winning photographs, plus the latest articles from around the globe. Special areas for kids, parents, and teachers. Easy to navigate and packed with great information, National Geographic is an obvious Best of the Best selection.

WorldAtlas.com

http://www.worldatlas.com/aatlas/world.htm

★★★★★

 All

Cool interactive globe. Click a continent and then a country to get a quick overview of its borders and geographical features plus a wealth of information about the country's economy, language, climate, currency, and more. Great resource for kids.

MAPS

Cultural Maps

http://xroads.virginia.edu/~MAP/map_hp.html

★★★★

Through this map site, visitors can gain access to many map collections and view them online. Historical and topographical maps are available here from numerous U.S. collections.

A
B
C
D
E
F
G
H
I
J
K
L
M
N
O
P
Q
R
S
T
U
V
W
X
Y
Z

A
B
C
D
E
F
G
H
I
J
K
L
M
N
O
P
Q
R
S
T
U
V
W
X
Y
Z

David Rumsey Historical Map Collection

http://www.davidrumsey.com

★★★★★

With a focus on rare eighteenth and nineteenth century North and South American cartographic historical materials, this online collection features more than 6,400 maps, which you can view by using your Web browser, via Java, or by using a special GIS viewer that features map overlays. The collection also features historical maps of the world, Europe, Asia, and Africa. A great place for geography teachers to introduce students to cartography.

Expedia.com

http://www.expedia.com/

★★★★

Plan your next trip at Expedia.com. If you're driving, click the Maps tab to obtain a detailed map, complete with driving directions, from your point of departure to your destination.

Exploring Maps

http://interactive2.usgs.gov/learningweb/teachers/exploremaps.htm

★★★★★

Map lesson plans and activities from the U.S. Geological Survey, geared toward grades K–12.

Finding Your Way with Map and Compass

http://mac.usgs.gov/mac/isb/pubs/factsheets/fs03501.html

★★★★

Detailed instruction on the use of maps and compasses from the U.S. Geological Survey Department. Also includes the fundamentals of topographical map making and scale.

The Geography of Cyberspace

http://www.geog.ucl.ac.uk/casa/martin/geography_of_cyberspace.html

★★★

This site tries to answer the question "what does cyberspace look like?" You'll find many links and articles related to the question, as well as maps of computer networks. An interesting question-and-answer site.

GraphicMaps.com

http://www.graphicmaps.com/graphic_.htm

★★★★

🚻 All

This site was developed by a custom mapping company and offers answers to geography questions, a map of the week, as well as several other types of maps for viewing. Also features a geography quiz and clip art.

International Map Trade Association

http://www.maptrade.org

★★★

Offers links to member stores' websites and a geographical directory of map and travel book retailers.

Related Site

http://www.worldtime.com/

MapBlast

http://www.mapblast.com/

★★★★★

Microsoft Network's map site that helps you create maps of your own. You can also get maps of popular destinations, such as major U.S. cities, national parks, state capitals, attractions, and U.S. regions.

[Best] MapQuest

http://www.mapquest.com/

★★★★★

Excellent and resourceful guide for those who are planning to travel in North America. Has travel guides, trip information, clickable maps, directions, and so much more. Share plans and tips with fellow vacationers, get relocation information, or order a road atlas on CD-ROM. When you're planning your next trip across town or across the country, don't forget to check out this site.

Maps.com

http://www.maps.com/

★★★★★

Huge map and travel store, where you can purchase and download printable maps or order printed maps.

Maps of the United States

http://www.lib.utexas.edu/maps/united_states.html

★★★★

High-quality electronic maps cataloged by state from the Perry-Castañeda Library Map Collection. Most maps in PDF format.

Mr. Beller's Neighborhood

http://www.mrbellersneighborhood.com

★★★★

Visit Mr. Beller's neighborhood (Manhattan island) and its various divisions, including Greenwich Village, Soho, Little Italy, Harlem, and Central Park. Explore an aerial view of Manhattan and click the red dots to read some interesting articles and stories.

OSSHE Historical and Cultural Atlas Resource

http://darkwing.uoregon.edu/~atlas/

★★★

This site was developed for students and aids their learning experience. It offers maps of North America, Europe, the Middle East, and North Africa. Normal maps can be viewed with any JPEG viewer. You need to download Macromedia's Shockwave plug-in—see the Requirements link and click Macromedia—to be able to view the interactive maps, which are indicated by an icon.

National Geographic's Map Machine

http://plasma.nationalgeographic.com/mapmachine/

★★★

Unique interactive map that can zoom in on any location in the United States. A little difficult to maneuver, but interesting to check out.

Rare Map Collection at the Hargrett Library

http://www.libs.uga.edu/darchive/hargrett/maps/maps.html

★★★

The Hargrett Library, at the University of Georgia, offers more than 800 rare maps from the sixteenth through the early twentieth century. Early maps depict the New World, whereas others chart Colonial and Revolutionary America, the Civil War, and Georgia's Revolutionary period, cities, and coastal areas. File sizes are large, so downloads are slow.

Road Map Collectors Association

http://www.roadmaps.org/

★★★

Organization of North American and British collectors to promote road map collecting and network with trading partners.

SkiMaps

http://www.skimaps.com/

★★★

Trail maps, resort locators, and resort bookings.

UM Weather Maps

http://yang.sprl.umich.edu/wxnet/

★★★★

Very interesting site that enables you to interact with weather maps. You can view such things as relative humidity, wind, and temperature—and then better understand the meteorological events that come into play with each other. When you select a type of weather map, you can click an area of that map (all U.S. areas) and get the status of a city's weather.

U.S. Census Bureau Maps

http://tiger.census.gov/

★★★

Allows you to generate a high-quality, detailed map of anywhere in the United States using public geographic data. Maintained by the U.S. Census Department.

Related Sites
http://www.oldmapsne.com/home.html

http://www.mapsonus.com/

http://grads.iges.org/pix/head.html

A
B
C
D
E
F
G
H
I
J
K
L
M
N
O
P
Q
R
S
T
U
V
W
X
Y
Z

GIFTS

ArtisanGifts.com

http://www.artisan-gifts.com/

★★★★

Choose distinctive, handcrafted gifts and have them wrapped and sent with just a few keystrokes. Pick by the occasion, or your budget, or select a category to get started.

Ashford.com

http://www.ashford.com

★★★★

Ashford offers fine personal accessories, such as watches, writing instruments, jewelry, and more, as well as information on what gifts are hot to help you make your selection.

Baby Shower Gifts

http://www.adorablebabygifts.com/

★★★★

Thoughtful gifts for. a new baby. Specializes in baby clothing, gift baskets, children's jewelry, christening gifts, baby shower games, and information on baby names.

BK Puff & Stuff

http://www.bkpuffnstuff.com/

★★★

Over-the-hill gifts, Christmas treats, baby gifts, golfer gifts, and Winnie the Pooh, too.

Blue Mountain

http://www.bluemountain.com/

★★★★★

Blue Mountain. is well known for its online greeting cards. Here you can find cards for every occasion and holiday, customize your cards, and email them to friends and family. Printable cards also are available.

Brookstone

http://www.brookstone.com/

★★★★★

When you need a gift for the person who has everything or if you just love cool gadgets, check out Brookstone's website, where you can find everything from foot massagers and CD players to robotic vacuum cleaners.

Consumer Direct Warehouse

http://www.consumer-direct.com/

★★★

Choose from gifts that start under $10. This site offers a large selection of items and different shipping options.

Einstein Gifts

http://www.einsteingifts.com/

★★★★★

Still popular after all these years, Albert Einstein is proof that it's cool to be smart. Check out the Einstein collection of gifts, including coffee mugs, posters, T-shirts, and scientific novelties.

FragranceNet.com

http://www.fragrancenet.com/html/

★★★★

Featuring more than 3,500 genuine, brand-name fragrances for both women and men, plus scented candles and other gifts. Discounts range from 20% to 60% off. Free shipping on orders over $60.

The Gift Collector

http://www.giftcollector.com/

★★★★

With more than 8,000 items, this online store features figurines, crystal, china, and other collectibles from Waterford, Swarovsky, Department 56, Herend, Lladro, Harmony Kingdom, TY Beanie Babies, and more.

GiftCertificates.com

http://www.giftcertificates.com/

★★★★

Want to send a gift certificate to someone special but don't have the time to drive to the store to pick it up? Then, this site is for you. Choose from more than 700 merchants, enter the value you want to purchase, and choose the gift-wrapping and card you want sent along with it. Your shopping is done, and an original gift certificate will arrive at the recipient's door in no time.

The Gift.com

http://www.1800flowers.com/flowers/gift/h_index.asp

★★★

Gifts for all occasions, including anniversary, baby birth, business gifts, congratulations, engagement, get well, graduation, housewarming, romance, wedding, and many more.

Best | Gifts.com

http://www.gifts.com

★★★★★

Find great gifts and great gift ideas here. Seasonal gifts and ideas for special holidays are featured. You can find a large number of special gift ideas for him, for her, even for pet owners, for any occasion. Gifts range from plants to jewelry to gift baskets filled with food, wine, bath items, golf-related items, and more. Just about anything a gift giver could want can be found on this Best of the Best site!

Gifts24.com

http://gifts24.com/g/

★★★

Offers a wide range of interesting gifts for all occasions. All in-stock FedEx orders received by 8 p.m. Eastern Standard Time, Monday through Friday, ship same day.

giftTree

http://www.gifttree.com/main.html

★★★

Offers comprehensive gift services and solutions. Handcrafted, professionally designed gift baskets, floral designs, and creative gift ideas for all occasions and every pocketbook. Nationwide coverage, quality guarantee, and devotion to customer service.

Great Plains Gifts

http://www.greatplainsgifts.com/

★★★

Great Plains Gifts features an assortment of unique and popular gift items, including *Harry Potter* and *Lord of the Rings* collectors' items, home decor, yard decorations, professional gifts, and more.

A
B
C
D
E
F
G
H
I
J
K
L
M
N
O
P
Q
R
S
T
U
V
W
X
Y
Z

A
B
C
D
E
F
G
H
I
J
K
L
M
N
O
P
Q
R
S
T
U
V
W
X
Y
Z

Gump's
http://www.gumpsbymail.com/

★★★★

Shop the famous Gump's department store online or request a catalog. Search by type of product or get ideas at the site for home furnishings, decorative accessories, and special occasion gifts.

Hammacher Schlemmer
http://www.hammacherschlemmer.com

★★★★★

Search for unusual gifts for business and personal gift giving here.

Harry and David Gourmet Food Gifts
http://www.harryanddavid.com/

★★★

Order gourmet food items and have them shipped to you or a friend. Specializes in fresh fruit and gift baskets.

Kosher Gourmet Gift Baskets
http://www.koshercornucopia.com/

★★★

Kosher Cornucopia is the largest mail order catalog of kosher gourmet gifts in the United States, offering an extensive selection for all holidays and occasions. This site offers an online catalog or the option to call an 800 number and request that a catalog be mailed to you.

MarthaStewart.com
http://www.marthastewart.com

★★★★★

Shop Martha By Mail for special gift ideas, as well as flowers, all from this site. She specializes in entertaining and keepsakes, so that's a lot of what you'll find here.

Nautical Gifts
http://www.compass-rose.com/

★★★

Compass Rose offers 500 nautical gifts and decorating accessories.

Netique
http://www.netique.com/

★★★

Why send ordinary flowers, gift baskets, or chocolate when you could send an extraordinary gift? Just place your order, and Netique does the rest—gift-wraps, prepares the enclosure card, and ships.

PenExpress.com
http://www.penexpress.com/

★★★

PenExpress claims to be the largest online reseller of fountain pens and other fine writing instruments, including Parker, MontBlanc, Cross, Pelikan, and more. Great discounts on top-of-the-line merchandise.

Perfect Present Picker
http://presentpicker.com/ppp/

★★★★

This expert shopping program will select a gift that's just right, based on someone's profession, interest, life, age, sex, and personality. Links to a large variety of online retailers.

Perfumania.com
http://www.perfumania.com/

★★★★

"America's largest online fragrance store," this site carries fragrances for women, men, and children, plus bath and body products and gift sets. Order online to have products shipped to your door.

RedEnvelope Gifts: The Right Gift, Right Away

http://www.redenvelope.com/

★★★★

Promotes the last-minute approach to gift giving. RedEnvelope offers an extensive collection of imaginative, original gifts for every occasion, recipient, and budget through its website and catalog. The company's merchants travel the world for unique products and often commission artists and vendors to create exclusive gifts just for RedEnvelope shoppers.

SeniorStore.com

http://store.yahoo.com/seniorstore/

★★★★

Products, birthday gifts, gift ideas for adults age 50+, seniors, grandparents, and grandchildren.

Sharper Image

http://www.sharperimage.com

★★★★★

Select gifts from this catalog site, known for its unusual, harder-to-find personal and home items. Great place for gadget shoppers or for those seeking the perfect gift for the person who has everything.

Spencer Gifts

http://www.spencergifts.com/home.asp

★★★★★

 Not for kids

Looking for a gift that's out of the ordinary? Then check out Spencer Gifts' huge line of odd and irreverent gifts. Living dead dolls, bobble-head Spiderman figurines, dorm room accessories (such as black lights and lava lamps), gag gifts, light-hearted birthday party accessories, erotic gifts, and more. Shop online, so you won't have to face the embarrassment of visiting the store in person.

Sports Flags and Banners

http://www.anyflag.com/sports/

★★★

Collection of flags and banners for sports teams and sporting events, along with American flags and more. All sports flags are authorized and licensed products. These flags make excellent gifts for your favorite sports fan.

Surprise.com

http://www.surprise.com/

★★★★★

At Surprise.com, you get gift ideas from other users. You can shop for ideas by the person's relationship to you (brother, sister, friend, kid's coach), by occasion (birthday, Halloween, graduation), or by category (unusual sense of humor, dog owner, loves to cook). Follow the trail of links to the item you want and then purchase it online.

Target

http://www.target.com/

★★★★★

Shop for gifts at Target without ever leaving your home. If you're engaged or expecting a baby, you can register online, making it very easy for friends and family members to shop for gifts.

USA Glad

http://www.usaglad.com/

★★★

USA Glad features a wide selection of gifts you can order online to have delivered.

Wish-List.com

http://www.wish-list.com/index/

★★★

Want to give the perfect gift? Find your friends' wish lists and purchase a gift you know they'll love. Even better, you can make your own wishes come true by filling your own wish list with gifts from all over the Internet, including your favorite retailers. If it's out there on the Internet, you can register it at Wish-List.com.

A B C D E F G H I J K L M N O P Q R S T U V W X Y Z

A B C D E F **G** H I J K L M N O P Q R S T U V W X Y Z

The 19th Hole

http://19thhole.com/

★★★

Serves as a place where fans and participants of the sport can gather, share a few stories, and settle a bet or two. Provides daily golf news, an almanac, and an art section. Also includes classified ads. Shop the bookstore and purchase books through links to Amazon.com.

AugustaGolf

http://sportsillustrated.cnn.com/augusta/

★★★

Multimedia views from the tournament, interviews with players, and statistics sortable by score or player name.

BadGolfMonthly.com

http://www.badgolfmonthly.com/

★★★★★

The golf site "for the golfer who really sucks," this site is more of a serious vacationer's guide to golf courses from TravelGolf.com. Some humorous articles provide a little levity for an otherwise frustrating sport.

Ben Hogan Golf Products

http://www.benhogan.com/

★★★★

Whether you're a Ben Hogan fan or you just like to swing his golf clubs, you'll love this site. Fans can find a complete timeline of Ben Hogan's career from 1938 to 1959 and view a few of his closest friends reminisce about their experiences with Ben Hogan. Customers and dealers can learn about the complete line of Ben Hogan golf clubs and accessories; Demo Days, when and where products will be demonstrated; and meet the staff pros. Very polished site.

CNN/SI Fantasy Golf Challenge

http://fantasy.si.cnn.com/

★★★

Grab your clubs and reserve your tee time today. With CNN/SI Fantasy Golf, you can play golf free all summer long, competing on a tournament-by-tournament basis as well as on a universal level. The site ranks every competing team for the individual tournament, as well as provides an overall cumulative ranking based on weekly results. Features player profiles, tournament updates, and in-depth interviews. Register a new foursome every week and make your mark on the pro tour! Site features various fantasy sports options that vary depending on the season.

ESPN Fantasy Golf

http://games.espn.go.com/golf/frontpage

★★★

ESPN Fantasy Golf is the closest thing you can find to managing professional golfers. All decisions are yours to make. Each team owner is supplied with all the tools—multiple draft methods, live statistics, unlimited waivers and trades, free agency, an all-empowering commissioner, chat rooms, league bulletin boards, sortable statistics for all players, and more.

FootJoy

http://www.footjoy.com/

★★★★

FootJoy is the #1 shoe in golf, offering 143 shoe styles. Check out FootJoy's products in its online catalog or enter your ZIP code to find the nearest golf shop that sells FootJoy products.

Golf Channel Online

http://www.thegolfchannel.com/

★★★

A cable TV channel dedicated to golf. Visitors to the site will find a program schedule, player statistics, tips on improving their game, and information on getting the Golf Channel on their cable systems.

Golfcourse.com

http://www.golfcourse.com/

★★★★

Golf Magazine's directory of golf courses, this site provides information on thousands of golf courses throughout North America and the world. The site includes comprehensive course descriptions and a list of the world's best courses.

GolfGuideWeb.com

http://www.golfguideweb.com/golfcourses.html

★★★★

Comprehensive list of golf courses across the nation listed by state and city. GolfGuideWeb.com provides stats for most golf courses and reviews for many. If you're planning on visiting a particular state or city and would like to know what's available in the way of golf courses, this is the site for you.

GOLFonline: Beginner's Guide

http://sportsillustrated.cnn.com/golfonline/beginners/

★★★

 All

Just what the title suggests: elementary golf terms, a kids' section, steps to avoid humiliation, instruction, equipment—all the basics and more. Created and maintained by *Sports Illustrated* and *Golf Magazine*.

Golfsmith

http://www.golfsmith.com/

★★★★★

Golfsmith International began more than 30 years ago and is now the largest direct marketer and superstore retailer of golf equipment in the world. The company makes and fits clubs and sells more than 20,000 different golf-related products. It even runs its own golf academy.

Golf Tips Magazine

http://www.golftipsmag.com/

★★★★

Excellent collection of golf tips from the experts. Tips for driving, using irons, working on your short game, and putting. Some very helpful video clips that show you just what to do.

Best ⛳ GolfWeb

http://www.golfweb.com/

★★★★★

Here, you can access the regular golf stuff: tournament results, online pro shops, and so on. But you can also link to the Lesson Tee for golfing tips, go to a link for women in golf, and write a personal message to the winner of a current tournament. This site has an easily accessible design and is packed with useful information and golf tips, making it an easy selection as best golf site.

LINKS Magazine

http://www.linksmagazine.com/

★★★

Information on 50 courses golf fans must play, a guide featuring places to golf while on vacation, and a section dedicated to golf course architecture.

LPGA.com

http://www.Lpga.com

★★★★★

👥 14-18

Get complete LPGA tournament coverage at the site, as well as an animated online lesson. You'll find schedules, player bios, headline golf news, and lots more about the LPGA at this official site. Area for junior golfers as well.

The Masters

http://www.masters.org/

★★★★

Official site of the Masters, including everything you want to know about the history of the Masters tournament and this year's event.

A
B
C
D
E
F
G
H
I
J
K
L
M
N
O
P
Q
R
S
T
U
V
W
X
Y
Z

A
B
C
D
E
F
G
H
I
J
K
L
M
N
O
P
Q
R
S
T
U
V
W
X
Y
Z

The Open Championship

http://www.opengolf.com/

★★★★

The world's oldest championship, one of golf's four major annual events, and the only one outside America. Find out all the details about this year's Open at this official Open Championship site.

PGA.com

http://www.pga.com/

★★★★★

👥 14-18

PGA.com is the Official website of the PGA. PGA works with IBM as an alliance partner for the website. In addition, through IBM's role as official scoring and information system of the PGA, PGA.com continues to provide the world's best real-time golf event scoring system. PGA.com is one of the most highly trafficked golf sites on the Web, delivering millions of page views surrounding PGA major championships including the PGA Championship, Ryder Cup, PGA Seniors' Championship, and the MasterCard PGA Grand Slam of Golf.

PING American College Golf Guide

http://www.collegegolf.com/

★★★

This site explains and promotes the PING American College Golf Guide, which contains information on every four-year and two-year men's and women's intercollegiate golf program in the United States. If you think your college kid has pro possibilities, this site will prove invaluable.

USGA

http://www.usga.org/

★★★★

👥 14-18

The United States Golf Association (USGA) has served as the national governing body of golf since its formation in 1894. It is a nonprofit organization run by golfers for the benefit of golfers. The USGA consists of more than 9,100 golf facilities. The USGA's Members Program has grown to more than 800,000 golfers who help support the game and the association.

Related Sites

http://www.callawaygolf.com/
http://www.cobragolf.com/
http://www.liquidmetalgolf.com/
http://www.macgregorgolf.com/
http://www.maxfli.com/
http://www.nevercompromise.com/
http://www.orlimar.com/
http://www.taylormadegolf.com/
http://www.titleist.com/
http://www.topflite.com/

GROCERIES

A B C D E F **G** H I J K L M N O P Q R S T U V W X Y Z

Albertsons.com

http://www.albertsons.com/

★★★★

Online grocery store featuring more than 25,000 items including meat, produce, and bakery goods. Specially trained order selectors pick the freshest items for you and deliver them right to your door. Available only in the following West Coast cities: Los Angeles, San Diego, San Francisco, Portland, Seattle, and Vancouver.

At Your Service

http://www.internetgroceries.com/default.asp

★★★★★

Buy your groceries, plus find recipes and nutritional guides at this site. Links to Internet florists and online electronic retailers.

Bashas' Online

http://www.bashas.com/

★★★

"Groceries on the Go" home delivery program. You can order your groceries online for delivery in the metro Phoenix area.

eGrocer Canada

http://www.egrocer.ca/

★★★

Online grocery shopping in Canada. You can virtually roam through the online store from the comfort of your own desk, at work or at home, and arrange for your groceries to be delivered to you.

EthnicGrocer.com

http://www.ethnicgrocer.com/eg/hm/eg.jsp

★★★

EthnicGrocer is an online source of ethnic food ingredients and consumer products from around the world, available for shipment overnight. Shop by country, by dish, or by recipe—all available at the site.

GroceryNetwork.com

http://www.grocerynetwork.com/

★★★

Supermarket magazine that covers all aspects of the supermarket industry.

Grocery Shopping List

http://www.organizetips.com/grocer.htm

★★★

Use this printable grocery list to remind you what you need from the store. Using this list might also jog your memory about other items you need.

Grocery Shopping Network

http://www.groceryshopping.net/

★★★

Searchable directory of online grocery stores, pharmacies, weekly ads, and recipes.

Kroger

http://www.kroger.com/

★★★

No online shopping or grocery delivery, but you can visit Kroger's website to learn about weekly specials, order prescription refills, and find a store near you.

A
B
C
D
E
F
G
H
I
J
K
L
M
N
O
P
Q
R
S
T
U
V
W
X
Y
Z

MegaFoods Pick 'n Save Supermarket

http://www.megafoods.com/

★★★

Online grocery shopping.

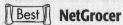 NetGrocer

http://www.netgrocer.com/

★★★★★

Thousands of food and general merchandise products to choose from. A great way to make sure your mother, grandmother, and child in college gets the food they need, no matter where you live. Just shop for food at NetGrocer and enter shipping information at the checkout page. You can even set up a recurring order that sends your shipment at an interval you choose. With this Best of the Best site, you may never need to go grocery shopping again!

NoMeat.com

http://www.nomeat.com

★★★★

Vegetarians and people trying to eat more healthy foods will want to check out this site, which offers vegetarian meat products, recipes, and tips for healthy eating.

Peapod

http://www.peapod.com/

★★★★

This site bills itself as America's Internet grocer—and with one million orders delivered, that's easy to believe. Shop online any time of day or night. Delivery is available seven days a week; you pick the time convenient for you. Orders are packed so perishables stay fresh and frozen items stay frozen. Available in Chicago, Boston, Long Island, and a few other select cities.

Pink Dot

http://www.pinkdot.com/

★★★

"Your Supermarket That Delivers." This supermarket offers grocery delivery service for the greater Los Angeles area.

Price Chopper Supermarkets

http://www.pricechopper.com/

★★★

Price Chopper is a medium-size chain of supermarkets in the Northeast, with headquarters in Upstate New York. This store currently offers a HouseCalls program (online grocery shopping), established for the Albany/Capital City area.

Ralphs: First in Southern California

http://www.ralphs.com/

★★★

Ralphs offers things you won't find at other stores, but it does not offer online shopping. Some of its perks include a Club Card, giving you discounts all over Southern California on everything from car rentals to fine dining. You'll also save on your favorite wines with Ralphs Wine Club. Ralph's was recently purchased by Kroger.

Safeway

http://www.safeway.com/

★★★

If you live in Sacramento, California (or the San Francisco Bay Area; Portland, Oregon; or Vancouver, Washington), you can tack on an extra ten bucks to your grocery bill and avoid the hassle of having to shop and carry your groceries yourself.

TeleGrocer

http://www.telegrocer.com/

★★★

Canadian online grocery shopping service.

ThaiGrocer

http://www.thaigrocer.com/

★★★★

Learn about and shop for Thai foods. This site provides Thai and oriental groceries, and a cooking school, too.

Wegmans Food Markets Inc.

http://www.wegmans.com/

★★★

Since its beginnings in 1916, Wegmans has grown to include more than 50 stores across New York state and Pennsylvania. Its latest expansion is in Princeton, New Jersey. Currently, the store does not offer online grocery shopping. Nevertheless, this site offers plenty of reasons to visit. You'll find recipes, produce information, diet and nutrition tips, holiday gift ideas you can order online, and much more. People from all over the world come to visit Wegmans. If you can't do that, do the next best thing and treat yourself to a visit to this site.

Your Grocer.com

http://www.yourgrocer.com/

★★★★

Bulk online groceries for Manhattan and Connecticut.

A B C D E F G H I J K L M N O P Q R S T U V W X Y Z

GYMNASTICS

GymInfo

http://www.troester.com/gym/

★★★

Check out team rankings, statistics, and rosters for NCAA men's and women's gymnastics teams.

Gymnastics Summer Camp Yellow Pages

http://ascx.com/gcd/

★★★

An alphabetical listing of camps in the United States. Also offers a supplies directory and a link to Magic Melodies Studios for gymnastics music.

gym-routines.com

http://www.gym-routines.com/

★★★

Great site for coaches and gymnasts of every age to check out some actual gymnastics routines from some of the top gymnasts.

⟦Best⟧ Inside Gymnastics Magazine

http://www.insidegymnastics.com/

★★★★★

👥 All

This new gymnastics magazine and website makes its debut in this book as the Best of the Best. Covers all areas of gymnastics, including elite world- and Olympic-level competitions, NCAA, club-level, cheerleading, tumbling, trampoline, acrobatics, and recreational. Every issue of the magazine includes news, event coverage, feature articles, athlete profiles, style, and journal entries. If you're a gymnast, cheerleader, fan, coach, acrobat, or general enthusiast, you don't want to miss an issue! Here you can preview the magazine online, check out the headlines, and even look up past issues.

International Gymnast Online

http://www.intlgymnast.com/

★★★★★

The online version of *International Gymnast Magazine*, which features gymnastics news, information, and competition results from around the world. Read interviews of your favorite gymnasts, check out the message boards, shop for apparel online, flip through the photo galleries, and much more. Very well-done site.

NCAA Men's Gymnastics

http://www.ncaachampionships.com/sports/mgym/

Ⓢ

★★★★

National College Athletic Association official site. Includes schedules, ticket information, TV coverage, records, results, and previews.

NCAA Women's Gymnastics

http://www.ncaachampionships.com/sports/wgym/

★★★★

Official guide to the National College Athletic Association championships. Includes schedule, TV coverage, previews, results, and records.

USA Collegiate Gymnastic Links on the WWW

http://www.ajspancott.com/links.html

★★★

Links to many gymnastics-related sites. You'll find historical information, photos, and results.

USA Gymnastics

http://www.usa-gymnastics.org/

★★★★

 All

The National Governing Body for the sport of gymnastics in the United States, USA Gymnastics records the history of gymnastics, steers its growth, and provides department descriptions and a list of constituent organizations. Here, you'll find an event calendar, information on event tickets and special events, publications, summer camp information, and more. Check out the USA Gymnastics store for apparel and other offerings.

Related Sites
http://www.welwyngymbook.com/

http://www.usgyms.net/index.htm

A
B
C
D
E
F
G
H
I
J
K
L
M
N
O
P
Q
R
S
T
U
V
W
X
Y
Z

A B C D E F G H I J K L M N O P Q R S T U V W X Y Z

HEALTH

AIDS/HIV TREATMENT AND PREVENTION

AIDS Education and Research Trust

http://www.avert.org/

★★★★

14-18

This site contains HIV and AIDS statistics, information for young people, personal stories, a history section, information on becoming infected, a young and gay section, free resources, and lots more. This site can also be translated into several different languages.

AIDSinfo

http://www.aidsinfo.nih.gov/

★★★★

Sponsored by six Public Health Service agencies, this site provides information about federally approved treatment guidelines for HIV and AIDS. Check the What's New page for updates on the latest news on antiretroviral agents, protease inhibitors, and other treatment possibilities. Check the Treatment Information page for history, glossary, current treatment information, and more.

AIDS.ORG

http://www.aids.org/index.html

★★★★

Nonprofit organization that provides AIDS education and prevention programs and essential HIV resources. Here, you can find information about AIDS testing and treatments and join a community of people in supporting AIDS patients, preventing the spread of AIDS, and finding new treatments.

AIDS Outreach Center

http://www.aoc.org

★★★★

This organization, based in Fort Worth, Texas, has one of the most complete resource listings available online for HIV/AIDS. Links are indexed by category and alphabetically for quick access. AOC also offers a variety of services; information on each is available from the website.

The Body: A Multimedia AIDS and HIV Information Resource

http://www.thebody.com/

★★★

In addition to selected coverage of AIDS, HIV, and related issues in the news, this site provides various forums with questions answered by a team of medical experts. Connections to government, commercial, and service sites. Also includes a section with many photos from the thought-provoking Loel A. Poor photographic essay, "AIDS: The Challenge to Educate."

Children with AIDS Project

http://www.aidskids.org/

★★★★

Children with AIDS Project of America is a publicly supported 501(C)(3) nonprofit organization, providing support, care, and adoption programs for children infected with HIV/AIDS. Find details on services and fees, register to become an adoptive parent, and learn how to help the cause.

HIV InSite: Gateway to AIDS Knowledge

`http://hivinsite.ucsf.edu`

★★★

Lots of answers to HIV questions, ranging from basic to more involved and including the latest information on therapies and clinical drug trials.

HIV Stops with Me

`http://www.hivstopswithme.org/`

★★★★★

This site provides an online home for a community of positive people dedicated to preventing the spread of HIV. This site features *spokesmodels*, who express their observations and insights via video or text about the current question of the month and what it's like to live with HIV. You can find articles on a wide range of health and social issues that affect the gay community.

The International Council of AIDS Service Organizations (ICASO)

`http://www.icaso.org/`

★★★

This organization's purpose is to unite and support community-based and nongovernmental AIDS organizations around the world. Emphasis is on support and activity within the community, although international conferences, meetings, and events are listed.

Magic Johnson Foundation, Inc.

`http://www.magicjohnson.org/`

★★★★

👫 14-18

The Magic Johnson Foundation is dedicated to raising money to support organizations that provide HIV/AIDS education, prevention, and care for young people. Information on educational resources, available grants, and ways you can help. Be sure to sign up for the newsletter.

Marty Howard's AIDS Page

`http://www.smartlink.net/~martinjh/`

★★★

Marty Howard is a man living with AIDS. He designed and updates this page to help you find as much HIV/AIDS-related information as possible from one starting place. The links will take you all over the United States and the world to many additional links where information in English can be found. Marty also invites site visitors to chat with him via the AOL Instant Messaging. This excellent site gives a name and face to AIDS.

Project Inform

`http://www.projinf.org/`

★★★★

Project Inform has maintained one primary focus: to remain dedicated to providing free, confidential, and empowering information about HIV/AIDS to anyone who asks, as well as speeding the search for a cure. Project Inform has earned an international reputation as a vocal, active, and effective advocate for the HIV/AIDS community it serves. This comprehensive site provides reliable, up-to-date information. You can also make donations online through secure donation pages.

The Safer Sex Page

`http://www.safersex.org/`

★★★

👫 Not for kids

Safer sex information for everyone (gay/lesbian/bisexual/heterosexual), with an excellent selection of articles on subjects ranging from condoms to counselor information.

A
B
C
D
E
F
G
H
I
J
K
L
M
N
O
P
Q
R
S
T
U
V
W
X
Y
Z

Stop AIDS Project

http://www.stopaids.org/

★★★★

[icon] Not for kids

Based in San Francisco, this organization's aim is to reduce the transmission of HIV and help the community of "self-identified gay and bisexual men." Educational materials and training manuals are free for downloading and adaptation (crediting the site, of course). Calendar of events and meetings, news updates, answers to common questions, an extensive list of resources, and more.

Related Sites

http://www.cdc.gov/hiv/dhap.htm

http://www.unaids.org/

CPR

CPR

http://216.185.112.41/

★★★★

[icon] 14-18

The American Heart Association guidelines and information booklets on CPR methods and technique. Special area for teenagers.

CPR for AIDS Patients

http://www.americanheart.org/presenter.jhtml?identifier=4417

★★★★

You must take some specific precautions when performing CPR on patients with AIDS. This site explains these precautions.

CPR Saves Lives

http://www.jhbmc.jhu.edu/cardiology/rehab/cpr.html

★★★

Everyone needs to know cardiopulmonary resuscitation because it can literally save lives. This short site gives a comprehensive how-to lesson in CPR.

CHILDREN

American Academy of Pediatrics

http://www.aap.org/

★★★★★

Home of the American Academy of Pediatrics, this site is primarily designed for pediatricians, parents, and childcare workers to keep them informed of the latest healthcare issues related to children.

Child Health Guide

http://www.ahcpr.gov/ppip/ppchild.htm

★★★

Online guide that teaches parents how to address the physical health needs of their children. Covers everything from doctors' appointments and immunizations to oral hygiene and tobacco use.

Child Health Research Project

http://www.childhealthresearch.org/

★★★★

Learn the latest about international child health issues and case management tools. This site is primarily for doctors and other healthcare providers and for ministries of health in countries all around the world.

Children's Hospital Boston

http://web1.tch.harvard.edu/

★★★★★

According to a survey by *U.S. News and World Report*, Children's Hospital Boston is the top pediatric healthcare center in the nation, and has been for 13 years straight. This hospital offers "a complete range of healthcare services for children from 15 weeks gestation through 21 years of age (and older in special cases)." The site includes a searchable children's health encyclopedia, specialist locator, list of clinical resources, a map of the facility, and information for healthcare providers.

The Children's Hospital of Philadelphia

http://www.chop.edu/consumer/index.jsp

★★★★

Opened in 1855 as the first hospital devoted exclusively to administering to the healthcare needs of children, the Children's Hospital of Philadelphia continues to be one of the best pediatric healthcare facilities in the world. This site provides useful information for parents and childcare providers about common childhood medical conditions, along with information about the hospital itself.

Children's Hospital and Regional Medical Center, Seattle

http://www.seattlechildrens.org/

★★★★

Since 1907, Children's Hospital and Regional Medical Center has provided healthcare for children in the Pacific Northwestern United States. Children's is "the only regional pediatric referral center devoted to the medical, surgical and developmental needs of children ages birth to 21 in the four-state area of Washington, Alaska, Montana, and Idaho." Visit this site to learn more about the hospital and its staff, programs, and research. You can also access general information about child healthcare issues.

drSpock.com

http://www.drspock.com

★★★★★

Staying in the spirit of world-renowned pediatrician, Dr. Benjamin Spock, this site is dedicated to providing parents with the expert information they need to raise healthy, happy children. Search this site for medical information, product alerts, and parenting advice from some of the world's top experts in childcare.

KidsHealth

http://www.kidshealth.org

★★★★★

👫 All

Created by the medical experts at the Nemours Foundation, KidsHealth has trainloads of information on infections, behavior and emotions, food and fitness, and growing up healthy, as well as cool games and animations! This site is sectioned off into three areas for Parents, Kids, and Teens.

National Institute of Child Health and Human Development

http://www.nichd.nih.gov/

★★★★

👫 All

Primarily provides news and information about the National Institute of Child Health and Human Development, but also provides helpful information for parents on nutrition and care of their children. Features areas designed especially for children that include games and other activities.

Riley Hospital for Children

http://www.rileyhospital.org/

★★★★

👫 All

Located in Indianapolis, Indiana, Riley Hospital for Children is consistently ranked as one of the top children's healthcare facilities in the United States. At this site, you can learn more about the hospital and its pediatricians, find general information about childcare and common childhood diseases, email a patient, and take a virtual tour of the hospital.

St. Jude Children's Research Hospital

http://www2.stjude.org/

★★★★

Located in Memphis, Tennessee, St. Jude Children's Research Hospital is "one of the world's premier centers for research and treatment of catastrophic diseases in children, primarily pediatric cancers." At this site, you can learn about the St. Jude Children's Research Hospital and staff, its research programs, various treatment options, and much more.

Your Child's Health

http://yourchildshealth.echn.ca/

★★★★

👫 0-8

One of three components of the electronic Child Health Network (eCHN), this section contains information about eCHN, its components, and its relationship to the Child Health Network (CHN). Also provides information for parents on common childhood conditions, including potty training, asthma, car safety, tonsillectomy, and more. Special area just for kids teaches them about health and safety issues.

A B C D E F G H I J K L M N O P Q R S T U V W X Y Z

A
B
C
D
E
F
G
H
I
J
K
L
M
N
O
P
Q
R
S
T
U
V
W
X
Y
Z

CRYOGENICS

Alcor

http://www.alcor.org

★★★

Learn more about the possibilities for resuscitation through cryogenics, the process of CryoTransport, and what long life could mean in the future. The Alcor Life Extension Foundation provides information about cryogenics and the opportunity to arrange for cryogenic stasis. This is the facility responsible for preserving the body of baseball great Ted Williams.

Cryogenic Society

http://www.cryogenicsociety.org

★★★

The Cryogenic Society of America, Inc. (CSA) is a nonprofit technical society serving all those interested in any phase of cryogenics. Check out this website to get current information about workshops, seminars, and technology.

Diversified Cryogenics: Cryogenic Tempering

http://www.diversifiedcryogenics.com/

★★★

Company that helps other companies increase the life and performance of their metal products through a process of cryogenic tempering.

Elsevier

http://www.else4.nl/

★★★

Elsevier is the world's leading journal focusing on all aspects of cryoengineering and cryogenics. Papers published cover a wide variety of subjects in low-temperature engineering and research.

Quality Cryogenics, Inc.

http://www.vjpipe.com/

★★★

A leading designer, manufacturer, and installer of custom-engineered piping solutions for the transfer of cryogenic liquids.

DISABILITIES

Ability Online Support Network

http://www.ablelink.org/public/default.htm

★★★

👫 All

An electronic bulletin board that connects young people with disabilities or chronic illnesses to disabled and nondisabled peers and mentors.

ADD Action Group

http://www.addgroup.org/

★★★

Dedicated to helping people with ADD find a variety of solutions for coping with and treating their condition. A helpful FAQ plus some articles on the potential causes and treatments of ADD.

Arkenstone

http://www.arkenstone.org

★★★

Arkenstone is a provider of reading systems for people with visual and reading disabilities. This site offers products for sale, as well as links to other reading-related web pages.

Blind Children's Learning Center, Inc. Home Page

http://www.blindkids.org/

★★★

This nonprofit organization provides resources and assistance to visually impaired children and their families. Offers information on an educational preschool program, family services, the current newsletter, and a calendar of upcoming events. Also lists links to other related sites.

Brain Injury Association

http://www.biausa.org

★★★

Learn more about the anatomy of a brain injury, preventive measures, treatment and rehabilitation, and research being done to correct problems associated with such injuries.

Disability Net

http://www.disabilitynet.co.uk/

★★★★

A nonpolitical service for people with disabilities, run by people with disabilities. Not only can you find information here on travel, money, health, and equipment, but you can also choose and correspond with a pen pal.

iCan Online

http://www.icanonline.net/

★★★★

iCan is an online community for people with disabilities of all types, providing a place to gather information, chat with friends, and learn about others facing similar circumstances.

Job Accommodation Network

http://janweb.icdi.wvu.edu

★★★

Organizations unsure about making their workplace accommodating to people with disabilities might want to spend some time at this site. Here, you can find guidance and ideas for making workplaces more accessible to workers with disabilities.

LD Online

http://www.ldonline.org/

★★★★

 0-8

Leading Web site for parents, teachers, and others to obtain information and resources relating to learning disabilities. Learn the basics, go into more depth, or view Dr. Silver's Q&A list. Features a Kids Zone with some fun activities as well as a discussion forum and a list of agencies and organizations where you can go for help. Links for books and videos point you to Amazon.com, where you can place your order.

Learning Disabilities Association of America

http://www.ldanatl.org

★★★

This nonprofit organization's website seeks to assist individuals and families of people with learning disabilities to improve their general quality of life by providing news, information on research, and networking opportunities.

National Association for Visually Handicapped

http://www.navh.org/

★★★★

People with vision impairment or their caregivers will want to visit this site for information on helpful products, events, and interesting articles. You can also purchase low-vision aids here, from writing aids to reading magnifiers.

National Association of the Deaf

http://www.nad.org/

★★★

Read news about the deaf community, learn about membership in this nonprofit organization, and check out links to other deaf-related sites. New NAD store promises to bring online shopping to the site soon.

Paralyzed Veterans of America

http://www.pva.org

★★★★

This nonprofit organization serves as an advocate for veterans with spinal cord injuries, working to ensure quality healthcare and benefits and to increase opportunities to this group of military heroes.

A B C D E F G H I J K L M N O P Q R S T U V W X Y Z

A B C D E F G H I J K L M N O P Q R S T U V W X Y Z

Tourette Syndrome Association

http://www.tsa-usa.org/

★★★★

 All

TSA gives Tourette Syndrome sufferers and their family and friends a place to turn in moments of crisis. Visit this site to learn how to become a member and receive informative newsletters, medical and scientific updates, discounts on publications and conferences, invitations to local and national events, and more. Some special offerings to teach children and teenagers about Tourette Syndrome.

UCPnet

http://www.ucpa.org/

★★★★

United Cerebral Palsy's site provides information—after you type in your ZIP code—about your local chapter, its mission and activities, FAQs, and grant and research overviews.

World Association of Persons with Disabilities

http://www.wapd.org/

★★★★

WAPD is an activist organization devoted to "advancing the interests of people with disabilities at national, state, local and home levels." Features membership information, a newsletter, chat rooms, a well-stocked directory of resources broken down by disability, and more.

DISEASES AND CONDITIONS

American Lyme Disease Foundation

http://www.aldf.com/

★★★

Information about Lyme Disease, including how to spot early symptoms and general precautions for avoiding ticks—thus avoiding the disease altogether.

Arthritis: Doctor's Guide to the Internet

http://www.pslgroup.com/arthritis.htm

★★★

Medical news and alerts about arthritis. Includes an overview of arthritis and a study of rheumatoid arthritis; and provides links to discussion groups, newsgroups, and other sites that have arthritis-related information.

Association of Cancer Online Resources

http://www.acor.org/

★★★★★

This site offers access to more than 130 electronic mailing lists as well as links to a variety of unique websites. The mailing lists are specifically designed to be public online support groups, providing information and community to more than 60,000 patients, caregivers, or anyone looking for answers about cancer and related disorders.

Cancer Page

http://www.cancerpage.com

★★★

This comprehensive site was created for people struggling with cancer, to provide a place for them to learn about prevention, detection, and treatment of a wide range of types of cancers. In addition to medical information, this site offers an active chat room.

Cardiovascular Institute of the South

http://www.cardio.com/

★★★

Center for the advanced diagnosis and treatment of heart and circulatory disease. Offers a wide range of reports covering the full spectrum of prevention, diagnosis, and nonsurgical and surgical treatment of circulatory problems.

Caring for People with Huntington's Disease

http://www.kumc.edu/hospital/huntingtons/

★★★

Although not intended to be an authoritative work, this page provides valuable information about Huntington's disease. The helpful tips on this page include communication strategies, help for eating and swallowing, and more. Also provides links to other HD sources.

Down Syndrome WWW Page

http://www.nas.com/downsyn/

★★★★★

Information on Down Syndrome, including articles, healthcare guidelines, a worldwide list of organizations, and education resources. The site also features a brag book containing photos of a number of children with the syndrome.

Endometriosis

http://www.ivf.com/endohtml.html

★★★

A variety of information on the puzzling disease, endometriosis, a common cause of infertility. The site includes a lengthy FAQ, case studies, and a number of articles on the subject. A photo gallery is also included.

Eye Diseases and Conditions

http://www.aao.org/

★★★

The American Academy of Ophthalmology has developed a collection of FAQs answering questions about a variety of eye diseases. Here, you can find information about cataracts, glaucoma, amblyopia, and more.

Gastroenterology Consultants

http://www.gastro.com/

★★★

Doctors Peter Gardner and Stuart Waldstreicher provide an informational page about gastroenterology and liver disease, as well as their own practice treating such disorders. You'll find links to descriptions of symptoms, videos of intestinal surgery, facts and statistics on digestive disease, and more patient information.

Introduction to Skin Cancer

http://www.maui.net/~southsky/introto.html

★★★★

Intended as a general introduction to skin cancer, this page provides basic information such as determining what causes skin cancer, what it is, what your personal risks are, and how to reduce those risks.

Jeffrey Modell Foundation

http://www.jmfworld.com/

★★★

The Jeffrey Modell Foundation (JMF) is a nonprofit research foundation devoted to primary immune deficiency, an inherited defect in the immune system. This site provides information about the warning signs, research, news, and updates.

Medicine OnLine

http://meds.com

★★★★

Serves as a commercial online medical information service, providing healthcare professionals and consumers with a convenient place to obtain medical information and serving as a gateway to access other health information services on the Internet. Currently focuses on HIV/AIDS and cancer information.

A
B
C
D
E
F
G
H
I
J
K
L
M
N
O
P
Q
R
S
T
U
V
W
X
Y
Z

A
B
C
D
E
F
G
H
I
J
K
L
M
N
O
P
Q
R
S
T
U
V
W
X
Y
Z

The Merck Manual

http://www.merck.com/pubs/

★★★

A definitive source of information about disease. Topics covered range from infectious diseases to nutritional and metabolic disorders to neurological and psychiatric disorders. The manual has an extensive list of tables and figures, and is very technical in nature. Access to the *Merck Manual of Medical Information*, *Geriatrics*, and *Diagnosis and Therapy* is available via this site.

Muscular Dystrophy Association

http://www.mdausa.org/

★★★★

Learn all about the MDA and what it does to help combat neuromuscular diseases. Also learn what you can do to help besides just watching the Jerry Lewis telethon. Donate online using your credit card.

National Osteoporosis Foundation

http://www.nof.org/

★★★

The NOF seeks to reduce the incidences of osteoporosis by making the public more informed about it. This site provides background information on the disease, information about who's at risk, and prevention and treatment ideas.

National Prostate Cancer Coalition

http://www.4npcc.org/

★★★★★

Includes pages on screening for prostate cancer, understanding diagnoses and treatments, and finding support groups.

NewsRx

http://www.newsrx.com/

★★★

The world's only weekly news dedicated entirely to medical and health news. Headlines and glimpses of the stories are available for free, but to get the full articles, you must subscribe. Sample issues are available.

The Skin (Diseases) Page

http://www.pinch.com/skin/

★★★

The home to archives of various skin disease–related Usenet newsgroups. Also provides descriptions of the various skin diseases and links to other skin-related sites.

StopPain.org

http://www.stoppain.org/

★★★★

Excellent collection of articles and other resources dealing with pain management. Describes the various conditions that often require pain management, including chronic lower back pain, fibromyalgia, headaches, and shingles and provides a list of general treatment options. The site also features a list of frequently asked questions and an area for caregivers and professionals.

Sudden Infant Death Syndrome (SIDS) Information Home Page

http://sids-network.org/

★★★★

Provides information about Sudden Infant Death Syndrome, recent research, and ongoing information sharing among parents who have been affected by the syndrome. You can also make a donation to the SIDS Network through PayPal.

World of Multiple Sclerosis

http://www.ifmss.org.uk/

★★★

FAQs, publications, research, products, services, forums, book reviews, a glossary of terms, and other information of interest to anyone involved in any way with multiple sclerosis.

FITNESS

Aerobics!

http://www.turnstep.com

★★★

This site is designed for step aerobics instructors and contains a FAQ sheet, a library of aerobics patterns, and a calendar of fitness events.

The Blonz Guide to Nutrition, Food Science, and Health

http://blonz.com/

★★★

Authored by Ed Blonz, Ph.D., this site is designed to help you discern the valuable nutrition sites on the Web from those that are mere cyberjunk. The page provides many links to the sites that are considered the best and is also available in a version that contains frames and Java.

Food and Nutrition Information Center

http://www.nalusda.gov/fnic/

★★★

Provides information about healthy eating, dietary guidelines, food labeling, and other nutritional information. Contains links to many nutritional sites.

IFIC Foundation

http://www.ific.org

★★★

The home page of the International Food Information Council. Provides information for health professionals, educators, parents, and consumers. Includes FAQs and other publications.

Mirkin Report

http://www.drmirkin.com/

★★★★

Breakthroughs in health, fitness, nutrition, and sexuality are covered at this site. Dr. Mirkin's radio broadcasts are also available for listening each day, and you can also purchase Dr. Mirkin's books, CDs, and videos through the secure server.

Nutricise

http://www.nutricise.com/

★★★

Nutricise is weight-loss and fitness program designed to help people get in shape and stay in shape. Nutricise takes a holistic approach that addresses nutrition, fitness, behavior, and lifestyle issues and tailors the program to the individual's needs. Here you can learn more about the program and sign up to become a client, but you won't find many freebies.

NutriGenie

http://members.aol.com/nutrigenie/home.html

★★★

A nutrition software publisher, including titles for weight loss, disease and nutrition, high blood pressure, heart disease, special diets, sports, allergies, and much more. Also includes other health-related sites and information for downloading.

Peak Performance

http://www.siteworks.co.uk/pperf/

★★★

Peak Performance is a scientific newsletter devoted to improving stamina, strength, and fitness. It presents high-quality information on the latest sports science research from around the world and shows you how to apply it. Read these exclusive extracts for yourself at this comprehensive site or subscribe to the newsletter to keep abreast of the latest performance-boosting products and techniques.

Walking for Fitness

http://walking.about.com/

★★★★

This site is a jam-packed resource of recreational walking tips and hints. You can find information about the correct type of walking shoes, the importance of staying hydrated, and walking/diet plans.

A B C D E F G H I J K L M N O P Q R S T U V W X Y Z

A
B
C
D
E
F
G
H
I
J
K
L
M
N
O
P
Q
R
S
T
U
V
W
X
Y
Z

GENERAL RESOURCES

AMA Health Insight

http://www.ama-assn.org/ama/pub/category/3457.html

★★★

Find out more about general health issues, learn more about specific conditions you're experiencing—such as back pain or indigestion—or create a custom personal health history and gather information related to your situation. This site was created to help improve the doctor-patient collaboration by providing consumers with access to more medical information. A great starting point for information about good health.

amIhealthy.com

http://www.amihealthy.com/

★★★

Log in to take various online surveys to determine your level of health or whether you are at risk for developing certain conditions.

Brain.com

http://www.brain.com/

⑤

★★★★

Take the five-minute IQ test and find out how you compare to people of the same age, or learn more about other aspects of your brain, such as your memory. You can also buy brain-enhancing products and get information on brain functioning.

eCureMe Self Diagnosis

http://www.ecureme.com/

⑤

★★★★

Answer a few questions to obtain a diagnosis online. Site also features general health resources, including a medical encyclopedia, health charts, and information about prescription medications and treatments.

Healthtouch

http://www.healthtouch.com/

★★★

Provides updates on health, diseases, and wellness and illness; a resource directory guide to organizations and government agencies; access to pharmacies in your community; and a drug search program that enables you to find information about prescription and over-the-counter drugs.

Healthy Ideas

http://www.prevention.com

★★★★★

Prevention's Healthy Ideas is stocked with herbal remedies, vitamin databases, alternative medicine news, advice from naturopathic doctors, and interactive forums. Check weekly for new features on women's health.

Healthy Ontario

http://www.healthyontario.com/

★★★★★

This Canadian health site is a great resource for individuals, families, and healthcare professionals to research health concerns, medications, treatment options, and preventions. Special areas for children, men, women, and seniors. Also features a page for looking up various conditions and locating health services in Canada.

MayoClinic.com

http://www.mayoclinic.com/

★★★★★

This is the website of the famed Mayo Clinic in Rochester, Minnesota. Here, you can look up information on a range of subjects from allergies to cancer to digestive issues and more, or you can catch up on the latest medical news.

Medscape

http://www.medscape.com

★★★★

Targeted at healthcare professionals, this site offers journal articles, up-to-date research, and daily summaries, as well as access to articles, discussions, images, and self-assessment tools.

Minority Health Network

http://www.pitt.edu/~ejb4/min/

★★★

Lists minority health resources by minority group, subject, and disease. Also includes lists of upcoming events and publications.

MSN Health

http://www.health.msn.com

★★★

Search for medical news and articles, find out the latest thinking in various treatments and preventive measures, and chat with others about issues on your mind, such as diabetes, hypertension, or whatever is the topic of the day.

National Safety Council

http://www.nsc.org/

★★★★

Information at this site is focused on preventing accidents, such as those involving cars and other machinery. You'll find a phone number you can call to report someone who routinely lets his or her children ride without a seat belt. And you can learn more about preventing injuries from everyday situations, such as using lotion to reduce the chance of skin cancer.

Quackwatch

http://www.quackwatch.com

★★★★

Skeptical that the claims made by a product are untrue? Heard unbelievable information about a medical procedure or practice? Check out this site to learn more about medical frauds and to find out how to recognize one in the future. You can also report fraudulent activity here.

WebMD

http://www.webmd.com

★★★★★

You'll find articles, news, and tips for improving your health and well-being. Searchable database packed with information, including definitions of diseases, prescription information, and treatments. A comprehensive encyclopedia of health and medicine.

World Health Network

http://www.worldhealth.net/

★★★★

Dedicated to health, vitality, and longevity. Contains information on anti-aging, nutrition and exercise, and traditional and alternative healthcare.

Your Surgery

http://www.yoursurgery.com/index.cfm

★★★

Before you go under the knife you'll want to visit this site to learn more about a procedure. You can read about it, hear how it's done, and watch animated images of exactly what will occur during your surgery. Then again, you might want to avoid this site.

HEALTHCARE

ACHE: American College of Healthcare Executives

http://www.ache.org/

★★★

A professional membership society for healthcare executives. Offers publications, policy statements, and educational programs. Ask the Expert section regularly hosts leading specialists who can field any specific questions you might have.

Achoo Gateway to Healthcare

http://www.achoo.com/

★★★★

Comprehensive, searchable directory of healthcare websites designed to help doctors, patients, and healthcare providers track down the information they need.

A B C D E F G H I J K L M N O P Q R S T U V W X Y Z

A
B
C
D
E
F
G
H
I
J
K
L
M
N
O
P
Q
R
S
T
U
V
W
X
Y
Z

Best Aetna InteliHealth

http://www.intelihealth.com/

★★★★★

This is a comprehensive and easy-to-navigate site that covers all aspects of human health, including health for children, men, women, and seniors. Site is organized into four sections: Diseases & Conditions, Healthy Lifestyles, Your Health, and Look It Up. Special features include health commentaries, dental health, a drug resource center, ask the expert, and interactive tools. Great site to bookmark for all your health needs and concerns.

American Physical Therapy Association

http://www.apta.org/

★★★★

A national professional organization representing more than 64,000 physical therapists across the nation, this group's goal is "to foster advancements in physical therapy practice, research, and education." Calendar of events, continuing education resources, information about practicing physical therapy, a list of FAQs, and much more make this a valuable site for any physical therapist. Also provides some job leads.

Aspen Publishers, Inc.

http://www.aspenpub.com/

$

★★★★

For more than 40 years, Aspen Publishers has served the needs of legal, business, and health-care professionals with timely books, periodicals, and information services by leading authorities. You can find product reviews here, as well as browse and order from the extensive publishing list.

Center for Rural Health and Social Service Development

http://www.siu.edu/~crhssd/

★★★

Seeks to bring together university resources and healthcare agencies to address health concerns. The center conducts research and training, tests new models of healthcare delivery, and develops policy recommendations to improve the health of rural populations.

Chiropractic Online

http://www.chiro-online.com/dcaddfr.html

★★★

Chiropractic OnLine Today offers two interactive forums and one chat area for posting questions and/or commentary, and can help in opening up discussions in the areas of chiropractic and healthcare.

Colorado HealthSite

http://www.coloradohealthsite.org/

★★★

Provides information on chronic illnesses, complementary therapies, healthcare plans, and state and federal agencies.

Health Economics

http://www.healtheconomics.com/

★★★★

Lists national and international links to biotech firms, medical libraries, journals, employment opportunities, and health databases.

Healthcare Information and Management Systems Society

http://www.himss.org/

★★★

A not-for-profit organization dedicated to promoting a better understanding of healthcare information and management systems.

InfoHealth Management Corp.

http://www.infohealth.net/

★★★

Consulting and support services for those in the healthcare industry. Develops software-solutions to help healthcare professionals provide better treatment for their patients in a more cost-effective manner. Also provides support for networking and Internet-related issues that healthcare providers face.

MedMarket.com

http://www.medmarket.com/

★★★

Provides a database of medical product sales and technical information for healthcare providers. Many links to retail sites.

National Institutes of Health

http://www.nih.gov/

★★★★★

The U.S. Department of Health and Human Services National Institutes of Health provides an often overlooked goldmine of health information for healthcare providers and consumers alike. Here you can find information on the latest proven treatments for a wide variety of conditions, learn about clinical trials and alternative treatment options, find health hotlines and prescription drug information, and much more. This site also features information about grants, the latest news and events, scientific resources, and visitor information.

Prior Health Sciences Laboratory

http://bones.med.ohio-state.edu

★★★★

As part of Ohio State University, this site (formerly BONES, Biometrically Oriented Navigator of Electronic Services) provides faculty, staff, and students in the health sciences with a starting point for Internet exploration. Databases, articles, and reference materials are available at this site.

Quackwatch.com

http://www.quackwatch.org/

★★★★★

Have you ever read a health article or had a friend suggest a remedy that sounded too good to be true? Then check it out at Quackwatch.com before you shell out any money or risk your health to try it. Here you will find a skeptical friend to help you sort out what's true from what is not when it comes to your physical well-being.

Society for Medical Decision Making

http://www.smdm.org/

★★★★★

Focuses on promoting rational and systematic approaches to decisions about health policy and the clinical care of patients. Includes decision analysis, applications of quantitative methods in clinical settings and medical research, studies of human cognition and the psychology of clinical reasoning, medical ethics, medical informatics and decision making, artificial intelligence, evaluation of medical practices, and cost-effectiveness or cost-benefit assessments.

SPA in Italy

http://www.travel.it/ter/teren.htm

★★★★

Promotes the belief that the natural hot springs in Italy can bring relief from every type of problem, from allergies to metabolism to stress.

HEALTH INSURANCE

AFLAC

http://www.aflac.com/

★★★

Provides guaranteed renewable supplemental health insurance. Get information on insurance options, locate an agent near you, and learn about the company at this site.

HealthInsuranceFinders.com

http://www.healthinsurancefinders.com/

★★★★★

When you don't know where to look for health, dental, life, or travel insurance, go to HealthInsuranceFinders.com to get some suggestions. Here, you can obtain quotes from several top providers.

Related Sites
http://www.insure.com/
http://www.health-medical-insurance-company.com/

A B C D E F G H I J K L M N O P Q R S T U V W X Y Z

A
B
C
D
E
F
G
H
I
J
K
L
M
N
O
P
Q
R
S
T
U
V
W
X
Y
Z

International Medical Group

http://www.imglobal.com/

★★★

Provides medical insurance to individuals, families, and groups who are living or traveling abroad.

Related Site
http://www.medibroker.com/

PacifiCare

http://www.pacificare.com/

★★★

This site is geared to anyone who wants to assess his or her own health or learn more about HMOs.

INSTITUTES

Arkansas Children's Hospital

http://www.ach.uams.edu/

★★★★

 All

Private, nonprofit institution. Offers children comprehensive medical care from birth to age 21. Available to every county in Arkansas and many nearby states, regardless of a family's ability to pay. Special area for kids because it addresses health and safety issues.

Catholic Health Association

http://www.chausa.org

★★★

Nonprofit association that represents more than 2,000 Catholic health care sponsors, systems, facilities, and related organizations. CHA unites members to advance selected strategic issues that are best addressed together, rather than as individual organizations. The site provides information about the association's purpose, educational programming, newsletters, and ethical information.

Dartmouth's Interactive Media Lab

http://iml.dartmouth.edu/

★★★

Part of the Dartmouth Medical School. Specializes in using computers, media, and communications technologies for medical simulations.

Missouri Institute of Mental Health

http://www.mimh.edu/

★★★

Highlights the research, education, and multimedia efforts with which the Missouri Institute of Mental Health is currently involved.

New England Medical Center

http://www.nemc.org/home/

★★★

Provides information about the tradition and history of the prestigious New England Medical Center, which offers comprehensive inpatient and outpatient care for adults and children. You can also keep up to date with the New England Medical Center's weekly newsletter as well as the latest news from Tufts.

OSHA (Occupational Safety and Health Administration)

http://www.osha.gov

★★★★

OSHA establishes and enforces protective standards and offers technical assistance to protect the American workplace. Research, reports, and worker safety announcements can be found on this site.

Radiation Effects Research Foundation

http://www.rerf.or.jp/

★★★

Dedicated to studying the effects of the atomic bombings of Hiroshima and Nagasaki during World War II to enable people to better understand the effects of radiation from atomic bombs and other sources.

MEDICAL HISTORY

Historical Center for the Health Sciences (HCHS)

http://www.med.umich.edu/medschool/chm/

★★★

Based at the University of Michigan, this site contains archival, manuscript, and museum materials; images of documents, photographs, graphic art, and artifacts; exhibits and galleries on special topics; educational products; and online assistance.

Images from the History of Medicine

http://wwwihm.nlm.nih.gov/

★★★

National Library of Medicine's exhibit of more than 60,000 images dealing with the history of medicine.

Indiana Medical History Museum

http://www.imhm.org/

★★★

Central Indiana Hospital's Pathology Building, originally a facility for research and physician education, has been transformed into a unique historic structure that houses the Indiana Medical History Museum. Take a virtual tour of the museum and learn about its featured exhibits.

TRAVEL RESOURCES

Center for Disease Control: Travel Health

http://www.cdc.gov/travel/

★★★★★

Are you planning a trip abroad? Then check out this site before you go to determine whether you need to be aware of any diseases you may encounter on your trip and recommended vaccines or medicines you should obtain before you leave.

Gimponthego.com

http://www.gimponthego.com

★★★★★

Pick up travel tips for disabled individuals on the go and hear hotel/motel and restaurant feedback from people who've visited. Find out which chains are the best in terms of wheelchair accessibility.

Outdoor Action Guide to High Altitude Acclimatization and Illness

http://www.princeton.edu/~oa/safety/altitude.html

★★★

Sponsored by Princeton University, this page discusses symptoms, the causes of high-altitude illnesses, and ways to prevent them. Also covers the different types of illnesses.

OutdoorEd.com

http://www.outdoored.com/articles/default.asp

★★★

This page is sponsored by the Outdoor Action Program at Princeton University. It covers workshops and conferences and lists first-aid resources for planning a wilderness trip.

Travel Medicine

http://healthlink.mcw.edu/travel-medicine/

★★★

Includes tips on traveling while pregnant and packing a travel medicine kit, lists environmental hazards such as altitude and motion sickness and auto accidents, and gives an overview of different diseases and vaccinations.

HERBS

The Banyan Tree

http://www.healthlibrary.com/reading/banyan1/index.htm

★★★★

Huge online textbook covering holistic health practices. The online HELP navigation system is a medical search system, developed and based in India. If you're looking for something specific in the natural or holistic healing genre, this site is for you.

A
B
C
D
E
F
G
H
I
J
K
L
M
N
O
P
Q
R
S
T
U
V
W
X
Y
Z

A
B
C
D
E
F
G
H
I
J
K
L
M
N
O
P
Q
R
S
T
U
V
W
X
Y
Z

Digestive System

http://www.healthy.net/hwlibrarybooks/hoffman/digestive/digest.htm

★★★★

This site offers a varied and comprehensive look at alternative medicines and herbal therapies for treating and curing digestive ailments. Shop for everything here, from teas to eyedrops.

Food and Nutrition

http://www.holisticmed.com/food.html

★★★

Great resource explaining how to start eating a more natural diet. This site offers information on how to shop for a healthier diet, makes suggestions on what foods to cut out or increase, and features a detailed question-and-answer section.

Harvest Moon Health Foods

http://www.harvesthealth.com/

★★★★

This site features online shopping for vitamins, minerals, herbs, and specialty health items. Check here for the latest deals.

Henriette's Herbal Home Page

http://www.ibiblio.org/herbmed/

★★★

Henriette has the best FAQs for medicinal herbs on the Net. This site is absolutely huge and very informative. Check out the culinary herb FAQ while you are here.

Herb Research Foundation: Herbs and Herbal Medicine for Health

http://www.herbs.org/

★★★★

This nonprofit foundation studies the use of herbs in health, environmental conservation, and international development. Provides frequently updated links to the latest herb-related news, features, information, and other related sites. You can also join and subscribe to the foundation's magazine.

Herb.org

http://www.herbnet.com/

★★★★

For anything herb-related, you'll want to stop here. Read the herb magazine that is posted the first Monday of each month and learn more about the healing properties of various herbs. Comprehensive Herbalpedia has information on just about every herb you might encounter.

Herbal Alternatives

http://www.herbalalternatives.com/

★★★★

You'll find up-to-date information on herbs, vitamins, and alternative medicine that can ease the effects of menopause, among other topics. Online shopping from this site planned in the near future.

Herbal Encyclopedia

http://www.naturalark.com/herbenc.html

★★★★★

Search for information on a particular type of medicinal herb by clicking on the appropriate letter, or start by reading short articles on how to use herbs, how to collect and store them, and more. A complete herb site with an appropriate cautionary warning up front about the proper use of herbs.

Herbs First

http://www.herbsfirst.com/

★★★★

This site strives to educate people on the proper use of herbs. Also offers high-quality, affordable herbal health food products, books, videos, and tapes.

Herbs and Pregnancy

http://www.gardenguides.com/herbs/preg.htm

★★★

This site provides specific suggestions for the use of herbs to lessen discomfort associated with pregnancy, delivery, and postpartum issues; it also provides a list of herbs to avoid while pregnant. Interesting information, but consult your physician first.

Related Site
http://pregnancytoday.com/reference/articles/herbspreg.htm

Hilton Herbs

http://www.hiltonherbs.com/

★★★

Promotes the use of natural herbal healthcare for horses and dogs. Includes aromatherapy, homeopathy, and phytotherapy pages as well.

Inner Self: Herbal Guide

http://www.innerself.com/Magazine/Herbs/HERBS_and_THEIR_USES.htm

★★★

Click on an herb name and find out about its medicinal benefits. You can also read articles about herbs and holistic health, as well as buy products at a discount from linked retailers.

Medicinal Herbs Online

http://www.egregore.com/

★★★

The Medicinal Herbs Online site was created to help educate visitors about the often forgotten wisdom in the old ways of treating illnesses.

Moonrise Herbs

http://moonriseherbs.com/

★★★

This site promotes a complete lifestyle in balance with the cycles of nature. The goal is to use herbs and natural products to aid the healing process. Customer satisfaction is guaranteed. Links to a retail site where you can buy herbal products, books, and more.

PlanetHerbs

http://www.planetherbs.com/

★★★

Dr. Michael Tierra combines the best of Eastern with Western herbalism and more. You can learn about herbal therapies here, as well as keep updated on workshops and seminars. Purchase items from magnets to herbal compounds.

Related Sites
http://nature.webshed.com/
http://www.richters.com/
http://world.std.com/~krahe/

Reference Guide for Herbs

http://www.realtime.net/anr/herbs.html

★★★

Quick, short, user-friendly information on selected herbs.

Rocky Mountain Herbal Institute

http://www.rmhiherbal.org/

★★★

A wealth of information and education on herbs based around traditional Chinese medicine.

Spiritual Herbal Medicine for Healing

http://home.switchboard.com/herbalspirit

★★★

Honoring the healing energy of our medicinal plant relatives, this site offers herbal information and an herbal tip of the week.

The Whole Herb Company

http://www.wholeherbcompany.com/

★★★

The Whole Herb Company prides itself on superior quality botanical herbs. Check out the company and its products at this site.

A
B
C
D
E
F
G
H
I
J
K
L
M
N
O
P
Q
R
S
T
U
V
W
X
Y
Z

HISTORY

American and British History Resources

http://www.libraries.rutgers.edu/rul/rr_gateway/research_guides/history/history.shtml

★★★

Annotated directory of scholarly resources of American and British history available on the Internet.

American Memory

http://memory.loc.gov/

★★★★★

👫 All

The Library of Congress' American Memory provides access to "primary source materials relating to the history and culture of the United States." 100 collections feature more than 7 million artifacts in digital format. You can explore the site by selecting one of the collections, searching for a specific item or topic, or choosing any of several guided lessons. The home page also features a link to learn a historical event that happened on this day. Another link gives you quick access to the site's FAQs list.

Ancient Greece at the World History Compass

http://www.worldhistorycompass.com/greece.htm

★★★★

Search for information about ancient Greek literature, art, and culture. Huge directory of links to other resources on Athens, Archimedes, medicine, art, architecture, astronomy, mathematics, and much more.

Art History Resources on the Web

http://witcombe.sbc.edu/ARTHLinks.html

★★★★

Find out all you need to know about prehistoric, ancient, middle ages, baroque, renaissance, eighteenth, nineteenth, and twentieth century art at this site, which also features information on museums and galleries, as well as links to other art history sites. A well-done site for anyone researching art history.

Avalon Project

http://www.yale.edu/lawweb/avalon/avalon.htm

★★★★

Digital documents relevant to the fields of law, history, and diplomacy.

Biography

http://www.biography.com

💲

★★★★★

👫 All

Learn more about the backgrounds of your favorite historical figures or celebrities; they're all profiled here on the Biography site, which also includes information on the TV show and magazine of the same name. Many of the *Biography* television shows are available on videotape and are for sale at this site.

CIA History for Kids

http://www.cia.gov/cia/ciakids/

★★★★★

👫 All

Maintained by the United States Central Intelligence Agency, this site provides a behind-the-scenes look at the history and development of the CIA. It also provides some fun stuff for kids, including a challenge to break a secret code and solve puzzles.

Computer History Museum

http://www.computerhistory.org/

★★★

Learn about the history of computers from 1945 to 1990. Check the historical timeline, learn about its collections and exhibits, and find out about upcoming events.

Conversations with History

http://globetrotter.berkeley.edu/conversations

★★★★

Important figures in recent history, including politicians, diplomats, news professionals, authors, and more, are featured in unedited interviews conducted in past years. Search the database of interviews by name, profession, topic, or other keyword.

EyeWitness to History

http://www.eyewitnesstohistory.com/

★★★★★

Read eyewitness experiences of historical events, sorted by date, to get a better idea of what life was like during specific time periods. Covers everything from ancient history to World War II and features snapshots, audio recordings of voices from the past, an index and the EyeWitness Store. Very cool site that's easy to navigate and packed with interesting, first-hand historical reports.

The Halifax Explosion

http://www.cbc.ca/halifaxexplosion/

★★★★★

On December 6, 1917, the world witnessed one of the largest and most devastating man-made explosions it had ever seen—the Halifax Explosion, leaving nearly 2,000 people dead and 9,000 injured. Visit this site to experience some of the horror of that day and see what survivors have to say about it.

History Channel

http://www.historychannel.com

★★★★★

 All

Select a decade back to 1800 and search for information on events during that time period at this site. Read articles about historical events, find out about upcoming TV reports on the History Channel, and chat with other history buffs. Don't miss the History Channel store; see what books and videotapes are available for purchase. Also features guides for history teachers.

History House

http://www.historyhouse.com

★★★

A history site devoted to digging up and reporting the dirt of historical events and characters, helping to make history come alive. Search the archives for past articles and stay tuned for more interesting historical trivia.

History Net

http://history.about.com/

★★★★

A huge site full of information on ancient history, U.S. history, historical personalities, events, eyewitness accounts, and more. Hefty collection of links to other sites as well.

History of Ancient Egypt

http://www.cofc.edu/~piccione/index.html

★★★

Collection of materials for the study of ancient Egypt, compiled for a course at Northwestern University. This site also offers a number of corresponding and related sites.

History of Medicine

http://wwwihm.nlm.nih.gov/

★★★

Nearly 60,000 images, including portraits, pictures of institutions, caricatures, genre scenes, and graphic art in a variety of media, illustrating the social and historical aspects of medicine.

A
B
C
D
E
F
G
H
I
J
K
L
M
N
O
P
Q
R
S
T
U
V
W
X
Y
Z

A
B
C
D
E
F
G
H
I
J
K
L
M
N
O
P
Q
R
S
T
U
V
W
X
Y
Z

History of Photography

http://www.rleggat.com/photohistory/

★★★★

Information on some of the most significant processes used during the early days of photography, in addition to pen-portraits of many of the most important photographers of the period.

History Matters

http://historymatters.gmu.edu/

★★★★★

👥 14-18

Developed by the American Social History Project/Center for Media & Learning, City University of New York, and the Center for History and New Media, George Mason University, this site provides resources for high school and college-level history teachers. Provides sample syllabi, reference texts, teaching materials, and links to dozens of other resources on the Web. Whether you teach history for a living or just enjoy studying it, this is a fantastic site.

History On-Line

http://www.history.ac.uk/

★★★★

Developed by the Institute of Historical Research (IHR), this site is devoted to "promoting high quality resources for the teaching and learning of history in the UK." Here, you can learn about the Institute for Historical Research, search History On-Line, or check out a useful collection of links to resources on researching and teaching specific topics.

History Place

http://www.historyplace.com

★★★

👥 14-18

Find images, documents, speeches, and more historical information compiled for students and educators, but available to anyone. Students can come here to get help with their history homework.

History of the Web

http://www.w3.org/History.html

★★★

A chronological history of the World Wide Web from 1945 through 1995. Check out the related links for a more complete view of how the Web took shape.

⌜Best⌝ HyperHistory

http://www.hyperhistory.com/online_n2/History_n2/a.html

★★★★★

Comprehensive guide to the last 3,000 years of world history, this ever-growing tome attempts to provide a balanced view of history, covering not only wars and political events, but also scientific, cultural, and religious facets. A 116-chapter book by Frank A. Smitha provides a more cohesive view of world history. Innovative navigational tools make it easy to move through this Best of the Best site.

Related Site

http://www.hyperhistory.com/

Irish History on the Web

http://larkspirit.com/history/

★★★★

Irish History on the Web provides a unique resource for anyone interested in learning about or researching a wide variety of Irish history topics. Like a sourcebook, most of the links found here will lead to primary documents, original essays, bibliographies, or specific informational sites.

Media History Project

http://www.mediahistory.umn.edu/

★★★★★

Promoting the study of media history from petroglyphs to pixels, the goal of this site is to encourage media historians to use and learn from the Internet—to consider this particular area both a gateway to useful information and an entrance to a laboratory.

NASA History Office

http://www.hq.nasa.gov/office/pao/History/
index.html

★★★

Documents tracing U.S. space exploration from the National Aeronautics and Space Administration.

National Security Archive

http://www.gwu.edu/~nsarchiv/

★★★★★

For those interested in the history of U.S. foreign policy, this site provides a gold mine of declassified National Security documents—more than 2 million pages in over 200 collections.

National Trust for Historic Preservation

http://www.nthp.org/

★★★

Opportunities to learn about the latest preservation issues. This site lists the 11 most endangered historical sites and offers you a way to help preserve these sites through your donation. Information is also available on how to make a positive impact by doing more than just providing a donation of money.

National Women's History Project

http://www.nwhp.org/

★★★★

Committed to providing education, promotional materials, and informational services to recognize and celebrate women's contributions to society.

Smithsonian Natural History Museum

http://www.mnh.si.edu/

★★★★★

 All

The National Museum of Natural History is part of the Smithsonian Institution in Washington, D.C., and is dedicated to understanding the natural world and our place in it. This site provides an abundance of online resources about the natural sciences. Be sure to spend a few minutes browsing the online store at smithsonianstore.com!

Smithsonian National Museum of American History

http://americanhistory.si.edu/

★★★★★

 All

The National Museum of American History is part of the Smithsonian Institution in Washington, D.C. Here, you can check out many of the museum's most popular exhibits online, including the history of the presidency and the *Star Spangled Banner*; visit the music room, to learn about musical performances at the museum; and check out the timeline of United States history.

Today in History

http://memory.loc.gov/ammem/today/today.html

★★★

Learn about significant historical events that happened in the past on today's date.

Women's History

http://womenshistory.about.com/

★★★★

Highlights women's achievements in all fields of endeavor. Learn the history of suffrage and abortion rights, meet the First Ladies, encounter the goddesses and female legends of history, and read articles about some of the most notable female figures in history. Powered by the History Net and hosted by About.com.

HISTORICAL DOCUMENTS AND LANDMARKS

AMDOCS—Documents for the Study of American History

http://www.ukans.edu/carrie/docs/amdocs_index.html

★★★★

Select from a vast collection of documents related to U.S. history dating from the fifteenth century to the present. Included are excerpts from Christopher Columbus's journal to George W. Bush's inauguration speech.

A B C D E F G H I J K L M N O P Q R S T U V W X Y Z

A
B
C
D
E
F
G
H
I
J
K
L
M
N
O
P
Q
R
S
T
U
V
W
X
Y
Z

American Memory

http://lcweb2.loc.gov/

★★★

👫 All

This site is part of the National Digital Library Program, which is an effort to digitize and deliver electronically the distinctive, historical Americana holdings at the Library of Congress, including photographs, manuscripts, rare books, maps, recorded sound, and moving pictures. Here, you can view maps, images, and materials related to our country's history.

Black Heritage Trail

http://www.afroammuseum.org/trail.htm

★★★

Details of the famous walking tour that explores the history of Boston's early African-American community—with text and map. The trail consists of 14 sites, all located in the Beacon Hill area.

California State Historical Landmarks

http://www.donaldlaird.com/landmarks/

★★★★

This site is named a Recommended Site by the History Channel. Visit more than 1,000 California historical landmarks or use the site's search engine to see your favorite historical California landmark. The author has photographed many of them and has been to more than 900 of the sites already.

A Chronology of U.S. Historical Documents

http://www.law.ou.edu/hist/

★★★★

A huge list of historical documents in chronological order, with explanations of the significance of each.

Ellis Island—Through America's Gateway

http://www.internationalchannel.com/education/ellis

★★★★

👫 All

Learn about the history of New York's Ellis Island, the people who arrived in the United States through it, and how it shaped our country.

Emily Dickinson Homestead

http://www.dickinsonhomestead.org/

★★★

Home of Emily Dickinson, a National Historic Landmark owned by the Trustees of Amherst College. Dickinson wrote most of her poems and letters while living at the homestead.

EuroDocs: Western European Primary Historical Documents

http://library.byu.edu/~rdh/eurodocs/

★★★

Search this database of European historical documents by country. Within each listing, the documents are posted chronologically. The items help to explain the significance of the historical happenings of the times.

European Walking Tours

http://gorptravel.gorp.com/xnet/picks.tcl?destination=101

★★★

Take a walking tour and see historic landmarks in Italy, Austria, Finland, Lapland, Norway, Scotland, England, Switzerland, Canada, Yellowstone, and the Beartooths. Brochures are available upon request.

Frank Lloyd Wright Building Guide

http://www.geocities.com/SoHo/1469/flwbuild.html

★★★

This site lists more than 420 buildings designed by the great architect Frank Lloyd Wright. The index lists the buildings by region and state. You'll find links for individual buildings and the most notable buildings.

Frank Lloyd Wright Home and Studio

http://www.wrightplus.org/

★★★★★

 All

Take a tour of Frank Lloyd Wright's home and studio. He and his family lived there from 1898 to 1909. See where the Prairie School of Architecture was born. Check out where Wright experimented with designs in his home and studio before he shared them with clients. If you're in the Oak Park, Illinois, area, you can visit the house in person; the site lists the tour hours.

George Washington's Mount Vernon

http://www.mountvernon.org

★★★

Tour, archaeological, membership, and lesson-plan information about the home of the first president of the United States.

Guggenheim Museum

http://www.guggenheim.org

★★★★★

 14-18

Read about the New York museum's history and architecture; its numerous programs, including tours; upcoming exhibitions; ways to become a member and all the benefits of membership; and the museum store, where you can buy art books, gifts, jewelry, children's books and toys, and signature Guggenheim products. Also available is information on the other four international museum locations.

Hearst Castle

http://www.hearstcastle.org

★★★

14-18

Once the home of newspaper publisher William Randolph Hearst, today a state historical monument in the Santa Lucia Mountains of California.

Henry Ford Estate: Fair Lane

http://www.umd.umich.edu/fairlane/

★★★★

Visit the estate of automotive pioneer Henry Ford. You can take a virtual tour of the estate and visit the beautiful rooms. If you're in the Dearborn, Michigan, area, you can visit the estate in person; check out the list of tour times. Christmas is a special time at Fair Lane, with activities for the whole family, including Ginger Bread House making, breakfast with Santa, tea, a sumptuous traditional Christmas dinner, and a candlelight tour. Be sure to check out the new gift shop page for books, jewelry, and gifts.

History Web Sites

http://www.msubillings.edu/history/Historysites.htm

★★★

Includes historical sites, history information, world history, European history, Asian history, American history, the seven wonders, world events, and world history sites.

House of the Seven Gables

http://www.7gables.org/

★★★

This historic site, the inspiration for Nathaniel Hawthorne's novel, is located on Salem Harbor (16 miles north of Boston, Massachusetts), and constitutes its own national historic district with a collection of six houses on The National Register of Historic Places.

Thomas Jefferson's Monticello

http://www.monticello.org/

★★★

All

This site offers historical facts and information on visiting Jefferson's beautiful home, now a museum in the Virginia Piedmont.

A
B
C
D
E
F
G
H
I
J
K
L
M
N
O
P
Q
R
S
T
U
V
W
X
Y
Z

Mount Rushmore

http://www.travelsd.com/parks/rushmore/

★★★

 All

History of the sculpture, current and historical pictures, and tourist information.

National Archives

http://www.nara.gov

★★★

Citizens can access significant documents, such as speeches, reports, and proof of our rights, in the form of governmental decrees and documents. The National Archives is the organization responsible for maintaining public access to these national treasures. This site also features some useful classroom resources for teachers.

National Civil Rights Museum

http://www.civilrightsmuseum.org

★★★

 All

Virtual tour of exhibits of the museum located on the site of Martin Luther King, Jr.'s assassination in Memphis.

National Parks and Monuments

http://www.nps.gov/

★★★★

Information on the United States national parks and monuments. Pick a park to learn about its main attractions and the history of the park, or print out a tour guide.

The National Parks Service Links to the Past

http://www.cr.nps.gov/

★★★

Learn about the Civil War, visit historical sites, find out about historical lighthouses and preserved vessels, read about the Native American Graves Protection and Repatriation Act, and learn about the National Park Services Tribal Preservation Program. Find out about tax credits and grants related to historic preservation.

Oyster Bay Historical Society

http://www.servenet.com/OBHistory/

★★★

This Long Island–based site lists plenty of activities for everyone. Read about the museum's hands-on tour for children, where they can visit Oyster Bay in the eighteenth and nineteenth centuries and see how early residents lived. Under construction is a railroad museum and rail excursions on restored Long Island Rail Road Locomotive #35. If you visit the museum in person, you might see the ghost of Teddy Roosevelt in the library.

San Francisco Architectural Heritage

http://www.sfheritage.org

★★★★

San Francisco Heritage is the historical preservation society for San Francisco. Landmarks are nominated, and architectural assistance is given for preservation topics. Pictures and descriptions of architectural styles are provided.

Santa Cruz Beach Boardwalk

http://www.beachboardwalk.com/

★★★

Check out upcoming events at the historic beach boardwalk in Santa Cruz, California, including concerts and a Christmas Craft and Gift Festival. Here, you can read about more fun things to do at California's seaside amusement park.

State Historic Preservation Offices

http://usparks.about.com/msubhistpres.htm?once=true&terms=historical+landmarks&COB=home

★★★

Stop by this listing of state historic landmarks and parks to find those of interest for each state.

Susan B. Anthony House Museum and National Landmark

http://www.susanbanthonyhouse.org/

★★★★

[👥] 14-18

Take an online tour of the Susan B. Anthony house located in Rochester, New York. Learn about this great women's suffrage leader and antislavery activist. Be a part of history and donate to the capital campaign drive to help preserve and expand the house so that people might visit for years to come. Visit other historical links to learn more about famous women in history.

Underground Railroad

http://www.nps.gov/undergroundrr/contents.htm

★★★

[👥] All

History and geography of the escape network and consideration of the National Park Service's commemoration proposals for sites, museums, and activities.

A B C D E F G H I J K L M N O P Q R S T U V W X Y Z

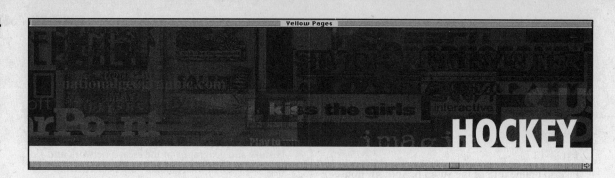

HOCKEY

A
B
C
D
E
F
G
H
I
J
K
L
M
N
O
P
Q
R
S
T
U
V
W
X
Y
Z

AHL: Official American Hockey League Web Site

`http://www.canoe.ca/AHL/home.html`

★★★★

 All

Fans of the American Hockey League should visit this site, which provides team and player information, broken down by conference and division. Also provides minute-by-minute game updates and scores, information on future games, player profiles, AHL record book data, hockey forums, and all the other good stuff related to the AHL.

American Hockey League Eastern Conference Team Sites

Albany River Rats	`http://www.albanyriverrats.com/`
Binghamton Senators	`http://www.binghamtonsenators.com/`
Bridgeport Sound Tigers	`http://www.soundtigers.com/`
Hamilton Bulldogs	`http://www.hamiltonbulldogs.com/`
Hartford Wolf Pack	`http://www.hartfordwolfpack.com/`
Lowell Lock Monsters	`http://www.lockmonsters.com/`
Manchester Monarchs	`http://www.monarchshockey.com/`
Manitoba Moose	`http://www.moosehockey.com/`
Portland Pirates	`http://www.portlandpirates.com/`
Providence Bruins	`http://www.providencebruins.com/`
Saint John Flames	`http://www.sjflames.com/`
Springfield Falcons	`http://www.falconsahl.com/`
St. John's Maple Leafs	`http://www.sjmapleleafs.ca/`
Worcester Ice Cats	`http://www.worcestericecats.com/`

American Hockey League Western Conference Team Sites

Chicago Wolves	`http://www.chicagowolves.com/`
Cincinnati Mighty Ducks	`http://www.cincinnatimightyducks.com/`
Cleveland Barons	`http://www.clevelandbarons.net/`
Grand Rapids Griffins	`http://www.griffinshockey.com/`
Hershey Bears	`tp://www.hersheypa.com/events/hershey_bears/`
Houston Aeros	`http://www.aeros.com/`
Milwaukee Admirals	`http://www.milwaukeeadmirals.com/`
Norfolk Admirals	`http://www.norfolkadmirals.com/`
Philadelphia Phantoms	`http://www.phantomshockey.com/`
Rochester Americans	`http://www.amerks.com/`
San Antonio Rampage	`http://www.sarampage.com/`
Syracuse Crunch	`http://www.syracusecrunch.com/`
Utah Grizzlies	`http://www.utahgrizzlies.com/`
Wilkes-Barre/ Scranton Penguins	`http://www.wbspenguins.com/`

Crease Monkey Hockey

http://hometown.aol.com/todnielson/
creasemonkey.html

★★★

A sort of online hockey scrapbook for fans. You can watch the hockey scores scroll by at this site, which also offers player profiles, message boards, features, a photo gallery, and general hockey links. The site focuses on the AHL and NCAA Division I college hockey.

ESPN Hockey Site

http://sports.espn.go.com/nhl/index

★★★★★

 All

ESPN's hockey page includes hockey headline news, the latest scores, team standings, statistics, trades, and much more.

First Base Sports' Ice Hockey Glossary

http://www.firstbasesports.com/hockey_glossary.html

★★★

A handy glossary of hockey terms. Jump to the desired description by clicking the first letter of the term and then scrolling down. If you're not sure what the crease lines are or exactly what part of the ice constitutes the neutral zone, this is one way to find out.

Hockey Hall of Fame

http://www.hhof.com/index.htm

★★★★★

 All

Play the Hockey Hall of Fame trivia game, track down statistics and rankings, and learn more about the best hockey players in history.

The Hockey News Online

http://www.thn.com

★★★★

The online version of *The Hockey News* magazine. Take a look at the latest issue, take part in this week's poll/drawing, and access all sorts of other timely and interesting online articles.

Hockey's Future

http://www.hockeysfuture.com/

★★★

Want to know who's rumored to be the top draft pick? Keep up on trade tips and rumors, read columnist opinions, and stay current on the latest hockey news.

HockeyNewsLink

http://www.hockeynewslink.com/

★★★

This is your source for all things hockey—your connection to resources and information. Jump to newspaper coverage of various teams, daily news, statistics, periodicals, leagues, associations, people, and other hockey-related links.

The HockeyNut.com

http://www.hockeynut.com/

★★★

Hockey news, scores, standings, team links, and more from a self-proclaimed hockey nut. Good information on the World Hockey Championship.

InTheCrease.com

http://www.inthecrease.com/

★★★

Catch all the latest scores, rankings, league headlines, and hockey news here. Covers the NHL, AHL, ECHL, UHL, WCHL, and CHL. Check out the ITC auction to find hockey memorabilia for sale. Photo gallery and message boards also featured.

Internet Hockey Database

http://www.hockeydb.com/

★★★★

Huge browsable directory of hockey information, including player statistics, team standings, records, draft picks, trading cards, and more.

Joy of Hockey

http://www.joyofhockey.com/

★★★★

Created and managed by an avid NHL fan (David "Sid" Joy) for avid NHL fans, this site features the current season's schedule, links to team sites, player index, and statistics.

A
B
C
D
E
F
G
H
I
J
K
L
M
N
O
P
Q
R
S
T
U
V
W
X
Y
Z

A
B
C
D
E
F
G
H
I
J
K
L
M
N
O
P
Q
R
S
T
U
V
W
X
Y
Z

LCS Guide to Hockey

http://www.lcshockey.com/

★★★

Get some of the best hockey news and reports in an entertaining format.

MyHockeyWorld.com

http://www.myhockeyworld.com/

★★★

If you routinely set up a hockey pool at the office, you can now use this site to manage it. See how you're doing versus other pools and stay current with team results.

National Hockey League Players' Association

http://www.nhlpa.com/

★★★★

 All

The official players' association page has links to past and present Player of the Day profiles, along with other NHL player information.

[Best] NHL: Official National Hockey League Web Site

http://www.nhl.com/

$

★★★★★

 All

This is the official NHL website where you can get all the news about NHL hockey you could want. Check out individual teams and NHL schedules, and take the most recent poll. The gift shop is also worth a look for items ranging from hats to official NHL jerseys of your favorite player. This comprehensive site delivers a lot of hockey information, a no-brainer choice as Best of the Best in the Hockey category.

National Hockey League Eastern Conference Team Sites

Atlantic Division

New Jersey Devils	http://www.newjerseydevils.com/
New York Islanders	http://www.newyorkislanders.com/
New York Rangers	http://www.newyorkrangers.com/
Philadelphia Flyers	http://www.philadelphiaflyers.com/
Pittsburgh Penguins	http://www.pittsburghpenguins.com/

Northeast Division

Boston Bruins	http://www.bostonbruins.com/
Buffalo Sabres	http://www.sabres.com/
Montreal Canadiens	http://www.canadiens.com/
Ottawa Senators	http://www.ottawasenators.com/
Toronto Maple Leafs	http://www.mapleleafs.com/

Southeast Division

Atlanta Thrashers	http://www.atlantathrashers.com/
Carolina Hurricanes	http://carolinahurricanes.com/
Florida Panthers	http://www.floridapanthers.com/
Tampa Bay Lightning	http://www.tampabaylightning.com/
Washington Capitals	http://www.washingtoncaps.com/

National Hockey League Western Conference Team Sites

Central Division

Chicago Blackhawks	http://www.chicagoblackhawks.com/
Columbus Blue Jackets	http://www.bluejackets.com/
Detroit Red Wings	http://www.detroitredwings.com/
Nashville Predators	http://www.nashvillepredators.com/
St. Louis Blues	http://www.stlouisblues.com/

Northwest Division

Calgary Flames	http://www.calgaryflames.com/
Colorado Avalanche	http://www.coloradoavalanche.com/
Edmonton Oilers	http://www.edmontonoilers.com/
Minnesota Wild	http://www.wild.com/
Vancouver Canucks	http://www.canucks.com/

Pacific Division

Mighty Ducks of Anaheim	http://www.mightyducks.com/
Dallas Stars	http://www.dallasstars.com/
Los Angeles Kings	http://www.lakings.com/
Phoenix Coyotes	http://www.phoenixcoyotes.com/
San Jose Sharks	http://www.sj-sharks.com/

Science of Hock436ey

http://www.exploratorium.edu/hockey/

★★★★★

The Science of Hockey takes you inside the game of hockey, utilizing RealAudio and video to bring you science bits from leading physicists and chemists. It also gives you insights from NHL players and coaches from the San Jose Sharks. Want to know why ice is slippery or how to shoot a puck 100 miles per hour? Check it out.

SLAM! Hockey Forums

http://www.canoe.ca/Hockey/hockeysession.html

★★★

Get news, standings, playoff information, and hockey discussions here. Check out the live scoreboard and extensive photo gallery. NHL, CHL, and other league activity is reported here.

SLAM! Women's Hockey Home Page

http://www.canoe.com/HockeyWomen/home.html

★★★

Gives you women's hockey news stories, plus such interactive offerings as the LIVE! Scoreboard, Photo Gallery, Hockey Talk (NHL), Puck Talk (junior), Fan Breakaway (AHL), and Cup Talk (playoffs). You can also get news, scores, and standings from the World Women's Championship.

U.S. College Hockey Online

http://www.uscollegehockey.com/

★★★★

Men's and women's college ice hockey news, schedules, scores, recaps, polls, and players of the week are available here. You can also check out your favorite college team's players and rankings.

USA Hockey

http://www.usahockey.com/

⑤

★★★★

 All

The official site of USA Hockey. The Main Menu asks you to pick from Players Only, Coaches & Officials, National Teams, USA Hockey InLine, News & Information, Rinks & Arenas, Fan Forum, Merchandise, and National Team Development Program. Come skate through this site for yourself. Also features areas for youth players.

Women's Hockey Information

http://www.cs.utoronto.ca/~andria/general/

★★★

Women's hockey FAQ, mailing lists, newsgroups, women's college hockey, and a look at women's hockey internationally.

A B C D E F G H I J K L M N O P Q R S T U V W X Y Z

HOLIDAYS AND CELEBRATIONS

A
B
C
D
E
F
G
H
I
J
K
L
M
N
O
P
Q
R
S
T
U
V
W
X
Y
Z

Allenbys.com

http://www.allenbys.com/

 $

★★★★

This site features a large selection of unique and affordable gifts for family and friends. A great place to shop to avoid spending all your money and losing your holiday spirit!

April Fools Day

http://wilstar.com/holidays/aprilfool.htm

★★★

This site features some theories about the origins of April Fools Day. Also provides several interesting quotes about fools in general.

Birthday Traditions from Around the World

http://www.kidsparties.com/traditions.htm

★★★

Learn how the tradition of birthday parties started, how they are celebrated in other cultures, and get some gift ideas here. Link to Amazon.com so you can order books and videos.

Chanukah on the Net

http://www.holidays.net/chanukah/

★★★

Fun and informative entertainment about this special holiday, including stories, tasty recipes, pictures for the kids to print and color, crafts to make, holiday games to play, and animated dreidels.

Christmas Around the World

http://christmas.com/worldview/

★★★★

 All

Asia, Europe, Latin America, the Middle East, and the Netherlands are among the regions with Christmas traditions explained on this site. Here, you'll also learn how to say "Merry Christmas" in more than 30 languages, and you'll find a list of other holidays that fall around the Christmas season.

ChristmasDepot.com

http://www.christmasdepot.com/

$

★★★★

An online Christmas store complete with trees, wreaths, ornaments, collectibles, letters to Santa, and gift ideas. The View Shopping Cart feature ensures that you don't overload!

Cinco de Mayo

http://www.mexonline.com/cinco.htm

★★★

An important date (May 5th) in Mexican and Chicano communities, it marks the victory of the Mexican Army over the French at the Battle of Puebla, which came to symbolize Mexican unity and patriotism. Visit this site for the complete history and photos.

Easter in Cyberspace: A Christian Perspective

http://www.njwebworks.com/easter/

★★★

 All

This page reminds Easter celebrants of the true meaning of the holiday. You might not find jelly beans or bunnies, but you will find a collection of links about the death and resurrection of Jesus Christ.

Famous Birthdays

http://www.famousbirthdays.com/

★★★

 All

Type in your birth date and find out which famous people share it. Kids area provides links to other sites for young children.

The Fourth of July

http://wilstar.com/holidays/july4.htm

★★★★

 All

This patriotic site is filled with links to historic documents such as the Magna Carta, Declaration of Independence, Constitution, Emancipation Proclamation, and more. Also contains flag-flying rules.

Hallmark.com

http://www.hallmark.com/

★★★★

The home page of the company known for spreading holiday cheer. Here, you can shop for cards and gifts, send flowers, and send eCards.

Hanukkah Festival of Lights

http://www.ort.org/ort/hanukkah/index.html

★★★

 All

Learn more about what Hanukkah represents—its history, games, and holiday songs associated with the eight-day celebration.

Happy Christmas

http://www.happychristmas.com/

★★★★

 All

Keep the merry in your Christmas holiday by visiting this site for funny stories, gift ideas from silly to practical to useless, lists of holiday movies, and more. You'll even find a list of pizza places that are open on Christmas Day, just in case!

Heather's Happy Holidaze Pages

http://www.heathersholidaze.com/

★★★★

 9-13

Most national holidays as seen through the eyes of a 12-year-old girl. This site has won several awards, and it is easy to see why: The links are complete and relevant! An entertaining site to visit whether you have kids or not.

Holidays and Celebrations from Around the World

http://www.topics-mag.com/internatl/holidays/festivals.htm

★★★

 All

Learn about holidays celebrated all around the world—from Christmas in Angola to Independence Day in Zaire!

⌐Best⌐ Holidays on the Net

http://www.holidays.net/

★★★★★

Collection of multimedia presentations for nearly every holiday of the year. Each presentation provides a brief history of the holiday, its meaning and significance, suggested activities, and a way to send an eCard to a friend or relative. Site includes holiday calendars, crafts, and recipes, a holiday store, and even ideas for holiday travel! Don't miss the fun and wacky daily holidays. If you're into celebrating holidays, bookmark this Best of the Best Holidays site and visit daily.

A
B
C
D
E
F
G
H
I
J
K
L
M
N
O
P
Q
R
S
T
U
V
W
X
Y
Z

A
B
C
D
E
F
G
H
I
J
K
L
M
N
O
P
Q
R
S
T
U
V
W
X
Y
Z

Home Page for the Holidays

http://www.merry-christmas.com

★★★

👬 9-13

Activities, games, list of Christmas movies, Kringle tales, Christmas coloring book, recipes, and Santa's email address.

Jewish Holidays and Festivals on the Net

http://www.jewishpost.com/holidays/

★★★★

A colorful site featuring the names and brief explanations of Jewish holidays. Categories include high holy days, Shavuot, Purim, and others.

Kids Domain Holidays

http://www.kidsdomain.com/holiday/index.html

★★★★

👬 9-13

Link to sites that explain and explore the meaning of a whole list of annual holidays to kids, from Veterans Day to Fathers Day, Valentine's Day, and just about every other major day. Even Guy Fawkes Day is explained here!

Kwanzaa Information Center

http://www.melanet.com/kwanzaa/

★★★

Here, you'll find reams of information about the background and purpose, symbols, and principles of the recently developed Kwanzaa holiday, as well as a schedule for Kwanzaa celebration.

Martin Luther King Jr. Day

http://www.holidays.net/mlk/

★★★★

👬 14-18

This site is dedicated to the memory of slain civil rights leader Dr. Martin Luther King, Jr. and the national holiday that honors him. It features a biography, links to his famous "I Have a Dream" speech, and more.

Passover on the Net

http://www.holidays.net/passover/

★★★★★

This beautifully illustrated and easy-to-navigate site offers the story of Passover, information about the Seder meal (plus recipes), and a collection of downloadable Passover songs in MIDI format.

The Plunge

http://www.theplunge.com/

★★★★★

Planning a holiday celebration or a party for a special event? Then check out The Plunge, where you can find everything you need—from party themes to printed postcards, to websites and party supplies. The opening page presents links for holidays and special events. Just click the link and follow the onscreen instructions to order everything you need!

Starnet Happy Holidays

http://www.azstarnet.com/public/holiday/holiday.html

★★★

👬 All

Forget those snail-mail cards! This site sends your electronic holiday greeting via the Internet.

Yahoo! Holidays and Observances

http://dir.yahoo.com/Society_and_Culture/Holidays_and_Observances/

★★★

Search this specialized Yahoo! directory to track down sites pertaining to just about any holiday—including Bastille Day, Juneteenth, and other cultural events.

The Yom Tov Page

http://www.torah.org/learning/yomtov/

★★★★

YomTov classes focus on a variety of aspects concerning Jewish holidays and commemorations, such as the philosophy behind the holiday, historical background, customs and practices, and relevant laws. All this and more can be found at this site.

Related Sites
http://www.smart.net/~mmontes/ushols.html
http://usacitylink.com/cupid/default.html
http://www.holidays.net/ramadan/
http://virtual-markets.net/vme/memorial/dvm_mem.html
http://www.joi.org/celebrate/rosh/
http://www.shamash.org/

A B C D E F G H I J K L M N O P Q R S T U V W X Y Z

HOME

BUILDING

Best Ask The Builder

http://www.askbuild.com/

$

★★★★★

Search the archives of this syndicated columnist (Tim Carter) to learn the best way to tackle a problem around the house. Project archives will tell and show you (using streaming video) how to clean a deck, for example. Straightforward advice. You can also purchase books, CDs, and other related merchandise here. This site's personal touch, excellent design, and comprehensive information make it our choice as Best of the Best in the Home Building category.

B4UBUILD.com

http://www.b4ubuild.com/

★★★★

 9-13

For home builders, this site offers more than 11,000 home plans, home-building guides, a sample construction schedule, information about construction contracts, and a complete overview of the home-building process. It also offers links for kids, to get them involved in the process, too.

Backwoods Home Magazine

http://backwoodshome.com/

 $

★★★

Backwoods Home Magazine offers practical ideas and articles on self-reliant living, including building, alternative energy, gardening, farming, and much more. Books and subscriptions are for sale here, too.

Bricsnet

http://www.aecinfo.com

★★★★

World's largest and most active database for architecture, engineering, construction, and home building. Site features interactive discussion forums, products, firms, services, news, events, projects, articles, classifieds, specifications, and schools.

Build.com

http://www.build.com/

★★★

Find suppliers and contractors through this site, broken down by categories relating to the type of project you want to undertake. You'll find flooring, paint and wall covering, decks, kitchens, baths, and just about every other potential home project.

Builder Online

http://www.builderonline.com/

★★★★

The online version of *Builder* Magazine, the site offers trade and consumer information, such as building plans and projects, products, contractors, industry news, and links to other home improvement sites.

Building Industry Exchange

http://www.building.org/

★★★★★

Extensive directory of contractors, subcontractors, and suppliers for the building industry. Includes listings for architects, concrete workers, electricians, plumbers, and just about any other service required in the building industry. Also features discussion forums and job leads for construction professionals.

eplans.com

http://store.yahoo.com/eplans/

★★★★

Full line of building plans for everything from house plans and landscaping to storage sheds and designing with light. Excellent selection with the added convenience of being able to order online.

Habitat for Humanity

http://www.habitat.org/

★★★★

Home of Habitat for Humanity International, a nonprofit, nondenominational, Christian housing organization devoted to "building simple, decent, affordable houses in partnership with those in need of adequate shelter." Learn more about Habitat for Humanity and find out how you can help.

HomeBuilder.COM

http://www.homebuilder.com/

★★★★

Shop for a new home in the area where you plan to settle. Just specify the state, area, ZIP code, and price range to view new home listings in the area. Here, you can also find custom builders, lots for sale, and everything you need for home improvement projects and home furnishings. Online shopping lets you compare prices at several stores.

Home Planners

http://www.homeplanners.com/

★★★

Design your dream home online using some of the most popular home plans, take a look at the design in 3D, and then price out the work and put together a construction calendar.

Housing Zone

http://www.housingzone.com/

★★★

Search more than 2,500 home building sites from this one location, as well as look at popular home designs, catch up on building industry news, and learn more about affording a home through HUD.

iNest

http://www.inest.com/

★★★

Buy your next home through iNest and receive 1% of the purchase back in cash. Visit this site to learn more about this unique program. This site also features some useful articles and tools, including school information about various areas, a salary calculator that analyzes cost-of-living issues, a moving expenses calculator, and a rent-versus-buy calculator.

New Home Web

http://www.newhomeweb.com/

★★★★

Find a home builder in any U.S. state or look at floor plans. Offers links to home products, mortgage sites, and a facility to add to your site. Links for products carry you to dealer websites where you can shop online.

New Home Source

http://www.newhomesource.com/

★★★★

Search more than 250,000 homes and house plans by the top builders in your area. Specify your state, area, and ZIP code; enter the desired price range; and receive a list of the top home builders in your area from the New Home Source. Click a button to view a snapshot of a home's exterior or the floor plans.

Sound Home Resource Center

http://www.soundhome.com/

★★★

Ask the Sound Home consultant a question about your home-building project, or check the articles and FAQs posted here on the topic. The glossary of terms will also help put you on par with your contractor.

A B C D E F G H I J K L M N O P Q R S T U V W X Y Z

A B C D E F G H I J K L M N O P Q R S T U V W X Y Z

CONSTRUCTION/ WOODWORKING

Building Online
http://www.buildingonline.com/

★★★

An excellent search engine with search capabilities to find contractors, architects, project plans, and links to many product suppliers and useful sites.

Dirtpile.com
http://www.dirtpile.com

★★★★

Looking for some heavy construction equipment for your construction company or project? This is the site for buying or selling heavy equipment, as well as checking up on industry news and weather reports.

Fine Woodworking
http://www.taunton.com/finewoodworking/index.asp

$

★★★★★

Tauton Press has put together this Fine Woodworking site with the real craftsman in mind. Online features include free project plans, descriptions of useful tools, techniques and tips, online video tips, and much more.

WoodNet
http://www.woodnet.net/

★★★★

More than 100 woodworking tips and techniques are available here to help you finish that project. You can also find out more about which tools are best for your job, exchange ideas in the discussion forums, and check out links to other woodworking sites.

WoodWeb
http://www.woodweb.com/

★★★★

Excellent directory of woodworking websites, provides links to woodworking information, resources, and products. Everything from adhesives and tools to software is available.

DECORATING/PAINTING

American Society of Interior Designers
http://www.interiors.org/

★★★★

An online referral service for the largest organization of professional interior designers in the world. Find information about the organization that has more than 30,000 designers, educators, and media members; more than 7,000 student members; and 3,500 industry foundation members. Learn how designers work or find the right designer for your project.

Antique Arts Home Page
http://antiquearts.com/

★★★

Bills itself as the Internet's antiques marketplace. Take a stroll down Antique Alley, stopping to enjoy the online catalogs of the shops that catch your fancy. Or use the powerful search engine to find what you want. You can also access a list of more than 35,000 antique shops and dealers across the nation, many of which support online shopping.

Ask a Designer
http://www.canadianhouseandhome.com/askHome.php

★★★

Pose your building, remodeling, or redecorating question to the pros at this site, and receive a reply with no required fee. The Dear Designer column is updated with answers to questions that have been submitted.

Ballard Design
http://www.ballarddesigns.com/home.jsp

★★★★★

Mail-order source for fine home furnishings and accents. You can find everything here from beds and bedding to office furniture.

Baranzelli Home

http://www.baranzelli.com/

★★★★★

Designer-quality home furnishings including fabrics, trims, furniture, and decorative accessories are now available directly to you through the Net; this site also serves as an information source for your decorating needs as well as a compendium of events and activities in the world of home décor.

Bed Bath & Beyond

http://www.Bedbathandbeyond.com

★★★★

Shop the online store for bed, bath, kitchen, and home accessories, and check the latest circular for the best deals.

Better Homes and Gardens

http://www.bhg.com/

★★★

A home and garden magazine for home decorating. You can find tips and advice here, as well as purchase books and magazine subscriptions.

Related Site
http://www.thegifthouse.net/

cMYVision

http://www.cmyvision.com/

★★★

Interactive design software that allows users to experimentally make changes to any digital photograph of a home, room, or yard to create a new look. Home decorators can drag and drop different paints, doors, trim, plants, siding, flooring, and so on, into their chosen image.

Country Sampler Decorating Ideas

http://www.sampler.com/decideas/decideas.html

★★★

Online version of the print magazine. Find do-it-yourself home decorating projects, get tips, and get help with techniques. Chat with others and share your decorating stories, or take a look at highlights from the current month's newsstand issue.

CrateandBarrel.com

http://www.crateandbarrel.com

★★★★

This retail store now provides online access to its furniture, bedding, kitchen and bar accessories, and home goods. The gift registry makes selecting purchases even easier.

Cuddledown.com

http://www.cuddledown.com/

★★★★

Offers fine home fashions and more—down comforters, bed linens and other sewn items, furniture, and accessories. Special discounts on discontinued and overstocked items.

Cyber Feng Shui

http://www.universalfengshui.com/

★★★★

Feng Shui is the ancient Chinese art of the proper and auspicious arranging and placement of furnishings and accessories. This site helps you apply the concepts of Feng Shui to your own interior designs and room arrangements.

Décor Delights

http://www.decordelights.com

★★★

Tole painting and decorative painting, free patterns, plus you can purchase books, videos, and pattern packet reviews, and more.

A B C D E F G H I J K L M N O P Q R S T U V W X Y Z

A
B
C
D
E
F
G
H
I
J
K
L
M
N
O
P
Q
R
S
T
U
V
W
X
Y
Z

Decorate Your Home

http://www.homestore.com/

★★★

Homestore.com provides hundreds of easy projects and step-by-step tutorials for beautifying your home. You can also find homes for sale as well as local places to shop for your home needs.

Designer Stencils

http://www.designerstencils.com/

★★★

Presented by The Stencil Shoppe, Inc., this site offers products for beginners or those experienced with stencils. View and order stencils from the collections, or order a catalog of designs.

Design Within Reach

http://www.dwr.com/

$

★★★★★

If you're looking to modernize your home without putting much thought into it, check out this site. Peruse beautiful home furnishings by genre (seating, tables, lighting, rugs), by room, or by collections and designers. Shop online and have everything shipped right to your door.

Design Addict

http://www.designaddict.com/

$

★★★★★

As this site proclaims, you can "discover the design world through Design Addict." More than 350 of the world's top designers are in the spotlight here, representing thousands of beautifully crafted home furnishings… and the collection grows daily as new designers visit the site and add their work to the gallery. When you're looking for a look, look here.

EatMyHandbagBitch.com

http://www.eatmyhandbagbitch.co.uk/

★★★★

Whether you're looking for the latest fashions in art, desks and tables, lighting, seating, storage, or art objects, visit this site. The focus here is on Italian, Scandinavian, and British designs.

EZblinds.com

http://www.ihomedecor.com/

$

★★★★

Incredible selection of window coverings. Follow the interactive four-step process to choose your blinds and order them online.

Fortunoff

http://www.fortunoff.com/

$

★★★★

Home of one of New York's oldest and largest department stores, this site features an incredible selection of goods ranging from wedding rings and other jewelry to home furnishings and appliances. You can even find items for your backyard, including grills and picnic tables. Convenient online shopping makes it almost too easy to spend money.

FurnitureFind.com

http://www.furniturefind.com

$

★★★★

Search for furniture for virtually every room in your house here and get free national delivery after placing your order. Lots of options from which to choose.

FurnitureOnline.com

http://www.furnitureonline.com/

$

★★★

An online catalog of office and limited home furnishings. Check out the weekly specials for discounted prices on individual pieces and accessories.

Garbe's Lighting and Home Furnishings

http://www.garbes.com/

★★★

Features distinctive lighting and home décor items. Departments include decorative hardware, door chimes/mailboxes, ceiling fans, everything for the bath, architectural products, and wall décor. Take a virtual tour and learn the FAQs of light.

Home and Garden Television (HGTV)

http://www.hgtv.com/

★★★★★

Home and Garden Television's website is arranged in "villages," letting participants home in on decorating, gardening, remodeling, craft, and entertainment information.

Home Décor Ideas

http://www.garbes.com/decor.html

★★★

Create elegance for the home with Garbe interior decorating and home décor ideas.

Home Decorating on a Shoestring

http://www.pamdamour.com/

★★★

A newsletter format from Pam Damour, with excerpts from the show *Home Matters* on the Discovery Channel. An Ask Pam feature and resources for decorating problems, including reviews of books and videos, are included.

Home Decorator

http://www.homefurnish.com/hmdeco_m.htm

★★★

Offers home decorating and interior design information, tips, and ideas. Subjects include furniture placement and room arrangement, accessorizing your home, color themes, pattern combinations, and monthly design topics. Interesting article on Feng Shui, the ancient oriental approach to interior design.

Home Fashion Information Network

http://www.thehome.com/

★★★★

Find information on a variety of home furnishing topics under one roof, displayed in rooms for convenience. Topics include tips and tricks, information on how to select items, and assistance with your bridal registry.

Interior Mall

http://www.interiormall.com/

★★★★

A full online home decorating purchasing agent. Products include fabrics, furniture, wallpaper, architecture, accessories, linens, drapery rods, art, lighting, screens, floor coverings, glassware, and more.

The International Interior Design Association

http://www.iida.org

★★★

There are more than 10,000 international members of this organization, which was formed through the unification of three influential interior design associations. Connect with the interior design community through this site, which has event listings and resources available.

iVillage Home & Garden

http://www.ivillage.com/home/

★★★

This site offers a variety of home-related sections. You can get advice on redoing a particular room, general decorating tips, and home repair help. Great place to find tips on home improvement projects.

J.R. Burrows & Company

http://www.burrows.com/

★★★

A source for English traditional home furnishings, including arts and crafts movement items, Victorian designs, and Scottish lace curtains. History, online catalog, and ordering information are included.

A B C D E F G **H** I J K L M N O P Q R S T U V W X Y Z

A B C D E F G H I J K L M N O P Q R S T U V W X Y Z

KozyHome

http://www.shop-the-malls.com/kozyhome.htm

★★★

Scan the KozyHome catalog and view your selections in a virtual room using 3D imaging software. Get 15% off your purchases for 30 days after registering at the site.

Longaberger Baskets

http://www.longaberger.com/

★★★★★

Introduces you to the Longaberger company and all the Longaberger products, including baskets, pottery, fabrics, home décor, and home accessories. The site does not allow you to purchase products directly, but it does help you locate an independent sales consultant. Jump to the kitchen, dining room, library, and living room areas to see the goods available and get valuable information.

Mainely Shades

http://www.mainelyshades.com/

★★★

Add to your home decoration with lampshades (cut and pierced, traditional, Victorian) that you create. Complete kits available through mail order.

No Brainer Blinds and Shades

http://www.nobrainerblinds.com

★★★

Get guaranteed low prices and custom cut shades that are shipped to you same day.

Paint and Decorating Retailers Association

http://www.pdra.org

★★★

Provides consumer information on decorating products and industry information for decorating product retailers and manufacturers.

Pier 1 Imports

http://www.pier1.com/

★★★★★

Pier 1 Imports is well known for its line of exotic home décor, and now you can shop Pier 1 online, use its bridal registry feature, check out specials, and peruse its furniture guide.

Pottery Barn

http://www.potterybarn.com/

★★★★★

The pottery barn has everything you need to fill those empty rooms with beautiful furniture and home décor. Products are grouped by furniture, bedding & bath, rugs, pillows & windows, accessories, lighting, tableware & entertaining, rooms, and sale items. You can shop online, set up a gift registry, or purchase items for a friend or relative who has set up a registry here.

Room by Room

http://www.roombyroom.com/

★★★★★

Room by Room is an HGTV show about how real people decorate. Click on *Room by Room* episodes (episodes are listed by room type, with a brief description of the episode, where items were purchased, its Tool Box Project, and the next airing time and date), or find out how you can have a room considered for an upcoming episode. Now that's decorating I like—someone else with the expertise transforms my room(s) for me!

Rustic Creations Home Page

http://www.everythingrustic.com/

★★★

Find rustic, handcrafted products for the home. You'll just have to see for yourself the things this master craftsman has made, including an antique stagecoach replica made of old barn wood and one-of-a-kind rustic stick chairs. Site also has various links, such as log home links and home remodeling links.

Stencil Ease Home Décor and Craft Stencils

http://stencilease.com/

★★★

Flip through the Stencil Ease catalog and order online. Stencils, paints, brushes, decorating stamps, and accessories are available. One page also gives detailed instructions on how to stencil. You can also order the Stencil Ease Decorator catalog.

Steptoe & Wife Antiques, Ltd.

http://www.steptoewife.com/

★★★★★

Architectural restoration products from iron staircases to drapery hardware are offered by this Canadian company whose motto is "100 years behind the times." Listings of products and distributors are provided.

Sudberry House

http://www.sudberry.com/

★★★★

Displays fine wood accessories used for mounting needlework and crafts, as well as an online color catalog, a factory tour, and many needlework designs.

Suzanne Seely's "Make it Beautiful" Decorating Newsletter

http://www.aiminc.com/seely/

★★★

Suzanne Seely brings her knowledge of style, design, color, resources, and years of interior decorating experience to Internet subscribers in her newsletter.

Traditional Home Magazine

http://www.traditionalhome.com/

★★★

Take a look at major design styles and then get ideas of how to implement them in your home. This is a great resource for home designers. You can also subscribe to the magazine from this site.

unicaHOME

http://www.unicahome.com/

★★★★★

This site features thousands of hard-to-find items that can give your home just the right touch. Very modern, very cool, and well-designed for anyone who likes to browse the aisles looking for home décor. Shop by company, designer, or genre (barroom, bathroom, kitchen, bedroom, and so on).

Related Site
http://www.jamilin.com

UrbanScapes

http://www.widerview.com/urban.html

★★★★

Great-looking modern furniture, lighting, kitchen tools, bath ware, and playful kitsch. These designs will add a touch of urban sophistication to your loft or city apartment.

Village Products

http://www.villagehome.com

★★★

Designer and manufacturer of home decorating products, created for the do-it-yourselfer, offers decorating products and advice. Even the website design is beautiful!

Wiltjer Pottery

http://www.maine.com/shops/wiltjer/welcome.htm

★★★★

Unique ceramic clay designs. View the gallery of pottery vases and bowls, and see the hand-thrown sinks. Also, take advantage of the offered links.

A
B
C
D
E
F
G
H
I
J
K
L
M
N
O
P
Q
R
S
T
U
V
W
X
Y
Z

A
B
C
D
E
F
G
H
I
J
K
L
M
N
O
P
Q
R
S
T
U
V
W
X
Y
Z

ELECTRICAL

DoItYourself.com Electrical Wiring

http://doityourself.com/electric/

★★★★★

DoItYourself.com provides useful information on all aspects of home ownership and maintenance. This particular page contains dozens of links to very informative how-to articles on electrical wiring inside your home. Here you can learn the basics, plus find specific instructions for wiring ceiling fans, dimmer switches, and track lighting. Learn how to use an electrical meter, and much more.

Electrical Safety Foundation

http://www.esfi.org/

★★★★★

Electrical wiring is an integral part of any home, but it can be quite dangerous if the wiring is faulty or unsafe products appliances are used. To make sure your house is wired safely and that you are using appliances safely, check out the information provided here, or download or order your ESFI Electrical Safety kit today.

MSN's Homeowner's Handbook: Electricity

http://houseandhome.msn.com/improve/electrical.aspx

★★★★★

MSN's Homeowner's Handbook offers a nicely illustrated beginner's guide to electricity in the home. It shows just how a typical home is wired and introduces you to the essential components: the types of wires, circuit breakers and fuses, outlets, light fixtures, and power cords. You can go more in-depth by clicking the links. When you click a link for one of the components, a screen appears with three tabs—one that explains the component, one that describes common problems, and a third that explains common fixes or repairs.

Home Electricity FAQ Question and Answer

http://www.faqfarm.com/Home/Electrical/

★★★

This site provides a great list of questions and answers about home wiring and electricity that just might be able to help you identify a problem in your home and help you repair it.

Home and Garden Television: Electrical

http://www.hgtv.com/hgtv/rm_electric_appliances/

★★★★

This site provides some excellent articles, instructions, and tips on electrical home appliances and home wiring. Learn how to install or replace a light fixture, install a new light switch or outlet, install a phone jack, use a circuit tester, and more.

Your Internet Home Electrical "How-To" Guide

http://www.electrical-online.com/

★★★

This site is a great place for do-it-yourself homeowners to learn about basic wiring. Site provides safety precautions for working with electricity, along with instructions on how to wire a light switch, ceiling fan, grounded outlet, and more. Nothing fancy here, just good solid instructions and advice.

FLOORING

Armstrong Flooring

http://www.armstrong.com/

★★★★★

The leader in vinyl and linoleum flooring provides products for residential and commercial use. Visit this site to explore your flooring options. Also features laminate "hardwood" flooring.

FloorFacts

http://www.floorfacts.com/

★★★

Take a look at the Flooring Guide before making your selection; then scan the offerings of manufacturers linked to the site to gather more information.

Pergo Laminate Flooring

http://www.pergo.com/

★★★★

Home of the fake wood floors that look like real hardwood floors. Consumers can check out the showroom, check out different products, and plan a project.

Woodfloors.org

http://www.woodfloors.org/

★★★★

National Wood Flooring Association maintains this site for consumers and professional installers. Consumers can visit this site to learn about the benefits of real hardwood floors and how to care for wood floors. Professionals can check out the NWFA site to learn more about membership and conferences.

HOME AUTOMATION

Home Automation

http://www.homeautomationmag.com/

★★★

Which home automation products are to die for and which can you do without? The online reviews at this site will tell you, as well as give you ideas for new technology you might want to install. A bimonthly e-zine with information on the newest in automation.

SmartHome.com

http://www.smarthome.com/

★★★★★

Take the guided tour of home automation products before viewing the catalog and considering products. You can also learn about the latest technology and why you need it. Incredible selection of home automation products.

X10

http://www.x10.com/homepage.htm

★★★★

Find out who's responsible for all those annoying X10 pop up ads that harass you when you're wandering the Web. X10 is the home of one of the largest digital camera stores in the world. If you need a camera for surveillance or for telecommunicating over the Internet, this is the place to get it. Also sells a variety of home automation products.

X-home.com

http://www.x-home.com/

★★★

Find out about some cool, smart products for your home or office. Learn what's new in networking and remote products that make your life easier and safer.

HOME IMPROVEMENT AND RESTORATION

Ace Hardware

http://www.acehardware.com/

★★★★★

Find a hardware store close to you, get answers to frequently asked questions, and learn hardware hints and tips at this site. You can also participate in seasonal contests and find out about store specials.

A B C D E F G H I J K L M N O P Q R S T U V W X Y Z

Better Homes and Gardens Home Improvement Encyclopedia

http://www.bhg.com/bhg/househome/

 ★★★

Calculate the total cost of your dream home improvement project and then search the encyclopedia for ways to complete it for less money. Learn about plumbing, wiring, carpentry, decks, masonry, and concrete. Or start with the introduction and nail down the basics first.

[Best] BobVila.com

http://www.bobvila.com/

 $

★★★★★

Bob Vila, host of the popular TV show *This Old House* and *Bob Vila's Home Again*, is almost synonymous with home restoration and improvement projects. Here you can visit Bob and his crew online, check out the TV shows, peruse his how-to library, sample his software design tools, post a question, and even shop for home improvement tools and products. This Best of the Best home improvement and restoration site shows little room for any improvement—it's easy to navigate, offers plenty of useful information, and its graphics are crisp and clear.

CornerHardware.com

http://www.cornerhardware.com

$

★★★

The How To section at this site is a great resource for all those little jobs around the house you weren't sure how to do. Learn how to unclog a toilet or edge your garden bed, as well as get tips for selecting the right appliances. Tons of helpful hints.

Do It Yourself, Inc.

http://www.remarketing.com/diy/

 $

★★★

One of the country's oldest and largest producers of educational videos, including award-winning titles on home improvement and woodworking. Most are accompanied by a fully diagrammed support booklet. Hosted by Amazon.com, so you can order these products online.

Faux Painting Finishing Techniques

http://faux-painting.finishing-techniques-effects.com/

 ★★★

Are you new to faux painting? Then read the introductory ebook online, check out faux techniques and painting supplies, find faux painting classes near you, and pick up a few expert tips.

Fiberglass Insulation by Owens Corning

http://www.owenscorning.com/

 $

★★★★

Get in the pink with information about the fiberglass insulation products this company has developed for homes, as well as other products, including roofing, vinyl siding, windows, and patio doors. Join the Owens Corning Homeowner Club at Panther Place, a centralized resource for home-related information, fun, and games.

Home Depot

http://www.homedepot.com

 $

★★★★

Get project help and information on Home Depot store locations and products. Check out store specials and also see whether you are in the Home Depot online ordering area. Hints, tips, and tricks are also available at this site.

Home Ideas

http://www.homeideas.com

 ★★★

Offers articles to help you plan home projects, a guide to Internet sites, and a request section to get free catalogs and brochures sent to you by mail. A joint project between *Home Mechanix* magazine and Build.com.

Hometime

http://www.hometime.com/

★★★★

Home page of the popular PBS television series. Offers text and still-frame highlights from the show and step-by-step instruction on several home improvement projects.

Ian Evans' World of Old Houses

http://www.oldhouses.com.au/

★★★★

If you're in the process of fixing up an old house, this site could become your best friend. Get advice on bringing a house back to its original form, track down old parts and accessories, and commiserate with fellow older-home owners from around the world.

ImproveNet.com

http://www.improvenet.com

★★★

The step-by-step guide to improvement projects, available in the Dream and Design section, is a good starting point to narrowing down what you want done. Then you can collect recommendations for contractors from the site, as well as product information.

Livinghome

http://www.livinghome.com/

★★★

Find a project design, get an instant estimate of the total project cost based on where you live, and hunt down lots of helpful advice and guidance for your project, as well as get the names of qualified contractors to take over when you feel overwhelmed.

Lowe's Home Improvement Warehouse

http://www.lowes.com/

★★★★★

Lowe's Companies, Inc., is one of America's top 30 retailers serving home improvement, home décor, home electronics, and home construction markets. Lowe's website offers step-by-step guides for home improvement projects, featured products, and tips from Lowe's Home Safety Council. You'll also find a store locator, recent corporate financial data, and a list of employment opportunities. You can also order merchandise from this site through a secure server.

The Old House

http://www.oldhouseweb.com

★★★★★

If you've purchased an older fixer-upper, the very first step you should take is to visit The Old House website, where you can find products and suppliers, do-it-yourself guides, feature articles, online forums, and much more. If you're looking for something more in-depth, check out the store for books and how-to videos.

On the House with The Carey Brothers

http://www.onthehouse.com/

★★★★

On the House is a weekly syndicated radio talk show offering advice, hints, and solutions relating to all aspects of home maintenance, repair, and improvement.

Pella Windows and Doors

http://www.pella.com/

★★★★★

Research the world of windows and find the latest products this company has to offer. Terminology and energy efficiency are explained.

A B C D E F G H I J K L M N O P Q R S T U V W X Y Z

A
B
C
D
E
F
G
H
I
J
K
L
M
N
O
P
Q
R
S
T
U
V
W
X
Y
Z

Remodel Online

http://www.remodelonline.com/

★★★★

Comprehensive directory of home remodeling instructions, help, and tips. Here, you can find links to guides for home owning, remodeling, and gardening. Other resources include newsletters, forums, classifieds, and books. Great place to pick up the how-to guide you need for completing that next home-improvement project.

Remodeling Online

http://remodeling.hw.net/

★★★★

Home of *Remodeling* magazine, a publication devoted to remodeling experts. Check out the reputations of the 50 top remodelers, research building codes, apply for building permits online, learn about conferences and special events, and more.

This Old House

http://www.thisoldhouse.com/toh/

★★★★★

An interactive doorway into *This Old House*, featuring articles and columns from the magazine, as well as topics related to building, renovation, and restoration. Current news, information on personal appearances by the TV series crew, and project house updates are posted regularly.

Tools of the Trade

http://www.toolsofthetrade.net/

★★★★

Online buyer's guide for construction and building tools. Find out about the newest tools on the market and see how they fare when run through a series of toughness tests.

Your New House with Michael Holigan

http://www.michaelholigan.com/

★★★★

One-stop resource center for building, buying, and remodeling homes, this site features advice from Michael Holigan, an expert in all things related to home improvement. Here, you can find project plans, step-by-step tutorials, online video demonstrations of popular products, floor plans, and more.

INSPECTION

Environmental Hazards in the Home

http://www.hsh.com/pamphlets/hazards.html

★★★

An EPA-sponsored site that is designed to warn you about potential hazards present in houses you might be considering purchasing. Get the low-down on substances such as radon, asbestos, lead, water contamination, and other harmful substances.

Home Inspection Supersite

http://www.inspectamerica.com

★★★

Learn more about the process of having a home inspected, what to look for in a home inspector, and then track down a licensed professional in your area.

HomePro Online

http://www.home-pro.com/

★★★

This home inspection company is one of the largest in the nation with offices in many major cities. Find out more about its services and whether it has an office in your town.

Home Inspector Locator

http://www.homeinspectorlocator.com/

★★★★

Enter your ZIP code, and the database of more than 3,000 inspectors will provide a list of professionals in your area.

MORTGAGES AND FINANCING

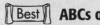 **ABCs of Real Estate**

http://realestateabc.com/

★★★★★

Whether you are buying your first house or trying to become a real estate broker, this site has all the information and resources you need to be successful. Check out the learning library to learn all about mortgages and financing; use the calculators to crunch your numbers; read the latest news about interest rates and the direction they're going; check out the directories to locate properties or find and agent. This site's basic design and comprehensive resources make it an easy pick for Best of the Best site.

ABN-AMRO

http://www.mortgage.com/

★★★★

Your "home for home loans" provides online access to the wide array of home lending products and services offered by ABN AMRO Mortgage. At mortgage.com, you can apply for a new mortgage, refinance your home, access information on your current mortgage, check current rates, and much more. Features a low-cost closing, so you know what you'll be paying up front.

Amortization Schedule

http://www.mortgageloan.com/

★★★★

No-frills site that's packed with useful information and tools. Scan current interest rates by state or use one of several financial calculators. Here, you can learn how much your monthly mortgage payment will be based on the amount financed, the interest rate, and the amount of the loan. Use the Early Mortgage Payoff calculator to see if you can pay off your mortgage early. The site can also put you in contact with several mortgage companies to have them bid for your business.

Related Site
http://www.cmacmi.com/

The Appraisal Institute

http://www.appraisalinstitute.org/

★★★★★

This highly regarded group represents real estate appraisers and produces the professionally oriented *Appraisal Journal*. The site provides a number of services to its members and the public, such as the yearly curriculum of courses and seminars, a section on industry news, a bulletin board service, and an online library featuring real-estate papers, articles, and publications.

bankrate.com

http://www.bankrate.com/brm/

★★★

Financial news plus bank rates on everything from mortgages to credit cards and car loans.

BestRate

http://www.bestrate.com/

★★★★

Tired of groveling for money? Do you want lenders to compete for *your* business? Then try BestRate. Just fill out a form online, and BestRate picks four of the best offers from more than 600 lenders nationwide to present to you.

California Association of Realtors Online

http://www.car.org

★★★

The official publications of the California Association of Realtors offer articles, industry news, legal information, and more. The site also provides an index to previous issues and links to other publications.

Countrywide Home Loans, Inc.

http://www.countrywide.com/

★★★★

One of the largest mortgage companies in the United States, Countrywide allows consumers to apply for mortgages online. You can also find information about homeowner's insurance and home refinance here.

A B C D E F G H I J K L M N O P Q R S T U V W X Y Z

A
B
C
D
E
F
G
H
I
J
K
L
M
N
O
P
Q
R
S
T
U
V
W
X
Y
Z

Ditech

http://www.ditech.com/

★★★★★

One of the most popular online loan services on the Web, Ditech features the tools and forms you need to research and secure a first or second mortgage or other type of loan from the convenience of your home. At this site, you can check the current rates, apply for a loan, and check your loan status 24 hours a day.

E-Loan

http://www.e-loan.com

★★★★

Apply for a mortgage or refinance online and learn whether you qualify. Rates are competitive and the process is fast. Good collection of financial calculators to show you how different interest rates and payment schedules can affect your monthly payment.

Fannie Mae Home Page

http://www.fanniemae.com/

★★★★

The nation's largest source of home mortgage funds, Fannie Mae works to expand affordable housing opportunities for all. The Fannie Mae site is as diverse as the company. Viewers can search the listing of Fannie Mae properties for sale, read up on the latest news for lenders, or review the latest housing and market outlook.

Federal Home Loan Banks

http://www.fhlbanks.com/

★★★★

Sponsored by the government but privately financed, Federal Home Loan Banks supports thousands of banks, credit unions, and savings companies as they supply mortgage loans to consumers. They provide lending support for most of the mortgages written in the United States.

Freddie Mac Home Page

http://www.freddiemac.com/

★★★★

Established to support home ownership and rental housing, Freddie Mac has helped to finance one in six American homes. The site explains Freddie Mac's role in housing finance, offers investor information on mortgage-backed securities, offers a listing of Freddie Mac homes for sale throughout the country through its HomeSteps link, and much more.

HUD Housing FHA Home Page

http://www.hud.gov/offices/hsg/index.cfm

★★★★

Information at this site is geared toward businesses and consumers, with lots of helpful information on buying or renting single and multifamily dwellings. Visitors to the site might also search a directory of HUD housing, participate in online forums, or review a number of related websites.

Inman News Features

http://www.inman.com/

★★★

A wellspring of real estate news and trends, *Inman News* offers extensive coverage of the industry with features and daily mortgage reports. Another plus: Featured articles from past issues are archived for weeks at a time on this site.

Interest.com

http://www.interest.com/rates.html

★★★

Comparison shop mortgage rates for your area and then consider all your options. Tips and advice at the site will help you decide when to refinance, whether you'll qualify for a standard mortgage, and what kinds of incentives might be available if you're a first-time home buyer.

LendingTree.com

http://www.lendingtree.com/

★★★★★

LendingTree.com can fix you up with a great deal on a loan, whether you need money to finance a mortgage, purchase a car, pay tuition, consolidate your debt, or start a business. Just fill out a brief application online, and LendingTree.com will provide you with offers from four lenders. LendingTree.com can also help you find homeowner's insurance, an automobile warranty, or a real estate agent. Features some resources that can help make you a more well-informed borrower.

LoanWorks.com

http://www.loanworks.com

★★★

Apply online and get an answer in five minutes regarding your mortgage status. The Quick Price feature gives you an instant rate quote. An excellent service for real estate professionals to go to secure loans for their clients.

Metro Area Mortgage Statistics

http://www.hsh.com/metstsmp.html

★★★★

HSH Associates surveys current loan rates from thousands of lenders throughout the United States and provides this data to consumers, lenders, the media, and others. Find out what average mortgage rates are for your area on this site.

MonsterMoving.com

http://www.mortgagequotes.com/

★★★★

Everything you need to move across town or across the country. Get free mortgage quotes, find a mover, search for childcare, locate a real estate agent, get tax advice, and more.

Mortgage 101

http://www.mortgage101.com/

★★★

Search interest rates by ZIP code; apply for pre-approval; or check out the E-Guides for information on calculators, appraisals, bankruptcy, credit, and down payments. Excellent place for first-time home buyers to go to better understand the home-buying process.

Mortgage Bankers Association

http://www.mbaa.org/

★★★★

Mortgage Bankers Association provides its members with the tools and resources they need to maintain and grow their lending institutions. Section on Buying a Home is excellent for consumers who are looking to purchase or refinance a home.

Mortgage Payment Calculator

http://www.homefair.com/homefair/usr/
mortcalcform.html

★★★★

You can use this page to help determine the amount of your monthly payment. Simply enter the amount of your proposed mortgage, the term of the loan, and your interest rate to check your approximate monthly payment. Then try it at different rates and different terms to see how they will affect your budget.

Mortgage-Net

http://www.mortgage-net.com/

★★★★

Use this page to determine the amount of income you need to afford the home of your choice, verify local mortgage rates, get a copy of your credit report, and more. This site has a wealth of mortgage trend information.

A
B
C
D
E
F
G
H
I
J
K
L
M
N
O
P
Q
R
S
T
U
V
W
X
Y
Z

MortgageSelect.com

http://www.mortgageselect.com/

★★★★

Easy-to-use mortgage finder displays today's current interest rates and lets you quickly apply for a loan online. Answer a few questions to have a loan officer call you with additional information. Click the Homebuyer's Toolbox link to obtain helpful information about shopping for a home and financing your mortgage. Rate Tracker helps you keep track of mortgage rates, so you can decide when to lock in.

PlanetMortgage

http://www.planetloan.com/

★★★★★

Search tool for finding local mortgage lenders. You simply select your state of residence and specify the type of loan desired (for example, Purchase, Refinance, or Auto). Planet Mortgage displays a list of local lenders. Select a lender and enter the requested information to have the lender contact you with more information. Some excellent articles and tools to help you make well-informed financial decisions.

QuickenMortgage.com

http://www.quicken.com/mortgage/

★★★★

Figure out what to expect given today's rates and your available funds.

Weichert Relocation

https://www.wrri.com/

★★★★

Weichert Relocation Resources is a global relocation company that helps thousands of employees sell, buy, finance, and rent residences around the world each year. WRR helps to bring the *best total solution* to its employee relocation needs worldwide, specifically tailored to each client's unique business environment, objectives, and budget.

SunTrust Mortgage

http://www.suntrustmortgage.com/

★★★★

Current mortgage interest rates, pre-qualifying information, calculators, a library of information, and more. You can also locate a loan officer near you.

Uncle Sam Offers Financing Breaks to Those Who Serve

http://mortgages.interest.com/content/govloan/vaintroduction.asp

★★★

If you are a veteran, you'll want to read this article, which details the history of VA loans, why and how they work, and who can benefit.

Related Sites
http://www.lendamerica.com/
http://www.mgic.com/
http://www.alaska.net/~premier/
http://www.first.co.uk/

PLUMBING

Kitchen-Bath.com

http://www.kitchen-bath.com/

★★★

Ideas and new products for updating your kitchen or bath. Provides information about kitchen and bathroom sinks, fixtures, floors, tile, ovens, stovetops, and much more.

PlumbNet

http://www.plumbnet.com/

★★★★

Built for plumbers and home improvement industry pros, the site also offers great advice and the chance to submit your challenging plumbing questions.

Toiletology 101

http://www.toiletology.com/index.shtml

★★★★★

Everything you ever needed to know about fixing and maintaining your toilet. Helpful guidance and instruction.

HOMESCHOOLING

A to Z Home's Cool Homeschooling Web Site

http://homeschooling.gomilpitas.com/

★★★★★

Created and maintained by Ann Zeise, an enthusiastic homeschooling advocate, this site is a huge directory of articles and resources on homeschooling. This site offers something for everyone, from those considering the homeschooling option to those in the trenches. Learn the basics, the laws, places to find study materials and lessons, methods to homeschool gifted children, and much, much more.

All-in-One Homeschool Resource Center

http://www.come-over.to/homeschool/

★★★

 9-13

Long list of book titles and links to some of the best homeschool information and resources on the Web. Links for some books connect you to Amazon.com, where you can order books. Some links to fun/educational sites for kids.

California Homeschool Network

http://www.californiahomeschool.net/

★★★★

A California-based organization devoted to protecting the rights of families to educate their children without government interference and to provide support for parents who choose to homeschool their children. Although the CHN is dedicated to families in California, this site offers some valuable resources for all homeschoolers, including articles on how to develop social skills and how to deal with irate relatives.

Eclectic Homeschool Online

http://www.eho.org/

★★★★

This site promotes creative homeschooling through "unique resources, teaching methods, and online helps." Shows how to teach important skills through daily activities and other innovative approaches.

Home Education Magazine Support Groups

http://www.home-ed-magazine.com/wlcm_groups.html

★★★

Get a free homeschooling guide and locate a support organization in your area through this site, which publishes a homeschooling magazine called *Home Education*.

Best Home School World

http://www.home-school.com/

★★★★★

This award-winning site features a Home Life catalog, a listing of homeschool support groups, directories of courses and lesson plans, and a mammoth homeschool mall where shoppers can find hundreds of items. This site also offers online book purchases from its secured server. If you're a parent who's home schooling your children or considering home schooling, bookmark this Best of the Best site and return to it whenever you need assistance.

A
B
C
D
E
F
G
H
I
J
K
L
M
N
O
P
Q
R
S
T
U
V
W
X
Y
Z

Homeschool Central

http://www.homeschoolcentral.com/

★★★★

This directory of resources for homeschoolers features an excellent article for new homeschoolers that lays out an overall education plan. Also includes a link to the Homeschool Central Mall (at http://homeschoolcentralmall.com/) where you can shop online for curriculum, software, and supplies. Message boards, online chat, and pen pal links help you keep in touch with other homeschoolers and help your child keep in touch with other children.

Homeschool.com

http://www.homeschool.com/

★★★★★

 All

Homeschool store that carries a wide selection of products for homeschoolers, including a Getting Started kit, books, CDs, videos, software, and online courses. If you want to homeschool your child but you don't know where to start, start here. Also features adult learning materials.

Home Schooling Magazines and Articles

http://learninfreedom.org/hsarticles.html

★★★

Periodicals and selected newspaper and magazine articles about homeschooling.

Home Schooling Resources: Science

http://www.eskimo.com/~billb/home.html

★★★

Homeschooling resources dealing primarily with science. Some information about the HOME-ED LIST-SERV and links to homeschool and alternative education sites.

HomeSchoolZone.com

http://www.homeschoolzone.com/

★★★★

 All

A community for homeschoolers (parents and kids), providing libraries of activities and events, as well as information and advice.

Kaleidoscapes

http://www.kaleidoscapes.com/

★★★

 All

Collection of message boards for kids and home education specialists, especially those focusing on self-directed and eclectic studies. Message boards include Monthly Topic, Newbie FAQ, Curricula, Unit Studies, and Kaleidoscapes' Kids Place. High school- and college-level message boards are also available.

Keystone National High School

http://www.keystonehighschool.com/

★★★

Keystone High School offers a fully accredited distance education program for 9th through 12th grade students. Its online site details the homeschooling program and features a parent planning guide, course descriptions, policies and guidelines, and other information.

The Link

http://www.homeschoolnewslink.com/

★★★

A national homeschooling online newspaper. This newspaper is also available in printed form. You can fill out the order form online and request a subscription be mailed to you.

Oregon Home Education Network

http://www.ohen.org/

★★★★

A nonprofit organization established to support Oregon's homeschooling families, the Oregon Home Education Network (OHEN) acts as a clearinghouse for homeschooling activities and resources at the local, state, and national level. The website includes FAQS about homeschooling, Oregon administrative rules, and a number of homeschooling resources.

PAIDEIA Productions

http://www.paideiaproductions.com/products.html

★★★

Videos and lesson plans for teaching a variety of science-related topics, focusing primarily on physics.

Teaching Home

http://www.teachinghome.com

★★★

Learn how to subscribe and become part of this Christian homeschooling publication that provides regular tips and opportunities for families across the country to submit articles.

Unschooling.com

http://www.unschooling.com

★★★

Read FAQs and essays about "unschooling," a self-directed, hands-on approach for helping children educate themselves. Pick up resources and tools, and chat with fellow families who have taken this approach to educating their children.

A B C D E F G H I J K L M N O P Q R S T U V W X Y Z

A
B
C
D
E
F
G
H
I
J
K
L
M
N
O
P
Q
R
S
T
U
V
W
X
Y
Z

HORSES

American Paint Horse Association

http://www.apha.com/

★★★★

Official site of the American Paint Horse Association. Obtain information on APHA membership and products, and the history, breeding, training, racing, showing, sales, and enjoyment of American Paint Horses. Lots of equine links, too. Order merchandise from the secure server.

The American Saddlebred Horse

http://www.american-saddlebred.com/

★★★★★

Anyone interested in horses—and show horses in particular—will enjoy viewing the video clips of the various gaits displayed during competitions. Detailed descriptions and diagrams of the horses' structure and history of the breed are also featured. The site includes a small photo gallery and links to saddlebred horse museums and national organizations. Be sure to submit your favorite saddlebred picture for consideration in the annual calendar. Anyone interested in horses and horseback riding should visit this and return to it often.

Arabian Home Page

http://www.ahlegacy.com/arabian.htm

★★★★

At this site, which is dedicated to Arabian horses, you'll find Arabian horse history, videos, photographs, biographies, art, collectible knives, books, jewelry, gifts, and more.

The Art of Classical Riding

http://www.geocities.com/gerrypony/

★★★★★

Maintained by "Egyptian Webmistress" Duaa Anwar, this site provides some excellent tutorials on the art of classical riding. Fully illustrated tutorials address the classical seat, posture, and positions of the hands and legs.

BarrelHorses.com

http://www.barrelhorses.com/

★★★★★

For barrel horse racing information, no site is better than this. It is packed with informative articles, show results, organizations, events, and much more. The Ask a Vet section enables you to post an equine health question and have it answered by a veterinarian. You can also check out horses for sale, post and read messages on the bulletin boards, locate barrel trainers, and learn some of your own training tips.

Breeds

http://www.ansi.okstate.edu/breeds/horses/

★★★★

 All

This site features a long list of horse breeds along with a description and photograph of each breed. Great place to learn about the various breeds of horses and other livestock, including cattle, goats, sheep, and swine.

Business of Horses

http://www.horseadvice.com/

★★★

Interested in learning more about the horse industry? Start here to read about managing your stables and horses.

Certified Horsemanship Association

http://www.cha-ahse.org/

 ★★★

CHA is a not-for-profit organization promoting equine safety through instructor certification, camp accreditation, education, and educational and safety materials.

Churchill Downs

http://www.kentuckyderby.com/

★★★★★

Official home of the Kentucky Derby, this site provides coverage of the Derby, complete with a list of contenders, the latest news, the history of the Derby, and online shopping. Even includes a recipe for Mint Juleps!

CuttingHorses.com

http://www.cuttinghorses.com/

$

★★★

This site primarily features ads for cutting horses and various related products and services.

Equine Info

http://www.equineinfo.com/

★★★★

EquineInfo is a comprehensive searchable collection of articles and links to any site related to horses. Cataloged by subject, and links annotated with descriptions.

EquineAdvertising.com

http://equineadvertising.com/

★★★★

Scan photos of horses for sale and adoption here, or place an ad to sell one.

EquiSearch

http://www.equisearch.com/

★★★

Pick up equine news, check out advertisements for horses and related products, take a look at funny bloopers, and chat with fellow horse lovers.

The HayNet

http://www.haynet.net/

★★★★

A directory of horse-related sites, organized by category. You'll find kids' sites, sites with classified ads, sites for mailing lists, and much more. Well-organized site makes it easy to navigate.

Best HorseCity.com

http://www.horsecity.com/

★★★★★

 All

HorseCity.com is a portal for the Best of the Best equine information and resources. According to management, more than 6 million pages and 18 million ads are available and are accessed each month by more than 750,000 visitors! The opening page features a collection of informative articles, along with links to additional articles, bulletin boards, shopping opportunities, and entertainment. This site, together with the sites it links you to, is our blue ribbon choice as the Best of the Best equine site on the Web!

Horse Exchange

http://www.hhhorse.com/

★★★

Watch streaming videos of horses for sale to get a much better sense of their talent and skill.

Horse Land

http://www.horseland.com

★★★

 All

Play the most fun horse game on the Web. Own, breed, and sell imaginary horses. Run shows and meet new horse lovers!

Horse World Club Online

http://www.horseworld.net/

★★★

Find ads for many stables and services here, sponsored by one of the leading equine publishing companies.

A B C D E F G **H** I J K L M N O P Q R S T U V W X Y Z

A
B
C
D
E
F
G
H
I
J
K
L
M
N
O
P
Q
R
S
T
U
V
W
X
Y
Z

Horse Worldwide

http://www.horseworldwide.com/

★★★

Designed for horse lovers, this site aims to provide lots of information about horses and horse-related products for sale.

TheHorse.com

http://www.thehorse.com/

★★★★

Online magazine devoted to helping horse owners and healthcare providers stay informed. Articles cover general health issues, injuries, and preventive care. Check back regularly for any health alerts in your area.

The Horseman's Advisor

http://www.horseadvice.com/advisor/

★★★★

Serves as a clearinghouse for articles and products on horse-related topics. Includes a discussion forum, classifieds, and links to other sites.

Horses, Horses and More Horses

http://horses.co.uk/

★★★

A multimedia horse photo album with more than 800 photographs of horses doing a variety of things, including jumping, showing, foaling, polo, and dressage.

Horsesites.com

http://www.horsesites.com/XcDirectory.asp

★★★

Get race results and racing news, track down suppliers, and investigate the pedigree of promising-looking horses here, where you'll find links to a host of horse sites.

Mane Points

http://www.manepoints.com

★★★

Search this horse information center for information about horse care and safety, as well as many other topics of interest to horse lovers. Must register to enter and have content customized for your geographical location.

RopeHorses.com

http://www.ropehorses.com/

★★★★

This site features ads for rope horses and related products and services. For more general information about horses, see the parent site, HorseCity.com.

United States Dressage Federation

http://www.usdf.org/

★★★★

Learn more about the sport of dressage, locate upcoming competitions and instructors to help you prepare, and find the results of recent events. Merchandise available (some freebies), but you must print and mail the order form.

WesternHorseman.com

http://www.westernhorseman.com/

★★★★★

 All

This is the homepage of *Western Horseman* magazine, which provides articles and information on everything related to Western horsemanship. Here you can find equine healthcare advice, training tips, and information about various events updated daily. Site also features a cartoon of the day, featured articles, a virtual vet, bulletin boards, and an online poll. Excellent site.

WWW Library: Horse Section

http://www.ansi.okstate.edu/library/equine.html

★★★★

Provides a listing of horse resources, including information on breeds and selection; horse publications; publications on diseases, disorders, and parasites of the horse; and general information such as behavior and training, buying a horse, care, shoeing, nutrition and feeding, and more.

Air Guitar

http://www.mirrorimage.com/air/

★★★

Tired of watching your friends play air guitar at the Steve Miller concert and wishing you had that talent? Well, take an online lesson here. Also has 100 links to other entertaining sites.

The Amazing Pecking Chicken

http://www.vanderbilt.edu/dotedu/staff/cluck/

★★★

Investigate this site of extreme silliness for images of a disco chicken, a pecking chicken, and the history of the pecking chicken home page. Read the top five "super-neato quotes from cluck worshipers" and find out how the power of the chicken has changed the lives of countless (okay, about 12) others.

The Anti-Telemarketer Source

http://www.antitelemarketer.com/

★★★

Do you hate it when telemarketers bother you? This site is about the revenge of the customer. Offers techniques, stories, and more about dealing with telemarketers. Finally, a site that's both funny and useful!

The Bathrooms of Madison County

http://www.nutscape.com/

★★★★

A well-done parody of the popular novel *The Bridges of Madison County* that includes pictures and a story told in seven parts about, literally, the bathrooms of Madison County in Iowa. The backgrounds used on some of the pages are a subtle touch; they look like bathroom tiles, outhouse siding, and so on.

The Bob Rivers Show

http://www.twistedtunes.com/

★★★★

🚫👶 Not for kids

This site is a must for anyone who enjoys song parodies. Features parodies of popular songs, updated weekly. Seasonal favorites are available, too. Also provides links to other funny and entertaining sites.

Bob's Fridge Door

http://www.bobsfridge.com/

★★★

Created by Bob Hirschfield, this page offers satirical, humorous coverage of the news and other topics. Check out the sections NOT for Dummies, Skewpoint, Parody Section, and, of course, Bob's Fridge Door.

Bureau of Missing Socks

http://www.funbureau.com/

★★★★

Finally, support has arrived for the matching sock deprived among us. The Bureau of Missing Socks is the first organization "devoted solely to solving the question of what happens to missing single socks." It explores "all aspects of the phenomenon, including the occult, conspiracy theories, and extraterrestrials."

Centre for the Easily Amused

http://www.amused.com/

★★★★★

A phenomenal site where you can waste huge amounts of time browsing. The site's links are organized by category, such as Sites That Do Stuff and Random Silliness, to make up one of the best lists of odd humor on the WWW. You'll also find trivia games, daily jokes, and chat rooms.

A
B
C
D
E
F
G
H
I
J
K
L
M
N
O
P
Q
R
S
T
U
V
W
X
Y
Z

Chickenhead

http://www.chickenhead.com/

★★★★

 Not for kids

Chickenhead is "a sickening repository of tasteless and self-congratulatory garbage, produced by a detestable clique of New York City losers, who toil needlessly in abject poverty and well-deserved obscurity." Need I say more? Kids should stay away, but college students and older folks looking for sick humor should definitely visit.

College Dropouts Alumni Association

http://www.geocities.com/CollegePark/7734/cdoaa.html

★★★

This humorous site lists famous alumni who dropped out of college, including Rosie O'Donnell, Bill Gates, and William Faulkner! Includes stories, articles, and other offbeat items about dropping out of college and supplies membership information.

Comedy Central

http://www.comedycentral.com

$

★★★★

Not for kids

Visit Comedy Central for the online version of *South Park, Primetime Glick, The Man Show*, and other humorous shows with lots of extras. Shop the online store for T-shirts and other Comedy Central show-related merchandise!

Comedy.com

http://www.comedy.com/

★★★

Comedy.com is your ticket to comedy clubs and the hottest new acts. Keep up on funny people, cool venues, and the joke of the day for a chuckle. Also features a 10,000-joke archive.

Comedyorama

http://www.comedyorama.com

★★★

Read biographies of some of the great comedians; hear clips of funny moments; and enjoy the memories of comedians of old, such as Phil Silvers, Jack Benny, and Daws Butler.

Comedy-Zone.net

http://www.comedy-zone.net/

★★★★★

Huge collection of funny stuff, including jokes, T-shirts, trivia, cartoons, games, TV comedy, stand-up comedy, and a humor directory with links to hundreds of additional funny sites.

CONK! Daily: Humor in the News

http://www.conk.com/index.htm

★★★★

Browse through this site for a hilarious take on the daily news. You'll also find daily fun facts and quotes, games and puzzles, more than 100 of your favorite comic strips, and more ways to goof off than you thought possible.

Conversational Cheap Shots

http://www.vandruff.com/art_converse.html

★★★★

I don't know about you, but I plan to email several copies of the guidelines suggested at this site to friends, loved ones, and not-so-loved ones. The author has grouped the most common conversational pitfalls into the categories of Ad Hominem Variants, Sleight of Mind Fallacies, Delay Tactics, Question as Opportunity, and General Irritants. Examples of each type of faux pas are given, too, but I'm sure you're not guilty of any of them—right?

Cruel Site of the Day

http://www.cruel.com/

★★★★

 Not for kids

Tired of a Pollyanna outlook? This site offers a cynical look at the Web by awarding sites that are the most perturbing and cruel, yet entertaining. This site provides a great starting point for what's warped, obscure, and peevish on the Web.

Cursing in Swedish

http://www.santesson.com/curshome.htm

★★★★★

 Not for kids

Study sharp, succinct swearing in Swedish. According to the introduction, the Swedish language is remarkably limited when it comes to using four-letter words. If you're Swedish and short-tempered, or just interested in expanding your repertoire, let this page help you take out your aggressions. WAV files are supplied so you can learn to pronounce your curses properly.

Darwin Awards

http://www.darwinawards.com/

$

★★★★★

14-18

The Darwin Awards honor "those who improve our gene pool by removing themselves from it in really stupid ways." When I last checked, winners of the Darwin Award included a man who blew himself up trying to booby-trap his home to blow up his family. Order your T-shirt online.

Dave's Web of Lies

http://www.davesweboflies.com/

★★★

Dave's crack team of researchers haunt the Web looking for lies packaged as the truth (and if you believe that…). Choose the Lie of the Day, go for A Week of Lies, or—better yet—search the Database of Lies by topic or by liar to find a lie useful for almost any situation. For special occasions, you might want to consult the Celebrity Liar.

Best | Despair, Inc.

http://www.despair.com

$

★★★★★

Ever get tired of seeing those posters and note cards with soaring eagles and sappy motivational sayings? Despair, Inc., has an answer to these annoying props. Check out the posters, calendars, and coffee mugs, and sign up for the newsletter. This is one of the cleverest sites to come along in a long time.

Dilbert Zone

http://www.dilbert.com/

$

★★★★

 14-18

The official online hangout for *Dilbert* fans, this site features the Dilbert comic strip archive, where you can select and email a strip to friends or relatives. Includes games, character biographies, downloadable desktop wallpaper and mouse pointers, and more.

Doonesbury

http://www.doonesbury.com/

$

★★★★★

Official site of the *Doonesbury* comic strip, this site is mapped out into four areas: The Strip, where you can read comics and character biographies; Arcade, where you can solve puzzles, play games, send e-greetings, play a trivia game, or ask Duke questions; Media Center, which includes a straw poll and daily briefing; and a Bookshop, where you can purchase posters and books and get some free stuff.

Fade To Black

http://www.fadetoblack.com/

$

★★★★

  Not for kids

Check out the latest news, the dumb quote of the day, and the unintentionally funny site of the day; then look at the list of organizations currently boycotting the site. Also find the results of a poll regarding which celebrities are most likely to die in the near future, as well as many other jokes, puns, and articles of black humor.

A B C D E F G H I J K L M N O P Q R S T U V W X Y Z

A B C D E F G H I J K L M N O P Q R S T U V W X Y Z

Frolic

http://www.frolic.org

★★★

 Not for kids

Downright silly in the extreme, the Naked Dancing Llama (NDL) is its own cottage industry, giving advice and running for the office of U.S. President (the Constitution doesn't actually say a llama can't hold the land's highest office).

The Gallery of Advertising Parody

http://parody.organique.com/

★★★

This site offers many different ad parodies for popular products, including Starbuck's Coffee, Prozac, and Calvin Kline.

Goofiness Dot Com

http://www.goofiness.com/

★★★★

Who knew wasting time could be so much fun? At Goofiness Dot Com, you'll discover all kinds of new ways to fritter away your productive hours. Supply captions for pictures, take personality tests, read the Random Prediction and Random Quote of the Day, and see the winners of the Ball of Goof Award.

Humor.com

http://www.humor.com/

★★★★★

 Not for kids

One of the best humor sites on the Web, this site features jokes, articles, cartoons, animations, diversions (games and such), and more. Some of the material is great for kids and adults alike, but some material is definitely off limits for kids. Also features a mall where you can find humorous gifts, T-shirts, posters, and other items.

HumorSearch

http://www.humorsearch.com/

★★★★★

Internet search engine for humorous sites and resources on the Web. Includes a gallery of Osama bin Laden cartoons, tax jokes, Clinton jokes, games, and more.

JibJab

http://www.jibjab.com/

★★★★★

 14-18

This site features political parodies, e-cards you can send to your friends via email, screensavers, and much more. Some very funny cartoons, including the Geezers Musical, Bubba's Brownies, and The Babysitter.

Jokes.com

http://www.jokes.com

★★★★★

 Not for kids

Search the free jokes database to find just the right one or read the daily headlines to see what craziness is being reported. The headlines are real, although the stupidity of many will make you wonder. Sign up to receive a free joke every day via email or request a more targeted joke, such as a sports joke, college joke, or Osama bin Laden joke.

JokeWallpaper.com

http://www.jokewallpaper.com

★★★

Download free joke wallpaper to liven up your computer screen. Choose from political statements, news and popular culture, celebrities, or a laundry list of others. Make your cursor do funny things, too.

LaughNet

http://www.laughnet.net/

★★★★

Not for kids

Directory of humor sites that organizes sites into categories, including Crude Humor, Workplace Humor, Computer Humor, Political Humor, and more than a dozen other categories. Some of the humor is fine for kids of all ages, other sites are acceptable for teenagers, and others are definitely for adults only.

Legodeath—A Museum of Horrors

http://www.legodeath.com

★★★★

Not for kids

Over the years, LEGO building blocks have been used to create buildings, cars, airplanes, and other human inventions. Now, at this site, you can see LEGOS used to create an entire museum dedicated to the humanly morbid topics of execution, torture, occupational hazards, domestic incidents, and accidents abroad.

Lip Balm Anonymous

http://www.kevdo.com/lipbalm/home.html

★★★

This site promotes the casting out of all lip balms based on their psychologically addictive tendencies. Read about the history of lip balm and "The Industry of Addiction," and please…share this site with someone you love.

Mefco's Random Joke Server

http://www.randomjoke.com/topiclist.html

★★★★

Choose the type of joke you want from a large list of categories, including Light Bulb Jokes, Murphy's Law, Jokes for Nerds, and so on. Read some funny stories, too, or submit your own joke, if you like.

Modern Humorist

http://www.modernhumorist.com/

★★★★

14-18

Modern Humorist is an entertainment company founded by John Aboud and Michael Colton in 2000. In addition to creating comedy for radio, TV, and other media outlets, the company created this online magazine, which showcases the work of some of the top humorists in America. Although the site is no longer updated with new content, it still provides archived content that can keep you laughing for hours.

National Lampoon

http://www.nationallampoon.com/

★★★★★

Not for kids

Home of *National Lampoon* magazine, the same folks who brought us the *Vacation* movies, *Animal House*, and other edgy comedies. Here, you can find a humorous look at the news, flashbacks, joke analysis, and true facts. Very funny site.

One Liner Diner

http://www.gwally.com/humor/oneliner.php

★★★

Check this site daily for a pithy or amusing one-liners you can use throughout the day. And if you don't think the first one's funny, click Another Line.

The Onion

http://www.theonion.com

★★★★★

Not for kids

An irreverent version of local, national, and international news, this site provides hilariously funny satirical reports that are both timely and acerbic. If you're easily offended, however, steer clear of this site.

A
B
C
D
E
F
G
H
I
J
K
L
M
N
O
P
Q
R
S
T
U
V
W
X
Y
Z

A
B
C
D
E
F
G
H
I
J
K
L
M
N
O
P
Q
R
S
T
U
V
W
X
Y
Z

The (un)Official Dave Barry Site

http://www.davebarry.com/

★★★★★

Check out this site to get information about the latest books and articles written by humor columnist, Dave Barry. Brief biography of Dave Barry, plus a list of Barry's books with a brief synopsis of each. Links to Amazon.com, where you can purchase the books. Links to other fan sites as well. Check out Dave's blog at http://weblog.herald.com/column/davebarry/.

The Oracle of Bacon at Virginia

http://www.cs.virginia.edu/oracle/

★★★

Fans of the game *Six Degrees of Kevin Bacon* will love this site, where the concept began. Enter the name of any actor or actress who has ever been in an American film, and the Oracle will show how that actor or actress is linked to Kevin Bacon. Orson Welles, for instance, was in *The Muppet Movie* in 1979 with Steve Martin, who was in *Novocaine* with Kevin Bacon in 2001.

PElvis

http://www.princeton.edu/~pelvis/

★★★

 Not for kids

The King lives in the mind and jeans of the Princeton students who created this page. Gives you a cynical look at drugs and alcohol, with several Elvis-related links and a not-so-serious look at the man behind the white jumpsuit.

Ray Owen's Joke a Day

http://www.jokeaday.com/

$

★★★★

 Not for kids

Visit this site for a free laugh, updated daily, or subscribe (for a fee) to gain access to archives of letters, Dweeb Letters, last week's jokes, babes, hunks, Video Minutes, Twisted Tunes, Weird Pictures, and lots more! You can also sign up to have jokes delivered daily via email.

Red Vs. Blue

http://www.redvsblue.com/

$

★★★★★

 14-18

Red Vs. Blue is an animated tongue-in-cheek science fiction adventure consisting of 4–5 minute episodes. You can check out the archived episodes online, join discussions with fans in the forum, submit and see viewer-submitted art, and shop online for T-shirts, hats, and other stuff.

Rodney Dangerfield Home Page

http://www.rodney.com/

★★★★

Not for kids

Rodney's home page features a joke of the day and the "no respect" contest. You can also download sound files and an answering-machine message in Rodney's voice.

SatireWire

http://www.satirewire.com

$

★★★★★

Not for kids

More sarcastic than. satirical, this site provides a tongue-in-cheek view of current events that will keep you laughing for hours. No subject is safe; SatireWire will even poke fun at itself.

Spatula City

http://pixelscapes.com/spatulacity/

★★★

You'll find more than just pancake flippers at this cool virtual spatula store. The site offers a wealth of information, organized into groups of The Silly Zone, Fiction and Faction, Black Light Special, and Kitchenware 'n' Candy Bars. Go to the Checkout Lane to see a list of links to related sites. More than three years old, but still funny.

The Squat

http://www.thesquat.com

★★★

If you're hooked on the twenty-something beach-house soap opera called *The Spot*, don't hesitate to drop in on its landlocked ugly cousin, *The Squat*. (No relation, really.) *The Squat* kids live in a smelly trailer in Paradise Park.

The Straight Dope Archives

http://www.straightdope.com/

★★★★

 Not for kids

For years, a character named Cecil Adams has been writing a newspaper column in which he answers any question that his devoted and unnaturally inquisitive readers see fit to put to him. *Any* question is fair game, it seems.

Un-Cabaret

http://www.uncabaret.com

★★★★

 Not for kids

This cyber-companion to L.A.'s *Un-Cabaret*, the "mother-show of the alternative comedy scene," where "writer-performers can experiment in long-form comedy storytelling and monologue," is rife with audio and video clips from the likes of Bobcat Goldthwaite, Julia Sweeney, Moon Zappa, Andy Dick, and Merrill Markoe, to name a few.

Whitehouse.org

http://www.whitehouse.org/

★★★★★

Not to be confused with www.whitehouse.gov or www.whitehouse.com, this site is packed with satire directed at the national political scene. See your favorite and least favorite politicians lampooned. See national policies dragged through the mud. Take a tour of the White House, if you can afford it. And, if you have any time left, visit the Office of Fraternal Affairs.

Working Wounded

http://www.workingwounded.com/

★★★★

 Not for kids

Brainchild of author and columnist Bob Rosner, this site is designed to provide no-nonsense advice to workers concerning issues they face at work. Real-life stories, office webcams, confessionals, gallery of cubicles, bad boss stories, and much more.

A
B
C
D
E
F
G
H
I
J
K
L
M
N
O
P
Q
R
S
T
U
V
W
X
Y
Z

472

A
B
C
D
E
F
G
H
I
J
K
L
M
N
O
P
Q
R
S
T
U
V
W
X
Y
Z

HUNTING

American Firearms Industry

http://www.amfire.com/

★★★

 Not for kids

"The World's Largest and Oldest Professional Firearms Retailers Association." Read about hot products, access the Buyer's Guide, get information on the Firearms Trade Expo, and more.

Bowhunting.Net

http://www.bowhunting.net/

★★★★

Not for kids

Catch up on the latest news in bowhunting here, as well as pick up some tips for improving your form and for increasing your hunting domain. You'll also find competition information.

The Bowsite

http://www.bowsite.com

★★★★

Not for kids

Anyone looking for statistics related to bowhunting need only stop at this site for details. Facts regarding the need for hunting, as well as benefits of the sport, are provided, as are tips for the hunter.

Browning Home Page

http://www.browning.com

★★★★

Not for kids

Shotguns, rifles, archery equipment, hunting wear, gun cases, knives—Browning makes it all, and you can find ready access to local dealers and price information on the company's home page. Order a catalog or check out job opportunities. You'll also find links to other hunting-related sites here.

BuckLore Hunting Adventures

http://www.bucklore.com/

★★★

Not for kids

Thinking of planning a hunting trip? This site for BuckLore Hunting will tell you all you need to know about arranging a trip at this lodge in the Adirondacks. In addition to hearing about the native animals, you can investigate the accommodations and food.

Buckmasters Magazine Online

http://www.buckmasters.com/

$

★★★★

Not for kids

Whitetail deer hunters can get hunting season information, jump into a chat room, check the message boards, view the trophy gallery, buy hunting gear, pick up hunting games, and read whitetail magazine articles at this rich site.

"The Burner" Jerry Barnhart

http://www.jerrybarnhart.com/

★★★

Not for kids

To say this guy is good would be a serious understatement. Mr. Barnhart is a champion shooter of too many competitions to list. You can ask him questions, view his equipment, and read tips about all aspects of target shooting perfection.

Burris Sports Optics

http://www.burrisoptics.com/

★★★

 Not for kids

With 25 years in the business, Burris has earned a consistent reputation as the most innovative and consumer-responsive company in the sports optics business. See the company's current line, check out the FAQs, get a free catalog, and find out why you should choose Burris over others.

Cabela's

http://www.cabelas.com/

$

★★★★★

Not for kids

Shop this outfitter for apparel, footwear, or equipment before your next hunting outing.

Clay Pigeon Shooting Association

http://www.cpsa.co.uk/

★★★★

Not for kids

Become a member of the CPSA; check out scores, news, and links; and learn where the next competitions will be held.

Crock Pot Venison and Game Recipes

http://southernfood.about.com/library/crock/blgame.htm

★★★

Not for kids

After you've field-dressed your deer or cleaned your birds, what do you do with all that meat? If you're getting tired of just plain old venison roasts or deer meat chili, the folks at Southern American Cuisine have gathered some wild game recipes here. This research was done during deer season, so the recipes are mostly for venison, but check it out during other seasons for quail, pheasant, and rabbit recipes.

Doug's Shooting Sports Interest Page

http://www.users.fast.net/~jasmine/

★★★★

 Not for kids

Doug provides information about skeet, trap, pin, reloading, and more. He also provides links to the NRA, the USA shooting team, and firearm laws—and, to keep things light, there's a Joke of the Week.

Ducks Unlimited

http://www.ducks.org/

 $

★★★★

Not for kids

Home base for the world's leading organization for conserving wetlands.

Easton Archery

http://www.eastonarchery.com/

$

★★★★

 Not for kids

Investigate all of Easton's archery products and buy them online after you've made your selection.

Eders.com

http://www.eders.com/

 $

★★★★

Not for kids

This online hunting catalog has an amazing selection of equipment, from bows to calls to bows and scents.

Fast Draw Resource Center: Guide to the Fastest Timed Sport in the World

http://www.gunfighter.com/fastdraw/

★★★

 Not for kids

 What's the world record for drawing, cocking, aiming, firing a gun, and hitting a target? You won't believe it! Fast Draw has gained in popularity in recent years, and this site chronicles every aspect of it. This site includes official rules and records, as well as lists of upcoming contests.

A B C D E F G H I J K L M N O P Q R S T U V W X Y Z

A
B
C
D
E
F
G
H
I
J
K
L
M
N
O
P
Q
R
S
T
U
V
W
X
Y
Z

Field & Stream Online

http://www.fieldandstream.com/

★★★★★

☒ Not for kids

The outdoorsman's bible has a site on the Internet. The current issue is here with features, articles, and editorials. You can even pick an area of the country and find out what's in season and where to hunt.

Fishing-Hunting.Com

http://www.fishing-hunting.com/

★★★

☒ Not for kids

Directory service for the fishing and hunting industry. The site is undergoing changes, so stay tuned for new features.

GunHoo

http://www.gunsgunsguns.com/gunhoo/

★★★

☒ Not for kids

GunHoo is an all-inclusive search engine for every conceivable topic on guns: accessories, ammunition, the Second Amendment, literature, safety, and more. Just as with Yahoo!, you can enter keywords and conduct Web searches.

Hunting Information Systems: An Online Guide

http://www.huntinfo.com/

★★★★

☒ Not for kids

Lots of products and outfitters listed here, and the site is updated often. Check out the recommended outfitters or suggest one of your own. You'll find the latest hunting news here, including alerts, state and regional information, news about swap hunts, and lots more.

Hunting.Net

http://www.hunting.net/

★★★★★

☒ Not for kids

The ultimate hunting site on the Web covers everything from turkey hunting to Elk hunting, bowhunting, sporting dogs, hunting outfitters, and hunting gear. Chat areas, message boards, auctions, and swaps put you in touch with other hunters online.

Hunting New Zealand

http://www.fishnhunt.co.nz/hunting.htm

★★★

☒ Not for kids

The Chat Room here is an interesting place to go, with Canadian hunters talking to New Zealand hunters talking to you. You'll find all sorts of information about hunting in New Zealand and in general, along with jokes and tips. Be sure to check out the list of guides and safaris in New Zealand.

Hunting Pennsylvania

http://www.huntingpa.com/index.shtml

★★★

☒ Not for kids

HuntingPA is a one-stop shop to find hunting spots and outfitters in the state. Hunters can also share information via chat and message boards, as well as report on their recent successful hunting trips.

Hunting Trail WebRing

http://www.hunting-trail.com/

★★★★

☒ Not for kids

A community of websites all relating to the topic of hunting. Find articles, newsletters, product reviews, chat rooms, message boards, and more.

Idaho Archery

http://www.idahoarchery.com/

★★★★

🚸 Not for kids

The best feature of this site is its archive of stories from bowhunters. If you're wondering what prompts someone to drive sometimes hundreds of miles into the wilderness and then walk more miles, all before the break of day, check out these stories from hunters in the field. You'll find the usual pictures of hunters with their prey, with the addition of the events that led up to the kill, and information about the exact equipment used. There's much more at this site, including deer and elk forecasts, upcoming competitions, and links to other pages, but the real-life stories are the best.

International Bowhunting Organization (IBO)

http://www.ibo.net/

★★★

🚸 Not for kids

Although the site is primarily for current and potential IBO members, the archery-related websites are an excellent starting point.

Kleen-Bore Gun Cleaning Products

http://www.kleen-bore.com/

★★★

🚸 Not for kids

A family-owned firearms maintenance company that provides rifle, shotgun, and pistol cleaning rods for the U.S. military. Has grown into one of the major international providers of gun cleaning and care products for sports shooting, hunting, military, and law enforcement.

Maine Guides Online

http://www.maineguides.com/

★★★★

🚸 Not for kids

Considering a hunting trip to Maine? Check out this site and then go to either the Big Game Hunting, Small Game Hunting, or Bowhunting section. You'll find everything you need right here: places to stay, places to hunt, guides, hunting equipment retailers, and things to do when you're not hunting. A very well-maintained site.

National Association of Shooting Sports Athletes (NASSA)

http://www.nassa.org/

★★★

🚸 Not for kids

Family-oriented organization designed to coach junior shooters to become world-class Olympic athletes. Learn about the full range of coaching, training, and support services offered to members. NASSA sponsors monthly postal matches for Air Pistol, which are open to everyone (including non-members and adults). It offers the opportunity to compete with some of the best shooters in the country—and possibly the world—and NASSA's staff will analyze your shooting performance and offer suggestions on how to improve it!

Best National Rifle Association

http://www.nra.org/

$

★★★★★

🚸 Not for kids

Keep up to date with the latest in gun legislation at this site. The NRA is one of the strongest advocates of the Second Amendment to the Constitution, guaranteeing the right to bear arms in the United States. The NRA offers programs benefiting gun safety, marksmanship, personal safety, hunting, and more. Find out about its services, latest news, and legislative activities at this site. This site also has a new online store where you can buy hats, shirts, and other NRA merchandise.

Outdoor Adventures Network

http://www.outadventures.com/

★★★

🚸 Not for kids

Outdoor adventure site that covers everything from backpacking to hunting and fishing. Features a tip of the day, information about various types of outdoor adventures, and links to other resources. Area for Outdoor Women is currently under construction.

A B C D E F G **H** I J K L M N O P Q R S T U V W X Y Z

A
B
C
D
E
F
G
H
I
J
K
L
M
N
O
P
Q
R
S
T
U
V
W
X
Y
Z

Outdoor Resources Online

http://www.outdoor-resources.com/Hunting/

★★★

Not for kids

Investigate hunting locations and products, as well as outfitters and guides for your next outing.

Outdoor Sports Web

http://www.osweb.com

★★★

Not for kids

Although the site is built for adults, the Kidz Korner is full of activities for children. They can print out coloring pages, get instructions for building a bird house, and learn new games at this site. For those users interested in the outdoor sports, the site is a resource for locating hunting and fishing guides and products. The tips and articles are submitted by fellow hunters; providing a first-hand look at outdoor adventures.

Pearson Archery

http://www.benpearson.com/

★★★

Not for kids

Learn more about Ben Pearson bows and dealers at this site, and locate a dealer close to you.

Sagittarius Twente, University Archery Club

http://www.student.utwente.nl/~sagi/

★★★

Not for kids

This site, from the Netherlands, has a unique site map in the form of an archery target. It's well constructed with pages of articles by and for archers. View pictures, hear humorous excuses, and discuss the sport of archery in the newsgroups.

The Shooting Sports Web Site

http://www.shootingsports.com/

★★★★

Not for kids

This site provides links to every other website you can imagine about guns, shooting, and related sports. It also has its own articles, including a bunch of recipes for pheasant and partridge.

Shotgun Sports

http://www.shotgunsports.com/

★★★

Not for kids

Every aspect of the shooting life is covered here. This site provides guides for clay and wing shooting, dog clubs, game bird breeders, gun rights groups and other organizations, shooting news, and more. Enter the talk groups with all your questions and comments.

Southern Duck Hunter

http://www.duckcentral.com/

★★★★

Not for kids

Huge collection of resources for duck hunters, ranging from hunt report forums to a recipe book. Check out the featured product, research state guidelines, listen to duck calls for various species, check river stages, and much, much more.

Sportsman's Choice

http://www.sportsmanschoice.com/

★★★

Not for kids

Sportsman's Choice is a family-owned business dedicated to providing a comprehensive resource for hunters and anglers, helping them locate detailed information regarding guides and services across the globe. Provides thousands of names of guides, outfitters, lodges, resorts, clubs, charters, marinas, taxidermies, and hunting preserves, along with links to DNR and government sites in the United States.

Sportsman's Guide

http://www.sportsmensguide.net/

$

★★★

Not for kids

An online catalog of clothing and hunting gear that is searchable by category.

Trapshooters.com

http://www.trapshooters.com/

★★★

 Not for kids

This website is devoted to informing the public about the sport of trapshooting. It helps you find the information you need to get involved in the sport of trapshooting, such as how to trapshoot, where to go to trapshoot, and lots more.

Ultimate Hunts

http://www.dovehunt.com/

★★★★

 Not for kids

Learn more about bird hunting and share photos of your successes at the site.

United States Practical Shooting Association

http://www.uspsa.org/

★★★★

 Not for kids

This nonprofit group oversees the sport of practical shooting, which is basically the shooting of targets that represent what guns of all makes and power will reasonably be expected to strike during their intended use. The site has a huge number of links for USPSA rules, information, classifications, and much more.

The Unofficial Tommy Gun Page

http://www.nfatoys.com/tsmg/

★★★★

 Not for kids

Not only will you find links and pages related to collecting Tommies, you'll also find a detailed history of the gun, which was so ahead of its time that the Armed Forces didn't start adopting it until 1930, nine years after the first Model 1921 came off the line. The original could fire 1,200 rounds per minute.

Related Sites
http://www.huntinginfo.org/training.html
http://links.shooters.com/

The U.S. and International Archer

http://www.bowhunting.net/usarcher/

★★★★

 Not for kids

At this website, you'll find the entire contents of the *U.S. Archer* magazine, a bimonthly publication. The current magazine and archived issues are here in their entirety, but there's also the offer of free books with a subscription. You'll find articles, editorials, photographs—everything you'd find in the real magazine. You'll also find links to all the official archery organizations and other sites of interest to archers. This magazine covers all aspects of archery, from field and target archery to 3D shoots to bowhunting.

U.S. Fish and Wildlife Service

http://www.fws.gov/

★★★★★

 Not for kids

Dedicated to conserving nature in the United States, this site helps hunters get appropriate permits and learn more about safe hunting. It also aims to teach kids what it means when a species is endangered.

U.S. Sportsmen's Alliance

http://www.wlfa.org/

★★★★★

 Not for kids

This is the place to go if you want to get serious about wildlife management and the future of hunting, fishing, and trapping. This is the only organization whose sole mission is the conservation of natural resources. Learn about its mission and how to join.

The Virtual Wild Turkey Hunting Network

http://www.bowhunting.net/wildturkey.net/default.htm#top

★★★

 Not for kids

This site is filled with goodies. You'll find seminars on many aspects of turkey hunting, such as tips for beginners, information about turkey behavior, and taxidermy tips, along with links to other great sites. Bonus items: downloadable turkey calls, free wallpaper for your PC, and killer recipes—Cajun fried turkey sounds incredible.

A
B
C
D
E
F
G
H
I
J
K
L
M
N
O
P
Q
R
S
T
U
V
W
X
Y
Z

A
B
C
D
E
F
G
H
I
J
K
L
M
N
O
P
Q
R
S
T
U
V
W
X
Y
Z

Waterfowler.com

http://www.waterfowler.com/

★★★

 Not for kids

Great place for bird hunters to communicate with one another, this site features an online lodge (members only); field reports from members; a bulletin board where you can buy, sell, and trade gear; and an online shop.

Wisconsin Hunters

http://wisconsinhunters.tripod.com/

★★★★

 Not for kids

This site provides access to information and resources for outdoors sports persons, including campers, hunters, and anglers. No fancy stuff here, just excellent information.

Yahoo! Sites on Archery and Bow Hunting

http://dir.yahoo.com/Recreation/outdoors/hunting/bow_hunting

★★★

 Not for kids

Yahoo! pulls together a lengthy list of archery and bow hunting sites, serving as a gateway to even more information about the sport. A handy reference site.

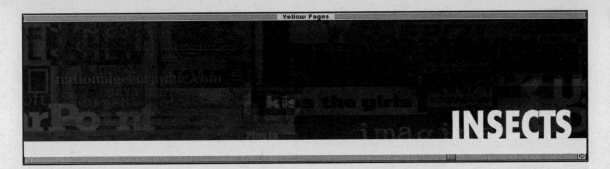

INSECTS

3D Insects

http://www.ento.vt.edu/~sharov/3d/3dinsect.html

★★★

👫 All

Watch insect movies in 3D here. Great entertainment for kids and insect-lovers.

BugBios.com

http://www.insects.org

★★★★★

👫 All

Bug fans will consider this insect heaven. The colorful and information-packed site offers incredible pictures and descriptions of insects. The digest section offers information on how insects are present in every facet of our life. You'll also find an ordinal key to help you identify insects. Explore this site's links to other websites and resources. BugBios.com has even taken the time to categorize and review them. The site is very eye-appealing and well organized, making it an easy Best of the Best pick.

BugInfo (Smithsonian Institution)

http://www.si.edu/resource/faq/nmnh/buginfo/start.htm

★★★

👫 All

Created and maintained by the Smithsonian Institution, the BugInfo page features links to a couple dozen information sheets on some of the more common (and popular) bugs and bug-related topics. Here, you can learn fun facts about beetles, common household pests, and other bugs.

The Butterfly Website

http://butterflywebsite.com/

★★★★

👫 All

Join a discussion group, learn how to attract butterflies with a butterfly garden, or become part of the effort to preserve butterfly habitats. The impressive photo gallery will help you identify the various species of moths and butterflies, and you can visit many butterfly gardens and zoos.

Coleoptera Home Page

http://www.coleoptera.org/

★★★

This site is for entomologists (who work on coleoptera/beetles), researchers and museum workers, ecologists, environmentalists, and others who are interested in insects, beetle collecting, wildlife, and nature. The page includes links and information on beetles, a bibliography, an image and sound library, an entomological glossary, and more.

eNature.com Insects

http://www.enature.com/guides/select_Insects_and_Spiders.asp

💲

★★★★★

👫 All

National Wildlife Federation's eNature.com is a comprehensive encyclopedia of animal life. This site provides thorough coverage of common and uncommon insects. For each insect, eNature.com displays a picture, a physical description, and information about the insect's food, life cycle, habitat, and range.

A B C D E F G H I J K L M N O P Q R S T U V W X Y Z

Entomology Index of Internet Resources

http://www.ent.iastate.edu/List/

★★★

Iowa State has provided a searchable database of websites pertaining to insects and related organisms.

Insects Hotlist

http://sln.fi.edu/tfi/hotlists/insects.html

★★★★★

More information than you probably ever thought you needed about insects—beetles, butterflies, ants, moths, roaches, and more—from the Franklin Institute.

Insects on WWW

http://www.isis.vt.edu/~fanjun/text/Links.html

★★★★

All

Impressive directory of insect sites and resources on the Web broken down into categories that cover every insect from A to T (ants to ticks). Learn about common pests, common insects, and insect anatomy and behavior. Miscellaneous links to kids sites, suppliers, bug food, and more.

Related Site
http://www.insectclopedia.com/

Introduction to the Arthropoda

http://www.ucmp.berkeley.edu/arthropoda/arthropoda.html

★★★★

The arthropods, the largest animal phylum, includes insects, spiders, crustaceans, and many more! This is the famous Berkeley site.

Iowa State's Entomology Image Gallery

http://www.ent.iastate.edu/imagegallery/

★★★★

All

They might not win an Academy Award, but the tick and beetle movies that you can view at this website provide a fascinating look at the lives of these industrious creatures. The site also contains an entomology index and special features on mosquitoes, lice, and corn borers. To view the movies, look for an icon featuring a strip of film. Many still images, too.

Spiders

http://www.powerup.com.au/~glen/spider.htm

★★★★

9-13

Check out this site to learn more than you ever wanted to know about our creepy friend, the spider. All information was written and pictures gathered by the 5th grade class at Rochedale State School in Australia. And if you have some spider pictures you'd like to share, the kids will put them on their website!

The Yuckiest Site on the Internet

http://yucky.kids.discovery.com/

★★★★

9-13

"Yuckiest" is not a distinction many websites would want, but Wendell the Worm and Ralph the Roach take great pride in introducing you to their world. Read all the exciting facts about the creepy crawlers and then take the Roach Quiz. Let Ralph give you the lowdown on all his friends, including the earthworm and the bearded worm. This informative site is a lot of fun. When you're finished exploring bugs, branch out and explore your "gross and cool body." This site offers a tremendous Parent's Guide that will lead you to great resources for kids of all ages, especially young kids.

1stQuote.com

http://www.1stquote.com/

★★★

Comparison shop for life, auto, and health insurance online through this site, which also collects quotes from hundreds of insurance companies

About Insurance

http://insurance.about.com/

★★★★

Directory of insurance-related sites and resources covering a variety of topics. Learn how to lower your insurance costs, research insurance companies, access research and statistics, contact insurance consultants, and more. The place to go for insurance information when you're not sure where to go.

Adjusters Online

http://www.adjustersonline.com/

★★★★

Premier site for insurance adjusters and claims managers. Helps claims managers find qualified adjusters by state, county, or province. Provides resources for adjusters, including weather reports, lists of state agencies, and job opportunities.

All About Dental Insurance

http://www.bracesinfo.com/insurance/

★★★

This site offers consumers a complete understanding of dental insurance—the costs, the benefits, and ways to maximize what you get for what you pay.

A.M. Best Company

http://www.ambest.com/

★★★

Check insurance company ratings and get information on insurance products at this site.

The American College

http://www.amercoll.edu/

★★★

The American College is an independent, accredited, nonprofit educational institution that provides graduate and professional education in the field of financial services and insurance. It administers the CLU and ChFC designations and offers self-study course materials for individuals preparing to take those exams. Find out more about the American College and the materials it offers at this site.

American Insurance Association

http://www.aiadc.org/

★★★★

The leading property/casualty trade association for more than 125 years. Find out about AIA, access current workers' compensation laws online, read its publications, get membership information, and find lots of insurance resources and links.

Association of Professional Insurance Women

http://www.apiw.org/

★★★

APIA is dedicated to the advancement of women in the insurance industry. This site offers information about APIA, membership information, a member chat area, key dates to remember, links, and more.

A
B
C
D
E
F
G
H
I
J
K
L
M
N
O
P
Q
R
S
T
U
V
W
X
Y
Z

Business Insurance Online

http://www.businessinsurance.com/

★★★

The site to visit for weekly reports on corporate risk, employee benefits, and managed healthcare news.

Captive.com

http://www.captive.com/

★★★★

Anyone looking for alternative insurance information and services will find the right stuff at this site. This site seeks to address the needs of captives, insurance companies, self-insureds, risk-retention groups, purchasing groups, associations, reciprocals, and public entity pools.

Casualty Actuarial Society

http://www.casact.org/

★★★

Want to know what an actuary is or how to become an actuary? This site can help you. Find out what the Casual Actuarial Society does and get hooked in to its calendar of events, actuarial discussions, publications, membership directory, and more.

Chartered Property Casualty Underwriters Society

http://www.cpcusociety.org/

★★★

A not-for-profit association founded in 1944 to promote and ensure excellence in insurance and risk management.

Claims

http://www.claimsmag.com/

★★★

An insurance industry magazine that covers major news stories, articles on the "business of loss," and upcoming conference information. You can also check the editorial calendar for information on upcoming articles.

Independent Insurance Agents of America

http://www.independentagent.com/

★★★

Pick up useful information on crash test results and general insurance tips, and locate an independent agent in your city through the site.

Insurance Information Institute

http://www.iii.org/

★★★★

This site provides a free resource open to the media, individuals, and organizations seeking insurance facts, figures, and general industry information.

Insurance Institute for Highway Safety

http://www.hwysafety.org/

★★★★★

Learn more about vehicle ratings, find out which cars are rated safest, and read the latest crash test results online.

Best Insure.com

http://www.insure.com

★★★★★

If you're trying to decide which insurer to go with, visit this site first. Insure.com provides free ratings from Standard & Poor's and Duff & Phelps Credit Rating Co. Their ratings will help you evaluate the quality and financial soundness of the insurers you are considering. You'll also find in-depth articles, and insurance tips on auto, homeowners, health, life, and business insurance. Perhaps best of all, this site does not sell insurance and is not owned or operated by an insurance company.

InsWeb

http://www.insweb.com/

★★★★★

Online insurance shopping service. You provide input and receive quotes from a variety of insurers. Comparison shop and choose what suits your needs best. InsWeb compares quotes from more than 15,000 insurance companies to find the most affordable insurance options for you. Site also features a Learning Center that can help you become a more educated shopper.

IntelliQuote.com

http://www.intelliquote.com/

★★★

Answer simple health and age questions to get term life insurance quotes or complete online forms for quotes on home and auto insurance. The glossary, FAQs, and How To information are also helpful.

National Association of Independent Insurers

http://www.naii.org/sitehome.nsf/home?openpage

★★★

Learn more about the NAII and its diverse membership. This organization claims to be "the nation's largest full-service property-casualty trade association with more than 700 members in the United States."

National Association of Insurance and Financial Advisors

http://www.naifa.org/

★★★★

Home to the National Association of Insurance and Financial Advisors, a federation of state and local associations representing 70,000 life and health insurance and financial services professionals. Learn about the part the NAIFA plays in encouraging legislation that safeguards policyholders and promoting a well-regulated insurance marketplace.

National Association of Insurance Commissioners (NAIC)

http://www.naic.org/

★★★

Many sites are devoted to the interests of insurance professionals. This one is home to the National Association of Insurance Commissioners (NAIC), an organization of insurance regulators from the 50 states, the District of Columbia, and the four U.S. territories. The function of NAIC is to protect the interests of insurance consumers. Visit this site to learn more about the NAIC and what this organization does on your behalf.

National Council on Compensation Insurance

http://www.ncci.com

★★★

Chances are very good that any workers compensation data you've read has originated from this company. Find out more about the NCCI and the wide array of products and services it provides to businesses, associations, state and federal agencies, regulatory authorities, and insurance companies.

National Safety Council

http://www.nsc.org/

★★★

Learn how to reduce insurance claims by driving and living more safely. Interesting articles on understanding the hazards of radiation, fall-proofing your home, and creating an emergency plan for your home or business.

Nationwide Insurance

http://www.nationwide.com/

★★★★★

For more than 75 years, Nationwide has provided quality insurance options for homes, cars, families, and the incomes of those who choose to retire. Features three core businesses: domestic property and casualty insurance, life insurance and retirement savings, and asset management. Learn more about the various products and services at this site.

Property and Casualty.com

http://www.propertyandcasualty.com/content/homepage/default.asp

★★★

Information on machinery, disasters, and claims. The site also includes liability news, editorials, insurance reference tools, and how-to articles for people in the business.

QuickQuote

http://www.quickquote.com/

★★★

Information on various forms of insurance, plus the ability to get quotes.

A
B
C
D
E
F
G
H
I
J
K
L
M
N
O
P
Q
R
S
T
U
V
W
X
Y
Z

A
B
C
D
E
F
G
H
I
J
K
L
M
N
O
P
Q
R
S
T
U
V
W
X
Y
Z

ReliaQuote.com

http://www.reliaquote.com/

★★★

Read the Insurance 101 file for helpful background information and then compare the prices of hundreds of life, auto, home, renters, and home warranty insurance plans from several insurance companies.

Risk and Insurance

http://www.riskandinsurance.com/

★★★

Get the inside track on trends and events in risk management, insurance, reinsurance, alternative risk transfer, self-insurance, and benefits through your free subscription to this trade journal. View the current issue online and sign up to become a print subscriber.

AUTOMOBILE

AAA

http://www.aaa.com

$

★★★★

Register at this national automotive organization and get access to maps, road condition reports, and discount travel arrangements. By joining, you also get discount insurance and other member benefits.

Allstate

http://www.allstate.com/products/auto/

★★★

Learn more about auto insurance, common terms, and what they mean. Also, get information on Allstate's products and services here.

eSurance

http://www.esurance.com

★★★

Determine what kind of coverage you need using the online planning tools and then get a quote from this online insurance company. Policyholders can also access customer service and their account from the Internet.

GEICO Direct

http://www.geico.com/

★★★

Get a free quote from GEICO or report anything to do with your existing account, such as an accident, at this site.

National Motor Club

http://www.nmca.com/

★★★

Like AAA, the NMC provides automotive travel services such as discount accommodations, maps, travel planning assistance, and emergency service on the road.

Progressive

http://www1.progressive.com/

★★★★

Request an insurance quote for your car, locate a local office, and make a claim online at Progressive's site.

Quotesmith.com

http://www.quotesmith.com/

★★★★★

Get insurance quotes from hundreds of different insurance companies. Compare prices and coverage at one site. This site also provides a great collection of articles and tools to help you make well-informed decisions when selecting a particular policy.

RelianceDirect

http://www.reliancedirect.com

★★★

Read Reliance's insurance tips for a car or motorcycle before making insurance decisions, and you'll probably save some money. Then get an online quote for your insurance needs.

State Farm

http://www.statefarm.com/

★★★★

Look at the financial management section of this site to help you save money in a number of areas of your life, such as deciding whether to refinance your mortgage right now, and then request an insurance quote or locate a local State Farm agent.

COMPANIES

AIG

http://www.aig.com/

★★★

AIG agents write insurance for both consumer and business needs, from marine insurance to property, life, and financial. Learn more about the company here.

Farmers Insurance

http://www.farmers.com/

★★★★★

Calculate your need for auto, flood, home, life, business, or healthcare professional liability insurance at Farmers' site. Excellent collection of online calculators to help you determine your insurance needs and better manage your personal finances. Checklists for bicycle safety, home inventory, and emergencies. Lots of great information and tools. Plus, you can get an insurance quote or file a claim right online.

Fidelity

http://www.fidelity.com/

★★★

Fidelity wants to help you determine whether you have enough life insurance with an online questionnaire. The site also provides information on annuities and helps you decide whether they're right for you. Fidelity Investments is better known for mutual funds, although it also sells insurance.

The Hartford

http://www.thehartford.com/

★★★

Find an agent, request a quote, or report a claim at The Hartford's personal insurance area of the site.

MassMutual

http://www.massmutual.com/

★★★

MassMutual offers retirement help, disability insurance, estate planning, and life insurance services.

MetLife

http://www.metlife.com/

★★★

Get advice on financial issues in the Advice Center and then research MetLife products that fit your needs. The IRAs section is especially helpful for understanding your options and contribution limits.

Prudential

http://www.prudential.com/

★★★

Search for information on all of Prudential's products and services, from real estate to financial services, such as loans, to life, auto, and property insurance.

The Travelers

http://www.travelers.com/

★★★

Get information about auto, property, life, and small business insurance at this site from Travelers.

A B C D E F G H I J K L M N O P Q R S T U V W X Y Z

A B C D E F G H I J K L M N O P Q R S T U V W X Y Z

INTERNET

European Telecommunications Standards Institute

http://www.etsi.org/

★★★★★

This European group is dedicated to setting standards for the telecommunications industry to help ensure its stability and growth. ETSI has "699 members from 55 countries, and brings together manufacturers, network operators, and service providers, administrations, research bodies and users—providing a forum in which all key players can contribute."

Grid Cafe

http://gridcafe.web.cern.ch/

★★★★★

Learn about the latest developments in distributed computing over the Internet. With distributed computing, users all over the world contribute their computer power (when they're not using the computer) to a collective pool that scientists, artists, and anyone else can tap into for additional computing power. Here, you can learn more about the potential for this technology and what experts in the field have to say about it.

Internet Architecture Board

http://www.iab.org/

★★★★★

Internet Architecture Board is a committee of the Internet Engineering Task Force and an advisory body of the ISOC (Internet SOCiety). In these roles, it seeks to steer the future development of the Internet and ensure its continued growth and stability by way of establishing standards.

Internet Storm Center

http://isc.sans.org/

★★★★★

The Internet Storm Center tracks Internet activity and analyzes trends to help the Internet community and law enforcement agencies predict and prevent Internet attacks. Here, you can obtain information supplied from more than 3 million sources daily.

InterNIC

http://www.internic.net/

★★★★

InterNIC provides public information regarding Internet domain name registration services. If you need information about domain-name registration or want to find out whether a particular company is licensed to sell domain names, this is the site to visit.

ISOC (Internet SOCiety)

http://www.isoc.org/

★★★★

The Internet Society is an international organization of more than 16,000 individuals and 150 organizations representing more than 180 different countries. ISOC functions as a global clearinghouse of information about the Internet, past, present, and future, and helps guide the future development of the Internet.

Wi-Fi Planet

http://www.wi-fiplanet.com/

★★★★★

If you are interested in wireless broadband technology, this is the place to learn about it. This site features news, reviews, insights, tutorials, a comprehensive glossary, forums, and many more resources devoted to wireless broadband.

ANTI-SPAM

ActivatorMail

http://www.activatormail.com/

★★★★

Free anti-virus email account that filters out spam and porn. Unique filter system that relies on blacklists and user reports to identify unsolicited messages and prevent them from reaching your computer.

Anti Spam!

http://members.hostedscripts.com/antispam.html

★★★★

Grassroots activist site that promotes submitting fake email addresses to known spammers to clutter their databases.

Anti-Spam Home Page

http://www.arachnoid.com/lutusp/antispam.html

★★★

Lots of helpful advice on reducing unwanted email. Also features a list of known spammers.

Brightmail

http://www.brightmail.com/

★★★

Sign up to have Brightmail connected to your existing POP email account and make use of its anti-spam technology, which filters out potential junk emails and sets them aside for you in case you want to review them. This is not a standalone email account.

BugMeNot

http://bugmenot.com/

★★★★

Are you annoyed when a site requires you to register to access its information? Then check out BugMeNot to get phony login information for the site. BugMeNot encourages users to submit phony login information that other users can share to access a site. This prevents companies from gathering accurate demographic information about users and from passing information on to spammers.

CAUCE

http://www.cauce.org/

★★★

A site devoted to fighting unwanted email, the Coalition Against Unwanted Commercial Email (CAUCE) provides information about the problems of junk email, proposed solutions, and resources for the Net community to make informed choices about the issues surrounding junk email.

Fight Spam on the Internet

http://spam.abuse.net/

★★★

Learn more about how to market without using spam and what to do about unwanted email (and what not to do). Also, read views on why spamming is so bad.

SpamCop

http://spamcop.net/

★★★★

SpamCop helps you learn how to report spam and punish the sender by alerting the hosting ISP of what the spammer is doing. In many cases, the offending company will lose hosting privileges if too many people complain. Read the introduction first to learn how the process works.

A
B
C
D
E
F
G
H
I
J
K
L
M
N
O
P
Q
R
S
T
U
V
W
X
Y
Z

A
B
C
D
E
F
G
H
I
J
K
L
M
N
O
P
Q
R
S
T
U
V
W
X
Y
Z

Yahoo! Spam Wars

http://dailynews.yahoo.com/full_coverage/tech/spam_
wars/

★★★

Keep up-to-date on the latest news involving spam and unwanted email at this site, which also lists related anti-spam sites you can go to.

Related Sites

http://www.summersault.com/chris/techno/qmail/
qmail-antispam.html

http://www.dgl.com/docs/antispam.html

http://www.exit109.com/~jeremy/news/antispam.html

http://www.elsop.com/wrc/nospam.htm

CHATS. CLUBS. AND CONFERENCES

CyberTown

http://www.cybertown.com/

★★★★★

 Not for kids

Cutting-edge, 3D virtual community where you can settle down online and become a citizen. Think of it as an online version of *The Sims*. You select a 3D character to represent you. You can then build a house, get a dog, find a job, create your own clubs, dance in the Black Sun nightclub, gamble at casinos, and much more. Very innovative online-community site. Not the easiest site to navigate if you have a standard modem connection.

DevChannel

http://devchannel.org/

★★★

DevChannel is the "central news and reference resource for developers interested in core technology topics." Here, you can find articles, interviews, daily news updates, access to SourceForge projects, Freshmeat downloads, and Slashdot discussions. Come here to share information and resources with other developers.

Electronic Messaging Association

http://www.ema.org/

★★★

EMA promotes the use and usefulness of the electronic messaging industry. Find out about breakthroughs in new electronic messaging technology and upcoming events within EMA, and view articles and publications related to the electronic messaging industry.

Epinions.com

http://www.epinions.com

★★★★

Read and share opinions of products at this site, where you can even make money by writing product reviews. Share your opinion of restaurants, cars, cigars, or lawn tools. Just about any product imaginable is rated here, which can be very helpful when you're the one considering a purchase.

evite

http://www.evite.com

★★★★★

Online gathering place for friends, relatives, and colleagues. To start an Evite session, you enter your online identity, name the event, pick a theme, and invite your friends and family to join in. Features a reminder service, polling, payments collection, restaurant and concert listings, and event shopping (sponsored by Ticketmaster).

ExpertCentral.com

http://www.expertcentral.com/

★★★

Feel like asking for an expert opinion? At this site, you can post your question in the category to which it pertains and have a volunteer expert provide you with answers or advice. Lots of subject experts, from business consultants to career advisers to technology gurus and more.

Google Groups

http://groups.google.com/

★★★★

Comprehensive list of Usenet newsgroup messages accessible via the Web.

ICQ: World's Largest Internet Online Communication Network

http://web.icq.com/

★★★★★

Download ICQ's time-limited beta for chatting, sending messages and files, and setting up other real-time communication. Developed by Mirabilis Ltd., this is a very comprehensive site, offering lots of valuable information on the ICQ suite of Internet tools. The site also features message boards, chat rooms, a search directory, and tools for communicating with cellular phones and other wireless devices.

MediaGate

http://www.mediagate.com/

★★★★

MediaGate is a company that specializes in developing advanced communication and messaging systems. For example, one of its products, iPost Universal Courier, is a monthly service system that allows you to check your voice, fax, or page messages through your existing email account. Also provides services that enable you to retrieve data using a cell phone or hand-held computer.

mIRC

http://www.mirc.co.uk/

★★★★

This program enables you to connect to the Internet Relay Chat (IRC) network. Learn more about mIRC and IRC and download the latest version free.

MSN Communities

http://communities.msn.com/

★★★★

Provides a place for family members, graduating classes, hobbyists, and any other group of people who share a common cause or common interests to gather. The group's leader must set up a community and then send email invitations asking others to join. Members can then post messages to the group, upload digital photos, post a calendar of events, and even chat online.

REBOL Internet Operating System

http://www.rebol.com/ios-intro.html

★★★★

Home of REBOL, an innovative new Internet operating system that enables you to set up and maintain your own private network via the Internet. With REBOL, you can establish a communications network and share resources with hundreds of other users of your network. Great for businesses both large and small. Free trial is available.

Talk City

http://www.talkcity.com/

★★★★

Not for kids

Gain free access to chat rooms and start meeting thousands of other users at Talk City. Upgrade to Safe Chat (for $12 per year) for premium service.

Topica

http://www.topica.com

★★★

Join email discussion lists to exchange opinions and ideas with others interested in the same topic. Sign up for daily tips, such as book reviews or online auction news.

World Wide Web Consortium

http://www.w3.org/

★★★★

Offers information about the upcoming WWW International Conference. Also contains a wealth of information on various Web issues, such as security, HTTP, and graphics standards.

Worlds 3D Ultimate Chat Plus

http://www.worlds.net/3dcd/

★★★★★

Not for kids

Provides a 3D multiuser chatting system. Allows you to use images and sound while you chat with others, interacting through your computer instead of with it. Links to online shopping, too.

Related Sites

http://www.worlds.net/

http://www.cube3.com/framebut.html

A
B
C
D
E
F
G
H
I
J
K
L
M
N
O
P
Q
R
S
T
U
V
W
X
Y
Z

A
B
C
D
E
F
G
H
I
J
K
L
M
N
O
P
Q
R
S
T
U
V
W
X
Y
Z

Yahoo! Chat

http://chat.yahoo.com

★★★★

With hundreds of chat rooms and thousands of registered chatters, Yahoo! is one of the best places to meet people on the Internet.

Yahoo! Groups

http://groups.yahoo.com/

★★★★★

Enables family members, graduating classes, organizations, and other groups of people to organize on the Web. Group moderator can broadcast messages, alerts, and newsletters to group members, and all members can post messages, digitized photos, and other information to the group.

CONNECTING FREE

Address.com

http://www.address.com/

★★★

Offering unlimited connect time, free web-based email, and access to a comprehensive search directory, Address.com is gaining popularity. What's the catch? You have to put up with pop-up ads, and you can't just dismiss them with a click of your mouse; you must let them run in order to continue browsing. For $9.95 per month, you can upgrade to premium (no-ads) service.

Consume

http://consume.net

★★★

Grassroots organization dedicated to building a new Internet free from the control of corporations and anyone else whose main interest in maintaining a presence on the Internet is to make money. Here, you can learn how to join the group and contribute your talents, time, and equipment to building a more independent Internet.

Free ISP Directory

http://www.findanisp.com/free_isps.php?src=
findwhatfree

★★★★★

Use this site to find free and low-cost Internet connection services.

The Free Site

http://www.thefreesite.com/Free_Internet_Access/

★★★★

Lists a variety of free Internet connections, as well as other free Internet services. Worth a look.

Going Platinum

http://www.goingplatinum.com/

★★★★

Innovative business model that rewards you for generating revenue on the Internet. You register as an affiliate and pay $9.95 per month to join. Every time you click an ad, respond to an advertiser's poll, search for a product, or purchase products through the Going Platinum portal, your account is credited a certain amount. When your account reaches $5.00 in commissions, your $9.95 monthly fee is credited back to your account. You can even earn a profit.

Juno

http://www.juno.com/

★★★★

Get free Internet access minus customer support, or pay a flat monthly rate for Juno Premium service and get 24-hour customer service and priority connections. NetZero (covered next) and Juno were both acquired by United Online in 2001, and each ISP provides the same free service: receive 10 hours per month free or pay about $10 per month for unlimited connect time and fewer pop-up ads.

NetZero

http://www.netzero.net/

★★★★★

One of the few truly free ISPs that survived the great Internet bust. Users can get totally free Internet access, email, chat, and instant messaging for 10 hours per month. For about $10 a month, you get unlimited connect time and fewer pop-up ads.

NoCharge.com

http://www.nocharge.com

★★★★

Western Washington's premier free Internet service provider offers free Internet access and email to users in selected communities in Western Washington state. No limitations on connect time and no ads. Premium service offering more reliable connections and support.

CONNECTING (FOR A FEE)

Cable Modem Service Customer Reviews

http://www.cable-modem.net/dbase.html

★★★

Customer reviews of various ISPs that provide cable modem service. Good place to go before you sign up for service with your local cable company.

CNET ISP List

http://www.cnet.com/internet/

★★★

Check out CNET's ratings of major ISPs before making your selection.

The Directory

http://www.thedirectory.org/

★★★

Claiming to be the largest directory of ISPs on the Web, the Directory provides thousands of listings of Internet providers as well as web hosting companies, telephone prefix locators, and mailing lists.

ISP Check

http://www.ispcheck.com/

★★★★

Search this site for ISPs and web hosting companies, or take a look at the Best Deal advertised here.

ISP Planet

http://www.isp-planet.com/

★★★

Industry information for Internet service providers. Articles address topics such as the cost of setting up a fixed wireless business, ways to fight spam, and ways to market your ISP.

ISPs.com

http://www.isps.com/

★★★

Search this database of thousands of ISPs to find one in your area.

The List of ISPs

http://thelist.internet.com/

★★★

Extensive database of ISPs allows you to search by state and area code for a local ISP to serve your needs.

CONNECTION SPEED

Broadbandwidthplace Speed Test

http://bandwidthplace.com/speedtest/

★★★★★

Wondering how fast your Internet connection is? Then come here and test your connection speed. This site performs a test, displays the results, rates your connection speed, and provides links to products that can improve the speed.

Broadband Home Central

http://www.broadbandhomecentral.com/

$

★★★★★

Sandy Teger and Dave Waks host Broadband Home Central, where you can learn about the latest in broadband technology, its practical applications, and products and services that can help you tap the full potential of broadband. Site leans toward the more technical aspects of broadband, but all users can benefit from the more general articles.

A B C D E F G H I J K L M N O P Q R S T U V W X Y Z

A
B
C
D
E
F
G
H
I
J
K
L
M
N
O
P
Q
R
S
T
U
V
W
X
Y
Z

DSL Reports Speed Test

http://www.dslreports.com/stest

★★★★★

DSL Reports is a great place to pick up tips and utilities for increasing the speed of your Internet connection. Here, you can also test your connection speed to determine whether it needs fixing.

PC Pitstop Internet

http://www.pcpitstop.com/internet/default.asp

★★★★★

PC Pitstop can test the speed, performance, and security of your computer to determine whether it is running at its peak performance. The site then makes recommendations concerning how you can address particular issues that might be slowing it down or making it less secure.

EMAIL

Access Quality Toys Birthday Reminder

http://www.accessqualitytoys.com/birthday.cfm

★★★★

👫 0-8

Never again forget the birthdays of children who are important to you! Sign up for this email reminder service and get a reminder four weeks prior to the date. This gives you plenty of time to find and order a special toy from the Access Quality Toys site.

Accessing the Internet

http://www.faqs.org/faqs/internet-services/access-via-email/

★★★★

FTP, the WWW, Veronica, and more. You can do it all with a plain email account. This highly recommended document tells you how.

Bigfoot

http://www.bigfoot.com/

★★★★★

Bigfoot provides a free web-based email account that blocks spam (junk mail) and enables you to manage your email account from a computer anywhere in the world that's connected to the Internet. 5MB of free storage is offered per account.

FindGift

http://www.findgift.com/

★★★★

FindGift will send you hints for important occasions. As an added bonus, the same site provides gift ideas.

Free Email Address Directory

http://www.emailaddresses.com/

★★★

Directory of more than 1,000 free email service providers and lots of other free Internet services.

Related Site
http://www.fepg.net/usa.html

Harness Email

http://www.learnthenet.com/english/section/email.html

★★★★

Excellent tutorial on email, covering everything from learning how it works to managing your email account. Learn how to follow the rules of email etiquette, join mailing lists, work with file attachments, keep email private, and more.

iName Email

http://www.iname.com/

★★★★

Free email that you can access from any Internet connection, anywhere in the world. This email service offers some distinctive addresses, such as writeme.com or engineer.com.

Lycos Mail

http://mail.lycos.com/

★★★

Get free email with 5MB of space set aside for you, as well as a handy-dandy reminder service and a spam-blocking service to keep unwanted junk mail out of your mailbox.

Mail.com

http://corp.mail.com/

★★★

Sign up for personalized free email or have your website's email processed by this site.

MSN Hotmail

http://www.hotmail.com

★★★★

Start here to learn more about setting up a free email account through MSN's Hotmail, a web-based email service, which allows users to access their email from anywhere.

My Own Email

http://www.myownemail.com/

★★★

Free email account provides you with an email address that reflects your personality, such as yourname@hehe.com. More than 200 domain names from which to choose. Also features spam filtering, outgoing email encryption, and the ability to send and receive email from anywhere.

Netiquette

http://www.albion.com/netiquette/corerules.html

★★★★

The core and much more: business Netiquette, social Netiquette, philosophical issues, *everything*. This online version of a book (originally published in 1994) is a must-read.

PeopleWeb

http://www.peopleweb.com/

★★★★★

PeopleWeb provides free accounts, including free web-based email, instant messaging, file management, and more.

Talking Email

http://www.4developers.com/talkmail/

★★★★

Have your email messages read to you by animated characters rather than reading them yourself. The ultimate multitasker tool. Features talking reminders that notify you of upcoming meetings and appointments, a talking clock, and a talking clipboard.

Yahoo! Mail

http://mail.yahoo.com

★★★

From the Yahoo! home page, you can sign up for free email. As an added bonus, you'll gain access to other Yahoo! services. You can also link your Yahoo! email address to a pager.

ZapZone Email

http://www.zzn.com/

★★★

Gives businesses large or small a way to provide free email service to their customers and clients.

INSTANT MESSAGING AND INTERNET PHONE

America Online Instant Messenger

http://aim.aol.com/

★★★★★

Get the most popular instant messaging program on the planet, register for a screen name, and start chatting online with all your friends and relatives who already use AOL's Instant Messenger.

ICQ.com

http://www.icq.com

★★★★★

Download the free trial ICQ (I Seek You) software so that you can immediately identify when a friend or family member logs on to the Internet. The software eliminates the need to regularly search for people you want to talk to. After you find someone you want to chat with, you can send text or voice messages in real-time.

A
B
C
D
E
F
G
H
I
J
K
L
M
N
O
P
Q
R
S
T
U
V
W
X
Y
Z

A
B
C
D
E
F
G
H
I
J
K
L
M
N
O
P
Q
R
S
T
U
V
W
X
Y
Z

Instant Messaging Planet

http://www.instantmessagingplanet.com/

★★★★

Instant Messaging Planet provides an information kiosk for instant messaging developers and providers. Articles examine "how companies use instant messaging and associated technologies to conduct business, and the specific obstacles/problems they face with using IM technology in our connected world." Covers both wired and wireless forms of IM.

Jabber

http://www.jabber.com

★★★★

Jabber is an XML-based, open-source system and protocol for real-time messaging and presence notification. The first application of Jabber is an instant messaging (IM) system similar to AOL Instant Messenger, ICQ, MSN Instant Messenger, or Yahoo! Messenger. However, Jabber is also being applied in the realms of wireless communications, embedded systems, and Internet infrastructure.

MSN Messenger Service

http://messenger.msn.com/

★★★★★

The free MSN instant messaging software allows you to see which of your friends are online and then send instant messages to them. You can also have group meetings or play a real-time game.

Net2Phone

http://www.net2phone.com/

★★★★★

Free PC-to-PC "phone calls" to anywhere in the world and free limited time PC-to-phone calls to any phone in the nation, plus low rates on PC-to-phone calls to other countries. With Net2Phone, users can talk to each other over Internet connections and phone lines using their PC's sound card equipped with a microphone.

Odigo.com

http://www.odigo.com/

★★★★★

Odigo, Inc., is the leading provider of Instant Messaging (IM) and Presence Solutions. Odigo's services include IM clients, IM and Presence Servers, and hosting of IM and Presence services. The company is a founding member of IMUnified and the PAM Forum, two coalitions that are working to establish industry standards for IM and Presence interoperability.

PalTalk

http://www.paltalk.com/

★★★

Using free PalTalk software, you can have voice conversations with other users around the world, send text-based instant messages, have group voice conversations, and leave voice messages for other PalTalk users. Download the software at this site. PalTalk is working to make its software interoperable with America Online's Instant Messenger.

Trillian

http://www.trillian.cc/

★★★★★

Trillian is an instant messaging program that enables you to communicate with all your instant-messaging friends using a single program. In Trillian, you can enter account information for AIM, MSN Messenger, Yahoo! Messenger, and ICQ. You can also use Trillian to send and receive messages to all of these services.

Yahoo! Messenger

http://messenger.yahoo.com/

★★★★

Using Yahoo!'s free instant messaging software, you can send instant messages to friends and sign up for free news and stock alerts.

ONLINE TELEPHONE DIRECTORIES

411 Locate
http://www.411locate.com/

★★★

Find people through white page searches or email address searches and businesses through yellow page searches, or track down public information at this site.

Alumni.NET
http://alumni.net

★★★

Locate fellow alumni from your high school or college through a search of public alumni directories.

AT&T AnyWho Info
http://www.anywho.com/

★★★★

Find a person or business that has a listing in the phone books by typing the name or category of business.

Bigfoot
http://www.bigfoot.com

★★★★

Search for anyone in the United States or add yourself to Bigfoot so friends and family can find you by searching this huge directory. You can also sign up for free email.

Infobel World
http://www.infobel.com/

★★★★

Telephone directories on the Web can help you track down the phone number for a person or business in virtually any country. More than 400 directories can be searched from this one site.

Internet Address Finder
http://www.iaf.net/

★★★

Find a person's email address by entering his or her name and other information, such as the company that person works for or the domain name of his or her ISP.

Switchboard.com
http://switchboard.com

★★★

Find people or businesses and learn their email addresses through a search on this directory.

WorldPages
http://www.worldpages.com/

★★★★

Do a search for people or businesses and then pull up a map of how to get to where they are.

YellowPages.Com
http://www.yellowpages.com/

★★★★

Search YellowPages.Com for any business anywhere in the country.

OPT-IN EMAIL

1-2-3 Opt-in Email Marketing
http://www.123opt-in.com/

★★★

Sells email addresses of customers who choose to receive email ads to companies that want to market their products on the Internet.

PostMasterDirect.com
http://www.postmasterdirect.com/

($)

★★★

Direct mail companies looking to do email marketing will want to consider buying addresses of people who have agreed to receive those messages. PostMasterDirect.com manages those lists and sells them. Get more information here.

A B C D E F G H I J K L M N O P Q R S T U V W X Y Z

A
B
C
D
E
F
G
H
I
J
K
L
M
N
O
P
Q
R
S
T
U
V
W
X
Y
Z

PRIVACY

AD Muncher

http://www.admuncher.com/

★★★★

AD Muncher significantly reduces banner ads and pop-up promotional messages that come through the Web. Download a free trial version here, $15 to purchase the program.

Anonymizer.com

http://www.anonymizer.com/

★★★★

If you're concerned about the amount of personal information you share every time you visit a website, come to this site first and type in the address you want to visit. Your identity will be protected at no cost. Or sign up for paid services to protect your identity and prevent cookies from being shared every time you visit a site.

BBBonline

http://www.bbbonline.com/

★★★

Pick up tips for protecting your personal information at this site, sponsored by the Better Business Bureau. You can also search the database to find out which online companies subscribe to the organization's code of conduct.

Center for Democracy and Technology

http://www.cdt.org

★★★★

Keep current on issues and legislation regarding Internet privacy issues through regular updates at this site. The opt-out forms available on the site are a godsend to consumers who want their names removed from corporate mailing lists.

CookieCentral.com

http://www.cookiecentral.com/

★★★★★

Visit this site to better understand what cookies are, how they collect information, and what you can do to prevent or eliminate them.

CyberPatrol

http://www.cyberpatrol.com

★★★

Download a free trial of this filtering system that pulls together lists of inappropriate sites and restricts access via your computer. Three variations of the software are available, for home, business, or school, with lists of good and bad sites customized depending on the application. Parents can also revise the lists, adding or subtracting sites children can view.

Electronic Frontier Foundation

http://www.eff.org

★★★

This site describes the mission and work of this nonprofit organization dedicated to protecting the rights of privacy and free expression on the Internet. Learn why these issues are so significant and what you can do to support the organization's work.

Fight Identity Theft

http://www.fightidentitytheft.com/

★★★

This site provides information and tools to help you avoid becoming a victim of identity theft, determine whether you have been a victim, and repair any damage if you are a victim.

ID Theft Affidavit

http://www.ftc.gov/bcp/conline/pubs/credit/affidavit.pdf

★★★★

If you are a victim of identity theft, contacting the banks and other companies where fraudulent debts and accounts have been set up in your name can be a nightmare. Visit this site to download and complete a single form that informs multiple companies that you have been a victim of identity theft.

Internet Watcher

http://www.internetwatcher.com/

★★★★

Download a free trial version of Internet Watcher, an Internet-filtering program that blocks many of the ads that pop-up on your computer as you browse the Web. Also provides tools for sharing a broadband connection among networked computers, increasing the speed of your Internet connection, censoring sites, blocking cookies, and more.

mValue.com

http://maxpages.com/surfpay/mValue

★★★

mValue gives you the opportunity to protect your identity but still make money by sharing information about yourself and your buying habits. You download an advertising bar that appears at the bottom of your screen every time you go online, and you're paid 50 cents an hour, to a maximum of $20 for this. You can also earn more money by referring friends to do the same.

Privacy Rights Clearinghouse

http://www.privacyrights.org/

★★★★

Privacy Rights Clearinghouse is a nonprofit consumer education and advocacy group that is dedicated to helping keep personal information private. Here, you can learn tips and tricks for keeping your personal information secure both on and off the Internet.

PrivacyTimes.com

http://www.privacytimes.com

★★★

Read Internet privacy-related articles from this trade publication written primarily for attorneys and professionals involved in privacy issues. Topics such as identity theft, direct marketing, and the Freedom of Information Act are regularly covered.

SmartParent.com

http://www.smartparent.com

★★★★

 All

SmartParent is dedicated to teaching parents how to safeguard their children from dangerous contact with people on the Internet. The site provides information on blocking and filtering software, protection tips, and links to parent and child-friendly sites, as well as links to agencies and organizations that focus on Internet-related issues.

SpyBot

http://www.safer-networking.org/

★★★★★

Are you afraid that somebody or some website has installed spyware or annoying adware on your computer that is following your Web wanderings and inundating your computer with annoying pop-up ads? Then download SpyBot from this site, install it, and check your system. SpyBot can track down most spyware and adware and automatically remove it from your computer.

SpyWare Info

http://www.spywareinfo.com/

★★★★

Many less reputable companies on the Internet install unsolicited spyware and adware on your computer to follow your movements on the Web and bury you in annoying pop-up ads. This site provides the information, resources, and utilities you need to fight back.

TRUSTe

http://www.truste.com

★★★★★

A site for web publishers and consumers, advising everyone on privacy issues. Consumers can learn how to best protect themselves from sharing too much information when online, and publishers can learn how to safeguard information provided by visitors.

A B C D E F G H I J K L M N O P Q R S T U V W X Y Z

A
B
C
D
E
F
G
H
I
J
K
L
M
N
O
P
Q
R
S
T
U
V
W
X
Y
Z

Webroot
http://www.webroot.com/

★★★★

Webroot sells software that protects your identity and provides security by preventing websites from viewing the cookies and history of previous web searches that reside on your computer. You can download a 30-day free trial of the Window Washer software to clean your hard drive and then pay $29.95 to use it beyond that point. Features several other Internet security, censoring, and privacy programs, too.

Zero-Knowledge Systems
http://www.zks.net/

★★★★

Get a 30-day free trial of Freedom software that prevents personal information from being shared when you're online, and consider buying it after that for $59.95 per year.

SAFETY FOR KIDS

The Children's Partnership
http://www.childrenspartnership.org/pub/pbpg98/partII98.html#safe
★★★★

How do you keep your child safe online? This site, from the Children's Partnership, the National PTA, and the National Urban League, can help

CYBERsitter
http://www.solidoak.com/

★★★

CYBERsitter enables parents to limit their children's access to objectionable material on the Internet. Parents can choose to block, block and alert, or simply alert them when access is attempted to these areas. Working secretly in the background, CYBERsitter analyzes all Internet activity. Download a free trial from the website, and then you can choose to purchase it later.

Family Connect
http://www.familyconnect.com/

★★★

Family Connect effectively blocks pornographic and detrimental sites, and is automatically updated daily to include the new sites. It requires no maintenance, and the system is virtually tamper-proof. Try it free and then choose to purchase later.

ICRA
http://www.icra.org/
★★★
 All

The Recreational Software Advisory Council is an independent, nonprofit organization based in Washington, D.C., that empowers the public, especially parents, to make informed decisions about electronic media by means of an open and objective content-advisory system. Useful information specifically for kids, too.

International Child Center (ICC)
http://www.icc-911.com/
★★★

ICC is the Internet's central bank of child protection information, resources, and services.

Net-Mom
http://www.netmom.com/

★★★

An excellent resource site from Jean Armour Polly, author of *Internet Kids* and *Family Yellow Pages*. Her book can be ordered via links to Amazon.com or Borders.com. You'll also find the 100 Hot Family Sites.

Parenthood Web
http://www.parenthoodweb.com/articles/phw557.htm
★★★★★

This site is the home of a parenting e-zine article titled "Child Safety on the Information Superhighway", provided by the National Center for Missing and Exploited Children and the Interactive Services Association.

SafeTeens.com

http://www.safekids.com/safeteens/

★★★★★

 14-18

A guide to teen safety on the Internet. This site not only offers ways to keep teens safe while using the Internet, but it also supplies many good websites that teens will find interesting or helpful. You can also subscribe to a free newsletter when you visit this site.

Web Wise Kids

http://www.webwisekids.com/

★★★★★

 All

Internet safety and computer usage tips from Tracey O'Connell-Jay, founder and director of Web Wise Kids. She offers some really good tips, such as keeping your computer in an easily supervised area and establishing rules for computer use and Internet surfing.

Search Engines

About.com	http://www.about.com
AltaVista.com	http://www.altavista.com
Big Hub	http://www.thebighub.com
Dogpile	http://www.dogpile.com
Go2Net	http://www.go2net.com
Google.com	http://www.google.com
Hotbot.com	http://hotbot.lycos.com
Lycos.com	http://www.lycos.com
Mamma	http://www.mamma.com
MSN.com	http://www.msn.com
Northern Light	http://www.northernlight.com
Profusion	http://www.profusion.com
Yahoo!	http://www.yahoo.com

Child-Safe Search Engines

Ask Jeeves for Kids	http://www.ajkids.com/
Yahooligans	http://www.yahooligans.com/
SearchEngines.com	http://www.searchengines.com/kids/
Kids Search Tools	http://www.rcls.org/ksearch.htm
CyberSleuth Kids	http://cybersleuth-kids.com/
LycosZone	http://www.lycoszone.com/
Kids Click!	http://sunsite.berkeley.edu/KidsClick!/

SECURITY/VIRUS HOAXES

McAfee Anti-Virus

http://www.mcafee.com/

$

★★★★★

Home of McAfee VirusScan, one of the most popular anti-virus programs on the market. Here, you can learn about the latest virus scares, find out if a reported virus is really a hoax, and download the latest virus definitions. You can also check out McAfee's firewall program to protect your system from hackers.

PestPatrol Research Center

http://www.pestpatrol.com/pestinfo/

★★★★★

PestPatrol Research Center serves the Internet community by providing information on more than 20,000 non-virus Internet pests, including spyware, adware, and Trojan horses. Site features a utility that can scan your system and let you know whether it's suffering from an infestation.

Best | Symantec AntiVirus Research Center

http://www.symantec.com/avcenter/index.html

$

★★★★★

Download detailed information on the latest virus definitions, find out what to do about them, browse the encyclopedia of online viruses and hoaxes, and visit the reference area for answers to commonly asked questions. If someone sends an email to you, warning you of a new virus, be sure to check this site to make sure the virus warning isn't a hoax. This is a very extensive listing. You can purchase Symantec products here, from firewalls to virus scanners, as well as purchase updates to your existing Symantec products. You can also purchase a family Internet security system that helps defend your PC against Internet threats and protects your children against inappropriate online content.

A B C D E F G H I J K L M N O P Q R S T U V W X Y Z

A
B
C
D
E
F
G
H
I
J
K
L
M
N
O
P
Q
R
S
T
U
V
W
X
Y
Z

TruSecure

http://www.trusecure.com/

★★★

Publisher of *Information Security Magazine*, this site also serves as a hub of current information about viruses, hoaxes, and other Internet security risks.

WildList

http://www.wildlist.org

★★★★

This organization keeps a list of which viruses have been spotted and who's tracking and reporting on them. It also provides an archive of past viruses as well as FAQs regarding how to deal with them.

WEB PAGE CREATION

1-2-3 ASPX

http://www.123aspx.com/

★★★★

Huge directory of ASP information, technology, and tools. Find books, tutorials, discussion groups, code libraries, and other resources

ASP Resource Index

http://www.aspin.com/

★★★

A type of focused search engine for programmers, providing Active Server Pages (ASP) components, applications, scripts, tutorials, and references. Users can search the information reviews, ratings, price, or software version.

ASP Today

http://www.asptoday.com/

★★★★

This online programmers' tool provides useful ASP columns written by programmers for programmers. Articles offer practical ASP-related techniques, tips, and tricks that don't take much time to read.

ASPWire

http://aspwire.com/

★★★

Stay current on ASP-related news at this site, which offers new product announcements, product reviews, articles, books, seminars, and ASP website announcements.

CGI Resource Index

http://www.cgi-resources.com/

★★★

Access hundreds of premade CGIs, articles, and documentation.

developerWorks: Java Technology

http://www.ibm.com/developerworks/java/

★★★

Learn more about Java technology and how to use it at IBM's site. Pick up tools and code, read instructional articles, and stay current on the latest Java announcements.

DevX

http://www.devx.com/

★★★★

Serving the programming community, DevX is a commercial site that provides developers with the information, technology, and resources they need to create websites, applications, and e-commerce solutions for their clients. Resources for .NET, ASP, C++, DHTML, Java, XML, wireless, and more.

Dreamweaver

http://www.macromedia.com/software/dreamweaver/

★★★

You'll find articles, tutorials, and other resources to help you with Macromedia's Dreamweaver.

Dynamic HTML Guru Resource

http://www.htmlguru.com/

★★★★

The purpose of this site is to help you explore new possibilities in DHTML development using new tools and techniques. Take tutorials, look at reference material, and jump into discussion threads to see what new tricks you can add.

EITplanet.com

http://www.enterpriseitplanet.com

★★★

Claims to be the single largest independent resource for Microsoft-related BackOffice technologies, where you'll find information on SQL Server, Exchange, SMS, Windows 2000, and more.

FreeCode

http://www.freecode.com/

★★★

Find free code software in the archives at this site. CGI programming, email, Internet protocols, chat, HTML authoring, and more are all here for your review and use.

FreeScripts

http://www.FreeScripts.com/scripts/

★★★

Download free CGI scripts here. You'll be able to add a footer, have visitors rate an item on your site, and much more.

The HTML Writers Guild

http://www.hwg.org/

★★★

A nonprofit organization for web authors, the Guild provides members with tools and resources to improve their skills, including a lengthy list of web authoring classes available online. Be sure to check out all the upcoming events, seminars, and workshops.

Jars.com

http://www.jars.com/

★★★

Search this Java review site for product and site information. You can also sign up to be a Jars reviewer and help to rate resource submissions.

Java.sun.com

http://java.sun.com/

★★★

Go to the source for Java information, including support, tutorials, product information, and discussions, as well as plenty more.

Javascripts.com

http://webdeveloper.earthweb.com/pagedev/webjs/

★★★

Access thousands of JavaScripts, complete with tutorials and open discussions with the more than 500,000 registered users at this site. Events, training, IT jobs, and more are also listed here.

Matt's Script Archive

http://www.scriptarchive.com/

★★★★

Search this site for free CGI scripts and link to other sites in search of what you're looking for. Check out the bulletin boards, web discussion forums, Matt's free Perl CGI scripts, and free C++ CGI scripts. Also, get help from this site.

.NET

http://www.microsoft.com/net/

★★★★

Learn all about Microsoft's new software technologies for "connecting your world of information, people, systems, and devices." Microsoft's .NET initiative is designed to blur the lines between personal computers, networks, the Internet, and wireless communication devices, including cellular phones.

A
B
C
D
E
F
G
H
I
J
K
L
M
N
O
P
Q
R
S
T
U
V
W
X
Y
Z

A
B
C
D
E
F
G
H
I
J
K
L
M
N
O
P
Q
R
S
T
U
V
W
X
Y
Z

Page Resource.com
http://www.pageresource.com/

★★★★

Novice web page creators will want to drop in for tutorials on HTML and JavaScript. Information on DHTML, CGI, and Perl, plus web design guidelines.

PASS
http://www.sqlpass.org/

★★★

Find out about this year's PASS conference at this site, including where and when it is being held. You also can find SQL news, discussion forums, and the schedule of upcoming PASSchats.

Perl.com
http://www.perl.com/

★★★★

O'Reilly and Associates' Perl site is the premier site for learning about Perl. Provides links for documentation, training, downloads, books, FAQs, and other resources focusing on Perl.

Quadzilla.com
http://wdvl.internet.com/Quadzilla/

★★★

A site dedicated to helping you improve the look and quality of your site, with the goal of being a one-stop HTML authoring and design site. You'll find lots of help in developing and maintaining a site here.

ScriptSearch
http://www.scriptsearch.com/

★★★

Search by keyword, language, or category to find free CGI scripts. Incidentally, this site claims to be the largest archive.

SiteExperts.com
http://www.siteexperts.com/

★★★★

Online community of web page and website developers. Variety of discussion groups and resources for developers.

SQL Server Magazine
http://www.sqlmag.com/

★★★★

This online magazine provides programmers with SQL news, how-to articles, and resources. Book and product reviews are just two of the helpful listings here. This site also links to Fatbrain.com, where you can purchase books and other printed materials.

SQLWire
http://sqlwire.com/

★★★

Like its sister site, ASPWire, this site provides up-to-date news and articles regarding SQL servers. Current and archived news and reviews are available, and be sure to sign up for the free newsletter.

WEB PAGE SOFTWARE AND RESOURCES

CoffeeCup Software
http://www.coffeecup.com/

★★★★

A complete line of web page design, creation, and management software, including CoffeeCup HTML Editor, Firestarter, WebCam, and GIF Animator. Download free shareware versions of these programs to take them for a test drive or order full versions online.

Corel XMetal
http://www.softquad.com/

★★★★

Formerly the home of SoftQuad's HotMetal program, a popular website creation and management program. SoftQuad has been acquired by Corel, and this site is now the home of Corel XMetal. XMetal makes creating web pages as easy as creating documents in a desktop publishing program. Here, you can download a shareware version of the program or purchase a copy. Additional resources also available.

DevEdge Online

http://developer.netscape.com

★★★

Site designing resources, tips, technology reviews, code-level advice, support, and newsgroups can all be found here. Sample code and manuals are available, too.

Developers Network

http://www.msdn.microsoft.com

★★★

Developers Network contains plenty of news, feature, and how-to articles, as well as technical notes, training information, and guidance.

FrontPage

http://www.microsoft.com/frontpage/

★★★★

The home of Microsoft's website creation and management software provides a brief introduction to FrontPage, a gallery of ideas, how-to articles, tips and tricks, free downloads, and online technical support.

HTML Goodies

http://www.htmlgoodies.com/

★★★★

Tutorials, tips, and advice for both beginners and experts presented in a very simple and straightforward manner.

Pagetutor.com

http://www.pagetutor.com/

★★★★

Excellent collection of HTML tutorials written in plain English. Download the shareware version of PageTutor.

Slashdot

http://slashdot.org

★★★★

At this site billed as News for Nerds, you can pick up techie news, articles, and reviews. Lots of reviews and a lengthy message thread here.

Web Reference

http://www.webreference.com/

★★★

Website design and programming tutorials are available here. You can download tools and turn to the experts for advice when you need it. The newsletters are especially helpful and timely.

Webmonkey.com

http://hotwired.lycos.com/webmonkey/

★★★★

A comprehensive resource for web developers, filled with how-to articles on web design, authoring, multimedia, e-commerce, programming, and jobs.

Webmonkey for Kids

http://hotwired.lycos.com/webmonkey/kids/

★★★★★

 All

Children can learn how to create their very own websites here. This site features four sections: Lessons, Projects, Playground, and Tools.

A
B
C
D
E
F
G
H
I
J
K
L
M
N
O
P
Q
R
S
T
U
V
W
X
Y
Z

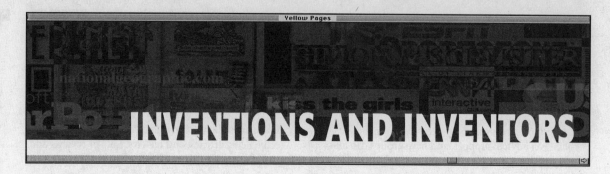

INVENTIONS AND INVENTORS

The American Experience

http://www.pbs.org/wgbh/amex/telephone/sfeature/

★★★★

 All

Sponsored by PBS, this site offers short essays on several inventions, such as the can opener, blue jeans, the Frisbee, the feather duster, the gas mask, the blood bank, and the oil burner. You can also find links to the rest of the PBS site, including the PBS shop and programming schedule.

American Inventors and Inventions

http://www.150.si.edu/150trav/remember/amerinv.htm

★★★

 All

At this site, learn more about inventions developed before 1880 that are on display at the Smithsonian Institution in Washington, D.C. Read about inventors and their inventions here.

Edison National Historic Site

http://www.nps.gov/edis/home.htm

★★★

 All

Visit the site of one of the greatest inventors of our time, go on a virtual tour of his laboratory, read his biography, check his long list of patents, visit the photo gallery, and much more.

Engines of Our Ingenuity

http://www.uh.edu/admin/engines/engines.htm

★★★★

 All

Produced by Oxford University, John H. Lienhard's radio program series about engines tells the story of how our culture is formed by human creativity and invention. You can purchase the book *The Engines of Our Ingenuity* from this site.

Federation of Inventions: Youth

http://www.invention-ifia.ch/ifiayouth.htm

★★★

All

The International Federation of Inventors' Association encourages inventiveness among young girls and boys. Join the IFIA, participate in contests, and read about the concept of inventiveness here.

George Washington Carver

http://inventors.about.com/library/weekly/aa041897.htm?once=true&pid=2821&cob=home

★★★★

All

George Washington Carver invented peanut butter, adhesives, bleach, chili sauce, ink, instant coffee, linoleum, mayonnaise, paper, plastic, pavement, shaving cream, and talcum powder. This site not only gives a comprehensive biography of Carver, but also offers links to various schools and other related sites.

History of Invention

http://www.cbc4kids.ca/general/the-lab/history-of-invention/default.html

★★★★

👥 All

Who made what when? Use this invention timeline produced by the Canadian Broadcast Corporation to find out. You can also suggest what invention you'd like to see added to the timeline. Great site for students, teachers, and parents.

Invention Dimension

http://web.mit.edu/invent/

★★★★

👥 All

Visit MIT's invention website, where you can learn about the Lemelson-MIT award program, find out who's the inventor of the week, check on high school programs, and find links to dozens of other inventor resources. This site also features a game and trivia area.

Inventions for Sale & License

http://www.inventionsforsale.com/

★★★

Search the database of close to 1,000 patented inventions for something you might like to license, such as beauty, aircraft, or health-related products. All are available for sale or license.

InventNet

http://www.inventnet.com/

$

★★★

News summaries and postings on topics of interest to inventors, including law and politics. This site supports inventor's rights.

Inventors

http://inventors.about.com/library/blindex.htm?once=true&pid=2821&cob=home

★★★★

Archived list of more than 50 interesting inventors, dates, and inventions. This site offers a lengthy article on each written by your About guide, as well as links to many related sites.

Inventors Assistance Resource Directory

http://www.inventored.org/

★★★

👥 All

A decent list of inventor support groups with local USA contact information. References listed here include how to promote your invention and how to contact an attorney to protect your invention.

Best | Inventors Online Museum

http://www.inventorsmuseum.com/

★★★★★

👥 All

Well-organized, visually pleasing, and full of useful information, this site was built as an online museum so people from all over the world could explore the world of invention and innovation. Sign up as a Museum affiliate and you will be kept informed about the museum, inventors' issues, new features, and news. Inventors, students, and teachers visiting this site will soon realize why it's our top pick in this category.

Inventors' Digest Online

http://www.inventorsdigest.com

$

★★★★

👥 All

This site is designed for anyone who has ever said, "I've got a great idea…now what do I do?" It's also THE spot for anyone who's searching for the next HOT product! Check out the magazine site and then follow the links to the wonderful world of invention! Clothing items available here, too.

Inventure Place

http://www.invent.org/

★★★

👥 All

Museum, programs, and activities related to inventing and inventors. The National Inventors Hall of Fame is located here.

A
B
C
D
E
F
G
H
I
J
K
L
M
N
O
P
Q
R
S
T
U
V
W
X
Y
Z

A
B
C
D
E
F
G
H
I
J
K
L
M
N
O
P
Q
R
S
T
U
V
W
X
Y
Z

Lemelson Center

http://www.si.edu/lemelson/

★★★★★

The Jerome and Dorothy Lemelson Center for the Study of Invention and Innovation is a branch of the Smithsonian Institution. The Center's mission is to "document, interpret, and disseminate information about invention and innovation, to encourage inventive creativity in young people, and to foster an appreciation for the central role invention and innovation play in the history of the United States." Here you can find exhibits on everything from Thomas Edison to electric guitars and quartz watches. Special areas are available for students, teachers, historians, inventors, and reporters.

National Inventors Hall of Fame

http://www.invent.org/hall_of_fame/1_1_search.asp

★★★

👫 All

Alphabetical index of inventors. Each link has a short biography, picture, and patent numbers of the inventor.

PatentCafe.com

http://www.patentcafe.com/

★★★

👫 All

Learn more about patenting and protecting your idea with information from this site, as well as locating professionals to assist you. Find manufacturers, government assistance, and attorneys. Click the link for the Kids' Cafe or go directly to http://kids.patentcafe.com/ to visit the area specifically designed for K–12 inventors.

U.S. Patent and Trademark Office

http://www.uspto.gov/

★★★★

👫 All

For more than 200 years, the basic role of the U.S. Patent and Trademark Office (PTO) has remained the same: to promote the progress of science and the useful arts by securing for limited times to inventors the exclusive right to their respective discoveries. Check out this site to see how to register your invention idea and get a patent.

Related Site
http://www.uspto.gov/go/kids/

Wacky Patent of the Month

http://colitz.com/site/wacky.htm

★★★★

👫 All

Featuring crazy inventors and their strange inventions, this site is devoted to recognizing selected inventors and their remarkable and unconventional patented inventions. The law office of Michael J. Colitz, Jr., registered patent attorney, sponsors this site.

JAILS

360degrees
http://www.360degrees.org

★★★★★

Collection of interviews and taped audio diaries gathered from inmates, correctional officers, lawyers, judges, parole officers, parents, victims, and others whose lives have been affected by the criminal justice system. As you listen to each individual's story, you can take a 360-degree tour of the individual's personal space—the jail cell, office, living room, or other environment in which the person spends most of his or her time.

American Jail Association
http://www.corrections.com/aja/

★★★★★

This site is the Internet home of the American Jail Association (AJA), a "national, nonprofit organization that exists to support those who work in and operate our nation's jails and is the only national association that focuses exclusively on issues specific to the operations of local correctional facilities." Here, you can find information about the organization and its conferences, training materials, and awards.

Corrections.com
http://database.corrections.com/

★★★★

Corrections professionals will want to visit this site to stay abreast of current issues, learn new techniques, and keep in touch with other people who work in corrections. Information on education, food service, healthcare, new technology, and more, plus message boards, chat rooms, and listserv newsletters.

[Best] Corrections Connection
http://www.corrections.com/

★★★★★

This site is a weekly news source and online community for corrections professionals. Here, you can find articles about corrections institutions, a buyer's guide covering more than 1,000 industry products and services, hundreds of job openings, open discussion forums, and more. The directory features categories including Education, Food Service, Health Care, International, Juvenile, Privatization, Student, and Technology. This one-stop site provides everything a corrections professional needs laid out in an easily accessible format, making it our choice for Best of the Best jail site.

CrimCast
http://www.crimcast.com/

★★★

A "turnkey training automation system" designed to help criminal justice associations and agencies train their people and develop their own interactive courseware. Students can register for and take courses online.

Federal Bureau of Prisons
http://www.bop.gov/

★★★

Home of the U.S. Department of Justice Federal Bureau of Prisons, this site describes the mission and vision of the Bureau and provides an inmate search tool to help visitors find out where a particular inmate is incarcerated. Visitors may be monitored, so be careful what you look for.

A
B
C
D
E
F
G
H
I
J
K
L
M
N
O
P
Q
R
S
T
U
V
W
X
Y
Z

Jail.Net

http://www.jail.net/

★★★

Information and resources for law-enforcement professionals. General information and links to other resources, including the FBI's and U.S. Marshal's Most Wanted lists, law libraries, corrections training centers, and a general resource library. Also features a directory of corrections and legal resources listed by state.

Officer.com

http://www.officer.com/

★★★★

Created and owned by officer James Meredith, this comprehensive law enforcement resource site is dedicated to serving the law-enforcement community. Hundreds of links to agencies, associations, departments of correction, most-wanted lists, police supply stores, and much more.

U.S. Bureau of Justice Statistics

http://www.ojp.usdoj.gov/bjs/correct.htm

★★★★★

This site tracks and makes available to the public statistics concerning adult correctional populations, jail facilities, trends, and other information pertinent to crime and correctional institutions in the United States. Also covers capital punishment, probation, and parole.

JANITORIAL

Janitorial Bidding Guide

http://www.janitorialbidding.com/

★★★

Thinking of starting your own janitorial service? Then visit this site to find out about a video that can help you land lucrative service contracts.

Janitorial Books

http://www.janitorialbooks.com/

★★★

Huge selection of books, videos, and manuals that show you how to start, promote, and manage a successful cleaning business.

SERVICES

ABM Janitorial Services

http://www.abm.com/

★★★★

One of the largest janitorial and building maintenance companies in the country, ABM caters to large corporations. Provides services to companies in more than 40 states and employs more than 43,000 people. ABM also provides other services, including engineering, elevator, parking, and security.

Coverall Cleaning Concepts

http://www.coverall.com/home.html

★★★

Site of one of the nation's leading commercial cleaning franchise companies with more than 6,000 franchise owners worldwide servicing more than 35,000 customers. Find out about Coverall services near you or check on franchise opportunities.

The Maids

http://www.maids.com/

★★★

Popular home-cleaning service available in several states. Here, you can check whether the service is available in your area, read a few cleaning tips, and even get an estimate for cleaning your house. If the service is unavailable where you live, you might consider applying for a franchise.

Molly Maid

http://www.mollymaid.com/

★★★

Another home-cleaning franchise devoted to handling the housework for its clients. Search for a Molly Maid near you or check out the franchise opportunities.

Vanguard Cleaning Systems

http://www.vanguardcleaning.com/

★★★

Featuring office-cleaning services for businesses and corporations, Vanguard provides commercial-cleaning services to more than 1,000 corporate customers through more than 200 independent franchises.

SUPPLIES

Carolina Janitorial & Maintenance Supply

http://www.cjms.com/

★★★★

Complete selection of cleaning equipment and supplies for professionals. Brooms, mops, paper products, disinfectants, deodorizers, window-cleaning supplies, and anything else you need to keep things clean and shiny. Good customer service reputation, too.

A B C D E F G H I J K L M N O P Q R S T U V W X Y Z

A
B
C
D
E
F
G
H
I
J
K
L
M
N
O
P
Q
R
S
T
U
V
W
X
Y
Z

CyberClean

http://www.cyberclean.com/

★★★★

Well-stocked collection of cleaning supplies and equipment. Everything from brooms to wastebaskets. Shop online and have your order shipped directly to you.

HighPower Supplies

http://www.higherpowersupplies.com/

★★★

Pressure washers and supplies, painting equipment, janitorial equipment and supplies, storage containers, safety equipment, and more.

Jani-Mart.com

http://www.jani-mart.com/

★★★★

Online janitorial supply warehouse featuring a complete stock of cleaning supplies. Trash cans and liners, paper products, mops and buckets, and more. Food service items available, too. Ships orders from any of 22 locations nationwide.

J&R Supply

http://www.jandrsupply.com/

★★★★★

J&R Supply has all the janitorial equipment and supplies you need, along with great service and prices and an excellent return policy. Best of all, the site is easy to navigate. After opening the home page, scroll down for links to various categories of equipment and supplies: Brooms, Brushes, and Accessories; Chemicals; Facility Maintenance; Floor Maintenance; and more. Free shipping on any orders over $1,200.

National Equipment Company

http://www.natequipment.com/front.htm

★★★

Incredible collection of janitorial supplies and equipment and food service equipment.

Fantasy Watersports

http://www.fantasywatersports.com/jetski/

★★★

This site of a Miami-based boat rental company is primarily designed to serve tourists visiting the Miami area, but it features some excellent information on recreational boating. Good article providing general riding instructions and watercraft courtesy tips.

Personal Watercraft Illustrated

http://www.jetskiers.org/

★★★★

Online version of the popular magazine for personal watercraft enthusiasts. The site offers articles, product reviews, message boards, and online shopping (mostly for videos). Also provides some information on upcoming events.

Powerski Jetboard

http://www.powerski.com/

★★★★

Powerski manufactures an interesting device called the Jetboard, which is like a motorized surfboard with a handle.

PWC Underground

http://www.jetski.com/

★★★

Dedicated to everything dealing with personal watercraft, this site provides a list of places to ride, a customizable ride calendar for logging events, model specs, club information, chat rooms, message boards, classifieds, and much more.

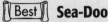 Best   Sea-Doo

http://www.sea-doo.com/

★★★★★

Home of some of the most popular lines of jetskis and waverunners on the market. Visit the virtual showroom to check out the current offerings. From the showroom, you can click a jetski or waverunner to view a brief description of it and check out the manufacturer's suggested retail price, check out the specs, view photos of the craft from different angles, check out reviews, or download a printable brochure. This site is very sleek and easy to navigate.

Wavetech.inc

http://wavetech1.com/

★★★

This personal watercraft parts store is the place to go for jetski replacement parts and personal watercraft accessories.

What's the Best Jetski?

http://www.whatsthebest.net/jetski

★★★★

Before you go shopping for a jet ski, check out this buyer's guide. Also features a jet ski forum.

A B C D E F G H I J K L M N O P Q R S T U V W X Y Z

JEWELRY

Blue Nile

http://www.bluenile.com/

★★★★★

Fine jewelry with a focus on wedding and engagement rings. Great place to shop for that special gift. Some excellent information on how to select quality jewelry, evaluate diamonds and pearls, and understand the differences of various precious metals.

Diamond-Guide

http://www.diamond-guide.com/

★★★★★

From the home page, click the learning center link to access illustrated tutorials that show you how to evaluate diamonds, pearls, and colored stones. Also provides tips on caring for and traveling with jewelry.

Best DiamondReview.com

http://www.diamondreview.com/

★★★★★

Providing independent, unbiased research on diamond jewelry, this site is the favorite hangout for many diamond jewelry enthusiasts and professionals. Features a four-step process to becoming an enlightened buyer: read the tutorial, ask questions, find a jeweler, and then research prices. Easy to navigate and packed with useful information for consumers, this site is an easy Best of the Best pick.

ice.com

http://www.ice.com/

★★★★

Shop by price or browse the online catalog to check out ice.com's wide selection of rings, necklaces, bracelets, watches, and other jewelry. Free shipping on orders more than $100, plus a 30-day money back guarantee.

Mondera

http://www.mondera.com/

★★★★★

Collection of fine jewelry worn by royalty and celebrities worldwide. Here, you can create your own custom ring by selecting a stone and setting. Get expert advice on how to choose quality jewelry and spot the phony stuff.

APPRAISAL

American Society of Appraisers

http://www.appraisers.org/

★★★★

Home of the ASA, one of the top two organizations responsible for setting guidelines for professional appraisers. Click Find an Appraisal Expert to search for an ASA approved appraiser in your area.

CARAT: Professional Jewelry Appraisal Software

http://www.jewelryware.com/

★★★

Professional Jewelry Appraisal Software enables you to print out a professional appraisal report complete with pictures. Download the free trial version or print the mail-in form to order the full version.

International Society of Appraisers

http://www.isa-appraisers.org/

★★★★

Home of the ISA, one of the top two organizations responsible for setting guidelines for professional appraisers. Click Search Database to search for an ISA approved appraiser in your area.

Jewelry Appraisal Services

http://www.jewelryappraisalservices.com/

★★★

Features a comprehensive list of services ranging from mail-in services to phone consultations and appraisal seminars. Some good general information for consumers on selecting diamonds, shopping for gold and platinum jewelry, and estimating your ring size.

Karen Jensen Gem and Jewelry Appraisals FAQ

http://www.kjappraisals.com/
essentialinfodetails.htm

★★★

Excellent FAQ addresses most questions consumers have concerning appraisals. Explains what an appraisal is and how to choose a qualified appraiser. Back up to Karen's home page to arrange for her to do your appraisal.

DESIGNERS

Abrasha's Gallery

http://www.abrasha.com/

★★★★★

Intriguing gallery of jewelry created from combinations of precious and nonprecious metals, stones, and other materials.

Castor Jewelry.com

http://www.castorjewelry.com/

★★★★

Browse the collection of beautiful and unique jewelry pieces or contact Tom Castor to have him draw up a design for you. Computerized illustrations provide you with a clear image of the design before you decide whether to have it made.

GRS Tools

http://www.grstools.com/main.htm

★★★

Tools for engraving, stone-setting, and jewelry-making. Also features courses on learning the basics.

Jewelry Design Professionals Network

http://www.geocities.com/~jdpn/

★★★

Founded "to promote greater communication between jewelry designers through out the industry," this site features a calendar of events, message boards, a member gallery, and information about design competitions. Also contains links to museums, galleries, schools, and other resources.

JewelrySupply.com

http://www.jewelrysupply.com/

★★★★

Create your own earrings, necklaces, rings, and other jewelry. At JewelrySupply.com, you can find all the tools and materials you need to start designing and creating your own custom jewelry.

A B C D E F G H I J K L M N O P Q R S T U V W X Y Z

A
B
C
D
E
F
G
H
I
J
K
L
M
N
O
P
Q
R
S
T
U
V
W
X
Y
Z

Payne's Custom Jewelry

http://www.paynesjewelry.com

★★★★

Tired of the same old standard jewelry? Then contact Tony Payne to design and create a piece for you.

Top Ten Trends in Jewelry

http://www.alrashidmall.com/jic/jewelry-top-ten.htm

★★★

Visit this site to find out what's hot in the world of jewelry fashion.

REPAIR

Art of Gold

http://www.artofgold.com/

★★★

Based in Denver, Colorado, Art of Gold provides quality jewelry repair and service. Also features some unique designs of its own.

Fast-Fix Jewelry Repairs

http://www.fastfix.com/

★★★

Specializing in watch and jewelry repair, this site provides a form you can fill out to obtain an estimate. Describe what you want done, and a representative will provide an estimate and arrange a way for you to send the item you want repaired. Fast-Fix resizes rings, repairs chains, retips prongs, fixes watches and watch bands, cleans watches, replaces watch batteries, and more.

RGM Watch Repair and Restoration

http://www.rgmwatches.com/repair.html

★★★★

Repair and restoration service for high-quality Swiss watch brands.

JOBS

2002–03 Occupational Outlook Handbook

http://www.bls.gov/oco/home.htm

★★★★

Excellent career resource. Find out information about different occupations, industry outlooks, and more. Information is provided by the Bureau of Labor Statistics.

Adventures in Education

http://adventuresineducation.org/

★★★★

👫 14-18

Adventures in Education designed this site to help junior high and high school students and their parents plan their careers and educational paths, calculate the costs, and secure financial aid.

Career Center

http://www.emory.edu/CAREER/Students/CareerDev.htm

★★★★

👫 14-18

A step-by-step procedure that can help you define your career planning process. It is recommended that each step be followed sequentially.

Career Development Manual

http://www.cecs.uwaterloo.ca/manual/index.htm

★★★

A complete career tutorial is available here and can be reproduced for classroom situations.

Career Discovery

http://www.careerdiscovery.com

★★★

This career assessment site offers an assessment tool for $95, with $20 discounts available to alums of specific colleges and universities.

Career Exploration Links

http://www.uhs.berkeley.edu/Students/CareerLibrary/

★★★

👫 14-18

This site provides access to the complete A–Z career database. To explore your career and educational options, select a general heading from the list provided. Pick a career and then pick a major.

Career Interests Game

http://career.missouri.edu/

★★★

👫 14-18

This online "game" is designed to help people match their interests and skills with various careers. If you're not sure what you want to do when you grow up, this site can provide you with a few career ideas that fit your personality. You can find the Career Interests Game by going to this site and clicking its link under Quick Links.

CareerJournal from The Wall Street Journal

http://www.careerjournal.com/

★★★★★

Excellent collection of articles and tips on finding your dream job. Salary and hiring information, job search tool, resume database, discussion groups, and more.

A
B
C
D
E
F
G
H
I
J
K
L
M
N
O
P
Q
R
S
T
U
V
W
X
Y
Z

Career Key

http://www.careerkey.org/english/

 ⑤

★★★★

 14-18

Visit this site to fill out an online form that helps determine the type of career that's right for you. This site also offers plenty of additional advice on how to make the best career choice. Includes information on various careers, including salary, job outlook, and training.

CareerMakers

http://www.careermakers.com/

★★★

A two-week career-planning seminar focused on networking, career transition, career management, and interview coaching.

Career Path Assessment

http://www.math.unl.edu/~nmsi/tQ2/assessment.html

★★★

 14-18

A guide to help you make a decision about your career path so you can develop an educational plan.

Career Paths

http://www.ipl.org/div/pathways/

★★★★

14-18

Career Paths is a directory of career planning tools to help visitors, especially teenagers locate careers that interest them. The directory is divided into three sections: Career Choices, Career Biographies, and Career Preparation.

Career Paths Online

http://careerpathsonline.com/

★★★

14-18

Career Paths is designed to help users make career and education plans. This site profiles people with interesting careers, reports on labor market information, highlights innovative programs, and examines all aspects of the career/life-planning process. Take advantage of the 10-step Career Planning Guide and career articles.

Career Resource Home Page

http://www.careerresource.net/

★★★★

This site is filled mainly with links. You can look at career services at universities, use an Internet job surfer, learn about professional societies, and more.

Careers.org

http://www.careers.org

★★★

This site is a great resource center if you're looking for a job or a new career. Many links with many inspiring ideas!

The Enneagram Institute.com

http://www.enneagraminstitute.com/index1.html

 ⑤

★★★

Sign up and purchase the personality analysis service independently validated using scientific means and learn more about yourself. You'll receive a summary and access to more information about your score.

⌐Best⌐ JobStar–Specific Career Information

http://jobstar.org/tools/career/spec-car.htm

★★★★★

14-18

This site offers career guides packed with information about planning your career. What kind of training or education is required for a particular career? What can you earn? What kind of environment will you work in? What's hot? What's not? Some career guides include personal stories from folks working in the field: How did they move (or stumble) into their current work situation? What advice would they give newcomers? Whether you're planning for college, trying to select a career after graduating, or planning a career change, you'll find just the information you need at this site, our unanimous choice for best career site.

JobWeb

http://www.jobweb.com/

★★★

👥 14-18

An excellent resource for career choice information on a variety of occupations. Information on different careers is provided by participating universities and employers. Get advice on what you want to do before you invest in your university education.

Keirsey Temperament Sorter

http://www.advisorteam.com/user/ktsintro.asp

★★★★

👥 14-18

Online personality test that scores results according to the Myers-Briggs system.

Mapping Your Future

http://www.mapping-your-future.org/

★★★

👥 14-18

Mapping Your Future's mission is to counsel students and families about college, career, and financial aid choices through a state-of-the-art, public-service website. This site is also available in Spanish.

Monster Message Boards

http://discussion.monster.com/messageboards/
Index.asp

★★★★

Don't let your career. just drift aimlessly. Get advice on planning and managing your career and any specific problems you have in one of the many message boards. Sponsored by Monster.com.

Self-Assessment Career Survey

http://mois.org/moistest.html

★★★★

👥 14-18

If you are interested in finding out what careers you might like to pursue, take a few moments and complete this brief survey of career cluster area interests.

Self-Directed Search

http://www.self-directed-search.com

★★★

Take the self-directed search for just $8.95 and in 15–20 minutes you'll have a personalized report that suggests types of jobs that match your skills and interests.

Workplace Fairness

http://www.workplacefairness.org/

★★★★★

If your boss or company is giving you the shaft, visit this site to learn your rights as an employee and find out where to go to get help. This site organizes its content into four distinct areas: your rights, news and issues, resources, and take action. Workplace Fairness is a not-for-profit group dedicated to establishing and enforcing workplace policies that are fair and productive for all involved.

COMPANY INFORMATION

Guide to Researching Employers

http://cdc.richmond.edu/career/rsrchemp.html

★★★

Before you head into your next interview, do a background check on the company and develop your own list of questions. Find out if the company can meet *your* expectations.

Jobstar.org

http://www.jobstar.org

★★★★★

If you're looking for a job in California, this is a great starting place. Learn about putting together a good resume, networking, and interviewing, as well as accessing databases of available jobs across the state.

A B C D E F G H I J K L M N O P Q R S T U V W X Y Z

A B C D E F G H I J K L M N O P Q R S T U V W X Y Z

Vault.com

http://www.vault.com

★★★★

Search for jobs by city or job function, research specific companies, get up-to-date industry news, and sign up to receive Vault.com's e-newsletters. Find out what you're worth, too, and network with other members. More information on specific companies and what you can expect to make than you'll find almost anywhere else.

Wet Feet

http://www.wetfeet.com/asp/home.asp

$

★★★★

Before starting your job search, stop by Wet Feet to research various career choices and get the inside scoop on specific industries, such as consulting and hiring companies.

EMPLOYEE INCENTIVES

CTM Incentives

http://www.ctm-incentives.com/

★★★★

A leading developer of online rewards and loyalty programs, NetCentives provides you with a way to build stronger relationships with customers and employees, by recognizing and rewarding the behavior you want to continue.

RewardsPlus

http://www.rewardsplus.com

★★★

In addition to standard employee benefits, such as health insurance, you can now offer your staff up to 25% savings on life and auto insurance, mortgages, and legal services as added perks. RewardsPlus negotiates group discounts that it passes along to its clients, who then offer them to employees as incentives and benefits.

Twenty-Four Seven Incentives

http://www.247incentives.com/

$

★★★

Shop for gifts to perk up your employees.

HUMAN RESOURCE ASSISTANCE

Evolve

http://www.evolve.com/

$

★★★

This company "provides enterprise software for optimizing people and projects at leading services organizations worldwide."

HR-Guide.com

http://www.hr-guide.com/

★★★

Huge directory of information and sites relating to human resource management. Information on just about every aspect of human resources, including staffing, compensation, legal issues, training, employee behavioral problems, and safety issues.

National Workforce Assistance Collaborative

http://www.ed.psu.edu/nwac/

★★★

U.S. Department of Labor initiative to help small and mid-size businesses develop effective workplace practices that attract and retain skilled workers.

Top Echelon

http://www.topechelon.com

★★★★

Top Echelon serves recruiters, companies, and job seekers by pooling information on candidates and trying to link them with matching potential employers.

Workforce Online

http://www.workforce.com/

★★★★

HR professionals will find news, gossip, tips, and other pros to share information with. Participate in chats and learn from each other here.

Workstream

http://www.workstreaminc.com/

★★★

Workstream is a workforce management company that provides services to all those involved in the workforce: HR professionals, their suppliers, third-party recruiters, and job seekers. Workstream offers recruitment services, outplacement services, job databases, and more.

JOB HUNTING

6Figurejobs.com

http://www.6figurejobs.com

★★★★★

Research jobs, find recruiters, and have your resume seen by some of the top companies at this site for experienced professionals

Academic Employment Network

http://www.academploy.com

★★★★

Search for education positions by state or position at this teaching-focused employment site.

America's Job Bank

http://www.ajb.dni.us

★★★★

One of the largest job banks around, this site provides access to the job listings of the public employment services in each state. Search by word, keyword, or state to find many potential jobs.

Black Collegian Online

http://www.black-collegian.com

★★★★

Career site for African-American students and professionals. Searchable jobs database, resume bank, internship listings, graduate schools, and study abroad.

Career Builder

http://www.headhunter.net/index.htm

★★★★★

Billed as a "Mega Job Search," careerbuilder.com has an active, continuously updated database of hundreds of thousands of jobs from more than 25,000 companies. Search the database, post your resume, and build your career.

Career Magazine

http://www.careermag.com

★★★

This online magazine brings you articles on finding and landing your dream job, as well as plenty of links and search tools all in one spot. Great place to search for jobs by profession.

CareerShop.com

http://www.careershop.com

★★★★

A job search site that offers to email you jobs that match your qualifications and interests, as well as allow you to search the jobs database. You'll also find streaming video job tips and news.

College Recruiter

http://www.adguide.com/

★★★

Jobs for college students, graduates, and recent grads. Entry-level work and career opportunities. Searchable database of jobs categorized by job type and location.

A B C D E F G H I J K L M N O P Q R S T U V W X Y Z

Computer Jobs

http://www.developers.net

★★★

IT professionals can create a job profile and then receive emails regarding jobs posted that match their profile. Limited to programming and computer positions.

Dice.com

http://www.dice.com

★★★

If you're interested in working in high-tech, you'll want to post your resume here for companies and recruiters to see. You can also receive emails regarding job opportunities.

FlipDog.com

http://www.flipdog.com/

★★★★★

Featuring a database of hundreds of thousands of jobs from more than 30,000 employers, FlipDog has become one of the most popular sites for jobhunters. Search the database, post your resume, or contact a headhunter. Useful tutorials on resume writing and distribution.

FreeAgent.com

http://www.freeagent.com/Myhome.asp

★★★

Freelancers and independent professionals looking for assignments will find FreeAgent a good place to look. You can find consulting projects and partners at this site.

Futurestep

http://www.futurestep.com/

★★★★

Executive search service for management professionals, this site is created and maintained by Korn/Ferry International, the world's largest executive search firm. Join Futurestep and let its management professionals help you succeed.

Related Sites
http://my.chief.monster.com/

http://www.heidrick.com/

http://www.execunet.com/

HotJobs.com

http://www.hotjobs.com

★★★

Search thousands of jobs by keyword, location, or company in just about every type of job.

Internet Job Source

http://www.statejobs.com

★★★

Source for jobs at major U.S. companies, and state and federal government agencies.

Job Bank USA

http://www.jobbankusa.com

★★★★

Employment and resume information services to job candidates, employers, and recruitment firms. Job meta-search feature accesses large Internet employment databases.

Jobfind.com

http://www.jobfind.com

★★★

Search the job database by location and function to receive a list of opportunities.

JobHuntersBible

http://www.jobhuntersbible.com/

★★★★

This site is designed to function as a supplement to the bestselling self-help book *What Color Is Your Parachute?* by Dick Bolles. Resources are generally divided into two sections: the Net Guide, which provides information on how to manage your job hunt, and The Parachute Library, which contains articles from Dick Bolles and his friends.

jobhunt.org

http://www.job-hunt.org/

★★★★

jobhunt.org provides a directory that's designed to filter out the crummy job search sites and provide links to only the best job hunting sites and resources on the Web.

JobOptions

http://www.joboptions.com

★★★

Browse links to research job openings and job fairs, and read useful articles on changing careers. The Job Alert function emails you new job opportunities that meet your criteria.

Jobs.com

http://www.jobs.com

★★★★

Have your resume broadcast to thousands of head-hunters and employers across the nation, and then sit back and wait for the offers to roll in.

Linkedin

https://www.linkedin.com/

★★★★★

Linkedin is an online networking service that enables you to leverage the power of your current contacts to establish your ultimate contacts. Whether you are looking for a new job or are trying to expand your business, Linkedin can help you find and get in touch with the people you need to contact.

Best Monster.com

http://www.monster.com

★★★★★

Receive daily emails of job summaries that match what you're looking for, from part-time to full-time in a range of career fields. You can search up-to-date databases for job openings nationwide in virtually any field and make online applications to those jobs. Post your resume on the site and have prospective employers come to you! This site's popularity in itself is enough to warrant it the Best of the Best designation, but it also features an easy-to-use interface and some of the best career information around.

Monstertrak

http://www.monstertrak.com/

★★★★

One of the few sites established especially for new college grads, Monstertrak is the result of a partnership with more than 800 career centers and alumni associations. Find listings and network with helpful grads.

NationJob Network

http://www.NationJob.com

★★★

Get a critique of your resume before submitting it Also, search jobs or sign up for email alerts for jobs of interest.

Netshare

http://www.netshare.com/

★★★★★

More than 1,800 elusive six-figure executive positions are listed here. By subscribing to the site, you have access to all the best-paying jobs plus some helpful information on how to tailor your cover letter and resume and give yourself the best chance of landing that dream position. Recruiters can post job openings for free. Visitors can search the database for free, but contact information is blocked; you must subscribe to the service to obtain all of the available information.

Net-Temps

http://www.net-temps.com

★★★

For contract professionals, Net-Temps has a job search agent, relocation tools, resume statistics, chat rooms, classifieds, and auctions to help you land assignments that fit your needs.

Quintessential Careers

http://www.quintcareers.com/

★★★★★

Whether you are entering the job market for the first time or are thinking about changing jobs for any reason, you can find the information and resources you need to execute a successful employment search. The opening page enables you to search for specific positions wherever you plan to live and work. It also provides links to other areas of the site, where you can access the career toolkit, obtain tips for writing resumes, get the latest job market data, ask the Career Doctor for advice, and much more.

A B C D E F G H I J K L M N O P Q R S T U V W X Y Z

A B C D E F G H I J K L M N O P Q R S T U V W X Y Z

Ryze

http://www.ryze.com

★★★★

Business networking site that enables registered users to "meet other people in the high-tech, finance and digital media industries and develop long-term business relationships with them." The site includes an events calendar, message board, private messaging facilities, home pages, and a contact manager.

Spencer Stuart Talent Network

http://www.spencerstuart.com/

($)

★★★★★

Spencer Stuart is a global headhunter, a talent-management organization that specializes in senior executive searches and board director appointments. It is focused on the long-term success of its clients. You can learn more about the available services, join the talent pool, or become a Spencer Stuart client online at this site.

Telecommuting Jobs

http://www.tjobs.com

★★★★

Check here for current news on the telecommuting phenomenon and find potential job opportunities online.

TrueCareers

http://www.truecareers.com/

★★★★

Dedicated to the new job hunter, TrueCareers provides information on job fairs, available positions, and has an online resume builder. Great place for new college grads to find premium openings at major corporations.

WetFeet

http://www.wetfeet.com/

★★★★★

WebFeet is an online job recruitment service that helps companies more effectively fill their openings with qualified personnel and helps job seekers find rewarding, well-paying positions. If you're about to enter or re-enter the job market or are thinking about changing careers, WebFeet can provide the information, resources, and job prospects you need.

JOB SHARING

Innovative Work Arrangements

http://www.advancingwomen.com/jobshare.html

★★★

Learn about women who balance family life and their careers by using different job-sharing strategies. Look here for innovative strategies to meet your work and home needs.

Jobsharing.com

http://www.jobsharing.com/

★★★★★

Created by a company called Job Sharing Resources, this site is devoted to helping companies make job sharing part of their corporate culture by making it easier for companies to find job-share partners. Here, businesses can search for employees who want a job-sharing arrangement, and job seekers can add their names to a database.

U.S. Department of Labor

http://www.dol.gov/dol/topic/workhours/jobsharing.htm

★★★★

Short article by the U.S. Department of Labor that describes job sharing and some of the benefits those who promote job sharing claim it offers.

What Is Job Sharing?

http://www.ivillage.co.uk/workcareer/worklife/
flexwork/articles/0,9545,202_156231,00.html

★★★

This site is dedicated to explaining job sharing and exploring the advantages and disadvantages of this type of working environment.

Woman's Work

http://www.womans-work.com/

★★★★

Featuring more than 25,000 professional flexible jobs, including job-share, telecommuting, and work-at-home opportunities, this is a great place for working mothers and anyone seeking alternative work arrangements to start searching for a job. Search the database or post your resume. Some excellent articles on job sharing and salary and benefit expectations as well.

Work/Life Options Job Sharing Guide

http://www.opm.gov/wrkfam/jobshare.asp

★★★★★

From the U.S. Office of Personnel Management, this job-sharing guide is designed to assist other government agencies in establishing family-friendly workplaces by making full utilization of all the personnel flexibilities and resources available.

WorkOptions.com

http://www.workoptions.com/jobshare.htm

★★★★

Devoted to promoting alternative work arrangements, WorkOptions.com provides information on job sharing, part-time positions, compressed work weeks, telecommuting, and flex time. For about $30, you can order the Flex Success Proposal Blueprint to pitch your work arrangement idea to your current employer.

A
B
C
D
E
F
G
H
I
J
K
L
M
N
O
P
Q
R
S
T
U
V
W
X
Y
Z

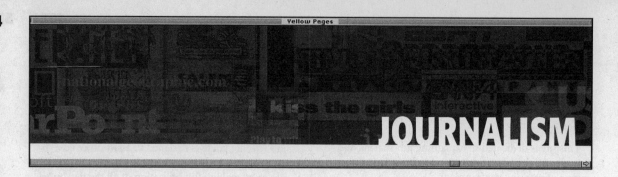

JOURNALISM

A
B
C
D
E
F
G
H
I
J
K
L
M
N
O
P
Q
R
S
T
U
V
W
X
Y
Z

Columbia Journalism Review

http://www.cjr.org/

★★★★

Home of "America's premiere media monitor." CJR is a watchdog organization that monitors the press in all its broadcasting forms: newspapers, magazines, radio, television, and the Internet. Tries to keep the press honest. Great collection of links to online versions of the most popular newspapers, magazines, and TV stations.

Fund for Investigative Journalism

http://fij.org/

★★★

Organization that provides financial support for journalists who are working outside major news organizations.

[Best] High School Journalism

http://www.highschooljournalism.org/

★★★★★

👥 14-18

Presented by the American Society of Newspaper Editors, this site is designed to encourage and support high school journalists and journalism teachers. Students can find articles on journalism, post questions to professional journalists, take a journalism quiz, and find links to high school newspapers. Teachers will find journalism lesson plans, links to support organizations, and other resources for teaching the craft. Visitors can also check into scholarships and colleges that offer journalism degrees. This Best of the Best site has something to offer anyone interested in journalism.

JournalismJobs.com

http://www.journalismjobs.com/

★★★★

In partnership with the Columbia Journalism Review, this site is dedicated to helping journalists find jobs. Job listings for newspapers, magazines, radio, TV, and online broadcasters are available. Articles on freelancing, salary expectations, journalism style, and more.

National Diversity Newspaper Job Bank

http://www.newsjobs.com/

★★★

Devoted to making the media more diverse, this site is devoted to helping women and minorities find jobs in the media.

North Gate: Berkeley's Graduate School of Journalism

http://journalism.berkeley.edu/

★★★

Journalism news from around the world, plus information on Berkeley's Graduate School of Journalism, including admissions policies, students, faculty, and resources.

Pew Center for Civic Journalism

http://www.pewcenter.org/

★★★

Devoted to encouraging journalists to report in such a way as to re-ignite the desire in people to become more involved in their communities, this site features newsletters, articles, videos, and other resources for journalists.

Poynter.org

http://www.poynter.org

★★★★★

👥 14-18

Home of the Poynter Institute, "a school for journalists, future journalists, and teachers of journalism." Here, you can learn more about the Poynter Institute's many seminars, find out about journalism conventions across the country, access online journalism tutorials, read award-winning reports and commentary, and much more.

Project for Excellence in Journalism

http://www.journalism.org/

★★★★

Devoted to improving the quality of journalism, the Project for Excellence in Journalism has put together a Citizen's Bill of Journalism Rights. The site also highlights daily news stories that represent issues in journalism and provides an extensive collection of articles relating to journalism. Discussion forums allow members to debate and discuss current issues.

Society of Professional Journalists

http://www.spj.org/

★★★★★

Dedicated to the preservation of the free press as a cornerstone of democracy in the United States, this site is maintained to help defend the First Amendment rights and to promote high standards in journalism. Here, you can catch the top news stories regarding journalism topics, find out more about careers in journalism, learn about SPJ's programs for journalists, and even enter a contest for a chance to win a prestigious SPJ award in journalism.

USC Annenberg Online Journalism Review

http://www.ojr.org/

★★★

Reviews of online journalism, where it's headed, how it's growing, and related news reports from around the world.

Walter Cronkite School of Journalism & Mass Communication

http://cronkite.asu.edu/

★★★★

Named after the former managing editor of *CBS Evening News with Walter Cronkite*, the Cronkite school is one of the largest of its kind in the nation. This site features information about the school plus a collection of articles dealing with current issues relevant to journalism.

Writers Write Journalism Resources

http://www.writerswrite.com/journalism/

★★★★

Excellent collection of articles and links to other sites where journalists can find additional resources. Find journalism schools, read headlines, or join a discussion group.

A B C D E F G H I J K L M N O P Q R S T U V W X Y Z

526

A
B
C
D
E
F
G
H
I
J
K
L
M
N
O
P
Q
R
S
T
U
V
W
X
Y
Z

JUNK

1-800-GOT-JUNK?

http://www.1800gotjunk.com/

★★★

Need to get rid of some junk? Contact America's largest junk removal service to have it hauled away. Here, you can find service center locations or even sign up for your own franchise.

Junk Yard Dog

http://www.junkyarddog.com/

★★★★

Free search tool for finding used auto, truck, and motorcycle parts. Fill out a part request and have Junk Yard Dog submit the request to its nationwide network of junk yards. Great way to locate those hard-to-find parts without rummaging through your local junk yard.

Junk Yard Parts Online

http://www.junk-yard-hotline.com/

★★★★

Looking for a part for your '67 Chevy? Then turn to Junk Yard Parts Online, a huge database of used car parts from junk yards all across the country. You specify the part you want and how much you're willing to pay, and this site contacts dealers to have them contact you via email, fax, or phone with their quotes.

Best] Junkyard Wars

http://www.junkyard-wars.com/

★★★★

Home of the Emmy-nominated television show, where engineers, mechanics, and the average Joe face off to see who can turn the most miserable pile of junk into something that does what it's supposed to do in 10 hours or less. Apply online to become a contestant. In an age when recycling is becoming more and more a necessity, this Best of the Best site provides a hands-on view of how recycling can be fun and challenging.

Recycled Crafts

http://www.sciswa.org/crafts.html

★★★

👥 All

Learn how to turn junk into home decorations. Great place for parents and teachers to go to learn how to teach children another option for recycling trash.

Stop the Junkmail

http://www.stopthejunkmail.com/

Ⓢ

★★★★

Service that sends email notices to specified companies on your behalf to tell them to stop sending flyers, catalogs, credit card applications, and other unsolicited junk to your home. Costs $19.95 to join.

Thrifty Planet

http://www.thriftyplanet.com/

★★★

Some junk is recyclable, if you only knew where to take it. Visit Thrifty Planet and search for recycling centers and thrift stores near you.

ACTIVITIES

Amazon Interactive

http://www.eduweb.com/amazon.html

★★★

 All

Avoid the mosquitoes and piranhas. Explore the Amazon online. Here, you'll find answers to the most common questions about the Amazon, such as, "How rainy is the rainforest?" and "Who lives there?"

Animaland

http://www.animaland.org/

★★★★

 All

Great site for young children to start exploring the wonderful world of animals. Everything from stories about animals to animal cartoons, pet care tips, career ideas, and Ask Azula's Q&A section.

Arts and Kids

http://www.artsandkids.com

★★★★

 All

Enter the art contest and have your artwork featured in an online gallery for everyone to enjoy. Or play the puzzle game by putting all the pieces together in the correct order. A good site for encouraging kids to paint and draw.

Artsonia

http://www.artsonia.com/

 $

★★★★

 All

Huge museum of artwork all done by children.

Aunt Annie's Crafts

http://www.auntannie.com/

★★★

 All

New craft projects every week for kids and adults. Focuses on learning and creativity. Purchase software and other products online through Digibuy.com.

Awesome Library

http://www.awesomelibrary.org/

★★★★

 All

A World Wide Web digital library for children in grades K–12. Contains information in the categories of art, science, social studies, miscellaneous, and so on. Within each category, several specific topics are featured to simplify searching.

Best Kid's Sites

http://www.geocities.com/EnchantedForest/Dell/4988/kid.html

★★★

 All

This site hosted by rodent librarian Mrs. Becky Mouseneaux, provides links to dozens of the best websites for kids.

A
B
C
D
E
F
G
H
I
J
K
L
M
N
O
P
Q
R
S
T
U
V
W
X
Y
Z

Bill Nye the Science Guy's Nye Labs Online

http://www.billnye.com

★★★★★

👫 All

A companion site to the educational television show *Bill Nye the Science Guy*, Nye Labs Online features daily home science demonstrations, a forum for asking Bill questions, episode guides, teaching materials, and related show resources.

BONUS.com

http://www.bonus.com/

★★★★★

👫 All

This supersite for kids features a huge range of games and activities, from word games to alien combat to pictures to print and color, and much more. Brain teasers and sports information are also part of this "busy" site. There is even a parent/teacher page that offers curriculum enhancers and homework help. But most importantly, your kids will be entertained for hours at this site.

Boston Baked Theatre

http://www.basictheatre.org/

★★★

👫 0-8

An online version of a children's theater in Massachusetts. Boston Baked Theatre creates humorous and musical productions of fairy tales. Shows include *The Princess and the Pea*, *Beauty and the Beast*, and *Snow White and the Seven Dwarfs*. You can even meet the actors.

BrainEvent

http://www.brainevent.com/be

★★★

👫 All

Online newspaper written by and for teenagers and young adults. Includes book and music reviews, a write-in advice column, puzzles and brainteasers, an online novel, and more.

Broderbund Software

http://www.broderbund.com/welcome.asp

$

★★★★

👫 All

This developer and marketer of educational software offers quality software for children. You'll find ABCs for preschoolers, skill-building math, reading programs, and history and geography software.

Build-A-Monster

http://www.goobo.com/monster/

★★★

👫 0-8

Mix up creatures into a creature of your own; easy and fun to do!

Captain Planet

http://www.turner.com/cpf/

$

★★★

👫 All

Information about the cartoon's characters and an episode guide. Learn more about the Captain Planet Foundation, whose mission is to fund and support hands-on environmental projects for children and youth. The objective of this foundation is to encourage innovative programs that empower children and youth around the world to work individually and collectively to solve environmental problems in their neighborhoods and communities.

Best | Cartoon Network

http://www.cartoonnetwork.com/

$

★★★★★

👫 All

This is the web site of the Cartoon Network, home of *Dexter's Laboratory*, *Scooby-Doo*, *Powerpuff Girls*, *The Justice League*, and other popular shows. This site features Kids Next Door, which provides video clips, art, and episode guides for every show. Also features a viewer poll, a huge collection of games, and a refrigerator that showcases kids' artwork. You can also buy Cartoon Network clothing and merchandise, sorted by show or category.

Channel One

http://www.channelone.com

★★★★★

 All

Online version of the popular Channel One broad-casting service that pipes news and current events into classrooms across America. At this site, kids can find information and commentary on various issues that relate to their generation. Check out the latest headline news, listen to music, find out the latest sports scores and highlights, play online games, enter contests, and much more.

Chem4Kids

http://www.chem4kids.com/

★★★

 All

A tour of key concepts in chemistry written for kids. The site also contains separate sections for physics, biology, astronomy, and geography that visitors can go to for similar instruction. Interesting and enter-taining.

Children's Express UK

http://www.childrens-express.org/

★★★★

All

Online children's news organization, based in the UK, and devoted to helping children ages 8 to 18 learn through journalism. Over 7 years, the staff has published more than 600 stories. Read some of the latest stories here.

The Children's Literature Web Guide

http://www.ucalgary.ca/~dkbrown/

★★★

All

This site provides online children's stories ranging from folklore to classics. It also offers an area devot-ed to stories written by children. It contains dozens of links to children's books, as well as links for par-ents, teachers, storytellers, and writers.

Children's Music Web

http://www.childrensmusic.org/

★★★

All

A nonprofit organization that provides links to any-thing musical from music reviews to online song-books. This site also provides a children's concert calendar and a section for music teachers.

Children's Site

http://www.totacc.com/children.html

★★★

All

This Total Access site lists a number of sites that are appropriate for children, such as Yahooligans! and The Cyber Zoomobile. Click the links to go to each site.

Children's Television Workshop

http://www.sesameworkshop.org/

★★★★★

0-8

Kid city! This site features stickers, games, gadgets, and puzzles. The Parent's Toolbox offers tips and tac-tics from *Sesame Street Parents*, plus email from Elmo, games, stories, coloring, Muppet profiles, show information, and trivia. You'll also find activities, crafts, and recipes.

Colgate Kid's World

http://kids-world.colgate.com/

★★★★

All

This site contains information about cavity preven-tion, games, stories, a coloring book, interesting information, and pictures from around the world.

A
B
C
D
E
F
G
H
I
J
K
L
M
N
O
P
Q
R
S
T
U
V
W
X
Y
Z

CollegeBound Network

http://www.collegebound.net/

★★★★★

👫 14-18

Working in partnership with colleges, universities, corporations, military branches, and educational companies, CollegeBound Network has created a stimulating community for teenagers to hang out and expand their horizons. Great resource for high school students who are considering college.

Coloring.com

http://coloring.com/

★★★★

👫 0-8

Kids can find coloring pages for major occasions (Christmas, Easter, Thanksgiving, and so on) as well as animal and football pictures. After they pick a picture, they are shown a palette of colors that they use to fill in the image. My 5-year-old loves to color; this site would be a big hit with him!

Compuserve.com Kids

http://www.compuserve.com/gateway/kids/games.asp

★★★

👫 All

Directory of great games for kids.

Cool LEGO Site of the Week

http://www.lugnet.com/cool/

★★★★

👫 All

Check out LUGNET to see the amazing things kids and adults are creating with LEGO bricks these days—not just the Lunar Lander you had as a kid. Also features links to other LEGO pages.

Crafts for Kids

http://www.craftsforkids.com/

★★★

👫 9-13

Explore the many crafts that children can create, including crafts for holidays and special occasions.

The Crayola Home Page

http://www.crayola.com/

★★★★★

👫 All

Everything you always wanted to know about crayons and all the fun things you can do with them. You can buy Crayola products, from crayons and markers to clothing items you can color. You'll also find a gift idea link to help you choose an age-appropriate gift. Great site!

Cyber Stacks for Kids

http://www.boulder.lib.co.us/youth/links.html

★★★

👫 14-18

A site provided by the Boulder, Colorado, Public Library that includes links for learning about cultures, reference resources, games, a meeting place, and a science center. Also links to other fun places for children.

Cyberhaunts for Kids

http://www.freenet.hamilton.on.ca/~aa937/Profile.html

★★★

👫 All

This site contains links for children of all ages to visit. Features itemized link categories on space, sound, literature, general children's pages, sports, communications, art, computer, science fun, music, animals, games, and more. A great place to start when browsing the Internet.

Cyberkids

http://www.cyberkids.com

★★★

👫 9-13

Lots of fun stuff for kids. Check out the newest articles, reviews, and fiction. Kids can even submit their own work to be published. There's fun stuff, too, such as magic tricks and a game section full of goodies.

Discovery Channel: Discovery Kids

http://kids.discovery.com/

★★★★★

 All

The Discovery Channel provides some of the best and most interesting educational programs for children and teens, including *Prehistoric Planet, Croc Files, Operation Junkyard, Strange Days*, and *Scout's Safari*. This site features information about each show, plus games, activities, and other fun, educational material.

Disney

http://disney.go.com/

★★★★★

 All

Great place for young kids to explore, this site is packed with online games, information about Disney TV shows and movies, kids clubs, family crafts and party planners, vacations, and more.

Download-A-Dinosaur

http://www.rain.org/~philfear/download-a-dinosaur.html

★★★

 All

Looking for a quick kids' craft activity? Look no further. Here, you can download printable dinosaur cutouts to create some prehistoric decorations.

Dr. Seuss: Seussville

http://www.randomhouse.com/seussville/

★★★★

All

Home of *The Cat and the Hat* and all the other beloved Dr. Seuss stories, this site carries visitors to Suessville, where they can read Dr. Suess's biography, have fun on the playground, shop online, or check on upcoming events. Very well-designed, engaging site.

Eco-Kids

http://www.futuresolutionsinc.com/Kids/activities.html

★★★

All

This site features ecological activities to teach children about recycling and composting.

edbydesign.com

http://www.edbydesign.com/kidsact.html

★★★★

All

This site features educational games designed for children between the ages of 5 and 12. Here, you can play scrambler puzzles; practice mathematical skills; and publish your own stories, jokes, riddles, and poems online. Also provides resources for teachers and parents of children with special needs.

Eddy the Eco-Dog

http://www.eddytheeco-dog.com/

★★★

All

Eddy the Eco-Dog teaches kids about the environment. Kids can go to four "surfermania" areas by guessing the right password. After they're in, they can find all sorts of cool places to go. They can send postcards to friends, learn more about Eddy, and sign Eddy's guest book so he can write to them.

Exploring Leonardo

http://www.mos.org/sln/Leonardo/

★★★

All

Learn all about Leonardo da Vinci, the great scientist, artist, and inventor. See sketches of his inventions and his beautiful masterpieces.

FamilyFun

http://family.go.com/

★★★

All

Home of *FamilyFun* magazine, this site offers unlimited activities you and your children can share. You will also find articles on any and every topic you might imagine that relates to your children.

A
B
C
D
E
F
G
H
I
J
K
L
M
N
O
P
Q
R
S
T
U
V
W
X
Y
Z

A B C D E F G H I J K L M N O P Q R S T U V W X Y Z

Fiona's Shark Mania

http://www.oceanstar.com/shark/

★★★

🏃 All

A site for the shark maniac! Areas include shark art, stories about sharks, and a shark mailing list. Many links are also provided.

Flash Cards for Kids

http://www.edu4kids.com/math/

★★★★

🏃 All

Children can improve their math skills by using these online flash cards. They can try their hand at addition, subtraction, multiplication, and division. Flash cards are simple (two numbers) to complex (up to 10 numbers).

Fox Kids Cyberstation

http://www.foxkids.com/

★★★★★

🏃 All

The Fox Kids Network site provides information and activities for kids. It has details about programs geared for kids and includes show times, activities, contests, and more. Free wallpaper and screenshot downloads for some shows. Lots to do here at this site!

The Froggy Page

http://www.frogsonice.com/froggy/

$

★★★★

🏃 All

Everything that kids want to know about frogs! Kids can listen to frog sounds, read frog tales from all over the world, and look at frog pictures. Older kids will appreciate the scientific amphibian section, which includes frog anatomy and dissection as well as detailed scientific information on frogs and other amphibians from all over the world. Be sure to check out the creative and unique T-shirts and sweatshirts available for purchase.

FunBrain

http://www.funbrain.com/

★★★★★

🏃 0-8

Fun games that train the brain, this site focuses on the K–8 crowd but offers games for high schoolers as well. Great place for teachers and parents to go for resources, too.

F.U.N. Place Chat

http://www.thefunplace.com/

★★★

🏃 All

FUN, short for Families United on the Net, is a gathering place for parents and children to share thoughts, ideas, and talents. This site also provides links to plenty of resources, including a parenting guide, recipe database, and bulletin boards.

Games Kids Play

http://www.gameskidsplay.net/

★★★★

🏃 All

Looking for some games to teach your kids? Or perhaps you want to find out the complete verse to a rhyme that's stuck in your head. Well, you've come to the right place. This site provides rules for hundreds of children's games, as well as rhymes to accompany some of them. A great parenting, camping, or scouting resource.

A Girl's World Online Clubhouse

http://www.agirlsworld.com/

★★★

🏃 14-18

A world created especially for girls, this site features advice, pen pals, online diaries, chat, and a class on babysitting. Articles on women's health issues, a recipe collection, and games are also featured.

GoCityKids

http://www.gocitykids.com/choose/

★★★★★

Are you looking for places to take your kids that are fun and educational? Then look to GoCity Kids for information on parks, stores, professional services, restaurants, babysitters, places to stay, entertainment, and other great places and services. GoCityKids can help parents navigate large metropolitan areas without spending a great deal of time researching. Whether you live in or near one of the cities the directory includes, or are planning a trip to one of them, you will find the directory most useful.

Goosebumps

http://place.scholastic.com/goosebumps/index.htm

★★★★

 All

Home of the popular collection of spooky *Goosebumps* books for kids by R. L. Stine. Visit this site to contact the author, play games, watch video clips, and more.

Headbone Zone

http://www.headbone.com/

★★★★

 All

Play games, enter contests, ask questions and get advice, read about celebrities, express your opinions, and chat with friends—all from headbone.com. Parents should supervise activity in the chat areas.

Hotlist: Kids Did This!

http://sln.fi.edu/tfi/hotlists/kids.html

★★★

 All

A "hot list" of sites produced by kids for kids. Kids can choose from seven topics, such as science, art, and school newspapers. Visiting kids select a topic to connect to the hot list of their choice.

Just 4 Girls

http://jfg.girlscouts.org/

★★★★★

 All

This Girl Scout–sponsored page helps girls learn how to do things, such as build their own web page and become a scout. And they can chat with friends online at the site.

Kaitlyn's Knock-Knock Jokes and Riddles

http://www.geocities.com/kaitlynbayne/

★★★

 All

Do you like knock-knocks and riddles the way we do? If so, here's your site.

Kidland

http://www.kidland.com/

★★★

All

Kids can leap from site to site with Webbie, an animated frog. This site contains an index of kids' sites, activities, books, cartoons, educational information, games, and other topics related to children.

Kids-Korner.com

http://www.kidskorner.com/

★★★★

All

Hangout for kids age 14 and under, this site features an entertainment center, complete with games, movie reviews, and book reviews. Also features a game of the week, site of the week, and search tool for finding kid-safe sites.

Kids on the Web

http://www.zen.org/~brendan/kids.html

★★★

All

This growing list of sites offers information for and about kids. Among other things, it includes a lot of stuff for kids to play with, information for adults, and information about schools and education.

A B C D E F G H I J **K** L M N O P Q R S T U V W X Y Z

A B C D E F G H I J K L M N O P Q R S T U V W X Y Z

KidSites.com

http://www.kidsites.com/

★★★★

👫 All

Directory of hundreds of the best websites for kids.

Kids' Place

http://www.eduplace.com/kids/

★★★★

👫 9-13

Houghton Mifflin's Kids' Place is designed specifically for children in grades K–8. Features three distinct areas—School Books, Games, and Brain Power—that provide many fun and educational activities.

Kids' Space Connection

http://www.ks-connection.org/

★★★

👫 All

Check out the Penpal box and read letters from other children. Kids can also post their own letters and become a pen pal. Other sections invite kids to read stories from other children and write their own. The emphasis is on bringing together children from around the world. Section for helping teachers keep in touch with one another, too.

KidsCom

http://www.kidscom.com

★★★

👫 All

Fun Web source for younger surfers. Find cool links from around the world. Get involved creatively in weekly polls and stories. You'll find lots of games here, too.

Kids Domain

http://www.kidsdomain.com

★★★

👫 All

Kids will enjoy playing online games or learning some new craft projects at this site, which has lots of children's activities.

KidsHealth.org

http://kidshealth.org/

★★★

👫 All

This site contains interactive articles about medicine, surgery, parenting, and children's healthcare. The site is divided into sections for parents, teens, and kids, with the content tailored accordingly. It's a nice option for parents who want to give their kids good health information that they can access without Mom and Dad.

Knowledge Adventure

http://www.vugames.com/vug/studio.do?studioName=Knowledge_Adventure

💲

★★★

👫 All

Knowledge Adventure produces children's edutainment software (entertainment software with an educational component). Kids will enjoy the game section and the encyclopedia. Parents will get exposed to this company's line of products and find demos to download as well as technical assistance.

The LEGO Company

http://www.lego.com/

💲

★★★

👫 All

The official LEGO universe: products, services, LEGOLAND, company history, and recent press releases. You can purchase LEGO toys from this site and have them shipped worldwide!

Links and Stuff for Kids

http://www.bltg.com/link4kid.html

★★★

👫 All

This site contains many children's links and descriptions to assist the young surfer. Also features a section for parents that addresses web safety and offers links to the top Internet security software and websites.

Little Explorers Picture Dictionary

http://www.EnchantedLearning.com/Dictionary.html

★★★

 All

Click on a letter of the alphabet and connect to not one but numerous pictures of words with that letter and hot links to websites about that word.

Lois Walker's Take Part!

http://www.loiswalker.com/

★★★

 All

Lois has developed a rather large site devoted to all sorts of entertainment for kids, from limericks and silly jokes to sing-along stories and arts and crafts.

MaMaMedia.com

http://www.mamamedia.com/

★★★★★

 All

A kid-safe, entertaining site that offers kids the chance to create website collections, design their own multimedia characters and stories, and enjoy computer clubs and interactive chat with other kids. Links to another site for older kids.

Mark Kistler's Imagination Station

http://www.draw3d.com/

★★★

 All

Learn how to draw in 3D with online drawing lessons from this famous public television art teacher.

MidLink Magazine

http://longwood.cs.ucf.edu:80/~MidLink/

★★★

 All

This award-winning electronic magazine is written by kids for kids. It's for children ages 8 to 15, and links children all over the world. Children tell about their role models and can send in stories, poetry, and dramas of their own.

Money Matters for Kids

http://www.mmforkids.org/

★★★★

 All

Created and maintained by Larry Burkett, this site is devoted to helping kids and young adults learn how to make and manage their money. Pick the section that best describes your age and experience: Just for Kids, Just for Teens, College and Trade Students, or Mom and Dad.

Mr. Rogers' Neighborhood

http://pbskids.org/rogers/

★★★★

 0-8

The famous Mr. Rogers has a website, sponsored by PBS. You can take a peek inside Mr. Rogers' house, sing along with the song list, and visit the neighborhood of make-believe. This site also includes a video tribute to Mr. Rogers, along with information for parents on how to help their children approach this site and the *Mr. Rogers' Neighborhood* series since the death of Mr. Rogers.

MysteryNet's Kids Mysteries

http://Kids.MysteryNet.com/

★★★

 All

Offers mysteries, stories, tricks, and contests for kids. Also features online Nancy Drew mysteries and maze adventures.

Nabisco Kids

http://www.nabiscokids.com/

★★★

 All

Great collection of online games divided into categories including arcade, sports, puzzle & board, and multiplayer. Register for prizes or just find out about Nabisco's collection of tasty snacks.

A
B
C
D
E
F
G
H
I
J
K
L
M
N
O
P
Q
R
S
T
U
V
W
X
Y
Z

A
B
C
D
E
F
G
H
I
J
K
L
M
N
O
P
Q
R
S
T
U
V
W
X
Y
Z

Noggin

http://www.noggin.com/

★★★★★

 0-8

Noggin, from the creators of Nickelodeon, bills itself as preschool on TV and on the computer. Of course, on the Internet, it is much more interactive, featuring games, stories, puzzles, and other interactive educational features to keep kids entertained while teaching them the basics.

The NoodleHead Network

http://www.noodlehead.com/

★★★★

 All

The NoodleHead Network is an award-winning video company based in Burlington, Vermont. It produces, markets, and distributes educational videotapes created from a kid's view. Kids play an integral role in the creation of each tape—from script development to acting to editing. Then a group of "ex-kids"—writers, producers, and educators—translate those ideas into unique videos that educate and inspire.

OLogy

http://www.ology.amnh.org

★★★★★

 All

If you think science is no fun, then check out this site sponsored by the American Museum of Natural History. Here, you can study genetics, astronomy, and paleontology in a fun-filled environment, and learn some interesting facts by playing a robust selection of trivia games.

Pasadena Kids' Pages

http://www.e-znet.com/kids/

★★★

 All

Contains a daily calendar of events for children in Pasadena, California, and surrounding suburbs.

Paw Island

http://www.pawisland.com/

★★★★

 0-8

Paw Island is a magical island world inhabited by cats and dogs. In this special world, all the adult pets have jobs, roles, or responsibilities on the island. More importantly, they are all able to teach the island's younger pets the difference between right and wrong. Features activities, games, cartoons, and online shopping.

PBS Kids

http://pbskids.org/

★★★★★

 All

Sing and dance to PBS tunes with your favorite characters, play any of the 47 different games available, or print out pages to color featuring more PBS characters. This site is rich with PBS characters and activities.

Pinhole Spy Camera

http://www.pinholespy.com

★★★★

 All

Download plans and instructions for building and using your very own pinhole spy camera. With this simple cardboard-constructed camera, you can learn photography basics while "snapping" your own surveillance photos.

Pojo.com

http://www.pojo.com/

★★★

All

Harry Potter and Pokémon players and fans will want to visit this site for game playing, card trading, news, and updates regarding Harry Potter, Pokémon, and other game tournaments and events.

The Prince and I

http://nfbkids.ca/kids/index.html

★★★

 All

Children visit a kingdom with the queen, search for treasure, submit their own drawings and stories, solve puzzles, and play games. The emphasis is on reading, fun, and creativity for kids in grades K–6.

Reach for the Sky: Careers for Teens

http://rfts.sky.com/

★★★

 14-18

Site developed for young adults (ages 11–18) to provide helpful information in their career decisions. Features actual career stories and information to help teens in choosing an appealing career to pursue.

Reading Rainbow

http://gpn.unl.edu/rainbow/

$

★★★★

 All

Home page of the *Reading Rainbow*, devoted to encouraging reading and writing in young children. Find a complete *Reading Rainbow* book list plus lesson plans and study guides. Books, videos, and other items available online.

Rocks for Kids

http://www.rocksforkids.com/

★★★

All

Young rock collectors and aspiring geologists will want to check out this site. Learn about the various types of rocks and how to identify them.

SFS Kids

http://www.sfskids.com

★★★★★

 All

Created and maintained by the San Francisco Symphony, this site is dedicated to providing a place for kids and families to learn more about music. Here, you can check out a selection of instruments, learn the basics of reading music, compose your own tunes, and send audio postcards to your friends and family via email.

Silly Billy's World

http://www.sillybilly.com/

★★★

All

Reading and writing are the focus of this site. It contains a reading series, learning links, stories for kids, and a creative writing area. The site also contains a section for teachers dedicated to children's reading.

SmartGirl

http://www.smartgirl.org/

★★★

 14-18

This all-girl teenage hangout features articles dealing with issues that many teenagers face, including sexuality, sports, school issues, family problems, and depression. Also provides reviews of books, beauty aids, music, and magazines. Creative writing forum where teen girls can showcase their works, plus an anonymous Speak Out section.

Soap Bubbles

http://www.exploratorium.edu/ronh/bubbles/

★★★★

All

Bubbles! Bubbles everywhere! Kids love bubbles, and this educational site will teach them everything about the chemistry that makes up bubbles. Get your summer bubble recipe here. The site also includes links to other bubbly sites.

A
B
C
D
E
F
G
H
I
J
K
L
M
N
O
P
Q
R
S
T
U
V
W
X
Y
Z

Sports Illustrated for Kids
http://www.sikids.com/splash.html
★★★★
All

Very cool site with sporting information geared toward kids and youths. Just like the adult *Sports Illustrated* magazine, this online version offers detailed articles about sporting events, sports heroes, and more. This version not only covers football, baseball, and other mainstream sports, but skateboarding and other "X" sports, too.

Stone Soup
http://www.stonesoup.com/
$
★★★★
9-13

Magazine written and illustrated by writers and artists ages 8 to 13. Children can send in their own manuscripts for possible publication. It inspires young writers and contains beautiful stories written by young people.

Story Fun
http://www.mit.edu/storyfun
★★★
All

Kids fill in the blanks using parts of speech such as nouns, adjectives, verbs, and adverbs that are then inserted into a story with hilarious results. A great educational tool and a lot of fun.

StreetPlay.com
http://www.streetplay.com/
$
★★★★★
All

Drop that mouse, turn off the TV, and hit the streets for some good old-fashioned fun with your neighborhood pals. This site celebrates the games your parents grew up with—stickball, handball, hopscotch, jump rope, and marbles, to name a few. Provides rules for most games and videos that show you how to play many of the featured games.

Terrific Web Sites for Middle School Kids
http://www.eastchester.k12.ny.us/schools/ms/kids/kids.html
★★★
14-18

This site, developed by the Eastchester Middle School, provides both educational and entertaining links for middle school students, broken down into several categories: Arts, Computers & Technology, English, Health, Mathematics, Science, Social Studies, Sports, County & State, and Fun & Entertainment. There are long lists of topics within each category, so you can locate particular interests quickly.

Thomas the Tank Engine Page
http://www.thomasthetankengine.com/
★★★
0-8

Calling all *Thomas the Tank Engine* fans! Read stories, play games, and have fun. You can also design your own My Thomas page.

TIME for Kids
http://www.timeforkids.com/TFK/
★★★★★
All

This online magazine is written and produced by the *Time Magazine* folks. This is a site where your kids can get the latest on their favorite music, film, or TV artists, as well as get the latest news on current events. They can also add their opinions in Kids' Views on the News.

Universal Studios Kids
http://www.universalkids.com/
★★★★
All

A safe, fun, and creative place for children of all ages learn about the latest movies from Universal, play games, and learn about some of Universal's best-loved film characters.

VolcanoWorld

http://volcano.und.nodak.edu/

★★★★

👫 All

An educational place for kids to learn all about volcanoes. This site contains experiments, images, and data (all pertaining to volcanoes), and an area where kids can learn where the latest volcanic eruptions have occurred. The Kids Door opens into a world of art, quizzes, and virtual field trips.

What Kids Can Do

http://www.whatkidscando.org/

★★★★

👫 14-18

Stories from around the country about kids who work with teachers or other adults for the public good.

The White House for Kids

http://www.whitehouse.gov/kids/

★★★★

👫 All

Kids tour the White House and learn about the location and history of the White House. Kids can learn about children and pets who grew up and lived in the White House, and even write to the President, the Vice President, and the First Lady using special email addresses!

Why Files

http://whyfiles.org

★★★

👫 All

Each week a new report is presented and explained using scientific theory—"the science behind the news." Search the archives to read past articles and send in your own questions.

🎟 Best 🎟 Wild World of Wonka

http://www.wonka.com/

★★★★★

👫 All

Willie Wonka and his chocolate factory have built a home on the Web. Visit the wacky Wonka, take a tour of the Chocolate Factory, read the joke of the day, play several games, or download the free screensaver or wallpaper. You and your kids both will love this Best of the Best site!

World Village Kidz

http://www.worldvillage.com/kidz/

★★★★

👫 All

Online activities for kids 3 to 13. This site contains pages for preteens and teenagers and pages for preschool and elementary students. The playground has areas for games, comics, e-pals, and puzzles, and provides links to other kid-friendly places on the Internet.

Yahooligans

http://www.yahooligans.com/

★★★★

👫 All

Website search engine for children that contains sections devoted to history, the arts, politics, computers and games, entertainment, sports and recreation, daily news, events, weather, and comics. Also features a school section that contains programs and homework answers.

A
B
C
D
E
F
G
H
I
J
K
L
M
N
O
P
Q
R
S
T
U
V
W
X
Y
Z

The Yuckiest Site on the Internet

http://yucky.kids.discovery.com/

★★★★★

[xx] All

Yuckiest is not a distinction many websites would want, but Wendall the Worm and Ralph the Roach take great pride in introducing you to their world. Read all the exciting facts about the creepy crawlers and then take the Roach Quiz. Let Ralph give you the lowdown on all his friends, including the earthworm and the bearded worm. This informative site is a lot of fun. Parents should check out the Just for Adults section for lots of great resources and links.

Related Sites
http://www.sass.ca/
http://www.ala.org/parentspage/greatsites/
http://scholastic.com/magicschoolbus/home.htm

KIDS' INTERNET GAMES

Alive Software

http://www.alivesoft.com/

★★★

[xx] All

Alive Software publishes games and educational software. Download free, fully functional copies of Snow White, Billy The Kid, Animal Quest, Magic Crayon, Scubaman's Quest, Dinosaur Predators, and more.

All Mixed Up

http://www.allmixedup.com/

★★★★

[xx] All

A collection of classic online games (hangman, tic-tac-toe, Connect Four, and lots more) that are challenging, fun, and suitable for kids of all ages.

Ambrosia Software

http://www.ambrosiasw.com/

$

★★★

[xx] All

Find all kinds of shareware games that you can download and play. Ambrosia also has mailing lists to tell you about upcoming games and such.

Billy Bear's Fun and Games

http://www.billybear4kids.com/games/online/games.htm

★★★

[xx] All

Play online jigsaw puzzles, tic-tac-toe, checkers, a solitaire marble game, Pipe Dreams, and other common favorites at the Playground.

Buzz's Animated Adventures

http://www.sikids.com/buzz/adventures/buzzmall2.html

★★★

[xx] All

Cool skateboarding game in Shockwave.

Centipede

http://www.wzzm13.com/games/centipede.html

★★★

[xx] All

Looks just like the arcade version of Centipede.

The Codebook

http://www.codebook.se/

★★★★

[xx] All

Serious Macintosh game players survive with cheats that get them extra lives, unlimited funds, hints, walkthroughs, and so on. Check this site for the cheats you need for your game.

Coolmath.com

http://www.coolmath.com/

★★★

[xx] All

"An amusement park of mathematics" that offers the Fractal of the Day, as well as helpful details and images to explain concepts from algebra, geometry, and calculus. Special areas for kids up to the age of 12 and for older kids ages 13–100.

Escape from Knab

http://www.escapefromknab.com/

★★★★

👫 All

A money-management Shockwave game for kids.

Funbrain.com

http://www.funbrain.com/

★★★

👫 0-8

More than 30 different online games. Kids can click on their age group or search by category to find a game they want to play.

Games-911

http://www.games-911.com/internet_games_for_
kids.htm

★★★

👫 All

Comprehensive directory of computer games, online games, and cheats.

Games for Kids

http://www.kidsgames.org/

★★★

👫 0-8

Choose from more than 500 games for kids ages 6–10. You'll find everything from arcade games to puzzles and mazes.

Games Kids Play

http://www.gameskidsplay.net/

★★★

👫 All

Take a break from the computer and go outside to play. Here, you'll find dozens of classic schoolyard games, such as Capture the Flag, Hopscotch, Marbles, and more, complete with rules.

Gustown Online Game Directory

http://www.gustown.com/ToyStore/Games/Games.html

★★★

👫 All

A few fun arcade games for young children. For access to more resources at Gustown, go to the Gustown home page at http://www.gustown.com/.

Junior Achievement TITAN

http://titan.ja.org/

★★★

👫 14-18

Kids over 13 are invited to play Junior Achievement's business simulation game, where they can play the role of CEO and compete against other young business tycoons.

KidsCom Games

http://www.kidscom.com/games/games.html

★★★★

👫 All

Lots of fun stuff for kids of all ages! This is the place to find video game information. You'll find easy games, challenging games, Shockwave games, Java games, and more. Share tips and tricks about your favorite games on the GameTalk message boards.

Lycos Zone

http://www.lycoszone.com/

★★★★

👫 All

Choose to play mind games, action games, arcade games, goofy games, or strategy games at this site, which has lots of other information and things to do.

playkidsgames.com

http://www.playkidsgames.com/

★★★★

👫 All

Educational games that kids can play with their parents. Play Subtraction Pinball, Whack a Mole Alphabet, Musical Memory Turtle, and more.

A B C D E F G H I J **K** L M N O P Q R S T U V W X Y Z

A
B
C
D
E
F
G
H
I
J
K
L
M
N
O
P
Q
R
S
T
U
V
W
X
Y
Z

Rocket Downloads Kids Software

http://www.rocketdownload.com/frmsrc/
kidsmaindate.htm

★★★★

 All

This URL takes you to the kids' portion of a larger software download site. Choose to have the huge selection displayed alphabetically or by most recent to least recent. Each item listing offers a review, program facts, and the option to download the program. You will have to pay to get the whole program, but at least you can try it before you buy it.

Seussville Games

http://www.randomhouse.com/seussville/games/

★★★★★

 0-8

Some of the best games on the Internet can be found in Seussville, which features interactive games that are all about your children's favorite characters! They're all here—Horton, Mayzie, and, of course, the Cat in the Hat.

Top 20 Games

http://www.top20games.com/

★★★★

 0-8

This site provides a directory of computer games in several categories, including PlayStation, Nintendo 64, Xbox, Board and Card Games, and Kids' Games.

Warner Brothers Games Gallery

http://www.warnerbros.com/wboriginals/

★★★★

 All

Find popular Warner Brothers characters such as the Animaniacs, Wile E. Coyote, and the rest of the Looney Toons clan. You'll also find many Shockwave games.

WebChess

http://www.june29.com/Chess/

★★★★

 All

WebChess is a website that allows two individuals to play chess over the Web. You can come and join in a game, wait for an opponent, or just watch the other games being played.

You Rule School

http://www.youruleschool.com/

★★★

 All

From General Mills, this site has fun games featuring Lucky Charms, Trix, Cheerios, and Fruit Roll Ups. This site also offers other activities kids will enjoy.

Zeeks.com

http://www.zeeks.com/

★★★

 All

Lots of activities for kids, from games to puzzles to projects and more. In addition to games, kids can chat, create their own calendar, and get answers to questions they submit.

PEN PALS FOR KIDS

A Girl's World Free Pen Pal Spectacular

http://www.agirlsworld.com/geri/pen-pal/

★★★

 All

Get a pen pal without publishing your email address and make changes to your online profile anytime you want. It's fun, free, and only for girls 7–17.

AltaVista Translation Site

http://babelfish.altavista.com/translate.dyn

★★★★★

 All

This amazing site lets you write a letter to someone in eight popular languages. You cut and paste what you wrote and translated and then "translate it" back to English to see how it reads in another language. Hilarious! Send someone a romantic letter in French and include the URL to this site so he or she can figure out your message.

Christian Pen Pals

http://christianpenpals.com/

★★★

 All

Check out pen pal ads or put in your gender and age range, and a pen pal will be chosen for you. This site claims it supports more than 30,000 Christian pen pals and is growing daily. Registration is required to help prevent members from receiving unsolicited mail and to enable the management to kick any riff-raff out of the club.

epals.com Classroom Exchange

http://www.epals.com/

★★★★★

 All

An excellent way for classroom teachers to connect their students with pen pals from other classrooms throughout the world. This classroom-to-classroom connection and web-based, teacher-monitored email accounts make exchanging email messages much safer. The site does not support direct email exchange between individuals outside the classroom setting.

The Kids on the Web: Pen Pals

http://www.zen.org/~brendan/kids-pen.html

★★★

All

This site provides an important caution to kids about establishing pen pal relationships over the Internet and provides links to several sites where you can find potential pen pals.

Kidworld

http://www.bconnex.net/~kidworld/

★★★

 All

Magazine for kids under 16 with jokes and riddles, games, quizzes, stories, and a pen pals/key pals corner. As with other sites that ask you to list your email address, this isn't the safest way to find a pen pal.

Student Letter Exchange

http://www.pen-pal.com/

★★★★★

Student Letter Exchange is a service that matches up students aged 9–18 around the world. Its database of more than a quarter million students is being constantly updated, ensuring that you will be able to find a pen pal from the country of your choice. Visit this site for details on having your name added to the databases. Children 13 years old and younger are encouraged to ask for parental permission first. The service does charge a fee of $1.25 for each pen pal, or $1 per pen pal for any orders of 15 names or more.

Surfing the Net with Kids: Safe Pen Pals

http://www.surfnetkids.com/penpals.htm

★★★

 All

Excellent article on exchanging email messages with pen pals in a safe, secure way

Tiggy's Pen Pals

http://www.geocities.com/SoHo/Coffeehouse/9025/PenPal.html

★★★★

 All

This site provides a list of people age 6–25 who are seeking pen pals. List is sorted by age.

A B C D E F G H I J K L M N O P Q R S T U V W X Y Z

A
B
C
D
E
F
G
H
I
J
K
L
M
N
O
P
Q
R
S
T
U
V
W
X
Y
Z

World Pen Pals

http://www.world-pen-pals.com/

★★★★

To connect with other kids around the world and foster a sense of friendship and understanding with people of other countries, visit this site to learn how to apply for a pen pal. This site provides access to a form you fill out and mail in with $3. The name and address of your pen pal will be mailed to you.

SAFE SURFING

Ask Jeeves for Kids

http://www.ajkids.com

★★★★

 All

If you type in a question in plain English, Ask Jeeves for Kids finds one website that answers the question. In some cases, you need to rephrase your question slightly to get the answer you want, but Ask Jeeves will prompt you.

Ben's Guide to U.S. Government for Kids

http://bensguide.gpo.gov/subject.html

★★★★★

 All

This site features an extensive directory of websites created by various U.S. government agencies specifically for kids. Browse through the directory or click a link for the desired age group: K–2, 3–5, 6–8, 9–12, or P&T (parents and teachers).

Related Site
http://www.afterschool.gov/kidsnteens.html

Cyber Patrol's CyberGuide

http://www.route616.com/

★★★

 All

A guide to the World Wide Web for kids, parents, and teachers. Features links to sites that are safe for kids ages 6–16+. A great way for teachers and parents to safely introduce children to the Internet.

GetNetWise

http://www.getnetwise.org

★★★★

 All

More than just a search engine, GetNetWise is a resource for parents to help kids have safe, educational, and entertaining online experiences. You'll find a glossary of Internet terms, a guide to online safety, directions for reporting online trouble, a directory of online safety tools, and links to safe sites for kids to visit.

JuniorNet

http://www.juniornet.com

★★★

All

This site provides lots of games and activities by established publishers for children ages 3–12. Only registered members from within a closed network can access JuniorNet.

KidsClick!

http://sunsite.berkeley.edu/KidsClick!/

★★★★

All

Search engine created by librarians for kids to help children and teenagers do their research on the Web in a safe, secure environment. Hundreds of links to interesting sites arranged in easy-to-navigate categories and subcategories.

Mayberry USA

http://www.mbusa.net/

★★★

All

Join this protected online community and block access to pornographic sites that your kids might stumble onto. Rates vary based on connection time and speed.

Net Nanny

http://www.netnanny.com

★★★★

 All

A software filter that prevents pornographic material from being shown on your computer and restricts access to files on your computer desktop. You can order the software at this site for $39.95 and download it immediately, or have it shipped to you.

OneKey

http://www.onekey.com/

★★★

 All

Powered by Google, OneKey has scoured the Net and developed a search engine with more than 500 categories. Using network TV standards, the site filters out sites that don't measure up, so your kids are protected from material inappropriate for their eyes.

Safe Surf

http://www.safesurf.com

★★★★

All

SafeSurf has developed an Internet rating system that alerts parents when inappropriate material is available on a website and then filters out sites that the parents do not want their kids to see. Excellent tip on shutting down your browser when being harassed by a never-ending barrage of pornographic windows.

SafeKids.Com

http://www.safekids.com

★★★★

 All

Find tips, advice, and information on searching safe sites, as well as links to family-friendly sites and search engines.

SurfMonkey Kids Channel

http://www.surfmonkey.com

★★★★

 All

Using Surf Monkey, kids can meet one another, learn, play, shop, and safely explore online. Parents can either set up Surf Monkey as a toolbar that filters out inappropriate material, or use the site as a browser, which will also filter. Service costs $3.95 per month.

SITES BY KIDS

Awesome Math Stuff

http://www.geocities.com/EnchantedForest/5411/math.html

★★★★★

 All

Test your math skills at Annie's home page while you enjoy some cool tunes.

B.J. Pinchbeck's Homework Help Page

http://school.discovery.com/homeworkhelp/bjpinchbeck

★★★

 All

Links to 450 Internet sites with school-related information.

Brianna

http://hometown.aol.com/ydb739094/brianna.html

★★★★★

 All

Learn all about Brianna and the medical challenges she has faced since birth. You'll get to know her and gain an appreciation for all that she faces on a daily basis. A cute girl, and a touching site that can teach kids about children who are different.

A B C D E F G H I J K L M N O P Q R S T U V W X Y Z

Elizabeth's Snow White Page

http://www.ecn.bgu.edu/users/gjmuzzo/lizzie1.htm

★★★★★

👫 All

Elizabeth has Down Syndrome and cerebral palsy, but that doesn't slow her down. Come see her Snow White Page. Elizabeth also has added many cool links to her site, from Disney links to other children's sites.

Kailua-Lanikai

http://www.lanikai.k12.hi.us/WATER/watermenu.htm

★★★

👫 All

Created by a 6th grade class at Lanikai school in Hawaii, this site features a multimedia presentation on the Mokulua Islands, the water, the wildlife in the area, recreational activities, and more.

Kathleen's Home Page

http://www.geocities.com/EnchantedForest/Dell/1902/

★★★

👫 All

Kathleen's page will teach you a lot about babysitting tactics, such as what to do in emergency situations.

My Dinomite Site

http://members.aol.com/cahaston/index.htm

★★★

👫 All

Bobby's website is dedicated to providing information about dinosaurs. Here, you'll find dinosaur quizzes, jokes, art, games, and more.

Neil's World

http://www.windycreek.com/Neil.html

★★★

👫 All

Neil's World has stuff about *Star Wars*, home schooling, Mars, and cats. Stop by and join his Book Club and see his Duck Tape Page.

Tori's Page

http://www.geocities.com/Heartland/6586/Tori.html

★★★

👫 All

Meet Tori, an 11-year-old Tae Kwon Do flute player and her family. Check out her list of cool sites.

KNITTING

Artfibers Fashion Yarn

http://www.artfibers.com/

★★★★

Displays hundreds of unique fashion yarns in knit swatches and offers ideas for using these yarns to create stylish projects.

Frugal Knitting Haus

http://www.frugalhaus.com/

★★★★

This online knitting store offers a wide selection of knitting and crocheting patterns, as well as needles and supplies. In addition, you can find knitting pattern books that give ideas for the use of leftover yarn. The store also offers free patterns.

Guide to Free Knitting Patterns on the Web

http://knitting.miningco.com/hobbies/knitting/

★★★

A list of links assembled by The Mining Company to help you find free knitting patterns.

Knit 'N Style

http://www.knitnstyle.com/

★★★

This is the online version of the knitting magazine, complete with pattern photos and information, as well as knitting links and articles.

The Knitting Guild of America

http://www.tkga.com/

★★★

Communicate and share with knitters online! Visit the national association of hand and machine knitters. Convention news, contests, *Cast On Magazine*, bulletin board, chat, and free patterns are available, too.

Knitting Tutorials

http://www.sweaterscapes.com/instruc1.htm

★★★★

Excellent collection of online knitting tutorials to help you learn various techniques. Some tutorials even come with a free pattern.

Related Sites

http://www.dnt-inc.com/barhtmls/knittech.html

http://www.craftown.com/knitlesson.htm

http://www.woolworks.org/hints.html

http://arcadiaknitting.com/knit.htm

http://www.knitting.co.nz/

Best Knitting Universe

http://www.knittinguniverse.com/

$

★★★★★

This is a comprehensive site for anyone interested in knitting. Learn about yarns; get tips, tricks, and techniques; and shop for yarns and patterns online. Download free patterns, too. You can also subscribe to *Knitter's Magazine*. Excellent resource for beginners and experts alike!

Machine Knitters Source Magazine

http://www.mksource.com/

★★★

Magazine full of machine knitting information.

Patternworks

http://www.patternworks.com/

$

★★★

Shop here for knitting needles, yarn, patterns, kits, and tools.

A
B
C
D
E
F
G
H
I
J
K
L
M
N
O
P
Q
R
S
T
U
V
W
X
Y
Z

Staceyjoy's Knitting Stitch Portfolio

http://www.redlipstick.net/knit/

★★★

Features an index of downloadable Fair Isle patterns and notes—with cable and machine tuck patterns.

Vogue Knitting

http://www.vogueknitting.com/

★★★★

Preview the next issues of *Vogue Knitting* and *Family Circle Knitting* magazines. This site also posts corrections to their published patterns. Also check out the crochet section.

Webs: America's Yarn Store

http://www.yarn.com/

★★★★

Located in Northampton, Massachusetts, Webs offers hand knitters, machine knitters, and weavers a complete selection of yarns and equipment for their crafts by mail order from its store.

Wool Works

http://www.woolworks.org/

★★★★

A noncommercial resource for knitters that can put you in touch with fellow knitters for discussion. In addition, it offers resource ideas to provide guidance and tells you about suppliers, as well as patterns, stores, and more. This site is frequently visited and has lots of useful information.

The Woolery

http://www.woolery.com/

★★★★

Since 1981, The Woolery has been a catalog mail-order supplier of spinning wheels, looms, related supplies, books, dyes, and fibers for crafters and artists. Now all its resources are at your disposal online. You can even read the site in French if you prefer.

Yesterknits

http://www.yesterknits.com/setup.html

★★★★

You'll find tens of thousands of vintage knitting and crocheting patterns at this Scotland-based company's site. Search the patterns, or just look at the most popular ones, and then buy them via mail.

LANGUAGES/LINGUISTICS

American Sign Language Linguistic Research Project

http://web.bu.edu/ASLLRP/

★★★★

This collaborative research project involves researchers at Boston University, Dartmouth College, Rutgers University, and Gallaudet University. Information is provided at this site on the two main parts of this project: investigation of the syntactic structure of American Sign Language (ASL) and development of multimedia tools for sign language research.

The Association for Computational Linguistics

http://www.cs.columbia.edu/~acl/

★★★

Includes background information on the association, conference schedules, abstracts from the *Computational Linguistics* journal, plus links to related sites.

Australian National Dictionary Centre

http://online.anu.edu.au/ANDC/

★★★

This center provides information on research in the usage of Australian English. Features a selection of Australian words, their meanings, and their etymologies, including the meaning and origin of Aussie words such as *bodgie*, *drongo*, *ocker*, and *wowser*.

Center for Applied Linguistics

http://www.cal.org/

★★★★

CAL is dedicated to "improving communication through better understanding of language and culture." Here, you can find a comprehensive list of past and ongoing projects at CAL, plus a database packed with language resources and an online store for purchasing books. Some CAL publications are free.

Center for Machine Translation

http://www.lti.cs.cmu.edu/Research/CMT-home.html

★★★

The Center for Machine Translation (CMT) at the School of Computer Science at Carnegie Mellon University conducts advanced research and development in a suite of technologies for natural language processing. At this site you will find project details, personnel profiles, technical reports, and more.

Center for Spoken Language Understanding

http://cslu.cse.ogi.edu/

★★★

This group from the Oregon Graduate Institute of Science and Technology has a mission to perform basic research leading to advances in the state of the art of spoken language systems. This website follows that mission by providing research summaries, publications—including the full text and illustrations of the Human Language Technology Survey—and more.

A
B
C
D
E
F
G
H
I
J
K
L
M
N
O
P
Q
R
S
T
U
V
W
X
Y
Z

Child Language Development

http://www.kidsource.com/ASHA/child_language.html

★★★

Q&A list discussing issues concerning language development in children. Addresses everything from the concept of language to the parents' role in helping children develop. Sponsored by the American Speech, Language, Hearing Association.

Colibri Home Page

http://colibri.let.uu.nl/

★★★

Colibri is an electronic newsletter and WWW service for people interested in the fields of language, speech, logic, or information. A searchable index of current and past issues is available, along with subscription directions and many links to related topics.

Corpus Linguistics

http://www.ruf.rice.edu/~barlow/corpus.html

★★★

Superb directory of corpora, news, and news sites broken down by language. Links to software, other sites, and additional resources.

English as a Second Language Home Page

http://www.rong-chang.com/

★★★★

 All

This home page is a starting point for ESL learners who want to learn English through the World Wide Web. Many people have created ESL learning materials for the Web. This home page links you to those ESL sites and other interesting places. The variety of materials will allow you to choose something appropriate for you. Includes a directory of kids language sites.

Ethnologue: Languages of the World

http://www.sil.org/ethnologue/

★★★★

If you've ever wanted to know what people are saying all over the world, this is the place to come. This site includes a detailed study of the names, number of speakers, location, dialects, linguistic affiliation, multilingualism of speakers, and much more information on more than 1,000 languages. A searchable database and clickable maps are provided to help you find just the language you are looking for.

FoLLI, the European Association for Logic, Language and Information

http://www.folli.uva.nl/

★★★

This site contains information on FoLLI's background, current and future projects, and publications. Also find out how to join FoLLI and receive its journal.

Best⁏ iLoveLanguages

http://www.ilovelanguages.com/

★★★★★

 14-18

This site contains more than 2,000 links to language resources, such as online language lessons, translating dictionaries, native literature, translation services, software, and language schools. This frequently accessed tool for students and teachers of foreign languages is a unanimous selection as best language/linguistics site.

Language Miniatures

http://home.bluemarble.net/~langmin/

★★★

Biweekly essays about the social, political, historical, and structural aspects of language. Past articles have addressed such topics as Female Grammar, animal language, and computer speech recognition.

Lexeme-Morpheme Base Morphology (LMBM)

http://www.facstaff.bucknell.edu/rbeard/

★★★

The LMBM lexicon is exclusively the domain of lexemes, which are defined specifically as noun, verb, and adjective stems, and the lexical categories that define them (number, gender, transitivity, and so on). LMBM distinguishes itself from other lexeme-based theories in that it maintains a pristine distinction between lexemes and grammatical morphemes and consequently predicts this distinction at every level of language and speech.

Linguistic Data Resources on the Internet

http://www.sil.org/linguistics/etext.html

★★★

Extensive directory of linguistic data resources on the Web arranged by topic: Text, Lexical Resources, and Grammar.

Loglan

http://www.loglan.org/

★★★★

Loglan is an artificial human language originally designed/invented by the late James Cooke Brown in the late 1950s. This site details the construction and usage of this language. An HTML primer to learn Loglan is also available.

The Mayan Epigraphic Database Project

http://jefferson.village.virginia.edu/med/home.html

★★★

The Mayan Epigraphic Database Project (MED) is an experiment in networked scholarship with the purpose of enhancing classic Mayan epigraphic research. MED is an Internet-accessible database of primary and secondary sources of epigraphic, iconographic, and linguistic data in a multimedia format.

Model Languages

http://www.langmaker.com/

★★★★

The electronic newsletter contains discussions and articles on made-up languages. Includes subscription information and a software package (Windows) for making your own language.

Semiotics for Beginners

http://www.aber.ac.uk/media/Documents/S4B/semiotic.html

★★★

As the title suggests, this site provides an online course in the study of signs and communication in society (semiotics). Here, you get the history of this discipline, current applications and research, and lists of suggested reading material.

Universal Grammar in Prolog

http://www.nyu.edu/pages/linguistics/ling.html

★★★

This page is part of a larger website that discusses the design and implementation of a computer programming language that works using real English syntax—not the cryptic commands of languages such as C++. This page relates the linguistic theories of Noam Chomsky to the larger project.

UCREL: University Centre for Computer Corpus Research on Language

http://www.comp.lancs.ac.uk/computing/research/ucrel/

★★★

The University Centre for Computer Corpus Research on Language is a Lancaster University research center shared between the Department of Linguistics and Modern English Language and the Department of Computing. Its objective is to carry out computer-based research on the analysis and processing of natural language data. This site provides details on the center's research, including data summaries, online papers, and conference schedules.

University of Chicago Press Cognitive Science and Linguistics Catalog

http://www.press.uchicago.edu/Subjects/virtual_linguistics.html

★★★

This page is the entry-point into the University of Chicago's online catalog and ordering system for linguistics texts. Search by author and subject or read the whole catalog, including book summaries.

A
B
C
D
E
F
G
H
I
J
K
L
M
N
O
P
Q
R
S
T
U
V
W
X
Y
Z

Virtual Foreign Language Classroom

http://www.nvcc.vccs.edu/vflc/links.htm

★★★★

This virtual classroom from the Virginia Community College System and Distance Learning facility provides links to other sites relating to culture, instruction, and other language resources designed to enhance the learning of foreign languages. Links are organized into three categories: Courses and Instruction, Language Resources, and Culture. Registered faculty members can read and post messages in the Forum.

WordSmith Tools

http://www.lexically.net/wordsmith/

★★★

Wordsmith Tools is an integrated suite of programs for looking at how words behave in texts. It is intended for linguists, language teachers, and others who need to examine language as part of their work. Download a full demo version from this site at the Oxford University Press.

Xplanation

http://www.xplanation.com/

★★★

Provides information on the EUROLANG Optimizer software package. This program is designed to work with the most popular word processors and RDBMS to provide language translation. Download the demo version from this site. Pages are available in French or English.

CONSTRUCTED LANGUAGES

Constructed Human Languages

http://www.quetzal.com/conlang.html

★★★

This site contains listings and links to further information on constructed human languages. Constructed human languages are planned languages created by humans, such as the various languages developed by J.R.R. Tolkien in his novels. The site is a good starting point for anyone interested in non-natural languages.

Esperantic Studies Foundation

http://esperantic.org/

★★★

This site is an index to English language sites on planned or international languages. It focuses on Esperanto because there have been more than 900 attempts to create an international language, but only Esperanto has been successful. Esperanto is thus used as a tool in the branch of linguistics known as interlinguistics (the study of how languages are used to communicate between two different groups).

Esperanto Access

http://www.webcom.com/~donh/esperanto.html

★★★

Esperanto is the most successful created language and is spoken by some two million people worldwide. Check out this site for a good introduction to Esperanto. The introductions are made available in English, Swedish, Dutch, Spanish, and many other languages.

The Klingon Language Institute

http://www.kli.org/

★★★★★

This site is for "scholars" wanting to study the Klingon language from the *Star Trek* TV series. Lots of information is available on the language, and you can even learn to speak Klingon using the site.

Vin Tengwar

http://www.elvish.org/VT/

★★★

Tengwar is the written language of the Elven people described in the books of J.R.R. Tolkien. Here, you can find information regarding this interesting constructed language. It includes explanations of Tengwar writing and links to Tengwar fonts for Windows and Macintosh computers.

ENGLISH LANGUAGE

Australian Slang

http://www.koalanet.com.au/australian-slang.html

★★★★

A site containing an Australian-English slang and phrase dictionary. You'll find hundreds of colorful Australian phrases here. If you're planning a trip to Australia any time soon, or just want to how far "Back of Bourke" is, check out this site.

BritSpeak

http://martinamis.albion.edu/britspeak.htm

★★★★

👫 Not for kids

Have you ever heard anyone say, "I'll knock you up tomorrow morning"? This statement would be shocking only if you didn't realize that, to the British, the term *knock up* means to awaken someone by knocking on that person's door. This site attempts to clear up these miscommunications, and provides a dictionary that converts British words and phrases to American and vice versa. Includes a link to the *Dictionary of British Cultural References.* Some foul language.

The Collective Nouns

http://www.ojohaven.com/collectives/

★★★★

If a group of fish is called a *school*, and a group of lions equals a *pride*, then what is the name of a group of whales? Would you believe a *pod*? This fun site catalogs many collective nouns—many of them humorous. For example, you might see a colony of penguins, a siege of herons, a bunch of things, or a giggle of girls.

Cyberbraai

http://www.fortunecity.com/marina/cyprus/125/cyberbraai/cyberi.htm

★★★★

A collection of lists of words and phrases in South African English, with explanations of their meanings. A very humorous and entertaining site.

English Everywhere

http://englisheverywhere.homestead.com/

★★★★

👫 All

Dedicated to helping students learn English through the media, this site provides a directory of resources organized by media type, including Television, Radio, Films, Newspapers, Magazines, and Music. Features areas for students and teachers.

Grammar and Style Notes

http://andromeda.rutgers.edu/~jlynch/Writing/

★★★★★

Quick! What's the difference between *affect* and *effect*? Jack Lynch has the answer, and he's offered it up on this site, an online guide to the complexities of English grammar. Lynch clearly explains the differences between commonly confused words, defines terms such as *dangling participle*, and offers his own opinions on a variety of style issues.

History of the English Language

http://ebbs.english.vt.edu/hel/hel.html

★★★

Home page for the History of the English Language mailing list (HEL-L), this page includes many resources for English language history studies. Anything from Anglo-Saxon texts to modern American English can be found here.

WordNet

http://www.cogsci.princeton.edu/~wn/

★★★

A lexical reference work, WordNet is designed to map out the relationships and connections between words and their synonyms. Created by the Cognitive Science Laboratory at Princeton University, this site was developed as an educational tool for improving vocabulary and reading comprehension.

A
B
C
D
E
F
G
H
I
J
K
L
M
N
O
P
Q
R
S
T
U
V
W
X
Y
Z

A B C D E F G H I J K L M N O P Q R S T U V W X Y Z

GENERAL LANGUAGE AND LINGUISTICS

ERIC Clearinghouse on Languages and Linguistics

http://www.cal.org/ericcll/about.html

★★★★

The ERIC Clearinghouse. on Languages and Linguistics is operated by the Center for Applied Linguistics, a private nonprofit organization. This site provides a wide range of services and resources for language educators, including a frequently asked questions list, directory of resources, online newsletter, and information teachers need to know about teaching languages.

European Minority Languages

http://www.smo.uhi.ac.uk/saoghal/mion-chanain/

★★★

Dedicated to lesser-known European languages, this site includes information on languages such as Breton, Basque, and various Celtic languages that are spoken by small groups of people throughout Europe. Contains links to other sites that specialize in particular minority languages.

Gaelic and Gaelic Culture

http://www.ibiblio.org/gaelic/

★★★★

This site contains a good introduction to the Gaelic languages spoken in Ireland, Scotland, and Wales. Information on Gaelic culture and history can also be found here. Many of the resources listed here are actually in Gaelic, so non-Gaelic speakers/readers beware.

Hindi: The Language of Songs

http://www.cs.colostate.edu/~malaiya/hindiint.html

★★★★

Spoken by millions around the world, Hindi is one of the major languages of India. As the site's title implies, a large archive of Hindi songs is available through this site. It also contains links to Hindi language and literary resources.

The LINGUIST List

http://www.linguistlist.org/

★★★

LINGUIST List is an electronic network hosted by Wayne State and Eastern Michigan Universities. Linguists worldwide use LINGUIST List for research and discussion through its electronic mailing list and website. Archives of past discussions are maintained on the site.

MERCATOR

http://www.mercator-central.org/

★★★

The MERCATOR Project is an initiative set up by the European community to promote the interests of the minority/regional languages and cultures within the European Union. The site also contains links to three MERCATOR departments and a bibliographic database.

The Translator's Home Companion

http://www.rahul.net/lai/companion.html

★★★

Sponsored by the Northern California Translators Association, the Translator's Home Companion provides a guide to resources for professional translators. Links to online translation resources, such as dictionaries, are listed on this site. Translation news, product information, and reviews can also be found here. Looking for work? Subscribe to the translator jobs newsletter.

Yamada Language Center Non-English Font Archive

http://babel.uoregon.edu/yamada/fonts.html

★★★

If you've ever needed foreign language fonts, this is the site to visit. This archive contains a large number of fonts for foreign languages. Graphic designers and linguists can both benefit from this archive.

LEARNING LANGUAGES

Chinese Language Information Page

http://www.webcom.com/bamboo/chinese/

★★★

An index of online resources on the Chinese language, including a featured Chinese site each month. Link categories include literature, software, and Chinese language radio broadcasts.

CLAP: Chinese Learner's Alternative Page

http://www.sinologic.com/clas/

★★★★

CLAP offers the Chinese learner great resources. In addition to the standard fare of vocabulary words and dictionaries, CLAP offers information on the latest happenings in Chinese language and culture. For example, one section details English words in common Chinese usage.

CyberItalian

http://www.cyberitalian.com/

★★★★

 All

Free trial tutorials from the site's Italian with Pinocchio course. To continue your studies, you must become a member.

Dutch 101

http://www.dutch-101.info/

★★★

Learn basic Dutch vocabulary and grammar. Unfortunately, this site provides little direction on proper pronunciation.

Esperanto Hypercourse

http://wwwtios.cs.utwente.nl/esperanto/hypercourse/inleiding.html

★★★

If you've ever had a desire to learn the Esperanto language, this site is for you. The site features a WWW version of a hypercard stack that will guide you through an introductory course on Esperanto. The lessons are available in English only.

French Language Course

http://www.jump-gate.com/languages/french/

★★★★

An online course in the French language. The course consists of nine lessons and some additional vocabulary. In addition to the lessons, you'll find a section describing French expressions and idioms. Also included are pointers to other French language and culture sites.

Focal an Lae: The Word of the Day in Irish

http://www.lincolnu.edu/~focal/

★★★

Focal an Lae, literally *the word of the day* in Gaelic, is a site devoted to the Gaelic language spoken in Ireland. It includes back issues of *Focal an Lae* in case you have missed them, or just want to build your vocabulary. The site also features other valuable Gaelic language resources such as a list of useful phrases and links to other Gaelic information sites.

Foreign Languages for Travelers

http://www.travlang.com/languages/

$

★★★★

A useful site featuring phrases in several languages that can be used by people who are planning trips abroad. Languages covered include Spanish, Portuguese, German, French, and Dutch. Sound clips demonstrating pronunciation can also be found on the site. Markets a line of text-based and voice-recognition translating devices and other translation tools.

Gaelic Languages Info

http://www.ceantar.org/

★★★

Collection of resources and pointers for learners and speakers of Irish Gaelic. Resources include links to Irish Gaelic websites, software, and online dictionaries. Although this site mainly lists information relevant to Irish Gaelic, it also includes some information on other Gaelic languages such as Scottish and Manx.

A
B
C
D
E
F
G
H
I
J
K
L
M
N
O
P
Q
R
S
T
U
V
W
X
Y
Z

A
B
C
D
E
F
G
H
I
J
K
L
M
N
O
P
Q
R
S
T
U
V
W
X
Y
Z

Learn Catalan

http://www.cookwood.com/personal/learncatalan.html

★★★

Catalan is a romance language spoken by millions of people along the eastern coast of Spain in the provinces of Catalunya and Valencia. Here, you will find an introduction to the language and five lessons that teach the fundamentals of Catalan.

Learn Spanish

http://www.studyspanish.com/

★★★★

Learn some basic Spanish vocabulary, grammar, and phrases. Premium pay services are available for the more serious language student. CDs and audio tapes are also available.

A Welsh Course

http://www.cs.brown.edu/fun/welsh/Welsh.html

★★★

A course in the Welsh language. Welsh is a language related to the Gaelic languages of Ireland and Scotland, primarily spoken in Wales. The course is geared toward beginners. The site also provides links to other Welsh resources on the WWW.

LAW

A
B
C
D
E
F
G
H
I
J
K
L
M
N
O
P
Q
R
S
T
U
V
W
X
Y
Z

CRIME AND CRIMINAL LAW

Crime Spider
http://www.crimespider.com/

★★★

This crime and law search engine provides those interested in the criminal justice system with lots of information about various aspects of the law, divided by subject area. So, if you're interested in bank robberies, you can easily search the subcategories under that heading. Or review information on crime-related TV shows and movies. A well-organized site that will make gathering information a snap.

Federal Bureau of Investigation
http://www.fbi.gov/

★★★★

 All

Take a look at the FBI's most wanted list or the monthly list of new criminals at this site, where you can also learn about the agency's activities and where kids can have fun finding out more about crime detection and law enforcement. Up-to-date information on the FBI's mission to combat terrorists as well. A well-organized, comprehensive site. For kids areas, click the For the Family link and then click the desired age group: K–5th Grade or 6–12 Grades.

Best National Crime Prevention Council
http://www.ncpc.org/

★★★★★

Most famous for its McGruff, the crime dog, campaign to prevent crime, the NCPC provides information about its programs and upcoming public service announcements. It has a section just for kids, as well as training tools and program ideas to help keep you and your family safe. Excellent site design combined with relevant information for regular people make this an easy Best of the Best pick.

National Institute of Justice
http://www.ojp.usdoj.gov/nij/

★★★

The NIJ is the research and development arm of the Department of Justice and is responsible for studying crime and developing programs to counter its spread. The site provides visitors with information about the organization's structure and its programs.

CYBER LAW AND CYBERSPACE ISSUES

Allwhois.com
http://www.allwhois.com/

★★★★

Type in a website URL and find out who owns it, who registered it, and where the organization is located. A handy resource for anyone needing to know more about a particular site.

A
B
C
D
E
F
G
H
I
J
K
L
M
N
O
P
Q
R
S
T
U
V
W
X
Y
Z

Copyright Website

http://www.copyrightwebsite.com

★★★★

Learn the basics .of copyright law and how it applies to Web-based media. You can even register here to have your entire website copyright protected, for a fee.

Cyber Law Encyclopedia

http://www.gahtan.com/cyberlaw/

★★★

This site contains more than 1,200 links to cyber law-related topics, arranged by subject. Some include email and spamming, copyright law, news, organizations, privacy, and more.

Cyber-Liberties

http://www.aclu.org/Cyber-Liberties/
Cyber-LibertiesMain.cfm

★★★

An ACLU site that provides the latest news and information on court cases, and it reports on cyber liberties issues. Sign up for the biweekly update online.

Electronic Commerce and Internet Law Resource Center–Perkins Coie, LLP

http://www.perkinscoie.com/

★★★

The case digest at Perkins Coie's website aims to provide background information on international cases that impact cyber law issues. The resource center offers recent articles on Internet law. You can also find out about recent litigation in which the firm represented Internet-related clients.

Kuesterlaw Technology Law Resources

http://www.kuesterlaw.com/

★★★★

This site is a comprehensive resource for "technology law information, especially including patent, copyright, and trademark law." Created and maintained by Jeffrey R. Kuester. Also provides a directory of helpful government resources.

GENERAL RESOURCES

ClassActionAmerica.com

http://www.classactionamerica.com/

★★★★

Learn about ongoing and upcoming class action lawsuits and see if you're eligible to cash in on the billions of dollars a year that go unclaimed.

divorceLAWinfo.com

http://www.divorcelawinfo.com

★★★

If you're contemplating divorce, you may want to read through the FAQs regarding divorce at this site, which is managed by a legal forms company. You can also hear more about how to represent yourself in a divorce, purchase divorce and separation agreement forms online, and learn about other services available from this company to assist you in getting a divorce.

FindLaw.com

http://www.findlaw.com/

★★★

Like Yahoo! for the law, FindLaw gives you access to virtually any information that's law related, some free and some at a fee. Download forms, search databases of past cases, scope out professional development opportunities, and a lot more at this site. Also provides a search tool for finding a lawyer in your area.

FreeAdvice

http://www.freeadvice.com/

★★★★

Explore a wide range of legal topics, research a particular issue, post a message in one of the many Q&A forums, or join a legal chat. Great place for the general public to find information on legal issues.

Internet Legal Resource Guide

http://www.ilrg.com/

★★★

Visitors will find more than 4,000 Web links to sites around the globe related to the law and the legal profession.

Law Books

http://www.claitors.com/

★★★★

Purchase law books as well as legal products and supplies at this site. Claitor's also offers one of the largest inventories of government books and papers available for purchase.

LawGuru.com

http://www.lawguru.com/

★★★★

Have a legal question you'd like the answer to? You'll probably find it at this site in the FAQs section, by searching more than 35,000 legal questions and answers in the bulletin board section (BBS), by searching the more than 500 search engines at the site, or by asking an attorney directly on the BBS system.

Lawyers.com

http://www.lawyers.com/

★★★★★

Excellent site for tracking down lawyers near you who specialize in various aspects of the law, such as disability, divorce, bankruptcy, and so on. Lawyer.com also provides information on how to select and work effectively with a lawyer who's right for you, and how to better understand whatever law issue you are currently facing.

Pritchard Law Webs

http://www.priweb.com/internetlawlib/1.htm

★★★

A legal resource originally established by the U.S. House of Representatives as a means of making the law more accessible to average citizens, the website is now managed by a private company. On it you'll find searchable databases to seek out legal cases of interest, check laws by subject, read laws sorted by state or country, as well as find several other ways to track down law information of interest.

WWW Virtual Library–Law

http://www.law.indiana.edu/v-lib/

★★★

Search the Indiana University virtual law library by typing in a keyword, or start with a pop-up menu of standard topics, such as business law, contracts, or family law. Or search by information type, such as state government or federal government. A straightforward way to start looking for information.

LAW SCHOOLS

Association of American Law Schools

http://www.aals.org/

★★★

 14-18

A nonprofit association of 162 law schools. The purpose of the association is "the improvement of the legal profession through legal education."

Columbia Law School

http://www.law.columbia.edu/

★★★★

14-18

Learn more about the resources, students, and faculty at Columbia through the law school's website. A scrolling Columbia Law news function enables you to click on a story to learn more.

Harvard Law School

http://www.law.harvard.edu/

★★★★★

14-18

Whether you're considering a legal career and want to know more about attending the oldest law school in the country or are interested in finding out about jobs at Harvard Law School, this website can tell you just about anything you need to know. Learn more about the admissions process, career counseling, students, faculty, facilities, programs, and publications.

A B C D E F G H I J K L M N O P Q R S T U V W X Y Z

A
B
C
D
E
F
G
H
I
J
K
L
M
N
O
P
Q
R
S
T
U
V
W
X
Y
Z

Jurist

http://jurist.law.pitt.edu/

★★★

👥 14-18

The University of Pittsburgh School of Law manages this site, which was set up to assist students and teachers of law stay current on legal information and to share ideas on legal events and rulings of the day.

Kaplan Test Prep and Admissions

http://www.kaptest.com/

★★★★

👥 14-18

From Kaplan, everything you need to know about the LSAT and law school—including scoring, sections, and dates and registration—is available. The site also includes links to help you through law school admission and financial aid. Access to law schools and law student resources can also be found on the page.

Law School Admission Council Online

http://www.lsac.org/

★★★

👥 14-18

Features Reggie, the online LSAT registration service. Link to this website and get information on law school forums, LSAT preparation materials, and law school financial aid. The page also includes links to WWW sites at LSAC-member law schools.

Law School Discussion.org

http://www.lawschooldiscussion.org/

★★★

👥 14-18

Law school discussion forums cover topics such as selecting a law school, taking the LSAT, finding law school rankings, and obtaining letters of recommendation. Links to other resources and book reviews.

LawSchool.com

http://www.lawschool.com/

★★★★

👥 14-18

Impressive collection of news reports, articles, and resources relating to law schools. Find law school rankings, tips on preparing for exams, law reviews, bar exam information, and more. Links to additional resources on pre-law and other topics.

Stanford Law School

http://lawschool.stanford.edu/

★★★

👥 14-18

Admissions, administrative, and faculty information are available at Stanford Law School's site, which also provides school news.

University of Chicago Law School

http://www.law.uchicago.edu/

★★★

👥 14-18

A complete guide to applying to and attending the University of Chicago Law School, with information about the process for prospective students, as well as information for current students on upcoming events at the school.

Writing for Law School Admission

http://www.accepted.com/law/

★★★

👥 14-18

Are you looking for tips on good writing? Advice on developing your personal statement? Perhaps you're in a sweat because a person you've asked for a recommendation has requested that you write the letter of recommendation so he or she can simply sign it? This site can get you started.

Related Site
http://www.writingweb.com/index.htm

Yale Law School Home Page

http://www.law.yale.edu/

★★★

👥 14-18

Find everything you wanted to know about this competitive law school at its website, which features admissions information, faculty and student data, a library overview, law school publications, and information about student programs.

LEGAL ORGANIZATIONS

ACLU Freedom Network

http://www.aclu.org/

★★★★★

The home page for the American Civil Liberties Union takes you to the latest happenings from Congress and what's happening in the nation's courts. You can also join the ACLU, browse its cyberstore, and read about current events. Other links take you to highlights of cases in which the ACLU is involved.

American Bar Association

http://www.abanet.org/

$

★★★★

The ABA network connects you to any information you need pertaining to this world's largest voluntary professional association. Links to information about the various entities of the ABA (each entity has its own link), a calendar of events, and public information are just a few starting points on this website that is ranked in the top 5%.

American Corporate Counsel Association

http://www.acca.com/

★★★

At the official site of the American Corporate Counsel Association, members of the organization can network with fellow corporate attorneys, find a local chapter, investigate professional conferences, and access information services.

American Immigration Lawyers Association

http://www.aila.org/

★★★

Links to information about the AILA, membership information, and AILA conferences can be found here. Also, writings about immigration as it pertains to America, the role of immigration lawyers, and recent legislative affairs that affect immigration law. Provided, too, is a searchable index of AILA members and immigration lawyers on the Web.

Association of Trial Lawyers of America

http://www.atlanet.org/

★★★★

Exchange information and ideas with fellow members of the ATLA, look into conferences and professional development opportunities, get up-to-date information on recent decisions, and learn more about the member benefits at this site.

ElderWeb

http://www.elderweb.com/

★★★★

ElderWeb was established to provide guidance and resources to professionals and family members grappling with the issue of long-term care and its legal ramifications. The site has nearly 4,500 links to senior resources with information constantly being added.

National Association of Attorneys General

http://www.naag.org/

★★★

Learn more about the role of the attorney general in your state, and catch up on recent legal decisions and actions taken by the AG's office. Members of the AG's office can use the site to share information and collaborate with other departments.

National District Attorneys Association (NDAA)

http://www.ndaa-apri.org/

★★★

Members of the NDAA can find out about upcoming conferences, publications, and resources available through this national organization.

A
B
C
D
E
F
G
H
I
J
K
L
M
N
O
P
Q
R
S
T
U
V
W
X
Y
Z

A
B
C
D
E
F
G
H
I
J
K
L
M
N
O
P
Q
R
S
T
U
V
W
X
Y
Z

LEGAL PUBLICATIONS

ALSO! Main Page

http://www.lawsource.com/also/

★★★

Provides a comprehensive, uniform, and useful compilation of links to all online sources of American law that are available without charge. Source documents are stored in various file formats in many separately maintained databases located in several countries.

European Journal of International Law

http://www.ejil.org/

★★★

Website of one of the world's leading international law journals. An integral part of the *European Journal of International Law*, this website provides many features unavailable in the printed version of the journal, including a discussion area.

Federal Communications Law Journal

http://www.law.indiana.edu/fclj/

★★★

The official journal of the Federal Communications Bar Association. This site includes links to electronic versions of currently available issues. Access is also available to information about the Federal Communications Bar Association and Indiana University School of Law. The journal is maintained by a student editorial board at Indiana University School of Law.

Hieros Gamos

http://www.hg.org/

★★★★★

Comprehensive resource for legal professionals, law students, and persons seeking law-related information. Links include bar associations, legal associations, law schools, publishers, law firms, law sites, government sites, vendors, and online services. The site is available in English, Spanish, German, French, and Italian. There are more resources than can be listed.

Indiana Journal of Global Legal Studies

http://ijgls.indiana.edu/

★★★

Published by the Indiana University School of Law, this site contains all back issues of the journal, information on how and why it was started, subscription information, and editorial board information. A search engine is available to help you locate the information you need.

Journal of Information, Law, and Technology

http://elj.warwick.ac.uk/jilt/

★★★

This site, home to the e-journal *JILT*, enables you to access past and present issues and link to what is new. You'll also find regular features, special features, and information about the people who put *JILT* together. Also link to information about *JILT*, how it was started, what its purpose is, and why it is maintained the way it is.

Law.com

http://www.law.com/

★★★

Updated daily, this journal highlights current events that affect the legal and political professions. Articles on high-profile cases and suits, courtroom updates, and new rulings are just some of the interesting and resourceful links on this page. Also included is access to national legal journals online, the marketplace, an employment center, and law firms online.

Law.Net

http://law.net/

★★★

A resourceful page that links to a directory of lawyers and law firms categorized by specialization. Also includes information on how to join, a newsletter, access to the library, articles of interest, and more.

Law Library of Congress

http://www.loc.gov/law/public/law.html

★★★★★

Internet home of the world's largest law library, with a collection of more than two million volumes spanning the ages and covering virtually every jurisdiction in the world.

LawMall

http://www.lawmall.com/

★★★

A virtual mall for the legal profession specializing in anti-trust lawsuits, this site is devoted to helping fight unlawful price discrimination, Wal-Mart expansion, globalization, and related issues.

TheLawyer.com

http://www.the-lawyer.co.uk/

★★★★

This U.K.-based legal site offers news on the profession, reports on special sectors, and job openings.

Lawyers Weekly

http://www.lawyersweekly.com/

★★★

Lawyers Weekly USA brings tens of thousands of readers up-to-the-minute news on the cases and developments that directly affect their practice. This site also provides insight from the country's leading experts on how to win more cases, avoid malpractice traps, practice more efficiently, and prosper. Focuses on small law firms.

National Law Journal

http://www.nlj.com/

★★★

Stay current on legal issues through this print and online publication by reading the latest news and searching past issues.

Nolo Press

http://www.nolo.com/

$

★★★★★

Publishing legal information in plain English for more than 30 years, Nolo Press has empowered average citizens to understand and fight for their rights. Here, you'll find Nolo's Legal Encyclopedia, a law FAQ, financial calculators, resources for various types of cases and legal issues, and a wide selection of Nolo Press books, which you can purchase online. Because this site provides legal information for average people in an easily accessible format, it is a hands-down winner as the best legal site on the Web.

United States Code

http://www4.law.cornell.edu/uscode/

★★★

Search the entire U.S. code by title and section at this site. This version is generated from the most recent version made available by the U.S. House of Representatives.

Web Journal of Current Legal Issues

http://webjcli.ncl.ac.uk/

★★★

This site connects you to past and present issues of the *Web Journal of Current Legal Issues*, covering current legal issues. The site also includes other legal links, a welcome message, and information on becoming an author for the *Journal of Current Legal Issues*.

A B C D E F G H I J K L M N O P Q R S T U V W X Y Z

LITERATURE

American and English Literature Resources

http://library.scsu.ctstateu.edu/litbib.html

★★★★★

This extensive bibliography of resources pertaining to American and English literature attempts to zero in on the best resources available on the Web, including where you can find electronic versions of classic texts and the home pages of various authors. Sites are organized first by American literature and then by English literature. These main categories are further subdivided by genre.

ÉCLAT

http://ccat.sas.upenn.edu/Complit/Eclat/

★★★★★

ÉCLAT (Essential Comparative Literature And Theory) is a directory of comparative literature sites, programs, and resources on the Web.

Literary Criticism

http://www.ipl.org/div/litcrit/

★★★★★

This is the Internet Public Library's directory of literary criticism, which points the way to critical and biographical websites about authors and their works that you can browse by author, by title, or by nationality and literary period. Great site for researching the existing criticism about a specific literary work.

Literary Resources on the Net

http://andromeda.rutgers.edu/~jlynch/Lit/

★★★★

This directory of literary resources maintained by Jack Lynch of Rutgers University features links related to various literary periods and nationalities, including Classical, Biblical, Medieval, Renaissance, Romantic, Victorian British, American, and Women's Literature and Feminism. Also includes links to literary theory.

AUTHORS

Alcott, Louisa May

http://www.empirezine.com/spotlight/alcott/alcott.htm

★★★

Explains why a moon crater was named after the author of *Little Women* and what her life was like in a commune. This site provides links to photos and other Alcott sites.

American Authors on the Web

http://www.lang.nagoya-u.ac.jp/~matsuoka/AmeLit.html

★★★

Search the lengthy list of American authors alphabetically to learn more about the individuals and their work. Some authors feature ongoing discussion groups that you can join.

Andrews, V.C.: The Garden in the Sky

http://www.simonsays.com/subs/txtobj.cfm?areaid=11&pagename=bio

★★★

 14-18

As close as you'll get to an Official V.C. Andrews website, this site, maintained by Simon & Schuster, provides a visual biography of Cleo Virginia Andrews thanks to V.C.'s younger brother, Gene, who furnished many of the memories and mementos of V.C. Andrew's younger years. Also provides a complete book list.

Asimov, Isaac

http://www.asimovonline.com/

★★★★

👥 14-18

Isaac Asimov's many books and stories continue to entertain and challenge the minds of science fiction fans. Here you can find a well-stocked directory of links to Asimov's books and short stories, a lists of his works, bookstores where you can purchase his books, FAQs, and other online resources.

Related Sites
http://www.asimovs.com/
http://www.asimov.org

Atwood, Margaret

http://www.owtoad.com/

★★★★

Official Margaret Atwood site provides biographical information, a list of books by and about Margaret Atwood, essays on writing, a schedule of lectures and readings, and a frequently asked questions list.

Austen, Jane

http://www.pemberley.com/janeinfo/janeinfo.html

★★★

You'll find access to many Austen e-texts at this site, as well as discussions of longer works, and biographical information of interest to Jane Austen fans. It is a large and rich site, although it looks pretty basic.

Authentic Author Signatures

http://home.earthlink.net/~criswell/authors/agraphs.htm

★★★

Click on the name of an author and an image of the person's signature will appear. Use it to authenticate true signatures or just to know a bit more about an important literary figure. Brought to you by My Book House.

Bear, Greg

http://www.gregbear.com

★★★

👥 14-18

Biography, bibliography, and some original work by Bear himself, exclusive to the Web ("for the time being"). Also contains bitmaps of some of Bear's paintings.

Bibliomania

http://bibliomania.net/

★★★★

This ultimate source of information for book buyers, sellers, and collectors is "intended to inform and educate book enthusiasts so that they can make wise decisions in their internet transactions."

BookNotes

http://www.booknotes.org/home/index.asp

★★★

"A companion Web site to C-SPAN's Sunday author interview series, BookNotes." Find out which author will be appearing on this week's show, watch a video clip of the interview, and scan the online resource section to read first chapters of featured books or to look at transcripts of past interviews.

BookWire Index–Author Indexes

http://www.bookwire.com/

★★★

An index of author and literature sites that can be searched and accessed via BookWire. A huge resource of useful sites.

Borges, Jorge Luis

http://www.themodernword.com/borges/

★★★

Everyone's favorite literary metaphysical thinker gets the Labyrinthian treatment at *The Garden of the Forking Path*.

A B C D E F G H I J K L M N O P Q R S T U V W X Y Z

A
B
C
D
E
F
G
H
I
J
K
L
M
N
O
P
Q
R
S
T
U
V
W
X
Y
Z

Brautigan, Richard

http://www.riza.com/richard/

★★★★

One of the few sites dedicated to this truly American surrealist, this page has a library and a "Trader's Corner." Configured for Netscape-compatible browsers. This site links to Amazon.com so you can order Brautigan titles.

The Brontë Sisters

http://www2.sbbs.se/hp/cfalk/bronteng.htm

★★★

This site provides several links to Brontë-related works, as well as biographical data about Anne, Charlotte, and Emily.

Burroughs, William S.

http://www.hyperreal.org/wsb/

★★★★

Whenever someone begins to study William S. Burroughs, there are usually words of warning or at least a caveat lector. This site keeps with that tradition but gives great insight into the life of the writer of books such as *Naked Lunch* and *Junky*. This site offers a Web memorial to Burroughs.

Candlelight Stories

http://www.candlelightstories.com/

★★★★

 0-8

This award-winning site is a repository for children's online literature. From *Rumpelstiltskin* to *Thumbelina*, you can read your children these online classics. Included is a bookstore, international gallery, and spelling machine game. Story and illustration submissions are welcome. This site links to Amazon.com, where you can purchase books.

Carver, Raymond

http://world.std.com/~ptc/

★★★

This site has biographical information and essays about Raymond Carver. His stories have become very popular recently, perhaps because of Robert Altman's film *Short Cuts*; however, Carver died of cancer in 1988.

Cather, Willa

http://www.gustavus.edu/oncampus/academics/english/cather/

★★★

A well-formatted site available from the Harvard Web server, this page has information about Cather, her work, and scholarly conferences in her honor. Her very astute picture of America in the early twentieth century should be impetus enough for a reader to look at the information included at this site.

A Celebration of Women Writers

http://digital.library.upenn.edu/women/

★★★

In an effort to educate the public about the variety and breadth of women writers' contributions to literature, this site offers links and information about some of the most notable women writers.

Cervantes, Miguel de

http://www.csdl.tamu.edu/cervantes/english/

★★★

A project of the Cervantes International Bibliography Online and the Anuario Bibliográfico Cervantino, this site is dedicated to solve the "problem of currency, thoroughness, and accessibility which now hampers research on Cervantes." This site includes a record of the books, articles, dissertations, reviews, and other points of interest here to this end.

Christie, Agatha

http://www.nd.edu/~rwoodbur/christie/christie.htm

★★★★★

 All

Provides a chronological listing of most of Christie's works, grouped optionally by featured detective. This site also offers a collection of plays and short stories. The maintainer of the page promises that all the books and plays listed will eventually have complete descriptions (including whodunit, for the impatient!).

⌐Best⌐ Clancy, Tom

http://www.penguinputnam.com/static/packages/us/tomclancy/

★★★★★

👥 14-18

This official Tom Clancy site includes a brief biography of the author, a list of his fiction and nonfiction works, a description of his latest book, and links to book reviews and fan sites.

Classic Short Stories

http://mbhs.bergtraum.k12.ny.us/cybereng/shorts/

★★★

👥 All

This site, devoted to lovers of short stories and short prose, includes an impressive selection of short stories from Edgar Allan Poe, Virginia Woolf, and more. You can search by story name as well as by author.

Crichton, Michael

http://www.globalnets.com/crichton/crichton.html

★★★

The writer of such novels as *Jurassic Park, The Eaters of the Dead,* and *Congo,* as well as all-around American media entrepreneur, Michael Crichton finds a welcome home at this page. You'll find many good links to information about his life, books, and other entertainment efforts.

Dickens, Charles

http://lang.nagoya-u.ac.jp/~matsuoka/Dickens.html

★★★★

The home page includes a painting of Charles Dickens by William Powell Frith (1859). This site is absolutely exhaustive in resources about Dickens, author of such fabulous books as *The Pickwick Papers* and *Great Expectations.* The site's dynamic quality is that it is constantly being updated to include new information about Dickens. You can link to archives dating back to April 1997, and all the historical information is very up to date and useful.

Dostoevsky Research Station

http://www.kiosek.com/dostoevsky/contents.html

★★★★

Great site, brought to you by Christiaan Stange, about the stellar Russian author of *Crime and Punishment* and *The Brothers Karamazov.* Covers the life of Dostoevsky and provides a bibliography of his works, quotations about him, online versions of the text, an image gallery, and more.

The Electronic Text Center at the University of Virginia

http://etext.lib.virginia.edu/

★★★★

This excellent and thorough site contains thousands of texts, in modern, early modern, and middle English, plus French, German, Japanese, and Latin. Here, you'll find fiction, science fiction, poetry, theology, essays, histories, and many other types of materials. Although a huge number of these texts are freely available, some texts are available only to users at the University of Virginia; the licensors of these texts have not permitted the university to make them widely available.

Faulkner, William

http://www.mcsr.olemiss.edu/~egjbp/faulkner/faulkner.html

★★★★

The site to visit for any sort of information about William Faulkner. John B. Padgett, currently a graduate student at the University of Mississippi (located at Oxford, whence Faulkner hailed), maintains this comprehensive site. You can find information on his letters, novels, poetry, speeches, interviews, screenplays, and essays. You can also find commentaries and complete synopses on his writings.

Fitzgerald, F. Scott

http://www.sc.edu/fitzgerald/

★★★★

Based at the University of South Carolina, this site, dedicated to F. Scott Fitzgerald, was created in celebration of the centennial of his birth. The mission statement of this page states that "this site celebrates his writings, his life, and his relationships with other writers of the 20th century." True to this, you'll find a biography, writings, and beautiful photos of the famous author from the Roaring '20s.

A B C D E F G H I J K L M N O P Q R S T U V W X Y Z

A
B
C
D
E
F
G
H
I
J
K
L
M
N
O
P
Q
R
S
T
U
V
W
X
Y
Z

Fleming, Ian: Mr. KissKissBangBang Web Page

http://www.ianfleming.org/index.shtml

★★★★

 14-18

The premier site of James Bond and Ian Fleming, his creator. Here, you'll find current articles and analysis of 007 themes, news clips, upcoming events, and new items to hit the market. Sign up for the newsletter to keep abreast of the most current information.

Hardy, Thomas

http://pages.ripco.net/~mws/hardy.html

★★★

This large site about the author includes what you might expect—biography, e-texts, and pictures—as well as some very entertaining sound bites of excerpts from works by Hardy and Monty Python's take on him. A nice selection of links is available, too.

Hawthorne, Nathaniel

http://www.underthesun.cc/Classics/Hawthorne/

★★★

Dedicated to presenting information about the life and works of Nathaniel Hawthorne, this site has complete texts of his most famous novels and stories. You'll find readings, pictures, and information about this nineteenth-century American author.

Hemingway, Ernest Foundation of Oak Park

http://www.hemingway.org/

★★★

Learn more about the life of Ernest Hemingway and find out how his work affected the community of Oak Park by touring his restored birthplace. You can also learn about and discuss his most important works.

HyperLiterature/HyperTheory

http://ebbs.english.vt.edu/hthl/HyperLit_Home.html

★★★

HyperLiterature/HyperTheory has an annotated bibliography, some readings, and some works by students who are studying this exciting new field.

Internet Classics Archive

http://classics.mit.edu/

★★★

A nice archive of 441 classic works, mostly ancient Greek and Roman, with several Persian works thrown in for fun.

Joyce, James

http://www.2street.com/joyce/

★★★★

There are many joys to this site: pictures of the author, his family, and those people mentioned in his work; important songs and readings by Joyce himself; links to articles and Internet groups who study Joyce; and maps of the places mentioned in his work.

Kafka, Franz

http://www.pitt.edu/~kafka/intro.html

★★★

Provides a bibliography (both of Kafka and critical works), biography, pictures, and more about the author of works such as *The Castle*, *The Trial*, *Metamorphosis*, and *Amerika*. Includes a listing of Kafka's library and links to other related sites.

Kerouac, Jack

http://www.cmgww.com/historic/kerouac/

★★★★

The official website of Jack Kerouac provides a biography, a bibliography, excerpts, and pictures of this beat author. Kerouac is known as the person who coined the term *beatnik*. His prose and style are still popular among the Bohemian culture today. Links to Amazon.com to purchase specific titles.

King, Stephen

http://www.stephenking.com/

★★★★★

Stephen King's official site features the latest media reports surrounding King and his novels, his biography, his past, current, and future works, a photo gallery, a newsletter, and even a discussion group you can join in to share your interest with other fans.

Koontz, Dean

http://dkoontz.freshlinks.net/fanclub/index.htm

★★★★

This site is written and maintained by a Koontz fan club, so you know the members are really charged with the excitement of his writing. This is not just a static Web experience (although you'll find some great links to other Koontz sites and online information). From this site you can chat with Koontz fans, join a club, send a Koontz postcard, join a discussion group, or play a trivia contest.

L'Amour, Louis

http://www.veinotte.com/lamour/

★★★★

This site is designed to be as simple and free-flowing as Louis L'Amour's elegant prose. Here, you can find an introduction to the man and his works, along with a biography of his life, a long list of movie adaptations, and a forum where you can discuss his works with other fans. Check out the Book of the Month for suggested reading.

Lewis, C.S. (Into the Wardrobe)

http://cslewis.Drzeus.net/

★★★

 All

Into the Wardrobe has many tidbits and large chunks of useful information for the scholar, reader, and fan of C.S. Lewis. One of the best parts of this site is its attitude toward studying Lewis and his work—it even includes a Useful Contacts page.

Literati.net

http://literati.net/

★★★

A great place to seek out information on well-known and lesser-known authors, including their bios, lists of books published, and upcoming appearance schedules.

Little Women

http://xroads.virginia.edu/~HYPER/ALCOTT/lwtext.html

★★★

The complete text of this classic book, written by Louisa May Alcott, linkable by chapter.

The Martian Chronicles Study Guide

http://www.wsu.edu:8080/~brians/science_fiction/martian_chronicles.html

★★★

Maintained by Washington State University, this useful page provides help for those wanting to study and critique Ray Bradbury's writing style.

Melville, Herman

http://www.melville.org/

★★★

Melville is very important to the American tradition. Look here, and you'll find comprehensive information about the author of one of the greatest American novels.

Michener, James

http://www.achievement.org/autodoc/page/mic0int-1

★★★

The Academy of Achievement has put together this tribute to James Michener, consisting of his profile, biography, and an illustrated interview.

Michigan Electronic Library

http://mel.lib.mi.us/

★★★

A project sponsored in part by Michigan's libraries, this site includes collections of online excerpts, stories, and reports in categories such as education, humanities and the arts, and science and the environment. It also includes a reference desk, as well as a periodicals section.

Morrison, Toni

http://www.luminarium.org/contemporary/tonimorrison/toni.htm

★★★★

Anniina Jokinen's site provides a biography, bibliography, and interviews with 1993 Nobel Prize–winning author Toni Morrison. It includes articles about Morrison's books, such as *Tar Baby*, *Song of Solomon*, *Sula*, *Beloved*, and many more. Links to Amazon.com to purchase these great books.

Related Site
http://www.gsu.edu/~wwwtms/

A
B
C
D
E
F
G
H
I
J
K
L
M
N
O
P
Q
R
S
T
U
V
W
X
Y
Z

The Mystery Books

http://www.bookspot.com/mystery.htm

★★★

Bookspot's mystery books features links to a mystery guide, a bloodstained bookshelf, The Thrilling Detective, and other mystery literature sites you might find interesting.

Related Site
http://www.cluelass.com/

Nabokov, Vladimir (Zembla)

http://www.libraries.psu.edu/nabokov/

★★★★

A formidable presence on the World Wide Web in terms of layout, content, and conciseness, Zembla offers a great amount of information concerning Vladmir Nabokov, the author of novels such as *Lolita* and *Bend Sinister*.

Native American Authors

http://www.ipl.org/ref/native/

★★★

 All

For information about contemporary Native American authors, this is your site. Here, you'll find bibliographies of published works, biographical information, and links to online resources including interviews, online texts, and tribal websites. This site also features special areas for kids and teenagers.

Nobel Laureates

http://www.nobel.se/literature/laureates/

★★★★★

Complete list of winners of the Nobel Prize in Literature from 1901 to the present. Click an author's name to access the author's biography, bibliography, acceptance speech, and other resources.

Oates, Joyce Carol (Celestial Timepiece)

http://www.usfca.edu/fac-staff/southerr/jco.html

★★★★

Celestial Timepiece gives a full view of author Joyce Carol Oates. You can find a great amount of information on Oates, who is the author of many novels, including *You Must Remember This* and *The Triumph of the Spider*. This site features a well-laid-out table of contents that covers her life and gives access to resources for research on Oates and her writing.

Orwell, George

http://www.levity.com/corduroy/orwell.htm

★★★

Had Orwell known that someday Big Brother might be watching him in the form of his picture and life story being on the Web for the world to see...well, he might have been pleased. This site provides a biography of Orwell's life and has a few links to related sites.

Parker, Dorothy

http://www.levity.com/corduroy/parker.htm

★★★★

This site features a photo of Dorothy Parker, a couple of her more caustic quotes, a brief biography, and links to other related Parker sites. A good place to start, but you need to read Parker's works to really appreciate her wit.

Project Gutenburg

http://www.gutenberg.org/

★★★★

This award-winning site contains a collection of electronically stored books, mostly classics, that can be downloaded free and viewed offline. Gopher searches for your favorite author reveal various options for downloading.

Pulitzer Prizes

http://www.pulitzer.org/

★★★★

Search the archive to find names of Pulitzer Prize winners since the awards' inception, read about the history of the awards, and download entry forms for consideration this year.

Rand, Ayn

http://www.aynrand.org/

★★★★

Dedicated to Rand's novels and philosophy, this site contains many links to biographies, bibliographies, mission statements, and objectivism. The philosophy of reason and self-interest lives here.

Rice, Anne

http://www.annerice.com/

★★★★

The official site of the horror writer from New Orleans. Anne Rice's books have become very popular in the past few years, and this site is testimony to that. You'll find pictures, biographies, bibliographies, sounds, and even information about the home she owned and restored in New Orleans that inspired many of her best books.

The Romance Reader

http://www.theromancereader.com/

★★★★

Before you buy that next romance novel, scan the thousands of reviews available at this site, which is dedicated to romance novel fans worldwide. While you're at the site, you can read biographical information, learn more about other members' interests and feedback, and share your thoughts on the quality of recent romance titles you've read.

Rowling, J.K.

http://www.scholastic.com/harrypotter/home.asp

★★★★

 All

This official Harry Potter home page provides information about the various books in the series; information about the author, J.K. Rowling; a discussion chamber; a portrait gallery; free screensavers; and more.

de Saint-Exupéry, Antoine

http://www.westegg.com/exupery/

★★★

Perhaps known mostly for his book *The Little Prince*, Antoine de Saint-Exupéry was also a pilot and an author of novels that appeal more to an adult audience. At this site you'll find links to quotes, a bibliography, and e-texts available in several languages.

Salinger, J.D.

http://www.salinger.org/

★★★

Provides information about J.D. Salinger, the author of *The Catcher in the Rye, Franny and Zooey,* and other novels and short stories. The site includes articles, essays, and more about Salinger's writing.

Shelley, Mary

http://www.kimwoodbridge.com/maryshel/maryshel.shtml

★★★

This site houses information about Mary Shelley, Percy Bysshe Shelley, the Romantics, and, of course, Mary Shelley's popular novel *Frankenstein.* Newly updated, this site has a gothic air, including a musical background.

Tan, Amy

http://www.luminarium.org/contemporary/amytan/

★★★

This site, created by Anniina Jokinen, gives excerpts, sound bites, interviews, links, and pictures of this influential contemporary American author. Amy Tan's work has been widely translated and deserves recognition for the greatness that it has attained.

Twain, Mark

http://www.boondocksnet.com/twainwww/

★★★

Comprehensive Mark Twain library that not only provides information about his books and his life, but also features letters, essays, manuscripts, quotes, and links to Mark Twain associations.

A
B
C
D
E
F
G
H
I
J
K
L
M
N
O
P
Q
R
S
T
U
V
W
X
Y
Z

Twain, Mark: Huckleberry Finn

http://etext.lib.virginia.edu/twain/huckfinn.html

★★★

👥 All

Browse the complete text, chapter by chapter if you like, and look at the first edition illustrations. Also included are early reviews and "the obscene sales prospectus illustration."

Updike, John: The Centaurian

http://userpages.prexar.com/joyerkes/

★★★

Provides information and a discussion area for the works of American author John Updike. Some of his best-known works include *Witches of Eastwick, A Month of Sundays,* and *Rabbit, Run.* This site also contains a bibliography (of criticism and of Updike's works), a biography, essays, articles, and pictures.

Verne, Jules

http://www.online-literature.com/verne/

★★★

This site opens with a brief biography of Jules Verne, but its real value is hidden behind the links it displays to a collection of Jules Verne's works. Here, you can obtain electronic texts of *20,000 Leagues Under the Sea, Journey to the Center of the Earth,* and other Jules Verne classics.

Victorian Women Writers

http://www.indiana.edu/~letrs/vwwp/

★★★

From Indiana University, this great site features scads of nineteenth-century texts. The works, selected with the assistance of the university Advisory Board, include anthologies, novels, political pamphlets, religious tracts, children's books, and volumes of poetry and verse drama.

Walker, Alice

http://www.luminarium.org/contemporary/alicew/

★★★

Essays, articles, criticism, poetry, short stories, excerpts—you name it, you'll find it here. This site includes a wealth of information about Alice Walker, the author of *The Color Purple* and many other titles. The site is created and maintained by Anniina Jokinen.

Wilde, Oscar

http://www.oscariana.net/index.html

★★★★

A textual and visual tour of Oscar Wilde's biography. During this tour, you will read about his life, see photographs, and view letters and telegrams to and from Wilde. When you get to the end, select About This Project to see other Wilde links on the Web.

The Wonderful Wizard of Oz

http://www.literature.org/authors/baum-l-frank/the-wonderful-wizard-of-oz/

★★★★

👥 All

Part of the Knowledge Matters Ltd., literacy series, this site offers the complete text of *The Wonderful Wizard of Oz,* linkable by chapter. Also offered are other titles by L. Frank Baum in the Wizard of Oz series.

MAGIC

Abbott's Magic Company

http://www.abbottmagic.com/

★★★

 All

Percy Abbott and magician friend Harry Blackstone formed Abbott's Magic Company nearly 100 years ago. Abbott's Magic Company is still the world's largest producer of handmade illusions. This site also features secrets to dozens of cool illusions.

Abracadabra Magic

http://www.abra4magic.com/

★★★

 All

An online magic store that allows you to search for tricks by type or age group, and then backs them up with technical support from fellow magicians.

All Magic Guide

http://allmagicguide.com/

★★★

 14-18

Learn new magic tricks, find out about upcoming TV and radio programs on magic, shop for magic tricks, and get firsthand advice on performing magic from fellow magicians.

Charlie's Electronic Magic Store

http://www.magicstore.net/

★★★

Subscribe to a free email magic newsletter and search past issues at the site, where you can read helpful product reviews before investing in magic tricks. You can also buy these tricks here.

Daytona Magic

http://www.daytonamagic.com/

★★★

Daytona Magic is a place for anyone who loves magic. You'll find thousands of magic tricks, clown supplies, jokes, gags, and makeup.

Discount Magic

http://www.discountmagic.com/

★★★

Search the site for magic tricks and pranks for sale and then purchase them at a discount.

Earth's Largest Magic Shop

http://www.elmagicshop.com/

★★★★

You'll find lots of stuff for everyone, from the beginner to the professional. Check out the Beginner's section and the Free Trick area.

A
B
C
D
E
F
G
H
I
J
K
L
M
N
O
P
Q
R
S
T
U
V
W
X
Y
Z

HappyMagic.com

http://www.happymagic.com/

★★★★

The folks at HappyMagic have done the sifting for you; you don't have to worry about getting a trick that you will just throw in a drawer and never use again.

International Conservatory of Magic

http://www.magicschool.com/

★★★★

This site contains more than 2,000 pages of magic. I.C.O.M Online provides comprehensive, first-class instruction in the art of being a magician, offering personal live instruction via lecture tours, 24-hour-a-day website–based text and virtual lessons, Internet chat, and live Web audio lectures. All aspects of magic are covered, including sleight of hand, illusion, presentation, showmanship, promotion, and theory.

MAGIC

http://www.magicmagazine.com/

★★★

The largest-selling magic journal in the world. Get a taste of the magazine here. If you like what you see, you can subscribe easily.

Magic Auction

http://www.magicauction.com/

★★★

Search this weekly auction site for used magic tricks and illusions, or make yours available for sale.

Magictricks.com

http://www.magictricks.com/

★★★★

Online magic store with many sources of magic history, museums, facts, and places to visit.

The Society of American Magicians

http://www.magicsam.com/

★★★

Magicians in the know are members of this organization. Find out about SAM, including its history, members, current news, and membership info/benefits.

Trickshop Magic Shop

http://www.trickshop.com/

★★★

Online source for today's hottest magic tricks, books, videos, and audiotapes, for street, close-up and stand-up performances.

TV Magic Guide.com

http://www.tvmagicguide.com/

★★★

 All

Here, you can check the TV listings for the upcoming week to learn about scheduled magic programs and interviews with magicians. Some free video clips are available to advertise videos that are for sale.

[Best] World of Magic

http://www.worldofmagic.net/magictricks.htm

★★★★★

 All

Magic tricks for kids and so much more: clown supplies, Halloween costumes, gags, pranks, makeup, gifts, toys, juggling equipment, masks, hats, deluxe children's costumes, wigs, special-effect lighting, and FunPaks for kids and adults. This is definitely one-stop shopping for your magic needs!

MARKETING

Ad-Guide

http://www.ad-guide.com/

★★★★

Internet advertising, marketing, and electronic commerce are all included in this site. Lots of comprehensive marketing information available here.

BusinessatHome

http://www.gohome.com/

★★★

Features interviews with home-based entrepreneurs and advice on running a home office. This site covers laws, taxes, financing, technology, marketing, and other business concerns.

ClickZ Network

http://www.clickz.com/

★★★★★

Download a free guide to email marketing at this site, where you can also participate in online forums regarding a host of marketing issues, such as pricing on the Net. You can also read articles and columns written by marketing gurus.

CommerceNet

http://www.commerce.net/

★★★★

Provides its users with a list of more than 20,000 commercial Web URLs, an 800-number directory, and a list of Internet consultants. Daily news updates keep users informed of events on the Internet.

DMPlaza

http://www.dmplaza.com/

★★★

Organizes and indexes Web information relating to the direct marketing industry.

Direct Marketing Association

http://www.the-dma.org/

★★★★★

The Direct Marketing Association (The DMA) is the largest trade association for businesses that are interested and involved in direct, database, and interactive global marketing. Here, you can learn more about the DMA, become a member, and access its services.

ESOMAR

http://www.esomar.org/

★★★

ESOMAR is an international organization of marketing and opinion research and professions. ESOMAR is devoted to promoting the use of opinion and market research to improve decision making in both business and society at large.

EventWeb

http://www.eventweb.com/

★★★

Interactive marketing guidance to meeting conference and trade show promoters.

The GreenBook

http://www.greenbook.org/

$

★★★★

Looking for a marketing research firm? Then the *GreenBook* should be your first stop. It is the annual directory of marketing research firms that can be ordered in print form here or searched free online.

A
B
C
D
E
F
G
H
I
J
K
L
M
N
O
P
Q
R
S
T
U
V
W
X
Y
Z

Guerrilla Marketing

http://www.gmarketing.com/

★★★★

Read daily or bimonthly material from Jay Conrad Levinson, Mr. Guerrilla Marketing, as well as search the site's archives for useful guerrilla marketing strategies detailed by other marketing pros. You'll find plenty of information here, as well as details on Jay's latest book.

Iconocast

http://www.iconocast.com/

★★★★

Weekly newsletter that tracks trends in marketing and advertising. Links to archives and other resources.

JimWorld

http://www.virtualpromote.com/

★★★★

JimWorld provides advice and strategies for promoting commercial websites. It includes tutorials on site promotion, articles on the effectiveness of banner advertising, and more. More than two million site reviews, plus links to GazetteWorld, NewsKlatsch, PrivacyWorld, TipWorld, and more.

Journal of Business & Industrial Marketing

http://www.emeraldinsight.com/jbim.htm

★★★

Explores how leading-edge theory can be applied to solve real-world problems in business and industrial marketing.

Journal of Consumer Marketing

http://www.emeraldinsight.com/jcm.htm

★★★

Examines issues and trends at the leading edge of consumer marketing and franchising.

JustSell.com

http://www.justsell.com/

★★★

Articles, tips, tools, and discussions focused on sales and marketing.

KnowThis.com

http://www.knowthis.com/

★★★★★

A reference site consisting of thousands of sites having to do with marketing, advertising, and promotion. Get a basic course in marketing or delve deep to find out what an effective website looks like. Whether you're a marketing student or professional, you'll find plenty of excellent, up-to-date information at this site, our Best of the Best selection in the Marketing category.

LitLamp

http://www.litlamp.com/

★★★★

Learn how to promote your business by sponsoring an organization. LitLamp is a community of more than 30,000 sponsors and agencies that offer advertising in exchange for sponsorships.

Marketing

http://www.marketingclick.com/

★★★

Marketing professionals can access the latest industry news, feature articles, and other information about Internet marketing, direct marketing, public relations, promotions, and advertising at this site, which provides a research library, discussion forums, and buyers' guides.

Marketing Online

http://www.marketing.haynet.com/

★★★

This is an e-zine produced by *Marketing Magazine*. The site includes news from the marketing industry, career planning, and links to other marketing and sales information on the Internet.

MarketingPower.com

http://www.marketingpower.com/

★★★

This is the home of the American Marketing Association's MarketingPower.com. It offers an overview of the projects and resources available to marketing professionals. Conference information and member-to-member job classified ads are also available.

Marketing Resource Center

http://www.marketingsource.com/

★★★

Features a searchable database of business associations, statistics, articles, and other resources for traditional and Internet marketing.

MRA: Marketing Research Association

http://www.mra-net.org/

★★★★

Dedicated to "advancing the practical application, use, and understanding of the opinion and marketing research profession," MRA features research tools, publications about marketing and opinion polls, software tools, and more. Distance-learning programs, video training, and a career guide are also available.

National Mail Order Association

http://www.nmoa.org/

★★★

Formed in 1972 to help small to midsize businesses and entrepreneurs that are involved or want to become involved in the area of mail-order marketing.

Professional Marketing Resource Services

http://www.pmrs-aprm.com/

★★★★

Home of PMRS, a nonprofit marketing organization for research professionals. Provides assistance in marketing, advertising, and social and political research. Founded in 1960, PMRS now serves more than 1,800 members across Canada from chapters in Halifax, Montreal, Ottawa, Toronto, Manitoba, Alberta, and Vancouver.

Reveries.com

http://www.reveries.com/

★★★★

Available only online, this marketing magazine groups its content into one of the following categories: Discussions, White Papers, Experts, Surveys, Essays, and Archives. You'll find case studies, marketing ideas, celebrity profiles, and more.

Sales and Marketing Executives International

http://www.smei.org/

★★★★

The world's largest association of sales and marketing managers. More than 200,000 searchable articles covering all areas of sales and marketing.

Sales and Marketing Magazine

http://www.salesandmarketing.com/smmnew/

★★★

Sign up for a free weekly email marketing tip from this industry magazine, which offers online articles and news at its online site. You can also get information on and subscribe to the print version here.

Target Marketing Online.com

http://www2.targetonline.com/

★★★

Target Marketing will email you a free weekly tip regarding direct marketing just for subscribing online at its site, which offers visitors a buyers' guide, resource directory, and direct marketing industry news.

Technology Marketing

http://www.technologymarketing.com/

★★★

Focuses on the marketing, branding, and advertising of technology and new media.

Web Marketing Tips, Tricks, Techniques and Tools

http://www.smart-web-promotion.com/

★★★

Provides hundreds of tips and information on promoting products on the Internet.

A
B
C
D
E
F
G
H
I
J
K
L
M
N
O
P
Q
R
S
T
U
V
W
X
Y
Z

A
B
C
D
E
F
G
H
I
J
K
L
M
N
O
P
Q
R
S
T
U
V
W
X
Y
Z

MARTIAL ARTS

GENERAL RESOURCES

American Center for Chinese Studies

http://www.kungfu.org/

★★★

This Web page is dedicated to those who want to pursue a better way of life through the cultivation of the mind, body, and spirit.

Century Fitness

http://www.centuryfitness.com/

★★★★

Mega-store for exercise and fitness products, this site features a martial arts section, where you can shop for everything from uniforms and sparring gear to weapons and nutritional supplements.

Doshin Martial Arts Supplies

http://www.doshinmartialarts.com/

★★★

Order martial arts supplies and read publications on various forms of martial arts at this site, which also offers an events and tournaments calendar.

Journal of Asian Martial Arts & Books

http://www.goviamedia.com/

★★★

This site offers information on a variety of Asian martial arts, including karate, tae kwon do, judo, aikido, taiji, shaolin, and other forms of self-defense. Also offers current books and videos on various martial arts theories and practices.

Martial Arm Martial Arts Centre

http://www.martialarm.com/martial-directory.html

★★★

Martialarm is a training device to help students develop entry and trapping skills. The device mounts on a wall and simulates an extended arm, as if an opponent is throwing a punch. This site features a huge collection of links organized by martial arts movies, directories (of resources), martial arts styles, martial arts supplies, and military supplies.

Martial Arts Books and Videos

http://www.turtlepress.com/

★★★

Dozens of free martial arts video clips, book excerpts, and articles, plus martial arts books and videos for sale.

Martial Arts Equipment

http://www.martialartsequip.com/

★★★

Good site to visit for martial arts clothing, books, and videos. You can also find an impressive assortment of sparring gear, training equipment, and weapons. Join the mailing list to get the latest martial arts news as well as special sales information.

Martial Arts Resource Page

http://www.martialartsresource.com/index.html

★★★

This site features information about Korean and Filipino martial arts. Be sure to sign up for email digests for either or both disciplines.

MartialArtsMart.com
http://store.yahoo.com/martialartsmart/

 $

★★★★

More than 3,000 pieces of martial arts equipment, accessories, and supplies are available here. Choose from Chinese, Japanese, Filipino, Korean, and Thai martial arts.

 MartialInfo.com
http://www.martialinfo.com/

 $

★★★★★

This huge information kiosk for everything related to martial arts, features articles, biographies, descriptions of the various styles, photo galleries, videos, and much more. Search for instructors, shop for equipment and clothing, read product reviews, and much more. If you're interested in martial arts, be sure to bookmark this site for quick return visits.

Qi: The Journal of Traditional Eastern Health and Fitness
http://www.qi-journal.com/

★★★★★

Features in-depth information on Chinese culture, traditional medicine, and research; links; a calendar of events; *Qi Journal* articles; and a very complete catalog of items related to the internal martial arts, Chinese culture, and the traditional healing arts.

Real Combat Online
http://www.kungfuonline.com/

★★★

 Not for kids

This site is for hardcore, brutal, hand-to-hand combat.

SouthEast Asian Martial Arts Reference Site
http://www.seama.com/

★★★

For those interested in the martial arts of Southeast Asia, such as silat, kali, escrima, arnis, and muay thai.

TigerStrike.com
http://www.tigerstrike.com/

 $

★★★★

Whether you need uniforms, sparring gear, weapons, or other martial arts equipment or apparel, this site claims that it can provide your order faster and cheaper than anyone else can.

JUDO

American Judo and Jujitsu Federation
http://www.ajjf.org/

★★★

AJJF news and general information, with links to regional activities and dojo listings.

British Judo Association
http://www.britishjudo.org.uk/

 $

★★★

At this home of the British Judo Association, you can learn more about the organization, read articles on the origin of judo and how to begin your study of judo, and sign up to become a member.

International Judo Federation
http://www.ijf.org/

★★★

This site has background information on the federation, as well as judo regulations, history, national bodies, and tournament results.

Judo Information Site
http://judoinfo.com/

★★★

This site offers links to national and international judo clubs, organizations, resources, and tournaments. Also links to Amazon.com, where you can purchase books and videos, as well as other online retailers where you can buy clothing and other related merchandise.

A B C D E F G H I J K L M N O P Q R S T U V W X Y Z

A
B
C
D
E
F
G
H
I
J
K
L
M
N
O
P
Q
R
S
T
U
V
W
X
Y
Z

Kodokan Judo Institute

http://www.kodokan.org/

★★★★

Home of the Kodokan Judo Institute, this site provides information about the institute and the origin of Kodokan Judo. Links to other judo sites, information about upcoming events, and an online store are all featured here.

United States Judo Federation

http://www.usjf.com/

★★★

This is USJF's home site, with information on affiliates, contact information, and locations.

USA Judo

http://www.usjudo.org/

★★★★

The national governing body for the sport of judo in the United States, USA Judo is responsible for selecting and preparing teams for international competition. Here, you can learn more about the organization, its teams and coaches, tournament results, and more.

World Judo Site

http://www.geocities.com/Colosseum/Field/5026/

★★★

Dedicated to judo around the world, this site features lists of clubs and organizations, belt descriptions, and the history of the sport.

JUJITSU

Jujitsu America

http://www.jujitsuamerica.org/

★★★

Dedicated to improving understanding of the art and sciences of jujitsu among its members, Jujitsu America is an organization that sets standards for instructors and students. Here, you can learn more about the organization and its members, locate an approved dojo, learn how to become a member, and more.

Small Circle Jujitsu International

http://www.smallcirclejujitsu.com/

★★★

Dedicated to the preservation and propagation of the Small Circle Jujitsu techniques developed by Professor Wally Jay. Features the history and principles of Small Circle Jujitsu, list of official dojos and instructors, and descriptions of books and videos on the subject.

United States Ju-Jitsu Federation

http://www.usjujitsu.net/

★★★

Home of the national governing body of jujitsu in the United States. Here, you can read USJJF news, read about upcoming events, find clubs near you, and find other jujitsu resources on the Web.

KUNG FU

Chinese Kung Fu Wu Su Association

http://www.kungfu-wusu.com/

★★★★

One of the few martial arts academies in the West that offers instruction in traditional Chinese kung fu. View a schedule of events and FAQ and meet Grandmaster Alan Lee and other masters of the temple. Additional information on Chi-Kung, Shaolin, Bhodidharma, and Taoism is in the works.

Kung Fu Magazine

http://ezine.kungfumagazine.com/

★★★★

This online version of *Kung Fu* magazine provides information and entertainment related to the Chinese martial and healing arts. Online features of the magazine include the e-zine, Kungfu Forums, Kungfu resources, and more.

Shaolin International Federation

http://www.shaolin.com/

★★★

Dedicated to preserving and promoting the understanding and practice of Shaolin kung fu, this site features information about Shaolin style kung fu. Resources are presented in four sections: Training, Library, Shopping, and Extras.

SHOTOKAN

Shotokan Karate for Everyone

http://www.shotokanforeveryone.com/

★★★

This site focuses on Shotokan karate and educates visitors about its history, philosophy, techniques, and traditions.

Shotokan Karate of America

http://www.ska.org/

★★★★

A nonprofit karate organization founded in 1955 by Tsutomu Ohshima, who is also recognized as the chief instructor of many other national Shotokan organizations worldwide.

TAE KWON DO

General Tae Kwon Do Info

http://www.barrel.net/

★★★

Covers tae kwon do techniques, competitions, history, and belt requirements; includes links.

International Tae Kwon Do Association

http://www.itatkd.com/

★★★

Information on the International Tae Kwon Do Association and its affiliates.

Philosophy of Tae Kwon Do

http://www.itatkd.com/tkdphil.html

★★★

An informative site from the International Tae Kwon Do Association that explains the complete philosophy of this martial art discipline.

Tae Kwon Do History

http://www.tkd.net/tkdnetwork/history.html

★★★

Provided by the Tae Kwon Do Network, this brief history of tae kwon do explains the beginnings of the discipline.

Tae Kwon Do Network

http://www.tkd.net/

★★★

Excellent directory of tae kwon do information and resources on the Web, including books, videos, schools (arranged by state), tournaments, and gear. Also hosts online chat areas and message boards.

Unofficial Tae Kwon Do Hyung Resource Page

http://ryanshroyer.tripod.com/

★★★

Descriptions of many of the forms you need to know to master tae kwon do. Includes a Korean/English dictionary of terms.

TAI CHI

Boston Kung-Fu Tai-Chi Institute

http://www.taichi.com/

★★★

Site includes information on kung fu, taiji and the internal arts, san shou, special programs, general information, instructors, and videotapes.

A B C D E F G H I J K L **M** N O P Q R S T U V W X Y Z

A
B
C
D
E
F
G
H
I
J
K
L
M
N
O
P
Q
R
S
T
U
V
W
X
Y
Z

ChiLel Qigong

http://www.chilel-qigong.com

★★★★

Information about qigong and tai chi. This site lists instructors, workshops, and retreats, and offers books and videotapes.

China's Living Treasures

http://www.onehand.com/

★★★

This site is composed of demonstrational and instructional movements. The range of the instructional topics is beginning, intermediate, and advanced, including tai chi chuan, chi kung (qigong), pa qua chang, and hsing i chuan, to name a few.

Good Chi Tai Chi Chuan

http://www.denver-taichi.com/

★★★

This site features information about tai chi cam and tai chi chat, offers an online video, and has a very cool Yangstyle tai chi animated film.

International Taoist Tai Chi Society

http://www.taoist.org/

★★★★

Founded by Master Moy Lin-Shin, this international society is dedicated to making Taoist tai chi available to everyone.

Qigong and Taiji

http://www.healthy.net/clinic/therapy/qigongandtaiji

★★★

Information about the practices, the paths you can take, images, and more.

Sing Ong Tai Chi

http://rembrandt.gen.nz/taichi/

★★★

Information, photos, and contact information for instruction of tai chi.

Tai Chi

http://lifematters.com/taijin.html

★★★

A collection of information on the practice, including animated graphics.

Tai Chi for Older People Reduces Falls

http://www.nia.nih.gov/news/pr/1996/05%2D02.htm

★★★

An NIH press release about the benefits of tai chi for older people.

Tai Chi Magazine

http://www.tai-chi.com/

★★★

Some general information about Chinese internal martial arts and information on subscribing to the magazine.

Taoism and the Philosophy of Tai Chi Chuan

http://www.chebucto.ns.ca/Philosophy/Taichi/taoism.html

★★★★

Comprehensive history of Taoism showing the connection between Taoism and tai chi.

Wudang.com

http://www.wudang.com

★★★★

This beautiful site contains information about the history, practice, and philosophy of tai chi.

MATHEMATICS

A
B
C
D
E
F
G
H
I
J
K
L
M
N
O
P
Q
R
S
T
U
V
W
X
Y
Z

American Mathematical Society

http://www.ams.org/

★★★★

Home of the American Mathematical Society. Offers professional memberships. Publishes electronic journals; books on math; and the fee-based MathSci database, which features comprehensive coverage of research in mathematics, computer science, and statistics.

Applied and Computational Mathematics

http://www.acm.caltech.edu/

★★★

Information about Cal Tech's Applied and Computational Mathematics program. At the bottom of the home page, click the Mathematics Resources link to view links to various math resources, including Matlab, GAMS, and Netlib. Also contains links to math-related Gopher sites, newsgroups, math institutes, and a math software index.

Ask Dr. Math

http://mathforum.org/dr.math/dr-math.html

★★★★

All

Math question and answer page, where you can post your math question to have it answered by a student or professor at Drexel University. Before posting a question, browse the archive to see if it has already been answered.

Calculus & Mathematica Home Page

http://www-cm.math.uiuc.edu/

★★★

Calculus & Mathematica is a calculus-reform project started at the University of Illinois and Ohio State University. It uses Mathematica, a software package from Wolfram Research, to teach calculus to high school and college students.

Chaos Theory and Fractals

http://www.mathjmendl.org/chaos/

★★★

Excellent overview of chaos theory, from its very beginnings to its current application in regard to fractals. Features a collection of fractals plus links to other sites that discuss chaos and fractals.

Chaos at Maryland

http://www-chaos.umd.edu/chaos.html

★★★★★

Provides information on the various applications of chaos theory, including dimensions, fractal basin boundaries, chaotic scattering, and controlling chaos. Includes online papers, a searchable database, and general references. Also offers the Chaos Gallery. Be sure to check here for dissertation help!

Common Weights and Measures

http://chemistry.berkeley.edu/links/weights/index.html

★★★

Contains information on converting to and from metric and U.S. measurements.

CSC Mathematical Topics

http://www.csc.fi/math_topics/

★★★

Provides information about mathematical software and guidebooks available at Finland's Center for Scientific Computing (CSC). Also points to application specialists at CSC for help on specific topics. Provides several kinds of search mechanisms to help find documents. Displays examples of mathematical animations and visualizations made at CSC. Also contains some guidebooks and newsletters published by CSC.

A
B
C
D
E
F
G
H
I
J
K
L
M
N
O
P
Q
R
S
T
U
V
W
X
Y
Z

CyberKids Math Page

http://www.cyberkids.com/lp/math.html

★★★

👥 All

Links to several math sites designed specifically for elementary, junior high, and high school students.

Dynamical Systems and Technology Project

http://math.bu.edu/DYSYS/dysys.html

★★★

Provides information on contemporary mathematics, such as fractals and chaos. Includes computer demos, as well as movies, on some famous fractal sets.

eFunda

http://www.efunda.com

★★★★

Short for engineering **funda**mentals, eFunda provides more than 30,000 pages packed with basic information about engineering, along with a collection of engineering calculators. Here, you'll find information about materials, designs, manufacturing processes, along with unit conversions, formulae, and basic mathematical principles.

Egyptian Mathematics

http://www.eyelid.co.uk/numbers.htm

★★★

Learn about the Egyptian math system and how the Egyptians used math in their architecture. Free Egyptian temples screensaver. Links to Amazon.com for online shopping.

[Best] Eric Weisstein's World of Mathematics

http://mathworld.wolfram.com/

$

★★★★★

👥 14-18

This comprehensive encyclopedia of mathematics includes hundreds of definitions and explanations of topics ranging from algebra and geometry to calculus and discrete math. Excellent reference book for math students and teachers. Hosted and sponsored by Wolfram Research, Inc., makers of *Mathematica*, "the world's most powerful and flexible software package for doing mathematics."

Eisenhower National Clearinghouse DCL

http://www.enc.org/

★★★

Supports improving teaching and learning of math and science in secondary schools. Offers links to other Internet resources. Presents online catalog and databases, as well as a collection of Internet software and information.

ExploreMath.com

http://www.exploremath.com/

★★★★

👥 All

This site features online, interactive math activities that cover linear equations, quadratic equations, complex numbers, trigonometry, and more.

Fractal Microscope

http://www.ncsa.uiuc.edu/Edu/Fractal/

★★★

Provides information on basic fractals, the reasons they should be discussed, their purposes in the real world, and the reasons supercomputers are necessary for fractals.

Galaxy Mathematics

http://www.galaxy.com/galaxy/Science/Mathematics.html

★★★

This site offers a substantial number of links to various mathematical disciplines, such as algebra, calculus, fractals, and more.

GAMS: Guide to Available Mathematical Software

http://gams.nist.gov/

★★★

Gateway to NIST guide to available mathematical software. Allows searching by package name or, more interestingly, by what problem it solves.

History of Mathematics

http://www-groups.dcs.st-and.ac.uk:80/~history/

★★★

Contains biographies of mathematicians, searchable by alphabetical or chronological index (some entries include pictures).

IMSA Home Page

http://www.imsa.edu/

★★★

Provides information about the Illinois Mathematics and Science Academy, a residential public high school for students talented in the fields of math and science.

Interactive Mathematics Online

http://library.thinkquest.org/2647/main.htm

★★★★

Learn more about what you can do with algebra, geometry, trigonometry, and chaos theory at this fun site. Check out the Cool Java Stuff page and make your own stereograms.

Larson Interactive Math Series

http://www.meridiancg.com/

★★★★

Math books and interactive software designed to help K–12 students learn basic math. At this site, you can learn about the various programs, order free teacher demos, get technical assistance, and more.

Math Forum–Internet Mathematics Library

http://mathforum.org/library/index.html

★★★

👥 14-18

Whether you're a math teacher looking for lesson plans, puzzles, or textbooks, or a student in need of some online coaching, this site can provide descriptions of many math topics and teaching assistance for elementary through college-level math problems.

Math Tutor

http://www.csun.edu/~vcact00g/math.html

★★★

👥 All

Contains a math-tutoring program developed for classroom computer labs aimed at primary and secondary school students.

Mathematics Archives WWW Server

http://archives.math.utk.edu/

★★★

Provides FTP access to shareware and public domain software for teaching math on the college level. Also includes considerable information on software, especially for people interested in math or looking for secondary school software.

Mathematics of Cartography

http://math.rice.edu/~lanius/pres/map/

★★★

Learn more about the link between mathematics and map-making at this site, which offers some useful information on the history of maps and some problem-solving games.

Mathlab

http://www-math.utsc.utoronto.ca/mathlab/

★★★

A mathematics computer lab. Features downloadable undergraduate level courseware (designed to run under Unix and Mathematica) on geometry, graph theory, and complex analysis.

MathSearch

http://www.maths.usyd.edu.au:8000/MathSearch.html

★★★

Allows you to search a collection of more than 200,000 documents on mathematics and statistics servers.

A
B
C
D
E
F
G
H
I
J
K
L
M
N
O
P
Q
R
S
T
U
V
W
X
Y
Z

A
B
C
D
E
F
G
H
I
J
K
L
M
N
O
P
Q
R
S
T
U
V
W
X
Y
Z

MathSoft

http://www.mathsoft.com/

★★★

Provider of math, science, and engineering software. Offers technical support, news, and a product catalog.

MathType

http://www.mathtype.com/mathtype/

★★★

Houses an equation editor for Mac and Windows machines. Offers technical support, registration, and product information.

MathWorks Home Page

http://www.mathworks.com/

★★★

Offers MATLAB, a high-end mathematics software package, as well as links to jobs, news, and books. Also presents products and services and an online copy of the MATLAB newsletter.

National Council of Teachers of Mathematics

http://www.nctm.org/

★★★★

The National Council of Teachers of Mathematics is dedicated to providing vision, leadership, and resources to math teachers of primary and secondary students to ensure quality math instruction for all students. This site provides tips and curriculum guidelines for elementary, middle school, and high school math teachers.

Netlib Repository at UTK/ORNL

http://www.netlib.org/

★★★

Contains a large number of downloadable math-related programs (most of the software is shareware), papers about different research on mathematical topics (many of which involve computers), and links to other math-related databases.

Quantum Books Home Page

http://www.quantumbooks.com/

★★★

Online technical bookstore specializing in computer topics such as the Internet, programming, and graphics, as well as books pertaining to mathematics and physics.

S.O.S. Mathematics Algebra

http://www.sosmath.com/algebra/algebra.html

★★★★

Get basic definitions and tools for various math topics, from integers to quadratic equations and factors. This is a very comprehensive site with lots of good information and links, designed primarily as a refresher course for adults who forget what they once knew.

University of Washington N-Body Shop

http://www-hpcc.astro.washington.edu/

★★★

Directory of science and mathematics education resources from the University of Washington.

Waterloo Fractal Compression Page

http://links.uwaterloo.ca/

★★★

Provides information on fractal compression software and papers on fractal compression.

World Wide Web Virtual Library: Mathematics

http://euclid.math.fsu.edu/Science/math.html

★★★

Provides links to all things mathematical. Includes links to math software, Gophers, newsgroups, electronic journals, preprints, bibliographies, TeX Archives, and high school and university math sites.

MEDIATION

adrworld.com

http://www.adrworld.com/

★★★

Primarily for alternative dispute resolution professionals, but the news and resources on the subject provided here might be of interest to others as well.

Best Conflict Research Consortium

http://www.colorado.edu/conflict/

★★★★★

The Conflict Research Consortium takes a multidisciplinary approach to conflict resolution, focusing on "finding more constructive ways of addressing difficult, long-term, and intractable conflicts, and getting that information to the people involved in these conflicts so that they can approach them in a more constructive way." Here, you can find conflict resolution sites, databases, publications, conference information, and links. This comprehensive resource on the subject of conflict resolution for difficult situations is well deserving of its Best of the Best designation.

Federal Mediation and Conciliation Services (FMCS)

http://www.fmcs.gov/

★★★

Agency of the U.S. government that handles arbitration and mediation of labor disputes and contract negotiations.

Guide to Alternative Dispute Resolution

http://www.hg.org/adr.html

★★★

From Hieros Gamos, "the comprehensive legal site." This site offers current legal and mediation news. Many links to other mediation information sites.

JAMS ADR

http://www.jamsadr.com

★★★★

Learn about alternative dispute resolution (ADR), find out about JAMS, discover why you should use the JAMS service, determine when you should contact JAMS, and find an office or panelist near you.

Mediation Essays

http://adrr.com/adr1/

★★★

From advanced topics to basic explanations, this site covers what mediation is, how to use it, and when to avoid the process.

Mediation Information and Resource Center

http://www.mediate.com/

★★★★

Everything from defining mediation to guidelines for choosing a mediator. An international searchable directory with links to mediators' Web pages.

Mediation Training Institute

http://www.mediationworks.com/mti/

★★★

For those interested in becoming mediators, this site offers seminars and training programs on mediation. View course descriptions and brochures.

National Mediation Board Forms

http://www.nmb.gov/documents/docsup.html

★★★

Provides details on how to obtain common NMB forms such as mediation services applications and requests for arbitration panel.

A
B
C
D
E
F
G
H
I
J
K
L
M
N
O
P
Q
R
S
T
U
V
W
X
Y
Z

Victim Offender Mediation Association

http://www.voma.org/

★★★

Victim Offender Mediation Association (VOMA) is an international membership association that supports and assists people and communities working to create justice systems in which offenders compensate their victims in some equitable way.

MEDICINE

DRUGSTORES

AdvanceRx.com

http://www.advancerx.com/

★★★★

Get your prescriptions filled, purchase cosmetics, and buy any other product that you would normally find in a traditional drugstore. Also provides tools for researching prescription medications.

CVS/Pharmacy

http://www.cvs.com/

★★★★

A quicker way to get your CVS prescription refilled—online. Log onto the site and specify the prescription you want refilled and the store that has the record, and your order will be ready for pickup when you arrive. While you're at the site, you can also check prices on other prescriptions and in-store specials, read health-related articles, and find the CVS nearest you.

drugstore.com

http://www.drugstore.com/

★★★★

Purchase health, beauty, and nutrition products, as well as prescription medicines, online at this site. A great selection of products, from shampoos to suntan lotion to vitamins, at reasonable prices. Helpful articles and tips help you improve your health and appearance.

Eckerd.com

http://www.eckerd.com/

★★★★★

Get your prescription filled and delivered directly to your doorstep from Eckerd's, where you can also research medicines or ask the pharmacist a question. Health and beauty supplies are offered here, too, as well as vitamins, household goods, and baby care items. You can also locate a store near you at the site.

familymeds.com

http://www.familymeds.com

★★★★★

Click on a common health problem, such as snoring or a sprain, and get more information on typical causes and suggested solutions to each from the site's pharmacist. You can then order the recommended products right from the site.

Medicine Shoppe

http://www.medshoppe.com/

★★★★★

In addition to ordering health products at this site, you can learn more about various diseases and illnesses and ways you can avoid them, read health news, and search the Reuters Drug Database. The emphasis is on learning to stay healthy rather than on product sales, which is nice.

A B C D E F G H I J K L M N O P Q R S T U V W X Y Z

A
B
C
D
E
F
G
H
I
J
K
L
M
N
O
P
Q
R
S
T
U
V
W
X
Y
Z

more.com

http://www.more.com

★★★★

Get answers to health questions and scan buyers' guides in the Resource Center at this site, or look for health information based on your gender or age (there's a seniors section as well as sections for men and women). Order health and beauty products, too, after checking the coupon section for special deals.

Rite Aid

http://www.riteaid.com/

★★★★

In addition to having a prescription filled, asking a pharmacist a question online, buying products, and scanning health databases online, you can also locate a nearby Rite Aid location and check for current specials and discounts.

SavOn.com

http://www.americandrugstores.com/default.asp

★★★★★

A fully stocked online drug store. Get product information here and then purchase the products online from this site. Lots of merchandise to choose from, including baby supplies, cosmetics, and vitamins.

Walgreen's

http://www.walgreens.com/

★★★★★

Search the Mayo Clinic Health information database for medical information and have your prescriptions filled online or at your local Walgreen's location.

DRUG INFO

DrugInfoNet

http://www.druginfonet.com/

★★★

Find information and links to healthcare and pharmaceutical websites from this handy site.

FDA Drug Approvals List

http://www.fda.gov/cder/da/da.htm

★★★★

Come to this site for weekly updates on recently FDA-approved health products. You can search as far back as 1996 for past approvals as well.

PharmWeb

http://www.pharmweb.net/

★★★★

This site is a great resource for pharmaceutical professionals or students. It provides information on job openings, college degrees, and coursework, as well as discussion forums, chat rooms, a virtual library, and access to a directory of fellow pharmacists.

RxList.com

http://www.rxlist.com/

★★★★

Excellent for researching specific prescription medications. Provides information on indications, dosages, side effects, warnings, interactions, and more.

Scholz Healthcare

http://www.ditonline.com/monograph/

★★★

Search for medication alphabetically at this pharmaceutical database.

WebMD Drug and Herb Reference

http://webmd.lycos.com/drugs_and_herbs

★★★

Learn about the potential side effects and health hazards of a wide range of drugs and herbal supplements, and access articles and other tools.

FIRST-AID INFORMATION

1st Spot First Aid
http://1st-spot.net/topic_firstaid.html

★★★★

 All

Find out how to treat basic injuries or conditions, such as heatstroke or frostbite, with the help of this site. You'll also find basic first aid guidance and answers to first aid questions. This site also offers invaluable information about what to keep in a first aid kit.

American College of Emergency Physicians
http://www.acep.org/

★★★★★

Everything you need to know about preventing emergencies and responding to emergencies when they happen. Find out what you need to pack in a first aid kit for your home and learn how to prepare an emergency-response plan.

Related Site
http://www.acep.org/1,402,0.html

Anaphylactic Treatment Guidelines
http://www.anaphylaxis.com/

$

★★★

Learn about the preferred treatment for severe allergic reactions. Links to EpiPen, an auto-injector that administers epinephrine, the definitive emergency treatment for severe allergic reactions.

First Aid Products Online
http://firstaidproductsonline.com/

$

★★★

Purchase items needed for first aid, including basic first aid kits for home or business. A comprehensive online catalog of products.

Hypothermia Prevention, Recognition, and Treatment
http://www.hypothermia.org/

★★★

Learn life-saving skills through helpful articles on preventing and treating hypothermia.

Snakebite Emergency First Aid
http://www.sarinfo.bc.ca/Library/Medical/snakebit.med

★★★

A step-by-step instruction on what to do (and what NOT to do) if bitten by a venomous snake.

MEDICAL RESOURCES

The AAMC's Academic Medicine Website
http://www.aamc.org/

★★★★

The Association of American Medical Colleges site lists and provides links to accredited U.S. and Canadian medical schools, major teaching hospitals, and academic and professional societies. It provides the latest information on news and events, includes AAMC publications and information, and presents research and government relations resources. Also includes information and links to education, research, and healthcare.

Alternative Medicine Home Page
http://www.pitt.edu/~cbw/altm.html

★★★

The Alternative Medicine Home Page is a jump station for sources of information on unconventional, unorthodox, unproven, or alternative, complementary, innovative, integrative therapies.

A B C D E F G H I J K L M N O P Q R S T U V W X Y Z

A
B
C
D
E
F
G
H
I
J
K
L
M
N
O
P
Q
R
S
T
U
V
W
X
Y
Z

American Academy of Pediatric Dentistry

http://www.aapd.org/

★★★★

Parents can open and read 24 brochures that answer commonly asked questions on topics such as emergency care and diet and snacking. Includes *E Today*, the electronic newsletter of the AAPD. Also enables you to subscribe to several related magazines. Includes a directory of advanced education programs in pediatric dentistry, with links to each program. Kids can investigate the entertainment section provided just for them.

American Lung Association

http://www.lungusa.org/

★★★★

Here, you can find information on the ALA (including research programs, grants, and awards), as well as The American Thoracic Society (the international professional and scientific society for respiratory and critical care medicine). Read the ALA's annual report. Check out information on asthma, emphysema, and other lung diseases; tobacco control; and environmental health. This is a great resource for parents of children with asthma. You'll also find information on volunteer opportunities, special events, and promotions, as well as an extensive list of related links.

BBC Science & Nature: Human Body & Mind

http://www.bbc.co.uk/science/humanbody/

★★★★★

This site takes you on a virtual tour of the human body and mind. Here you can build your own skeleton, stretch muscles, arrange internal organs, take the senses challenge, play the nervous system game, and much more. Also explores issues dealing with psychology and the functioning of the human brain.

CareGuide.com

http://www.careguide.com/

★★★

Find information and resources for providing quality elder and childcare at this site. This site provides articles, directories of support organizations, and tools you can use to make your job easier.

CDC: Diabetes and Public Health Resources

http://www.cdc.gov/diabetes/

★★★★

This division of the Centers for Disease Control and Prevention (CDC) is responsible for translating scientific research findings into health promotion, disease prevention, and treatment strategies. Learn about diabetes and what the CDC is doing to reduce the burden of this disease. You'll want to investigate the diabetes articles from the CDC and the helpful FAQs.

Centers for Disease Control and Prevention

http://www.cdc.gov/

★★★★★

Provides links to the CDC's 12 centers, institutes, and offices, and a search engine to quickly locate your point of interest. Includes geographic health information and pinpoints certain disease outbreaks in the world. Also makes vaccine and immunization recommendations. Provides information on diseases, health risks, and prevention guidelines, as well as strategies for chronic diseases, HIV/AIDS, sexually transmitted diseases, tuberculosis, and more. Also offers information on specific populations, such as adolescent and school health, infants' and children's health, and women's health. Offers helpful links to publications, software, and other products. Also provides scientific data, surveillance, health statistics, and laboratory information.

Department of Otorhinolaryngology at Baylor College of Medicine

http://www.bcm.tmc.edu/oto/page.html

★★★

Provides information from the Department of Otorhinolaryngology (head and neck surgery) and communicative sciences. Potential patients can find information and answers to their questions here. Includes a faculty and resident directory, research updates, residency and fellowship information, audiology program information, grand rounds archives, subscription information for the OTOHNS-Online Otolaryngology discussion group, and links to other otolaryngology resources. Also includes back issues of the *Head and Neck* newsletter.

HealthAtoZ
http://www.healthatoz.com/

★★★

A comprehensive navigation tool for health and medicine, in which all sites have been manually cataloged by a team of medical professionals.

Healthfinder
http://www.healthfinder.gov/

★★★★★

 All

Healthfinder is an informational site from the U.S. government. It leads you to selected online publications, clearinghouses, databases, websites, and support and self-help groups. It also gives you access to government agencies and not-for-profit organizations that produce reliable information for the public. Includes FAQs on children, older adults, women, minority health, and more. Also includes FAQs on many conditions from AIDS to food and drug safety. Provides a link to Kids Healthfinder.

Healthtouch
http://www.healthtouch.com

★★★

Enables you to look up information on health, wellness, diseases, and illnesses. Topics include prevention and treatment information on allergies, dental health, drug and alcohol abuse, and numerous other health areas. Includes background information about the disease or healthcare issue and product information. You can also look up information about prescription or over-the-counter medications to learn about the proper use of medicines and possible side effects.

Immunologic Diseases
http://www.mic.ki.se/Diseases/c20.html

★★★

A huge mixture of links on a variety of immunology-related subjects, including autoimmune diseases and allergies.

Internet Health Resources
http://www.ihr.com

★★★

Provides access to Internet-wide health information and local information for the San Francisco Bay Area. Includes resources for dealing with infertility, a wide range of health topics (from allergies to women's health), links to healthcare publications, Internet health newsgroups and LISTSERV groups, and state and national healthcare organizations. Also includes resources for healthcare providers, including related topics, schools, and publications.

Library of the National Medical Society
http://www.ccspublishing.com/

★★★

Read current issues of more than 20 medical-related publications and look over the subscription information. Issues include the *Journal of Pediatric Medicine Online*, *Journal of Psychiatry Online*, *Emotional and Mental Health Library*, and *Women's Health Library*.

Medical Matrix
http://www.medmatrix.org/

★★★

Users can register for a free 24-hour trial membership to use this extensive database of medical journals, articles, and reports on a wide variety of topics. It costs $79 per year to use the service beyond the trial period.

MedLine Plus
http://medlineplus.nlm.nih.gov/medlineplus/

★★★

Find information on diseases, conditions, and health issues by searching the comprehensive database. You can also track down drug information, hospitals, doctors, and organizations that specialize in a particular condition.

A
B
C
D
E
F
G
H
I
J
K
L
M
N
O
P
Q
R
S
T
U
V
W
X
Y
Z

A
B
C
D
E
F
G
H
I
J
K
L
M
N
O
P
Q
R
S
T
U
V
W
X
Y
Z

National Organization for Rare Disorders, Inc. (NORD)

http://www.rarediseases.org/

★★★

NORD consists of more than 140 not-for-profit voluntary health organizations serving people with rare disorders and disabilities. Read the Orphan Disease Update newsletter or search the rare disease database, the NORD organizational database, or the orphan drug designation database for information on specific rare disorders. A rare or orphan disease affects fewer than 200,000 people in the United States. There are more than 5,000 rare disorders that affect 20 million Americans. This site includes links to various support groups.

New England Journal of Medicine

http://content.nejm.org/

★★★★

A comprehensive site from the famed journal. You can find present and past issues of the journal here, as well as up-to-date medical information on a wide variety of topics. This site is a must for anyone interested in the medical field.

Plink: The Plastic Surgery Link

http://www.nvpc.nl/plink/

★★★

 Not for kids

Offers a collection of plastic surgery-related links, targeting physicians and interested laypersons. Includes hospital web pages, journals, books, and general information. Also provides information on societies, departments, physicians, private clinics, conferences, research, and residencies.

Student Doctor Network

http://www.studentdoctor.net/

★★★

The Student Doctor Network (SDN) is "a nonprofit web site, dedicated to the pre-health and health professional student community," whose mission it is to help students select and prepare for various professional careers in health. Site includes plenty of useful resources, but also acts as a forum where professionals and students can meet to exchange information.(d)Telemedicine Info Exchange (TIE).

Telemedicine Info Exchange (TIE)

http://tie.telemed.org/

★★★

TIE is a not-for-profit research organization, and its site offers a database of information on *telemedicine*, which is the use of electronic signals to transfer medical data (radiological images and patient records, for example) from one site to another. This is part of an effort to improve access to medical care. This site also includes Yellow Pages of companies that provide telemedicine products and presents product reviews and technology descriptions. You can also browse through abstracts from current issues of telemedicine journals and newsletters.

Three Dimensional Medical Reconstruction

http://www.crd.ge.com/esl/cgsp/projects/medical/

★★★★★

This site lets you view 3D MPEG-format movies of the human brain, skull, colon, lung, heart (and its arteries), and torso. It also provides a simulation of a baby delivery, MR particle flow visualization (in this case, the artery structure of the brain and a visualization of data flow captured by an MR scanner), and a focused ultrasound. Very cool stuff!

U.S. Department of Health and Human Services

http://www.os.dhhs.gov/

★★★★

Browse through press releases and fact sheets, speeches, public service campaigns, congressional testimony, and policy forums. Also check out the information on the research, policy, and administration provided by HHS, as well as other federal government research. Use the search feature to find topics from the federal HHS agencies and the government information Xchange.

U.S. National Library of Medicine

http://www.nlm.nih.gov/

★★★

In addition to accessing MedLine for more medical information, you can access libraries and learn more about research programs here.

U.S. News Best Hospitals

http://www.usnews.com/usnews/nycu/health/hosptl/tophosp.htm

★★★

Search *U.S. News and World Report*'s database of the top hospitals nationwide by specialty, region, name, or metro area.

Virtual Environments and Real-Time Deformations for Surgery Simulation

http://www.cc.gatech.edu/gvu/visualization/surgsim/

★★★

Focuses on simulating the perceived environment a surgeon encounters during endoscopic surgery. This prototype focuses on abdominal procedures that target the removal of the gall bladder. Offers a large downloadable MPEG movie.

Visible Human Project

http://www.nlm.nih.gov/research/visible/visible_human.html

★★★

Three-dimensional representations of the human body, with visualizations of the dissectible human, software tools, and other areas.

Best WebMD

http://www.webMD.com

★★★★★

A site connecting consumers and health professionals, WebMD aims to provide patients with more information about their healthcare, as well as to help prevent problems by providing useful health-related articles and advice. Online support groups are also available here for topics such as quitting smoking and dieting. This essential medical encyclopedia makes it easy to research symptoms, diseases, prescription medications, and other health-related topics. An easy Best of the Best pick in the Medical Resources category.

The WWW Virtual Library: Biosciences: Medicine

http://www.ohsu.edu/cliniweb/wwwvl/

★★★

Browse through the extensive listings of and links to institutions and what they offer in their health/medicine fields. Use the search units provided to find answers to questions about topics such as pharmacy, epidemiology, veterinary medicine, and more.

PAIN MANAGEMENT

American Academy of Pain Management

http://www.aapainmanage.org

★★★★

A site for healthcare professionals and consumers suffering from chronic pain, providing both with the opportunity to connect and learn more about pain management techniques. Consumers can search the database for a qualified pain management professional.

American Academy of Pain Medicine

http://www.painmed.org/

★★★

This site presents public information published by the American Academy of Pain Medicine, the primary organization for physicians practicing the specialty of Pain Medicine in the United States.

American Chronic Pain Association

http://www.theacpa.org/

★★★

The American Chronic Pain Association (ACPA) is a nonprofit, tax-exempt organization whose members provide a support system for those suffering with chronic pain through education and self-help group activities. Find out how to join by visiting this site.

A B C D E F G H I J K L **M** N O P Q R S T U V W X Y Z

The American Pain Society

http://www.ampainsoc.org/

★★★

A multidisciplinary educational and scientific organization dedicated to serving people in pain. The organization includes more than 3,200 physicians, nurses, psychologists, dentists, scientists, pharmacologists, therapists, and social workers who research and treat pain, and work as advocates for patients with pain.

American Society of Pain Management Nurses

http://www.aspmn.org/

★★★

The American Society of Pain Management Nurses is "an organization of professional nurses dedicated to promoting and providing optimal care of individuals with pain." This organization accomplishes its goals through education, standards, advocacy, and research.

Ask NOAH About: Pain

http://www.noah-health.org/

★★★

Defines basic types of pain, care and treatment, and related concerns.

Center to Improve Care of the Dying

http://www.gwu.edu/~cicd/

★★★

CICD is a unique, interdisciplinary team of committed individuals, engaged in research, public advocacy, and education activities to improve the care of the dying and their families. Dr. Joanne Lynn, an ethicist, hospice physician, and health services researcher, serves as Center Director.

International Association for the Study of Pain

http://www.iasp-pain.org/

★★★

An international, multidisciplinary, nonprofit professional association dedicated to furthering research on pain and improving the care of patients with pain. Membership in IASP is open to scientists, physicians, dentists, psychologists, nurses, physical therapists, other health professionals actively engaged in pain research, and to those who have special interest in the diagnosis and treatment of pain. Currently, IASP has thousands of members from nearly 100 countries.

International Pelvic Pain Society

http://www.pelvicpain.org

★★★

Newly available surgical and medical therapies might offer hope for women suffering from chronic pelvic pain. This site serves as a forum for professional and public education.

Pain.com

http://www.pain.com/

★★★★★

This site offers a world of information on pain, including information about pain products and the companies that make them, pain resources, a collection of original full-text articles on pain and its management by noted pain professionals, and much more! Site offers CME/CPE/CE credit for healthcare professionals.

Pain Net

http://www.painnet.com/

★★★

Pain Net provides expert pain management solutions and training for physicians, hospitals, and caregivers.

Patient Education Institute

http://www.patient-education.com/

★★★

X-Plain, an interactive multimedia computer system used by patients in clinical settings, provides information to patients about diagnosis, alternative treatments, and benefits and risks of treatment. More than 1,000 titles covering health promotion, diagnostic tests, disease management, risks and benefits of surgery, pre-op instructions, discharge instructions, and medications.

Primary Biliary Cirrhosis Organization

http://pbcers.org/

★★★

The Primary Biliary Cirrhosis Organization invites you to discuss medical information, medications, new research, and pain management; and to ask questions, vent your anger and fears, build friendships, and speak freely on the ups and downs of daily living with liver disease.

TALARIA: A Hypermedia Assistant for Cancer Pain Management

http://www.talaria.org/

★★★

Online interactive program designed to help medical professionals provide better pain management care for their patients.

A
B
C
D
E
F
G
H
I
J
K
L
M
N
O
P
Q
R
S
T
U
V
W
X
Y
Z

MEN AND MEN'S ISSUES

American Coalition for Fathers & Children

http://www.acfc.org/

★★★

An organization that works to eliminate gender bias in court cases, such as divorce and custody, giving the father equal access and responsibility for raising his children. The site provides information on the organization's mission, membership, legislation, recent rulings and research, as well as access to legal information.

Backlash.com

http://www.backlash.com/

★★★

Read articles and quotes on issues related to gender, race, feminism, and a host of other categories. A provocative site that will make you think.

Fathering Magazine

http://www.fathermag.com/

★★★★

A site that indexes a huge range of fatherhood topics, from custody issues to second families, to a father's relationship with a son or daughter. News, information, and discussions galore. Well worth a visit.

Father's Forum

http://www.fathersforum.com

★★★

The Fathers' Forum is an "experiment in trying to help fathers connect with one another and reflect on what it means to become a parent." The site offers information on setting up a local Fathers' Forum chapter, as well as material that the host uses in providing counseling and mentoring to fathers in his local area. Links to Amazon.com to shop for books.

Father's Network

http://www.fathersnetwork.org/

★★★

A site with information, networking, and sharing opportunities in support of fathers and families raising a child with special needs.

The Mankind Project

http://www.mkp.org/

★★★★

A nonprofit training organization that seeks to help men make better decisions about how they live their lives, to help them connect with their feelings, and to lead lives of integrity. The site provides information on upcoming Warrior training weekends and the organization's mission.

Best | Men Stuff

http://www.menstuff.org/

★★★★★

An educational website with information on more than 100 topics related to men's issues, such as circumcision, divorce, fathers, and sexuality. Provides a nonjudgmental environment where men can learn more about becoming better fathers, husbands, and human beings; find out more about male health issues, including testicular cancer and sexual dysfunction; and stay informed about other current issues relating to male health and well-being. When dealing with just about any issue related to being a man, there's no better site in this category.

The Men's Defense Association

http://www.mensdefense.org/

★★★

An organization that supports men's rights in divorce. Find sites that are male positive via this site.

Men's Journal

http://www.mensjournal.com/

★★★

Search past articles from this men's magazine and find out what's in store in this month's issue.

National Center for Fathering

http://www.fathers.com/

★★★

A site devoted to helping men become better fathers through articles, research, tips, and sharing with other fathers.

National Coalition of Free Men

http://www.ncfm.org/

★★★

This organization examines how sex discrimination affects men, providing visitors with downloadable articles and research to better information. Links to Amazon.com, where you can order topic-related books.

National Fatherhood Initiative

http://www.fatherhood.org/

★★★

In an effort to counteract the trend toward father-lessness in families, this site provides support, information, and advice to fathers to help get and keep them connected to their children.

National Organization for Men

http://www.tnom.com/

★★★

A nonprofit organization that works to protect men's rights, offering articles on fathering and men's issues at the site. Read the regular newsletter and enjoy a laugh on the Lighter Side.

Promise Keepers

http://www.promisekeepers.org/

★★★

A national Christian men's organization and movement that offers opportunities to connect with one another and share how God has shaped their lives through Promise Keepers. This site also offers organizational news and information.

Single & Custodial Father's Network

http://www.scfn.org/

★★★

An organization devoted to helping men become better fathers through articles, research, publications, discussions, and chats with other fathers.

Slowlane.com

http://www.slowlane.com/

★★★

Stay-at-home dads will enjoy the articles, publicity clips, and support available at this site about being the stay-at-home parent. The site also provides access to research, articles, and discussions.

MEN'S HEALTH

HairSite.com

http://www.hairsite.com

★★★

A site for men (and women) concerned about hair loss, potential reasons for the condition, and treatments. In addition to medical resources and information, you can find discussion forums and chat here, as well as purchase hair regrowth products.

Male Health Center

http://www.malehealthcenter.com

★★★

 Not for kids

A site devoted to providing the same type of information and self-care guidance that women would receive from an OB/GYN. Sections on exercise, diet, sex, and symptoms of male health problems are informative and helpful.

A
B
C
D
E
F
G
H
I
J
K
L
M
N
O
P
Q
R
S
T
U
V
W
X
Y
Z

Men's Fitness

http://www.mensfitness.com/

★★★

 Not for kids

The online edition of this monthly men's magazine offers personal health articles and discussion areas, including training, nutrition, sex and behavior, sports and adventure, and gear. You can also subscribe to the print version from this site.

Men's Health

http://www.menshealth.com/

$

★★★

 Not for kids

Sign up for weekly health and fitness tips to be emailed to you free; check out the results of the latest online men's survey; and investigate articles and information on topics ranging from fitness, health, sports, style, food, and sex. You can search the back issue archive for more guidance if the current online issue isn't enough.

Men's Health Network

http://www.menshealthnetwork.org/

★★★★★

 14-18

Men's Health Network (MHN) is a non-profit organization dedicated to keeping men, boys, and families informed about various health issues related to the male population. Physicians, researches, public health workers, and other individuals and health professionals contribute to the site. Here, you can find out more about the organization, subscribe for its newsletter, and find links to other helpful sites.

Men's Health Topics–Virginia Urology Center

http://www.uro.com/mhealth.htm

★★★

 Not for kids

Find out more about common men's health conditions, such as penile warts, kidney stones, and urinary tract infections, among others at this informational site.

Prostate Cancer

http://www.cancer.med.umich.edu/prostcan/prostcan.html

★★★

 Not for kids

This University of Michigan site is designed to be a resource for prostate cancer-related information regarding diagnosis, treatment options, specialists, investigational studies, and current research. You'll find articles, information on clinical trials, and treatment options here.

Regrowth.com

http://www.regrowth.com

★★★

This site for men facing hair loss provides reference material, chat opportunities, product reviews, news, and hair loss research to keep you informed of promising treatments.

Viagra

http://www.viagra.com/

★★★

 Not for kids

Take the self-screening questionnaire at this site to find out whether you're likely to be suffering from erectile dysfunction. If you are, you'll want to read more at the site about Viagra, how it works, and whether it's likely to help or if you should take it.

MENTAL HEALTH

A B C D E F G H I J K L **M** N O P Q R S T U V W X Y Z

The American Academy of Experts in Traumatic Stress

http://www.aaets.org/

★★★

Read articles from *Trauma Response,* the official publication of the Academy. Articles cover a wide range of trauma: trauma as a result of combat, domestic violence, plane disasters, terrorist acts, natural disasters, rape, divorce, school violence, and more. You can examine case studies and profiles, learn exactly what post-traumatic stress disorder is, look at what causes it, and learn about the various treatments that have been administered.

Anxiety Panic Internet Resource

http://www.algy.com/anxiety/

★★★★

A self-help guide for those suffering from anxiety and/or panic disorders. This site addresses the causes of and treatments for panic attacks, phobias, extreme shyness, obsessive-compulsive behaviors, and generalized anxiety that disrupt the lives of an estimated fifteen percent of the population. If you or someone you love suffers from an anxiety or panic disorder, visit this site for relief and help.

AtHealth.com

http://www.athealth.com/

★★★

For the general public, this site features a Consumers area, where you can find excellent descriptions of nearly every mental disorder, including a description of the disorder and possible treatments, organized in a Q&A format. The Practitioner area provides more in-depth information on prescriptions and other treatment recommendations, but it requires you to register.

Behavior OnLine

http://www.behavior.net/

★★★

Mental health and behavioral science professionals might find this site a useful place to join in discussions regarding various types of therapies and theories, as well as read the *Journal of Online Behavior,* which is available at the site.

Bipolar Disorders Portal

http://www.pendulum.org/

★★★★

If you need information about bipolar disorder (manic depression), you should start here. Links to diagnostic criteria, psychotropic medications, alternative treatments, articles, and dozens of other resources on the Web.

Center for Anxiety and Stress Treatment

http://www.stressrelease.com/

★★★

Get resources and services for the treatment of anxiety, stress, panic, phobias, and worry. Includes an online sale of books and audiotapes. Also provides links to treatment centers, workshops, and counseling services.

A
B
C
D
E
F
G
H
I
J
K
L
M
N
O
P
Q
R
S
T
U
V
W
X
Y
Z

The Center for Mental Health Services

http://www.mentalhealth.org/

★★★★

The CMHS National Mental Health Services Knowledge Exchange Network (KEN) provides information about mental health via toll-free telephone services, an electronic bulletin board, and publications. KEN is for users of mental health services and their families, the general public, policy makers, providers, and the media. It gives you information and resources on prevention, treatment, and rehabilitation services for mental illnesses.

David Baldwin's Trauma Information Pages

http://www.trauma-pages.com/

★★★

David Baldwin's site features very useful information about dealing with post traumatic stress disorders. Through these papers, Baldwin explores what goes on in the brain biologically during traumatic experiences, which psychotherapies are most effective in dealing with these disorders and why, and how one can best measure the clinical effectiveness of these treatments. Excellent bibliography with links to Amazon.com for online shopping.

Dr. Bob's Mental Health Links

http://www.dr-bob.org/

★★★

A large index of links to mental health information.

 ### Internet Mental Health

http://www.mentalhealth.com/

★★★★★

Find what you need to know about mental health, including the most common mental health disorders, diagnoses, and most-prescribed medications. Also check out the several links to related sites and information. This site also has an online magazine with editorials, articles, letters, and stories of recovery. If you or a loved one is suffering from a mental illness, you need information and hope; this Best of the Best site offers both in an easily accessible format.

Mental Health InfoSource

http://www.mhsource.com/

★★★★

This site contains sections regarding disorders and drugs, 600 links on mental health, a mental health professional directory, and more. Use the search tool to track down information on the particular mental health topic in which you're interested.

Mental Health Law

http://www.bazelon.org/

★★★

Legal and policy resources on the civil rights of people with mental disabilities, including healthcare, education, housing, federal benefits, insurance, and employment.

Mental Health Matters

http://www.mental-health-matters.com/

★★★

A directory of resources related to mental health and mental illness, including alternative treatments, emotional support, mental health law, community and government agencies, statistics, support groups, and more. The listings are updated regularly to stay current.

Mental Health Net

http://mentalhelp.net/

★★★★

Get information on disorders such as depression, anxiety, panic attacks, chronic fatigue syndrome, and substance abuse. You can also get access to professional resources in psychology, psychiatry, and social work; journals; and self-help magazines. Plus, you can read articles containing the latest news and developments in mental health.

mentalwellness.com

http://www.mentalwellness.com/

★★★★

An online resource for people suffering from schizophrenia or other mental illnesses, where you can find a support group, locate other community resources available to assist you, as well as read about the disorder and others who are afflicted with it.

National Alliance for the Mentally Ill (NAMI) Home Page

http://www.nami.org/

★★★★

Browse through a host of articles brought to you by NAMI. Learn about the latest treatments and therapy; health-insurance issues; the role of genetics; typical Q&As; and related bills, laws, and regulations. Look into NAMI's campaign to end discrimination against the mentally ill and ways you can help. Take advantage of Helpline Online, where volunteers talk with you about mental illnesses and the medications that treat them. Examine the scientific aspects of mental illness. Get the facts on depression, schizophrenia, brain disorders, and several more.

National Institute of Mental Health

http://www.nimh.nih.gov/

★★★

The NIMH site provides news about mental health research, reports, and clinical trials, both for mental health professionals and members of the public.

National Mental Health Association

http://www.nmha.org/

★★★

Information about the organization and its network of hundreds of affiliates. This site includes mental health fact sheets, pamphlets, news releases, legislative alerts, and more.

Obsessive-Compulsive Foundation

http://www.ocfoundation.org/

★★★★

👥 14-18

Learn about the different classifications of OCD and the treatments that have been effective. Find out the causes and symptoms of the disease, as well as how to get help. Find out whom to contact for more information.

Online Dictionary of Mental Health

http://www.shef.ac.uk/~psysc/psychotherapy/

★★★★

Global information resource and research tool covering all the disciplines contributing to our understanding of mental health.

Who's Who in Mental Health on the Web

http://wwmhw.com/

★★★★

A database of more than 2,000 mental health professionals around the world, and their practice and networking interests.

World Federation for Mental Health

http://www.wfmh.com/

★★★

Read about upcoming programs and conferences related to mental health and check out mental health links made available through this advocacy group's site.

PSYCHOLOGY

American Academy of Child and Adolescent Psychiatry

http://www.aacap.org/

★★★

Get information on child and adolescent psychiatry, fact sheets for parents and caregivers on more than 50 psychiatric disorders, and updates on the current research and legislation. You'll find clinical practice guidelines, managed care information, and public health information. You also get links to many related publications.

American Psychological Association

http://www.apa.org/

★★★

Some good articles on general psychological and mental health issues of current interest, plus a consumer health guide, searchable psychologist directory, and information about the APA.

A B C D E F G H I J K L M N O P Q R S T U V W X Y Z

A
B
C
D
E
F
G
H
I
J
K
L
M
N
O
P
Q
R
S
T
U
V
W
X
Y
Z

Behavior Online

http://www.behavior.net/

★★★

Excellent site for behavior analysis. This site offers links to an editorial corner, resources, and organizations. You can also find ongoing discussions about anything from Gestalt theory to organizational development to classical Adlerian psychotherapy. Before you get too serious, though, check out the Diversions section.

Cognitive and Psychological Sciences on the Internet

http://www-psych.stanford.edu/cogsci/

★★★

An overall resourceful site that links to academic programs, organizations, journals and magazines, newsgroups, publishers, software, and much more—all related to psychology. Learn more about Essex University's Data Archive or join a discussion list.

Community Psychology Net

http://www.cmmtypsych.net/

★★★★

Educators, undergraduate and graduate students, and faculty members will find that the Community Psychology Network site is full of information regarding professional membership societies, graduate schools, community psychology course materials, funding sources, position announcements, books and suggested reading material, as well as links to other related sites.

Cyber Psychologist

http://www.cyberpsych.com/

$

★★★

This site offers you a free way to get the support of a licensed psychologist, Dr. Rob Sarmiento. You can access information and coping strategies for a wide variety of issues: depression, stress management, addictive behaviors, relationship issues, career and work problems, and more. The Q&A forum allows you to post a question you want answered by the doctor. Unless you want a private response, there is no charge for this service.

Dr. Grohol's Psych Central

http://psychcentral.com/resources/

★★★

Search psychology topics organized alphabetically to find articles on subjects such as manic depression, obsessive-compulsive disorder, abuse, and many others. You can also jump into live chats at the site for more discussion.

Encyclopedia of Psychology

http://www.psychology.org/

★★★★

Excellent online directory for psychiatrists, psychologists, students, and patients. Not technically an encyclopedia, this site provides links to other sites.

Galaxy Psychology

http://www.galaxy.com/galaxy/Social-Sciences/Psychology.html

★★★

Links to a variety of online psychology sites. Also listed are hypnosis, psychologists, and self-help site links.

Health Psychology and Rehabilitation

http://www.healthpsych.com/

★★★

Focuses on psychomedical disorders and recovery, with information on medicine, therapy, pain management, and rehabilitation. Offers a page of statistical information ("factoids") from studies done about health/psychology disorders. Also has a forum in which professionals can discuss their points of view about various disorders. This page also offers a few links for further help on the subject.

Jung: C.G. Jung Institute of Boston

http://www.cgjungboston.com/

★★★

At this great site, you can find anything Jung-related that you need. Get information on LISTSERVs and newsgroups, link to related sites, and browse more than 300 books about Jung. You can join a discussion area, take personality tests, and join a mailing list. This site also links to several dream-analysis websites.

Kids Psych

http://www.kidspsych.org/

★★★

👫 0-8

This psychology site for kids provides some games to help parents spend quality time with their children, and to help them with cognitive thinking skills, deductive reasoning, and also just to have some fun! Parents are encouraged to talk with their children about the skills used in each activity.

Mind Control Forum

http://www.mindcontrolforums.com/

★★★

Do you feel controlled by outside sources? Do you think that somebody is controlling your thoughts? Or are you just interested in the concept of mind control? Then check out this website, where users provide personal accounts of their experiences with mind control.

NetPsychology

http://www.netpsych.com/

★★★

NetPsychology aims to make connections between psychologists and individuals using the Internet, so you'll find chat opportunities, billboard ads, email, and discussion forums available to generate discussions.

New York Psychoanalytic Institute and Society

http://www.psychoanalysis.org/

★★★

This site focuses on Freud and psychoanalytical studies. The many links and information here are very useful for students and professionals alike. Click the link for the A. A. Brill Library to check out the Freud archives, from which you can read many of Freud's writings, including *The Interpretation of Dreams*.

PSYbersquare

http://www.psybersquare.com/

★★★★

A site for worriers to come to acquire skills and tools they need to be more satisfied with their lives. "Whether you need help at home or at work, in the bedroom or the board room, the exercises and events at PSYbersquare can help you achieve and win in the game of life," claims Dr. Mark Sichel, an experienced therapist and the originator of the site. Links to Amazon.com, where you can purchase recommended books.

Psyc Site

http://kenstange.com/psycsite/

★★★

Sponsored by Nipissing University's Department of Psychology, this site serves as a resource for those interested in the science of psychology. Its vast number of links include those to information sources, LISTSERVs and newsgroups, downloadable psychology-related software, university and student centers, a message board, research sites, and a chat room.

Psychology.com

http://www.psychology.com/

$

★★★★

Find a therapist or ask a therapist a question online at this site, which also offers tests and games to help you learn more about yourself, articles on useful concepts and techniques, and tips on dealing with stress and other issues.

Psychology.net

http://www.psychology.net/

★★★★

Headline news about current events and issues relating to psychology. Links to Amazon.com to search for books on various psychology topics.

A
B
C
D
E
F
G
H
I
J
K
L
M
N
O
P
Q
R
S
T
U
V
W
X
Y
Z

A
B
C
D
E
F
G
H
I
J
K
L
M
N
O
P
Q
R
S
T
U
V
W
X
Y
Z

Quantitative Study of Dreams

http://psych.ucsc.edu/dreams/

★★★

This site from the University of California, Santa Cruz offers analytical studies of dreams and the reasons we dream. See the DreamSAT database, which is downloadable. This site also includes links to tools, a look at Jungian and Freudian studies, and research examples (including case studies and variables such as norms).

School Psychology Resources Online

http://www.schoolpsychology.net

★★★★

Good resource for school-related psychology programs. The links are vast and include mental retardation, eating disorders, substance abuse, the gifted and talented, mood disorders, and much more. This site also offers links to journals and articles, as well as many links to related sites.

Self-Help Magazine

http://www.shpm.com/

★★★★

E-zine that has more than 75 professionals who contribute to its issues. Offers articles, classifieds, reviews, banner ads, and many links to related information. This site also has *psychtoons* and postcards. You can subscribe to a free newsletter, too.

ShrinkTank Web

http://www.shrinktank.com/

★★★

This site is great, offering links to articles and discussions, other related sites, and online personality and psychological tests. This site also features tons of downloadable software, most of which is straightforward and of the self-help variety.

MOTIVATIONAL AND SELF-IMPROVEMENT INFORMATION

ABCs of Personal Growth

http://www.helpself.com/

★★★

This self-help/self-improvement site offers thought-provoking psychology tests and articles about love, sex, hate, blame, parenting, anger, weight loss, self-esteem, and more.

Awakenings

http://www.lessons4living.com/

★★★

Clinical psychologist Dan Johnston has translated his professional and personal experiences into a site that he hopes will help others in their personal journey toward psychological and spiritual maturity.

Bob Sheinfeld's Success Breakthroughs

http://www.invisiblepath.com/

Ⓢ

★★★★

Discover the next generation in personal success systems. Produce more powerful and consistent results in less time, with less effort and a lot more fun. Success, personal growth, and spirituality books, tapes, and personal seminars are available, as well as personal coaching.

The Cameron Method

http://www.compumind.com/

Ⓢ

★★★

This site promotes a program called The Cameron Method, which refers to a book that is the cornerstone of this philosophy. You can read the first four chapters online. If you're interested, you can sign up for the free email newsletter or download a trial version of the CompuMind SalesPower software. You can also purchase books from a secure server.

Creative Awareness Guided Imagery Self-Hypnosis Tapes

http://www.upword.com/Creative_Awareness/imagery.html

★★★

Experience the body/mind connection through guided imagery and self-hypnosis audiocassettes. Guided imagery has been associated with positive stimulation of the immune system, which helps to create healthy energy cycles within the body. Award-winning hypnotherapists Kim and Steven Falcone have skillfully woven a mixture of imagery, music, and natural sounds to reduce pain and discomfort. Order books and tapes online from this site.

Best Deepak Chopra

http://www.chopra.com/

Ⓢ

★★★★★

This is a one-stop shopping website for those seeking self-improvement. Pick up the tip of the day, the quote of the day, the vegetarian recipe of the week, and plenty of other spiritual guidance at Deepak Chopra's site, which includes information about his personal growth workshops and materials. You can also ask him a question and learn more about the Center for Well Being. Order books, candles, spices, and food supplements here.

A
B
C
D
E
F
G
H
I
J
K
L
M
N
O
P
Q
R
S
T
U
V
W
X
Y
Z

A
B
C
D
E
F
G
H
I
J
K
L
M
N
O
P
Q
R
S
T
U
V
W
X
Y
Z

Dr. Phil

http://www.drphil.com/

★★★★★

A popular guest on the Oprah Winfrey show until he received his own show, Dr. Phil's in-your-face approach encourages people to "Get Real, Get Smart, and Get Going." Here, you can learn more about the show and about Dr. Phil and his books; you can shop for merchandise online; and you can even learn what to do to get on the show.

Freeing the Mind

http://www.trans4mind.com/personal_development/

★★★

This site contains many articles on mental and spiritual development, as well as philosophy and computer topics. Links to Amazon.com, where you can purchase books and tapes.

Harvey Mackay: Business Motivational Speaker

http://www.mackay.com/

★★★

This site promotes powerhouse business motivational speaker Harvey Mackay, his products, and his speaking services.

InnerSelf Magazine: Behavior Modification

http://www.innerself.com/Magazine/Behavior_Modification/

★★★★

This site offers an extensive list of behavior modification articles. From here, you can click on the link to the *InnerSelf Magazine* home page and find lots of other articles and topics to explore. The entire premise behind this site is to "assist in creating the life you want."

John Gray

http://www.marsvenus.com/

★★★★

Take John Gray's Personal Success Block Buster questionnaire to get feedback on what areas of your life are holding you back from total success. Then read about all of his books, upcoming conferences, and recent magazine columns on relationships and parenting. Purchase books, audio and video tapes, CDs, and games at this site.

Les Brown

http://www.lesbrown.com/

★★★

Find a quote that speaks to you in Les's Success Quotes section of the site, or read Les's bio, find out about upcoming speaking engagements, read essays, and post a message on the message board.

LifeQuest

http://www.lifequest-freshstart.com/

★★★

This site markets four products to help you achieve a better sense of health, well-being, and confidence.

Motivation 1-2-3

http://www.motivation123.com/

★★★

Motivation 123 provides hundreds of simple tips and ideas that are guaranteed to motivate you. Free motivation idea kit is available.

Motivational Mecca

http://www.onlineconsulting.com/excite.html

★★★

Plenty of free motivational information and guidance here, including free goal-setting software, free rentals of several motivational audiotapes, free e-books, and tips and quotes from motivational speakers.

MotivationalQuotes.com

http://www.motivationalquotes.com/

 ★★★★

Huge collection of motivational quotes, prayers, and positive affirmations. The site is devoted to promoting positive thinking.

Related Site

http://www.motivationalquotes.com/links/

Motivational Speakers

http://www.speakersla.com/

⑤

 ★★★

Learn about the Distinguished Speakers Series and "Experience a season of heroes and legends. You'll be moved, you'll be challenged, you'll leave INSPIRED!" Purchase tickets to the series from this website.

Personal Success Radio Network

http://www.personalsuccessradio.com/

 ★★★★

Internet radio station that focuses on "personal success, positive living, and self-improvement." Features top motivational speakers giving free advice.

Quest for Success

http://www.questforsuccess.com/

⑤

 ★★★

This site sells a variety of framed motivational images, from posters to notecards. Purchase the products online directly from this website.

Self-Improvement Online

http://www.selfgrowth.com/

★★★

This site offers a plethora of self-help and personal growth resources. You'll find articles, more than 4,000 links, IQ tests, a free newsletter, inspirational quotes, and much, much more.

Study Skills Self-Help Information

http://www.ucc.vt.edu/stdysk/stdyhlp.html

 ★★★

 14-18

Maintained by the Virginia Polytechnic Institute, this site is designed to help students better manage their time, improve their study skills and concentration, sharpen their memories, read difficult books, and hone other skills required to be successful in school.

Successories.com

http://www.successories.com/

⑤

 ★★★★★

Successories is dedicated to helping organizations and individuals realize their full potential. This company believes that motivation originates with attitude, grows in response to goals, and endures when reinforced through exposure to insightful ideas in your environment. The unique collection of themed merchandise is designed to promote a positive outlook; celebrate human achievement; and inspire excellence in your career, your business, and your life.

Suze Orman

http://www.suzeorman.com/home.asp

⑤

 ★★★★★

This site is the home of money-management guru Suze Orman, author of *The Laws of Money, the Lessons of Life*, which provides practical advice on holding on to what you have and achieving your personal financial goals and other goals relating to your family. At this site, you can find books and other products, sign up to receive a newsletter, check out her program schedule, and much more.

A
B
C
D
E
F
G
H
I
J
K
L
M
N
O
P
Q
R
S
T
U
V
W
X
Y
Z

A
B
C
D
E
F
G
H
I
J
K
L
M
N
O
P
Q
R
S
T
U
V
W
X
Y
Z

Tony Robbins: Resources for Creating an Extraordinary Quality of Life

http://www.tonyrobbins.com/

★★★★

Home page of motivational guru Anthony Robbins. Learn about upcoming events; browse through his products and order them online, read the results he's achieved, visit daily for the day's "Daily Action," find out about coaching support, and more.

Zig Ziglar

http://www.zigziglar.com/

★★★

Sign up to get a free Zig newsletter, listen to clips from the speaker, and get more information on Zig Ziglar and his programs here. Books, videos, and gifts can all be purchased from the website.

1-Stop-Guide-Motorcycle Section

http://www.1-stop-guide.com/motorcycles/
motorcycles.html

★★★

Specializes in trucks, trailers, hitches, and related products. If you need a trailer for pulling your motorcycle, this is the place to go. If you're looking for motorcycles, you won't find them here.

2WF.com

http://www.2wf.com/

★★★★

Huge resource for everything related to motorcycles, this site covers racing, culture, bike tests, repair and maintenance, stunt riding, and more. Staffed by motorcycle owners and enthusiasts, dedicated to providing the best information in an irreverent and entertaining format. Discussion groups are also available.

AFMWeb (American Federation of Motorcyclists)

http://www.afmracing.org/AFM1.html

★★★

Focuses on motorcycle road racing. Offers a new racer school, practice information, and a schedule of races. Also includes a FAQ, a rulebook, links, membership information, race results, and a classified section.

Allen Vintage Motorcycle Museum

http://www.allenmuseum.com/

★★★

Find out more about the Allen Vintage Motorcycle Museum, located just outside Boston, and its collection of vintage racing and touring motorcycles from 1955 to the current era. At the site you can also investigate buying or selling vintage bikes and find other motorcycle links.

AMA Superbike

http://www.amasuperbike.com/

★★★★

An unofficial AMA superbike site containing news, feature articles on racers, point summaries, and a racing calendar for the upcoming year.

American Motorcyclist Association

http://www.ama-cycle.org/

★★★★

Promotes the interests of motorcycle enthusiasts. The site includes AMA pro and amateur racing information, travel, and more.

BMW Motorcycles

http://www.bmwmotorcycles.com/

★★★★★

The official BMW motorcycles website, this visually appealing site is full of fun animation and solid information about BMW motorcycles. Learn about the complete line of BMW bikes, check out the gear and accessories, find a local dealer, and get financing information.

A
B
C
D
E
F
G
H
I
J
K
L
M
N
O
P
Q
R
S
T
U
V
W
X
Y
Z

Buell American Motorcycles

http://www.buell.com

★★★★

Learn all about the history of bikes made by Buell, part of the Harley-Davidson family. The site also includes a locator for finding a local dealer and information about clothing and other accessories.

 Best **Harley-Davidson**

http://www.harley-davidson.com/

 $

★★★★★

Official site of Harley-Davidson—the products, the company, and the experience. Check out the current models; find a dealer; and see what kind of new clothing, accessories, and gifts are available. You can even get information about investing in the Harley-Davidson company. This site's sleek design and comprehensive offerings make it the best commercial motorcycle site on the Web.

Honda Motorcycles

http://www.hondamotorcycle.com/

★★★

Get a preview of the newest Honda models, and get your racing news and schedule here, as well as information on special deals and events sponsored by Honda. You can also learn more about patented Honda racing innovations.

Horizons Unlimited

http://www.horizonsunlimited.com/

 $

★★★★★

When motorcycle travelling is in your blood, there's not much you can do to quell the urge, so visit this site for some ideas on where you can explore next. This site is dedicated to fostering a community of motorcycle travellers and providing them with the information and resources they need to find the best places to go and the best places to stay and eat along the way. This site provides plenty of information on trip planning, traveller's tales, links to other sites, and online forums in several languages.

Indian Motorcycles

http://www.indianmotorcycles.com/

$

★★★★

Home of America's oldest brand of motorcycle. Check out the latest line of Indian motorcycles, view a history of the company from 1900 to present, find a dealer, or copy free ride maps.

Kawasaki.com

http://www.kawasaki.com

$

★★★

Find out about special deals on Kawasaki wheels, order Kawasaki clothing and accessories online, and stay on top of Kawasaki news and promotions.

MotoDirectory.com

http://www.moto-directory.com/

★★★

A site for a collection of links on motorcycle items, from servicing to products to dealers.

motogranprix.com

http://www.dorna.com/

★★★★

If you follow the Motorcycle Grand Prix, you'll want to bookmark this page. Features calendar of races, race results, current standings, news, information about the riders and teams, and much more.

Motorcycle Online

http://www.motorcycle.com/

★★★

Motorcycle Online includes feature articles and classifieds, plus a museum and bulletin board. Read product reviews, get repair tips, share information with other motorcycle enthusiasts, and hear about next year's models at this site.

Motorcycle Riders Foundation

http://www.mrf.org/

★★★★

This Washington, D.C.–based bikers advocacy site offers news from D.C., MRF reports, a message board, national motorcycle laws, and links for information and research.

Motorcycle Safety Foundation

http://msf-usa.org/

★★★

This nonprofit group was created to provide safety information for motorcyclists—both new and experienced. The site offers links to training courses around the country and information on protective gear.

Motorcycle Tips and Techniques

http://www.msgroup.org/TIPS.asp

★★★★

A collection of tips to keep the potentially dangerous hobby of motorcycling as safe as possible. The site also provides a case study on women motorcyclists and links to a variety of other motorcycle pages.

Motorcycle USA

http://www.motorcycle-usa.com/

★★★

👫 14-18

Compare the newest bikes, post messages on the boards, place classified ads, and get the latest racing news at this site. Some games and moto trivia that teenagers will find particularly interesting.

MotorcycleShopper.com

http://www.motorcycleshopper.com/

★★★

An interactive electronic magazine that allows motorcycle enthusiasts, riders, and collectors to communicate with one another and place free ads. Links to thousands of parts, accessories, and other merchandise.

MotoWorld.com

http://www.motoworld.net/

★★★

This site offers racing news, results, clips, and interviews, as well as action photos and a calendar of upcoming TV race coverage. Links to other sites for online shopping.

Ronnie Cramer's Motorcycle Web Index

http://sepnet.com/cycle/

★★★

Links to an array of motorcycle-related sites, with such categories as Bikes, Parts, Apparel, Clubs, Dealers, and Publications, as well as other motorcycle websites.

Yamaha

http://www.yamaha-motor.com/

★★★★

Home of Yamaha Motor Company, makers of motorcycles, snowmobiles, jetskis, boats, golf carts, and other popular recreational motor vehicles. Here, you can check out the latest motorcycle models and find a dealer near you.

A B C D E F G H I J K L M N O P Q R S T U V W X Y Z

Agony Booth

http://www.agonybooth.com/

★★★★

If you have ever been subjected to an awful movie and kind of enjoyed wallowing in it by discussing its failures on so many levels, then the Agony Booth might just be the place for you. Here, rogue reviewers trash the worst that the movie industry has to offer—all in good humor, of course.

All Movie Guide

http://www.allmovie.com/

★★★★★

This site was designed with the movie buff in mind. It provides search tools for tracking down movies by title and actors and directors by name. The opening screen displays the titles of new films and movies, the names of actors born on this day, currently featured links, and snippets of movie trivia. Also provides a useful link for checking out new releases on VHS and DVD. Whatever you're looking for that's related to movies, you can find it at this site.

AtomFilms

http://atomfilms.shockwave.com/

★★★★★

AtomFilms features on-demand viewing of more than 1,500 world-class film and animation titles, ranging from 1 to 30 minutes in length. Genres include animation, comedy, music, extreme, action, and drama. Collectively, more than 20 million entertainment fans visit the AtomFilms and Shockwave sites each month to check out what they have to offer. Very cool streaming video.

BMW Films

http://bmwfilms.com

★★★★

 14-18

If you're interested in short films created by some of Hollywood's finest talents, check out this site. If you have a fast Internet connection, you can download and view the films online; otherwise, consider ordering clips on DVD. If you own a BMW (lucky you), the DVD will be shipped to you for free. If you don't own a BMW, you must pay a small fee to cover shipping and handling.

Dogville

http://www.tvropa.com/Dogville/

★★★★★

This site takes you behind the scenes of the filming of *Dogville*, staring Nicole Kidman as a woman on the run from the mob. She finds herself in a small town, where she makes a deal with the locals to assist her. Personal politics come into play as the plot unfolds. This site feature short film clips, interviews, actor bios, a gallery of still shots, and more. This site is everything a movie website should be—attractive, easy to navigate, and packed with substance.

The Dreamers

http://www.the-dreamers.com/

★★★★

Not for kids

The Dreamers is a film about a young American student studying in Paris in 1968 who forms a friendship with a French brother and sister. Together, they explore and test the limits of their dreams, where "nothing is impossible" and "nothing is forbidden." This site can be a little difficult to figure out at first; pretend that you are playing an adventure game. You need to explore each page to figure out where to click. Use your mouse pointer as your guide.

E! Online

http://movies.eonline.com/

★★★★★

You're sure to be up to speed on all the movie industry dirt with the help of this site, which offers celebrity news, movie release information and rankings, movie synopses, and box office reports.

Film.com

http://www.film.com/

★★★★★

Read reviews of top movies and new releases, watch clips and movie trailers, read interviews with the stars, and find out about upcoming projects.

Film Affinity

http://www.filmaffinity.com/

★★★★★

At Film Affinity, you register and enter your ratings for a selection of movies. The site searches its database of other registered users, finds your movie soulmates, and consults their ratings to find other movies that might appeal to your tastes. Pretty cool concept, and very cool site.

Fog of War

http://www.sonyclassics.com/fogofwar/

★★★★★

Fog of War is the official website of the documentary of the same name, about the difficult lessons that Robert McNamara, former United States Secretary of Defense, learned about the nature of war through his experiences and observations. This site features a clickable timeline of McNamara's career, along with video clips from the film.

IFILM

http://www.ifilm.com

★★★★★

Online video library packed with short downloadable movies and movie clips broken down into several categories, including Action, Animation, Comedy, Drama, Erotica, Gay & Lesbian, and Sci-Fi. Check out the top short films and trailers, or browse the categories for a complete selection.

Best Internet Movie Database

http://www.moviedatabase.com/

★★★★★

The online authority for all things related to movies and film, this comprehensive directory allows you to track down movies and trivia by movie title, director, or actor. Want a list of all the movies in which Robert De Niro appeared? Then search for "Robert De Niro" to pull up a list of this master's films. Check out the new releases, top videos on DVD and VHS, top rated movies of all time in various categories, and independent movies. You can tour the photo gallery, play movie trivia games online, and visit the message boards to keep in touch with fellow movie buffs. With its no-frills presentation, excellent search tools, and comprehensive database of movie trivia, this site has no equal.

Metacritic

http://www.metacritic.com

★★★★★

Are you looking for a movie review for a newly released flick? Then look no further. For every movie featured on the site, Metacritic pulls together reviews from the top film critics, provides a brief synopsis of each critic's opinion of the flick, and provides a link for accessing the full review. Metacritic also tallies the ratings to determine a "metascore" that reflects the collective rating from all critics. Recently, Metacritic has started rating CDs and games, as well.

Movie Clichés List

http://www.moviecliches.com

★★★

You'll find this list of the most annoying and common logic flaws and stereotypes found in movies to be entertaining. And you're welcome to add those that bug you to the list on the site.

Movies.com

http://movies.go.com/

★★★★★

Are you planning a movie night? Then get it right at Movies.com. Here, you can find movie reviews, trailers, theater times and locations, DVDs and videos, and everything else related to movies. This site focuses on new releases.

A B C D E F G H I J K L M N O P Q R S T U V W X Y Z

A
B
C
D
E
F
G
H
I
J
K
L
M
N
O
P
Q
R
S
T
U
V
W
X
Y
Z

Richmond Moving Image Co-Op

http://www.rmicweb.org/

★★★★★

Flicker festivals have cropped up all around the nation, providing budding filmmakers the chance to produce their own short flicks (under 15 minutes) and show them to real live audiences. This site is the home of the Richmond Flicker, located in Richmond, Virginia, and the James River Film Festival. Here, you can learn about upcoming festivals, check the schedule, and even download programs from past festivals. Do you have a movie you want to show? Click the SUBMIT YOUR FILM link and learn where to mail your footage. *RMIC* is a great source of information about alternative films. You can read about filmmakers, find out what's showing where, and download images from films.

Spellbound

http://www.spellboundmovie.com/

★★★★★

This is the official site of the award-winning documentary, *Spellbound*, that follows a group of master spellers through their competition in the National Spelling Bee held in Washington D.C. Here you can read the story, view a trailer, learn about the filmmakers, and even play a round of hangman. Very cool 3D animations and graphics.

Sundance Film Festival

http://www.sundanceonlinefilmfestival.org/

★★★★★

Robert Redford's Sundance Film Festival now has a website, where you can learn more about this important festival and check out what's happening at Sundance when the festival is in full swing.

MUSEUMS

Devices of Wonder

http://www.getty.edu/art/exhibitions/devices

★★★★

 All

Sponsored by the Getty Museum, this site features the Devices of Wonder exhibit, a unique collection of the ancestors of modern cinema, cyborgs, computers, and optical devices.

Exploratorium

http://www.exploratorium.edu

Ⓢ

★★★★

 All

Website of the Exploratorium, a unique museum housed inside San Francisco's Palace of Fine Arts, which features more than "650 science, art, and human perception exhibits." Founded by noted physicist Dr. Frank Oppenheimer, this site is devoted to nurturing people's curiosity about the world around them. Here, you can check out various online exhibits and learn more about the museum.

MUSÉE

http://www.musee-online.org/

★★★★★

 All

International directory of museums allows visitors to search by type of museum, alphabet, or geographical location. Rates each museum on a scale of one to five and provides information about each museum, including its hours of operation, educational materials, fun stuff to do, and visual content.

MuseumLinks Museum of Museums

http://www.museumlink.com/

★★★

14-18

Excellent directory of museums divided into three groups: Canadian Museums, U.S. Museums by State, and International Museums. Also features a list of online museums.

MuseumStuff.com

http://www.museumstuff.com/shop/

★★★★

All

Directory of online museum stores, many of which feature online shopping. Search for a museum store by entering a keyword or browse by categories, such as Art and Design, History, and Science.

ARCHITECTURE

The Chicago Athenaeum: The Museum of Architecture and Design

http://www.chi-athenaeum.org/

★★★

14-18

The Chicago Athenaeum features "Landmark Chicago," the first permanent exhibition celebrating Chicago's position as the world capital of historical and contemporary landmarks of modern architecture. This site contains information and photos from this exhibit, as well as other details about the museum, its exhibits, and its upcoming schedule.

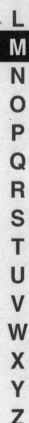

A
B
C
D
E
F
G
H
I
J
K
L
M
N
O
P
Q
R
S
T
U
V
W
X
Y
Z

Getty Center

http://www.getty.edu/

★★★

👥 14-18

Home of the Getty Center, in Los Angeles, "one of the largest privately funded architectural complexes ever designed and constructed in a single architectural campaign." Check out a gallery from more than 600 photographers whose work is in the Getty Museum's collection.

National Building Museum

http://www.nbm.org/

★★★★

👥 14-18

The National Building Museum presents permanent exhibitions about the world we live in, from our homes and offices to our parks and cities. This site has online excerpts of exhibits past and present, as well as information about books that complement them. It also offers summaries from "The Urban Forum," a program designed to explore issues related to the design, growth, and governance of American cities. Stop by this site to find the museum's hours of operation and location.

Netherlands Architecture Institute

http://www.nai.nl/e/index.html

★★★

👥 14-18

This site contains exhibitions and other activities from this museum, which houses a vast collection of works from Dutch architects and many others. It contains everything about the epicenter of Dutch architecture, including a link to *Archis*, a Dutch/English monthly magazine about architecture, urban design, and visual arts.

The Skyscraper Museum

http://www.skyscraper.org/

★★★

👥 14-18

This not-for-profit corporation is devoted to the study of high-rise buildings, past, present, and future. The site celebrates New York City's rich architectural heritage. Here, you can learn more about the organization and its projects and events.

The Vitoslavlitsy Museum of Wooden Architecture

http://faculty.washington.edu/dwaugh/rus/novgorod/novgwood.html

★★★

👥 14-18

Russian museum of wooden architecture located south of Novgorod and not far from the outlying Iur'ev Monastery. Old wood buildings from surrounding areas have been dismantled and rebuilt on the grounds here. Check out a video gallery of the exhibits.

Wharton Esherick Museum

http://www.levins.com/esherick.html

★★★★

👥 14-18

This site features the life and work of this "Dean of American Craftsmen." Photos include the world-famous spiral oak staircase from his studio in Pennsylvania, and Esherick's regional influences are discussed.

ART

The African/Edenic Heritage Museum

http://www.kingdomofyah.com/museum.htm

★★★★

👥 14-18

This traveling exhibit highlights the indigenous African presence in the Holy Land. Exhibit features "450 square feet of informative maps, provocative text, and exclusive photographs of the indigenous African/Edenic people of Israel." Here, you can learn more about the museum and how to contact the organizers.

Agung Rai Museum of Art

http://www.nusantara.com/arma/

★★★★

👥 14-18

This Indonesian museum houses a collection of works by Balinese, Javanese, and foreign artists. Select works shown on the site provide an intriguing display of history and culture.

American Visionary Art Museum

http://www.avam.org/

★★★

 All

The world's largest grassroots art exhibition, located in Baltimore's Inner Harbor. Some stuff for kids, such as the Make Your Own Robot game.

The Andy Warhol Museum

http://www.warhol.org/

★★★★★

 14-18

This site is part of the Carnegie Museums of Pittsburgh; it features a guided tour of the museum itself (opened in 1994), which features images and biographical information regarding Andy Warhol. It also describes the work of the Archives Study Center, which collects and preserves anything to do with Warhol's life and work. A calendar details upcoming exhibitions and events. Links to various Andy Warhol stores, where you can purchase T-shirts, posters, prints, and more.

Artcyclopedia

http://www.artcyclopedia.com/

★★★

 14-18

An art search engine that lets you track down art information by artist, movement, medium, subject, or nationality. It also offers information on museums and other art links.

The Art Institute of Chicago

http://www.artic.edu/

★★★★★

 All

Comprising both a museum and an art school, the institute's site contains everything you always wanted to know about the museum, including information about exhibits and collections, the history and layout of the museum, publications and press releases, gift shop items, and Institute membership information. You can also view art and play games related to art here. Special area for kids and families.

Asian Art Museum of San Francisco

http://www.asianart.org/

★★★

This is the largest museum in the Western world devoted to the arts and cultures of Asia. This site provides information about exhibits and programs at the museum, as well as job openings there. Art is organized by country or region.

Canadian Wildlife and Wilderness Art Museum

http://www.magma.ca/cawa/cawaintr.html

★★★

 14-18

Contains representative works of Canada's internationally acclaimed wildlife and wilderness painters, sculptors, and carvers. Includes a gallery of artwork, as well as a bio of and artwork by Robert Lougheed, one of North America's best-known wildlife and Western artists.

The Chrysler Museum of Art and Historic Houses

http://www.chrysler.org/

★★★

14-18

Learn about the museum's American and European paintings and sculptures, glass, photography, and decorative arts collections of more than 30,000 objects spanning almost 4,000 years.

Cincinnati Art Museum

http://www.cincinnatiartmuseum.com/

★★★★

All

This site features a virtual tour of the museum's collections, children's activities, general information, and much more. Be sure to check out the museum's online gift store for gift items.

A B C D E F G H I J K L M N O P Q R S T U V W X Y Z

A
B
C
D
E
F
G
H
I
J
K
L
M
N
O
P
Q
R
S
T
U
V
W
X
Y
Z

The Columbia Museum of Art

http://www.colmusart.org/

★★★★

⛐ All

The museum's exhibits contain European and American fine and decorative art representing a time period of nearly seven centuries. Its public collections of Renaissance and Baroque art include works by Botticelli, Boucher, Canaletto, Tintoretto, and many others. The museum's online magazine, *Collections*, will alert you to recent acquisitions, a calendar of events, staffing changes, and additional newsworthy tidbits about the museum, located in Columbia, South Carolina.

Farnsworth Art Museum

http://farnsworthmuseum.org/

$

★★★

⛐ 14-18

This regional art museum boasts a specialized collection focusing on Maine's role in American art. The new Wyeth Center provides a glimpse at many of the works of N.C., Andrew, and Jamie Wyeth. The online gift store is worth taking a few minutes to browse through.

Fine Arts Museums of San Francisco

http://www.thinker.org/

$

★★★

⛐ 14-18

Search more than 75,000 images from the deYoung Museum and the Legion of Honor, the two museums that comprise the Art Museums of San Francisco, as well as browse information about current and upcoming exhibitions. You can even create your own online gallery using any selection and arrangement from the collection of 75,000 images.

The Finnish National Gallery

http://www.fng.fi/

★★★

Visit the collections at the Finnish National Gallery's three specialist museums—Sinebrychoff, the Museum of Foreign Art; Ateneum, the Museum of Finnish Art; and Kiasma, the Museum of Contemporary Art—which cover a period of eight centuries. The site contains links to the galleries, as well as the capability to search for information about a particular artist or work.

Best | J. Paul Getty Museum

http://www.getty.edu/museum

$

★★★★★

⛐ 14-18

Learn about the Getty Museum's collection of artworks, which include antiquities, decorative arts, medieval manuscripts, European paintings, sculptures, drawings, and photographs. Get an overview of the exhibitions and check out the calendar of upcoming events. The online gift store offers everything from hats and T-shirts to calendars, cards, and posters. This site's excellent design, superior graphics, and exquisite content make it an easy choice as Best of the Best.

Guggenheim Museums

http://www.guggenheim.org/

$

★★★★

⛐ 14-18

Site contains information about five museums: the Solomon R. Guggenheim Museum on Fifth Avenue in New York City; the Guggenheim Museum SoHo on Broadway in New York City; the Guggenheim Museum in Bilbao, Spain; the Peggy Guggenheim Collection in Venice, Italy; and the Deutsch Guggenheim Berlin. Includes some great photos of the museums and their exhibits. Some information on programs for children and families.

Harvard University Art Museums

http://www.artmuseums.harvard.edu/

★★★

👥 14-18

This is the website for the Harvard University Art Museums—the Fogg Art Museum, the Busch-Reisinger Museum, the Arthur M. Sackler Museum, and the Strauss Center for Conservations—all in Cambridge, Massachusetts.

Indianapolis Museum of Art

http://www.ima-art.org/

★★★

The nation's seventh largest general art museum has permanent collections of African, American, Asian, contemporary, decorative, and European art, as well as a textiles and costumes collection, prints, drawings, and photographs. The IMA complex is surrounded by a 152-acre park, including 50 intensively landscaped acres that are accessible to the public.

Isamu Noguchi Garden Museum

http://www.noguchi.org/

★★★

👥 14-18

This museum was conceived and designed by the artist himself. It contains an extensive collection of sculpture, drawings, and documentation, and includes an online tour through the gardens. Also includes biography information about the artist and links to other sites that display his work.

The Kemper Museum of Contemporary Art

http://www.kemperart.org/

★★★

This site includes a calendar of events, the history and architecture of the museum, images from the collection, and a guest book. The museum boasts a notable Georgia O'Keeffe collection, several watercolors of which can be viewed at this site.

Le Louvre

http://www.louvre.fr/

★★★★★

👥 All

This official site of the famous museum, the home of the *Mona Lisa*, includes information about the museum's seven departments: Oriental Antiquities (with a section dedicated to Islamic Art); Egyptian Antiquities (with a section dedicated to Coptic Art); Greek, Etruscan, and Roman Antiquities; Paintings; Sculptures; Objets d'Art; and Prints and Drawings. The site includes many details (small sections of paintings, enlarged so you can see them better) from the museum's collections. Take some cool QuickTime virtual tours of the museum.

The Leonardo Museum

http://www.leonet.it/comuni/vinci/

★★★

👥 All

A museum devoted to the works of Leonardo da Vinci. In addition to his more famous works, the site also includes some of his drawings and sketches, his engineering and futuristic designs, and historical details about his life.

Metropolitan Museum of Art, New York

http://www.metmuseum.org/

💲

★★★★★

👥 14-18

One of the largest art museums in the world, The Met's collections include more than two million works of art—several hundred thousand of which are on view at any given time—spanning more than 5,000 years of world culture, from prehistory to the present. Stay updated on upcoming exhibitions and buy museum products online.

A B C D E F G H I J K L **M** N O P Q R S T U V W X Y Z

A
B
C
D
E
F
G
H
I
J
K
L
M
N
O
P
Q
R
S
T
U
V
W
X
Y
Z

Musée des Arts et Métiers

http://www.arts-et-metiers.net/

★★★

👫 14-18

This French site contains a QuickTime virtual visit to Foucault's pendulum in the Pantheon, a RealAudio tape of a dulcimer player, and a link to online radio. It also has a database of 45,000 objects online. The site can be a little confusing at times, but there are many neat links to follow.

Museum of Bad Art

http://glyphs.com/moba/

Ⓢ

★★★★

The Museum of Bad Art is dedicated to the collection, preservation, exhibition, and celebration of bad art. The site contains many examples of bad art, including one rather amusing piece entitled "Sunday On The Pot With George." Be sure to check out the MOBA gift store, where you can purchase miniature art reproductions!

Museum of Fine Arts, Boston

http://www.mfa.org/

Ⓢ

★★★★★

👫 All

This museum prides itself on exhibiting art that is "past and present, old and new, plain and fancy," including masterpieces by Renoir, Monet, Sargent, Turner, Gauguin, and others. The site hosts an online exhibition and contains links to samples from upcoming exhibits. Learn about upcoming exhibitions and purchase museum products online.

Museum of Fine Arts, Houston

http://mfah.org

★★★★★

👫 All

The Museum of Fine Arts, Houston site, includes visuals and information about the permanent collection, traveling exhibitions, events, and educational programs. Collections with online links include African sculpture, American painting, ancient art, decorative arts, Impressionist painting, and twentieth-century sculpture.

Museum of Modern Art, New York

http://www.moma.org/

★★★★★

👫 All

This site displays samples from current and future exhibits, as well as from MOMA's permanent collection, which includes paintings and sculptures, drawings, prints and illustrated books, architecture and design, photographs, and film and video. The collection includes exceptional groups of work by Matisse, Picasso, Miró, Mondrian, Brancusi, and Pollock. It also contains links to online projects as well as other websites created in conjunction with the Museum of Modern Art and its exhibits. A wealth of information is available about this New York City landmark. Be sure to check out the online gift store.

National Gallery of Art

http://www.nga.gov/

Ⓢ

★★★★★

👫 All

The National Gallery of Art is located in Washington D.C., but no matter where you live, if you have a computer and an Internet connection, you can tour the gallery's vast collection right here. Peruse the collection by category, take a guided tour, check out the exhibitions, learn more about the collection, and even shop online. Younger kids will find the special NGA for Kids area quite appealing.

National Gallery of Canada

http://national.gallery.ca/

★★★★

👫 All

The National Gallery of Canada is the permanent home of Canada's exceptional national art collection, which includes Canadian art, Inuit art, contemporary art, as well as European, American, and Asian art. With text descriptions in both French and English, this well-designed site showcases this large gallery housing the Canadian national art collection.

National Gallery, London

http://www.nationalgallery.org.uk/

★★★

 All

This gallery's collection of 2,300 Western European paintings includes works dating as far back as 1260. At the site, learn more about upcoming exhibitions, which are always free to the public; the gallery's permanent collection; and its artists.

The National Portrait Gallery

http://www.npg.si.edu/

★★★

 All

The portraits in the Gallery's permanent collection number more than 10,000, including portraits of 42 presidents (President George W. Bush's hasn't been added yet), all of which can be viewed at this site. Other permanent collections include "The Age of Revolution" and "Native Americans" and are supplemented by other special exhibits.

Royal Ontario Museum

http://www.rom.on.ca/

★★★

 All

This large museum has Greek, Roman, and Far Eastern art, archaeology, and natural sciences collections, as well as Native ethnology and natural history collections. Virtual exhibits include educational activities such as games, quizzes, and QuickTime movies, as well as online artifact identification and curatorial research.

The San Francisco Museum of Modern Art

http://www.sfmoma.org

★★★★

 14-18

Information about the museum's collection of modern and contemporary artwork is available, including exhibition details, a calendar of events, and educational programs. Information about the rental gallery can also be found here.

Sheldon Memorial Art Gallery and Sculpture Garden

http://sheldon.unl.edu/

★★★

Together, these two comprise more than 12,000 works of art, and the garden contains 33 sculptures exhibited year-round. The site contains a few photos of the sculptures, a schedule of upcoming exhibits, and an artist index.

The Smithsonian Institution

http://www.si.edu/

★★★★★

 All

The 150-year-old Smithsonian Institution comprises the National Portrait Gallery, the National Museum of American Art, the National Air and Space Museum, the Sackler Gallery, the Cooper-Hewitt Museum of Design, the National Museum of American History, the National Museum of Natural History, and more. You can search this comprehensive site using an A–Z subject index and learn about events and activities. Special areas just for kids.

The University of Memphis Institute of Egyptian Art and Archaeology

http://www.memphis.edu/egypt/

★★★

 All

This site includes photos and information from its Egyptian artifacts exhibit, and you can take a virtual tour of more than a dozen ancient Egyptian sites along the Nile River. Also contains links to other sites that provide information about Egypt.

The Victoria and Albert Museum

http://www.vam.ac.uk/

★★★

The Victoria and Albert Museum is the largest museum of the decorative arts in the world. Today the beautiful Victorian and Edwardian buildings house 145 galleries containing some of the world's greatest collections of sculpture, furniture, fashion and textiles, paintings, silver, glass, ceramics, jewelry, books, prints, and photographs.

A
B
C
D
E
F
G
H
I
J
K
L
M
N
O
P
Q
R
S
T
U
V
W
X
Y
Z

A B C D E F G H I J K L M N O P Q R S T U V W X Y Z

Web Gallery of Art

http://www.kfki.hu/~arthp/index1.html

★★★★★

The Web Gallery of Art boasts a collection of over 11,600 digital reproductions of European paintings and sculptures from 1150 to 1800 A.D., along with commentary and biographies of many of the artists. Search for a specific piece or take a guided tour through the gallery. This site is somewhat off the beaten track, but well worth the detour.

Webmuseum

http://www.ibiblio.org/louvre/

★★★

All

Site includes a small tour of Paris, a unique Famous Paintings collection, and an exhibition of medieval art, *Les Très Riches Heures du Duc de Ber*. The site always features at least one special exhibit—such as a great collection of works by Post-Impressionist Paul Cézanne.

Whitney Museum of American Art

http://www.whitney.org/index.shtml

★★★

This site contains selections from the permanent collection of twentieth-century American art, as well as links to other art museums. The museum also sponsors artists working on the Web and provides links to some artists' Web projects. View the online exhibition or gather information about entrance to the Manhattan museum.

HISTORY AND CULTURE

Bosnia and Herzegovina Pavilion at XIX Triennale di Milano

http://www.iht.it/arte/bih/bos-id-e.htm

★★★

14-18

Contains pictures and a wealth of historical information from *Reconstruction of Bosnia and Herzegovina*, shown at the Triennale di Milano XIX Esposizione Internazionale. The page—available in Italian, English, and Bosnian—contains links to other websites concerning Bosnia-Herzegovina.

Morikami Museum and Japanese Gardens

http://www.morikami.org/

★★★

The only museum in the United States dedicated exclusively to the living culture of Japan, this museum contains a rare Bonsai collection of miniature trees and has beautiful Japanese-style landscaping. Sample photos from the museum's exhibits of Japanese arts, crafts, and artifacts are included at this site.

Museum of Tolerance

http://www.wiesenthal.com/mot/

★★★

14-18

Take an online tour of this interactive museum that focuses on prejudice and racism in America, as well as the horrors of the Holocaust, as examples of inhumanity. Read biographies of children of the Holocaust, which are updated daily, and make arrangements to visit the Los Angeles museum in person.

National Civil Rights Museum

http://www.civilrightsmuseum.org/

★★★

All

The National Civil Rights Museum presents a timeline of the civil rights struggle relating to African-Americans, with emphasis on the significant events of the 1950s and 1960s. Take an online tour or get more information about the facility at the website.

UCLA Fowler Museum of Cultural History

http://www.fmch.ucla.edu/

★★★

14-18

UCLA's Fowler Museum "celebrates the world's diverse cultures and rich visual arts, especially those of Africa, Asia, Oceania, Native, and Latin America," through exhibitions and publications.

University of Hartford Museum of American Political Life

http://www.hartford.edu/polmus/polmus1.html

★★★

 All

The more than 60,000 artifacts related to presidential life in America form the basis of presentations, exhibits, and discussions at the museum. Great place for American history buffs of all ages.

United States Holocaust Memorial Museum

http://www.ushmm.org/

(S)

★★★★

 All

This museum is an international resource for the development of research on the Holocaust and related issues, including those of contemporary significance. Includes a photographic, film, and video archive. The site contains links to museum resources and activities, as well as to related organizations and an internship program.

Wright Brothers Aeroplane Company and Museum of Aviation

http://www.first-to-fly.com/

★★★★

All

Enjoy hands-on aviation fun at this museum, which offers virtual adventures and expeditions in four Wright brothers' planes, as well as historical information. The site contains a lot of information about planes and aviation that is perfect for students.

NATURAL HISTORY

American Museum of Natural History

http://www.amnh.org/

(S)

★★★★

 All

The museum's collections include the world's largest collection of fossil mammals, dinosaurs, insects, invertebrates, and more. The site lists a few of its thousands of research projects, along with some photos. The museum displays a wide range of temporary exhibits, which also can be explored at this site. Search the site to find specific information about animals of interest.

Related (Kid) Site
http://www.ology.amnh.org/

The Carnegie Museum of Natural History

http://www.carnegiemuseums.org/cmnh/

★★★★

 All

Founded in 1895, the Carnegie Museum of Natural History is one of the nation's leading research museums and is renowned for its Dinosaur Hall. This page was established to provide news of the museum's events, as well as developments in the field of natural history in general. It is divided into 13 different and wide-ranging scientific sections, from anthropology and birds to minerals and nature reserves.

The Cleveland Museum of Natural History

http://www.cmnh.org/

★★★★

 All

This museum has more than one million specimens in the fields of anthropology, archaeology, astronomy, botany, geology, paleontology, zoology, and wildlife biology. It also has educational programs and links to exhibits and museum news.

A
B
C
D
E
F
G
H
I
J
K
L
M
N
O
P
Q
R
S
T
U
V
W
X
Y
Z

A
B
C
D
E
F
G
H
I
J
K
L
M
N
O
P
Q
R
S
T
U
V
W
X
Y
Z

The Field Museum

http://www.fmnh.org/

★★★★★

 All

Use this site to find out what's new at Chicago's Field Museum, which has featured Sue, the largest, most complete T-Rex exhibit in the world; the Dead Sea Scrolls; and maneless tigers, called Tsavos. This is one of the largest and most diverse museums in the world.

Florida Museum of Natural History

http://www.flmnh.ufl.edu/

★★★

 All

With more than 16 million specimens, this is the largest museum of natural history in the southern United States. This site features descriptions of its collections in both the Department of Anthropology and the Department of Natural Sciences, which include mammals, birds, fossils, plants, and more.

Natural History Museum of Los Angeles County

http://www.lam.mus.ca.us/

★★★

 All

Descriptions of current and upcoming exhibits at the museum, plus a calendar of events, information on membership and group visits, and a few online presentations.

Natural History Museum in the United Kingdom

http://www.nhm.ac.uk/

★★★

 All

This site defines and explains each of the museum's five main departments and also discusses its six focus areas for research. For each department (Botany, Zoology, Entomology, Paleontology, and Mineralogy), the site provides photos and details about several ongoing research projects at the museum.

Smithsonian National Museum of Natural History

http://www.mnh.si.edu/

★★★★★

 All

This extensive site has everything you ever wanted to know about this museum. Read about museum exhibitions, such as the return of Ishi, Echinoderms, and the giant squid. Online exhibits relate to global warming, hologlobes, and crossroads of continents, among others.

Swedish Museum of Natural History

http://www.nrm.se/

★★★

 All

The largest museum in Sweden, it has more than 18 million objects and is one of the 10 largest natural history museums in the world. The page is divided into the following categories: Research, Exhibitions, Events and Education, Cosmonova (one of the most modern Omni-max theaters in the world), and Administration and Service.

Related Sites
http://www.cyberspacemuseum.com/
http://www.dallasdino.org/

PAPERMAKING, PRINTING, AND TYPESETTING

American Museum of Papermaking

http://www.ipst.edu/amp/

★★★

This renowned resource on the history of paper and paper technology features a collection of watermarks, papers, tools, machines, and manuscripts. You can go on a virtual tour of the museum and learn about topics such as forerunners to paper, the invention of the paper machine, and recycling in the paper industry.

Melbourne Museum of Printing

http://home.vicnet.net.au/~typo/

★★★★

This is a working and teaching museum of type and printing. Its collection includes machines, information about fonts, and other printing items. It also has links to books and records that have to do with printing and businesses of that type (no pun intended).

Paper, Printing, Publishing, and Typesetting/Typography

http://www.trans-link.com/printing.html

★★★★

This site provides a comprehensive directory of links to sites that specialize in all areas of printing and publishing. Several links to various glossaries.

PHOTOGRAPHY AND FILM

Berkeley Art Museum/Pacific Film Archive

http://www.bampfa.berkeley.edu/

$

★★★★

The visual arts center of the University of California at Berkeley, the UAM/PFA is noted for its thought-provoking exhibitions of both art and film. The museum website contains online versions of current and former exhibitions.

California Museum of Photography

http://www.cmp.ucr.edu/

★★★★

14-18

This site contains photos, descriptions, and other information from exhibits at this museum, as well as links to a museum store, with copies of featured photos from the exhibit for sale. (Items in the store link to Amazon.com, where you can place your order.)

George Eastman House: International Museum of Photography and Film

http://www.eastman.org/

★★★

14-18

Take a look at the timeline of photography, learn more about the photographic and film exhibitions, and find out about upcoming workshops at this museum.

International Center of Photography

http://www.icp.org/

★★★★

14-18

Established to collect twentieth-century works, this center has a special emphasis on documentary photography. The center, located in New York City, also teaches all levels of photography. Site contains photos from special exhibits.

National Museum of Photography, Film, and Television

http://www.nmpft.org.uk/

★★★★

All

This museum contains varied displays, interactive features, large and small screens, and constantly changing special exhibitions, events, theater, and education. Catch up on online research projects and learn about upcoming exhibitions here.

Smithsonian Photographs Online

http://photo2.si.edu/

★★★

All

This site makes the photographic offerings of the Smithsonian available online. Browse the contents or search a huge library of photographs by keyword.

A B C D E F G H I J K L **M** N O P Q R S T U V W X Y Z

A
B
C
D
E
F
G
H
I
J
K
L
M
N
O
P
Q
R
S
T
U
V
W
X
Y
Z

Underwater Photography: Philip Colla

http://www.oceanlight.com/

★★★★★

 All

Gallery of some of the most beautiful underwater photos covering all aspects of marine life and ecology by Philip Colla. If you have a publication that requires some top-notch undersea photos, this is the place to purchase a license for some of the best photos you'll find.

ORGANIZATIONS

American Association of Museums

http://www.aam-us.org/

$

★★★

This organization provides a focal point for professionals in museum and museum-related fields, and currently has more than 16,000 members. Every type of museum is represented in its membership, from arboretums to youth museums. Site links to membership information, newsletters, and a bookstore.

Group for Education in Museums

http://www.gem.org.uk/

★★★

Group for anyone concerned with education in museums. Site contains links to excerpts from the quarterly newsletter, the annual *Journal of Education in Museums*, and other publications. Also contains links to lists of museums.

James Renwick Alliance

http://www.jra.org/

★★★

A national nonprofit organization created to support the Renwick Gallery of the Smithsonian American Art Museum of the Smithsonian Institution, Washington, D.C. The site links to the history of the gallery, membership information, a newsletter, and more.

The Museum Security Network

http://www.museum-security.org/indexdefinitief.html?

★★★

This initiative by security managers of leading Dutch museums aims to present a global platform for all aspects of museum and art security. The site has articles about security matters, law links, and searchable databases. Also links to other similar sites.

Museum Trustee Association

http://www.mta-hq.org/

★★★

The only organization in the nation that "provides ongoing board education programs, services and resources for the special needs of museum trustees." Learn more about the history of MTA, register for its newsletter, available workshops, and membership benefits.

SCIENCE AND TECHNOLOGY

Adler Planetarium and Astronomy Museum

http://www.adlerplanetarium.org/

$

★★★★

 All

This Web home of the Alder Planetarium and Astronomy Museum features astronomy FAQs, a Skywatchers Guide, and information about what you can see at this Chicago facility. Though it's no substitute for a visit to the museum, this site provides a preview of what you can find at the museum and in your own star-gazing adventures.

The Exploratorium

http://www.exploratorium.edu/

$

★★★★

All

The Exploratorium is a collage of 650 interactive exhibits in the areas of science, art, and human perception. It provides access to and information about science, nature, art, and technology. The site has online versions of exhibits and tons of other scientific information.

Kelsey Museum of Archaeology

http://www.lsa.umich.edu/kelsey/

★★★

👫 All

This site contains maps of the ancient world and other online resources for classical art and archeology. It also shows photos of objects on display in the museum's two main galleries, The Greek and Roman Gallery and The Egyptian and Near Eastern Gallery.

The Museum of Contemporary Ideas

http://toolshed.artschool.utas.edu.au/moci/home.html

★★★★

👫 14-18

This unique museum delves into the worlds of the visual arts, the philosophy of science, architecture, technology, performing arts, and off-planet systems.

The Museum of Science and Industry, Chicago

http://www.msichicago.org/

$

★★★★★

👫 All

This site contains online exhibits that provide a sample of the experiences available at the museum. It also provides Omnimax film clips and educational resources for teachers, as well as exhibit schedules and general information about the Chicago area.

National Museum of Science and Technology, Canada

http://www.science-tech.nmstc.ca/

★★★★

👫 All

This museum was created to explore "the transformation of Canada." Different subjects of the museum include agriculture, communications, energy, forestry, graphic arts, transportation, and many others. Links and descriptions are provided for all subjects as well as for behind-the-scenes information such as restoration.

Oregon Museum of Science and Industry

http://www.omsi.edu/

$

★★★★

👫 All

Observe vibrations and sound waves in the museum's Electronics Lab or weave your own piece of the Web in the Computer Lab. This site provides links to all the museum's main areas, complete with photos and descriptions of many exhibits. You'll find a lot of great information at this site.

Questacon: National Science and Technology Centre

http://www.questacon.edu.au/

★★★★★

👫 All

This site includes fun activities and links for Australia's national science museum. You can take a virtual tour of the galleries and explore the hands-on zone, all without leaving the comfort of home (or paying for a trip to Australia).

Shedd Aquarium

http://www.sheddnet.org/

★★★★★

👫 All

Find out about animals and exhibits at this Chicago aquarium, where you can Ask Shedd about an aquatic topic, such as caring for a home aquarium, or a particular animal at the aquarium.

Stephen Birch Aquarium Museum

http://www.aquarium.ucsd.edu/

★★★★★

👫 All

Part of the Scripps Institution of Oceanography, this aquarium offers volunteer opportunities, educational programs, and summer learning adventures. This home page provides information about all these, plus links to what's new at the aquarium and membership information.

A B C D E F G H I J K L M N O P Q R S T U V W X Y Z

A
B
C
D
E
F
G
H
I
J
K
L
M
N
O
P
Q
R
S
T
U
V
W
X
Y
Z

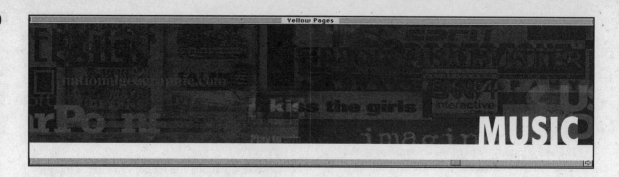

BUYING RESOURCES

AllCheapMusicEtc.com

http://allcheapmusicetc.com/

★★★★

This company purchases CDs from music stores that are going out of business and resells them at bargain prices. You won't find many new releases here, but you will find a bargain bin of $1.99 and $2.99 CDs and many other older CDs at bargain prices.

AlphaCraze.com

http://www.alphacraze.com/

★★★★

Discount retail store offers great prices on CDs and DVDs as well as on books, consumer electronics, and software. Before you purchase a CD, check this site to see whether you can find a better price.

Amazon.com

http://www.oceanlight.com/

★★★★★

Amazon.com started out selling books online. Now it sells CDs, DVDs, and just about anything else a major retail store sells. Good prices and great service.

Barnes & Noble.com

http://music.barnesandnoble.com/

★★★★

This popular bookstore has been selling CDs for quite some time, check out the selection and prices and place your order online.

BeatPort

http://www.beatport.com/

★★★★★

BeatPort is an online music store designed to help DJs find great dance music at affordable prices. Here, you can sample thousands of tracks and purchase only the tracks you really like. Site is very easy to navigate and search.

BestBuy.com

http://www.bestbuy.com/

★★★★★

The largest consumer electronics store in the nation now delivers a huge collection of CD and DVD titles at competitive prices.

Bleep

http://www.warprecords.com/bleep/

★★★★★

Warp Records in Britain features this online music store where you can purchase entire albums or individual tracks in MP3 format for less than the cost of those same tracks on CD. Check out the featured albums, choose to browse by artist, or search for a particular artist or album.

Blue Vision Music

http://www.bluevisionmusic.com/

★★★★

 All

Specializing in original contemporary music for kids, this online store offers a small collection of tapes, CDs, and books featuring the work of James Coffey. Sample some of the songs directly from the site (in AU format—requires a plug-in or player). The Kid's Club section offers some interesting activities for the younger set (QuickTime or other movie viewer required).

Buy.com

www.buy.com

★★★★

Pick a category of music and then search for particular artists or albums. On the right side of the site, you can find out which albums and singles are at the top of the charts. Buy.com provides free shipping, too.

CD Baby

http://www.cdbaby.com/

★★★★

Online music store specializing in CDs from independent artists. If you recorded a CD, CD Baby can help you sell it online. You can even sample one or two songs from a CD before you decide to purchase it.

CDnow

http://www.cdnow.com/

★★★★

CDnow claims to be the world's largest music store, and this site seems to back up that statement, with an amazing number of titles available. Plenty of RealAudio sound clips. Gift certificates for those who have everything; the personalized gift program can also recommend 10 gift ideas based on the names of four artists.

CD Universe

http://www.cduniverse.com/

★★★★

CD Universe promises the most music at the best prices. The interface is particularly easy to use, with graphics augmented by text to explain the purpose of each section (you don't need to spend as much time roaming around to find the section you want). Interested in the top-flight artists in each genre? Check out the Charts section.

CHEAP-CDS

http://cheap-cds.com/surf/finds1

★★★

Glitz-free store offering new CDs for less than $13.

eFolkMusic.com

http://www.efolkmusic.org/

★★★

Download MP3 folk, Celtic, and bluegrass music for just 49 cents. You'll also find free MP3s, in addition to music news and information about your favorite folk artists.

GEMM: Global Electronic Music Marketplace

http://gemm.com

★★★

Enables you to search for information about artists, albums, and companies from more than 16 million listings. Lets you register to be notified when a particular item you want is mentioned elsewhere in the marketplace.

A
B
C
D
E
F
G
H
I
J
K
L
M
N
O
P
Q
R
S
T
U
V
W
X
Y
Z

A
B
C
D
E
F
G
H
I
J
K
L
M
N
O
P
Q
R
S
T
U
V
W
X
Y
Z

getmusic.com

http://www.getmusic.com/

★★★

Get prerelease news, audio and video clips of your favorite artists, as well as access to plenty of music here. Download clips and free MP3s and then buy that release you've been thinking about here. The site covers just about every type of music.

Gracenote

http://www.cddb.com/

★★★

Download a free CDDB-enabled CD player so that you can play CDs on your computer and access information about the music that appears on the screen at the same time.

iTunes

http://www.apple.com/itunes/store/shop.html

★★★★★

One of the most popular online music stores, Apple iTunes provides a simple interface for searching for and downloading complete albums or selected tracks for about a dollar per tune. You can sample any tune before purchasing it. Great way to stock your CD and MP3 library. iTunes also has audiobooks available.

Raag: Indian Music

http://www.webcom.com/raag/

★★★

Audio CDs, cassettes, and videos (on DVD and laser disc) from India and around the world. According to the site, this store features "Classical, Carnatic, Hindustani, Hindi, Tamil, Telugu, Bengali, Malayalam, Punjabi, Bhangra, Gujarati, Marathi, Ghazals, Bhajans, Meditation, Kundalini, Chakras, etc." Quite a selection! Check out the Buyers' Club page for special discounts.

Musicplasma

http://www.musicplasma.com/

★★★★

Musicplasma features one of the more interesting music search interfaces on the Web. Here, you enter the name of your favorite artist, and Musicplasma displays a solar system of artists and groups whose sound might appeal to you. You can then click links to order CDs online. Cool concept, but when we visited, we could not bring some parts of the web page into view, making it difficult to navigate.

Sam Goody Music

http://www.samgoody.com/

★★★★

Just about every type of music for every possible taste is available here. This online extension of Sam Goody's brick-and-mortar stores offers CDs, tapes, and videos, as well as sheet music.

Siren Disc Online Music Store

http://www.sirendisc.com/

★★★

Specializes in imported and alternative music. The site also boasts a nicely done catalog; you can search the database alphabetically or browse as you like. Be sure to check the Treasure Chest section for one-of-a-kind or specialty items each time you stop in.

SonyMusicDirect.com

http://www.sonymusicdirect.com/

★★★★

 All

A division of Sony Music Entertainment, Inc., that's dedicated to delivering thousands of CD and DVD titles directly to the consumer at bargain prices. Children can click the Kids Corner link for special selections.

TowerRecords.com

http://www.towerrecords.com/

★★★★★

Search for particular bands or types of music, or just browse the listings to find something of interest. The site offers CDs for under $7 and new releases you'll want to pay attention to. You can also listen to tracks before you buy them.

Virgin Megastore

http://www.virginmega.com/

★★★★

Get digital downloads and exclusive music news and clips, as well as a huge selection of music for sale in just about every category, at Virgin Records.

World Wide Music

http://www.worldwidemusic.com/

★★★

Online music store allows you to listen to 30-second sound samples from more than 50,000 albums before you buy.

INFORMATION. NEWS. AND REVIEWS

Alternative Press Online

http://altpress.com

★★★★

 14-18

Read reviews of your favorite alternative bands, buy a back issue of an AP or preorder an upcoming one, make a custom CD, or add your two cents to the online reviews and discussions here.

AMG All Music Guide

http://allmusic.com/

★★★★

14-18

All Music Guide offers music and game reviews, biographies of performers, ratings, images, titles, and credits for current and out-of-print works. Links to Barnes & Noble to provide online shopping.

Artistdirect.com

http://www.artistdirect.com/

★★★★

14-18

This site represents a network of music-related offerings: MP3 and more, UBL.com, imusic.com, and the Artistdirect superstore. Visitors will find an overview of what each category has to offer and links to connect directly to anything that appeals. Find out what your favorite artists are listening to, read the latest music news, preview new music, buy official merchandise, and lots more.

BBC Music News

http://news.bbc.co.uk/1/hi/entertainment/music/default.stm

★★★★

14-18

Get the latest news about musicians, performers, and their music at this site. Primarily focuses on the music scene in Britain, but covers the international scene as well.

Billboard Online

http://www.billboard.com/

★★★★

14-18

This site offers fast and easy access to *Billboard Magazine*'s huge electronic library. Charts and articles from the current issue are available to visitors.

A B C D E F G H I J K L **M** N O P Q R S T U V W X Y Z

Black Beat Magazine

http://www.blackbeat.com/

★★★★

Online version of *Black Beat* magazine, the magazine for urban music and culture, primarily rap music.

CD Shakedown

http://www.cdshakedown.com

★★★

 All

Every week this site posts reviews of new music releases, including pop, rock, indie, alternative, and folk. Also included are concert information and some children's reviews.

Entertainment Weekly Online

http://www.ew.com/ew/

★★★

👫 14-18

This weekly magazine focuses on movie and television features as well as music information. A good source for general music news.

The Grindstone Magazine

http://www.grindstonemagazine.com/

$

★★★

A funky '50s retro-style guide to roadhouse, roots, and rockabilly. Call the hotline phone number to get the latest information on concerts and artists, and be sure to check out the merchandise page where you can order Grindstone Magazine T-shirts.

Hyperreal

http://www.hyperreal.org/

★★★

 Not for kids

Presents an online collaborative publishing effort that covers rave culture and electronic music. Provides links to myriad different rave and electronic music sites. Includes an archive of various sound samples, artwork, articles, and more.

ICE Online

http://www.icemagazine.com/

★★★

Based on the printed publication. The site offers a free trial subscription and provides information and exclusive articles on upcoming album releases. Also includes release dates that are updated weekly.

iMUSIC

http://imusic.artistdirect.com/

★★★★

 Not for kids

News, features, CD reviews, bulletin boards, chat rooms, and even an online music store—this site has it all. Tons of links to individual artists and bands grouped by musical category. Parents should monitor any activity on the message boards.

Jelly

http://www.jellyroll.com/

★★★

👫 14-18

This site has something for almost everyone: jazz, blues, country, soul, and rock. Issues are put online only after the latest issue comes out. If you want the most current issue, you have to subscribe.

Latin Music Online

http://www.lamusica.com/

★★★

👫 14-18

The popularity of Latin music continues to grow in the United States. This site is well designed and packed with quality news and features surrounding Latin music. Links to CDNow for shopping.

Launch Your Yahoo! Music Experience

http://launch.yahoo.com/

$

★★★★★

👫 14-18

This is Yahoo!'s pop music site, where you can find articles about your favorite musicians, groups, and CDs. Features music videos, exclusive online radio stations, downloadable music clips, and much more.

MishMash.com
http://mashmusic.tripod.com/

★★★

 14-18

Check out indie music reviews here with the latest information about up-and-coming artists. You can also order T-shirts and other MishMash merchandise online.

MTV
http://www.mtv.com/

★★★★★

👥 14-18

Weigh in with your vote for who should be cast in the next *Real World/Road Rules* crew, read interviews with top groups and artists, skim reviews of upcoming releases, and get the music news of the day here, where you can also find out about the TV schedule. Buy digital music on this site. One of the first of its kind, MTV's website remains the best of its kind.

Music Critic
http://www.music-critic.com/

★★★

👥 14-18

You'll find reviews of music, movies, games, and beer at this site. Links to Amazon.com, where you can purchase many of the items reviewed.

Music Station
http://www.musicstation.com/

★★★

👥 14-18

Learn which artists will be appearing on TV this week by clicking either on the name of the performer or the day of the week you're interested in hearing about. You can also catch up on music news and music club information. This site is divided into three areas: RockOnTV, MusicNewswire, and The CD Club Web Server.

Music Yellow Pages
http://musicyellowpages.com

★★★

Search the more than 40,000 listings in 400 categories related to the music, pro audio, lighting, and entertainment industries. Find suppliers online free or order the print edition for a fee.

NME
http://www.nme.com/

★★★★★

 Not for kids

The online home of *NME* (New Musical Express) magazine, this site features music news, reviews, concert information, charts, and much more. Bulletin boards and chat provide a means of interacting with fellow fans, and NME Radio plays in the background, so you can listen while you explore the site. The site has an attitude that's not the best for young children.

NY ROCK
http://www.nyrock.com/

★★★

Daily rock-and-roll updates, reviews, and articles with that New York flair. Categorized by band, this site also offers gossip, news, and RealAudio sound clips.

RootsWorld
http://www.rootsworld.com/

★★★★★

RootsWorld features music, art, and culture from around the world. Here you can read reviews of various artists' work, sample audio clips, and find out where to order CDs. Most reviews display an ear icon. Click the ear to listen.

A B C D E F G H I J K L M N O P Q R S T U V W X Y Z

A
B
C
D
E
F
G
H
I
J
K
L
M
N
O
P
Q
R
S
T
U
V
W
X
Y
Z

VH1.COM
http://www.vh1.com/

★★★★

👫 14-18

Read daily reviews at the online version of this cable station, where you can also get music news, find concerts coming to your area, and learn what's on tap tonight on VH1.

VIBE
http://www.vibe.com/

💲

★★★

👫 14-18

A hip-hop online magazine that features daily entertainment updates, preview videos and audio clips, and archives of past issues.

Wilson and Alroy's Record Reviews
http://www.warr.org/

★★★

Provides reviews of thousands of records, mostly rock and pop. Includes links to hundreds of other related sites. Includes some music book reviews, rock timelines, and other assorted features.

World Café
http://worldcafe.org/

💲

★★★★

Home of the *World Café*, a public radio show that provides an avenue for up-and-coming musicians to showcase their stuff. Hosted by David Dye, the show consists of a low-key interview intermixed with songs. Links to interviews that you can listen to online. Search for artists, buy CDs, enter contests, or find a local radio station that plays the show.

Worldwide Internet Music Resources
http://www.music.indiana.edu/music_resources/

★★★★

Hosted by the William and Gayle Cook Music Library at Indiana University. Contains links to almost every imaginable music-related site—artists/ensembles, composers, genres, publications, the music industry, general and miscellaneous resources, Usenet groups, research, and more.

LYRICS

Bob Dylan Music
http://orad.dent.kyushu-u.ac.jp/dylan/song.html

★★★★

👫 14-18

Are you sometimes not sure what the words are when Bob sings? Here are the lyrics to just about every Dylan song ever recorded, alphabetized by song title.

The Cyber Hymnal
http://www.cyberhymnal.org/

★★★★

👫 All

At this site, you'll find the lyrics to hundreds of gospel songs and hymns. With a sound card and speakers, you can hear the music, too. There are special areas of children's, Christmas, and Easter songs, along with biographies of song writers and hymn trivia.

Burt Bacharach: A House Is Not a Home Page
http://www.bacharachonline.com/

★★★★

Provides lyrics, biography, news, audio files, lyrics, chord sheets, and news about songwriter Burt Bacharach. Includes articles, pictures, and a list of hit songs. Also provides links to sites where you can purchase Bacharach's music.

Led Zeppelin Lyrics
http://www.alwaysontherun.net/ledzep.htm

★★★

👥 14-18

This site contains the lyrics to many Led Zeppelin songs. Just click the song title and read the lyrics. The links will take you to a master index of lyrics for many groups.

Music Database
http://www.cs.nott.ac.uk/~ef//music/database.htm

★★★

👥 14-18

A collection of more than 1,000 traditional British-related folk dance tunes, divided into jigs, reels, hornpipes, and other categories. Most are chords only; some have the score in GIF format. Scores are downloadable in PostScript format in case you want to print them.

Musicnotes.com
http://musicnotes.com/

💲

★★★★★

Download digital sheet music to your PC for a small fee, print it, and play it. Choose from a huge selection of today's pop hits to classical selections. Search by title, artist, or composer to find exactly what you're looking for.

National Anthems
http://www.lengua.com/hymnen.htm

★★★

👥 14-18

The national anthems of many countries are available here. You'll find them in their original form or with an English translation. Click the speaker to hear the anthem you've chosen. This is a growing site, so you might want to contribute any information you have about other national anthems, their lyrics, music, or history.

Phil's Home Page
http://www.iinet.net.au/~pgb/

★★★★

👥 14-18

Phil has chosen quite a few songs to provide lyrics for, and they're all meaningful. He even suggests certain times when each song would be appropriate. Want to tell someone how you feel, but you're at a loss for words? Check these lyrics.

Schoolhouse Rock Lyrics
http://www.apocalypse.org/pub/u/gilly/Schoolhouse_Rock/HTML/grammar/grammar.html

★★★

👥 0-8

Here are the lyrics to those cute Schoolhouse Rock songs. Remember *Conjunction Junction*? Just click the title and see all the words.

Scout Song Book
http://www.emf.net/~troop24/scouting/songbook.html

★★★

👥 0-8

If you're in need of some Scout songs, including campfire singalongs, slower ballads, or inspirational tunes, visit this site for many selections.

Twisted Tunes
http://www.twistedtunes.com/

★★★

👥 Not for kids

Bob Rivers as Weird Al Yankovic. Features downloadable hits such as *Livin' La Vida Yoda* and *Dirty Deeds Done with Sheep*.

A B C D E F G H I J K L M N O P Q R S T U V W X Y Z

MP3-RESOURCES

Artist Direct Free MP3
http://listen.artistdirect.com/

★★★★

👥 14-18

Register at DownloadsDirect to be able to download the hottest music from every conceivable genre for a small fee. Some of it is even available at no charge. There is a huge selection of music. You can also read columns written by critics.

audiogalaxy
http://www.audiogalaxy.com/

★★★★

👥 14-18

Home of Rhapsody, a subscription service ($10 per month) that enables you to download music clips, listen to radio stations online, and burn CDs (CD burning costs an additional $.99 per track). Royalties are paid to the various music companies and artists, making this all legal. More than 19,000 albums from more than 8,000 artists.

emusic
http://www.emusic.com/

★★★★

👥 14-18

Download music tracks for one low monthly fee. Try it free for one month. More than 200,000 MP3s to choose from.

Epitonic.com
http://www.epitonic.com/

★★★

Choose to download clips or entire songs at this site, all free. Most bands you might not have heard of—yet. But the site offers a wide array to choose from.

Furthur Network
http://www.furthurnet.com/

★★★★★

Many performers and bands encourage their fans to share their recordings of live shows. Furthur Network enables fans to do this online via special peer-to-peer network sharing. Visit this site to download the software and hook up with thousands of fans to share your recordings of live shows. If you're a taper or want to hook up with some tapers, this is the place to be.

Heavy.com
http://www.heavy.com/

★★★★

👥 14-18

Heavy.com features some free MP3 audio clips, video games, jokes, and other self-described cultural material to keep you entertained. This site features its Sumosonic collection of CDs that are a must for any serious music fan, which you can order online.

iMesh
http://www.imesh.com/

★★★★

This site features file-swapping software, similar to KaZaA and Morpheus, that enables users to swap files (usually MP3 music files) and chat online.

KaZaA
http://www.kazaa.com

★★★★★

👥 14-18

Internet file-sharing program enables users to swap files, including games, audio clips, video clips, and shareware over the Internet. Relies on the honor system to prevent users from breaking copyright laws.

listen.com

http://www.listen.com/

★★★★

Listen.com provides a music-on-demand subscription service. You pay a monthly subscription fee and then pick the artists and songs you want to hear. Listen.com provides you with unlimited playback time for the selected songs.

Morpheus

http://www.morpheus.com/

★★★★★

A program similar to Napster that allows users to swap MP3 files on the Internet. As of the writing of this book, Morpheus was the only online file-sharing program that was ruled legal in the United States.

MP3.com

http://www.mp3.com/

★★★★

👥 14-18

The leader of the MP3 phenomenon that has more than 250,000 songs available for you to sample for free.

MP3 Nexus

http://www.bigg.net/

★★★★

Download players, search other MP3 sites for music, get the latest digital music news, and download songs for your personal enjoyment.

MP3Nut

http://www.mp3nut.com/

★★★★★

Huge, searchable database of MP3 files. A little difficult to maneuver at first, but if you read the screens and follow the instructions, this might just turn out to be your favorite MP3 site on the Web.

MPEG.ORG

http://www.mpeg.org

★★★

A directory of links to MP3 sites with downloadable music, as well as MP3 news and information.

Napster

http://www.napster.com

★★★★

Originally the most popular place on the Internet for swapping MP3 music clips with other music lovers, this service has undergone major renovation to make it legal. Napster no longer is an MP3 file-sharing program, but a service that enables you to download a certain number of tracks for a monthly fee. Select from more than 500,000 tracks!

MP3—SEARCH ENGINES

theinfo.com

http://www.theinfo.com/music/

★★★

👥 14-18

A music search engine that allows you to put all your criteria in one screen. You can also find music and links to buy it direct from online stores such as Amazon.com.

LYCOS: MP3 Search

http://music.lycos.com/downloads/

★★★

Search for music using the Lycos search engine. You can find not only music but also software to play back that music by using this fast and easy-to-use interface. Music is categorized by genre.

Media Crawler

http://search.mp3.de/

★★★★★

 14-18

Excellent search engine for finding music clips and other media files. Simply type the artist or group name or the name of the desired song in the Search box and click the Show Results button.

A
B
C
D
E
F
G
H
I
J
K
L
M
N
O
P
Q
R
S
T
U
V
W
X
Y
Z

Search MP3
http://www.searchmpthree.com/

★★★

14-18

This search engine allows you to search for songs and music videos created by various artists and placed on the site for promotional purposes. You can also purchase CDs through links to Amazon.com.

MUSIC EVENTS

Blues Festivals
http://www.bluesfestivals.com/

★★★★

14-18

A fantastic site full of listings and links to blues festivals nationwide. Bookmark this one; it's a must for any true blues fan

CC.com
http://sfx.com/

$

★★★★

14-18

Formed through the merger of Sunshine Promotions and SFX Entertainment, this site provides information about some of the hottest live shows on the circuit, including Nick Cave, The Cranberries, Paul McCartney, U2, and Jamie Foxx. Links to Ticketmaster to purchase tickets.

Live Online: Music Events Calendar
http://www.live-online.com/

★★★

A listing of online live concerts, chats, and listening parties, complete with the date, time, and name of the featured band. Offers options, such as Everyone's a Critic, where you can voice your opinion on a Web-only prerelease preview. If the folks behind this site like your critique, they'll post it and you could win some cool stuff.

Mardi Gras Official Website
http://www.mardigrasday.com/

★★★

Although it is now known primarily as a drunkfest, Mardi Gras includes some fantastic music and draws musicians from all over to join in the festivities. Check out this site for details and schedules of music events.

Mojam
http://www.mojam.com

★★★

Find music events by searching the database for cities, venues, or artists. Or click on one of the lists of top tours, or new tours, to find out where the groups are headed. You can also learn more about what events are coming up in major U.S. cities simply by clicking on the city name. If you're a band or promoter, you can add information about an upcoming event to the calendar as well.

Musi-Cal
http://www.musi-cal.com/

★★★

This site provides access to worldwide live music information about concerts, festivals, and musical events. Search by performer, venue, city, or event.

Music City Attractions
http://musiccityattractions.com/

★★★

Traveling shows originating from Nashville, Tennessee. Check the tour calendar to see when the show will be coming to a town near you.

Pollstar: The Concert Hotwire
http://www.pollstar.com/

★★★★

This online weekly media magazine geared for the concert industry publishes several industry directories, performer tour histories, mailing labels, and directories on disk. Search the site for upcoming concert information by band name or venue.

Ticketmaster.com

http://www.ticketmaster.com/

★★★★★

Find music and sporting events, as well as upcoming theater and comedy performances, by searching the Ticketmaster site by keyword, artist, or location. You can then charge your tickets by phone or purchase your tickets online.

Related Site
http://tickets.msn.com/

TicketWeb

http://www.ticketweb.com

★★★★

Online box office that simplifies the process of obtaining tickets to concerts, plays, museums, and other interesting and entertaining places and events.

tkt.com

http://www.tkt.com/

★★★

Scalper website, where you can buy or sell tickets to some of the top events at astronomical prices.

Related Site
http://www.tixx.com/
http://www.ticketsnow.com/

MUSIC GENRES—ALTERNATIVE

Alien Ant Farm

http://www.alienantfarm.com/

★★★★★

👥 14-18

Features spiffy Flash presentation of the band, showcasing its unique sounds and performances. Fans can read the latest news headlines, check out concert information, access biographies, check out links to related sites, and even shop for memorabilia online.

Brave Combo

http://brave.com/bo/

★★★

👥 All

"Nuclear polka" is probably the best way to describe this Texas-based group. This great-looking site with content to match is an excellent reflection of the group's talent. You'll find a discography, band profiles, a calendar of upcoming appearances, and more.

The Color Red

http://www.thecolorred.com/

★★★★

👥 14-18

Sample music from the latest album of this West Coast rock band, read about how the members got together, and find out where some of the upcoming shows are.

The Cramps

http://www.geocities.com/thecrampspage/

★★★★

👥 14-18

Rockabilly band with some punk flavor and a taste for fetish-wear, The Cramps were big on the alternative scene before there was an alternative scene (in the early and mid 1970s). Visit this site for photos of the band and other interesting tidbits.

Creed

http://www.creednet.com/

★★★★

👥 14-18

Check out Creed's home page, where you'll find music and video clips, a well-stocked photo gallery, concert information, and much more.

A
B
C
D
E
F
G
H
I
J
K
L
M
N
O
P
Q
R
S
T
U
V
W
X
Y
Z

A B C D E F G H I J K L M N O P Q R S T U V W X Y Z

The Cure

http://www.thecure.com

★★★

👥 14-18

One of the first bands to be considered "alternative," The Cure evolved from very basic punk rock beginnings to become darker and more melancholy and then eventually somewhat twisted. This official site provides some very scant information about the band and a few photos. When I visited, none of the links to sound clips functioned. Try http://www.sirenscure.com/resources.html for links to other sites.

D'CuCKOO

http://home.earthlink.net/~sabean2/bandlife.html

★★★★

👥 All

The techno-tribal band is made up of six women from Oakland who build and play their own percussion instruments, including 6-foot bamboo "trigger sticks." This site features information about the band, its famous MidiBall, and RiGBy, the computer-generated puppet. The band's music mixes sophisticated pop vocals and lyrics with techno, dance, and world music influences.

Dave Matthews Band

http://www.dmband.com/

★★★★★

👥 14-18

Join the announcement list to receive word of news and updates regarding this popular band. You can also investigate the band's history, check its tour schedule, read about the members and view their photos, or order Dave Matthews Band merchandise.

Depeche Mode Home Page

http://www.depechemode.com/

Ⓢ

★★★

👥 14-18

This official site of eclectic alternative band Depeche Mode includes news about the band, upcoming releases, concert information, video clips, and more.

does not

http://www.doesnot.com/

★★★★

👥 14-18

Very high-tech site plays multimedia clips of several of the band's songs. Also features music videos, audio clips, bios, and more.

The Fall

http://www.visi.com/fall/

★★★

👥 14-18

Here, you'll find articles, interviews, a history, and a discography of the U.K. rock group, The Fall. Includes lyric transcriptions, bibliography, discography, and much more.

GreenDay.com

http://www.greenday.com/

Ⓢ

★★★★

👥 14-18

The official site of Green Day. Here, you can find news about the band and its upcoming tours, check out its CDs and video clips, visit the photo gallery, and even join the "Idiot Club." Online shopping for apparel and other merchandise.

Ink Blot Magazine: Deep Coverage of Great Music

http://www.inkblotmagazine.com/

★★★

👥 14-18

Ink Blot online music magazine features album reviews, band interviews, music industry gossip, RealAudio music clips, pictures, and much more. This e-zine is biweekly and free.

Intellectually Alternative Music

http://www.iarmusic.com/

★★★

 14-18

Located in Alexandria, Virginia, the folks behind this site promote new music, intellectually alternative rock music, and new artists that they believe in. This site allows you to listen to the music they promote via MP3/Real Player before it's even for sale. Register your radio station to receive the next promotional CD, and if you are a local, find out how you can use the group's studios for a nominal fee.

Korn

http://www.korn.com/

★★★★

 Not for kids

Watch KornTV—a.k.a. Kornography—at the band's site, browse the photo gallery, read and post messages on the many message boards, and find out when the band will be playing near you. You can also find which shows are going to be rescheduled.

Limp Bizkit

http://www.limpbizkit.com/

$

★★★★

Not for kids

Take a look at tour pictures, use the lyrics section to double-check those lyrics you weren't sure of, order merchandise, and link to the band's site.

Lou Reed and the Velvet Underground

http://www.rocknroll.net/loureed/

★★★★★

14-18

You'll find information about Lou Reed, the Velvet Underground, and more here. Includes, among other things, a bootleg gallery, a discography, an image gallery, and comments on the latest tour.

Nettwerk Productions

http://www.nettwerk.com/

★★★

14-18

Home of Nettwerk Records. Check out the Unforscene Music section for information on alternative artists and groups signed with this label.

Nick Cave Online

http://www.nick-cave.com/

★★★★

This official home page of the gothic blues rock music of Nick Cave and the Bad Seeds includes current news, articles, interviews, and links to other related sites in a well-organized format.

No Doubt

http://www.nodoubt.com/

$

★★★★

14-18

Home of No Doubt, creators of the smash hit "Hey Baby," this site features a huge collection of tidbits about the band and its members, plus several music and video clips, a photo gallery, tour information, links to related sites, and more.

The Offspring

http://www.offspring.com/

$

★★★★

14-18

Tons of information about the rock band The Offspring. Includes pictures, videos, lyrics, discography, articles, images, sound clips (in WAV and RealAudio), and interviews, plus chat rooms and message boards where you can stay in touch with fellow fans.

A B C D E F G H I J K L M N O P Q R S T U V W X Y Z

A
B
C
D
E
F
G
H
I
J
K
L
M
N
O
P
Q
R
S
T
U
V
W
X
Y
Z

Pearl Jam

http://www.pearljam.com/

★★★★★

👫 14-18

Pearl Jam's official home page, this site features news about the band, a discography, tour information, music videos, message boards, and even a Pearl Jam store where you can purchase "consumables" online.

Phish

http://www.phish.com

★★★★

👫 14-18

Find out everything you need to know about the band Phish—from where the band will be playing to when its next album will be released. Band news also includes information about individual members and where they'll be showing up live, onstage.

Rage Against the Machine

http://www.ratm.com/

★★★

🚫👫 Not for kids

Home of activist group Rage Against the Machine, read up on the latest happenings and band-support protests and boycotts. Plenty of music clips and photos to stoke the enthusiasm of fans and keep you coming back for more. Links to ArtistDirect for online shopping.

Red Hot Chili Peppers

http://redhotchilipeppers.com

★★★★

🚫👫 Not for kids

Get on the official Red Hot Chili Peppers email list for updates regarding albums, tours, and news. Read Flea's messages from the road and listen to Chili Peppers' music at the site.

R.E.M.

http://www.remhq.com/

★★★★★

👫 14-18

This official R.E.M. website includes news and reviews, a link to the official fan club, discography, videography, and a "Thriftstore," where you can purchase CDs, T-shirts, and other memorabilia.

rockfetish.com

http://www.thepunkpage.com/

★★★

👫 14-18

Warehouse of rock and alternative apparel, mainly T-shirts, plus caps, stickers, and patches.

Sonic Youth

http://www.xs4all.nl/~bigron/sonic/

★★★

👫 14-18

Features eight bands and five artists. Find out the story behind the lyrics, hear music, read the latest news, and explore the links. Also offers a biography of the New York City–based band Sonic Youth.

Stone Temple Pilots

http://www.stonetemplepilots.com/

★★★★★

👫 14-18

Official home page of the hard-hitting alternative rock band Stone Temple Pilots, this site features news, tour dates, discography, biographies of the band and its members, multimedia shows, a photo gallery, and more. Purchase memorabilia online.

Stunt Monkey

http://www.stuntmonkey.net/

★★★

👥 14-18

Get the latest news about this pop trio, including member bios, music clips, merchandise, and an archived listing of past shows and festivals (if you want to know where they've been).

Sub Pop Records Online

http://www.subpop.com/

$

★★★

👥 14-18

This site, the online home for Sub Pop Records, covers the underground Seattle music scene. Get reviews and hear samples of hot upcoming bands and artists, find out about tours and appearances, and check out the links to fun stuff.

Sunhawk.com

http://www.sunhawk.com/

★★★★

👥 14-18

Download, print, and play back engraving-quality sheet music! This site offers Free Solero interactive music software and a new free song every week. Thousands of best-selling titles to choose from! Digital alternative music is just one option of many.

Third Eye Blind

http://www.3eb.com/

$

★★★★★

👥 14-18

Information about the band, albums, articles, tour dates, sound and video clips, and email. Interesting graphics, by the way. Occasionally, the site goes into hibernation when the band is preparing to go on tour.

Tom Waits

http://www.officialtomwaits.com/

★★★★

👥 14-18

This official Tom Waits site features background information and insights into this enigmatic artist. Not much in the way of audio and video clips, but if you'd like to know more about Tom Waits and his variety of creative projects, this is the place to go. Provides a complete list of Waits albums, movies in which he acted, and interviews.

Tori Amos

http://www.toriamos.com/

★★★

👥 14-18

Check on Tori Amos concert dates and headlines at her official site.

The Tragically Hip: Tales from the Hip

http://www.thehip.com/

$

★★★

👥 14-18

Check out this official home for the Canadian band The Tragically Hip. You'll find lots of pictures from past tours, find out how to join the mailing list, get on the Tragically Hip web ring, read bios and reviews, and more. Check out the section on the band's latest release.

Ubu Web: Difficult Choices

http://www.dnai.com/~obo/ubu/

★★★

👥 14-18

Here's a detailed, well-crafted site with cool graphics (especially the garage!). You can find the history, discography, and graphics of the Cleveland-based "Avant-Garage" rock group Pere Ubu. The site includes album artwork, articles, FAQs, interviews, links to related sites, and ordering and contact information.

A B C D E F G H I J K L **M** N O P Q R S T U V W X Y Z

A
B
C
D
E
F
G
H
I
J
K
L
M
N
O
P
Q
R
S
T
U
V
W
X
Y
Z

Violent Femmes

http://www.vfemmes.com/

★★★★

 14-18

Check out Violent Femmes interviews, lyrics, discography, photo gallery, tour information, and more at the band's official home site. Even features a cookbook, in case you get hungry at the site.

Weird Music

http://www.weirdomusic.com/

★★★★★

Beyond alternative is weird music—"wacky, odd, and just plain bizarre music." And you can find a little of each type right here, from library music to space age pop, from sitar strumming to the best musical comedy scores, this site covers it all. Check the artist index, read the columns, sample some free MP3 downloads, and shop online.

Zwan

http://www.zwan.com/

★★★★

 14-18

Leaning toward the heavy side of alternative rock, this site is packed with free audio clips, images, and video clips. Visit the discussion forum to read and post messages about the band and its concerts. Zwan is a relatively new band formed by Billy Corgan, formerly of Smashing Pumpkins.

MUSIC GENRES—BLUEGRASS

Amazing Grass

http://www.amazinggrass.net/

★★★★

 14-18

Amazing Grass is a bluegrass band from Northeastern Wisconsin. It plays "an eclectic mix of traditional bluegrass mixed with newgrass, some original material." Here, you can check the calendar to see when and where the band is playing, view photos of members, and listen to sound clips. Don't forget to sign the guestbook!

Banjo Tablatures and Bluegrass Information

http://www.bluegrassbanjo.org/

★★★

Banjo newsletter recommended for all banjo pickers features tablatures for three-finger, clawhammer, and jazz banjo players.

Beppe Gambetta

http://www.beppegambetta.com/

★★★

An accomplished Italian acoustic guitarist who performs his traditional American guitar playing all over the world. Schedule him for your next acoustic music festival, workshop, or concert by contacting his national managing agent. Note his list of credentials, discography, and published works.

Blistered Fingers

http://www.blisteredfingers.com/

★★★

Site of all information related to June and August Blistered Fingers Family Bluegrass Festival (Waterville, Maine). In addition to festival information, you can send information if you'd like to be part of the open stage segment, find other links, and subscribe to the newsletter.

The Bluegrass Connection

http://www.gotech.com/

★★★★

Online resource where you can locate festivals and bluegrass music products and information. Also find out about record companies, manufacturers of bluegrass equipment, and instrument-supply companies.

Bluegrass Music Listings: The Country Grapevine

http://www.countrygrapevine.com/music/bluegrass/listings.htm

★★★★

Florida country music fans will enjoy tracking down their favorite bluegrass bands at this site, where you can find out about upcoming auditions, check the schedule of local bands, and join in country chat.

Bluegrass Unlimited

http://www.bluegrassmusic.com/

★★★★

This home of *Bluegrass Unlimited* magazine provides an image of the current month's issue along with a list of the top five songs, bluegrass music awards, reviews, pictures, and more.

BlueGrassRoots Master Catalog Search

http://members.tripod.com/~kc4vus/roots.html

★★★★

Enormous database of bluegrass musicians and record labels. Search the database for your favorite musician, band, or album. You can also search by the label or the year. A master catalog is available for download.

Bluegrass World

http://www.bluegrassworld.com

$

★★★★

You'll find bluegrass musicians, festivals, merchandise, record companies, catalogs, radio stations, and bluegrass music links all in one place.

Canyon Country Bluegrass Festival

http://www.canyoncountrybluegrass.com/

★★★

This is home to Canyon Country Bluegrass Festival information. Located in Pennsylvania's "Grand Canyon," this festival has been celebrated for more than 10 years.

Central Texas Bluegrass Association

http://www.centraltexasbluegrass.org/

★★★

Offers information about the Central Texas Bluegrass Association, a nonprofit corporation. Includes a calendar of events, as well as workshop and membership information.

Edgar Meyer

http://sonyclassical.com/artists/meyer/

★★★

Considered by some to be "the best bassist alive," Edgar Meyer offers downloadable clips of recent pieces at his site, as well as information about upcoming albums and collaborative efforts. Meyer performs not only bluegrass, but classical music, too.

Huck Finn's Country and Bluegrass Jubilee!

http://www.Huckfinn.com/

★★★

This country and bluegrass festival in Southern California lasts three days and also includes horseback riding, clogging, catfish fishing, boating, and crafts. Make a reservation, check the maps on how to get there, and check out the activities available.

iBluegrass Magazine

http://www.ibluegrass.com/

★★★

Listen to Bluegrass music as you scope out this site for chat, news, and festival information from its vast database, or search for a new band to listen to. You can also list festivals or bands you're involved with free by uploading information to the onsite database.

A
B
C
D
E
F
G
H
I
J
K
L
M
N
O
P
Q
R
S
T
U
V
W
X
Y
Z

Intermountain Acoustic Music Association

http://www.xmission.com/~iama/

★★★

Nonprofit organization devoted to promoting and preserving acoustic music, including bluegrass, folk, and old-time music. The IAMA sponsors various seminars, workshops, and concerts; check out the event calendar for dates and locations. There's also a monthly newsletter for members—become one by filling out the online form and sending in your membership fee.

International Bluegrass Music Association

http://www.ibma.org/

★★★

The IBMA's mission is to promote bluegrass and expand its popularity. Obtain membership information, read the latest news, or visit the International Bluegrass Museum.

Prime Cuts of Bluegrass Radio

http://www.primecutsofbluegrass.com/

★★★

This company markets bluegrass music to radio stations. The site explains the company's services for artists and DJs. It also provides a release schedule for the year, products available for purchase, a what's new section, and much more.

Rural Rhythm Classics

http://www.ruralrhythm.com/

★★★

Collection of old-time country and bluegrass albums. Click the Jukebox icon to pull up Uncle Jim's Rural Rhythms jukebox, a Shockwave jukebox on which you can select from several classic folk, country, and bluegrass tunes.

Society for the Preservation of Bluegrass Music in America

http://www.spbgma.com/

★★★★★

SPBGMA is dedicated to preserving the tradition of bluegrass music in the United States. At this site, you can find a printable order form for the *100 Classic Bluegrass and Folk Songs* book, a calendar of events and festivals, current awards, a Hall of Greats, information about the organization.

Top 100 Bluegrass Sites

http://www.bluegrassrules.com/top100.asp

★★★★

Directory of the "best" 100 bluegrass sites is a great place to start looking for information about various bands and festivals.

Tottenham Bluegrass Festival

http://www.tottenhambluegrass.ca/

★★★

Everything you want to know about the Tottenham Bluegrass Festival (Ontario, Canada). Find out location, ticket price, and performance schedule.

Washington Bluegrass Association

http://www.washingtonbluegrassassociation.org/

★★★

Extensive listing of links to bluegrass performance schedules, artists, and associations. You can also find teachers and membership information.

Welcome to Planet Bluegrass!

http://www.bluegrass.com/

★★★★

Blue Planet Music, organizers of the legendary Telluride Bluegrass Festival, is now online. The site contains a festival schedule and information, as well as information about Blue Planet recordings and its mail-order operation. You can also buy posters, T-shirts, tickets, and other merchandise from the secure server.

MUSIC GENRES— CHRISTIAN MUSIC

CCM Magazine.com
http://www.ccmcom.com/

★★★

👥 14-18

Read about provocative Christian musicians in the news section or read music reviews, listen to clips by Christian bands, or join in discussions going on at the site. You can also find interesting feature articles about bands on tour and Christian musicians in general.

CC Music
http://www.ccmusic.org/

★★★

👥 14-18

Search the extensive directories of Christian musicians and music web pages and offer your opinions of Christian musicians in the discussion groups. You'll also find links to Christian band sites.

Christian Music Resources
http://www.guitarsite.com/christian.htm

★★★★

👥 14-18

Excellent collection of links to various Christian music resource sites on the Web.

Christian Tuner
http://www.christiantuner.com/

★★★★

👥 14-18

This site provides live links to more than 600 Christian radio stations, as well as lists of Christian TV and radio stations and MP3 clips available for download. Find programs of interest on a wide range of topics just by searching the site for stations carrying subjects that you're interested in.

Jamsline: The Christian Music Info Source
http://www.jamsline.com/

💲

★★★★

👥 14-18

Cool-looking site that offers hundreds of titles for purchase, including Amy Grant, Jars of Clay, Anointed, and more.

Jars of Clay
http://www.jarsofclay.com/

★★★★★

👥 14-18

Official site of the Christian rock group Jars of Clay. Here, you'll find band and tour information, sound bites, and more. Links to Amazon.com and other online retailers where you can purchase related materials. Great-looking page! Be sure to sign up for the mailing list!

The Official Michael Card Website
http://michaelcard.com/

💲

★★★

👥 14-18

Official site for the Christian composer and musician. Offers lyrics, music, bio information, new release information, song titles, and more. Great site and well organized.

Susan Ashton
http://www.christianitytoday.com/music/artists/susanashton.html

💲

★★★

👥 14-18

Christianity Today's portrait of Susan Ashton provides a discography complete with links to her CDs, a short biography, and message boards where you can keep in touch with other Susan Ashton fans.

A B C D E F G H I J K L M N O P Q R S T U V W X Y Z

MUSIC GENRES—CLASSICAL

All Classical Guide
http://allclassical.com/

★★★

This All Media Guide to classical music offers music reviews, musician biographies, ratings, images, and titles. Simply type in the composer, work title, or album title to bring up information culled from the site's vast music database.

American Classical Music Hall of Fame
http://www.americanclassicmusic.org/

★★★★★

The official home of the American Classical Music Hall of Fame features photos and biographies of inductees along with a sampling of their musical achievements. You can also learn about the Hall of Fame and obtain instructions on how to explore this site more fully.

BMG Music
http://www.bmgmusic.com/

$

★★★★

A large online store where you can order almost any recording currently in circulation, including classical music.

The Classical Guitarist
http://www.guitarist.com/cg/cg.htm

★★★

The Classical Guitarist features classical guitar sheet music and MIDI files, a beginner's page, a guide to classical guitar in Portland Oregon, and a directory of links to other classical guitar sites.

The Classical MIDI Connection
http://www.classicalmidiconnection.com/cmc/

★★★

Contains a load of classical MIDI sequences for your perusal. You can browse the site and listen to or save any of the sequences available. This site is well organized, and you can search via composers as well as musical style.

Classical Music of the WWW Virtual Library
http://www.gprep.org/classical/

★★★

A huge resource of information available for you to read, just like at a traditional library. Search the database to learn more about particular classical composers or music, learn about classical music organizations, find out about discussion forums, brush up on music techniques, or peruse many other subcategories.

Classical USA
http://classicalusa.com/

★★★★

This site features reviews of more than 1,000 CDs, 4,800 files, and more than 2,600 links to other classical music websites. Very comprehensive directory to all things classical on the Web, including film and video, opera theater and song, and music publications.

CLEF: Classical Music Education Foundation
http://www.clef.org/

★★★

CLEF states its purpose as singular: to bring music to the ears of anyone who will listen. This elegant-looking site includes a well-organized list of related links.

Franz Schubert Page
http://home1.swipnet.se/~w-18046/schub.html

★★★

Listen to a continuous Schubert loop as you browse this page, which includes information on Schubert's life, works, and the historical times surrounding this young composer's life.

Gramophone
http://www.gramophone.co.uk/

★★★★★

Online version of the internationally acclaimed magazine, this site features incisive articles on current classical music recordings, orchestras, and performances. Interviews, profiles, editor's choice top 10 recordings, information about competitions and industry news, and more. Also provides online discussion forums.

Great Women Composers

http://www.geocities.com/EnchantedForest/3744/

★★★

This site offers a biographical account of the many forgotten women opera librettists, singers, and harpsichordists. Includes pictures, music, writings, and biographies of these women.

Klassiknet

http://www.culturekiosque.com/klassik/

★★★★

An online magazine for classical music fans, including articles, performer and composer interviews and biographies, reviews, and schedules. Some articles appear in both French and English. Don't leave without checking out the list of the 101 best vintage recordings.

Leonard Bernstein

http://www.leonardbernstein.com/

★★★★★

Here, you can learn more about Bernstein's life and his work, find books about him, listen to excerpts from his recordings, look at photos of Bernstein and his family and friends, scan music from his personal collection, and read about some of his philanthropic projects. You can also purchase recording and sheet music, as well as books written by the famous composer/conductor.

Medieval and Renaissance Music

http://home.hkstar.com/~mulcheng/

★★★★

This is a site for beginners rather than scholars; it provides history and a timeline for both medieval and renaissance music. Includes lists of literature and manuscript resources for more information about this music.

MusicOnline Classical Music Directory

http://www.musicalonline.com/

★★★★

Comprehensive directory to classical music resources on the Internet, including schools, museums, journals, music theory, scholarly works, competitions, scholarships, and much much more.

National Association of Composers, USA

http://www.music-usa.org/nacusa/

★★★★

NACUSA, founded in 1933, is devoted to the promotion and performance of music by Americans. The site includes member links, recent and upcoming concert schedules, chapter information, and a plethora of links to other music-related sites.

New York Philharmonic

http://www.newyorkphilharmonic.org/

★★★★★

👫 All

Information for fans and friends of the New York Philharmonic, including educational guides, historical information, ticket information, and news releases. Kids are welcome to visit this site or the site designed specifically for them at http://www.nyphilkids.org/.

OrchestraNet

http://www.orchestranet.co.uk/

★★★

An excellent point of entry for classical music searches, this site says it's an unbroken chain of hundreds of classical music websites ranging greatly in content and style. Includes lists of orchestras, concerts, CDs, books, and music-related news. Links to Amazon.com to purchase CDs and books.

Piano Nanny

http://www.pianonanny.com/index.html

★★★★

👫 All

Always wanted to learn how to play the piano but never had the time to learn? This site provides piano lessons online. Each lesson takes about 35 minutes to complete (you must have QuickTime installed).

A B C D E F G H I J K L M N O P Q R S T U V W X Y Z

A
B
C
D
E
F
G
H
I
J
K
L
M
N
O
P
Q
R
S
T
U
V
W
X
Y
Z

The Piano Page

http://www.ptg.org/

★★★

A site solely devoted to the piano, including news, events, conventions, music, teachers, manufacturers information, images, advice on buying a piano, and more! Louis Moreau Gottschalk's *Souvenir d'Andalousie* plays in the background as you browse the site. Piano lovers shouldn't miss this one; the links alone are worth the time.

Sony Classical

http://www.sonyclassical.com/

★★★★★

Sony Entertainment's classical music site, where you can learn about Sony's classical artists, check out their CDs, listen to sample sound clips, view photos, and find out about upcoming tours.

Symphony Orchestra Information

http://www.hoptechno.com/symphony.htm

★★★

Find information on the major symphony orchestras in the world. Organized by geographical area, this site includes historical background, websites, email addresses, and concert schedules of many major symphony orchestras.

XLNC1.org

http://www.xlnc1.org/

★★★

Excellency One is an Internet radio station based in Chula Vista, California, that plays classical music from its database of more than 400 pieces. Check in here to find the best stream for your location.

Related Sites

http://music.acu.edu/www/iawm/pages/

http://www.chopin.org/

http://www.edepot.com/beethoven.html

http://www.e-universe.com/lmfhome/

http://www.sai-national.org/phil/composers/composer.html

MUSIC GENRES—COUNTRY

Alan Jackson

http://www.alanjackson.com/

★★★★★

Official site for fans of this popular entertainer. Offers tour and fan club information, and introduces you to his band. Check out the Alan Jackson merchandise available, from clothing to beanie bears. Did you know his favorite TV show is *The Andy Griffith Show*?

Brooks & Dunn Online

http://www.brooks-dunn.com/

★★★★

Provides tour information and the opportunity to order merchandise and albums. Also provides an email address.

Charlie Daniels Band

http://www.charliedaniels.com/

★★★

Everybody knows *The Devil Went Down to Georgia*, but there's more to Charlie Daniels than that. Check out his latest album, meet the band members, tack a message to the message board, or join the fan club. You can also purchase music, apparel, and collectibles at this site.

The Clint Black Website

http://www.clintblack.com/

★★★★

See what this dimpled crooner has been up to lately and when he'll be appearing near you. Listen to sound clips, brush up on your lyrics, watch videos, or read recent articles about him.

CMT.com

http://www.cmt.com/

★★★★

Read feature articles on country music stars, find new albums slated for release, download country music clips from your favorite artists, and read country music news. Also features audio and video clips.

Dixie Chicks

http://www.dixiechicks.com

★★★

 14-18

Get the latest news on this hot girl band here. Check out the current touring schedule, post messages on the bulletin board, and watch band videos.

Faith Hill

http://www.faithhill.com/

$

★★★★★

 14-18

See Faith's latest album cover, read about her most recent awards, scan music and tour reviews, and learn more about this superstar performer at her official site. You can also buy apparel, mousepads, keychains, and other Faith Hill–related products. This is truly a lovely site, well constructed, and easy to navigate.

Garth Brooks: Planet Garth

http://www.planetgarth.com/

$

★★★★

14-18

Provides the latest on country sensation Garth Brooks. Includes tour information, reviews, chord chart positions, song lyrics, pictures, and downloadable songs in RealAudio format. This site also has an extensive store where you can purchase all kinds of Garth Brooks merchandise.

George Strait Online

http://www.georgestraitfans.com/

$

★★★

Visit the George Strait General Store to pick up items such as pillowcases, ornaments, clocks, and notepads—all bearing the likeness of your favorite hat act! Or you can visit the Swap Shop, read the latest fan newsletter, or chat with other fans. Snapshots, audio clips, and video clips are also featured at this site.

History of Country Music

http://www.roughstock.com/history/

★★★

Focuses on influential country artists as far back as the beginning of country music itself. Features history on artists such as Roy Acuff, Hank Williams, Gene Autry, Patsy Cline, Charley Pride, and more. Includes country styles such as Western swing, urban cowboy, honky-tonk, the Nashville sound, and others.

Johnny Cash: The Official Page

http://www.johnnycash.com/

$

★★★★

Contains a long list of career highlights and a summary of Johnny Cash's biography (published in October of 1997). Check out the selection of classic audio clips from this legendary country performer.

Martina McBride

http://www.martina-mcbride.com/

★★★

14-18

Contains many sections of information and clips from this popular singer. The From the Vaults section contains an Internet-only radio production brought to you exclusively by this official site. You can join the mailing list and fan club here, as well as catch up on news and TV appearances. Links to other stores for buying memorabilia.

A B C D E F G H I J K L **M** N O P Q R S T U V W X Y Z

A
B
C
D
E
F
G
H
I
J
K
L
M
N
O
P
Q
R
S
T
U
V
W
X
Y
Z

Mary Chapin-Carpenter

http://www.sonynashville.com/MCC/

★★★

Sony Music Entertainment's official site for country/folk singer Mary Chapin-Carpenter. Site includes news, a biography, discography, pictures, and an active discussion forum.

Oak Ridge Boys

http://www.oakridgeboys.com/

★★★★

This award-winning group has had members come and go in its 50-year history, but most people know the current members whose hits include *Elvira* and *Y'All Come Back Saloon*. Site contains tons of photos, clips, group history, and everything a fan could want.

Patsy Cline: A Tribute

http://www.patsy.nu

★★★

Viewers can share stories and memories about this artist who died prematurely in a 1963 plane crash. Read quotes about Patsy from people who knew her and view the events calendar commemorating the achievements of her life and career.

Patty Loveless

http://www.sonynashville.com/PattyLoveless/

★★★★

Listen to some of Patty's songs, read through her detailed bio, and join the fan club. This CMA Female Vocalist of the Year winner has earned her following by producing hit after hit. Check out this site to see why.

Randy Travis

http://www.randy-travis.com/

★★★

Brush up on your Travis trivia at this site, which includes both his musical accomplishments and his recent foray into acting (which includes an appearance in *The Rainmaker*). Also contains clips from his *Greatest Hits Volumes I & II*.

Reba McEntire

http://www.reba.com/

★★★★

The official site for devotees of the country music singer. Links include the Album, Chat, the Book, and Off The Record. Check out the store to see what CDs and videos are available for sale. You can even shop for your favorite Reba movies and videos. Online shopping available through Amazon.com.

Shania Twain

http://www.shania-twain.com/

★★★

👫 14-18

The home page for country diva Shania Twain. You can read about the success of her last album, what projects she has forthcoming, and also what people in her hometown think of her (they're building a facility in her honor).

Tim McGraw

http://www.timmcgraw.com/

★★★★

👫 14-18

Become a mcgrawfunaddict (in other words, join the fan club) at this site. Contains all the latest information about this hunky singer and his wife, country singer Faith Hill. You can also buy T-shirts and other "McGrawWear" items here.

Trace Adkins Official Website

http://traceadkins.com/

★★★★

Listen to a message from Trace or the songs from his latest album. Also contains the usual bio, tour dates, gift shop, and fan club information.

trishayearwood.com

http://www.trishayearwood.com/

★★★★★

Visit the official site of Trisha Yearwood, listen to her sing, watch her perform, meet other fans, check concert dates, and more. Links to Amazon.com for CDs.

Vince Gill

http://vincegill.com/

★★★

Contains information on upcoming concerts and special appearances. You can listen to his latest hit single and read bios about Vince and his band and staff. Also offers the words to many of his hits. Read Vince Gill's thoughts on his latest album.

Willie Nelson's Page

http://www.sonymusic.com/artists/WillieNelson/

★★★

This is the official site from Sony, Willie's current label. Read about his more than 100 albums and the twists and turns of his long career.

Related Sites
http://www.countrystars.com/artists/mccready.html
http://www.diamondrio.com/
http://www.geocities.com/Nashville/4244/
http://www.bogguss.com/
http://www.cbvcp.com/c2/john.html
http://www.claywalker.com/
http://www.leeroy.com/

MUSIC GENRES—ETHNIC

African Music Encyclopedia

http://africanmusic.org/

★★★★

Comprehensive list of African musicians searchable by artist or country, plus a glossary of terms relating to African American music. This site also provides a list of books with links to Amazon.com for purchase.

Afro-Caribbean Music

http://www.afromix.org/

★★★

Yes, you'll find reggae music here, but you'll also find everything from Afro Funk to Ziglibithy to suit your musical tastes. Explore Africa and the Caribbean by artist, geographical location, and style. You'll also find a list of African/Caribbean nightclubs and restaurants in Paris. This site, available in both English and French, is nicely organized, with colorful 3D musical notes indicating the sections. You'll find an excellent page of links to related web resources, too.

Ari Davidow's Klezmer Shack

http://www.klezmershack.com/

★★★

Focuses on the klezmer musical blend of traditional Jewish folk music, blues, and jazz. You'll find articles, artist profiles, CD reviews, concert and festival information, a guide to radio programs, and contact information for klezmer musicians. You'll also find links to sites where you can buy klezmer CDs and a great annotated section on other klezmer-related resources on the Web.

Charts All Over the World

http://www.lanet.lv/misc/charts/

★★★

This site features links to more than 800 music charts from all over the world, organized by country.

Cultures of the Andes

http://www.andes.org/

★★★

Music, pictures, and literature from the Andes mountains of South America; offerings in English, Spanish, and the Quechua Indian language. You can also see movie clips of dances. English translations of the lyrics are available, and most sound clips are available in both AU and WAV format.

A
B
C
D
E
F
G
H
I
J
K
L
M
N
O
P
Q
R
S
T
U
V
W
X
Y
Z

Dirty Linen

http://www.dirtynelson.com/linen/73toc.html

★★★

Dirty Linen is an online magazine for folk and world music. At its home page, you can find a table of contents, a list of back issues, a "gig guide," and more. Well worth checking out. You can also subscribe to the regular magazine and have it delivered to you every other month.

The Flamenco Guitar

http://www.guitarist.com/fg/fg.htm

★★★

More information on flamenco, with an introduction for beginners. Discographies for both dancers and guitarists and MIDI sound files are available. You'll also find dozens and dozens of links to related sites.

Folk Australia

http://folk.mountaintracks.com.au/Folk_Australia/

★★★

This site covers Australian folk music and even offers a search feature. You'll also find interviews, news of local folk clubs in the Sydney area, and links to folk music sites in Australia, Ireland, the UK, and the USA. You'll find short bios of Australian folk musicians, news of upcoming festivals and events, and "folksie" organizations, all in a clear, nicely organized format.

Gateway to Scottish Music

http://www.musicinscotland.com/

★★★

This Scottish music promotes music and musicians who have a Celtic connection to a worldwide audience, including Scottish, Irish, Cape Breton, French, and Spanish musicians. This site provides an excellent introduction to Scottish music and provides links to many additional resources.

Hawaiian Jamz

http://www.mauigateway.com/~jamz/

★★★

Great site on Hawaiian music and culture; however, you need RealAudio to hear the clips and shows. Clean, clear graphics and organization. Each show is about an hour long and revolves around a particular theme, such as "Traditional Hawaiian Falsetto." There's also a list of related sites.

Irish and Celtic Music on the Internet

http://www.celticmusic.com/

★★★

CelticMusic.Com, an online magazine, focuses on Celtic music. Check out the site's magazine index for a helpful listing of back issues and links to the home pages of featured artists. The site also includes sheet music for traditional tunes, reviews of recent CDs, audio excerpts (for the titles with dancing musical notes next to them), and more in the Virtual Tunebook section.

Japanese Kabuki Music

http://www.fix.co.jp/kabuki/sound.html

★★★

Fascinating information on kabuki and the instruments commonly used in kabuki, such as the taiko drum and the three-stringed shamisen. You can also hear samples of some of the instruments and examples of kabuki fans shouting out support for their favorite actors; these shouts are called *kakegoe*.

KiwiFolk: Folk and Acoustic Music in New Zealand

http://kiwifolk.org.nz/

★★★

This site organizes a wealth of information about New Zealand folk and acoustic music. You'll find upcoming events, festival news, bios of "kiwi" artists, and links to related pages.

Mbira

http://www.mbira.org/

★★★★

This page is an excellent introduction to mbira, the traditional music of Zimbabwe. It also covers Shona traditions, customs, and literature as they relate to mbira. You can listen to a sampler of mbira music and check out the calendar of events.

MIZIK

http://www.mizikmizik.com/

★★★

Here's an eclectic collection of world music information and extensive links to other ethnomusicology-related sites. Includes discographies (with images from the CD covers), sound samples, reviews, and more. You'll hear music from Asia, the French Antilles, and Africa, to name a few.

Norwegian Music Information Centre

http://www.mic.no/

★★★

You'll find all kinds of information on Norwegian music here—biographies on many composers; articles covering Norwegian music history, early and church music, and more recent pop, rock, and jazz; information on festivals and other events; and links to many related sites.

Peruvian Music

http://www.musicaperuana.com/english/song.htm

★★★

 All

This page has sound files of Andean flute and guitar music as well as links to related Peruvian music topics. The opening page offers three language selections: Spanish, French, and English.

Puro Mariachi

http://www.mariachi.org

★★★

You'll find just about everything you wanted to know about mariachi music here, including a history of mariachi, recommended books and CDs, and the lyrics to just about every Mexican song ever written, alphabetized by first line of the song. There are also dozens and dozens of links to Mexican music and cultural sites.

Shimamura: English Index

http://www.shimamura.co.jp/english/index.html

★★★

At first, this site looks like an advertisement for the music store and its locations; however, if you go down to the links on traditional music and instruments, you'll find some excellent information.

Songs of Indonesia

http://www.geocities.com/SoHo/1823/

★★★

This is an archive of Indonesian songs, divided into pop, traditional, and national songs, some in MIDI format. You'll find links to related sites as well.

Tara Publications: The World of Jewish Music

http://www.jewishmusic.com/

$

★★★★

Offers a wide variety of Jewish music selections. You'll find an online catalog and links to other Jewish music sites. There are a few articles, too, and an artists section with links to their home pages. Check out the RealAudio library.

Temple Records

http://www.templerecords.co.uk

$

★★★★

Provides home site and online ordering for Temple Records, which specializes in Scottish traditional music. Includes an online catalog, artist descriptions, and ordering information.

A B C D E F G H I J K L M N O P Q R S T U V W X Y Z

A B C D E F G H I J K L M N O P Q R S T U V W X Y Z

The Unofficial Clannad Website
http://www.jtwinc.com/clannad/main.html

★★★★

Excellent site, organized into sections with a discography, lyrics, images, interviews, sound bytes, and information about the Irish band Clannad. You'll also find links to other Clannad sites.

Welcome to Bali & Beyond
http://www.balibeyond.com/

★★★★

Bali & Beyond is a Los Angeles–based performing arts company inspired by the culture of Indonesia. The ensemble tours nationwide, featuring a variety of music, theater, and educational presentations. This colorful site contains lots of information about upcoming concert schedules and events. Check out the Kechat section for background on the Indonesian culture and music, and Maria's Corner for all kinds of interesting gift items.

MUSIC GENRES—JAZZ

52nd Street Jazz
http://www.52ndstreet.com/

★★★★

In addition to reading about featured "CDs in the Spotlight," here you can find reviews of the latest CDs featuring every kind of jazz—from contemporary to avant-garde. The site also offers a searchable archive of more than 1,000 previous reviews and a bulletin board to share and learn the latest jazz news. Links to CDNOW, where you can purchase jazz music online.

Down Beat Magazine
http://www.downbeat.com/

★★★★

The place to go for the latest news, reviews, and information about your favorite jazz bands and artists.

JAZZ
http://www.pbs.org/jazz/

★★★★★

 All

This is the home of the PBS-sponsored movie *JAZZ*, by Ken Burns, where you can find biographies of famous jazz musicians, transcripts of many of the interviews, audio samples (in the Jazz Lounge), a jazz timeline, and a special area just for kids.

Jazz Corner
http://www.jazzcorner.com/

★★★★

This comprehensive jazz kiosk provides links to individual artists' home pages, a calendar of jazz events for most states, a photo gallery, interviews, reviews, news, and a discussion area.

Jazz Online
http://www.jazzonln.com/

★★★

Watch live online video of some of your favorite jazz performers, such as Chick Corea and Kenny Garrett, among others; listen to jazz clips; check out the hottest jazz albums on the top five lists; read feature articles on jazz performers; and get the latest music news. Features a Jazz 101 class for beginners.

The Jazz Review
http://www.jazzreview.com/

★★★★

Listen to audio reviews, post your own review of particular pieces, read others' reviews, check out a featured artist, and listen to featured performers as part of the "CD of the Week."

Jazz Roots
http://www.jass.com/

★★★

A great history site offering a musical timeline showing the extension of jazz music nationally, as well as archives containing bios of musicians and photos. A nice overview of the growth of this musical genre.

Miles Davis

http://www.milesdavis.com/

★★★★★

Official home page of the famous jazz trumpet player and composer, this site features a biography of Miles Davis, a brief history of his musical career, and a sampling of MP3 clips.

Related Site
http://www.sonymusicstore.com/store/catalog/
MerchandiseDetails.jsp?merchId=1480

Red Hot Jazz Archive

http://www.redhotjazz.com/

★★★

Search for information on jazz bands, musicians, and films at this site, which provides plenty of information about the rise of jazz prior to 1930. You can also search for information about essays.

Scott Joplin

http://www.scottjoplin.org/

★★★

Home of the famous Ragtime artist Scott Joplin. Here, you can read about his life, find out about the upcoming Ragtime festival, and learn more about the Scott Joplin International Ragtime Foundation.

MUSIC GENRES—OPERA

The Aria Database

http://www.aria-database.com/

★★★

Would you like to be able to search for information on a particular aria, opera, or composer? This is the place. Search by name, opera, language, or voice type. The database includes MIDI files of some of the music, libretti, translations, and more. Mozart and Verdi are featured, but many other composers are also included. Related links also featured.

Báthory Erzsébet: Elizabeth Báthory

http://bathory.org/

★★★★

If you're at all interested in how an opera came to be, visit this site. In the Cologne Journal section, Dennis Báthory-Kitsz describes the plans for this semihistorical opera in progress. Check out the history, the bibliography, and, of course, the castle photos.

Bob's Opera Madness

http://www.geocities.com/Vienna/1059/

★★★

This 3D Opera Gallery is best viewed with 3D glasses. You'll find plenty to see and do here—a collection of opera singers' advertisements for various products, photo essays of singers (some drawn from home movies), and even a list of appearances by opera singers in the movies.

FanFaire

http://ffaire.com/

★★★★

A web-zine by and for fans of opera and classical music, updated quarterly, with reviews, slideshows, pictures, and embedded sound files. For best viewing, you'll need a fairly fast modem and a recent version of Netscape or Internet Explorer. Be prepared for sound at a substantial volume; the Java applets might reset your volume levels.

The Metropolitan Opera

http://www.metopera.org/

★★★★

Before you head out to see Aida or Carmen—or any other major opera, for that matter—turn to the Stories of the Operas section at this site to get the lowdown on what's going to happen. You can also check the Metropolitan Opera's concert schedule, take the Met quiz, and learn more about the Met's history.

A
B
C
D
E
F
G
H
I
J
K
L
M
N
O
P
Q
R
S
T
U
V
W
X
Y
Z

A
B
C
D
E
F
G
H
I
J
K
L

M
N
O
P
Q
R
S
T
U
V
W
X
Y
Z

Monsalvat

http://home.c2i.net/monsalvat/

★★★

This personal site belongs to a Wagner fan, and is devoted to *Parsifal* with quite a few articles on various aspects, including a chronology, the libretto (in German), a discography, and so on. You'll find many links to related opera sites—both performers and companies alike.

Musical Online Companies

http://www.wynn.com/mol/music.on.line.html

★★★

Come to Musical Online when you're in search of professional companies or musicians. This site contains strictly listings and links, except for a musical chat room. The opera company list reaches outside the United States into Canada and Europe.

New York City Opera

http://www.nycopera.com/

$

★★★

Information and current schedules for the world-famous New York City Opera. Includes performer biographies.

OPERA America

http://www.operaam.org/

★★★

OPERA America is an organization that serves the field of opera by providing informational, technical, and administrative resources to the public in regard to opera. Its mission is to promote opera as exciting and accessible to individuals from all walks of life. The site includes information about advocacy and awareness programs, professional development, an artists' database of OPERA America members, and a season and schedule database.

Opera Dictionary

http://joshua.micronet.it/italian/mariobiondi/opere/diz_opera_.html

★★★

An online opera dictionary compiled by Mario Biondi. If you're interested in some particular composer or opera, simply search in this page using your browser's Find feature or the indexed alphabet.

Opera Glass

http://rick.stanford.edu/opera/main.html

★★★

Enjoy this ever-expanding site of links to opera information on the Web. Opera companies, opera people, and more help to comprise this comprehensive site.

Opera News Online

http://www.operanews.com/

★★★★

An electronic publication of the Metropolitan Opera Guild, Inc. Historical and musical analyses, performance reviews, profiles and interviews, and more. Visitors are welcome to pop in and scope out selected news and articles before subscribing. A subscription gives you access to the full magazine online and via mail.

The Opera Schedule Server

http://www.fsz.bme.hu/opera/

★★★

A searchable database providing information about what's playing at opera houses all around the world.

Opera Works

http://patriciagray.net/operahtmls/works.html

★★★★

This unusual site, a production of Rhodes College in Memphis, Tennessee, provides a pronunciation dictionary, complete with a brief description and a sound file, for dozens of names associated with opera—names of composers, names of operas, and so on. Also connects to the Opera Memphis home page.

Opera World

http://www.operaworld.com/

★★★★

Sign up for a distance learning class to learn more about opera, or order educational material about operas to study on your own, and pick up information on upcoming opera broadcasts you can tune into. You can also search for and purchase opera CDs and merchandise, such as performance posters.

Operabase

http://www.operabase.com/

★★★★

Detailed information on broadcast and performance schedules, festivals, and events; opera houses; reviews; and links. Includes opera timelines for viewers seeking a little history. Databases are searchable by singer, conductor, producer, composer, and more. A complete and complex site, available in six languages.

Opera for Kids

http://www.operaforkids.org/

★★★★

 All

Information about FBN Productions' operas for kids. This site is designed more for teachers to learn about productions that they can offer to their students.

OperaNet Magazine

http://www.culturekiosque.com/opera/

★★★

An online magazine for opera fans, featuring performer interviews, articles, schedules, and reviews of performances and recordings.

San Francisco Opera

http://www.sfopera.com/

★★★★

 All

This site features information about the San Francisco Opera, including upcoming performances, ticket information, and opera basics.

Seattle Opera

http://www.seattleopera.org/

★★★

Get free previews of upcoming performances, learn more about opera stories, find ticket information, and make arrangements to attend a performance at the Seattle Opera, all from the company's website.

Related Site
http://www.terririchter.com/

Sydney Opera House

http://www.sydneyoperahouse.com/

★★★★

 All

Learn more about this Australian cultural landmark, its history, and its future performances. This site also sports a nice shopping site where you can purchase CDs, videos, and Australian-related music gifts. Children can go to http://www.sydneyoperahouse.com/kids/ to view special areas for kids.

MUSIC GENRES—POP MUSIC

Alanis Morissette: Intellectual Intercourse

http://www.alanismorissette.com/

★★★

 14-18

This official home page of Canadian singer Alanis Morissette includes song lyrics, photos, concert information, selections from Morissette's personal journal, and more. Also features online shopping for Alanis Morissette T-shirts and CDs. Good collection of music video clips.

Related Site
http://www.charlieanderson.com/Alanis.htm

A B C D E F G H I J K L M N O P Q R S T U V W X Y Z

A
B
C
D
E
F
G
H
I
J
K
L
M
N
O
P
Q
R
S
T
U
V
W
X
Y
Z

Backstreet Boys

http://www.backstreetboys.com/

★★★★

👥 14-18

Be the first to hear about the Backstreet Boys' upcoming projects, such as a book and comic, as well as check out photos and bios of the members, and sign up for their free fan newsletter. Free music clips and music videos. Check out the shopping site for Backstreet Boys merchandise.

The Beatles: Songs, Pictures, and Stories of the Beatles

http://www.rarebeatles.com/

★★★★

👥 14-18

Find out what that Beatles memorabilia is worth by taking a look at information and links at this site. Trying to locate that album cover that's missing from your collection? You're likely to find it here, where Beatles fans gather.

Bee Gees Fan Club

http://www.beegeesfanclub.org/

★★★★

The ultimate disco group. A great site for true fans to enjoy the Brothers Gibb. Don't forget to order your Bee Gees calendar and read the touching tribute to Maurice Gibb.

Britney Spears

http://www.britneyspears.com/

★★★★

👥 14-18

Check out the moves of this pop star maven, check out her latest CD, and keep up on the latest tour dates and concert information. A good collection of photos, audio clips, video clips, and other entertaining material will keep fans busy for hours. Also features online shopping for Britney Spears apparel and memorabilia.

Buddy Holly

http://www.buddyholly.com/

★★★★★

👥 14-18

Learn more about the life, career, and music of Buddy Holly at the Official Buddy Holly website. Here, you read his biography and achievements, learn some fast facts and quotes, view photographs, listen to audio clips, check out his complete list of albums, and even find links to other great Buddy Holly sites. Nicely designed site packed with great information and resources.

Christina Aguilera

http://www.christina-a.com/

★★★★

👥 14-18

Check out the official site of Christina Aguilera and find out just how this sexy superstar has skyrocketed to fame in the world of pop. Here, you can listen to audio clips, view video clips, tour Christina's photo gallery, read her biography, join the fan club, and much more.

Chicago

http://www.chicagotheband.com/

$

★★★★

The official website for the legendary music group Chicago. Learn about the group's music, what's new, talk to the band, look at images, and so on. You can also order band merchandise from this site.

Emerson, Lake, and Palmer (ELP)

http://www.brain-salad.com/

★★★

Provides Emerson, Lake, and Palmer (ELP) information. Includes online back issues of the ELP digest and links to other ELP sites.

Janet Jackson

http://www.janet-jackson.com/

★★★★

🚷 Not for kids

This site focuses on Janet Jackson, and includes the latest news, tour information, sounds, image gallery, lyrics, and more. Links to Artist Direct, where you can purchase Janet merchandise ranging from tour buttons to autographed CDs.

Jimmy Buffett's Margaritaville

http://www.margaritaville.com/

★★★★★

This is truly the quintessential Jimmy Buffett site. You can find current tour information, learn the lyrics to every Buffett tune, shop online for Jimmy Buffett apparel and other memorabilia, learn about the band members, and keep in touch with fellow Parrot Heads! Great site for hard-core Buffett fans!

> **Related Site**
> http://www.cobo.org/main.html

Kid Rock

http://www.kidrock.com

$

★★★★

🚷 Not for kids

Visit the official website of the bad boy of pop, Kid Rock. Check out the latest headline news concerning the band, check tour dates, read Kid Rock's biography, check out the photo gallery, listen to free audio clips, and more. Free Kid Rock desktop wallpaper and AOL chat icons available.

Madonna

http://www.madonna.com/madonna/

$

★★★★★

👫 14-18

Catch up on the history of this pop icon, learn the lyrics to her most popular songs, listen to sample audio clips, view music videos, check out the photo gallery, or shop online for Madonna memorabilia. This site opens with a very cool video timeline of Madonna's career.

Mariah Carey

http://www.mariahcarey.com/

$

★★★★★

👫 14-18

For some time, the hottest performer in pop, Mariah's career took a dive in the '90s, but she's on the rise and has one of the best voices in the business. Check out her official website and sample her latest cuts, video clips, and information about upcoming projects and performances.

Michael Jackson

http://www.michaeljackson.com/

$

★★★★★

👫 14-18

High-tech site from the legend of pop showcases this incredible performer's career. View MJ's biography, check out his discography and list of short films, and keep abreast of the latest news regarding Michael Jackson.

Natalie Merchant

http://www.nataliemerchant.com/

$

★★★

The official home page of Natalie Merchant, former 10,000 Maniacs lead singer and songwriter. Here, you can view a pictorial timeline of Miss Merchant's life and career, read selected letters, ask her a question, tour the photo gallery, or hang out and chat in the parlor with other Natalie Merchant fans.

Nicks Fix

http://nicksfix.com/

★★★

👫 14-18

This site, which features Fleetwood Mac's Stevie Nicks, contains Stevie news, album and video information, song lyrics, photos, and more. Also includes several links to other Stevie-related pages.

A B C D E F G H I J K L M N O P Q R S T U V W X Y Z

A
B
C
D
E
F
G
H
I
J
K
L
M
N
O
P
Q
R
S
T
U
V
W
X
Y
Z

NSYNC.com

http://www.nsync.com/

★★★★★

👫 14-18

Very cool site! Get a look behind the scenes at an NSYNC concert, or find out when and where the next one is. You can also review bios and pictures of band members, and check out new music and videos.

The Official Hootie and the Blowfish Website

http://www.hootie.com/

★★★★

👫 14-18

This site gives you a whole lotta Hootie! A good site with a distinctly collegiate feel. Check it out for more information on this longtime college party band. You can see latest tour photos, find song lyrics, and stop by the Hootie store for Hootie merchandise.

Olivia Newton-John

http://www.onlyolivia.com/

★★★

Provides information about Olivia. Offers links to albums, singles, music videos, movie information, a photo collection, and much more. Also offers information on how to join the fan club.

Pop-Music.com

http://www.popmusic.com

★★★★

👫 14-18

Check the charts to see how your favorite group is doing, search for information about pop groups, chat with fellow fans, and get the latest news here. You'll find just about everything you want to know about your group here, whether it's NSYNC, the Backstreet Boys, or Madonna.

Ricky Martin

http://www.rickymartin.com/

★★★★

👫 14-18

This Ricky Martin site, which is full of photos, details the former Menudo performer's background and music. Good collection of audio and music video clips. You can also sign up to be on his mailing list.

Shakira

http://www.shakira.com/

★★★★★

👫 14-18

Official home page of one of the hottest new pop stars, Shakira. Read her biography, check out the latest headlines, listen to audio clips, view video clips, and keep abreast of concert news and information. The site also features chat and message boards to keep in touch with fellow fans.

Toni Braxton: Sweet, Soft, and Sensual

http://www.musicfanclubs.org/tonibraxton/

★★★

👫 14-18

A site full of images, lyrics, and audio of this sultry and talented singer. Also includes her story, her news, and related links.

MUSIC GENRES— RAP/HIP HOP

Beastie Boys

http://www.beastieboys.com/

Ⓢ

★★★

👫 14-18

Get the lyrics to your favorite Beastie Boys songs, chat with other fans, and check out the message boards.

Unofficial Busta Rhymes Website

http://www.ewsonline.com/music/busta/

★★★★★

 Not for kids

This unofficial home page of Busta Rhymes features his album reviews, a picture gallery, lyrics, audio and video clips, and more.

Destiny's Child Fan Club

http://www.dc-unplugged.com/

★★★★★

 14-18

The Official Destiny's Child Fan Club, this site features news about the group, biographies of the girls, a photo gallery, downloadable wallpaper and AOL chat icons, and a few music videos. Check out the online store for apparel and memorabilia.

Eminem

http://www.eminem.com

★★★★★

 Not for kids

Official home of Eminem, multi-platinum hip-hop artist, Grammy award winner, and Academy Award winner (for best song), this site showcases Eminem's music and performances. Check out his biography and discography, play audio and video clips, tour the photo gallery, exchange messages with other fans in the discussion forums, and much more. Online store links to Artist Direct, where you can shop for Eminem memorabilia.

Ice Cube

http://www.icecube.org/

★★★

 Not for kids

Home of the Web's leading authority on Ice Cube, this site features news about Ice Cube's upcoming tours, movies, and other projects. Also provides sample audio clips, a photo gallery, and lyrics.

Lauryn Hill

http://www.lauryn-hill.com/

★★★

Sony Music Entertainment's official website of Lauryn Hill, hip-hop diva. Here, you can read Lauryn Hill's biography, listen to some of her most popular songs, learn the lyrics to her songs, and check out some of the awards she's won. Message board also available.

Lil' Kim

http://www.lilkim.com/home.html

★★★★

 Not for kids

Lil' Kim fans will want to bookmark this page to keep abreast of the latest news, concert information, audio and video clips, and hot photos of this sexy hip-hop star. Message board available for fans who want to keep in touch with one another and share their enthusiasm for Lil' Kim.

Public Enemy

http://www.publicenemy.com/

★★★★★

 Not for kids

Official high-tech site of one of Rap's most notorious bands features a photo gallery, an archive of song lyrics, band member bios, links to videocasts and webcasts, an enemy board (for reading and posting messages), and more. Shop online at the PE shop for books, caps (hats), and T-shirts.

Will Smith

http://www.willsmith.com/

★★★★

 14-18

Sony Entertainment's official Will Smith website features links to Will Smith's discography, where you can listen to some of his tunes from the *Willenium* and *Big Willie Style* CDs. Links to the Sony Music store, where you can purchase CDs online. This site also provides links to Will Smith's movie sites, including the *Men in Black II* site where you can view movie trailers.

A
B
C
D
E
F
G
H
I
J
K
L
M
N
O
P
Q
R
S
T
U
V
W
X
Y
Z

A
B
C
D
E
F
G
H
I
J
K
L
M
N
O
P
Q
R
S
T
U
V
W
X
Y
Z

MUSIC GENRES—
ROCK AND ROLL

AC/DC

http://www.elektra.com/elektra/acdc/index.jhtml

★★★

👫 14-18

Elektra's official home page of one of the first and most popular heavy metal bands ever to take the stage. Take a look at a history of the band, as well as a discography, photo gallery, and collection of audio and video clips. Online chat and message boards are available for the many fans to hook up with one another and discuss their favorite topics.

Related Site

http://acdcband.kicks-ass.net/

Aerosmith

http://www.aerosmith.com/

★★★★★

👫 14-18

This official Aerosmith site features tour dates, biographies of the band members, audio and video clips, a discography, and a chat room. Very imaginative, interactive site.

Blink 182

www.blink182.com

★★★★

👫⃠ Not for kids

A ton of information about the band, from tour dates to personal information about band members. Watch videos and hear the latest releases from this site. Lots of free audio and video clips for downloading.

Bob Dylan

http://www.bobdylan.com/

💲

★★★★

👫 14-18

Visit Bob Dylan's official home on the Web to learn more about his albums, read lyrics to his songs, and check out links to other Bob Dylan sites. Features a great collection of audio clips and lyrics, so you can read along as Dylan sings.

Bruce Springsteen

http://www.brucespringsteen.net/

★★★

👫 14-18

Provides news, concert information, pictures, lyrics, songs, albums, and an online store where you can purchase albums and other merchandise.

Related Site

http://www.brucespringsteen.com/

Electric Magic: The Led Zeppelin Chronicle

http://www.led-zeppelin.com/

★★★

👫 14-18

Online edition of the fan magazine and rated the best Zeppelin site on the Net. Features photo and article archives, a video vault, information about the band's appearance on the MuchMusic special and the Montreux concerts, plus much more.

Dave Emlen's Unofficial Kinks Website

http://kinks.it.rit.edu/

★★★

👫 14-18

Includes information on The Kinks—everything from pictures, sounds, and videos to a complete discography and lyrics database.

Related Site

http://www.thekinks.com/

Eric Clapton

http://www.repriserec.com/ericclapton/

💲

★★★★★

👫 14-18

Sign up to receive advance notice of Eric Clapton's releases and be able to buy his music and videos at prerelease prices. You can also check out tour information as well as upcoming television appearances. Chat with other Clapton fans at the interactive fans page.

Grateful Dead
http://www.dead.net/

★★★★

 14-18

The official site for the Grateful Dead provides information about the band and its music, an online store of band paraphernalia, and sections created and maintained by individual band members.

Iggy Pop
http://www.iggypop-virginrecords.com/

★★★

 Not for kids

Browse through the discography, lyrics, current news, and articles about rock singer and songwriter Iggy Pop. Includes a biography, photos, and links to related sites. Also includes video clips, sound bytes, and much more.

Jack's "The Who"
http://www.riverdale.k12.or.us/students/jackr/who.html

★★★

 14-18

Get information on the rock-and-roll band The Who. You'll find pictures, information on the band, and information on the Broadway production of its rock opera, *Tommy*. You can also read a history of The Who.

Official Site
http://www.mcarecords.com/artistMain.asp?artistid=236

Jethro Tull Music Archive
http://remus.rutgers.edu/JethroTull/

★★★

 14-18

Find out how this band that was formed in 1968 got its name. You'll get information on album releases and tour dates. Check out the discography, which includes song titles and lyrics. Learn about Jethro Tull with the extensive FAQ. Includes back issues of *St. Cleve Chronicle*—a digest on news, opinions, and anything to do with Tull.

Official Site
http://www.j-tull.com/

Kiss
http://www.kissonline.net/

★★★★

 Not for kids

Win tickets to see Kiss live, read the transcript of interviews with band members, buy and sell Kiss memorabilia, listen to audio clips, view video clips, and just generally get to know the band better at this site. Contests, clubs, message boards, and other features make this a prime site for Kiss fans.

The Los Angeles Rock and Roll Roadmap
http://www.net101.com/rocknroll/page2.html

★★★

 14-18

Check out L.A.-area maps, addresses, and pictures of hangouts where you can run into or reminisce about your favorite musicians and bands. Visit Chateau Marmont, former "home" of the Doors' Jim Morrison; or, visit The Rainbow, the hangout of the likes of Led Zeppelin, Keith Moon, and John Lennon.

The Official Van Halen Site
http://www.van-halen.com/

★★★

14-18

The official site for the venerable rock band features news about the group, trivia, and more. Great collection of audio clips, music videos, and song lyrics, plus tour dates, downloadable wallpaper and screensavers, message boards, and links to other Van Halen sites.

The Original (Unofficial) Elvis
http://metalab.unc.edu/elvis/elvishom.html

★★★★

14-18

Listen to songs from early rock-and-roll star Elvis Presley. Includes a tour of Graceland, photos, lyrics, articles, and much more. Also includes links to related sites and an Elvis TV schedule. You'll also find an extensive list of Elvis pen pals you can hook up with. You can read Elvis' last will and testament, and—of course—keep up to date on all the latest Elvis sightings.

Official Site
http://www.elvispresley.com/

A B C D E F G H I J K L **M** N O P Q R S T U V W X Y Z

A
B
C
D
E
F
G
H
I
J
K
L
M
N
O
P
Q
R
S
T
U
V
W
X
Y
Z

Past Masters: A Virtual Beatles Tribute

http://members.aol.com/hahahahno/private/frames.htm

★★★

👥 14-18

Read the lyrics for each song on each of The Beatles albums. Visit the bulletin board or listen to some guitar tabs. Check out pictures from the photo gallery or play one of the trivia games. Use the search engine to find more Beatles pages. Listen to sound clips in Wave format or RealAudio.

Pink Floyd

http://www.pinkfloyd.co.uk/

★★★

👥 14-18

Visit this site. for information on and pictures of this cutting edge rock band that still appeals to listeners young and not-so-young. Check out the 30th Anniversary tribute to *Dark Side of the Moon*, *Echoes*, images, album stats, and more. Plan to spend some time checking out the site—it's not the most intuitive to navigate, but the audio and video elements are incredible. Would you expect anything less? Very cool. From the home page, you can also access the official Floyd forum.

Plugged: The Unofficial Paul McCartney

http://www.mcbeatle.de/macca/

★★★★

👥 14-18

A personal home page dedicated to rock icon Sir Paul McCartney. The site has current news, pictures of McCartney, details on his investiture, a complete discography, links to many other McCartney- and Beatles-related pages, and much more.

Official Site

http://www.paulmccartney.com/

Best Rock+Roll Hall of Fame

http://www.rockhall.com/

$

★★★★★

👥 14-18

This is the website for the Rock and Roll Hall of Fame and Museum, located in Cleveland, Ohio. Take a virtual tour of the museum to meet the legends of rock. Read about the songs that made them superstars and the events that made them notorious. Learn how the inductees are chosen and find out who is being inducted this year. You can also view a list of all the past inductees by induction year. Click on any inductee to get a bio, description of impact, song clips, and musical influences. This is a great source of information on all the major influences in rock. And be sure to check out the online shop for some great gift ideas!

Rockmine

http://www.rockmine.music.co.uk/

★★★

👥 14-18

A searchable database of information on rock music and artists. Includes special sections on the Beatles, Bob Dylan, the Doors, Jimi Hendrix, Elvis, David Bowie, and others. Also features trivia quizzes and rock star news.

RollingStone.com

http://www.rollingstone.com/

★★★★

👥 14-18

This is the online home of *Rolling Stone* magazine. The site contains most of the news, reviews, charts, and interviews available in the print edition. It also includes an area where users can comment on movies, music, and more. Free downloadable MP3 clips, video clips, and a huge photo gallery make this one of the best hangouts for rock fans.

Rolling Stones

http://www.rollingstones.com/

★★★★★

 14-18

This official website of the Rolling Stones contains a vast collection of sounds, pictures, video, and interviews. Check out the discography, chronology, and biography.

Related Site

http://www.stones.com/

Santana

http://www.santana.com/

★★★★★

 14-18

Listen to music by Santana, learn more about the man and the musicians who support him, as well as awards and news about the band's tour schedule here. The official Santana store offers autographed posters, jewelry, apparel, and other band-related items.

Sting

http://www.sting.com/

★★★★★

 14-18

Try to keep up with Sting at his site, which features information and the sounds of his latest album, as well as details of his career and background. You can buy T-shirts, music, tour merchandise, and other Sting stuff from this website.

Teenage Wildlife: The Interactive David Bowie Fan Page

http://www.teenagewildlife.com/

★★★★

 14-18

Chronicles the life of David Bowie. Get information and ratings about his albums, movies, and videos, and purchase merchandise at the online store. Find out where you can chat with other David Bowie fans. Also, learn about where he'll be touring and making appearances. Includes a search engine so that you can locate the lyrics of specified David Bowie songs.

Official Site

http://www.davidbowie.com/

This Day in Rock and Roll History

http://www.arrowfm.com/cgi/history.pl

★★★

14-18

What happened this day in rock and roll history? A calendar of music events covers every day of the year.

Tom Petty

http://www.tompetty.com/

★★★★★

14-18

A fantastic site featuring tons of information about Tom Petty and the Heartbreakers. Get bio information about all band members, check out the most current tour information, and learn the lyrics of all Tom Petty songs. Plenty of sample audio and video clips. Links to Artist Direct to shop for memorabilia.

The Van Morrison Website

http://www.harbour.sfu.ca/~hayward/van/van.html

★★★

14-18

Provides lyrics, a discography, reviews, and articles about the Irish soul and rock singer Van Morrison. Includes information about Van Morrison's songs, as well as who played what instrument on what song. Also provides interviews and a bibliography.

A B C D E F G H I J K L **M** N O P Q R S T U V W X Y Z

A
B
C
D
E
F
G
H
I
J
K
L
M
N
O
P
Q
R
S
T
U
V
W
X
Y
Z

zappa.com

http://www.zappa.com/

★★★★

 14-18

Browse through the complete discography, articles, and answers to FAQs. Get information about Frank's sons'—Dweezil and Ahmet—musical endeavors. Listen to the "Frank Zappa: American Composer" audio page, a two-hour radio documentary that originally aired on U.S. radio in the summer of 1996. Includes a brief biography and interview with Gail Zappa (Frank Zappa's wife) from *SECONDS Magazine.* Also includes an online store for Zappa's label, Barfko Swill Records.

MUSIC SOFTWARE

Magix Music Maker

http://www.magix.com/

★★★★

Find lots of software to make your own music, including children's music, music for your website, or to learn how to play an instrument. You can also download MP3 files.

Media Player

http://www.microsoft.com/windows/mediaplayer

★★★★

Download Windows Media Player here so that you can play virtually any format of music file, including MP3, WAV, AVI, MPEG, and Windows Media. You also can access streaming radio stations and improve the quality of videos you view onscreen. Plus, you can get the latest upgrade and technical support at this site, if you've downloaded previous versions and need assistance.

MusicMatch

http://www.musicmatch.com/

★★★★★

Home of one of the most popular MP3 players, rippers, and burners around. With MusicMatch, you can transform audio clips on CDs into MP3 clips, arrange MP3 clips to create your own playlists, and burn your playlists to create custom CDs.

QuickTime

http://www.apple.com/quicktime/

★★★★

Download QuickTime at this site so that you can view videos on your computer. You'll also find some of the top music videos available for downloading and viewing here.

RealPlayer

http://www.realplayer.com

★★★★

Get 2,500 radio stations, clear audio and bright video, free upgrades, and more when you purchase RealPlayer from realplayer.com. This site also offers other Real products that can enhance your listening and viewing experience. Check it out!

RioPORT.com

http://www.rioport.com/

★★★

Download music or spoken files, such as news and books, at this site, which also provides the software necessary to play the MP3 or other format files. You also have the opportunity to buy players, such as the Rio Player, at the site.

Roxio

http://www.roxio.com

★★★★

Home of Roxio's popular Easy CD Creator software, which allows you to duplicate CDs, copy data files to recordable discs, transform CD tracks into MP3 clips, play MP3 clips on your PC, and burn your own custom playlists to audio CDs. Excellent program for managing your digital music collection and very easy to use.

Shareware Music Machine

http://www.hitsquad.com/smm/

★★★

A large collection of downloadable music software for use in recording and playing music with your computer. Instructions and assistance provided by the webmasters.

Shockwave.com

http://www.shockwave.com

★★★★

Download Shockwave and Flash Player here so that you can view games, presentations, and animations in all their glory on other sites. The software is free, too.

MUSIC: INSTRUMENTS

8th street.com

http://www.8thstreet.com/

★★★★

Search the online database for virtually any type of musical instrument or equipment and find guaranteed lowest prices as well as free shipping when you order from the site. Whether you need amps, drums, or professional recording gear, you'll find it at this site.

Accordions International

http://www.accordioninfo.com/

★★★

Accordion music has come a long way since Lawrence Welk. This manufacturer even offers MIDI kits for electronic accordions. Read about the Concerto, the world's first digital/acoustic accordion. Other types of new—as well as used—instruments are also available. Order merchandise by phone, fax, or mail.

The American Nyckelharpa Association

http://www.nyckelharpa.org/

★★★

This traditional Swedish folk instrument has been around for hundreds of years, but you might not be familiar with it. The author of this page knows of 124 nyckelharpa players in North America. If you're one of them—or you're just curious about this instrument and its players and music—check out this page for details on the association, sound files, and more.

American Recorder Society

http://ourworld.compuserve.com/homepages/recorder/

★★★

Did you think recorders were just for junior high kids and new age fanatics? Find out more about this instrument and its proponents—more than 3,500 of them in nearly 30 countries. This site is primarily membership-based, but a list of related sites is available as well.

The Barrel Organ Museum

http://www.organito.com.ar/

★★★

The barrel organ has a fascinating history that constitutes more than just the prototypical organ grinder. If you've never seen a barrel organ (other than in the movies), be sure to visit this museum, located in Argentina. Scroll down the opening page and click the link for the desired language: Spanish, Italian, English, French, German, Dutch, or Japanese.

The Ethnic Musical Instruments Co.

http://www.mid-east.com/

★★★★

This site offers a large selection of ethnic musical instruments: sitars, bagpipes, lyres, ocarinas, doumbeks, and many others. Specials, seconds, and repairs—some at great prices—have their own page. Addresses of regional showrooms and related links are also included.

Gibson Musical Instruments

http://www.gibson.com/

★★★

Get information on Gibson guitars, locate local dealers, and buy and sell Gibson equipment online at the Gibson site.

A
B
C
D
E
F
G
H
I
J
K
L
M
N
O
P
Q
R
S
T
U
V
W
X
Y
Z

Guitarsite.com

http://www.guitarsite.com/

★★★★

If you're into guitar music—playing, recording, or listening—check out this site. You'll find hundreds of listings for guitar shops, guitar chords, guitar dealers, guitar publications, guitarists…you get the idea. But it's not just guitars—everything musical seems to be included. (Note: The screen colors might be a little extreme on some browsers.)

Guitar: WholeNote.com

http://www.wholenote.com/

★★★★★

WholeNote is dedicated to fostering a community of guitar aficionados for sharing musical knowledge. WholeNote provides an ever-evolving, always expanding music instruction book that you can play at your own speed. Site features a guitar store, composer software, groove builder, instruction, MP3s, and much more. Whether your pick, pluck, or strum a guitar, this site is for you, no matter what your level of expertise.

Hubbard Harpsichords, Inc.

http://www.hubharp.com/

★★★★

Hubbard sells complete harpsichords but also sells kits. The company's weekend workshops can help you to put together your own kit, with Hubbard's help, at a price that's substantially reduced from that of a completely assembled instrument. This site offers details about all the Hubbard products and services, as well as books, CDs, news, events, and general information.

The Internet Cello Society

http://www.cello.org/

★★★

With more than 10,000 members in more than 80 different countries, this organization is an international "cyber-community of cellists." Learn about the society, connect with other musicians, check out the links, and play the many RealAudio sound files.

LOOPLABS

http://www.looplabs.com

★★★★

Featuring an online music mixer, this site enables visitors to mix their own collection of recorded sounds to create original recordings. You'll feel like you're in a professional recording studio! After you have recorded your tune, you can upload it to share with others online.

The Music House

http://www.musichouse.com/

★★★

Based in Lake Forest, California, this company provides a wide variety of instruments and sheet music to commercial establishments or educational institutions. The service is particularly useful to small music stores that don't have the space or capital to keep a large inventory. Music House School Affiliates can rent or purchase band and orchestral instruments and receive funding assistance.

Rhythm Fusion—Musical Instruments from Around the World

http://www.rhythmfusion.com/

★★★★

Looking for sound makers from around the world? Then this is your site. You can purchase doumbeks, African drums, rattles, wind instruments, gongs, and much more by clicking on the icon of each type of instrument.

Things Musical

http://www.thingsmusical.com/

★★★★

More than 18,000 musical instruments are available at this site, at prices up to 40% off. Search by clicking on the first letter of the type of instrument you're interested in or scroll down to look at the long list of items available.

Unicorn Strings Music Company

http://unicornstrings.com/

★★★

This company specializes in bowed psalteries. You might have seen these unusual instruments in magazines and on TV, such as on the popular science fiction show *Babylon 5*. From this site, you can learn about the company, the instrument and how it's played, the music it produces, and, of course, how to get one.

UCSC Electronic Music Studios

http://arts.ucsc.edu/ems/music/

★★★

This University of California, Santa Cruz site provides a wealth of information on using electronic instruments, some of it in amazing detail. Definitely for serious musicians and the detail-oriented.

ORGANIZATIONS AND CLUBS

AMC: American Music Conference

http://www.amc-music.com/

★★★

AMC is a nonprofit educational organization dedicated to promoting music, music making, and music education to the general public through several educational institutions nationwide. Visit the site to learn more about the group's research and educational programs.

American Federation of Musicians of the United States and Canada

http://www.afm.org/

★★★

Professional union of musicians, full- and part-time, as well as students, in all genres. The AFM's goal is to improve musicians' working conditions and wages, and to support the arts and arts education. The Current Events section includes important industry news; the Hiring Musicians section describes how to hire a musician and provides links to booking agents and local musicians. Check the site list for links to related organizations, affiliates, and more.

American Society of Composers, Authors, and Publishers

http://www.ascap.com/

★★★

Read *Playback Magazine*, ASCAP's member magazine at the site, which addresses licensing issues of interest to independent creative artists. You can also get membership information. You'll certainly want to visit the ASCAP café online, where you can pick up survival tips, hear success stories, and solicit expert opinions from those who've been there.

BMI.com

http://bmi.com/

★★★

BMI is a nonprofit organization representing hundreds of thousands of songwriters, composers, and music publishers in all genres. This site provides a searchable database of its more than three million works. Check the Legislative Update section to keep up to date with the latest on copyright laws and other legislation related to intellectual property. The Recommended Reading section tracks all sorts of information on the BMI membership, along with books and articles of interest to the community. The Licensing and Songwriters' Toolboxes provide a wealth of useful material for the professional involved in the music field.

CD Club FAQ

http://www.blooberry.com/cdfaq/

★★★★

If you're considering joining (or rejoining) a music club such as Columbia House or BMG, read this FAQ first. It provides details on the best deals from the various clubs, strategies on how to get the most for your money, and rules/restrictions of club memberships. Answers to most-asked questions are available in a brief yes/no format, as well as a detailed listing.

Canadian Music Organizations

http://www.canehdian.com/organizations.html

★★★

A mammoth site filled with information about Canadian musicians, musical organizations, music news and events, album reviews, MP3 downloads, and more about the entertainment industry in general.

A B C D E F G H I J K L **M** N O P Q R S T U V W X Y Z

A
B
C
D
E
F
G
H
I
J
K
L
M
N
O
P
Q
R
S
T
U
V
W
X
Y
Z

Columbia House Music Club

http://www.columbiahouse.com

★★★

An extensive list of music in a wide variety of categories, but you must be a member to order. Join the club at this location. The current offer is 12+ CDs or cassettes free when you sign up; note that you pay for shipping and handling. Catalogs will come to members by mail, but you can also shop online (members get a special site and ordering number).

Country Music Awards

http://www.cmaawards.com/

★★★★

 14-18

Home of the Country Music Awards, this site provides information about the top-rated country music stars and songs. Here, you can find out about the upcoming Country Music Awards, check out the nominees, and look up the winners of awards.

Creative Musicians Coalition

http://www.aimcmc.com/

★★★

This international organization represents independent artists and record labels producing music in more than two dozen different styles. On the site, you'll find a directory of artists and the *AfterTouch* catalog. Search by artist, style, or label. The Showcase section offers reviews and samples of new music (some might require plug-ins). Are you ready to experiment?

Grammy.com

http://www.grammy.com/

★★★★

 14-18

Home of the Grammy Awards, the premier awards organization in the recording industry. This site provides information about the National Academy of Recording Arts & Sciences, Inc., also known as the Recording Academy. This group is "dedicated to improving the quality of life and cultural condition for music and its makers." Here, you can find out about the upcoming Grammy Awards, check out the nominees, and look up the winners.

Hearnet

http://www.hearnet.com/

★★★

Listening to loud music can seriously damage your hearing. If your kids cringe at the idea of turning down the sound, check out this website for news that might give them—and you—something to think about. Hearing Education and Awareness for Rockers (H.E.A.R.) is intent on preventing today's *Third Eye Blind* fans from turning into tomorrow's hearing-aid wearers. This nonprofit organization has the support of some heavy medical and musical folks.

Incorporated Society of Musicians

http://www.ism.org/

★★★

The professional organization for musicians, music students, and teachers in the UK, the ISM works to further the interests of its members by protecting copyrights, providing legal assistance and networking opportunities, and promoting its members to potential hiring organizations.

NAMM

`http://www.namm.com/`

★★★

Home of the International Music Products Association, NAMM represents more than 7,700 retailers, manufacturers, wholesalers, and publishers in the United States and 85+ other countries. Here, you can learn about upcoming events, including trade shows and the summer session; access resources; and learn about NAMM's current and upcoming projects.

Recording Industry Association of America

`http://www.riaa.com/`

★★★

The RIAA is a trade association representing the U.S. sound recording industry. The thrust of this site is the themes of antipiracy and artistic freedom. Plenty of interesting reading on these and other topics, as well as a searchable database of gold and platinum record winners, and a short list of related links. This site also features information for parents.

Wolverine Antique Music Society

`http://www.shellac.org/wams/`

★★★★

Presents the Wolverine Antique Music Society. Focuses on the preservation of music originally recorded for 78rpm records. Offers much to the 78 collector and early jazz aficionado. Contains many articles on the music, collecting, and all sorts of technical and resource information pertaining to antique audio. Also contains information on the early record labels, 78 album cover art, and sound clips.

Women In Music

`http://www.womeninmusic.com/`

★★★★

Women In Music (WIM) is a nonprofit organization with the goal of supporting the efforts and careers of women in the music industry. Numerous programs are offered at this site, including referrals, newsletters, seminars and workshops, insider's tips, and more. Events and industry news sections provide useful updates on music-related activities. You can also order apparel and other merchandise from this site, join the organization, and make donations online.

RADIO SITES

All Songs Considered

`http://www.npr.org/programs/asc`

★★★★★

Home of National Public Radio's music broadcasts, this site provides an on-demand archive of musical pieces featured on NPR's popular radio show. Features a handful of music videos, as well.

BBC Radio 4 Website

`http://www.bbc.co.uk/radio4`

★★★★★

The British Broadcasting Company is famous worldwide for its news coverage as well as in-depth reports on science, nature, history, religion, and more. Its comedy specials and dedication to preserving drama and the other arts also add to its allure. At this site, you can access much of what the BBC has to offer via its radio programming; plus you can quickly link to its television offerings as well.

BRS Web-Radio Directory

`http://www.web-radio.com/`

★★★★

Directory of thousands of radio stations that broadcast on the Web. You can view the complete directory or browse stations by call letters, states, countries, or format, or view a list of stations that broadcast exclusively over the Internet.

Related Site
`http://www.radiotower.com/`

CBC Radio

`http://www.cbcradio3.com/`

★★★★★

This is the online radio station of CBC Radio-Canada, Canada's National Public Broadcasting network. As soon as you connect, the music starts playing. Click the Table of Contents link on the left of the page to view additional content, including articles, photos, and links to other online music sites.

A B C D E F G H I J K L M N O P Q R S T U V W X Y Z

A
B
C
D
E
F
G
H
I
J
K
L
M
N
O
P
Q
R
S
T
U
V
W
X
Y
Z

Earth & Sky Radio Series

http://www.earthsky.com/

★★★

Every day Deborah Byrd and Joel Block discuss scientific issues that affect our lives on this science radio series heard by millions of Americans on more than 950 commercial and public stations across the country. The online shop offers many gift ideas that you can buy from the website.

Hearts of Space

http://www.hos.com

★★★★

Home of Hearts of Space, a combination record label and radio show syndication company. Here, you can sample the works of various recording artists, listen to Internet radio stations, and learn more about the company and its services.

KEXP

http://www.kexp.org/

★★★★★

At this site, you can listen to KEXP out of Seattle, check its daily programming schedule, listen to archived programs and live performances, read reviews of new albums, find out about upcoming concerts and events, and much more.

The KFJC Edge of Obscurity Music Database

http://www.spies.com/misc/kfjc/md/db/

★★★

KFJC, 89.7 FM, Los Altos Hills, California, plays a mix of music completely determined by the "on-air host" (note, not DJ). You might hear psychedelic, rock, pop, reggae, hip-hop, western, jazz, experimental—all mixed together. The database follows the same philosophy, providing a wide array of music, some of it fairly obscure. Search by label, artist, reviewer, or genre.

KPIG Radio Online

http://www.kpig.com/

★★★★

Tune into the web version of this California radio station that aims to be a throwback to the '60s and '70s when DJs added personality to their broadcasts. Check the site for the station's playlist, which varies from '50s music forward, information on DJs, and an active community of fans you can chat with. Be sure to check out the calendars and T-shirts available for purchase from this site.

JazzWeb (WNUR-FM)

http://www.wnur.org/jazz/

★★★

Based in Northwestern University in Evanston, Illinois, WNUR-FM plays a variety of interesting music of all genres. The JazzWeb page is devoted to the jazz spectrum. You'll also find fairly complete discographies of many popular (and some more obscure) artists. Search for your particular favorites or roam around in the other sections for something new.

KAOS: Welcome to KAOS!

http://www.kaosradio.org/

★★★★

KAOS is a radio station located at Evergreen State College in Olympia, Washington. It offers traditional and popular music of America and the world, including jazz, classical, swing, blues, soul, rap, R&B, Celtic, new acoustic and electronic music, Native American, Spanish language, rock, and Broadway music. You'll also hear comedy, radio theater, stories from *Pacifica News* and the *Monitor Press*, and news on public affairs. The site includes an on-air schedule, bios of the programmers, and descriptions of the programs. You'll also see KAOS's listing of the current top 30 songs.

Live365

http://www.live365.com

★★★★★

Live365 features the largest network of Internet radio stations on the Web providing everything from music stations to talk radio and special broadcasts. To start browsing, simply click the link for the desired genre, including Alternative, Comedy, Hip Hop, Classical, Reggae, Pop, and Rock. Click the More link for a complete offering of links, including Talk and Government. When you don't know where to tune in, stop here for a complete directory.

Live Radio on the Internet

http://www.live-radio.net/

★★★

Directory of thousands of live radio stations from all over the world that broadcast over the Internet. Stations are grouped by geographical location rather than by genre, making it a little tough to find what you want, but if you're looking for a news or weather report, this organization scheme works well.

MITList of Radio Stations on the Internet

http://www.radio-locator.com/cgi-bin/home

★★★

Find stations broadcasting on the Web by typing in a city and state, or the call letters, and you'll quickly find out where you can tune in to the broadcast. The database contains more than 10,000 stations, so there's a fair chance the one you want is here.

NPR: National Public Radio Online

http://www.npr.org/

★★★★★

This site lets you listen to NPR news on the hour. View summaries of programs and then listen to them, or check out some of the special highlighted stories that you might have missed. Check out the information on the news magazines, talk shows, and cultural and information stories you can listen to— among them, *All Things Considered, Morning Edition, Car Talk,* and *Jazz from Lincoln Center.*

Premiere Radio Networks

http://www.premrad.com

★★★

You'll find a large selection of syndicated talk, music, and entertainment shows that air on Premiere Radio Networks' radio waves here on their web version. Search the channels to find the type of programming you want to listen to and then tune in.

Public Radio Exchange

http://www.prx.org/

★★★★★

PRX (Public Radio Exchange) is a service that links public radio program producers with stations to assist in the distribution and peer review of programs. Register and you can listen to new shows before they are broadcast on the radio and offer your own feedback. Station managers can choose to license shows.

Public Radio Fan

http://www.publicradiofan.com/

★★★★

This site features a public radio programming guide for stations across the United States. Many program listings contain links that take you directly to the radio station's website, where you can "tune in" to the program. When you connect, make sure you enter your time zone to obtain an accurate programming schedule.

Radioio.com

http://radioio.com/

★★★★★

Radioio is one of the best sites to tune into alternative music in various genres, including acoustic, ambient, beat, boogie, classical, jazz, pop, and rock. If Mike, Radioio.com's resident deejay, finds a recording has the right mix of "rough edges" and "fluid motion," he plays it. Radioio features the work of more than 1,200 of the most creative musical artists in the past and present.

A
B
C
D
E
F
G
H
I
J
K
L
M
N
O
P
Q
R
S
T
U
V
W
X
Y
Z

A
B
C
D
E
F
G
H
I
J
K
L
M
N
O
P
Q
R
S
T
U
V
W
X
Y
Z

Transsom

http://www.transom.org

★★★★

Billing itself as "A Showcase & Workshop for New Public Radio," Transom features a diverse collection of in-depth, behind-the-scenes reports about real-life events and concerns. When you're tired of hearing the same old news reports and nightly specials, check out Transom for some more unique offerings. You can even record your own stories and submit them for inclusion on this site.

World Radio Network Online

http://www.wrn.org/

★★★★

WRN offers a global perspective on current world events and updates you on news from your homeland. It also covers arts and culture, music, sports, science, and more. WRN via cable, satellite, local AM/FM, and the Internet is used as an educational resource by schools, colleges, and universities. You'll also find WRN schedules and learn how to listen to live newscast audio streams in RealAudio and StreamWorks 24 hours a day from many of the world's leading public and international broadcasters.

WTOP

http://www.wtopnews.com/

★★★★★

WTOP online is Washington D.C.'s source for news, sports, and weather on the Internet. At this site, you can read local, national, and world news stories; check Washington's traffic, weather, and sports; look into science, health, and entertainment; and tune in to WTOP to listen to its live broadcast.

Yahoo! Launchcast

http://launch.yahoo.com/launchcast/

★★★★★

Yahoo! Launchcast enables you to tune in to 50 exclusive commercial-free radio stations, create your own custom radio station based on the genres you prefer, and search for song lyrics while you listen.

Youth Radio

http://www.youthradio.org

★★★★★

Youth Radio is dedicated to providing young people with the training and opportunities to become successful as radio producers, broadcasters, and in other radio broadcasting roles. Here, you can check out the work of some of the talented individuals involved with Youth Radio.

NATURE

BBC Nature Site

http://www.bbc.co.uk/sn/

★★★★

All

The British Broadcasting Company's Nature site is packed with articles and presentations about animals and the environment. Check out this week's nature special, take the daily quiz, subscribe to the newsletter, check out the birdcam, or browse the site for nature information that catches your eye.

Becoming Human

http://www.becominghuman.org

★★★★★

14-18

Documentary, news, commentary, and reference library designed to help visitors more fully comprehend human evolution.

Best eNature

http://www.enature.com

$

★★★★★

All

This for-profit site, owned and operated by the National Wildlife Federation, features a huge collection of wildlife resources for novice and expert alike. Find field guides for a wide range of animal and plant species, learn about birding, find out how to create your own nature habitats in your yard, get answers from the experts, and much more. This site covers the birds, the bees, the butterflies, the lizards, and every other known creature, plant, and living organism on this planet, making it our pick for Best of the Best nature site.

Kratts' Creatures

http://www.pbs.org/kratts/

★★★

All

Join Martin and Chris on their adventures into the wilderness to search for your favorite creatures. Explore Creature World, check in on the Creature of the Week, visit the Creature Clubhouse, and check out your favorite adventure with the Episode Guides.

Nature

http://www.nature.com/

$

★★★★

All

This online version of *Nature* journal provides free access to many of the features and articles covered in the journal. Subscribers obtain full access to the site. Covers the latest nature news, giving a more scientific perspective.

The Nature Conservancy

http://www.panda.org/

$

★★★

All

With an emphasis on saving existing habitats, including both plants and animals, this is a great place for environmental activists to visit. Learn about the group's activities and programs and how you can join the Nature Conservancy in its conservation efforts.

A
B
C
D
E
F
G
H
I
J
K
L
M
N
O
P
Q
R
S
T
U
V
W
X
Y
Z

The Nature Study Online Project

http://www.backyardnature.net/nsop/welcome.htm

★★★

 All

Grab your field guides, binoculars, magnifying glasses, and mosquito repellant, and join the Nature Study Online Project to gather information and share it with other budding naturalists online. Here, you can learn nature-study basics, post lists of plants and animals you found, look up life-cycle information, and join a mailing list to keep abreast of your colleagues' findings.

PBS Nature Site

http://www.pbs.org/wnet/nature/

★★★★★

 All

For more than 20 years, the PBS *Nature* series has informed and entertained its viewers through its premier nature programming. You can now access much of the information presented in these shows online. The site features a searchable database of past programs, information on upcoming programs, a video database, puzzles, interactive games, and e-postcards you can send to friends and relatives.

RainforestWeb.org

http://www.rainforestweb.org/

★★★★

 All

Concerned about preservation of the rainforests? Then visit this site to learn more about rainforests and the projects that threaten their very existence. Learn why rainforests are important, what's happening to them, why they're being destroyed, and what you can do to help.

Sierra Club

http://www.sierraclub.org/

★★★★

 All

The Sierra Club is one of the oldest grass-roots environmental activist groups. Its website encourages you to enjoy the great outdoors, take action to preserve our natural resources, and join or donate to the Sierra Club to help the organization fight for environmental-friendly legislation. Great place for environmental activists to keep abreast of current issues.

Whale Net

http://whale.wheelock.edu/Welcome.html

★★★

 All

Sponsored by Wheelock College in Boston, Massachusetts, this program tags and tracks whales. The website features a WhaleNet tour to help you navigate the site.

NETWORKING

3Com

http://www.3com.com/

★★★★

3Com Corp., a manufacturer of networking hardware, allows people who visit the company's site to learn about employment opportunities, browse company products, and get customer support.

About Computer Networking

http://compnetworking.about.com/

★★★

About's computer networking directory provides links to hundreds of resources on the Internet that provide information on networking. Links to sites that cover everything from basic networking terminology to setting up a network.

ATM Forum

http://www.atmforum.com/

★★★★

This group seeks to accelerate the use of asynchronous transfer mode technology in computer networks. Included at this site are answers to frequently asked questions about ATM technology, a glossary of terms, and membership criteria for the organization.

Cable Datacom News

http://www.cabledatacomnews.com/

★★★★★

Tracks the development of high-speed cable data services and contains monthly news reports. Users can also subscribe to CDN's email newsletter.

CastleTronics

http://www.castletronics.com/

★★★

Home of CastleTronics, a networking company based in Phoenix, Arizona, that specializes in networking, surveillance systems, and automation systems for homes and small businesses

CheapBytes.com

http://www.cheapbytes.com/

★★★★★

One of the more favorable places to seek out Linux software, books, novel items, and information on the world's best operating system. If you want to install a networking system using Linux or you need information on networking, this is the ultimate place to find it

[Best] Cisco Connection Online

http://www.cisco.com/

★★★★★

Cisco Systems, Inc., is the worldwide leader in networking for the Internet. Cisco products include routers, LAN and ATM switches, dial-up access servers, and network management software. Cisco Systems news and product/service information are available on this site. The opening page is packed with links for information, products, services, technology, and training, and its one-stop approach to networking makes this site the Best of the Best.

A
B
C
D
E
F
G
H
I
J
K
L
M
N
O
P
Q
R
S
T
U
V
W
X
Y
Z

Consortium for School Networking

http://www.cosn.org/

★★★★

The Consortium for School Networking (CoSN) is a national nonprofit organization that promotes the use of information technologies and the Internet in K–12 education to improve education. School districts, state and local education agencies, nonprofit educational organizations, and other companies and individuals in the Consortium work together to achieve its goals.

Related Site
http://www.ncrel.org/tandl/k-12infra/k-12infra.htm

Digital Tool Group

http://www.dtool.com/

★★★★

Learn more about networking and system security through troubleshooting tips provided at the site, as well as networking resources and support information offered by the site's "wizardlettes."

DSL Forum

http://www.adsl.com/

★★★

A forum where digital subscriber line (DSL) access network systems are discussed.

Emulex Network Systems

http://www.emulex.com/

★★★★

This company designs and produces hardware and software for network access, communications, and time management. Products specialize in the management of data between computers and peripheral equipment. The site includes detailed product listings, upgrade programs, technical support, and a company profile.

HELIOS Software

http://www.helios.de

★★★★

Developers of color-management and client/server software, including Helios EtherShare, PCShare, EtherShare OPI, and Helios ColorSync 2 Xtension. Check out the FAQ section, read the latest news, and see the specials HELIOS is offering.

High Speed USB

http://www.usb.org/

★★★

Information about the Universal Serial Bus interface. Also features technical specifications and other resources for developers

Hitachi Data Systems (HDS)

http://www.hds.com

★★★★★

Learn about Hitachi Data Systems products and services targeting the IT needs of large enterprises.

Home Network Security

http://www.cert.org/tech_tips/home_networks.html

★★★★

How secure is your home network? Check this site to find out and to learn about network security in a home or small-business environment. This site begins with an introduction to home security and then discusses available technology, specific risks, and actions you can take to secure your network

Hughes Network Systems

http://www.hns.com/

★★★★★

Hughes Network Systems' home page presents the company's networking and telecommunications products and services. Job listings, general corporate information, and online customer support are also provided.

Hummingbird Ltd.

http://www.hummingbird.com/

★★★

Delivers enterprise software solutions to simplify business transactions on the Internet and empower users to get their jobs done more easily and accurately.

IBM Networking Hardware

http://www.networking.ibm.com/

★★★★★

Read IBM's Networking Primer to learn more about the basics of computer networking and then get information about the company's Token Ring Network products and upgrades.

Interactive Network Design Manual

http://www.tele.sunyit.edu/NETWORK.PDF

★★★★

Whether you're considering building a network or are in the initial planning stages, this interactive manual is the first source you should explore. Here, you will find a basic introduction to networking along with some plain English explanations of key concepts.

Interphase Corporation

http://www.iphase.com/

★★★★

Products for mass storage and high-speed networks. You'll find links to products, support, news, and employment opportunities

InterWorking Labs

http://www.iwl.com/

★★★★★

Offers Test Suite software products that test SNMP network hardware, such as routers, printers, hubs, servers, and UPSs. Find out about the company's products, download a free SNMP test suite demo, and contact IWL staff.

Intranet Journal

http://www.intranetjournal.com/

★★★★★

Visitors to this site can learn about current intranet standards, intranet security and software, planning, tools, and more. An intranet FAQ, message boards, and an events calendar keep you abreast of what's happening in the world of intranet technology and development.

ITPRC.com

http://www.itprc.com/nms.htm

★★★

The goal of this site is to provide a one-stop shop for information technology professionals to find technical information on data networking. You'll find links to a large collection of networking-related information as well as links to career management information and professional discussion forums.

Jini Connection Technology

http://wwws.sun.com/software/jini/

★★★★★

Official page of Sun Microsystems' networking technology, Jini. This site features technical specifications, white papers, and tutorials. Jini network technology provides a simple infrastructure for delivering network services and for creating spontaneous interaction between programs that use these services. The site has many articles and stories about Jini, as well as more extensive definitions.

KarlNet

http://www.karlnet.com/

★★★★

Bridges and routers to solve your network security problems. Pictures and links to products and information, applications, and pricing are available.

Kinesix

http://www.kinesix.com/

★★★★

Manufacturer of Sammi, which enables you to integrate network applications without writing any network or graphical user interface code. The site has several links to places where you can learn more about Sammi, including current users, tech support, employment opportunities, and more.

Lancom Technologies

http://www.lancom-tech.com/

★★★★

Lancom Technologies provides all the courseware you need to become CNA or CNE certified. Provide this courseware for your students or yourself at reduced costs.

A
B
C
D
E
F
G
H
I
J
K
L
M
N
O
P
Q
R
S
T
U
V
W
X
Y
Z

A
B
C
D
E
F
G
H
I
J
K
L
M
N
O
P
Q
R
S
T
U
V
W
X
Y
Z

LANology Enterprise Network Solutions

http://www.lanology.com/

★★★★★

Networking and IT staffing service, LANology is a headhunting service for computer professionals. If you need a networking guru or IT professional and don't know where to look, visit this site.

Linksys Online

http://www.linksys.com/

★★★★★

This site is the home page for Linksys, a manufacturer of high-speed networking and connectivity products, specializing in wireless networking configurations. Visitors to this site can learn about company products and receive technical support and free software upgrades.

Lucent

http://www.lucent.com/

★★★★

Lucent has been one of the main producers of networking and telecommunications equipment and technology. Visit this site to learn more about Lucent's products and services.

Microsoft Servers

http://www.microsoft.com/servers/

★★★★★

Interested in Microsoft's networking products? Then visit this site, where Microsoft showcases its network server software. Here, you can find information about Microsoft's .NET Enterprise family of servers, including BizTalk, Commerce, Exchange, Internet Security, and Mobile Information servers. Obtain product information, find out where you can purchase products, get technical support, download patches, and much more.

Myricom, Inc.

http://www.myri.com/

★★★

This site explains Myrinet technology, software, and support, and it offers information on Myricom. Myrinet is a cost-effective, high-performance, packet-communication and switching technology that is widely used to interconnect clusters of workstations, PCs, servers, or single-board computers. Clusters provide an economical way of achieving high performance and high availability.

Netgear

http://www.netgear.com

★★★★★

Whether you have a large corporate network or just a home or small office network, you will find what you need here. This site complements itself with many useful and informative articles and documents on the subject of networking.

NETiS Technology, Inc.

http://www.netistech.com/

★★★★

NETiS is a manufacturer and service provider for all your individual, business, and institutional computer needs. Check out the company's corporate profile, services and support, product info and press releases, promotions, and more.

NetWare Connection

http://www.nwconnection.com/

★★★

Magazine for Novell networking professionals. Covers products, technical issues, and industry news. The site includes current and archived issues, a magazine subscription form, and an online bookstore.

Network Computing Magazine

http://www.nwc.com/

★★★★★

IT professionals will want to bookmark this online version of *Network Computing* magazine. Here you can find the latest networking news and reviews, learn how to perform specific networking tasks, download networking tools and toolkits, and much more. Additional benefits are available for subscribers.

Network Professionals Association

http://www.npanet.org/

★★★★

NPA is a nonprofit association for network professionals that encourages adherence to a Code Of Ethics, self-regulation, and vendor neutrality. The NPA focuses on helping network professionals fully develop their skills and talents and ensures the integrity of the profession.

Network Security Library

http://secinf.net/

★★★★

This site features a directory of network security information and resources, including hundreds of articles, FAQs, white papers, and books. Network professionals are encouraged to submit additional resources to grow the library.

Network World Fusion

http://www.networkworld.com/

★★★★★

A huge online community that provides networking product reviews and buyer's guides, online chat and discussion forums, headline news and networking-specific news, as well as topical columns and career info.

NetworkMagazine.com

http://www.networkmagazine.com/

★★★★

Read the current issue of the online version of this print publication for networking professionals or search the archives for back issues. The resource section contains helpful news and information for individuals looking for a new job.

NeuroDimension, Inc.

http://www.nd.com/

★★★

A neural network simulation environment that supports any neural models. Check out the product and simulation demos, press releases, screen shots, and more.

Nortel Networks

http://www.nortelnetworks.com/index.html

★★★★★

Nortel offers secure networks to ensure privacy. Check out the networking solutions and training programs to benefit your organization

Novell, Inc.

http://www.novell.com

★★★★

A leader in networking software provides information on new products, online technical support, and different networking solutions for business and government.

Paradyne Corporation Power Pages

http://www.paradyne.com/

★★★★

Paradyne Corporation manufactures network access products. This website contains information about the company and its products and services, as well as support. You'll also find an interactive form for checking on the status of an order.

Plaintree Systems

http://www.plaintree.com

★★★

Produces wireless network connectivity and optical wireless products. If you're looking for a wireless surveillance solution, this is the place to go.

A B C D E F G H I J K L M **N** O P Q R S T U V W X Y Z

A
B
C
D
E
F
G
H
I
J
K
L
M
N
O
P
Q
R
S
T
U
V
W
X
Y
Z

Practically Networked

http://www.practicallynetworked.com/

★★★★★

This excellent resource for IT and networking professionals features articles and reviews of the latest equipment and technologies along with dates and reports about important conferences. Includes separate sections for IT Management, Networking & Communications, Web Development, Hardware & Systems, and Software development.

Proxim

http://www.proxim.com/

★★★

This site will explain what wireless LAN technology is and introduce you to Proxim and its products and services. Proxim claims to be "the world's most popular wireless LAN" and offers you the option to read what several independent market research firms say about the company.

SoftLinx, Inc.

http://www.softlinx.com/

★★★★★

Provides network fax and Internet messaging products for mid-size to large corporations and service providers.

System Resources Corporation

http://www.srcorp.com/

★★★

Provides many different services and network system solutions for corporate, government, and defense clients. The site includes a company profile, philosophies, and services offered. Also includes contact information and information about what's new.

TechFest—Networking Protocols

http://www.techfest.com/networking/prot.htm

★★★★

Read reference material on networking, from the basic to the very advanced. Also find out which books are recommended references through the Good Book listings.

Telindous

http://www.k-net.co.uk/

★★★★

UK networking and telecommunications consultants, trainers, and service. Features manufacturer-independent solutions.

TENET Computer Group, Inc.

http://www.tenet.com

★★★★

A Canadian Novell NetWare network reseller and installer. Find out about Tenet, its products, certifications, and more. This site also offers IT links.

Vicomsoft

http://www.vicomsoft.com/

★★★★

This software company develops and markets several products for networking PCs, primarily in a home- or small-business environment. Click Resources and then click KnowledgeShare to access some interesting tutorials on basic networking topics

WaiLAN Communications Inc.

http://www.wailan.com/

★★★

This site provides information about the company's line of networking and Internet connectivity products.

NEW AGE

A B C D E F G H I J K L M N O P Q R S T U V W X Y Z

Access: New Age

http://www.accessnewage.com/

★★★

This site contains all things new age. It has one of the most comprehensive link indexes. The site focuses mostly on astrology, but it also provides other features such as a Moon Table, a Zodiascope, a section on Tarology, and even a Humor section.

AquarianAge

http://www.aquarianage.org/

★★★

Established to provide a central resource of information about astrology and new age studies, this site is constantly updated as part of a cooperative effort to share information and understanding of the topic.

AzNewAge

http://www.aznewage.com/

★★★

A vast amount of new age religion and philosophy information with links to other Arizona sites. It will take you hours to go through all the information provided by this site, which covers religion, healing, philosophy, theology, politics, sex, and even income taxes.

Full Circle New Age Book Shop

http://members.tripod.com/~vijaykumarjain/

★★★

Contains an extensive list of books on spirituality, Janism, Hinduism, self-realization, and meditation. Order the books through Amazon.com. The pop-up ads at this site can become annoying.

How To Talk New Age

http://www.well.com/user/mick/newagept.html

★★★★

Learn the new age lingo, from a humorous standpoint. Serious followers of new age disciplines probably should avoid this site.

I Ching Bookmarks

http://www.zhouyi.com/

★★★

Check this list of links on the background, resources, tools, freebies, and software related to the I Ching.

International Center for Reiki Training

http://www.reiki.org/

★★★★

The International Center for Reiki Training promotes becoming more in tune with spiritual consciousness (REI) in order to properly guide our life energy force (KI) to affect positive personal and global change. Visit this site to learn more.

Llewellyn Online

http://www.llewellyn.com/

 14-18

Get a free copy of *New Worlds*. This publisher's color catalog covers the widest range of new age subjects, from astrology and psychic development to yoga, healing, personal transformation, modern magic, the paranormal, Wicca, and beyond. Includes a special area for teens and young adults.

A
B
C
D
E
F
G
H
I
J
K
L
M
N
O
P
Q
R
S
T
U
V
W
X
Y
Z

New Age Books

http://www.newagebooks.com/

★★★★

Browse a catalog of more than 30,000 books or the site's wide selection of incense, tarot cards, pendants, cards, and calendars.

New Age Directory

http://www.newagedirectory.com/

★★★

Here is a good-size directory of new age sites sorted by topics, including Dream Interpretation, ESP & Telepathy, Crystals/Gemstones, Prophecy & Prediction, and much more.

New Age IQ Test

http://www.iqtest.net/newage/

★★★

Take this fun, interactive, and informative IQ test covering a wide range of new age topics.

NewAgeJournal.com

http://www.newagejournal.com/

★★★★

This online magazine features articles about various New Age topics, along with free daily horoscopes and a brief primer on New Age beliefs and lifestyles. This site is divided into five sections: New Age Web Works, New Age Travel, New Age Retreats, New Age Bazaar, and Astrologers-R-Us.

New Age Net

http://www.newagenet.com/

★★★

The purpose of this site is to promote the power of prayer in all religions. You can submit your prayer request at this site.

New Age Online Australia

http://www.newage.com.au/

★★★★★

This site contains a huge amount of free-to-read new age and spiritual information covering astrology, Wicca and Pagan spirituality, UFOs and ETs, ascension, earth changes, channelings, crystals, dreams, divination, angels, magic, karma, meditation, healing, and much, much more. With icons for just about every new age topic you can imagine, great graphics, a clean design, and an easy-to-navigate interface make this site the Best of the Best.

New Age Retailer

http://www.newageretailer.com/

★★★★

This site is the Internet home of the top-selling publication for retail distributors of new age products— *New Age Retailer* magazine. The mission of this magazine is to present information and resources for new age stores.

New Age Web Works

http://www.newageinfo.com/

★★★★

A site that provides information about New Age, UFO, Pagan, Occult, and Alternative Spirituality communities. At the site you can buy products, read articles and newsletters, and share ideas.

Real Music

http://www.realmusic.com/

★★★★★

Real Music features more than 100 new age albums from more than 20 international artists. Its artists regularly chart on Billboard' Magazine's New Age Chart. If you are looking for relaxing, spiritually uplifting music, this is the site for you.

Salem New Age Center

http://www.salemctr.com/newage/

★★★★★

Offers FAQs on the new age movement and meditation, lists of popular new age books, articles on ET human origins, and a free email newsletter.

NEWS

A B C D E F G H I J K L M N O P Q R S T U V W X Y Z

MAGAZINES

Arts & Letters Daily

http://www.aldaily.com

★★★★

Comprehensive digest and directory of news, book reviews, essays, and opinions gathered from the top newspapers, magazines, radio programs, news services, and other media sources around the world. Features gobs of information in an easy-to-access format.

Atlantic Unbound

http://www.theatlantic.com/

$

★★★★

Sample in-depth articles on politics, society, arts, and culture from this print magazine. Back issues are archived.

Congressional Quarterly

http://www.cq.com/

$

★★★★

Comprehensive news and analysis of what's happening in the corridors of power. The site follows Congress, the federal government, and political events.

Harper's

http://www.harpers.org/

$

★★★★

Aims to provide readers with a window on the world by exploring non-mainstream topics. Find a magazine index and subscription details here.

Internet Public Library

http://www.ipl.org/div/serials/

★★★★★

 All

The Internet Public Library offers this directory of online magazines that fall into several categories, including Arts & Humanities, Business & Economics, Computers & the Internet, Education, and Health & Medical Services. Links to Kids and Teens areas.

Khabar

http://www.geocities.com/SouthBeach/Port/8282/khabar.htm

★★★

This site provides links to all major newspapers and magazines from India, Pakistan, Bangladesh, Sri Lanka, Afghanistan, Nepal, Bhutan, and the Maldives.

The MagazineBoy—Online Magazine Directory

http://www.themagazineboy.com/

$

★★★

The MagazineBoy provides the Web's biggest collection of quality searchable links to thousands of online magazines from around the world. Every subject is covered, with something for everyone's taste. Why waste time at the corner drugstore or newsstand when you can find just about every magazine you will ever want to read here? The MagazineBoy site provides the Web's biggest collection of quality searchable links to thousands of online magazines from around the world. Every type of magazine is covered, including fashion, automotive, business, news, and computers, to name a few. You'll also find a nice search feature where you enter the subject to find the magazine or select from a handy categorized list. You can order online.

Related Site
http://www.thepaperboy.com/

A
B
C
D
E
F
G
H
I
J
K
L
M
N
O
P
Q
R
S
T
U
V
W
X
Y
Z

MagazinesAtoZ.com

http://www.magazinesatoz.com/

★★★★

Use this directory of more than 1,300 magazines and periodicals to track down the desired publication. This site also features a search tool to find specific articles within magazines.

National Journal

http://nationaljournal.com/

$

★★★★

Formerly *PoliticsNow*, *National Journal* contains many of the features that made *PoliticsNow* one of the most popular sites on the Web, including the Poll Track database, the "Buzz" insider columns, and the *Almanac of American Politics*. Also, it contains *Earlybird*, an early morning digest of hot political news; *Buzz Columns*, a "daily dose of analysis and commentary on Congress"; and *Daybook*, a daily planner for upcoming political and policy events in the capitol.

National Review

http://www.nationalreview.com/

$

★★★★

This site is filled with opinions and features from the popular United States conservative magazine, with commentary from William F. Buckley, Jr.

The Nation

http://www.thenation.com/

$

★★★

Weekly selected articles from the well-known liberal magazine, sound files of the show *RadioNation*, and discussion forums are available at this site.

The New Republic

http://www.thenewrepublic.com/

$

★★★

Award-winning weekly journal of opinion offers selected articles from the Thursday print edition. A full table of contents plus various links are included.

News Directory

http://newsdirectory.com/

★★★★★

This site features an extensive directory of magazines grouped by categories, including Arts & Entertainment, Business, Science, Sports, and Travel. Also features a directory of newspapers grouped by country and broadcasting stations. Excellent site for tracking down a broad selection of offerings.

Best **Newsweek**

http://www.msnbc.com/news/NW-front_Front.asp

$

★★★★★

Read this week's top stories; check daily news updates; log in with your questions for upcoming Live Talk segments on controversial topics; and read regular columns about international issues, business, society, political campaigns, and more. You'll definitely be caught up on current events after visiting this Best of the Best site!

Popular Science

http://www.popsci.com/

$

★★★★

This website comes to you compliments of the editors of *Popular Science Magazine*. Find out what's new in the automotive, computer, electronics, home technology, and science fields. Plus, get other articles from the magazine, various buying guides, and helpful links.

TIME

http://www.time.com/

★★★★★

 All

Puts the news in context with full text of the print magazine each week. This site is updated throughout the day and cross-referenced. Like the magazine, this site is more focused on celebrities, entertainment, science, and the human-interest viewpoint than on more serious news events and investigative journalism. Includes a link to *TIME for Kids*.

U.S. News

http://www.usnews.com/usnews/home.htm

★★★★★

Online version of the popular current affairs magazine. The Washington Connection is included for the latest political news and election coverage.

USA Weekend

http://www.usaweekend.com/

★★★★

This Gannett magazine is carried by nearly 500 United States newspapers; it features entertainment, fitness, finance, and current events.

The Utne Reader

http://www.utne.com/

★★★★★

The reader's digest of the alternative press, *The Utne Reader* wanders off the mainstream track to provide articles about topics you won't find covered in *Time* or *Newsweek*.

The Weekly Standard

http://www.weeklystandard.com/

★★★★★

The online version of this right-leaning magazine contains samplings of news and commentary. Features from previous issues are included, along with an excellent collection of current editorials.

ZDNet–PC Magazine

http://www.pcmag.com/

★★★★★

You will find all kinds of current information about computers on this site, including late-breaking news, articles, product reviews, and free downloads. By becoming a registered member, you will receive free email, software, and the free magazine. The site is very well designed, with the information presented in a way that makes it easy to find and easy to navigate.

American Journalism Review

http://www.ajr.org

★★★

This site provides a comprehensive review of news media, including magazines, newspapers, TV, radio, and websites; more links to industry-related sites; and a job search tool for journalists.

E&P Media Links

http://www.editorandpublisher.com/

★★★★★

Editor and Publisher has collected a vast listing of newspapers available on the Web, accessible via a clickable map or the Quick Links option.

EmergencyNet News

http://www.emergency.com/ennday.htm

★★★★

An international news source reporting on worldwide incidents that pose potential threats to safety and security. Search the archives for past reports, link to other news channels, and find out what's going on in countries across the world. Recent articles reported on bomb scares, Internet security breaches, and child kidnapping, among others.

The Feedroom

http://www.feedroom.com/

★★★★★

Picture yourself surrounded by monitors, each broadcasting a different news story from around the world. You click a monitor to tune in to the story you want. News on demand? This is the closest thing, although you might get more in-depth coverage at some of the "print" news sites.

indianz.com

http://www.indianz.com/

★★★★

You'll find news, information, and entertainment provided from a Native American perspective. In addition to national news, this site offers headlines from tribes across the country, as well as more in-depth reports on issues that directly impact Native American communities.

A
B
C
D
E
F
G
H
I
J
K
L
M
N
O
P
Q
R
S
T
U
V
W
X
Y
Z

Mirror Syndication International

http://www.mirpix.com/

★★★★★

Features more than 250,000 newspaper pictures online plus an offline library of more than 3 million pictures, which it offers for sale to businesses and private customers. The site accepts credit cards.

News and Newspapers Online

http://library.uncg.edu/news/

★★★

Lists hundreds of newspaper and magazine links organized by continents and countries. Also offered are FAQs and an advanced search.

Newseum

http://www.newseum.org/

★★★★★

Visit the Newseum .to read the headlines of more than 250 newspapers around the world, play the Newsmania Quiz Game, and check out the Newseum's virtual exhibits of the media coverage surrounding many of history's top stories.

News Express

http://www.foreignmedia.com/

★★★★

Providers of foreign books, newspapers, and magazines. If you are doing research, this is a good place to find material on every news-related subject in many countries.

NewsLink

http://newslink.org/

★★★

An index of national and foreign newspapers, campus newspapers, dailies, non-dailies, and alternative press. Covers both newspapers and magazines.

Newsstand Connection

http://www.geocities.com/~paulstan/u.html

★★★

Find links to news, weather, sports, business media resources, recipes, and more. In addition, this site offers a search capability, free downloads, and Web directories.

oneworld.net

http://www.oneworld.net/

★★★★★

This supersite of information is dedicated to reporting on global development issues, such as education, migration, or children's rights. In addition to news reports, you'll find searchable archives, opportunities for chat, and discussion forums. Links to various editions worldwide in several different languages.

ONLINE Magazine

http://www.onlinemag.net/

★★★

This site provides numerous articles, product reviews, case studies, evaluations, and informed opinions about selecting and using electronics products. Written for the busy information professional.

PBS Global Connections

http://www.pbs.org/wgbh/globalconnections/

★★★★

When you're trying to understand international events from a global perspective, check out PBS Global Connections. This site focuses on the hot spots around the world and places the events in a historical, cultural, and political context. Great place for students, teachers, and parents to help foster a deeper understanding of current events.

TotalNEWS

http://www.totalnews.com/

★★★★

Comprehensive, searchable directory of news sites, covering everything from entertainment and sports to international news and business. Local news, weather, politics, human interest stories, and opinions are also covered.

The Write News

http://www.writenews.com

★★★★

This site features news, information, and resources for professionals in the media and in publishing. Provides more than 1,000 links to the most valuable resources on the Web.

WWW News Resource Web

http://sun3.lib.uci.edu/~dtsang/netnews1.htm

★★★

This site features an extensive directory to various news resources, including Alternative News, Campus News, Conservative News, Ethnic News, and newspapers inside and outside the United States.

SERVICES

allAfrica.com

http://allafrica.com/

★★★★★

This leading provider of African news and information posts more than 700 stories daily in English and French and features a searchable archive of more than 400,000 articles. Visit this site to access the latest African headline news, sports, and editorials, along with business and stock market reports, currency information, health alerts, and more.

Aljazeera

http://english.aljazeera.net/HomePage

★★★★★

Aljazeera is the news service of choice for most of the Arabic world. Here you can find news from around the world, commentary, special reports, political cartoons, polls, and other newsworthy items.

Bay City News

http://www.baycitynews.com/

★★★

An online regional news service from the San Francisco Bay area that offers entertainment news, general news, and legal news. The site also offers info about the news service itself and a fax/email headline service.

Best BBC News

http://news.bbc.co.uk/

★★★★★

Updated every minute, the British Broadcasting Channel (BBC) site has a definite international slant to its reporting, which runs the gamut from international politics to sports and celebrities. Its balanced coverage, comprehensive approach, excellent design, and easy-to-navigate layout make this site the Best of the Best.

Business Wire

http://www.businesswire.com/

★★★★

Business News distributes news to the media locally, nationally, and worldwide. This wire service offers customized news-release distribution to the news media, online services, the Internet, and the investment community.

Crayon

http://crayon.net/

★★★★

Nifty free tool for managing news on the Web. Create your own newspaper with links to sources that interest you.

Desktop News

http://www.desktopnews.com/

★★★★

Get streaming news, weather, sports, and stock information on your Windows desktop. Download the free Desktop News Ticker Toolbar and customize it to view just the news you want.

Federal Communications Commission

http://www.fcc.gov/

★★★★

Federal Communications Commission (FCC) online serves as a forum for public discussion concerning FCC issues (including broadcasting). It contains current legislation, full text of relevant speeches, agenda, and the FCC daily digest, along with lists of email addresses to which you can send comments and concerns about television.

A B C D E F G H I J K L M N O P Q R S T U V W X Y Z

A
B
C
D
E
F
G
H
I
J
K
L
M
N
O
P
Q
R
S
T
U
V
W
X
Y
Z

HotBot: News Channel

http://news.lycos.com/

★★★★

Wired News' search service looks at some major newspapers and a variety of other news sources.

IMEDIAFAX

http://www.imediafax.com

★★★★

This online news distribution service faxes your business message to the media. Users create a proprietary media list from a vast selection of magazines, newspapers, syndicates, and broadcast stations. Click on industry and classification, key editors, states, market area, or circulation, and then enter your news release and click to send. IMEDIAFAX news releases can contain graphics, letterheads, logos, or pictures. The cost is 25¢ per faxed page (minimum order of $50). News releases are better targeted, and another bonus is that there are no international phone or fax charges.

Individual.Com

http://www.individual.com/

★★★

Gives you a daily. business briefing, with news from the computing and media worlds, as well as other key industries. The site also provides breaking general news and access to CompanyLink, where you can look up news, research, and contacts for more than 65,000 companies. And you can register to create your own individualized NewsPage. Access 20,000 daily news stories, from more than 600 sources. Register for this free service.

InfoBeat

http://www.infobeat.com/

★★★★

Find out about InfoBeat's personalized news service. This service will deliver email news customized to your stated preferences.

Media Monitors

http://www.mediamonitors.com.au/

★★★★

Learn about Australia's leading provider of customized news and information services, read today's top stories, and join the mailing list.

NCNS: Network Computing News Service

http://www.ncns.com/andmore2.html

★★★

You get three things at this site: computer-related photo links, computer-related news at a glance, and hot links (to such sites as alphaWorks and WebTV). The news selections include stories on Internet networking, Netscape Navigator, and Microsoft, to name a few.

NewsHub

http://www.newshub.com/

★★★

NewsHub integrates and reports headlines from the world's premier news sources every 15 minutes.

The Paperboy

http://www.thepaperboy.com/

★★★★

Check this service's "top drawer" to find top news sources or browse newspaper listings by country. Excellent collection of the world's most popular newspapers, plus the search tools you need to track down the stories you want.

PBS: Online NewsHour

http://www.pbs.org/newshour/

★★★★

News features and analysis, complete with online forums for discussion of the issues of the day. Subscriptions for email news delivery also are available.

A B C D E F G H I J K L M N O P Q R S T U V W X Y Z

The Positive Press

http://www.positivepress.com/

★★★★

This online service posts positive news stories from publications around the United States, plus positive quotations, affirmations, stories, and more. This free site is updated frequently.

PR Newswire

http://www.prnewswire.com/

★★★

PR Newswire describes itself as "the leading source of immediate news from corporations worldwide for media, business, the financial community, and the individual investor." The site seems to live up to this claim, with a long list of content that's worth scrolling through.

RadioSpace

http://www.radiospace.com/index.html

★★★

Serves as a resource for radio-station programming and news staffs. It provides ready-for-broadcast sound bites, news, and programming.

Reuters

http://www.reuters.com/

★★★★★

Reuters, a leading news and information company, fulfills the business community's and news media's financial, multimedia, and professional information needs. At this site, you can get online news or learn more about Reuters.

RocketNews

http://www.rocketnews.com/

★★★★★

RocketNews broadcasts current news and delivers business news and information to its subscribers. Several categories of news are available here, including Breaking News, World, Business & Finance, Technology, Entertainment, Health, Science, Sports, and Arts & Literature.

South African Broadcasting Corporation

http://www.sabc.co.za/

★★★★★

The South African Broadcasting Corporation (SABC) is South Africa's national public service broadcaster. This site gives details on the company, its services, answers to FAQs, and more.

Sympatico NewsExpress

http://www1.sympatico.ca/news/

★★★

Canada's news service featuring news headlines, editorials, stories, and features, plus updates, local coverage, and current affairs and events.

WebClipping.com

http://www.webclipping.com/

★★★★

Monitor the Web and newsgroups for name, brand, or trademark. Prices, services, and research tools are listed.

World Radio Network

http://www.wrn.org/

★★★★★

The World Radio Network (WRN) provides you with access to the world's leading broadcasters. You'll find constant news flow and current events. WRN carries live newscast audio streams in RealAudio, WindowsMedia, and StreamWorks 24 hours per day. Listeners can hear the news live in English and other languages direct from the source.

U.S. NEWS MEDIA

abcNEWS.com

http://abcnews.go.com/

★★★★★

This home site of ABC's award-winning *World News Tonight* with Peter Jennings puts the day's top stories within reach of a single mouse click. Check U.S. and international news, stock market updates, politics, weather, sports, and more. Links to other ABC news shows, including *Good Morning America*, *20/20*, and *Primetime*.

A
B
C
D
E
F
G
H
I
J
K
L
M
N
O
P
Q
R
S
T
U
V
W
X
Y
Z

Associated Press

http://www.ap.org/

★★★★★

The Associated Press online offers full access to the AP news wires.

CBS News

http://www.cbsnews.com/

★★★★★

Visit Dan Rather's home on the Web to check out today's headline news. Focuses mainly on U.S. news, but covers international issues, business and stock market news, and investigative stories as well. Use the navigation bar at the top of the home page to find more information on World news, Science and Technology, HealthWatch, and Entertainment. Links to *60 Minutes*, *48 Hours*, and *The Early Show*.

Christian Science Monitor

http://www.csmonitor.com/

★★★★

Comprehensive national and international coverage from the online version of this award-winning newspaper. Use the navigation bar at the top of the page to check out World News, US News, Commentary, Work & Money, Learning, Living, and more. This newspaper provides a very balanced view on most issues.

CNN Interactive

http://www.cnn.com/

★★★★★

Get all the top news stories at your fingertips, or delve into weather, sports, science and technical news, travel, style, show business, health, and earth topics. Many stories have accompanying QuickTime video segments. This site also describes what CNN has to offer on television.

CNN/Time AllPolitics

http://www.cnn.com/ALLPOLITICS/

★★★

Comprehensive coverage of all the latest political news.

Disaster News Network

http://www.disasternews.net/

★★★★

Comprehensive source of primarily United States disasters, response news, and volunteer needs. Some coverage of international disasters and relief efforts as well. You'll find organization links, ways you can help, and the latest stories.

ESPN.com

http://espn.go.com/

$

★★★★★

 14-18

You can view game scores and statistics, get sports news, participate in fan polls, interact with other sports lovers, buy tickets online for sports events, visit the training room, and much more.

FoxNews.com

http://www.foxnews.com/

★★★★★

For a more conservative approach to the news and editorials of the day, visit the FoxNews website. Here, you can check out national and international news, get weather forecasts for your area, keep abreast of the current political scene, and check in on entertainment options. Hardcore conservatives should check out the link to the *O'Reilly Factor*.

Los Angeles Times

http://www.latimes.com/

★★★★★

Includes local news as well as national coverage of major stories, in-depth features, pictures, and classifieds. This website's no-frills approach to headline news coupled with a comprehensive list of links to various feature articles make it our choice as Best of the Best. However, there are so many excellent candidates in this category that we had a tough time selecting only one.

MSNBC

http://www.msnbc.com/news/

★★★★

You can personalize the MSNBC news page to get the news you want, the way you want it. Or you can stick with the standard page for a wide variety of news options. You can also choose news audio headlines to hear the news read to you by newscasters (some video and illustrated audio are also available).

News of the Weird

http://www.newsoftheweird.com/

★★★

Chuck Shepherd's weird news stories collected from various newspapers and other sources across the nation. When you get tired of "normal" news, take a break and visit this site.

New York Daily News

http://www.nydailynews.com/

★★★

Get a daily dose of gossip about movie stars, politicians, and sports heroes. Also, read the latest news about New York City.

New York Times

http://www.nytimes.com/

★★★★★

Home of one of the world's most famous broadsheets, featuring local and national sports and news, as well as coverage of international issues. Covers the entire range of news, including national and international news, business, sports, weather, politics, science, technology, entertainment, education, health, and editorials.

NPR

http://www.npr.org/

★★★

National Public Radio broadcasts. Listen to the most recent or past broadcasts including *All Things Considered, Morning Edition, Science Friday, Talk of the Nation*, and NPR's hourly newscast.

San Jose Mercury News

http://www.bayarea.com/mld/mercurynews/

★★★

Up-to-the-minute news on computers and technology, sports, national issues, and business from this Silicon Valley community paper.

Top 100 Newspapers

http://www.interest.com/top100.html

★★★★★

Composed by a leading home finance company, this site offers direct access to many popular United States newspapers on the Web.

United Press International (UPI)

http://www.upi.com/

★★★★

Avoid the middlemen and get the news where the news services get their news, the UPI wire service. This site posts up-to-the-minute news on business, sports, current events, politics, science, technology, and more.

Best USA Today

http://www.usatoday.com/

★★★★★

The first full-color national paper to hit the market, this online version of *USA Today* features the top news, money, sports, and life reports across the nation. When you'd rather look at pictures than read lengthy reports, *USA Today* is the place for you.

Wall Street Journal Interactive

http://online.wsj.com/public/us

Ⓢ

★★★★★

If you think the *Wall Street Journal* is for guys who wear expensive suits, visit this site to have your preconceptions erased. WSJ features some of the best investigative reporting, analysis, and writing of any newspaper in the United States, and you can access much of it online. You must subscribe, for about $60 per year, but you can check it out for free.

A B C D E F G H I J K L M N O P Q R S T U V W X Y Z

A
B
C
D
E
F
G
H
I
J
K
L
M
N
O
P
Q
R
S
T
U
V
W
X
Y
Z

Washington Post

http://www.washingtonpost.com/

★★★★★

Includes most of the print features from this daily, which is known for its political coverage. This site also offers weather, style, technology, and a place for chat.

WEBZINES

Asia Pacific News

http://www.apn.btbtravel.com

★★★★

Browse through the top 50 news agencies and newspapers in the Asia Pacific region. Also offered are links to shopping and employment sites.

Blueprint

http://members.aol.com/bluemagzin/whatsnew.html

★★★

News bulletin offers alternative perspective on culture, politics, and science. Send an email directly to the editor.

Boston Bull's Union News

http://www.geocities.com/Area51/Corridor/4030/

★

Read the latest union news, add your union's news, read membership letters, and add your two cents to the mix. You'll also find union links, along with the option to add your union. Want to be notified of strikes? This site offers that service, too.

Drudge Report

http://www.drudgereport.com/

★★★

Internet scandalmonger Matt Drudge tracks the latest gossip from Capitol Hill, Hollywood, and beyond. Links to international news sources and columnists can also be found here.

The Economist

http://www.economist.com/

★★★

This site features a selection of articles from the current print issue of this UK-based weekly magazine. Subscription details are available.

Emerging Markets

http://www.emergingmarkets.org/

★★★

Offers daily records for the joint annual meetings of the International Monetary Fund and the World Bank. Subscribe to the mailing list.

Jane's Defence Weekly

http://jdw.janes.com/

★★★

Oriented toward defense issues in the Middle East and Asia, this magazine offers in-depth articles and features.

Jane's Foreign Report

http://www.foreignreport.com/

★★★

Offers predictions and analyses on foreign diplomacy, political developments, economic policies, and business. Subscribe for weekly briefings.

Salon.com

http://www.salon.com/

★★★★

An intelligent, provocative online magazine that presents the latest news, reviews, and analysis in a variety of content areas including Arts & Entertainment, Life, News, People, and Politics. Winner of several awards for site design and content as well as journalism.

Slate

http://slate.msn.com/

★★★★

Hard-hitting online magazine that pulls no punches when it comes to criticizing politicians and policies. Behind-the-scenes reviews of international happenings and their effects on life in the United States. Features business, sports, and technology sections, as well.

The Smoking Gun

http://www.thesmokinggun.com

★★★★

This online tabloid masquerading as the home of an investigative journalism site provides background reports covering the latest celebrity and political scandals. Check out the day's featured document or click the Archives link for a list of previous investigations.

Veterans News and Information Service

http://www.vnis.com/

★★★★

Browse through this comprehensive news and information resource for military veterans. It includes news from the Navy, the Marines, and the Coast Guard.

WorldNetDaily

http://www.worldnetdaily.com/

★★★★

Compiles stories from wire services, networks, and international papers, plus offers some original reporting. Asks some of the more probing questions that the mainstream news media avoid.

A B C D E F G H I J K L M N O P Q R S T U V W X Y Z

NONPROFIT AND CHARITABLE ORGANIZATIONS—RESOURCES

RESOURCES FOR NONPROFIT ORGANIZATIONS

BoardSource

http://www.boardsource.org/

★★★

If you need to assemble a board of directors for your nonprofit agency, this is the place to go. Features books, training, Board Q&As, and membership information.

The Chronicle of Philanthropy

http://philanthropy.com/

★★★★

Summaries of articles published in the *Chronicle*'s print version. Browse the site to find information on gifts and grants, fundraising, management, and technology of interest to nonprofit organizations.

Council on Foundations

http://www.cof.org/

★★★★★

A membership association composed of more than 1,300 nonprofit foundations (independent, corporate, and public). Its programs are issues such as education, health, human services, science and research, and so on. The site also promotes accountability among member foundations.

Foundation Center

http://www.fdncenter.org/

★★★★

For grant seekers and grant makers, this site contains information on libraries and locations, training and seminars, funding trends and analyses, the fundraising process, and publications and CD-ROMs. Also, it includes a searchable database and an online reference desk.

Foundation Finder

http://lnp.fdncenter.org/finder.html

★★★

This Foundation Center search page can help you find addresses and phone numbers for more than 7,000 foundations in the United States.

Foundation News and Commentary

http://www.cof.org/newsroom/index.htm

★★★★

A Council on Foundations publication with feature articles about foundations and funding. Only selected articles are available online.

Fund$Raiser Cyberzine

http://www.fundsraiser.com/

★★★★★

Fundraising ideas, information, and resources. Only the current issue is online. Back issues may be ordered on disk.

Getting Major Gifts

http://www.tgci.com/magazine/96spring/gifts1.asp

★★★

More excellent advice from Kim Klein, the author of *Fundraising for Social Change* and the publisher of *The Grassroots Fundraising Journal*. This article, reprinted with permission, is excerpted from a collection of articles that originally appeared in *The Grassroots Fundraising Journal*.

Internet Nonprofit Center

http://www.nonprofits.org/

★★★★

Based on an IRS database, the Internet Nonprofit Center is a project of the Evergreen State Society of Seattle, Washington. It offers information for and about nonprofit organizations in the United States.

Internet Prospector

http://www.internet-prospector.org/

★★★

This excellent site has links to many online databases and search engines to help you find your "high-roller" prospects. You'll also find an online newsletter.

John D. and Catherine T. MacArthur Foundation

http://www.macfdn.org/

★★★

One of the nation's 10 largest foundations, MacArthur today has assets of $4 billion and issues grants totaling more than $175 million annually. The Foundation seeks the development of healthy individuals and effective communities, peace within and among nations, responsible choices about human reproduction, and a global ecosystem capable of supporting healthy human societies. It pursues this mission by supporting research, policy development, dissemination, education and training, and practice.

Joseph & Matthew Payton Philanthropic Studies Library

http://www.ulib.iupui.edu/special/ppsl.html

★★★

Houses one of the world's largest and most comprehensive collections of books, periodicals, dissertations, and audio-visual resources on the subject of philanthropy. Included are books on social movements, ethical and moral issues, nonprofit organizations, religion in American public life, critiques of philanthropy across the political and ideological spectrum, fundraising, and philanthropy and education.

National Committee on Planned Giving

http://www.ncpg.org/

★★★★

The National Committee on Planned Giving is the professional association for people whose work includes developing, marketing, and administering charitable planned gifts. Those people include fundraisers for nonprofit institutions and consultants and donor advisors working in a variety of for-profit settings.

NonProfit Gateway

http://www.nonprofit.gov/

★★★★★

Learn more about government support for nonprofit groups by clicking on federal government agency names at this simple site.

Nonprofit Genie

http://www.genie.org/

★★★★

Sponsored by C-MAP, the California Management Assistance Partnership, this site is dedicated to providing the nonprofit community the information and resources it needs to succeed. Features a hot topic and cool site of the week, a useful collection of nonprofit FAQs, a monthly newsletter, and links to other nonprofit resources on the Web.

A B C D E F G H I J K L M N O P Q R S T U V W X Y Z

A
B
C
D
E
F
G
H
I
J
K
L
M
N
O
P
Q
R
S
T
U
V
W
X
Y
Z

The NonProfit Times

http://www.nptimes.com/

★★★

This home site of "The Leading Business Publication for Nonprofit Management" presents a sampling of articles from the current edition of the print magazine plus special reports and items of interest to nonprofit organizers.

NPO-NET

http://npo.net/

★★★★

This site is primarily a resource for Chicago-area nonprofit organizations, but also enables you to search for grants and grant makers, information on fundraising and philanthropy, training for nonprofit management, nonprofit discussions, and more.

Philanthropy News Digest

http://fdncenter.org/pnd/

★★★

Short articles on major philanthropic gifts. This is a good place to see what the major charity players are doing. If you're looking for something in particular, the site is searchable.

Philanthropy.org

http://www.philanthropy.org/

★★★★

This site is the home of the Center for the Study of Philanthropy (CSP), which was founded in September 1986. CSP is devoted to providing an ongoing national and international forum for research, discussion, and public education on philanthropic trends. The home page contains links to Research on Philanthropy, Multicultural Philanthropy, International Philanthropy, and Women's Philanthropy.

PRAXIS

http://www.ssw.upenn.edu/~restes/praxis.html

★★★★

From Richard J. Estes, professor at the University of Pennsylvania, this page provides resources for social and economic development. It contains a reference room and links to development assistance agencies, organizations, policies, descriptions of levels of social development practice, home pages, news services, and more.

Schoolpop

http://www.schoolpop.com/

★★★★★

Hundreds of shops are linked through this site, which provides up to 60% of the purchase proceeds to fund the work of more than 60,000 nonprofit organizations. Choose an organization to support, or pick a shop to buy from and whenever you purchase anything from one of the member stores, a percentage of your purchase goes to the nonprofit of your choice. Major retailers are involved, including eBay, Staples, Best Buy, and Coldwater Creek, and there is no additional cost to the consumer.

Tech Soup

http://www.techsoup.org/

★★★★★

Nonprofits need. technology, too, and this site shows them where to obtain hardware, software, and technical advice free or at bargain rates. A wide range of users will find the technical support area useful, and if you would like to donate used computer equipment, this site can help you find centers that accept used equipment and deliver it to nonprofits that need it.

UK Fundraising

http://www.fundraising.co.uk/

★★★

This site offers a lot of information about fundraising in the UK. It offers information on charity and nonprofit fundraising in the UK and beyond.

NONPROFIT ORGANIZATIONS

Academy of Education Development

http://www.aed.org/

★★★

👥 All

AED is a nonprofit organization devoted to "solving critical social problems in the U.S. and throughout the world through education, social marketing, research, training, policy analysis, and innovative program design and management." Here, you can learn more about the organization and its various programs.

Adobe Community Relations

http://www.adobe.com/aboutadobe/philanthropy/main.html

★★★★

This corporate philanthropy arm of Adobe is primarily interested in supporting nonprofit health and human service organizations that, in turn, provide help to disadvantaged youth, the homeless, victims of abuse, and so on.

The Alliance

http://www.allianceonline.org/

★★★★

The Alliance for Nonprofit Management is devoted to helping nonprofits fulfill their missions by providing them with the information, resources, and leadership they need.

AT&T Foundation

http://www.att.com/foundation/

★★★

This site is the company's philanthropic arm that helps people to lead self-sufficient, productive lives. AT&T is particularly interested in projects that involve technological innovation. Its four program areas are education, civic programs, arts and culture, and community service.

Ben and Jerry's Foundation

http://www.benjerry.com/foundation/

★★★

Ben and Jerry's Foundation seeks programs concerned with societal, institutional, and environmental change. The foundation's particular areas of interest are children and families, disenfranchised groups, and the environment. The site also describes restrictions, types of grants, and ways to apply.

Benton Foundation

http://www.benton.org/

★★★★

Concerned with the information infrastructure. Among the foundation's projects: communications policy and practice, a report on public opinion of library leaders' visions of future, children's programs, the arts, and public interest organizations.

Carnegie Foundation

http://www.carnegie.org/

★★★

Grant-making foundation dedicated to enhancing knowledge. Currently supports education and healthy development of children and youth, preventing deadly conflict, strengthening human resources in developing countries, and other special projects. Learn how to submit a proposal, search for grant opportunities, and check out the proposal guidelines. If you're planning on writing a grant proposal, check out this site before you start. You'll save yourself some time and frustration.

Children's Miracle Network (CMN)

http://www.cmn.org/

★★★

Find out what this organization does to help nonprofit children's hospitals. Learn how you can become involved in supporting its mission. Search for your community's local CMN affiliate if you are most interested in giving where you live and in helping critically ill children.

A B C D E F G H I J K L M N O P Q R S T U V W X Y Z

A
B
C
D
E
F
G
H
I
J
K
L
M
N
O
P
Q
R
S
T
U
V
W
X
Y
Z

Commonwealth Fund

http://www.cmwf.org/

★★★★

Conducts research on health and social policy issues. Programs include improving healthcare services, improving the health of minority Americans and the well-being of the elderly, developing the capacities of children and young people, and improving public spaces and services.

Goodwill Industries International

http://www.goodwill.org/

Ⓢ

★★★★★

Provides employment and training services, and removes barriers for people with disabilities. The site contains information on the THAP Project, current news, and more. Also, it enables you to find a donation center, a retail location, and a Goodwill store in your area.

Habitat for Humanity International

http://www.habitat.org/

Ⓢ

★★★★

Learn about the efforts of this organization to build affordable homes for the needy. You'll find information on where the organization builds, how it works, and how you can support its work—either by volunteering locally or donating.

Junior Achievement

http://www.ja.org/

★★★★

 All

Find out more about Junior Achievement's efforts to introduce students in grades K–12 to the free enterprise system by establishing for-profit businesses in local communities. Search the site to find a JA chapter near you.

Project HOPE (Health Opportunities for People Everywhere)

http://www.projhope.org/

★★★

Dedicated to improving healthcare throughout world. This site provides education, policy research, and humanitarian aid. Also, it contains links to the group's research on health policy, programs, and journal. The HOPE website has a searchable database.

Real Change: Seattle's Homeless Newspaper

http://www.realchangenews.org/

★★★

Features the past two issues, subject index of stories in archives, and directions on organizing a homeless paper in your own city. In addition, it contains poetry by those who are homeless.

Starlight Children's Foundation

http://www.starlight.org/

★★★

Find out how you can volunteer or donate to this children's organization that works to make the lives of critically ill or injured children more enjoyable by granting wishes and providing audio-visual programming on a monthly basis.

United Way of America

http://national.unitedway.org/

★★★★★

An organization embracing local community–based United Way groups, made up of volunteers, charities, and contributors. This site contains information on several of the United Way's programs, including Mobilization for America's Children and the United Way partnership with the National Football League. The site also includes news, a United Way FAQ sheet, and a description of how United Way works.

CHARITABLE CONTRIBUTIONS

American Institute of Philanthropy

http://www.charitywatch.org/

★★★★

Find out about this organization, the charities it tracks, and its philosophy on rating. You'll also find articles on charitable giving. Request a free copy of *Tips for Giving Wisely*.

BBB Wise Giving Alliance

http://www.give.org/

★★★

Find out how your favorite charity is spending your donation. This organization carries information for hundreds of top nonprofits that solicit contributions across the United States. You can also look at the organization's Standards in Philanthropy.

Canadian Charitable Organizations

http://www.charityvillage.com/

★★★★

This Charity Village page has Canadian nonprofits listed by type. Click on your choice, and you are taken to more links. From there, you can connect directly to the organization of your choice.

Charitable Choices

http://www.charitablechoices.org/

★★★★

Look here for information on more than 300 non-profit organizations. Most of the charities listed are based in the Washington, D.C., area. Many international organizations are also represented.

The CharityNet

http://www.charitynet.org/

★★★★

This supersite provides resources for the international nonprofit community and its contributors.

GuideStar

http://www.guidestar.org/

★★★★

Links to the latest articles in the popular press about nonprofits and philanthropy. Also, access the Search For A Non-Profit database, which contains more than 800,000 nonprofit organizations. You can search by type, city and state, revenue range, or keyword.

The Hunger Site

http://www.thehungersite.com/

★★★★★

By just visiting this site and clicking a button, you can help donate food to needy areas and countries. The site's sponsors fund the work of the group, so there is no cost to you. The site has delivered millions of tons of food through the United Nations World Food Program.

Independent Charities of America

http://www.independentcharities.org/

★★★★

A nonprofit organization that prescreens high-quality national and international charities and presents them for your giving consideration. Click on a category (Children, Animals, Environment) or click on Charity Search to search by name or keyword.

Best ⭐ JustGive.com

http://www.justgive.org/

$

★★★★★

If you would like to make a donation to a nonprofit organization but are not sure just who to give to and which organizations are legitimate, check out this site. JustGive is a nonprofit organization dedicated to connecting people with the charities and causes they care about. JustGive also features charity baskets, each of which distributes your overall contribution to four related charities. Baskets include Animals, Hunger, Peace, Earth, and Children. Site serves more than 850,000 legitimate nonprofit organizations and ensures that your contribution goes toward a good cause. The site's clean design and overall usefulness makes it our choice for Best of the Best in the nonprofits category!

A
B
C
D
E
F
G
H
I
J
K
L
M
N
O
P
Q
R
S
T
U
V
W
X
Y
Z

Network for Good

http://www.networkforgood.org/

★★★★★

Network for Good aims to be a central resource connecting individuals who want to volunteer or donate financially to local organizations of interest. Search for a charity from among the 850,000 listed at the site based on your location or the type of work you want to do.

Philanthropy Roundtable

http://www.philanthropyroundtable.org/

★★★★

This site offers articles of interest to donors and observers of the philanthropic world.

Planned Giving Design Center

http://www.pgdc.net/pub/

★★★★

This site offers research and planning resources to planned giving specialists and financial advisors. It is sponsored by a group of charitable organizations and requires registration. There is no charge for using the site.

Tax Exemption Information

http://www.irs.gov/charities/

★★★★★

This IRS page is a good place to begin learning about tax-exempt nonprofit organizations.

Urban Institute

http://www.urban.org/

★★★★

Studies policies surrounding social and economic problems. At this site, you'll find the institute's annual report, text of current and back issues of publications (for example, *Future of the Public Sector*), and a list of the institute's sites. This site is also searchable.

World Vision

http://www.worldvision.org/worldvision/master.nsf/

★★★★

Sponsor a child, read about disaster relief opportunities, and check out the WV annual report. Features a newsletter and a domestic projects database.

VOLUNTEERING

20 Ways for Teenagers to Help Other People by Volunteering

http://www.bygpub.com/books/tg2rw/volunteer.htm

★★★★★

 14-18

This page shows teenagers 20 ways to volunteer their time to help other people. Have you ever thought of giving some of your time to helping others? There is a lot to be gained from doing this. For one thing, you can gain valuable experience that will help you in later life, and better yet, you will make someone else happier. The world will be a better place to live with your contribution. Imagine yourself working at a homeless shelter, for the Red Cross, or the Salvation Army. When you get older, you can travel the world by joining the Peace Corps.

Advice for Volunteers

http://www.serviceleader.org/advice/index.html

★★★★

14-18

Information on finding the right volunteer opportunity and making the most out of your volunteer activities and efforts can be found on this site.

Alliance for National Review

http://www.ncl.org/anr/

★★★

Dedicated to helping communities rebuild, this coalition of more than 200 national and local organizations includes the National 4-H Council and the American Association of Retired Persons. At this site, you can find out more about the organization, sample its publications, keep abreast of news and events, and learn how to become a member.

America's Charities

http://www.charities.org/

★★★★★

This site features an index of U.S. charitable organizations, searchable by charity type (education, environment, health, human services, civil and human rights, and so on).

Association for Volunteer Administration

http://www.avaintl.org/

★★★★

The Association for Volunteer Administration is dedicated to helping its members become more competent managers and administrators of volunteer organizations. Here, you can learn more about the AVA and its programs.

Business Volunteers Unlimited

http://www.businessvolunteers.org

★★★

This resource center links businesses and nonprofits to communities in need of volunteers. Lists its members, services, events, and resources.

Corporation for National and Community Service

http://www.cns.gov/

★★★★

Official site of the AmeriCorps, Senior Corps, and Learn and Serve America, this government site is dedicated to encouraging and supporting volunteerism in America.

FIU Volunteer Action Center

http://www.fiu.edu:80/~time4chg/

★★★★

Sponsored by Florida International University, this site provides opportunities for volunteers, service learning, and advocacy in southern Florida. It includes lists of nonprofit agencies in the area. In addition, it enables students to assist faculty in service learning programs. It also links to the Volunteer Action Center reading room.

Global Volunteers

http://www.globalvolunteers.org/

★★★★★

Global Volunteers is an effort to achieve worldwide peace by partnering volunteers with local hosts and sponsors, who all work together on a project. The site provides information on the work of this organization and includes a volunteer application.

Idealist

http://www.idealist.org/

★★★★

 All

Global clearinghouse of nonprofit and volunteering resources. Search or browse through 26,000 organizations in more than 150 countries. Find volunteer opportunities worldwide, particular programs, services, books, videos, articles, or materials for nonprofits, and more. Idealist is a project of Action Without Borders and includes a special area for kids and teens.

Landmark Volunteers

http://www.volunteers.com/

★★★

👥 14-18

Looking for a summer adventure that enables you to serve a worthy cause? Then check out Landmark Volunteers, where you can learn about summer service programs at 65 of the top U.S. landmarks.

National Volunteer Fire Council

http://www.nvfc.org/

Ⓢ

★★★★

The National Volunteer Fire Council (NVFC) is a nonprofit membership association representing the interests of the volunteer fire, emergency medical, and rescue services. The NVFC serves as the information source regarding legislation, standards, and regulatory issues.

Best | Peace Corps

http://www.peacecorps.gov/

★★★★★

👥 14-18

U.S. government–supported volunteer organization with participants involved in projects in more than 80 countries. President Kennedy founded the Peace Corps in 1961 to provide help and assistance to underdeveloped countries. Since then, thousands of people from diversified cultural groups have served in the Peace Corps. The Peace Corps has three main goals: to help people in countries that are interested, to promote a better understanding of Americans, and to promote a better understanding of other people in other countries and societies. On this site you can find out how and why you might want to volunteer.

A
B
C
D
E
F
G
H
I
J
K
L
M
N
O
P
Q
R
S
T
U
V
W
X
Y
Z

A
B
C
D
E
F
G
H
I
J
K
L
M
N
O
P
Q
R
S
T
U
V
W
X
Y
Z

Presidential Freedom Scholarships

www.nationalservice.org/scholarships/index.html

★★★

[icon] 14-18

Information about volunteering and scholarships through the Presidential Freedom Scholarships program.

SERVEnet

http://www.servenet.org/

★★★★

[icon] 14-18

Enter your ZIP code at the SERVEnet site to post and find volunteer and career opportunities in your local area. In addition to searching for volunteer opportunities that make the best use of your interests and skills, you can find service news, events, best practices, and other resources.

Service Learning

http://csf.colorado.EDU:80/sl/

★★★

A compendium of Web resources on "service learning," this is a cooperative effort enabling academic programs and communities to interact. The site contains articles, bibliographies, dissertations, theses, films and videos, handbooks and manuals, and much more. Also, it links to archives of two service-learning–related LISTSERVs and is searchable.

Virtual Volunteering Project

http://www.serviceleader.org/vv/

★★★★

Allows anyone to contribute time and expertise to nonprofit volunteer organizations via the Internet. Offers a project profile, news, and resources.

VISTA—Volunteers in Service to America

http://www.friendsofvista.org/

★★★★★

[icon] 14-18

One of America's oldest volunteer organizations, founded during the Kennedy years, this site provides the volunteer with useful information about what the organization does and how you can join. A great way to volunteer your time.

Volunteer Opportunities for Older Americans

http://www.aoa.gov/eldfam/Volunteer_Opps/Volunteer_Opps.asp

★★★

This article outlines ways seniors can enrich their lives through volunteering with programs such as foster grandparenting.

Volunteer Today

http://www.volunteertoday.com/

★★★★

This monthly gazette features news, articles, event schedules, and an archive, as well as recruiting, retention, and training information.

Volunteering

http://seniors-site.com/retiremt/volunter.html

★★★

Discover how volunteering can benefit you and your community. This site includes links to volunteer organizations.

Volunteerism in Canada

http://www.volunteer.ca/index-eng.php

★★★★

This site features some of the benefits of volunteering and provides a directory of organizations in Canada that are in need of volunteers.

VolunteerMatch

http://www.volunteermatch.org/

★★★★★

This ambitious project has more than lived up to its potential, enabling volunteers to find many thousands of volunteer opportunities all over the United States. Organizations might post both ongoing and one-time projects, allowing volunteers from several key cities to find just the opportunity they are looking for.

VolunteerMatch–Find a City Near You Needing Volunteers

http://www.impactonline.org/citymatch

★★★★

Learn about local opportunities for which you can volunteer online and sign up now. You can search a huge database to find a city near you that has such organizations in need or search the Non-profit database. The VolunteerMatch organizations service utilizes the power of the Internet to help individuals nationwide find volunteer opportunities posted by local and public sector organizations. You can locate an organization needing you and then sign up automatically by email. Makes the process informative, fun, and easy.

Volunteers of America

http://www.voa.org/

★★★★★

Services, news, and policy positions from one of America's largest and most comprehensive charitable, nonprofit human service organizations.

Wilderness Volunteers

http://www.wildernessvolunteers.org/

★★★★

This nonprofit organization promotes volunteer service in U.S. wildlands, parks, and reserves. The site details registration information, leadership qualities, meals, and activities. Must be 18 or older to volunteer.

A B C D E F G H I J K L M N O P Q R S T U V W X Y Z

A
B
C
D
E
F
G
H
I
J
K
L
M
N
O
P
Q
R
S
T
U
V
W
X
Y
Z

Yellow Pages

NURSING

American Association of Neuroscience Nurses

http://www.aann.org/

★★★★

American Association of Neuroscience Nurses (AANN) is a specialty organization serving nurses worldwide. Its site offers membership info, a bulletin board, resources, and more.

AllHeart.com

http://www.allheart.com

★★★

A shopping site for nurses and the medical profession. Order scrubs, stethoscopes, and much more from this site. You can also request a bid on a volume order.

allnurses.com

http://allnurses.com/

★★★★

Gain access to medical databases, career information, guidance, and a network of your peers at this site.

American Association of Colleges of Nursing

http://www.aacn.nche.edu/

★★★★★

Overview of the American Association of Colleges of Nursing. Upcoming conferences, educational standards and special projects, CCNE accreditation and publications, position statements, and a CareerLink are all included.

American Nurses Association

http://www.nursingworld.org/

★★★★★

The ANA represents the nation's 2,600,000 registered nurses. The site lists addresses of state nursing associations, meetings and events, and links to important reference sources.

Cybernurse.com

http://www.cybernurse.com/

★★★★

Resource page for nurses, with extensive information related to careers, a search function, and related links.

Ensearch Management Consultants

http://www.ensearch.com/

★★★

Places advanced practice and administrative nurses in neonatal and pediatric fields. Pore over its nationwide job listings or meet the company's staff.

Health Care Innovations

http://www.hcinnov.com/

★★★★

Displays openings for nurses in hospitals, doctors' offices, schools, businesses, and homes. Examine the vacancies and submit a profile.

Interfaith Health Program

http://www.ihpnet.org/

★★★★

This site explains IHP and offers a searchable database to access real-life examples of the healthcare model it supports. You'll also find an archive of articles, news on the program's research, and health resource links.

National Institute of Nursing Research

http://www.nih.gov/ninr/

★★★

Government organization dedicated to supporting research on health-related issues, ranging from the proper treatment of the ill to preventive health maintenance. Learn more about the NINR and its research funding and programs. Access NINR press releases, learn about upcoming events, and check out the latest scientific advances related to healthcare.

National League for Nursing

http://www.nln.org/

★★★

NLN is the leading accrediting body for all types of nursing education programs within the United States and its territories. Visit this site to learn about NLN's educational programs, conferences, online courses, books, and other products and services.

National NurseSearch

http://www.nursesearch.net/

★★★★

Fills a wide variety of nursing positions in hospitals nationwide. Subscribe to the job announcement newsletter or register with the firm.

NP Central

http://www.npcentral.net/

★★★★

Information for and about nurse practitioners, including a directory of links to sites, job announcements, education resources, and professional bodies.

Nurse Options USA

http://www.nurseoptions.com/

★★★★

Sign up for an email listing of positions for RNs and nurse management or learn about extra income opportunities. Submit your profile.

NurseWeek.com

http://www.nurseweek.com

★★★★★

This site contains nursing articles, editorials, continuing education programs, nursing events, career advancement information, and employment opportunities. Excellent place for nurses to go for career information, information on continuing education courses, and news relating to the nursing field.

Best NursingCenter.com

http://www.nursingcenter.com/

★★★★★

Packed with articles, inside information, and links to the best nursing resources on the Web, this site lives up to its billing as "The Web's most comprehensive resource for nurses." Includes recommended reading, information on professional development and continuing education, career guides, a job center, links to the nursing community, and links to online stores where you can purchase nursing apparel and other nursing-related items.

Nursing Desk Software

http://www.community.net/~sylvan/MacNursing.html

★★★★

Offers shareware and freeware, nursing links, and hospital unit information systems.

Nursing Education of America

http://www.nursingeducation.org/

$

★★★★

This site offers info on NEA and its accredited continuing education programs for nurses.

NursingNet

http://www.nursingnet.org/

★★★

This site provides a detailed index of nursing-related issues, groups, and resources, as well as a chat room and an employment message board.

A
B
C
D
E
F
G
H
I
J
K
L
M
N
O
P
Q
R
S
T
U
V
W
X
Y
Z

A
B
C
D
E
F
G
H
I
J
K
L
M
N
O
P
Q
R
S
T
U
V
W
X
Y
Z

Nursing Standard

http://www.nursing-standard.co.uk/

★★★

Hailing from the UK, this site is *Nursing Standard* magazine's home on the Web. Specializes in helping nurses find resources on professional development, nursing courses, and jobs.

Procare USA

http://www.procareusa.com/

★★★★

Places American and Canadian RNs throughout the United States. Read about the employment search and hiring packages.

StarMed Staffing Group

http://www.healthtour.com/

★★★★

Family of companies that specialize in the placement of nursing and allied health professionals nation-wide. The site provides information for specific job types.

WholeNurse

http://www.wholenurse.com/

★★★★

Provides information to nurses, patients, and medical personnel of all types in an effort to keep up with the growing amount of information posted online.

OCEANS

Aquatic Network

http://www.aquanet.com

★★★★

This site functions as an information server for the aquatic world, providing information on aquaculture, conservation, fisheries, marine science and oceanography, maritime heritage, ocean engineering, and seafood. You can purchase everything from books to fish on this site!

Beneath the Sea

http://www.beneaththesea.org

★★★

Beneath the Sea is a not-for-profit organization that works toward increasing awareness of the earth's oceans and the sport of scuba diving. BTS helps promote the protection of marine wildlife via grants to other nonprofit groups. This site includes links to seminars, workshops, mailing lists, and other diving-related sites.

Enchanted Learning's Guide to the Oceans

http://www.enchantedlearning.com/subjects/ocean/

★★★★

 All

This site is one of the best sites for children to begin their exploration of the oceans and the plant and animal life that live below sea level. Here, kids can learn about waves, tides, coral reefs, tidal zones, ocean explorers, and much more. They can also print diagrams to label and color and download instructions for fun and interesting projects.

How Sharks Work

http://www.howstuffworks.com/shark.htm

★★★★★

 All

This site provides an incredibly clear, illustrated description of shark anatomy and physiology. If you find sharks fascinating, then check out this site to learn more about shark anatomy, eating habits, and sensory organs as well as some of the threats to their survival.

National Oceanic and Atmospheric Administration

http://www.noaa.gov

★★★★

This home of the NOAA is packed with information not only about ocean weather patterns and currents but also about fisheries, fishery management, preservation of coastal environments and coral reefs, and explanations of navigational tools and techniques. This site is very easy to navigate and features a hefty collection of colorful photos.

NOAA's Coral Reef Online

http://www.coralreef.noaa.gov

★★★★

At this site you will find links to dozens of resources, including coral reef photos, areas where coral bleaching is a problem, locations of NOAA marine sanctuaries, information about biodiversity in coral reefs, and much more.

A
B
C
D
E
F
G
H
I
J
K
L
M
N
O
P
Q
R
S
T
U
V
W
X
Y
Z

Ocean Weather

http://www.oceanweather.com

★★★

Ocean Weather uses a unique hind-casting approach to forecast ocean weather including winds, waves, and surf. At this site, you can obtain current ocean data for various areas worldwide.

⫸Best⫷ Ocean.com

http://www.ocean.com

★★★★★

 All

This site features the latest news, studies, and warnings about the condition of the earth's oceans. Here, you'll find information about ocean travel, a gallery of ocean photos, Poseidon's library of sea stories, and links to hundreds of sites featuring everything from ocean gear to conservation groups. Well-designed, easy to navigate, and packed with useful information and links to other resources, this site is my personal favorite.

Related Sites
www.whoi.edu
sio.ucsd.edu
www.aquarium.ucsd.edu

OceanLink

http://oceanlink.island.net

★★★★

 All

OceanLink is packed with information and resources for enthusiastic ocean explorers of all ages. Click Ocean Info to access more than a dozen links for a variety of fascinating ocean topics; click AquaFacts for the latest news and trivia about ocean life; or click Records to find out which marine creature is the largest or smallest, which can dive the deepest, which is the fastest, and which is the slowest. This site also features an excellent glossary.

Oceans Alive

http://www.abc.net.au/oceans/alive.htm

★★★★

All

This site focuses on marine life in the waters surrounding Australia and provides information on whale watching and marine biodiversity hot spots. It also provides general ocean information, including a list of ocean facts, information about seal training, links to schools that offer studies in marine biology, and links to other oceanic resources.

The Ocean Alliance

http://www.oceanalliance.org

★★★★

All

The Ocean Alliance is focused on protecting and conserving whales through research and international education initiatives. Here, you can follow the voyage of the Odyssey as it carries out its five-year mission to study the seas; you can learn more about the Ocean Alliance and its goals; you can contribute to the organization; and you can even shop online.

PADI: Professional Association of Diving Instructors

http://www.padi.com

★★★

Updated daily, this site offers dive center listings, bulletin boards, product catalogs, news, course listings, and a wide range of information beyond what you can find at most scuba diving sites. PADI also offers a fish quiz to test your knowledge, a map of the ocean floor from NOAA, dive insurance, and more. If you plan on becoming a scuba diver, visit this site often.

Scripps Institution of Oceanography

http://sio.ucsd.edu

★★★★

This is the Internet home of the world famous Scripps Institution of Oceanography, a part of the University of California, San Diego campus. Scripps has a 100-year history of helping various countries around the world research and solve problems relating to the oceans. Here, you can find information about the various programs and research projects that the Scripps Institution is involved in and explore its diverse collection of marine species and geophysical data. Its library is also searchable online.

Scuba Yellow Pages

http://www.scubayellowpages.com

★★★★

Scuba Yellow Pages enables you to search a worldwide directory to find contacts and suppliers for all your scuba diving needs—from tour operators to airlines to clubs and certifications. The site also offers tons of information, a diver's directory, a search feature to help you quickly locate information, email, and lots of diver resources. If you are interested in diving for fun or profit, this is the place for locating equipment you need and other resources to make your dive much more successful, whether you dive for recreation or professionally.

SeaWeb

http://www.seaweb.org/

★★★★

SeaWeb is dedicated to raising awareness of the world oceans and sea life and the threats they face in the modern world in the hopes that greater awareness will inspire people to do what they can to conserve the world's oceans. Here you can learn more about SeaWeb and its programs, read the latest information about the oceans, and find out what you can do to help.

SeaWorld

http://www.seaworld.org

 $

★★★★★

👥 All

This site is a great place for kids to learn about animals both in the oceans and on land. It's also a great place for teachers to obtain resources for their biology and science classes. Downloadable, printable teacher guides are available for all ages of students from kindergarten up to 12th grade and cover a variety of topics ranging from arctic wildlife to sharks, wetlands, and species diversity. Parents can also obtain information about various adventure camps designed for kids.

Stephen Birch Aquarium Museum

http://www.aquarium.ucsd.edu

★★★★

👥 All

Stephen Birch Aquarium Museum is part of the Scripps Institution of Oceanography. This aquarium has information about volunteer opportunities, educational programs, and summer learning adventures. Here, you can also find links to what's new at the aquarium, membership information, ocean quizzes, and articles and videos about various species of marine animals.

Surfrider Foundation USA

http://www.surfrider.org

★★★

👥 14-18

Surfrider Foundation is a nonprofit group dedicated to protecting, preserving, and restoring the world's oceans and beaches. Its site includes daily surf reports, *Coastal Factoids*, policy updates, and an online membership form.

A
B
C
D
E
F
G
H
I
J
K
L
M
N
O
P
Q
R
S
T
U
V
W
X
Y
Z

A
B
C
D
E
F
G
H
I
J
K
L
M
N
O
P
Q
R
S
T
U
V
W
X
Y
Z

Titanic, the Official Archive

http://www.titanic-online.com/

★★★★

 14-18

This site explores the history of the Titanic from its conception and building to the time it sank and its discovery at the bottom of the ocean. This site also provides information about the passengers and crew and descriptions and photos of many of the artifacts collected during the discovery. You can shop for Titanic-related merchandise online.

Whales Online

http://www.whales-online.org

★★★★

 All

This information site is dedicated to the "conservation of whales, dolphins, and porpoises in the Southern Hemisphere." Here, you can find information about whales, dolphins, and porpoises by region; obtain information about responsible whale and dolphin watching; and learn about the numerous threats that our oceans and whales face.

Woods Hole Oceanographic Institution

http://www.whoi.edu

★★★★★

 All

Woods Hole Oceanographic Institution is a private, not-for-profit organization that studies the oceans and attempts to develop solutions for the most serious problems threatening the health of our oceans. At this site, you can learn about the Woods Hole programs and research projects, about the many interesting research vessels and vehicles (submersibles), and about its educational program offerings. This site also features fascinating articles about current expeditions and other ocean-related topics.

OFFICE MANAGEMENT

A B C D E F G H I J K L M N O P Q R S T U V W X Y Z

OFFICE EQUIPMENT

abcoffice.com

http://www.abcoffice.com/

★★★★★

This online office supply store carries more than paper and staples. It also carries some of the heavy-duty items that large offices require, including display cases, payroll clocks, shrink wrap equipment, and much more.

BuyerZone.com

http://www.buyerzone.com/office_equipment/

★★★★★

Resources for becoming a more-informed purchaser of office equipment, focusing primarily on electronic equipment, including copiers, printers, fax machines, and shredders. Features buyer's guides, articles, and newsletters. Obtain free quotes on equipment purchases from several online stores. Whether you manage your own small office or offices for a large corporation, you'll find plenty of excellent information and deals on this Best of the Best site.

Home Office Direct

http://www.homeofficedirect.com/

★★★★

Online office furniture warehouse features a wide selection of desks, computer desks, computer carts, office chairs, and accessories.

OfficeFurniture.com

http://www.officefurniture.com/

★★★★

Search for modular furniture, filing cabinets, seating, and accessories for your office at OfficeFurniture.com, where you should have no problem finding an office furniture solution that fits your budget.

OFFICE SUPPLY STORES

Action Office Supplies, Inc.

http://www.actoff.com/

★★★

Based in Adelphia, New Jersey, Action offers a wide variety of office equipment and supplies. For details on the company's offerings, fill in a request for a catalog (several types are offered). Catalogs are sent via snail mail, but you can order online from this site, which also includes links to major office equipment and supply manufacturers.

BusinessSupply.com

http://www.business-supply.com/

★★★★★

This site offers convenient, one-stop shopping for the business supplies, office machines, and business furniture you need to keep your small business or large office. Browse the store by category or search for specific items.

A
B
C
D
E
F
G
H
I
J
K
L
M
N
O
P
Q
R
S
T
U
V
W
X
Y
Z

Boise—Worldwide Office Supply Services

http://www.boiseoffice.com/

★★★★★

If you travel a lot or you need to order products while you are at different locations, this is a good resource to know about. Even if you order locally, this company may help if you can't find your products locally. Worldwide Office Supply Services has just about every office supply and any office equipment you need. It is a worldwide distributor of business supplies and services, computer supplies, office furniture, and promotional products. It's a valuable resource you can't ignore.

The City Organiser

http://www.cityorg-pdq.co.uk/

★★★★

Is stationery your bag? How about Mont Blanc pens? This is the place to come for desk products, including engraving, gift wrapping, and worldwide delivery. The site has a large variety of products. It is based in London; therefore, prices are in pounds.

Independent Stationers Online

http://www.office-plus.com/

★★★★

This online newsletter promises to keep you up to date on the latest in the office products industry—hot topics, products, reviews, and more. Also, get the details on the OP Office Plus cooperative and its network of dealers.

Levenger

http://www.levenger.com/

★★★★

This website features quality stationery, pens, desks, chairs, reading lamps, and desk accessories. Other office supplies for sale include leather goods and corporate gifts. It bills itself as the site "for serious readers." You can order online using secure credit card services.

Office Depot

http://www.officedepot.com/

★★★★★

Office Depot offers a wide range of office supplies including office furniture, office stationery, and mailroom supplies. Shoppers can search for items by Office Depot's product number, the manufacturer's model number, or the UPC or barcode number found on products. The site also features an online Office Depot credit card application and a store locator to help shoppers find the Office Depot closest to them.

PRIME Office Products

http://www.petaluma.primeop.com/

★★★★

This online office supply superstore features two catalogs: Perfectly Priced (for your everyday office needs) and Total Source (for any additional office supplies or equipment). Simply enter your contact information and start shopping to have your office supplies and equipment delivered right to your door.

OfficeMax OnLine

http://www.officemax.com/

★★★★

Register at this business-to-business secure site. (Registration is required, and you must supply name, address, and billing information to enter the site.) Shop through various categories of office equipment, supplies, and services in the OfficeMax, CopyMax, and FurnitureMax sections. If your business has more than 50 office employees, you can sign up to join the OfficeMax Corporate Direct program for perks and savings.

onlineofficesupplies.com

http://www.onlineofficesupplies.com/

★★★★

No-frills office warehouse packed with all the office supplies and equipment you may ever need. The site has a very basic home page that groups various office supplies and equipment into categories, thus making it easy to browse the store to find what you need.

Quill Office Products

http://www.quillcorp.com/

★★★★★

Quill Corporation is a business-to-business direct marketer of office supplies, computer supplies, and office machines. It serves schools, businesses, associations, institutions, and professional offices in the United States.

Reliant Business Products

http://www.rbp.com/

★★★

Catering to the corporate customer, Reliant features more than 50,000 office equipment products and office supplies. Corporate customers can set up accounts for individual departments or for the entire company and access tools that simplify the shopping process.

 ## Staples, Inc.

http://www.staples.com/

★★★★★

Although most people are familiar with this office-products superstore, not as many are aware of the company's website. Locate the store nearest you, look over special deals for contract and commercial customers (government, healthcare, and educational accounts), and don't forget to check out the job postings! Fill in your snail mail info for a copy of the Staples catalog or order all your supplies and equipment online and have them shipped to your door. Reasonable prices, a wide selection, and easy-to-use order forms combine to make this the best office equipment site on the Web.

USPS Shipping Supplies Online

http://shop.usps.com/

★★★★★

If you have a busy office—at home or otherwise—this site will save you a lot of time. You can order supplies and packing materials, and you can send Priority Mail, Express Mail, Global Mail, and even Global Express Guaranteed. This provides a convenient way to do your shipping and receiving functions.

Viking Direct

http://www.viking-direct.co.uk/

★★★★★

If you visit Europe frequently, perhaps on business trips, or you live in the area, this is a great place to order your supplies. You can also order from any other country. Just keep in mind that, if you are traveling, this resource is available to you. Viking is an online mail order facility offering everything from office supplies to office machines.

RESOURCES

123 Sort It

http://www.123sortit.com

★★★★

If you feel as though you could use some help in organizing your home or office, you'll definitely want to visit this site. Here, you'll find some great ideas for getting more organized—finding your desk, reducing clutter, and managing your paperwork more efficiently. You can also buy some tools to help you stay on top of your mess.

A
B
C
D
E
F
G
H
I
J
K
L
M
N
O
P
Q
R
S
T
U
V
W
X
Y
Z

A
B
C
D
E
F
G
H
I
J
K
L
M
N
O
P
Q
R
S
T
U
V
W
X
Y
Z

Better Buys for Business

http://www.betterbuys.com/

★★★

Guides to the major types of office equipment relating to the printing, copying, transmission, and storage of documents. Each year, Better Buys publishes a series of 10 guides covering subjects such as copiers, fax machines, multifunctional equipment, color devices, printers, duplicators, and electronic filing systems. You can pay for the subscription for this service online using secure credit card resources.

CheckWorks.com

http://www.checkworks.com/

★★★★

Order your business or personal checks straight from the printer and get a huge selection of styles at a very reasonable price.

Epinions.com on Office Equipment

http://www.epinions.com/offc

★★★

Ratings and reviews on a wide variety of office equipment, everything from printers and copiers to paper shredders and multimedia projectors.

Office.com

http://www.office.com/

★★★★

This site pulls together news specific to your industry, ways to network with your peers, business management advice, and details on which suppliers to use. With this site's help, you can save time and money looking for qualified vendors. You can also learn more about getting started with e-commerce.

PriceSCAN.com

http://www.pricescan.com/home_office.asp

★★★★

Get free price quotes from several companies so that you can comparison-shop for office equipment online.

seeuthere.com

http://www.seeuthere.com/default.asp

★★★★

Managing special events or parties is now easier with seeuthere.com. This site enables you to create and distribute invitations, accept event registrations (including payment), or process RSVPs online.

SmallBizManager

http://smallbizmanager.com/

★★★★

This site acts as an information kiosk for small-business owners, providing links to everything from office supply stores to legal services. If you're running a small business and can't find what you need, this is a great place to start.

SO-HO.com

http://www.so-ho.com/

★★★

A collection of useful, objective information about products and services for the small office/home office.

United States Postal Service ZIP Code–Look-Up

http://www.usps.gov/ncsc/lookups/lookups.htm

★★★★★

Type in the address, city, or office location and the U.S. Postal Service's ZIP code look-up software will provide the ZIP-plus-four code. Using this service is much easier than using the print directory—and you can be sure it's always up to date.

Zairletter

http://biz.zairmail.com/

★★★★

Direct mail service. Download templates from this site to create professional-looking letters, postcards, flyers, and brochures; then have them printed, folded, and mailed, all by Zairletter. You design the message and let the experts at the site get it out quickly and economically.

ADOLESCENTS

ADOL: Adolescence Directory On-Line

http://education.indiana.edu/cas/adol/adol.html

★★★★★

This electronic guide to information on adolescent issues is a service of the Center for Adolescent Studies at Indiana University.

ABC's of Parenting

http://www.abcparenting.com/

★★★★

This site contains a parenting and pregnancy index with reviews of thousands of sites with articles on child, infant, health, and women's issues. You can shop online at this site, which has great gift ideas and links to other related sites.

About Parenting Teens

http://parentingteens.about.com/mbody.htm

★★★★

You can learn a lot about parenting on this site from expert human guides and get hot news, helpful advice, and invaluable links to other sites that contain similar information.

Being a Teenager

http://www.fcs.wa.gov.au/templates/being_a_teenager/

★★★★

👫 14-18

Great site for teenagers to learn more about themselves, their rights, and their responsibilities. Good place for parents to go to learn more about what's on the minds of their teenagers.

Campaign for Our Children

http://www.cfoc.org/

★★★

👫 14-18

News, facts, and statistics about teenage pregnancies, with resources for parents and teachers.

Canadian Parents Online

http://www.canadianparents.com/

★★★★

This excellent resource covers everything from pre-conception tips to raising tweeners and teenagers. Chat rooms and message boards help parents join forces in the challenging field of parenting. Online experts offer tips and hints on topics such as packing a healthy lunch and raising children with special needs. Links to stores where you can purchase products online.

Child.net

http://www.child.net/

★★★★

👫 All

Sponsored by the National Children's Coalition, this site is an excellent resource for parents and kids. Features three sections (near the bottom of the page): For Kids, For Teens, and For Parents & Teens. The Kids sections offers safe search tools, kids chat, games, and more. The Teens section covers everything from drug and alcohol avoidance to study tips and free classifieds. The Parents section provides a directory to resources on tough love, volunteer opportunities to help kids, and drug and alcohol awareness.

A
B
C
D
E
F
G
H
I
J
K
L
M
N
O
P
Q
R
S
T
U
V
W
X
Y
Z

Dear Lucie

http://www.lucie.com/

★★★★

👥 14-18

Lucie Walters writes a syndicated teen advice column. This site offers advice to teens on subjects such as sexuality, depression, alcohol, pregnancy, romance, eating disorders, and parents. The site contains an archive of past columns.

Drug Testing

http://rapiddrug.com/parents_test_package.htm

★★★★

Are your kids on drugs? This site offers drug testing kits that include simple dip sticks to test for marijuana and five-panel test kits to check for THC, cocaine, opium, meth, and amphetamines.

Early Childhood Parenting Collaborative

http://ecap.crc.uiuc.edu/info/

★★★

The Early Childhood Parenting Collaborative is a clearinghouse of educational resources for parents and those who work with parents. This site offers links to information and resources.

Facts for Families

http://www.aacap.org/info_families/

★★★★

👥 14-18

The American Academy of Child and Adolescent Psychiatry (AACAP) developed *Facts for Families* to provide concise and up-to-date information on issues that affect children, teenagers, and their families. Find out about depression in teens, ways to help your teen with stress, manic-depressive illness in teens, normal adolescent development, ways to deal with teens and eating disorders, and so on.

Family Development Program: Parenting Teens Publications

http://ceinfo.unh.edu/famdtpub.htm

★★★

This site lists publications about parenting teens. Each publication focuses on a specific aspect: physical changes, emotional changes, cognitive changes, and changes in relationship dynamics.

Girl Power! Campaign

http://www.girlpower.gov/

★★★★★

👥 9-13

This is the official site of Girl Power, a national public education campaign sponsored by the Department of Health and Human Services to encourage 9- to 13-year-old girls to make the most of their lives.

KidsHealth.org: For Teens

http://kidshealth.org/teen/

★★★★★

👥 14-18

Brought to you by AI duPont Hospital for Children in Delaware. Teens can come here and get answers to questions or concerns that they haven't wanted to talk about. Topics include issues such as health, sex, food, sports, and school. A separate section has been created for parents who need a resource for concerns about their own teen.

Kotex.com

http://www.kotex.com/

★★★★

👥 14-18

This is a great commercial site. Take your daughter here when the time is right or let her explore it on her own.

National Families in Action

http://www.nationalfamilies.org/

★★★★

National Families in Action is a national drug education, prevention, and policy center based in Atlanta, Georgia. The organization was founded in 1977. Its mission is to help families and communities prevent drug abuse among children.

ParenTalk Newsletter: Adolescence

http://www.tnpc.com/parentalk/adoles.html

★★★

Advice about parenting your teen: keeping the lines of communication open, talking about sex and drugs, dealing with rebellion, dealing with divorce, discussing suicide, and more.

Parenting.com

http://www.parenting.com/parenting/

$ⓢ$

★★★★★

Parenting.com is dedicated to "making pregnancy and parenthood smarter, saner, and easier." This site focuses on parenting in the early years, but is planning to expand its coverage to raising teenagers. This site also features chat areas and message boards.

Parenting.org

http://www.parenting.org/

★★★★

Created and maintained by the Girls and Boys Town National Resource and Training Center, this site is designed to help parents deal with the day-to-day care taking, guidance, and development of their children. Resources are organized by age group, as follows: precious beginnings (0–4), discovery years (5–9), tween years (10–14), and taking flight (15–19). Also features a site for professionals.

ParentsPlace.com

http://www.parentsplace.com/

★★★★★

Lots of parenting info for children of all ages. Select the Age/Stages option, from birth to teenage years, and follow the prompts to get to the topic that interests you. There is also some information to help parents after the great event, such as how to put the spice back into your romance after the baby is born.

Positive Parenting

http://www.positiveparenting.com/

★★★★

The Positive Parenting site is dedicated to providing resources and information to make parenting more rewarding, effective, and considerably easier.

Talking with Kids About Tough Issues

http://www.talkingwithkids.org

★★★★★

Tips and resources for talking with your kids about tough issues, especially violence, alcohol, sex, HIV/AIDS, and terrorism. Request booklets and read Q&As to see the recommendations for helping teens deal with these important issues.

Teen Challenge World Wide Network

http://www.teenchallenge.com/

$ⓢ$

★★★

Education about drug culture and abuse, including the latest statistics, outreach programs, and local information.

Teen Help

http://www.vpp.com/teenhelp/

★★★

👫 14-18

Support network for teenagers and parents dealing with issues confronting adolescents. Includes links and a hotline.

Teen Hoopla

http://www.ala.org/teenhoopla/

★★★★

👫 14-18

An Internet guide for teens. Links to sites on topics such as teen magazines, homework help, music, art, comics, sports, and library services.

Teens Today

http://www.thefamily.com/teens/teenindex.html

$ⓢ$

★★★★

Articles written by parents who have successfully raised their teens and want to share their experience and wisdom with you.

A
B
C
D
E
F
G
H
I
J
K
L
M
N
O
P
Q
R
S
T
U
V
W
X
Y
Z

A
B
C
D
E
F
G
H
I
J
K
L
M
N
O
P
Q
R
S
T
U
V
W
X
Y
Z

 The WholeFamily Center: Teen Center

http://www.wholefamily.com/aboutteensnow/index.html

★★★★★

👥 14-18

Forum for learning strategies for resolving the tensions arising in family life. Each center has real-life dramas you can listen to on RealAudio. The site features just about all the information that families and teens, especially, have questions about. You'll find sections on school, sexuality, a crisis center, ways to deal with relationships, feelings and emotions, substance abuse, and what kids like to do—just hang out. The Best of the Best site is easy to navigate and well designed and offers something of interest to everyone in the family.

BABIES AND TODDLERS

Baby Bag Online

http://www.babybag.com/

★★★★

This website is a resource for parenting and childcare. Visitors can post birth announcements, read stories, and access articles and links on topics ranging from health and safety to pregnancy and childbirth. Some excellent advice from experts.

Baby Catalog of America

http://www.babycatalog.com/

★★★★★

Baby supply store with online catalog and ordering, shower registry, and gift certificate ordering. Books, videos, furniture, toys, skin care, and safety items are featured.

BabyCenter

http://www.babycenter.com/

$

★★★★

Offers information on pregnancy, baby care, and nutrition as well as a guide to baby names and a pregnancy timeline. Users can personalize the page by entering their baby's due date or birth date.

babyGap

http://www.gap.com/

$

★★★★★

Gap store designed for babies/toddlers. Buy clothes online, locate a store near you, or see what's on sale. To get to the babyGap, open the Gap's home page and click the BABYGAP link.

BabyPlace

http://www.baby-place.com/

$

★★★

This site features more than 60,000 pages of baby-related content and more than 2,500 links to other sites that its editors have personally reviewed. Offers information on pregnancy, parenting, health, games, and even jokes. Baby Place Mall provides links to online stores where parents can shop.

BabysDoc.com

http://www.babysdoc.com/

★★★

Online healthcare resource for sick babies. Parents can visit to look up information about common symptoms, illnesses, and remedies. Check growth charts, body mass indexes, and development charts. Find out which vaccinations your baby needs and when baby should get them. Poison center, Parents Q&A, and articles from pediatricians make this one of the prime sites for parents of babies and toddlers.

Better Baby Care

http://www.betterbabycare.org/

★★★★

The Better Baby Care Campaign is a "nationwide effort to improve the quality of care for children under age three." Visit this site to learn about the campaign, to search for quality childcare, or to join in the movement. If you're a parent getting ready to search for quality childcare, visit this site to learn how to evaluate a childcare provider.

CribLife 2000

http://www.criblife2000.com/

★★★

Dedicated to helping parents reduce babies' exposure to harmful chemicals and other dangers related to cribs. Read a history of Sudden Infant Death Syndrome (SIDS) and learn about safe crib practices and products.

Dr. Greene: Toddlers

http://www.drgreene.com/toddlers.html

★★★★

A pediatrician dispenses advice on handling temper tantrums, surviving the terrible twos, teaching sharing, stopping biting, and all sorts of other questions and concerns that specifically apply to toddlers.

Early Childhood Educators' and Family Web Corner

http://users.stargate.net/~cokids/

★★★★

Provides resources for both teachers and families on the subject of early childhood education. Resources include articles, websites, a calendar of events, and more.

eToys

http://www.etoys.com/

★★★★★

 All

Huge online toy store, featuring recommendations, bargains, a catalog, and a searchable database. Items are sorted by age group and by category: dolls, collectible toys, video games, and so on. Great place for kids to go shopping, too; just make sure your child doesn't have your credit card number.

Family Education Network: A Parenting and Education Resource

http://www.familyeducation.com/home/

★★★★

 All

Articles and advice from experts. Psychologists and pediatricians answer questions from parents. Users can find schools in their area that provide online access by using the search feature at this site. Kids can obtain homework help and check out some interesting activities.

FamilyTime

http://www.familytime.com/

★★★★

Articles and advice from experts on how to better organize your family and the time you spend together. Tools for meal planning, keeping a calendar, and saving money are featured, along with plenty of useful tips.

FindCareNow

http://www.findcarenow.com/

★★★★

This site features a childcare search tool to match parents with nannies and other childcare providers.

iParenting.com

http://www.iparenting.com/

★★★★★

From conception to birth to teen years, you'll find helpful articles and guidance from other parents who've dealt with similar issues.

KidSource: Toddlers

http://www.kidsource.com/kidsource/pages/toddlers.html

★★★★

Advice and reference material on health, learning, and development. The site also includes information on positive discipline.

A B C D E F G H I J K L M N O **P** Q R S T U V W X Y Z

A
B
C
D
E
F
G
H
I
J
K
L
M
N
O
P
Q
R
S
T
U
V
W
X
Y
Z

Live and Learn

http://www.liveandlearn.com/

★★★★

Contains links to education resources, free software, and online games, plus information on age-appropriate toys and child safety. In addition, the site provides a good list of teaching sites.

National Organization of Mothers of Twins Clubs

http://www.nomotc.org/

★★★★

Find facts and figures related to the incidence of multiple births as well as local support organizations and resources to aid in meeting the distinctive developmental needs of twins. Information on the organization's annual conference is also available.

The National Parenting Center

http://www.tnpc.com/

★★★★

Founded in July 1989, The National Parenting Center (TNPC) has become one of America's foremost parenting information services. Dedicated to providing parents with comprehensive and responsible guidance from the world's most renowned child-rearing authorities, The National Parenting Center invites parents to expand their parenting skills and strengths. Also learn about product recalls at this site.

Pampers Parenting Institute

http://www.pampers.com

★★★★

Advice for parents about child development, health, and skincare—plus a guide to the Pampers range of diapers.

ParenTalk Newsletter: Toddlers

http://www.tnpc.com/parentalk/toddlers.html

★★★★

Choose from all sorts of articles on toddler topics: ways to survive the terrible twos, advice on potty training, age-appropriate learning and development, and more.

Parenthood.com

http://www.parenthood.com/

★★★★

Lots of articles on parenthood, as well as chat, shopping, and special offers. You'll also find a useful how-to section that teaches even the newest parents the basics of caring for a child.

Parents.com

http://www.parents.com

★★★★★

Feature articles from this print publication cover topics such as parents-to-be, travel, development, health and safety, fun, and food. "Ask the Expert" gives you the chance to have your specific question answered.

K–6

About Child Parenting

http://childparenting.about.com/

★★★★

About's Child Parenting section covers just about every topic imaginable that's related to raising children K–6. Learn some arts and crafts ideas, get help for raising children with special needs, and learn how to deal with specific problems that commonly arise.

AdvanceAbility Speech Therapist

http://www.aability.com/

★★★★

Submit questions to a practicing speech/language pathologist. The site also includes a section for parents on teaching children to read.

Boy Scouts of America

http://www.scouting.org/

★★★★★

This organization's home page describes the Cub Scouts and Boy Scouts and their programs. The site also covers joining and volunteering for parents and kids, and offers a catalog of merchandise. Find a BSA council in your area using the locator provided.

FamilyFun.com

http://familyfun.go.com/

★★★★★

 All

This is a great place for parents and kids to go when they're "bored." This site is packed with ideas for fun crafts and activities. When I visited just before April Fool's Day, the site featured a collection of 35 pranks that parents could play on their children. Very current information presented in an easily accessible and very fun format! Site also features basic parenting tips.

Kids Camps

http://www.kidscamps.com/special_needs/learning_disab_add.html

★★★★

The Internet's most comprehensive directory of traditional and specialty overnight camps. The camp caters to those with learning difficulties and offers tours and experiences for children, teenagers, and families.

Childhood Years: Ages Six Through Twelve

http://www.ces.ncsu.edu/depts/fcs/human/pubs/child6_12.html

★★★★

This is a National Network for Child Care article reprinted by the North Carolina Extension Service.

ClubMom

http://www.mom.com/

★★★★

Read interesting articles on raising children today, chat with moms facing similar situations as you, and get and give advice on parenting subjects. Also, tune in to live chats with experts.

Developmental Assets: An Investment in Youth

http://www.search-institute.org/assets/

★★★★

The Search Institute promotes investing time in our youth. It offers ideas for families, communities, churches, and schools.

Expect the Best from a Girl

http://www.academic.org/

★★★★

Provides ways to encourage your daughter to develop competence and self-confidence—particularly in science, math, and technology.

FamilyFun

http://family.go.com/

★★★★

 All

Lots of helpful information for running a household. The site gives problem-solving advice, tools, recipes, crafts, and gift suggestions.

Good Housekeeping: The Latchkey Solution

http://www.homearts.com/gh/family/10lachf1.htm

★★★★

This site addresses self-care as an option for school-aged children, along with suggestions about preparing your child for being on his or her own and what you should know before leaving your child home alone.

HELP for Parents

http://www.helpforfamilies.com/frameparent.htm

★★★★

A great resource from Dr. Tim Dunnigan, where you can learn effective discipline techniques. Visiting this site is just like going to a good parenting class—without having to leave your house.

KidsHealth.org

http://www.kidshealth.org/

★★★★

All

Looking for expert health information for the entire family? KidsHealth.org has the latest on everything from chicken pox to dyslexia, in easy-to-read articles for kids, teens, and parents.

A B C D E F G H I J K L M N O P Q R S T U V W X Y Z

A
B
C
D
E
F
G
H
I
J
K
L
M
N
O
P
Q
R
S
T
U
V
W
X
Y
Z

Looking After Kids

http://www.fcs.wa.gov.au/templates/looking_after_
kids/default.cfm

★★★★★

Thorough discussion of your school-age child's development. This attractive site from Australia's Family and Children Services covers all stages of development from babies to teenagers. Includes tips on having fun together, protecting kids, and foster care.

MOST—Mothers of Supertwins

http://www.mostonline.org/

★★★

Mothers of triplets or more will want to commiserate with other moms in the same situation through this site's message boards. The site also has a quarterly online magazine and access to shopping sites that will fit your particular needs. You must become a member in order to shop at the online store.

NCF—National Center for Fathering

http://www.fathers.com/

★★★★★

The NCF mission is to inspire and equip men to be better fathers through fathering research and inspiration.

National Network for Child Care: School Age Child Development

http://www.nncc.org/

★★★★

Excellent collection of articles on all stages of childhood development from infant to primary school, plus groupings of articles on special topics, such as brain development, aggression, social skills, depression, and assessing a child's abilities.

Parenting Pipeline

http://www.ext.nodak.edu/extnews/pipeline/

★★★★

Online newsletters from the North Dakota State University Extension Service. Very good developmental information for parenting elementary-age and junior high school children.

Parent News

http://www.parent.net/

★★★★

Parent News provides a parenting tip of the day, family movie reviews, articles about childcare, a section on children's health, and links to educational Internet resources.

Parent Soup: Chat Descriptions

http://www.parentsoup.com/

★★★★

This site offers a wide selection of current articles on parenting and issues that parents face. As mother's day or father's day approaches, the site focuses its coverage on mothers or fathers respectively. Site also features links to dozens of other articles and resources addressing specific topics.

Parents Planet

http://www.parents-planet.com/

★★★★

This site features a searchable directory of thousands of parenting and educational resources for parents and teachers.

ReadnDiscover K–6

http://www.readndiscover.com/Parenting/K-6%20Kids/

★★★

This site provides several articles on raising and teaching children in grades K–6, including Child Development, Discipline, Education, Emotional and Behavioral Problems, and Health and Nutrition.

SINGLE PARENTING

Christianity Today: Single Parenting

http://www.christianitytoday.com/parenting/
features/single.html

★★★

Christianity Today's Single Parenting area provides several articles to help single parents raise their children and deal with common issues, especially those relating to teenagers.

Divorce Online

http://www.divorceonline.com/

★★★★★

A well-organized website with articles on different aspects of divorce such as financial and legal issues.

Federal Child Custody Laws

http://wwwsecure.law.cornell.edu/topics/child_custody.html

★★★★

Information about federal statutes and judicial decisions from the Legal Information Institute at Cornell University.

Making Lemonade

http://makinglemonade.com/

★★★★

Read articles in the archives, check out single parent-related links, and share your war stories with other single parents at this site.

Mothers Without Custody

http://www.women-resources-divorce.com/

★★★★

A support and resource organization for this much-overlooked segment of the single-parent population. Provides a forum for discussing issues.

Parenting SOLO for Singles

http://www.solosingles.com/ssparent/

★★★

Extensive directory of information and resources for single parents covers everything from making time for yourself to building your child's self-esteem.

Parents Without Partners

http://www.parentswithoutpartners.org/

★★★

Locate a PWP chapter near you. The site has many features and is concerned with problems of bringing up children alone—especially the emotional conflicts of divorce, never being married, separation, or widowhood. PWP is an international organization that provides real help in the way of discussions, professional speakers, study groups, and publications. The site is well designed, and you will enjoy looking through it. You'll find a news section, a newsletter, and you can shop at the Mall from such companies as Amazon.com.

Power Parenting Tools

http://www.parentingtoolbox.com/timecush.html

★★★★

Learn time-management and child-rearing tips for nontraditional families. The site is updated regularly.

Single and Custodial Fathers' Network

http://www.scfn.org/

★★★★

Support organization for single and remarried fathers with custodial care. Find information on work and parenting issues, a mailing list, and chat.

Single Parent Central

http://www.singleparentcentral.com/

★★★★

Get news and information about trends in single-parenting families, share advice and wisdom, learn about ways to save money, and find links to other related sites.

Single Parent Resource Center

http://www.singleparentusa.com/

⑤

★★★

Based in Manhattan, this resource center is a "clearinghouse for information on single parent organizations in the United States and around the world." Search for a single-parenting organization near you or order recommended publications from the bookstore.

A B C D E F G H I J K L M N O P Q R S T U V W X Y Z

A B C D E F G H I J K L M N O P Q R S T U V W X Y Z

Single Parents Association

http://www.singleparents.org/

★★★★

Single Parents Association (SPA) is a nonprofit organization devoted to providing single-parent families educational opportunities and fun activities through its national headquarters and local chapter network.

Single Parents World

http://parentsworld.com/

★★★★

Explore commentary on child support, dating, and parenting. Visit the site's bookstore. Also find a forum for meeting and talking with other parents.

SPECIAL NEEDS

Alliance of Genetic Support Groups

http://www.geneticalliance.org/

★★★★

This organization helps individuals and families with genetic disorders. The site includes publications and membership forms.

American Hyperlexia Association

http://www.hyperlexia.org/

★★★

This site offers information, advice for parents, an international email network, and materials that can be ordered.

Arc

http://www.thearc.org/

★★★★★

Formerly the Association for Retarded Citizens, this national organization provides support for children and adults with mental retardation and their families.

Autism: Cure Autism Now Foundation

http://www.canfoundation.org/

★★★★★

The Cure Autism Now foundation is made up of parents, physicians, and researchers who are working together to find effective treatments and a possible cure for autism. Visit this site to find out the latest developments and to lend a hand.

Autism Research Institute

http://www.autism.com/ari/

★★★

Autism Research Institute (ARI) conducts research on the causes of autism and on methods of preventing, diagnosing, and treating autism and other severe behavioral disorders of childhood. Check this site to learn more about ARI's research projects and the results of its research.

Related Site
http://www.autism.org/

Autism Resources

http://www.autism-resources.com/

★★★

Extensive directory of information and resources relating to autism, organized in categories that include Links, Frequently Asked Questions Memo, Advice to Parents, Book Information, and More Material.

Autism Society of America

http://www.autism-society.org/

★★★★

This organization offers information and referral packages for parents and educators. Membership and society details are included.

Center for the Study of Autism

http://www.autism.org/

★★★★★

This Oregon-based center provides information to parents and professionals. It also conducts research into various treatments.

Child Amputee

http://www.amp-info.net/childamp.htm

★★★★★

👫 All

New mailing list giving information and support contacts. The site includes a host of links to prosthetic technology sites.

Children with AIDS Project

http://www.aidskids.org/

★★★★★

Services for children infected and affected by AIDS. Kids can chat online and get support. Adults can read about becoming an adoptive parent.

Children with Spina Bifida

http://www.waisman.wisc.edu/~rowley/sb-kids/index.htmlx

★★★★

Promotes information sharing between parents. The site provides news and research updates, details of problems, and a list of related organizations.

Cleft Lip: Wide Smiles

http://www.widesmiles.org/

★★★★★

Formed to ensure that parents of cleft-affected children do not have to feel alone. Chat online with parents or read the files.

Cleft Lip and Palate Surgery

http://www.plasticsurgery.org/public_education/procedures/index.cfm

★★★★

Introduction for parents to common palate surgery procedures. The site is sponsored by the American Society of Plastic and Reconstructive Surgeons.

ConductDisorders.com

http://www.conductdisorders.com/

★★★★

You can join the parents' support group here. Also, read articles that may help you understand and better deal with your child's conduct difficulties. Find out about treatment programs and scan the bookstore for suggested resources you may want to read.

Council for Exceptional Children

http://www.cec.sped.org/

★★★★

The Council for Exceptional Children is an organization dedicated to improving educational outcomes for students with disabilities. Users can access a database of professional literature, information, and resources.

Deaf Education

http://www.deafed.net/

★★★★

Comprehensive directory of sites that provide information and resources relating to educational issues for the deaf.

Related Site
http://www.oraldeafed.org/

Disabilities Rights Education and Defense Fund

http://www.dredf.org/

★★★

Advocacy group for people with disabilities, including children. This is a great place to go if you're having trouble obtaining the proper treatment for your child at school. The DREDF is devoted to improving conditions for disabled individuals through legislation, litigation, advocacy, education, technical assistance, and training.

Down Syndrome

http://www.downsyndrome.com/

★★★★

This forum for sharing experiences and information about Down Syndrome features a family chat area, a bulletin board, and an online magazine.

Dyslexia: The Gift

http://www.dyslexia.com/

★★★★

Provides information about the positive side of learning disabilities and remedial teaching methods suited to the dyslexic learning style.

A
B
C
D
E
F
G
H
I
J
K
L
M
N
O
P
Q
R
S
T
U
V
W
X
Y
Z

A
B
C
D
E
F
G
H
I
J
K
L
M
N
O
P
Q
R
S
T
U
V
W
X
Y
Z

Family Village

http://www.familyvillage.wisc.edu/

★★★★★

Virtual community for persons with mental retardation and other disabilities, their families, and those who provide services and support. From the shopping mall you can buy anything from canes and walkers to clothing, computers, software, and footwear.

HANDITEL

http://www.socialnet.lu/handitel/

★★★★

This central site for international resources includes organizations, mobility devices, aids, publications, and prosthetics.

Hydrocephalus Association

http://www.hydroassoc.org/

★★★★

This site provides publications, conference details, and links for people with hydrocephalus, their families, and health professionals.

Individualized Educational Program (IEP)

http://www.familyvillage.wisc.edu/education/iep.html

★★★

If you are the parent of a child who has special needs in school, the first step you want to take is to develop an Individualized Educational Program (IEP) for your child. This site provides a directory of resources to help you understand what an IEP is and what it should contain.

Internet Resources for Special Children

http://www.irsc.org/

★★★★★

This site features a catalog for parents and professionals in relation to child disabilities, disorders, and healthcare. Huge collection of links broken down into categories including Adaptive Equipment & Technologies, Diseases & Conditions, Sports & Recreation, Learning Disabilities, and more than a dozen more. Great place to start researching any topics relating to children with special needs.

Make-a-Wish Foundation of America

http://www.wish.org/

★★★★

This site outlines the history of this organization, which grants wishes to children with life-threatening medical conditions. You'll also find details about activities in the works.

Mountain States Genetics Network: MoSt GeNe

http://www.mostgene.org/

★★★★

An A-to-Z listing of online groups and organizations providing information and support for those who live with or treat genetic illnesses. Focusing primarily on Arizona, Colorado, Montana, New Mexico, Utah, and Wyoming.

National Academy for Child Development (NACD)

http://www.nacd.org/

★★★★

The NACD provides data and support for learning disorders, including ADD and mental retardation. Find out more about the organization and its products and services at this site. You can order CDs, audio tapes, and special software from the site.

National Information Center for Children and Youth with Disabilities (NICHCY)

http://www.nichcy.org/

★★★★

The National Information Center for Children and Youth with Disabilities provides facts about referrals, education, and family issues. The site can help you locate the organizations and agencies within your state that are working on disability-related issues.

Online Asperger Syndrome Information & Support (OASIS)

http://www.udel.edu/bkirby/asperger/

★★★

Links to information about diagnosis, classroom management, research, projects seeking participants, and parent support.

PCI Publishing

http://www.pcicatalog.com/

★★★★

This site offers a catalog for children and adults with special needs. Topics include life skills, transition, inclusion, and communication. The site sells a variety of learning products for children, including games and books. You can purchase online.

Post-Traumatic Stress Disorder Directory

http://www.brokenspirits.com/resources/ptsd.asp

★★★★

Excellent directory of sites dealing with post-traumatic stress disorders.

Sibling Support Project

http://www.thearc.org/siblingsupport/

★★★★

Dedicated to brothers and sisters of people with special health and developmental needs. The site also conducts workshops.

SNAP Online: Special Needs Advocate for Parents

http://www.snapinfo.org/

★★★★

An online resource for information, education, advocacy, and referrals for families with special needs children of all ages and disabilities.

United Cerebral Palsy

http://www.ucpa.org/

★★★★★

This national group provides education and research services to people with disabilities, their families, the public, and other organizations. Good place to go for information and assistance with all disabilities, not just cerebral palsy.

STAY-AT-HOME PARENTS

Bizy Moms: A Complete Resource for Work-at-Home Moms

http://www.bizymoms.com/

★★★★

Business ideas for moms working from home. Also included are FAQs and insights into the book *The Stay at Home Mom's Guide to Making Money from Home.*

Chat: Stay-at-Home Parents

http://homeparents.about.com/mpchat.htm?once=true&

★★★★

Meeting place for stay-at-home parents. The site has so many features that it would be impossible to list them all here, but you'll find articles, a forum, a chat room, a contact guide, newsletter, and a nice FAQ, to name a few. You can find extensive information on arts and crafts, links to other family sites, scrapbooks, home schooling, and a lot more. You can order a wide variety of products such as books and baby-related items from the online shopping mall.

Dr. Laura

http://www.drlaura.com/

★★★★

This is the official site of Dr. Laura Schlessinger, the controversial radio and TV talk host who believes strongly in stay-at-home parents.

A
B
C
D
E
F
G
H
I
J
K
L
M
N
O
P
Q
R
S
T
U
V
W
X
Y
Z

A
B
C
D
E
F
G
H
I
J
K
L
M
N
O
P
Q
R
S
T
U
V
W
X
Y
Z

The Entrepreneurial Parent

http://www.en-parent.com/

★★★★

Tips on how to manage your career and your family from your home, with resources and links.

Family and Home Network

http://www.familyandhome.org/

★★★

Formerly Mothers At Home (MAH), this national nonprofit organization is committed to supporting the choice of one parent to stay at home and other alternatives to providing for the needs of children. The site offers a monthly publication supportive of at-home mothers and fathers.

Feeling Respected As a Stay-at-Home Mom

http://www.suite101.com/article.cfm/home_mom/17880

★★★★

From *Suite101*, author Kelli Cole discusses her life as a stay-at-home mom.

Feminist Mothers at Home

http://feministmothersathome.com/

★★★

Mailing list offering a positive feminist voice on mothering issues. It also has links to feminist sites.

Home-Based Working Moms

http://www.hbwm.com/

★★★★

Association for mothers and fathers working from home. Find out about membership and get tips and ideas for your business.

HomeEcon Research

http://www.homeecon.com/research.html

★★★★

Lots of links to help parents. Although many links are oriented strictly to stay-at-home parents, the site contains even more links that parents in general will find useful.

HomeJobStop

http://homejobstop.com/

★★★★

HomeJobStop.com is devoted to helping telecommuter wannabees achieve their dreams of establishing a successful career working at home. Think of it as a placement service for telecommuters.

Main Street Mom

http://www.mainstreetmom.com/

★★★★★

An online network for stay-at-home moms. Lots of good articles and links are available.

Miserly Moms: Stay-At-Home Mom (SAHM) Links

http://www.miserlymoms.com/

★★★★

The author of this site says "Staying at home with your children is one of the best things you can do for them. In order to help you with this goal, I have compiled the following list of some of the best SAHMs links that can be found." This attractive, well-organized site is full of useful stuff.

Moms at Home

http://MomsAtHome.ca/

★★★

This great site has articles and information for stay-at-home parents. Use the links at the bottom of the page to navigate this site.

Mothers and More

http://www.mothersandmore.org/

★★★★★

Find local chapters, advocacy efforts, and more. Particularly well suited to the mother who is neither a working mom nor an at-home mother but rather a mix of both.

National Center for Fathering

http://www.fathers.com/

★★★★

Founded to address the epidemic of fatherless families, this site is dedicated to encouraging fathers to establish strong and lasting bonds with their children in all situations that require a man to act as a father. Features excellent articles gathered from a variety of sources.

Parent's Home Office

http://www.parentshomeoffice.com/

★★★★

This site provides information and tips on how to become more organized and more productive in a home office setting. Includes articles on how to balance your home and work lives and manage your kids while you work.

Slowlane.com

http://www.slowlane.com/

★★★★★

Searchable online resource for stay-at-home dads and primary caregivers and their families. Includes articles primarily written by stay-at-home dads. Also includes media clips and links to hundreds of other resources on the Web. Online chat and discussion groups to help stay-at-home dads keep from becoming agoraphobic.

Stay-at-Home Moms and Dads

http://www5.kidsource.com/forums

★★★

A great discussion forum. Find out what other stay-at-home parents are thinking (and saying) about their kids.

WAHM (Work at Home Moms)

http://www.wahm.com/

★★★★

For mothers working from home, this site offers advice on balancing mothering and work as well as access to a network of "web moms."

Work at Home Jobs

http://www.workathomejobs.com/

★★★★

Do you want to stay home with your kids, but you can't figure out a way to finance your dream? Then check out this site to get some ideas of how you can make money working out of your home.

Work at Home Parents

http://www.work-at-home-parents.com/

★★★★

Work at Home Parents provides you with the resources you need to choose the right business opportunity for you. Also provides information about scams and ways to avoid falling for a scam.

Work@HomeParents.com

http://www.workathomeparents.com/

★★★★

Work@HomeParents.com is focused on inspiring parents to start their own businesses and work at home to earn a living. Here, you will find plenty of information, ideas, and resources to get started.

STEPPARENTING

Building a Blended Family

http://www.homeandholidays.com/love-at-home/blend1.shtml

★★★★

This site begins with a blueprint for a blended family that's designed to help divorced couples who have children successfully merge their families into a working family unit. Seven additional articles follow the blueprint.

ParentsPlace: Stepfamilies

http://www.parentsplace.com/family/archive/0,10693,239452,00.html

★★★★

Ask the family counselor a question or read previous Q&A columns about stepchildren and stepparents. This site includes stepfamily discussion forums.

A B C D E F G H I J K L M N O **P** Q R S T U V W X Y Z

A B C D E F G H I J K L M N O P Q R S T U V W X Y Z

Second Wives Club

http://www.secondwivesclub.com/

★★★

Support and advice with a healthy attitude for women who are involved in blended families or living as second wives.

Shared Parenting Information Group

http://home.clara.net/spig/

★★★★

Find guidelines for separated parents, parenting plans, and FAQs about joint custody. The site includes articles and resources on shared parenting.

Stepfamily Association of America

http://www.stepfam.org/

★★★★

Support organization for stepfamilies and blended families. The site includes featured articles, book reviews, and some interesting facts.

The Stepfamily Network Bookstore

http://www.stepfamily.net/review.shtml

★★★★

Find links to books about stepfamilies that can be purchased through Amazon.com. Send comments or suggest other books via email.

The Stepfamily Connection

http://www.stepfamily.com/

💲

★★★★

Use the stepparent directory to track down someone in your area who may be a resource and sounding board for you as you face the challenge of stepparenting. Read the diary of a stepparent and nominate someone for Stepparent of the Month. You'll also want to check out the entertainment section of the site, which has nothing to do with stepparenting but can reduce your stress level.

Stepfamily in Formation

http://www.stepfamilyinfo.org/

★★★

Provides links to message boards, stepfamily organizations, newsletters, and support group resources. Also, the site contains downloadable articles.

Stepfamily Network

http://www.stepfamily.net/

★★★★

👫 14-18

Includes some useful links on how to get support. Find info on the volunteer network and get answers to your questions at this site.

Stepparenting and Stepfamily Links

http://www.janiceandkevin.com/stepparent.html

★★★

Janice and Kevin's Stepparenting and Stepfamily Links provides information and resources that are useful in the trenches. This site also features an article on 10 Ways to Be a Bad Parent/Stepparent. Scroll down to the bottom of the page for a robust collection of links to other resources.

Stepparenting Tips

http://www.familyfirst.net/parenting/steptips.asp

★★★

Here, you'll find 16 wise tips from Charmayne Balames on how to be an effective stepparent and increase your chances of being accepted by your stepchild.

StepParent's Web

http://www.cyberparent.com/step/

★★★

Learn what it means to take on the role of a stepparent and learn how to build a family unit. Share insights, ideas, and frustrations with other stepparents through discussions.

TeensHealth: Blended Families

http://www.kidshealth.org/kid/feeling/home_family/blended.html

★★★

👫 14-18

TeensHealth provides a collection of articles about blended families, including an explanation of just what a blended family is. Articles also cover common issues and the benefits of blended families.

Related Site

http://kidshealth.org/kid/feeling/home_family/blended.html

American Park Network

http://www.americanparknetwork.com/

★★★★

Consult maps and look at the scenery for any of America's national parks. Historical and educational notes are included for each park. Participate in online discussions about camping and exploring these national resources.

Arches National Park

http://www.americanparknetwork.com/parkinfo/ar

★★★★

The geological wonders of the Arches National Park in Utah are showcased here, along with information on accommodations, flora and fauna, and outdoor adventures in the region.

Canyonlands

http://www.canyonlands-utah.com/

★★★★★

Utah's largest national park is profiled at this site. You'll find accommodations, various area destinations, tours, campgrounds, and travel resources via the site.

Colorado State Parks and Outdoor Recreation

http://parks.state.co.us

$

★★★★★

 All

Information on parks in Colorado, including recreational activities and fees. This site also provides information on seasonal jobs, a park finder, trail maps, news, and online activities for kids.

Death Valley National Park

http://www.desertusa.com/dv/du_dvpmain.html

$

★★★★

Visitors to this website will find a virtual visitor's center for Nevada's Death Valley National Park. Information on weather, temperature, activities, accommodations, and fees is included, as are maps and a guide to desert wildlife. You can also communicate with others at the Desert Talk message board and mailbag. Be sure to visit the Trading Post for some shopping fun!

Discover Banff

http://www.discoverbanff.com/

★★★★★

A comprehensive guide to travel in Banff, Canada, is available at this site. It offers information on Banff and Jasper Parks, dining, tours, accommodations, equipment rentals, seasonal activities, and links to related sites.

Fodor's National Parks

http://www.fodors.com/parks

★★★★★

Information on lodging, camping, and dining facilities at America's national parks from Fodor's, featuring maps and photos of each park.

A
B
C
D
E
F
G
H
I
J
K
L
M
N
O
P
Q
R
S
T
U
V
W
X
Y
Z

Glacier National Park

http://www.nps.gov/glac/

★★★

This site describes Glacier National Park, which covers more than one million acres of forests, lakes, meadows, and high rocky peaks in the northwest part of Montana. You'll learn that 70 species of mammals and 260 species of birds contribute to the spectacular diversity of life preserved in the park. You can select any state on this site to locate a national park of your choice.

GORP: Great Smoky Mountains National Park

http://www.gorp.com/gorp/resource/US_National_Park/
tn_great.HTM

★★★★

Your first stop for information on the Great Smoky Mountains and the park. Find out about traveling through the Smokies by car, cycling, camping, fishing, hiking and backpacking, and horseback riding; also learn about the accommodations, the mountain people, and naturalist activities. You can also access information on trips and other Internet resources.

GORP: U.S. National Parks and Reserves

http://www.gorp.com/gorp/resource/US_National_Park/
main.htm

★★★★

Features a state-by-state list of national parks in the United States. Users can click on a park to obtain specific information on visitor centers and facilities such as hiking, climbing, and camping.

GORP: Wilderness Area List

http://gorp.away.com/gorp/resource/US_Wilderness_
Area/main.htm

★★★★

Tourist information and tips about U.S. national forests and wildlife refuges.

Grand Canyon Official Tourism Page

http://www.thecanyon.com/

★★★★★

This site provides all the tourism information you'll need when visiting Grand Canyon National Park. You'll get all the standard information on what to do and where to go, stay, eat, and shop. Plus, read news bits, get weather info, see photographs, read anecdotes, and learn all about the local area. A great resource. The site also offers a great shopping mall where you can buy everything from wonderful jewelry to Native American art, and you can shop online as well as at the park.

Haleakala

http://www.maui.net/~kelii/MIA/parks/hale.html

★★★

This site offers information on Haleakala National Park in Hawaii, plus precautions for hikers and campers exploring the area.

Harper's Ferry NHP Virtual Visitor Center

http://www.nps.gov/hafe/home.htm

★★★

The John Brown–led insurrection against slavery, in Harper's Ferry in 1859, later spawned the National Park Service's Harper's Ferry (West Virginia) Virtual Visitor Center, which is located at the confluence of the Potomac and Shenandoah rivers. These pages help you learn about or plan a trip to the area, plus give you insightful lessons on a part of our national heritage.

John Donohue's National Park Photos

http://www.serve.com/wizjd/parks/parks.html

★★★★

Get a look at a wide array of national parks by viewing photos of their various splendors. Watch a slideshow of the photographer's favorites, or pick a park and see all the related photos. Nice photography.

L.L. Bean's Park Search

http://www.llbean.com/parksearch/

★★★

A park-search service covering 1,500 U.S. national and state parks, forests, wildlife refuges, and other public recreation lands. You can search by park name, activity, or state. A handy site with volumes of information and many photos.

Maps of United States National Parks and Monuments

http://www.lib.utexas.edu/maps/national_parks.html

★★★★

The University of Texas at Austin has put its map collection online. Maps are listed alphabetically or by park region. The site also contains maps of national historic and military parks, memorials, and battlefields.

Mesa Verde National Park

http://www.mesaverde.org/

★★★★

This site provides a wealth of information on the Mesa Verde National Park in Colorado, delves into the archaeology of the ancestral Puebloans, and covers the ancient—as well as the modern—culture of the area. Check out the electronic bookstore, which sells park-related materials.

Mount Rainier National Park

http://www.mount.rainier.national-park.com/

★★★★

This unofficial guide to Mount Rainier National Park features information on the park's history, visitor services, trails, and more.

New Mexico State Parks

http://www.emnrd.state.nm.us/nmparks

★★★★

The New Mexico State Parks site contains information on and a detailed map of each park, as well as month-by-month listings of park events, fees, and regulations for park and boating use.

North Cascades Conservation Council

http://www.northcascades.org

★★★★

This site is the unofficial guide to North Cascades National Park, in northwestern Washington, providing basic park facts and visitor services. Learn about the natural history of the area, obtain park management information, and link to related websites; get everything from the latest conditions to boating information to details on the alpine plants.

Northwest Trek

http://www.nwtrek.org/

★★★

 All

This wildlife park is located in Tacoma, Washington; its site contains a virtual tour of the park, news on current special events, an animal trivia quiz, and general park information.

Oak Mountain State Park

http://www.bham.net/oakmtn/

★★★★

The Oak Mountain State Park site features information about the park (located in Alabama) and its services. Visitors can access information about trails, park regulations, and the fishing center.

Olympic National Park

http://www.northolympic.com/onp/

★★★★★

This site provides dozens of links to information on Olympic National Park in the Pacific Northwest, which has 4,000,000 visitors annually. Also included is a link to a virtual tour of the park. All the information you need in one spot.

A B C D E F G H I J K L M N O P Q R S T U V W X Y Z

A
B
C
D
E
F
G
H
I
J
K
L
M
N
O
P
Q
R
S
T
U
V
W
X
Y
Z

Best | PARKNET: The National Park Service Place

http://www.nps.gov/

★★★★★

All

A mandatory stop for anyone interested in our national parks. This is the National Park Service's home page, a searchable site that links to NPS sites for all the parks. Besides finding data on any individual park, you can read special travel features and learn about such topics as natural resources in the parks and America's histories and cultures—plus visit the Park Store. If you're planning a nature vacation, be sure you check out this Best of the Best site.

Passport to Your National Parks

http://www.geocities.com/Yosemite/4434/
passport.html

★★★★

Visit this site to learn about obtaining and using the *Passport to Your National Parks*, an information book and personal travel scrapbook available at national parks. The Passport offers color-coded maps, illustrations, visitors' information, and photos—and it can be stamped with an official park "cancellation mark" each time you visit.

Petrified Forest National Park

http://www.nps.gov/pefo/

★★★★

All

The Petrified Forest National Park protects one of the largest, most spectacular tracts of petrified wood in the nation. This site gives a history of the area as well as other useful information.

South Carolina State Parks

http://www.discoversouthcarolina.com/stateparks/
index.asp

★★★★

Listing of state parks in South Carolina with photos, descriptions, and recreational information on each. This site also has listings of bed and breakfasts and other lodging, and a calendar of events.

Texas State Parks

http://www.tpwd.state.tx.us/park/parks.htm

★★★

This page lists Texas' state parks and historic sites, providing information about accommodations, activities, and regulations in each park.

The Total Yellowstone Page

http://www.yellowstone-natl-park.com/

★★★★

This is a one-man tour de force of information about Yellowstone National Park. Absolutely a must-visit site if you are planning a trip to Yellowstone National Park!

U.S. National Parks

http://www.us-national-parks.net/

★★★★

List of national parks in the United States with photos and information on each, including the address; camping, hiking, and lodging guides; park details; maps; and skiing, rafting, and visitors' guides.

Wyoming State Parks and Historic Sites

http://spacr.state.wy.us/

★★★★

Information on Wyoming State Parks, historic sites, and the State Trails program. Includes snowmobile regulations, regional trails, campground locations, a trading post, and a listing of annual events and things to do.

Yellowstone Net

http://www.yellowstone.net/

★★★★

Site recommended by *USA Today* and others. Visit Yellowstone Net for all kinds of information on the park, news, photos, specialty stores, reservations, related links, and access to the Yellowstone Net community. Check it out.

Yosemite Park

http://www.yosemitepark.com/

★★★★★

Official website of Yosemite National Park in central California. This appealing site offers a park overview, information about Yosemite lodging, park activities, dining and shopping, special events, gifts and memories, special offers, news releases, and search/index categories for you to explore.

A
B
C
D
E
F
G
H
I
J
K
L
M
N
O
P
Q
R
S
T
U
V
W
X
Y
Z

A B C D E F G H I J K L M N O P Q R S T U V W X Y Z

Achoo Healthcare Online

http://www.achoo.com/main.asp

★★★★

A medical search engine that acts as a jumping point. The site is an information resource for the medical community and all other Internet users interested in healthcare information.

American Academy of Pediatric Dentistry

http://www.aapd.org/

★★★★

Provides information about children's dental care at this site, which has sections for parents, kids, and pediatric dentists. The page also has tips, publications, a search engine for finding a pediatric dentist in your area, and links to related sites.

[Best] American Academy of Pediatrics

http://www.aap.org/

★★★★★

Established primarily for pediatricians seeking to provide the best care for their patients, the AAP site provides research papers; free access to Medline, the medical database; and information on professional opportunities. Parents will find the section on You and Your Family particularly useful; it's packed with safety information, product recalls, parenting guidelines, and tips to help make your parenting experience more fulfilling and successful.

American Board of Pediatrics

http://www.abp.org/

★★★★

The American Board of Pediatrics is dedicated to establishing high standards for pediatricians and evaluating pediatricians who apply for certification. At this site, pediatricians and medical students can learn more about the board, residency training, and the certification process. Parents can use the search tool to find a certified pediatrician by location. The site also provides links to other resources.

Children with Diabetes

http://www.childrenwithdiabetes.com/index_cwd.htm

★★★★

All

Anyone who has diabetes or who has a child with diabetes needs to visit this site. It is packed with information and has real-time chat rooms. This site strives to be "the online community for kids, families, and adults with diabetes.

DISHES Project for Pediatric AIDS

http://www.dishes.org/

★★★★

The DISHES Project is the modeling industry's first 501(c)(3) nonprofit foundation. At the heart of the project is the desire to raise funds and awareness for direct care, education, and emotional support for pediatric AIDS.

Dr. Greene's HouseCalls

http://www.drgreene.com/

★★★★

Get helpful hints from this pediatrician. Need some advice from a kid pro? Submit a question online, search through topics relating to developmental stages, or just read up on Dr. Greene's featured articles. This site is a friendly resource for any parent.

Dr. Plain Talk

http://www.childrenshc.org/DrPlainTalk/

★★★★

This site is maintained by Dr. Rob Payne, who has been a pediatrician for more than 20 years. At this site, you can find plain and simple information about complex medical issues relating to babies and children.

DRs 4 Kids

http://www.drs4kids.com/

★★★

A pediatrician answers parents' questions about infants and children at this site. Individual questions may be asked via email.

drynights.com

http://www.drynights.com/

★★★★

Gives information about bedwetting and encourages you to get your child medical help.

GeneralPediatrics.com

http://generalpediatrics.com/

★★★★

Designed to be a starting point for general pediatrics information on the Web. Find resources suitable for patients and physicians.

Harriet Lane Links

http://derm.med.jhmi.edu/poi/

★★★★

Extensive list of links to resources for parents. Topics include birth, SIDS, disabilities, and allergies such as asthma. Johns Hopkins Department of Pediatrics maintains this site.

I Am Your Child

http://www.iamyourchild.org/

★★★★

Designed to give information about children from before birth through three years of age, this quality site has much to offer parents of young children. The site is tuned in to the issues of child development in this age group and offers information from "The Experts."

India Parenting

http://www.indiaparenting.com/

★★★

Comprehensive healthcare guide for parents and pediatricians. Explains common childhood diseases and treatments, provides home remedies and commonsense treatments, and provides guidelines on nutrition and prescription medications. The preponderance of pop-up ads at this site is annoying.

Journal of Pediatrics

http://www.harcourthealth.com/scripts/om.dll/serve?action=searchDB&searchDBfor=home&id=pd

★★★★

The Journal of Pediatrics site describes the contents of the journal and offers other pertinent information. Everything from preventive healthcare to treatment of childhood diseases to emergency care is covered in the Journal. It serves as a practical guide for the continuing education of physicians who diagnose and treat disorders in infants and children. You'll find many useful articles with helpful information. Abstracts are available free, but to access full-text articles, you must subscribe (for about $160 per month).

kidsDoctor

http://www.kidsdoctor.com/

★★★★★

This site's for you if you like expert opinions on how to keep your kid(s) healthy. You'll find a list of topics written by a doctor, parents' Q&As, and a searchable database so you can zero in on the specific health information you want.

A B C D E F G H I J K L M N O **P** Q R S T U V W X Y Z

A
B
C
D
E
F
G
H
I
J
K
L
M
N
O
P
Q
R
S
T
U
V
W
X
Y
Z

KidsMeds

http://www.kidsmeds.com/

★★★★★

Provides pediatric drug information to parents of infants and children. A pediatric pharmacist is online at this site to answer specific questions.

KidSource Online

http://www.kidsource.com/

★★★

👫 All

Good collection of articles and other resources relating to child rearing and healthcare. Covers everything from summer planning and homework helpers to health and safety issues. Some book reviews that might interest kids.

La Leche League International

http://www.lalecheleague.org/

★★★★

Home to the international, nonprofit, nonsectarian organization that promotes the health benefits of breastfeeding and provides lactation support for women who want to breastfeed. The site also provides healthcare professionals with continuing education opportunities and the latest research on lactation management. Find information about local chapters of La Leche League, too.

MedlinePlus Doctor and Dentist Directories

http://www.nlm.nih.gov/medlineplus/directories.html

★★★★

Enables you to locate dentists, physicians, healthcare providers, and hospitals in your area based on your specific healthcare needs.

MedMark Pediatrics

http://medmark.org/ped/

★★★★

Extensive list of organizations and resources that cover children's hospitals, emotional well-being, and kids' health issues.

Medscape: Pediatrics

http://www.medscape.com/pediatricshome

★★★★★

Medscape, part of WebMD, provides medical information and educational resources for physicians and the general public. Its Pediatrics Home Page focuses on specific issues and conditions that pediatricians must deal with in their practices and health concerns that parents may have concerning their children.

National Childhood Cancer Foundation

http://www.nccf.org/

★★★★★

This site gives details of the programs and activities of this organization, which supports pediatric cancer treatment and research projects.

OncoLink

http://www.oncolink.com/

★★★

Sponsored by the University of Pennsylvania Cancer Center, this site acts as an information guide to all topics relating to pediatric and adult cancer, including leukemia. Excellent source for information on the latest treatments.

Pediatric-Doctor.com

http://www.pediatric-doctor.com/

★★★

Shopping guide for baby- and childcare products. Here, you'll find information on digital ear thermometers, skin care products, diaper rash formulas, security monitors, and more. Some general information on what to expect during various developmental stages, a list of baby names, and child safety tips.

Pediatrics in Review

http://pedsinreview.aapjournals.org/

★★★★

Pediatrics in Review provides continuing education articles and resources for pediatricians. By subscribing, pediatricians can gain full access to the journal, which includes special features, such as Back to Basics (refresher courses), Consultation with the Specialist (specialists' perspectives on a range of topics), What's New (breakthroughs), and Index of Suspicion (to test diagnostic skills).

Virtual Children's Hospital

http://www.vh.org/VCH/

★★★★

👫 All

Digital library of authoritative pediatric information for primary care providers and patients. The site offers a database of resources on illnesses and links.

A
B
C
D
E
F
G
H
I
J
K
L
M
N
O
P
Q
R
S
T
U
V
W
X
Y
Z

746

A B C D E F G H I J K L M N O P Q R S T U V W X Y Z

PETS

AllPets.com

http://www.allpets.com/

★★★★

Well-stocked online pet store offers just about everything any pet owner needs, from beds and bones to pet ramps and training aids. The only thing this store doesn't carry is food. Shop online and have your order shipped to your home, so you can spend more time with your pet.

AnimalNetwork

http://www.animalnetwork.com/

★★★★★

 All

Looking for a magazine about your favorite pet? Then check out this site. Here, you'll find magazines for every pet imaginable, from dogs and cats to fish and reptiles. You can even find magazines about horses. Free trial subscriptions available if you subscribe online.

mypetstop.com

http://new.mypetstop.com/

★★★★

 All

This multilingual site provides more information than you can shake a tail at. Pick your country, click the species (Dogs, Cats, Fish, Birds, Horses, or Other Animals), and you're on your way to learning everything you need to know to properly care for your pet and enjoying your time together. You can ask questions ranging from ailments to nutrition. You'll also find some information on animal psychology.

CATS

American Cat Fanciers Association

http://www.acfacat.com

 ★★★★

Rated one of Links2Go's top feline sites, this site showcases ACFA, a national cat registry sponsoring shows internationally and annually ranking top-scoring cats. ACFA also records Household Pets. The site guides you to local cat shows and breeders and contains photos and forms to register and join this ever-growing organization.

Bad Kitty!

http://www.badpets.net/BadPets/BadKitty.html

 ★★★

A very long list of promises that a family cat makes to its owners, including which annoying habits will stop, how bathroom etiquette is to be observed, how bodily functions will no longer interfere with their lives, and much more. The site also includes lists for birds, dogs, rodents, and miscellaneous (iguanas, horses, and other semi-domesticated beasts).

Beware of Cat!

http://www.geocities.com/Heartland/Meadows/6485/

 ★★★★

 All

Surfing all these cat sites may make you a cat lover. If you decide to add cat pages to your own site, come here to find a wide array of feline graphics, animation, backgrounds, and icons.

Big Cats Online

http://dialspace.dial.pipex.com/agarman/

★★★★

👥 All

This site offers information regarding all aspects of nondomestic cats, including their conservation. Many links to other sites are provided.

Cat Fanciers

http://www.fanciers.com/

★★★★

👥 All

Provides cat-related information. This site offers numerous FAQs on different cat breeds, feline health, and care issues. It also offers links to show schedules, cat organizations, FTP and gopher sites, as well as links to commercial sites, picture sites, and cat owners' home pages.

Cat Fanciers Association

http://www.cfainc.org/

★★★★★

👥 All

The world's largest purebred cat registry features its top award-winning felines and information on each recognized breed. This site encourages responsible cat ownership and advises how you can show purebred and household pet felines and participate in local CFA cat clubs and shows throughout the world.

Cat House (EFBC/FCC)

http://www.cathouse-fcc.org/

★★★★

👥 All

Contains pictures and some audio clips straight from the cat's mouth. The Cat House (a.k.a. the Feline Conservation Center) is a desert zoo that contains a variety of wild cat species. More than 50 cats, representing 13 species, live at the compound. Photos of recent births are included.

Cats Protection League

http://www.cats.org.uk/

★★★★

Learn more about caring for cats through online guides at this nonprofit organization's site that is dedicated to providing new homes for cats throughout the UK. At the site you can track down a location near you and find out how to adopt a kitten or cat that's been rescued.

Catsbuzz Bookstore

http://members.aol.com/catsbuzz/

★★★★

Books, books, and more books about cats. On this site, you'll find books about specific breeds, books with general information, books for kids, and books for Christmas. Link over to Catsbuzz Central and check out cats in the news, great cat links, and cat poetry.

Best CatToys.com

http://www.cattoys.com/

💲

★★★★★

👥 All

Check the list of recommended toys for your particular breed of cat and then purchase it online here. You'll want to visit frequently to see what the new specials are each week. One of the most fun things you can do with cats is to watch them play with that new toy you just bought them, and this site will allow you to order many types of toys for them online. If you're a cat lover, you must visit this Best of the Best site.

Cindy's Cat Pages

http://www.cindydrew.com/cats/

★★★

👥 All

Contains resources for feline information but also has extensive reviews of other cat sites. Check out the cat poetry, the Black Panther Awards, cat "tales," book reviews, and more. Forms are provided for application to membership into CLAW, the most exclusive club for cats.

A
B
C
D
E
F
G
H
I
J
K
L
M
N
O
P
Q
R
S
T
U
V
W
X
Y
Z

Feline Information

http://www.animalclinic.com/catpage.htm

 ★★★

This page offers extensive info and advice concerning major diseases that cats suffer, from leukemia to diabetes. The style is in a familiar question-and-answer format, so even nonveterinarians can understand.

Feline Information Page

http://sirlou.thebeatuk.com/cat/feline.html

 ★★★

This fun site is filled with stories, photos, and factual information on the care and feeding of cats. In addition, you can study the history and evolution of cats as a species and read some cat haiku.

Happy Household Pet Cat Club

http://hhpcc.org/

 ★★★

The Happy Household Pet Cat Club (HHPCC), an international organization founded in 1968, is geared toward cat owners who want to exhibit their feline companions in cat shows. HHPCC's website offers access to a bimonthly newsletter, membership information, and advice on how you can get the most out of showing your household cat in shows.

How to Toilet Train Your Cat

http://www.karawynn.net/mishacat/toilet.shtml

★★★★

If you're tired of buying cat litter and emptying it, it may be time to consider toilet training. No, really, you can toilet train your cat! This site offers its own advice and techniques. Karawynn explains the basics, while Misha demonstrates the techniques and positions.

Mystic Molly of the Web

http://web.ukonline.co.uk/Members/keith.dumble/

 ★★★

Molly is a furry fortune teller and horoscope reader. Lottery players will appreciate her methods for picking this week's numbers. Occasionally, Molly makes live Web appearances. Be sure to get your Mystic Molly T-shirt!

Sheba

http://www.sheba.com/

 ★★★

 All

Sheba cat food's hangout caters to cat lovers. Here, you can enter your cat's picture in a photo contest, play cat games, chat about cats with other cat enthusiasts, and learn cat care basics.

The Tame Beast

http://www.tamebeast.com/7c.htm

 ★★★

In addition to the traditional information about cats, this site offers extensive links to clubs, services, and products. A long list of shelters and vets will help you to find a place to keep your cat while away or a place to find more cats when you're ready to adopt another.

Virtual Kitty!

http://www.virtualkitty.com/

 $

 ★★★★

 All

Very much like the popular Tamagotchi pets, Virtual Kitty lets you adopt your own online cat (or dog). You can read the Owners Manual to get some tips for caring for your kitty, and you can mail a kitty to a friend as a gift. The site also offers you a free-for-life email address.

The Virtual Pet Cemetery

http://www.mycemetery.com/pet/index.html

★★★★

 All

All pet owners must eventually deal with the loss of a pet. The Virtual Pet Cemetery offers a place to give your pet a virtual burial and to say your good-byes. This site has numerous touching accounts of people and the pets they lost. The site has won many awards.

Why Cats Paint

http://www.monpa.com/wcp/

★★★

👥 All

Did you know that the Egyptians knew of some cats' ability to paint 3,000 years ago? Or that some cats' work is sold at auction? One painter sold paintings for up to $7,000. This site explores the creative aspects of the feline, recently reinspired by the international best-seller, *Why Cats Paint*.

DOGS

The Actual Dog Show

http://www.showdogsupersite.com/actualshow/

★★★

This site dedicates itself to dog fanciers who show their dogs. Learn what happens at dog shows, why you should want to go, and why *bitch* is not a dirty word. You'll find out what the grooming area, the obedience ring, and the breed ring are.

Adopt a Greyhound

http://www.adopt-a-greyhound.org/

★★★★

Greyhounds may have been famous for their speed and grace on the track, but recently, people have begun to adopt them upon retirement from the races—saving them from euthanasia or worse. This site provides a huge amount of information, as well as links to other sites. Check out the many adoption agencies specializing in greyhounds.

Akbash Dog

http://www.turkishdogs.com/akbash/

★★★★

The Akbash is a livestock-protection dog found in rural Turkey. This site enables you to view pictures of Akbash dogs, read their history and breed description, and learn about Akbash Dog Association International and its rescue program.

American Kennel Club (AKC)

http://www.akc.org/index.cfm

★★★★★

👥 All

Find out more about this organization, read about different breeds, and locate an AKC near you. You'll also enjoy the informational brochures covering everything from boarding your dog to showing your dog. This site is packed with information! Besides the great graphics layout, ease of use, and all the information, the site enables you to purchase everything concerning dogs from books, videos, and apparel to artwork.

Canine Vaccination Schedule

http://critterfixer.com/pages/canine.asp

★★★

If you're a pet owner, you know how difficult it can be to keep up with your pet's inoculation schedule. However, there is an easier way: Visit this site, which contains a schedule for canine vaccinations from age 6 weeks up to 18 months. The site also provides descriptions on how each vaccine is administered and describes the illness the vaccine treats.

Caucasian Mountain Dog (Ovcharka)

http://www.flockguard.org/cauctoc.htm

★★★★

Focuses on the Caucasian Mountain dog, a flock guardian that has served as a livestock guard, a home guardian, and a fighting dog. This site includes breed standards, a photo gallery, and links to many other resources.

A
B
C
D
E
F
G
H
I
J
K
L
M
N
O
P
Q
R
S
T
U
V
W
X
Y
Z

⌷Best⌷ Dog Breed Info Center

http://www.dogbreedinfo.com/

★★★★★

👫 All

Before investing in a new pet, visit this site to select the best breed for your family situation, temperament, living space, or whatever criteria you want to use. It's a good place to assess whether you're ready for the responsibilities of being a dog owner. This site is very well organized and offers the information you need to have before taking that big step of owning a dog. The site has great graphics, is easy to navigate, and will help you in the selection process, which is important because you want to make sure you select an animal you will be happy with.

Dog.com

http://www.dog.com/

★★★★

Search more than 17,000 dog-related sites to find the information you need, including details of a breed's personality. You can also catch up on the latest dog news headlines and shop for the dog lover in your life.

Dog Owner's Guide

http://www.canismajor.com/dog/

★★★★

Read articles about choosing the right breed, caring for a dog, training it, selecting a vet, as well as learning about the law and dogs, and staying out of trouble. The site has plenty of information on a wide range of topics.

Dog Term Glossary

http://www.ecn.purdue.edu/~laird/dogs/glossary

★★★★

Presents terminology both common and uncommon to the canine field. This site provides many links to additional sites, as well as pointers to other parts of the glossary. Also, it contains contact information for Humane Societies and the American Kennel Club. Great place to go to for a description of most dog breeds plus links to other sites that focus on specific breeds.

Dog-Play

http://www.dog-play.com/

★★★★

👫 All

Literally an A–W (no X, Y, or Z) of fun things to do with your dog, this site also gives pet owners something different to think about: animal-assisted therapy. The author of this site details the experience of using dogs to help reach out to the elderly and confined individuals. The site includes links to organizations involved in animal-assisted therapy, books and publications on therapy dogs, and links to other dog-related sites.

Dogs in Review

http://www.dogsinreview.com/

★★★

👫 All

Whether you show dogs or just like to watch dog shows, *Dogs in Review* magazine can provide you with the information you need—articles written by some of the top dog experts in the country. Check this site to find out what's in this month's issue or to subscribe to the magazine.

GORP: Great Outdoor Recreation Pages

http://www.gorp.com/gorp/eclectic/pets.htm

★★★★

👫 All

Tired of walking the dog just around the block or to the local park? These pages detail countless destinations that will cater to you and your canine. Complete lists by activity, region, interest, and lodging are provided. Includes information about emergency care for your dog.

iLoveDogs.com

http://www.i-love-dogs.com/

★★★★★

👫 All

Exhaustive directory of dog sites listed in categories that include All About Dogs, Dog Award Sites, Dog Breeders, Dog Shopping, and Dog Humor.

Index of Famous Dogs, Cats, and Critters

http://www.citizenlunchbox.com/famous/animals.html

★★★★

👫 All

A surprising number of dogs and other animals have important roles in TV and movies or are owned by famous people. This site is dedicated to listing most if not all of them. You'll even find the obscure ones. For example, what is the name of the dog who pulls down the bikini of the little girl in the old Coppertone ads? What was the name of Santa's Little Helper's wife? How about all their puppies? You can get the answers at this website.

NaturalDogFood.com

http://www.naturaldogfood.com/

★★★

Ever wonder whether the canned food you feed your dog is actually good for him? This site's Webmaster is sure that her dog's diet of people food helped it live a healthy life, and she cites experts to prove her point. The site provides some recipes, a FAQ section, suggested reading, and more.

Net Pets

http://www.netpets.com/

★★★★

👫 All

Excellent directory of sites that can provide the information and resources you need to take care of your domesticated roomies. Covers dogs, cats, birds, horses, and fish. Net Pets' main purpose is to rescue animals, so be sure to check out this site to see how you can help.

Pomeranian Dog

http://www.personal.u-net.com/~galley/

★★★

👫 All

Provides information on the Pomeranian. This site includes links to pictures, history, and breed standards, as well as information on other links related to the Pomeranian.

Portuguese Water Dog Index

http://www.ecn.purdue.edu/~laird/dogs/PWD/

★★★

Offers information on the Portuguese Water Dog, also referred to as the Fisherman's Dog. This site also offers links to other related sites, including the Pacific Northwest Portuguese Water Dog Club site.

SaraQueen: Queen of All Dogs in the Universe

http://members.aol.com/saraqueen/

★★★

👫 Not for kids

A humorous account of existence through the eyes of SaraQueen. She has a chat room, a doggy Prozac alternative, Devotee of the Month, a Dogs Against Gates campaign (yes, both kinds of "Gates"), and more.

The Schipperke Pages

http://www.caninetoday.com/breed/schipperke/

★★★★

Includes information and pictures on the Schipperke breed of dog (pronounced *schipperkey*), including an index of breeders, medical information, and breed standards. Check out the message boards to get in touch with other fans of this breed.

Shy Dogs Links Page

http://www.geocities.com/Heartland/9820/

★★★

Not all dogs are as brave as Rin Tin Tin or as outgoing as Lassie. Among other dog-related links are pages dedicated to the quiet, soft-spoken dogs—the ones the neighbors don't even know exist. Perhaps a visit from a few more web surfers will help these dogs break out of their furry shell.

Siberian Husky

http://www.execpc.com/~bbackman/index.html

★★★

Find out how to prepare for your new husky and what it will need. Browse through the photo gallery and cool sites. Learn about training huskies, keeping them from being bored, and adding them to your family. The site includes warnings against pet stores, irresponsible breeders, and puppy mills.

A B C D E F G H I J K L M N O **P** Q R S T U V W X Y Z

A B C D E F G H I J K L M N O P Q R S T U V W X Y Z

Three Dog Bakery

http://www.threedog.com/

★★★★

 All

After stocking up on your own sticky buns and cake, remember to stop by this website to order some treats for Spot. The bakery's doggie treats were a knee-jerk reaction to commercial biscuits that had up to 50 ingredients, and pups all over the world love them, including Oprah's! Fresh baked and all natural ingredients.

PET CARE

American Animal Hospital Association (AAHA)

http://www.healthypet.com/

★★★★

AAHA offers pet care tips, answers to FAQs on care and illnesses, and a library of articles on topics from behavior to nutrition. At first glance, the site looks a little sparse, but click on the Pet Care Library link, and you'll see links to all sorts of tutorials and articles on pet care and training. Click the Coloring link to view printable posters for kids to color. Check the FAQ for answers to common questions or subscribe to the Pet Planet newsletter.

American Pet Association

http://www.apapets.com/

★★★★

 All

The American Pet Association is dedicated to promoting responsible pet ownership through action, services, and education. You will find lots of useful information here to help you assist your pet in leading a more peaceful, safe, and enjoyable coexistence with you. Information here is interesting, informative, and useful for pet owners of all types.

Animal Health Information

http://www.avma.org/careforanimals/
animatedjourneys/pethealth/pethealth.asp

★★★★

 All

Get info on dental care, pet population control, and vaccinations. Learn how to deal with diseases such as heart disease, heartworm disease, cancer, Lyme disease, parasites, toxoplasmosis, and rabies.

The AVMA (American Veterinary Medical Association) Network

http://www.avma.org/

★★★★★

 All

The American Veterinary Medical Association answers questions on pet care, selection, and loss, and how your veterinarian helps you enjoy your pet. The Kids' Korner includes pictures you can print out for your kids to color. Each picture includes an activity or advice on feeding, training, or basic care. This site is extremely attractive, well organized, and offers a wealth of information.

CyberPet

http://www.cyberpet.com/

★★★★

 All

Directory to resources on the Web for cat and dog owners and breeders, including healthcare, selection and training articles, products, and services. Pet fanciers, exhibitors, owners, and breeders will find something here.

DoctorDog.com: Cat and Dog Supplies and Pet Health Care

http://www.doctordog.com/

★★★★

Huge collection of dog and cat healthcare and pet supplies, including leashes, toys, shampoos, rug cleaners, and more, plus some resources on general healthcare issues.

FINS: Fish INformation Service

http://fins.actwin.com/index.php

★★★

 All

Provides a global, alphabetical listing of fish stores, along with a description of what each store offers, plus general information about caring for fish, setting up attractive aquariums, and more.

Friendly Ferrets

http://www.blarg.net/~critter/dscott.html

★★★

Offers articles, pictures, and links relating to ferrets.

HomeVet Natural Pet Care

http://www.homevet.com/

💲

★★★

Brief information about veterinary house calls, as well as advice about pet care, medical news, and ways to deal with the loss of a pet. Even if you don't live in Weston, Connecticut, to be able to take advantage of this at-home service, you'll benefit from the other info offered at this site.

I Love My Pet

http://www.ilovemypet.com/

💲

★★★★★

The I Love My Pet site offers tips, a pet club, online vet, specialty foods, discounts, and a breeder registry. Both pet owners and pet fans will find useful information here. If you're looking for information on pet diets, healthcare, or just fun and games, this is the place to find it. While you're here, check out all the selections from the online catalog.

NetPets

http://www.netpets.com/

★★★★

 All

A resource for dog, cat, horse, fish, and bird owners. The site includes information about pet health and nutrition, and offers an events calendar, a library of articles, and a list of animal shelters by state.

Pet Care Library

http://www.healthypet.com/Library/

★★★★

All

Complete library of reference materials for taking care of pets. Includes volumes on Behavior, Illnesses and Disease, Common Health Problems, and more.

Pet Care and Wildlife Information

http://www.klsnet.com/

★★★★

All

This reference provides information on caring for all sorts of pets, including exotic fish, reptiles, and amphibians. Also provides information about caring for dogs, cats, and other furry creatures.

ThePetCenter.com

http://www.thepetcenter.com/

★★★★

All

Information about general healthcare issues relating primarily to dogs and cats. Some specific information about various diseases and treatments and what you can expect if your pet must undergo surgery. Excellent tutorials on how to attract natural wildlife to your back yard. Animal lovers of all types should check out this site. Links to other sites to purchase pet supplies.

Pet Columns from University of Illinois College of Veterinary Medicine (CVM)

http://www.cvm.uiuc.edu/ceps/

★★★★

Search by keyword or by most recent to least recent articles for authoritative articles on pet care, common problems, and their management. Also, the site provides links to the University of Illinois CVM and the Continuing Education Public Extension Service.

A
B
C
D
E
F
G
H
I
J
K
L
M
N
O
P
Q
R
S
T
U
V
W
X
Y
Z

A
B
C
D
E
F
G
H
I
J
K
L
M
N
O
P
Q
R
S
T
U
V
W
X
Y
Z

PetEducation.com

http://www.peteducation.com/

★★★★★

⚎ All

This site was created by vets to provide information on caring for your pet, so you'll find tons of articles to scan. There are also pet services directories, a veterinary dictionary, answers to frequently asked questions, quizzes, and the latest pet news.

Pet First Aid

http://www.petfirstaid.org/

$

★★★

You probably keep a first aid kit on hand for yourself or your family, but what about for your pet? Pet First Aid carries first aid kits for dogs, cats, other pets, and even barn animals. Kits come complete with instructions on what to do during common emergency situations.

Pet Plan Insurance

http://www.petplan.com/

★★★★

Pet Plan Insurance offers health insurance policies for your cat and dog to protect them in the event of accident, illness, or disease. Having pet insurance is becoming increasingly common, because people don't want to have to choose between saving their beloved pet or putting it down because they can't afford the medical price tag.

PetNet

http://www.petnet.com.au/

★★★★

⚎ All

Australia's Petcare and Advisory Service has information for pet lovers everywhere, including Selectapet, plus a guide to local services. By using Selectapet, you can be sure that you are ready to get a pet and find which breeds are best suited to your lifestyle, budget, and temperament.

PetPlace.com

http://www.petplace.com/

★★★★

⚎ All

Whether your pet is well or sick, you'll find this site a handy reference. Wellness tips will help keep your pet healthy, and the illness information will assist in assessing what might be wrong when Fido starts acting funny. You can also store your pet's medical information at the site for easy access in a central spot.

Pets Need Dental Care, Too

http://www.petdental.com/

$

★★★★★

⚎ All

This site makes you aware of potential problems with your pets caused by dental situations, just as with humans. Dental problems can cause serious health problems in addition to painful tooth loss or gum disease. If your pet is acting strangely or seems to be ill for no apparent reason, you should check out this site.

PetSage—Pet Care Products

http://www.petsage.com/

$

★★★★

⚎ All

The PetSage site introduces you to products that will enhance pet care. The goal of this company is to inform you of changes and choices available in pet care, in the hopes that together with your veterinarian, they can help you raise a healthy and loving companion. The site offers a lot of information about raising and caring for pets.

Petsville

http://www.petsville.com/

★★★

 All

This active online community provides a place where pet owners, enthusiasts, and pet care specialists can keep in touch with one another for the primary purpose of rescuing animals and finding them homes. Features some general information on pet care, an online adoption center, and a shopping mall. Donate online or shop at some of the recommended stores; all benefits go to the organization.

Practical Pet Care

http://www.practical-pet-care.com/

★★★★

 All

Excellent resource for pet owners, as well as for veterinarians, this site provides dozens of links to articles ranging from basic pet care and training to diagnosis and treatment of specific illnesses. Features pet information, pet pictures, ask an expert area, and freebies.

Professor Hunt's Dog Page

http://www.cofc.edu/~huntc/dogpage.html#Message

★★★★

Get info on rescues, animal health, and socially responsible activities. This site has a special emphasis on herding (working) breeds.

Purina Pet Care Center

http://www.purina.com/

★★★★

 All

More than just nutrition from this pet food company. Pet care advice, training, kennel management, and some fun games. Purina's hope is that you'll find this site to be a very useful resource and the goodwill generated will translate into lots more sales of Purina products.

Veterinary Oncology

http://www.vetmed.lsu.edu/oncology/

★★★★

This veterinary hospital of Louisiana State University has information for owners about the diagnosis and treatment of cancer in animals.

Vetinfo

http://www.vetinfo.com/

★★★

Search for veterinary medical information on dogs and cats, and learn more about your veterinarian and careers in animal care.

Waltham World of Pet Care

http://www.waltham.com/

★★★★★

 All

This pet nutrition company provides advice on caring for dogs, cats, birds, and fish. Provides excellent information about each animal that's covered, including breed selection, basic care instructions, training and feeding tips, and more.

PET SUPPLIES

Doolittle's

http://www.doolittles.com/

★★★★★

At Doolittle's, you'll find a unique combination of distinctive gifts for pets and pet lovers, fine quality pet supplies, premium pet foods, gourmet treats, and a full-service pet grooming salon.

MyPetPrescriptions.com

http://www.mypetprescriptions.com/

★★★

Does your pet have a long-term illness requiring treatment with expensive medications? Then check out this site, where you can order prescriptions for your pet online. Also offers a few nonprescription products.

A B C D E F G H I J K L M N O **P** Q R S T U V W X Y Z

A
B
C
D
E
F
G
H
I
J
K
L
M
N
O
P
Q
R
S
T
U
V
W
X
Y
Z

Nature's Pet Marketplace

http://www.naturespet.com/

★★★★

Offers natural and holistic products. This site includes homeopathic remedies, dog and cat food, vitamin and herbal supplements, grooming and skin care products, and flea and tick remedies. Also, it offers a natural line of bird food and supplements. The site includes descriptions and explanations of holistic products as well as other information.

Noah's Pet Supplies

http://noahspets.com

★★★★★

This site offers more than 6,000 items for pets. You'll also find a Q&A section where you can get answers to your pet questions. The selection is so large that the company even offers a section highlighting the newest product additions.

Pet Botanics by Cardinal Labs, Inc.

http://www.cardinalpet.com/natural/naturepro.html

★★★★

Try tea-tree spray for flea-bite dermatitis, hot spots, and dry skin irritation, or check out the oatmeal shampoo for dry, itchy skin and skin irritations. Or maybe your pet just needs the herbal shampoo for cleaning and deodorizing. The cedar shampoo and cedar spray kill infestations of insects (these are natural, nontoxic alternatives to chemical insecticides). Try the herbal collar to repel insects. A glossary of herbs and botanicals is included. These products are not sold online, but you can look at a list of local outlets that sell them.

Pet Experts

http://www.pet-experts.com/

★★★★★

About pets, animals, wholesale pet products, and discount animal supplies. Dog, cat, bird, fish, reptile, iguana, and even ferret supplies can be found here.

Pet Market

http://www.petmarket.com/

★★★★

Search for discount pet supplies and learn about the most popular products for your dog, cat, bird, or other friend.

PetFoodDirect.com

http://www.petfooddirect.com/store/

★★★★★

Order pet foods and accessories online and have them shipped to your doorstep. Food, health products, toys, and treats are all found here.

Petopia.com

http://www.petco.com/

★★★★★

Read articles about dog care, such as how to safely trim your pooch's nails. Learn whether putting your pet in a kennel is harmful and search for pet services and products all at this one place.

ThatPetPlace.com

http://www.thatpetplace.com/

★★★★★

This pet supply superstore carries everything for almost every pet imaginable at great prices. Features accessories for dogs and cats, fish, birds, reptiles, and other small creatures. Includes a few articles on caring for and training pets. Easy to navigate.

PETsMart

http://www.petsmart.com/

★★★★★

Huge online pet store and pet information kiosk. Whether you own a dog, cat, bird, fish, reptile, or rodent, you can find all the supplies and accessories you need right here. Features basic care instructions, feeding calculators, information on illnesses and treatments, instructions on choosing the right animal for you, and much more.

Pet Warehouse

http://www.petwarehouse.com

★★★★★

A mail-order catalog company that specializes in aquatic, bird, dog, cat, reptile, small animal, and pond products at factory direct prices.

Wyld's Wingdom, Inc.

http://www.wingdom.com

★★★★

Specializes in exotic pets and pet bird products. Offers bird food, bird toys, and bird-related products. Wyld's doesn't sell directly to the public, but these products may be at your local pet store.

Related Sites

http://www.petsafe.net/

http://www.pet-expo.com/birdbird.htm

http://www.coolpetstuff.com/

A B C D E F G H I J K L M N O **P** Q R S T U V W X Y Z

A
B
C
D
E
F
G
H
I
J
K
L
M
N
O
P
Q
R
S
T
U
V
W
X
Y
Z

Yellow Pages

PHOTOGRAPHY

CAMERAS

Abe's of Maine

http://www.abesofmaine.com/

★★★★★

Promising prices of up to 50% off retail, Abe's specializes in selling camera equipment and supplies online from the store in Brooklyn, New York.

Ace Index

http://www.acecam.com/

★★★★

Use the Ace index to find manufacturer sites, dealer sites, used equipment sites, photo labs, and much more.

AGFA Digital Cameras

http://www.agfa.com/

★★★★★

Which digital camera is right for you? Check out AGFA's product line. This site has a search feature that allows you to search for information, and the company offers commercial services such as those offered to the newspaper industry.

Amazing Fish Cam!

http://www.netscape.com/fishcam/fishcam.html

★★★

The Amazing Fish Cam! is a camera (two cameras, actually) trained on a tropical aquarium. Every five minutes, a fresh (or maybe saltwater) image is posted. For Netscape users, there's the Continuously Refreshing Fish Cam.

Apogee Photo: The Internet Photo Magazine

http://www.apogeephoto.com/

★★★★★

 All

Dedicated to entertaining and informing photographers of all ages, this site offers high-quality articles and columns about photography. Features basic instructions on taking pictures, techniques for novice and advanced photographers, information about digital imaging, and more. Also provides links to workshops, books, and schools that may be of interest to readers.

Beach Photo & Video

http://beachphoto.com/

$

★★★★

Whether you need a photo restored or are in the market for a used camera, Beach Photo is likely to provide the services you need. Buy new or used equipment here, and have film processed or printed, too.

Bender Photographic

http://www.benderphoto.com

$

★★★

Thinking about making your own camera? Benders sells kits for 4×5 and 8×10 view cameras from kiln-dried cherry and brass hardware. By building your own camera, you can invest more on a good lens, which will improve the quality of your photos. Learn more about building a camera and then order the kit at this site.

Camera Review.com
http://www.camerareview.com/

★★★★★

Specify the features you're looking for in a camera, and the database will provide a list of camera models that meet your criteria. You can also look at the online rankings of the most popular cameras, according to people who own and use them. Then compare features of two or more cameras side-by-side to help in making your purchase decision.

Cameras Etcetera
http://www.cameras-etc.com/

★★★★★

This site focuses on selling "quality used photo equipment at fair prices." Links to eBay where you can purchase the equipment.

CameraWorld
http://www.cameraworld.com/

★★★★

This enormous online camera warehouse is stocked with everything a novice or expert photographer needs: digital cameras, film cameras, a wide variety of camcorders, lenses, film, light meters, books, and more.

Complete Guide to Digital Cameras and Digital Photography
http://www.shortcourses.com/

★★★★

A free online course on digital photography. A gallery of images taken with a digital camera is included. This is an information-packed site!

Digital Camera Imaging Resource Page
http://www.imaging-resource.com/

★★★★★

Digital cameras, features, specs, reviews, and sample images for most brands and models are available at this site.

Digital Camera News
http://www.steves-digicams.com/diginews.html

★★★★

A great overview of the latest digital camera products. The site also includes information on related software and updates. It includes the Picture of the Day, submitted by viewers. The site comes from Steve's Digicams.

Digital Camera Resource Page
http://www.dcresource.com/

★★★

The Digital Camera Resource page posts current information and reviews. This is a popular site for digital camera buffs, current owners, and potential owners. It is well designed and easy to navigate. In the site's own words, "The Digital Camera Resource Page, founded in 1997, is designed to be an unofficial resource for current or future owners of digital cameras. It is aimed more towards the consumer end, rather than the high end." This site does not sell anything or promote anything but rather offers current information on digital cameras.

Digital Photography Review
http://www.dpreview.com/

★★★★★

A complete digital camera resource that carries information about hundreds of digital cameras and accessories. Includes product news, galleries, forums, a buying guide, and a glossary.

EarthCam
http://www.earthcam.com/

★★★★

Want to watch the world go by while sitting at your computer? Then tune in to these Webcams positioned at major metropolitan areas around the world: New York, Chicago, Las Vegas, Moscow, and Quito, to name a few. You can also poke around people's kitchens and offices, tattoo shops, and anywhere else people choose to photograph other people and places and broadcast them on the Web.

A B C D E F G H I J K L M N O P Q R S T U V W X Y Z

A
B
C
D
E
F
G
H
I
J
K
L
M
N
O
P
Q
R
S
T
U
V
W
X
Y
Z

Focus Camera & Video

http://www.focuscamera.com/

★★★★★

Bills itself as the #1 deep discount source for every photographic, sports optic, astronomical, and video camera item for more than 30 years. One of America's largest-stocking photo and optics dealers, with thousands of items in stock.

HowStuffWorks: How Digital Cameras Work

http://www.howstuffworks.com/digital-camera.htm

★★★★★

 All

If you're curious as to how digital cameras capture and store images, this site provides an easily understandable explanation.

Kodak Digital Cameras

http://www.kodak.com/global/en/digital/easyShare/

★★★★

The Kodak family of digital cameras and related products.

Megapixel.net

http://www.megapixel.net/

★★★★

Like most good photography sites, this one offers photography articles, discussion forums, product reviews, and tips and techniques for improving your skill.

PC Photo Review

http://www.pcphotoreview.com/

★★★★★

Digital camera site offers news, reviews, guides, tips, and forums.

Photo.net

http://www.photo.net/

★★★★★

Pages and pages of camera-related commentary. For example, "What Camera Should I Buy?" explores some options (view cameras, medium-formats, SLRs, and even lowly point-and-shoots are covered) and some opinions. This site contains a ton of handy tips: recommended films, ritzy frame shops, places to shop for cameras, places to send your slides for processing, and so on.

Ritz Camera

http://www.ritzcamera.com

★★★★★

A network of e-commerce websites, including Ritz Camera, Wolf Camera, Photography.com, and other businesses, this site offers a huge selection of cameras and provides easy browsing. Stop by the Learning Center to learn more about various photographic products and services and then check out the special coupons and deals available at Ritz Camera.

DIGITAL PHOTO PRINTS AND SHARING

Club Photo

http://www.clubphoto.com/

★★★★★

Club Photo can. transform film into digital images or work directly with the digital image files stored on your digital camera. Simply send in your film or upload the files, use Club Photo's software to edit and enhance the photos, and then share them online with friends and family or order prints, cards, calendars, mugs, T-shirts, and other items right online. This site introduces you to the process and makes it very easy to upload and edit photos and order prints and other products.

Digital Photography Challenge

http://www.dpchallenge.com/

★★★★★

Join Digital Photography Challenge to pick up photography tricks and techniques, enter your photos in competitions, and challenge your knowledge of photography. Site features several photo galleries, forums where you can read and post messages, tutorials, advice, and much more. Members can even sell their prints online!

HP Digital Photo Projects

http://h30036.www3.hp.com/photos/us/home/home.php

★★★★★

If you have a printer that's capable of photo printing, check out some of what HP has to offer in papers and other products that can help you transform your photos into creative keepsakes.

Image to Art

http://www.imagetoart.com/

★★★★★

Image to Art is a service that can transform a photograph into an oil-on-canvas work of art with more depth and definition than is possible in a photo. Service also features religious icons, decorative pillows, and artistic room-divider screens. A little pricey, but unique.

Ofoto.com

http://www.ofoto.com/

★★★★★

With Ofoto, Kodak's online photo sharing and print service, you can send in a roll of film or upload digital photos from a digital camera to the service. The site allows you to share your photos with others by creating an online photo album and/or order prints, greeting cards, and other items. Kodak offers free software to help you upload your photos to the service, and to crop and enhance your photos before ordering prints.

PhotoWorks

http://www.photoworks.com/

★★★★★

Another popular online digital photo processing site, PhotoWorks allows you to send in a roll of film or upload photos you have taken with your digital camera and then edit, enhance, and share photos online. If desired, you can order photo prints, greeting cards, custom calendars, and other items that display your photos. This service is great for creating keepsakes and gifts!

SmugMug

http://www.smugmug.com/

★★★★★

SmugMug is a digital photo/video sharing service that enables you to share photos and video clips with friends and relatives and/or market them online. For about $30 per year, you can store an unlimited number of photos and have up to 2 gigabytes of traffic per month—that's about 20–30 thousand photo views per month. This site has an elegant design that is very easy to navigate. For another $20 per year, you can bump up your storage, double your traffic, and add video clips.

Snapfish.com

http://www.snapfish.com/

★★★★★

Whether you snap photos using a 35mm camera with film or a high-tech digital camera, Snapfish can develop your film for you, create a set of prints, put together an online photo album, and provide the tools you need to create professional photo albums, mugs, greeting cards, T-shirts, and other creative items. Snapfish even provides the software you need to enhance your images before you make prints!

A
B
C
D
E
F
G
H
I
J
K
L
M
N
O
P
Q
R
S
T
U
V
W
X
Y
Z

A
B
C
D
E
F
G
H
I
J
K
L
M
N
O
P
Q
R
S
T
U
V
W
X
Y
Z

RESOURCES

American Museum of Photography

http://www.photographymuseum.com/

★★★★

This site provides a beautifully displayed collection along with information and services for researchers and collectors. It also contains information on preservation and a newsletter.

Apogee Photo

http://www.apogeephoto.com

★★★★

All

Check Apogee's buyer's guide and product reviews before making another camera equipment purchase, and enjoy the free online magazine to learn more about the art and process of taking good photos. Industry news, articles, columns, and other tidbits round out the site, which is for professionals and amateurs. Also includes links to resources for young photographers.

Best BetterPhoto.com

http://www.betterphoto.com/home.asp

$

★★★★★

This excellent source for novice photographers features scads of information about photography basics, plus online workshops that lead you step-by-step through the process of learning new techniques. Created and maintained by Jim Miotke, author of *Absolute Beginner's Guide to Taking Great Photos*, this site also provides a Q&A section, discussion forums, and a buyer's guide. Links to Amazon.com, where you can purchase cameras and accessories online.

City-Gallery.com

http://www.city-gallery.com/

★★★

Post information and ask questions about old photography methods and materials.

F32: Online Photography Magazine

http://www.f32.com/

★★★

F32 is the online interactive photography magazine for photographers from professional to hobbyist.

Focus on Photography

http://www.azuswebworks.com/photography/

★★★★★

 All

Lots of information on the processes and techniques of modern photography. A wealth of technical information is available. This site is wonderful in its simplicity because the information is easy to find. This makes it a gem for the amateur and professional alike. You'll find everything from the basics to the more complicated techniques such as lighting and composition. You'll also find a section with sample pictures, references, and an excellent FAQ.

George Eastman House: Timeline of Photography

http://www.eastman.org/5_timeline/5_index.html

★★★★

An overview of the history of photographic images from the fifth century B.C. until the present. The information is presented in list style or by time periods. The site is from the George Eastman House.

Getty Images

http://creative.gettyimages.com/photodisc

$

★★★★

Looking for high-quality digital images for use in an upcoming marketing campaign? Then search this site by keyword to find images that may fit your needs. You can purchase more than 100,000 images on disc using secure card services.

International Center of Photography

http://www.icp.org

★★★★★

ICP's mission is to "present photography's vital and central place in contemporary culture, and to lead in interpretation issues central to its development." View online exhibitions and learn more about the work of this organization.

International Freelance Photographers Organization (IFPO)

http://www.aipress.com/

★★★

The International Freelance Photographers Organization (IFPO), founded in 1988, offers help, information, and assistance to freelance photographers as well as others in the business. By joining, you get professional training, press passes, information, and much more. This is one of the best known and respected organizations in the business, and many members are known throughout the world. IFPO publishes a magazine that includes not only the members' pictures but information that can help you in your career.

Jeff Harris

http://www.jeffharris.org

★★★

Personal website of Canadian-based photographer Jeff Harris, who has had his picture taken every day since January 1, 1999. Here, you can flip through the complete photo journal of Jeff Harris.

KODAK: Taking Great Pictures

http://www.kodak.com/US/en/nav/takingPics.shtml

★★★★★

 All

This handy guide to taking better pictures provides tips, techniques, and "problem picture remedies," for any level photographer. Online tutorials discuss fundamentals of photography, including lighting, composition, and basic darkroom techniques. Sample photos show you how the pros do it, and a selection of reference materials is always on-hand to help you with technical terminology and concepts.

Masters of Photography

http://www.masters-of-photography.com/

★★★★

Browse the list of famous photographers and click on someone of interest to view his or her photos and read articles on that individual's background and training.

Online Photography Courses

http://www.photo-seminars.com/pscampus.htm

★★★

Online courses and workshops. This site also offers one-on-one instruction—lessons on all subjects and photography on all levels. You can purchase books, videos, and other related items through the online store using secure card services.

PanOguide.com

http://www.panoguide.com/technique/

★★★

James Rigg put together this how-to guide for shooting panoramas. If you're interested in the "big picture," you can visit this site to learn how to shoot a panorama manually or compose panoramas using any of several special software programs. Features instructions, tips, and a photo gallery.

Photo Arts

http://www.photoarts.com

★★★★

View exhibitions of work by contemporary and fine art photographers; take a look at what some online galleries have to offer; and read the *PhotoArts Journal* for up-to-date news, reviews, and more beautiful photo art.

Photo Info Highway

http://128.111.124.127/ssr/PhotoInfoHighway.htm

★★★

The Photo Info Highway is a list of photo links that can be used to guide beginning and amateur photographers. The collected links include basic photo information resources, such as cameras, lenses, tripods, ballheads, filters, flashes, camera bags, photo equipment manufacturers, places to buy equipment, a mail order survey, lens tests and reviews, and general photography information.

A
B
C
D
E
F
G
H
I
J
K
L
M
N
O
P
Q
R
S
T
U
V
W
X
Y
Z

Photography Review

http://www.photographyreview.com/

★★★★

Learn photography skills from fellow photographers, check out product reviews of cameras by consumers and professionals, as well as other photography equipment, and then scan the online swap sheet to find good used gear. The site is "By photographers for photographers," leaning more toward an advanced audience.

Photolinks Database

http://www.photolinks.net/

$

★★★★

Searchable directory of photography-related websites. Because this site focuses on photography, it can provide a more up-to-date and comprehensive listing of photography sites than you'll find at a general search site, such as Google. Free listings for photography-related websites are available.

PhotoSecrets

http://www.photosecrets.com

$

★★★

Learn how to take and sell travel photos at this site, which offers travel photography guide books for sale. The tips are definitely worth a look.

PhotoSig

http://www.photosig.com

★★★★

PhotoSig was designed by Willis Boyce to "give photographers the opportunity to display their photographs, have them evaluated and critiqued by others, and improve their photographic skills through constructive criticism." Amateur and expert photographers are welcome to post their photographs, hone their skills, and help other photographers improve their techniques.

PhotoWorks.com

http://www.photoworks.com/

★★★★★

Send your photos to PhotoWorks for processing and have them stored on a personalized, password-protected website for viewing by anyone you like—at no charge. The photos can be either digital or film-based. From the online store, you can purchase anything from photographic supplies and cameras to T-shirts and mugs with your photos on them.

Professional Photographers of America

http://www.ppa.com/

★★★★

Search the database of member professional photographers to find one you like. Learn about upcoming educational opportunities and events, as well as PPA member benefits. You can also pick up creative ideas for making your family photos more memorable and your wedding photos smashing.

Shutterbug Online

http://www.shutterbug.net/

★★★★

Read articles, scan product reviews, study the Lesson of the Month, and enter contests. You'll have fun learning at this online version of the print publication.

Site Photography

http://www.sightphoto.com/

★★★

Online photography magazine highlighting photographers and reviews of photographic work on the Web.

Top Nature and Landscape Photography Pages

http://members.aol.com/elgallery/topphotos.html

★★★

Links to the best nature and landscape photography sites on the Web. Scroll down the page to see the photography of featured artists.

The Atlantic: Poetry

http://www.theatlantic.com/unbound/poetry/

★★★★★

The Atlantic has a long tradition of providing literary criticism, reviews, and author interviews. Here, in its online poetry section, you can read about your favorite poets, check out reviews of poetry collections or books about poetry or poets, and even listen to some poetry that appears in the magazine read out loud by the poets themselves.

Bad Poetry Page

http://www.coffeeshoptimes.com/badpoet.html

★★★★

Coffee Shop Times is an online cultural hangout for the alternative crowd. Here, the folks of CST treat you to some really bad poetry. If you come across a really bad poem somewhere else, consider posting it here for consideration.

Bartleby.com Verse

http://www.bartleby.com/verse/

★★★★★

Thousands of poems by hundreds of famous poets are available at this site, where you can search for poets by name or poems by title or browse throught the available collections and anthologies. Best of all, access to the poems is completely free!

Fooling with Words with Bill Moyers

http://www.pbs.org/wnet/foolingwithwords/

★★★★★

This online version of the PBS special provides an overview and lesson plans that can help teachers encourage student interest in poetry. An overview and three lesson plans are available. More than a dozen contemporary poets are featured, along with videos of the poets reading their poems. This excellent introduction to poetry benefits not only younger students, but also anyone interested in gaining a greater appreciation of poetry.

Giggle Poetry

http://www.gigglepoetry.com/

★★★★

 All

Giggle Poetry introduces young children to poetry in a way that most kids find to be fun and engaging. This site features colorful cartoons, poetry games and ratings, school poems, favorite poems, instructions on writing nursery rhymes and limericks, and much more.

Internet Poetry Archive

http://www.ibiblio.org/dykki/poetry/

★★★

This site provides access to the selected poetry of a number of contemporary poets. The archive includes the work of living poets from around the world. The project started with eight poets and promises to grow over time.

A
B
C
D
E
F
G
H
I
J
K
L
M
N
O
P
Q
R
S
T
U
V
W
X
Y
Z

Poets.org

http://www.poets.org/

★★★★★

Poets.org, created and managed by The Academy of American Poets, features more than 1,400 poems, essays about poetry, biographies of more than 450 poets, and RealAudio recordings of more than 100 poems read by the composing poet or other poets. Here you can learn about the Academy and its programs, share your own work, find local poetry resources and events, and explore the rhythms and sounds of the contemporary poetry scene.

Poetry Archives

http://www.emule.com/poetry

★★★★★

 All

The Poetry Archives is devoted to preserving and making available to students, educators, and others interested in poetry the works of the classic poets. You can search the database by first line, author, or poem title. Active discussion forums can help you track down other poetry and learn more about poetry. The Top Poems list ranks poems by popularity, and the Top Authors list ranks poets by popularity. All original poems are no longer copyrighted, but any translations included may be copyrighted. Also includes a shopping area for purchasing classic poetry collections.

Poetry.com

http://www.poetry.com/

★★★★★

Sponsored by the International Library of Poetry, Poetry.com's goal is to "eliminate the traditional barriers that prevent most people from having their message heard." Visit this site to enter your poems in one of the biggest poetry contests in the world for a chance to win cash prizes. Site also features information about rhyming and poetry techniques, a list of the 100 greatest poems ever written, a quiz to test your poetry IQ, and much more.

Poetry Daily

http://www.poems.com/

★★★★★

This site features a new poem every day from a contemporary poet and provides information about the poet and any poetry that he or she has published. You can browse the archives for previous featured poetry.

Poetry Express

http://www.poetryexpress.org/

★★★★

Poetry Express features 15 poems that you can write simply by following the step-by-step instructions given at this site. The site uses various techniques to inspire you to create something that is your own unique poetic expression.

Poetry Magic

http://www.poetrymagic.co.uk/

★★★★

Poetry Magic provides information and resources for both beginning and advanced poets. Beginners can learn the basics, including a general understanding of poetry and its different forms, and then progress to the writing cycle to learn how to compose their own original poetry. Advanced poets can scroll down the page to learn more about literary criticism, craftmanship, various poetry movements, and more.

Poetry Slam, Inc.

http://www.poetryslam.com/

★★★★★

Poetry Slam is the art of spoken word performance poetry, and this site is its official home on the Web. Poetry Slam, Inc. encourages performance poets and organizers to join in its grassroots movement by creating registered poetry slams in their towns or cities. Here you'll find a Slam FAQ (frequently asked questions), information about the current year's National Poetry Slam, a list of Poetry Slam venues around the country, free audio and video clips of top performers, discussion forums, chat rooms, and much more. You can even shop online for Slam CDs, books, t-shirts, and other paraphernalia.

Related Sites
http://www.nuyorican.org
http://www.abqpoetryslam.org
http://www.austinslam.com
http://www.chicagopoetry.com
http://www.gotpoetry.com
http://www.e-poetry.de
http://www.slamnation.com
http://www.poetrycircus.org

The Poetry Society of America

http://www.poetrysociety.org/

★★★★★

The Poetry Society of America is dedicated to stirring up interest and enthusiasm in all forms of poetry—written and spoken word. Its Poetry in Motion project places poems in buses and subways, and currently reaches more than 10 million Americans on a daily basis. Here you can learn more about the organization and its members and programs, enter the chapbook contests, learn about upcoming events, and order books online.

slampapi.com

http://www.slampapi.com/

★★★★★

This is the official digital hangout of Marc Smith, who catalyzed the Slam Poetry movement and continues to spread the (spoken) word. Here you can check out information about upcoming events at the Green Mill, read a selection of poems, learn about Slam shows and other performance poetry events around the country, submit an article for publication on the site, or contact Marc personally. This site provides a good feel for the family nature of the Poetry Slam and its commitment to allowing people to voice their opinions, even if those opinions are highly critical of slam.

World of Poetry

www.worldofpoetry.org

★★★★★

Billing itself as "the first digital poetry anthology," The World of Poetry is a project that's designed to pick up where *The United States of Poetry* left off. The project pairs up filmmakers with poets from across the country and around the world to record poets composing, performing, and teaching their art. The ultimate goal is to create a digital video library of hundreds of the best, most original contemporary poets. Selected clips, along with narration, will be compiled into a one-hour PBS special called *World of Poetry*. Here, you can learn more about the project and access the official website for *The United States of Poetry*.

A B C D E F G H I J K L M N O **P** Q R S T U V W X Y Z

A
B
C
D
E
F
G
H
I
J
K
L
M
N
O
P
Q
R
S
T
U
V
W
X
Y
Z

POLITICS

Capitol Hill Blue

http://www.chblue.com/

★★★★★

Capitol Hill Blue provides no-holds-barred coverage of late breaking stories in Washington politics. When you want insider information with some savvy commentary, this is the site to visit. Capitol Hill Blue takes a skeptical view of Washington politics, trusting very few of the policymakers who run the lives of the U.S. citizens.

Contacting the Congress

http://www.visi.com/juan/congress/

★★★★

Find a Congressperson's email address, website, or ground address by typing in that person's name or clicking on the state he or she represents. You can also key in your ZIP code to identify your representative and find his or her email address. There are more than 500 email addresses on the site and 500 more web page addresses.

Council on Foreign Relations

http://www.cfr.org

★★★★★

Are you interested in United States foreign relations? Then check out this official site of the Council on Foreign Relations, where you can find out the latest information on the United States' relationships with other countries, including Russia, Britain, Egypt, Saudi Arabia, Pakistan, and others. Learn what current and former presidents, national security advisors, and other leaders are thinking about U.S. foreign policy and politics.

FactCheck.org

http://www.factcheck.org/

★★★★★

When you want the facts without the spin about various politicians, go to FatCheck.org. This non-profit organization is dedicated to keeping politicians honest, or at least making sure that the voters have access to the facts. When one politician quotes another, did he or she get the quote right? Does a particular political advertisement properly present the facts? Find out all that and more at this site.

The Hill

http://www.thehill.com

★★★★★

Web home of *The Hill*, "a non-partisan, nonideological weekly newspaper that describes the inner workings of Congress, the pressures confronting policy makers and the many ways—often unpredictable— in which decisions are made." If you're interested in the inner workings of Congress and other government leaders and are looking for behind-the-scenes coverage of current political events, this is the site for you.

Meetup

http://www.meetup.com/

★★★★★

Meetup is a service that enables local interest groups to set a time and place for their meetings. Although not strictly political, in election years many of the more popular groups that arrange to meet on Meetup are interested in a specific candidate. All sorts of local groups form at Meetup, including poker groups, goths, movie buffs, and subculture groups.

National Political Index

http://www.politicalindex.com/

★★★★

Designed to be a one-stop shop for substantive political information, this site provides ways to contact federal and local politicians. It also provides access to think tanks, news media, contests, and areas for discussions and debates.

Office of the Clerk On-line Information Center

http://clerkweb.house.gov/

★★★★

Take a virtual tour of the House Chamber, obtain copies of bills and House documents, and find historical information about the House of Representatives.

opensecrets.org

http://www.opensecrets.org

★★★★★

Are your senators and congressional leaders in the pockets of large corporations and special interest groups? Check this site to find out. This site is created and maintained by the Center for Responsive Politics, a watchdog group that follows the money in Washington, D.C., to find out where it's going and why, and to keep citizens informed.

Related Site
http://www.capitaleye.org/

Political Money Line

http://www.fecinfo.com

★★★★★

Home of the Federal Election Commission, this site provides citizens with information on campaign contributions from corporations, PACs, and other sources. If you're wondering where the money flows in Washington, check out this site.

Politics1.com

http://www.politics1.com

★★★★★

A bipartisan site that aims to inform Americans regarding the political process and issues being discussed. Get campaign information, updates on current debates, and sign up for the Politics1 newsletter.

Public Affairs Web

http://www.publicaffairsweb.com/

★★★

If you need information about issues and organizations concerning local, state, and national governments and organizations, this is the place to find it. The PAW is dedicated to bringing you the best and latest information and ideas from around the United States concerning candidates, public issues, legislation, state and local ballot measures, and news about public officials.

President Match

http://www.presidentmatch.com/

★★★★★

In a presidential election, who should you vote for? This site can help you decide by determining which candidate best represents your stand on most of the important issues.

Best SpeakOut—Politics, Activism, and Political Issues Online

http://www.speakout.com/

★★★★★

SpeakOut.com is an opinion research company started by Ron Howard, a guy who wanted to speak out and make his opinions known to the government but didn't have a clear idea about how to go about expressing himself to the people who could really help him. So, Ron started this site to help other aspiring activists figure out how to make their voices heard. SpeakOut gives you an opportunity to let your thoughts and opinions be known using the site's online polls. The site provides you with the information and activism tools needed to speak out on such subjects as political and social issues, elections, political parties, the government, and democracy. When you feel as though you can't sit still and remain silent while other people are making decisions that negatively affect your life, check out this Best of the Best site and get involved!

A B C D E F G H I J K L M N O P Q R S T U V W X Y Z

A
B
C
D
E
F
G
H
I
J
K
L
M
N
O
P
Q
R
S
T
U
V
W
X
Y
Z

Vote.com

http://www.vote.com/

★★★★★

Vote.com presents a list of current hot issues you can read about and cast a vote for or against. Vote.com passes the poll results on to Congress and other leaders, so your voice can be heard.

washingtonpost.com OnPolitics

http://www.washingtonpost.com/politics

★★★★★

Home of the *Washington Post*, one of the most popular newspapers on Capitol Hill, this site provides headline news about what's going on in the Capitol. In addition, you can find out about upcoming elections, election results, lobbying efforts, campaign contributions, and other political topics. You can even cast your vote in the daily poll.

Welcome to the White House

http://www.whitehouse.gov/

★★★★

 All

A rich site filled with information about the White House, including background information on the president and vice president and their families. It provides access to government services, news regarding what's happening at the White House this week, historical information, and access to White House documents.

POLITICAL CAMPAIGNS

California Voter Foundation

http://www.calvoter.org

★★★★

If you're a California citizen and you feel obligated to cast your vote in the next election, visit this site first to get the information you need to make an informed choice. Here, you can find the most current voter guide along with information about the latest initiatives. Pull up the campaign promises archive to see whether your local politicians are delivering on their word.

Campaigns and Elections

http://www.campaignline.com/

★★★★

Campaigns and Elections Online is a magazine for political professionals. You can check out the changing odds on major national, state, and local races across the country. Browse any of the following sections: National Directory of Public Affairs; Lobbying; and Issues Management Consultants, Products, and Services. Or, check out the Political Analysis section. Get a subscription to *Campaign Insider*, a weekly newsletter for political consultants and committees. The site also includes *C&E's Buyers Guide*, information on telephone services, media placement, direct mail services, fundraising, and more.

Campaign Finance Reform

http://www.brookings.org/GS/CF/CF_HP.HTM

★★★★

This site's goal is to improve the quality of debate on campaign finance reform so that a workable approach can be passed by Congress and signed into law by the president. Examine new approaches to reform. Check out articles analyzing the proposed reforms, related opinion pieces, and proposals to Congress. Go to the Public Forum on Campaign Finance Reform to view others' ideas, analyses, and opinions.

Center for the American Woman and Politics

http://www.rci.rutgers.edu/~cawp/

★★★

The Center for the American Woman and Politics (CAWP) is a university-based research, education, and public-service center. Its mission is to promote greater understanding and knowledge about women's relationships to politics and government, and to enhance women's influence and leadership in public life. CAWP is a unit of the Eagleton Institute of Politics at Rutgers, The State University of New Jersey. Learn about CAWP job opportunities and look at general information. Read publications and press releases. Get highlights from reports and order from the list of recommended books. Sample and learn how to order the *CAWP News & Notes* newsletter, and read about female candidates in the latest elections.

Federal Election Commission (FEC)

http://www.fec.gov/

★★★★★

This is the official site for the Federal Election Commission (FEC), which was established to administer and enforce the Federal Election Campaign Act (FECA). The site is filled with tons of useful information that can be searched by state, party, office, or name. Very useful for research on political subjects, for entertainment, or just for informative reading on how the political system works.

C-SPAN Networks

http://www.c-span.org

★★★★

Check out the C-SPAN schedules (C-SPAN and C-SPAN2) and content, explore the Public Affairs Video Archives, or listen to the *Washington Journal* program. Explore today's headlines from papers such as the *Washington Post, San Francisco Examiner, Chicago Sun-Times*, and more. C-SPAN in the Classroom is a great link for teachers and students. C-SPAN's Majic Bus travels on tours such as one chronicling the history of civil rights in the Deep South. *C-SPAN Online Live* lets you watch events as they are happening (such as news conferences). Check out the *Booknotes* program, which presents America's finest authors discussing reading, writing, and the power of ideas. Get information on the U.S. House schedule and weekly committee hearings.

Elections

http://www.multied.com/elections/

★★★★

 All

This presidential elections statistics site is presented by MultiEducator. Check out colorful graphs of the electoral votes cast in presidential elections from 1789 to the present. Download photos of scenes from American history and read selected documents (such as the Articles of Confederation and the Civil Rights Act of 1957). The MultiEducator American History product lets you access events chronologically, alphabetically, or by topic. Access facts about major events in U.S. history and get extensive information about each of the presidents. Audio-visuals highlight major periods in U.S. history, and video clips showcase achievements and tragedies. This site links to HistoryShopping.com, where you can purchase learning materials online.

The Gallup Organization

http://www.gallup.com/

★★★

The people who practically invented the political public-opinion poll bring you a site that lets you study all the political trends for the entire election season. Gallup Polls, press releases, and special reports on key social and business-related issues are presented. Get information and poll results on current events.

MotherJones.com

http://www.mojones.com/

★★★★

Mother Jones is a magazine of investigation and ideas for independent thinkers. Provocative articles inform readers and inspire action toward positive social change. Colorful and personal, this magazine challenges conventional wisdom, exposes abuses of power, helps redefine stubborn problems, and offers fresh solutions. The discussion forum encourages visitors to share their views with one another on a variety of issues. Winner of several awards for excellence in publishing and journalism.

A B C D E F G H I J K L M N O P Q R S T U V W X Y Z

A B C D E F G H I J K L M N O P Q R S T U V W X Y Z

The National Journal

http://nationaljournal.com/

★★★★

The National Journal provides commentary, news, and resource materials on politics and policy. It offers online delivery of most National Journal Group daily publications—*CongressDaily, The Hotline, American Health Line, Greenwire,* and *Technology Daily.* It includes a database of polling results and trends. It also offers the *Almanac of American Politics,* as well as schedules for Congress.

OnPolitics.com

http://www.washingtonpost.com/wp-srv/politics/talk/talk.htm

★★★★

OnPolitics.com is a site that provides you with the *Free Media* weekday political talk show from the washingtonpost.com site. Post reporters and editors and the people they cover put the news of the day in perspective. The site also has a huge article archive, graphics photo library, cartoons, and political news. Great for entertainment or just to be informed.

Pew Research Center

http://people-press.org/

★★★

Independent organization that "studies attitudes toward press, politics, and public policy issues." This site includes survey results and an index of public attention to major news stories.

Political Information

http://www.politicalinformation.com/

★★★★

If you're looking for information on politics for whatever reason, this site provides a quick way to find almost everything that you need. The political information site is just that, a site where you can look up information about political campaigns, who's who, and other useful information. The site is really a search engine geared toward political subjects.

Project Vote Smart

http://www.vote-smart.org/

★★★★★

Project Vote Smart tracks the performance of more than 12,000 political leaders—the president, congresspersons, governors, and state legislators. Get information on issue positions, voting records, performance evaluations, campaign finances, and biographies. Enter your ZIP code, and the search engine looks up who represents you and gives you the relevant details and statistics. Alternatively, track the performance of the Congress. Find out how candidates stood on issues before they were elected and see how your Congressperson voted on a bill. Track the status of legislation as it works its way through Congress; read the text of a bill; and find out whether a bill has had committee action, whether it is scheduled for a hearing or a vote, and whether your Congressperson is a cosponsor.

Questia

http://www.questia.com/

 $

★★★★★

Questia provides an extensive online library packed with books and journal articles that contain valuable information relating to political campaigns. Subscribe to the service to access more than 70,000 resources.

Roll Call

http://www.rollcall.com/

★★★★

Biweekly newspaper covering Congress.

Smith & Harroff Political Advertising

http://www.smithharroff.com/polcampaigns.htm

 $

★★★★

If you're gearing up to campaign for office, where do you go to put together the required advertising? Smith & Harroff is one company that you can try. Visit this site to browse through a list of clients and to find out what the company has to offer.

So You Want to Buy a President?

`http://www.pbs.org/wgbh/pages/frontline/president/`

★★★

This site contains a transcript of the program "So You Want to Buy a President," which aired on the show *Frontline* (a weekly public-affairs series on PBS). See what *Frontline* learned about the rules of the game. See profiles of the interlocking business and political relationships that dominated past presidential fundraising games. Read excerpts from conversations with a U.S. senator, a former presidential candidate, and political analysts. Get information and resources about politics, campaign financing, and reform.

THOMAS: U.S. Congress on the Internet

`http://thomas.loc.gov/`

★★★★★

 All

What's going on in the United States Congress? THOMAS can tell you. The THOMAS World Wide Web system, developed and maintained by the Library of Congress, provides free access to congressional records and bills that have passed or are in the process of being developed and approved.

Votenet

`http://www.votenet.com/`

★★★★★

Search the Votenet site using its search engine and find just what you're looking for in the world of politics. Find out who's giving what to different campaigns, read today's headlines, and use political content provided here to inform and educate others.

WhiteHouse '04

`http://www.niu.edu/newsplace/whitehouse.html`

★★★

The site discusses current issues about the present political structure, issues concerning the next political campaign, possible candidates for the next election, and other political information. It also has a lot of reform information for 2004 that is quite interesting.

Related Sites

`http://www.spectator.org/`

`http://www.townhall.com/`

POLITICAL PARTIES

The American Party

`http://www.theamericanparty.org/`

★★★★

Home of The American Party, a very conservative organization devoted to free trade, clean living, and strong families. Visit this site to learn more about the party and its principles, read the party's platform for the upcoming election, view a calendar of events, and check out the list of officers.

The Christian Coalition

`http://www.cc.org/`

★★★★

CC members fight for laws they feel promote the Christian agenda and fight against those that do not. This site has reports on every relevant law, as well as how each member of Congress voted. The pages include family resources, articles on American Christians, and more.

College Republican National Committee

`http://www.crnc.org/`

★★★★

 14-18

Home of the nation's largest, oldest Republican student organization, this site features information about the CRNC, news related to the organization, and membership information. Use the online form to register to vote.

Constitution Party

`http://www.constitutionparty.com/`

★★★

The Constitution Party subscribes to Henry David Thoreau's claim "That government is best which governs not at all." The party's platform includes abolishing the IRS, replacing mandatory welfare with voluntary charity, making English the official national language, and abolishing the United States Department of Education.

A B C D E F G H I J K L M N O P Q R S T U V W X Y Z

A
B
C
D
E
F
G
H
I
J
K
L
M
N
O
P
Q
R
S
T
U
V
W
X
Y
Z

The Democratic National Committee

http://www.democrats.org/index.html

★★★★

Read news from the DNC, browse through the archives, and learn where the Democratic Party stands on various issues. You can also read through the current year of DNC press releases. This site includes information on various Senate hearings, as well as a guide to Republican campaign finance abuses. The site also includes Democratic National Committee FAQs. The Get Active! section tells you how to join the DNC, volunteer, and register to vote.

Democratic Socialists of America

http://www.dsausa.org/

★★★

The DSA believes that capitalism has failed and that the working peoples of the world are being oppressed and suppressed by a tiny percentage of rich. The DSA works to establish its own humane vision of international economic and social order.

Directory of U.S. Political Parties

http://www.politics1.com/parties.htm

★★★★

Excellent directory of political parties in the United States. This site covers the two major parties, Republican and Democrat, along with lesser-known parties.

Green Party USA

http://www.gpus.org/

★★★

This site is one in a chain of Green Party sites. It revels in some of the past actions of the Green Party, such as Ralph Nader's candidacy for president, but it also reaches beyond that election to highlight current Green Party issues, activism, and campaigns. If you're interested in supporting environmental causes and consumer activism, check out this site.

Labor Party

http://www.thelaborparty.org/

★★★

This party for the working people of the United States advocates an amendment to the Constitution that guarantees every citizen a job with a living wage. Also supports labor unions, family leave, universal access to quality healthcare, and other pro-worker, pro-family legislation.

Libertarian Party Headquarters

http://www.lp.org

★★★

The Libertarian party is dedicated to lessening the influence of government on people's lives and helping people take more responsibility for their actions. This site is dense with Libertarian issues and positions.

The John Birch Society

http://www.jbs.org/

★★★★

The JB Society makes Republicans look like a bunch of long-haired liberals. This site discusses their opinions of "less government, more responsibility," and offers a FAQ, a newsletter, commentary on pending legislation, and more.

Natural Law Party of the United States of America

http://www.natural-law.org/

★★★★

Describes America's fastest growing alternative political party (for those interested in government that is conflict-free, prevention-oriented, and that utilizes proven, field-tested solutions). With a foundation in nature and quantum physics, the Natural Law Party is trying to build a government that's in concert with the flow of nature. Sounds a bit like Buddhism.

New Party

http://www.igc.apc.org/newparty/

★★★

A grassroots, progressive political party running candidates for local elections around the country. The party fights for living wage jobs, campaign finance reform, and public education.

Reform Party Official Website

http://www.reformparty.org/

★★★★

If there's an aspect to politics and government that can be reformed, this party wants to reform it. The party's platform is wide, but highlights include disallowing all gifts and junkets, requiring the White House and Congress to have the same retirement and healthcare plans as the rest of us, shortening campaigns to four months, changing Election Day to a Saturday or Sunday so working people can vote more easily, and more.

Republican National Committee

http://www.rnc.org/

★★★★

The RNC has a pretty interesting home page. It looks like a small town main street, and the icons are the storefront windows. You can link with candidates and get their email addresses and, of course, join the party.

Workers World Party

http://www.workers.org/

★★★★

This anti-capitalist, pro-socialist party believes that capitalism rests on the foundation of the wealthy few oppressing the multitudes of poor. The party basically calls for the workers of the world to unite against imperialist policies worldwide.

Young Democrats of America

http://www.yda.org/

★★★★

👫 14-18

This site offers a map of the United States that you can click to find contact information and upcoming Young Democrats events for your area.

A B C D E F G H I J K L M N O **P** Q R S T U V W X Y Z

A
B
C
D
E
F
G
H
I
J
K
L
M
N
O
P
Q
R
S
T
U
V
W
X
Y
Z

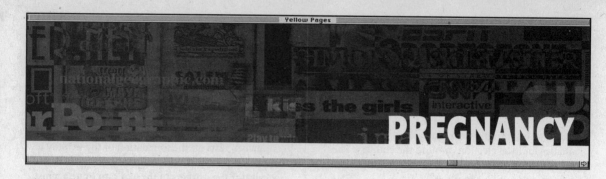

PREGNANCY

INFERTILITY

About Infertility

http://infertility.about.com/

★★★★

Not for kids

Directory of articles and resources relating to infertility and techniques and drugs that can increase your chances of conceiving.

American Infertility Association

http://www.americaninfertility.org/

★★★★

Not for kids

Dedicated to increasing the awareness and understanding of infertility and related issues, AIA features support groups for couples who have trouble conceiving. AIA also advocates health insurance to cover infertility. At this site, you can learn more about the AIA support groups, join discussion forums, chat with other couples who are dealing with infertility, and read the Facts and FAQs for additional information.

Ask Fertilitext

http://www.fertilitext.org/

★★★★

Not for kids

A guide to getting pregnant. This site contains a comprehensive guide to conception and pregnancy. Excellent information on reproductive health, ovulation, and the male factor.

Electronic Infertility Network

http://www.ein.org/

★★★

Not for kids

A nonprofit organization based in Europe that works to inform and support people who are dealing with infertility issues. Some general information about infertility and tips for increasing your chances of conceiving, plus an Ask the Doctor section, where you can submit a question. Links to other articles and resources as well.

Environmental Causes of Infertility

http://www.chem-tox.com/infertility/

★★★

Not for kids

This site features a collection of information regarding environmental conditions that are commonly thought to affect fertility, including coffee, alcohol, cigarettes, and auto emissions.

Fertility Plus

http://www.fertilityplus.org/toc.html

★★★★

Not for kids

Read articles about basic fertility issues, such as low-tech ways to conceive and ovulation predictor kits, as well as more advanced topics. Check out fertility FAQs, see the fertility resource list, and chuckle at the humor section.

Ferti.Net

http://www.ferti.net/

★★★

🧒 Not for kids

This worldwide fertility network features the latest news and information about fertility and infertility, including treatments and other options. Includes a library, glossary, message boards, and articles from FertiMagazine.

Infertility: A Couple's Survival Guide

http://www.drdaiter.com/table.html

★★★★

🧒 Not for kids

Learn the basics regarding infertility, ovulation, the pelvis, and sperm here—to increase your odds of getting pregnant.

Infertility.to

http://www.infertility.to

★★★

🧒 Not for kids

Directory organizations, clinics, sperm and egg banks, and pharmacies, plus a message board where you can read and post questions, answers, and other messages regarding infertility

Infertility Treatments

http://www.ihr.com/infertility/

★★★★

🧒 Not for kids

Take a quick online tour of infertility treatments and options. Or gather more in-depth information on the various options. You can also get book references and check out links. You'll find lots of useful medical overviews.

 Best The InterNational Council on Infertility Information Dissemination (INCIID)

http://www.inciid.org

★★★★

🧒 Not for kids

This nonprofit consumer advocacy group aims to inform couples of their options regarding infertility treatments. Features essays, articles, commentaries, and fact sheets on infertility, plus a searchable directory of fertility experts. The site also includes interactive discussion forums and chat rooms. This site's excellent information and straightforward presentation combine to help it reign in the honor of the best site in its category.

IVF.com

http://www.ivf.com/

★★★★

🧒 Not for kids

Dr. Mark Perloe has compiled information in areas of women's health including infertility, polycystic ovaries, IVF, endometriosis, and pelvic pain treatment options. Information is offered in the form of articles. Discussion transcripts are available to aid couples in understanding their treatment options.

National Library of Medicine's Infertility Resources

http://www.nlm.nih.gov/medlineplus/infertility.html

★★★★★

🧒 Not for kids

Reading room packed with news and articles pertaining to infertility divided into categories including News, General Overviews, Anatomy/Physiology, Clinical Trials, Diagnosis, Treatment, and much more. Excellent place to start researching infertility and finding ways to treat it.

A
B
C
D
E
F
G
H
I
J
K
L
M
N
O
P
Q
R
S
T
U
V
W
X
Y
Z

A
B
C
D
E
F
G
H
I
J
K
L
M
N
O
P
Q
R
S
T
U
V
W
X
Y
Z

Oh No Not Again (ONNA)

http://www.onna.org/

★★★★

⊞ Not for kids

Full of information on fertility and getting pregnant, this site is for anyone—from those who have just started trying to have a baby to those who have been diagnosed with infertility.

A Patient's Guide to Male Infertility

http://www.ivf.com/shaban.html

★★★

⊞ Not for kids

A thorough, professional overview of the causes and treatments of male infertility.

RESOLVE: The National Infertility Association

http://www.resolve.org/

★★★★

⊞ Not for kids

You'll find infertility support and information at this organization's site. You can read the online guide, access a helpline to find local organizations to assist you, as well as contact a community of people to help you make choices regarding fertility treatments, adoption, surrogacy, or the decision to remain child-free.

Shared Journey

http://www.sharedjourney.com/

★★★★

⊞ Not for kids

A valuable collective resource for information on infertility. Here, you can find answers to your questions as well as support and information regarding current technology being used to achieve the goal of parenthood.

MIDWIFERY

American College of Nurse-Midwives

http://www.midwife.org/

★★★

⊞ Not for kids

Dedicated to supporting and improving healthcare to women through the practice of midwifery, this ACNM site acts as an information kiosk for the organization. Here, you'll learn about advocacy activities the ACNM is involved in, plus any upcoming conferences and events. A Consumer section provides information about midwifery, basic information on pregnancy and baby care, and a searchable directory of midwives.

Doulas of North America

http://www.dona.org/

Ⓢ

★★★★

⊞ Not for kids

This site explains what doulas are, how to find one, and what their role is. You'll also find certification/training information and more.

Midwife Archives

http://gentlebirth.org/archives/

★★★★

⊞ Not for kids

Offers a midwife perspective on pregnancy, childbirth, and women's healthcare. You'll also find links to other related sites.

Midwifery Information

http://www.moonlily.com/obc/midwife.html

★★★★

⊞ Not for kids

Whether you're interested in becoming a midwife or are one already, you'll enjoy this site's wealth of information on the topic. It offers articles, links, current news and information, and lots of resources.

Midwifery Resources on the Internet

http://website.lineone.net/~ics001/midwifery.htm

★★★★

 Not for kids

This site features FAQs, mailing lists, chat, news-groups, links, a bulletin board, visitor pictures, and stories of their experiences.

Online Birth Center

http://www.moonlily.com/obc/

★★★★

Not for kids

Lots of information about being a parent, keeping your child safe, and the benefits of breastfeeding.

MISCARRIAGE

Honored Babies

http://www.kjsl.com/~honored/

★★★★

 Not for kids

For mothers and grandmothers who have experienced the loss of a child, whether as an infant death, stillbirth, neonatal loss, termination, or miscarriage, this site helps women by providing support and a place to memorialize their children. Women can submit journal entries for inclusion in a book and join email forums.

Hygeia

http://www.hygeia.org/

★★★★

 Not for kids

Hygeia is an international community of families grieving from the loss of a child. Here, you'll find original poetry of loss and hope, medical information about maternal and child health, and the opportunity to share your stories and share your experience of lost parenthood with thousands of registered families worldwide.

M.I.S.S.—Mothers In Sympathy & Support

http://www.missfoundation.org/

★★★★

 All

At this site, you can find a support group, a place for sharing experiences, as well as articles, poetry, and information for professionals and families in grief. Special areas to help bereaved children cope.

Miscarriage Support & Information Resources

http://www.fertilityplus.org/faq/miscarriage/resources.html

★★★★

 Not for kids

You'll find medical information sources as well as newsgroups, mailing lists, online support groups, and memorial sites. You'll also find a list of books that may help you in your time of need.

Recurrent Miscarriage (Pregnancy Loss)

http://www.drdaiter.com/pregtable.html

★★★★

 Not for kids

Learn more about the causes of pregnancy loss, its frequency, and the grieving process. This site provides plenty of medical information to help you understand.

SHARE

http://www.nationalshareoffice.com/

★★★

 Not for kids

Sign up for the SHARE newsletter for grieving parents, link with other parents suffering the same loss, read articles that may help, and find support groups.

A
B
C
D
E
F
G
H
I
J
K
L
M
N
O
P
Q
R
S
T
U
V
W
X
Y
Z

PREGNANCY/BIRTH

About.com–Pregnancy/Birth

http://pregnancy.about.com/health/pregnancy/

★★★★

📷 Not for kids

Even if you're just starting to think about getting pregnant, this site is a great resource. From conceiving to experiencing pregnancy and getting ready for the big day, this site just about has it all. You'll find lots of information, opportunities for sharing and learning from other parents, and places to buy all the baby stuff you'll need.

Anne Geddes

http://www.annegeddes.com

★★★★

📷 Not for kids

Enjoy looking at photos of babies taken by this renowned baby photographer. Buy products with her photos, such as photo albums, calendars, and stationery for your enjoyment. And learn more about keeping children safe at the section on child help.

Ask NOAH

http://www.noah-health.org/english/pregnancy/pregnancy.html

★★★★

📷 Not for kids

A very thorough guide to all aspects of pregnancy from the New York Online Access to Health.

BabyUniverse.com

http://www.babyuniverse.com/

★★★★

📷 Not for kids

Get advice on what you *really* need for a baby; then read product reviews and order just about everything from this site. You'll find strollers, car seats, cribs, gift ideas, and lots more.

BabyZone

http://babyzone.com/drnathan/glossary.htm

★★★★★

📷 Not for kids

A handy reference tool from preconception to parenting. You can also shop online with a large selection of baby clothes, educational toys, and some baby gift ideas in case you can't make up your mind about what to get. You can also read about adoption, birth stories, and baby names, and you can ask an expert.

Birth Psychology

http://www.birthpsychology.com/

★★★★

📷 Not for kids

Provides information on prenatal and perinatal psychology and health. Find out what affects the psychology of the fetus inside the womb, traumas that can damage the vulnerable psyche, and treatments to help heal mental and emotional damage. This site features personal stories, expert articles, and late-breaking news.

Breastfeeding.com

http://www.breastfeeding.com/

★★★★★

📷 Not for kids

Wow, you'll be amazed at all the information you can find here on breastfeeding. You'll find answers to questions about supply, technique, development, working while breastfeeding, and much more. You can even buy breast pumps, watch video clips of babies, find a local lactation consultant, and join discussions with other moms and dads.

Childbirth.org

http://www.childbirth.org/

★★★★★

📷 Not for kids

Search this huge site to get answers to all your questions about childbirth, including episiotomies, doulas, depression, and diapering. You'll find all these topics here.

Coping with Common Discomforts of Pregnancy

http://www.babybag.com/articles/fisher.htm

★★★

 Not for kids

A nice article that briefly discusses many common discomforts of pregnancy.

ePregnancy.com

http://www.epregnancy.com/

$

★★★★★

 Not for kids

As this site claims, "from before pregnancy to after birth," you'll find helpful articles, interactive features to chat with and meet other women like you, links to useful resources, as well as shopping solutions for you and your baby.

Fit Pregnancy

http://www.fitpregnancy.com/

★★★★

 Not for kids

Read articles at this site and learn about eating right, exercising, keeping your mind and body fit, and understanding you and your baby. You can also Ask the Experts for pregnancy advice. This site is for pregnant women and those trying to get pregnant.

Labor of Love

http://www.thelaboroflove.com/

★★★★

 Not for kids

Pregnancy and parenting website with message boards, tips, birth stories, pen pals, and an online magazine.

Myria: The Magazine for Mothers

http://myria.com/

★★★★

 Not for kids

Pregnancy resources, boards, and much more from *Myria*, an online magazine created to support, inform, and encourage women who are mothers. You'll find information on pregnancy skincare, a due date calculator, and more!

OBGYN.net

http://www.obgyn.net/women/pregnancy/pregnancy.htm

★★★★

 Not for kids

A range of pregnancy information from amniocentesis to toxoplasmosis.

Parenthood.com

http://www.parenthood.com/

★★★★★

 Not for kids

Parenthood.com brings you a one-stop source for articles, expert advice, and feedback from other parents on issues related to pregnancy, labor, and baby care. Experts, chat, and greeting cards are available at this site. You can even register to get an email newsletter tailored to your stage of pregnancy or your baby's age.

Pregnancy and Women's Health

http://www.womens-health.co.uk/

★★★

 Not for kids

At this site, information is provided about pregnancy problems and common gynecological conditions such as miscarriage and infertility.

Pregnancy Calendar

http://www.parentsplace.com/pregnancy/calendar/

★★★★

 Not for kids

Create a day-by-day customized calendar detailing the development of a baby from before conception to birth.

Pregnancy Centers Online

http://www.pregnancycenters.org/

★★★★

 Not for kids

Find a pregnancy center near you and places to get help after an abortion. Learn about fetal development and email questions.

A
B
C
D
E
F
G
H
I
J
K
L
M
N
O
P
Q
R
S
T
U
V
W
X
Y
Z

A
B
C
D
E
F
G
H
I
J
K
L
M
N
O
P
Q
R
S
T
U
V
W
X
Y
Z

National Campaign to Prevent Teen Pregnancy

http://www.teenpregnancy.org/

★★★★

 14-18

The National Campaign to Prevent Teen Pregnancy is dedicated to reducing the number of teen pregnancies by one third between the years 1996 and 2005. This site provides information for teenagers, parents, teachers, and healthcare workers. You can also visit this site to obtain posters, stickers, and other materials for your school or organization.

Pregnancy Daily

http://pregnancydaily.com/

★★★★★

 Not for kids

Sign up to receive your pregnancy daily update, telling you how old your fetus is in days and what's going on with your pregnancy that day. More than 500 entries guide you from pregnancy to birth.

Pregnancy-info.net

http://www.pregnancy-info.net/

★★★

 Not for kids

This site features links to dozens of articles for expecting parents, including articles on complications, childcare, and becoming a first-time father. Also features a list of the top 10 pregnancy articles and top 10 parenting articles.

Pregnancy Information

http://www.w-cpc.org/pregnancy/

★★★★★

 Not for kids

Pregnancy help, fetal development, health tips, and resources are available here.

Pregnancy.org

http://www.pregnancy.org/

★★★★★

 Not for kids

Online community of parents who gather to support each other and educate one another to raise their children. Here, you'll find pregnancy information, a pregnancy calendar, growth charts, fun games, bulletin boards, question and answer areas, and much more.

Pregnancy Place

http://www.pregnancy-place.com/

★★★★

 Not for kids

Pregnancy Place features links to resources, services, products, and communities that can help answer any questions you have about your pregnancy and address any of your pregnancy needs.

Pregnancy Today

http://pregnancytoday.com/

★★★★★

 Not for kids

Pregnancy information including news, discussion boards, resources, lifestyle issues, expert advice, and more.

Sidelines

http://www.sidelines.org/

★★★

 Not for kids

Women in high-risk pregnancies will find Sidelines a supportive organization, providing emotional and informational resources. Find a chapter of this non-profit organization in your area or chat online with families in similar circumstances.

Signs of Pregnancy

http://www.childbirth.org/articles/pregnancy/
signs.html

★★★

 Not for kids

This site provides a list of possible, probable, and definite signs of pregnancy.

StorkNet

http://www.storknet.com/

★★★★

 Not for kids

One-stop web station for pregnancy, childbirth, breastfeeding, and parenting information.

Weight Gain Estimator

http://www.babycenter.com/calculator/1522.html

★★★★

 Not for kids

Type in your height (in inches) and weight (in pounds) to obtain an estimate of how much weight you will gain by the time you are ready to give birth.

A
B
C
D
E
F
G
H
I
J
K
L
M
N
O
P
Q
R
S
T
U
V
W
X
Y
Z

A B C D E F G H I J K L M N O P Q R S T U V W X Y Z

PUBLICATIONS

JOURNALS AND E-ZINES

Anagram

http://www.jhu.edu/~anagram/

★★★

This literary journal is based at The Johns Hopkins University and dedicated to Asian Americans. Although most of the contributors are students at Johns Hopkins, writers from other venues are also presented.

The Angling Report Newsletter

http://www.anglingreport.com/index.htm

★★★★

This newsletter from the traveling fisherman covers tackle, fishing equipment, fishing info, and fishing hot spots. Great information for light-tackle and fly-fishing enthusiasts.

BestEzines—Choose Your Ezines Wisely

http://www.bestezines.com/

★★★★

Why waste time searching for e-zines on the Internet when you can find them on BestEzines.com? This site offers hundreds of free e-zine subscription opportunities. You can choose from the best ones, but first you should check out the many articles and advice on the subject. Don't clutter your mailbox with worthless junk when you can have the best and most useful to you.

De Proverbio

http://www.utas.edu.au/docs/flonta/

★★★

This is an electronic journal of international proverb studies. Several issues are available to be accessed and read, and other links are available to reach the editors and editorial board of the periodical.

Dimension2

http://members.aol.com/germanlit/dimension2.html

★★★

This is a journal of contemporary German-language literature. It is available in both the original German and in English. Also present at this site is original artwork by a contemporary German artist.

Early Modern Literary Studies

http://www.shu.ac.uk/emls/emlshome.html

★★★

Dedicated to the English language, literature, and literary culture from the sixteenth and seventeenth century, this journal is very interactive, featuring the capability to respond to its published papers in a reader's forum.

Exemplaria

http://web.english.ufl.edu/exemplaria/

★★★★

A journal of theory in medieval and Renaissance studies, *Exemplaria* is based at the University of Florida. Read articles concerning literature and culture from the formative Middle Ages.

eZineSearch

http://www.site-city.com/members/e-zine-master/

★★★

Scan the list of more than 600 business e-zines and sign up for those of interest absolutely free.

Ezine-Universe.com

http://ezine-universe.com/

★★★★

Searchable and browsable directory of e-zines. E-zines are grouped into categories including Arts and Humanities, Business and Economy, Entertainment, Government, Health, and more.

E-zineZ

http://www.e-zinez.com/

★★★★

The E-ZineZ site is dedicated to helping you produce and publish an Internet email newsletter. It begins by offering an online tutorial and individual articles on planning, producing, and promoting your e-zine. This site is very helpful!

The Gay and Lesbian Review

http://glreview.com/

★★★★

 Not for kids

Considered the premier journal for gay and lesbian studies, *The Gay and Lesbian Review* is now online. You'll find indexes, articles, and excerpts in the area of sexuality from big-name scholars, such as Camille Paglia and Edmund White.

The Journal of African Travel Writing

http://www.unc.edu/~ottotwo/

★★★

The Journal of African Travel Writing presents and explores past and contemporary accounts of African travel, including scholarly articles, true narratives, fiction, poetry, reviews, and so on.

Ovid

http://www.ovid.com/

★★★★★

This site scans medical journals daily and compiles them into reports on specific medical topics that are then emailed to individuals who've requested them. Sign up here to be on the list for the most up-to-date medical information on AIDS, women's health, cardiology, and several other topics.

Pet Bird Magazine

http://www.birdsnways.com/wisdom/

★★★

Pet Bird Magazine, an e-zine about exotic birds and pet parrots, includes magazine articles on the care and breeding of pet birds.

Romanticism on the Net

http://www.ron.umontreal.ca/

★★★

A great site about British Romanticism in general, this online journal presents many articles, links, and the ability to publish online—that is, if you have something to say about Romanticism.

Best Science Fiction Weekly

http://www.scifi.com/sfw/

★★★★★

This electronic sci-fi magazine covers books, movies, TV, games, artwork, merchandise, and even some interviews. This popular site among sci-fi buffs includes a "news of the week" feature, which informs readers about current events in the sci-fi world. The site is very easy to navigate and features interesting letters from readers and other visitors. Though the site design is not stellar for a science-fiction site, the content here is top notch, earning this site our Best of the Best designation.

Wine and Dine E-Zine

http://www.winedine.co.uk/

★★★★

This site covers wine and restaurant reviews. One item of particular interest is the New Restaurant review, which is quite extensive.

A B C D E F G H I J K L M N O P Q R S T U V W X Y Z

A
B
C
D
E
F
G
H
I
J
K
L
M
N
O
P
Q
R
S
T
U
V
W
X
Y
Z

MAGAZINES

Advertising Age

http://www.adage.com/

★★★★★

This site presents images for viewing and contains archives, ad market information, and a daily top story. It also enables you to join the AdAge mailing list.

Astronomer Magazine

http://www.theastronomer.org/index.html

★★★

A British publication online that targets the advanced amateur but still contains items for the beginner. It also contains information on comets, asteroids, supernovae, and a variety of other topics that pertain to astronomy.

BYTE Magazine

http://www.byte.com/

★★★★

Contains a five-year, searchable archive of *BYTE Magazine*. Enter a search term, and presto! Articles that include the term you entered appear in an easy-to-retrieve format. You can download files and share-ware mentioned in *BYTE* articles and download *BYTE*'s benchmark tests. This valuable site is worth a bookmark in your browser software.

Car Collector

http://www.carcollector.com/

★★★★

Car Collector Magazine online features back issues, advertising information, subscription information, and automotive news.

Computer Games Magazine

http://www.cgonline.com/

★★★

 14-18

Computer Games magazine is a print publication that keeps up with the daily happenings in the computer games industry. It contains everything from in-depth previews and reviews of the latest games to daily news. At this site, you can preview the magazine and register for a free issue.

Computer Shopper Online

http://shopper.cnet.com/

★★★★★

Check out the top stories for the latest edition of *Computer Shopper*. It is considered to be the monthly computer bible for computer buyers. To access the magazine, go to cnet's shopping page, using the link above, and then click the link for *Computer Shopper Magazine*.

Computerworld Online

http://www.computerworld.com/

★★★★★

Stay current on all the news of the computer industry with this rich site.

Cosmopolitan

http://www.cosmomag.com/

★★★★★

 Not for kids

Pick up weekly tips to improve your love life and career, check your horoscope, and offer advice to other readers facing agonizing situations. This site is an encapsulated version of the print magazine, but entertaining nonetheless.

Discover Magazine

http://www.discover.com

★★★★★

 14-18

Discover Magazine online is a science magazine that includes text of issues, photos, links related to articles, and a subscription service.

Editor & Publisher

http://www.editorandpublisher.com/

★★★★

Editor & Publisher Magazine online offers selected articles from the printed version of the magazine, as well as Web-only content. It also offers comprehensive coverage of new media news and trends affecting the newspaper industry.

Electronic Green Journal

http://egj.lib.uidaho.edu/

★★★

This environmental journal online contains information about environmental issues. It also lists the contents of the journal's recent issues.

Esquire

http://www.esquireb2b.com

★★★★★

 Not for kids

Online version of one of the most popular men's magazines—*Esquire*. Find out what's stylish and what's not and who's hot and who's not.

E.W. Scripps

http://www.scripps.com/

★★★

Presents the media giant on the Web. Scripps-Howard owns 21 daily newspapers, 10 TV stations, and a host of other stuff you might want to check out.

Fantasy and Science Fiction Magazine

http://www.sfsite.com/fsf/

★★★★

 14-18

Founded in 1949, *Fantasy and Science Fiction Magazine* is "the award-winning SF magazine which is the original publisher of SF classics like Stephen King's *Dark Tower*, Daniel Keyes's *Flowers for Algernon*, and Walter M. Miller's *A Canticle for Leibowitz*." Visit this site to find out what's in the current issue or to subscribe to the magazine or order back issues.

Folk Roots

http://www.frootsmag.com/

★★★★

14-18

This site provides the condensed, electronic version of *Folk Roots*. It features its guide to folk and world music events in Britain and Europe, CD reviews, charts of best-selling music, a play list from *Folk Roots* radio program on the BBC World Service, a complete table of contents from the current issue, and much more.

Forbes

http://www.forbes.com

★★★★★

Stay up to date on the day's financial and investing news with Forbes.com, analyze your holdings, get stock advice from Streetwalker, and play the Forbes Investment Challenge to earn a chance at a new laptop computer.

Fortune

http://www.fortune.com

★★★★★

Daily business reports and articles from the print magazine. Get company profiles, tips on investing, small-business information, and career leads. Also features top executives, top companies, and a list of the best companies to work for.

Free Computer-Related Publications

http://www.soci.niu.edu/~huguelet/TLOFCRP/

★★★

If you've ever been buried by catalogs arriving right before Christmas, you'll appreciate this site. Jim Huguelet provides an alphabetical list of addresses and phone numbers for magazines he receives free, yet never asked for. Several publishers that discovered this list requested to be removed—they are listed here, too.

A B C D E F G H I J K L M N O P Q R S T U V W X Y Z

A B C D E F G H I J K L M N O P Q R S T U V W X Y Z

Glamour

http://us.glamour.com/

★★★★★

👫 14-18

Read some of this month's articles online, check out fashion do's and don'ts, and post your opinion for the benefit of *Glamour*'s editors.

HotWired

http://hotwired.lycos.com/

★★★★★

The slickest magazine in the industry has a web page with articles on the arts, politics, and technology. Before you can access much of anything, however, you have to join (free of charge). If you decide to sign up and are looking for something to do, check out the Arts and Renaissance articles first.

Internet Public Library

http://www.ipl.org/div/serials/

★★★★★

Internet Public Library contains a directory of online magazines organized by category. Follow the trail of links to locate the desired publication.

Internetweek Online

http://www.internetweek.com

★★★★★

A colorful site with news for corporate network managers. This publication provides testing, reviews, industry news, and funny tidbits on the world of networking and information management.

MacWorld

http://www.macworld.com/

★★★★★

MacWorld is the premier magazine for Macintosh computers, users, and buyers. *MacWorld* online enables you to search past issues and read articles. It also provides Internet tips, product reviews, industry news, newsletters, forums, and a pricefinder. If you own a Mac, bookmark this site.

Magatopia.com Free Online Magazines

http://www.magazine-rack.com/

★★★★

Find hundreds of magazines online, all free at this site that allows you to click and read magazines on just about any subject. Why pay when you can read for free?

Magazine City.net

http://www.magazinecity.net

★★★★

Search to find your favorite magazines or locate ones in subject areas of interest and then subscribe at the "guaranteed lowest price."

Magazine CyberCenter

http://www.magamall.com

★★★★

Get information on magazines, such as where to buy them locally, how to subscribe, and how to get back issues. Search by magazine name or topic to find what you're looking for.

Magazines A-Z

http://www.magazinesatoz.com/

★★★★

This site has a directory of Magazines Online including automotive, arts and entertainment, bridal, business and finance, computers, and a few other subjects. Find your favorite magazine here for sure. You can use the shopping feature to shop dozens of online stores such as Amazon and each of the magazine offerings, which are presented in a more orderly fashion than normal.

Metagrid

http://www.metagrid.com/

★★★★

Metagrid is a searchable, browsable directory of more than 4,000 online newspapers and 2,500 online magazines. It looks very much like the Yahoo! search page but focuses exclusively on magazine sites.

Motorcycle Online

http://www.motorcycle.com/

★★★★

[icon] Not for kids

This online magazine covers all aspects of motorcycles, including new model reviews, daily news, technical help, pictures, and tours.

NewsLink

http://newslink.org/

★★★★

Find online versions of many of the most popular newspapers and magazines or search for a topic to find articles in one or more of the online publications.

Newsweek

http://www.msnbc.com/news/NW-front_Front.asp

★★★★★

Catch this week's news on the *Newsweek* online site, which contains articles and commentary.

PC-TRANS

http://www.kutc.ku.edu/pctrans/

★★★★

Provides home site for *PC-TRANS*, a trade magazine for PC users in the transportation industry. The site provides technical support, a discussion forum, and a bulletin board. It includes contact information for the group and the magazine.

People

http://people.aol.com/people/

★★★★★

Get a rundown of the articles in this week's issue of the popular entertainment magazine, *People*, as well as special subscription offers.

PM Zone

http://popularmechanics.com/

★★★★★

Popular Mechanics online provides movies, pictures, and information about new and useful products and technology.

Popular Science

http://www.popsci.com/

★★★★★

Articles from the magazine's current issue, links, and message forums are available here.

Rolling Stone

http://www.rollingstone.com/

★★★★★

[icon] 14-18

Stay in tune to top musical acts, read music news, and even upload your demo tape for review by *Rolling Stone* critics! You'll also find video-on-demand of stars you love and a schedule of upcoming music Webcasts.

Runners World

http://www.runnersworld.com/

★★★★

Race results, tips from top athletes, info on biomechanics and injury prevention, and articles from the print magazine are at this site.

Science Magazine Home

http://www.sciencemag.org/

★★★★★

You will find many interesting articles from this magazine and learn how to subscribe to the print magazine. The site contains current articles and an archive of previous articles.

ScienceDaily Magazine–Your Link to the Latest Research News

http://www.sciencedaily.com/

★★★★★

ScienceDaily is a free, advertising-supported online magazine that presents late-breaking news about the latest discoveries and hottest research projects in everything from astrophysics to zoology. The site also provides a nice search feature and a picture of the day.

A B C D E F G H I J K L M N O P Q R S T U V W X Y Z

A B C D E F G H I J K L M N O **P** Q R S T U V W X Y Z

Scientific American

http://www.sciam.com/

★★★★★

Scientific American is the premier science magazine for the general public. Features the latest news in the world of science, covering everything from anthropology to zoology. Good collection of articles on recent discoveries in space, on earth, and undersea. Covers medical breakthroughs, environmental debates, strange phenomena, and daily occurrences that you might not understand, such as what happens when you get a sunburn. If you're a scientist at heart, this is the site for you.

SciTech Daily Review

http://www.scitechdaily.com

★★★★★

Comprehensive digest and directory of science and technology articles pulled from the top scientific publications around the world. Covers everything from the latest feats accomplished by computer hackers to the way a doctor's bedside manner can affect the recovery rates of his or her patients. This publication takes no sides and presents a balanced selection of the latest data in science, technology, and medicine.

Scientific Computing and Instrumentation Online

http://www.scamag.com/scripts/default.asp

★★★★★

A colorful website for a magazine devoted to computer analysis software for scientists and engineers. Read articles from the latest issue, link to related sites and to sites of software developers such as IBM and National Instruments, or access chemical databases.

Serif: The Magazine of Type and Typography

http://www.serifmagazine.com/

★★★

Online magazine that targets the desktop publisher. The site features sample articles, subscription information, and desktop publishing links.

Shutterbug

http://www.shutterbug.net/

★★★★

Photography information and source magazine, with articles, reviews, and back issues available online.

SkiNet

http://www.skinet.com/

★★★★

The editors of *Ski Magazine* and *Skiing Magazine* present snow reports, resort profiles, gear information, and news.

Sky & Telescope Online

http://skyandtelescope.com/

★★★★★

Sky Publishing Corporation provides astronomical news and calendars, product reviews, viewing tips, and special pages.

Smoke Magazine

http://www.smokemag.com/

★★★★

🚫 Not for kids

The distinctive lifestyle magazine is geared to the cigar and pipe enthusiast.

South Carolina Point

http://www.mindspring.com/~scpoint/point/

★★★

Provides online site for *South Carolina Point* news monthly. The site includes current and back issues along with contact information.

Surfer Magazine

http://www.surfermag.com/

★★★★

At this site, you can read recent surfing headlines, ask the surf doctor, see QuickTime movies, and select stories from the print magazine.

Tai Chi

http://www.tai-chi.com/

★★★

Some general information about Chinese internal martial arts and information on subscribing to the magazine.

TechUpdate

http://techupdate.zdnet.com/

★★★★

This site provides computer news, special reports, downloads, and more.

Tennis Magazine

http://www.tennis.com/

★★★★

Comprehensive tennis resource that includes the latest news and results from grand slams and other tournaments, along with rankings, and stats.

Time Magazine

http://www.time.com/time/

★★★★★

Time Warner's site offers links to *Time* online, *Sports Illustrated* online, *Money Magazine* online, and more.

TravelASSIST Magazine

http://travelassist.com/mag/mag_home.html

★★★★

This online magazine contains articles on travel and travel spots around the United States and the world. It includes back issues for online reading.

Twins Magazine

http://www.twinsmagazine.com/

★★★★

This site includes tidbits, resources, articles, and more from the magazine's current issue.

Typofile Magazine

http://www.will-harris.com/type.htm

★★★

This online magazine focuses on type and its uses. The site includes articles and links to other type and desktop publishing sites.

U: The National College Magazine

http://www.colleges.com/

★★★★★

 14-18

News, sports, fun, and special offers for college students, including contests and scholarship money.

Vogue

http://www.vogue.com/

★★★★

 14-18

Home of *Vogue* magazine. See a listing of the current month's magazine content with brief descriptions. The site also offers links to nutrition, fitness, and weight loss information. It includes forums, a chat room, and other Conde Nast publications.

Whole Earth

http://www.wholeearthmag.com/

★★★★

Whole Earth is dedicated to empowering individuals with vision to take control of their lives and work to build the communities of their dreams. It works to break down common, stale views and reveal possibilities of improving our lives and our environment. Here, you can learn more about the print publication and read some of its articles and book reviews.

Windows and .NETMagazine

http://www.winntmag.com/

★★★★★

Lab and book reviews, features, and other exclusive stories are available on the magazine's website. These Web-exclusive articles will not be published in the print edition.

Wine Spectator

http://www.winespectator.com/

★★★★

A comprehensive magazine covering wine, food, and travel.

A B C D E F G H I J K L M N O **P** Q R S T U V W X Y Z

A
B
C
D
E
F
G
H
I
J
K
L
M
N
O
P
Q
R
S
T
U
V
W
X
Y
Z

Wood Online

http://www.woodmagazine.com/

★★★★

Wood magazine covers the world of woodworking from A to Z and includes how-to project instructions, techniques, tool reviews, wood technology, and lumber kits.

Worth Online

http://www.worth.com/

★★★

Provides daily market snapshots, a message board, and financial intelligence online.

ZDNet

http://www.zdnet.com/

★★★★

One of the PC world's premier websites, ZDNet features product reviews, industry news, downloadable shareware, and great leads on computing deals.

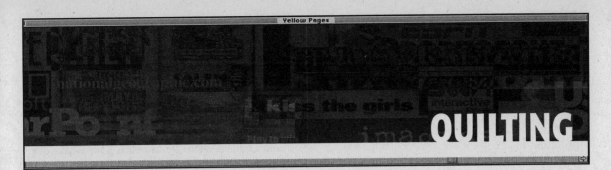

QUILTING

The AIDS Memorial Quilt

http://www.aidsquilt.org/

★★★★★

Description of the AIDS Memorial Quilt project, including its history, purpose, and display schedule. You'll find a nice gift shop or online store from which you can purchase clothes, videos, books, posters, postcards, and other such items. The site is very well designed and easy to navigate and features information about the AIDS Memorial Quilt project.

The Antique Quilt Source

http://www.antiquequiltsource.com/

★★★★

Browse the current catalog and order quilts online. Based in, and inspired by, Pennsylvania's famed quilt country.

American Quilts

http://www.americanquilts.com

★★★★

Search the database to find an Amish or antique quilt from among the 1,200 in inventory. Large, small, finished, and custom are available.

Applewood Farm Publications

http://applewd.com/

★★★★

Offers quilting patterns, classes, seminars, and mystery quilts by Beth Ferrier.

Canadian Quilters' Association

http://www.canadianquilter.com/

★★★★

Learn about this association, check out the schedules for upcoming events, paste a message on the quilting board, and peruse the extensive list of quilting links.

Cats (and People) Who Quilt

http://www.catswhoquilt.com/

★★★★

Sew a cat on your quilt! This site has no patterns or instructions, but lots of images and links to Net resources, all featuring cat quilts. Also provides some safety tips to prevent cats from harming themselves by swallowing thread or needles.

David Walker, Artist, Teacher, Quiltmaker

http://davidwalker.us/

★★★★

Gallery of work by this artist and quiltmaker, as well as a workshop and lecture schedule. Also features an artist of the month.

Favorite Quilting Magazines

http://www.quiltmag.com/

★★★★

Information on five U.S. quilting magazines, with article abstracts and notes from the editors, plus subscription information. The site has a many links to other sites where you can order quilting supplies.

A B C D E F G H I J K L M N O P Q R S T U V W X Y Z

A
B
C
D
E
F
G
H
I
J
K
L
M
N
O
P
Q
R
S
T
U
V
W
X
Y
Z

Fiona's Craft Page

http://www.geko.net.au/~fthorne/craft/

★★★

The many links to crafting sites in the USA, Australia, and Europe make this a one-stop resource for keen quilters.

From the Heartland

http://www.qheartland.com

★★★★

Share ideas and information with other quilters in the online discussion forum at the site, and learn more about upcoming TV and online specials hosted by Sharlene Jorgenson. You also can search for local quilting shops.

Grandmothers' Quilts

http://www.womenfolk.com/grandmothers/

★★★★

History and heritage, includes images of heirloom quilts and a comprehensive article about the Victorian crazy quilt.

Handquilter

http://www.handquilter.com

★★★

Read Candy's top handpiecing tips or locate other topics in the archive. A nice introduction to hand-piecing of quilts.

Jan Patek Quilts

http://janpatekquilts.com/

★★★

This site shares the author's quilts and offers sections devoted to projects, fabrics, and events. Although you cannot buy items from this site, you will see a list of resources in the "Where to Buy" section.

Jeanne's Quilt Page

http://showcase.netins.net/web/quilting/

★★★

Offers quilt pictures and workshops for people interested in learning to quilt. Check out the quilter's recipes.

Jinny Beyer Studio

http://www.jinnybeyer.com/

★★★★★

Quilting instruction, monthly patterns, quilting tips, and a quilters' showcase, as well as Jinny Beyer's own range of quilting fabrics.

Keepsake Quilting

http://www.keepsakequilting.com/

★★★★

Online warehouse packed with a wide selection of fabric, batting, patterns, books, and other quilting supplies. Project corner features free patterns. Before you leave, check out a picture of the shop, inside and out, and say hello to Cisco.

Martingale & Company

http://www2.martingale-pub.com/

★★★★

Looking for books on quilting? Then this site is your source. Search for a particular book or scan the database of titles. You'll also find free quilting patterns for download.

McCall's Quilting Magazine

http://www.quiltersvillage.com/mccalls/

★★★★★

You can get free quilting patterns, articles, and information about quilting shows, as well as find out how to subscribe to the magazine. This site also features a Kids' Korner, where quilters can find quilt designs for kids' rooms.

National Online Quilters

http://www.noqers.org/

★★★

Take a few lessons in the classroom and discover new quilting tips, and get a chance to keep up with the latest news from the group.

National Quilting Association

http://www.nqaquilts.org/

★★★★

The National Quilting Association, a nonprofit organization that was founded in 1970, works to promote every aspect of quilting, including everything from creating quilts to collecting and preserving quilts. Visit this site to learn more about the organization and its programs and services.

Piecemakers

http://www.piecemakers.com/

★★★★★

You'll definitely want to check out the calendar quilts this group designs and sells; they're extraordinary. At this site you can buy quilting supplies and kits, pick up free stuff, and just learn more about quilting. California residents might want to find the group's location and class schedule.

Planet Patchwork

http://planetpatchwork.com/

★★★★★

This comprehensive site for quilters includes reviews of quilting software, books, and products, plus links and excellence awards.

Planet Patchwork's Web Excellence Awards

http://www.tvq.com/topten.htm

★★★★

Looking for the best quilting sites? Check out Planet Patchwork's picks. Read a brief description for each site and then link directly to it.

QuiltArt

http://www.quiltart.com/

★★★★

View images from the gallery, find out about online chat groups for quilters, and more.

Quilt-A-Way Fabrics

http://www.quiltaway.com/

★★★

A good variety of quilting fabrics that you can search by design theme, as well as books, notions, and so on.

Quilt Care FAQs

http://www.bryerpatch.com/faq/storage.htm

★★★★

Learn how to hang, store, and clean quilts of any age. Get workshop information or look at the free quilting pattern.

The Quilt Channel

http://www.quiltchannel.com/

★★★★★

This quilting hub provides a searchable database for quilting-related queries, or you can click on one of the subject categories to get started. You'll find connections to anything quilting related you could desire: people, sites, tips, organizations, shopping resources, and more.

The Quilt Emporium

http://www.quiltemporium.com/

★★★★

This shop in California offers classes, patterns, quilting supplies, and a selection of books.

Quilting Arts Magazine

http://www.quiltingarts.com/

★★★★

Quilting Arts Magazine features articles on artists, quilting, embroidery, doll making, and other creative activities that require sewing. This site features a FAQ list, information about quilting contests, a quilters' bazaar, message boards, and more.

A
B
C
D
E
F
G
H
I
J
K
L
M
N
O
P
Q
R
S
T
U
V
W
X
Y
Z

A
B
C
D
E
F
G
H
I
J
K
L
M
N
O
P
Q
R
S
T
U
V
W
X
Y
Z

Quilting with Children

http://www.thecraftstudio.com/qwc/

★★★★

 All

Learn about the joys of quilting with children from Heddi Craft, who has been quilting with children for more than nine years. This site provides ideas, techniques, and resources for quilting with children.

Quilting with a Passion

http://quiltingpassion.com/

★★★★

Comprehensive directory of free patterns and other quilting resources on the Web. Find more than 2,100 free patterns! Subscribe to the Quilting Passion newsletter, check out the forum gallery, download a free quilted calendar Windows desktop, or take a quilting class. You'll find plenty to keep you busy (and interested) at this site!

Quilting and Sewing with Kaye Wood

http://www.kayewood.com

$

★★★★

Quick and easy, accurate quilting with Kaye's strip-piecing techniques and tools. This site has a lot of information on quilting and sewing books, tools, and notions for sale. All designed to make your quilting a pleasure, not a pain.

Quilting Guilds Around the World

http://quilt.com/QuiltGuildsPage.html

★★★★

This site features a listing of quilting guilds and clubs in U.S. regions and some international locations.

Quilting How To's

http://ttsw.com/HowToPage.html

★★★

Helpful advice on block-piecing methods, appliqué, rotary cutting, drafting, machine quilting, binding, basting, and more.

Quilt Software Network

http://www.quiltsoftware.net/

★★★★

This commercial site reviews software for quilters, including quilt design software, patterns, fabric selection guides, and print enhancement software for printing the patterns you design.

Best | Quilters Online Resource

http://www.nmia.com/~mgdesign/qor/

★★★★★

Meet pen-pals, look at patterns, scan project ideas, read software reviews, or enjoy the photo gallery. Check out the beginners' section. If you are a busy quilter, this site is probably your best bet because it is quick loading, with only a few graphics, but the ones here are effective in leading you to the information you need. This site is easy to navigate and has many useful features. These features include a section for beginners (well suited for a general quilting audience), a project section, pen-pals section, an email card section, quilting styles section, and a pattern page. You'll also find links to sites where you can make online purchases, too.

Quilters Village

http://www.quiltersnewsletter.com/

★★★

This magazine shop for quilters provides links to Primedia's four quilting magazines: *Quilter's Newsletter Magazine*, *McCall's Quilting*, *Quiltmaker*, and *Quick Quilts*. Click the cover of the magazine you want to preview or scroll down the page and click the Basic Lessons link to learn some basic quilting techniques. Also features a message board for quilters to share ideas and skills.

QuiltTalk

http://www.quilttalk.com/

★★★

This site offers quilting chat and lots of quilting activities. Check out the paper patterns to print out and sew, participate in a lesson, find a quilting pal, plus lots more.

QuiltWear.com

http://www.quiltwear.com/

★★★★★

Advertises women's and children's clothing patterns and embellishments of interest to quilters, sewers, and crafters.

World Wide Quilting Page

http://www.quilt.com/MainQuiltingPage.html

★★★★

This, the oldest and largest quilting site on the Web, has hundreds of pages of instructions, patterns, show listings, store listings, guild listings, famous quilters' pages, a bulletin board, a trading post, classifieds for quilters, and lots more.

A
B
C
D
E
F
G
H
I
J
K
L
M
N
O
P
Q
R
S
T
U
V
W
X
Y
Z

A B C D E F G H I J K L M N O P Q R S T U V W X Y Z

QUOTATIONS

Ability.org

http://www.ability.org/quotat.html

★★★★

Many links to famous and not-so-famous quotes.

Advertising Quotes

http://advertising.utexas.edu/research/quotes/

★★★★

Jef Richards, associate professor of Advertising at the University of Texas at Austin, has collected a set of quotations about the world of advertising. The index includes more than 60 subcategories. Highlights along the way include Billboards, Critics, Evil, Fantasy and Dreams, Honesty, Manipulation, Morality and Ethics, Puffery, Sex, and Value.

Amusing Quotes

http://www.amusingquotes.com/

★★★★

Read some funny quotes from some of the funnier people in history, including W.C. Fields, Will Rogers, Erma Bombeck, and Bill Cosby.

Annabelle's Quotation Guide

http://www.annabelle.net/

★★★★★

Browse quotes by topic or author, sign up to receive a weekly featured quote, and check out the quotation bookstore to find just the right book of sayings.

Bartlett's Familiar Quotations

http://www.bartleby.com/100/

★★★★★

The 10th edition of John Bartlett's famous book, published in 1901, has been converted to HTML format and posted to the Web by Project Bartleby, an extensive Web-based literature library established by Columbia University.

Creative Quotations

http://creativequotations.com/

★★★★★

A comprehensive quotation site that can be searched/perused in multiple ways: by different thematic concepts, keyword, or author. Also included are areas for quotational poetry, a thematic quotation calendar, quotations from famous individuals born on the current date, and a "Test your QQ (Quotational Quotient)" section. Well worth a visit.

Daremore Quotes

http://www.daremore.com/quosoft.html

★★★★

This site offers daily inspirational messages for women, providing a different quote on the users' desktops every day. You can download new messages monthly, or you can drop by the site at any time to peruse the entire list.

Famous Quotations

http://www.famous-quotations.com/

★★★★★

Search quotations alphabetically, by author, or by subject, or browse the category listings. You can find proverbs here, too. Learn about the lives of select authors, check out the top 10 quotation sites, and even get free email for life.

Follow Your Dreams

http://www.followyourdreams.com/food.html

★★★★

Inspirational quotations. Includes hundreds of quotations about courage, persistence, happiness, the purpose of life, and more from famous people throughout history.

Freeality Search

http://www.freeality.com/phrases.htm

★★★★★

Search for words, phrases, and quotations at a list of sites, which should provide a wide range of quotes to choose from.

Good Quotations by Famous People

http://www.cs.virginia.edu/~robins/quotes.html

★★★

Collection of Dr. Gabriel Robins' favorite quotations. Some good computer and math quotes you might not find in a standard book of quotations.

MemorableQuotations.com

http://www.memorablequotations.com

★★★★★

Huge collection of quotations categorized by discipline (or profession), country, historical period, and author. No search tool to zero in on a specific quote, but a great place to browse for wise tidbits and sage advice.

qotd.org

http://www.qotd.org/

★★★

Visit this site to view the randomly selected quote of the day or search through its collection of more than 22,500 quotes by subject or author.

Quotable Quotes

http://www.quotablequotes.net/

★★★

Search the database of more than 1,500 thought-provoking quotes and sign up for the quote of the day.

Quotation Center

http://cyber-nation.com/victory/quotations/subjects/quotes_subjects_a_to_b.html

★★★★★

Provided by Cyber Nation, this collection of more than 13,000 quotes meant to empower and motivate is quite impressive. You can choose from just about any topic available, alphabetized by category.

Quotation Search

http://www.starlingtech.com/quotes/search.html

★★★★★

Search this site for quotations from famous people with more than 10,000 quotes to choose from. You can browse by subject, author, or keywords.

Quotations

http://www.jsu.edu/depart/library/graphic/quote.htm

★★★

List of links to seven online quotation sites.

Quotations of William Blake

http://www.memorablequotations.com/blake.htm

★★★

This page offers, in somewhat of a hodgepodge, a list of quotations by the radical poet.

Quotations Page

http://www.quotationspage.com/

★★★★

This searchable collection of quotations includes quotes of the day, links to other quotation resources, and the opportunity to submit quotations.

⌐Best⌐ QuoteWorld.org

http://www.quoteworld.org/

★★★★★

Tens of thousands of famous quotations. Search for a specific quote by author or subject, check out the quotation of the day, browse the quotations by topic or author, see quotes in context, or check out the discussion area to post a quote or ask someone for help in tracking down a quote. This site's comprehensive collection of famous quotes combined with its powerful search tools make it the Best of the Best quotation sites on the Web.

A B C D E F G H I J K L M N O P Q R S T U V W X Y Z

A
B
C
D
E
F
G
H
I
J
K
L
M
N
O
P
Q
R
S
T
U
V
W
X
Y
Z

Quotegeek.com
http://www.quotegeek.com/

★★★★

Find quotes for term papers or school work, or just for fun, from Literature and Personalities to Movies and TV. Scan quotes relevant for the season and find which are the most popular.

quoteland.com
http://www.quoteland.com/

★★★★

Identify who said it or ask for help in tracking down an appropriate quote. You can search databases or turn to discussion groups for assistance.

Quotez
http://www.geocities.com/Athens/Oracle/6517/

★★★★★

This site features more than 5,000 quotations arranged into more than 500 subjects by some 800 authors (including more than 100 by Shakespeare alone). Can't find what you're looking for? Fill out the form provided; the folks at this site will conduct a search for you and post your request to the alt. quotations newsgroup for quotation nuts to respond to as well.

TPCN–Quotation Center
http://www.cybernation.com/victory/quotations/directory.html

★★★★

You'll find more than 12,000 great quotations on this site indexed by author and by subject. You will be inspired by these words of wisdom designed to empower you to achieve your dreams and fantasies.

Women's Quotes
http://wisdom_quotes.tripod.com/blqulist.htm

★★★★

Free online database of quotations by historic and contemporary women. Browse by subject or author.

Zappa Quote of the Day
http://www.amusingquotes.com/h/1/548.htm

★★★

Offers a new random quote each day from one of the geniuses of rock music, Frank Zappa.

RAILROADS

AAR: Association of American Railroads

http://www.aar.org/

★★★★★

Representing North America's freight railroads and Amtrak. Strives to help make the rail industry increasingly safe, efficient, and productive. Here, you can examine statistics, position papers, and links collections.

Amtrak

http://www.amtrak.com

★★★★★

Check departure and arrival times for Amtrak trains, find the station nearest to you, check fares and schedules, plan a trip, and search for specials. If you like riding the train, you'll love the convenience of this site.

Federal Railroad Administration

http://www.fra.dot.gov/

★★★★

Home of the United States government's organization for ensuring and improving railroad safety. Visit this site for a brief history of the administration and see what it's doing to make train travel safer.

Freightworld

http://www.freightworld.com/railroads.html

★★★★

Provides links to websites for freight railroad companies throughout the world, organized by region.

 ## Gateway Division NMRA

http://www.gatewaynmra.org/library.htm

★★★★★

This online modeler's reference library of tips, techniques, photos, clinics, and articles is sponsored by the Greater St. Louis area chapter of the National Model Railroad Association. One of the most useful sites I've found for information about model railroading, with a complete online library and a section on modeling topics as well as recent news about the subject. The site is well organized with easily searched topics. There is even a section on the annual train show. Novices and experts will both agree that this site is well deserving of its Best of the Best designation.

Golden Gate Railroad Museum

http://www.ggrm.org/

★★★

Tucked away in San Francisco, this little-known museum is "dedicated to the preservation of steam and passenger railroad equipment, and the interpretation of local railroad history." Here, you can find information about the museum and many of its restoration projects. Cool Rent-a-Locomotive project lets you or a group rent a locomotive by the hour and drive it (with the help of a certified engineer, of course).

A B C D E F G H I J K L M N O P Q **R** S T U V W X Y Z

A
B
C
D
E
F
G
H
I
J
K
L
M
N
O
P
Q
R
S
T
U
V
W
X
Y
Z

Great American Station Foundation

http://www.reconnectingamerica.org/

★★★★★

Dedicated to fostering community growth and enhance railroad travel, the Reconnecting America is responsible for organizing the restoration and rebuilding of many train stations in major metropolitan areas across America, as well integrating the various transportation networks that help us get around. Visit this site to learn more about the organization and its ongoing projects.

The Historical Website

http://www.rrhistorical.com

★★★★

If you are interested in railroading, this is the first site you should visit because it contains extensive information about railroading, including information about the history of railroading, clubs, organizations, and technical societies.

Illinois Railroad Museum

http://www.irm.org/

★★★

Online home of America's largest railroad museum, this site features information about the museum and its collection; an online photo gallery; feature articles; and an online schedule showing when the electric, steam, or diesel engines are running.

Model Railroading Magazine

http://www.modelrailroadingmag.com

★★★★

A model train magazine by modelers, for modelers. Includes prototype and modeling information. The site offers several books that you can order online using secure credit card resources. The site is beautifully designed and easy to navigate using the convenient and easy-to-understand menus.

NMRA on the Web: The National Model Railroad Association

http://www.nmra.com/

★★★★

Claims to be the "largest organization devoted to the development, promotion, and enjoyment of the hobby of model railroading." Find out all about the NMRA and also enjoy the Directory of World Wide Rail Sites featuring more than 3,700 links.

NTRAK Modular Railroading Society, Inc.

http://ntrak.org

★★★

Provides specifications and information about NTRAK modules for N scale (1:160) and includes links to NTRAK local and regional clubs.

NYO&W WebTrain

http://nyow.railfan.net/webtrain/

★★★★★

Operated by the New York, Ontario, and Western Modelers Special Interest Group, this site serves to connect websites that either feature the NYO&W and the railroads that served the NYO&W's territory or companies that offer products related to these railroads. All stations on the NYO&W WebTrain are family friendly and child safe.

Pacific Northwest LEGO Train Club

http://www.pnltc.org/

★★★★

The Pacific Northwest LEGO Train Club (PNLTC) is a great resource for model train builders who prefer the LEGO medium. Read articles about creating the perfect layout or view galleries of past club displays.

Railroad Network

http://www.railroad.net/

★★★★

Railroad Network is a creation of Mike Roque, whose love for trains was inspired by the commuter trains in his hometown of Mount Vernon, New York. Mike later moved to upstate New York, where he became interested in freight trains and model railroading. This site features online forums, articles, photos, event announcements, links, and a store where you can shop for shirts, coffee mugs, and other souvenirs.

RailServe

http://www.railserve.com/

★★★★

A railroad site's catalog that enables visitors to search by a specific keyword to find all rail-related sites or to browse by category, such as antiques, newsgroups, or passenger transit. Thousands of links.

Trains.com

http://www.trains.com/

★★★★

 All

Incredible collection of articles, specs, and other resources concerning model trains, railroading, rail travel, and railroads for kids. Even provides links to railroading magazines and online stores where you can purchase model railroads, tracks, and accessories.

TrainWeb

http://trainweb.com/

★★★

Information and photographs relating to passenger, freight, and model trains, plus late-breaking news stories regarding train travel.

Union Pacific Railroad

http://www.uprr.com/

★★★★★

The official Union Pacific site, containing service reports, the INFO Online magazine, facts, and figures and history, as well as plenty of corporate information regarding getting a job here and doing business with the company.

Walthers Model Railroad Mall

http://www.walthers.com

★★★★★

Brings you the best in model railroading, including a searchable catalog, containing more than 85,000 items, plus online ordering from your local hobby shops.

Webville and Hypertext Railroad Company

http://www.spikesys.com/webville.html

★★★

You'll find all kinds of railroading stuff here: songs, slogans, documents, forums, trivia, links, rail-related software, and more.

Z-World

http://www.z-world.com

★★★★

Provides information about Z scale (1:220) model railroading for collectors, operators, and dealers.

A
B
C
D
E
F
G
H
I
J
K
L
M
N
O
P
Q
R
S
T
U
V
W
X
Y
Z

Yellow Pages

REAL ESTATE

BUYING/SELLING

Ads4Homes

http://www.ads4homes.com/

★★★★★

Lists homes by state, enabling you to locate ads for homes that might interest you. Provides links to relocation information. Also, you can place an ad for your home, get the latest interest rate listings, and find a bank.

Americas Virtual Real Estate Store

http://www.americas-real-estate.com/

★★★★★

In the site's own words, this is the Internet's most complete source for finding homes for sale and free home valuations.

bestagents.com

http://www.bestagents.com/

★★★

Provides information for home buyers and sellers. Serves as a network of exclusive real estate agents who become your personal advisors, consultants, and negotiators.

Century 21

http://www.century21.com

★★★★★

Aimed at property buyers and sellers. An online Property Search lets you search by state, city, or ZIP code. You provide input, and every listing matching your criteria pops up. Click on Tips and Terms and find answers to FAQs and the Real Estate Glossary, which defines more than 900 real estate–related terms.

Coldwell Banker

http://www.coldwellbanker.com/

★★★★★

Before you invest time in searching for a new home, try out Coldwell Banker's Personal Retriever service that assists you in determining what features you need in a home. Then search the Coldwell Banker database of more than 200,000 homes and make use of the online concierge service to get settled with less hassle.

The Commercial Network

http://www.tcnre.com/

★★★★

A comprehensive resource for securing corporate real estate and facility requirements worldwide, including North America, the Pacific Rim, Latin America, and Europe, among others. In addition to listing properties for sale or lease in more than 150 locations, the site offers an online referral information service and a database that helps members pinpoint market values and property trends worldwide.

Consumer Information Center

http://www.pueblo.gsa.gov/

★★★★★

Free federal consumer publications covering mortgages, mobile homes, inspections, buying, insurance, and many other topics. Most of the online versions of the publications are free, but you can order the print versions of most publications for 50¢ to $3.00. After you reach the home page, by entering the address given above, click the Housing link to view a list of publications related to housing.

Best | Domania.com

http://www.domania.com/

★★★★★

Before selling or buying a home, do your homework at this site. Check comparable home prices, determine how much equity you have built up in your home, check mortgage rates, use the online calculators, and much more. Cool tool helps you find out the actual sales price of recently purchased homes in your area. This site is attractive, easy-to-navigate, and packed with powerful tools and great information for both sellers and buyers, making it our pick for Best of the Best.

HomeBuilder.com

http://www.homebuilder.com/

★★★★

Find a new home, or a home builder, from the database of builders at this site. You also can make arrangements for financing, moving, and performing many other home-buying–related activities at the site.

HomeFair.com

http://www.homefair.com

★★★★★

The calculators and research tools available at this site will be a big help to anyone looking for a home, including crime statistics, moving estimates, and school reports, to name just a few. You also can get information on home-related services, such as decorating, home improvement, financing, gardening, and more.

HomeGain

http://www.homegain.com

★★★★★

Use HomeGain's Valuation Tool to find out what your home's worth and then select an agent that's just right for you using the Agent Evaluator. You'll also find consumer guides to home buying and selling in the site's library. Note that you will have to register to use the site's resources.

Homeseekers.com

http://www.homeseekers.com/

★★★★★

Search for a home in a particular city or region and track down an agent to assist you in finding a new home, or use the information pulled from 175 multiple listing services to assess the value of your home before deciding to put it on the market. You also can shop for a mortgage and other home-related services.

HUD: U.S. Department of Housing and Urban Development

http://www.hud.gov/

★★★★

Created and maintained by the U.S. government, HUD's online site provides some valuable information for anyone who's planning to buy or sell a home. Check out a list of questions you should ask before purchasing a home, learn your rights as a home buyer, find out how much house you can afford, and much more.

International Real Estate Digest

http://www.ired.com

★★★★★

Looking for an independent and all-inclusive source of real estate information? This mega-site is it. The IRED Real Estate Directory offers nearly 10,000 links to real estate websites worldwide and can be searched by state, country, or category. If you're buying a home, selling a home, or just interested in real estate information in general, this site offers just about everything you want to know.

Land.Net

http://www.land.net/

★★★★

Very extensive real estate site. Buyers can search for homes and also post requests to be contacted when a property matches their requirements. Special sections cater to real estate professionals.

A
B
C
D
E
F
G
H
I
J
K
L
M
N
O
P
Q
R
S
T
U
V
W
X
Y
Z

A
B
C
D
E
F
G
H
I
J
K
L
M
N
O
P
Q
R
S
T
U
V
W
X
Y
Z

LoopNet

http://www.loopnet.com

★★★★★

This site is geared for commercial realtors, offering a commercial listing service, marketing program, financing assistance, and buyer/seller matching service. With its more than 450,000 members, this is one of the largest commercial real estate sites.

MSN HomeAdvisor

http://homeadvisor.msn.com/

★★★★★

HomeAdvisor provides a searchable database of U.S. real estate listings, complete with neighborhood demographics. It contains information on the home-buying process, including negotiating and financing. Visitors can pre-qualify or apply for a loan online. Also features advice on home decor, cooking and entertainment, and home improvement and repair. Very comprehensive, nicely designed site.

NewHomeNetwork.com

http://www.newhomenetwork.com/

★★★★

A site for new home builders and buyers, visitors can search the database of available homes in cities across the country. In addition to basic home and community information, you can learn about school districts and mortgage estimates and see floor plans and photos.

Nolo.com–Real Estate

http://www.nolo.com/category/re_home.html

★★★★★

This self-help legal site can assist you in learning more about the process of buying and selling real estate, as well as commercial space and rental property. Read articles, do research, and turn to Auntie Nolo, with questions you can't seem to find the answer to. Features online mortgage calculators, as well.

Owners.com

http://www.owners.com/

★★★★★

Owners.com provides a searchable, national database of homes for sale by owners. It also provides reports on school districts, real estate glossaries, and mortgage calculators. Excellent real estate hub for buyers and sellers alike.

PikeNet

http://www.pikenet.com/pike?func=showHome

★★★

You'll find access to more than 3,500 commercial real estate sites and services at this starting point, which organizes information into categories to make it easier for you to find what you're looking for, from listings to research to demographic data. You also can sign up for a free newsletter.

Real Estate Center Online

http://recenter.tamu.edu/

★★★★

This is the comprehensive source for all things related to Texas real estate. An excellent site design allows viewers to browse efficiently through myriad materials, including numerous publications, statistical data, an extraordinary collection of real estate articles—even annual and monthly building permit statistics for all 50 states.

realtor.com

http://www.realtor.com

★★★★

Home buying is broken down into a well-organized, six-step process: Getting Started, Buying, Selling, Offer/Closing, Moving, and Owning. Lots of tools, tips, and advice within each step.

Realty Locator

http://www.realtylocator.com/

★★★

Directory of 100,000 links related to real estate, including realtors, rentals, new homes and builders, appraisers and inspectors, and more. Covers 10,000 cities and towns in all 50 states.

REMAX Real Estate Network

http://www.remax.com/index.html

★★★★

The corporate site of this nationwide real estate agency offers a lot of material useful to both agents and consumers. Browsers can search a listing of home properties or REMAX agents, review commercial or mortgage information, or find out about relocation services.

SellMyHome101.com

http://www.sellmyhome101.com/

★★★★★

Whether you plan to do it yourself or hire a realtor, this site offers advice about how to prepare your home to sell—including how tidying up the garage and adding fresh flowers in strategic spots to help you market your house.

Wine Country Weekly Real Estate Reader

http://www.rereader.com/

★★★★

A delightful online magazine with a wealth of information on California wine country real estate. Beyond its extensive listings (recreational, commercial and estate properties, vacation rentals, developments, and homes), the magazine offers real estate articles and sales data.

RELOCATION SERVICES

 America Mortgage Online

http://amo-mortgage.com/relocate.htm

★★★★★

This site focuses on offering you mortgage information and tools in addition to relocation services. You can find relocation links for all 50 states and register to receive a free relocation package. You also can look through the Mortgage Library, read the Real Estate News, order your credit report, do a home inspection, search for homes, and look at other real estate links. The site is very well designed and easy to navigate, and the information is very useful.

Apartments for Rent Online

http://www.forrent.com/

★★★★★

Apartments for Rent Online is a listing of apartments and homes available across the United States. Users can search alphabetically; by amenities; or by state, city, and neighborhood. Visitors also can submit online ads.

Employee Relocation Council (ERC)

http://www.erc.org/

★★★★

This site covers myriad relocation and human resource issues, from transfer costs to family concerns. Sections include information on ERC, a Relocation Career Hotline, Research and Publications, and more.

ExecuStay Inc.

http://www.rent.net/ads/execustay/

★★★★

Find temporary housing accommodations nationwide at this site. ExecuStay (by Marriott) offerings range from fully furnished apartments to private homes, complete with linens, electronics, and cable television.

MonsterMoving.com

http://www.monstermoving.com/

★★★★★

MonsterMoving.com, from the same folks who created MonsterJobs.com, is an online relocation guide that contains more than 100,000 links. Users can find links to real estate, careers, education, travel, taxes, insurance, mortgage, and rental sites. The database can be searched by subject, city, or state. You'll even find resources for childcare information and links for making the move easier for your kids. If an international move is in your future, this site can help with that, too.

A
B
C
D
E
F
G
H
I
J
K
L
M
N
O
P
Q
R
S
T
U
V
W
X
Y
Z

A
B
C
D
E
F
G
H
I
J
K
L
M
N
O
P
Q
R
S
T
U
V
W
X
Y
Z

The Relocation Wizard

http://www.homefair.com/homefair/wizard/?NETSCAPE_LIVEWIRE.src

★★★★★

Answer the questions and submit your information to the wizard and receive a suggested timeline. Find out what to do to help make your move go smoothly. Good selection of calculators for analyzing salary issues, moving costs, home affordability, and more. Links to school reports, city reports, and crime reports for most cities and towns.

RelocationCentral.com

http://www.relocationcentral.com/

★★★★★

Comprehensive directory to everything you need to know to make wise relocation decisions. The home page is minimal, offering four main links: State Selector, National Relocation Directory, Tools & Tips, and Search. Click State Selector to begin your research, and then pick the destination state and city. RelocationCentral displays links for all sorts of services in the specified city, including apartment locators, real estate agents, local phone companies, moving and storage companies, and much more.

Rent.net

http://www.rent.net/

★★★★★

This site offers a variety of rental and relocation resources broken into different categories of interest. Visitors will find a section geared to seniors, another on vacation rentals, one on furnished suites, and more. There are also sections on movers, truck rental, furniture rental, city guides, insurance and auto information, and lots more.

RentCheck

http://www.rentcheck.com/

★★★★

Search listings of more than 300,000 apartment units, temporary furnished suites, houses, condominiums, and vacation rentals for floor plans, photos, and customized neighborhood views at this site.

Salary Calculator

http://www.homefair.com/homefair/calc/salcalc.html

★★★★

If you make $45,000 per year living in Atlanta, Georgia, and would like to move to Seattle, Washington, how much would you need to make per year to maintain your current lifestyle? This site will tell you…and probably shock you.

The School Report

http://www.homefair.com/sr_home.html

★★★★

Offers school comparisons by city or county. Pick a state and a city or county, and up pops a report listing the various school districts, along with information about the total number of students, average student-to-teacher ratio, and average class size.

SchoolMatch

http://www.schoolmatch.com

★★★

Find a school or system anywhere in the United States using the free online directory here, or buy an instant school evaluation.

TIMESHARES

Century 21 TRI-Timeshares

http://www.tri-timeshare.com/

★★★★

Bid on timeshare auctions here or search through available timeshare opportunities for more information. This site also provides a timeshare advisor to assist you in finding a good vacation match.

Hotel Timeshare Resales

http://www.htr4timeshare.com/index.html

★★★★

This site's entire focus is Marriott hotel timeshares. It offers listings to browse and information explaining why you should choose this company to buy a timeshare property.

RCI vacationNET

http://www.rci.com/

★★★★★

Resort Condominiums International (RCI) offers a searchable online directory of more than 3,000 resorts around the world affiliated with its timeshare exchange program. The site also includes travel tips, a tour of featured resorts, and a section explaining vacation ownership.

Stroman

http://www.stroman.com/

★★★★★

Search this site to learn more about available timeshares for sale by looking through the catalog of properties and reading up on the buying and selling process. Thousands of resort timeshares are also available.

TimeLinx

http://www.timelinx.com/

★★★★★

Fully searchable database, containing information on more than 3,500 timeshare resorts worldwide for exchange, resale, and rental. Includes membership details and featured resorts.

The Timeshare Beat

http://www.thetimesharebeat.com/

★★★★

Timeshare Beat is an online magazine for those who own and manage timeshare properties all over the world. This magazine has feature articles about the best areas to own timeshare properties along with up-to-date travel information.

Timeshare Resales of the Americas

http://tra-resales.com/

★★★★

Timeshare Resales of the Americas is a service company that enables timeshare owners to resell their timeshares and purchase additional timeshares in other parts of the world.

TimeSharing Today

http://www.timesharing-today.com/

★★★★

The online edition of this magazine includes extensive classifieds, sample articles, and resort reviews. This site features valuable articles about resort destinations, plus tips and advice on exchanging, buying, and selling time-shares. Also offers straightforward resort reviews from owners on exchange, and much more. The classified ads list hundreds of units for sale, rent, or trade.

A
B
C
D
E
F
G
H
I
J
K
L
M
N
O
P
Q
R
S
T
U
V
W
X
Y
Z

REFERENCE

DICTIONARIES AND THESAURI

Acronym Finder

http://www.acronymfinder.com/

★★★★★

All

The Acronym Finder provides more than 341,000 common acronyms, abbreviations, and initialisms for a wide range of subjects in a searchable database.

Acronyms and Abbreviations

http://www.ucc.ie/cgi-bin/acronym

★★★★

All

Can't remember an acronym's meaning, like whether you should call AA or AAA when your car won't start? This easy-to-use site can help you out of your dilemma. Just type in the letters you're trying to decipher, and the acronym lookup site gives you an immediate definition.

ARTFL Project: Roget's Thesaurus Search Form

http://humanities.uchicago.edu/orgs/ARTFL/forms_unrest/ROGET.html

★★★★

The American and French Research on the Treasury of the French Language (ARTFL) Project, located at the University of Chicago, has provided this online version of Roget's Thesaurus. The interface is simple: Type the word you want, and the form will return synonyms and antonyms. Back up to http://humanities.uchicago.edu/orgs/ARTFL/ for more resources.

The Astronomy Thesaurus

http://msowww.anu.edu.au/library/thesaurus/

★★★

This extensive thesaurus lists words related to astronomy. Just click a word and the list of synonyms appears onscreen. The thesaurus is available in English, French, German, Spanish, and Italian.

AVP Virus Encyclopedia

http://www.avp.ch/avpve/

★★★★★

The makers of AntiViral Toolkit Pro present this encyclopedia, featuring descriptions of hundreds of computer viruses. Search by virus name or type.

A.Word.A.Day

http://www.wordsmith.org/awad/index.html

★★★

Become a subscriber to the mailing list and receive a word, with its definition, every day. Increase your vocabulary the fun, easy way. The site also contains an anagram solver. Just submit a word you'd like to have an anagram for and await the results.

The Climbing Dictionary

http://home.tiscalinet.de/ockier/climbing_dict.html

★★★

Browse the only dictionary of rock/mountain-climbing terms in English, along with translations in German, French, Dutch, Italian, Spanish, Swedish, and Polish.

Dictionary of Cell and Molecular Biology

http://www.mblab.gla.ac.uk/~julian/Dict.html

★★★★

Searchable cell biology index. The online counterpart to *The Dictionary of Cell and Molecular Biology, Third Edition*, plus some additions.

Dictionary.com Definitions

http://dictionary.reference.com/

★★★★★

👥 All

Type a word and press Enter to view a list of definitions for that word.

Dictionary.com Translation

http://www.dictionary.com/translate/

★★★★

Translate any word, phrase, or sentence from English to a long list of languages, including French, German, Italian, Spanish, and Portuguese, or to English from the same languages.

The Free Online Dictionary of Computing

http://foldoc.doc.ic.ac.uk/foldoc/index.html

★★★

Searchable dictionary of computer terms. Also includes a list of links to other reference sites.

Merriam-Webster Online

http://www.m-w.com/

★★★★★

👥 All

In addition to a dictionary and a thesaurus, you'll find a word of the day, a game to play, and other interesting word-related items. Check out Words from the Lighter Side if you enjoy knowing the latest slang terms and their meanings.

On-line Dictionaries and Glossaries

http://www.rahul.net/lai/glossaries.html

★★★★★

Access dictionaries to assist in translating documents in foreign languages to English, or from English to something else. A long list of languages covered.

OneLook Dictionaries

http://www.onelook.com/

★★★

This site works like all the searchable dictionaries, with one slight difference: It searches more than 600 dictionaries. You'll find links to all the dictionaries and some related sites.

RhymeZone

http://www.rhymezone.com/

★★★

👥 All

Trying to write a poem? Stymied for a word that rhymes with *hunger*? Check out this page. Simply type the word you want to find a rhyme for and click the Submit button. RhymeZone also features other fun and educational sections, including a section on Shakespeare, grammar quizzes, nursery rhymes, and quotations.

SpellWeb

http://www.spellweb.com/

★★★

👥 All

Use the Internet to determine which spelling of a word is more popular, although not necessarily correct. You also can use the site to ask questions regarding relative popularity of certain items, such as cats or dogs.

Thesaurus.com

http://www.thesaurus.com/

★★★★★

👥 All

This is the complete thesaurus. You can browse alphabetically, choose one of the six classes of words, or type in a word to search. Then click the word and receive a list of synonyms.

TravLang's Translating Dictionaries

http://dictionaries.travlang.com/

★★★★★

Access a long list of translating dictionaries at this site, offering translations to and from many foreign languages.

A B C D E F G H I J K L M N O P Q **R** S T U V W X Y Z

A B C D E F G H I J K L M N O P Q R S T U V W X Y Z

A Web of Online Dictionaries

http://www.yourdictionary.com/

★★★★★

Here, you're likely to find just about any answer to a translation or language question through the online translating dictionaries, thesauri, grammar checkers, and linguistic tools.

Webopedia.com

http://www.webopedia.com/

★★★★★

Is there a computer acronym, term, or concept that has you stumped? Then turn to the Webopedia to decipher it. Just type the entry and press Enter to find a complete definition. Most definitions also include a collection of links to other resources where you can find additional information.

The Word Wizard

http://wordwizard.com/

★★★★★

Not a dictionary in the strictest sense, but a site where words are celebrated. You must register to participate, but there are contests with prizes and just plain fun stuff to do with words. You also can Ask the Word Wizard for help with definitions, usage, or word origins.

WordNet 1.7 Vocabulary Helper

http://www.notredame.ac.jp/cgi-bin/wn

★★★

This is a simple but powerful site. Just type in a word, any word, and you'll be rewarded with every possible meaning of the word: synonyms, antonyms, hyponyms, coordinate terms—the list goes on.

LIBRARIES

The American War Library

http://members.aol.com/veterans/

★★★★

This library contains data on every military conflict in which the United States has been involved since the founding of the country. It also offers a veterans' registry, a photo archive section, and many other areas of benefit to veterans and their families.

Awesome Library for Teens

http://www.awesomelibrary.org/student5.html

★★★★

 14-18

Directory of links for teenagers and teachers organized by categories, including Games, Projects, English, Mathematics, Science, Leadership, Friends, and more.

Berkeley Digital Library SunSITE

http://sunsite.berkeley.edu/

★★★

This site contains "digital collections and services while providing information and support to others doing the same." Essentially an online library.

Bibliomania: The Network Library

http://www.bibliomania.com/

★★★★

With more than 2,000 complete classic novels, articles, poems, and short stories in HTML and PDF formats, this is a great place to get that classical education you always wanted but never found the time for. You can purchase some of these books online using secure card resources.

Center for Research Libraries

http://wwwcrl.uchicago.edu/

★★★★

An international not-for-profit consortium of colleges, universities, and libraries that makes available scholarly research resources to users everywhere.

Christian Classics Ethereal Library

http://www.ccel.org/

★★★

With hundreds of fiction and nonfiction titles, hymns and choral music, and even a study Bible, this site offers an extensive collection of excellent spiritual titles, all in the public domain.

The C. Christopher Morris Cricket Library and Collection

http://www.haverford.edu/library/cricket/

★★★

This library, located at Haverford College, has the largest collection of cricket literature and memorabilia in the Americas. With more than a thousand volumes, plus related cricket material, the library serves as the leading resource to preserving the history of the sport of cricket in the United States and Canada.

Global Reports, LLC

http://www.global-reports.com/

★★★

A collection of more than 500,000 full-color, annual reports from more than 10,000 companies located in more than 65 countries.

Related Site
http://www.zpub.com/sf/arl/

HighBeam Research

http://www.highbeam.com

★★★★★

This unique library assistant, made up of partnerships with newspapers and magazines, provides a searchable index of articles from both current and past issues. You simply enter a keyword or phrase, and the e-librarian tracks down the resources for you. Provides free abstracts, but to access entire articles, you must subscribe to the service (about $20 per month or $100 per year). Free seven-day trial.

Internet Public Library

http://www.ipl.org/

★★★★★

All

Includes resources for children, teenagers, and adults. The reference center allows you to ask questions of a real librarian (not a computer). The youth services and teen divisions have links to both books and other resources, such as writing contests, college information, science projects, and author question-and-answer sessions. A section is also devoted to information for librarians and other information professionals. Other features include tutorials, an exhibit hall, a reading room with browsable full-text resources, links to web search engines, and a multi-user object-oriented (MOO) environment for browsing the library.

The Library of Congress

http://www.loc.gov/

★★★★★

All

Provides access to the Library of Congress' online catalog and other databases. For librarians, this site includes valuable information about Library of Congress standards for cataloguing, acquisitions, and book preservation. You'll find frequently asked reference questions; links to international, federal, state, and local government information; links to Internet search engines and meta-indexes; a link to the U.S. Copyright Office home page; and information about Library of Congress special events and exhibits.

Library Spot

http://www.libraryspot.com/

★★★★★

All

This online reference desk provides access to libraries, as well as answers to questions about a host of subjects, organized into categories. Established for students and teachers, but accessible to everyone.

A B C D E F G H I J K L M N O P Q R S T U V W X Y Z

A
B
C
D
E
F
G
H
I
J
K
L
M
N
O
P
Q
R
S
T
U
V
W
X
Y
Z

Libweb–Library Servers on the WWW

http://sunsite.berkeley.edu/Libweb/

★★★★

 All

Find information from libraries in more than 100 countries. Use a keyword to locate a particular library location or system, or scan the long list.

Medical/Health Sciences Libraries on the Web

http://www.lib.uiowa.edu/hardin-www/hslibs.html

★★★★

A state-by-state listing of all medical and health science libraries on the Net. You'll find sections for foreign countries, plus an extensive listing of links.

National Archives and Records Administration

http://www.nara.gov/

★★★★

Includes both searchable and browsable services for locating government information via the Government Information Locator Service (GILS). Has links to the Federal Register, the National Archives and Records Administration Library, and the presidential libraries. The presidential libraries' page also includes the addresses, phone numbers, fax numbers, email addresses, and links to the home pages for the presidential libraries. Also has links for genealogical research.

National First Ladies' Library

http://www.firstladies.org/

★★★★

Explores lives of our first ladies and their contributions to history. Contains bibliographies, press releases, a newsletter, a photo album, and Saxton McKinley house information.

The National Sporting Library

http://www.nsl.org/index.htm

★★★

Containing more than 13,000 volumes on such topics as horse racing, breeding, shooting, foxhunting, angling, polo, sporting art, and more, the NSP serves as a resource for both the interested browser and the serious researcher. With books going back to the 1500s, the library is a storehouse of historical information on these sports. The emphasis is on horse-related sports, plus other sports closely related to the country life, so team sports such as baseball are not included.

North American Sport Library Network

http://www.sportquest.com/naslin/

★★★★

NASLIN was developed to facilitate the spread of sports information among sports librarians, archivists, and others through publications, conferences, and educational programs. SPORTDiscus Online, the largest database of its kind, offers coverage of sports, fitness, and recreation-related publications. SPORTDiscus contains more than 400,000 bibliographic citations and "a wide range of information published in magazines and periodicals, books, theses, and dissertations, as well as conference proceedings, research papers, and videotapes." Click the Sports link to access a huge directory of links for nearly every sport imaginable.

OCLC Online Computer Library Center, Inc.

http://www.oclc.org/home/

★★★★★

Contains information that is especially useful for librarians and other information professionals. Has links to OCLC documents and forms, a search engine for searching OCLC information, and demonstrations of OCLC services. Actual logon to some OCLC services is available by subscription only.

Perry-Castañeda Library Map Collection

http://www.lib.utexas.edu/maps/united_states.html

★★★★★

An online map library, with one of the most extensive collections of maps in the world. The online collection is more than just a listing of maps in the library; you can view, download, and print out the maps as you require. Be sure to read the FAQ before viewing or printing any of the maps to be sure that your machine is capable of the task (some of the maps are very large). The site also has links to other map-related sites around the world.

Portico: The British Library

http://www.bl.uk

★★★★★

👥 All

Portico is the online information server for the British Library. From this point, you gain access to the online catalogs, lists of services, collections, and digital library. The site is beautifully rendered, with some documents (including images of actual pages) already available or in progress.

Smithsonian Institution Libraries

http://www.sil.si.edu/

💲

★★★★★

👥 All

Includes links to the various Smithsonian Museums, a search engine for locating information within the Smithsonian, information about visiting Washington, D.C., information explaining how to become a member of the Smithsonian, a map showing the locations of most of the Smithsonian Museums, and a browsable shopping area.

Special Libraries Association

http://www.sla.org/

★★★

The SLA consists of special librarians who are employed as information specialists by private businesses, governments, colleges, museums, and associations. This site is designed to promote the Special Library and to promote and advertise SLA membership benefits.

Lightspan

http://www.lightspan.com

★★★★

👥 All

Lightspan features a proven model available for educators that gives them an integrated set of products to assess students, align curricula to meet state standards, instruct students to successfully meet or exceed the standards, evaluate your program, and continue professional development in your system.

The Sunnyvale Center for Innovation, Invention & Ideas

http://www.sci3.com/

★★★

Established by a unique arrangement between the United States Patent and Trademark Office and the City of Sunnyvale, California, the center is able to provide patent and trademark information and research to the entire western United States as well as to Pacific Rim countries. This is the only office of its kind in the western United States that can provide PTO information outside the Washington, D.C., area.

U.S. Department of Education (ED)

http://www.ed.gov/index.jsp

★★★★★

👥 All

Explore the U.S. Department of Education's home page, discover information about its offices and programs, and learn how to get assistance from the department. Lots of information and resources for research and education.

U.S. National Library of Medicine

http://www.nlm.nih.gov/

★★★★★

Search the library's free online health information library, Webline, or clinical trials information database for a better understanding of issues surrounding your personal health.

A B C D E F G H I J K L M N O P Q R S T U V W X Y Z

A
B
C
D
E
F
G
H
I
J
K
L
M
N
O
P
Q
R
S
T
U
V
W
X
Y
Z

WWW Library Directory

http://www.webpan.com/msauers/libdir/

★★★★

Click a country name to locate a list of links to libraries in that country. Most of the countries currently represented are European (both East and West) and North American, although a few Asian, Middle Eastern, and South American countries are represented, also. Also has links to other library-related resources.

WWW Virtual Library

http://vlib.org/Overview.html

★★★★

Directory of reference materials organized by category, including Agriculture, Computing, Education, Humanities, Law, Science, and Society.

RESEARCH HELP

555-1212.com Area Code Look Up

http://www.555-1212.com/

★★★★

Search by city or state name for U.S. or Canadian area codes, or browse by area code or state name. Returns area code and corresponding city/state. Area code links lead to a business directory that can be browsed by category or searched by business name.

Academic Info

http://www.academicinfo.net/

★★★★

A subject directory of Internet resources tailored to the university community. Each subject entry contains an annotated list of links to general websites for the field and links to more specialized resources.

Academy of Achievement

http://www.achievement.org/

★★★★★

 All

The Academy of Achievement features the stories of influential figures from the twentieth century who have been successful in their fields. Video and sound clips are included, inspirational books are cited, and an online mentor program is available.

Airline Toll-Free Numbers and Websites

http://www.geocities.com/Thavery2000/

★★★

Browse this list of both domestic and international airlines with corresponding 800 numbers and links to websites if available. Includes the most current information.

American Sign Language Browser

http://commtechlab.msu.edu/sites/aslweb/browser.htm

★★★★★

Click on a word to get a short description of the motion of the sign, which is also illustrated by a video clip.

AnyWho Toll Free Directory

http://www.tollfree.att.net/tf.html

★★★★

Toll-free phone number directory set up by company name, city, state, and/or category. Also includes information about AT&T.

Ask an Expert Sites

http://njnie.dl.stevens-tech.edu/askanexpert.html

★★★★

 All

Directory of sites where you can post questions to have them answered by experts in science and math, medicine and health, computing and the Internet, history and social studies, and other subjects.

Ask Jeeves

http://www.ask.com/

★★★★★

 All

Ask a question of the Internet butler in plain English and get references to sites that are likely to be able to answer it.

Ask Jeeves for Kids
http://www.ajkids.com/

Atomica.com—Research Assistance for Companies

http://www.atomica.com/

★★★

Information about Atomica (formerly guru.net), which is a company providing information retrieval to other businesses and companies. Its mission is to help leading companies gain a competitive edge by providing their employees the right information at the right time. This site has a great search engine (you have to register first) that can quickly provide you with the answers you seek.

Biographical Dictionary

http://www.s9.com/biography/

★★★★

Short biographies of more than 28,000 remarkable men and women who have shaped the world from ancient times to the present, searchable by name, birthday, date of death, profession, famous works, achievements, and other key words.

Biography.com

http://www.biography.com/

$

★★★★

 All

Search a database of biographical information on more than 20,000 famous people and historical figures at this site. A program guide, trivia games, discussion forums, and an online store are also available.

Britannica.com

http://www.britannica.com/

$

★★★★★

 All

Search the complete Encyclopedia Britannica at this site, as well as learn historical information and catch up on the day's news. Browse topics of interest or search for specific nuggets of knowledge.

CAIRSS for Music

http://imr.utsa.edu/CAIRSS.html

★★★★

Bibliographic database of music research literature covering music education, psychology, therapy, and medicine. Database includes citations from more than 1,300 different journals, including 18 primary journals.

Car Talk

http://cartalk.cars.com/

★★★★

The online version of NPR's radio show provides advice and information on cars, mechanics, and repairs. The site also features *Car Talk* trivia, a puzzler, virtual postcards, online classifieds, and *Car Talk* hate mail.

Central Notice

http://www.notice.com/

★★★★

Central Notice posts listings of product recalls, class action lawsuits, and missing children. It also offers help and answers to consumer problems, tips on finding a lawyer, and more.

CIA World Factbook

http://www.odci.gov/cia/publications/factbook/

★★★★★

 All

The CIA World Factbook provides ethnographic, scientific, political, and geographic information about the world's countries and regions.

The Consumer Information Center

http://www.pueblo.gsa.gov/

★★★★★

Federal consumer publications are available at this site. Choose from eight categories or view those most recently featured by the media. Full-text versions are available online and can be viewed at no charge. You also can purchase printed copies. The site also offers a search option to make retrieving information easier.

A B C D E F G H I J K L M N O P Q R S T U V W X Y Z

A
B
C
D
E
F
G
H
I
J
K
L
M
N
O
P
Q
R
S
T
U
V
W
X
Y
Z

The Cook's Thesaurus

http://www.switcheroo.com/

★★★★

Search this database for more information about ingredients and cooking tools. You'll find definitions, uses, pictures, and common substitute information for each category.

The DataStar Information Retrieval Service

http://ds.datastarweb.com/ds/products/datastar/ds.htm

★★★

This service of Knight-Ridder Information provides a searchable index to hundreds of databases including information such as automotive industry data; import/export trade statistics; pharmaceutical, biomedical, and healthcare information; and European news organizations.

Dismal Scientist

http://www.dismal.com/

★★★★

If you're looking for global economic news and analysis, this is the site to visit. Here, you'll find tools, analyses, and message boards to share your thoughts and opinions with others.

eHow

http://www.ehow.com/

★★★★

 14-18

Interesting search tool that helps you track down instructions on how to perform more than 15,000 tasks. Covers everything from checking the oil in your car to delivering puppies.

Encarta Online

http://encarta.msn.com/

★★★★★

 All

Microsoft's Encarta Concise Free Encyclopedia is available at this site. The encyclopedia is available in several languages and includes more than 55,000 articles. Lesson plans featuring Encarta content and other teaching resources are also provided. For a monthly fee, you can access articles from encyclopedias, magazines, reference books, and many other sources.

FedWorld.gov

http://www.fedworld.gov/

★★★★

👥 14-18

This site provides a list of links to various United States federal offices and administrations to make it easier for citizens to find the information they need.

FinAid: The Financial Aid Information Page

http://www.finaid.org/

★★★★★

👥 14-18

A clearinghouse of information on college funding. Learn about loans, scholarships, grants and fellowships, and prepaid tuition plans. You also can calculate future college costs and estimate financial aid awards.

The Flag of the United States of America

http://www.usflag.org/toc.html

★★★★

👥 All

Provides flag etiquette, a history of the U.S. flag, text of the Declaration of Independence, and words to the National Anthem and the Pledge of Allegiance to the flag (in English, German, and Spanish). Information about obtaining a flag that was flown over the U.S. Capitol and links to other flag-related sites, poetry, songs, and more.

General Research Resources

http://www.uwc.edu/library/subject.htm

★★★★

👥 14-18

This University of Wisconsin online library of resources is organized by subject, including everything from Anthropology to Zoology. Provides links to additional university databases and search tools as well.

Geographic Nameserver

http://geonames.usgs.gov/pls/gnis/web_query.gnis_web_query_form

★★★

This index is searchable by ZIP code or city name. Results returned include city, county, state, country, and ZIP code; latitude, longitude, population, and elevation are returned if available. If more than one city matches the search criteria, information on all matching cities is returned.

How Stuff Works

http://www.howstuffworks.com/

★★★★★

👥 All

Learn how everyday machines and contraptions work. This site provides in-depth explanations, illustrations, and answers to frequently asked questions. Nicely designed site that's easy to navigate and provides excellent (and interesting) information.

infoplease.com

http://www.infoplease.com/

★★★★★

Comprehensive, searchable research library provides convenient access to various almanacs, a dictionary, an encyclopedia, and an atlas. Research history and geography and look up information on any country in the world. Also features biographies, weather reports and information, business and entertainment news, and more.

InfoSpace.com

http://infospace.com

★★★★★

An information portal that gives you access to several information resources, from White and Yellow Page listings to maps and directions, city guides, weather, and many shopping options, all in one spot.

The Internet 800 Directory

http://inter800.com/

★★★★

Searchable by keyword and state. Returns businesses matching the search criteria and their corresponding 800 telephone numbers, up to a maximum of 100 businesses.

Internet FAQ Archives

http://www.faqs.org/faqs/

★★★★★

Thousands of websites feature FAQs (frequently asked questions lists) designed to help new visitors get up to speed in a hurry with the design or content of the site. The Internet FAQ Archives is a searchable/browsable directory of these FAQs.

iTools.com

http://www.itools.com/

★★★★★

Using fill-in-the-blank forms, you can search through dictionaries and thesauri; find acronyms or quotations; translate words between English and French and English and Japanese; find maps, area codes, and 800 numbers; look up currency exchange rates and stock quotes; and even track packages through the United States Postal Service, UPS, and FedEx.

Listology

http://www.listology.com/

★★★

Before renting your next movie, buying a book to read, or picking up the newest CD, check the personal lists of best and worst compiled by Listology members. It's a sort of review site combined with message boards to give you a good sense of what you're getting yourself into before you plunk down your hard-earned cash for some entertainment.

A
B
C
D
E
F
G
H
I
J
K
L
M
N
O
P
Q
R
S
T
U
V
W
X
Y
Z

Martindale's: The Reference Desk

http://www.martindalecenter.com/

★★★★★

The Martindale Center features a rich directory of reference resources including a language center, science center, computer and Internet center, conversion tables, translators, world maps, constitutions, historical links, and just about anything else you might need to complete a research project. This site points you to some of the best educational resources that the Web has to offer. It's not fancy, but if you need information and don't know where to find it, Jim Martindale's links can point the way.

MegaConverter

http://www.megaconverter.com/

★★★★★

A collection of calculators and converters of measures, weights, and units is available at this site. For instance, users can convert miles to kilometers, gallons to liters, and years to seconds. Ancient measuring systems also can be converted.

ModemHelp

http://www.modemhelp.com/

★★★★

Installation instructions, upgrade information, and links to various modem resources. You'll also find a great tutorial on how to set up and install a home or small-office network.

Morse Code and the Phonetic Alphabets

http://www.soton.ac.uk/~scp93ch/morse/

★★★★

Contains the phonetic alphabets in British English, American English, international English, international aviation English, Italian, and German—and the Morse code equivalent for all letters plus some punctuation marks.

National Address and ZIP+4 Browser

http://www.semaphorecorp.com/cgi/form.html

★★★★

Searchable by company name, street address, city, state, and ZIP code. Returns closest matches along with ZIP+4 code. After information is returned, you are given the option to browse addresses in the same geographical location. Also includes list of state code abbreviations.

National Geographic Map Machine

http://www.nationalgeographic.com/resources/ngo/maps/

★★★

 All

The *National Geographic* Map Machine features an animated political map of the world. It also includes an online atlas featuring other political maps, physical maps, individual country maps, flags of the world, and country profiles.

The Nobel Foundation

http://www.nobel.se/

★★★★★

 14-18

In addition to offering a list of present winners, this official site presents a searchable database for past winners, games for teenagers, simulations, and more. Also offers a bio of Alfred Nobel and discusses his motivations for founding the prizes, in addition to explaining how Nobel Laureates are nominated and selected.

Old Farmer's Almanac

http://www.almanac.com/

★★★★★

The Old Farmer's Almanac is North America's oldest continuously published periodical, providing information on weather and soil conditions since 1792. The online version offers weather forecasts, agricultural reports, and other seasonal features.

Period.Com Airlines

http://www.period.com/airlines/

★★★

Airline toll-free 800 phone numbers and links to airline websites. Click on any letter, A–Z, to get started. Search for airfares, car rental information, hotels, and rail passes as well.

PhoNETic

http://www.phonetic.com/

★★★

Enter a phone number to receive all possible letter combinations for that phone number or enter letters to receive the phone number corresponding to those letters. Also includes information about obtaining phonetic telephone numbers and an explanation for why calculator and telephone keypads are different.

Best refdesk.com

http://www.refdesk.com/

★★★★★

This site bills itself as a "one-stop reference for all things Internet." Although it is mainly a collection of links, it maintains a thorough and comprehensive database of references on a vast array of subjects. This site is one of my favorites, especially because I am a writer and it provides quick reference to everything from grammar usage to the Library of Congress. Reported to be used by many professional people as well as just about everyone else, including government officials. If you need to do some quick and accurate research, I highly recommend this site as being your first stop.

Reference Tools

http://www.washington.edu/tools/

★★★★★

All

This extensive collection of links to a variety of reference materials from libraries to encyclopedias includes categories for particular grades, including Grads, Undergraduates, and Visitors & K12.

RxList: The Internet Drug Index

http://www.rxlist.com/

★★★★★

Users can search this site for prescription drugs by brand or generic name. There is also a Top 200 list and information on side effects, toxicity, and other concerns related to the use of specific drugs.

Smithsonian Institution Research Information System

http://www.siris.si.edu/

★★★★★

SIRIS searches the research catalogs of the Smithsonian Institution that include the institution's libraries, art collections, archives, manuscripts, and specialized research bibliographies. This is a huge resource.

Standard Industrial Classifications (SIC) Index

http://www.wave.net/upg/immigration/sic_index.html

★★★

Browse this list of the latest available edition of the SIC index, arranged alphabetically by subject.

SuperPages.com

http://www.superpages.com/

★★★★

Find the names and locations of businesses using this search engine, which accepts the business name, category, city, and/or state. Search also can be narrowed by using the ZIP code, area code, street name, or map location. Search returns the name, address, and telephone number of businesses matching search criteria. Option is available for seeing business locations on a map.

A B C D E F G H I J K L M N O P Q R S T U V W X Y Z

A
B
C
D
E
F
G
H
I
J
K
L
M
N
O
P
Q
R
S
T
U
V
W
X
Y
Z

Switchboard

http://www.switchboard.com/

★★★★★

Search for either businesses or people. For people searches, enter the last name, first name, city, and/or state to receive the name, address, and phone number of all people matching the search criteria. For business searches, enter the company name, city, and/or state to return the name, address, and phone number of all businesses matching the search criteria. Registered users might also personalize and update their own listings. This is another highly recommended site for researchers and those persons interested in finding quick information about companies and businesses.

THOR: The Virtual Reference Desk

http://thorplus.lib.purdue.edu/

★★★★★

This information-rich site at the Purdue University Library provides references to many web resources, including government documents, information technology, dictionaries and language references, phone books and area codes, maps and travel information, science data, time and date information, and ZIP and postal codes.

United States Postal Service

http://www.usps.com/

★★★★★

Includes information about stamp releases, pictures of stamps available, a searchable index for ZIP+4 codes, state and address abbreviations, preferred addressing methods, size standards for mail, postage rates for both domestic and international mail delivery, history of the USPS, news releases, a calendar of events, and other postal-related information. The business section of this website includes information addressing the mailing needs of businesses and the purchasing needs of the USPS.

U.S. Census Bureau

http://www.census.gov/

★★★★★

The U.S. Census Bureau provides population figures, economic indicators, and demographic information at this site. The site features an internal search engine to allow users to find census data more easily.

UTLink: Resources by Subject

http://www.library.utoronto.ca/

★★★

The University of Toronto Library maintains this site, which offers lists of resources, at U of T and beyond, in academic fields ranging from aboriginal educational resources to zoology.

Virtual Reference Desk

http://www.vrd.org/

★★★★

Developed primarily for K–12 educators, the Virtual Reference Desk is an Internet-based question-and-answer service that connects users with subject matter experts who respond to questions personally. What makes this type of site unusual is that an actual person answers a question so you don't need to rely on the results posted by a computer database.

Vital Records Information: United States

http://vitalrec.com/

★★★★★

This page contains information about where to obtain vital records from each state, territory, and county of the United States. You can also search public records (birth, death, marriage certificates, divorce decrees, and so on) for just about any citizen of the United States. To obtain records, you must pay up front for the search.

VoiceOfThePeople.com

http://www.globalseeker.com/voxpop/

★★★★

 All

This site gives you a voice in government. Here, you can cast your vote on any of several hot issues and find contact information for various leaders at the White House.

Wikipedia

http://en.wikipedia.org/

★★★★★

Wikipedia is a free, comprehensive online encyclopedia that students young and old will find indispensable. Wikipedia features more than 200,000 articles in the English version alone, and continues to grow as volunteers contribute additional information. Here you can search for specific articles, browse by topic, and contribute to the encyclopedia with your own unique knowledge and expertise. Because volunteers contribute articles, some content is open for debate, but you can find many insightful articles that include facts you can find nowhere else.

World Population

http://www.census.gov/main/www/popclock.html

★★★★

This site offers an estimate of the current world population at the time you access it.

Worldtime

http://www.worldtime.com/

★★★

Worldtime features an interactive world atlas, information on local times (including sunrise and sunset times in several hundred cities), and a database of worldwide public holidays.

The WWW Virtual Library

http://vlib.org/Overview.html

★★★★★

This web-based library offers hundreds of subjects in science, mathematics, art, literature, music, culture, museums, religion, spirituality, sports, finance, and transportation.

A
B
C
D
E
F
G
H
I
J
K
L
M
N
O
P
Q
R
S
T
U
V
W
X
Y
Z

RELIGION AND PHILOSOPHY

Academic Info: Philosophy

http://www.academicinfo.net/phil.html

★★★★

An extensive directory of sites on the study of philosophy. Includes sections on specific philosophical topics and general reference sources.

Academic Info: Religion

http://www.academicinfo.net/religindex.html

★★★★

This site contains an extensive directory of websites devoted to world religions. Especially useful for the academic study of comparative religions.

Adherents—Religion Statistics and Geography

http://www.adherents.com/

★★★★★

This site offers insight into the growing collection of church memberships and religion inherent statistics. It provides more than 41,000 statistics for more than 4,200 faith groups from all major and most minor religions. Very statistical.

BBC World Service—Religions of the World

http://www.bbc.co.uk/worldservice/people/features/world_religions/

★★★★★

👥 All

Learn more about the major religions of the world at this site, which brings together information about Islam, Hinduism, Christianity, Buddhism, Judaism, and Sikhism.

beliefnet

http://beliefnet.com/

★★★★★

👥 14-18

Non-sectarian religious site devoted to keeping believers and non-believers informed about their beliefs. Covers everything from atheism and Christianity to earth-based (pagan) religions. Additional sections explore the link between religions and marriage, sexuality, politics, and more. Take online quizzes, check out the message boards, or join a meditation or prayer group online.

Family Christian Stores

http://www.familychristian.com/

$

★★★

👥 All

Huge online shopping store stocked with a complete line of Christian products. Carries everything from Bibles to T-shirts.

Gays for God

http://www.rslevinson.com/gaylesissues/gfg/blgfg.htm

★★★

A resource list for gays and lesbians seeking religious fellowship, this site is home to a great list of links to supportive congregations and organizations from all religious faiths and traditions.

Heroes of Faith

http://www.myhero.com/faith/faith_content.asp

★★★★★

This site, which promotes no specific religion, features founders of the world's great religions along with individuals whose words and deeds qualify them to be considered heroes of faith.

religion-online.org

http://www.religion-online.org/

★★★★

This site features the full text of more than 5,200 articles and chapters of books composed by some of the most recognized religious scholars in the world. The texts cover a wide range of topics, including the Old and New Testament, Theology, Ethics, History and Sociology of Religion, Communication and Cultural Studies, Pastoral Care, Counseling, Homiletics, Worship, Missions, and Religious Education.

Religion and Philosophy Websites

http://www.chowan.edu/acadp/Religion/websites.htm

★★★★

Links to many religion and philosophy websites compiled by Chowan College.

ANCIENT

Best | Antiquity Online

http://fsmitha.com/h1/

★★★★★

Search this site or scan the major subcategories for information about ancient history, philosophy, and religions, with an emphasis on historical significance and events of the times. The site has many documents and other information tracing the religious philosophy from ancient times to later years. The site is easy to navigate and has maps, images, and testimonials about the information provided here. You can read how religious ideas more than likely developed in "cave-dweller" days of ancient persons and how they evolved over time. Although not one of the "flashier" sites, it provides an intriguing look at the historical aspects of religion.

The Egyptian Book of the Dead

http://www.touregypt.net/bkofdead.htm

★★★

Learn all about the ancient Egyptians' view on death and the afterlife. The Book of the Dead is here in its full-translated glory, everything from "Hymn to Osiris" to "Making the Transformation to the Crocodile God."

ATHEISM

American Atheists

http://www.atheists.org/

★★★★

Information about atheism, separation of church and state, legal battles, school prayer, and Biblical contradictions. Features an online store and a magazine.

Atheism Central for Secondary Schools

http://www.eclipse.co.uk/thoughts/

★★★★

This excellent introduction to atheism explains the basis for most atheists' beliefs in the non-existence of God (or of a god who intervenes in our lives).

Atheist Alliance

http://www.atheistalliance.org/

★★★★

Reach out to other atheists through this site, which aims to educate the public about the dangers of authoritarian religions through articles, books, links to other websites, and reference material.

The Secular Web

http://www.infidels.org/

★★★★★

A page of interest to atheists, agnostics, humanists, and freethinkers. Links to a variety of Internet resources, including Usenet newsgroups, IRC channels, and other web pages. The library contains several documents, historical and otherwise.

A B C D E F G H I J K L M N O P Q R S T U V W X Y Z

A
B
C
D
E
F
G
H
I
J
K
L
M
N
O
P
Q
S
T
U
V
W
X
Y
Z

BUDDHISM

Access to Insight
http://www.accesstoinsight.org/

★★★

👥 14-18

Focuses on supporting and deepening Buddhist meditation practice. Emphasizes teachings from the Theravada Buddhist tradition, but represents other Buddhist traditions as well.

Buddhanet.net
http://buddhanet.net/

★★★★★

👥 14-18

This site, affiliated with a nonprofit organization, has a huge amount of information about the teachings of Buddha, links, chat, books about Buddhism, articles, and much more. You're likely to find everything you wanted to know about Buddhism here.

International Meditation Centres
http://www.webcom.com/~imcuk/welcome.html

★★★

Offers information on 10-day Vipassana meditation courses as well as a newsletter, Theravada Buddhist publications, and images of pagodas.

New Kadampa Tradition
http://www.kadampa.net/

★★★★

This Mahayana Buddhist organization aims to preserve and promote the essence of Buddha's teachings in a form suited to the Western mind and way of life. This site offers information on books, meditation programs, and a directory of NKT centers.

An Overview of Buddhism
http://www.religioustolerance.org/buddhism.htm

★★★

👥 14-18

This short article provides an overview of the Buddhist religion, the four main teachings of Buddha, and the way Buddhists view themselves and the world. Interesting information without being overwhelming.

Resources for the Study of Buddhism
http://online.sfsu.edu/~rone/Buddhism/Buddhism.htm

★★★★★

Learn about basic Buddhist teachings through links and web references offered at this site, which contains helpful sites for children and adults.

tharpa.com
http://www.tharpa.com/

💲

★★★★

Online bookstore for some of the best books on Buddhism and meditation. The site also features weekly snippets of wisdom, informative articles, and 500 glossary terms with definitions.

CHRISTIANITY

About.com–Christianity
http://christianity.about.com/

★★★

This site culls the latest news and information about Christianity, centralizing it on this one site. Information is organized by subtopic, making it easy to track down what you're looking for. You'll also see headline news and chat and discussion opportunities linked to each.

American Baptist Churches USA Mission Center Online
http://www.abc-usa.org/

★★★★

Contains information about local American Baptist churches and American Baptist Green Lakes Conferences, as well as national, international, and educational ministries.

Answers in Action

http://answers.org/

★★★

Seeks to train Christians to "adopt and promote a Christian world view in every area of their lives." Features book reviews, information on contemporary issues, the Bible, Christian apologetics, and cults.

Augustine

http://ccat.sas.upenn.edu/jod/augustine.html

★★★★★

Contains translations and texts of Augustine, one of Christianity's most gifted and disciplined thinkers. Also includes other research materials and reference aids, and papers from an online seminar and images.

Baker Book House

http://www.bakerbooks.com/

★★★

Baker Book House publishes approximately 200 Christian books a year in the categories of fiction, nonfiction, children's books, academic textbooks, and references. It also sells BakerBytes reference software. Published authors include Ruth Bell Graham and Robert Schuller, among others. Read excerpts from the latest publications online.

The Best Christian Links

http://www.tbcl.com/

★★★★★

Comprehensive directory of the best Christian sites on the Web divided into categories including Art & Culture, Churches, Fellowship & Fun, and Spiritual Growth.

Bible Gateway

http://bible.gospelcom.net/

★★★★

👥 14-18

This award-winning site provides a search form for the Bible and handles many common translations. Lets you conduct searches and output verses in French, German, Swedish, Tagalog, Latin, or English. Also features audio versions of the Bible and its many passages, both old and new testaments.

Catholic Online

http://www.catholic.org/

★★★★

👥 14-18

Bills itself as the "world's largest and most comprehensive Roman Catholic information service." Provides message centers, forums, and research materials related to Roman Catholicism. You'll also find information about Catholic organizations, dioceses and archdioceses, publications, software, and doctrines.

Related Site
http://www.catholic.org/shopping/

Center for Paleo-Orthodoxy

http://capo.org/

★★★★

This consortium of scholars, think-tanks, and publications is committed to shedding ancient (hence "Paleo") light on modern issues. Links to the award-winning e-journal, *Premise.* Also links to various institutes (Calvin, Kuyper, Van Til) and PCA mail.

Center for Reformed Theology and Apologetics (CRTA)

http://www.reformed.org/

★★★★

A nonprofit organization committed to the dispersal of online resources for the edification of believers of a Calvinist leaning. Links to articles on apologetics, the Bible, reformed books and commentaries, Calvinism/soteriology, Christianity and science, and so on. Searchable.

Christian Articles Archive

http://www.joyfulheart.com/

★★★★★

Contains articles for Christian newsletters, religious periodicals, brochures, and sermon illustrations. Also provides information about using Internet email conferencing for Christian teaching and discipleship.

A B C D E F G H I J K L M N O P Q R S T U V W X Y Z

A
B
C
D
E
F
G
H
I
J
K
L
M
N
O
P
Q
R
S
T
U
V
W
X
Y
Z

Christian Interactive Network

http://www.cin.com/

★★★★

A huge web resource for Christians. Contains links to information on various ministries, missions, publishing, family issues, radio/TV, education, sports, business, shopping, and more. Enables you to enter your business into the directory at no charge.

The Christian Missions

http://www.sim.org/

$

★★★★

This site offers the Great Commission Search Engine, which enables you to search for Christian missions all over the world.

Christianbook.com

http://www.christianbook.com/

$

★★★★

All

Huge online bookstore specializing in books and other publications dealing with Christianity and related topics. Sells CDs, videos, and Christian gifts as well.

Christianity Online

http://www.christianitytoday.com/

★★★★★

All

Christianity Online is a Christian service featuring news about current events and politics, interviews with Christian musicians, and links to other Christian magazines. Visitors also can search a database of thousands of Christian websites.

Creation Science

http://emporium.turnpike.net/C/cs/

★★★

14-18

A site that provides arguments for creationism and against evolutionism. It poses questions to evolutionists and contains a list of recommended books on the subject of creation and a list of creationist bulletin boards.

Creationism Connection

http://members.aol.com/dwr51055/Creation.html

★★★

14-18

A wealth of information for creationists, this page provides synopses of creationist books, lists other creationist sites and newsgroups, and maintains a list of creationist organizations sorted by state.

crosswalk.com

http://www.crosswalk.com/

$

★★★★★

All

Crosswalk offers Christians access to a directory of more than 20,000 Christian sites, news, information, Bible study tools, chat and discussion forums, a Bible search directory, and much more. But there's also a community to join and entertainment to be had here through the learning and sharing that takes place.

D.M. Lloyd-Jones Recording Trust

http://www.mlj.org.uk/

$

★★★

Designed to promote, restore, and distribute works by the famous English minister. The Trust has a collection of his sermons on tape. Material by other prominent teachers is available.

The ECOLE Initiative

http://www2.evansville.edu/ecoleweb/

★★★

The Early Church Online Encyclopedia (ECOLE) Initiative is a cooperative effort on the part of scholars across the Internet to establish a hypertext encyclopedia of early Church history (to the Reformation) on the Web.

Evolution Versus Creation Science

http://www.religioustolerance.org/evolutio.htm

★★★

 14-18

Explains the differences between the various theories of creationism and evolution. Examines what the Bible has to say about creation, how creation scientists believe the Earth was formed, and how evolutionists might interpret the Bible.

Fire and Ice: Puritan and Reformed Writings

http://www.puritansermons.com/

★★★★

In this case, the site name is highly suggestive of the contents. Contains many works of various Puritan writers, from John Owen to Cotton Mather. Also contains history and biography, poetry, new and recommended works, and a quote of the week.

First Church of Cyberspace

http://www.godweb.org/

★★★

In an effort to bring together an online Christian congregation, this site offers sermons, scripture studies, a multimedia Bible, and movie reviews.

The Five Points of Calvinism

http://www.gty.org/~phil/dabney/5points.htm

★★★★

R.L. Dabney discusses Calvinism without making use of the well-known acrostic. He discusses original sin, effectual calling, God's election, particular redemption, and perseverance of the saints. Footnotes follow.

Glide Memorial Church

http://www.glide.org

★★★★

 14-18

San Francisco's "church without walls" has a long history of serving the downtrodden outcasts of our society from the hippies and Black Panthers in the sixties, Vietnam protestors in the seventies, AIDS victims in the eighties, crack addicts in the nineties, and all people suffering from socio-economic problems into the twenty-first century. Here, you can learn more about Glide and how you can help.

Gospelcom.net

http://www.gospelcom.net/

★★★★★

One of the best all-around Christian websites in this section, Gospelcom.net features a verse of the day, a daily devotional, mission news, ministry features, articles on how to become closer to God, and suggestions for youth ministry. Very solid site that's easy to navigate and serves the needs of the modern Christian.

GraceCathedral.org

http://www.GraceCathedral.org

$

★★★★

Visit San Francisco's Grace Cathedral Episcopal Church online, listen to services via its Webcast, check out the media center, read interviews with spiritual leaders, and even take a virtual tour of the church without stepping foot in San Francisco.

Greater Grace World Outreach

http://www.ggwo.org/

$

★★★★

An international ministry with links to associated ministries such as *The Grace Hour International Radio Show*, missionary outreaches, and the Maryland Bible College and Seminary. This site also contains daily faith thoughts and information about upcoming conferences.

A B C D E F G H I J K L M N O P Q **R** S T U V W X Y Z

A
B
C
D
E
F
G
H
I
J
K
L
M
N
O
P
Q
R
S
T
U
V
W
X
Y
Z

Greek Orthodox Archdiocese of America

http://www.goarch.org/en/resources/

★★★★★

Provides information about Orthodox Christianity, the Greek Orthodox Archdiocese, the online chapel, Orthodox Christian resources, Orthodox Christian organizations, the Ministry Outreach Program, and more.

Harvest Online

http://www.harvest.org/

★★★★

Provides the history of the Harvest Christian Fellowship. Includes dates for upcoming Harvest Crusades, along with information about *A New Beginning with Greg Laurie* broadcasts.

ICMC

http://www.icmc.org/

★★★

👥 14-18

The International Christian Media Commission's vision is to proclaim the Good News through all types of existing media. This site provides an electronic magazine that members can use to browse directories. Maintains a list of links to resources for Christians.

Jesus Army

http://www.jesus.org.uk/

★★★★★

👥 14-18

What is the Jesus Revolution? Find out on this award-winning British-based site. Contains an electronic magazine and many pictures.

Jesus Fellowship

http://jf.org/

★★★★

 All

A family church, a Christian teaching center, a covenant community, a worldwide outreach center, a campus ministry, a neighborhood Bible fellowship, and much more. Links to Miami Christian University, where you can earn theological degrees online.

Jesus Film Project

http://www.jesusfilm.org/

★★★★

 All

Presents the Campus Crusade for Christ's Jesus Film project. Includes well-designed graphics pages. Offers links to other Campus Crusade for Christ sites in the United States and abroad.

Leadership U

http://www.leaderu.com/menus/truth.html

★★★★

👥 14-18

An interdisciplinary, non-specialized journal for the academic community (students, professors, scholars) with a distinctly Christian perspective. Seeks to provide a critical analysis of crucial contemporary intellectual issues. The issues discussed are scientific, philosophical, literary, historical, or theological in nature.

Logos Research Systems

http://www.logos.com/

★★★★

An electronic publishing firm that offers CD-ROMs of biblical translations, ranging from the King James to the Revised Standard Version. Also includes many other titles.

Monastery of Christ in the Desert

http://www.christdesert.org/pax.html

★★★★★

Benedictine monks share their monastery via a beautiful website. Read up on their lives, listen to their chants, research their monastic studies, and even shop at the online gift store for books, prints, and other items.

Orthodox Christian Page

http://www.ocf.org/OrthodoxPage/

★★★★

What is Greek Orthodox Christianity all about? This site tells you and provides links to European and American Orthodox sites. You'll find pages covering scriptures and liturgy, icons, prayers, readings, and links to other resources.

Our Daily Bread

http://www.gospelcom.net/rbc/odb/

★★★

Presents a short, daily devotional guide for Christians. Includes an archive page for access to previous months' devotions.

Presbyterian Church USA

http://www.pcusa.org/

★★★★

Contains news from the Presbyterian News Service, reports and proceedings of the General Assembly, mission news, religious humor, and the PresbyNet conferencing system. There also are links to other Presbyterian-related sites, such as the web pages of local churches.

Project Wittenberg

http://www.iclnet.org/pub/resources/text/
wittenberg/wittenberg-home.html

★★★★

This award-winning site provides the thoughts of Martin Luther online. Plans to accumulate all of Luther's work, along with that of other theologians.

The Quiet Place: Reformed Baptist WWW Resources

http://www.iserv.net/~mrbill/Quiet.html

★★★

This site is a veritable cornucopia of resources for the Reformed Baptist web-head. Here, you can find home pages of Baptist churches across the country. You also can fellowship with other Reformed Baptists.

Religion News Service

http://www.religionnews.com/

★★★★

The Religion News Service provides a daily newsletter featuring unbiased coverage of religion, ethics, and Christian spiritual issues from a secular viewpoint.

Religious Society of Friends WWW site

http://www.quaker.org/

★★★★

 All

Offers a list of links about Quakers on the Web. Includes links to sites focusing on Quaker schools, journals, The American Friends Service Committee, genealogy sites, Quaker history, newsgroups, and more.

Scrolls from the Dead Sea

http://www.ibiblio.org/expo/deadsea.scrolls.
exhibit/intro.html

★★★★

This exhibit from the Library of Congress (reorganized by Jeff Barry) is a great scholastic site, containing the published text of the Quamran scrolls, commonly known as the Dead Sea Scrolls. Bible scholars have studied these works extensively. The site offers a link to the Expo Bookstore, where you can purchase a printed copy of the exhibition catalog.

A
B
C
D
E
F
G
H
I
J
K
L
M
N
O
P
Q
R
S
T
U
V
W
X
Y
Z

A
B
C
D
E
F
G
H
I
J
K
L
M
N
O
P
Q
R
S
T
U
V
W
X
Y
Z

SDAnet
http://www.sdanet.org/

★★★

👥 14-18

This is the site for the Seventh Day Adventist (SDA) WWW server. Links to Gopher sites, SDA institutions, and Bible study forums can be found here.

The Spurgeon Archive
http://www.spurgeon.org/

★★★★

👥 14-18

This award-winning site is a collection of resources by and about Charles H. Spurgeon, the English preacher and theologian. Contains information on his personal library, the full text of his sermons, his writings, and excerpts from *The Sword and the Trowel* and *The Treasury of David*.

Talk.Origins Archive
http://www.talkorigins.org/origins/faqs.html

★★★

👥 14-18

A large collection of FAQs generated by the Usenet newsgroup talk.origins. The site maintains FAQs on creationism, evolution, flood geology, catastrophism, and more. The collection is basically an argument for evolutionism.

Vatican
http://www.vatican.va

★★★★★

👥 14-18

Online home of the Roman Catholic Church, this site takes you on a virtual tour of the Vatican, where you can access the latest news, perform research in the Vatican library and secret archives, tour the Vatican museums, read about past popes, and much more.

White Mountain Education
http://www.wmea-world.org/

★★★

Provides articles, lectures, the online publication *Meditation Monthly International*, esoteric astrology, and psychology.

World Religions Index
http://wri.leaderu.com/osites.html

★★★★

👥 14-18

This site provides you with an insight into the many religions and religious organizations of the world and offers to answer many interesting questions that you may have—for example, "Do all religions point to the same truth and do all religions lead to God?"

CULTS

AFF Cultic Studies
http://www.csj.org/

💲

★★★

🚫 Not for kids

Studies psychological manipulation and cultic groups and aims to assist those who have been victims of such groups. Books and periodicals such as *Cultic Studies Journal*, *Cult Observer*, and *Young People & Cults* are available for order online.

Cults "R" Us
http://www.mayhem.net/Crime/cults1.html

★★★★

🚫 Not for kids

This "hit list" from the pages of the Internet Crime Archives gives general information about a number of cult figures whose cultish practices included murder, human sacrifice, and suicide.

F.A.C.T.Net
http://www.factnet.org/

★★★★★

🚫 Not for kids

Read news reports and suggestions of mind control and cult activity at this site, which aims to protect the freedom of the mind. Learn about psychological coercion, cult groups, and mind control here.

Ms. Guidance on Strange Cults

http://www.t0.or.at/msguide/devilgd1.htm

★★★★★

⚏ Not for kids

A plethora of links to all sorts of cult subjects. Several cult categories are addressed, including generic magic, paganism, freemasons, Gnostics, and many more.

DEISM

Aldeism

http://www.aldeism.com/

★★★

Learn about Aldeism, a manifestation of deism based on the following three principles: Altruism, Deism, and Reason.

French Deism

http://www.utm.edu/research/iep/d/deismfre.htm

★★★

Read up on the famous French Deists Voltaire and Rousseau and the Encyclopedists. See how their views differ and how they contributed to defining and developing the philosophy of deism.

The Human Jesus and Christian Deism

http://www.onr.com/user/bejo/

★★★

If "Christian Deism" sounds like a contradiction to you, visit this site to learn how John Lindell, creator of the site, merges the two religions.

United Deist Church

http://www.deism.org/

★★★★

Learn what Thomas Jefferson thought about traditional religions, including Christianity, and the theology of deism. Read the basic tenets of deism and research its history.

World Union of Deists

http://www.deism.com/

★★★★

Excellent introduction to deism, the belief that there is a god, but that god does not directly intervene in the world through revelations or actions. Read thought-provoking essays by Thomas Paine, read a comparison of deism to Christianity and atheism, and research some of the beliefs of this humanist approach to spirituality.

HINDUISM

Bhagvat Gita

http://www.iconsoftec.com/gita/

★★★★

For students of Hinduism's most revered scripture, this site offers the Bhagvat Gita in the original Sanskrit, available in both PostScript and PDF formats. Also offers Arnold's complete English translation.

Friends of Osho

http://www.sannyas.net/

★★★★

⚏ All

Introduction to the work of Osho (Bhagwan Shri Rajneesh), popular and controversial teacher of Tantra Yoga.

Hare Krishna

http://www.webcom.com/~ara/

★★★★

Official ISKCON site, detailing the religion of Krishna Consciousness founded by A.C. Bhaktivedanta Swami Prabhupada. Identifies spirit as primary and matter as secondary.

Hindu Resources Online

http://www.hindu.org/

★★★★★

Comprehensive directory to information and resources related to Hinduism. The opening page provides an excellent definition of what it means to be Hindu.

A B C D E F G H I J K L M N O P Q R S T U V W X Y Z

A
B
C
D
E
F
G
H
I
J
K
L
M
N
O
P
Q
R
S
T
U
V
W
X
Y
Z

Hindu Universe: Hindu Resource Center

http://www.hindunet.org/

★★★★

 All

Learn about upcoming events, get the latest news about Hinduism and India, and stay connected to Hindu practices and teachings.

Hinduism Online

http://www.himalayanacademy.com/

$

★★★★

Created and maintained by the Himalayan Academy, this site provides a basic introduction to Hinduism, plus links to *Hinduism Today* magazine, Hindu books and art, the Hawaii Ashram, and other resources.

Hinduism Today

http://www.hinduismtoday.com/

★★★★

Learn all the basics of Hinduism at this informative site, which also offers books and other resources on the subject. Shopping mall provides links to stores where you can shop online for everything from books to gemstones.

Kundalini Research Foundation, Ltd.

http://www.siriuslink.com/client/krf/
foundation.html

★★★

Concerned with the Kundalini Paradigm, an offshoot of Tantra Yoga and Shaivism. Center for scholarly study of the "serpent energy" and its relationship to higher consciousness. Founded by Gopi Krishna.

ISLAM

Al-Islam

http://www.al-islam.org/

★★★★★

This site serves as a means of introducing Islam to you, and provides you with options for exploring this religion further. If you are a Muslim, this site serves as a repository for advancing your knowledge about Islam.

International Association of Sufism

http://www.ias.org/

★★★★★

Offers a look into the teachings and precepts of Sufism. Offers many pages of information, pictures, and links intended to spread Sufi teachings of the brotherhood of man. This site focuses specifically on providing accurate English translations of Sufi texts.

Islam World

http://www.islamworld.net/

★★★

If you want to learn more about Islam or about becoming a Muslim, visit this site, which is educational, inspirational, and sincere. This site voices a firm belief that Islam is the one true religion.

Islamic Studies

http://www.arches.uga.edu/~godlas/

★★★★

With the turmoil in the Middle East, more and more people are becoming interested in the Islamic faith. To learn about Islam for yourself, check out this site. Here, you can find the basic beliefs and traditions explained and explore some of the teachings of one of the world's largest religions. This site also describes the various Islamic sects, provides statistics about some of the more populous Islamic areas around the globe, and provides galleries of Islamic art and architecture.

IslamiCity in Cyberspace

http://www.islam.org/

★★★★

Includes overview of doctrine, Qur'an; news, culture, education, and political information; downloadable radio/TV broadcasts (free software download); online shopping; a chat room; a virtual Mosque tour; web links; and a matrimonial service. Heavy coverage of Middle East politics.

Muslim Life in America

http://usinfo.state.gov/products/pubs/muslimlife/

★★★★

Maintained by the U.S. Department of State, this site is dedicated to promoting a greater understanding of Muslim people in the United States and elsewhere. Features a photo gallery, electronic journals, and links to other websites and publications.

Online Islamic Bookstore

http://www.sharaaz.com

$

★★★★

Provides information about the store's books, tapes, and software. Offers links to Islamic sites and book reviews of important books. Its aim? "To encourage the Muslim community to read again. To assert the importance of spiritual knowledge especially in this modern age."

JUDAISM

Chabad-Lubavitch in Cyberspace

http://www.chabad.org

★★★★★

 All

Offers information pertaining to Chabad philosophy and Chassidic Judaism. Includes Kosher recipes and children's links, multimedia, a LISTSERV, and Gopher resources.

Conversion to Judaism

http://www.convert.org/

★★★

Anyone considering a conversion to Judaism should read the material offered on this site, which is organized in a FAQ format, making it easy to track down answers to some of the basic questions about Judaism and the process of conversion from another religion.

Jewish America

http://www.jewishamerica.org/ja/index.cfm

★★★★

Links to Jewish sites, humor, and news are available through this site, which aims to connect Jewish people to each other.

Jewish Theological Seminary

http://www.jtsa.edu/

★★★★

Represents this conservative seminary online. Provides a wealth of resources and links to conservative Jewish synagogues and institutions.

JewishFamily.com

http://jewishfamily.com/

★★★

 All

Learn how to integrate Jewish teachings and beliefs into everyday life with your children and family with the help of articles and teachings at this site. The tone is friendly and helpful.

Jews for Judaism

http://www.jewsforjudaism.org

★★★

Through education and community, this site is working to counter attempts by Christians to convert Jewish believers. It provides resources, links, and information about local groups and counseling for those who might be interested.

Judaism 101

http://www.jewfaq.org/

★★★★

This site is an online encyclopedia of Judaism, covering "Jewish beliefs, people, places, things, language, scripture, holidays, practices and customs." The purpose is simply to inform and educate Jews and non-Jews about the religion.

A B C D E F G H I J K L M N O P Q R S T U V W X Y Z

A
B
C
D
E
F
G
H
I
J
K
L
M
N
O
P
Q
R
S
T
U
V
W
X
Y
Z

Judaism and Jewish Resources

http://shamash.org/trb/judaism.html

★★★★

Quite possibly the most complete source of Jewish information and Jewish-related links on the Web. Lists of links include media, singles groups, communities, newsgroups, reading lists, and museums, as well as commerce sites.

MavenSearch

http://www.maven.co.il/

★★★★★

Searchable directory for links to all things Jewish. Type a keyword or phrase to search the directory or browse by category. Categories include Communities, Travel and Tourism, Israel, Holocaust, Shopping & Gifts, and much more.

Middot: Spiritual Study of Personal Qualities

http://www.ashrei.com/

★★★★

This is the home of a community of worshippers who study Middot, a practice that encourages followers to focus on characteristic traits that can be improved in one's life. This site also features psalms and spiritual biographies.

MyJewishLearning

http://www.myjewishlearning.com/

★★★★★

This transdenominational website is dedicated to helping visitors deepen their knowledge and understanding of all aspects of Judaism. Here you can find sections on History & Community, Daily Life & Practice, Holidays, the Jewish Lifecycle (rituals for various stages in one's life), Texts, Ideas & Beliefs, and Culture. Site also features a glossary and a discussions area.

ORT

http://www.ort.org/

★★★★★

Coined from the acronym of the Russian words *Obschestvo Remeslenovo i zemledelcheskovo Trouda*, meaning The Society for Trades and Agricultural Labour, ORT is a worldwide education and training organization. At this site, you can learn more about ORT and its programs and schools.

Project Genesis—Torah on the Information Superhighway

http://www.torah.org/

★★★★

This site provides Jewish educational material through article and reference archives, program and speaker information, and popular email classes.

Shamash

http://shamash.org/

★★★★★

This award-winning site run by the Jewish Internet Consortium offers links to various Jewish religious organizations ranging from Hillel to the World Zionist Organization. Includes FAQs pertaining to various facets of Judaism.

Shtetl: Yiddish Language and Culture

http://metalab.unc.edu/yiddish/shtetl.html

★★★

"Shtetl" means "small town" in Yiddish. This site aims to be a virtual small town on the Web. Provides information on Yiddish culture, as well as resources that point toward a wide range of links ranging from recommended books to kosher recipes.

Society Hill Synagogue of Philadelphia

http://www.societyhillsynagogue.org/

★★★

An independent, conservative, egalitarian synagogue that offers numerous programs covering all aspects of Jewish religious and cultural life. The site includes detailed descriptions, a brochure, a monthly newsletter, and some nice graphics.

Virtual Jerusalem

http://www.virtualjerusalem.com/

★★★★

Virtual Jerusalem offers updated news and information about Judaism and Israeli life, with departments for news, travel, technology, holidays, and entertainment. Bulletin boards and a Jewish email directory.

Zipple.com

http://www.zipple.com/

★★★★★

This "Jewish SuperSite" provides Jewish information, news, chat, discussions, a business directory, an events calendar, and much more. Shopping links point to stores where you can purchase products online.

PHILOSOPHY

BEARS in Moral and Political Philosophy

http://www.brown.edu/Departments/Philosophy/bears/homepage.html

★★★

Brown Electronic Article Review Service on Moral and Political Philosophy. Contains short reviews of articles and books that have appeared in the past six months. Provides information on contributors and a list of reviews.

Comic Relief for the Pathologically Philosophical

http://www.christian-thinktank.com/comic.html

★★★

Come here and unload at this site for the truly zany (or just bored). Philosopher light bulb jokes, teleology of chicken and road, weightless philosophy, causes of death, and more topics that you have never thought of before.

Dictionary of Philosophy of the Mind

http://www.artsci.wustl.edu/~philos/MindDict/

★★★★

Exhaustive glossary of philosophical terms and brief biographies of the most famous philosophers, along with explanations of what made them famous. Enables you to submit entries and error corrections. Also contains philosophy links.

Environmental Ethics

http://www.cep.unt.edu/

★★★

Provides information on environmental ethics. Focuses on environmental ethics resources. Provides book reviews and site summaries and links of interest to environmental philosophy.

EpistemeLinks.com: Philosophy Resources on the Internet

http://www.epistemelinks.com/

★★★★★

Site features thousands of sorted links to philosophy-related sites. Links are divided into categories including philosophers, philosophy texts, publications, newsgroups, and job postings. Shop for books via a link to Amazon.com. Excellent starting point for any philosophical research project.

Ethics Updates

http://ethics.sandiego.edu/

★★★

A directory of resources for both ethics instructors and their students. Provides updates on current ethics-related issues. Covers both ethical theory and applied ethics. Takes you to additional resources.

Internet Encyclopedia of Philosophy

http://www.utm.edu/research/iep/

★★★★

Search this philosophy encyclopedia by keyword or by clicking on the first letter of the topic you want to explore. Entries cover most philosophers, philosophies, and philosophical terms.

A B C D E F G H I J K L M N O P Q R S T U V W X Y Z

A
B
C
D
E
F
G
H
I
J
K
L
M
N
O
P
Q
R
S
T
U
V
W
X
Y
Z

Methodological Naturalism

http://www.id.ucsb.edu/fscf/library/plantinga/mn/home.html

★★★

At this site, Plantinga discusses "methodological naturalism," which is the idea that "science cannot involve religious belief or commitment." He tackles the issue, in part, by addressing whether science is religiously neutral.

Nietzsche Page at Stanford

http://plato.stanford.edu/entries/nietzsche/

★★★★

Excellent overview of Friedrich Nietzsche's life, publications, and ideas. Features a substantial bibliography plus links to other useful Nietzsche sites. Part of Stanford's Encyclopedia of Philosophy.

Perseus Project

http://www.perseus.tufts.edu/

★★★

This award-winning site is adapted from the Perseus disk. It includes Greek and translated texts by Aristotle, Plato, and Sophocles; art and archaeology; a Greek lexicon; and more.

The Philosophical Gourmet Report

http://www.philosophicalgourmet.com/

★★★

Contains the national rankings of graduate schools of analytic philosophy in the United States. Also includes foreign rankings. Highly detailed.

Philosophy Around the Web

http://users.ox.ac.uk/~worc0337/phil_index.html

★★★★

Striving to be a central gateway to philosophy information on the Web, users can learn the basics of philosophy, find useful links, check out sites by topic, scan educational institution and individual web pages, and much more.

Plato's Dialogues

http://plato-dialogues.org/

★★★★

Brief biography of Plato's life, including his works, plus English translations of Plato's dialogues, including *The Crito*, *The Phaedo*, *The Phaedrus*, *The Symposium*, and *The Republic*.

PSYCHE

http://psyche.cs.monash.edu.au/

★★★★

PSYCHE is an interdisciplinary journal of research and consciousness. The site provides direct access to *PSYCHE*'s archives. Also contains a FAQ associated with the journal.

Socrates

http://www.philosophypages.com/ph/socr.htm

★★★

Brief biography of Socrates' life and teachings, plus a recommended reading list to learn more about this most famous philosopher and links to other Socrates resources on the Web.

Stanford Encyclopedia of Philosophy

http://plato.stanford.edu/

★★★★★

Features an indexed dynamic encyclopedia in which each entry is maintained and kept up to date by an expert or group of experts in the field of philosophy. This is a work in progress, and many of the philosophers and concepts listed in the comprehensive index are not covered in the encyclopedia. However, the coverage that is provided is exceptional.

The Thinking Man's Minefield

http://www.theabsolute.net/minefield/index.html

★★★★

Contains all kinds of worldly insights, including philosophic works, male and female psychology, poetry, quotations, travel in India, atheist archives, and links to articles from *Life and Death Magazine*.

Theosophical Society

http://www.theosociety.org/

★★★★

The society was founded in 1875 in an effort to promote the expressed awareness of the Oneness of Life. This site links to descriptions of foundational, esoteric texts by Blavatsky and others. Acts as a guide for personal exploration of truth.

PRAYER

Bible Prayer Europe

http://www.bible-prayer-europe.com/

★★★★

 All

This site encourages Bible study and prayer throughout Europe and the world and offers Bible-based advice on how to live properly and treat other people.

Book of Common Prayer

http://justus.anglican.org/resources/bcp/

★★★

A comprehensive resource for the *Book of Common Prayer*, including sections formatted as the original.

Catholic Prayers

http://www.webdesk.com/catholic/prayers/

★★★★★

All

A treasury of Catholic prayers.

International Prayer Network

http://www.victorious.org/needpray.htm

★★★★★

All

The 24-hour International Prayer Network is one of the world's largest Christian prayer fellowships, with worldwide volunteers interceding for prayer requests from all over the globe.

Lutheran Prayer Ministries

http://web.wt.net/~wayne/halpm.html

★★★

Learn how to start a prayer ministry and find useful resources and links at this site.

National Day of Prayer

http://www.ndptf.org/

★★★★

14-18

The first Thursday in May is the National Day of Prayer. This site encourages people to pray on this day and to organize other groups to pray. Includes a recommended prayer written specifically for this day.

Presidential Prayer Team

http://www.presidentialprayerteam.org/

★★★★

Join the Presidential Prayer Team and pray with others for the President of the United States.

The Prophet's Prayer

http://www.qss.org/articles/salah/toc.html

★★★★★

This Islamic Society provides information on the Prophet's Prayer and other Islamic prayers and practices.

Sacred Space

http://www.jesuit.ie/prayer/

★★★★★

Visit this site for an invitation to pray along with a group of Irish Jesuits. Features a prayer of the day in 11 languages plus a link to a site where you can pray with the Pope.

World Ministry of Prayer

http://www.wmop.org/

$

★★★★

This site allows you to pray with a live person over the telephone or by email. It also has a prayer requests section as well as a catalog from which you can order from a large selection. Offers support through prayer.

World Prayer Network

http://www.worldprayer.org/

★★★

This site is interested in uniting the world in prayer. Offers you the opportunity to pray with thousands of others with the same concerns and problems.

A B C D E F G H I J K L M N O P Q R S T U V W X Y Z

RETIREMENT

4Retirement

http://4retirement.4anything.com/

★★★

Find all the retirement information you need in one place, on 4retirement.com! Whether you're looking for the perfect community or resort where you can spend your quiet years or are in need of a financial investor to help you make your nest egg grow, this site is a good place to begin.

401K Center for Employers

http://401kcenter.com/

★★★★

Helps employers formulate a 401K plan by providing information on the six plan functions. Features plan overviews, Q&As, and contact numbers.

401Kafe.com

http://www.mpowercafe.com/

★★★★★

Participants in 401Ks with questions or concerns about their investments will want to stay up to date regarding 401K news. Here, you'll find tips, reports, and useful information about this particular investment vehicle.

Best | AARP WebPlace

http://www.aarp.org/

★★★★★

The home page for the American Association of Retired Persons provides information on the group's membership benefits, public policy positions, and volunteer programs. It also includes fact sheets on health, money, retirement, and other topics. As soon as you retire (possibly even before you retire), become a member of AARP and start taking advantage of what it has to offer. AARP is one of the most vocal advocates of senior citizen rights in the country.

The Advisor

http://finance.americanexpress.com/finance/fshub.asp

★★★★

This instructional site, maintained by American Express, provides information on retirement savings, tax planning, and insurance buying.

American Association of Homes and Services for the Aging

http://www.aahsa.org/

★★★★

The American Association of Homes and Services for the Aging is an advocacy group composed of more than 5,600 nonprofit nursing homes, retirement communities, and other senior housing facilities. This site features a database of available senior housing.

ElderNet

http://www.eldernet.com/

★★★★★

This comprehensive web index offers links to sites for the elderly, along with descriptions of each site. Incorporates health, finance, law, retirement, and lifestyle advice for seniors. Use tutorials, find activities, search resources, and read tips.

Guide to Retirement Living

http://www.retirement-living.com/

★★★★

Comprehensive listing of living and healthcare options for retired people in the mid-Atlantic states.

InvestorGuide: Retirement

http://www.investorguide.com/Retirement.htm

★★★

Handy mix of basic explanations and web links covering 401K plans, IRAs, Social Security, retirement, and estate planning.

Railroad Retirement Board

http://www.rrb.gov/

★★★★

The Railroad Retirement Board is an independent federal agency whose job it is to "administer comprehensive retirement-survivor and unemployment-sickness benefit programs for the nation's railroad workers and their families, under the Railroad Retirement and Railroad Unemployment Insurance Acts." Here, you can learn more about the agency and tap its resources.

Retire Early

http://www.retireearlyhomepage.com/

★★★

Aided by software and spreadsheets, this magazine offers details on ways to retire early. News, articles, and a planner are listed.

Retirement Calculators

http://www.bhbt.com/pgs/calc_frame.html

★★★★

What will your expenses be after you retire? Are you saving enough to retire comfortably? What will your income be after you retire? Find answers to all of these questions and more by using Bar Harbor Bank and Trust's online retirement calculators.

Retirement Net

http://www.retirenet.com/

★★★★★

Retirement Net claims to be the "world's leading online retirement resource." This site enables you to search for retirement communities that match your interests and lifestyle. Browse through categories by lifestyle or search for a specific community.

Retirement Research Foundation

http://www.rrf.org/

★★★★

This is the nation's largest private foundation devoted to aging and retirement issues. Explore funding interests, guidelines, FAQs, and what's new.

SeniorsSearch

http://www.seniorssearch.com/

★★★★

This directory provides links to more than 5,000 sites geared toward the over-50 age group. Topics include history, health and fitness, hobbies, grandparenting, genealogy, travel, senior discounts, retirement, volunteering, and more.

Seniors-Site.com

http://www.seniors-site.com/

★★★★

Features information and bulletin boards on topics for seniors, including finance, education, death and dying, retirement, nursing homes, and nutrition.

A
B
C
D
E
F
G
H
I
J
K
L
M
N
O
P
Q
R
S
T
U
V
W
X
Y
Z

A
B
C
D
E
F
G
H
I
J
K
L
M
N
O
P
Q
R
S
T
U
V
W
X
Y
Z

Social Security Online

http://www.ssa.gov/

★★★★★

This official site includes an online earnings and benefit statement, a guide for employers, and many other resources.

Third Age

http://www.thirdage.com/

★★★★★

An e-zine aimed at those baby boomers who are starting their fifth decade. It includes articles on investing, love and relationships, health and fitness, hobbies, and technology. It also includes a chat room, discussion forums, and advice columns.

ROCK CLIMBING

About.com: Rock Climbing

http://rockclimbing.about.com/

★★★

Advice and links on mountain and rock climbing, including locations, photography, training techniques, and gear reviews.

American Mountain Guides Association

http://www.amga.com/

★★★

The AMGA's site is aimed mostly at the climbing professional, with pages about certification, but it is helpful to regular climbers with a page of referrals to certified guides.

American Safe Climbing Association

http://www.safeclimbing.org/

★★★★

Dedicated to making the sport of climbing safer, the ASCA replaces unsafe bolts and anchors at many popular climbing sites, such as Yosemite, Red Rock, and Joshua Tree, and educates climbers on safe climbing techniques. Check out this site for bolt information, fall forces, rebolting techniques, safe climbing techniques, and more. The site also provides a list of climbing routes that the ASCA has rebolted.

Archive of Rock Climbing: Moves and Tips

http://climbing.tropic.org.uk/

★★★

Extensive list of tips and techniques for rock climbers who range in experience from total newbie to world-class climber.

Big Wall Climbing Web Page

http://www.bigwalls.net/

★★★★★

👥 14-18

Diehard climbers will appreciate a home page dedicated to intense, multi-day climbs; read about different walls, as well as stories of individual climbs. Answers the big question: What about when you need to go?

Bouldering

http://www.bouldering.com/

★★★★★

👥 14-18

Read interviews with master climbers, take a look at photos from amazing vantage points, and stay in touch with the rock-climbing community through news and information here.

Climb New Hampshire

http://climbnh.com/

★★★★

👥 14-18

Provides information on places to climb in the Granite State, lists places to eat and stay, and includes a bibliography of guide books for the region.

Climber's First Aid

http://www.outdoor-resources.com/cfa.html

★★★

👥 14-18

This web page is aimed at outdoor enthusiasts—climbers, hikers, bikers—and promotes the purchase of *Climber's First Aid: What to Do While Waiting for Help.* The book is printed on tear-resistant, water-resistant stock so that it will be rugged enough to take along on your wilderness adventures.

A
B
C
D
E
F
G
H
I
J
K
L
M
N
O
P
Q
R
S
T
U
V
W
X
Y
Z

[Best] **Climbing Online**

http://www.climbing.com/

★★★★★

[14-18]

Climbing magazine's home on the web features the latest climbing news, feature stories, product reviews, and online tutorials. Learn the basics or go beyond the basics with the latest techniques. Special how-to sections on dealing with rock and dealing with ice, plus dozens of technical tips and links to other rock-climbing resources on the Web make this site the pinnacle of sites in this category.

Climbing Quotes

http://www.gdargaud.net/Humor/QuotesClimbing.html

★★★★★

Not for kids

Inspirational and not-so-inspirational climbing quotes, plus stunning photos of conquered summits from around the world.

GORP–Climbing

http://www.gorp.com/gorp/activity/climb.htm

★★★★★

Read articles organized by topic, such as gear, know-how, and location, to improve your skill level and prepare for your next climb. You'll also find information on trips you might want to consider. Lots of inspiring photos and helpful tips.

GPS Rock Climbing Guide

http://www.colororange.com/

★★★

This site, maintained by climber Jacques Rutschmann, provides geographic coordinates of rock-climbing areas (and hot springs) in the USA, Europe, and the world.

Joshua Tree Rock Climbing School

http://www.rockclimbingschool.com/

★★★★

[14-18]

Learn how to climb from some of the top climbers in the world at one of the most popular climbing sites in the world, Joshua Tree National Park, located in southern California. This site provides information on the various rock-climbing courses offered at the school, plus brief biographies of the instructors and information about accommodations.

Online Climbing Guide

http://www.onlineclimbing.com/

★★★★

[14-18]

This site, created by rock climbers for rock climbers, represents a community effort by climbers to provide a comprehensive directory of places to climb. Includes directions to favorite climb sites, photos, difficulty ratings, and more. Search for sites by state. Also features a directory of climbing gyms organized by state.

Mountain Online

http://www.mountaineers.net/mountain/

★★★

This online mountaineering and climbing magazine offers everything you would expect in a magazine, including articles, reviews, profiles, interviews, updates, contests, classifieds, and maybe even information on your kitchen sink if you look hard enough.

Nova Online: Lost on Everest

http://www.pbs.org/wgbh/nova/everest/

★★★★★

[14-18]

PBS's *Nova* followed an expedition up the world's highest mountain, and every aspect of the climb can be found on this site. The series originally followed the climbers live in real-time.

Rock & Ice: The Climber's Magazine

http://www.rockandice.com/

★★★★

 14-18

Home of *Rock & Ice* magazine, this site provides a preview of the contents of the current issue and enables you to subscribe online.

RockClimbing.com

http://www.rockclimbing.com/

★★★★

A super climbing website complete with climbing routes, gear shopping, partner connecting, discussions, photos, and information on climbing techniques to improve your skill.

RockList

http://www.rocklist.com/

★★★

 14-18

Long lists of cliffs, climbing gyms, alpine clubs, e-zines, literature, expeditions (including Everest), gear manufacturers, mountain information, and more. Search by geographical area anywhere in the world. Great site for finding places to climb.

Thedeadpoint.com

http://www.thedeadpoint.com

★★★★★

 14-18

Read about climber triumphs, take a look at the photo gallery, read articles on rock climbing and bouldering, join in discussions, and post reviews.

A
B
C
D
E
F
G
H
I
J
K
L
M
N
O
P
Q
R
S
T
U
V
W
X
Y
Z

American Junior Rodeo Association

http://home1.gte.net/ajra/

★★★★★

 All

The AJRA was begun when its founder went to rodeos and thought how unfair it was that kids were competing with adults, and so would never win, despite giving it their all. This page has a history of the AJRA, information about the coliseum the association uses, a schedule, and more.

Billy Joe Jim Bob's Rodeo Links Page

http://www.gunslinger.com/rodeo.html

★★★★★

Perhaps the most complete rodeo index on the Web. Billy Joe Jim Bob takes great care to include links for every rodeo, rodeo association, and rodeo site he could find, which ends up being a whole lotta links!

Janet's Let's Rodeo Page

http://www.cowgirls.com/dream/jan/rodeo.htm

★★★★

 14-18

Janet's page has pictures, links to other rodeo sites, a long list of articles, and countless answers to her question, "What do cowgirls dream about?"

Jeff's Rodeo Links

http://www.jeffevans.net/html/links.html

★★★

This site provides links to riders' sites, rodeos and associations, stores, and other resources.

[Best] Pro Rodeo Online

http://www.prorodeo.com/

$

★★★★★

 All

The Professional Rodeo Cowboys Association's official website, ProRodeo.com provides up-to-date information about the latest rodeo competitions across the country. Read about your favorite rodeo riders, find the tour standings and scoreboard, check out the injury reports, learn of upcoming televised events, and even flip through some action photos. For novice fans, the Sport link introduces you to the sport of rodeo, describes the various events and how they are scored, and provides an online record book and a link to the ProRodeo Hall of Fame. You can shop online at ProRodeo Merchandise, become a member, and even check out the media library. Packed with useful information in an easy-to-navigate format, this site is the hands-down winner of the Best of the Best award.

Related Site

http://www.pikes-peak.com/rodeo/

ReadTheWest.com

http://www.readthewest.com/rodeo.html

★★★

Check on the standings of your favorite rodeo cowboys and girls, find out about the schedule of upcoming events, learn about rodeo books you might want in your library, and get results from recent competitions here.

SLAM! Sports Rodeo

http://www.canoe.ca/SlamRodeo/home.html

★★★★

Interested in what happened at rodeo tournaments last night or want to know more about your favorite rodeo stars? Check Slam! Sports Rodeo for all your rodeo news needs. Slam also covers other sports.

Women's Pro Rodeo Association

http://www.wpra.com/

★★★★

The Women's Professional Rodeo Association formed in 1948 by a group of Texas ranch women who wanted to "add a little color and femininity to the rough-and-tumble sport of rodeo." At this site, you can view standings, results, a schedule of competitions, information about the division tour, and a history of rodeo.

A
B
C
D
E
F
G
H
I
J
K
L
M
N
O
P
Q
R
S
T
U
V
W
X
Y
Z

A B C D E F G H I J K L M N O P Q R S T U V W X Y Z

SCI-FI AND FANTASY

Ambit

http://www.ambitweb.com/

★★★

👥 14-18

When you can't find the TV listings for your favorite sci-fi show, check Ambit. It has a 10-day listing for all the regular broadcast and cable shows, but unfortunately lists shows in syndication with no scheduling information (says to check local listings for those). The site includes a sci-fi TV newsletter discussing what's going on and upcoming episodes. The site also has access to search engines, non–sci-fi material, and much more.

Analog Science Fiction and Fact

http://www.analogsf.com/

★★★★★

👥 14-18

The popular *Analog* magazine is online here, offering samples of its columns and stories. *Analog* places equal emphasis on the terms "science" and "fiction," in an attempt to provide a more realistic view of how science might develop in the future and be applied to improve the human condition. At this site, you can check out some columns and story excerpts from the magazine.

Asimov's Science Fiction

http://www.asimovs.com/

★★★★★

👥 14-18

Home of *Asimov's Science Fiction* magazine, which reviews the Best of the Best new science fiction publications and presents some of its own. Learn about the awards it has won, its authors, and other information about the magazine. Read some science fiction short stories from some of the best sci-fi writers in the business.

Broadsword

http://www.broadsword.org/

★★★

The web page for *Doctor Who, the New and Missing Adventures*. This e-zine includes interviews with actors, a writer's guide, articles on the missing adventures, and a list of books published about *Doctor Who*. Don't click New Adventures if you don't want to know what happens in these stories.

Caroline's Hercules Page

http://www.angelfire.com/co/greekbard/

★★★★

👥 14-18

This fan's *Hercules* site has an interesting page where she compares the TV character to the one in classical mythology. Includes games based on the show, plus upcoming episodes. Has links to other *Hercules* and *Xena* pages.

The Centre

http://www.neon-hummingbird.com/centre/

★★★★★

👥 14-18

Based on the TV show *The Pretender*, this site has episode guides, bios on the staff, and an excellent FAQ that answers most of the questions you might have if you haven't watched every episode. Lots of photos of the program and some audio files.

Dark Planet Science Fiction Webzine

http://www.sfsite.com/darkplanet/

★★★★★

👥 14-18

The official site of the *Dark Planet Science Fiction, Fantasy, and Horror Webzine*. This e-zine accepts submissions from writers and has a nice archive of stories and articles. The graphics are great, and the site is very well worth the visit if you like to read science fiction and horror stories.

Dark Shadows

http://members.aol.com/darkkshad/super/natural.htm

★★★

👥 14-18

Premiering in 1966 on ABC television, this show was a soap opera based on ghouls, goblins, vampires, and the like. There are story lines, photo galleries, fan fictions, and other points of interest for *Dark Shadows* fans at this website.

Official Site
http://www.scifi.com/drkshad/

FANDOM—Star Trek Central

http://www.cinescape.com/0/Fanspeak.asp

★★★★

👥 14-18

Star Trek fans will love this site, which provides actor interviews, Trek news, show and movie information, photos, polls, discussion forums, and products for sale.

FanGrok

http://www.roblang.demon.co.uk/fangrok/

★★★★

👥 Not for kids

A UK online e-zine that satirizes sci-fi television. The site essentially reprints an article or two from the paper magazine *FanGrok*. Some of the articles are very funny; be sure to check out the *Spice Docs* issue. And, naturally, you can get instructions on how to subscribe to *FanGrok* so you can get the complete issue.

Feminist Science Fiction, Fantasy, and Utopia

http://www.feministsf.org/femsf/index.html

★★★★

Created and maintained by Laura Quilter, this site provides information about feminist themes in science fiction literature; reviews; a checklist of feminist science fiction, fantasy, and utopian stories; a list of anthologies; links to research guides; and much more.

Global Episode Opinion Survey

http://www.geos.tv/

★★★

You hate (or love) a particular episode of your favorite sci-fi television show. Are you curious whether others agree or disagree? Then join GEOS, where you and others around the world can give opinions and rate the shows and their episodes.

Lord of the Rings Movie Site

http://www.lordoftherings.net/

★★★★★

👥 14-18

Home of one of the most popular movie series of all time, this site provides a virtual tour of the films and the legend. Check out movie trailers; learn more about the cast and crew; find late-breaking news and upcoming events; explore the well-stocked photo library; and even download free screensavers, desktop wallpaper, and other goodies.

Lurker's Guide to Babylon 5

http://www.midwinter.com/lurk/lurker.html

★★★

👥 14-18

This site provides information about the TV show *Babylon 5*. Watch out for spoilers if you haven't seen a show yet. Includes information on the making of the show, its cast and characters, images of the amazing special effects, and episode information.

A
B
C
D
E
F
G
H
I
J
K
L
M
N
O
P
Q
R
S
T
U
V
W
X
Y
Z

A
B
C
D
E
F
G
H
I
J
K
L
M
N
O
P
Q
R
S
T
U
V
W
X
Y
Z

 The Matrix Reloaded

http://whatisthematrix.warnerbros.com/

★★★★★

 14-18

Fans of *The Matrix* will want to enter this virtual tour of the movie set to experience *The Matrix* in a completely new way. Read interviews with the cast and crew, view photos from the set, take 3D tours of the deck of the *Nebuchadnezzar*, flip through the comics, and more. One of the best new science fiction movies has the best science fiction website as well. It will keep visitors of all ages busy for hours.

Mystery Science Theater 3000

http://www.mst3kinfo.com/

★★★★

Have your friends been talking about the weird TV show where they make fun of old sci-fi and horror movies from a space station? Would you like to know what they're talking about? Then come to the *MST3K* site and see what all the hype is about. The site has audio and video files, a FAQ, plus information on the stars and writers and lots of other goodies.

The Netpicker's Guide to The X-Files

http://bedlam.rutgers.edu/x-files/

★★★★★

This site points out the *netpicks* in each episode. A netpick is "a writing/research error, a technical glitch, or a continuity error that made it through post production." A very interesting site, but it covers only the first three seasons.

Poltergeist: The Legacy

http://www.scifi.com/poltergeist/

★★★★

14-18

Home of the SciFi Channel's *Poltergeist: The Legacy* TV show. The Legacy is a "secret and ancient society" that wages war against the forces of evil.

Science Fiction Book Club

http://www.sfbc.com/

$

★★★★

14-18

Save up to 65% on science fiction books by becoming a member of the Science Fiction Book Club. This book club carries top titles and the latest publications.

SciFan

http://www.scifan.com/

★★★★

14-18

SciFan offers science fiction fans plenty of reading material, from magazine subscriptions and books. Search the sci-fi author database to track down those titles you haven't read yet and then link to a bookstore to order it.

SCIFI.COM

http://www.scifi.com/

★★★★★

14-18

Lots of sci-fi adventures to choose from here. Between online programming and TV and movie reviews, you'll find plenty of unique and fascinating story lines to follow. You can also get sci-fi news, clips of animated features, and movie trailers; plus, you can connect with other sci-fi fans through chat or bulletin board postings. With so much to offer, this site is one of the top science fiction sites on the Web.

The Sci-Fi Site

http://www.sfsite.com/

★★★★

14-18

Book reviews, news, and resources. This great site has lots of book reviews, opinion pieces, author interviews, fiction excerpts, author and publisher reading lists, and a variety of other wonderful features. You'll find a comprehensive list of links to author and fan tribute sites, SF conventions, movies, TV, magazines, e-zines, writer resources, publishers, and small press sites.

Science Fiction and Fantasy Research Database

http://library.tamu.edu/cushing/sffrd/

★★★★

👥 14-18

Compiled by Hal W. Hall, this database provides online access to more than 55,000 historical and critical items about science fiction, fantasy, and horror (in that order).

Science Fiction and Fantasy World

http://www.sffworld.com/

★★★★★

👥 14-18

Featuring more than 10,000 pages of science fiction and fantasy, this is one of the largest science fiction sites on the Web. Read some of the latest short stories and poems, check out the interviews, or visit the discussion forums to share your science fiction enthusiasm with other fans. The site also provides a directory of TV and movie listings, book reviews and excerpts, e-zines, and more. You can even submit your own writings for consideration.

Science Fiction and Fantasy Writers of America (SFWA)

http://www.sfwa.org/

★★★

Sci-fi writers will find this site, and this nonprofit organization, a big help in improving their writing skills and improving the financial rewards of writing science fiction. The site provides writing tips as well as model contracts to follow, document formatting guidance, and a regular bulletin for members.

Science Fiction Resource Guide

http://www.sflovers.org/SFRG

★★★★

An extensive collection of links to sci-fi resources on the Net. Subject areas include other archives and resource guides, authors, bibliographies, movies, and more.

Science Fiction Weekly

http://www.scifi.com/sfw/

★★★★★

Weekly news, articles, features, interviews, and reviews. The site also features a games column, letters from fans, On Screen information about programs on television and in the movies, a Cool Stuff column, and a site-of-the-week feature.

SFF Net

http://www.sff.net/

★★★★

This is the science fiction and fantasy website "for people who like to read," particularly for people who like to read genre fiction, including science fiction, fantasy, horror, romance, mystery, and young adult fiction. SFF Net's goal is to bring together writers, editors, publishers, and readers in an online community that benefits them all.

Smallville Ledger

http://www2.warnerbros.com/web/smallville/ledger/home.jsp

★★★★

👥 14-18

Smallville, the latest TV series based on the Superman legend, has its own neighborhood newspaper on the Web. Check out the front-page news, the community calendar, the local classifieds, and more. You can even check out the *Smallville Torch*, the Smallville high school newspaper. Very entertaining stuff, especially for *Smallville* fans.

Space Opera

http://www.bright.net/~tomb/reviews/space.html

★★★

If you remember Tom Corbett Space Cadet or Video Ranger, this is the site for you—dedicated to the science fiction shows of the 1950s. You can find listings of articles from various magazines on these shows (sorted by decade) as well as information on the programs; special emphasis is given to Tom Corbett Space Cadet.

A
B
C
D
E
F
G
H
I
J
K
L
M
N
O
P
Q
R
S
T
U
V
W
X
Y
Z

A
B
C
D
E
F
G
H
I
J
K
L
M
N
O
P
Q
R
S
T
U
V
W
X
Y
Z

Star Trek

http://www.startrek.com/

★★★★★

Provides a good amount of information and links to many sites that cover the television, film, and cultural phenomenon that is *Star Trek*. This site includes pictures, sounds, quotes, fan information, and much more. Links to Amazon.com for online shopping.

Starship Store

http://www.uncomyngifts.com/Main/Recreation_Room/StarTrek/

★★★

Includes collectors' items, memorabilia, and clothing of every *Star Trek* series. Order T-shirts with pictures of your favorite characters, keychains, toys, and other items.

Star Wars Official Site

http://www.starwars.com/

★★★★★

Star Wars fans will want to bookmark this site, which serves up everything you need to know about the *Star Wars* series. Features movie clips, well-stocked photo galleries, interviews with the creators and cast, and much more. Material is organized by episode, making it easy to find what you want. You can even shop online for *Star Wars* apparel and collectibles.

The TV Sci-Fi and Fantasy Database

http://www.pazsaz.com/scifan.html

★★★★★

If you can't remember the name of a particular episode, or when it ran, just check with the database. It lists the name and original air date of more than 70 different shows. Note that no information about the episode is given. Comes in full graphical and less graphical versions.

The Ultimate Science Fiction Web Guide

http://www.magicdragon.com/UltimateSF/SF-Index.html

★★★★

If you're looking for websites about science fiction, you'll be in the right place at the Ultimate Science Fiction Web Guide because it features more than 6,000 links to such resources.

Virus

http://www.virusthemovie.com/

★★★★

This official site offers information on the cast and crew of this action–science fiction movie. Photos, movie trailer, and games.

SENIORS

A B C D E F G H I J K L M N O P Q R **S** T U V W X Y Z

AARP

http://www.aarp.org/

★★★★★

This very user-friendly site contributes to AARP's goal of allowing senior citizens to lead the rich and fulfilling lives that they are accustomed to—not only by staying well informed, but also by staying active.

Administration on Aging (AOA)

http://www.aoa.dhhs.gov/

★★★★★

AOA is a federal agency serving as an advocate for older Americans and issues that concern them. The site provides a lot of background information on the Older Americans Act, as well as practical information for senior citizens and their caregivers—a resource directory, list of local agencies providing senior services, news, and health information.

Age of Reason Recommended Senior Living Facilities

http://www.wiredseniors.com/ageofreason/

★★★★

Complete information, including online experts about living and vacationing in several senior-friendly facilities.

Best AgeNet

http://agenet.agenet.com/

★★★★★

Seniors and their family members will find information at this site both interesting and useful. Topics covered include health, insurance, finance, drugs, and caregiver support. You can use the Social Security estimator, for example, to estimate the value of benefits you should receive at retirement or try out some brain exercises to improve your mental faculties. This site's comprehensive collection of resources for seniors combined with a very inviting presentation makes this our choice as the Best of the Best senior sites on the Web.

The Aging Research Centre (ARC)

http://www.arclab.org/

★★★

Researchers and laypersons alike can find usable information on aging from the University of Toronto Centre for Studies of Aging. The site includes links to additional university resources.

Alliance for Retired Americans

http://www.retiredamericans.org/

★★★★

The Alliance is a new national organization for retired citizens of the United States. Created by the AFL-CIO, the Alliance works to promote legislation that "protects the health and economic security of seniors, rewards work, strengthens families and builds thriving communities." Think of it as a union for retired workers, a way for retired workers to fight for their rights and have their voices heard.

A
B
C
D
E
F
G
H
I
J
K
L
M
N
O
P
Q
R
S
T
U
V
W
X
Y
Z

Alzheimer's Association

http://www.alz.org/

★★★★★

This national nonprofit organization provides support to those afflicted with Alzheimer's as well as their caregivers. AA funds Alzheimer's research, which is documented at the site, and offers support and resources to help families cope with this illness.

Alzheimer's Disease Education & Referral Center

http://www.alzheimers.org

★★★★

This site has a wealth of information for anyone interested in assessing his or her risk of being afflicted with the disease, researching treatments, as well as learning to cope with caring for someone with the disease.

American Association of Homes and Services for the Aging

http://www.aahsa.org

★★★★★

Visit this site for a listing of member facilities. Includes assisted living, nursing homes, and retirement communities.

Assisted Living Described

http://www.alfa.org/

$

★★★★★

Detailed description from the Assisted Living Federation of America (ALFA). This organization represents more than 6,000 for-profit and not-for-profit providers of assisted living, continuing care retirement communities, independent living, and other forms of housing and services. Founded in 1990 to advance the assisted living industry and enhance the quality of life for the approximately one million consumers it serves, ALFA broadened its membership in 1999 to embrace the full range of housing and care providers who share ALFA's consumer-focused philosophy of care. The site includes an online bookstore from which you can order ALFA's books and other related items.

Assisted Living Online

http://www.assistedlivingonline.com/

★★★

Continuously growing national listing of assisted-living facilities that includes a description of each facility. Links to senior-related resources, tips on selecting a facility, and more.

Burma Shave Signs

http://seniors-site.com/funstuff/burma.html

★★★

This is a senior site because if you remember Burma Shave signs, you are a senior citizen. Refresh your memory or share with your grandchildren. If you can remember a sign that isn't listed here, submit it to the site to share with others.

Caregiver Network Inc.

http://www.caregiver.on.ca/

★★★★

The Canadian woman who maintains this site became a caregiver overnight. She is very aware of what resources you need to take care of someone you care about. Most links are in the United States, and many will refer you to services in your own area.

Choosing an Assisted Living Facility

http://www.aahsa.org/public/al.htm

★★★★

What assisted living is, how to choose, what the costs are, and what the standards are—information provided by the American Association of Homes and Services for the Aging.

Elderhostel

http://www.elderhostel.org/

★★★★★

With the fundamental belief that no one should ever stop learning, this site provides access to resources around the world to continue your education (for adults age 55 and over). Currently, you must register through postal mail, but all of the registration information is at the site.

Friendly4Seniors Websites

http://www.friendly4seniors.com/

★★★★★

This site simply offers links to sites that are of interest to seniors. Choose your topic—Government, Financial, Housing, Medical, and many more—click and find what you're looking for. More than 2,000 senior-related listings that are reviewed and approved before being added to the list.

Grand Times

http://www.grandtimes.com/

★★★

An e-zine dedicated to the needs of active retirees. Sample topics include travel; useful products; beating the casino; high-tech bird feeders; and relief from arthritis, back pain, and migraines.

HomeStore.com Senior Living

http://www.springstreet.com/seniors/

⑨

★★★★★

This site has gathered a wide range of lifestyle options so family members and seniors can easily sort through retirement communities, assisted living, nursing homes, and home healthcare. Search through more than 55,000 listings!

HUD for Senior Citizens

http://www.hud.gov/groups/seniors.cfm

★★★★★

The United States Department of Housing and Urban Development has created this section specifically to inform senior citizens of their housing options and help them find suitable places to live. Information to help seniors stay in their current homes, find apartments to rent, find retirement or nursing homes, locate organizations to stay active, and much more. Features related information on senior jobs, links to other resources on the Web, and links to other government agencies that address the needs of seniors.

Life Extension Foundation

http://www.lef.org/

★★★★★

Anyone looking to slow the aging process will want to visit this site for research and medical news regarding life extension and aging. You can also purchase products and learn about membership in LEF.

LivOn

http://www.livon.com/

★★★★

Look for senior housing, care, and services in the United States and abroad. More than 60,000 listings are available.

Maple Knoll Village—Pioneer in the Alzheimer's Experience

http://www.mapleknoll.org/

★★★★

Web home of Maple Knoll Village Retirement Home, one of the top 20 retirement communities in the nation. Here, you can learn more about Maple Knoll and what it has to offer. Explore the history of the home or request more information online. Maple Knoll Village Retirement Home is located just outside Cincinnati, Ohio.

The National Senior Citizens Law Center

http://www.nsclc.org

★★★★

The National Senior Citizens Law Center advocates, litigates, and publishes on low-income elderly and disability issues including Medicare, Medicaid, SSI, nursing homes, age discrimination, and pensions.

New LifeStyles

http://www.newlifestyles.com/

★★★★

New LifeStyles Online, a complete guide to senior housing and care options, lists all state-licensed senior housing facilities in the major metropolitan areas nationwide.

A B C D E F G H I J K L M N O P Q R **S** T U V W X Y Z

A
B
C
D
E
F
G
H
I
J
K
L
M
N
O
P
Q
R
S
T
U
V
W
X
Y
Z

Nursing Home and Long Term Care Topics

http://www.geocities.com/HotSprings/2021/

★★★

This site covers a variety of subjects for those working in long-term care from the perspective of a nursing home administrator. Recommended reading for seniors and families.

Nursing Home Information Site

http://members.tripod.com/~volfangary/

★★★

This site is dedicated to providing information about nursing homes and tips for selecting a home that's right for you.

Senior.com

http://www.senior.com/

★★★★★

There's lots of interest to seniors on this site, including a chat room and message center devoted to the senior citizen community. You'll find articles of interest and links to other pages. Be sure to read the Solutions column and definitely check the Personals.

Senior Center

http://www.seniorcenter.com/

★★★★★

Excellent collection of information for seniors organized by categories, including News, Living, Health, Money, Travel, Services, and Weather.

The Senior Citizens League

http://www.tscl.org/

★★★

Senior citizens advocacy group that works to ensure that senior citizens have a voice in government. The Senior Citizens League lobbies for legislation that protects the rights of senior citizens. Site features information on Social Security and finances as well as coverage of health topics.

The Senior Citizens' Website

http://www.intecon.com/senior/

★★★★

This website for active seniors features sections on Crisis & Grief, Education, Financial, Recreation, Government, Health, and more. Complete directory of organizations and places of interest for seniors organized by state.

Senior Cyborgs

http://online96.com/seniors/

★★★★★

Extensive listing of online resources for adults age 50 and older. Includes information about health, medicine, legal issues, housing, retirement, and finance.

The Senior Information Network

http://www.senior-inet.com/

★★★★

This site has everything you need to know about being a senior. The Senior-inet (Senior Information Network) site is the premier high-tech source in obtaining information about Senior Support Services across the United States. The body of the community web pages is designed to provide you with a list of those people and agencies that can provide services for seniors in each community. The website has a lot of information about seniors for seniors.

Senior Sites

http://www.seniorsites.com/

★★★★★

This site lists more than 5,000 nonprofit housing and services for senior citizens in the United States, Guam, and Puerto Rico. Also includes national and state resources.

SeniorJournal.com

http://www.seniorjournal.com/

★★★★

This news and information kiosk for seniors covers everything from health to politics. Check here for information on healthcare for seniors, legislation, Social Security and Medicaid information, and much more.

SeniorNet

http://www.seniornet.org/

★★★★★

SeniorNet's mission is to "provide older adults education for and access to computer technology to enhance their lives and enable them to share their knowledge and wisdom." The site supports this effort through online programs, discussions, news, and special offers available only on the Internet.

seniorresource.com

http://www.seniorresource.com/

★★★★★

A resource for seniors considering all their housing options, with information about alternatives and links to supporting services, such as financing, mortgages, and retirement communities.

The Seniors Page–FirstGov for Seniors

http://www.seniors.gov/

★★★★★

Senior citizens are not only the fastest-growing segment of the population but also the fastest-growing user base on the Internet. This site gives seniors information on everything from the specifics of Alzheimer's to tips for preparing income taxes. You'll also find dozens of links of interest to seniors.

SeniorsSearch.com

http://www.seniorssearch.com/

★★★★★

A comprehensive search engine developed specifically for the over-50 crowd. Find merchants, information sources, and services organized by category. You'll also find senior media, such as senior radio, that provide programming information.

Seniors-Site

http://seniors-site.com/

★★★

If you're already acquainted with Yahoo!, this site will look very familiar to you. The many links here keep senior citizens in mind, though, from travel information to fraud, scams, and abuses.

Social Security Online

http://www.ssa.gov/

★★★★★

Official website of the Social Security Administration. Includes announcements and reports on issues related to Social Security, contact information, and regular updates.

Third Age

http://www.thirdage.com/

★★★★★

This site is a must-visit for baby boomers. It provides information, insights, interactive guides, and assessments on finances, beauty and health, personal growth, spirituality, relationships, and much more. Members can join in the lively online chats and post and peruse personal ads.

Transitions, Inc. Elder Care Consulting

http://www.asktransitions.com/

★★★★★

Transitions locates and arranges services for older adults and their caregivers. Company representatives assess needs, hold seminars, and provide eldercare counseling.

Wired Seniors

http://www.wiredseniors.com

★★★★

This is a directory of businesses and services that are geared to the senior or that offer special senior citizen discounts. You'll find hundreds of links to businesses you'll want to know about.

A
B
C
D
E
F
G
H
I
J
K
L
M
N
O
P
Q
R
S
T
U
V
W
X
Y
Z

SEWING

Cranston Village

http://www.cranstonvillage.com/

★★★★★

Home of the oldest fabric printing company in the United States, this site features suggestions for crafts and quilts, plus a history of the Cranston Print Works Company.

The Fabric Club

http://www.fabricclub.com/store/

★★★★

Order a wide variety of fabrics from this site, which advertises wholesale prices. Search by type of fabric or use, such as home decorating or quilting, and order as many or as few yards as you need.

Fabrics.net

http://www.fabrics.net

★★★★★

An information resource for sewers in search of particular fabrics, as well as individuals and vendors who have fabrics to sell. You can learn all about various types of fabrics and then look for sources in the database or shop online.

Fashion Fabrics Club

http://www.sewingfabrics.com

★★★★★

Looking for unique, high-quality fabrics for your next sewing project? Then visit the Fashion Fabrics Club and check out its selection.

Fashion Supplies

http://www.umei.com/

★★★★

Fashion accessories, supplies, buckles, buttons, trims, chains, lace, fittings, zipper pulls, and more.

Fiskars

http://www.fiskars.com/

★★★★★

You'll find plenty of information about the many types of Fiskars brand scissors at this site, which also has many project ideas and tips. You'll also find links to related sites, such as crafts, special rebates or deals, and news about Fiskars.

[Best] Home Sewing Association

http://www.sewing.org/

★★★★★

 All

Dedicated to "Get People Sewing," this site encourages visitors to take up a needle and thread and start stitching their own clothes. This site is packed with tutorials covering sewing techniques for both novice and intermediate stitchers, plus plenty of sewing projects, tips, and advice for sewers of all ages. Excellent place for both children and adults to learn how to start sewing. With its appeal to such a wide audience and its comprehensive sewing information and instructions, we couldn't help but name this site Best of the Best in the Sewing category.

Jo-Ann etc.
http://www.joann.com/

★★★★★

 All

If you're looking for a sewing project, come to the Jo-Ann etc. site for free craft, sewing, home decorating, and quilting projects to choose from. After you've selected a project, you can search the Jo-Ann catalog for the supplies you need. There's also a discussion forum to connect you with fellow sewers who might have the advice you need.

Lily Abello's Sewing Links
http://www.lilyabello.com

★★★★

For sewing links and books, or button crafts, visit Lily's simple but abundant site.

Nancy's Notions
http://www.nancysnotions.com/

★★★★★

A catalog of sewing, serging, and quilting notions. Also the home of *Sewing with Nancy* (the longest-running sewing show on PBS) and Nancy's Video Library, your rental source for sewing and other creative arts ideas.

Patternshowcase.com
http://www.patternshowcase.com/

★★★★★

Huge collection of sewing patterns listed by manufacturer, style, or size. Shop online for your patterns and have them delivered to your door.

Sew News
http://www.sewnews.com

★★★★

Read articles from this sewing magazine, share information and ideas with others through the discussion forums, and link to other sewing sites through this one.

Sewing.com
http://www.sewing.com/

★★★★★

Find sewing instruction from other sewing community members as well as links to sites providing lessons. You'll also find book reviews, articles, and discussions. Comprehensive sewing dictionary, too.

The Sewing Place
http://thesewingplace.com/

★★★

Resource for the sewing hobbyist. Great place to shop for patterns, stencils, trim, and other sewing accessories.

A Sewing Web
http://www.sewweb.com/

★★★★

Provides quality industrial sewing supplies to professional sewers all over the world, including industrial sewing thread, sewing machine presser feet, sewing accessories, and more.

Threads Magazine
http://www.taunton.com/threads/index.asp

★★★★★

Threads is the creative forum where people who sew and love to work with fabrics and fibers share their knowledge. The Feature Library offers links for Sewing Basics, Garment Construction, Fabric, Fitting, and more. Packed with step-by-step instructions, tips from the experts, and online videos that show you how it's done.

Wild Ginger Software
http://www.wildginger.com/

★★★★

Home of Wild Ginger Software, a company that develops sewing software for customizing patterns. You can download a free demo at this site.

A
B
C
D
E
F
G
H
I
J
K
L
M
N
O
P
Q
R
S
T
U
V
W
X
Y
Z

MACHINES

Baby Lock

http://www.babylock.com/

★★★★

Learn more about Baby Lock brand machines, find projects you can complete with your Baby Lock, and locate local dealers and events.

Bernina USA

http://www.berninausa.com/

★★★★★

Official corporate site for Bernina sewing machines. Product information, dealer listing, new products, and more.

Creative Feet

http://www.creativefeet.com/

($)

★★★★★

Founder of the company, Clare Rowley-Greene, invented Creative Feet in order to enable visually impaired individuals to sew using a standard sewing machine. Since creating the first presser feet designs, Clare has widened her focus to create presser feet that simplify the sewing of specialized stitches. The site offers information about the presser feet designs, as well as other sewing products, such as books and videos.

Elna USA

http://www.elnausa.com/

★★★★

Developers of sewing machines, sergers, embroidery machines, presses, and sewing accessories. Product information, dealer locations, and more.

Husqvarna Viking

http://www.husqvarnaviking.com/

($)

★★★★

Learn more about Husqvarna, its products, and dealers, as well as educational retreats and free projects available at the site.

Pfaff Sewing Machines

http://www.pfaff.com/

★★★★★

Official corporate site for Pfaff sewing machines.

Sewing Equipment Warehouse

http://www.a1sew.com/

★★★

Worldwide access to new and used industrial sewing machines, equipment, and parts. Also provides a list of home use machines for sewing, serging, and knitting.

Sewing Machine Outlet

http://www.sewingmachineoutlet.com/

★★★★★

Source for new and used sewing machines, needles, sewing machine parts, and more.

Singer Machines

http://www.singersew.com/

★★★★★

Wide variety of Singer-brand sewing machines, prices, product information, and more.

PATTERNS

Butterick Home Catalog

http://www.butterick.com

★★★★★

Preview the Butterick Home Catalog or subscribe from this site.

Free Patterns Online

http://sewing.about.com/hobbies/sewing/msubfree.htm

★★★★★

Visit this Mining Company site to find a number of free patterns available for downloading.

Kwik Sew

http://www.kwiksew.com/

★★★

An index of all the books that Kwik Sew has published for special sewing details and learning.

McCall's Pattern Catalog

http://www.mccall.com/

★★★★

Order your own copy of McCall's catalog and receive free patterns.

Sewingpatterns.com

http://www.sewingpatterns.com/

★★★★★

Huge collection of sewing patterns from several of the most popular companies, including McCall's, Simplicity, Kwik Sew, and Wallies.

Simplicity

http://www.simplicity.com/

★★★★★

Flip through the latest Simplicity pattern book for ideas for this season's fashions and get sewing help online here.

A
B
C
D
E
F
G
H
I
J
K
L
M
N
O
P
Q
R
S
T
U
V
W
X
Y
Z

A
B
C
D
E
F
G
H
I
J
K
L
M
N
O
P
Q
R
S
T
U
V
W
X
Y
Z

Adult Sexuality Web

http://www.minou.com/adultsexuality/

★★★

 Not for kids

This website features articles about several of the most common concepts and issues related to adult sexuality in order to improve sexual relationships.

Albert Ellis Institute

http://www.rebt.org/

⑤

★★★★

Not for kids

The Albert Ellis Institute provides an excellent international referral list of mental health professionals trained in Rational Emotive Behavior Therapy (REBT). REBT is an extremely effective short-term, results-orientated, cognitive behavioral approach to relationship and sexuality issues, anxiety, depression, anger, and life-change issues. This site features a comprehensive free catalog of workshops and seminars, books, audio and video programs, and other self-help materials.

AltSex

http://www.altsex.org/

★★★★★

Not for kids

A website dedicated to sharing and exploring information related to sexuality and sexual issues, such as homosexuality, sexual conduct, and transgender issues.

The American Association of Sex Educators, Counselors, and Therapists (AASECT)

http://www.aasect.org

★★★★

Not for kids

AASECT's website features a therapist locator as well as a list of FAQs about human sexuality, links to other sites, and information about how to become a certified sex educator, counselor, or therapist.

American Board of Sexology

http://www.sexologist.org

★★★★

Not for kids

Searchable database of certified sex therapists, as well as information about the history of sexology and research in the field.

Coalition for Positive Sexuality

http://www.positive.org/Home/

★★★★

Not for kids

Subtitled "sex ed for your head," this site is an honest affirmation of safe sex between consenting individuals, primarily teenagers.

Dr. Ruth Online!

http://www.ivillage.com/relationships/experts/drruth

★★★★★

Not for kids

Ask Dr. Ruth Westheimer a question that's been bugging you, or read her responses to others who've written in for sex guidance. There are daily tips, too.

Gay and Lesbian Politics

http://www.indiana.edu/~glbtpol/

★★★

Not for kids

Annotated guide to the resources on politics, law, and public policy. Designed for students, scholars, journalists, activists, and citizens.

Gender and Sexuality

http://eserver.org/gender/

★★★★★

Not for kids

This page publishes texts that address gender studies and homosexuality studies, with a particular focus on discussions of sex, gender, sexual identity, and sexuality in cultural practices.

Go Ask Alice!: Sexuality

http://www.goaskalice.columbia.edu/Cat6.html

★★★★

Not for kids

Read frequently asked questions about male and female anatomy and sexual response at this site.

Gottman Institute

http://www.gottman.com

$

★★★★★

Not for kids

The Gottman Institute offers weekend and week-long workshops to help couples remain satisfied and fulfilled in their long-term monogamous relationships. The website includes quizzes and tips on relationships and an online store where you can shop for books, audiocassettes, videos, and other helpful products.

Guide to Love and Sex

http://www.loveandsex.com/

★★★★★

Not for kids

Tips on love, sex, romance, dating, and birth control. Offers free stuff such as product samples and electronic post cards.

HisandHerhealth.com

http://www.hisandherhealth.com/

★★★★

Not for kids

Read current research findings regarding male and female reproductive health and sexuality, as well as joining in chat, asking the doctor for guidance, and scanning articles and news.

HealthySex.com

http://www.healthysex.com

$

★★★★

Not for kids

At this site, Wendy Maltz, MSW, offers information and articles about healthy sexuality, sexual fantasies, mid-life sexuality, sex abuse, and more. You can also order books and tapes online.

Helen Fisher

http://helenfisher.com

Not for kids

This website discusses Dr. Fisher's findings on love, sex, and evolution.

HowToHaveGoodSex.com

http://www.howtohavegoodsex.com

$

★★★★

Not for kids

Founded by Alex Robboy, LCSW, HowToHaveGoodSex.com features sex education and tips, a glossary of common terms, questions and answers, plus information about workshops and an online store where you can order videos and toys.

Impotence Specialists

http://www.impotencespecialists.com

★★★★

Not for kids

Find an impotence specialist online, read through FAQs about impotence and potential treatments, or post a question for a doctor on the bulletin board and check back for an answer.

A B C D E F G H I J K L M N O P Q R **S** T U V W X Y Z

A
B
C
D
E
F
G
H
I
J
K
L
M
N
O
P
Q
R
S
T
U
V
W
X
Y
Z

intimategifts.com

http://www.intimategifts.com/

★★★★★

 Not for kids

Order sex toys, books, lubricants, videos, and other accessories and gifts for loving couples here.

National Institute on Aging Page–Sexuality in Later Life

http://www.nia.nih.gov/health/agepages/sexuality.htm

★★★

 Not for kids

This site contains lots of information about the sexuality of the aging person and how you can enjoy a normal sexual relationship in your later years. Most older persons want and are able to enjoy an active, satisfying sex life, and you can find information on this site to help you reach and maintain that goal.

Nerve.com

http://www.nerve.com

★★★★★

 Not for kids

Online magazine that celebrates the beauty and absurdity of sex through thought-provoking and very funny articles on various topics relating to human relationships and sexuality. View photographs, read personal essays, check out Nerve's fiction and poetry, check out the personals, get advice, or visit the message boards to view questions and opinions from other fans of Nerve.

Network for Women's Sexual Health

http://www.newshe.com

★★★★★

Not for kids

This is the official website of Drs. Jennifer and Laura Berman, experts in female sexual dysfunction and other areas of human sexuality that specifically affect women.

Oxygen's Relationships and Sex

http://www.oxygen.com/

★★★★

 Not for kids

Articles on all topics of sexuality, plus chat, message boards, quizzes, polls, and contests.

Parents and Loved Ones of Sexual Abuse and Rape Victims

http://www.geocities.com/HotSprings/2656/

★★★

 Not for kids

This site provides support and information for parents, partners, families, and friends of those who have been sexually abused or raped. Users can find helpful articles, read others' stories, locate books, and get answers on how to deal with various aspects.

Pat Love & Associates

http://www.patlove.com

★★★★★

 Not for kids

This is the home page of Dr. Pat Love, author of *Hot Monogamy*. At this site, you can learn more about Dr. Love and her approach, research current studies on relationships and sexuality, take relationship quizzes, and find out more about available seminars and workshops.

⌜Best⌟ Sexual Health infoCenter

http://www.sexhealth.org/

★★★★★

 Not for kids

Online reading room and multimedia center for everything related to human sexuality. Guides on how to have better sex, sex and aging, STDs, safe sex, sexual dysfunction, and birth control. Discussion forums make it easy to obtain answers to your most pressing and personal questions. Links to intimategifts.com for online shopping. With its extensive coverage of nearly every topic relating to human sexuality, this site is well deserving as one of our Best of the Best sites.

SexualHealth.com

http://www.sexualhealth.com/

★★★★

🚹 Not for kids

You'll find lots of questions regarding sex, as well as answers from professionals, to help you understand your own issues and options. You can post your own questions, get recommended reading, and scan articles on sex topics.

Sexuality.org

http://www.sexuality.org/

★★★★

🚹 Not for kids

You'll find articles and material designed to educate and inform visitors regarding sexuality issues. This site offers technique tips, book reviews, and event information.

Sexuality Database

http://www.sexualitydata.com

$

★★★★★

🚹 Not for kids

Search the online sexuality database to get more information about topics you're interested in or concerned about. This site also features FAQs and the opportunity to ask a question of a doctor. Created and maintained by the Sinclair Intimacy Institute.

Sexuality Forum

http://www.askisadora.com/

★★★★

🚹 Not for kids

Check the article archive for sexuality subjects you're interested in and, if you don't find what you're looking for, post a question to the public forum. You can also buy products that have been carefully selected by Isadora, the site's host.

Sexuality Information and Education Council of the U.S.

http://www.siecus.org/

★★★★★

🚹 14-18

SIECUS is a national, nonprofit organization which affirms that sexuality is a natural and healthy part of living. Provides information for parents and teens in an easy-to-understand format that's designed to educate visitors about sexuality and safe sex practices.

SexWithoutPain.com

http://www.sexwithoutpain.com

★★★★★

🚹 Not for kids

This site takes a multidisciplinary approach to the causes and treatments of pain associated with sexual intercourse.

Society for the Scientific Study of Sexuality (SSSS)

http://www.ssc.wisc.edu/ssss/

★★★

🚹 Not for kids

The SSSS is an international organization dedicated to the advancement of knowledge about sexuality. It is the oldest organization of professionals interested in the study of sexuality in the United States.

Woman Spirit

http://www.Womanspirit.net

$

★★★★

🚹 Not for kids

Dr. Gina Ogden, author of *Women Who Love Sex: An Inquiry into the Expanding Spirit of Women's Erotic Experience* provides information on female sexuality and spirituality. Here, you also can join a reader's forum to exchange ideas with others, find a calendar of events and information about books and articles, access resources for counseling, and check out links to other websites.

A B C D E F G H I J K L M N O P Q R S T U V W X Y Z

SHOPPING

ActivePlaza

http://www.activeplaza.com/

★★★★★

ActivePlaza provides a "unique combination of online shopping mall, product catalog, and comparison shopping." At this site, you can search for products carried by the top online merchants to help you find the best deals.

All-Internet Shopping Directory

http://www.all-internet.com/

★★★★

This site provides a directory of the top stores on the Web. Simply click the category of the desired product and follow the trail of links to the desired store.

Amazon.com

http://www.amazon.com/

★★★★★

This well-known online bookstore offers just about every title under the sun, as well as videos, music, software, electronics, gardening equipment, toys, kitchen paraphernalia, and more. The Amazon auction site provides a wide variety of items available from Amazon members.

BargainDog

http://www.bargaindog.com/

★★★★

Bargain Dog hunts down the best bargains on the Internet and sends you an email notice, so you'll never miss a deal you can't pass up.

Buy.com

http://www.buy.com/

★★★★★

Buy videos, music, software, books, games, computers, electronics, and travel services at a discount from this site. Pick a category and search the database to find the product you're looking for.

CatalogLink

http://www.cataloglink.com/

★★★★

Select the catalogs you want to receive from the categories at this site to help you with your home shopping. You'll also find several links to the companies' home pages for online shopping.

Half.com

http://half.ebay.com/

★★★★★

Buy used items at 50% off or more from individuals who have them available. At this site, unlike an auction, you're guaranteed to get the product if it's advertised. Books, music, movies, and games are available.

Home Shopping Network

http://www.hsn.com/

★★★★★

If you traded in your TV for a computer, you can still shop at the Home Shopping Network by visiting this site online. Shop by category, search for specific items, or browse through the most popular, featured products.

iQVC

http://www.qvc.com/

★★★★★

The granddaddy of home shopping networks. You can buy clothing, jewelry, electronics, home décor items, office supplies, fitness equipment, and more at this site.

Lycos Shopping Network

http://shop.lycos.com/

★★★★★

A good point of entry, this site includes an impressive list of shopping categories as well as special features such as Aardvark, the online shopping experience with gifts for pets and the people who love them, and Andy's garage, gift ideas for men. Find the department store you're looking for from here.

msn Shopping

http://eshop.msn.com/

★★★★★

The Microsoft Network features its own online shopping site, where you can find deals on just about any product, including computers and electronics, apparel, furniture, books, jewelry, and automotive equipment, just to name a few.

[Best] Netmarket.com

http://www.netmarket.com/

★★★★★

Search this database of hundreds of thousands of items to find what you're looking for. Daily special deals offer great prices, and you can sign up for a personal shopper to take care of your shopping for you. The site's goal is to save you time by bringing together tons of merchandise. And, because it achieves both goals and does so in style, we award it our Best of the Best designation.

Outlets Online

http://www.outletsonline.com/

★★★★

Provides nationwide information on outlet and factory store shopping. Includes Virtual Outlets, which allow you to order merchandise or request catalogs from online outlet stores. An online magazine and Q&A from other readers let you get in touch with fellow shoppers.

CLOTHING

BabyStyle

http://www.babystyle.com/

★★★★★

This website features clothing and accessories for expectant mothers and their babies. This store also carries books, toys, bedding, and other items for babies and kids.

Bloomingdale's

http://www.bloomingdales.com/

★★★★

Includes online shopping, shopping by catalog, and shopping by personal shopper. The events page tells about upcoming sales and seasonal happenings in its various stores. Get design and style tips from the home design experts page.

Coldwater Creek

http://www.coldwatercreek.com/

★★★★

Coldwater Creek specializes in casual clothing, accessories, and gifts that reflect the wide-open nature of the Rocky Mountains and the echoes of Native America.

A B C D E F G H I J K L M N O P Q R S T U V W X Y Z

A
B
C
D
E
F
G
H
I
J
K
L
M
N
O
P
Q
R
S
T
U
V
W
X
Y
Z

DELiAs.com

http://www.delias.com

★★★★

Request a catalog or shop online referring to catalog pages or a clothing item. You can also hang out in the lounge and chat, look at pictures, and enter contests. Popular with high school girls.

Designer Outlet.com

http://www.designeroutlet.com/

★★★★★

Every two weeks new designer fashions are made available at this site, which aims to bring designer samples and overstocks to the world. Search by category, look at photos of items for sale, or sign up for a personal shopper to keep her eyes open for that perfect item.

Eddie Bauer

http://www.eddiebauer.com/

★★★★

Search the site to check out Eddie Bauer's latest casual wear for men and women, request a catalog, or see what's on sale this week.

Fashionmall.com

http://www.fashionmall.com/

★★★★★

Shop by brand, category, or style for fashions from a wide variety of merchants online. You can also enter drawings for free merchandise, check out recommended purchases, and tune in for chats with designers and celebrities.

HerRoom.com

http://www.herroom.com/

★★★★★

No matter what kind of undergarment you prefer, underwire bras, thongs, or half-slips, this is the site you'll want to check out. Search for products by brand, style, or size.

L.L.Bean

http://www.llbean.com/

★★★★★

Search L.L. Bean's selection of apparel and sporting gear online.

Land's End

http://www.landsend.com/cd/frontdoor/

★★★★★

Land's End, owned by Sears Roebuck and Company, offers decorations, kids' stuff, pet gifts, home accessories, and more. A good-quality mail order merchandiser with a nicely designed website.

Lane Bryant

http://www.lbcatalog.com/

★★★★★

For women who wear sizes 14W and up, Lane Bryant is one of the more popular stores to shop. Here, you can access the Lane Bryant catalog and place your order online.

Neiman Marcus

www.neimanmarcus.com

★★★★★

Neiman Marcus is *the* store for fashion apparel, shoes, handbags, jewelry, and accessories. The site features a personal shopper who can provide fashion advice via chat or email. Check out the latest trends in fashion and order right online.

COMPARISON BOTS

BizRate

http://www.bizrate.com/

★★★★★

Comparison-shopping service that helps you find the best prices from online merchants who carry the products you want. Features customer ratings, too, to help you find online stores that offer reliable customer service.

mySimon

http://www.mysimon.com

★★★★★

Search for products by keyword or brand and then let MySimon provide you with a list of online merchants who carry it and their quoted price.

NexTag

http://www.nextag.com

★★★★★

Unlike other comparison shopping sites, this site lets you negotiate with sellers after collecting total quoted prices from several. Sellers are online merchants and individuals.

Pricegrabber.com

http://www.pricegrabber.com/

★★★★★

Find the stuff you want for the best price on the Web. Search for specific products or browse through several categories. Pricegrabber finds the store that offers the item for the best price. Enter your ZIP code to add shipping and handling charges.

PriceScan

http://www.pricescan.com/

★★★★

Click on a category and specify the particular product you're looking for, and PriceScan will provide a list of all online merchants who have it, organized by total cost, which includes shipping and handling fees.

Productopia

http://www.productopia.com

★★★★★

Read user reviews and join in product discussions before searching the site for a purchase. You'll also find recommended gifts to get you started.

RoboShopper.com

http://www.roboshopper.com

★★★★

Pick a category, pick a product, and RoboShopper will present you with the merchants carrying that product and the associated price. You can then jump from site to site, comparing total product cost information.

Shopping.com

http://www.shopping.com/

★★★★

Choose a product, and Shopping.com will search for the best prices among many online merchants and auctions. If you're not ready to buy right away, Shopping.com will keep you posted on specials and new options.

DISCOUNT STORES

Costco

http://www.costco.com

★★★★★

Learn all about Costco and its member benefits, locate a Costco near you, purchase a membership, and shop securely with Costco Online. Also find out what's new at the club and sign up to be notified of special offers by email.

A B C D E F G H I J K L M N O P Q R **S** T U V W X Y Z

A
B
C
D
E
F
G
H
I
J
K
L
M
N
O
P
Q
R
S
T
U
V
W
X
Y
Z

Overstock.com

http://www.overstock.com

★★★★★

Search for brand-name bargains at this site, which offers just about everything—from computers to home décor to clothing—at a discount. Overstocked merchants mean great deals for consumers. But beware—the selection is limited.

Sam's Club

http://www.samsclub.com/eclub/main_home.jsp

★★★★★

Learn all about Sam's Club and member benefits, locate a Sam's Club near you, purchase a membership, and shop securely with Sam's Club Online. Also find out what's new at the club and join the Product Forum.

Target

http://www.target.com

★★★★★

A sharp site detailing all of Target's programs and offerings, such as the Lullaby Club, Club Wedd, Take Charge of Education, School Fundraising Made Simple, 5% Back to the Community, TREATSEATS, the Target Guest Card, and various guest services. You can even access sound clips of new music available at Target.

Wal-Mart Online

http://www.wal-mart.com/

★★★★★

Find Wal-Mart product and price information at this site, and order your goodies online. Search the store for what you want; you'll be rewarded with photos and details on each item. Also, locate the Wal-Mart nearest you.

JEWELRY

Antique Jewelry Exchange

http://www.antiquejewelryexch.com/

★★★★★

The Antique Jewelry Exchange Online Shop specializes in fine jewelry, featuring more than 6,000 unique items. Shop the store by category: Clearance, Jewel of the Day, Diamonds in Platinum, Diamonds in Gold, and so on. Each item has a brief description and is accompanied by a photo. Family-owned and operated for more than 25 years, this shop has a solid reputation for quality and service.

Ashford.com

http://www.ashford.com

★★★★★

Specializing in watches but also offering other luxury goods, Ashford provides guidance in selecting gifts and gives customers access to some of the top brands, all in one place.

The Disney Store Online

http://disney.store.go.com/

★★★★★

 All

The Disney Store Online allows you to shop for jewelry for the kids. This site has a wealth of other items for sale also, but the main focus is jewelry products featuring the characters from Disney films and videos. The site offers online buying. If you need a great gift for the kids, this is the place to get it, especially jewelry items.

Mondera

http://www.mondera.com/

★★★★★

Home of "Fine diamonds and timeless jewelry," this site features great deals on high-quality jewelry, plus advice from the experts. Great place to shop for wedding rings, anniversary gifts, or surprises for that special someone.

NetJewels.com

http://www.netjewels.com/

★★★★★

Excellent selection of rings, necklaces, bracelets, watches, and other jewelry at good prices. Use the navigation bar at the top of the screen to pick the type of jewelry you want. Shop online and have your order shipped to your home. Check back often for rebate deals and free gifts.

PERFUME

FragranceNet

http://www.fragrancenet.com/

★★★★

FragranceNet boasts that it is "The world's largest discount fragrance store." With more than 1,000 genuine brand names at up to 70% off retail, it might well be. The attractive, well-designed site also offers free gift wrapping and free shipping, a gift reminder service, a search engine, and the chance to enter to win a $100 shopping spree, and more.

Perfume Center

http://www.perfumecenter.com/main.htm

★★★★

This store offers more than 1,200 original brand-name fragrances for both men and women. You can place your order online or call the toll-free phone number, which is prominently featured on the opening page.

Smell This

http://www.smellthis.com/

★★★★★

The folks at this site are not shy about their philosophy, which is, in a nutshell, "perfume sucks." Smell This is the alternative line of fragrance products for the mind, body, and home. These scents are based on familiar smells we all identify with, such as baby powder, the beach, canned peaches, cut grass, soda pop fizz, fresh towels, chocolate brownies…you get the idea. You can order online, read through FAQs, find a store that carries the line, and more.

Uncommon Scents

http://uncommonscents.com/

★★★★

Specializing in luxurious, natural, custom-scented body care products for more than a quarter of a century. Choose from more than 70 fragrances inspired by nature or shop for natural bath and body care products from around the world. Toll-free phone *and* fax ordering available in addition to the online shopping option. Most products can be custom scented at no additional charge to you!

SEARCH ENGINES

Buyer's Index

http://www.buyersindex.com/

★★★★

Search 20,000 shopping sites and mail order catalogs offering more than 300 million products for consumers and businesses. Use keywords, product names, or company names to begin your search.

InternetMall.com

http://www.internetmall.com/

★★★★★

Comparison shop by searching through categories of products and services at this site, or link to other shopping sites of interest.

A B C D E F G H I J K L M N O P Q R S T U V W X Y Z

A
B
C
D
E
F
G
H
I
J
K
L
M
N
O
P
Q
R
S
T
U
V
W
X
Y
Z

ShopGuide

http://www.shopguide.com/

★★★★★

When you search this site, which consists of more than 20,000 online store sites all rolled into one, you'll find what you're looking for and learn about specials, discounts, coupons, freebies, and incentives.

Shopping.com

http://www.shopping.com/

★★★★★

Search the entire Web for the product you want or browse the directory by category. Features comparison prices for each product.

Yahoo! Shopping

http://www.shopfind.com/

★★★★

A search engine devoted to making your online shopping experience more satisfying. You simply enter items you want to purchase, and ShopFind returns a detailed list of places to start. The site is simple and easy to use.

SPECIALTY

Crate and Barrel

http://www.crateandbarrel.com/

★★★★

Opened in 1962 as a family business, Crate and Barrel is well known for carrying a wide range of unique, high-quality furniture and housewares. If you're getting married or expecting a baby, consider registering online to give your friends and relatives an easy way to purchase just what you need.

eBags.com

http://www.ebags.com/

$

★★★★

This site specializes in bags of all types—for computers, clothes, and sporting gear. You can find wallets, duffel bags, and bags for kids in all materials.

Fogdog

http://www.fogdog.com

★★★★

👫 14-18

Basketball, baseball, and football fans will want to check out this site for the equipment they need to play well. But there is plenty of other gear for sports enthusiasts who like golf, badminton, tennis, and just about every other sport around. Apparel, equipment, and footwear can all be found here.

Gothic Clothing and Jewelry

http://www.blackrose.co.uk/

$

★★★★

Not for kids

Complete line of gothic clothing and jewelry for both men and women, including dresses, corsets, lingerie, skirts, bags, and hats.

Harry and David

http://www.harryanddavid.com/

$

★★★★

This site belongs to the company that has the best pears found anywhere in the world. Anything you order here will be appreciated and devoured.

Ikea.com

http://www.ikea.com/

★★★★★

Request a copy of this year's catalog of inexpensive but well-designed furniture from IKEA or search the online product listings. You can also locate a store nearest you and get technical assistance in assembling your purchases.

Reel.com

http://www.reel.com/

★★★★★

Movie buffs will want to check out this site for access to more than 100,000 movies and DVD titles available for purchase through buy.com. The site provides lots of assistance to help you decide which movies to buy through the use of reviews, interviews with stars, trailers, and synopses.

Sailor Moon Specialty Store

http://japanimation.com/sm/

★★★★

One-stop shopping for apparel, jewelry, dolls, books, videos, games, and other Sailor Moon items.

The SPORTS Authority

http://www.thesportsauthority.com

★★★★

Brand-name sporting good merchandise is available at this site in more than 1,000 categories, for just about every activity imaginable. Apparel, equipment, and footwear are all here. You'll also find an auction section where you can bid on used equipment.

World Traveler Luggage and Travel Goods

http://www.worldtraveler.com/

★★★★★

A discount site for online ordering of sporting goods, luggage, business and computer cases, and travel accessories. Shop by product or by brand—whichever you find easier. Lowest, direct-to-consumer prices on major brands. Money-back guarantee.

A B C D E F G H I J K L M N O P Q R **S** T U V W X Y Z

SKATING

A B C D E F G H I J K L M N O P Q R S T U V W X Y Z

Black Diamond Sports

http://www.skatepro.com/

 $

★★★★★

 All

A huge selection of skates and parts are available at this site, as well as special deals and closeouts. Also provides a map of skate parks in and around Palo Alto, CA.

Riedell Skates

http://www.riedellskates.com

★★★★★

 All

Get information about Riedell skates for hockey, figure skating, inline skating, speed or roller skating, and pick up some tips and techniques for improving your performance and caring for your skates.

FIGURE SKATING

International Figure Skating Magazine (IFS)

http://www.ifsmagazine.com/

★★★★

 14-18

Get the scoop on the latest news in figure skating through the online version of this print magazine. Read about the stars, their challenges, results of recent competitions, and sporting news; then chat online with other fans.

Stars On Ice

http://www.starsonice.com/

 $

★★★★★

 All

Learn more about the cast of skaters in this year's Stars on Ice performance and get news regarding the tour. You can also get ticket information and performance dates.

INLINE SKATING

Get Rolling

http://www.getrolling.com/

★★★★

 All

Find out about skating books, classes, camps, workshops, magazines, and more through the resources section of this site, which was established to help all skaters improve their skill and enjoyment of the sport.

International Inline Skating Association

http://www.iisa.org/

★★★★

 All

Learn to skate, find places to skate safely, pick up rules of the road, meet fellow skaters—all through this site. In addition, you can get news and information about the sport. Lots of information you'll want to look into.

Skatepile.com

https://www.skatepile.com/

$

★★★★★

 All

One-stop shop for inline skates, parts, accessories, and videos. Features advice from the masters, profiles of some of the best inline skaters around, videos, trick tips, setup tips, and a photo gallery. For skates, accessories, and tips, there's no better place on the Web.

Skating.com

http://www.skating.com/

★★★★★

All

A place for sharing information about where to skate, what you think of particular brands and models of skates, as well as a place to sell old equipment, ask questions of more experienced skaters, read profiles of skating legends, and read the latest skating news.

Zephyr Inline Skate Tours

http://www.zephyradventures.com/

★★★★★

Get information about skating tours and vacations here, where you can request a guide by mail or scan the basic details online.

A
B
C
D
E
F
G
H
I
J
K
L
M
N
O
P
Q
R
S
T
U
V
W
X
Y
Z

A
B
C
D
E
F
G
H
I
J
K
L
M
N
O
P
Q
R
S
T
U
V
W
X
Y
Z

SKIN CARE/COSMETICS

Acne

http://www.mckinley.uiuc.edu/health%2Dinfo/
dis%2Dcond/misc/acne.html

★★★

 14-18

Basic information about treatments, their duration, myths, points to remember, and other concerns.

Acne Treatment

http://www.acnetreatment.com

★★★★

 14-18

Basic information about diet, prescription drugs, over-the-counter products, stress, and other factors.

Acne Treatment, Prevention, and Products

http://www.substance.com/skin/acne/

$

★★★★★

 14-18

Learn the myths, facts, and most effective treatment for acne at any age. This site features an acne FAQ, Acne 101 tutorial, tips on how to prevent and cure acne, tricks for concealing it without making it worse, acne treatments and products, and an acne message board where you can post a question or just vent.

Dermatology Images: University of Iowa

http://tray.dermatology.uiowa.edu/DermImag.htm

★★★★

 14-18

The Image Database of the Department of Dermatology of the University of Iowa provides you with information about common skin disorders and images of what they look like. This site will help you to identify most forms of skin problems, but you should consult your dermatologist if you think you have a problem. Nevertheless, the site is very informative. Not for those with weak stomachs.

⌨Best⌨ Dermatology Medical Reference

http://www.emedicine.com/derm/index.shtml

★★★★★

Information on acne, contact dermatitis, scabies, and other conditions. This site isn't the usual "flashy" web page, but it does have all or most of the information you would need to know about skin care, with many interesting articles on the subject. Just a few of the many subjects discussed include Allergy and Immunology, Bacterial Infections, Cosmetics, Diseases of the Dermis, Fungal Infections, and Pediatric Diseases. Each subject is categorized alphabetically, which makes it easy to find. This site is directed more toward professional dermatologists rather than the general public.

National Rosacea Society

http://www.rosacea.org

★★★★

Information on the skin problem, including the Rosacea Review, a hotline, links to websites, and other areas.

Neutrogena

http://www.neutrogena.com

★★★★★

👫 14-18

Skin care products, special offers, and advice. S.O.S. section lists links to common skin problems; click a link to find solutions and products that can help. If the problem you have is not listed, click the Ask Neutrogena link to post the question to a dermatologist.

Problems and Diseases of the Skin

http://cpmcnet.columbia.edu/texts/guide/ hmg28_0003.html

★★★★

Prevention, causes, home remedies, alternative therapies, and related information on disorders such as acne, hair loss, and more.

Skin Culture Peel

http://www.skinculture.com

$

★★★★

Manufactures and sells skin peel products. This site features an online form you can fill out to determine your skin type, information about skin peels, and an online store where you can purchase various skin peel products.

COSMETICS

Avon

http://shop.avon.com/

$

★★★★★

👫 14-18

Having trouble finding the Avon Lady in your neighborhood? Then go directly to Avon online. Avon carries a complete line of beauty aids, cosmetics, and jewelry. Shop online and have your order shipped to your door.

beautyjungle.com

http://www.beautyjungle.com/beautyjungle/main.asp

$

★★★★★

👫 14-18

Whether you like elite cosmetic brands or purely natural products, you're likely to be able to find them here among the 10,000 products available. You can also learn more about celebrity beauty routines so you can copy them.

Cosmetic Connection

http://www.cosmeticconnection.com/

$

★★★★

👫 14-18

Read feature articles on beauty trends, techniques, application tips, and other seasonable information in the articles section, and then search for product reviews in the library before investing your hard-earned money in products that don't work as you want them to. Sign up for the free cosmetics report newsletter to get the skinny on the products you've been hearing about.

Cosmetic Mall

http://www.cosmeticmall.com

$

★★★★

👫 14-18

Shop by brand or department, such as face or aromatherapy, for your favorite products. Or get advice and tips on what you should be using.

drugstore.com

http://www.drugstore.com/

$

★★★★

👫 14-18

Search for skin care products by use or brand here and have them shipped directly to you. Fragrances and cosmetics are also available here.

A
B
C
D
E
F
G
H
I
J
K
L
M
N
O
P
Q
R
S
T
U
V
W
X
Y
Z

A
B
C
D
E
F
G
H
I
J
K
L
M
N
O
P
Q
R
S
T
U
V
W
X
Y
Z

eve.com

http://www.sephora.com/

★★★★★

 14-18

Search for products to address your beauty challenges by typing in keywords, or looking by brand. You'll find advice, gift ideas, and product information galore. Sephora is the leading retail beauty chain in Europe. And now the company is here in the United States. Discover more about the company and its innovative stores, and learn more about Sephora's family of companies, including Sephora.com, Sephora USA, and the parent company, LVMH.

If you're looking for a Sephora store near you, look at the Store Directory and new store openings. There is a nice store with areas on Fragrance, Makeup, Magazines, Bath & Body, Tools & Accessories, Gifts, and Treatments.

Faceart

http://www.faceart.com/

★★★★

 14-18

Created by makeup junkies for makeup junkies, this site features articles on creative makeup projects. Sections on eye art, lip art, hair art, and more. Read the feature articles, find answers to your makeup questions, or visit the Makeupshop for how-to videos.

Mary Kay

http://www.marykay.com/

★★★★★

 14-18

Learn how to get the look you want with makeup through the Virtual Makeover section of this site, which shows you pictures of models having makeup applied in various ways. You can also learn more about various Mary Kay products and locate a local consultant, if you don't already have one.

SNOW SKIING

Altrec.com

http://www.altrec.com/shop/dir/ski/

★★★★

👫 14-18

Skiing, snowboarding, cycling, hiking, hunting, fishing, and other outdoor adventure sports. Altrec carries all the gear you need for most adventure sports, including skiing. The site also features some articles and comparison shops.

Austria Ski Vacation Packages

http://www.snowpak.com/snowpak/resorts/austriaresorts.html

★★★★

Part of the Snow Pak Online site. Get quotes for ski vacation packages in Austria and plan your dream vacation. Be sure to register for full-color brochures to be mailed to you and check out the live resort cams.

Boston Mills-Brandywine Ski Resort

http://www.bmbw.com/

★★★★

Located in the Cleveland/Akron area of Ohio, these two ski resorts operate jointly. Check out their website for powder and weather reports, available services, rental fees, night skiing information, and lots more.

Complete Skier

http://www.complete-skier.com

★★★

👫 14-18

Top skiing news, competition information, ski resorts and travel, equipment, techniques, and a forum.

Cool Works' Ski Resorts and Ski/Snowboard Country Jobs

http://www.coolworks.com/skirsrts.htm

★★★★★

Ever wondered how those ski instructors get such cool jobs? Check out this site. Pick a state. Pick a resort. Pick a job. Spend the winter playing at your dream job. You'll also find links to other cool jobs in state parks, on cruise ships, and in camps. Definitely check this out.

CRN: Colorado Resort Net

http://www.discovercolorado.com/

★★★★

Serves as a guide to Colorado resort communities, including hotels, restaurants, arts, events, real estate, and shopping information.

GoSki.com

http://www.goski.com/

★★★★

Get more information about ski resorts around the world, plan your next ski vacation, look at product reviews, check the weather, and check the headlines before you head out.

Hyperski

http://www.hyperski.com/

★★★

Find out about snow conditions and special packages. Also read the articles about picking the right pair of skis, snow-cat skiing, using skid chains, and skiing in Austria. This page has a little more than the usual.

A
B
C
D
E
F
G
H
I
J
K
L
M
N
O
P
Q
R
S
T
U
V
W
X
Y
Z

K2 Skis

http://www.k2skis.com/

★★★★

👥 14-18

Visit this site to check out the complete line of K2 skis or use the ski selector to find a pair that matches your needs. Use the Dealer Locator to find a dealer near you.

Las Lenas Ski Packages

http://www.snowpak.com/snowpak/resorts/
laslenas.html

★★★★

Skiing in Argentina might not be something you've considered before. Check out this page to discover what's available. Get a quote for your vacation plans. Check this one out. It's a little different, but you might like it.

National Ski Patrol

http://www.nsp.org

★★★

Skiing and snowboarding safety tips, a skier's and rider's checklist, information on dressing properly, and back-country avalanche safety.

Outdoor REVIEW

http://www.outdoorreview.com/

★★★★

Read or write your own reviews of skis, gear, and resorts. You can also pick up some basic skiing tips, chat with other skiers, check road reports, submit photos from mountains you've skied, and link to other hot sites.

Over the Hill Gang

http://www.skiersover50.com/

★★★★★

If you're over 50 and enjoy skiing and other outdoor activities, check out this site. The Over the Hill Gang provides discounts on everything from lift tickets to lodging and ski shop purchases. The group also plans trips to North American, South American, and European ski areas. In the summer, there's whitewater rafting, bicycling, hiking, and golf. If one spouse is over 50, you both qualify for membership.

Salomon Sports

http://www.salomonsports.com/

★★★★

👥 14-18

Home of some of the most popular skis and snowboards, this site provides product information, information about famous skiers, and links to Salomon ski magazines and sites.

Best | SkiCentral

http://www.skicentral.com/

★★★★★

👥 14-18

Check out the #1 search and index site for skiers and snowboarders on the Internet. You'll find 8,000 snow sports sites, ski reports, resorts, snowcams, travel packages, equipment, and more. So, before planning your trip to the "white mountains of fun and pleasure," check out what this site has to offer.

Categories include Snowsport Sites, Find Gear, Resort Lodging, Ski Packages, Free Ski Photographs, Resorts & Travel, Lodging, Trip Planning, Skiing, Snowboarding, Snow Reports, Snowcams, News & Views, Sites by Region, Contests, Employment, and even Trail Maps.

Skiing in Jackson Hole

http://www.jacksonholenet.com/ski/

★★★★★

Extensive information about travel and lodging, the usual weather and powder reports, and information about four different ski resorts: Snow King, Grand Targhee, Jackson Hole, and White Pine. You'll also find a unique bit of information about ski safety, road safety, and spring skiing safety—along with tips on keeping warm.

SkiNet

http://www.skinet.com/

★★★★★

👥 14-18

The editors of *Ski Magazine* and *Skiing Magazine* present snow reports, resort profiles, gear information, and news.

Snow Sports Destinations

http://www.skisnowboard.com/

★★★★★

If you're looking for a place to ski or snowboard, this should be the first place you turn. Here you can find the best resorts for skiing, snowboarding, cross-country skiing, snowshoeing, and other snow sports around the world.

St. Moritz Ski Page

http://www.ifyouski.fr/

★★★★★

Get an honest appraisal of the world's most luxurious ski accommodations. Find out what to really expect in St. Moritz, what's available to entertain the children, and what to do at night. There's also the usual information about trail conditions and weather, as well as links to other European ski areas.

Stowe Mountain Resort

http://www.stowe.com/

★★★★★

Find out about upcoming package deals at Stowe, Vermont. The latest weather and powder conditions are here, along with FAQs, information about lessons, and directions to the resort.

The U.S. Ski Home Team Page

http://www.usskiteam.com/

★★★★

👥 14-18

The official page for the U.S. Ski Team. Stay informed about all the doings of the ski team all the time, not just during the Olympics. There's also World Cup news, selection criteria, and more official news.

A
B
C
D
E
F
G
H
I
J
K
L
M
N
O
P
Q
R
S
T
U
V
W
X
Y
Z

A B C D E F G H I J K L M N O P Q R S T U V W X Y Z

SNOWMOBILING

American Snowmobiler Magazine

http://www.amsnow.com

★★★★★

 14-18

Up-to-date information about snowmobiling and the snowmobile industry. Includes current news, a racing guide, a travel guide, and more.

Arctic Cat

http://www.arctic-cat.com

★★★★★

Arctic Cat company's official site, with product information on snowmobiles, watercraft, and ATVs—plus safety information and dealer links.

Clean Snowmobile Facts

http://www.deq.state.mt.us/CleanSnowmobile/solutions/challenge/

★★★

If you're concerned about the effects of snowmobiling on the environment, visit this site to learn more about snowmobile modifications that are more environmentally friendly.

International Snowmobile Manufacturers Association

http://www.snowmobile.org

★★★★

 14-18

Timely information about the sport of snowmobiling in North America and Europe. Features articles, stats & facts, and information on snowmobile safety. Links to other sites as well.

Maine Snowmobile Connection

http://www.sledmaine.com

★★★★

 14-18

Accommodations, trail reports, clubs, sled rentals, and other information for would-be Maine snowmobilers.

Northern Michigan Snowmobiling

http://www.michiweb.com/snowmobile/

★★★★

Northern Michigan snow and trail reports, featured regions, rentals, stops, and more.

Polaris Industries

http://www.polarisindustries.com

★★★★

14-18

Maker of snowmobiles, watercraft, and ATVs. Product information, latest news, annual report, and employment opportunities.

Ski-Doo

http://www.ski-doo.com

★★★★

14-18

Official site for Ski-Doo snowmobile manufacturer. Includes product information, safety tips, and links.

Snowmobile Online

http://www.off-road.com/snowmobile/

★★★★★

Read the latest snowmobiling news, stay up to date on land use issues that threaten snowmobilers' access to parks and other areas, find places to ride, read product reviews and lots of other information about snowmobiling here. Snowmobilers will want to bookmark this Best of the Best snowmobiling site for quick return trips later.

Snowmobiling.net

http://www.snowmobiling.net

★★★★

Snowmobilers load up on links, classified ads, electronic shopping services, message boards, and news.

SnowRider Magazine

http://www.snowridermag.com

★★★

 14-18

E-zine devoted exclusively to snowmobiling. Includes recommendations on resorts and rides, technical advice, safety information, lots of links, and more.

Yamaha Motor Corporation

http://www.yamaha-motor.com/

★★★★★

 14-18

Official corporate site of Yamaha Motor Corporation, USA, maker of snowmobiles, watercraft, ATVs, boats, racing karts, and more. Includes product and competition information.

A
B
C
D
E
F
G
H
I
J
K
L
M
N
O
P
Q
R
S
T
U
V
W
X
Y
Z

A
B
C
D
E
F
G
H
I
J
K
L
M
N
O
P
Q
R
S
T
U
V
W
X
Y
Z

SOCCER

[Best] AlphaSoccer

http://www.alphasoccer.com/

★★★★★

👥 14-18

This is your one-stop place to find out about soccer, with various links to clubs, leagues, associations, players, and other interesting information about soccer. This comprehensive directory to everything related to soccer even provides links to various places online where you can purchase equipment, apparel, books, videos, and other soccer-related items. Though not the easiest soccer site to navigate, this site is the best directory of soccer information on the Web.

ATL World Soccer News

http://www.wldcup.com/

★★★★

👥 14-18

Offers world soccer news, commentary, statistics, and scores.

The Daily Soccer

http://www.dailysoccer.com/

★★★★

👥 14-18

The Daily Soccer e-zine features up-to-the-minute news, scores, and statistics from the world of soccer. Content is organized by country, although a searchable players database is available as well. The page also contains links to related sites.

ESPN Soccer

http://soccernet.espn.go.com/

★★★★★

👥 14-18

Provides links to soccer's hot zone, Europe, but also to World Cup qualification coverage worldwide. As Major League Soccer grows in the United States, expect ESPN's current coverage to grow with it.

FIFA Online

http://www.fifa.com/

★★★★★

👥 14-18

Official page of soccer's world governing body provides coverage of competitions, press releases, a newsletter, and rules updates.

FIFA World Cup

http://fifaworldcup.yahoo.com

$

★★★★★

👥 14-18

Home of the biggest soccer tournament in the world, this site provides coverage of the most recent World Cup soccer games. Provides a preview of upcoming matches, scores and coverage of recent matches, video highlights, online message boards, and more.

InternetSoccer.com

http://www.internetsoccer.com/

★★★★★

👥 14-18

Late-breaking soccer news and scores plus a searchable index of teams and players. Search for news by continents, countries, competitions, or leagues.

Major League Soccer (MLS)

http://www.mlsnet.com/

★★★★★

 All

Get stats, schedules, results, rankings, team information, and images of some of the best shots this season.

Soccer.com

http://www.soccer.com/

⑤

★★★

Get all the news and event information you need about European soccer, including feature articles about the sport; soccer-related screensavers you can download; and events, contests, and games you might want to participate in.

Soccer Camps

http://www.soccer-camps.com/

★★★★

Get the latest scores, schedules, recruiting details, information on camps, and much more at this site. You can search for a soccer camp; plus, you can find registration and pricing information, schedules, and just about anything else you need to know about soccer camps, with dozens of camps listed.

The Soccer Home Page

http://www.distrib.com/soccer/

★★★★

This cool page contains tons of information, from soccer clubs to current standings, events, and game information.

Soccer Information Systems

http://www.soccerinfo.com/

★★★★

👥 14-18

Contains a database of information relating to amateur soccer. Topics include high school soccer, coaching, recruiting, soccer writers, and camps.

Soccer-Sites

http://www.soccer-sites.com/

★★★★★

One of the best directory sites dedicated to thousands of soccer sites around the world. Soccer-Sites is your central starting point for the top soccer/football–related sites all over the world! Search the database using keywords to find a site quickly. Sites in the database are removed if not activated for seven days, so the database is always up to date. This means you waste much less time following dead links. Also, a new site can be added INSTANTLY. Some other search engines take weeks to add a site.

Soccer Times

http://www.soccertimes.com/

★★★★★

👥 14-18

Up-to-date news on the latest in U.S. and international soccer. Check on your favorite teams and players, explore NCAA soccer, get information on U.S. national teams, and keep abreast of the happenings at the World Cup Soccer tournament.

Soccer Tutor

http://www.soccertutor.com/

★★★★★

Whether you are a player or a coach, you will find the techniques, training, and tips to carry your soccer play to the next level. Here you can take a free tour of the service to see what it has to offer, sign up for a free trial, and then subscribe to the service when you see how much it really has to offer. Nice design and great content.

Soccer Yellow Pages

http://www.tdl.com/~chuckn/soc/soc.html

★★★★★

Lots of listings for soccer sites. This is a good place to go when you're searching for more information on soccer.

A
B
C
D
E
F
G
H
I
J
K
L
M
N
O
P
Q
R
S
T
U
V
W
X
Y
Z

A
B
C
D
E
F
G
H
I
J
K
L
M
N
O
P
Q
R
S
T
U
V
W
X
Y
Z

United States Soccer Federation

http://www.ussoccer.com/

★★★★★

The official site of the United States soccer governing body. It provides a history of soccer in the United States, an Olympic recap, a quarterly soccer e-zine, and more. Coaches and referees will find training advice and tips here as well.

U.S. Youth Soccer

http://www.usysa.org/

★★★★★

 All

History of the association, an events calendar, a catalog of U.S. Youth Soccer materials, and addresses of groups across the United States.

World Soccer Page

http://www.wspsoccer.com/

★★★★★

 14-18

The world soccer page gives you plenty of information about U.S. and international soccer teams, players, games, news, and merchandise.

SOCIAL WORK/SERVICES

A B C D E F G H I J K L M N O P Q R **S** T U V W X Y Z

AAMFT

http://www.aamft.org/

★★★★★

American Association for Marriage and Family Therapy. Information on marriage and family therapists, and a practice strategy newsletter.

ADEC

http://www.adec.org/

★★★

Association for Death Education and Counseling, for professionals, with conferences, workshops, certification, and publications.

The Carter Center

http://www.cartercenter.org/

★★★★★

Former U.S. President Jimmy Carter and his wife, Roslyn, have based their public policy institute in Atlanta, Georgia. Visit this site to get information about their current and past work, as well as to find out what you can do to help.

Catholic Charities USA

http://www.catholiccharitiesusa.org/

★★★★

Largest social services organization in America. The site provides descriptions of programs and contact details for local agencies.

Centers for Disease Control and Prevention

http://www.cdc.gov/

★★★★★

Tells about the agency and its services. Links to public health officials and agencies nationwide. Warns travelers of disease outbreaks worldwide. Gives data and statistics. Very informative.

Evaluation and Training Institute

http://www.otan.dni.us/webfarm/eti/

★

Established in 1974, ETI is a full-service, nonprofit consulting firm that conducts research, program evaluation, policy analysis, and training with a focus on educational and social services programs and public policy issues.

FamiliesUSA

http://www.familiesusa.org/

★★★

Home of one of the most active healthcare advocacy groups. FamiliesUSA works to provide high-quality, affordable healthcare and long-term care for everyone. This site features articles on the latest news and legislation affecting healthcare issues.

HandsNet

http://www.handsnet.org/

★★★

HandsNet is a resource for nonprofit community service groups. It aims to offer a way for these groups to share information and collaborate by providing a central online location they can access. Articles covering a wide range of community issues are posted and updated frequently.

Health and Social Services Job Profile Directory

http://www.jobprofiles.org/hea.htm

★★★

Career information. Real people tell what it is like to work their particular job—the rewards, the stresses, and challenges to overcome.

A
B
C
D
E
F
G
H
I
J
K
L
M
N
O
P
Q
R
S
T
U
V
W
X
Y
Z

National Association of Alcoholism and Drug Abuse Counselors (NAADAC)

http://naadac.org/

★★★★

Learn about the NAADAC and its membership, certifications, products, services, resource links, and more.

National Center for Missing and Exploited Children

http://www.missingkids.com/

★★★★★

Offers searchable database records by specific criteria. Short and long indexes of all missing children. Comprehensive site with photographs of some of the children. For even more, click the "Children at Risk" link. Service provided in an attempt to find missing children.

National Civic League

http://www.ncl.org/

★★★★

When Theodore Roosevelt founded this group with the goal of improving communities, he surely didn't realize how helpful and accessible it would become. This site will link you to mission statements, recent progress in the area, and ways you can assist your own community.

The National Coalition for the Homeless

http://www.nationalhomeless.org/

★★★

With the primary goal of abolishing homelessness in mind, this group relates tales of people's struggles with homelessness and provides links to information on recent developments and legislation that pertain to homelessness.

Native American Culture and Social System

http://www.greatdreams.com/native.htm

★★★★

This site contains more information than you can read in one night on the Native American social system and philosophy. There is information on every tribe that has ever existed, with detailed descriptions of their thoughts, beliefs, and the way they live. If you are doing research on Native Americans or you just want to understand their social system, this is a great place to start.

New York State Department of Family Assistance

http://www.dfa.state.ny.us/

★★★★★

Formerly the Department of Social Services. You have three categories to choose from: Office of Temporary and Disability Assistance, General Department of Family Assistance, and Office of Children and Family Services.

[Best] Social Work and Social Services Websites

http://gwbweb.wustl.edu/websites.html

★★★★★

This directory of services, put together by Washington University in St. Louis, features a robust list of links to social work and social services sites on the Web, categorized into dozens of groups covering everything from Abuse and Violence to Women's Issues. This comprehensive list of resources addresses health issues, psychiatric illnesses, disabilities, family crises, counseling, housing, veterans' issues, and much more. When you're looking for help, this is the Best of the Best places to start.

SocialService.com

http://www.socialservice.com/

★★★★

Social workers and other social service professionals looking for a job will want to start here to find a new position, whether you're looking for something in mental health, domestic violence, children, outreach, or just about any other specialty. Employers can also post openings for access by professionals nationwide.

U.S. Department of Health and Human Services

http://www.os.dhhs.gov

★★★★★

The government's principal agency for protecting the health of Americans and providing essential human services, especially for those who are least able to help themselves. The agency oversees more than 300 programs.

VISTA Web

http://www.friendsofvista.org/

★★★★

Volunteers in Service to America has been around since 1964, and it is now part of the larger AmeriCorps VISTA program. Find out about both groups' successes in the past, what they're planning to do in the future, as well as how to find someone with whom you might have worked in either group.

A
B
C
D
E
F
G
H
I
J
K
L
M
N
O
P
Q
R
S
T
U
V
W
X
Y
Z

A B C D E F G H I J K L M N O P Q R S T U V W X Y Z

SOFTBALL

All American Softball School

http://www.kj22.com/

★★★

 14-18

This site belongs to a school devoted exclusively to developing the skills of athletes interested in playing Olympic-style softball.

Amateur Softball Association

http://www.softball.org/

★★★★★

 All

If you're looking for information about the game of softball—fast pitch, slow pitch or modified, men's or women's, adult or youth—you've come to the right place. Lots of links to other softball sites too.

[Best] ISF: International Softball Federation

http://www.internationalsoftball.com/

★★★★★

 All

This bilingual site (English and Spanish) is the home of the governing body of international softball, "as recognized by the International Olympic Committee (IOC) and the General Association of International Sports Federations (GAISF)." This site features information about the organization, the rules it sets, and upcoming and ongoing tournaments it sponsors. Tournaments include the Olympic games, the Slow Pitch World Cup, the Seniors Softball World Cup, and the World Masters Games. Free subscription to the ISF newsletter, plus online shopping for ISF merchandise. With all it has to offer, this site is the Best of the Best softball sites on the Web.

National Pro Fastpitch

http://www.profastpitch.com/

★★★★

 14-18

This official site of the National Pro Fastpitch league provides information about the league, its president, and its future. This site will include information about teams, players, standings, and more.

NCAA Women's Softball

http://www.ncaasports.com/softball/womens

★★★★★

 14-18

National Collegiate Athletic Association's official site for women's softball. Includes a schedule, ticketing information, results, and previews. This site is well designed and easy to navigate and has great graphics with lots of information about softball. Some of the many features are rankings, teams, history, places to purchase tickets, and information about NCAA championships. Plus, you can purchase merchandise from an online store.

NZ Softball—New Zealand

http://www.softball.org.nz/

★★★★★

Get a new perspective on the old baseball game by visiting this site somewhere down under—namely, New Zealand. This is the official New Zealand website with plenty of interesting information and facts about softball.

Senior Softball

http://www.seniorsoftball.com/

★★★★

Learn more about tournaments, rules, tours, and news regarding senior softball here.

Slow Pitch Softball History Page

http://www.angelfire.com/sd/slopitch/

★★★★

 14-18

This site features softball national championship and World Series history. Also contains links to other softball-related sites.

Softball.net

http://www.softball.net/

★★★★

Offers a directory of 118 links related to softball. Find national and local Amateur Softball Associations (ASA), colleges and universities, commercial sites, fast pitch sites, general softball sites, non-ASA softball associations, slow pitch sites, and tournament information, too.

Softball on the Internet

http://www.softball.com/

★★★★★

 All

Softball information and an online catalog with products. Facts about gear, an Ask the Umpire section, and a toll-free number for ordering. Enter tournament dates into the directory.

SoftballSearch.com

http://softballsearch.eteamz.com/

★★★★★

 14-18

Tournament listings and results along with team announcements by state and country. Just click a state name to view current announcements.

U.S.A. Softball Official Site

http://www.usasoftball.com/

★★★★★

 14-18

Fans of the U.S.A. Men's and Women's softball teams should bookmark this site to keep abreast of the latest news and developments. Provides information about and coverage of the Olympic Games, Pan American Games, and ISF World Championships. Includes "rosters, player and coach biographies, competition schedules, statistics and live play-by-play updates," when available.

A B C D E F G H I J K L M N O P Q R **S** T U V W X Y Z

STRESS MANAGEMENT

American Institute of Stress

http://www.stress.org/

★★★

This organization is committed to understanding the role of stress in health and disease. Find a collection of articles and a Who's Who directory.

International Stress Management Association

http://www.isma.org.uk/

★★★★

Excellent resource for learning how to deal with stress. Features articles from *Stress News*, a complete list of recommended reading materials, a schedule of conferences and upcoming events, links to other useful sites, and some specific advice and suggestions on how to make your life more enjoyable and stress-free.

Lycos Health with WebMD—Stress

http://webmd.lycos.com/content/dmk/dmk_summary_account_1466

★★★★

If you're feeling stressed, this site might help you better understand what you're feeling and how you can deal with it in the short and long term. You can determine whether the symptoms you're exhibiting are likely to be caused by stress and read articles about coping with it.

Optimum Health Resources

http://www.optimumhealth.ca/

★★★★

Learn how to reduce your stress either at home or in the workplace to improve your health and well-being.

The Stress Doc

http://www.stressdoc.com/

★★★★★

Mark Gorkin, a licensed psychotherapist, known as "The Stress Doc," offers a wealth of stress management resources. In addition to finding information about his speaking programs, visitors will also find lots of articles and links to help them get a handle on their stress.

Stress Less

http://www.stressless.com/

Ⓢ

★★★★

Learn about and purchase stress reduction products, such as tapes, videos, and books, here.

Stress Management

http://www.ivf.com/stress.html

★★★★

This fact sheet from the Atlanta Reproductive Health Centre offers a definition of stress and several pointers on how to manage stress.

Stress Management & Emotional Wellness Page

http://www.imt.net/~randolfi/StressPage.html

★★★★

Well-stocked directory of links to various resources on the Web designed to help visitors reduce stress. Links point to sites covering everything from biofeedback and relaxation techniques to controlling stress in the workplace.

Stress Management and Stress Reduction

http://www.less-stress.com/

★★★★★

Stress management and information about the nature and causes of stress with online stress assessment service. The website provides an insight to the causes and effects of stress and offers a jargon-free understanding of the problems that arise from excessive levels of stress.

Most importantly, the website gives direct access to the Changing Times method of psychometric modeling and online stress reduction. The site provides a valuable tool for individuals who seek to tackle their own stress levels and to managers and executives who want to reduce stress in their organizations.

Stress Management for Patients and Physicians

http://www.mentalhealth.com/mag1/p51-str.html

★★★★★

This book by David B. Posen, M.D., is for anyone with a busy lifestyle; it covers all the major approaches of stress management, including humor.

Stress Management Techniques

http://www.mindtools.com/smpage.html

★★★★

Practical techniques for reducing stress and avoiding stressful situations.

StressStop.com

http://www.stressstop.com/

$

★★★★

Materials and ideas to make your stress management training the best it can be. Complete with tapes, articles, and online resources.

Wes Sime: Stress Management

http://www.unl.edu/stress/mgmt/

★★★★★

Dr. Wesley Sime teaches stress management at the University of Nebraska. Topics discussed include the physiology of stress and decision-making.

A
B
C
D
E
F
G
H
I
J
K
L
M
N
O
P
Q
R
S
T
U
V
W
X
Y
Z

A B C D E F G H I J K L M N O P Q R S T U V W X Y Z

TABLE TENNIS

Butterfly Online

http://www.butterflyonline.com/

★★★★★

 14-18

Butterfly is one of the major manufacturers of table tennis equipment in the world. At this site, you can find information about recent and upcoming tournaments, table tennis news, rules of the game, coaching tips, and player profiles; plus, you can browse through the huge collection of paddles, tables, balls, accessories, robots, and other equipment and accessories.

Classic Hardbat Table Tennis

http://www.hardbat.com/

★★★

Learn about hardbat table tennis—the rules, ratings, photos, and player profiles. Sign up for the newsletter or check out the upcoming events and tournament results at this site.

[Best] Denis' Table Tennis World

http://www.tabletennis.gr/

★★★★★

Prematch, match, and post-match tips by Dimosthenis E. Messinis, Ph.D. Huge collection of resources with an easy-to-use navigation bar on the left containing sections on Articles-Tips, Exercises, Basics, Equipment, Rules, and even video clips. Quizzes, FAQs, interviews, world rankings, awards, and more provide a one-stop kiosk for everything a table tennis enthusiast needs to know. The Best of the Best table tennis sites in the group.

English Table Tennis Association Limited

http://www.etta.co.uk/

★★★★★

Top resource for table tennis information in the UK. Information and entry forms for the Butterfly Grand Prix, information on TV coverage of table tennis tournaments, an events calendar, the latest news, details on county and national championships, and more.

International Paralympic Table Tennis Committee

http://www.ipttc.org/

★★★★

The official governing body for the disabled table tennis—both wheelchair and standing disabled.

International Table Tennis Federation

http://www.ittf.com/

★★★★

 14-18

Browse through this online magazine for the latest world competition results and profiled players. Also includes links to other table tennis sites.

Megaspin.net

http://www.megaspin.net/

★★★★★

Check out table tennis rules, rankings, links, the picture gallery, news, and updates. Subscribe to the free newsletter to keep abreast of the latest news and upcoming events, or shop online for paddles, balls, and other table tennis accessories. This excellent site was barely edged out in the running for the Best of the Best prize, so be sure to check it out.

North America Table Tennis, Inc.

http://www.natabletennis.com/

★★★★

Find out about the Stiga North American Teams Championships, one of the largest table tennis championships in the world, and about the Stiga North American Tour. Also provides information about the AAU Junior Olympics and the ACUI/NCTTA Collegiate events and other NATT events. Provides a calendar of events, plus an online store where you can register for tournaments and purchase NATT apparel and used tables.

The Sport of Table Tennis

http://library.thinkquest.org/20570/

★★★★

Excellent information organized in a Q&A format for anyone interested in taking up the game of table tennis. Answers the questions: What is table tennis? How do I play? What do I need? Where do I play? Also provides tips, table tennis facts, table tennis terms, and a discussion board.

Table Tennis

http://tabletennis.about.com/

★★★★★

Find out lots of interesting facts from this complete table tennis community with an expert guide, forum, chats, links, bimonthly newsletter, weekly features, coaching tips, and much, much more.

Table Tennis Links

http://www.hal-pc.org/~canupnet/ttlinks.html

★★★★

You will find thousands of links here relating to table tennis worldwide. Why waste time searching for this subject when you can do it from one convenient site.

USA Table Tennis

http://www.usatt.org/

★★★★★

 14-18

Check here for news on the USA Nationals and browse through the Tournament Information Guide. Investigate the information on clubs, hot spots to play, equipment, dealers, USATT rules, upcoming tournaments, and results. Learn how to become a USA Table Tennis member. You can get information on table tennis rules in the Stump the Ump section or browse through the current and past issues of *USA Table Tennis* e-zine.

World Table Tennis News

http://www.worldtabletennis.com/

★★★★

14-18

This site provides the latest news and information about competitive table tennis tournaments around the world.

World Wide Ping Pong

http://www.asahi-net.or.jp/~SZ4M-KS/wwpp.html

★★★

This site gives you a collection of links to table tennis home pages all over the world.

A B C D E F G H I J K L M N O P Q R S **T** U V W X Y Z

Yellow Pages

TAXES

Bankrate.com

http://www.bankrate.com/brm/itax/default.asp

★★★★★

Excellent income tax information and tips for individuals and small-business owners. Read articles that help you track down your refund, estimate your withholding tax, claim tax credits, realize the benefits of itemizing, deduct mortgage interest, and much more.

Citizens for an Alternative Tax System: CATS

http://www.cats.org/

★★★★★

Houses the national public interest group for an alternative tax system and tax reform. Describes the group's manifesto and related information, which basically consists of replacing the current federal income tax system with a retail sales tax.

Citizens for Tax Justice

http://www.ctj.org/

★★★★★

This nonprofit organization does research to support its advocacy of a fairer tax code for middle- and low-income families, closing corporate tax loopholes, reducing the federal deficit, and requiring the rich to pay their fair share.

The Digital Daily

http://www.irs.gov/newsroom/index.html

★★★★

The Digital Daily is the IRS's online newsletter. It provides news, places to go for help, online forms, links, information about record keeping, a commissioner's forum, and a site map.

eSmartForms

http://www.etaxforms.com/

★★★★★

Tired of filling out those paper forms and mailing your tax return? Then do it online. This site features two simple, inexpensive ways to file your tax return electronically: either complete the "paperwork" online using web-based forms or download the forms you need, in Microsoft Word format. Complete the forms and upload to submit them. Cost is $15 or less.

Essential Links to Taxes

http://www.el.com/elinks/taxes/

★★★★★

Taxpayer tips and information on income tax preparation assistance, rules, tax code, financial planners and tax preparers, forms (from W-2 to Form 1040), publications, instructions, deductions, and filing.

Fairmark Press—Tax Guide for Investors

http://www.fairmark.com/

★★★★

You'll find pages and pages of material to guide you in making smart investment choices in the Tax Guide section—more than 700 pages to be exact. Learn about the essentials of Roth IRAs, the basics of computing capital gains, or the tax guide for traders, as well as several other tax-related subjects.

Flat Tax Proposal

http://www.taxreform.com/flat_tax.html

★★★

How would you like to file your tax return on one side of a postcard? With the flat tax proposal sponsored by Representative Dick Armey, everyone would pay a 17% income tax, and we would be rid of deductions and tax loopholes for good. Of course, there are two sides to this issue, and at this site, you can learn both sides.

Best H&R Block

http://www.hrblock.com/

★★★★★

Although you'll find plenty of information here to help you get better rates on credit cards, mortgages, and loans, the tax information is the most helpful. Use the Withholding Calculator to figure out how much you should be having taken out of your paycheck. Or find out the status of your refund check. Features tax news and tips, a year-round tax planning guide, a tax calendar, information about new tax laws, a well-stocked library of tax forms and IRS publications, and hundreds of tax-saving tips. Very attractive site, easy to navigate, and packed with the great tax information.

IRS: Internet Revenue Service

http://www.irs.gov/

★★★★★

The IRS site provides everything you need to become an informed taxpayer. Search the site for specific information or for downloadable, printable tax forms you might have trouble finding at your local post office or library. The site also provides news about the IRS and tax legislation, along with information specifically for individuals, businesses, nonprofit organizations, and tax professionals. Learn about the earned income tax credit, tax scams and frauds, and your rights as a taxpayer.

IRS.com

http://www.irs.com/index.htm

★★★★★

IRS.com is the Internet's first consumer-oriented source for federal, state, and local tax-related developments. The site provides answers to general tax questions plus hyperlinks to current federal and state-sponsored tax information.

Kiplinger Online

http://www.kiplinger.com

★★★★★

For more than 80 years, Kiplinger has been providing cutting-edge information and advice for financial management and investment. Check out this site for some free offerings. Includes business forecasts, news of the day, financial advice, tax news and advice, and investment and retirement information. Additional services for paying members.

MoneyCentral on Taxes

http://moneycentral.msn.com/tax/home.asp

★★★★

Information on tax planning and preparation, tax estimators, deduction finder, tax IQ test, Q&A, and information on reducing your tax burden.

SmartPros Accounting

http://accounting.smartpros.com/

★★★★

Download federal and state tax forms and publications, file your taxes electronically, or find an accountant to handle your taxes for you.

State and Local Taxes

http://www.taxsites.com/state.html

★★★★

State tax resource with general locators, current tax issues, organizations, and more. This site has dozens of useful and informative links to information about tax preparation, tax changes and updates, and more.

A
B
C
D
E
F
G
H
I
J
K
L
M
N
O
P
Q
R
S
T
U
V
W
X
Y
Z

A B C D E F G H I J K L M N O P Q R S **T** U V W X Y Z

Tax.org

http://www.tax.org

★★★★

This nonprofit for tax professionals provides lists of its publications and discussion groups about various tax issues. Also provides the *Tax Notes Today*, updated three times daily.

Tax and Accounting Sites Directory

http://www.taxsites.com

★★★★

Guide to tax resources on the Web. Includes tax forms, electronic filing preparation, articles, and accounting information.

Tax Glossary

http://taxes.yahoo.com/glossary/

★★★

Long list of terms you might encounter on your tax return along with a precise definition of each term.

Tax History Project

http://taxhistory.tax.org/

★★★★

Visit the multimedia timeline of American taxation here and learn all about the history of taxation.

Tax Links

http://www.taxlinks.com

★★★

Online resource for IRS revenue rulings. Tax lawyers will find this site particularly useful for tracking down precedents that might help their clients or hinder their cases.

The Tax Prophet

http://www.taxprophet.com/

★★★★★

Read through helpful articles on taxes written by attorney Robert Sommers, as well as FAQs and tax-related links.

Tax Resources on the Web

http://taxtopics.net/

★★★

A simple-to-navigate yet very comprehensive site that allows you to click on keywords, such as kiddy tax or dividends, and find links to sites with useful information on the subjects.

Tax Sites

http://www.taxsites.com

★★★

A site full of web-based tax and accounting resources, which you an access by clicking on a keyword.

TaxFoundation.org

http://www.taxfoundation.org

★★★★★

Dedicated to translating the overly complex and cryptic income tax code into something the average taxpayer can understand, TaxFoundation.org publishes reports that explain in plain English what taxpayers need to know. The foundation also answers tax questions from individuals and the media. This site also features headline tax news and commentary.

TaxHelp Online.com

http://www.taxhelponline.com

★★★★★

Get tax help online to address your individual concerns and situation. Find out what to do if you owe back taxes, or if you haven't filed in years, as well as how to handle just about any situation, including the infamous audit.

TurboTax

http://www.turbotax.com/

★★★★★

This is the home of the most popular tax software in the United States. You can complete and submit your tax return right on the Web and use several of TurboTax's most popular calculators, including Tax Estimator. Site also provides access to IRS forms, a tax-prep checklist, tips and resources, information about tax law changes, and more.

United States Tax Code Online

http://www.fourmilab.ch/ustax/ustax.html

★★★★★

Provides interactive access to the complete text of the United States Internal Revenue Code.

Yahoo! Tax Center

http://taxes.yahoo.com/

★★★★★

Yahoo! provides an online kiosk where you can get all the tax forms, information, and tools you need to calculate your tax liability and pay your fair share of the taxes. Includes tax calculators, federal and state forms, a beginner's guide, tax tips, and a whole lot more.

A
B
C
D
E
F
G
H
I
J
K
L
M
N
O
P
Q
R
S
T
U
V
W
X
Y
Z

TEACHING

Activity Search

http://www.eduplace.com/activity/

★★★★★

A searchable database of 400 original K–8 classroom activities and lesson plans for teachers and parents.

American Federation of Teachers

http://www.aft.org/

★★★★★

Representing one million teachers and educational staff members, the AFT site (part of the AFL-CIO) provides teaching news, reports, and resources. This site also has many downloadable files concerning information that teachers will be interested in, plus information for parents.

Archive.edu

http://www.coe.uh.edu/archive/

★★★★

A storehouse of instructional materials on a variety of topics, including language arts, math, science, social studies, and technology.

ArtsEdge

http://artsedge.kennedy-center.org/artsedge.html

★★★★★

ArtsEdge, sponsored by the Kennedy Center and maintained by MCI, is devoted to helping educators teach the arts more effectively. Teachers will find a pre-established curriculum, lesson plans, teaching materials, and activities available for download, as well as helpful web links, publications, and professional development information. The site also features a NewsBreak section, which provides current, up-to-date information on what's happening in the arts and education. Well presented and packed with useful tools.

CEC Lesson Plans

http://www.col-ed.org/cur/

★★★

Search this directory of lesson plans to find material for science, language arts, math, social studies, and miscellaneous curricula. The plans are divided by age group—grades K–5, 6–8, and 9–12.

Classroom CONNECT

http://www.classroom.net/

★★★★★

This business unit within Harcourt, Inc., is dedicated to helping schools incorporate the Internet into their curricula. Provides professional development and online curriculum resources that foster the use of computers and the Internet in core subjects, including math, language arts, science, and social studies.

Collaborative Lesson Archive

http://faldo.atmos.uiuc.edu/CLA/

★★★

Forum for the creation, distribution, and archival of education curricula for all grade levels and subject areas.

Edheads

http://www.edheads.org/

★★★★★

 All

Edheads partners up with various schools to provide interactive educational programming for students that is designed to help students achieve state standards. Several engaging online presentations are available here, including virtual knee surgery, weather, and simple machines. Teacher guides are available to help teachers incorporate the programming into their curriculum.

EdLinks

http://webpages.marshall.edu/~jmullens/edlinks.html

★★★

Annotated directory of education links. This site contains dozens of useful links.

Education.com

http://www.education.com/

★★★★★

 All

This learning site for teachers, parents, and students provides the tools needed to help parents and teachers better educate students. Well-stocked collection of resources for students broken down by age groups: ages 0–6, ages 6–9, and ages 9–12. Homeschooling resources, including an online encyclopedia, are available, plus articles that teach parents what children should know at each stage of their educational careers. Register for access to additional features.

Education Place

http://www.eduplace.com/

★★★★★

 All

Focused on education for K–8 students, this site provides teachers with resources for professional development and offers some lively activities for the classroom. Special sections for students and parents as well.

Education Week on the Web

http://www.edweek.org

★★★★

News, special reports, a teacher magazine, and discussion forums.

Education World

http://www.education-world.com

★★★★★

 All

Education World is a powerful and free search engine focused on providing information to educators, students, and parents. Use the keyword search, browse by category, or join the Educators' Forum, a message board system to dialogue with educators around the globe. Reviews of 20 education sites are posted each month.

Best Educator's Reference Desk

http://eduref.org/

★★★★★

This site is a gold .mine for educators at all levels. Its resource collection contains links to more than 3000 resources, including Internet sites, educational organizations, and electronic discussion groups. Its Lesson plan collection features more than 2,000 lesson plans submitted by teachers from all across the United States. It's now the home of the ERIC Database, the world's largest source of educational information, including one million abstracts of documents and journal articles on education research and practice. Current information is provided in an easily accessible format at this Best of the Best site!

The Educator's Toolkit

http://www.eagle.ca/~matink/

★★★★

 All

The Educator's Toolkit is a great tool for busy educators. Here, you'll find a monthly Internet newsletter, lesson plans, theme sites, teacher resources, and more.

ENC Online–Eisenhower National Clearinghouse

http://www.enc.org

★★★★

Get K–12 math and science teaching support, including the newest ideas in approaches and material for teaching the subjects, and professional development support through publications and discussions.

A
B
C
D
E
F
G
H
I
J
K
L
M
N
O
P
Q
R
S
T
U
V
W
X
Y
Z

Federal Resources for Educational Excellence (FREE)

http://www.ed.gov/free/

★★★★

FREE makes hundreds of Internet-based education resources supported by agencies across the U.S. federal government easier to find.

Figure This!

http://www.figurethis.org

★★★★★

👫 14-18

A site that encourages family involvement in supporting math skill development through challenging online quizzes that middle school students and their families can take part in.

Gateway to Educational Materials

http://geminfo.org

★★★★

A project to provide teachers with one-stop access to Internet lesson plans.

Global SchoolHouse

http://www.gsh.org/

★★★★★

👫 All

One-stop shopping for Internet-based projects of interest to K–12 educators. Encourages and assists teachers in working collaboratively no matter where they're located geographically.

Harcourt School Publishing

http://www.harcourtschool.com/

$

★★★★★

👫 All

A site that blends interactive learning for kids in grades pre-K–6 with resources for teachers and parents—all to complement Harcourt Brace school publications.

How Stuff Works

http://www.howstuffworks.com/

★★★★★

👫 All

An innovative teaching tool that's fun, too. Want to know more about how something works? This is the site. From how car engines work to web pages, CDs, TVs, and toilets, this site has plenty of interesting and instructional information to share.

ICONnect

http://www.ala.org/ICONN/

★★★★★

Learn the skills necessary to navigate the information superhighway. Developed especially for school library media specialists, teachers, and students.

Intel Innovation in Education

http://www.intel.com/education/

★★★★

👫 All

Intel provides curriculum in support of math and science education, as well as information on competitions, scholarships, events, and more. Good information for teachers and students.

History/Social Studies for K–12 Teachers

http://home.comcast.net/~dboals1/boals.html

★★★★

K–12 teachers will find this history and social studies directory useful for tracking down lesson plans, collaborative projects with other classes and schools, newsgroups, links, and training resources. This site contains at least a couple of hundred links to resources of interest to teachers, parents, and students.

Lesson Plans Page

http://www.lessonplanspage.com

★★★★★

More than 2,000 lesson plans that are helpful for anyone in pre-K–12 education. Simply select your subject and your grade level to display a hefty list of links to lesson plans organized by category, such as math, science, English, music, computers and the Internet, social studies, art, physical education, and other subjects.

McGraw-Hill School Division

http://www.mmhschool.com

★★★★☆

👥 All

Web-based teaching resources for reading/language arts, mathematics, health, social studies, music, bilingual studies, and professional development. This site is the brainstorm of Macmillan/McGraw-Hill, the elementary school publishing unit of McGraw-Hill, and is one of the better-designed sites I've seen. McGraw-Hill is dedicated to educating children and to helping educational professionals by providing the highest quality services. The site is divided into sections called "islands," with one for parents, teachers, and students. Very well designed and worth the visit.

National Education Association

http://www.nea.org/

★★★★

The NEA site provides education statistics, reports, information on grants, events, legislative action, and much more information on the state of education.

National Geographic Education

http://www.nationalgeographic.com/education/

💲

★★★★★

👥 All

Geography teachers will want to bookmark this site. Here, you can find maps, facts, and photos of intriguing places from all around the globe, obtain free lesson plans for all grade levels, introduce students to a variety of online adventures and interactive games, become part of the National Geographic teaching community, and shop online for additional classroom materials.

New York Times Learning Network

http://www.nytimes.com/learning/

★★★★★

👥 All

Challenge your students to the daily news quiz or the word of the day. Science Q&A, Ask a Reporter, and a crossword puzzle are additional learning opportunities posted at this site. Teachers gain access to lesson plans and lesson plan archives.

Pitsco's Ask an Expert

http://www.askanexpert.com

★★★★★

👥 All

Select from 14 categories with more than 300 websites and email addresses where you can find experts to answer your questions about the Amish lifestyle to facts about zookeeping.

The Puffin House

http://www.puffin.co.uk

💲

★★★★★

👥 All

The Puffin House contains information about Penguin children's books. It includes activities for children, teachers' resources, and a searchable database of the full range of book titles.

Scholastic.com

http://teacher.scholastic.com/index.htm

★★★★★

👥 All

Lots of great information to be incorporated into lesson plans as well as news regarding the latest teaching tools and methods, such as software and books. Great place to visit for students, teachers, and parents.

Teachers.net

http://www.teachers.net/

★★★★★

Self-described as "The ultimate teacher's resource," this site encourages and supports teacher communication and collaboration. Features message boards, chat rooms, a schedule of online teacher meetings, libraries of teacher-submitted lesson plans and curricula, and more. To stay in touch with other teachers worldwide and work together to improve education, check out this site.

A B C D E F G H I J K L M N O P Q R S T U V W X Y Z

A
B
C
D
E
F
G
H
I
J
K
L
M
N
O
P
Q
R
S
T
U
V
W
X
Y
Z

U.S. Department of Education–Funding Opportunities

http://www.ed.gov/topics/topics.
jsp?&top=Grants+%26+Contracts

★★★★★

👥 All

Any teacher looking for funding will find it well worthwhile to visit this site for information about funding sources, tips on applying for an educational grant, contract information, and upcoming opportunities.

USA Today Education

http://www.usatoday.com/educate/home.htm

★★★★★

👥 All

Join Experience Today to get your students involved in reading and understanding issues covered in the media. A four-page lesson plan accompanies a subscription to *USA Today* to assist teachers in making use of editorial content.

TEENS

Alloy Online

http://www.alloyonline.com/

★★★★★

👥 14-18

Online magazine and community dedicated to entertaining and informing teenage girls. Check up on your favorite celebrities or keep abreast of the latest fashion crazes at this site.

Bolt

http://www.bolt.com

★★★★

👥 14-18

Bolt is a popular hangout for high school and college kids, where they can express their opinions freely on virtually any topic. They can share information through forums, chat, or instant messaging. Almost all the content comes from members, not adults.

CyberTeens

http://www.cyberteens.com/

💲

★★★★

👥 14-18

Contests, interviews, art, and chat. Anyone can visit the message boards and browse messages posted by members, but if you want to participate, you must register and then sign in.

Favorite Teenage Angst Books

http://www.grouchy.com/angst/

💲

★★★★

👥 14-18

The teenage years are a tough transitional period in which painful self-discovery leads to tremendous anxiety. Here, you can browse the bookshelves to check out books that express and explore teenage angst.

Girls Life Magazine

http://www.girlslife.com

💲

★★★★★

👥 14-18

A magazine for girls and teens, featuring entertainment, news, advice, and more. Subscription information is available. The site contains a one-stop shopping mall just for girls.

[Best] IPL Teen Division

http://www.ipl.org/teen/

★★★★★

👥 14-18

A large collection of teen resources for doing homework, researching papers, career pathways, clubs, dating, health, and much more. If you are a teen, this site has information on all the things you would normally be interested in, such as arts and entertainment, college, high school, books, music, clubs, organizations, computers and the Internet, money matters, and homework. If you're looking for some easy answers—and who isn't—this is the place you can come to and ease your mind. The site also hosts a teen advisor who will help you with your problems. One of the more positive hangouts for teens on the Web.

A B C D E F G H I J K L M N O P Q R S T U V W X Y Z

A
B
C
D
E
F
G
H
I
J
K
L
M
N
O
P
Q
R
S
T
U
V
W
X
Y
Z

LIQUIDGENERATION.com

http://www.liquidgeneration.com/

★★★★★

[icon] Not for kids

Edgy and irreverent, this site pokes fun at the establishment with its singing celebrity karaoke machine, disgusting how-to videos, and *LiquidGeneration EXPOSED* tabloid.

Listen Up!

http://www.pbs.org/merrow/listenup/

$

★★★★★

Listen Up! is a. PBS program that "connects youth producers and their adult mentors from around the country to exchange work, share experiences and learn from one another." You can find out more about Listen Up!, its national programs and distribution support, festival opportunities, and funding.

MyFuture

http://www.myfuture.com

★★★★

[icon] 14-18

Resources to help high school students plan for their future. Includes information about saving money, choosing careers, creating resumes, investigating military opportunities, understanding alcoholism, buying cars, finding scholarships, and dating.

TechnoTeen

http://technoteen.studentcenter.org/

★★★★★

[icon] 14-18

Super site for teens features a student center, relationship questionnaires, teen horoscopes and jokes, chat rooms and discussion forums, a date finder, and much more. Some stuff is not suitable for younger teens.

Teen Advice Online

http://www.teenadviceonline.org/

★★★★★

[icon] 14-18

Counseling center where you can get help from a team of nonprofessional counselors age 13 years and older. Meet the volunteer counselors, read articles on various teenage-related issues, or post your question to get some free advice.

Teen Chat

http://www.teen-chat.net

★★★★

[icon] 14-18

Designed as a safe place for teens to chat on the Net, you can find pen pals from around the world, hop into chat, or join ongoing discussions.

Teenager Driving Contract

http://www.legalnews.net/drivingK.htm

★★★★

Is your child enrolled in a driver's education course? Then before he or she receives a license, visit this site to obtain a legal agreement that spells out the rules of the road in detail. This agreement has plenty of built-in humor as well.

Teenager E-Books

http://www.hopcottebooks.com/ebooks/teenager.html

$

★★★★

[icon] 14-18

Electronic books written for the teenage audience. Includes a photo of each book's cover plus a brief description of the plot.

Teenager's Guide to the Real World

http://www.BYGPUB.com/books/tg2rw/

★★★

 14-18

Online site based on the book of the same name, designed to help teenagers see the freedom they have to control their lives and their destinies, and to help them make good decisions about the future. You can purchase the book *A Teenagers Guide to the Real World* on this site, which has some chapters you can read for free.

Teenagers Today

http://teenagerstoday.com/

★★★

14-18

Information for parents about raising their teenage children.

TeenLink

http://www2.nypl.org/home/branch/teen/

★★★★

14-18

Links from the New York Public Library.

Teenmag.com

http://www.teenmag.com/

★★★★

14-18

This e-zine for teenagers features news about teen celebrities and musical groups, an advice column, style tips, online questionnaires, and much more. Primarily suited for teenage girls.

TeenPeople.com

http://www.teenpeople.com/teenpeople/

★★★★★

14-18

People magazine for teenagers is online with this sleek site that features news about celebrities most teens care about. Celebrity news, hot styles, online games, and chat rooms make this a great teen hangout.

TeenReading

http://www.ala.org/ala/yalsa/teenreading/
teenreading.htm

★★★

14-18

This American Library Association website is devoted to encouraging teenagers to read. Includes a recommended reading list, a top-ten list, and tips on how to encourage teens to read.

TeenTalk

http://teentalk.com

★★★★★

14-18

Christian site where teens can post questions about problems and get advice from other teens. Topics include alcohol, appearance, dating, depression, school, and more.

Understanding Your Teenager

http://www.gospelcom.net/uyt/

★★★★

Is your teenage child running the house and driving you nuts? Then check out this site to learn more about the Understanding Your Teenager seminars. This group hosts seminars for churches, schools, and other organizations that work with teenagers.

WireTap

http://www.wiretapmag.org/

★★★★★

14-18

WireTap is an online news magazine created by socially conscious youth for socially conscious youth. It features "investigative news articles, personal essays and opinions, artwork and activism resources that challenge stereotypes, inspire creativity, foster dialogue and give young people a voice in the media." Here, visitors can read articles about environmental and political issues, learn about events sponsored by WireTap, check the classifieds for job opportunities, get involved in WireTap campaigns, read reviews of books, films, and albums, read poems and short stories, and peruse the gallery of photos, graffiti, and drawings.

A
B
C
D
E
F
G
H
I
J
K
L
M
N
O
P
Q
R
S
T
U
V
W
X
Y
Z

A
B
C
D
E
F
G
H
I
J
K
L
M
N
O
P
Q
R
S
T
U
V
W
X
Y
Z

Young Investor

http://www.younginvestor.com

★★★★★

 All

A place to learn about money and maybe even earn
some, too. Features a game room, where you can
learn about money in a fun environment; a parent-
to-parent section, where parents can have their questions answered; a survey, where you can find out how
you stack up against others in regard to how much
you know about money; and an online college savings calculator you can use to determine how much
money you need to save for college.

TELEVISION

BBCi

http://www.bbc.co.uk

★★★★★

Home of British Broadcasting Corporation's interactive website, BBCi provides the latest headline news and sports; TV and radio programming information; and information on concerts, nightclubs, and other entertainment offerings.

CSI: Crime Scene Investigation

http://www.cbs.com/primetime/csi/main.shtml

★★★★★

This interactive site, created and maintained by CBS, provides visitors with case files for the various episodes of the popular television series *CSI: Crime Scene Investigation*. Here, you can check the latest case file, obtain personnel records for the various investigators, access a handbook that explains many of the technical terms used on the show, tour the crime lab, and chat with other fans.

HBO: Home Box Office

http://www.hbo.com/

★★★★★

Home of the *Sopranos*, *Sex and the City*, *Six Feet Under*, and other award-winning shows, this site provides information about the various HBO original series, premier movies, sports specials, HBO documentaries and films, and much more. Here, you can get a sneak preview of your favorite shows and movies and go behind the scenes with your favorite HBO celebrities.

E! Online

http://www.eonline.com

★★★★★

👫 14-18

TV fans will want to bookmark this site, home of E!, the source for the latest news about everything in the entertainment industry. Here, you can find the latest news and gossip about your favorite celebrities and the hottest TV shows, movies, and recording artists. Read TV, movie, and CD reviews; take online quizzes and compete in trivia contests; check out the latest movie trailers and music clips; and find recent interviews with the top stars.

The Osbournes

http://www.mtv.com/onair/osbournes

★★★★

👫 14-18

Wondering what Ozzy Osbourne and his family are up to? Then drop in on them at their web home and find out. Here, you can learn more about this popular reality-based, family-oriented sitcom, meet the family, take a virtual tour of their home, and check the TV listings for the next episode. You can even download a free screensaver and flip through the kids' personal diaries.

Television Without Pity

http://www.televisionwithoutpity.com/

★★★★★

Satirical recaps of television shows for the pure pleasure of lambasting the very worst that TV has to offer.

A B C D E F G H I J K L M N O P Q R S T U V W X Y Z

A
B
C
D
E
F
G
H
I
J
K
L
M
N
O
P
Q
R
S
T
U
V
W
X
Y
Z

Titan TV

http://www.titantv.com/

★★★★★

Titan TV is a television programming guide with muscle. Here, you can search up to two weeks of program listings, complete with program descriptions, view the listing by category (news, sports, comedy, and so on), sign up for reminders, learn about new stations that might be available in your area, and much more.

TiVo

http://www.tivo.com

★★★★★

Are you busy whenever your favorite shows are on? Are you tired of programming your VCR to record them just so you can search your tapes later to find out what you recorded? Then consider TiVo, a system that lets you record up to 140 hours of TV shows to watch at your convenience and replay whenever you like. This site tells you what TiVo is all about, lets you order it online, and shows you how to set up the system.

[Best] TV Guide Online

http://www.tvguide.com/

★★★★★

Can't find your television guide? Then tune in to the home page of one of the most popular magazines in the country, *TV Guide.* Click the TV Listings link, enter your ZIP code, make a few other selections, and you get an onscreen listing of all the TV shows of the day. This site also features news about your favorite shows, gossip about your favorite stars, a movie guide, a guide to the soaps, and much more. Shop the online store for collectors' items, special CDs and DVDs, and other items. If you spend more than an hour a day in front of the tube, you'll want to bookmark this Best of the Best site for your future reference.

TV Land

http://www.tvland.com

★★★★★

 All

Do you miss those TV shows from yesteryear? Can't live without *The Dick Van Dyke Show, Leave It to Beaver,* and *Get Smart?* Then check out TV Land's home on the Web, where you can learn more about these shows, download complete TV listings, and even shop online for TV Land apparel and paraphernalia.

TV Party

http://www.tvparty.com/

★★★★

 All

Online museum of the best (and worst) in TV over the past 40 years. If you become nostalgic over the old TV shows, this is the site for you. Go behind the scenes with the site's creator and host, Billy Ingram, to listen to the gossip; explore the scandals; and view some of the best dancing, drama, comedy, and action clips from the shows that made TV what it is today.

Ultimate TV

http://www.ultimatetv.com/

★★★★

Ultimate TV provides television shows on-demand by recording your favorite shows to disk. You simply set up a schedule of what you want to record and then play back the show when *you're* ready to view it. Visit this site to learn more about this revolution in TV viewing.

Who Wants to Be a Millionaire

```
http://abc.abcnews.go.com/primetime/millionaire/
millionaire_home.html
```

★★★★★

Home of the most popular game show on the planet, the Who Wants to be a Millionaire website provides information about the show, show highlights, and an online version of the game. Join Regis Philbin online, play fastest finger, and see how much play money you could win playing a sample round of the game. This site also provides information on how to get tickets to the show and how to become a contestant.

TOP TV NETWORKS

ABC	http://abc.abcnews.go.com/
ABC Family	http://abcfamily.go.com/
A&E	http://www.aetv.com/
AMC	http://www.amctv.com/
Animal Planet	http://animal.discovery.com/
BET	http://www.bet.com/bethome
BRAVO	http://www.bravotv.com/
Cartoon Network	http://www.cartoonnetwork.com/
CBS	http://www.cbs.com/
Cinemax	http://www.cinemax.com/
CMT	http://www.cmt.com/
CNBC	http://moneycentral.msn.com/investor/home.asp
CNN	http://www.cnn.com/
Comedy Central	http://www.comedycentral.com/
Court TV	http://www.courttv.com/
C-SPAN	http://www.c-span.org/
Discovery Channel	http://www.discovery.com/
Disney Channel	http://disney.go.com/park/channels/tv/today/flash/
Encore	http://www.starzsuperpak.com/se/encore/index.html
E!	http://www.eonline.com/
ESPN	http://msn.espn.go.com/
Food Network	http://www.foodtv.com/
FOX	http://www.fox.com/
FoxNews	http://www.foxnews.com/
FoxSports	http://foxsports.lycos.com/
FX	http://www.fxnetwork.com/
Gameshow Network	http://www.gameshownetwork.com/
Golf Channel	http://www.thegolfchannel.com/
Hallmark Channel	http://www.hallmarkchannel.com/
History Channel	http://www.historychannel.com/
HBO	http://www.hbo.com/
HGTV	http://www.hgtv.com/
Indie Film Channel	http://www.ifctv.com/
Lifetime	http://www.lifetimetv.com/
MSNBC	http://www.msnbc.msn.com/
MTV	http://www.mtv.com/
NBC	http://www.nbc.com/
Nickelodeon	http://www.nick.com/
Outdoor Life	http://www.olntv.com/
Sci-Fi	http://www.scifi.com/
Showtime	http://sho.com/
STARZ!	http://www.starz.com/
SpeedTV	http://www.speedtv.com/
TBS Superstation	http://tbssuperstation.com/
TCM	http://turnerclassicmovies.com/
TLC	http://tlc.discovery.com/
TNN	http://www.thenewtnn.com/
TNT	http://www.tnt.tv/
Travel	http://travel.discovery.com/
TV Land	http://www.tvland.com/
USA	http://www.usanetwork.com/
VH1	http://www.vh1.com/
Weather	http://www.weather.com/
WE!	http://www.we.tv/
WGN	http://wgntv.trb.com/

A
B
C
D
E
F
G
H
I
J
K
L
M
N
O
P
Q
R
S
T
U
V
W
X
Y
Z

A
B
C
D
E
F
G
H
I
J
K
L
M
N
O
P
Q
R
S
T
U
V
W
X
Y
Z

TENNIS

American Tennis Professionals

http://www.atptour.com

★★★★★

 14-18

Tour news, events information, player profiles, and pro shop. In English and German. Links to the Tennis Warehouse (www.tennis-warehouse.com) for online shopping.

CBS SportsLine: Tennis

http://www.sportsline.com/u/tennis/

$

★★★★★

14-18

Daily news and tournament results, plus special features and columns relating to the game of tennis. Some areas require membership. The site has a shopping area where you can purchase tennis rackets and other tennis-related products.

GoTennis

http://www.gotennis.com

$

★★★★★

14-18

Find tournament information, results, player profiles, tips and techniques for improving your game, tennis-related shopping links, and audio and video news. The site has a Pro shopping area where you can purchase tennis rackets, shoes, and just about everything else.

⌐Best⌐ International Tennis Federation Online

http://www.itftennis.com

★★★★★

14-18

Official site of the world governing body for tennis. Includes results and rankings. Want the latest news about tennis-related events? This site has much to offer in the way of the latest news, rules and regulations, and even the latest facts and figures. Add all that to a great looking site, and you have the winner of our Best of the Best award for Tennis sites.

SLAM! Sports Tennis

http://www.canoe.ca/SlamTennis/home.html

★★★

14-18

Results, articles, player profiles, tournament schedules, rankings, and top servers list.

Steve G's ATP Tour Rankings

http://www.stevegtennis.com/

★★★★

14-18

Current rankings, archives, and tour calendar. Covers ATP, challengers, satellites, and futures.

Tennis Canada

http://www.tenniscanada.com

★★★★★

14-18

Canadian tennis rankings plus player information and tournament news. In French and English.

Tennis Industry News

http://www.tennisindustry.com/

★★★

Brief news stories concerning tennis facilities and manufacturers. Excellent site for the tennis industry, but not much here for the average player or fan.

Tennis: A Research Guide

http://www.nypl.org/research/chss/grd/resguides/tennis/

★★★★

Bibliography on general tennis works from The New York Public Library, with links to more specific bibliographies. References to biographies, histories of the game, tennis instruction and literature, and periodicals.

Tennis Resorts Online

http://www.tennisresortsonline.com

★★★

A guide to the top 100 tennis camps and resorts that can be sorted by location or type, such as junior camps.

Tennis Server

http://tennisserver.com

★★★★

 14-18

Features, equipment tips, and links to other tennis sites. The site has a nice selection of tennis products with lots of links to other sites where you can continue to shop if you don't see what you want on the Tennis Server site.

Tennis Worldwide

http://www.tennisw.com

★★★

Tennis chat site where fans discuss their favorite topics. A good list of recommended books, but not much additional content.

TennisONE

http://www.tennisone.com

★★★★

 14-18

Tennis lessons, fitness information, and products. This site also has a link to the Tennis Warehouse, where you will find most of the things you need to play tennis effectively.

United States Professional Tennis Association (USPTA)

http://www.uspta.org/

★★★★

Find a pro in your area for instruction, find out when this year's conferences and conventions are being held, and learn all about being a USPTA member here.

United States Tennis Association

http://www.usta.com/

★★★★★

 14-18

Web home of the USTA, this site is dedicated to promoting and developing tennis. The USTA is the first governing body for tennis. At this site, you'll find news about the latest tournaments, information about various tennis leagues, tennis rules and regulations, and even some online games.

USA Today: Tennis

http://www.usatoday.com/sports/tennis/tennis.htm

★★★★

14-18

Includes ATP and WTA results, rankings, money leaders, archived stories, and the latest news.

WTA Tour

http://www.wtatour.com

★★★★★

14-18

Official site with schedule, rankings, news, profiles, pro shop, and multimedia clips.

A
B
C
D
E
F
G
H
I
J
K
L
M
N
O
P
Q
R
S
T
U
V
W
X
Y
Z

Yellow Pages

THEATER AND MUSICAL

Actors' Page

http://www.serve.com/dgweb32/

★★★★★

An actor and member of the Screen Actors Guild and the American Federation of Television and Radio Artists has offered a practical and entertaining site for those interested in the acting arts, as well as those who want to find some contacts in show biz. You can add your URL to the page, check out lists of talent agencies and casting directors in New York City, and join a discussion called "The Actors' Roundtable." Click the Links button at the bottom of the home page to view an exhaustive list of links to theaters and actors.

Aisle Say

http://www.aislesay.com/

★★★

"The Internet magazine of stage reviews and opinion." Reviews, reviews, and more reviews of stage productions all over the United States and Canada.

Albany, New York Theatre and the Arts

http://metro-links.com/AlbanyNewYork/
EntertainmentTheTheaterTheArts.htm

★★★★★

This site provides a directory of arts and theater offerings in Albany, New York.

American Conservatory Theater

http://www.act-sfbay.org/

★★★★

This acclaimed training institution and regional theater offers information on its upcoming schedule, performers, past productions, and mission here. You can purchase single tickets online to some productions.

American Repertory Theatre

http://www.amrep.org/

★★★★

Interviews with casts and playwrights, previews of upcoming shows, and synopses of past productions.

American Variety Stage

http://lcweb2.loc.gov/ammem/vshtml/vshome.html

★★★★★

Vaudeville and Popular Entertainment, 1870–1920. Online exhibition from the Library of Congress.

Annie: Long John Silver's Reference Website

http://www.anniethemusical.com/

★★★★

Links to various articles and resources about *Annie: The Musical*, plus discussion forums for fans of this popular musical. Includes cast lists and biographies, cast member birthdays, audio clips, and links to other *Annie* sites.

Broadway Play Publishing, Inc.

http://www.BroadwayPlayPubl.com/

★★★★

This company, which adapts American plays, has a search engine and several related links. You can order books, plays, musicals, one-act collections, and play anthologies. See the adaptations of American classics and check out the photo gallery.

The Children's Theatre

http://www.thechildrenstheatre.com/

★★★★★

 All

The Children's Theatre in Cincinnati runs plays in a real theater space that are geared specifically for children. Here, you can learn more about this theater and what it has to offer. Links to Ticketmaster to purchase tickets.

Related Site
http://faculty-web.at.nwu.edu/theater/tya/
history.html

ChildrensTheatrePlays

http://www.childrenstheatreplays.com/

★★★★

 All

This site features stage plays for children, young audiences, and families, including *Snow White*, *Cinderella*, and *The Wizard of Oz*. This site is a great place for theater producers, directors, drama coaches, and teachers to find scripts for their productions.

Complete Works of William Shakespeare

http://the-tech.mit.edu/Shakespeare/

★★★★

In addition to providing the complete text of every Shakespeare play and poem, this site includes a discussion area, chronological and alphabetical lists of the plays, Bartlett's familiar Shakespeare quotations, and a funeral elegy by the old man himself. An unbelievable site!

Related Site
http://shakespeare.palomar.edu/

Current Theatre

http://www.nytimes.com/library/theater

★★★★

Theater reviews from the *New York Times*.

English Actors at the Turn of the Century

http://www.siue.edu/COSTUMES/actors/pics.html

★★★★★

This straightforward, interesting site provides colorful, full photographs of twentieth-century actors in their roles. Just click an actor or movie, and you're there. See many old actors including Maud Jeffries in *Herod*, Sir Henry Irving in *As You Like It*, and George Alexander in *If I Were King*.

Grand Theatre

http://www.grandtheatre.com/

★★★★

Check out this London, Ontario, Canada's theater website to learn more about the renovated theater and upcoming performances, and to catch a glimpse of the ghost of the theater's founder, Ambrose Small, who haunts the theater and the site, it seems. You can get ticket purchase information here and do a little shopping online.

Grease: The Musical

http://www.prigsbee.com/Musicals/shows/grease.htm

★★★

The Broadway Musical Home of Grease provides information about the original musical, including a cast list, synopsis of the story, and a list of musical numbers. Links to other sites to purchase music and videos.

Jimbo's Unofficial Rent Site

http://www.lifecafe.com

★★★

News and up-to-date information about *Rent*: the show, cast bios, articles, and chat. Even includes some interactive games!

Larry Stark's Theater Mirror

http://www.theatermirror.com/

★★★

Lengthy reviews of new plays in Boston are only part of this rich web resource. The page includes a calendar of shows, upcoming plays, the casting callboard, and notes on recent productions.

A B C D E F G H I J K L M N O P Q R S T U V W X Y Z

A B C D E F G H I J K L M N O P Q R S **T** U V W X Y Z

Lighting Dimensions
http://lightingdimensions.com/

★★★★★

Selected articles from the print version of the highly respected magazine for behind-the-scenes theater professionals, including lighting, sound, and production designers, and costume and makeup professionals.

London Theatre Guide Online
http://www.londontheatre.co.uk/

★★★★★

Use this handy page to find information on West End shows, the Royal National Theatre, and other London theaters. Includes addresses, seating arrangements, reviews of current shows, ballet and opera listings, and a monthly email update service. You can find out the current costs of tickets and where to purchase them as well as do some shopping by linking to other sites such as Amazon.com.

Mermaniac: A Show Tunes Weblog
http://www.mermaniac.com/

★★★★

This site, devoted to Broadway show-tune fans, is a serious collection of information on Broadway musicals and their composers, with pictures, cast lists, discographies, CD reviews, links to related sites, and more.

Musical (Dance) Films
http://www.filmsite.org/musicalfilms.html

★★★

This site is composed of a lengthy, incredibly detailed document that tells the history of musical films from *Don Juan* (1926) to *Tarzan* (1999). It includes pages on many of the films, with theatrical posters, pictures, and some synopses that tell in great detail the story of each film—including occasional song lyrics and dialogue. Lots of popups.

Musicals.net
http://musicals.net

★★★★★

This site lists about 75 popular musicals and plenty of new ones coming up. Click a musical's name to list links, lyrics, media clips, notes, synopses, and tons of other information.

Now Casting
http://www.nowcasting.com/

★★★★

Searchable database brings together actors, casting directors, managers, and agents to help filmmakers create films and to find appropriate jobs for actors.

Performing Arts Online
http://www.performingarts.net

★★★★

The Performing Arts Network has put together a great site, with links to dozens of performers and companies, sorted by genre—musical theater lists of current shows in production. A clickable Featured Artists button changes every few seconds to connect you to performers' sites. Hundreds of links to related sites.

[Best] Playbill Online
http://www.playbill.com/

★★★★★

The electronic version of the famous print publication that focuses on Broadway and Off-Broadway theatres. You can purchase tickets online, read reviews, and learn about the stars behind the top productions. Excellent site with a strong content offering.

The Public Theater
http://www.publictheater.org/

★★★★

The Public Theatre presents full seasons of new plays and musicals, as well as Shakespeare and other classics at its Manhattan location. Find out how to get there, what shows the troupe will be performing, who's in the cast, and how you can support this group.

Roundabout Theatre Company

http://www.roundabouttheatre.org/

★★★★★

Find out more about this classic theater group, upcoming shows, subscriptions that give members access to additional private performances (Theatre-Plus), its history, and ways you can subscribe. Links to other sites to purchase tickets.

Screen Actor's Guild

http://www.sag.com/

★★★★★

Online site of the Screen Actor's Guild, the largest professional actors' advocacy group. Read news about SAG and its events, view a calendar of upcoming events, and get leads on talent agents. Professional actors should bookmark it.

Shakespeare: Subject to Change

http://www.ciconline.org/bdp1/

★★★★★

This intriguing site, hosted by Cable in the Classroom, explores the various ways that Shakespeare's original texts might have been changed by typesetters, editors, directors, and others to provide us with the texts that many assume to be Shakespeare's original writings. Along the way, the site explores Shakespeare's language and points out some interesting facts about how well versed this playwright really was. This site is very well designed and features engaging Flash presentations.

Shakespeare Theatre

http://shakespearedc.org/

★★★★★

Information about the Washington D.C.–based Shakespeare Theatre, including upcoming performances, cast bios, job listings and internships, and acting classes. Links to Tickets.com for purchasing tickets.

SITCOM

http://www.dangoldstein.com/sitcom.html

★★★★

Information on the SITCOM program of improvised half-hour shows that mimic rehearsed and planned TV comedy. Provides a blend of structuralist literary criticism and artificial intelligence, a live show that converts audience suggestions into full-length, improvised TV sitcoms that unfold live on stage.

Tony Awards Online

http://www.tonys.org/

★★★★★

The Tony Awards program isn't strictly about musicals, of course—plenty of wonderful dramas and comedies take awards in their own categories—but the Tonys are always a guide to what's good in musicals on stage. Go to this site for a variety of entertainment: contests, games, a chat page, lists of award winners (and nominees, depending on the season), theater news, and other interesting sections. The site is very well designed and has a variety of information about the Tonys.

Vintage Vaudeville and Ragtime Show

http://www.bestwebs.com/vaudeville/

★★★

Get back to the old ragtime days with this modern site about vaudeville. First, check out the history of vaudeville. Then view some cool, old pictures. Also, get some biographical data on stars such as Ada Jones and Len Spencer. Best of all, sit back and enjoy some actual music, such as Arthur Collins singing *Ragtime*. There are several RealAudio files to enjoy.

World Wide Arts Resources: Theater

http://wwar.com/categories/Theater/

★★★

Huge directory of theater-related resources on the Web covering everything from actors to musicals and from opera to theater companies. Search by keyword or phrase, or browse through the many categories. Pop-up ads at this site can be very annoying.

A
B
C
D
E
F
G
H
I
J
K
L
M
N
O
P
Q
R
S
T
U
V
W
X
Y
Z

A
B
C
D
E
F
G
H
I
J
K
L
M
N
O
P
Q
R
S
T
U
V
W
X
Y
Z

WWW Virtual Library Theatre and Drama
`http://vl-theatre.com/`

★★★★

This site features a comprehensive directory of theater-related resources on the Web, including plays, monologues, conferences, journals, mailing lists, and message boards.

ALEX

http://www.alextoys.com

★★★

 0-8

A fun and creative site offering art supplies and activity kits. At this site, children can also hear animals talk, read the Alex newsletter, and find out about featured products.

Archie McPhee

http://www.mcphee.com/

$

★★★★

 All

Home of the FUZZ action figure, tailless monkey T-shirts, and nerd supplies, this novelty store carries a good collection of fun stuff that's a little on the wild side.

AreYouGame.com

http://www.areyougame.com/interact/default.asp

$

★★★★★

 All

Choose an age group; favorite type of activity, such as brain teasers; or game, such as Monopoly, and AreYouGame will recommend specific games and puzzles for your child, or child at heart. Learn about new games or order well-known favorites at this site, which has an extensive collection of games for almost any age group.

Big Fun Toys

http://www.bigfuntoys.com/

★★★★★

Fun toys and gag gifts abound at this site, where you can find everything from hula dancer honeys to the ever popular potato gun.

Boardgames.com

http://www.boardgames.com/

★★★★★

 All

A huge selection of board games is available here, from children's games to adult, strategy, or electronic handheld. You'll find current popular games such as Millionaire and Scrabble, but there are many, many others to buy or give as gifts. This site is well designed and easy to navigate. Better and easier than shopping at the mall. If you are into games of all kinds and would rather spend your time playing them than shopping in faraway crowded malls, this site is the place to get them. You can shop from the convenience of your own home, look at the games online, and read the descriptions at your leisure. You'll also find a lot of useful information about all the games here.

A
B
C
D
E
F
G
H
I
J
K
L
M
N
O
P
Q
R
S
T
U
V
W
X
Y
Z

BRIO

http://www.briotoy.com/

★★★★★

 0-8

Learn all about how BRIO wooden toys are con-structed, about the many types, and the awards the toys have won. You can request a catalog be mailed to you or conduct an online toy search here to find what you're looking for. The site contains a feature that enables you to find out where to buy BRIO toys near you.

The Copernicus

http://www.copernicustoys.com

★★★★

 All

A store specializing in toys of the imagination for adults: optical illusions, craft kits, puzzles, and the like. You can email for a complete catalog.

Creativity for Kids

http://www.creativityforkids.com

★★★★

 0-8

A wonderful craft activities supplier. Choose craft projects by age or type—such as glass beads, ceram-ics, or stitchery—to find a long list of products that match the criteria. Although you can't buy the prod-ucts at this site, if you enter your ZIP code, the site will create a list of local stores that carry what you're looking for, as well as online merchants.

Discovery Toys

http://www.discoverytoysinc.com/

★★★★

 0-8

Check out the latest toys from this company, which creates toys appropriate for a child's age and develop-mental state. Learn more about which toys are appropriate and find a local educational consultant you can buy from.

Disney Online Store

http://disney.store.go.com/

★★★★★

 All

Offers a full online catalog of Disney merchandise with secure online purchasing. You also can access the Disney Store "gift finder" service and a listing of Disney Store locations worldwide.

The Dummy Doctor

http://homepage.mac.com/asemok/dummies2.html

★★★★★

 All

A commercial site offering "hand-crafted profession-al ventriloquial figures," plus puppets and mari-onettes for both professionals and hobbyists. Also does repair and evaluation of vintage dummies and puppets.

EducationalToys.com

http://www.educationaltoys.com/

★★★★★

 All

This site sells Quercetti Intelligent Toys, which are designed to stimulate reasoning, creativity, and mobility skills. They can be used over and over with-out being repetitive because they inspire new discov-eries and inventions. Choose by age, category, activity, or recommendations and shop online.

Etch-a-Sketch

http://www.etch-a-sketch.com

★★★★

 All

Look at the Etch-a-Sketch art gallery, do your own Etch-a-Sketch online, and play games.

Best eToys

http://www.etoys.com

$

★★★★★

 All

Huge online toy warehouse featuring just about every toy imaginable. Shop for specific toys by keyword or phrase, or browse for toys by age, category, or brand name. eToys can even help you shop by providing a list of bestselling toys, video game reviews, and special offers. Order toys online and have your order shipped right to your door. If you need a hard-to-get toy fast, you'll find that this site is truly the Best of the Best.

Firebox.com

http://www.firebox.com/

$

★★★★★

 All

Toys for boys (older boys and men, that is). This site features an excellent collection of toys for older kids, including digital cameras, portable MP3 players, game pads, remote control vehicles, mini speakers, projection clocks, and all sorts of other gadgets. Shopping for the man who has everything? Then shop here.

Fisher-Price

http://www.fisher-price.com

$

★★★★★

 0-8

Select the perfect product from the personal shopper, create your own online baby and gift registry, view more than 300 products in the Fisher-Price showroom, and more.

The Gallery of Monster Toys

http://members.aol.com/raycastile/page1.htm

★★★★

 All

The creator of this site says it best: "Vintage monster toys are typically overlooked by collectors, largely because they seem obsolete in today's world. The toys in this gallery are not, for the most part, 'slick' or 'hyper-detailed.' They are humble and imperfect. They depict flawed, tortured creatures. These toys capture a time when horror was fun." After searching through all the "monsters" of past, present, and maybe the future, you may want one of these cuddly creatures for your very own. You'll find some information and links where you can purchase these prize creatures. This site is nice to visit if for no other reason than it is well designed and shows some great "monsters" that you might want to own.

Genius Babies.com

http://www.geniusbabies.com/

$

★★★★★

 0-8

Whether you're looking for an activity for your toddler or a baby shower gift, you're likely to find one in your price range here. Choose by age or type of toy, such as play mats or puzzles. You might want to find out about the top sellers, which are listed at the site, too.

Hasbro World

http://www.hasbro.com

★★★★★

 All

Home to the makers of Action Man, Battleship, Collector's Corner, Monopoly, Risk, Scrabble, Trivial Pursuit, Yahtzee, and many more favorites. You'll find a nice selection of Hasbro toys here, such as G.I. Joe and all his accessories and equipment. The site includes a search feature to help you locate places where you can buy the toys.

A B C D E F G H I J K L M N O P Q R S **T** U V W X Y Z

A
B
C
D
E
F
G
H
I
J
K
L
M
N
O
P
Q
R
S
T
U
V
W
X
Y
Z

Into The Wind

http://www.intothewind.com/

★★★★★

 All

Claiming to be the world's largest kite seller, this site will teach you about flying a kite and give you lots of types to choose from for purchase. From flags and banners to wind socks to traditional or stunt kites, this site has them all. You can also join a discussion forum to chat with fellow kiters.

KBKids

http://www.kbkids.com/index.html

★★★★★

 All

Shop by age, price, or brand for the toy you want, or find out about this week's sales before you decide. This online KB Toys site has a wide selection of toys for all ages.

Latoys.com

http://www.latoys.com/

★★★★

 All

A wide selection of toys and brands is available here with plenty of pictures to guide you.

Learning Curve International

http://www.learningcurve.com/

★★★★

 0-8

Learn about the toy product lines that build on your child's expanding mobility and development. Starting with soft Lamaze toys for infants, you can move to more solid Ambi toys and into several other toy lines as your child ages. Select the product line you're interested in and then view all the available toys. The site has a feature to help you find out where to purchase these toys.

The Official LEGO World Wide Website

http://www.lego.com/

★★★★★

 All

Aimed primarily at kids, this site lists the LEGO toy groups (LEGO, Duplo, and so on) and provides a parent guide, a web surfer's club (so kids can list or make their own LEGO sites), and games to play on the Internet. Also has listings of whom to contact to get the various toys in every country. You can also shop online if you prefer. One of the better sites on the Internet with great graphics and easy-to-navigate menus.

Little Tikes

http://www.littletikes.com/

★★★★★

 0-8

View and listen to Little Tikes toys being used at this site, which shows you the complete 200+ toy line. Then you can the nearest local store that carries what you need. You'll also find a list of hot toys and those on sale.

Mattel

http://www.mattel.com

★★★★★

All

The official site of one of the worldwide leaders in the design, manufacture, and marketing of children's products, including such brand names as Barbie, Hot Wheels, Tyco, Disney, and more. Guess what? You can conveniently shop online at this site for all those toys you couldn't find locally.

Nintendo

http://www.nintendo.com

★★★★★

 All

Home of the king of video games, this site is packed with information about the company and its products. Here, you can learn about the latest Nintendo game systems, explore the wide selection of available games, get technical support and customer service, and share your enthusiasm for Nintendo video games with other enthusiastic players. You can even play free online games, download free software, subscribe to the Nintendo newsletter, check out featured Nintendo sites, and get more information about Nintendo and its products than you could ever imagine. Very easy to navigate and packed with valuable resources for Nintendo fans.

Only Toys

http://www.onlytoys.com/

★★★★

 All

Search this online toy store for stuffed animals, dolls, wooden toys, and more. And if you don't find exactly what you're looking for, send an email to see whether Only Toys has that toy in its Tennessee store. Only Toys carries more than 5,000 products.

Rokenbok

http://www.rokenbok.com/

★★★★★

 All

Rokenbok Toys are for kids aged five and up and are designed to be expanded. You can build with them, add cars and trucks, as well as add radio-controlled pieces. Learn about the components and skills your child builds with each addition. A convenient deal locator will help you find your local source of toys and items for you to purchase.

Schylling

http://www.schylling.com/

★★★★

 0-8

If you're looking for classic toys like tea sets or Curious George playthings, you'll want to scan this online store first.

Sega

http://www.sega.com

★★★★★

All

Games, contests, product news, an online store, technical support, and more.

SmarterKids.com

http://www.smarterkids.com/

★★★★★

All

Choose toys for your child according to his or her developmental stage, learning style, or grade expectation, or by teachers' and parents' recommendations. This site has lots of toys to choose from, organized in many ways. And there are thousands of toys on sale at 50% off.

Teddy Bear Directory

http://www.bearsbythesea.com/

★★★

0-8

Listings of teddy bear stores and artists around the world. This site even has an online store to make your shopping easier.

Toys for Tots

http://www.toysfortots.org/

★★★★

The U.S. Marine Reserve program Toys for Tots is described in complete detail at this site. It goes into the history, the foundation that helps to support the program, its corporate sponsors, and most importantly, how you can help.

A
B
C
D
E
F
G
H
I
J
K
L
M
N
O
P
Q
R
S
T
U
V
W
X
Y
Z

The Virtual Toy Store

`http://www.uncomyngifts.com/`

Targeted toward science fiction and fantasy enthusiasts. Offers a fully interactive toy store, complete with sound and video clips. Specializes in hard-to-find gifts, toys, T-shirts, and jewelry.

TRACK AND FIELD

Armory Track & Field Center

http://www.armorytrack.com/

★★★★

👫 14-18

The Armory in northern Manhattan is one of the fastest indoor tracks in the world. It is also the future home of the National Track & Field Hall of Fame. At this site, you can tour this old facility, research its history, and learn more about its programs.

Athens 2004

http://www.athens.olympic.org/

★★★★★

👫 14-18

The official home pages of the 2004 Summer Olympics, to be held in Athens, Greece. You can view media releases, environmental guidelines, information about any of the events, and other information. Download free screensavers, desktop wallpaper, and e-cards. You can even learn about becoming one of the many volunteers who contribute to making the Olympics a success.

Athletics Canada

http://www.athleticscanada.com/

★★★★★

👫 14-18

As the governing body for Canadian track and field, Athletics Canada's page focuses on Canadian athletes, records, rankings, events, coaching, and news. Bilingual—English and French.

International Association of Athletics Federations

http://www.iaaf.org/

★★★★★

👫 14-18

This home of the International Association of Athletics Federations provides news, results, athletic journals, calendars, world rankings, and much more. This is a great site to visit to check out official world records for various track events.

Kelly's Running Warehouse

http://www.kellysrunningwarehouse.com/

💲

★★★★★

👫 14-18

At this site with more than 75,000 running shoes in stock at prices up to $50 off, runners will want to at least check the inventory here before their next purchase. You can shop online using 100% secure shopping.

Masters Track and Field

http://www.masterstrack.com/index.shtml

★★★

👫 14-18

Young whippersnappers aren't the only people enjoying themselves on the track. This page is dedicated to running seniors, some of whom, into their nineties, are still breaking records.

A B C D E F G H I J K L M N O P Q R S **T** U V W X Y Z

A
B
C
D
E
F
G
H
I
J
K
L
M
N
O
P
Q
R
S
T
U
V
W
X
Y
Z

Road Runner Sports Shoe Store

http://www.roadrunnersports.com

★★★★★

👥 14-18

Research and buy sports shoes, including name brands such as Nike, Reebok, Adidas, and Puma. If you like to shop online, this site has a very nice, well-organized, and easy-to-navigate online store.

Runner's Web

http://www.runnersweb.com/running.html

★★★★

👥 14-18

Information source for running competitions, news, and accessories.

Runner's World Online

http://www.runnersworld.com/

★★★★★

👥 14-18

Home of the popular *Runner's World* magazine, this site features some of the best articles about track and field events, cross-country, and marathons. Free training log and workout regimens, training plans, and calculators. Shoe and treadmill reviews, treatments for injuries, nutrition information, and much more.

Running4.com

http://www.running4.com/

★★★★

👥 14-18

Running4.com is an online training log by runners for runners. At this site, you can keep your own training log, read and post messages, or search the database for links to other running sites.

Running Network

http://www.runningnetwork.com/

★★★★★

👥 14-18

Get running tips, news, and links, as well as a track calendar and race results. This e-zine is dedicated to America's "grassroots runners." Here you will find national and local running news, features, photos, extensive race results, a searchable calendar, training tips, clubs, stores, product reviews and more.

Running and Track & Field

http://www.tflinks.com/

★★★★★

👥 14-18

This site features an excellent directory of articles, books, and links to other sites related to track and field.

Best Track and Field News

http://www.trackandfieldnews.com/

★★★★★

👥 14-18

Peruse past issues and check up on races, athletes, and records. The countless articles will keep die-hard runners busy until they're rested and ready to start running again. This site offers much for the online shopper as well. You can shop in a nice, easy-to-navigate online store and purchase everything from books to videos. You can review the latest issue of the magazine, see the men's world rankings by nation, search for articles of interest in the archive, and even check out the calendar and links to related sites. With all it offers and its pleasing presentation, this site grabs the gold.

Training for 400m/800m: An Alternative Plan

http://www.oztrack.com/plan.htm

★★★★

👥 14-18

This site shares information gathered by its author regarding better methods to prepare an athlete to run in either the 400- or 800-meter medium sprints. The information includes specific training regimens.

USA Track and Field

http://www.usatf.org/

★★★★★

 14-18

The official site of track and field's overseeing authority in the United States. These pages contain news, national and international records, race walking resources, masters racing, and race numerology.

Vault World (Pole Vault Paradise)

http://www.polevault.com/

★★★

 14-18

Get answers to your questions in the Coaching Area, see who the top vaulters are this year, link to related sites, view pictures and videos, and read articles about vaulting.

A
B
C
D
E
F
G
H
I
J
K
L
M
N
O
P
Q
R
S
T
U
V
W
X
Y
Z

Yellow Pages

TRAVEL AND VACATION

ADVENTURE

Adventure Center

http://www.adventurecenter.com/

★★★★★

Adventure Center provides safaris, treks, expeditions, and active vacations worldwide in Antarctica, South America, Europe, Africa, Asia, and the South Pacific. Tribal encounters are common, and you can see images of past trips at this site, where you can find out more about upcoming travel opportunities.

Adventure Travel Tips

http://www.adventuretraveltips.com/

★★★★★

This site provides links to more than 1,000 adventure vacations grouped by category, including animal treks, bicycling, bird watching, sailing, hunting, scuba diving, and much more.

Adventurous Traveler

http://adventuroustraveler.com/

★★★★★

This site features a huge collection of travel books, including hiking guides, travel guides, national parks, and ecotourism adventures.

Alpine Ascents

http://www.alpineascents.com/

★★★★★

For the extreme vacation adventure, check out Alpine Ascents Expeditions and Mountain Climbing School. You can learn about the school, its various expeditions and guides, the gear required and provided, and much more. Be sure to read the FAQ before signing up for your first expedition.

P.O.V. Borders

http://www.pbs.org/pov/borders/

★★★★★

This is the home of the PBS series *P.O.V. Borders*, which takes viewers on adventures across borders to see how people on the other side live. This site includes media from the series, interactive games, discussion areas where you can share your stories and ask questions, materials for teachers and parents, and much more.

EarthRiver Expeditions

http://www.earthriver.com/

★★★★★

EarthRiver Expeditions can lead you on an adventure in North or South America, the South Pacific, or Asia by raft, kayak, and/or on foot. Check out this site's interactive map for more details. From this point of departure, you can check out the available expeditions, check the calendar for a time that fits your schedule, learn about the guides, view expedition maps, take a virtual tour, and much more. Nicely designed site with beautiful graphics and excellent content.

Festivals

http://www.festivals.com/

★★★

Big-party goers will fancy this site, where they can learn about the major festivals around the world. A clickable map lets you search by geographical region, or you can enter a keyword to search for a specific location or festival. This is a pretty cool idea, and the site has a nice design, but tracking down specific festivals wasn't as easy as it looked. However, the site does have a navigation bar at the top that gives you quick access to festivals and events in the following categories: Arts, Culture, Kids, Motorsports, Music, and Sports.

Great Pacific Adventures

http://www.greatpacificadventures.com/

★★★★

Learn more about whale-watching tours in the Pacific Northwest with this company and view pictures from past trips.

Best iExplore

http://www.iexplore.com/

★★★★★

From the magazine that is know for its world-class expeditions comes iExplore, the premier site for adventure travel on the Web. This site is packed with interesting trip ideas to the world's hidden treasure destinations. Click the Travel Dream Machine link to check out some of the more intriguing trips, or scroll down the page to view the top destinations or explore trips by country. Online trip finders, destinations guides, and expert advice help you pick the trip that's right for you. You can also check out exclusive trips, great deals, and membership benefits. If you're looking for a journey that's off the beaten track, you'll find it here.

Mountain Travel Sobek

http://www.mtsobek.com/

★★★★★

You'll find a huge number of different types of adventure travel trips described at this company's site—from hiking adventures to river rafting, biking, small boat cruises, and many more. Look at photos from past trips and read the Travel Journal to hear from past travelers about some of their experiences.

Rod and Gun Resources

http://rodgunresources.com/

★★★★

An international hunting and fishing adventure travel company offering trips around the world. See the site for information about destinations and to see comments from past travelers.

Silver Lining Tours

http://www.silverliningtours.com/

★★★★

Ever wanted to see a storm up close? Then check out this site for information on storm-chasing adventures planned for next year. Learn about what you might see and how you can sign up for this very popular tour. This site has a lot of information about tornadoes and severe storms. If you don't want to pay for a tour, just move to the Midwest—if you don't already live there. The site has contact information you will need to sign up for the trip.

Smithsonian Journeys

http://www.smithsonianjourneys.org/

★★★★

Some people travel to relax. Other people like to learn something. Smithsonian Journeys, although they do provide plenty of relaxation, are more for those who like to return home from vacation a little more knowledgeable than when they left. At this site, you pick a departure date, an interest (such as archeology or philosophy), a tour type (such as countryside, private jet, hiking, or cruise), or a destination (say, France or China), and Smithsonian Journeys suggests several journeys that you might find appealing.

A B C D E F G H I J K L M N O P Q R S T U V W X Y Z

A
B
C
D
E
F
G
H
I
J
K
L
M
N
O
P
Q
R
S
T
U
V
W
X
Y
Z

Storm Chasing Adventure Tours

http://www.stormchasing.com/

★★★★

Another storm-chasing travel operator that will tell you about upcoming trips and accommodations. Trips are 13 days long. The site has contact information for helping you plan your tour online.

Tornado Alley Safari Tours

http://tornadosafari.com

★★★★★

Learn about the storms this travel company has encountered on its expeditions and get information on upcoming trips to witness serious storms and tornadoes. You can get contact information here for planning your tour. This site was featured on several top network news shows and is very well organized with lots of pictures and information about the tours. If you like tornadoes, lightning, and severe weather, then this site is well worth a visit. The site also features numerous pictures of previous tours that have resulted in encounters with tornadoes and severe storms.

Travel Source

http://www.travelsource.com/

★★★★

Use this travel search guide to find the adventure travel experience you're looking for with the activities and location you want.

Walking Adventures International

http://www.walkingadventures.com/

★★★★

Consider taking a walking tour of interesting places all around the world with this group, which travels through the United States, Europe, the Mediterranean, and many more places. Check the travel schedule to see when and where you might like to go. You'll find information to help you conveniently sign up for the tour.

AIR TRAVEL

Air Charter Guide

http://inetserver.guides.com/acg/

★★★★

The online edition of *The Air Charter Guide*, a limited version of the book. Serves as a guide for locating charter operators, arranged by state and name. Also includes tips on planning and pricing a charter.

Airlines of the Web

http://flyaow.com/

★★★★★

Provides information about airlines, organized by geographic region. Also provides information about cargo airlines, newsgroups, and airports.

AirlineSafety.com

http://www.airlinesafety.com/

★★★★

Devoted to making airlines safer for passengers to fly, this site attempts to provide an open forum about airline safety that's free from special interests and politics. Here, you can read articles on various airline safety topics that you won't see in the daily news.

Airpasses of the World

http://www.etn.nl/airpass.htm

★★★★

Links to airlines that offer airpasses. An airpass can be used only by a foreign visitor, and it is a fabulous bargain. If you are planning to visit outside your home country, check the possibility of using an airpass.

AirSafe.com

http://www.airsafe.com/

★★★★★

If you're worried about airline safety and security, this is the site for you. Here, you'll find tips on how best to deal with safety issues, terrorist threats, airport security, and baggage issues. Loads of tips available to make your air travel safer and make it proceed with fewer hassles. Get the latest safety statistics for various airlines and airplane models, plus additional travel advice. Before you head to the airport, head to this site.

Flight Arrivals

http://www.flightarrivals.com

★★★★★

Real-time arrival and departure times for flights throughout the United States and Canada. Just type in the flight information and learn whether it's on time. Just the tool you need before heading to the airport to depart or to pick someone up.

Seat Guru

http://seatguru.com/

★★★★★

Where should you sit on your next flight? Do you want a window seat? Quick access to the aisle? Plenty of legroom? A quiet seat? Tell Seat Guru the airline and aircraft you plan on flying, and let the Guru tell you where to sit.

AIRLINES

Aer Lingus

http://www.aerlingus.ie/

($)

★★★★★

Air Canada

http://www.aircanada.ca/

($)

★★★★★

Alaska Airlines

http://www.alaska-air.com

($)

★★★★★

America West

http://www.americawest.com

($)

★★★★★

American Airlines

http://www.aa.com/

($)

★★★★★

Ansett Australia

http://www.ansett.com.au/

($)

★★★★★

British Airways

http://www.british-airways.com/

($)

★★★★

Cathay Pacific

http://www.cathaypacific.com/

($)

★★★★

Continental

http://www.continental.com

($)

★★★★

Delta

http://www.delta.com/

($)

★★★★★

Hawaiian Airlines

http://www.hawaiianair.com

($)

★★★★★

Lufthansa

http://www.lufthansa.com/

($)

★★★★★

A B C D E F G H I J K L M N O P Q R S **T** U V W X Y Z

New England Airlines

http://users.ids.net/flybi/nea/

★★★★★

Northwest

http://www.nwa.com

★★★★★

Qantas Airlines

http://www.qantas.com/

★★★★

Southwest

http://www.southwest.com/

★★★★★

United

http://www.ual.com

★★★★★

US Airways

http://www.usairways.com

★★★★★

BUDGET TRAVEL

11th Hour Vacations

http://www.11thhourvacations.com

★★★★★

Browse the available trips and cruises with departure dates in the next couple of weeks to find great deals. Whether you want to see New York City or Greece, you have a huge number of options to choose from. And the prices are very reasonable. You can also enter your email to be alerted to deals on a particular destination.

Arthur Frommer's Budget Travel Online

http://www.frommers.com

★★★★★

Features and resources for all types of vacations and travel. Includes a travel planner and tips on booking travel.

ArtofTravel.com

http://www.artoftravel.com/

★★★

Read this online book to learn how to backpack around the world for less than $25 a day. You'll find tips, commentary, and humor here about backpacking and world travel.

Backpack Europe on a Budget

http://www.backpackeurope.com/

★★★★

Learn some of the strategies that can make it possible for you to backpack across Europe inexpensively. Find out about hostels, working abroad, and discount packages.

BargainTravel.com

http://www.bargaintravel.com/

★★★★★

Find the best prices on vacation packages, car rentals, airfare, cruises, and hotels at this site.

Bestfares.com

http://www.bestfares.com/

★★★★★

Sign up for the BestFares weekly email to be alerted to special discount opportunities for Thursday through Tuesday travel. Some great deals you wouldn't have found anywhere else.

Budget Hotels

http://www.budgethotels.com

★★★★★

Find accommodations around the world at discount prices, as well as other travel bargains on cars and airfares here.

Busabout Europe

http://www.busabout.com/

★★★★

The economical alternative to rail travel. Connects 50 cities in Europe and 41 destinations outside Europe by bus.

Council Travel

http://www.counciltravel.com/

★★★★

Offers discount and budget airfares, rail passes, hostel memberships, international student ID cards, and more, for student, youth, and budget travelers.

DiscountAirfares.com

http://www.discountairfares.com

★★★★

Lots of links to low-cost airfare sites.

Economy Travel

http://www.economytravel.com/

★★★★★

Lowest international airfares on the Web, booked online. Consolidator fares, private fares, and low published fares, all on one site.

Expedia

http://www.expedia.com

★★★★★

Search for travel deals, make reservations, and shop around for special packages at Expedia.

Hostels.com

http://www.hostels.com/

★★★★★

Find a hostel or low-cost hotel near where you're traveling and learn more about what to expect from experienced travelers at this site.

Hotwire.com

http://www.hotwire.com/

★★★★★

Hotwire is dedicated to helping travelers fly, drive, and sleep cheap. On the opening page, you can search for bargains on airfare, car rentals, motel rooms, and cruises. Hotwire.com features tabs for easy navigation, including tabs for weekend getaways, packages, and deals & destinations.

LastMinuteTravel.com

http://www.lastminutetravel.com/

★★★★★

A site where you can find last-minute deals on airfare, hotels, cars, and cruises. Search by departure date or desired destination.

Lowestfare.com

http://www.lowestfare.com/

★★★★

If you're planning a vacation, cruise, or just a short trip into the next state, you'll find a travel guide and a reservation section here and all at the lowest fares. Check out the fares here before planning your trip.

Moment's Notice

http://www.moments-notice.com

★★★

Check the daily specials to find last-minute travel deals at greatly reduced prices. Sign up for email alerts when travel bargains arise that meet your particular interests.

A
B
C
D
E
F
G
H
I
J
K
L
M
N
O
P
Q
R
S
T
U
V
W
X
Y
Z

A
B
C
D
E
F
G
H
I
J
K
L
M
N
O
P
Q
R
S
T
U
V
W
X
Y
Z

OneTravel.com

http://www.onetravel.com/index.cfm

★★★★★

This site tracks hot deals for airfare, cruises, resorts, and long weekends. You can search multiple departure cities at the same time and can request customized emails be sent to you weekly to keep you posted of specials that matter to you. Some excellent travel advice from the experts, too.

priceline.com

http://www.priceline.com

$

★★★★★

Place a bid on airfare, hotels, and car rentals and see whether a company will accept it. If so, you can save hundreds or even thousands of dollars.

Road Trips

http://www.roadtripusa.com/

$

★★★★★

With air travel and cruises, many people overlook the joyous adventures of affordable road trips. Here, you can check cross-country routes that have managed to avoid the devastation of development and retain their flavor.

SkyAuction.com

http://www.skyauction.com/

$

★★★★

Bid on airfares, resorts, hotels, and car rentals starting at $1.

Travel Discounts

http://www.traveldiscounts.com/

★★★★

A business travel–oriented site providing information about discounts on car rentals, railroads, tours, cruises, airlines, and specific tour packages arranged by region.

Travelocity

http://www.travelocity.com

$

★★★★★

Full online travel service with information on destinations, travel bargains, and travel tips. You can even sign up to be notified when fares to a particular destination drop.

CAR RENTAL

Alamo Rent A Car

http://www.goalamo.com/

$

★★★★★

Avis

http://www.avis.com

$

★★★★

Budget Rent a Car

https://rent.drivebudget.com/

$

★★★★

Dollar Rent A Car

http://www.dollar.com/

$

★★★★★

Economy Car Rental Aruba

http://www.economyaruba.com/

$

★★★★

Enterprise Rent-A-Car

http://www.enterprise.com/

$

★★★★★

Hertz

http://www.hertz.com

$

★★★★★

National Car

http://www.nationalcar.com/

$

★★★★★

Rent-A-Wreck

http://rent-a-wreck.com/

$

★★★★

Thrifty Car Rental

http://www.thrifty.com/

$

★★★★★

CAR TRAVEL

ASIRT: Association for Safe International Road Travel

http://www.asirt.org

★★★★★

Want to know which countries are the most danger-ous to drive in? You'll find such information here, as well as other road information and safety data.

Auto Europe Car Rentals

http://www.autoeurope.com/

$

★★★★★

Auto Europe offers auto rentals, discounted airfare, and hotel packages worldwide. Check the Travel Specials to find this week's bargains.

BreezeNet's Rental Car Guide and Reservations

http://www.bnm.com/

$

★★★★★

A one-stop car rental site for quick online reserva-tions to auto rental companies with airport service. Also includes coupons, discounts, and phone num-bers.

Route 66

http://www.historic66.com/

★★★★

Get your kicks on the famous roadway Route 66. This site is packed with photos, stories, and a wealth of helpful information. Also features a locator map.

Scenic Byways and Other Recreational Drives

http://www.gorp.com/gorp/activity/byway/byway.htm

★★★★★

Organized into categories such as Far West, Desert Southwest, Great Plains, and Great Lakes, this site helps you locate the scenic route to your destination. Contains links to a majority of the 50 states.

Traveling in the USA

http://www.travelingusa.com/

★★★★

These pages will help the U.S. traveler find informa-tion on parks, campgrounds, resorts, and recreation. From relief maps to kiddie activities, you'll probably satisfy your travel needs here. Also features links for Traveling Australia, Canada, and New Zealand.

A B C D E F G H I J K L M N O P Q R S T U V W X Y Z

A B C D E F G H I J K L M N O P Q R S T U V W X Y Z

CRUISES

Bargain Travel Cruises—Cheap Cruises
http://www.bargaintravelcruises.com/

★★★★

You can have a terrific vacation at the lowest possible cost by doing some research for the best possible deals available. You can take a bargain cruise by selecting from the best and cheapest available on this site. The site contains contact information on how to sign up for that trip of your dreams.

Carnival Cruises
http://www.carnival.com/

★★★★★

Home of one of the most popular cruise lines in the world, this site provides quick quotes on the cost of your cruise. Just select a destination, specify the desired length of the cruise (in days), and pick a month. The site also provides information about destinations and guest services, group travel rates, and ways to finance your cruise. Also learn about job openings at this site.

Cruise.com
http://www.cruise.com/

★★★★★

This site provides cruise reviews, statistics, and deals and offers to beat just about any offer you can find.

Cruise Shoppes America, Ltd.
http://www.cruiseshoppes.com/

★★★

Provides full-service cruise travel services. Includes destinations, monthly specials, and contact information. Includes an association directory with links to agencies by region.

Cruise Specialists
http://www.cruiseinc.com/

★★★★★

Provides information and profiles about many different cruises and destinations. Includes company backgrounds, photo albums, cruise reviews, and ordering information, as well as links to cruise lines on the Web.

Cruise Value Center
http://www.mycruisevalue.com/

★★★★

Find great values in cruises throughout the United States and the Caribbean here.

CruiseStar.com
http://www.cruisestar.com/

★★★★

In addition to cruise reviews and FAQs, you'll find discount cruises, last-minute deals, and bargains organized by cruise line.

Freighter World Cruises
http://www.freighterworld.com/

★★★★

Advertises Freighter World Cruises, Inc., a travel agency that focuses on freighter travel. Provides information on various freighter lines and their destinations. Cruise in economy style.

Holland America Line
http://www.hollandamerica.com/

★★★★★

This site has information on Holland America Line's cruises to Alaska, the Caribbean, Hawaii, Asia and the Pacific, South America, Canada and New England, and Europe. You might request literature and order a video on your desired cruise destination.

i-cruise.com

http://www.icruise.com/

★★★★★

Search for cruises by destination, travel date, or type of trip—singles, group, honeymoon, or linked with an adventure travel tour.

mytravelco.com

http://www.mytravelco.com/

★★★★★

You'll find all sorts of travel deals and information on getting discounts on cruises, airfare, and group tours here.

Norwegian Cruise Line

http://www.ncl.com/

★★★★★

Read about Norwegian Cruise Line destinations and music theme cruises, such as a big band cruise. Sample destinations are Mexico, Hawaii, Alaska, and the Caribbean. Find out about special deals.

Orbitz

http://www.orbitz.com/

★★★★★

Orbitz is your online travel guide for tracking down the best air fares, hotel rooms, car rentals, and especially cruises. You simply choose the desired destination, such as Alaska or Caribbean, pick the month you want to take your cruise, enter your ZIP Code, and Orbitz tracks down the available cruises, dates, and prices for you. You can even choose to book your cruise online and make travel arrangements to the cruise liner's departure point.

Princess Cruises

http://www.awcv.com/princess.html

★★★★★

Cruise on the Love Boat to the Caribbean. Find out about special discounts, 50% or more. You can book your cruise online.

Schooner Mary Day

http://www.schoonermaryday.com/

★★★★

The Schooner Mary Day is a sailing cruise ship (Windjammer) that carries couples, singles, and groups on three- to six-day cruises among the islands of Midcoast Maine. Here, you'll find online contact information for booking a cruise.

INFORMATION/TRAVEL TIPS

100% Pure New Zealand

http://www.newzealand.com/travel/

★★★★★

New Zealand is a land of mountains, volcanoes, rain forests, beaches, and some of the most breathtaking scenery in the world. Visit this official travel site to get a small sample of the land, its people, and its culture. This site provides a history of New Zealand, key facts about it, a list of interesting destinations and activities, information on accommodations, and much more.

A&E Traveler

http://travel.aande.com/

★★★★✓

Not your average travel agent, this travel site, maintained by A&E, The History Channel, and Biography, is designed to help you plan trips to some of the more interesting points on the globe. Pick a country and an interest to view a list of available tours.

A
B
C
D
E
F
G
H
I
J
K
L
M
N
O
P
Q
R
S
T
U
V
W
X
Y
Z

A
B
C
D
E
F
G
H
I
J
K
L
M
N
O
P
Q
R
S
T
U
V
W
X
Y
Z

Access-Able Travel Source

http://www.access-able.com/

★★★

Find out how to request special services; locate phone numbers for rental car companies, airlines, and hotels; and read FAQs to help you arrange and have a great trip. This site is devoted to helping people with special needs travel comfortably. You can purchase from a large selection of magazines online.

Abercrombie & Kent

http://www.abercrombiekent.com/

★★★★★

 All

Luxury travel at its best. Visit this site and see how the other half lives. Travel through Scotland on the Royal Scotsman, with tours through England and Wales, or ride aboard the Venice-Simplon Orient Express. Enjoy gourmet dining and impeccable service. Go ahead—splurge!

Away.com

http://away.com/index.adp

★★★★★

Are you tired of the standard vacations to Florida, Hawaii, and other popular tourist destinations? Then check out Away.com for some more unique ideas. Here, you can learn about trips to far-out places ranging from Alaska to Zimbabwe; search by activity to find archaeological trips, windsurfing hot spots, or ecological adventures; or search by interest to find inspirational destinations.

Citysearch

http://www.citysearch.com/

★★★★★

Whether you're going out of town or looking for the best dining, entertainment, and attractions near your home, let Citysearch be your guide. Here, you pick a city of your choice and view an online directory of restaurants, nightclubs, and events. Explore a little deeper and you can find the best bars, hotels, singles scenes, stores, spas, and health clubs.

Ecotourism Explorer

http://www.ecotourism.org/

★★★★

Official website of The International Ecotourism Society (TIES), this site provides information about finding and using ecology-friendly lodging and travel services. Learn how to make ecologically responsible travel decisions, check out some sample trips, and learn more about ecotourism.

Excite Travel

http://travel.excite.com

★★★★

This site provides a link to Expedia.com for tracking down deals on flights. Also features some useful travel tools, including a currency converter and airport survival guide, along with some general destination guides to various continents and countries.

FamilyTravelForum

http://www.familytravelforum.com/

★★★★★

 All

"Have Kids, Still Travel," is this site's motto, and members of FamilyTravelForum use this service to do just that. You can find help planning affordable family trips that everyone in your family will enjoy—or they'll at least need a pretty good excuse not to. Membership is about $4 per month ($10 for three months) and is well worth the cost, even if you use the service for a single trip.

Fodor's Travel Online

http://www.fodors.com

★★★★★

Features guides to cities worldwide, travel chat, and resources. Also lets you custom-tailor a guide to more than 90 destinations worldwide.

Gimponthego.com

http://gimponthego.com

★★★

Pick up disabled travel news, tips, and suggestions for packing at this site, which aims to connect disabled travelers to aid in sharing information.

IgoUgo

http://www.igougo.com

★★★★★

Looking for travel advice from real people who traveled where you plan to go? Then look no further. IgoUgo features personal travel journals for more than 2,000 destinations written by regular people who have actually visited those places. Find out about the best places to stay, the top restaurants offering the best value, interesting sites, and much more. Links to other services to book flights and cruises, rent automobiles, reserve a room, and more. Also features a good collection of photos of various destinations.

Journeywoman

http://www.journeywoman.com

★★★★

From where Queen Elizabeth buys her bras to how to stay healthy in Tibet to girls-only fly-fishing in the USA, *Journeywoman* dispenses valuable travel tips gathered from around the world. Written entirely from a female perspective.

Lonely Planet Online

http://www.lonelyplanet.com/

★★★★★

Lonely Planet guidebooks have always catered to the budget traveler. At this site you can explore U.S. and world destinations. Simply click on a region, a country, or a city to get started. The Optic Nerve gives you pictures of the area you're considering. Read a selection from a book related to a journey that might be of interest, post messages for other travelers to respond to, and lots more.

Luxury Link Travel Services

http://www.luxurylink.com/

★★★★★

Dedicated to the sophisticated traveler, this site features unique travel packages to countries all over the world. Here, you can find thousands of tours, cruises, specialty travel, hotels, resorts, inns, lodges, yacht charters, villas, spas, and more. Site features exclusive packages, best buys, and even auctions.

The North American Virtual Tourist

http://www.virtualtourist.com/North_America/

★★★★

An incredible resource for North American travel! One click on the image map of North America will lead you to every WWW resource available for the selected state or region. This site is heaven for those looking for an all-encompassing site in the United States, Canada, or Mexico. Make a bookmark and visit frequently!

One Bag

http://www.oratory.com/onebag/

★★★★

Learn how to travel light, with tips on what to pack and how to pack. You'll also find travel resource information and other tips on making travel easier.

Pets Welcome

http://www.petswelcome.com

★★★★★

Look through the Listings page to find hotels, bed and breakfasts, resorts, campgrounds, and beaches that are pet-friendly. Learn from other pet owners who've traveled with their friends and share your advice with others in the discussion forums.

Rough Guides

http://www.roughguides.com

★★★★

Read online articles at this publisher's site to find out more about traveling to exotic locations. Learn more about restaurants, landmarks, the people, and things to do for many cities.

A
B
C
D
E
F
G
H
I
J
K
L
M
N
O
P
Q
R
S
T
U
V
W
X
Y
Z

A B C D E F G H I J K L M N O P Q R S T U V W X Y Z

RV America

http://www.rvamerica.com

★★★

A site established to help connect fellow RVers to share information in discussion forums and chat. This site also provides a handy directory of 14,000 resorts and campgrounds.

Specialty Travel Guide

http://www.biztravel.com/

★★★★★

Interesting site that organizes trips an tours by category, including Romance, Affinity (artist tours, gay workshops, and so on), Family, Nature & Wildlife, Adventure, Spiritual, and so on.

timeout.com

http://www.timeout.com/

★★★★

Get the latest information about bars, restaurants, night life, and more for the top 34 cities in the world. Just click on London, Beijing, New York, Paris, or many others, to get the inside scoop on the scene.

Travel.com

http://www.travel.com/

★★★★

Get travel advisories, weather information, as well as recreational, shopping, and real-time flight information at this site, which is arranged as a travel search engine.

Travel Channel Online

http://travel.discovery.com/

★★★★★

Programming and schedules along with travel resources and travel chat from the folks who bring us *The Discovery Channel*. Choose to explore the site by destination or idea. Check out the live Webcams and the interactive gallery.

Travel Facts

http://www.travelfacts.com

★★★★

Provides detailed information and photos for dozens of destinations, hotel and restaurant databases, a chat room, feature articles, and more.

travel intelligence.net

http://www.travelintelligence.net

★★★

With more than 70 seasoned travel writers on staff and combing the world, this site features some insightful information about some of the most popular destinations around the globe. Subscribe to the Travel Intelligence newsletter, order travel reports online, or check the hotel hotlists directory for some of the best hotels in the world. Click the Destinations link for articles about a specific area you want to visit or would just like to know more about.

Travel Medicine

http://www.travmed.com/

★★★★

Provides information about diseases, environmental concerns, and immunizations for travelers. Includes tips on what to pack in your travel medicine kit and concerns for pregnant women who are traveling. Features the 2001 edition of *International Travel Health Guide* in PDF format.

The Travel Page

http://www.travelpage.com/

★★★★★

A thorough travel-planning site for visitors. Make hotel, airline, and cruise reservations online. Provides vacation recommendations ranging from the more popular to the truly unique.

The Travelite FAQ

http://www.travelite.org/

★★★★

Learn more than you probably ever wanted to know about packing tips. You'll find out about luggage, things to bring, packing methods, electrical appliances, accessories, and more.

Travelon

http://www.travelon.com

★★★★★

Travel resources ranging from trips offered by adventure and specialty travel companies to cruises and package vacations.

TravelSource

http://www.travelsource.com/

★★★★

Includes information about different vacation packages and locations. Also provides links to travel agents and other travel resources to fine-tune your vacation plans. Whether you're looking to scuba dive, whitewater raft, take a cruise, or simply kick back, this site is your one-stop vacation planner.

TripAdvisor

http://www.tripadvisor.com/

★★★★★

Unbiased reviews. of hotels, resorts, and vacations is TripAdvisor's specialty, but it does a great job of helping travelers come up with ideas for their next trips, too. You can check out trips to destinations all over the world, discover ways to travel more affordably, and find out the best places to stay. With TripAdvisor as your guide, you get the reliable advice you need to make the best choices.

Uniglobe.com

http://www.uniglobe.com/

★★★★

Designed for individuals and small-business travelers looking for a one-stop shop for airline, hotel, car rental, cruise, and vacation package information.

Virtual Tourist

http://www.virtualtourist.com/

★★★★★

Information and links about entertainment, media, business, culture, and traveling opportunities all over the world. Features separate tabs for travel guides, hotels, flights, and auctions. Also provides areas to hook up with other travelers and read and post messages.

World Hum

http://www.worldhum.com

★★★★

This unique travel site focuses less on commerce and more on human interaction, the stuff that makes most trips most memorable. Here, you'll find some of the best travel stories on the Web. This site encourages visitors to expand their horizons through travel and human interaction.

Zagat.com

http://www.zagat.com/splash.asp

★★★★★

You'll find more than 20,000 restaurant reviews for dining spots around the world. Choose a city and you'll get recommendations for places to dine that evening.

INTERNATIONAL TRAVEL

1000Tips4Trips

http://www.tips4trips.com/

★★★★

More than 1,000 travel tips submitted by real travelers. Search for tips by keyword or browse by categories, which include Air Travel, Cruises, Just for Men, Just for Women, Traveling with Children, Traveling with Pets, and more.

A B C D E F G H I J K L M N O P Q R S T U V W X Y Z

A
B
C
D
E
F
G
H
I
J
K
L
M
N
O
P
Q
R
S
T
U
V
W
X
Y
Z

AFRICANET

http://www.africanet.com/

★★★★★

Use the search feature to track down just what you're looking for in the way of Africa travel information. Get in-depth information on many African countries and learn about recommended African sites to check out.

Airhitch

http://www.airhitch.org/

$

★★★★★

This down-and-dirty site will help you learn how to travel to and within Europe for very little money; it also offers other amazing travel deals. You might not have the coziest of accommodations, but you can get there cheaply.

Australia Travel Directory

http://www.anzac.com/

★★★

Offers links to information on tourism, visas, individual states, and transportation.

CDC (Centers for Disease Control and Prevention)

http://www.cdc.gov/travel/

★★★★★

This U.S. government health agency is dedicated to preventing the spread of infectious diseases. This site provides useful, up-to-date information about health risks and disease outbreaks in areas all over the world. Find out which vaccinations you should receive and treatments you should pack before you leave for your trip. The site also provides up-to-date information about biological agents, such as anthrax.

China Circulate International Travel Service (CCITS)

http://china-times.com/ccits/ccits.htm

$

★★★

A travel service that will arrange your tour in China.

China Travel Specialists

http://www.chinaexplorer.com/

★★★

Find out how to arrange group or individual travel to China, getting as little or as much assistance from this travel group as you'd like.

Czech Info Center

http://www.muselik.com/

★★★★★

A well-organized guide to the Czech Republic. Includes general information, bulletin boards (to help you find ancestors, for example), helpful travel information, and a section on the city of Prague.

Europe Today Travel and Tourist Information

http://www.europe-today.com/

★★★

Travel and tourist information covering 16 European countries, regions, resorts, travel tips, excursions, tours, hotels, and competitions.

European Visits

http://www.eurodata.com/

$

★★★★

This "online magazine of European travel" offers articles on travel through Europe, as well as flight and hotel information. Get rail passes as well as guidebooks and maps online here, too.

Eurotrip.com

http://www.eurotrip.com

$

★★★★★

Anyone considering backpacking through Europe will want to start at this site for information on flying there cheaply, the hostels to stay in, things to see and do, packing tips, rail passes, and much more. Purchase your rail passes right online!

Foreign Language for Travelers

http://www.travlang.com/languages/

★★★

Discusses common words and phrases of just about any language you can imagine, including German, French, Italian, Russian, Czech, Turkish, Finnish, Danish, Esperanto, English, Spanish, Portuguese, Dutch, Polish, Romanian, Swedish, Norwegian, and Icelandic. Furnishes sound files for each language. Offers links to other sites that feature translation dictionaries and general information. Previously won a GNN Best of the Net award.

FranceEscape

http://www.france.com/

★★★★

Informative site on planning a vacation in France. Includes studies in France, festivals, transportation, and classifieds.

Help For World Travelers

http://www.kropla.com/

★★★★

Find out the basics of electricity and phone usage in countries around the world. You'll want to know this stuff so you can use your modem and blow dry your hair after you get there.

International Travel and Health

http://www.who.int/ith/

★★★★

This World Health Organization's publication on world health and infectious diseases is an invaluable resource for world travelers. This site features information on traveling by air, environmental health risks, travel accidents, infectious diseases, and more. Search by country to determine specific health risks for a particular region.

International Travel Guide for Mallorca and the Balearic Islands

http://www.mallorcaonline.com

★★★★

Check out this international travel guide for Mallorca and the Balearic Islands to plan your next trip to Spain.

International Travel Maps and Books

http://www.itmb.com/

★★★★

International Travel Maps and Books, Canada's largest supplier of maps, prepares detailed travel maps and guides of countries and regions around the world. Visit this site to order the map(s) and travel guides you need.

International Travel News

http://www.intltravelnews.com/

★★★★

This site provides travel tips, reviews of various travel services, and recommendations from real world travelers.

Mexico: Travel Trips for the Yucatan Peninsula

http://www.geocities.com/TheTropics/5087/

★★★★

Travel advice for people wanting to go to Mexico or the Yucatan Peninsula. Advice on choosing an airline, resorts, shopping, the best places to see, and many other things.

Monaco Online

http://www.monaco.mc/

★★★★

Presents the Principality of Monaco and its tourism, business, and motor racing. Includes English and French versions.

A
B
C
D
E
F
G
H
I
J
K
L
M
N
O
P
Q
R
S
T
U
V
W
X
Y
Z

MU-MU Travel Tips in Japan

http://www.asahi-net.or.jp/~py3y-knd/

★★★

Many important tips for travelers to Japan. Don't worry about the culture difference; just visit this home page for advice on food, money, and more.

OANDA.com

http://www.oanda.com/converter/classic

★★★★

Quickly convert U.S. dollars into any other currency using this handy online converter. You can also convert into U.S. dollars by specifying the international currency.

Peru

http://www.travelspots.com/peru.htm

★★★★

Anything you want to know about travel through Peru is probably here. How to get there, what to see, what to do, what to eat, how to dress, and what to listen to. It's all here and easy to click to.

Planeta

http://www.planeta.com

★★★★★

Environmentally aware travelers will want to check out Planeta, which is a guide to ecologically and environmentally responsible travel through South America and the Caribbean. This site serves as a central repository for travel that explores conservation and local development issues. Contributors include travel operators, environmentalists, and fellow travelers.

Rick Steves' Europe Through the Back Door

http://www.ricksteves.com/

$

★★★★★

Learn what Rick Steves means about traveling Europe through the "back door," at his site, which contains information gleaned from his travel books, as well as information on upcoming European trips that he manages.

Round the World Travel Guide

http://www.travel-library.com/rtw/html/faq.html

★★★

Planning a trip around the world? This is the site you will want to visit to get information about money matters, travel companions, and other subjects. Contains many links to travel-related information.

Salzburg, Austria

http://www.salzburg.com/tourismus_e/

★★★★

Provides seasonal tourist information about Salzburg, Austria, and its surrounding regions. Offers alternatives to traditional holiday plans when abroad (in German and English).

Sino.net

http://www.sino.net/

★★★

Serves as a guide to travel in the eastern half of the globe, including Japan, Australia, Indonesia, Vietnam, South Korea, and the Middle East. Each travel guide explains the customs, attractions, activities, currency, and other aspects of each country. Also provides valuable traveler tips. Check out the discount hotels for less expensive accommodations.

Sri Lanka Internet Services

http://www.lanka.net

★★★★★

All

The Sri Lanka web server page with links to travel and business guides, maps, gems, news, and Internet access information.

Sydney International Travel Centre

http://www.sydtrav.com.au/

$

★★★★★

Sydney International Travel is an integrated agency, combining corporate, wholesale, and retail departments, specializing in individual group arrangements and personalized tour programs. Here, you can plan and purchase your trip online.

Tour Canada Without Leaving Your Desk

http://www.cs.cmu.edu/Web/Unofficial/Canadiana/
Travelogue.html

★★★★

Take a virtual vacation in Canada and each of its provinces via the website links provided. This site is a good resource for anything you'd like to find out about Canada and what it has to offer for tourists.

Trotty

http://www.trotty.com/

★★★★★

For European travel, few travel sites are better than Trotty. Simply click the desired destination country, and Trotty presents you with a complete directory of available accommodations, restaurants, travel options, parks, museums, campgrounds, and additional information about that country. It's almost as though you have a friend living in that country acting as your guide—however, Trotty probably knows more than most friends do about what's available.

United Kingdom Pages

http://uk-pages.net/

★★★★

Provides information about the United Kingdom in many categories: Higher Education, Cities, Countryside, Culture, Government, Travel, Employment, and more. Provides more than a thousand links to other sites, primarily within the United Kingdom. Also lists bed-and-breakfast accommodations, picturesque pubs, and so forth. Offers several photo albums of downloadable images, including photographs of the Royals.

United States State Department Travel Warnings and Consular Info Sheets

http://travel.state.gov/travel_warnings.html

★★★★★

Provides up-to-date information for international travelers, including warnings, entry requirements, medical requirements, political status, and crime information for travel sites abroad. Also includes the location of the U.S. embassy in each country. Countries are easy to find in an alphabetical index.

Universal Currency Converter

http://www.xe.com/ucc/

★★★★★

Presents the exchange rate for 90 currencies. Don't be taken for an ignorant tourist and robbed blind when touring another country. If you need to know what Indian rupees are worth in Dutch guilders, this site will not let you down. Exchange rates are updated daily.

Vancouver, British Columbia

http://www.city.vancouver.bc.ca/

★★★★★

Provides FreeNet's information and links about Vancouver. Also offers links to the British Columbia home page and other Canadian home pages.

ISLAND TRAVEL

All-Inclusives Resort and Cruise Vacation Source

http://www.all-inclusives.com/

★★★★

This site offers information on Caribbean and Mexican cruises and resorts as well as vacation information about Alaska, the Panama Canal, and Hawaii. The All-Inclusives offer is to give you all services with one payment, and you can sit back and enjoy your trip without worrying about attached costs. Links to Magellan's, Amazon.com, and Sharper Image for online shopping.

America's Caribbean Paradise

http://www.usvi.net/

★★★★

Provides information about the Virgin Islands, including wedding and vacation information, holidays, carnivals and other events, and weather forecasts. Also offers a section on real estate, vacation rentals, recipes, and Caribbean products.

A B C D E F G H I J K L M N O P Q R S **T** U V W X Y Z

A B C D E F G H I J K L M N O P Q R S T U V W X Y Z

Bahamas Online

http://thebahamas.com/

 ★★★

Provides Bahamian facts, available accommodations, restaurants, banks, and bars. A good resource for those looking to visit the islands and drink some Goombay punch.

Club Med

http://www.clubmed.com/

 ⑤

★★★★★

Locate a Club Med! location that meets your needs for a particular type of vacation and activities, find out more about the atmosphere there, check on current deals, and even take a 360-degree look at some of the beaches.

Galveston Island Official Tourism Site

http://www.galvestontourism.com

 ⑤

★★★★★

Your official site for information about Galveston, including maps, weather reports, activities, attractions, restaurants, and entertainment. You can even reserve a room online or check out the scenery and activity around Galveston Island with the webcams!

Hideaway Holidays: Travel Specialists to the Pacific Islands

http://www.hideawayholidays.com.au/

 ⑤

★★★★

Specialist tour wholesaler to the exotic islands of the South Pacific. Air/land inclusive or land-only packages. Inquiries welcome from anyone.

Isles of Scilly Travel Centre

http://www.islesofscilly-travel.co.uk

 ⑤

★★★★

Sea and air services to the Isles of Scilly from southwest UK. Pictures and information about these subtropical islands.

Maui Interactive

http://www.maui.net/~kelii/MIA/MI.html

 ⑤

★★★

A full-blown interactive guide to Maui. Contains information on travel, entertainment, maps, photography, magazines, and art.

NetWeb Bermuda

http://www.bermuda.com/

★★★★

Offers links to Bermuda travel and cultural information. Also serves as an advertising site for Bermuda businesses.

The Strawberry Guava

http://www.hawaiian.net/~lauria/

★★★

The Strawberry Guava is a country bed and breakfast high in Lawai Valley on the quiet and beautiful island of Kauai, the Garden Island.

Tybee Island

http://www.tybeeisland.com

★★★★★

The complete Tybee Island information center. Includes information on rental units, hotels and motels, restaurants, night life, shopping, and more.

World Beaches

http://www.surf-sun.com/worldbeaches.html

★★★★★

This site can help you choose the perfect coastal destination. It links to sandy sites throughout the United States and around the world.

LODGING

123 Hotels

http://www.123hotels.net/

★★★

Click on a city and find great hotel rates and availabilities, even for "sold-out" dates. Sign up for the email bulletins that alert you to special deals each week. Savings can be as much as 65% per night through this travel service. Book your trip online now.

Alaskan Cabin, Cottage, and Lodge Catalog

http://www.midnightsun.com

★★★★

The Alaskan Cabin, Cottage, and Lodge Catalog is a comprehensive listing of all the wilderness cabins, cottages, and lodges in the state of Alaska. It includes a listing of nearly 200 USFS recreation cabins in the Tongass and Chugach National Forests.

all-hotels.com

http://www.all-hotels.com/

★★★★★

This site aims to provide a one-stop-shop for hotel reservations, centralizing information about hotels worldwide in one place. Get information on available hotels and rooms for cities around the world, and book online when you find what you want. More than 100,000 hotels all over the world in the database.

Bed and Breakfast Inns Online

http://www.bbonline.com/

★★★

Do large hotels get you down? Try this site to find that quaint little hideaway. Pictures and sketches help describe more than 4,800 of these travel gems in the United States, Canada, Mexico, and the Caribbean.

Bed and Breakfast Lodgings in the UK

http://www.visitus.co.uk/

★★★

Check out more than 6,000 accommodations in London, Scotland, Wales, and Northern Ireland. Use the handy map as a reference. Also lists specific cities and regions.

Choice Hotels

http://www.hotelchoice.com/

★★★★★

More than 5,000 of the Choice Hotels International are available from this site, which includes branches of Econolodge, Clarion, Comfort Inn, and more. Reservations are available from this site.

Colorado Vacation Guide

http://www.coloradoadventure.net/

★★★★

The leading source for Colorado campgrounds, cabins, and lodges. Includes Colorado recreation, vacations, adventures, and fun things to do. Come and experience beautiful Colorado!

Cyber Rentals

http://www.cyberrentals.com/

★★★★★

Looking for a really "quiet" and private vacation spot? Why not rent a home, condo, or villa for your vacation and enjoy a home away from home? This site provides you with plenty of resources for just such a vacation and many of them at bargain prices. Features available accommodations worldwide.

Holiday Junction

http://www.holidayjunction.com/

★★★

Holiday Junction is an online accommodation directory focusing on resorts, lodges, and private cottage rentals.

A B C D E F G H I J K L M N O P Q R S **T** U V W X Y Z

A
B
C
D
E
F
G
H
I
J
K
L
M
N
O
P
Q
R
S
T
U
V
W
X
Y
Z

Hotelguide.com

http://www.hotelguide.com/

 $

★★★★★

Look at a map of most major cities worldwide here to find the locations of hotels before booking a room. Then search the database to find available rooms and book online at one of more than 85,000 hotels listed for savings of up to 50%. You can also get information on vacation packages, such as golf outings, and link to other vacation and travel sites.

InnSite

http://www.innsite.com/

★★★★★

Search more than 50,000 pages of bed and breakfast listings to find one in 50 countries worldwide that meets your needs. For more detailed feedback about locations, you might want to visit the discussion groups to chat with fellow travelers.

International Bed and Breakfast Guide

http://www.ibbp.com/

★★★★★

National and international B&Bs dot this site. Countries featured other than the U.S. include Canada, Great Britain, New Zealand, and Argentina.

Lake Tahoe's West Shore Lodging

http://www.tahoecountry.com/wslodging.html

★★★★★

Bed and breakfasts, guesthouses, and lodges along Lake Tahoe's tranquil West Shore offer visitors peaceful settings and a taste of Old Tahoe.

Lodging Guide World Wide

http://www.lgww.com/

 $

★★★★★

It's not called the *Lodging Guide World Wide* for nothing. Reservations in most major cities around the world can be made here.

The National Lodging Directory

http://www.guests.com

★★★★

The National Lodging Directory, a user-friendly site, contains listings for hotels, motels, bed and breakfasts, and vacation rental property located in the United States. You can make online reservations on most client sites.

Professional Association of Innkeepers International

http://www.paii.org/

 $

★★★★★

You'll find more than just the *Innkeeping Weekly* at this site, but do look at that, too. The book *So You Want to Be an Innkeeper* is available from this site, as are stimulating articles such as "Cutting Deals with Unlikely Allies" and B&B management tips.

Travel Web

http://www.travelweb.com/

★★★★

This huge travel monster will provide information about more than just lodging. This site features a unique selection of independent hotels to help you keep away from the lodging machine of franchised establishments, if that's what you're looking for; however, you can find chain hotels here, too.

West Virginia Lodging Guide

http://wvweb.com/www/travel_recreation/lodging.html

★★★★★

West Virginia Lodging, a visitors guide to WV accommodations in the West Virginia Web, includes bed and breakfasts, camping, hotels, motels, resorts, and vacation properties.

TRAIN TRAVEL

All Aboard: The Complete North American Train Travel Guide

http://www.trainweb.com/books/bookloom.htm

★★★

If your vacation plans include traveling by rail, you will surely want to visit this site to get more information about train travel in America. Having the right information will allow you to travel in style. You can order the guide online.

Amtrak

http://www.amtrak.com/

★★★★★

The country's foremost train authority, Amtrak, is accessed through this page. Find everything from the latest high-speed train information to travel tips and reservations on this useful home page. Promotional offers, student discounts, senior discounts, child fares, disability discounts. Check the site regularly because seasonal fare specials vary.

European and British Rail Passes

http://www.eurail.com/

★★★

Provides information on the Eurail Pass and rail passes for other countries such as Germany, Austria, Italy, Czech Republic, and Scandinavia. This site is a must for those considering traveling Europe by Eurail.

Grand Canyon Railway

http://www.thetrain.com/

★★★★★

Read about the historic Grand Canyon Railway. This site lists timetables and fares, travel packages, and weather information. The opening graphic is wonderful, and when you "climb aboard," listen for the train whistle blowing.

Orient-Express Trains & Cruises

http://www.orient-expresstrains.com/

★★★★★

View a slide show to get a sense of the experience of traveling cross-country via the Orient Express and other trains and cruise ships. You can also look at the route each train travels and get information on upcoming trips. Whether you want a luxury ride through the United Kingdom, Southeast Asia, Australia, or Europe, there are several relaxed and luxurious rides to choose from.

VIA Rail Canada

http://www.viarail.ca/en.index.html

★★★★★

 14-18

Canada's rail system. Here, you'll find senior rates, student rates, a frequent traveler program, the CanRailPass, and information about various outdoor adventures in Canada.

U.S. TRAVEL

Access New Hampshire

http://www.nh.com/

★★★★★

A comprehensive guide to the state of New Hampshire, including information about tourism, historical legacy, local happenings, and everything else under the sun.

Alabama Wonder Full

http://www.touralabama.org/

★★★★★

This site created and maintained by the Alabama Department of Tourism & Travel is your travel guide to the best that Alabama has to offer you as a tourist. You can find out about activities that match your interests, special attractions and events, maps, accomodations, and more.

A B C D E F G H I J K L M N O P Q R S T U V W X Y Z

A
B
C
D
E
F
G
H
I
J
K
L
M
N
O
P
Q
R
S
T
U
V
W
X
Y
Z

Alaskan Travel Guide

http://www.alaskan.com/

★★★★★

Find out all about travel in and around Alaska here, from where to stay, what to see, which parks to visit, and much more. Use the travel planner to sketch out your visit, as well as consider specific types of vacations.

Best The Arizona Guide

http://www.arizonaguide.com/

⑤

★★★★★

 All

The official site for the Arizona Office of Tourism organized by region in text and imagemap format. Provides up-to-date weather information, maps, and state information. Features golf resorts and, of course, the Grand Canyon and the many touring packages for exploring it. Well worth visiting even if you're not planning a trip to Arizona any time soon. Extremely well done and beautiful site. The site contains a list of destinations and activities and offers a travel service, trip planner, interactive state map, and even a free travel kit. If you live in the United States, this would be a great "mini-vacation" for you to look forward to. If you live in another country, then it's still worth saving your money and taking a vacation here because Arizona has a lot to see. You can also learn many interesting things on the site, such as places to stay, eat, and sleep. If you're an Old West fan, you'll want to visit such historical places as Tombstone and Fort Apache.

Arkansas: The Natural State

http://www.arkansas.com/

★★★★★

This exhaustive tourism guide of Arkansas provides information on state parts, outdoor recreation, history and heritage, arts and entertainment, lodging and dining, and a calendar of events. Features some free Arkansas screensavers and desktop wallpaper, plus an area for kids stuff and information about group travel.

Atlanta Travel Guide

http://www.atlanta.net/

★★★

Take a virtual tour of Atlanta, Georgia, a big city filled with southern hospitatlity. This site features an area for tourists, as well as information about business conventions and relocating to Atlanta.

Blue Ridge Country

http://www.blueridgecountry.com/

⑤

★★★★

Read the current issue of this travel magazine dedicated to the Blue Ridge Mountain region, see photos of the area, get advice on travel routes, and read the birding guide to learn more about native species. Lots of interesting articles that will pique your interest in this area.

California Travel Guide

http://www.visitcalifornia.com/state/tourism/tour_homepage.jsp

★★★★★

If you're thinking of visiting or moving to California, visit this site first to find maps, activities and attractions, lodgings, information about national parks and museums, and much more.

Cambridge, Massachusetts

http://www.cambridgema.gov/

★★★★★

Features Cambridge resources and more. Offers information on the city's art, entertainment, museums, tourism, and more general information for those looking to relocate.

Cincinnati Vacation Gateways

http://cincinnati.com/getaways

★★★★★

If you're thinking about traveling in the United States, why not visit one of the most beautiful and exciting places in the Midwest—Cincinnati, Ohio? You can spend a day at Kings Island with the kids, stay at one of dozens of luxury hotels, and dine in some of the finest restaurants in the country. Stay awhile and watch the Bengals football team play or maybe even spend a day watching the world-famous Cincinnati Reds play baseball. In the site's own words, the service will customize an "à la carte" vacation that is just right for you. This service can provide you with hotel accommodations, tickets to events and attractions, sporting events, museums, and much, much more. This is your complete online shopping mall for a wonderful vacation in Cincinnati.

Colorado.com

http://www.colorado.com/

★★★★★

Request the official Colorado state guide to what's going on there or search the site for activities, view the state map to choose a destination, or search the city directory to find items of interest by location. There's also a seasonal directory to activities statewide. You'll definitely want to stop here before finalizing your plans for a trip to Colorado.

George Washington's Mount Vernon Estate

http://www.mountvernon.org/

★★★★★

Take a virtual tour of Mount Vernon or get information on visiting the estate in person. You can also find information from the library and archaeological digs on the premises.

TheGrandCanyon.com

http://www.thegrandcanyon.com

★★★★★

Need to know more about the Grand Canyon? You'll find maps, tour information, lodging and camping details, weather information, and more to help you get the most out of your trip here.

Gulf Getaway

http://www.gulfgetaway.com

★★★★★

Gulf Shores, Alabama, .is one of the more popular, up-and-coming vacation areas on the Gulf, and Gulf Getaway can get you there in style. This site features gulf-front condominium rentals, area attractions, vacation packages, live weather information, easy online booking, and a toll-free number. Don't miss the cool virtual tour of the condo.

Idaho

http://www.state.id.us/

★★★★

Provides information on regional attractions, state parks, and national forests; a calendar of events; and more general information on the state of Idaho.

Iowa Tourism Office

http://www.traveliowa.com/

★★★★★

One of the better state-run sites on the Web, this site features a navigation bar at the top that contains links for Things To Do, Accommodations, Getting Around, Facts and Fun, a Media Center, and much more.

Las Vegas

http://www.vegas.com

★★★★★

Includes a wide range of vacation-planning information concerning Las Vegas, ranging from hotel information and reservations to show schedules, sports, conventions, betting tips, employment opportunities, and business services.

Louisiana Travel Guide

http://www.louisianatravel.com/

★★★★★

Request a free travel kit to learn more about all there is to do and see in Louisiana, or search online for ideas for family outings, outdoor fun, landmarks, restaurants, and accommodations. Succulent photos of Cajun cuisine will make you hungry for a trip to Louisiana.

A B C D E F G H I J K L M N O P Q R S **T** U V W X Y Z

A
B
C
D
E
F
G
H
I
J
K
L
M
N
O
P
Q
R
S
T
U
V
W
X
Y
Z

Minneapolis

http://www.minneapolis.org

★★★★★

The official site of the city of Minneapolis, the city of lakes. Contains a searchable database for narrowing the scope of your search for travel information whether you're in town for a convention or on vacation with the family. From accommodations to dining and entertainment, it's all right here.

Nashville Scene

http://www.nashscene.com/

★★★★

An award-winning online newspaper providing the traveler a guide to dining and events in Nashville, Tennessee, in addition to offering some insight into the Tennesseean mindset.

Nebraska Travel and Tourism

http://visitnebraska.org/

★★★★★

A well-presented documentation of the attractions, campgrounds, hotels, and tourist sites of Nebraska presented in a colorful interface organized by locale and topic.

New Jersey and You

http://www.state.nj.us/travel/

★★★★★

Explore New Jersey at this website to find out about the main attractions, events, and accommodations. Features sections on the arts, family recreation, romantic getaways, historical sites, outdoor recreation, shopping, and sports.

New Mexico: America's Land of Enchantment

http://www.newmexico.org/

★★★★★

A traveler's guide to New Mexico. Provides information about culture, outdoor activities, area ruins, regional events, and skiing. Also includes maps and historical tidbits for travelers.

New York State

http://www.iloveny.com

★★★★★

Get travel ideas by region, as well as accommodation and activities suggestions at this site, where you'll see photos of the varied landscape in New York state. Check the schedule of state events and attractions, too.

Oregon Online

http://www.oregon.gov/

★★★★★

Provides information on the government, education, and commerce of Oregon. Of particular interest to the tourist is the section on communities, which provides links to the various regions of the state that might be more pertinent to your travel plans.

Travel Michigan

http://travel.michigan.org/

★★★★

Offers comprehensive information on what Michigan has to offer, such as local news and events, sightseeing, travel, entertainment, shopping, and more. Be sure to visit this site *before* you travel Michigan.

Santa Fe, New Mexico Travel Information

http://www.santafe.org/

★★★★★

 All

Excellent guide for tourism and business travel for Santa Fe, New Mexico. Includes a directory of restaurants, art galleries, museums, motels, and more.

Seattle.com

http://www.seattle.com/

★★★★★

Serves as a guide to events, restaurants, accommodations, shopping, sports, and nightlife in the greater Seattle area. Scroll down to the bottom to view a good collection of links to other cities organized by state.

South Dakota World Wide Website

http://www.state.sd.us/

★★★

The official state page of South Dakota, replete with travel information, including area attractions, available accommodations, events, state parks, outdoor recreation, and travel tips available from an accurate clickable imagemap. Also provides general information about South Dakota in addition to links to other South Dakota sites.

USA CityLink

http://www.usacitylink.com

★★★★★

A fantastic guide to touring the 50 U.S. states. This site is organized alphabetically by state and further broken down by city. Offers links to pertinent travel information for each city. A thoroughly indexed site for the virtual or planning tourist.

Utah! Travel and Adventure Online

http://www.utah.com/

★★★★★

Visit the Rocky Mountains, sand dunes, and Salt Lake of Utah via a virtual tour. This site also provides general tourist information, including maps and travel tips. Find out about a selection of vacation packages ranging from guided adventures to traditional family adventures. A visually breathtaking site not to be missed.

Virginia Is for Lovers

http://www.virginia.org/

★★★★★

An eye-pleasing site containing general tourism information in addition to recreational activities, places to stay, restaurants, local events, theme attractions, and other points of interest in the state for lovers.

Washington, D.C.

http://www.district-of-columbia.com

★★★★

Look at some of the most popular attractions and activities in Washington and get the editor's picks for hotels and restaurants. Recreation and travel into the area are also covered at this comprehensive site.

The Yankee Traveler

http://www.yankeemagazine.com/travel/

★★★★★

Provides a compilation of travel-related sources of New England. Includes state web pages, information on Cape Cod and the islands, bed and breakfast inns, and map links. Also provides information about real estate, local businesses, and more.

WEEKEND GETAWAYS

1st Traveler's Choice

http://www.virtualcities.com/ons/0onsadex.htm

★★★

Information on lodging across the United States, Canada, and Mexico. Search by state, province, type, or languages spoken by innkeepers. Includes *Country Inns* magazine, the *Inn Times*; virtual cities' trade show; and a gourmet directory of hundreds of recipes from innkeepers. New inns added weekly.

Balsam Shade Resort

http://www.balsamshade.com/

★★★

This country family resort is located in the foothills of the northern Catskill Mountains (Greenville, New York). Activities include springtime whitewater rafting down the Hudson River Gorge, bicycling, and hiking the trails of the Catskill Park. Several golf courses and museums are nearby. Other activities include horseback riding, visiting amusement parks, and taking a trip to Reptiland.

Concierge Travel

http://www.concierge.com/

★★★★

Concierge.com is dedicated to helping the sophisticated traveler envision, plan, and execute the ideal vacation or getaway. Concierge.com features award-winning magazine media, including the Condé Nast Traveler Gold List, Hot List, Spa Poll, and Ski Poll, along with in-depth insider guides.

A
B
C
D
E
F
G
H
I
J
K
L
M
N
O
P
Q
R
S
T
U
V
W
X
Y
Z

A
B
C
D
E
F
G
H
I
J
K
L
M
N
O
P
Q
R
S
T
U
V
W
X
Y
Z

EscapeMaker Weekend Getaway Ideas

http://escapemaker.com/

★★★★

When you need to get away for the weekend, but you're not sure where to go, visit EscapeMaker, where you can find ideas for weekend getaways on the East Coast of the United States.

GORP: California National Forests

http://www.gorp.com/gorp/resource/US_National_ Forest/CA.HTM

★★★★★

GORP (Great Outdoor Recreation Pages) describes all the national forests in California. Click the city you're interested in to view details on activities such as hiking, fishing and hunting, camping, picnicking, mountain biking, and sightseeing. Also includes descriptions of canyons. You'll also find the locations and phone numbers of the district ranger stations.

GORP: Great Outdoor Recreation Pages

http://www.gorp.com/

★★★★★

Your guide to U.S. parks, forests, wildlife areas, wilderness areas, monuments, rivers, scenic drives, national trails, beaches, recreation areas, historic sites, and archaeology sites. Get advice on equipment, apparel, and accessories; travel and lodging; maps and tours; and features and activities for each destination. Visit the photo gallery of beautiful outdoor scenes, get tips on staying healthy while you travel, and investigate places to take your kids and pets on your next outdoor adventure.

Mountain Vacations

http://www.mountainvacations.com/

★★★★★

Mountain Vacations is dedicated to providing information and resources to help individuals and families plan winter ski vacations. Here, you can find information and advice from experts who have actually visited the resorts and condominiums they recommend.

The Old Carriage Inn Bed and Breakfast in Shipshewanna

http://www.oldcarriageinn.com

★★★

This B&B is located in the midst of Indiana Amish farmlands. You'll have access to craft boutiques, country stores, specialty shops, and the Shipshewanna Flea Market. Features the art of storytelling—each weekend, the B&B hosts a professional storyteller. Also includes murder mystery weekends; you're an active part in the mystery as it unfolds. Or, attend a Rubber Stamp Art Workshop Weekend to learn new skills and make some great projects. Includes an Amish FAQ and a weather conditions and forecast page.

Sandals Resorts

http://www.sandals.com

★★★★★

Features information on tropical hideaways on the enchanted isles of Jamaica, Antigua, St. Lucia, and the Bahamas, created exclusively for couples.

site59.com

http://www.site59.com

★★★★★

If you're not the type to plan your trip ahead of time, Site59 is the place for you. Named after the 59th minute, this site assumes that you've waited till the last minute to start planning your trip. Just choose the desired destination, and Site59 will assemble a travel package for you, including airline tickets, car rentals, and room reservations at a reasonable price. The departure points are limited to major cities, but except for that minor drawback, the site features an interesting approach to last-minute travel plans.

St. Paul Recommends: Destinations (Minnesota)

http://www.mspmag.com/

★★★★★

Home of *Mpls.St.Paul Magazine,* this site's goal is to recommend "the very best the Twin Cities has to offer," including the people, places and events that make the Minneapolis/St. Paul community the wonderful place that it is. Site includes editors' recommendations for the best places to dine, visit, and explore.

This Week in the Poconos Magazine Online

http://www.thisweek.net/

★★★★

This e-zine includes information about B&Bs, country inns, lodging, dining, hiking, and more. It lists airports, upcoming events, church services, libraries, movie theaters, museums and galleries, and points of interest. Also features a guide to searching for antiques, tips on shopping, and information on state parks.

TotalEscape

http://www.totalescape.com/

★★★★★

Get away from it all by traveling to the most interesting sites in and around California. TotalEscape is California's guide to "local adventures, area activities, and cool places" off the beaten track, including areas where you can rent houseboats. Excellent collection of photos and links of the best places to go to and things to do to recharge your batteries. Links to Amazon.com for shopping.

Trip Spot

http://tripspot.com/

★★★★★

Travel planning central for your weekend getaways—airlines, hotels, maps, city guides, destination ideas, and much more!

Washington Post Weekend Getaways Guide

http://www.washingtonpost.com/wp-adv/specialsales/virtualvacation/weekend.html

★★★★★

Guide to weekend getaways in and around Washington, D.C. Provides information on scenic events, fun and educational activities, recreation, lodging, and restaurants. Features links to the most popular vacation spots in the Washington, D.C., area.

Weekend Getaway Packing Checklist

http://abcnews.go.com/sections/travel/FamilyAdventure/checklist_weekend.html

★★★★

What should you pack for your next weekend getaway? Visit this site for a complete checklist.

A B C D E F G H I J K L M N O P Q R S **T** U V W X Y Z

A
B
C
D
E
F
G
H
I
J
K
L
M
N
O
P
Q
R
S
T
U
V
W
X
Y
Z

UFOs

58 Signs of Abduction by Aliens

http://www.anw.com/aliens/52questions.htm

★★★

Alien abductions are more common than you might think. There are 58 signs to look for to see whether you might have been the guest of visitors from somewhere else. For example, you have a memory of flying through the air that could not be a dream, or you've had many dreams involving flying. Maybe you've had a dream of eyes, such as animal eyes (like an owl or deer) or remember seeing an animal looking in at you, or you have a fear of eyes. If you or any of your friends or family are experiencing something similar to the 58 signs listed on the site, please seek professional help.

Alien Abduction Experience and Research

http://www.abduct.com/

★★★

A page for and about abductees, this site has many nice features. Among these interesting items are a discussion group, news exclusively about UFOs, research reports, UFO book reviews, stories about personal experiences, and many other feature articles. Besides offering a wealth of information and interesting photos, the site also has some reviews of your favorite UFO-related movies.

Aliens and UFOs Among Us

http://www.bright.net/~phobia/

★★★★★

For those who wonder "Are we alone?" this site is for you. Take a look at the photos, participate in chats, and read through some of the information collected regarding UFOs.

Anomalous Images and UFO Files

http://www.anomalous-images.com/

★★★★

The site contains a lot of information about such abnormal things as lost cities on Mars, crashed spacecraft on Mars, a secret cave in the Grand Canyon that is supposed to be UFO related, the famous faces of Mars, and the latest Lost Island City on Mars. And all these things are documented with pictures to prove their existence. There are many great graphics, pictures, and information to pique your interest. Good site for a cold, dark, and wet night. It also has some interesting music that will put you in the mood for your visit.

Coast to Coast AM with George Noory

http://www.coasttocoastam.com/

★★★★★

Coast to Coast AM is the UFO/conspiracy theory radio program, made famous by radio talk show host Art Bell. Art Bell has since retired, but now George Noory is at the mike, continuing the tradition. This features program information, a comprehensive library and photo gallery, and audio recordings of past shows. Focuses on UFOs, extraterrestrial beings, paranormal phenomena, and conspiracy theories.

Best Center for UFO Studies

http://www.cufos.org

★★★★★

This organization is dedicated to exploring and studying reports of UFOs and is asking for help in keeping its files current. You can search the archive of articles and UFO sightings, as well as add to them with your own stories and reports. You can also read about famous sightings here.

The Center for UFO Studies (CUFOS) is an international group of scientists, academics, investigators, and volunteers dedicated to the continuing examination and analysis of the UFO phenomenon. The purpose of this organization is to promote serious scientific interest in UFOs and to serve as an archive for reports, documents, and publications about the UFO phenomenon.

Conspiracy Journal

http://members.tripod.com/uforeview/

★★★★

Conspiracy Journal will bring you the best UFO/conspiracy reports. The site also has a massive list of books and other items you can order online using a secure card resource as well as other interesting information about UFOs, Tesla, and other scientists and engineers who are interested in the UFO phenomena.

CSETI–The Center for the Study of Extraterrestrial Intelligence

http://www.cseti.org/

★★★★★

This is the site of the only worldwide organization dedicated to establishing peaceful and sustainable relations with extraterrestrial life forms. The organization was founded in 1990 for this specific purpose.

CSICOP

http://www.csicop.org/

★★★★

Hundreds of thousands of people have reported alien abductions, viewings of UFOs, visits by ghosts, and other paranormal experiences, but are these honest, verifiable accounts? The Committee for the Scientific Investigation of Claims of the Paranormal (CSICOP) checks these reports to determine their validity. This site keeps you informed of what the skeptical, scientific community has concluded about many of the most popular claims.

Famous UFO Cases

http://ourworld.compuserve.com/homepages/AndyPage/

★★★★

All the classic UFO cases of the past, in chronological order. The site also contains a list of books, articles, and other items that are of great interest to those interested in this field.

International Center for Abduction Research

http://www.ufoabduction.com/

★★★★

David Jacobs' International Center for Abduction Research (ICAR) is devoted to the dissemination of information about UFO abductions to help improve the understanding of such experiences.

International UFO Museum & Research Center

http://www.iufomrc.com

★★★★

Learn more about the infamous Roswell, New Mexico, incident of 1947 at this site, which hopes to educate and inform the public about UFOs. The library provides UFO-related articles and research. Sales in the gift shop support the work of this organization.

A B C D E F G H I J K L M N O P Q R S T **U** V W X Y Z

A
B
C
D
E
F
G
H
I
J
K
L
M
N
O
P
Q
R
S
T
U
V
W
X
Y
Z

Journal of Scientific Exploration

http://www.scientificexploration.org/jse.html

★★★★

"Advances are made by answering questions. Discoveries are made by questioning answers." The *Journal of Scientific Exploration* publishes articles about unusual scientific research in a scientific journal format.

Kidnapped by UFOs?

http://www.pbs.org/wgbh/nova/aliens/

★★★★★

The *Nova Online!* program on abductions is very likely the best, most balanced presentation available on the topic of UFO abductions. Features a balanced view by providing expert opinions from the two conflicting camps: believers and skeptics.

MUFON

http://www.mufon.com/

★★★★★

Dedicated to the "systematic collection and analysis of UFO data with the ultimate goal of learning the origin & the nature of the UFO phenomenon." Here, you can report a sighting, get the latest UFO news and information, find out more about MUFON, join MUFON, and purchase UFO books and other publications online.

National UFO Reporting Center

http://www.ufocenter.com

★★★★

The latest sightings reported to the National UFO Reporting Center. Have you seen a UFO? Then you can file a report at this site, too.

Rutgers UFO Site

http://bedlam.rutgers.edu/ufo.html

★★★

This site isn't the most attractive site of the lot, but it does provide an excellent directory of other UFO websites where you can obtain additional information.

Secrets of the Hidden Universe

http://www.geocities.com/Area51/Corridor/6280/

★★★

This site is dedicated to introducing the topic of UFOs and alien contact to those new to the subject. Discusses events and ideas that helped to shape the study known as UFOlogy, and also provides the latest news and information on the subject.

UFO Info

http://www.ufoinfo.com

★★★★★

Get updates regarding sightings and abduction reports, news from around the world, publications, books, TV and radio programs devoted to UFOs, links, and other related articles and information about the site and how it functions (with the help of volunteers around the world). You can purchase dozens of books, CDs, and DVDs related to this subject from the online e-store by using secure credit card ordering.

UFO Roundup

http://ufoinfo.com/roundup/

★★★★

The latest weekly sightings roundup from Joseph Trainor. This Australian site offers lots of books, CDs, and videotapes in its online store. Most of these are through such online retailers as Amazon.com. You'll also find about 20 UFO-related reports. These professional, authentic reports are factual, straightforward, and interesting. This is an excellent source for UFO-related materials.

UFO Seek

http://www.ufoseek.com/

★★★★★

Comprehensive directory of UFO and paranormal information and resources. Search the directory by keyword or phrase, or browse by categories including alien abductions, near death experiences, and millennium prophecies, to name just a few.

WWW Space and Mystery

`http://spaceandmystery.tripod.com/`

★★★★★

An excellent source for UFO news. This site is unique because it has information on just about everything concerning UFOs and the unusual. You'll find articles, books, and news about the mysteries of Mars, the Roswell Incident, the Egyptians and their culture, and much more. There are links where you can go to purchase books and other material on the subject.

Yellow Pages

U.S. GOVERNMENT INFORMATION/SERVICES

Center for Defense Information: Terrorism Project

http://www.cdi.org/terrorism/responding.cfm

★★★★★

As a result of the 9-11 tragedy, the United States government has been working diligently to wage a war on terrorism and protect the United States homeland. The Center for Defense information has been working just as diligently to keep track of the government's progress and to keep citizens informed. Here, you can find information about the war on terrorism, including reports about Operation Enduring Freedom, the President's special orders and mandates, reports from known terrorist hot spots, homeland security issues, updates about the situation in Iraq, and much more.

Related Site
http://www.whitehouse.gov/response/

Central Intelligence Agency

http://www.cia.gov

★★★★★

Learn all about the CIA, what it does, how to be considered for employment, which agencies report into it, what announcements the organization has made recently, and what publications it has produced. You'll also find FAQs and related links here.

Consumer Information Center

http://www.pueblo.gsa.gov/

★★★★★

The folks with all the free publications. Most can be obtained online from the website. You can read these free publications or order them online. You can get information on dozens of topics, including consumer help, education, employment, federal programs, food, health, housing, money, recalls, travel, and scams/frauds.

DefenseLINK

http://www.defenselink.mil/

★★★★★

The Department of Defense is responsible for providing the military forces needed to deter war and protect the security of our country. Visit this site to learn of the latest progress in the war on terrorism and on those countries that threaten our homeland security.

Department of Agriculture

http://www.usda.gov/

★★★★★

USDA enhances the quality of life for Americans by supporting agriculture, and ensuring a safe, affordable, nutritious, and accessible food supply.

Department of Commerce

http://www.doc.gov

★★★★★

Responsibilities include expanding U.S. exports, developing innovative technologies, gathering and disseminating statistical data, and predicting the weather.

Department of Education

http://www.ed.gov/

★★★★★

The mission of the Education Department is to ensure equal access to education and to promote educational excellence for all Americans.

Department of Energy

http://www.energy.gov/

★★★★★

DOE works to foster a secure and reliable energy system and to be a responsible steward of the nation's nuclear weapons.

Department of Health and Human Services

http://www.os.dhhs.gov/

★★★★★

Health and Human Services is responsible for protecting the health and well-being of Americans through programs such as Medicare, and disease research to aid in prevention. The website provides information about the wide range of HHS programs.

Department of Homeland Security

http://www.dhs.gov/

★★★★★

Created in response to the attack on 9-11, the Department of Homeland Security is responsible for ensuring the safety of U.S. citizens against attacks from foreign countries and from terrorists at home and abroad. This department is also responsible for keeping citizens informed and helping them prepare for potential attacks.

Department of Housing and Urban Development

http://www.hud.gov/

★★★★

HUD's mission is "To help people create communities of opportunity." HUD oversees all housing and Community Development Block Grant programs.

Department of the Interior

http://www.doi.gov/

★★★★★

The Department of the Interior protects and provides access to our nation's natural and cultural heritage. Part of this mission involves honoring our responsibilities to Native American tribes.

Department of Justice

http://www.usdoj.gov/

★★★★★

As the largest law firm in the nation, the Department of Justice serves as counsel for its citizens. It represents them in enforcing the law in the public's interest.

Department of Labor

http://www.dol.gov/

★★★★★

The Department of Labor helps to prepare Americans for work and attempts to ensure their safety while on the job.

Department of State

http://www.state.gov/

★★★★★

The Department of State is the institution for the conduct of American diplomacy, a mission based on the role of the Secretary of State as the president's principal foreign policy adviser.

Department of Transportation

http://www.dot.gov/

★★★★★

Serves as the focal point in the federal government for the coordinated national transportation policy and safety efforts.

Department of the Treasury

http://www.ustreas.gov/

★★★★★

The Department of the Treasury has a long history of managing the government's finances; promoting a stable economy; and helping to ensure a safer America promoting a prosperous and stable American and world economy, manage the government's finances, safeguard the financial systems, protect government leaders, secure a safe and drug-free America, and build a strong institution.

A
B
C
D
E
F
G
H
I
J
K
L
M
N
O
P
Q
R
S
T
U
V
W
X
Y
Z

A
B
C
D
E
F
G
H
I
J
K
L
M
N
O
P
Q
R
S
T
U
V
W
X
Y
Z

Department of Veterans Affairs

http://www.va.gov/

★★★★★

The Department of Veterans Affairs (VA) Internet World Wide web server is a resource of information on VA programs, benefits, and facilities worldwide.

Economic Analysis

http://www.bea.doc.gov/

★★★★

The Bureau of Economic Analysis reports the Gross Domestic Product (GDP), the Gross State Product (GSP), national personal income figures, and more.

Environmental Protection Agency

http://www.epa.gov

★★★★★

Learn about pending environmental legislation, recent reports and updates regarding hazardous substances, speeches and testimony, emerging environmental issues, and more at this site.

Federal Bureau of Investigation

http://www.fbi.gov

★★★★★

Learn all about the FBI. Read the FBI's *Most Wanted Fugitives* list, see what investigations are underway, learn about the Freedom of Information Act, and more.

Federal Job Search Links

http://www.careers.iastate.edu/Students/Job_Searching/federal_job_search_links.htm

★★★★★

This site is offered by the Liberal Arts and Sciences Career Services of Iowa State University. It has links to employment websites of various federal departments and to other sites where you can learn more about employment opportunities in the government.

Federal Trade Commission

http://www.ftc.gov/

★★★★★

Learn about what this agency does to protect consumers and educate yourself about protection through articles and publications, news releases, legal action reports, and other information about the inner workings of this organization.

FedStats

http://www.fedstats.gov/

★★★★★

👫 All

Statistics from more than 100 government agencies. Many agencies provide statistical reports in the form of downloadable PDF files only. Also provides links to several kids pages.

FedWorld Information Network

http://www.fedworld.gov

★★★★★

Search for documents, reports, and forms generated by U.S. government agencies through this searchable site.

〖 Best 〗 FirstGov

http://www.firstgov.org/

★★★★★

👫 All

Billing itself as "Your First Click to the U.S. Government," this site acts as an information kiosk to help citizens, businesses, and other government agencies find their way around Washington. Here, you can start your search to find out how to secure government benefits, find a government job, check your Social Security status, apply for student loans, and access other federal government services. This official site of the U.S. government is intended to put government within easy reach of its citizens and reduce some of the paperwork involved.

Health Statistics

http://www.cdc.gov/nchs/datawh/statab/pubd.htm

★★★★★

The National Center for Health Statistics (NCHS) presents a massive statistical study of the health of Americans. Categories include Obesity, Diseases, Births, and Deaths. Data is presented in easy-to-read tables.

Index to Government Websites

http://usgovinfo.about.com/newsissues/usgovinfo/blindex.htm

★★★

An alphabetically indexed list of links to more than 200 federal agencies, bureaus, commissions, and offices.

MarineLINK

http://www.usmc.mil

★★★★

Learn what it takes to be a marine; stay current on marine news; read about commemorative events for veterans, current leadership, history, and traditions; and find out how to be considered for the marines.

Motor Vehicle Registration and Licensing

http://www.usps.gov/moversnet/motor.html

★★★

This handy page from the Postal Service gives links to the DMV websites of almost every state in the union.

Peace Corps

http://www.peacecorps.gov

★★★★

Read stories of true Peace Corps volunteer adventures, learn about what it means to be a volunteer, and apply for the opportunity online.

The Public Debt to the Penny

http://www.publicdebt.treas.gov/opd/opdpenny.htm

★★★

The Bureau of the Public Debt shows us how much America owes right now. Guaranteed to make you feel better about your Visa bill.

U.S. Army

http://www.army.mil

★★★★

Read about the leadership and management of the Army, as well as news regarding current issues and events; find out what it means to be in the Army and where installations are; and get access to an archive of Army information you can search.

USA Secure

http://www.usasecure.org/

★★★★

USA Secure is a group of companies in the United States that provide products and services to ensure homeland security. This site provides a forum for all those involved in homeland security to trade information, obtain assistance, and work together to develop the best products and services possible.

U.S. Navy

http://www.navy.mil

★★★★★

Learn all about the Navy, its ships and submarines, job opportunities, and news here, where you can also post a question to be answered by a naval officer. You can also view photos of ships and subs.

United States House of Representatives

http://www.house.gov

★★★★★

Find out what issues are being debated on the House floor this week, check on the voting histories of current representatives, and find out who your local representative is. You can also write to that individual through the site.

United States Senate

http://www.senate.gov

★★★★

Search the site for your senator or for the specifics of a bill recently passed or under consideration, and view images of fine art on display in the Senate Art Collection.

A
B
C
D
E
F
G
H
I
J
K
L
M
N
O
P
Q
R
S
T
U
V
W
X
Y
Z

A
B
C
D
E
F
G
H
I
J
K
L
M
N
O
P
Q
R
S
T
U
V
W
X
Y
Z

Welcome to the White House

http://www.whitehouse.gov

★★★★★

Lots of information about the White House, the current president, and the vice president; access to White House documents, statistics and reports, and issues of the day; as well as information about how the government works and how to track down services you might be entitled to. You'll also find information about touring the White House, including a map and information for those who may be handicapped or have special needs. You will find information about the president and other government leaders, as well as news, history, and information for kids.

VETERAN AND MILITARY ORGANIZATIONS

Air Force Association

http://www.afa.org/

★★★★★

The AFA is "an independent, nonprofit, civilian aerospace organization that promotes public understanding of aerospace power and national defense." At the site, visitors can learn more about this organization; get information on legislative affairs; find out about membership; and access the online library, links, and event details.

American Battle Monuments Commission

http://www.abmc.gov/

★★★★

Visit this site to learn more about the work of this commission to honor our war dead, including accessing the names of the hundreds of thousands of war dead since 1917. The site also provides information on national commemorative events scheduled throughout the year.

The American Legion

http://www.legion.org/

★★★★★

 All

This site offers information about the Legion's patriotic programs, including education and scholarships, Boy Scouts, flag protection, and more. Also covers veteran health issues. The American Legion was chartered by Congress in 1919 as a patriotic, mutual-help, wartime veterans' organization. Since then, the Legion has offered many services to its members, such as making sure veterans are treated fairly in hiring, getting medical attention, and receiving their rights for serving their country. There are approximately 15,000 Legion posts worldwide with nearly three million members.

Army and Air Force Exchange Service

http://www.aafes.com/

★★★★★

AAFES operates close to 11,000 facilities worldwide, supporting 25 separate businesses in 25 countries, as well as in every state. Military personnel can access their accounts online, check out weekly specials, and find locations.

Defend America

http://www.defendamerica.mil/

★★★★★

Visit this site to learn the latest information about the United States war on terrorism and its efforts in reigning in rogue regimes. You can also visit this site to sign a card thanking our service men and women for fighting to protect the United States.

Department of Veterans Affairs

http://www.va.gov/

★★★★★

An up-to-the-minute report about where veterans can go to find out about benefits, facilities, and special programs available to them.

Disabled American Veterans

http://www.dav.org/

★★★★★

The DAV is a nonprofit organization of more than one million veterans disabled during war. The primary work of the DAV is fighting for and obtaining benefits from various government agencies on behalf of disabled veterans. Veterans need not be members to qualify for this free assistance. The website describes the work the organization does and how individuals can support it.

A
B
C
D
E
F
G
H
I
J
K
L
M
N
O
P
Q
R
S
T
U
V
W
X
Y
Z

Gulf War Veteran Resource Pages

http://www.gulfweb.org

★★★★★

This site is focused on providing useful information for Gulf War veterans. You'll find links to FAQs about chronic fatigue syndrome, Veterans Affairs medical centers, and information about chemical warfare and mustard gas. You'll also find a newsletter from Gulf veteran organizations and other support sources.

Korean War 50th Anniversary

http://korea50.army.mil/

★★★★

Learn more about the history of this conflict and commemorative events surrounding it at this site, where you'll also find images, first-hand interviews, and a Hall of Honor.

Military.com

http://www.military.com/

★★★★★

This choice for Best of the Best military sites would make any general proud. It is well designed, up-to-date, and packed with the best information, most interesting articles, and most insightful U.S. military commentary on the Web. Here, young men and women can learn the benefits of serving in the various branches of the military, and all those interested can check out the latest military news, intel, rumors, and opinions. Military books, humor, movies, and everything else you can think of that's related to the military is covered here. Military.com boasts a membership of more than 3 million and supports all branches of the military—those on active duty, veterans, retirees, reservists, members of the National Guard, defense workers, family members, prospective military personnel, and military enthusiasts.

Military Family Support Information

http://deploymentlink.osd.mil/deploy/family/family_support.shtml

★★★

This Department of Defense–sponsored site deals with how the entire family is affected by military service. Covers all branches of the military, including the Army, Navy, Air Force, Marines, Coast Guard, and National Guard. There are also links for military brats.

Military Order of the Purple Heart (MOPH)

http://www.purpleheart.org/

★★★★

The only Congressionally chartered veterans' organization exclusively for combat-wounded veterans.

Military USA

http://www.militaryusa.com/

★★★★

Military USA is an organization that locates veterans worldwide. The site includes the company's mission, a national reunion registry, and a Vietnam veteran database.

Military Women

http://www.militarywoman.org/

★★★

This organization provides information to women in the military, women contemplating military service, and female veterans.

National Coalition for Homeless Veterans

http://www.nchv.org/

★★★★

This site provides links to veteran and related organizations, including All Things Military, AMVETS Blinded Veterans Association, Disabled American Veterans, Gulf War Veteran Resource, Jewish War Veterans of the USA, Military Order of the Purple Heart, National Veterans Legal Service Program, and more.

National Veterans Organization of America

http://www.nvo.org/

★★★

Comprehensive list of links to information, resources, and available benefits for veterans of the United States Armed Services. Veterans can register online or simply check out what's available.

Office of the Inspector General

http://www.va.gov/oig/51/51-home.htm

★★★★

The Office of the Inspector General, Office of Investigations website. The office makes criminal investigations in veteran-related areas. The site includes a sample list of investigation areas.

Soldier City

http://www.soldiercity.com/

★★★★★

Online Army and Navy store. Scroll down the page and click Military Links to access dozens of military sites.

MOAA

http://www.moaa.org/

★★★★★

An independent, nonprofit organization, MOAA (Military Officers Association of America) is dedicated to serving the members of the uniformed services—active, inactive and retired, National Guard, and Reserve—and their families and survivors. MOAA works to preserve earned entitlements and maintain a strong national defense. Six out of 10 retired officers belong to MOAA, as do more than 30,000 active duty officers.

U.S. Department of Housing and Urban Development Veteran Resource Center (HUDVET)

http://www.hud.gov/offices/cpd/about/hudvet/index.cfm

★★★★

HUDVET provides assistance in securing home mortgages and receiving HUD services through local assistance centers. The website offers information on resources and publications of use to veterans.

Veteran and Military Organizations

http://www.fortnet.org/Post15/orgs.htm

★★★★

An A-to-Z listing of veteran and military organizations. Start by clicking on a letter of the alphabet to view a list of links; from there, you can connect directly to the organization of your choice by clicking on the link provided.

Veterans for Peace

http://www.veteransforpeace.org/

★★★★

Veterans for Peace is a not-for-profit activist organization that works to promote peaceful solutions to disagreements and to promote peace and justice through non-violence. Here, you can learn more about the organization and how to support it by donating or volunteering your time.

Veterans News and Information Service

http://www.vnis.com/

★★★★★

VNIS is a comprehensive Internet resource for military veterans who are searching for the latest news and information regarding the military veteran community, including Navy, Air Force, Marine Corps, and Army news.

VFW: Veterans of Foreign Wars

http://www.vfw.org/

★★★★★

Dedicated to remembering and supporting U.S. veterans, the VFW is the nation's oldest major veterans' organization. At this site, you can learn more about the organization and its programs and find links to other veterans' organizations and support groups.

A
B
C
D
E
F
G
H
I
J
K
L
M
N
O
P
Q
R
S
T
U
V
W
X
Y
Z

A
B
C
D
E
F
G
H
I
J
K
L
M
N
O
P
Q
R
S
T
U
V
W
X
Y
Z

Vietnam Veterans of America

http://www.vva.org/

★★★★★

Founded in 1978, Vietnam Veterans of America is "the only national Vietnam veterans organization congressionally chartered and exclusively dedicated to Vietnam-era veterans and their families." This not-for-profit group addresses issues that relate specifically to Vietnam veterans. At this site, you can learn more about the organization, its objectives, and the benefits that Vietnam vets are entitled to.

The Vietnam Veteran's Memorial Wall Page

http://thewall-usa.com/

★★★★★

This site contains a database of 58,195 names on The Wall in Washington, D.C. This is the most accurate database online.

Related Site

http://www.nps.gov/vive/

VETERINARY MEDICINE

AAHA HealthyPet.com

http://www.healthypet.com/

★★★★★

 All

This association of veterinary care providers seeks to help consumers identify qualified hospitals to care for their pets, as well as provide basic pet care information through its online library. Kids will enjoy printing out and coloring in the coloring page, and owners will appreciate the newsletter and FAQs.

American College of Veterinary Surgeons

http://www.acvs.org/

$

★★★★

Find out why your pet might need a specialist surgeon and what board certification means. Search the directory for a surgeon near you.

American Veterinary Medical Association

http://www.avma.org/

★★★★★

 All

The association's official site presents articles from the *Journal of American Veterinary Medical Association*, along with an animal health database, veterinary industry information, and pet care advice. This site features a lot of news and stories about animals and animal care as well as vet resources and has a members center and a list of allied organizations. The site is very well designed and easy to navigate, and you won't have any problems in finding information about animal care here.

Ask an Expert!

http://wwwiz.com/QandA/

★★★★

Have a question about your pet's health or behavior? Then submit it online and have the WWWiz Vet provide an answer, or search the Q&A archive to see whether your question has already been asked and answered.

AVA Online

http://www.ava.com.au/

★★★★★

The Australian Veterinary Association provides online employment, education, and conference references on veterinary medicine. The site also has the latest news stories, current issues, articles on the rural sector, a search engine, and related links.

Board-Certified Avian Veterinarians

http://www.birdsnways.com/articles/abvpvets.htm

★★★

Select a specialist avian veterinarian from this listing from the American Board of Veterinary Practitioners and Birds'n'Ways.

CAB International

http://www.cabi.org/

★★★

CAB International is a not-for-profit organization with three principal areas of activity: publishing, information for development, and bioscience. CAB International's activities in the animal sciences and veterinary medicine area are focused particularly on veterinary medicine, veterinary parasitology, animal breeding, genetics and biotechnology, animal nutrition, dairy science and technology, apiculture, and aquaculture.

A
B
C
D
E
F
G
H
I
J
K
L
M
N
O
P
Q
R
S
T
U
V
W
X
Y
Z

California Veterinary Diagnostic Laboratory System

http://sphinx.ucdavis.edu/

★★★

The California Veterinary Diagnostic Laboratory Systems (CVDLS) provides disease control and health maintenance for livestock. This site has a listing of the professionals in the field and information on bacteriology and disease syndromes.

Care for Pets

http://www.avma.org/care4pets/

★★★★★

 All

This American Veterinary Medical Association site contains pet care information, such as safety tips, breed statistics, articles on how to deal with the death of a pet, tips for selecting a veterinarian, and pet stories.

Careers in Veterinary Medicine

http://careerplanning.about.com/library/weekly/aa100400a.htm

★★★

This site has extensive information on the veterinary profession and animal-related news. If you're considering a career as a vet, this site may be your best bet.

Center for Animal Health and Productivity

http://cahpwww.vet.upenn.edu/cahp/index.php

★★★★

This site describes a research institution created by the School of Veterinary Medicine at the University of Pennsylvania. Here, lay people and experts can find information on livestock diseases, new treatments, and reference materials in animal medicine.

Center for Veterinary Medicine

http://www.fda.gov/cvm/default.html

★★★★

The U.S. Food and Drug Administration's Center for Veterinary Medicine (CVM) "regulates the manufacture and distribution of food additives and drugs that will be given to animals." Regulated items include pet foods and drugs as well as livestock feed and drugs for poultry, cattle, swine, and other farm animals.

Department of Animal Science: Oklahoma State University

http://www.ansi.okstate.edu/

★★★★★

This site provides information about the Oklahoma State School of Veterinary Science. A map of the campus, descriptions of current research, student resources, and course information are included.

E Medicine

http://www.emedicine.com/

★★★★

Free online medical textbooks for physicians, veterinarians, medical students, physician assistants, nurse practitioners, nurses, and the public.

International Association of Equine Professionals

http://www.neosoft.com/~iaep/menu.html

$

★★★

The International Association of Equine Practitioners site has information on healthcare for horses. At this site, you can learn about becoming a member and find a list of equine veterinary clinics and farriers nationwide.

Journal of Veterinary Medical Education

http://www.utpjournals.com/JVME/JVME.html

★★★

This site provides back issues of the *Journal of Veterinary Medical Education* in e-zine form. Users can search a database of previous articles from the journal, and author submission guidelines are included.

Kentucky Equine Research

http://www.wehn.com/

★★★★★

This site is a resource for equine veterinarians, featuring a bulletin board for exchanging ideas on equine health. Other resources include an archive of the journal *Equine Review* and a calendar of upcoming conferences.

Multilingual Dictionary of the Horse

http://www.microtec.net/bouletjc/vc2e/searvc2.htm

★★★★

This site is a searchable dictionary of equine veterinary terms in French, English, Spanish, and German.

Murdoch University: Division of Veterinary and Biomedical Sciences

http://wwwvet.murdoch.edu.au/vbs/vet/

★★★★★

This site, maintained by the Division of Biomedical Sciences at Murdoch University in western Australia, has information on the school, its programs, faculty, staff, students, studies, alumni, computer-aided learning, and activities, along with a search engine.

National Board Exam (NBE)

http://www.nbec.org

★★★★

In-depth information for candidates preparing for the National (U.S.) Board Exam, from the Professional Examination Service. You can also order a sample exam to study.

OncoLink: Veterinary Oncology

http://www.oncolink.com/types/section.cfm?c=22&s=69

★★★★★

This site, provided by the veterinary hospital of the University of Pennsylvania, has information about the diagnosis and treatment of cancer in animals.

ProVet

http://www.provet.com/

★★★★★

Well-stocked online warehouse of products for veterinary clinics and veterinarians. Features products from more than 150 manufacturers and offers services to help veterinarians find the products they need and manage their inventories more efficiently.

TalkToTheVet.com

http://www.talktothevet.com/

★★★★

 All

Get quick information about your pet by reading the numerous articles on this site. For about $25 per month, you can consult with a veterinarian via email about various health-related issues for your pet(s).

Veterinary Medicine

http://vetmedicine.miningco.com

★★★★★

This site contains a lot of material pertinent to animal care such as information about diseases, pets, animals, vaccinations, vet schools, vet professional careers, and much more. If you're interested in becoming a vet, you'll find information on this topic, also.

Veterinary Medicine Libraries

http://duke.usask.ca/~ladd/vet_libraries.html

★★★

This site offers extensive links to veterinary-related catalogs and libraries at many major universities, colleges, and other professional establishments. The collections are listed by geographic area such as Canada, USA, and Mexico. You can find information on just about every aspect of the subject here.

Veterinary Pet Insurance

http://www.petinsurance.com/

★★★★★

Find out why you might want to consider buying pet insurance and the types of insurance products available; then enroll online if you like.

Vetscape

http://www.vetscape.co.uk/

★★★★★

A veterinary resource site for professionals. Links to sites containing information on medical topics such as homeopathic medicine, exotic animals, professional journals, anesthesia, parasitology, and others.

A B C D E F G H I J K L M N O P Q R S T **U V** W X Y Z

A
B
C
D
E
F
G
H
I
J
K
L
M
N
O
P
Q
R
S
T
U
V
W
X
Y
Z

Washington State University College of Veterinary Medicine

http://www.vetmed.wsu.edu/

★★★★★

This site provides a virtual tour of veterinary hospital and service units. Admissions, undergraduate and graduate programs, continuing education, and research are also covered at this site.

World Organization for Animal Health

http://www.oie.int/

★★★

Databases on animal diseases and biotechnology. Online animal health texts are included.

VIDEO AND MULTIMEDIA

bThere

http://www.bthere.tv

★★★★★

 Not for kids

Hip, Web-based television station that gives you everything you can get on TV, including the commercials! Go behind the scenes with your favorite models and celebrities, cheer for the top athletes, or just kick back and listen to some tunes. See what the future of broadcasting has in store for you. You'll need a broadband Internet connection to fully experience this site, but it's well worth the visit. Some material is inappropriate for people under the age of 18.

Oddcast

http://www.oddcast.com

★★★★★

Oddcast is a multimedia service company that develops tools to help media moguls create and roll out interactive, on-demand media products for broadcasting over the Web. At this site, you can check out some of the many tools that Oddcast has developed, learn more about how the company has helped other media companies develop award-winning media products, and even enter some online contests.

Without a Box

http://www.withoutabox.com

★★★★★

Service designed for upcoming filmmakers, Without a Box helps aspiring filmmakers submit their films to various festivals, including Cannes. As a filmmaker, you can submit one video, one press kit, and a single application to Without a Box to have your film distributed to multiple film festivals around the world.

Best ZED

http://zed.cbc.ca/go.ZeD?page=home

★★★★★

ZED provides a place where artists can test the boundaries of genre, contributing work in any medium or collection of media they desire. ZED features music, film, video, performance art, visual art, word and spoken word forms of expression and exhibits these creations online at this site. Very easy to navigate, packed with original material, and ever evolving, ZED earns a spot as our Best of the Best Site for Video and Multimedia.

DVD

DVD Price Search

http://www.dvdpricesearch.com

★★★★★

A site that compares the total cost of purchasing a particular DVD across several sites, telling you which merchant offers you the best deal. The site doesn't sell movies; it just tells you which online merchant has the lowest price.

DVDDigital.com

http://dvddigital.vstoredvds.com/

★★★★★

Search for DVD movies or read the reviews of new releases to select those you want to purchase from this site.

A B C D E F G H I J K L M N O P Q R S T U V W X Y Z

A
B
C
D
E
F
G
H
I
J
K
L
M
N
O
P
Q
R
S
T
U
V
W
X
Y
Z

dvdfile.com

http://www.dvdfile.com/

★★★★★

Join in discussions about DVD movies, hardware, and software at this site, which also features industry news, movie release information, and a long list of movies currently available for rent or purchase in DVD format. Find out information on just about any movie, DVD, or software that you might have an interest in and order online. The site also has interesting information on the most current movies and music.

Netflix.com

http://www.netflix.com

★★★★★

This site offers a movie-recommendation search engine and Cinematch, which enables you to see movie suggestions that are geared to your specific preferences. In addition to offering movie reviews, the site also offers online rentals, access to what's playing when at your local theater, ticket sales, and streaming movies.

MULTIMEDIA SEARCH ENGINES

120Seconds.com

http://www.120seconds.com

★★★★

Offbeat Canadian radio station/media kiosk, where you can access all sorts of entertaining audio and video clips, animation shorts, games, news briefs, and funny stories. Even with a speedy cable-modem connection, downloads can take eons.

Real.com

http://realguide.real.com/

★★★★★

Search for videos and music at this site, which offers a wide range of things to listen to and watch. For movies, you can catch trailers and information about the latest releases, view interviews and animated features, or watch business and educational pieces. For videos, you can look for a particular title for download, or research top box office hits and site favorites.

Search Engine Colossus

http://www.searchenginecolossus.com/

★★★

The International Directory of Search Engines gives you quick, efficient access to hundreds of search engines from around the world with which you can search for the latest audio and video information as well as many other subjects.

Searchmedia

http://library.humboldt.edu/~ccm/searchmedia.html

★★★

You can use this search engine to search for anything multimedia such as videos, music, photos, and much more.

VIDEO

Blockbuster

http://www.blockbuster.com/

★★★★★

Search Blockbuster's database of videos and DVDs for purchase, get news on upcoming releases, learn who won the latest video awards, and watch short films online. There's also a news section called Latest Scoop to keep you in the know regarding the movie industry.

Buy.com

http://www.us.buy.com/

★★★★★

Search for videos to buy at a discount here, and find out about new releases and top rentals before making your selection.

Reel.com

http://www.reel.com

★★★★★

Information kiosk for movies on DVD and VHS. Find out about new releases, check out the movie reviews, and even go behind the scenes in Hollywood to learn about your favorite celebrities and their latest projects. Links to Amazon.com for purchasing videos.

A
B
C
D
E
F
G
H
I
J
K
L
M
N
O
P
Q
R
S
T
U
V
W
X
Y
Z

VITAMINS AND SUPPLEMENTS

anti-oxidant.com–Quick Reference Guide

http://www.klsdesign.com/anti-ox/

★★★★★

Find up-to-date health and wellness information and research articles at this site. This particular section invites the user to use a pull-down menu to obtain information on every antioxidant from Alpha-lipoic Acid to Zinc.

Champion Nutrition

http://www.champion-nutrition.com/

$

★★★★

Vitamins, minerals, and nutritional supplements for athletes.

eNutrition.com

http://www.enutrition.com

$

★★★★

Get tips for managing your weight and improving your health. Also find information on sports nutrition, body and senses, and vitamins through useful short articles at the site. And then buy the products you need to get the results you want, such as appetite suppressants, vitamins, meal replacements, and much more, organized by category.

healthshop.com

http://www.vitacost.com/healthshop.html

$

★★★★★

Use the site's Healthplanner to design a custom program for improving your health. Answer questions about medical history, lifestyle, and family history and receive an action plan to help overcome fatigue, illness, or other challenges, such as weight gain. The site provides information and all-natural products for sale. You can also ask an expert or have an online chat with a nutritionist for more support.

Best MotherNature.com

http://www.mothernature.com/

$

★★★★★

This site offers a plethora of "natural" products and services aimed at helping you have a healthier lifestyle. You can research health issues, use a Supplement Planner to determine what vitamins are best for you, read customer reviews of products, and purchase vitamins and supplements online. With its huge product line, excellent search tools, and simplified order forms, this site earns its place in the Best of the Best club.

Pharmaton

http://www.pharmaton.com/

$

★★★★

Features a collection of natural healthcare products and dietary supplements, including Ginsana, Ginkoba, and Flexium.

Puritan's Pride

http://www.puritan.com/

★★★★

Shop online for vitamins, minerals, and other dietary supplements. This site includes health, fitness, and consumer information; a nutrient database; and a listing of live chat events.

Quacks and Vitamin Pushers

http://www.quackwatch.org/01QuackeryRelatedTopics/spotquack.html

★★★

Interesting article against the use of vitamins and supplements from Stephen Barrett, M.D.

Thriveonline.com

http://thriveonline.oxygen.com/

★★★★★

Thrive offers a searchable health library, feature articles on topics ranging from stress to vitamins, and a chance to email a doctor with health questions.

Vita-Web

http://www.vita-web.com

★★★★

Everything you want to know about vitamins is here. Find out what your body needs, how it metabolizes different vitamins, what interferes with their absorption, what are the effects of deficiencies, and more. The site also provides links to current research and resources.

VitaminShoppe.com

http://www.vitaminshoppe.com/

★★★★★

Shop by brand name or product to find vitamins, nutritional supplements, and herbal products here. You can also catch up on health and nutrition news in the Learning Center.

A
B
C
D
E
F
G
H
I
J
K
L
M
N
O
P
Q
R
S
T
U
V
W
X
Y
Z

978

A B C D E F G H I J K L M N O P Q R S T U V W X Y Z

VOLLEYBALL

American Volleyball Coaches Association

http://www.avca.org/

★★★★★

👥 14-18

The AVCA site provides up-to-date results, job openings, available playing dates, educational materials, and articles on sports medicine and coaching.

American Wallyball Association

http://www.wallyball.com/

💲

★★★★★

👥 14-18

Wallyball is volleyball played on a racquetball court. Use this site to read the game's rules, order supplies, find out where you can play, and get details about different leagues and tournaments.

Association of Volleyball Professionals (AVP)

http://www.volleyball.org/avp/

★★★

👥 14-18

Members of the AVP are the best beach volleyball players in the country. This site houses their schedule, roster, rankings, awards, history, address, and more. The goal of the AVP, established in 1983, is to maximize the sport while protecting the commercial interests and integrity of the players. Links to purchase books through Amazon.

Cobra Volleyball

http://www.cobravolleyball.com/

★★★

The Cobra net is a popular system used on sand or grass; it sets up easily for all levels of play, from elementary school gym to professional tournaments.

Collegiate Volleyball Update

http://www.cvu.com/

★★★★★

👥 14-18

Visit this site to keep abreast of the latest news, scores, stats, and standings in college volleyball. Covers both men's and women's volleyball, featuring dozens of stories about college teams, players, and coaches across the nation. Also provides some information on high school volleyball.

English Volleyball Association

http://www.volleyballengland.org/

★★★

👥 14-18

Comprehensive site for volleyball in the U.K., this site provides information about junior and professional volleyball, beach volleyball, national teams, coaching, officiating, and other topics of interest.

🏆Best🏆 FIVB WWW Home Page

http://www.fivb.ch/

★★★★★

👫 14-18

The FIVB (Fédération Internationale de Volleyball) is the governing body of international volleyball. Use this site to learn more about upcoming events and tournaments, worldwide beach volleyball, FIVB meetings, program development, and educational and promotional material. As the home for the governing body of international volleyball, this site has an edge over the other sites in this category, but its design and content also contribute to making it the Best of the Best site in its class.

NCAA Men's and Women's Volleyball

http://www.ncaachampionships.com/

★★★★★

👫 14-18

The National College Athletic Association's official site includes information about all NCAA sports, including volleyball. After you pull up the NCAA home page, click the Volleyball link in the navigation bar on the left and click the desired section: Men's Volleyball or Women's Volleyball. Each section provides a schedule, ticketing details, results, and previews.

Schneid's Volleyball Page

http://www.volleyweb.com/

★★★★

👫 14-18

Schneid's excellent content includes the normal links and rules, but also tips on strategy, drills to improve your game, nutritional information for athletes, and advice on training and flexibility.

Spike Nashbar

http://www.spikenashbar.com/

 💲

★★★★

👫 14-18

Spike Nashbar carries anything and everything you might need to play and/or coach volleyball.

Todd's Volleyball Page

http://vbref.org/

★★★

👫 14-18

Todd provides comprehensive coverage of the game's rules, according to varying organizations. He also recommends his favorite equipment and discusses volleyball in the opposing towns of Austin, Texas, and Chicago, Illinois.

USA Volleyball Home Page

http://www.usavolleyball.org/

★★★★

👫 14-18

Links to youth and Junior Olympic teams as well as rosters for top men's and women's teams (U.S. and international).

Volleyball.com

http://www.volleyball.com/

💲

★★★★★

👫 14-18

You'll find indoor and outdoor volleyball gear for sale here; tips for improving your form; information on where to play locally; and rankings, schedules, bios, and stats on AVP, college, and Olympic volleyballers. The volleyball forum lets you express your opinion and get advice from fellow volleyball fans.

Volleyball Hall of Fame

http://www.volleyhall.org/

💲

★★★★

👫 14-18

Read the sport's and the hall's history, view photos, see who's been inducted into the hall, send feedback, buy a centennial volleyball, and study a map showing where the hall is located in Holyoke, Massachusetts.

A
B
C
D
E
F
G
H
I
J
K
L
M
N
O
P
Q
R
S
T
U
V
W
X
Y
Z

Volleyball Magazine

http://www.volleyballmag.com/

★★★★★

👥 14-18

Coverage of the sport from the beaches to the hardwood courts. Scores, player features, and forums for volleyball players are included in this site, along with information on subscription.

Volleyball Sites on the WWW

http://volleyball.org/www_sites/

★★★★

👥 14-18

Links to volleyball sites all over the world indexed by country.

Volleyball World Wide

http://www.volleyball.org/

★★★

👥 14-18

This site includes a fact page and links for both indoor and beach volleyball (men's and women's), and provides information for all levels of volleyball (amateur, collegiate, and professional). Links to related associations such as the U.S. Disabled Volleyball Team home pages are also provided.

America's Wars

http://www.multied.com/wars.html

★★★★

History Central provides overviews of the various wars and conflicts that the United States has been involved in, starting with the American Revolution and leading up to Operation Enduring Freedom. When you click a link for a particular war, a page appears with links that provide a brief overview or timeline of the war. Click a link for additional information. The coverage is not very comprehensive, but if you're looking for overviews, this is a great place to start.

DEBKAfile

http://www.debka.com/

★★★★★

To find out what's really going on in Israel and the rest of the Middle East, check out the DEBKAfile. This independent Internet publication features investigative reports and analysis focusing on "international terrorism, intelligence, international conflicts, Islam, military affairs, security and politics." Israeli-based, DEBKAfile is updated seven days a week in both English and Hebrew.

GlobalSecurity.org

http://www.globalsecurity.org/

★★★★★

GlobalSecurity.org is dedicated to making the world a more secure place by keeping people more informed about what's really going on. Here you can learn more about special weapons, intelligence, homeland security, space, and cyberspace security. Some of the information is understandably less than forthcoming, but this site does provide a great deal of useful military data.

Institute for War and Peace Reporting

http://www.iwpr.net/

★★★★★

In an attempt to present both sides of the story and provide a balanced view of what's going on in the hot spots around the globe, the Institute for War and Peace Reporting features perspectives that commonly pitch intent against reality. Site is accessible in several languages and seeks assistance from anyone who can contribute information or expertise.

Jane's Information Group

http://www.janes.com/

★★★★★

Jane's Information Group provides intelligence and analysis on national security issues, risks, and international defense to governments, militaries, business leaders, and academics in more than 180 countries. Here you can access some of the less classified information, see what Jane's Information Group has to offer, and perhaps even open an account.

Strategy Page

http://www.strategypage.com/

★★★★

If modern military strategy interests you, check out the Strategy Page, where you can find out what's currently working and not working in the war on terrorism and other conflicts. This site goes behind the scenes to provide visitors with the news that most sources don't make available to the public. The site's design is not award-winning, but the information available here is something you can't get anywhere else!

A
B
C
D
E
F
G
H
I
J
K
L
M
N
O
P
Q
R
S
T
U
V
W
X
Y
Z

AMERICAN CIVIL WAR

AmericanCivilWar.com

http://americancivilwar.com/

★★★★★

 14-18

Excellent site for learning about the people who were involved in the Civil War and the major events that define it. Feature indexes include a timeline of the Civil War, State Battle Maps, Women in the War, Battle Statistics, and more. A list of the major players and major battles is also included, plus a collection of recommended books and other resources.

The American Civil War Homepage

http://sunsite.utk.edu/civil-war/

★★★★

14-18

Huge directory of American Civil War resources on the Web includes links to music of the era, information about the secession crisis leading up to the War, articles about the presidential elections, images from the war, biographies of those involved, and much more. Nothing fancy here, but the site is updated regularly and features an extensive directory for serious researchers.

Civil War Book Review

http://www.cwbr.com/

★★★★

This site features reviews of books about the Civil War and interviews with the authors. The opening page displays a list of reviews available in the current issue, but you can click the Past Issues link to check out books that were previewed in earlier issues.

Best The Civil War Home Page

http://www.civil-war.net/

$

★★★★★

14-18

This site is dedicated to all the participants, both North and South, of the great American Civil War. It features a wide range of documents, such as Abraham Lincoln's Emancipation Proclamation and Sullivan Ballou's letter to his wife, a timeline of events leading up to the Civil War, a searchable database of more than 1,000 photos, an index to other Civil War sites on the Web, and much more. If you're looking to do some research on the American Civil War, make this Best of the Best site your first stop.

The United States Civil War Center

http://www.cwc.lsu.edu/

★★★★★

14-18

The United States Civil War Center (USCWC) promotes the study of the American Civil War from various perspectives and disciplines. Here, you can find an index of resources on the Web along with a cemetery database, events calendar, questions page, and virtual exhibits.

COLD WAR

CNN Interactive: Cold War

http://www.cnn.com/SPECIALS/cold.war/

★★★★★

If you never did grasp what the Cold War was all about, how it started, the tactics involved, and how and why it was eventually resolved, check out CNN Interactive's online special. Here you can navigate interactive maps, witness rare video footage, read the biographies of the key players, access declassified documents, and tour the Cold War capitals through 3D animations. You can explore this site in any number of ways: access the site one episode at a time, relive the Cold War experience, peruse the knowledge bank, discuss and debate topics online with other interested visitors, take the Cold War Challenge, or view the notes and tips for educators. This site is attractive, easy to navigate, and packed with intriguing information—a very close runner up in the race for Best of the Best.

The Cold War Museum

http://www.coldwar.org/

★★★★★

The Cold War Museum consists of a timeline of the Cold War from the 1940s to the 1990s. When you click a decade, a page pops up that includes the key events or individuals in that decade who shaped to the Cold War. Click an event or key player to read more. The site also features a Cold War Trivia game to test your history knowledge. Though the site doesn't provide much in-depth coverage, it does provide an excellent overview in a cool format that's easy to navigate.

Cold War Policies: 1945–1991

http://history.acusd.edu/gen/20th/coldwar0.html

★★★★

This site features a basic timeline of the Cold War, starting in Yalta, and ending with the aftermath in the Clinton era. Scan the timeline to get an overview of the events leading up to and contributing to the Cold War and then click individual links in the timeline to learn more. Most of the links call up pages with both text and photos to give you a clear understanding of a particular event.

 ## The National Archives Learning Curve: The Cold War

http://learningcurve.pro.gov.uk/coldwar/default.htm

★★★★★

This very cool, interactive site provides an overview of the Cold War that questions the date on which it really began along with other commonly held theories. The site's goal is to provide facts and various theories and then leave it up to you to draw your conclusions. Asking tough questions and taking a skeptical view of popular theories is what makes this site much more intellectually interactive than most of the Cold War sites you might encounter. That, coupled with the attractive design and easy-to-use interface, makes this site our pick as the Best of the Best in the Cold War category.

 KOREAN WAR

Korean War Commemoration

http://korea50.army.mil/

★★★

This site commemorates the 50th anniversary of the Korean War. Here, you can find a brief history of the Korean War along with some direct observations from veterans, a chronology of the War, biographies of some of the key figures, maps, photos, and other tidbits.

The Korean War

http://www.korean-war.com/

★★★★★

Ed Evanhoe, life member of the Special Forces and Special Operations Associations, created and maintained this site, which features an excellent collection of information about the Korean War. Learn the history and facts about the "Forgotten War," find out which countries were involved, join the discussion lists, and check out some additional recommended reading.

History Central: The Korean War

http://www.multied.com/korea/

★★★★★

History Central has done an outstanding job of chronicling the Korean War, from the causes leading up to it to the peace talks that followed it. Site consists of about 20 links, each of which opens a short article on the selected topic along with a photo or two. Not very in-depth, but it provides an excellent overview of the War.

Korean War: The Forgotten War

http://www.military.com/Content/
MoreContent1?file=index

★★★★★

Military.com provides an excellent overview of the Korean War from beginning to end. Links on the left provide an outline of the presentation, and text and photos appear on the right.

A B C D E F G H I J K L M N O P Q R S T U V W X Y Z

A
B
C
D
E
F
G
H
I
J
K
L
M
N
O
P
Q
R
S
T
U
V
W
X
Y
Z

Korean War Project

http://www.koreanwar.org/

★★★★

This site is dedicated to providing support for veterans and family members of the Korean War and to researchers and students of military history. Here, you can find help searching for those killed or missing in action and information about a particular unit. Find out about reunions and possibly even organize one yourself.

VIETNAM WAR

Vietnam Online

http://www.pbs.org/wgbh/amex/vietnam/

$

★★★★

This site looks back at the most unpopular war in U.S. history. It provides a brief introduction by David McCullough, a biography of the major players in the war, an interactive timeline, reflections from those who were involved at the time, specific notorious events, and a list of references. The tone of this site is one of regret and sadness at the losses both sides experienced.

The Vietnam Veterans Home Page

http://grunt.space.swri.edu

$

★★★

This home of the Vietnam veterans features tributes by family members and friends, a virtual visit to Vietnam (including pictures, stories, and maps), a list of veterans organizations and support groups, and links to other resources.

Vietnam Veterans Memorial

http://www.virtualwall.org/

★★★★★

The Virtual Wall is the online version of the Vietnam Veterans Memorial. Here, veterans are listed in alphabetical order, so you can quickly look up their names, remember their service to the United States, and contribute to their memorials.

 The Vietnam War Pictorial

http://www.vietnampix.com/

$

★★★★★

This site provides a highly graphical tour of the Vietnam War—"From the Delta to the DMZ, From Politics to Hippies, This Is the Fire in the Jungle." This site is not intended to provide an accurate documentation of the history of the war, but to provide a graphic tour of the conditions that both sides were subjected to. Tim Page took most of the intense photos that are displayed here. The tour leads you through six sections: Background, Machines, Faces, Hippies, Under Fire, and Life and Sorrow.

The Wars for Viet Nam: 1945–1975

http://vietnam.vassar.edu/

★★★★

This site, based on course materials developed by Robert Brigham for his senior seminar on the Vietnam war at Vassar College, gives students the opportunity to study official documents related to the war. This site provides an excellent overview of the Vietnam war, including events that led up to it, and features links to the official documents used in Robert Brigham's seminar. Don't miss the Resources link for additional information and resources accessible on the Web.

WORLD WAR I

Encyclopedia of the First World War

http://www.spartacus.schoolnet.co.uk/FWW.htm

$

★★★

If you're looking for a comprehensive resource on World War I and you don't mind getting bogged down at a site that's somewhat difficult to navigate, you will find this Encyclopedia of the First World War most informative. Here you can find a complete timeline of events leading up to and through the war, a list of the countries involved and their roles in the war, assessments of the allied armed forces and the central powers, and much more.

FIRST WORLD WAR.COM
http://www.firstworldwar.com/

★★★★★

This site features extensive coverage of World War I, starting with events leading up to the war and proceeding to its end. Site features text, commentary, photos, and even audio clips. A navigation bar on the left side of the page makes it easy to move through the various areas of the site: How It Began, The Battles, Who's Who, War Timeline, Maps, Encyclopedia, Weapons of War, Prose and Poetry, and more. Excellent site that promises to get even better over time.

The Great War
http://www.pbs.org/greatwar/

★★★★★

Home of the PBS special *The Great War And the Reshaping of the 20th Century*, this site features an interactive timeline of the war, maps and locations, interviews with 20 of the top World War I historians, and recaps of the eight episodes that made up this award-winning show. You can also order the video collection and/or book online.

War Times Journal: The Great War
http://www.wtj.com/wars/greatwar/

★★★★

This site features a list of archives and articles about World War I. Archives include High Adventure, The Grand Fleet, The Red Fighter Pilot, and Germany's High Seas Fleet. Articles cover the Königsberg Incident, The Western Front, The Eastern Front, and Dark Autumn: The 1916 German Zeppelin Offensive. Most articles include photos and illustrated maps.

World War One
http://www.bbc.co.uk/history/war/wwone/

★★★★★

The BBC has put together an incredibly informative and moving site dealing with all aspects of World War I. Once you land on the shores of this site, forget about the navigational links on the left—they're for other areas of the BBC's history site. The main area of the home page provides links to the major campaigns and battles, other geographical areas where the war was waged, revolutions in Russia, debates of the time, and more. Off to the right, you can find links to a timeline and a multimedia center, where you can view photos, listen to audio clips, and play animations of the battlefronts.

WORLD WAR II

The History Place: World War II
http://www.historyplace.com/worldwar2/timeline/ww2time.htm

★★★

The History Place features a timeline of events leading from the end of World War I to the suicide of Hermann Göring on October 16, 1946. Most of the items on the timeline are plain text that provide a one-sentence description of what happened on a particular date. Several of the items, however, are links that open pages with text and photos that go into more depth.

Second World War Encyclopedia
http://www.spartacus.schoolnet.co.uk/2WW.htm

★★★

Incredibly comprehensive resource on World War II that features a complete timeline of events leading up to and through the war, a list of the countries involved and their roles in the war, lists of U.S., British, French, Russian, German, and Japanese military leaders, information on the air war and the sea war, descriptions of French and German resistance, and much more. Without a navigation bar to help you quickly return to the main sections of this site, it is a little difficult to navigate, but if you're looking for in-depth coverage of World War II, you'll find it here.

A
B
C
D
E
F
G
H
I
J
K
L
M
N
O
P
Q
R
S
T
U
V
W
X
Y
Z

U.S. National World War II Memorial

http://www.wwiimemorial.com/

★★★★

The World War II memorial honors the 16 million people who served in the armed forces of the U.S. during World War II, the more than 400,000 who died, and the millions who supported the war effort from home. Visit this site to learn more about the memorial and what you can do to show your support.

War Times Journal: World War II

http://www.wtj.com/wars/wwtwo/

★★★★★

This site features a list of current and archived articles about World War II. Articles include "The Normandy Landing," "Marine Scout on Saipan," "The Sinking of the Hyuga and Tone," and "Thunder Gods and Kamikazes." Archived articles include "The Bombing of Hiroshima." Most articles include photos and illustrated maps. The Flash animated map of the Normandy invasion is particularly well done.

World War Two

http://www.bbc.co.uk/history/war/wwtwo/

★★★★★

The BBC has designed an engaging and informative site dealing with all aspects of World War II. Ignore the links on the left side of the home page—they're for other areas of the BBC's history site. The main area of the home page provides links to The War Abroad, The Battle of the Atlantic, The Battle of Britain, The Secret War, Politics and Personalities, The Holocaust, and more. Off to the right, you can find links to a timeline and a multimedia center where you can view photos, listen to audio clips, play animations of the battlefronts, and even watch brief video clips.

DIVING/SCUBA DIVING

Aloha Dive (Scuba)

http://alohadive.com/

★★★

The Aloha Dive Company in Hawaii offers a unique experience, in that you learn the historical and geological significance of each site as you visit it. Whether you want to see humpback whales, photograph creatures underwater, or just take lessons, you can find what you want at this family-run business.

Aqua Lung

http://www.aqualung.com/

★★★★

More than 60 (years ago when Jacques Cousteau and Emile Gagnan developed the first aqua-lung. Since then, an entire company has sprouted up, offering a complete line of diving equipment. Visit this site to check out Aqua Lung's product line, use the interactive equipment selector, or find a dealer near you.

Beneath the Sea

http://www.beneaththesea.org/

★★★★★

BTS is a not-for-profit organization that works toward increasing awareness of the earth's oceans and the sport of scuba diving. BTS helps promote the protection of marine wildlife via grants to other non-profit groups. Includes links to seminars, workshops, mailing lists, and other diving-related sites.

Deep Sea Divers Den

http://www.divers-den.com/

★★★★★

Based in Far North Queensland, Australia, Deep Sea Divers Den includes scuba diving to the Great Barrier Reef. Offers scuba diving courses in Cairns, Australia, at all levels as well as one-day trips to the Great Barrier Reef for snorkelers and divers. PADI certification is available. You are asked to email for information on registering or signing up for the courses and other activities.

Dive Buddy White Pages

http://www.divebuddy.com/

★★★

Promotes the #1 dive rule: Never dive alone. Offers a free registry of more than 4,000 divers so you can find a buddy to dive with anywhere you want to go. Encourages divers to register and exchange ideas and tips on underwater photography, dive gear, dive locations, and any other dive-related topic of interest.

Dive Connections

http://www.caldiveboats.com/

★★★

Home of the largest dive charter company in San Diego, this site provides a list of interesting dive sites around San Diego with a brief description of each one, plus a description of the various charter boats that are available. Information about rental gear and hotels in the area is also available.

DiverLink

http://www.diverlink.com/

★★★★

Pointers to dive sites on the Internet in categories such as clubs, manufacturers, and aquariums.

A
B
C
D
E
F
G
H
I
J
K
L
M
N
O
P
Q
R
S
T
U
V
W
X
Y
Z

DiversDiscount.com

http://www.diversdiscount.com/

★★★★★

Shop the online scuba catalog for gear you might need or ask the scuba experts for guidance. Read newsletter articles about diving and find resources and instruction here.

DiveWeb

http://www.diveweb.com/

★★★★★

Comprehensive resource for commercial diving, marine technology, underwater repair of vessels, and other underwater industries. Here, you can find headline news stories about a wide range of water-related issues and events around the world. You can also join discussion groups, learn about commercial diving equipment, and check the online calendar for conferences and shows.

Diving Equipment and Marketing Association

http://www.dema.org/

★★★

Dedicated to the dive industry, this site supplies information on how to become a diver, industry news, details on how to become a DEMA member for those involved in the commercial side of the dive business, and continuing education for certified divers. Also provides information on the annual DEMA trade show.

Doc's Diving Medicine

http://faculty.washington.edu/ekay/

★★★★★

Dedicated to undersea medicine and issues of diving safety for sport and professional divers.

The Franck Goddio Website

http://www.underwaterdiscovery.org/

★★★★★

Home of the Franck Goddio Society, an organization that "sponsors search and excavation projects around the world aimed at finding and recovering or preserving underwater shipwrecks and other underwater sites of special historical and cultural significance." Franck Goddio is the archaeologist version of Jacques Cousteau. Here, you can learn more about Franck Goddio and his society, find out about upcoming events and ongoing projects, visit the photo gallery, and more.

HSA: Handicapped Scuba Association

http://www.hsascuba.com/

★★★★

This organization is dedicated to making scuba more accessible to people with physical challenges, and its site appears to be updated frequently. It offers a quarterly journal, travel schedule, guides to wheelchair-accessible dive resorts, an HSA instructor locator page, and training course information for divers interested in becoming HSA dive instructors.

Luis Cabanas Scuba Diving and Instruction (Mexico)

http://www.cozumel.net/diving/luis/

★★★★

Luis, a PADI master scuba diver trainer, has logged in more than 250 dives to Punta Sur. His website includes quotes from satisfied customers, photographs of dives in progress, and descriptions of basic dives for beginners. Also offers fishing trips, jungle adventure tours, underwater camera rentals, fast boat dive trips, and cave diving. Group discounts available. You are asked to send email for registration.

Mad-Dog Expeditions

http://www.mad-dog.net/

★★★

If you want to experience a challenging dive adventure, check out Mad Dog for diving expeditions to the Arctic or to a sunken aircraft carrier, or dive with great white sharks in South Africa, among other planned trips. You'll also find more tame dives to popular Caribbean spots.

Maui Diving Scuba Center/Snorkel Shop

http://members.aol.com/div4me/frames.html

★★★

Promises cheaper rates than the hotels and caters the dive to your experience level. Claims to have the best safety record on all of Maui. Offers NAUI and PADI certification. For ages 12 and up.

PADI: Professional Association of Diving Instructors

http://www.padi.com/

★★★★★

👫 All

A fantastic site with current information. Updated daily, this site offers the usual dive center listings, BBSes, product catalogs, news, and course listings, and a wide range of information beyond the usual. Also provides plenty of information about PADI diving certification.

Rodale's Scuba Diving—The Magazine Divers Trust

http://www.scubadiving.com/

★★★★★

The complete source for answers about diving, including objective equipment evaluations, information on dive sites, and dive medicine answers to help you dive safely. Visitors are offered a free trial subscription to *SCUBA Daily News*. Also supplies a guide to dive-related books available on the Web, a humorous top-10 list, and a helpful *Scuba Divers Handbook*. Purchase books mostly through Amazon.com and learn about tours worldwide.

Scuba Central

http://scubacentral.com/

★★★

A good point of entry for all scuba divers, this site provides a directory of the top scuba links and travel resources.

Scuba Diving and Snorkeling Worldwide

http://www.batnet.com/see&sea/

★★★★

Information about dive travel, live-aboard diving, marine life, and underwater photography. Features an excellent directory of diving destinations around the world, complete with links to websites where you can learn more about each destination. Excellent photo gallery of Carl Roessler's diving adventures, plus tips on taking your own great underwater photos.

Scuba Radio

http://www.scubaradio.com/

★★★★★

Tune in online to the Internet radio show devoted to scuba diving. At the site you can also find information on learning to dive, archived shows, and lots of information on sites and guides.

⧉Best⧉ Scuba Yellow Pages

http://www.scubayellowpages.com/

 $

★★★★★

Search this worldwide directory to find contacts and suppliers for all your scuba diving needs—from tour operators to airlines to clubs and certifications. The site also offers tons of information, a divers directory, a search feature to help you quickly locate information, email, and lots of divers' resources. If you're interested in diving for fun or profit, this is the place to locate equipment you need and other resources to make your dive much more successful no matter what your reason for diving.

A B C D E F G H I J K L M N O P Q R S T U V **W** X Y Z

A
B
C
D
E
F
G
H
I
J
K
L
M
N
O
P
Q
R
S
T
U
V
W
X
Y
Z

ScubaDuba

http://www.scubaduba.com/index.html

★★★★★

Encourages active participation from divers. Requests that visitors submit diving-related articles or stories of interest. It offers classified ads, a buddy directory, a chat room, and photos.

Skin Diver Online

http://www.skin-diver.com/

★★★★★

With destination guides, gear info, instruction how-tos, and shopping options, you'll want to see what's here. Features interesting articles from *Skin Diver* magazine, Ask the Pro questions and answers, and medical information.

Sport Diver

http://www.sportdivermag.com/

★★★★★

Read feature articles from this magazine about dive spots, track down dive operators and hotels, and get gear and instruction information. Learn about diving and the beautiful places you might want to experience.

Sub-Aqua Association

http://www.saa.org.uk/

★★★★

This organization was founded more than 20 years ago by various British dive clubs to promote diving issues nationally. The site is extremely professional and detailed, including a URL minder service to notify you via email any time the site is updated.

YMCA Scuba Program

http://www.ymcascuba.org/

★★★★★

A good source of general information, such as a list of courses offered at the Y. This site also contains instructions on how to replace a lost C-card, which is a requirement for any diver. This site offers a quarterly journal, too.

RAFTING

American Whitewater Resources Online

http://www.americanwhitewater.org/

★★★★★

Find out all the specifics about the rivers you will be rafting on before planning your experience. The mission of the AWA is to conserve and restore America's whitewater resources and to enhance opportunities to enjoy them safely. You'll find all kinds of help and information here, especially on safety and what is being done to save the whitewater ways.

Find-a-Guide: Rafting Guides and Trips

http://www.findaguide.com/raft.htm

★★★★

Worldwide directory of links and contact information for professional rafting guides.

GORP: Paddlesports

http://www.gorp.com/gorp/activity/paddle.htm

★★★★★

GORP's paddlesports site is part of a larger network of sites devoted to outdoor recreation. Here, find out what is featured in the rafting news. Jump to river sites all over the country and the world. Learn how to keep from capsizing, get information on clubs, find books and other media about rafting, and join an online forum devoted to whitewater fans who have shared interests.

Grand Canyon River Running

http://www.azstarnet.com/grandcanyonriver/

★★★★★

This site gives information about private and commercial rafting trips through the Grand Canyon. Also shows beautiful pictures and helpful maps as it guides you through the beginning point, Lee's Canyon, to the ending point, Lake Mead. This site is well designed, with a Native American motif and easy-to-follow icons.

Northwest River Supplies

http://www.nrsweb.com/

★★★★

Shop the online rafting catalog or surf the online classifieds to locate used equipment. You can also join the discussions and check out other river rafting links here.

The River Wild

http://www.nationalgeographic.com/features/96/selway/

★★★★

Offers a cyber tour of the Selway River in Idaho. From the home page, you get full access to a map that shows the course of rafting the Selway. Pictures give you a feel for the lovely mountain scenery. The tour offers hints for camping, navigating the river, speaking in river lingo, and observing the nearby wildlife. Features a QuickTime movie of a rafter running through Lava Falls.

RIVERSEARCH

http://www.riversearch.com/

★★★★★

Click on the online map to locate the best rivers for rafting near you, as well as outfitters equipped to guide you.

Vince's Idaho Whitewater Page

http://www.myweb.cableone.net/rafter/

★★★★

A charming example of a personal website, this offers everything from music for your listening pleasure to a photo gallery. In frames, this site is laid out well and easy to navigate. Plus, it has some extra information not found in most rafting sites, such as political issues surrounding Idaho's rivers. Find out about flow and weather conditions, and read about Vince's personal rafting experiences.

White Water Photos

http://www.mywhitewaterphotos.com/

★★★★

A photographer's paradise. This site has a great photo gallery that features the American Rivers, Kern River, Merced River, and Pigeon River. If you plan on rafting any of these whitewater rivers, check out this site to learn more about photograph packages of your trip.

Wild and Scenic Rivers

http://www.nps.gov/rivers/

★★★★

The Wild and Scenic River Act in 1968 called for preserving rivers and their natural environments. This site tells you the history of the act. An exceptional part of this site's information, however, is in the listings of rivers by state, which is fairly exhaustive. Also, find out how you can get involved with agencies whose goal it is to uphold the Wild and Scenic River Act.

Windfall Rafting

http://www.windfallrafting.com/

★★★★★

Learn more about rafting at this Maine outfitter, which also can provide accommodations and a travel planner. Get more information here or request a brochure.

ROWING

Amateur Rowing Association

http://www.ara-rowing.org/

★★★★

14-18

Home of the governing. body of the sport of rowing in Great Britain, this site features information on coaching, development, and competitions. Features a brief article on the history of rowing, plus water safety codes and guidelines.

A B C D E F G H I J K L M N O P Q R S T U V W X Y Z

A
B
C
D
E
F
G
H
I
J
K
L
M
N
O
P
Q
R
S
T
U
W
X
Y
Z

iROW.com

http://irow.com/

★★★★

👥 14-18

Check the rowing calendar to find upcoming rowing regattas and competitions, read the Olympic diary of Chris Ahrens, learn more about the sport of rowing, including how the top schools rank, and join in online discussions.

No Frontiers: A Year in the Life of Fermoy Rowing

http://ireland.iol.ie/~tops/

★★★★

👥 14-18

This video follows eight young rowers going for three Irish titles and an Olympic medal in 1996. Be sure to visit; the European scenery is beautiful.

Paddling@about.com

http://paddling.about.com/

★★★★★

👥 14-18

This site offers comprehensive information about rowing that covers canoes, kayaks, and rafts. Features news, results, links, a chat room, a bulletin board, magazines, outfitters, stores, and more.

Regatta Sport

http://www.regattasport.ca/

$

★★★★★

👥 14-18

The primary apparel maker for the Canadian National Rowing Team, Regatta Sport also makes jackets, jewelry, and other accessories for the crew enthusiast.

River and Rowing Museum

http://www.rrm.co.uk/

★★★★

👥 14-18

Home of the River and Rowing Museum Henley on Thames, this site provides a brief introduction to the museum to encourage you to visit. Includes information about various educational programs provided by the museum.

Row Works

http://www.rowworks.com/

$

★★★★

👥 14-18

The Row Works Clothing Company makes top-quality suits, shorts, winter gear, insulating Lifa Bodywear, and other fine rowing accessories.

Row2K.com

http://www.row2k.com/

$

★★★★★

👥 14-18

Source of news, results, interviews, and general information about the sport of rowing.

Rower's World

http://rowersworld.com/

$

★★★★★

👥 14-18

Comprehensive rower's resource contains news and regatta results, a glossary of terms and rules, images and email postcards, and classifieds. The site is well designed and easy to navigate, which makes finding the information that you want almost as much fun as rowing itself. You'll find a nice search feature that will help you find what you want, a section with diaries and columns, and lots of stories, and you can even shop at an online store for items you may want to purchase.

Rowing FAQ

http://www.ruf.rice.edu/~crew/rowingfaq.html

★★★★★

👫 14-18

Extensive collection of basic rowing information and terminology. Includes contact information for some of the larger rowing associations.

Rowing from an Oarsman's Perspective

http://sports.tjhsst.edu/crew/old_site/Intro/

★★★★

👫 14-18

This site is great for people new to the sport. You can learn about its history, study the glossary to understand all the terminology, view illustrations of the different kinds of boats, learn about the ergonomics of rowing, understand what the coxswain does, and more.

The Rowing Service

http://users.ox.ac.uk/~quarrell/

★★★★

👫 14-18

This British page offers news, crew notices, race reports, coaching and technical information, and more. Site is a little archaic and not the easiest to navigate, but it features a treasure-trove of information and links to related resources on the Web.

RowingLinks—The Internet's Definitive Source for Rowing Links

http://www.rowinglinks.com/

★★★★★

👫 14-18

You can find all kinds of links to sites about the fine art of rowing your boat. Offers information about the sport all around the globe.

Simply OarSome

http://www.oarsome.com.au/

★★★★★

👫 14-18

This Australian company has been supplying the Australian Rowing Team since 1989. You can view its entire catalog and order all the gear online. You'll also find WWW rowing links and results from major rowing events.

USRowing

http://www.usrowing.org/

💲

★★★★★

👫 14-18

Home of the organization that's dedicated to promoting and supporting the sport of rowing in the United States. Here, you can learn more about the organization and its members, get the latest rowing news and results, view a list of upcoming USRowing events, obtain information about the national team, and more.

Vespoli USA

http://www.vespoli.com/

💲

★★★★

👫 14-18

This commercial site promotes Vespoli racing shells. It discusses the shells' speed and value, as well as the company's quality assurance and service.

A
B
C
D
E
F
G
H
I
J
K
L
M
N
O
P
Q
R
S
T
U
V
W
X
Y
Z

A
B
C
D
E
F
G
H
I
J
K
L
M
N
O
P
Q
R
S
T
U
V
W
X
Y
Z

Best WorldRowing.com

http://www.fisa.org/

★★★★★

👥 14-18

Home of the Fédération Internationale des Sociétés d'Aviron (FISA, in French), or the English equivalent International Federation of Rowing Associations. FISA is the international governing body of the sport of rowing. This site provides information about the organization, the events and competitions it sponsors, rowing news from *World Rowing Magazine*, competition results and standings, best times, and much more. Also features a photo gallery, a list of the top rowers, and an online version of FISA's rulebook. Links to stores where you can purchase FISA apparel online. Any rowing enthusiast should bookmark this page.

WWW Virtual Library: Rowing

http://archive.museophile.sbu.ac.uk/rowing/

★★★★

👥 14-18

Features a comprehensive rowing directory. It includes information about regattas, Olympic results, and links to rowing publications and newsgroups.

SURFING

Board Building

http://www.viser.net/~anthwind/

★★★★★

👥 14-18

This library of links related to surfboard building includes links to board design, shaping, repair, tools, and fins. Includes a section on CAD.

Closely Guarded Secrets of the UK Surfing World

http://www.britsurf.org/UKSurfIndex/

★★★★★

👥 14-18

A thorough and well-designed site for surfing in the UK. Features include listings of surf clubs and schools, an online surf shop, links to surfing magazines and the British Surfers Association, and much more.

Best Coastal British Columbia

http://www.surfingvancouverisland.com/

★★★★★

👥 14-18

This great site gives you all kinds of information about surfing. Even if you don't want to go surfing in British Columbia, you should check out the great pictures and information on this page. It has weather and wave information as well as good stories, photos, and other sporting information. If you like to surf and are interested in more information about some of the best surfing locations, enjoy a good story, and want to see photos of what you can expect when you get there, this is the site to find out about all that. It also has a free classified ad section for you.

International Surfing Museum

http://www.surfingmuseum.org/

★★★★★

👥 14-18

At this site, you can view the collection of surf films, surf music, surfboards, and memorabilia. Visit the current exhibit, too. If you like this site, consider becoming a member.

Nancy Emerson's School of Surfing

http://www.surfclinics.com/surfclinics/surfclinics.html

★★★

👥 14-18

This school, which is located in Australia, offers classes and clinics taught by international surfing champion Nancy Emerson and other top instructors. You can contact the school by telephone or email for information about setting up a class.

OceanBlue

http://www.oceanblue.com/

★★★★

👥 14-18

This site offers a guide to the best beaches and sea sports, and to taking care of the environment. Also contains information on windsurfing, body boarding, boogie boarding, and ocean kayaking. A picturesque site full of useful information.

Surf and Sun Beach Vacation Guide

http://www.surf-sun.com/

★★★★★

👥 14-18

This site strives to be the ultimate resource for beach information and vacation planning on the Internet. It offers information on more than 500 beach destinations. Definitely check out the Surf the Beach Guide.

Surfermag.com

http://www.surfermag.com/

★★★★★

👥 14-18

The *Surfermag* site features up-to-the-minute headlines and pictures, video clips of surfers in action, a bulletin board, product reviews, a surf report, an online surf shop, and subscription information.

Surfing in South Africa

http://www.wavescape.co.za/

★★★★★

👥 14-18

This site offers you an extensive guide to surfing in South Africa with travel information, surfing spots, photos, daily surf reports, stories, cartoons, and a lot more.

Surfline

http://www.surfline.com

★★★★★

👥 14-18

Billing itself as "The Best Place on the Net to Get Wet," this site provides up-to-date reports and live webcams of the best places to surf worldwide. The site also features some product reviews and plenty of articles about surfing and the world's top surfers.

Surfrider Foundation USA

http://www.surfrider.org/

★★★★

👥 14-18

The Surfrider Foundation is a nonprofit group dedicated to protecting, preserving, and restoring the world's oceans and beaches. Its site includes daily surf reports, Coastal Factoids, policy updates, and an online membership form.

SurfTrader

http://www.surftrader.com/

★★★

👥 14-18

This site features surf classifieds that link buyers and sellers of surfing collectibles, art, and memorabilia.

Windsurfer.com

http://www.windsurfer.com/newsite/index.cfm

💲

★★★★★

👥 14-18

A thorough windsurfing database divided into organized categories. Board reviews, travel reviews, weather information, wind calculator, and links too.

A
B
C
D
E
F
G
H
I
J
K
L
M
N
O
P
Q
R
S
T
U
W
X
Y
Z

A B C D E F G H I J K L M N O P Q R S T U V W X Y Z

SWIMMING

D&J Sports

http://www.djsports.com/

★★★★★

14-18

Speedo, Tyr, and Dolfin competition and fashion swimwear, plus caps, clothing, accessories, and other equipment. Use the secure online shopping cart.

FINA

http://www.fina.org/

★★★★★

14-18

FINA is the international governing organization of amateur aquatic sports. FINA, based in Switzerland, is a worldwide policy maker in all swimming, diving, synchronized swimming, water polo, open water, and Masters swimming sports. Read articles on the latest developments in aquatic sports. Check out the FINA calendar of events and find out the latest competition results. Learn about FINA's history, regulations, and members. You can also purchase related publications and videos from FINA.

International Swimming Hall of Fame

http://www.ishof.org/

★★★★★

14-18

The International Swimming Hall of Fame is a not-for-profit educational organization. It annually honors the world's greatest aquatic heroes and preserves the sport's history. It serves as a worldwide focal point of swimming, diving, water polo, and synchronized swimming. Learn about the history of the Swimming Hall of Fame, the membership, and ways to make a donation. Includes a calendar of events and information on programs and activities.

NCAA Men's Swimming and Diving

http://www.ncaasports.com/swimming/mens

★★★★★

14-18

National College Athletic Association official site. Includes schedules, ticket information, records, results, and previews.

NCAA Women's Swimming and Diving

http://www.ncaasports.com/swimming/womens

★★★★★

14-18

Official guide to the three divisions of the National College Athletic Association championships.

STORMFAX Safe Ocean Swimming Guide

http://www.stormfax.com/safeswim.htm

★★★

14-18

This site discusses the major causes of accidents and ways you can avoid injury while enjoying your favorite activity. You learn about various dangerous surf conditions and even get the average water temperatures (by month) for various spots on the Atlantic coasts. You also learn how to use the Beaufort Wind Scale, which includes World Meteorological Organization wind descriptions and their effects on land and sea.

SwimInfo

http://www.swiminfo.com/

★★★★★

14-18

Caters to recreational swimmers as well as world-class competitors. Includes water workouts for specific purposes, products, results, and records.

Swimmers Guide Online

http://www.swimmersguide.com/

★★★★

👥 14-18

Contains a database of international, accessible, full-size, year-round pools (6,000+ currently). Each listing includes the name and address of the facility, contact and admission information, and a description of the facility.

Swimming in Circles

http://www.usms.org/training/circles.htm

★★★

👥 14-18

Coach Emmett Hines, the head coach of H20uston Swims, talks about how the best swimmers create their art. Hines shares his observations of several world-class freestylers working out together. Check out his comparisons of several swimming styles and body positions.

Swimming Science Journal

http://www-rohan.sdsu.edu/dept/coachsci/swimming/index.htm

★★★★

👥 14-18

This journal is divided into several parts, including the following: Swimming Science Abstracts, the Carlile Coaches' Forum, the Swimming Science Bulletin, DRUGS: The Crisis in Swimming, and How Champions Do It. The articles presented are drawn from the personal files of the editor. The contents usually are changed monthly and might or might not be thematic.

Swimming Teachers' Association

http://www.sta.co.uk/

★★★★★

👥 14-18

The STA focuses on teaching aquatic skills, from basic water confidence to serious survival. Progressive challenges enable everyone—toddlers, teenagers, adults, the elderly, the handicapped, and the disabled—to get used to the water, enjoy it safely, and increase their fitness and water skills. Ambitious, able swimmers can proceed to competition lifeguard and teaching levels. The STA discusses new ideas on coaching in swimming, diving, water polo, and lifesaving. Read a history of the STA and learn about the examinations, certificates, and awards available. Learn about STA membership, the membership goals, and the fees.

SwimNews Online

http://www.swimnews.com/

💲

★★★★★

👥 14-18

This e-zine of the printed version presents breaking news, meet results, world rankings, and special events. Read the current issue of the magazine or browse through the archives of back issues. Use the search engine to specify a swimmer's last name or country and then view that swimmer's biography. Check out the swimming calendar of events or visit the Shopping Mall to order clothing, equipment, accessories, or training software.

United States Masters Swimming

http://www.usms.org/

★★★★★

An organized program of swimming for adults. Anyone can join USMS. It has grown to more than 40,000 men and women from age 18 to over 100 and offers a variety of programs for the swimming enthusiast.

A
B
C
D
E
F
G
H
I
J
K
L
M
N
O
P
Q
R
S
T
U
V
W
X
Y
Z

A B C D E F G H I J K L M N O P Q R S T U V **W** X Y Z

U.S. Diving Online

http://www.usdiving.org/

★★★★★

♐ 14-18

The official website of U.S. Diving, the national governing body of Olympic diving in the United States.

USA Swimming

http://www.usswim.org/

★★★★★

♐ 14-18

USS is the national governing body for competitive swimming in the United States. Get information on the USS, which formulates the rules, implements policies and procedures, conducts national championships, disseminates safety and sports medicine information, and chooses athletes to represent the United States in international competition. You'll also find the latest swimming news, meet results, records, Olympic games information, and several swimming discussion forums you can participate in.

WebSwim

http://www.webswim.com/

★★★★

♐ 14-18

Excellent directory of swimming resources on the Web as recommended by Donncha, the site's creator and maintenance crew. Site includes a FAQ that Donncha updates regularly based on questions asked and answered in the newsgroup rec.sport.swimming. The site also features links to online swim stores, a discussion of drugs in the sport of swimming, and a short list of Masters clubs and events around the world.

WATERSKIING

American Barefoot Club

http://barefoot.org/

★★★★★

♐ 14-18

A division of USA Water-ski, ABC is dedicated to promoting the sport of barefoot skiing for individuals at all ability levels. Here, you can learn more about the organization, get the latest news, check up on U.S. competitions, hang out in the Barefoot chat room, check rankings, and more.

International Water Ski Federation

http://www.iwsf.com

★★★★★

♐ 14-18

Includes information on the IWSF World Cup, a calendar, World Junior Championships, and more. Covers water-skiing, wakeboarding, racing, and barefoot skiing.

National Show Ski Association

http://showski.com/

★★★★★

♐ 14-18

If water-skiing with one foot hooked on the bar or as part of a pyramid sounds like fun to you, consider joining the NSSA. The association's site has a schedule of events, results of the Nationals tournament, show ski humor, news, photos, links, and more.

National Water Ski Racing Association

http://www.nwsra.net/

★★★★

♐ 14-18

News, schedule of events, results, and more. Sport division of the American Water Ski Association.

Planet Waterski

http://www.planetwaterski.com/

★★★★

👥 14-18

Up-to-date list of upcoming water-skiing competitions around the world covers racing, barefoot, kneeboard, wakeboard, cable, and tournament events. Features event results and recommended places to ski, plus links to other ski resources on the Web.

USA Water Ski/American Water Ski Association

http://www.usawaterski.org/

★★★★★

👥 14-18

The official site of the U.S. waterskiing's governing body. Keep up to date on upcoming competitions and read the latest news on who's making headlines in this sport. This site provides information on sport skiing, show skiing, wakeboards, collegiate skiing, kneeboards, ski racing, barefoot skiing, and disabled skiers.

Water Ski and Wakeboard Online

http://www.waterski-online.com/

★★★

👥 14-18

This site provides all the latest news, including video clips of new tricks, feature articles, editorials, classified ads, professional news, and a searchable database.

Water Skier's Web

http://waterski.net/

★★★★

👥 14-18

Every type of water-skimming sport is listed in this links page, including barefoot, air chair, wake boarding, and knee boarding. You can check out the Water Skier's Mall and follow Usenet discussions.

A
B
C
D
E
F
G
H
I
J
K
L
M
N
O
P
Q
R
S
T
U
V
W
X
Y
Z

WEATHER AND METEOROLOGY

AccuWeather.com

http://www1.accuweather.com/

★★★★★

Watch the animated weather map of the United States to see what patterns might affect your plans. You can also type in your ZIP code to get your local forecast. This site is the world's weather authority for weather information in your area, including five-day forecasts. Not only that but you can get weather forecasts for almost any city that you might be interested in traveling to. Lots of weather news and information using cool graphics.

Atlantic Tropical Weather Center

http://www.atwc.org/

★★★★

Provides the latest hurricane information and other weather information dealing with tropical cyclones. Also offers images, data, pictures, meteograms, models, and satellite loops.

Automated Weather Source Nationwide School Weather Network

http://www.aws.com/corp/default.asp

★★★★★

Provides national weather information from images to textual data. Also presents a photo gallery of severe weather by storm chasers throughout the country. Download the WeatherBug to have up-to-the-minute weather forecasts and information beamed to your desktop.

Related Site
http://www.aws.com

CNN Weather

http://www.cnn.com/WEATHER/

★★★★★

Get your weather from CNN with full weather-related stories, information, and maps.

Current World Weather

http://www.emulateme.com/weather.htm

★★★★

Offers many links to current U.S. and world weather conditions, other weather-related sites, and AccuWeather information. This site gives information provided by major weather organizations, such as CNN weather, The Weather Channel, and Earthwatch Communications, Inc.

Defense Meteorological Satellite Program

http://dmsp.ngdc.noaa.gov/dmsp.html

★★★★★

Two satellite constellations of near-polar orbiting, sun-synchronous satellites that monitor meteorological, oceanographic, and solar-terrestrial physics environments. Features currently occurring meteorological phenomena.

EarthWatch Weather on Demand

http://www.earthwatch.com/

★★★★

Contains many images of 3D satellite views from space. Also plugs its 3D software package that integrates 3D weather visualization with a global database to create a virtual world.

El Niño

http://www.enn.com/specialreports/elnino/

★★★★★

Tells what El Niño is, what past El Niños were like, and how they affect our weather. Also gives news reports on the current status of El Niño and discusses how El Niño systems are measured.

Florida Weather Monitor

http://www.hurricaneadvisories.com/

★★★★

Florida weather, radar, and satellite images; tropical weather information; and surf reports.

Intellicast

http://www.intellicast.com/

★★★★★

Serves as guide to weather, ski reports, and ocean conditions. Provides information for weather novices and professionals. New to Intellicast are health and travel reports. Also, check out its forecasts for national parks.

National Hurricane Center Tropical Prediction Center

http://www.nhc.noaa.gov/

★★★★★

Contains resources for the researcher, advanced student, and hobbyist interested in the latest information on tropical weather conditions, as well as archival information on weather data and maps. Provides links to other NOAA information and satellite data.

National Severe Storms Laboratory

http://www.nssl.noaa.gov/

★★★★★

Provides information about the laboratory, including current research and programs. Does not offer specific information on severe weather but does provide links to sites that do. Also includes an extensive list of links to Web literacy sites.

National Weather Center: Interactive Weather Center

http://iwin.nws.noaa.gov/iwin/graphicsversion/bigmain.html

★★★★★

A user-friendly interface to the weather, with raw data from a telecommunications gateway, satellites, and other multilayered links.

Best National Weather Service

http://www.nws.noaa.gov/

★★★★★

Provides all information output by the NWS, including national and international weather in graphical and textual formats, and information about regional offices. Also offers links to NOAA and other NWS programs. This is the official site of the National Weather Service, which is part of the National Oceanic and Atmospheric Administration. The site is clean, well organized, and easy to navigate. You don't have to wait for the latest weather bulletins from all around the country. The National Weather Service (NWS) provides weather, hydrologic, and climate forecasts and warnings for the United States and adjacent waters and oceanic areas. This is a good site to bookmark for quick weather forecasts and urgent bulletins such as tornado and severe storm information. This site can provide you with excellent information for such purposes as knowing when you are in danger from severe weather, planning trips, and for general interest.

Ocean Weather

http://www.oceanweather.com/

★★★★

Uses a unique hindcasting approach to forecast ocean weather, including winds, waves, and surf. At this site, you can obtain current ocean data for various areas worldwide.

Pilot Weather

http://www.lattery.com/pilotwx/

★★★

A means for pilots to easily obtain the latest and best weather data available on the World Wide Web before they receive a formal preflight briefing.

A B C D E F G H I J K L M N O P Q R S T U V **W** X Y Z

A
B
C
D
E
F
G
H
I
J
K
L
M
N
O
P
Q
R
S
T
U
V
W
X
Y
Z

Seismological Laboratory

http://www.gps.caltech.edu/seismo/

★★★★★

Southern California site that provides seismology-related resources, including the record of the day, recent earthquake activity, and publications. A new feature of this site is its Terrascope section, in which you can plot data or get EQ information for recent large earthquakes.

Space Science and Engineering Center (SSEC) Real-Time Data

http://www.ssec.wisc.edu/data/

★★★

Includes weather information and ocean temperatures. Also offers images, movies, and composites of weather events.

Storm Chaser Home Page

http://www.afn.org/~afn09444/weather/spotchas.html

★★★★

Includes information about storm chasers, a photo gallery of storms, and the latest news about the Storm Chasers group. Also provides information about storm chasing at home, including how to contact the NWS.

UM Weather

http://cirrus.sprl.umich.edu/wxnet/

★★★★

Tries to list every weather-related link on the Internet. Includes not only WWW sites, but also FTP, Gopher, and Telnet sites. Includes commercial sites as well as educational and governmental sites.

University Corporation for Atmospheric Research

http://www.ucar.edu/ucar/

★★★

Consists of several scientific divisions and programs working together with member universities on research activities to better understand Earth's climate systems. Includes information on resources, facilities, and services; research data archives; and weather-related information.

Vantage Point Network

http://vp.accuweather.com/vantagepoint/wx/cur_radar/

★★★★

Information kiosk for the agriculture industry, this site features online weather forecasts, powered by AccuWeather, plus updated futures prices.

Warren Faidley's Storm Chasing Home Page

http://www.stormchaser.com/

★★★

Presents photos of severe weather taken by Warren Faidley, full-time storm chaser.

Weather Channel

http://www.weather.com/

★★★★★

Includes information about the Weather Channel and also provides novice weather enthusiasts with simple weather maps. Provides up-to-date flight information, travel forecasts, and storm watches.

Weather and Climate Images

http://grads.iges.org/pix/

★★★

Offers short- and medium-range forecasts for North America and current weather maps and climate anomaly models for the rest of the world. Provides a key to the weather maps and a table of weather symbols. One of its new features is an El Niño forecast.

The Weather Underground

http://www.wunderground.com/

★★★★★

Nationwide weather forecasts and information, including temperatures, visibility, wind strength and direction, heat index, windchill factor, humidity, dew point, and more. Click the desired state on the map or find forecasts by city or ZIP code.

Weather World

http://www.ems.psu.edu/WeatherWorld/

★★★

Forecasts and special features about how weather works. From Penn State University.

WeatherOnline!

http://www.weatheronline.com/

★★★★

Get forecasts complete with weather graphics for any part of the United States. Just type in a ZIP code, city, or state to be provided with plenty of weather and condition information and forecasts for the region.

A
B
C
D
E
F
G
H
I
J
K
L
M
N
O
P
Q
R
S
T
U
V
W
X
Y
Z

A
B
C
D
E
F
G
H
I
J
K
L
M
N
O
P
Q
R
S
T
U
V
W
X
Y
Z

WEDDING PLANNING

After I Do

http://www.afterido.com

★★★★★

Learn more about an alternative to the standard wedding registry, which includes registering for a dream honeymoon that your guests can contribute to as their wedding gift. Work with travel planners to select your desired honeymoon and direct guests here to contribute. You'll also find links to other wedding service companies to help you plan your wedding day.

Ask Ginka

http://www.askginka.com/

★★★★★

Pick a nationality, religion, theme, or holiday and have Ginka track down the services, products, and resources you need to plan the wedding of your dreams. Ginka features a directory of more than 14,000 links!

The Best Man

http://www.thebestman.com/

★★★★★

Has your buddy designated you to be the best man at his wedding? If you've never done it before, you may be wondering just what you're supposed to do. This site provides a list of your duties as best man, help for planning the bachelor party, information on tuxedos, and tips on how to compose a successful toast.

Best blissweddings.com

http://www.blissweddings.com/

★★★★★

Before you walk down the aisle with your bride or groom, walk down the aisles of this directory of wedding products and services. This site features some excellent navigational tools—for instance, from the home page, you can open the Subjects list and click Ethnic Weddings to find all the resources you need for planning various ethnic weddings. Four such lists are available here: Subjects, Planners & Guides, Couples' Corner, and Ask the Experts. Just open a list, click your pick, and get with the plan. If we could hand out two Best of the Best awards for any category, this would be a definite pick!

Bridalink Store

http://www.bridalink.com/

★★★★

The Bridalink site is an online store known to have low prices on accessories, such as wedding cameras. In addition, visitors can register for monthly giveaways.

Brides and Grooms

http://www.bridesandgrooms.com

★★★★

Marriage and wedding guide with information on everything from honeymoons to marriage counseling.

Great Bridal Expo

http://www.greatbridalexpo.com/

★★★★★

This site features information about the Great Bridal Expo, a bridal show that tours to various cities throughout the United States. From this site you can find out more about the Expo's exhibitors, special events, dates, and locations throughout the United States. You can even order tickets for the show online!

Grooms Online

http://www.groomsonline.com/

★★★★★

The ultimate wedding site for men, Grooms Online provides a forum where men, both grooms and groomsmen, can discuss various wedding issues. It also provides helpful wedding information written in a tone especially designed for men.

The Knot: Weddings for the Real World

http://www.theknot.com

★★★★★

This site is an excellent wedding resource: 3,000+ wedding-related articles, 6,000 searchable gown pictures, how-tos, plus daily hot tips, a 24-hour chat room, and special personalized planning tools. This is definitely one of the most comprehensive, useful bridal planning sites on the Web. The site offers much in the way of helping you to plan your wedding, and you can even shop online for just about everything you will need.

Modern Bride

http://www.modernbride.com/

★★★★★

Features a peek at the current issue of *Modern Bride* magazine. Contains sections covering just about anything wedding-related, plus a chat room and a tip of the day. You can subscribe to the magazine online using secure credit card resources.

Ten Top Honeymoon Destinations

http://honeymoons.miningco.com/travel/honeymoons/msub8.htm?

★★★★★

The Mining Company has investigated and ranked the top 10 honeymoon locations for brides to consider. Links to each country (most are in the Caribbean) are right here on the page.

Time Out City Guides

http://www.timeout.com/

★★★★★

The latest (and hippest) word on what to do and where to go in major domestic and international cities.

Today's Bride Online Magazine

http://www.todaysbride.com/

★★★★★

Picked as a Yahoo! Pick of the Week, *Today's Bride* magazine's website is very user-friendly, including a search engine to help you find specific topics. The site even offers an online bridal consultant to help you with your toughest questions.

Town & Country Weddings

http://tncweddings.com/

★★★★★

From *Town & Country Magazine*, this site contains not only the special wedding issue, but also a wealth of other wedding information. Couples can specify where they are registered in the Registry section, and friends and family can access this information. Overall, this site is a complete source for wedding fashion, planning, and much, much more!

Ultimate Internet Wedding Guide

http://www.ultimatewedding.com

★★★★★

Comprehensive information for those planning a wedding in California. Includes products and services, bridal shows, engagement announcements, upcoming bridal shows, and links galore.

A
B
C
D
E
F
G
H
I
J
K
L
M
N
O
P
Q
R
S
T
U
W
X
Y
Z

A B C D E F G H I J K L M N O P Q R S T U V **W** X Y Z

USA Bride

http://www.usabride.com

★★★★★

Wedding planning help for brides and grooms, including gift and shower ideas, wedding songs, frugal wedding tips, and more.

Video In Production

http://www.videoinproduction.com/

★★★★★

If you're planning on getting married in the Chicagoland area and would like to have your wedding day memories preserved on video DVD or VHS tape, check out this site and give the guys at Video In Production a call. Video In Production professionally records your wedding day, edits the video and mixes it with music, still shots, and other media to give you a keepsake that will last a lifetime.

Wedding Bells

http://www.weddingbells.com/

★★★★★

Wed-zine that takes a thorough and stylish approach to wedding planning for both brides and grooms.

The Wedding Channel

http://www.weddingchannel.com

★★★★★

The Wedding Channel is an all-encompassing wedding resource. It contains the following wedding-related sections: Fashion and Beauty, Local Businesses, Honeymoon Suite, Home and Registry, Wedding Planner, and Groom's Corner. The Wedding Planner section has tips from wedding planning expert Beverly Clark, author of the best-selling book, *Planning a Wedding to Remember*.

Wedding Photography–Advice for the Bride and Groom

http://members.aol.com/anorama/

★★★★★

This site offers some advice about selecting a wedding photographer for the special event. You should choose with care because you get only one shot at it and you want the best pictures possible.

Weddings on Hawaii, Kauai, Maui, and Oahu

http://www.creativeleisure.com/hawaii/weddings/

★★★★★

Are you thinking of marrying in the Hawaiian Islands? This site offers special wedding packages for each of the islands. Your dream wedding could be only a website away!

WedNet

http://www.wednet.com/

★★★★

Contains numerous wedding-related articles with tips for every aspect of wedding planning. In addition, you can search for other Internet resources and wedding vendors, visit the WedNet library, and even register for a free subscription to a monthly newsletter.

Your Formal Wear Guide

http://www.tuxedos4u.com/

★★★★★

A complete guide to men's tuxedos. You can view the latest styles in tuxedos and use the "store finder" to locate the closest place to rent your tuxedo. In addition, the site has a Q&A section to help you select the appropriate tux for your occasion and a worksheet to help organize your tuxedo needs.

WEIGHT LOSS

A B C D E F G H I J K L M N O P Q R S T U V W X Y Z

American Dietetic Association

http://www.eatright.org

★★★★

Healthy lifestyle tips, nutrition resources, tips on finding a dietitian, and more. Includes information on food irradiation.

Best of Weight Loss

http://bestofweightloss.com/

★★★★

The Best of Weight Loss is a new directory maintained by specialists in weight-loss physiology, weight management, exercise programs, and Internet research.

CyberDiet

http://www.cyberdiet.com

★★★★★

Access a daily food planner and assessment tools, find your nutritional profile, grab recipes and exercise tips, and much more.

Doctor's Guide to Obesity

http://www.docguide.com/news/content.nsf/
PatientResAllCateg/Obesity?OpenDocument

★★★★

The latest medical news and information for patients or friends/parents of patients diagnosed with obesity-related disorders.

eDiets.com

http://www.ediets.com/

$

★★★★

Meal plans and fitness programs designed to help you lose weight and keep it off. Enter your email address, age, sex, height, and weight for a free profile and newsletter.

Fast Food Facts–Interactive Food Finder

http://www.olen.com/food/

★★★★

Click on a fast food restaurant name and type in a product to find out the breakdown of calories, fat, sodium, carbohydrates, and more. Or find out what products fit your diet by selecting a restaurant and setting limits on calories or sodium. Warning: You might lose your appetite after seeing how fattening some items are.

FDA: Nutrition and Weight Loss

http://vm.cfsan.fda.gov/~lrd/advice.html

★★★

What are the new government dietary guidelines for Americans? Can vegetables prevent cancer? What are some of the questionable weight-loss products? You can also ask your own questions at this site, and the FDA will answer.

FreeWeightLoss.com

http://www.freeweightloss.com/

★★★

This huge collection of free advice, articles, and tools for losing weight includes a calorie counter, body fat calculator, recipe database, and message boards. You can post a question to have it answered by an expert, learn fast food facts, and enter the sweepstakes.

Jenny Craig

http://www.jennycraig.com/

$

★★★★★

Home of one of the most popular weight loss programs, this site features Jenny Craig's story, success stories of people who have followed the program, weight-loss programs and support for members, and online shopping.

A
B
C
D
E
F
G
H
I
J
K
L
M
N
O
P
Q
R
S
T
U
V
W
X
Y
Z

Natural Nutrition

http://www.livrite.com/

★★★★

Learn all about natural nutrition, its basic philosophy, and tips for eating better with whole grains. This site contains lots of articles to read, recipes to copy, and directories of natural food stores and merchants online.

Nutrisystem

http://www.nutrisystem.com/

★★★★★

Home of the popular Nutrisystem weight loss program. Here, you can learn more about the program, sign up for a free membership, and shop online for products.

Prevention.com–Weight Loss and Fitness

http://www.prevention.com/

★★★★★

With 100 diet tips, a meal planner, calorie calculator, and workout and weight quizzes, you're sure to be inspired to start that weight-loss program you've been meaning to. Lots of helpful advice and strategies from the publishers of *Prevention Magazine*. After reaching the home page, click the Weight Loss or Fitness tab to start your journey.

Shape Up America

http://www.shapeup.org

★★★★★

Safe weight management and physical fitness programs for one and all. Although not one of the flashier sites on the Internet, this site does have a lot of helpful information that will assist you in losing and controlling weight. If you are serious about this undertaking, you can visit the Body Fat Lab to find out how to control your diet, exercise, and use other methods to control your weight. You'll find a handy BMI (Body Fat Lab), Library, Cyber Kitchen, Professional Help, Fitness Center, and an area for support.

Weight Loss Methods

http://fatloss.com/

★★★

An overview of various weight-loss methods.

Weight Watchers

http://www.weightwatchers.com

★★★★★

Learn about Weight Watchers programs around the world at this site, which will also tell you about Weight Watchers' proprietary 1-2-3 Success Plan. Find local organizations by searching the database.

WELLNESS

A B C D E F G H I J K L M N O P Q R S T U V W X Y Z

Ask Dr. Weil

http://www.askdrweil.com

★★★★★

Learn more about Dr. Andrew Weil's approach to health by combining Western thinking and traditional medical perspectives. At the site, you can learn how to eat healthier, how vitamins and herbs can improve your health, and where to find natural foods.

Health Ink & Vitality Communications

http://www.healthink.com

★★★★★

Publisher of consumer health newsletters provides this informative site with articles on children, teen, and adult health. Includes an Ask the Doctor section.

Best | HealthCentral

http://www.healthcentral.com

★★★★★

 All

If you're looking for health and wellness information, it's very likely you'll find it here, along with just about anything else you need to know about nutrition, health, eating right, vitamins, and more. There are columns, library articles, and many tools available to treat your body better.

This site has just about everything that you need to know and to purchase in the area of healthcare. Besides being well designed and easy to navigate, the site offers a full online drugstore, a library, drug interaction center, facts about vitamins, prescriptions, beauty products, and many health products. You can place a prescription at the drugstore or purchase other products. You'll find a lot of helpful information and access to professional help here.

HealthGate

http://www.healthgate.com

★★★★★

Read about health issues affecting consumers today and steps you can take to prevent serious illness or treat conditions you already have. Columns, news, and articles are all available to you.

Net Wellness

http://www.netwellness.org/

★★★★

This consumer health site provides a search tool for finding information about various maladies and health issues, an ask an expert forum, an online health encyclopedia, an area specifically focused on African-American health issues, and much more.

SeekWellness.com

http://www.seekwellness.com/

★★★★★

This thorough site covers everything from weight management and fitness to sexual health and various conditions.

StayHealthy

http://www.stayhealthy.com

★★★★

Links to a health resource directory, a drug information database, healthcare topics, expert advice, an American hospital directory, and more.

A
B
C
D
E
F
G
H
I
J
K
L
M
N
O
P
Q
R
S
T
U
V
W
X
Y
Z

Wellness Junction

http://www.wellnessjunction.com/

★★★★★

For consumers and healthcare professionals who want to stay on top of the research and trend information regarding wellness. Read the headlines for this week, learn more about wellness at home or office, and link to other useful sites. Professionals will also find professional development and networking opportunities.

WIRELESS WEB SITES

FINANCE

Financial Times

http://wap.ft.com

★★★★

This site provides market news, business news, stock quotes, and special features for subscribers.

MSN Money

http://mobile.msn.com/

★★★★★

MSN's Money page is now available for your wireless web-enabled phone. Here you can check out stock prices, quotes, indexes, and news.

RichQuote

http://richquote.com/wap/

★★★★

RichQuote.com features quotable quotes from books by Robert Kiyosaki, including *Rich Dad Poor Dad* and *Cashflow Quadrant*.

StockPoint

http://wml.stockpoint.com/index.wml

★★★★

This site features a stock tracker, global market news, and indexes. Site can also feed you information about U.S. IPOs.

Vipana

http://www.vipana.com/index.wml

★★★

Vipana is a business development and merchant trading company that engages in the import, export, distribution, and trading of consumables and equipment. Obtain information and contact information at this site.

Wall Street Journal

http://wap.wsj.com

★★★

This site provides the latest headline news in the world of business.

Yahoo! Finance

http://mobile.yahoo.com/finance

★★★★★

Connects you to Yahoo!'s financial page, where you can check your portfolio, receive current stock quotes, and check the status of the markets.

FUN, GAMES, AND DIVERSIONS

Fantastic Amoeba

http://tagtag.com/wasted

★★★★

👥 All

Provides daily insights from the fictional Fantastic Amoeba.

FourJokers.co.uk

http://www.fourjokers.co.uk/wap

★★★

🚫 Not for kids

FourJokers provides some side-splitting humor, including the joke of the day, funny "chatup" lines (pickup lines), beer jokes, and strange stories.

MSN Games

http://mobile.msn.com/wml/default.aspx/Games/Entertainment/Games

★★★

👫 All

As this was being written, MSN's wireless web gaming arcade consisted of one game—Bubble Blast. Check back later for more.

Murphy's Laws

http://murphys-law.mywap.genie.co.uk

★★★★

👫 All

If you ever wonder why it seems that everything that could possibly be going wrong is going wrong, check out this site and refresh your memory.

Rational Conspiracy

http://tagtag.com/conspiracy

★★★

This site takes a lighter look at conspiracy theories.

Skol Celebrity Pictures

http://wap.skol.ch/pics.wml

★★★

🚫 Not for kids

Skol's celebrity site features black-and-white photos of popular models and celebrities.

TwilightWap

http://wappy.to/funzone

★★★★★

🚫 Not for kids

In the WAP games category, you will find no site better than this. TwilightWap features Action, Casino Games, Sports, Adventure, Trivia, and More. X-Rated section is definitely not for kids.

Twilight Zone

http://tagtag.com/ctheron

★★★

🚫 Not for kids

This site features a fun zone with games, animations, and humor; a Charlize Theron fan club; some romance tips and tidbits; and a dating portal.

W@pomatic

http://wapomanic.com

★★★★

W@pomanic features a good collection of games online and off.

WebTender

http://wap.webtender.com

★★★★

🚫 Not for kids

WebTender is a searchable recipe database for mixing alcoholic beverages.

Best | Wireless Gaming Review

http://wgamer.com/

★★★★★

You'll have to use your computer's web browser to access this site, because it is not wireless web-enabled, but the reviews that are available here are for games designed to run on wireless devices, such as cell phones. Check out reviews of the top games, newest games, and newest devices. Read game articles, previews, and reviews, along with FAQs and instructions on how to make the most of your wireless device. This site is packed with useful information in an easily accessible format, making it our choice for Best of the Best.

Wireless Winnings

http://wirelesswinnings.com

★★★

🚫 Not for kids

Wireless Winnings is a wireless gambling service where you can play blackjack or poker for fun or for money.

WIRELESS WEB SITES   **1013**

HEALTH

Fat/Calories

http://tagtag.com/fat

★★★

This site displays the fat content and calories for a number of the most popular fast food and junk food items.

Living & Health

http://wap.livingandhealth.com

★★★

Living & Health features news and information about cholesterol, diabetes, and heart disease, along with risk factors.

LocalMed

http://www.localmed.co.uk/wap/index.asp

★★★★

When you're on the road and need emergency medical information, turn to this site. This site includes a basic CPR guide, self-help for various conditions, and a list of vaccinations you need before you travel.

mDiabetic

http://www.mdiabetic.com/

★★★★

mDiabetic provides mobility for diabetics and health care providers. At this site, you can use your mobile device to track your blood sugar levels and daily medication and share your records with your doctor.

National Mental Health Information Center

http://www.mentalhealth.org/wap

★★★★★

This site provides news and information about various mental health issues, primarily depression.

Pocket Doctor

http://wap.pocketdoctor.co.uk

★★★

Pocket Doctor is a searchable medical encyclopedia and resource tool for the traveler. Includes PocketFirstAid, a symptom analyzer, interactive tools, and even the phone number of a doctor on call.

MOVIES

Hollywood.com

http://wap.hollywood.com

★★★★

Hollywood.com provides a searchable listing of movies, movie times, ticket information, movie reviews, and movie news. This is a must site for movie buffs with cell phones.

LeoFun Movies & More

http://www.leofun.com/m/

★★★★

LeoFun offers wallpaper, screensavers, streaming media, and a couple of movie lists.

Yahoo! Movies

http://mobile.yahoo.com/movies

★★★★★

Yahoo! Movies enables you to search for movie theatres and show times in your area, look up movie titles and descriptions, and find box office hits.

MUSIC

Blue Audio

http://wap.blueaudio.com/

★★★

👥 14-18

This is the site of an electronic pop artist and producer John Wu. It features song lyrics and information on where you can go to download MP3 clips and order CDs.

A B C D E F G H I J K L M N O P Q R S T U V **W** X Y Z

A
B
C
D
E
F
G
H
I
J
K
L
M
N
O
P
Q
R
S
T
U
V
W
X
Y
Z

Reejo

http://tagtag.com/reejo

★★★

👥 14-18

Animated site that offers some wallpaper, games, ringtones, and audio clips you may or may not be able to play.

Virgin Radio

http://wap.virginradio.com

★★★

👥 14-18

Virgin Radio is the home page of a London Radio station, where you can view playlists, top albums, a program schedule, and more.

NEWS

7am.com

http://wap.7am.com

★★★★★

7am.com is a news and information kiosk, serving up international and headline news covering politics, business, science, and sports.

Ananova

http://wap.ananova.com

★★★★

👥 All

Ananova is an excellent source for news and information in the UK. Features coverage of news, sports scores, entertainment, business, weather, and even has a TV program guide.

InternetWire

http://wap.internetwire.com

★★★★★

InternetWire covers a wide variety of newsworthy items, providing headline news about technology, business, entertainment, lifestyles, travel, education, medicine, sports, and more.

Moreover.com

http://wap.moreover.com/index.wml

★★★★★

This site contains news feeds from around the world covering everything from international headlines and U.S. news to business and financial happenings and news from the entertainment world. Very extensive.

MSN News

http://mobile.msn.com/

★★★★★

MSN provides news, weather, and both national and local sports. From the opening menu, click Local and enter your ZIP Code to access local weather and news. Sports is provided via ESPN.

🏅Best Yahoo! News

http://mobile.yahoo.com/news

★★★★★

Yahoo! News provides headline news from around the world, business stories, technology breakthroughs, entertainment features, sports scores, and more.

PERSONALS/DATING

MobileDating.TV

http://mobiledating.tv

★★★★★

👥 Not for kids

MobileDating.TV is a wireless dating service where members can post their personal ads and check out the profiles of other members. Features live text chat and a list of pickup lines.

PickUp

http://www.wapdrive.com/pickup/

★★★★

👥 Not for kids

PickUp features chat pickup lines broken up into categories including Saucy, Smooth, and Desperate.

Romance Women

http://twilightwap.com/romance/

★★★

 Not for kids

This site provides tips and tricks for romancing the woman of your dreams. Includes personals, chat, dating tips, kissing tips, a list of love words, and a romance test.

REFERENCE

Did You Know?

http://tagtag.com/didyouknow

★★★★

👥 All

Did You Know? features factoids and trivia for various topics, including animals, inventions, music, movies, and sports.

LookWAYup

http://lookwayup.com/wap

★★★

👥 All

LookWAYup is a mobile dictionary and thesaurus. You type the word you want to look up and then select the option to view the word's definition or a list of synonyms.

SuperPages

http://superpages.com

★★★★

SuperPages features searchable phone directories—both yellow pages (for businesses) and white pages (for residential listings). Even provides a reverse lookup feature for finding the name of a business or person given the phone number.

RELIGION AND SPIRITUALITY

Fellowship Baptist

http://tagtag.com/fbc/

★★★

👥 All

This site is the mobile home of Fellowship Baptist Church in North Carolina. Here, you can find contact information, directions to the church, and the schedule of services.

GospelWAP

http://wap.gospelsearch.com

★★★

👥 All

GospelWAP features a Bible quote of the day and a tool for finding specific Bible passages.

MoBible

http://wap.mobile.org

★★★★★

👥 All

MoBible is an excellent mobile Bible resource, which includes a Psalm of the day, features for browsing and searching the Bible (both Old and New Testaments), a list of parables, a copy of the Lord's Prayer, and a Bible FAQ.

Unity of Man

http://www.unity-of-man.org/

★★★★

👥 All

This Islamic site focuses on the notion that all life is unified by an inner force. The site features the teachings of Sant Kirpal Singh.

SCIENCE AND NATURE

c|net News

http://wap.cnet.com

★★★★

👥 14-18

c|net's Wap site provides headline news from the world of technology.

A
B
C
D
E
F
G
H
I
J
K
L
M
N
O
P
Q
R
S
T
U
V
W
X
Y
Z

Rosses Place

http://www.wapdrive.com/rosshi

★★★

👥 All

This site features technical information about the various planets in our solar system.

Science Links

http://tagtag.com/sci-links

★★★★★

👥 All

Science Links is a directory of wireless websites organized by topic, including Physics, Astronomy, Chemistry, and Math.

Tabulka

http://wap.tabulka.cz

★★★★

👥 All

Tabulka features a periodic table of the elements searchable by the name, symbol, or proton number of the element.

SHIPPING

FedEx

http://mobile.fedex.com

★★★★★

This site enables you to track a package with its FedEx tracking number and find the location of the nearest FedEx shipping center near you.

UPS Tracking

http://wap.tanger.cz/ewups_e.wml

★★★★★

This site enables you to determine the location of a package based on its UPS tracking number.

SHOPPING/BUYING

eBay Anywhere

http://catalyst.2roam.com/www.ebay.com/

★★★★

eBay Anywhere keeps you posted concerning the latest activities on your online auctions.

Edmund's Auto Shopping

http://mobile.edmunds.com/wml

★★★★★

Shopping for a car or truck? Whether you're looking for something new or used, grab your wireless web-enabled phone and dial into Edmund's for advice. Here, you can check prices for new and used vehicles, find dealers, check financing options, warranties, and much more. Very cool site.

My Corner Shopping

www.mycorner.com/mycorner/wap/default.asp

💲

★★★★★

Shop on the road with My Corner for electronics, flowers, gifts, tickets, and more. Site was under construction at the time this was being written.

SPORTS

Challengers Baseball

http://wap.challengers.org

★★★★

👥 All

Challengers Baseball is the home page of the Challengers baseball team, a team out of Zurich.

Crash.net

http://crash.net/wap

★★★★

👥 All

Crash.net features news from the world of motorsports, including the major racing leagues—Formula One, IRL, NASCAR, F3, British Rally, and much more.

ESPN Mobile
http://mobile.espn.com

★★★★★

 All

ESPN Mobile is the mobile home of the largest sports network on the planet. Here, you can find links to the NFL, NBA, NHL, MLB, and other professional and college leagues, plus links to Golf, Boxing, Tennis, Horse Racing, and more.

Hockey 123
http://www.wapdrive.com/hockey123/index.wml

★★★

 All

Hockey 123 provides the latest NHL and NWHL hockey league results and standings.

IGolftheWorld
http://www.igolftheworld.com/phone

★★★

All

This site features an index of golf courses from around the world that you can search by country and city. This site also enables you to keep abreast of the major golf tournaments.

MySnowReport
http://attsnow.mobliss.com

★★★★

14-18

This site features updated snow reports and weather alerts plus an Excuse O'Matic that provides excuses for taking a ski or snowboarding trip.

Real Surf
http://wap.realsurf.com

★★★★

14-18

Real Surf features surf reports submitted by surfers for the waters surrounding Australia.

SoccerAge
http://wap.rete.it

★★★★

All

SoccerAge is a comprehensive site for soccer fans from almost every country. Provides current results and standings for the major soccer competitions and tournaments, plus scores and highlights of various matches.

TELEVISION

EuroTV
http://www.eurotv.com/wap

★★★★

All

EuroTV features TV program listings for countries throughout Europe, including the UK, Ireland, Belgium, France, Spain, the Netherlands, and Luxemburg.

Star Trek UK
http://tagtag.com/sttc

★★★

All

This is a fan club for the *Star Trek* series. Includes program listings for the UK, Star Trek news, episode descriptions, and special features.

TV Guide Wireless
http://wireless.tvguide.com

★★★★★

All

TV Guide Wireless provides TV listings for the United States that are searchable by ZIP code.

A B C D E F G H I J K L M N O P Q R S T U V W X Y Z

A
B
C
D
E
F
G
H
I
J
K
L
M
N
O
P
Q
R
S
T
U
V
W
X
Y
Z

TRAVEL & ENTERTAINMENT

10Best.com City Guides

http://wap.10best.com

★★★★★

This site provides a searchable index of some of the best restaurants, motels, nightclubs, shopping centers, and recreational activities for a wide range of cities and towns. This site also provides weather forecasts.

A1 Vacations

http://www.a1-w.com

★★★

A1 Vacations is a searchable index of vacation rentals from around the world.

Airline Phone Numbers

http://tagtag.com/patzig

★★★

This site features a searchable directory of airline company phone numbers for reservations and cargo. Most phone numbers are toll-free.

Connex

http://www.connexwap.net

★★★

Connex provides schedules and information about delays for commuter trains in England.

Dollar Rent a Car

http://mobile.dollar.com

★★★★★

Dollar Rent a Car enables you to check rental car rates, rent a car, check your reservation, and even cancel a registration from your wireless device.

HotelCatalogue

http://wap.hotelcatalogue.net

★★★★

HotelCatalogue features an index of hotels and motels from around the world that you can search by typing in the name of a city. You can even reserve a room online.

InterHike

http://www.interhike.com/wap

★★★

InterHike enables you to search for campsites all across Europe.

Maporama

http://wap.maporama.com

★★★★

Maporama provides maps, driving directions, and weather reports for various locations in the United States.

NextBus

http://www.nextbus.com

★★★

NextBus provides bus schedules for various bus companies from around the United States, including major cities on the east and west coasts and the central United States.

WEATHER

Online Weather

http://wap.onlineweather.com

★★★★

Online Weather features online weather forecasts and sailing advice for the United Kingdom.

Yahoo! Weather

http://mobile.yahoo.com/weather

★★★★★

Yahoo! Weather provides current weather forecasts searchable by city or ZIP code.

WOMEN/WOMEN'S ISSUES

A
B
C
D
E
F
G
H
I
J
K
L
M
N
O
P
Q
R
S
T
U
V
W
X
Y
Z

AFL-CIO: Working Women Working Together

http://www.aflcio.org/women/

★★★★★

  All

Working women will want to check out the AFL-CIO's site devoted to supporting working women for facts and figures regarding working women and the children they support. You can also get information on how to become more active in supporting legislation for working women. Fill out the survey and find out more about upcoming conferences, too.

American Association of University Women (AAUW)

http://www.aauw.org/

★★★★★

14-18

The American Association of University Women is a national organization that promotes education and equity for all women and girls. This website describes AAUW issues, research programs, grants and fellowships, membership information, and much more.

Amnesty International USA Women's Human Rights

http://www.amnestyusa.org/women/

★★★★★

Read about the poor conditions and situations women around the world face and learn more about what you can do to change it.

Artemis Search for Women's Studies Programs

http://www.artemisguide.com/

★★★★

A database of 324 U.S. women's studies programs, listed alphabetically with brief descriptions and the opportunity to link to the specific college or university for more information.

Aviva

http://www.aviva.org/

★★★

Aviva is an online women's magazine featuring news items from around the world. Users are invited to contribute to the site. *Aviva* also includes a directory of international women's groups and a calendar of events.

AWARE

http://www.aware.org

★★★★

Learn more about the importance of self-protection and defense, strategies you can use, and places to go for instruction.

BizWomen

http://www.bizwomen.com/

★★★★

BizWomen provides an online interactive community for successful women in business to communicate, network, exchange ideas, and provide support for each other via the Internet. BizWomen also provides you with an Internet presence with your online business card, a colorful online brochure, or interactive catalog to make your products and services available online.

A
B
C
D
E
F
G
H
I
J
K
L
M
N
O
P
Q
R
S
T
U
V
W
X
Y
Z

Brukoworld

http://www.brukoworld.com/

★★★★★

Visit Brukoworld, where you can tour the mind and soul of Bruko, a photographer and visual design artist who graciously shares her photos, journal entries, and visions.

 The Business Women's Network Interactive

http://www.bwni.com/

★★★★★

The Business Women's Network Interactive acts as an umbrella organization to unite, network, and promote the 2,300 women's business and professional organizations and websites profiled in the directory—a constituency representing more than 10 million women throughout the U.S. and Canada. BWN serves as a liaison between the Executive Branch, Small Business Administration, Congress, and other government divisions and working women—with an emphasis on women's business ownership.

CatalystWomen.org

http://www.catalystwomen.org/

★★★★

Catalyst reports on the state of women in business, providing research summaries and reports to help companies improve conditions and opportunities for women. Learn more about recent reports and recommendations made by Catalyst.

A Celebration of Women Writers

http://digital.library.upenn.edu/women/

★★★

Celebration of Women Writers recognizes the contributions of women writers throughout history. This site provides a comprehensive listing of links to biographical and bibliographical information about women writers, and complete published books written by women. See What's New! for the most recent authors and books added to the listing. This is not only a great site for writers but for those wanting to break into the writing field. It has a lot of useful information for others doing research in this field and for the general public.

Center for Reproductive Law and Policy

http://www.crlp.org/

★★★★★

 Not for kids

This site provides a review of women's reproductive freedom in six countries around the world: Brazil, China, Germany, India, Nigeria, and the United States. Each country's pertinent laws and policies are discussed on a wide range of topics.

Chistell Publishing

http://www.chistell.com/

★★★★

This site contains books written by African-American women about women's issues. Both informative and inspirational.

Christian+Feminist

http://www.users.csbsju.edu/~eknuth/xpxx/

★★★★

Many articles, reviews, and directories which support the premise that feminism can coexist peacefully with the historically patriarchal Christian religion.

Cybergrrl

http://www.cybergrrl.com/

★★★★★

Informing, inspiring, and celebrating women. Includes articles, movie and book reviews, family information, and more. The server for this site also houses many other feminism-related sites.

Diotima: Women and Gender in the Ancient World

http://www.stoa.org/diotima/

★★★★

This website is intended to serve as a resource for anyone interested in patterns of gender around the ancient Mediterranean and as a forum for collaboration among instructors who teach courses about women and gender in the ancient world. Includes research articles, course materials, a comprehensive bibliography, and more.

Expect the Best from a Girl

http://www.academic.org/

★★★★★

This site prepared by the Women's College Coalition contains information about what parents and others can do to encourage girls in academic areas, particularly math and the sciences. Includes a listing of programs and institutes that can be contacted.

Facts Encyclopedia: Women's Issues on the Internet

http://www.refdesk.com/women.html

★★★

Directory of websites that deal with various women's issues. Links are organized alphabetically.

Feminist.com

http://feminist.com/

★★★★★

Feminist.com is a site aimed at helping women network more effectively on the Internet. Includes the abridged text of articles and speeches, women's health resources, women-owned businesses, links, and *lots* more!

Related Site
http://feminist.com//market/wombus/

Feminist Arts-Music

http://www.feminist.org/arts/linkmusic.html

★★★★★

An annotated list of feminist musicians, with links to the artists' home pages and fan club pages where you can get more information.

Feminist Bookstores Index

http://users.rcn.com/seajay.dnai/fbn/fbn98/
stores.html

★★★

This page provides a comprehensive listing of women's bookstores in the United States and Canada arranged by state and province. Includes postal addresses and Internet links (where available).

Feminist Majority Foundation Online

http://www.feminist.org/

★★★★★

This site contains information on government actions for and against women, an online discussion group, publication information, and much more. There is also a shopping area where you can purchase feminist gifts, clothing, and other items.

Forum for Women's Health

http://www.womenshealth.org/

★★★★

Health and wellness page that focuses exclusively on women's health issues.

Girl Power!

http://www.health.org/gpower/

★★★★★

 9-13

The national public education campaign sponsored by the Department of the Health and Human Services to help encourage and empower 9- to 14-year-old girls.

Girl Scouts of the USA

http://www.girlscouts.org/

★★★★★

 All

For every girl who enjoys scouting and every adult woman whose life was enhanced by scouting. Girl Scouts can find out about special events and activities, order uniforms and equipment, and read about the history of Girl Scouting; adults can participate in an alumni search and learn how to volunteer.

Girls Incorporated

http://www.girlsinc.org/

★★★★★

 All

An organization dedicated to "Helping girls become strong, smart, and bold." This site includes research and advocacy information, membership information, and more.

A B C D E F G H I J K L M N O P Q R S T U V **W** X Y Z

A
B
C
D
E
F
G
H
I
J
K
L
M
N
O
P
Q
R
S
T
U
V
W
X
Y
Z

Global Fund for Women

http://www.globalfundforwomen.org/

★★★★

The Global Fund for Women is an international organization that focuses on female human rights. Includes information on supported programs, news articles, and a FAQ sheet and describes what you can do to help.

Good Vibrations

http://www.goodvibes.com/

★★★★

 Not for kids

Good Vibrations is a worker-owned cooperative with two retail stores, a publishing company called Down There Press, and two catalogs: Good Vibrations and The Sexuality Library. The company sells quality sex toys, books/audio, and videos at reasonable prices, in a straightforward, nonsleazy environment.

International Women's Issues

http://www.state.gov/g/wi/

★★★★

Maintained by the U.S. Department of State, this site provides information about various international women's issues, including treatment of Afghan women, the current U.S. administration policies that affect women, and other primarily political issues that affect women's lives.

iVillage.com: The Women's Network

http://www.ivillage.com/

★★★★★

Find information about many subjects of interest to women, including relationships, money, work, and career, plus getting pregnant, raising children, and more.

Library Resources for Women's Studies

http://metalab.unc.edu/cheryb/women/librcws.html

★★★★

As the site title indicates, this page provides links to university and research center libraries across the United States that contain "useful or unique collections" related to women's studies. Includes Telnet, Gopher, FTP, and web addresses.

Lifetime Online

http://www.lifetimetv.com/

★★★★★

This is the World Wide Web extension of Lifetime Television, the women's network. Provides information about Lifetime's television schedule and programs, as well as articles on health and fitness, parenting, sports, and more. Includes a searchable index of topics covered.

Machon Chana

http://www.machonchana.org/

★★★★★

A women's institute for the study of Judaism. This nicely done site helps educate Jewish women about their religion and culture.

National Association for Female Executives

http://www.nafe.com/

★★★★★

Offers links to online career and business resources as well as contacts for networking. The site also offers articles on entrepreneurial issues and information on the mission and benefits of the National Association for Female Executives.

National Museum of Women in the Arts

http://www.nmwa.org

★★★★

Home of the only museum in the world dedicated to recognizing the contributions of women artists, this site provides a history of the organization, an online gallery complete with biographies of each featured artist, a library and research center, and much more.

The National Organization for Women (NOW)

http://www.now.org

★★★★★

This home page for NOW offers press releases and articles, information on issues NOW is currently involved in, information on joining (with email or web addresses for many local chapters), and the history of NOW. Also provided is a search form if you're looking for a specific topic at NOW's site.

National Partnership for Women & Families (NPWF)

http://www.nationalpartnership.org/

★★★★★

Test your knowledge of work and family issues by taking the short online quiz here. Then find out more about public policy issues facing families and watch a video about NPWF.

National Women's Hall of Fame

http://www.greatwomen.org/

★★★★★

👫 All

Find out who this year's Hall of Fame inductees are, play games and participate in exercises to increase your knowledge of the contribution great women have made, learn more about the work of this organization, and buy Hall of Fame merchandise here.

National Women's History Project

http://www.nwhp.org

★★★★★

👫 All

Official website of the National Women's History Project, which originated Women's History month. Many interesting features here about the history of women and what they have contributed in the past. Educators might benefit from learning more about the significant impact women had on history and for which they have not received credit. This project aims to bring their contributions to light. The site offers information and resources, as well as an online catalog of products for sale.

NBCC–National Breast Cancer Coalition

http://www.natlbcc.org/

★★★★

Learn more about this nonprofit advocacy organization and its efforts to eradicate breast cancer through action and public policy change. Join the organization or just learn more about breast cancer here through the breaking news section.

NWSA–National Women's Studies Association

http://www.nwsa.org/

★★★★

👫 All

The NWSA supports and promotes feminist teaching, learning, research, and many other projects. It provides professional and community service at the pre-K through post-secondary levels. It also provides information about the inter-disciplinary field of Women's Studies for those outside the profession. The organization publishes a newsletter called *NWSAction* and other publications. The *NWSA Journal,* an official publication of the National Women's Studies Association, publishes the most up-to-date interdisciplinary, multicultural feminist scholarship linking feminist theory with teaching and activism. NWSA has an annual conference that provides opportunities for teachers, students, activists, and others to share research findings, strategies, and ideas for effecting social change.

Office of Women's Business Ownership

http://www.sbaonline.sba.gov/womeninbusiness/

★★★★

Produced by the U.S. Small Business Association, this page provides information and resource links for women currently running or seeking to run small businesses in the United States.

OWBO Online Women's Business Center

http://www.onlinewbc.gov/

★★★★

OWBO promotes the growth of women-owned businesses through programs that address business training and technical assistance. You'll find a wealth of information here if you are in business or thinking about it.

A
B
C
D
E
F
G
H
I
J
K
L
M
N
O
P
Q
R
S
T
U
V
W
X
Y
Z

Oxygen.com
http://www.oxygen.com/

★★★★★

The online site with information for, by, and about women. Discuss issues of great importance, such as making the world a better place, to less important but perhaps equally interesting issues such as shopping, relationships, learning, and more. Lots of chat and discussion opportunities, as well as interactive elements. The site also supports a shopping area for things you might need.

Shescape Online
http://www.shescape.com/

★★★★★

 Not for kids

Shescape is a dance show that celebrates lesbian culture. This site provides information about the show and includes an advice column, interviews, schedules of upcoming concerts and events, monthly horoscopes, health and fitness advice, and links to related sites.

Society of Women Engineers
http://www.swe.org/

★★★★

Information about the society, plus a résumé database and job search help for female engineers. You can also subscribe to the group's magazine and find out how to submit articles for publication in it.

Spinsters Ink
http://www.spinsters-ink.com/

★★★

Spinsters Ink publishes novels and nonfiction works that deal with significant issues in women's lives from a feminist perspective. Included on the website are book reviews, ordering information, and submission information.

Sports Illustrated for Women
http://sportsillustrated.cnn.com/siwomen/

★★★★★

 All

Stay up-to-date on hot women's sports stars and learn more about getting and keeping your body in shape.

TASC: The American Surrogacy Center, Inc.
http://www.surrogacy.com/

★★★

Comprehensive information on surrogate childbearing, including message boards, classified advertising, a directory of agencies and groups, and articles about surrogacy.

The United Nations and the Status of Women
http://www.un.org/Conferences/Women/PubInfo/Status/Home.htm

★★★★

This site from the United Nations provides information about what the UN has done since its inception to further the status of women. Included are conference findings, general articles, and commission reports.

WE: Women's Entertainment
http://www.we.tv/

★★★★

Home of the Women's Entertainment broadcasting company, which features programming specifically addressed to the female audience. Here, you can learn more about WE's various TV programs.

Web by Women, for Women
http://www.io.com/~wwwomen/

★★★★★

Lots of solid, unbiased, nonsleazy information about sexuality, pregnancy, contraception, and more.

WIDNET (Women In Development Network)

http://www.focusintl.com/widnet.htm

★★★★

The WIDNET site presents information pertaining to women's resources throughout the Internet. Also includes the *WIDNET* magazine, a searchable resource database, business contacts, and much more. Available in English and French.

WISE (Women's Initiative for Self Empowerment)

http://www.wise-up.org/wise_hist.htm

★★★★

This site focuses primarily on domestic violence issues and providing "holistic and sustainable support services to women and children survivors of domestic violence and sexual assault; education to the public-at-large; advocacy with critical stakeholders; and training to service providers on the issues of domestic violence and sexual assault."

WomanOwned.Com–Business Information for Women Entrepreneurs

http://www.womanowned.com

★★★★★

Learn how to start your own business, get it financed, and get support for your business. You'll find pages of helpful information as well as links to other related sites.

Women.com

http://www.women.com/

★★★

👫 Not for kids

This resource for young women has several sections including entertainment, sex & dating, horoscopes, style, and fun & games. Click the Girl Talk link to access the discussion boards.

The Women and Politics Institute

http://www.american.edu/oconnor/wandp/

★★★★★

Women and Politics is an academic journal published at West Georgia College in Carrollton, Georgia. The goal of the journal is to foster research and the development of theory on women's political participation, the role of women in society, and the impact of public policy upon women's lives. Included online are article abstracts, calls for papers, and subscription information.

Women in Aviation History: The Ninety Nines

http://www.ninety-nines.org/bios.html

★★★

👫 All

At this site you'll find biographies and tributes to the prominent women in the history of aviation, including Louise Sacchi, Fay Gillis Wells, and Bessie Coleman. Interesting!

Women in Islam

http://www.usc.edu/dept/MSA/humanrelations/womeninislam/

★★★★

Interesting basic information about how women fit into the Islamic religion, mostly oriented toward those unfamiliar with Islam.

Women Leaders Online (WLO)

http://wlo.org/

★★★★

WLO is an organization dedicated to stopping the Radical Right/Contract with America agenda. This website contains information about Women Leaders Online and a variety of other women-related issues.

Women's History

http://socialstudies.com/c/@0/Pages/womenindex.html

★★★★★

This website, part of the Social Studies School Service, provides teachers with several lessons, student exercises, and reviews of special materials that present exciting ways to bring women's history into their classrooms. Topics include Women in Wartime, American Women at Work, Amelia Earhart, and others.

A B C D E F G H I J K L M N O P Q R S T U V **W** X Y Z

A
B
C
D
E
F
G
H
I
J
K
L
M
N
O
P
Q
R
S
T
U
V
W
X
Y
Z

Women's Human Rights Net

http://www.whrnet.org/

★★★★★

A beautiful site designed with women's rights in mind. Lots of useful information for you to read and benefit from.

Women's Human Rights Resources

http://www.law-lib.utoronto.ca/Diana/

★★★★

A collection of websites, online documents, and bibliographies about women's human rights issues.

Women's Studies

http://www-unix.umbc.edu/~korenman/wmst/links.html

★★★

Directory of sites that provide resources on women's studies and issues that women face. Links are organized by categories including Activism, Arts & Humanities, Business/Work, Girls and Young Women, and Higher Education.

WomensNet

http://www.igc.org/

★★★

Supports women's organizations worldwide and provides articles and links to information and resources for women's issues.

WomenWatch

http://www.un.org/womenwatch/

★★★★

An overview of United Nations and regional programs dealing with women's rights and the advancement and empowerment of women, plus related news and statistics.

Working Moms Refuge

http://www.momsrefuge.com/

★★★★★

Pick up tips and strategies for making the most of your time, from quick recipes to ideas for choosing a financial planner, at this site. Much of the content is geared to moms juggling childcare and work responsibilities, with chat and discussions forums available for commiserating and advice.

WWWomen!

http://www.wwwomen.com/

★★★★★

A comprehensive search directory for information on issues of interest to women. WWWomen links users to chats, advice, site reviews, message boards, and websites about topics including health, religion, education, and feminism.

Yale Journal of Law and Feminism

http://www.yale.edu/lawnfem/law&fem.html

★★★★★

The Yale Journal of Law and Feminism is committed to publishing pieces about women's experiences, especially as they have been structured, affected, controlled, discussed, or ignored by the law. This website contains subscription information, Telnet access to past issues, and the chance to submit your own article or even order a T-shirt.

WRESTLING

Lords of Pain

http://www.wrestlingheadlines.com/

★★★★

Up-to-date headline news, results, and columns about professional wrestling.

ProWrestling.com

http://www.prowrestling.com/

★★★★

Locate information on upcoming pro wrestling matches and TV programming, and read articles, get headline news, and stay up to date regarding your favorite wrestler's career here.

SLAM! Sports Wrestling Ratings

http://www.canoe.com/SlamWrestling/rankings.html

★★★★

View a list of the top professional wrestlers ranked not only by their win/loss record but also by their effectiveness in generating the admiration or disapproval of the fans.

TheMat.com

http://themat.com/

★★★★★

Whether you're looking for collegiate, high school, youth, or women's wrestling, you'll find Olympic trial information, archives, results, and links here.

USA Wrestling

http://www.themat.com/newusaw/

★★★★

USA Wrestling is the national governing body for Olympic wrestling in the United States. At this site, you can learn more about the organization, event schedules, wrestling camps and clinics, international tours, and more. Shop online for USA Wrestling merchandise.

World Wrestling Entertainment

http://www.wwe.com/

★★★★★

World Wrestling Entertainment is one of the top professional wrestling organizations in the world. Visit this site to learn more about the organization, its superstars, and upcoming events both on television and on pay per view. Chat areas and video games are also available.

World Wrestling Federation

http://www.wwf.com/

★★★★★

Home of the World Wrestling Federation (WWF) and the most popular professional wrestling league in the world. Here, you can read the latest news, find out about upcoming events, and learn more about your favorite celebrity wrestlers. Details on pay-per-view offerings, TV appearances, videos, magazines, sweepstakes, and more. If you're a big fan of professional wrestling, be sure to bookmark this page.

WrestleZone

http://www.wrestlezone.com/

★★★★★

Read the extensive list of headline wrestling news, stay updated on results and upcoming fights, and check out pics of your favorite guys and gals here.

[Best] Wrestling USA Magazine

http://www.wrestlingusa.com/

★★★★★

Take a look at action photos, see results from college and high school matches, read articles, and find out about wrestling camps and just about anything else you might want to learn about junior high, high school, and collegiate wrestling. You can subscribe to the magazine, *Wrestling USA*, using a secured credit card connection. For coverage of real wrestling, this site has no match.

11 Rules of Writing

http://www.junketstudies.com/rulesofw/

★★★★

👫 14-18

Concise and practical tip list for punctuation, grammar, and clear writing. Also has links to other writing resources.

A+ Research and Writing

http://www.ipl.org/teen/aplus/

★★★★★

👫 14-18

This resource for high school and college students includes guides for researching and writing academic papers. Also has research links.

About.com—Freelance Writers

http://freelancewrite.about.com/careers/

★★★★

A great site for experienced and new freelance writers, providing writing gigs, tips for improving your writing abilities, contract help, and discussion opportunities. Go to the Jump Start section if you're new to freelancing or just jump right in to look for potential assignments. Find out what editors expect and learn from fellow writers based on their experiences.

⌐Best⌐ AuthorLink!

http://www.authorlink.com/

★★★★★

A website dedicated to authors, literary agents, and publishers. Contains book reviews, business news, competition info, links to publishers and agents, and insights into writing. Very comprehensive.

Authorlink, an award-winning Internet news/information/marketing service for the publishing industry, has been around for several years, which proves its viability. The service provides editors and agents fast access to prescreened professional fiction and nonfiction manuscripts that have been submitted by authors. Readers and writers can quickly order any titles from the secure e-store. These titles are available at major bookstores and online bookstores such as Amazon.com. Authorlink also has its own publishing imprint, Authorlink Press, which offers all the standard services including electronic press, short-run publishing services, and other services. If you are a writer or just interested in reading a good book, this is the site for you.

Bartleby.com

http://www.bartleby.com/

★★★★★

This site bills itself as "The preeminent publisher of literature, reference and verse providing students, researchers, and the intellectually curious with unlimited access to books and information on the Web, free of charge."

A
B
C
D
E
F
G
H
I
J
K
L
M
N
O
P
Q
R
S
T
U
V
W
X
Y
Z

BookLocker.com—Online Bookstore and Publisher

http://www.booklocker.com/

★★★

BookLocker sells print and ebooks on all subjects, from everyday to unusual and eclectic, by new authors and published authors. This is a great site for the first-time author to gain exposure and to learn about writing from the many articles, books, and links.

Business Writing Tips

http://www.basic-learning.com/wbwt/tip01.htm

★★★★

Basic Learning Systems presents *Bull's Eye Business Writing*, a self-paced workbook that can help managers and others improve their business writing and all other written communications such as email, reports, letters, and so on. You can order some of the publications through the secure online store.

Children's Writing Resource Center

http://www.write4kids.com/

★★★★★

Articles and recommendations for becoming a successful writer for children. Chat with other children's writers and illustrators.

FreelanceWorkshop.com

http://www.freelanceworkshop.com/

★★★★

A very rich graphical site providing links to the workshop materials, a chat room, and information on how to take the online magazine's Article Writing Workshop.

Guide to Grammar and Writing

http://webster.commnet.edu/HP/pages/darling/original.htm

★★★★★

 All

A great refresher regarding sentence structure and grammar, as well as a resource to turn to regarding correct usage of various parts of speech.

IAAY Expository Writing Tutorial

http://www.cty.jhu.edu/writing/

★★★★★

Home to John Hopkins' Institute for the Academic Advancement of Youth. This cool site provides expository writing instructions for kids in grades 6–12. Kids get to work with a more experienced writer as they explore the writing process. To participate, they must be enrolled in the tutorial to access the pages containing the assignments. Financial aid is available.

Laura Brady's Business Writing Basics

http://www.as.wvu.edu/~lbrady/105.html

★★★★

An academic site providing links to course work on business writing, examples, writing help sites, and related topics.

Paradigm Online Writing Assistant

http://www.powa.org/

★★★★★

This excellent site by Chuck Guilford provides extensive instruction on how to write essays for different purposes. Each essay type is presented via a link. A discussion group is provided for sharing writing ideas.

Purdue Online Writing Lab (OWL)

http://owl.english.purdue.edu/

★★★★★

Improve your writing with help from this online resource, where you'll also find handouts that might answer lots of your questions. But if not, turn to the Purdue experts for help.

RoseDog.com

http://rosedog.com/

★★★★★

Post your work and get feedback or just exposure that might help boost your career. You'll also find information on literary agents here, too.

Screenwriters Online

http://screenwriter.com/insider/

★★★

This is the only screenwriters' tutorial sponsored by professional screenwriters. It consists of a series of chat rooms, forums where screenplays are critiqued, the *Screenwriters Insider* newsletter, and interviews with professionals.

Self-Publishing

http://win-edge.com/SelfPublish.shtml

★★★

Learn how to write, publish, and market your own informational and how-to books and booklets at this site.

storybay

http://www.storybay.com/

★★★★★

Online meeting place for writers, editors, and consumers, this site features tools to help writers fast-track their careers by developing and showcasing their talents. Provides executives the opportunity to find and recruit writers for their various projects. For consumers, the site features novels, screenplays, and other literary works.

Computer Book Café

http://www.studiob.com

★★★★★

StudioB is a literary agency for computer book authors. It sponsors and maintains the Computer Book Café, which offers computer book writers articles about the computer book industry, its publishers, and fellow writers. It also provides financial information, tax advice, and a mailing list. StudioB also presents information on the organization and how to become represented.

Waterside Productions

http://www.waterside.com/

★★★★★

Waterside Productions Inc., an electronic rights, software, and literary agency, was founded in 1982. Since then, more than 5,000 contracts have been negotiated with more than 50 publishers. The site hosts links to agents, writers' resources, sample contracts, publishers, conferences, and information about how to be represented.

The Write News

http://writenews.com/

★★★★★

This site presents everything you ever wanted to know about the publishing business. An online industry newsletter with more than 1,000 links for writers, agents, and publishers.

The Writer's Place

http://www.awoc.com/AWOC-Home.cfm

★★★★★

Searchable writer's guidelines database of paying markets. Find advice, publications, and resources for making money as a writer.

Writer's Write

http://www.writerswrite.com/

★★★★★

Find writing jobs, improve your craft, and mingle with fellow authors here.

Writers on the Net

http://www.writers.com/

$

★★★★

Pay-for-use tutoring and editing classes, and workshops led by experienced, published writers.

A B C D E F G H I J K L M N O P Q R S T U V W X Y Z

A B C D E F G H I J K L M N O P Q R S T U V W X Y Z

Writing Assessment Services

http://members.aol.com/cmarsch786/

★★★★

These writing assessments are offered to home-schoolers to help evaluate children's writing progress. The assessments were created by a woman who was a college English instructor and is a current instructor for America Online's Online Campus. She's also a homeschooler herself.

Writing-World.com

http://www.writing-world.com/

★★★★

News articles, tips, and online classes for aspiring writers and for writers who want to further develop their talents.

Writing for the Web

http://www.useit.com/papers/webwriting/

★★★★

People read differently on the Web than they do when reading printed publications, so writers need to adapt their material to the Web. Here, John Morkes and Jakob Nielsen publish the findings of their research on how people access information on the Web. Some excellent writing guidelines for web authors.

Xlibris

http://www1.xlibris.com/

★★★★

14-18

If you have a manuscript and are not sure how to go about getting it edited, illustrated, published, and marketed, check out this site. Xlibris provides complete services to authors to help them get their manuscripts to market to start generating royalties.

Young Authors Workshop

http://www.planet.eon.net/~bplaroch/

★★★★

14-18

Resource for middle school students has sections for getting ideas, writing, editing, and publishing their work. Also has teacher resources.

YOGA

A B C D E F G H I J K L M N O P Q R S T U V W X Y Z

Body Trends

http://www.bodytrends.com/strech.htm

★★★★

You can order all your yoga-associated products from the BodyTrends.com site to get you started on the right stretch. The company offers such products as mats, bags, wedges, blocks, sandbags, straps, and numerous yoga-related videos.

Hatha Yoga: Yoga Synergy

http://www.yogasynergy.com.au/

★★★★★

Yoga Synergy was established in Newtown in 1984. The teaching represents a synthesis between traditional Hatha Yoga and modern medical science.

INDOlink: Health and Fitness

http://www.indolink.com/Health/main.htm

★★★★★

Find detailed information about yoga, along with other aspects of health and fitness such as herbal remedies.

Keyboard Yoga

http://www.ivillage.com/fitness/tools/yoga/

★★★

Basic yoga techniques you can do right at your keyboard! Great information on this overall stellar site, from iVillage.com.

Kundalini Support Center

http://www.kundalini-support.com/

★★★★

Kundalini yoga focuses on awakening the spirit and increasing self-awareness of its practitioners. In some cases, the awakening experience of Kundalini can be quite intense and lead to complications. Here, you can find support and information to help you through the awakening and achieve the heightened awareness that Kundalini strives for. This site includes a survival guide, a list of Kundalini links and spiritual links, and a bibliography.

Peace Learning Center

http://www.peacelearningcenter.org

★★★★

Located in Eagle Creek Park in Indianapolis, the Peace Learning Center develops and runs programs to help with conflict management and to help individuals and communities live more peacefully. The Center also offers yoga classes. Visit this website to learn more about the Center and the programs and curriculum it has to offer.

Peace Through Yoga

http://www.peacethroughyoga.com

★★★★

Peace Through Yoga is the yoga site for the Peace Learning Center, located in Eagle Creek Park (Indianapolis). Here, you can obtain yoga class schedules and prices.

A
B
C
D
E
F
G
H
I
J
K
L
M
N
O
P
Q
R
S
T
U
V
W
X
Y
Z

Sahaja Yoga Meditation

http://www.sahajayoga.org/

★★★★

Created by Shri Mataji Nirmala Devi in 1970, Sahaja Yoga is a "method of meditation which brings a breakthrough in the evolution of human awareness." At this site, you can learn more about. Sahaja meditation, read testimonials and health benefits, view a list of Q&As, check out the book reviews, and much more. Also provides information about Kundalini yoga

Siddha Yoga Meditation

http://www.siddhayoga.org/

⑤

★★★★★

Learn what Siddha Yoga is, and find out about courses, news, and reading that might be of help, as well as centers that specialize in this type of yoga. The site also provides information on upcoming events and programs for youth. It also includes a nice online bookstore from which you can order related books.

Sivananda Yoga "Om" Page

http://www.sivananda.org/

★★★★★

A clearinghouse for information on yoga and vedanta. The site has yoga exercise tips, a guide to higher consciousness, and biographies of Swami Vishnu and his guru, Swami Sivananda.

Step by Step Yoga Postures

http://www.santosha.com/asanas/

⑤

★★★★★

👥 All

This site has a lot of useful information. One of the highlights is the listing of both the Sanskrit name and English translation. Choose from a long list of asanas and read step-by-step directions on how to achieve these yoga positions. Also read about meditation.

A World of Yoga

http://www.yogaworld.org/

★★★★★

At this site, you'll learn more about yoga techniques and how it can help you reach a higher state of consciousness, according to the site's host, Graham Ledgerwood. Find out about the eight main types of yoga and how they relate to an individual's spiritual path.

Yoga and AIDS

http://www.yogagroup.org/kout.html

★★★

An excellent article by Paula Kout, complete with descriptions of each position.

[Best] Yogabasics.com

http://www.yogabasics.com/

⑤

★★★★★

This beautifully designed site makes it easy to learn yoga basics and then move on to learn how to use yoga as a healing art. Four tabs on the opening page provide easy access to the major features at this site: Practice, Learn, Explore, Connect. Each tab pulls up a list of options—for example, when you click the Practice tab, a navigation bar appears that enables you to check out yoga postures, breathing techniques, meditation, and pose sequences. Clear graphics make it easy to understand the various positions.

The Yoga Directory

http://www.yogadirectory.com/

★★★★★

The Yoga Directory contains a list of yoga teachers, yoga centers, organizations, music, yoga therapists, health products, and yoga retreats, giving you just about everything you need to practice yoga.

Yoga Journal
http://www.yogajournal.com/

★★★★★

Read online articles about Hatha Yoga here, as well as learn about other publishing products you might be interested in. The site also includes a directory of yoga teachers you can consult to find a local instructor. You can subscribe to the magazine online.

Yoga for Menopause
http://www.healthy.net/asp/templates/article.asp?id=1370

★★★★

This in-depth article, by Susan M. Lark, M.D., includes illustrations along with information on how to choose the right yoga technique.

Yoga Postures for HIV/AIDS
http://www.yogagroup.org/postures.html

★★★

The Yoga Group is a Colorado nonprofit organization providing free Yoga classes to persons living with HIV/AIDS.

Yoga Site
http://www.yogasite.com/

★★★★★

Great instructional material that tells and shows you, through drawings, about basic yoga positions. You also can read about yoga styles, review questions and answers posed regarding yoga, identify yoga-related organizations, and read about yoga therapy news. And if you still find you have unanswered questions about yoga, you'll find links to other yoga sites that might help.

YogaClass
http://www.yogaclass.com/welcome.html

★★★★

Online yoga instruction including breathing, exercises, stretches, and chants. Includes a chat room.

YogaFinder
http://www.yogafinder.com/

★★★★★

Use this national search system to find classes, facilities, and general information about yoga.

YREC: Yoga Research and Education Center
http://www.yrec.org/

★★★★★

This "Gateway to Traditional Yoga" provides information on yoga education and research as well as the therapeutic application of yoga in healthcare. Here, you can check on daily classes and teacher training, sign up for a yoga correspondence course, and learn how to give something back to yoga. The illustrated beginner's tour is especially helpful for novices and those interested in finding out more about yoga.

A
B
C
D
E
F
G
H
I
J
K
L
M
N
O
P
Q
R
S
T
U
V
W
X
Y
Z

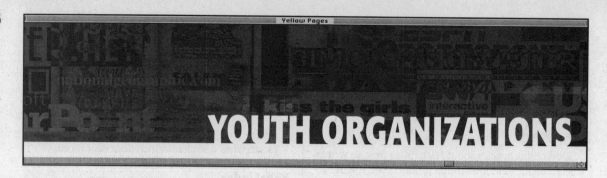

YOUTH ORGANIZATIONS

Boy Scouts of America

http://www.scouting.org/

★★★★★

All

If you're a scout, you can use this site to learn about scouting programs, events, publications, merchandise, and awards, as well as to play fun games online. Anyone considering becoming a scout, which includes boys age 7–20, or a scout leader, will find this site informative.

Boys and Girls Clubs of America

http://www.bgca.org/

★★★★★

All

The Boys and Girls Club Movement is a nationwide affiliation of local, autonomous organizations working to help youth from all backgrounds (with special concern for those from disadvantaged circumstances) develop the qualities needed to become responsible citizens and leaders.

B'nai B'rith Youth Organization

http://www.bbyo.org/

★★★★

All

B'nai B'rith is a "youth led, worldwide organization which provides opportunities for Jewish youth to develop their leadership potential, a positive Jewish identity and commitment to their personal development."

The CityKids Foundation

http://www.citykids.com/

★★★★

A multicultural organization dedicated to the survival, education, and self-expression of today's youth. Based in New York City.

CYO: Catholic Youth Organization

http://www.cyocamp.org/

★★★★

All

Home of the Catholic Youth Organization-sponsored camps. Learn more about the CYO camps, meet the staff, check up on employment opportunities, and learn how to contact personnel via email.

Best Girl Scouts

http://www.girlscouts.org/

$

★★★★★

All

Learn all about the world's largest organization for girls, its programs, research activities, traditions, publications, and, of course, Girl Scout cookies. The site also has a nice shopping mall where you can securely shop for most of the things any young woman would be interested in. There is also a helpful FAQ if you have unanswered questions. The Girl Scouts are where girls turn to discover fun, friendship, and the power of girls together. They promote the theory that Girl Scouting gives girls opportunities to build skills for lifetime success in sports, science, and even in a Girl Scout cookie sale.

Little League Baseball Online

http://www.littleleague.org/

★★★★★

Find out more about Little League baseball programs in your area, the history of the program, divisions, summer camp, forms and policies, equipment, and merchandise.

National 4-H Council

http://www.fourhcouncil.edu/

★★★★★

 All

Whether you're considering joining 4-H, or if you're a 4-H alumnus, this site has information for you about current programs and initiatives, getting involved, and reconnecting with past 4-Hers. 4-H is dedicated to helping youth develop leadership skills while understanding and addressing important community issues.

National PTA

http://www.pta.org/

★★★★★

Join one of America's oldest organizations to work on behalf of our youth. The site offers facts, photographs, archives, and information about the PTA.

Sierra Student Coalition

http://www.ssc.org/

★★★

The student activist arm of the environmental group, the Sierra Club, the SSC educates students about conservation and then sends them into their own communities to make a difference. The SSC site contains information about the organization, membership, campaigns, and resources.

YMCA

http://www.ymca.int/

★★★★★

 All

Locate YMCA offices and hotels at this site, where you'll also learn more about the mission of this Christian organization and its programs. You can review the online magazine, *YMCA World*, and catch up on organizational news. You'll also find a directory of national and local associations.

Youth and Children's Resource

http://www.child.net/

★★★★★

 All

Extensive list of links to support networks and services. Includes resources for parents and national hotlines.

YouthLink

http://www.youthlink.org/

★★★★★

 All

YouthLink, a division of the Foundation of America, is geared toward youths and encourages their participation within their own communities by rewarding those who are selected with Youth Action Award grants.

A
B
C
D
E
F
G
H
I
J
K
L
M
N
O
P
Q
R
S
T
U
V
W
X
Y
Z

ZOOS

The Albuquerque Aquarium

http://www.cabq.gov/biopark/aquarium/index.html

★★★★★

 All

Take a fascinating journey through the marine habitats of the oceans at this fantastic aquarium in New Mexico. Many other features are available here, such as information about the zoo, the city, and other items you may be interested in.

American Zoo and Aquarium Association

http://www.aza.org/

Ⓢ

★★★★

This is the flagship membership organization for zoological parks, aquariums, oceanariums, and wildlife parks in North America. Find out what they are all about, their members, publications, conferences, how to support their conservation and animal welfare work, and more.

Arizona-Sonora Desert Museum

http://www.desertmuseum.org/

★★★★

All

A zoo, a natural history museum, and a botanical garden make up this complex. Find information about visiting this Tucson institution and view exhibits at this site.

Big Cats Online

http://dialspace.dial.pipex.com/agarman/bco/ver4.htm

★★★★★

All

Find out everything you ever wanted to know about the world's wild cat species. No matter what question you have about these beautiful cats, you're likely to find it here. The site includes great pictures and lots of detailed information.

Brevard Zoo

http://www.brevardzoo.org/

★★★★

All

Visitors to this site can take a virtual tour of the Brevard Zoo in Melbourne, Florida. The site also includes general information and news updates from the zoo.

The Bronx Zoo

http://wcs.org/zoos/

★★★★★

All

The Bronx Zoo is home to more than 6,000 animals, including some of the world's most endangered species. The zoo has more than 265 wooded acres devoted to spacious naturalistic habitats. The site is almost as impressive with abundant information about the zoo and what it provides.

Calgary Zoo

http://www.calgaryzoo.org/

★★★★★

👥 All

Learn about the zoo (in Calgary, Alberta, Canada), conservation programs, special events, and employment and volunteering opportunities.

Cincinnati Zoo and Botanical Garden

http://www.cincyzoo.org/

★★★★★

👥 All

Wander through this site to experience the Cincinnati Zoo and the world of nature. Find current events and discover what's new, learn about conservation and how you can help, get information on exotic travel programs, educate yourself about wildlife, and participate in the weekly animal/plant guessing game.

Cleveland Metroparks Zoo

http://www.clemetzoo.com/

★★★★★

👥 All

Want to visit the rain forest? Tour the zoo? Learn about conservation? Get educated about the natural world? Read about research being conducted by zoo staff? You can do all this and more at the site of the Cleveland Metroparks Zoo.

The Cyber Zoomobile

http://www.primenet.com/~brendel/

★★★★

👥 All

This kid-oriented virtual zoo focuses on the curator's own favorite animals: the canidae (dogs), the ursidae (bears), and the felidae (cats), as well as sea life, primates, lizards, snakes, boas, and more. Big cats are the clear favorites, but you'll find lots of photos and facts exploring any of the categories that have been included. By signing in and providing feedback, you are registering to win a prize from the site's monthly drawing. This site also offers lots of good links and activities in the Stuff section. Definitely browse through the photomosaic images of animals, too.

The Dallas Zoo

http://www.dallas-zoo.org/home/home.asp

★★★★★

👥 All

One of the best-looking websites featuring all the main attractions you can find at most zoos plus an aquarium. There's tons of information about the zoo and related subjects. Be sure to visit here before you go to the zoo. It's worth the effort just to visit the site, and after you do, you'll probably want to visit the zoo in person.

Denver Zoo

http://www.denverzoo.org/

★★★★★

👥 All

Visitors can take a zoo tour and view short video clips of the animals, find operating hours and admission prices, or read about the conservation efforts of the Denver Zoo.

Double R Exotic Animals

http://www.rrzoo.com

★★★

👥 All

Traveling, educational exotic animal exhibit, petting zoo, and camel rides for hire, for fairs, and other events. Live Christmas nativity, including camels and a simulated stable.

The Electronic Zoo

http://netvet.wustl.edu/e-zoo.htm

★★★

👥 All

The Electronic Zoo is a directory of online animal sites, veterinary sites, and other animal-related resources.

A B C D E F G H I J K L M N O P Q R S T U V W X Y Z

A
B
C
D
E
F
G
H
I
J
K
L
M
N
O
P
Q
R
S
T
U
V
W
X
Y
Z

Fort Worth Zoo

http://www.fortworthzoo.com/

★★★★★

 All

Zoo hours, a zoo map, educational opportunities, and special events are presented here. Visitors also can print games and puzzles from the Delta's Kids Page.

The Good Zoo Guide Online

http://www.goodzoos.com/

$

★★★★

 All

This site offers you an exciting guide to all the zoos on the entire planet. It features the best zoos, wildlife parks, animal collections, and more than 200 pages of zoo reviews and discussions.

The Indianapolis Zoo

http://www.indianapoliszoo.com/

★★★★★

 All

Go to the Information Center for "who, what, when, where" details on the Indianapolis Zoo, or visit the virtual zoo for photos and information on the zoo's many inhabitants—both plants and animals. In the Virtual Zoo, you can use the search utility to put the information you want at your fingertips. This zoo is home to one of the few baby elephants born in captivity.

Kids World 2000: Animals, Zoos and Aquariums

http://now2000.com/kids/zoos.shtml

★★★★

 All

A place where young cyber-travelers can find 50+ links to animals, zoos, and aquariums in the United States and overseas. Just click a link to jump to the site of your choice and learn all about the flora and fauna.

Lincoln Park Zoo

http://www.lpzoo.com/

★★★★★

 All

This site provides an index of the more than 1,000 animals featured at this free Chicago zoo. You also can find information on adopting animals; endangered species; and educational programs for schools, families, and adults. A special feature is an online tour of the zoo.

The Los Angeles Zoo

http://www.lazoo.org/

★★★★

 All

Opened in November 1966, the Los Angeles Zoo is home to more than 1,200 animals. This site includes a history of the zoo as well as visitor information, animal facts, excerpts from the zoo's quarterly magazine, and a list of job opportunities.

Memphis Zoo Home Page

http://www.memphiszoo.org/

★★★★

All

This site provides basic information about the Memphis Zoo, such as hours and prices, educational programs, special events, membership, the gift shop, the animal hospital, and the zoo's history. Good information mainly for those interested in visiting in person.

National Zoo

http://natzoo.si.edu/

$

★★★★★

The Smithsonian Institution runs the National Zoological Park, the world's largest museum and research complex. The National Zoo is dedicated to "celebrating, studying, and protecting wild animals in their natural habitats." The actual zoo is a 163-acre zoological park in Rock Creek National Park in Washington, D.C., where the famous pandas, Tian Tian and Mei Xiang, call home. This website is packed with information about all sorts of wild animals, and the site is very attractive and easy to navigate. Visiting is like taking a trip to the zoo, except here you can learn much more about the various species. With its excellent site design and wealth of useful information, this site is well deserving of its ranking as the best online zoo on the Web.

The North Carolina Zoological Park

http://www.nczoo.org/

★★★★★

 All

If you'd like to get a glimpse of this zoo, click Visit the Zoo to get a park overview, a park map, visitors' hints, and gift and food information. One tip for real-world visitors: Wear good walking shoes because the zoo spans more than 1,400 acres and takes an estimated five hours to walk through.

Oregon Zoo

http://www.zooregon.org/

★★★★★

 All

You can search this Portland, Oregon, zoo's site or just jump to one of the offered areas: About Our Zoo, About Our Animals, Visitor Information, What's Happening, Get Involved, Saving Species, Teachers and Educators, No Adults Allowed!, and more. There's something for everyone here.

Perth Zoo

http://www.perthzoo.wa.gov.au/

★★★★

 All

Find out about upcoming events and exhibits at this West Australia zoo, as well as conservation efforts, research, and zoo schedules and operations at this site.

Philadelphia Zoo Online

http://www.phillyzoo.org/

★★★★★

 All

Besides the home page, this site offers an education page, a conservation page, an animals list, the PhillyZoo News page, and an online search engine. You also can enter the site index to get all kinds of information on animals, conservation activities, zoo facts, and more.

The Phoenix Zoo

http://www.phoenixzoo.org/zoo/

$

★★★★★

 All

Offers zoo trails to explore, a cool stuff section especially for kids, a calendar of events, animal information, zoo stats, general information, and links to other sites.

The St. Louis Zoo

http://www.stlzoo.org/home.asp

$

★★★★★

 All

You can do everything from plan your visit to the zoo to adopt an animal and much more. A beautiful site consisting of many rich features to make your visit more enjoyable.

A B C D E F G H I J K L M N O P Q R S T U V W X Y Z

A
B
C
D
E
F
G
H
I
J
K
L
M
N
O
P
Q
R
S
T
U
V
W
X
Y
Z

The San Antonio Zoo

http://www.sazoo-aq.org/

★★★★

 All

At this site, you can get a word from the director, learn what's new at the zoo, get general zoo information, tour the zoo, learn about the "adopt an animal" program, find out about zoo membership and employment opportunities, and access links to related sites.

San Diego Zoo

http://www.sandiegozoo.org/

★★★★★

 All

Known for its housing of some of the rarest pandas, the San Diego Zoo takes full advantage of this, hosting Panda Central on its site. Here, you can look at the photo album and check in on the panda family through Panda cam. Panda facts help educate children on the lives of these special animals. You also can get information on visiting the zoo and supporting its panda initiatives here.

San Francisco Zoo

http://www.sfzoo.org/

★★★★

All

For the past few years, the San Francisco Zoo has been undergoing some major renovations, including a recently expanded Children's Zoo and an all new Lipman Family Lemur Forest. At this site, you can learn about the latest developments; obtain visitor information; and learn about the various programs, exhibits, and activities sponsored by the zoo.

Sea World/Busch Gardens Animal Information Database

http://www.seaworld.org/

★★★★★

 All

Contains a searchable animal information database maintained by the Sea World/Busch Gardens theme parks. Find out how your classroom can take advantage of the *Shamu* TV series. The Animal Bytes section includes "Ask Shamu," a column that features answers to animal-related questions. The site offers a wealth of animal information, images, and resources. It also has sections devoted to camps, study trips, and zoological career information.

Wildlife Conservation Society

http://www.wcs.org/

★★★★★

 All

This society, founded in 1895 in New York City, works to save wildlife around the world. It also maintains five wildlife parks in New York, including the Bronx Zoo. This site provides information on the society, its wildlife parks, and other programs.

Woodland Park Zoo (Seattle, WA)

http://www.zoo.org/

★★★★★

All

The Woodland Park Zoo in Seattle, Washington, maintains this site with a virtual tour; information on admission, conservation, and education; special events, the zoo store, and exhibits.

ZooNet for Kids

http://members.aol.com/zoonetkids/

★★★

 All

This kid-friendly site will appeal to young animal lovers. They can zip from link to link, exploring such items as Muriel's Traveling Petting Zoo, Whale Times: Kid's Page, Rhinos and Tigers and Bears—Oh My! (Knoxville Zoo), the ZooNet Animal Speller, and Indianapolis Zoo Photos.

A
B
C
D
E
F
G
H
I
J
K
L
M
N
O
P
Q
R
S
T
U
V
W
X
Y
Z

A B C D E F G H I J K L M N O P Q R S T U V W X Y Z

A
B
C
D
E
F
G
H
I
J
K
L
M
N
O
P
Q
R
S
T
U
V
W
X
Y
Z

A B C D E F G H I J K L M N O P Q R S T U V W X Y Z

A
B
C
D
E
F
G
H
I
J
K
L
M
N
O
P
Q
R
S
T
U
V
W
X
Y
Z

B

A B C D E F G H I J K L M N O P Q R S T U V W X Y Z

A
B
C
D
E
F
G
H
I
J
K
L
M
N
O
P
Q
R
S
T
U
V
W
X
Y
Z

A
B
C
D
E
F
G
H
I
J
K
L
M
N
O
P
Q
R
S
T
U
V
W
X
Y
Z

Merrill Lynch, 137
Microsoft Corporation, 137
Mobil, 137
Molly Maid, 509
Motorola, 137
National Association for Female Executives, 50, 1022
National Equipment Company, 510
office equipment
    abcoffice.com, 717
    BuyerZone.com, 717
    Home Office Direct, 717
    OfficeFurniture.com, 717
Office of Women's Business Ownership, 1023
office supply stores, 717-719
OneSource, 136
OWBO Online Womens Business Center, 1023
Pachter & Assoicates, 301
patent information, 144-145
PR Newswire Home Page, 695
The Procter & Gamble Company, 137
Prudential Insurance Company of America, 137
SBC Communications, 137
Sears, Roebuck & Company, 137
Small Business - Products and Services, 145-146
Small Business - Webstorefront Support, 147
Standard Industrial Classifications (SIC) Index, 821
STAT-USA, 136
State Farm Insurance Companies, 137
SuperPages.com, 821
Switchboard: The Internet Directory, 136, 822
TechExpo on WWW, 136
Texaco, 13
They Rule, 5
TIAA-CREF, 137
Tradeshow List, 136
Travel-Watch, 136
United Parcel Service of America, Inc. (UPS), 137
Vanguard Cleaning Concepts, 509
Verizon.com, 137
Wal-Mart Stores, Inc., 137
Wall Street Journal Interactive, 697, 1011
The Walt Disney Company, 137
Web100: Big Business on the Web, 136
WhoWhere?!, 136
WIDNET (Women in Development Network), 1025
WomanOwned.com, 1025
Working Wounded, 471
business travel. *See* air travel; travel

C

California
Adventure City, 39
Asian Art Museum of San Francisco, 619
Bay City News Home Page, 693
Berkeley Art Museum/Pacific Film Archive, 627
California Association of Realtors Online, 455
California Homeschool Network, 459
California Museum of Photography, 627
California State Historical Landmarks, 430
California Travel Guide, 950
California Voter Foundation, 770
Fine Arts Museums of San Francisco, 620
Getty Architectural Complex, 618
Golden Gate Railroad Museum, 801
GORP: California National Forests, 954
J. Paul Getty Museum, 620
Joshua Tree Rock Climbing School, 844
LEGOLAND California, 40
Los Angeles Zoo, 1040
Mount Wilson Observatory, 54
Museum of Tolerance, 624
Napa Valley Virtual Visit, 349
Natural History Museum of Los Angeles County, 626
Pasadena Kids' Pages, 536
San Diego Zoo, 1042
San Francisco Architectural Heritage, 432
San Francisco Museum of Modern Art, 623
San Francisco Opera, 661
San Francisco Zoo, 1042
San Jose Mercury News, 697
Santa Cruz Beach Boardwalk, 432
Seismological Laboratory, 1002
TotalEscape, 955
UCLA Fowler Museum of Cultural History, 624
Ultimate Internet Wedding Guide, 1005
Wine Country Weekly Real Estate Reader, 807
Yosemite Park, 741
calories. *See also* weight loss
Fast Food Facts - Interactive Food Finder, 1007
Prevention.com - Weight Loss and Fitness, 1008
Calvinism. *See also* religion and philosophy
Center for Reformed Theology and Apologetics (CRTA), 827
The Five Points of Calvinism, 829
cameras. *See also* photography
Abe's of Maine, 758
Ace Index, 758
AGFA Digital Cameras, 758
Amazing Fish Cam!, 758
Beach Photo & Video, 758
Bender Photographic, 758
Camera Review.com, 759
Cameras Etcetera, 759
Cameraworld.com, 759
Complete Guide to Digital Cameras and Digital Photography, 759
Digital Camera Imaging Resource Page, 759
Digital Camera News, 759
Digital Photography Review, 759
EarthCam, 759

Focus Camera & Video, 760
How Digital Cameras Work, 760
Kodak Digital Cameras, 760
Megapixel.net, 760
PC Photo Review, 760
Photo.net, 760
Ritz Camera, 760
camping
Adventure Network, 148
Altrec.com, 148
American Camping Association, 148
American Park Network - Camping, 148
Backpacker Magazine, 151
backpacking, 151
Benz Campground Directory, 148
Camp Channel, 149
Camp-A-Roo, 148
Campground Directory, 149
The Camping Source, 149
Camping World Online, 149
Camping-USA, 149
CampNet America, 149
Christian Camping International, 149
Coleman.com, 149
Equipped to Survive, 149
Get Knotted, 149
GORP: Great Outdoor Recreation Pages, 150
hiking, 152-154
InterHike, 1018
Kids Camps, 150
KOA Homepage, 150
L.L. Bean Welcome Page, 150
Minnesota State Parks, 150
Nature Rangers, 150
Ocean City, MD's Frontier Town Campground, 150
Outdoor Action, 151
Summer Camps, 151
Visit Your National Parks, 151
camps (youths)
Catholic Youth Organization (CYO), 1036
Cool Works' Ski Resorts and Ski/Snowboard Country Jobs, 879
Dick Ritger Bowling Camps, 130
Kids Camps, 727
Soccer Camps, 885
Soccer Information Systems, 885
Canada
1st Traveler's Choice, 953
The Aging Research Centre (ARC), 853
Air Canada, 155, 931
Aisle Say, 914
Alzheimer Society of Canada, 37
Athletics Canada, 925
Birding in British Columbia, 107
Calgary Zoo, 1039
Canada.com, 155
Canadian Business Franchise Magazine, 137
Canadian Charitable Organizations, 705
Canadian Genealogical Projects Registry, 389
Canadian Music Organizations, 673
Canadian Parents Online, 721

A B C D E F G H I J K L M N O P Q R S T U V W X Y Z

A B C D E F G H I J K L M N O P Q R S T U V W X Y Z

A
B
C
D
E
F
G
H
I
J
K
L
M
N
O
P
Q
R
S
T
U
V
W
X
Y
Z

A B C D E F G H I J K L M N O P Q R S T U V W X Y Z

A
B
C
D
E
F
G
H
I
J
K
L
M
N
O
P
Q
R
S
T
U
V
W
X
Y
Z

A B C D E F G H I J K L M N O P Q R S T U V W X Y Z

F

A B C D E F G H I J K L M N O P Q R S T U V W X Y Z

A B C D E F G H I J K L M N O P Q R S T U V W X Y Z

A B C D E F G **H** I J K L M N O P Q R S T U V W X Y Z

A
B
C
D
E
F
G
H
I
J
K
L
M
N
O
P
Q
R
S
T
U
V
W
X
Y
Z

A
B
C
D
E
F
G
H
I
J
K
L
M
N
O
P
Q
R
S
T
U
V
W
X
Y
Z

A
B
C
D
E
F
G
H
I
J
K
L
M
N
O
P
Q
R
S
T
U
V
W
X
Y
Z

A B C D E F G H I J K L M N O P Q R S T U V W X Y Z

A B C D E F G H I J K L M N O P Q R S T U V W X Y Z

A B C D E F G H I J K L M N O P Q R S T U V W X Y Z

K

A B C D E F G H I J K L M N O P Q R S T U V W X Y Z

A B C D E F G H I J K L M N O P Q R S T U V W X Y Z

Consumer Law Page, 217
crime and criminal law, 557-558
cyber law and cyberspace issues, 558
Department of Justice, 961
ElderNet, 841
Federal Child Custody Laws, 729
Gay and Lesbian Politics, 863
gay/lesbians
    American Civil Liberties Union,
    384
    Gay and Lesbian Activist Alliance,
    384
    Gay and Lesbian Alliance Against
    Defamation (GLAAD), 384
    Gay Rights Newstrove, 384
    Human Rights Campaign, 384
    National Gay and Lesbian Task
    Force, 385
    National Lesbian and Gay Law
    Association, 385
general resources, 558-559
Greensboro Justice Fund, 177
Institute of Continuing Legal
  Education, 263
Internet Storm Center, 486
KuesterLaw Resource, 145
Law Research: The United States
  Department of Justice, 177
law schools, 559-561
LawCatalog.com, 123
Lawschool.com, 197
legal organizations, 561
legal publications, 562-563
LEXIS-NEXIS Communication Center,
  135
mediation, 587-588
Mental Health Law, 602
NARAL Pro-Choice California, 2
National Senior Citizens Law Center,
  855
Office of the Inspector General, 967
Patent Law Links, 145
Pre-Law – How to Get into Law School,
  198
Workplace Fairness, 517
law enforcement
  360degrees.org, 507
  American Jail Association, 507
  Corrections Connection, 507
  Corrections.com, 507
  CrimCast, 507
  Federal Bureau of Investogation (FBI),
    557
  Federal Bureau of Prisons, 507
  Jail.net, 508
  Officer.com, 508
law schools. *See also* **colleges and universi-
ties**
  Association of American Law Schools,
    559
  Columbia Law School, 559
  Harvard Law School, 559
  Jurist, 560
  Kaplan Law, 560

Law School Admission Council Online,
  560
Stanford Law School, 560
University of Chicago Law School, 560
Writings for Law School Admission, 560
Yale Law School Home Page, 561
lawn care
  Gemplers.com, 23
  John Deere—Agricultural Equipment,
    23
  Organic Lawn Care, 377
  Outdoor Power Equipment, 377
  Scotts Lawncare, 377
  Yardcare.com, 377
learning disabilities
  Ability Online Support Network, 412
  ADD Action Group, 412
  Arkenstone, 412
  Brain Injury Association, 412
  LD Online, 413
  Learning Disabilities Association of
    America, 413
legal organizations
  ACLU Freedom Network, 561
  American Bar Association, 561
  American Corporate Counsel
    Association, 561
  American Immigration Lawyers
    Association, 561
  Association of Trial Lawyers of America,
    561
  ElderWeb, 561
  National Association of Attorneys
    General, 561
  National District Attorneys Association
    (NDAA), 561
legal publications
  ALSO! Main Page, 562
  European Law Journal, 562
  Federal Communications Law Journal,
    562
  Hieros Gamos, 562
  Journal of Information, Law, and
    Technology, 562
  Law Library of Congress, 562
  Law.com, 562
  Law.Net, 562
  LawMall, 563
  Lawyers Weekly, 563
  National Law Journal, 563
  Nolo Press, 563
  The Lawyer.com, 563
  United States Code, 563
  Web Journal of Current Legal Issues, 563
lesbians. *See* **gay/lesbian/bisexual/trans
issues**
libraries
  American Library Association, 49
  American War Library, 812
  Awesome Library, 527
  Berkeley Digital Library SunSITE, 812
  Bibliomania: The Network Library, 812
  Board Building, 994
  BookCrossing, 118
  C. Christopher Morris Cricket Library
    and Colection, 813
  Center for Research Libraries, 812

Christian Classics Ethereal Library, 812
Deaf Library, 235
Global Reports, LLC, 813
HealthCentral, 1009
HighBeam Research, 813
Internet Public Library, 813
Joseph & Matthew Payton Philanthropic
  Studies Library, 701
Library of Congress, 813
Library of the National Medical Society,
  593
Library Resources for Women's Studies,
  1022
Library Spot, 813
Libweb—Library Servers on the WWW,
  814
Lightspan, 815
Medical/Health Sciences Libraries on
  the Web, 814
Michigan Electronic Library, 572
National Archives and Records
  Administration, 814
National First Ladies' Library, 814
National Library of Medicine's
  Infertility Resources, 777
National Sporting Library, 814
Network Security Library, 685
North American Sport Library Network,
  814
OCLC Online Computer Library
  Center, 814
Perry-Castaneda Library Map
  Collection, 815
Shape Up America, 1008
SignWritingSite, 236
Smithsonian Institution Libraries, 815
Smithsonian Photographs Online, 627
Special Libraries Association, 815
Sunnyvale Center for Innovation,
  Invention & Ideas, 815
Thriveonline.com, 977
U. S. Department of Education (ED)
  Home Page, 815
U.S. National Library of Medicine, 594,
  815
Veterinary Medicine Libraries, 971
WedNet, 1006
WWW Library Directory, 816
literary agents
  AuthorLink!, 1029
  Computer Book Cafe, 1031
  RoseDog.com, 1030
  Waterside Productions, 1031
literature
  America and English Literature
    Resources, 564
  authors, 564-572
  Essential Comparitive Literature and
    Theory, 564
  Literary Criticism, 564
  Literary Resources on the Net, 564
  WWW Virtual Library, 823
lodging
  123 Hotels, 947
  Alaska Cabin, Cottage, and Lodge
    Catalog, 947
  all-hotels.com, 947

A B C D E F G H I J K L M N O P Q R S T U V W X Y Z

A B C D E F G H I J K L **M** N O P Q R S T U V W X Y Z

A B C D E F G H I J K L **M** N O P Q R S T U V W X Y Z

A
B
C
D
E
F
G
H
I
J
K
L
M
N
O
P
Q
R
S
T
U
V
W
X
Y
Z

A
B
C
D
E
F
G
H
I
J
K
L
M
N
O
P
Q
R
S
T
U
V
W
X
Y
Z

A B C D E F G H I J K L M N O P Q R S T U V W X Y Z

A B C D E F G H I J K L M N O P Q R S T U V W X Y Z

A
B
C
D
E
F
G
H
I
J
K
L
M
N
O
P
Q
R
S
T
U
V
W
X
Y
Z

A B C D E F G H I J K L M N O P Q **R** S T U V W X Y Z

A B C D E F G H I J K L M N O P Q R S T U V W X Y Z

A B C D E F G H I J K L M N O P Q R S T U V W X Y Z

A
B
C
D
E
F
G
H
I
J
K
L
M
N
O
P
Q
R
S
T
U
V
W
X
Y
Z

A B C D E F G H I J K L M N O P Q R S T U V W X Y Z

A B C D E F G H I J K L M N O P Q R **S** T U V W X Y Z

A
B
C
D
E
F
G
H
I
J
K
L
M
N
O
P
Q
R
S
T
U
V
W
X
Y
Z

T

A
B
C
D
E
F
G
H
I
J
K
L
M
N
O
P
Q
R
S
T
U
V
W
X
Y
Z

A B C D E F G H I J K L M N O P Q R S T U V W X Y Z

A B C D E F G H I J K L M N O P Q R S T U V W X Y Z

A B C D E F G H I J K L M N O P Q R S T U V W X Y Z

A B C D E F G H I J K L M N O P Q R S T U V W X Y Z

A
B
C
D
E
F
G
H
I
J
K
L
M
N
O
P
Q
R
S
T
U
V
W
X
Y
Z